December 2–5, 2014
Sydney, Australia

Association for
Computing Machinery

Advancing Computing as a Science & Profession

CoNEXT'14

Proceedings of the 2014
Conference on emerging Networking Experiments and Technologies

Sponsored by:

ACM SIGCOMM

Supported by:

National Science Foundation, Cisco, NICTA, Technicolor, Google, Hewlett-Packard, & Microsoft Research

Association for
Computing Machinery

Advancing Computing as a Science & Profession

The Association for Computing Machinery
2 Penn Plaza, Suite 701
New York, New York 10121-0701

Notice to Past Authors of ACM-Published Articles
ACM intends to create a complete electronic archive of all articles and/or other material previously published by ACM. If you have written a work that has been previously published by ACM in any journal or conference proceedings prior to 1978, or any SIG Newsletter at any time, and you do NOT want this work to appear in the ACM Digital Library, please inform permissions@acm.org, stating the title of the work, the author(s), and where and when published.

ISBN: 978-1-4503-3279-8 (Digital)

ISBN: 978-1-4503-3439-6 (Print)

Additional copies may be ordered prepaid from:

ACM Order Department
PO Box 30777
New York, NY 10087-0777, USA

Phone: 1-800-342-6626 (USA and Canada)
+1-212-626-0500 (Global)
Fax: +1-212-944-1318
E-mail: acmhelp@acm.org
Hours of Operation: 8:30 am – 4:30 pm ET

Printed in the USA

Welcome to CoNEXT 2014

It is our pleasure to welcome everyone to *ACM CoNEXT 2014*, one of ACM's flagship conferences in networking, and Sydney, one of the world's greatest harbour cities.

Keeping with tradition, CoNEXT 2014 is organized as a single-track event over 3 days, and one day of workshops, sprinkled with several social events to facilitate networking. We have managed to make this happen entirely due to the work of a dedicated group of people working as a team. *Augustin Chaintreau* and *Luigi Rizzo, Technical Program Co-chairs,* took care of putting together an outstanding program committee, and as a result have come up with a high quality program. Sponsorship chair, *Sanjay Jha,* worked hard to get a record number of sponsorship for a conference in Australia, and *Sebastien Ardon,* the finance chair, navigated financial uncertainties like a true professional. *Sipat Triukose* and *Salil Kanhere,* the local arrangements chairs, managed the myriad nitty gritty details of getting the venue and organising the social events; *Guillaume Jourjon* managed the all the online content. The entire team made themselve available, at unscheduled times, and for numerous unanticipated tasks, to make certain everything ran as smoothly as possible. *Colin Dixon,* publication chair, and the folks at Sheridan Communications handled publication details and did a wonderful job of managing the many tasks with their associated deadlines. *Aruna Balasubramanian* and *Emmanuel Lochin* ensured wide publicity for the conference. *Gaogang XIE*, *Steve Uhlig* and *Mostafa Ammar*, working with *Mahbub Hassan*, *Ali C. Begen* and *Christian Timmerer* have organized an interesting workshop.

CoNEXT has always encouraged and financially supported student participation and we have continued this tradition. *Theophilus Benson* and *Xenofontas Dimitropoulos* served as travel grant chairs, managing student travel grants and successfully lobbying for support from the government agencies. Through their work and the generosity of our corporate supporters, students' registration costs and the number of travel grants awarded are at the same level as in past years.

We hope you will come a few days before or stay a few days after the conference and enjoy the city of Sydney and surrounding areas, and also find *CoNEXT 2014* a rewarding experience.

Aruna Seneviratne
CoNEXT'14 General Chair

Christophe Diot & Jim Kurose
CoNEXT'14 Vice General Chairs

Program Chairs' Welcome

Dear Attendees,

It is a great pleasure to welcome everyone to the 10th ACM International Conference on emerging Networking EXperiments and Technologies (ACM CoNEXT'14). At the close of a decade as one of the major forums for presentations and discussions of novel computing technologies that will shape the future of Internet-working, the conference travels to another continent.

The single track program including what we found the most promising submissions on computer and communication networks research at large is a reflection of commitment of all PC members to the three values of CoNEXT: recognizing farsighted excellence, promoting a broad definition of networking research, and assuring authors of submitted papers a fair and thorough review process. We hope it will bring new technical interactions and substantial novelty to the field of networking for the years to come.

- The program, 27 long papers and 10 short ones, was selected from the 187 papers we received (including 133 long and 54 short).
- The geographical diversity of our research community, with submission from authors in 25 countries, lead to 18 countries being represented by at least one author in the program. Often ill-represented as US-centric, our community is more balanced than one may have thought: although 21 papers have at least one author affiliated in North America, 19 and 5, contain one author affiliated in Europe or Pacific/Asia, respectively.
- Looked over topics, contributions in the program reflect our set of submissions: 12 papers on wireless, 10 on theory, 7 in novel application and other fields, and an expected high number 16 on papers on management, including on data-centers and SDN. Acceptance rate for all topics above are around 20%. The only exception we noticed is in systems and security, less represented in submissions and with a lower acceptance rate, ending with only 4 papers in our program.

As can be judged by these numbers, the competition has been worldwide and the selection drastic. We would like to report information on how the reviewing process was organized.

- Apart from two papers with clear content or formatting problems, each paper was formally reviewed by 3-5 reviewers, producing a full review and a binary 'accept/reject' suggestion. These reviews and suggestions have been used by the chairs and other PC members to start a discussion on the merits of the submission. The online discussion was vigorous (995 comments were posted by PC members, an average of 5 per paper) and members updated their review to reflect additional information gathered and discussed. A plenary PC meeting attended by the vast majority of PC members at SIGCOMM made final decisions on all controversial papers w.r.t. their merits and limitations.
- Multiple factors are important to select works to be presented, and we summarized them in two criteria: Impact and Technical Quality, graded on a scale from 1 to 4 with 4 being the strongest, allowing reviewers to specify what part of this paper they appreciated to justify their decisions.
- While the decision to include or not, each paper was done individually, and all papers have been considered independently of raw scores, we thought it might be important to share statistics on the 187 submissions we received:
  - 19 received only accept scores (of which 100% were accepted)

- ➢ 18 received a strict majority of accept (72% accepted)
- ➢ 16 received a tie (30% accepted)
- ➢ 134 ended with a strict majority of reject (0% accepted)

Distributions of impact scores (1, 2, 3, 4) was (9%, 57%, 33%, 1%);
technical quality (1, 2, 3, 4) was (11%, 45%, 38%, 6%).

- A minority of papers received interaction from PC members, a feature we encouraged whenever a short clarification could help reviewers assessing a particular fact about the paper. Note that this was not a rebuttal. In the end, 8 papers received such requests which were all answered promptly and used in the decision; 3 of those papers were accepted into the program. We think this was a useful approach and not one that causes excessive burden to authors and reviewers.

Following last year's CoNEXT, short papers were considered under the same term as long papers (i.e., mature work with novelty and impact), only with a more open mind towards criticism on the scope of evaluation or broadness of the topics. The acceptance ratio for long and short papers was nearly identical, and we will continue to support authors to use a variety of presentation formats while sticking to the same excellent standard of research.

We hope you will enjoy CoNEXT'14 program.

Luigi Rizzo
Program Co-Chair
Università di Pisa, Italy

Augustin Chaintreau
Program Co-Chair
Columbia University, USA

Table of Contents

CoNEXT 2014 Conference Organization

General Chair: Aruna Seneviratne *(NICTA/UNSW, Australia)*

Vice General Chairs: Christophe Diot *(Technicolor, France)*
Jim Kurose *(Umass, USA)*

Program Chairs: Augustin Chaintreau *(Columbia University, USA)*
Luigi Rizzo *(University of Pisa, Italy)*

Workshop Chairs: Gaogang XIE *(Chinese Academy of Science, China)*
Steve Uhlig *(Queen Mary, Engnland)*
Mostafa Ammar *(Georgia Tech, USA)*

Student Workshop Chairs: George Iosifidis *(CERTH and UTH, Greece)*
Eric Keller *(University of Colorado, USA)*
Sun Yi *(Chinese Academy of Science, China)*

Travel Grant Chairs: Theophilus Benson *(Duke, USA)*
Xenofontas Dimitropoulos *(ETH, Switzerland)*

Finance Chair: Sebastien Ardon *(NICTA, Australia)*

Local Arrangements Chairs: Sipat Triukose *(NICTA, Australia)*
Salil Kanhere *(UNSW, Australia)*

Webmaster: Guillaume Jourjon *(NICTA, Australia)*

Publicity Chairs: Emmanuel Lochin *(ISAE, France)*
Aruna Balasubramanian *(University of Washington, USA)*

Publication Chair: Colin Dixon *(Brocade, USA)*

Sponsorship Chair: Sanjay Jha *(UNSW, Australia)*

Steering Committee Chair: Max Ott *(NICTA, Australia)*

Steering Committee: Olivier Bonaventure *(Universite catholique de Louvain, Belgium)*
Bruce Davie *(VMware, USA)*
Constantine Dovrolis *(Georgia Tech, USA)*
Peter Key *(Microsoft Research, UK)*
Vishal Misra *(Columbia University, USA)*

Program Committee: Matthew Andrews *(Bell Labs)*
Theophilus Benson *(Duke University)*
Giuseppe Bianchi *(U. Roma Tor Vergata)*
Sem Borst *(TU Eindhoven/Bell Labs)*
Augustin Chaintreau (co-Chair) *(Columbia U.)*
Haibo Chen *(Shanghai Jiao Tong University)*
Kenjiro Cho *(Internet Initiative Japan)*
David Choffnes *(Northeastern U.)*
Chen Nee Chuah *(U. California Davis)*
Paolo Costa *(Microsoft Research)*
Vijay Erramilli *(Guavus)*
Nick Feamster *(Georgia Tech)*
Phillipa Gill *(Stony Brook U.)*
Leana Golubchik *(U. Southern California)*
Saikat Guha *(Microsoft Research)*
Orion Hodson *(Microsoft Research)*
Felipe Huici *(NEC)*
Gianluca Iannaccone *(Facebook)*
Stratis Ioannidis *(Technicolor)*
Dali Kaafar *(INRIA/NICTA)*
Thomas Karagiannis *(Microsoft Research)*
Christian Kreibich *(ICSI & Lastline, Inc.)*
Nikos Laoutaris *(Telefonica)*
Sam Leffler *(Google)*
Richard Ma *(National U. of Singapore)*
Harsha Madhyastha *(U. California Riverside)*
Bruce Maggs *(Duke U.)*
Ratul Mahajan *(Microsoft Research)*
Anirban Mahanti *(NICTA)*
David Malone *(Hamilton Institute)*
Marco Mellia *(Politecnico di Torino)*
Daniel Menasche *(U. Fed. Rio de Janeiro)*
James Mickens *(Microsoft Research)*
Alan Mislove *(Northeastern U.)*
Michael Mitzenmacher *(Harvard U.)*
Thomas Moscibroda *(Microsoft Research)*
Cristina Nita-Rotaru *(Purdue U.)*
Jitendra Padhye *(Microsoft Research)*
Joshua Reich *(AT&T Research)*
Robert Ricci *(U. Utah)*
Luigi Rizzo (co-Chair) *(U. Pisa)*
Vyas Sekar *(Carnegie Mellon U.)*
Kannan Srinivasan *(Ohio State U.)*

Program Committee (continued):

Peter Steenkiste *(Carnegie Mellon U.)*
Lakshmi Subramanian *(New York U.)*
Renata Teixeira *(INRIA)*
Andreas Terzis *(John Hopkins U. / Google)*
Patrick Thiran *(EPFL)*
Steve Uhlig *(Queen Mary/U. of London)*
Joerg Widmer *(IMDEA)*
Walter Willinger *(Niksen)*
Haifeng Yu *(National U. of Singapore)*
Minlan Yu *(U. Southern California)*
Zhi-Li Zhang *(U. of Minnesota)*

Additional reviewers:

Irfan Sheriff
Giovanni Stea
Michael Walfish
Xia Zhou

CoNEXT 2014 Sponsor & Supporters

Sponsor: acm sigcomm

Platinum Supporter: NSF

Gold Supporter: CISCO

Silver Supporters: NICTA technicolor

Google hp

Bronze Supporter: Microsoft Research

Analyzing and Boosting the Performance of Power-Line Communication Networks

Christina Vlachou*, Albert Banchs†, Julien Herzen*, Patrick Thiran*
* EPFL, Switzerland † IMDEA Networks Inst. and Univ. Carlos III of Madrid, Spain
* firstname.lastname@epfl.ch † banchs@it.uc3m.es

ABSTRACT

Power-line communications are employed in home networking to provide easy and high-throughput connectivity. IEEE 1901, the MAC protocol for power-line networks, employs a CSMA/CA protocol similar to that of 802.11, but is substantially more complex, which probably explains why little is known about its performance. One of the key differences between the two protocols is that whereas 802.11 only reacts upon collisions, 1901 also reacts upon several consecutive transmissions and thus can potentially achieve better performance by avoiding unnecessary collisions.

In this paper, we propose a model for the 1901 MAC. Our analysis reveals that the default configuration of 1901 does not fully exploit its potential and that its performance degrades with the number of stations. We derive analytically the optimal configuration parameters for 1901; this drastically improves throughput and achieves optimal performance *without* requiring the knowledge of the number of stations in the network. In contrast, to provide a similar performance, 802.11 requires knowing the number of contending stations, which is unfeasible for realistic traffic patterns. Our solution can be readily implemented by vendors, as it only consists in modifying existing MAC parameters. We corroborate our results with testbed measurements, unveiling a significant signaling overhead in 1901 implementations.

Keywords

Power-line communications; HomePlug AV; IEEE 1901; CSMA/CA; Performance Evaluation; Enhancement.

Categories and Subject Descriptors

C.2 [**Computer-Communication Networks**]: Network Protocols, Local and Wide-Area Networks.;
C.4 [**Performance of Systems**]: Modeling techniques

CoNEXT'14, December 2–5, 2014, Sydney, Australia.
Copyright 2014 ACM 978-1-4503-3279-8/14/12 ...$15.00
http://dx.doi.org/10.1145/2674005.2675016.

1. INTRODUCTION

Power-line communications (PLC) are developing rapidly. HomePlug, the leading alliance for PLC standardization, proposes different solutions for home automation and high data-rate local networks, with physical rates up to 1 Gbps. It is estimated that by 2013 over 120 million HomePlug devices had been shipped worldwide [3]. The annual growth rate for HomePlug AV devices (aimed for high data-rate networks) is expected to be about 30% until 2016 [4]. Although 95% of PLC devices follow the HomePlug specification [3], the MAC layer of this specification has received little attention so far in the research community, in contrast to the PHY layer. In particular, no work has investigated how far from optimality this MAC protocol is. This work explores and justifies the design choices adopted for the MAC layer of PLC networks.

As PLC technology is becoming an important component in home networks[1], residential buildings are expected to host networks with a high number of PLC stations. These PLC stations interfere with each other, because – in contrast to wireless technology that can employ different communication channels – PLC utilizes the entire available bandwidth (1.8 - 80 MHz) for communication. The recent HomePlug AV2 standard provides physical data rates of more than 1 Gbps, by employing efficient PHY layer techniques and parameters as well as small inter-frame timings [17]. However, in addition to data rate improvements, there is also the need for enhancements at the MAC layer, as an efficient MAC can further improve performance when many stations contend for the medium. Therefore, in this paper we focus on understanding the MAC layer dynamics, and on enhancing its performance building on this understanding.

Due to the shared nature of power lines, HomePlug devices employ a multiple-access scheme based on CSMA/CA that is specified by the IEEE 1901 standard[2] [7]. The 1901 CSMA/CA protocol bears some resemblance to the CSMA/CA mechanism employed by IEEE 802.11 that has been extensively studied in the literature (for instance, in [8, 14]). Nevertheless, 1901 differs from 802.11 in that its CSMA/CA mechanism is more complex, which makes its theoretical analysis challenging. In particular, in addition to using a backoff counter, it also uses a so-called *deferral counter*. The deferral counter significantly increases the state-space required to describe the backoff procedure, which contrasts

[1]PLC is also employed for hybrid networks comprising multiple technologies such as Ethernet and Wireless LAN.
[2]All HomePlug specifications, including 1.0, AV, AV2, and GreenPhy, employ the same CSMA/CA process.

with the comparatively small state-space required to analyze 802.11 (see, e.g., the Markov chain used in [8]). As a result, despite the commercial success and massive adoption of PLC technologies, the analysis of the 1901 CSMA/CA protocol has received little attention.

From a general perspective, it turns out that 1901 implements an approach to contention resolution that is drastically different from the usual 802.11 CSMA/CA procedure. In particular, 802.11 can only react to contention (by doubling its contention window) after detecting a collision. In contrast, 1901 can already react when it senses the medium busy during a certain number of time slots (decided by the deferral counter). Such a protocol design has two distinct advantages over 802.11:

1. The contention window can be increased as many times as required to reach appropriate backoff durations without suffering any collision. In contrast, with 802.11 the contention window can only be doubled after a collision, and thus one or more collisions might occur before the contention window reaches the appropriate value. As a result, 1901 can reduce the channel time wasted in collisions, potentially leading to better performance.
2. By appropriately selecting the number of busy slots that trigger an increase of the contention window, we can adjust with fine granularity the level of contention that triggers a reaction. In contrast, this is not possible in 802.11, where contention is detected by the binary signal given by channel occupation: either the channel is busy upon a transmission attempt, which yields a collision, or it is not, and any finer refinements are not possible.

Following the above reasoning, it seems that 1901 can substantially outperform 802.11 if properly configured. However, as we will observe, the default configuration of 1901 does not achieve the level of efficiency that one would expect given these premises, and indeed performance can be largely improved. One important cause of the (relatively) poor performance of the protocol is the lack of an accurate and simple analysis that provides an insightful understanding of its dynamics and that can be used to configure the protocol appropriately.

Motivated by the above, in this paper we propose a general framework for modeling and enhancing the CSMA/CA process of 1901. The main contributions of this paper are as follows:

- First, we introduce a model that accurately captures 1901 performance while reducing very substantially the required space-state; this model comes in the form of a fixed-point equation which we show that admits a unique solution. Our model is accurate as long as the number of stations is not too small, due to the assumptions upon which we rely to derive a simple model. In [19], we analyze the impact of these assumptions and propose an alternative model that is more accurate; however, the model of [19] is more complex and does not provide insights on the optimality of the protocol, which is one of the main contributions of this paper.
- Second, we employ our model to compute a configuration that improves the throughput of the network. Our configuration consists in simply setting existing MAC parameters – such as the contention windows – to appropriate values, and thus can be readily implemented by manufacturers of PLC devices. The proposed configuration provides drastic performance improvements.
- Third, we validate our analysis through simulation as well as by means of experimental results of a HomePlug AV testbed with 8 stations. Using our testbed, we unveil important details of 1901 implementations such as HomePlug AV, and we investigate the overhead of management messages exchanged between the PLC stations. This information can be useful for improving HomePlug AV2 implementations, as this specification aims at reducing various MAC layer overheads.

One of the most remarkable results of the paper is that, with the proposed configuration, 1901 provides a performance very close to that of an optimally configured MAC protocol without requiring to know the total number of contending stations N. This contrasts with similar methods for enhancing the CSMA/CA procedure of 802.11 networks that do require knowing N (see, e.g., [16]), which challenges their practicality in real deployments because N varies in time. Thus, with the configuration proposed here, the 1901 protocol represents an interesting step towards a practical and optimal MAC protocol.

The rest of this paper is organized as follows. In the next section, we present the 1901 backoff procedure. In Section 3, we review related work on models and enhancements for MAC protocols. We then present our model for 1901 in Section 4, and we propose enhancements for 1901 configuration in Section 5. Our model and proposed configurations are evaluated in Section 6. Finally, we give our concluding remarks in Section 7.

2. THE 1901 MAC MECHANISM

In this section, we present the relevant aspects of the 1901 CSMA/CA procedure [7]. We give insights on the requirements that established this intricate protocol, by comparing 1901 with 802.11.

The first HomePlug specification that included this CSMA/CA mechanism is HomePlug 1.0. HomePlug 1.0 employs a frame preamble comprising 7.5 OFDM symbols[3]. The slot duration was determined by the time required by a station to decide whether the medium is busy or idle (i.e., to detect a preamble transmission) [15], and it is equal to the duration of 7 HomePlug 1.0 symbols (i.e., 35.84 μs). Although newer technologies have different symbol durations, the slot duration has remained the same for all HomePlug standards for backward compatibility. Observe that the slot duration is large compared to the one of 802.11 (which is 9 μs for 802.11a/g/n/ac). In the next paragraphs, we explain the effect of the slot duration in the backoff process.

The backoff process of 1901 uses two counters: the backoff counter (BC) and the deferral counter (DC). In addition, there are four *backoff stages*[4]. We now discuss the common features of 1901 and 802.11, and we elaborate later on the deferral counter. When a new packet arrives for transmission, the station starts at backoff stage 0, and it draws the backoff counter BC uniformly at random in $\{0, \dots, CW_0 - 1\}$,

[3]HomePlug 1.0 provides rates up to 14 Mbps. Similar to all HomePlug standards, it employs an OFDM scheme at the PHY layer.

[4]In the standard [7], the backoff stage is determined by the so-called *backoff procedure counter* (BPC).

where CW_0 refers to the contention window used at backoff stage 0. Similarly to 802.11, BC is decreased by 1 at each time slot if the station senses the medium to be idle, and it is frozen when the medium is sensed busy. In case the medium is sensed busy, BC is also decreased by 1 once the medium is sensed idle again. When BC reaches 0, the station attempts to transmit the packet. Also similarly to 802.11, the station jumps to the next backoff stage if the transmission fails (unless it is already at the last backoff stage, in which case it re-enters this backoff stage). When entering backoff stage i, a station draws BC uniformly at random in $\{0, \ldots, CW_i - 1\}$, where CW_i is the contention window at backoff stage i, and the process is repeated. For 802.11, the contention window is doubled between two successive backoff stages, and thus $CW_i = 2^i CW_0$. For 1901, CW_i depends on the priority level, and is given in Table 1. There are four priority classes in 1901, CA0 to CA3. CA0/CA1 priorities serve best-effort applications, and CA2/CA3 the delay-sensitive ones.

Now, when there are few contending stations (i.e., 1 or 2), or when the traffic load is very low, the time spent in backoff is a large overhead and increases as the contention window increases. Given the large slot duration of 1901, the average delay due to backoff ($\sim (CW_0 - 1)/2$ time slots) can be reduced when there are few contending stations – that is, small collision likelihood – by choosing a small minimum contention window, e.g., $CW_0 = 8$, as specified for 1901 (Table 1). However, as expected, small contention windows yield higher collision probabilities when the number of stations increases or when the traffic load rises. The deferral counter DC was introduced as a countermeasure in the CSMA/CA process of 1901, to reduce collisions induced by small contention windows. This is achieved by triggering a redraw of the backoff counter BC *before* the station attempts a transmission.

Priority class:	CA0/CA1		CA2/CA3	
backoff stage i	CW_i	d_i	CW_i	d_i
0	8	0	8	0
1	16	1	16	1
2	32	3	16	3
3	64	15	32	15

Table 1: IEEE 1901 parameters for the contention windows CW_i and the initial values d_i of deferral counter DC, for each backoff stage i.

The main difference between 1901 and 802.11 is the introduction of DC in 1901, which allows a station to enter a higher backoff stage even if it did not attempt a transmission. The mechanism to decide when this occurs works as follows. When entering backoff stage i, DC is set at *an initial DC value* d_i, where d_i is given in Table 1 for each i. After having sensed the medium busy, a station decreases DC by 1 (in addition to BC). If the medium is sensed busy and $DC = 0$, then the station jumps to the next backoff stage (or re-enters the last backoff stage, if it is already at this stage), and it re-draws BC *without attempting a transmission.* Figure 1 shows an example of such a backoff process.

We now discuss the effect of the deferral counter on jitter, because this justifies the choice of rest of the parameters in 1901. As we have seen above, the deferral counter manages to reduce collisions. It can however introduce high jitter. The transmitting station has an advantage against the other stations because its CW is maintained at its initial value CW_0, whereas the other stations might increase their CW

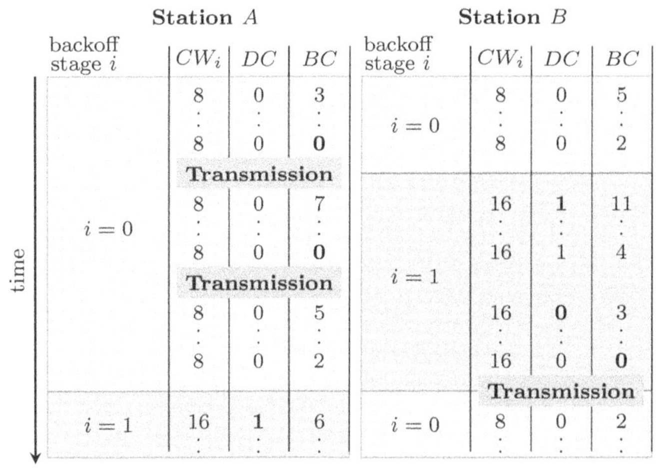

Figure 1: Evolution of the backoff process with 2 saturated stations A and B. Initially, both stations are at backoff stage 0. A transmits twice consecutively. Note the change in i when a station senses the medium busy and has $DC = 0$.

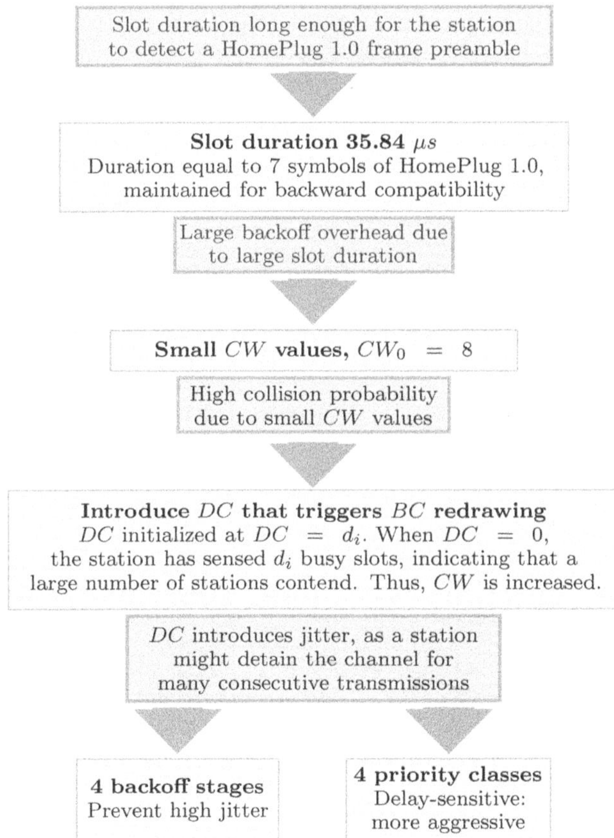

Figure 2: A discussion of the design choices of the 1901 MAC.

when $DC = 0$, as explained earlier. As a result, a station can grasp the channel for multiple consecutive transmissions until it releases the channel, and then wait for a long sequence of other station transmissions until obtaining the token again, which yields high jitter. To reduce the CW imbalance between the transmitting station and the others, 1901 employs a total of 4 backoff stages. Moreover, there are two different configurations for best-effort and delay-sensitive applications (see Table 1). The delay-sensitive class employs smaller contention windows, and the contention window is not doubled between backoff stages 1 and 2. This improves jitter, but yields a higher collision probability, i.e., lower throughput, compared to CA0/CA1 class. In this paper, we focus on modeling and enhancing 1901 performance for best-effort classes (targeting high throughput), whereas in [19] and [21], we investigate the short-term fairness aspects of 1901, related to jitter. Figure 2 summarizes the insights concerning the MAC parameters described in this section.

Let us underline a major consequence of the difference between 1901 and 802.11, which is due to the introduction of the deferral counter in 1901. A 1901 station can redraw its backoff counter *without* experiencing a collision, if its deferral counter is 0 and it senses the medium busy. This results in 1901 having the two distinct features that we mentioned earlier, and which offer new opportunities for access control:

- With 1901, the contention window can be increased without suffering from a collision, hence a station can adapt its transmission behavior to the level of contention in the network without wasting channel time in collisions.
- By appropriately configuring its deferral counter, 1901 can optimally adjust its level of reaction to contention with a fine granularity, which is contrary to 802.11, where the level of reaction cannot be tuned.

Figure 3 provides an evidence of the 1901 potential. We investigate the time evolution of the protocol dynamics and compare 1901 with 802.11 for two different values for the number of stations in the network, $N = 2$ and $N = 15$. Observe that for $N = 2$, 802.11 has large average CW only after consecutive collisions, whereas 1901 adapts CW even after successful transmission attempts. The 1901 average CW increases or remains constant as a given station keeps transmitting, and decreases only when the other station successfully wins the medium. Finally, notice that for $N = 15$, 1901 adapts CW before a collision, thus it wastes less time in collisions and the average CW converges much faster to the steady state. Hence, under dynamically changing traffic, 1901 can adjust faster CW to the load demand.

In Section 5, we show that the two above 1901 features make it possible to configure 1901 so that it efficiently adjusts to the level of congestion in the network, *without knowing the number of active stations.* In contrast, although many approaches to efficiently configure and optimize 802.11 have been proposed in the literature, these are limited to a given (known) number of active stations and, to the best of our knowledge, there exists no such 802.11 configuration that works when the number of stations is unknown.

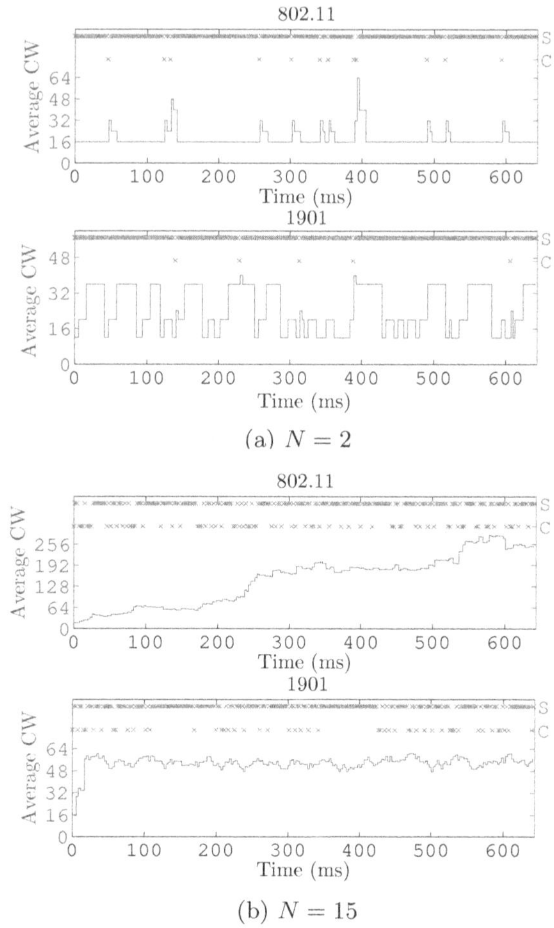

Figure 3: Time evolution of the contention window CW averaged over all stations in the network (left axis) and the binary outcome of transmission attempts (right axis), i.e. success (S) or collision (C), in simulation. Our simulator is validated experimentally in Section 6.2. All stations are saturated and start at backoff stage 0. 1901 is simulated with CA1 class, and 802.11 with $CW_0 = 16$ and 7 backoff stages (i.e., 802.11a/g/n), and we use the timings specified in Section 6.

3. RELATED WORK

Analytical models of 802.11 can provide insights for analyzing 1901. Indeed, 802.11 can be viewed as a simplified version of 1901 in which the deferral counter never expires. We review here major studies on 802.11 and some of the few studies on 1901.

Models of IEEE 802.11.

A large number of performance evaluation models have been proposed for 802.11 (e.g., [8, 14]). In particular, the model proposed by Bianchi in [8] for single contention domain networks is very popular. This work models the backoff process of 802.11 using a discrete time Markov chain. Importantly, Bianchi assumes that the backoff processes of the stations are independent, which is known as the *decoupling assumption.* In this case, the collision probability γ experienced by all stations is time-invariant, and can be found by solving a fixed-point equation that depends on the protocol parameters.

Kumar et al. [14] study the backoff process of 802.11 under the decoupling assumption using renewal theory. We employ a similar method for finding a fixed-point equation for 1901. However, due to the increased complexity of 1901, proving the uniqueness of the solution of this fixed-point equation is significantly more challenging than for 802.11 and it is the object of Theorem 1.

Models of IEEE 1901.

To the best of our knowledge, the only works analyzing the backoff process of 1901 are [12, 11, 20, 19]. The authors in [12] propose a model similar to Bianchi's model for 802.11 [8]. However, the paper does not provide the corresponding fixed-point equation for the collision probability, due to the increased complexity of the Markov chain introduced by the deferral counter. To compute the collision probability in this case, a costly system of more than a thousand non-linear equations has to be solved. Moreover, it has not been investigated whether this system of equations has a unique solution. The work in [11] discusses the validity of the decoupling assumption and simplifies the model in [12] in the case the stations are not saturated. Here again, the authors do not investigate the uniqueness of the solution(s) of their model. Our short paper [20] includes the model of Section 4, but without any proofs or enhancements.

We propose a model which is strictly equivalent to the model of [12] in terms of modeling performance. The key difference is that, in our case, the collision probability can be obtained by solving a single fixed-point equation. In this sense, our model can be seen as a drastic simplification of [12], and this simple form enables us to derive some efficient configuration parameters for 1901. In [19], we introduce an alternative model that does not rely on the decoupling assumption. However, this model is intricate and does not yield insights for enhancing performance.

Enhancements of IEEE 802.11.

There is a large body of work introducing enhancements for the 802.11 CSMA/CA procedure. In particular, Bianchi [8] computes τ_{opt}, the transmission probability that achieves maximum throughput. τ_{opt} is obtained by tuning the contention window, and it is a function of the number of contending stations N. Typically, N is unknown and varies, and practical implementations of such optimal configurations need to use some estimation techniques.

To apply Bianchi's analysis, several attempts have been made to estimate the number of contending stations [9, 16]. These methods typically rely on measuring the collision probability or the channel activity and on estimating N periodically. The main disadvantage of such approaches is that they introduce more complexity at the MAC layer, making them difficult to implement in practice. The improvements that we propose for 1901 do not require the knowledge of N, nor do they require that the CSMA/CA process itself be changed. Instead, they can be simply implemented, as they only consist in judiciously choosing the backoff parameters CW_i and d_i (and, optionally, the number of backoff stages m). In Section 6, we observe that they provide drastic performance improvements compared to the default 1901 and offer similar efficiency levels as an optimally-configured 802.11 network, but without knowing N.

Enhancements of IEEE 1901.

There are not many studies on enhancements of 1901 MAC. The authors in [10] propose a constant d_i equal to 0 for all backoff stages i, which means that whenever a station senses the medium busy it doubles CW. This technique decreases the collision probability, but it yields the most extreme case of 1901 unfairness; for small N, always doubling CW leads idle stations to have fewer chances of accessing the channel, compared to a station that just transmitted successfully (and whose CW is minimal). This yields a high variance of delay, as explained in Section 2. Moreover, the authors do not use an analytical model and do not investigate the different tradeoffs involved in the parameter setting to find the optimal configurations.

Another modification of 1901 is proposed in [13]. The authors provide a mechanism that keeps d_i and CW constant, but where CW depends on the number of stations N. Requiring the knowledge of N is impractical.

4. ANALYSIS

In this section, we introduce our model for the 1901 CSMA/CA process. We analyze the protocol under the following assumptions. First, there are N saturated stations in the network. Second, all stations belong to a single contention domain. Third, there is no packet loss or errors due to the physical layer. Therefore, transmission failures are due only to collisions. Fourth, the stations never discard a packet until it is successfully transmitted, hence the retry limit is infinite[5]. Finally, the 1901 standard specifies that only the stations belonging to the highest contending priority class participate in the backoff process[6]. We follow this property of 1901, and we assume that all the contending stations are in the same class and use the same set of parameters.

We now turn our attention to the modeling assumptions, which assert that the backoff process of a station is independent of the aggregate attempt process of the other $N-1$ stations, and are referred to as the *decoupling assumption*. In detail, this term refers to the following set of assumptions (see e.g., [8, 14]):

[A1] The stations attempt a transmission in each time slot with a *constant* transmission probability referred as the average attempt rate τ.

[A2] Given a tagged station, the probability that at least one of the other stations transmits is fixed (state independent) and is denoted by γ. Therefore, transmission attempts experience a fixed collision probability γ. Furthermore, a station with $BC \neq 0$ senses the medium busy at any time slot with probability γ, independently of the medium status at previous slots.

The above assumption, which considers that the collision probability of a station is independent of its state, has been proven to be accurate in 802.11. However, in [19, 21], it has been shown that a PLC network with few stations can be short-term unfair for some configurations, which implies that there is some coupling between the stations. Indeed, for such configurations, when a station is in a state with large backoff stage, the probability that some other station is at small backoff stage state is high, and as a result its collision probability is larger in that state, which contradicts the decoupling assumption. The simulation results of Section 6.2 confirm that, while the model has reduced accuracy for some configurations when there are few stations in the network, accuracy is high as long as the number of stations is not too small. To improve the 1901 modeling accuracy for small N, a theoretical framework without relying on the decoupling

[5]IEEE 1901 does not specify any retry limit, contrary to 802.11. However, there exists a vendor specific timeout on the frame transmission. This timeout is 2.5 s for the devices of our testbed presented in Section 6, and is very large compared to the maximum frame duration (2.5 ms), which is in line with our hypothesis.

[6]In practice, the contending class is decided using a simple system of busy tones called *priority resolution symbols*.

assumption is applied in [19]; however the resulting model is more complex and challenging. Here, our work invokes the decoupling assumption, which yields a simple model that is accurate for large N and can be employed for performance enhancements. As shown in the results of Section 6.3, our model indeed enables us to provide configurations that boost significantly the 1901 performance.

Our analysis requires to compute the expected number of time slots (a time slot can be idle or can contain a transmission) spent by a station at backoff stage i. Let k denote the value of BC drawn uniformly at random in $\{0, \ldots, CW_i - 1\}$, when the station enters stage i. If the station is running 802.11, BC always expires and the station spends exactly $(k+1)$ time slots in stage i, the $(k+1)th$ slot being used for transmission, because a station leaves backoff stage i only when it attempts a transmission. In contrast, in 1901 a station might leave backoff stage i either because of a transmission attempt, when BC expires (like in 802.11), or because it has sensed the medium busy $d_i + 1$ times, before BC has expired. In this latter case, the station spends a number of slots at backoff stage i, which is at least $d_i + 1$ and no more than k. More precisely, the station spends $d_i + 1 \leq j \leq k$ slots when it senses the medium busy d_i times in any of the first $j - 1$ slots, and in the jth slot.

Let us write bc_i for the expected number of time slots spent by a station at backoff stage i. To compute bc_i we need to evaluate the probability of the events that (i) a station attempts a transmission or (ii) senses the medium busy d_i+1 times within the k slots. Let T be the random variable describing the number of slots during which the medium is sensed busy among the k slots. Because of [A2], T follows the binomial distribution $\text{Bin}(k, \gamma)$. Now, let x_k^i be the probability that a station at backoff stage i jumps to the next stage $i+1$ in k or fewer time slots due to event (ii). Then,

$$x_k^i = \mathbb{P}(T > d_i) = \sum_{j=d_i+1}^{k} \binom{k}{j} \gamma^j (1-\gamma)^{k-j}. \quad (1)$$

We can compute bc_i as a function of γ via x_k^i. We distinguish two cases on k. First, if $k > d_i$, then event (i) occurs with probability $(1 - x_k^i)$, in which case the station spends $(k+1)$ slots in stage i. Now, event (ii) occurs with probability x_k^i. More precisely, event (ii) occurs at slot j, with $d_i + 1 \leq j \leq k$, with probability $(x_j^i - x_{j-1}^i)$ [7], in which case the station spends j slots in backoff stage i. Second, if $k \leq d_i$, then event (ii) cannot happen. Thus, the backoff counter expires, event (i) always takes place, and the station spends $(k+1)$ time slots in stage i. By summing all the possible cases described above, it follows that bc_i is given by

$$bc_i = \frac{1}{CW_i} \sum_{k=d_i+1}^{CW_i-1} \left[(k+1)(1-x_k^i) + \sum_{j=d_i+1}^{k} j(x_j^i - x_{j-1}^i) \right] + \frac{(d_i+1)(d_i+2)}{2CW_i}. \quad (2)$$

Let R be the random variable describing the number of transmission attempts experienced by a successfully transmitted packet. Similarly, let X be the random variable describing the total number of slots spent in backoff for a successfully transmitted packet. Then from the renewal-reward theorem, with R being the reward and X being renewal lifetimes [14], the average attempt rate is given by

$$\tau = \frac{\mathbb{E}[R]}{\mathbb{E}[X]}. \quad (3)$$

Let t_i be the probability that a station at backoff stage i ends this backoff stage by attempting a transmission. Similarly to (2), t_i can be computed as

$$t_i = \frac{d_i+1}{CW_i} + \sum_{k=d_i+1}^{CW_i-1} \frac{1}{CW_i}(1 - x_k^i). \quad (4)$$

Finally, let us introduce $s_i = (1-\gamma)t_i$, which is the probability that a station at backoff stage i ends this stage after a successful transmission. We are now ready to compute $\mathbb{E}[R]$ and $\mathbb{E}[X]$, and thus τ by (3).

LEMMA 1. *The expected number of slots spent in backoff per successfully transmitted packet is*

$$\mathbb{E}[X] = \sum_{i=0}^{m-2} bc_i \prod_{j=0}^{i-1}(1-s_j) + \prod_{i=0}^{m-2}(1-s_i)\frac{bc_{m-1}}{s_{m-1}}.$$

PROOF. Let X_i be the random variable describing the number of slots that a station starting in stage i spends in backoff before transmitting its current packet successfully. Using the law of total probability, we have

$$\begin{aligned}\mathbb{E}[X] = \mathbb{E}[X_0] &= s_0 bc_0 + (1-s_0)(bc_0 + \mathbb{E}[X_1]) \\ &= bc_0 + (1-s_0)\mathbb{E}[X_1].\end{aligned}$$

Repeating recursively for $\mathbb{E}[X_1]$, we have

$$\begin{aligned}&\mathbb{E}[X_0] = bc_0 + \quad (5)\\ &(1-s_0)(bc_1 + (1-s_1)(bc_2 + \ldots (1-s_{m-2})\mathbb{E}[X_{m-1}])).\end{aligned}$$

Now, $\mathbb{E}[X_{m-1}]$ is given by

$$\mathbb{E}[X_{m-1}] = bc_{m-1} + (1-s_{m-1})\mathbb{E}[X_{m-1}].$$

Solving for $\mathbb{E}[X_{m-1}]$, we obtain $\mathbb{E}[X_{m-1}] = bc_{m-1}/s_{m-1}$. Plugging this expression into (5) concludes the proof. □

LEMMA 2. *The expected number of transmission attempts per successfully transmitted packet is*

$$\mathbb{E}[R] = \sum_{i=0}^{m-2} t_i \prod_{j=0}^{i-1}(1-s_j) + \prod_{i=0}^{m-2}(1-s_i)\frac{t_{m-1}}{s_{m-1}} = \frac{1}{1-\gamma}.$$

PROOF. Similar to the proof of Lemma 1. □

Since γ is the probability that at least one other station transmits, it can be expressed as a function of τ:

$$\gamma = \Gamma(\tau) = 1 - (1-\tau)^{N-1},$$

where $\tau = \mathbb{E}[R]/\mathbb{E}[X]$ is also a function of γ, which we denote by $G(\gamma)$. The composition of the two functions $\tau = G(\gamma)$ and $\gamma = \Gamma(\tau)$ yields the fixed-point equation for the collision probability

$$\gamma = \Gamma(G(\gamma)). \quad (6)$$

Theorem 1 below establishes the uniqueness of the solution of this fixed-point equation, for configurations satisfying $CW_{i+1} \geq 2CW_i - d_i - 1,\ 0 \leq i < m-1$. Note that, from

[7]Observe that $(x_j^i - x_{j-1}^i)$ is the difference of two CCDFs and denotes the probability that (ii) happens exactly at slot j.

Table 1, these constraints on CW_i are compliant with the standard, except for the class CA2/CA3 at backoff stage $i = 1$. While our numerical experiments seem to indicate that uniqueness of the solution holds for a wider range of configurations, we leave the extension of this result to other configurations for future work.

THEOREM 1. *$\Gamma(G(\gamma)) : [0,1] \to [0,1]$ has a unique fixed-point if $CW_{i+1} \geq 2CW_i - d_i - 1$, $0 \leq i < m-1$.*

PROOF. By Brouwer's fixed-point theorem, since $\Gamma(G(\gamma))$ is a continuous function, there exists a fixed-point in $[0,1]$. Furthermore, if $\Gamma(G(\gamma))$ is monotone, this fixed-point is unique. As $\Gamma(\tau)$ is non-decreasing in γ, it is thus sufficient to show that $G(\gamma)$ is monotone in γ.

Let $Q(\gamma) = (1-\gamma)\mathbb{E}[X]$. Then, using Lemma 2, we have $G(\gamma) = 1/Q(\gamma)$. Now, $G(\gamma)$ is non-increasing in γ if and only if $Q(\gamma)$ is non-decreasing in γ. In the following, we show that $Q(\gamma)$ is non-decreasing.

Let B_i denote the expected number of backoff slots between two transmission attempts of a station that always stays at backoff stage i. At backoff stage i, according to Lemma 3 in Appendix, B_i is given by $B_i = bc_i/t_i - 1$. Replacing bc_i with $t_i(B_i+1)$ in the expression for $\mathbb{E}[X]$, $Q(\gamma)$ can be recast as

$$Q(\gamma) = \sum_{i=0}^{m-2} s_i(B_i+1)\prod_{j=0}^{i-1}(1-s_j) + \prod_{i=0}^{m-2}(1-s_i)(B_{m-1}+1).$$

The derivative of $Q(\gamma)$ with respect to γ is given by

$$\begin{aligned}\frac{dQ}{d\gamma} &= \sum_{i=0}^{m-2} s_i \frac{dB_i}{d\gamma}\prod_{j=0}^{i-1}(1-s_j) + \prod_{i=0}^{m-2}(1-s_i)\frac{dB_{m-1}}{d\gamma} \\ &- \sum_{i=0}^{m-2}\frac{ds_i}{d\gamma}\left[\sum_{j=i+1}^{m-2}\left((B_j+1)s_j\frac{\prod_{k=0}^{j-1}(1-s_k)}{1-s_i}\right)\right. \\ &\left. -(B_i+1)\prod_{j=0}^{i-1}(1-s_j) + \frac{\prod_{j=0}^{m-2}(1-s_j)}{1-s_i}(B_{m-1}+1)\right].\end{aligned} \quad (7)$$

We now show that $Q(\gamma)$ is non-decreasing. First, in Lemma 3 in Appendix we prove that $dB_i/d\gamma > 0$. Thus, the first two terms in (7) are positive and it follows that

$$\begin{aligned}\frac{dQ}{d\gamma} > &- \sum_{i=0}^{m-2}\frac{ds_i}{d\gamma}\left[\sum_{j=i+1}^{m-2}\left((B_j+1)s_j\frac{\prod_{k=0}^{j-1}(1-s_k)}{1-s_i}\right)\right. \\ &\left. -(B_i+1)\prod_{j=0}^{i-1}(1-s_j) + \frac{\prod_{j=0}^{m-2}(1-s_j)}{1-s_i}(B_{m-1}+1)\right].\end{aligned} \quad (8)$$

Now, in Lemma 3, we show that x_k^i is increasing with γ (see (25)). Thus, s_i is decreasing with γ, because, using (4),

$$\frac{ds_i}{d\gamma} = -t_i - (1-\gamma)\frac{\sum_{k=d_i+1}^{CW_i-1} dx_k^i/d\gamma}{CW_i} < 0.$$

Also, by Corollary 1 in Appendix, B_i is a strictly increasing sequence of i. Using these two properties (i.e., $ds_i/d\gamma < 0$, $B_{i+1} > B_i$) for $i = m-2$ in (8), we have

$$\begin{aligned}\frac{dQ}{d\gamma} > &- \sum_{i=0}^{m-3}\frac{ds_i}{d\gamma}\frac{1}{1-s_i}\left[\sum_{j=i+1}^{m-2}\left((B_j+1)s_j\prod_{k=0}^{j-1}(1-s_k)\right)\right. \\ &\left. -(B_i+1)\prod_{j=0}^{i}(1-s_j) + \prod_{j=0}^{m-2}(1-s_j)(B_{m-1}+1)\right].\end{aligned} \quad (9)$$

Using the same properties again in (9) and then, rearranging the factors in the products involving the s_i's, we have

$$\begin{aligned}\frac{dQ}{d\gamma} &> -\sum_{i=0}^{m-3}\frac{ds_i}{d\gamma}\frac{1}{1-s_i}\left[(B_i+1)\sum_{j=i+1}^{m-2}\left(s_j\prod_{k=0}^{j-1}(1-s_k)\right)\right. \\ &\qquad \left. -(B_i+1)\prod_{j=0}^{i}(1-s_j) + \prod_{j=0}^{m-2}(1-s_j)(B_{m-1}+1)\right] \\ &= -\sum_{i=0}^{m-3}\frac{ds_i}{d\gamma}\frac{\prod_{j=0}^{m-2}(1-s_j)}{1-s_i}(B_{m-1}-B_i) \geq 0,\end{aligned}$$

with equality at $\gamma = 0$. This completes the proof. □

We now explain how to obtain actual throughput figures from our model. Solving the fixed-point equation (6) gives the value for γ, which can be used to obtain τ. We can therefore compute p_s and p_e, the probability that a slot contains a successful transmission, or that it is empty, respectively. We have $p_s = N\tau(1-\tau)^{N-1}$, and $p_e = (1-\tau)^N$. Let p_c denote the probability that a slot contains a collision. We have $p_c = 1 - p_e - p_s$. We now have enough information to compute the normalized throughput S of the network as

$$S = \frac{p_s D}{p_s T_s + p_c T_c + p_e \sigma}, \quad (10)$$

where D is the frame duration, T_s is the duration of a successful transmission, T_c is the duration of a collision, and σ is the time slot duration.

5. ENHANCEMENTS OF THE IEEE 1901 MAC FOR HIGH THROUGHPUT

As highlighted in Section 2, 1901 has the advantage over 802.11 in that it reacts pro-actively to collisions. However, it can be configured more efficiently for high throughput. We employ our model to examine 1901 configurations that perform close to an optimal MAC protocol. Our model adopts the same assumptions as other models investigating optimal versions of 802.11 [8].

In the following, we propose a configuration of the 1901 MAC parameters that drives the system to the optimal collision probability γ_{opt}. Specifically, γ_{opt} is the collision probability that maximizes the achievable throughput of the network, as computed by (10). The optimal transmission probability τ_{opt} is the one that achieves γ_{opt}. It is computed in [8] as

$$\tau_{opt} \approx \frac{1}{N}\sqrt{\frac{2\sigma}{T_c}}. \quad (11)$$

Using the above, the optimal collision probability is

$$\gamma_{opt} = 1 - (1-\tau_{opt})^{N-1} = 1 - \left(1 - \frac{1}{N}\sqrt{\frac{2\sigma}{T_c}}\right)^{N-1} \quad (12)$$

which, as N gets large, can be approximated[8] by

$$\gamma_{opt} \approx 1 - e^{-\sqrt{\frac{2\sigma}{T_c}}}. \quad (13)$$

Following the analysis in Section 4, γ can be obtained from the following fixed-point equation:

$$1 - (1-\gamma)^{1/(N-1)} = \frac{\mathbb{E}[R]}{\mathbb{E}[X]}. \quad (14)$$

[8]For the 1901 parameters (shown in Section 6), the approximation is good for $N \geq 3$.

We can re-write the right-hand side of (14) as

$$\frac{\mathbb{E}[R]}{\mathbb{E}[X]} = \frac{1}{(1-\gamma)^2 \sum_{k=0}^{\infty} \gamma^k BC_k}, \tag{15}$$

where BC_k is the average number of slots spent in backoff at the k-th transmission attempt. BC_k is the average number of slots in backoff stages where the station does not transmit plus the average number of slots in the backoff stage where the k-th transmission occurs. To compute BC_k, we make the following *key approximation*: We assume that if the expectation of the backoff counter at a given backoff stage is smaller than the average number of slots required to reach the deferral counter, then the backoff counter always expires before the deferral counter expires; conversely, we assume that the deferral counter expires otherwise.

The above approximation is necessary in order to come up with a configuration that is close to optimal for any number of stations. The key idea behind the proposed configuration is as follows. The expected value of the backoff counter does not depend on γ, whereas the average number of slots required for the deferral counter to expire is decreasing with γ. We set the expected value of the backoff counter to be equal to the average number of slots required for the deferral counter to expire at $\gamma = \gamma_{opt}$. Then, when $\gamma < \gamma_{opt}$, a station always transmits before the deferral counter expires (according to this approximation), thus increasing γ. Similarly, if $\gamma > \gamma_{opt}$, a station never transmits, and γ decreases. As a result, this configuration drives the system to operate at $\gamma = \gamma_{opt}$, which (as seen above) corresponds to the optimal operation independent of the number of stations. While there are other configurations that have been proposed to provide optimal performance [16, 13], these require to know the number of stations and thus, need to be adaptively adjusted as the number of active stations in the network changes.

At the k-th transmission attempt, there is a unique backoff stage where the transmission occurs, and there might be some backoff stages where the deferral counter expires. Let l be the backoff stage where the transmission occurs, at the k-th transmission attempt. Then, there is a set of backoff stages S_k for which the deferral counter expires. With our approximation mentioned above, BC_k is given by

$$BC_k \approx \sum_{i \in S_k} D_i + C_l, \tag{16}$$

where D_i is the average number of slots required for the deferral counter to expire at backoff stage i, C_l is the expectation of the backoff counter at stage l, and S_k is the set of backoff stages for which $D_i > C_i$ at the kth transmission attempt. For simplicity, here we restrict ourselves to configurations where $CW_i = 2^i CW_{min}$ for each backoff stage $0 \le i \le m-1$. At stage i, with a configuration CW_i and d_i, we have $C_i = (2^i CW_{min} + 1)/2$, and $D_i \approx (d_i + 1)/\gamma$, because D_i can be expressed as the average number of attempts to achieve $d_i + 1$ successes of an event with success probability γ.

Now, we address the issue of finding the configuration of CW_{min}, m and d_i to ensure that the solution of (14) corresponds to the optimal collision probability γ_{opt} of (13). To do this, we proceed as follows. First, we set d_i such that $D_i = C_i$ for $\gamma = \gamma_{opt}$. The rationale behind this is as follows: to force the solution of (14) to be at γ_{opt}, we need that the right-hand side of (14) to sharply decrease from a large to a small value at this point, so that the two curves cross at $\gamma = \gamma_{opt}$ for all N. Since increasing γ decreases D_i, and not C_i, if we set D_i such that with γ_{opt}, we have $D_i = C_i$, then for a smaller γ, D_i will be larger and the stations will be more likely to transmit. Otherwise, they will be more likely to defer. Indeed, if we force $D_i = C_i$ for $\gamma = \gamma_{opt}$, we obtain that $\mathbb{E}[R]/\mathbb{E}[X]$ sharply decreases from a maximum to a minimum value at $\gamma = \gamma_{opt}$, i.e.,

$$\frac{\mathbb{E}[R]}{\mathbb{E}[X]} \simeq \begin{cases} \tau_{max}, & \gamma \le \gamma_{opt}, \\ \tau_{min}, & \gamma > \gamma_{opt} \end{cases} \tag{17}$$

where τ_{min} is the value of $\mathbb{E}[R]/\mathbb{E}[X]$ given by our previous analysis of Section 4, which is minimized at $\gamma = 1$, and τ_{max} is the corresponding maximum value, at $\gamma = 0$. An illustration of our analysis is given in Figure 4.

Following the above, we need to enforce $D_i = C_i$, $0 \le i \le m-1$, which gives the configuration of d_i,

$$d_i = \left\lceil \gamma_{opt} \frac{2^i CW_{min} + 1}{2} - 1 \right\rceil, \tag{18}$$

where the ceiling is used to avoid negative values of d_0.

The remaining challenge is to configure CW_{min}, and m. To ensure that the curve $1-(1-\gamma)^{1/(N-1)}$ crosses $\mathbb{E}[R]/\mathbb{E}[X]$ at $\gamma = \gamma_{opt}$, we need that τ_{max} be sufficiently large so that even with small N the curve is crossed at this point and, conversely, that τ_{min} be sufficiently small for large N.

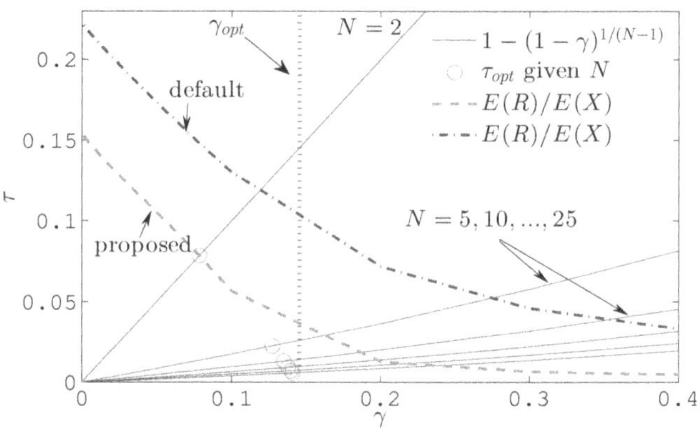

Figure 4: The analysis used for our enhancements. τ is plotted as a function of γ. The fixed-point is the intersection of $1-(1-\gamma)^{1/(N-1)}$ and $G(\gamma) = \mathbb{E}[R]/\mathbb{E}[X]$. We plot $1-(1-\gamma)^{1/(N-1)}$ for various number of stations N, and show $G(\gamma)$ for both the 1901 CA1 configuration, and our proposed enhancement from (18), (19) for $m = 6$. Finally, we also show γ_{opt} (obtained from (13)), and the corresponding τ_{opt} (obtained from (11)). Observe that the default 1901 configurations yield fixed-points having large collision probabilities. By contrast, our proposed 1901 configurations yield fixed-points that are much closer to τ_{opt}.

To guarantee that τ_{max} is sufficiently large even for $N = 2$, the CW at backoff stage 0, CW_{min}, needs to be as small as the optimal CW for $N = 2$. Accordingly, we set CW_{min} equal to the optimal CW value for $N = 2$ as if CW was constant, which gives $\gamma_{opt} = \tau = 2/(CW_{min} + 1)$, i.e.,

$$CW_{min} = \left\lfloor \frac{2}{1 - e^{-\sqrt{\frac{2\sigma}{T_c}}}} - 1 \right\rfloor. \tag{19}$$

Finally, we need to ensure that τ_{min} is sufficiently small for a large number of stations. Therefore, m should be sufficiently large. Following this, we choose the configuration $m = 6$; with this setting for m, the resulting τ_{min} is sufficiently small to ensure that $\tau = 1 - (1 - \gamma)^{1/(N-1)}$ crosses $\mathbb{E}[R]/\mathbb{E}[X]$ close to $\gamma = \gamma_{opt}$ even for N as large as 30.

Figure 4 shows the point of operation resulting from our configuration as well as the default one, given by the intersection between the curves $1-(1-\gamma)^{1/(N-1)}$ and $\mathbb{E}[R]/\mathbb{E}[X]$. While according to our approximation $\mathbb{E}[R]/\mathbb{E}[X]$ should decrease sharply at $\gamma = \gamma_{opt}$, in reality this decrease is much smoother due to the randomness associated to the deferral and backoff counters. Despite this, our configuration is still much closer to γ_{opt} (and hence to the point of optimal performance) than the default configuration.

6. PERFORMANCE EVALUATION

In this section, we present our experimental and simulation settings, and evaluate the performance of our proposed 1901 configurations. Using experimental results from a HomePlug AV and WiFi testbed, we show how throughput is affected by the number of stations in practice for these two MAC layers. We then validate our simulator using testbed experiments. Finally, we evaluate our 1901 configurations proposed in Section 5 and we observe that they perform similar to an optimally-configured 802.11 (which would be aware of the number of stations).

6.1 Experimental Setup and MAC Overhead

We built a test-bed of 8 stations, each comprising a Homeplug AV interface (a miniPCI card with Intellon INT6300 chip), and a 802.11n interface (a miniPCI card Atheros DNMA-92). The stations are Alix boards running the OpenWrt Linux distribution [6]. We conduct our testbed experiments with the default configuration of 1901 (i.e., CA1). Unfortunately, the firmware of all HomePlug devices is encrypted, and parameters such as the CW_i's and the d_i's are firmware based and they cannot be modified. So far, vendors have not released any information on how to modify these values[9].

Both WiFi and 1901 MAC layers introduce some overhead, due to backoff delays, headers, preambles, acknowledgments and inter-frame spaces. In addition, 1901 devices are subject to an additional overhead, due to the presence of management messages (MMEs). These MMEs are required for updating the modulation schemes between any two communicating stations. Both 802.11n and HomePlug AV use OFDM at the PHY layer. The difference between the two is that in 802.11n all carriers use the same modulation scheme, which is defined by the MCS index in the frame header [5], whereas in HomePlug AV each carrier can employ a different scheme, because different frequencies experience variable attenuation. As a result, the HomePlug AV stations have to exchange MMEs that indicate the modulation per carrier (917 carriers in total), and the receiver has to update the transmitter with this information each time the channel conditions (bit error rate) change [7]. The MMEs are sent with priority CA2/CA3 and they also use CSMA/CA and consume backoff time. The exact amount of messages exchanged is not specified in the standard and depends on the implementation.

We now conduct some experiments to measure MAC and MMEs overheads when the number of stations N varies. In particular, we consider N stations, with $1 \leq N \leq 7$, that send saturated UDP traffic using `iperf` to the same non-transmitting station. The stations are plugged to the same power-strip in order to avoid external interference and study the PLC MAC in isolation. We use the PLC tool `faifa` [2] to get the relevant statistics from the PLC interfaces. The guidelines to reproduce all the testbed measurements of this work are presented in [22]. Figure 5 shows the throughputs obtained with 802.11 and 1901, and the 1901 MME overhead (measured by the fraction of management frames among all data frames sent). Both MACs follow relatively similar trends for throughput degradation when N grows. However, for $N \geq 3$, the MMEs overhead represents about 10% of all frames sent. Further, for $N = 1$, we can compute the MAC layer overhead by computing the ratio of received throughput at the MAC layer and the physical data rates used on the links. We observed similar overheads for WiFi (about 40%) and PLC (about 38%). The fact that the throughput degradation is similar for WiFi and PLC – even though PLC is subject to a significant MMEs overhead – suggests that the 1901 MAC is otherwise more efficient than 802.11. This efficiency is revealed by the introductory example of Figure 3, in which 1901 suffers from fewer collisions than 802.11. Our results also indicate that a significant fraction of the overhead in 1901 is specific to MMEs. As the channel conditions are ideal in our tests, we expect that this overhead is larger for lossy links or links with electrical devices creating impulsive noise.

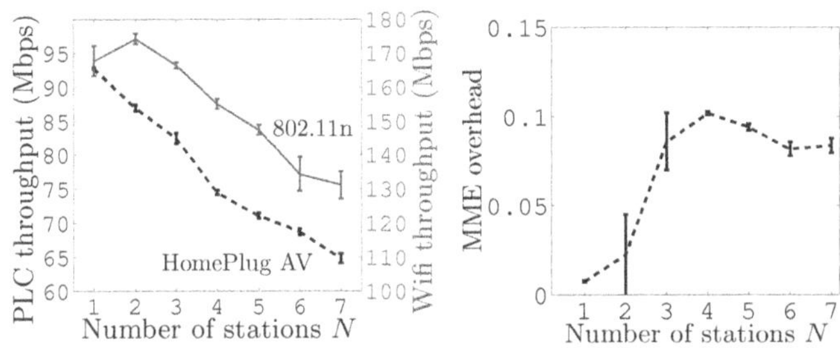

Figure 5: Total throughput of N saturated stations transmitting, for $1 \leq N \leq 7$, obtained by experiments with HomePlug AV and 802.11n devices (left), and MMEs overhead of the HomePlug AV tests (right). The measured physical rate for PLC is ~150 Mbps and for wireless ~300 Mbps. Both protocols include a large MAC overhead (about 40%), with HomePlug AV having the additional overhead of MMEs.

6.2 Simulator Validation - Model Evaluation

In this subsection, we validate our simulator with testbed experiments, and we evaluate our model using simulations. We use the collision probability and not throughput to verify our simulator, because we ignore overheads such as MMEs, as their arrival rate depends on the channel conditions and on the 1901 implementation. We compare the value of γ measured in the testbed with the value γ computed in simulation, and γ obtained by our model. To measure γ in testbed, we use the Atheros PLC toolkit [1] as explained in [22]. To simulate 1901, we wrote a Matlab simulator,

[9]For these reasons, we also wrote a Matlab simulator for 1901, which will be validated against experiments in the next subsection.

which implements the full CSMA/CA process of 1901 and is provided in [22]. Figure 6 shows the average collision probability obtained from 10 tests run as described in Section 6.1, and 10 simulation runs. We observe an excellent fit between the experiments and simulations. In addition, our model accurately predicts the collision probability.

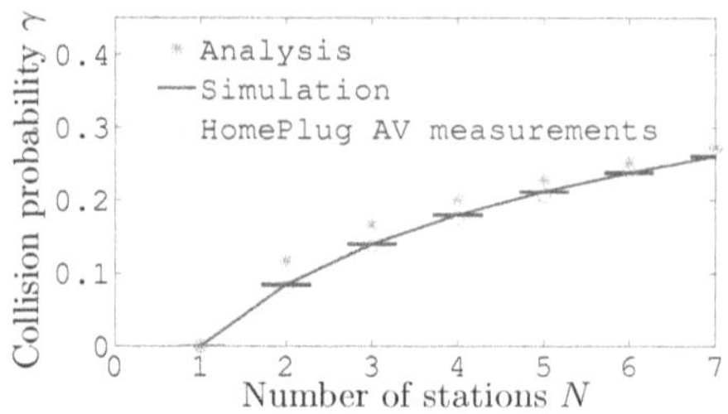

Figure 6: Collision probability obtained by simulation, our model of Section 4, and experiments with HomePlug AV devices.

We now present the normalized throughput obtained by our model and simulator. We ignore the bit loading of the frames, because in reality, the HomePlug AV physical rate varies in intervals of few ms [7]. We do not consider these rates as we propose later a MAC enhancement that can be used for different data-rate HomePlug specifications, since they all employ the same CSMA/CA process. To simulate the 1901 CSMA/CA method, we use the time slot duration and timing parameters as specified in the standard (see Table 2). A PLC frame transmission is preceded by two priority tone slots (PRS) and a preamble (P), and is followed by a response inter-frame space ($RIFS$), the ACK, and finally, the contention inter-frame space ($CIFS$). A PLC frame has a duration D. Thus, a successful transmission has a duration $T_s = 2PRS + P + D + RIFS + ACK + CIFS$. In case of a collision, the stations differ their transmission for $EIFS$ μs, where $EIFS$ is the extended inter-frame space used by 1901. Hence, a collision has a duration $T_c = EIFS$.

Parameter	Duration (μs)
Slot σ, Priority slot PRS	35.84
$CIFS$, $RIFS$	100.00
Preamble P, ACK	110.48
Frame duration D	2050.00
$EIFS$	2920.64

Table 2: Simulation parameters.

Figure 7 presents simulations of 1901 with the default parameters for the two priority classes CA1 and CA3 (CA0 and CA2 are equivalent). We show the normalized throughput of the network obtained by (10) and the collision probability predicted by our model.

We observe a good fit between analysis and simulation, especially when N is not too small, or when the CA2/CA3 priorities are used. The fact that the accuracy is somewhat reduced for small N in CA0/CA1 priorities is due to the decoupling assumption, which fails to capture the coupling introduced by the deferral counter. In [19], we study this coupling and we propose a different (and more complex) model that does not invoke the decoupling assumption and has a better accuracy.

6.3 Enhancement of the IEEE 1901 MAC

We now evaluate the enhancements proposed in Section 5. Given the parameters of Table 2 and using (18) and (19),

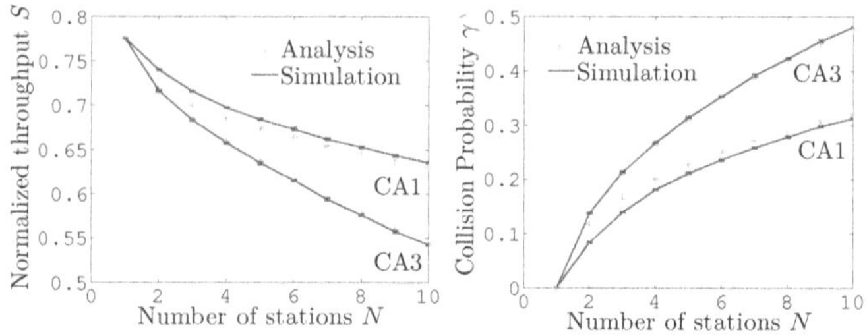

Figure 7: Performance metrics obtained by simulation and with our model, for the default configurations of 1901 (given in Table 1).

the parameters of the enhanced 1901 are $CW_{min} = 12$ and $d_i = \{0, 1, 3, 7, 14, 27\}$ for each backoff stage, with $m = 6$. Remember that our simulator is validated by testbed results and that the enhancements consist simply in modifying the parameters of the protocol.

Figure 8 compares the performance of (i) 1901 using default CA1 configuration, (ii) 1901 using our proposed enhanced configurations mentioned above, and (iii) "optimal" 802.11 for a varying number of stations. For the "optimal" 802.11, CW_{min} is computed from the fixed-point equation for the transmission probability of the 802.11 MAC (see [8, 16]) given τ_{opt} in (11) and γ_{opt} in (12). It appears that 1901 with our proposed configurations performs similarly – or better than – the optimally-configured 802.11, which requires knowing the number of stations N. Furthermore, the proposed configurations drastically boost the efficiency of 1901.

In Figure 9, we show similar results, but using $m = 4$ instead of $m = 6$ for the number of backoff stages. Here too, our proposed configurations yield substantial improvements. These improvements can offer tens of Mpbs of throughput gain, given the data rate (up to 1Gpbs) of HomePlug AV2.

In order to evaluate the sensitivity to the proposed configuration, we have conducted some experiments in which we perturbed the configuration of the various parameters around the proposed setting. Qualitatively, the results of these experiments showed that: (i) the proposed configuration is quite robust, as small perturbations of the parameters do not yield significant changes in the resulting throughput; (ii) the d_i parameter is particularly robust, as changing its configuration does not result in any noticeable variation in performance; (iii) the CW_i parameter is also quite robust, although in this case it can be noticed that, when increasing this parameter, throughput (slightly) decreases for small N and increases for large N.

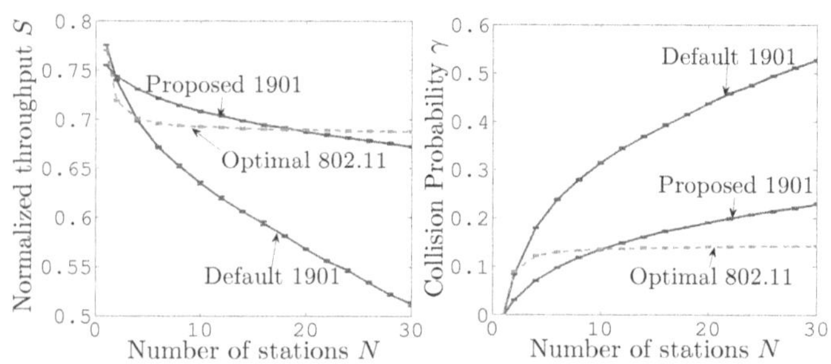

Figure 8: Simulations of 1901, enhanced 1901 proposed here, and optimal 802.11 for $m = 6$.

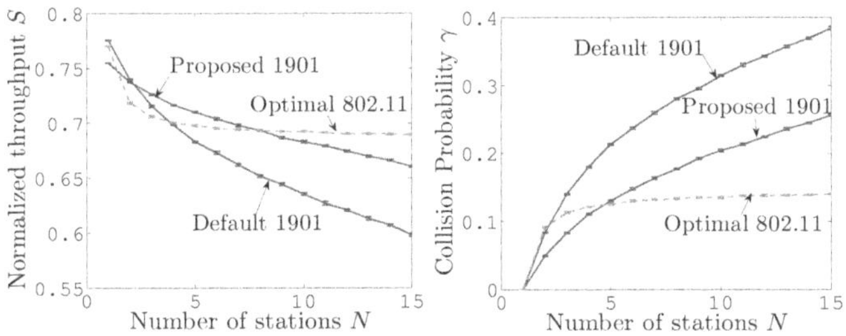

Figure 9: Simulations of 1901, enhanced 1901 proposed here, and optimal 802.11 for $m = 4$.

In the following subsections we discuss the impact of our proposed configuration on multiple contention domains and non-saturated stations scenarios.

6.4 Multiple Contention Domains

The performance of the 1901 MAC under multiple contention domain scenarios is quite different from the results presented in previous subsections. 1901 specifies an optional RTS/CTS mechanism, which is not enabled by default. Thus, without this mechanism, the performance degrades in scenarios such as hidden nodes. Our proposed configuration does not solve such performance issues, but it attenuates their effects as it uses larger a contention window than the default one (see [18] for a similar analysis in an optimal 802.11 approach). Note that the deferral counter is not triggered if two interfering stations are hidden to each other.

6.5 Saturated and Non-Saturated Stations

We now evaluate the performance of our proposed configurations in a mixed scenario of both saturated and non-saturated stations. The non-saturated stations have Poisson traffic with arrival rate λ. Figure 10 presents the normalized throughput for a scenario where half of the stations are saturated and half are not. Also, it depicts the same metric under a scenario where only 3 stations are saturated, whereas the number of non-saturated stations varies. We observe that under these scenarios, our proposed configurations perform better than the optimal 802.11 and the default 1901.

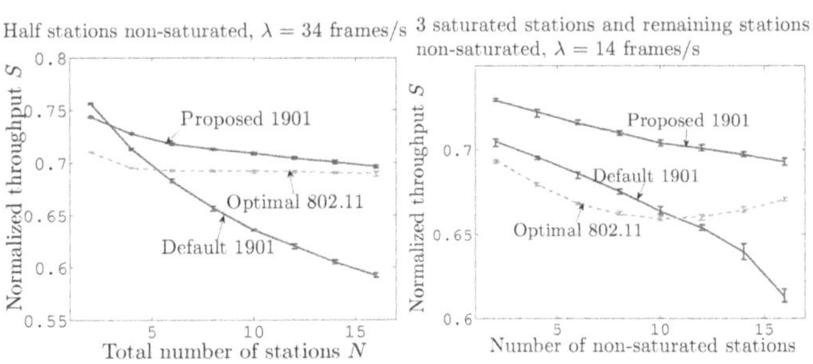

Figure 10: Simulations of 1901, enhanced 1901 proposed here, and optimal 802.11 for $m = 6$, in scenarios that include non-saturated stations.

7. CONCLUSIONS

The MAC layer of 1901 can react to contention with a fine granularity and without involving collisions, which offers the potential of strong gains in terms of throughput as compared to 802.11. Unfortunately, with the default parameter setting of 1901, the protocol operates far from optimality and does not fully exploit its potential. We believe that the cause of this is the lack of a simple model of 1901 that can be leveraged to find an appropriate setting of its parameters. Indeed, despite the commercial success of IEEE 1901 and its wide adoption in home networks, this protocol has remained largely unexplored by the research community.

One of the main challenges to model 1901 is the complexity of the protocol, which has a very large state-space. To reduce the state-space and come up with a simple model, we make the assumption that the backoff processes of the stations are independent. Building on the resulting model, we derive a procedure to steer the network towards its optimal point of operation. With this, we obtain a protocol that provides performance close to optimal independently of the number of stations, which is a result that has been long pursued by the research community.

Our proposal consists in only modifying some existing parameters, and does not require to change the CSMA/CA 1901 algorithm itself. Therefore, it can be easily incorporated into practical deployments. Our simulations confirm the drastic performance improvements. Moreover, we employed testbed measurements to validate our results and investigate MAC overheads of 1901 implementations.

Appendix

LEMMA 3. *Let B_i be the expected number of backoff slots between two transmissions attempts of a station that always remains at backoff stage i. Then, B_i is given by $bc_i/t_i - 1$, and B_i is an increasing function of γ for any i.*

PROOF. By its definition, B_i is given recursively by

$$B_i = \frac{d_i(d_i+1)}{2CW_i} + \sum_{j=d_i+1}^{CW_i-1} \frac{j(1-x_j^i) + \sum_{k=d_i+1}^{j}(k+B_i)(x_k^i - x_{k-1}^i)}{CW_i} \qquad (20)$$

Now observe that solving (20) over B_i, gives $B_i = bc_i/t_i - 1$, with bc_i and t_i given by (2) and (4).

To prove the second part of the lemma, we proceed as follows. (i) First, we compute $dB_i/d\gamma$. (ii) Second, we show that this derivative is positive at $\gamma = 1$. (iii) Third, we show that if the derivative is negative at some $0 < \gamma^* < 1$, it will also be negative at any value $\gamma > \gamma^*$. The proof then follows by contradiction: if the derivative was negative at some γ^*, it would also be negative at $\gamma = 1$, which would contradict our result (ii).

(i) After rearranging terms, (20) can be recast as

$$B_i = \frac{CW_i - 1}{2} + \frac{1}{CW_i} \sum_{j=d_i+1}^{CW_i-1} \left(B_i x_j^i - \sum_{k=d_i+1}^{j-1} x_k^i \right). \qquad (21)$$

The derivative of B_i can be computed as

$$\frac{dB_i}{d\gamma} = \sum_{k=d_i+1}^{CW_i-1} \frac{\partial B_i}{\partial x_k^i} \frac{\partial x_k^i}{\partial \gamma}. \qquad (22)$$

The partial derivative $\partial B_i / \partial x_k^i$ can be computed from (21) as

$$\frac{\partial B_i}{\partial x_k^i} = \frac{B_i - (CW_i - 1 - k)}{CW_i} + \frac{\partial B_i}{\partial x_k^i} \sum_{j=d_i+1}^{CW_i-1} \frac{x_j^i}{CW_i}, \qquad (23)$$

which yields

$$\frac{dB_i}{d\gamma} = \frac{\sum_{k=d_i+1}^{CW_i-1} (B_i - (CW_i - 1 - k)) \frac{\partial x_k^i}{\partial \gamma}}{CW_i - \sum_{j=d_i+1}^{CW_i-1} x_j^i}. \quad (24)$$

To compute $\partial x_k^i / \partial \gamma$, we observe that x_k^i is the complementary cumulative function of a binomial distribution. By taking its partial derivative, we obtain

$$\frac{\partial x_k^i}{\partial \gamma} = \frac{k!}{(k - d_i - 1)! d_i!} \gamma^{d_i} (1 - \gamma)^{k - d_i - 1}. \quad (25)$$

(ii) Next, we show that $dB_i/d\gamma > 0$ at $\gamma = 1$. At $\gamma = 1$, we have $B_i = CW_i - d_i/2 - 1$ from (20). Substituting in (24) yields $dB_i/d\gamma = d_i/2 + 1$, i.e., $dB_i/d\gamma > 0$.

(iii) Next, we show that if $dB_i/d\gamma$ is negative at some value γ^*, then it is also negative for any $\gamma > \gamma^*$. Observe that in (24) some terms are negative for $k < CW_i - 1 - B_i$. Let us assume that the derivative is negative at γ^*. Then, for some $\gamma = \gamma^* + \epsilon$, $\epsilon > 0$ we have $B_i(\gamma) < B_i(\gamma^*)$. This implies that in (24) some of the terms that were positive with $\gamma = \gamma^*$ become negative for $\gamma = \gamma^* + \epsilon$. Furthermore, from (25) we have that

$$\frac{\partial x_k^i / \partial \gamma}{\partial x_{k-1}^i / \partial \gamma} = \frac{k}{k - d_i - 1} (1 - \gamma). \quad (26)$$

Thus, in (24) the relative weight of the negative terms increases and that of the positive terms decreases. From the above, if $dB_i/d\gamma$ was negative at any γ^*, it would also be negative for all $\gamma > \gamma^*$. Since this contradicts result (ii), we conclude that $dB_i/d\gamma \geq 0$ for $\gamma \in [0, 1]$. □

COROLLARY 1. *B_i is a strictly increasing sequence of i if $CW_{i+1} \geq 2CW_i - d_i - 1$, $0 \leq i < m - 1$.*

PROOF. By Lemma 3, the minimum value of B_{i+1} is $B_{i+1}^{min} = (CW_{i+1} - 1)/2$ at $\gamma = 0$, and the maximum value of B_i is $B_i^{max} = CW_i - d_i/2 - 1$ at $\gamma = 1$. Setting $CW_{i+1} \geq 2CW_i - d_i - 1$, yields $B_{i+1}^{min} \geq B_i^{max}$, hence $B_{i+1} > B_i$ for all $\gamma \in [0, 1]$. □

Acknowledgment

This work is financially supported by a grant of the Smart-World project of the Hasler Foundation, Bern, Switzerland.

8. REFERENCES

[1] Atheros Open Powerline Toolkit. https://github.com/qca/open-plc-utils.

[2] Faifa. http://github.com/ffainelli/faifa.

[3] HomePlug Alliance (retrieved 9/2014). www.homeplug.org/media/filer_public/e4/cb/e4cbfc97-5e5e-4df1-9625-c226df16c93f/connected_home_summits_2013.pdf.

[4] HomePlug Alliance (retrieved 9/2014). www.homeplug.org/news-events/member-pr/358/.

[5] IEEE 802.11n-2009-Amendment 5: Enhancements for Higher Throughput.

[6] OpenWrt. https://openwrt.org/.

[7] IEEE Standard for Broadband over Power Line Networks: Medium Access Control and Physical Layer Specifications. *IEEE Std 1901-2010*, 2010.

[8] G. Bianchi. Performance analysis of the IEEE 802.11 distributed coordination function. *Selected Areas in Communications, IEEE Journal on*, 2000.

[9] G. Bianchi, L. Fratta, and M. Oliveri. Performance evaluation and enhancement of the CSMA/CA MAC protocol for 802.11 wireless LANs. In *Personal, Indoor and Mobile Radio Communications, 1996. PIMRC'96., Seventh IEEE International Symposium on.*

[10] M. E. M. Campista, L. Costa, and O. Duarte. Improving the multiple access method of CSMA/CA home networks. In *Proc. CCNC*, 2006.

[11] C. Cano and D. Malone. On Efficiency and Validity of Previous Homeplug MAC Performance Analysis. *arXiv preprint arXiv:1401.6803*, 2014.

[12] M. Chung, M. Jung, T. Lee, and Y. Lee. Performance analysis of HomePlug 1.0 MAC with CSMA/CA. *Selected Areas in Communications, IEEE Journal on*, 24(7):1411–1420, 2006.

[13] E. Kriminger and H. Latchman. Markov chain model of homeplug CSMA MAC for determining optimal fixed contention window size. In *Power Line Communications and Its Applications (ISPLC), 2011 IEEE International Symposium on.*

[14] A. Kumar, E. Altman, D. Miorandi, and M. Goyal. New Insights From a Fixed-Point Analysis of Single Cell IEEE 802.11 WLANs. *Networking, IEEE/ACM Transactions on*, june 2007.

[15] M. Lee, R. E. Newman, H. A. Latchman, S. Katar, and L. Yonge. HomePlug 1.0 powerline communication LANs—protocol description and performance results. *International Journal of Communication Systems*, 16(5):447–473, 2003.

[16] P. P. Patras, A. Banchs, P. Serrano, and A. Azcorra. A control-theoretic approach to distributed optimal configuration of 802.11 WLANs. *Mobile Computing, IEEE Transactions on*, 10(6):897–910, 2011.

[17] A. Schwager. An Overview of the HomePlug AV2 Technology. *Journal of Electrical and Computer Engineering*, 2013.

[18] P. Serrano, P. Patras, A. Mannocci, V. Mancuso, and A. Banchs. Control theoretic optimization of 802.11 wlans: Implementation and experimental evaluation. *Computer Networks*, 57(1):258–272, 2013.

[19] C. Vlachou, A. Banchs, J. Herzen, and P. Thiran. On the MAC for Power-Line Communications: Modeling Assumptions and Performance Tradeoffs. In *IEEE International Conference on Network Protocols (ICNP)*, 2014.

[20] C. Vlachou, A. Banchs, J. Herzen, and P. Thiran. Performance Analysis of MAC for Power-line Communications. In *ACM Sigmetrics*, 2014.

[21] C. Vlachou, J. Herzen, and P. Thiran. Fairness of MAC protocols: IEEE 1901 vs. 802.11. In *2013 17th IEEE International Symposium on Power Line Communications and Its Applications.*

[22] C. Vlachou, J. Herzen, and P. Thiran. Simulator and Experimental Framework for the MAC of Power-Line Communications. Infoscience EPFL, Technical Report, 2014.

Filtering Noisy 802.11 Time-of-Flight Ranging Measurements

Andreas Marcaletti
ETH Zurich
Zurich, Switzerland

Maurizio Rea
ETH Zurich
Zurich, Switzerland

Domenico Giustiniano
IMDEA Networks Institute
Madrid, Spain

Vincent Lenders
Armasuisse
Thun, Switzerland

Aymen Fakhreddine
IMDEA Networks Institute &
UC3M
Madrid, Spain

ABSTRACT

Time-of-Flight (ToF) echo techniques have been proposed as a way to estimate the range between regular Wi-Fi stations. Recent works either did not address practical questions for deployability, or made evaluations in basic setups, or used advanced 802.11 hardware designs. We build an approach solely deployed using ToF measurements and relying on software access point (AP) upgrades of simple commercial off-the-shelf 802.11 chipsets. Our solution filters noisy measurements collected by WiFi chipsets of six dollars each, it has been tested across different and heterogeneous setups and testbeds, and has the potential to enable ToF ranging in every Wi-Fi chipsets.

Categories and Subject Descriptors

C.2.1 [**Computer-Communication Networks**]: Network Architecture and Design—*Wireless Communication*

Keywords

Indoor Localization; 802.11; Time of Flight; Design; Implementation; Evaluation

1. INTRODUCTION

In the attempt to find an alternative to error-prone signal-strength based ranging measurements [3, 5, 10, 13, 16], Time-of-Flight (ToF) echo techniques have recently received attention by the research community. The underlying principle of ToF is that the distance between two devices is estimated using the time that the signal travels between two devices, with the advantage of being much less susceptible to the diversity of the obstacles between the devices [8, 14]. The intuition is that electromagnetic waves travel at a speed that is close to the speed of light for most propagation media in typical indoor environments, and thus the signal propagation speed is fairly independent on the environment, obstacles, etc.

CoNEXT'14, December 2–5, 2014, Sydney, Australia.
Copyright 2014 ACM 978-1-4503-3279-8/14/12 ...$15.00.
http://dx.doi.org/10.1145/2674005.2674998.

Despite of these advantages, ToF measurements are very sensitive to noise since, at the speed of light, a measurement error of 1 μs already results in a distance estimation error of 300 meters. This noise is further exacerbated when using Commercial Off-The-Shelf (COTS) WiFi devices for a cost-effective and wide-spread implementation. Recent efforts could increase the accuracy of ToF at the cost of leveraging advanced hardware designs available in more recent WiFi chipsets [14]. However, most of the Access Points (APs) in the world are still deployed with older hardware, and it is economically not possible to change all the APs with newer hardware in the near future (and also not appealing in terms of electronic garbage).

We leverage the existing 802.11 protocol timing specification (and nothing more than that) to build a system that runs on COTS APs to estimate the distance to target stations. We rely on a customized firmware operating in the core of the 802.11 MAC state machine of a low-cost Wi-Fi chipset (cost per unit of less than six dollars). To deal with the intrinsic challenges of noisy ToF measurements, we develop an adaptive filter which manages to predict the distance despite the large noise introduced by the devices and the multipath reflections in indoor environments.

Our approach has been tested across various setups and testbeds. We show that our filtering technique needs just a few samples to estimate the distance range with a median error of 1.7 – 2.4 m and a 80-percentile error of 3.7 – 5.8 m, comparable to [14] (median error of ≈ 1 m and 80-percentile error of ≈ 5 m) that required advanced inputs from the hardware such as channel state information per antenna. Our solution further outperforms recent works such as [8].

Given its simplicity, the principles discussed in our work can be applied to any old and new 802.11 AP already deployed, just with software upgrades.

2. BACKGROUND AND CHALLENGES

This section describes the basics of WiFi ToF ranging and highlights various real-world challenges that arise when applying this technique with simple off-the-shelf devices.

2.1 WiFi ToF Ranging Technique

While traditional ToF-based echo techniques as employed in radar systems rely on uncoded RF signals and their reflections, WiFi echo techniques use regular frames of communication. In WiFi communication, every DATA frame is acknowledged by the receiver with an ACK frame. Since

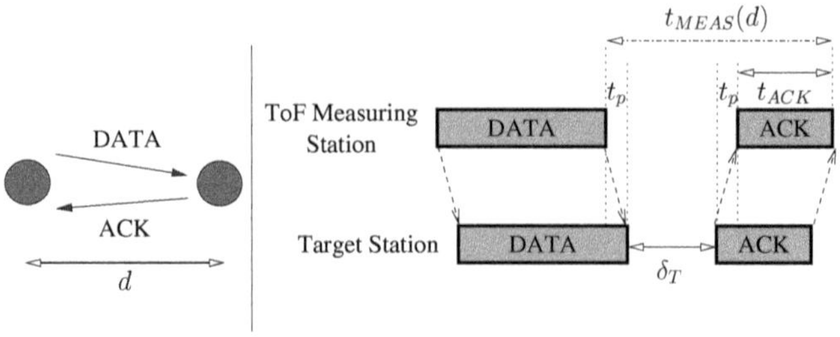

Figure 1: Principle of the Wi-Fi ToF echo technique. In the example, δ_T offset is originated at the target device, and it depends on the hardware delay to schedule the ACK at the target device. Not shown in the figure, time offset may be also generated at the measuring device.

the interframe time between the DATA and ACK frames is fixed by the 802.11 standard (the Short InterFrame Symbol, SIFS, time), the delay between DATA and ACK frames can be used to infer the distance between two nodes. However, ToF-based ranging estimation is affected by severe noise and has thus long been considered impracticable for WLAN localization. Back then, [12] suggested that the accuracy of spacing between a DATA and ACK frame that are defined to be separated by a SIFS time is up to 2 μs, equal to 600 m of error, and too high for indoor localization. However, the technique was studied in [6,9,11,15] (subjected to variable jitter and very high dispersion), and later refined in [7,8,14] showing that better accuracy is achievable than the wort-case bound dictated by the maximum SIFS tolerance.

ToF ranging can be formulated as follows. If d is the distance between a local station and a target, the measured time-of-flight $t_{MEAS}(d)$ between a sent DATA frame and a received ACK frame is expressed as

$$t_{MEAS}(d) = 2 \cdot t_P(d) + t_{ACK} + \delta, \tag{1}$$

where $t_P(d)$ is the signal propagation time between the transmitter of the DATA frame and the target (channel reciprocity is assumed), t_{ACK} is the time needed to transmit the ACK, δ is an offset depending on the target and local sender. The distance to the target device is then inferred as

$$\hat{d}_n = \frac{c}{2} \cdot (t_{MEAS}(d) - t_{ACK} - \delta), \tag{2}$$

where c is the speed of signal propagation which is close to the speed of light in air. Assuming that N consecutive samples $\{\hat{d}_n\}$ are collected, the distance between the local station and the mobile device is finally estimated as:

$$\hat{d} = f(\hat{d}_n), \tag{3}$$

where f is either the expected value on the input data or any other estimator.

Firmware integration. To alleviate any unnecessary source of noise or instability, the time measurements $t_{MEAS}(d)$ have to work as close as possible to the radio hardware. The best location to fully control the measurement is therefore in the firmware of the WiFi radio chipset, rather than in the driver as proposed in [8]. To measure $t_{MEAS}(d)$ in the firmware, we have customized the open-source 802.11 openFWWF firmware[1]. This firmware is written in assembler and runs on off-the-shelf 802.11 Broadcom chipsets, such as the ones widely used in Linksys APs. Our customized firmware reports $t_{MEAS}(d)$ for each successful transmission of an 802.11 DATA frame. The timing is regulated by the general purpose timer, running on the wireless card's internal clock at a rate of 88 MHz. The timer starts to count clock cycles just after the 802.11 processor sets up a register to indicate that a frame has been sent. Once the ACK frame has been received (or the ACK timeout has elapsed), another register is updated and the timer gets stopped. Every time a measurement is made, the firmware writes $t_{MEAS}(d)$ into a defined address of the shared memory (SHM). The measurement architecture is shown in Fig. 2. Since the driver has also access to the shared memory block, it can retrieve the measurement every time an ACK is received[2]. In the driver, we gather additional data about the incoming ACK such as the data rate, MAC addresses, etc, and store them all in a buffer. Once this buffer is full or a timeout elapsed, the data is transferred to the user space with the help of UDP sockets.

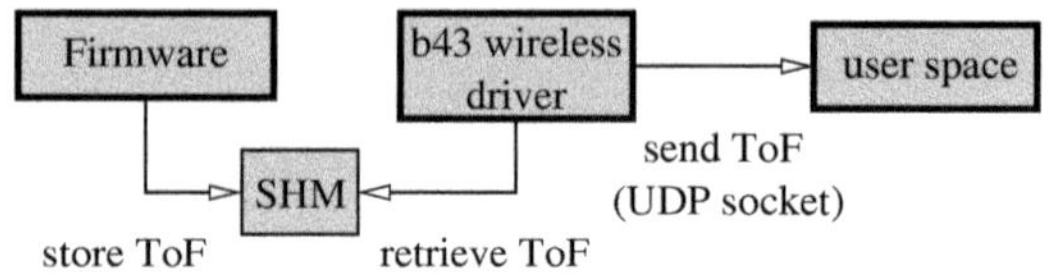

Figure 2: ToF measurement architecture. The figure shows the interaction between firmware, driver and user space. Measured data from the firmware is transferred to the driver through shared memory. Buffered ToF measurements are then sent to user space.

2.2 Real-world Challenges

In the real-world, ToF measurements are affected by large noise coming from the timing imprecision of off-the-shelf WiFi devices. The offset δ is given by:

$$\delta = \delta_T + \delta_L, \tag{4}$$

where δ_T and δ_L are the offsets of target station and local sender, respectively. In addition, the multipath signal propagation characteristics of complex indoor environments play an important role to ToF measurements. In the following, we describe the main sources of noise and how they affect the accuracy of ToF ranging.

Target and measuring noise. The 802.11 standard specifies the SIFS time between the reception of a DATA and the transmission of an ACK at the receiver as a fixed interval. In 802.11b, for example, this time is specified as 10 μs [2]. However a relatively high tolerance of 1 μs is tolerated which can result in significant noise and distance estimation errors up to 300 meters if the target would fully exploit this specified tolerance level. While most chipsets may not fully exploit this tolerance, the dispersion is still quite significant. To illustrate this, Fig. 3 on the left represents the resulting dispersion of a typical Broadcom WiFi chipset as target device. The shown histogram was obtained by estimating the distance $\hat{d}_n$ according to Eq. (2) for 10000 packets. To

[1]`http://www.ing.unibs.it/openfwwf/`

[2]We operate in promiscuous mode which allows us to know in the driver when an ACK has been received and thus a new data is available in the SHM.

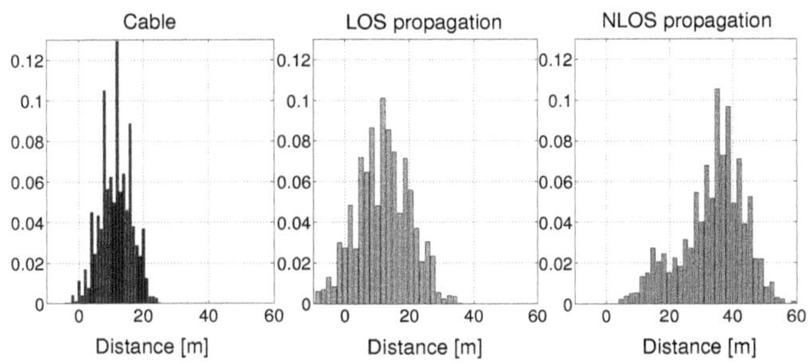

Figure 3: Noise introduced by ToF ranging. Tests with controlled environment (Cable) show that the there are sources of large dispersion in the estimation. Tests over the air (LOS and NLOS propagation) show that the distribution greatly depends on the channel conditions. All the tests are in addition subject to quantization noise and other spurious noise sources.

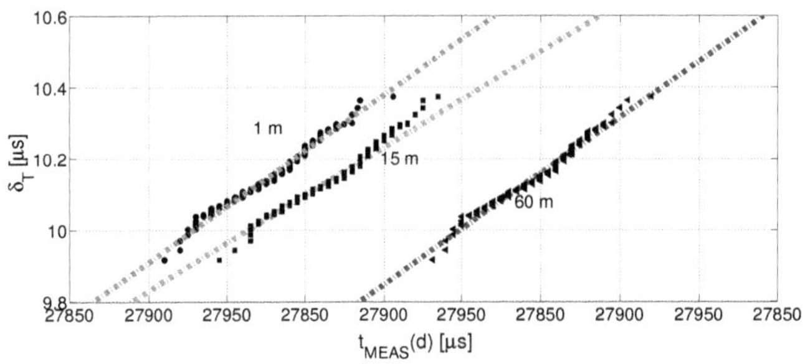

Figure 4: QQ plots for LOS links. The plots show that the error of the local offset has a negligible impact on the noise of $t_{MEAS}(d)$.

avoid any dispersion from environmental effects, the measurements were performed over a coaxial cable of 13.5 meters length. As we can see, there is heavy noise in the measurement setup that leads to distance estimations ranging from 0 to 25 meters.

Environmental noise. It is well known that signal propagation in complex indoor environments is subject to multipath effects in which multiple copies of the transmitted signal arrive at the receiver over different reflected paths. It is even possible that the direct component is entirely attenuated and the signal is received only over indirect paths. Since signals that travel over indirect paths will take longer to arrive at the receiver, they introduce an error in the distance estimation when considering the time-of-flight. This situation is shown in Fig. 3 in the middle and on the right where the same experiment as on the left was repeated but for a line-of-sight (LOS) and non-line-of-sight (NLOS) signal propagation link over omnidirectional antennas. The dispersion spans a range of 40 and 60 meters for the LOS and NLOS links respectively. In addition, the NLOS link shows a skewed distribution, suggesting that the signals are received from different propagation paths over the duration of the experiment. Multipath effects must therefore be taken into consideration in order not to overestimate the distance when dealing with reflected signal propagation paths. Finally, multipath may also happen in LOS links, and thus a method robust to the propagation conditions must be designed.

Additional sources of noise. Off-the-shelf WiFi chipsets have not been designed to provide accurate ToF measurements. Additional noise therefore comes from the coarse clock resolution of the radios. For example, the Broadcom chipset operates with a reference clock of 88 MHz, corresponding to a maximal distance resolution of 1.7 meters. In addition to this quantization noise, off-the-shelf chipsets introduce all sorts of considerable additional noise. As we could see in the histograms of Fig. 3, the shape of the distribution is far from being smooth despite using 10000 samples to create the histograms, suggesting that the radios must have some bias when measuring the time. The measurement noise must therefore also be factored in to estimate the distance.

3. TARGET AND MEASURING NOISE

To dissect the relative importance of the noise of the target station with respect to the local noise, we use a wideband oscilloscope (Infiniium 90000A Oscilloscope) with a fast sampling rate of 10 GS/s to measure the target offset δ_T. A horn antenna is connected to the oscilloscope which serves as a passband filter for the 2.4 GHz band. The target device is in close proximity to the horn antenna, so that radio signals of received 802.11 DATA and transmitted 802.11 ACK are immediately captured by the oscilloscope, and effects of signal reflections are minimized. The noise of our high-end oscilloscope can be regarded as low such that reported measurements are not affected by any measuring noise but dominated by the target noise [4].

We use above setup to statistically compare the effective ToF to the measured time $t_{MEAS}(d)$ as being locally reported by our firmware on the Broadcom chipset. To compare both distributions, we use the method of the quantile-quantile (QQ) plot. We collect samples in LOS settings at $d = \{1, 15, 60\}$ m. Results are summarized in Fig. 4. We observe a linear pattern, which indicates that the noise of the target station and the data measured locally by the 802.11 firmware have very similar distributions. Hence, the dispersion of the local offset has a negligible impact on the noise of $t_{MEAS}(d)$, and most of the dispersion comes from the target device. This further demonstrates that our approach to implement the ToF measurement in the firmware allows to minimize the impact of the local dispersion of the noise for LOS links with limited multipath. In the next section, we look at the impact of richer multipath.

4. ENVIRONMENTAL NOISE

Environmental noise is tricky to deal with. The reasons are the following:

- multipath reflections introduce a skewness of the sample distribution which cannot be easily smoothed out by averaging over a set of biased samples,
- the target noise introduces large offset noise which adds to the noise created by multipath,
- environmental noise is highly unpredictable as the reflected paths are location-specific.

We therefore need an adaptive filter that is calibrated to the actual multipath characteristics of the experienced location-specific environment.

Our goal is to design a filter that takes a series of N consecutive measurements $\{\hat{d}_1, \hat{d}_2, \ldots, \hat{d}_N\}$, and selects the p-percentile $\hat{d}(p)$ of the series that minimizes the estimation error. Intuitively, in absence of multipath, the median $p = 50$ could fairly represents the distance, while taking the median in presence of multipath reflections will cause an over-estimation of the distance due to the added traveled distance of the signals. By selecting a percentile $p < 50$ to estimate the distance, we can therefore counterbalance those biased values in the estimation process.

4.1 Data Integrity

First, to guarantee data integrity in our evaluation, we removed sequences of samples which experienced undesired side effects for a systematic evaluation. In particular, for statistical relevance of the results, consecutive ToF measurements are supposed to be independent and identically distributed (i.i.d.). While this assumption holds in most tests, this condition does not hold in general. We perform cable tests and they show that the autocorrelation is very low for lag greater than zero. We observe however that there are links with high autocorrelation when DATA is transmitted over the air. This could be explained with the presence of more than one path between transmitter and receiver, which may imply that the circuitry continuously jumps between two states in an attempt to tune the frame synchronization. We therefore discard those sequences which were subject to a high absolute lag-one autocorrelation (above 0.2) for the analysis. Removing measurements with a high autocorrelation is a valid assumption in the real-world as this kind of test can easily be performed by the AP.

4.2 Estimating Multipath Noise

The second step is to estimate the noise caused by multipath reflections on a link. Since we cannot directly measure the individual multipath components at the signal-level on off-the-shelf WiFi radios, we propose to use a higher-level estimator f for this. We explored various options in an extensive evaluation in one of our testbeds (Testbed I, Fig. 7) with all links with low lag-one autocorrelation (83% of the links). As estimators, we considered the first three moments (median, standard deviation, and skewness) for the ToF as well as for the Received Signal Strength Indicator (RSSI). For each of these six estimators, we evaluate two variants, leading to a total of twelve candidate estimators. In the first variant, we determine the moments directly on the raw samples. In the second variant, we attempt to pre-filter obvious outliers that arise from the device-related measurement noise prior determining the moments. These outliers are filtered out applying the Thompson Tau technique, a statistical method for deciding whether to keep or discard samples based on the expected value and the expected deviation of the sequence of samples.

We evaluate the precision of these estimators by determining their correlation to the optimal percentile p_{opt}, defined as the percentile that provides the minimum absolute distance estimation error as:

$$p_{opt} = \underset{0 \leq p \leq 0.5}{\text{argmin}}\, |d - \hat{d}(p)| \qquad (5)$$

	unfiltered	pre-filtered
median of RSSI	0.62	0.63
standard deviation of RSSI	0.04	0.05
skewness of RSSI	0.23	0.24
median of ToF	0.76	0.76
standard deviation of ToF	0.19	0.21
skewness of ToF	0.20	0.51

Table 1: Absolute value of Pearson correlation coefficient between different moments of the RSSI and ToF versus the optimal percentile p_{opt} (0=no correlation, 1=maximal correlation).

that is, the a-posteriori optimal percentile for each link given the true distance of each link in our experiments.

To quantify the correlation between the different moments and p_{opt}, we use the Pearson correlation coefficient on the entire set of links of Testbed I. The Pearson correlation coefficient is an indicator of the linear correlation of the variables, where absolute values close to zero indicate a low correlation and absolute values close to one represent a high linear dependence of two variables. A value close to one thus indicates that a moment is a good estimator to predict a percentile that will filter out the multipath noise effectively.

Table 1 shows the resulting correlation coefficient for all twelve variants. The best correlation is provided by the median of the ToF, followed by the median of the RSSI and the skewness of the ToF. All other moments have a correlation coefficient below 0.5 which indicates a low correlation. Most of the moments profit from pre-filtering to remove the outliers. In particular, the skewness of the ToF increases from 0.20 to 0.51 and is therefore considerably better when pre-filtering the outliers.

One may wonder why the skewness of the ToF has a worse correlation than the median ToF. Intuitively, the skewness of the distribution should be a good indicator of the multipath, given that links with strong reflected (delayed) components are left-skewed, with p_{opt} smaller than for right-skewed link. Our results suggest that the combined device-related noise of the receiver and the measuring station have a strong negative effect on the correlation on the skewness. This is reflected in the pre-filtered version of the skewness which has a considerably better correlation than the unfiltered version. In contrast, the median of the ToF is much more robust to this device-related noise and therefore outperforms the skewness. In addition, it reflects the tendency of having more links affected by multipath for longer distances.

4.3 Filter Design

Motivated by the good correlation of the median ToF and the optimal percentile, we designed a filter that relies on this correlation to select an appropriate percentile of the sample ToF measurements when estimating the distance. The filter relies on a linear model which is derived from the empirical distribution of the median ToF versus p_{opt}. We call it offline calibration, since it would be usually performed before actual tests. This distribution on all the 207 links of Testbed I is shown in the top of Fig. 5. We note that the value of the optimal percentile is widely distributed between $0 \leq p_{opt} \leq$ 50%. Therefore, it does not exist one value of percentile

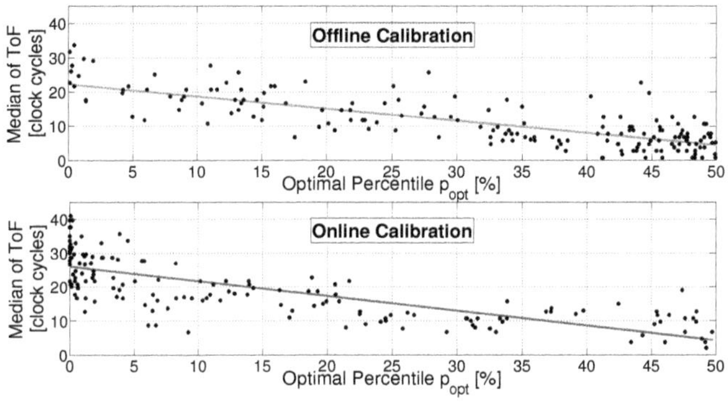

Figure 5: Median ToF versus optimal percentile p_{opt} for all links of Testbed I - Offline and online calibration.

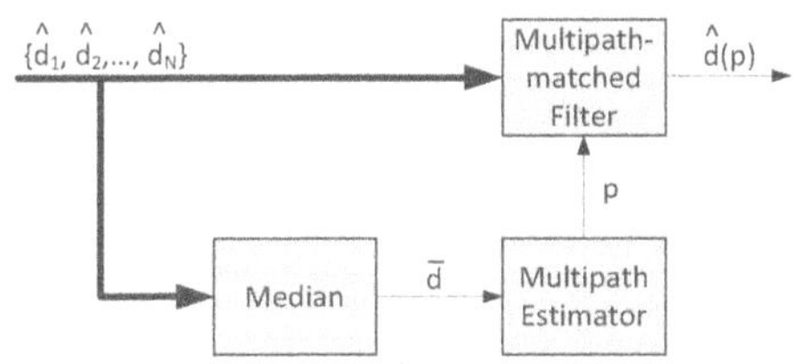

Figure 6: Adaptive filter design.

p that it is optimal, but it rather changes from link to link. We therefore perform a linear regression on these data points and obtain the linear link-dependent model, as represented by the continuous line in the figure. Since the correlation coefficient of the median ToF versus the optimal percentile is not improved by pre-filtering outliers, we apply this model on the raw, unfiltered samples. (For the estimator based on the skewness of ToF we instead use the pre-filtered version).

Since it is desirable to avoid offline calibration, we then run the same methodology measuring the median ToF between pairs of APs, which can be performed online (as long as the distance between APs is known a priori). The results are shown in the bottom of Fig. 5. We find that the calibration results in a very similar linear regression.

We illustrate our filter design in Fig. 6. In practice, our filter works as follows. For a given series of N consecutive measurements $\{\hat{d}_1, \hat{d}_2, \ldots, \hat{d}_N\}$, we first determine the median ToF, $\bar{d}$. The median ToF is then used to estimate the amount of multipath using a linear model. The output of the estimator is the percentile value p. We apply linear interpolation to the sequence of measurements $\{\hat{d}_1, \hat{d}_2, \ldots, \hat{d}_N\}$ and select the p-percentile $\hat{d}(p)$ of the series that minimizes the error.

5. EVALUATION METHODOLOGY

This section presents the system and environmental setup we used to evaluate the performance of our filter.

5.1 System Setup

AP infrastructure. We have build a prototype ToF system to evaluate its performance in real-world conditions. Our system is based on COTS APs from Soekris (net5501 embedded machine with a 500 MHz AMD Geode LX single chip processor). The APs are equipped with Broadcom AirForce54G 4318 mini PCI type III cards which we operate with our customized firmware and b43 driver presented in Section 2.1. As operating system on the APs we use Ubuntu server 10.04 with a Linux kernel version 2.6.32.60. In order to operate the embedded device as WLAN AP, we use the software suite hostapd. The APs are connected to the central localization unit over Gigabit Ethernet.

Target devices. As target devices we use Dell Inspiron 5150 laptops equipped with Broadcom AirForce54G 4318 mini PCI type III cards. The operating system on the laptops is Ubuntu 10.04 with its original Linux kernel version 2.6.32-21.32. The wireless cards are operated in client mode.

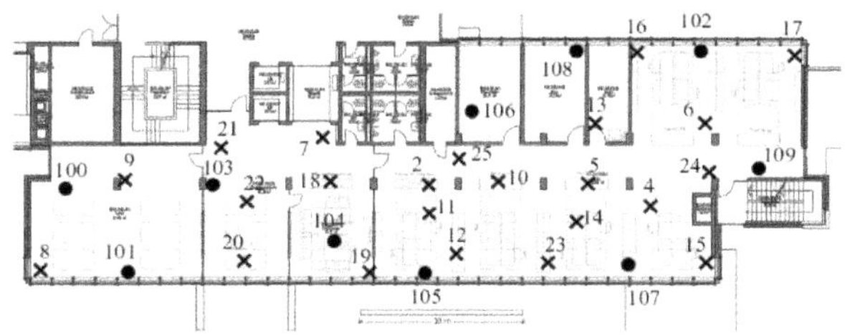

Figure 7: Testbed I. Circles correspond to AP locations and crosses to target locations.

5.2 Deployment Scenarios

Testbed deployment. We perform experiments in three indoor testbeds deployed in different environments. We deploy 10 APs in Testbed I and III and 9 APs in Testbed II. Testbed I and Testbed II are office environments. The environment of Testbed I is shown in Fig. 7 and it covers a surface of almost 1000 m^2. We use 25 randomly selected locations (marked with a cross) to test our algorithms. We conducted tests over two different days, with some position repeated again with different location of some furniture, and collected a total of 207 wireless links. Testbed II features 180 links and it covers a smaller space of around 200 m^2. The target station is in 20 different positions. Testbed III has been deployed at the facilities of the IEEE/ACM IPSN Microsoft Indoor Localization Competition [1]. The testbed features 200 links and it covers 320 m^2. The target device is placed at 20 different positions across two rooms and a hallway.

In all the testbeds there exists a mixture of line-of-sight and non-line-of-sight wireless links. The testbeds also contain several propagation obstructions, including concrete walls, tables and glasses. All experiments are conducted with other active WLAN networks. We operate the three testbeds on a fixed frequency channel of the 2.4 GHz ISM band. The PHY automatic selection rate is active, such that the measurements include probes sent at different rates.

6. EVALUATION RESULTS

This section evaluates the performance of different ranging estimators in our testbeds.

6.1 Filter Performance

Distance Ranging Accuracy. To test our filter, we have evaluated its performance on all the links of Testbed I. For each link, we first compute the distance estimation error with 20 samples, and then calculate the average error

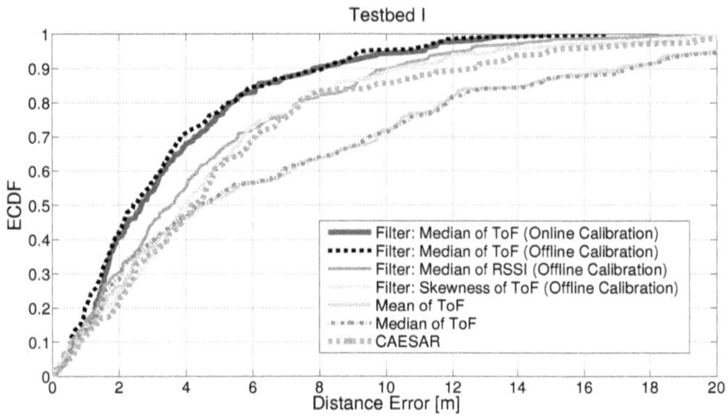

Figure 8: ECDF of the distance estimation error for our adaptive filter compared to other schemes (Testbed I). For each scheme, we use sequences of 20 samples.

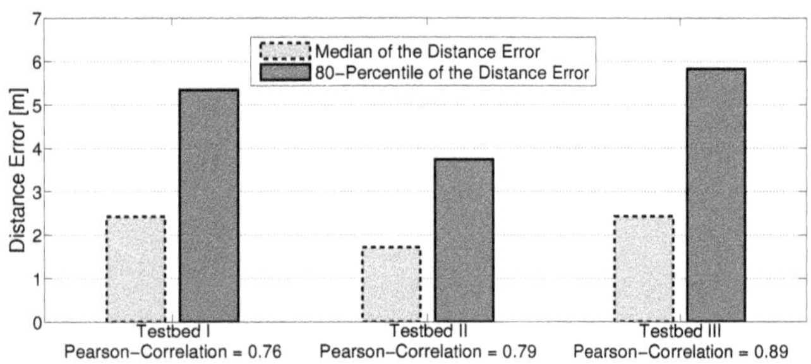

Figure 9: Performance in the three different testbeds.

using 500 sequences. We consider our filter that uses the median ToF to estimate the optimal percentile, and two other versions of the filter that rely on the median of the RSSI (pre-filtered) and the skewness of the ToF (pre-filtered), as they provided the second- and third-best correlation coefficients in Section 4.2. In addition, we also provide the error for naive approaches such as the mean and median of the ToF (without any filter).

Figure 8 shows the Empirical Cumulative Distribution Function (ECDF) of the distance ranging error. Our three new estimators clearly outperform the mean or the median. The mean and median have roughly equal estimation error. Their median error is approximately 4.5 m and the 80-percentile error is approximately 11.8 m. The error of the filter that uses the median RSSI slightly outperforms the skewness of the ToF. This is not surprising since Table 1 shows a higher correlation coefficients of the filter with median RSSI. The best performance is achieved with our filter using the median ToF. In Testbed I, we obtain a median error of 2.4 m and a 80-percentile error of 5.3 m.

Comparison with [8]. Fig. 8 also shows that our three estimators outperform CAESAR, introduced in [8], which achieves a median error of 4.3 m and a 80-percentile error of 7.4 m. Our evaluation of CAESAR is also very consistent to the one recently presented in the indoor evaluation of [14].

Online calibration. We then compare online versus offline environmental calibration for the filter of median of

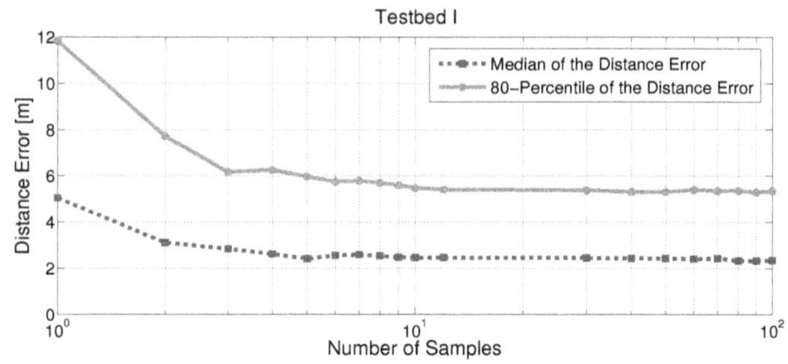

Figure 10: Median and 80-percentile error of our estimator that filters the noise based on the median of ToF. Results are provided for different number of samples.

ToF (similar results are achieved with our other filters). As reported in Fig. 8, the online calibration achieves similar results with respect to the offline tests, with median error of 2.6 m and a 80-percentile error of 5.4 m. Thus, the environmental calibration can be executed online without significant performance loss.

Robustness to different environments/testbeds. Fig. 9 shows the median and 80-percentile of the distance error for the three different testbeds using sequences of 20 samples. As shown in the x-label of the figure, we measure a high Pearson correlation coefficient between the median of ToF and the optimal percentile (0.76 – 0.89). The median distance error is in the range 1.7 – 2.4 m and the 80-percentile error is in the range 3.7 – 5.8 m. Concluding, the estimator is robust across different environments.

Impact of Number of ToF Samples. A further parameter we evaluate with regard to our filter is the number of ToF measurement samples N that are used for the estimation of the distance. Figure 10 shows the error for our filter that relies on the median of the ToF as a function of the number of samples. It is remarkable that the error is stable with five or more samples for the median of the distance error, and with ten or more samples for the 80-percentile of the distance error.

7. CONCLUSION

We have designed a cost-effective ranging technique such that it does not require any special hardware, special antennas, or software-defined radio architectures. Our solution can be deployed as a software upgrade to current WLAN infrastructures. While our best performing estimator may be a bit counter-intuitive, we have shown its robust performance in a variety of different setups and testbeds. Since ToF-based WLAN localization is still at its infancy, we believe that further research in this area might help to even further improve the accuracy of our results in the future.

Acknowledgments

We are grateful to Francesco Gringoli for sharing the openFWWF code and supporting the project with his enlightening comments. The work was supported by Armasuisse. The research leading to these results has received funding from the European Research Council under the EU's Seventh Framework Programme, ERC Grant Agreement no. 617721.

8. REFERENCES

[1] Microsoft indoor localization competition, http://research.microsoft.com/en-us/events/ipsn2014indoorlocalizatinocompetition/.

[2] IEEE std 802.11-2012 (revision of IEEE std 802.11-2007), IEEE standard for information technology, 2012.

[3] BAHL, P., AND PADMANABHAN, V. RADAR: an in-building RF-based user location and tracking system. In *Proc. IEEE INFOCOM'00* (Mar. 2000).

[4] BOURCHAS, T., BEDNAREK, M., GIUSTINIANO, D., AND LENDERS, V. Poster abstract: Practical limits of wifi time-of-flight echo techniques. In *Proceedings of the 13th International Symposium on Information Processing in Sensor Networks* (Piscataway, NJ, USA, 2014), IPSN '14, IEEE Press, pp. 273–274.

[5] CHINTALAPUDI, K., PADMANABHA IYER, A., AND PADMANABHAN, V. N. Indoor localization without the pain. In *In Proc. of ACM MobiCom '10* (2010), pp. 173–184.

[6] CIURANA, M., BARCELO-ARROYO, F., AND IZQUIERDO, F. A ranging system with IEEE 802.11 data frames. In *Radio and Wireless Symposium, 2007 IEEE* (2007), pp. 133–136.

[7] GALLO, P., GARLISI, D., GIULIANO, F., GRINGOLI, F., AND TINNIRELLO, I. WMPS: A positioning system for localizing legacy 802.11 devices. In *Transactions on Smart Processing and Computing,* (October 2012).

[8] GIUSTINIANO, D., AND MANGOLD, S. CAESAR: carrier sense-based ranging in off-the-shelf 802.11 wireless lan. CoNEXT '11, ACM, p. 10.

[9] GOLDEN, S. A., AND BATEMAN, S. S. Sensor measurements for Wi-Fi location with emphasis on time-of-arrival ranging. *IEEE Trans. Mobile Comput. 6*, 10 (Oct. 2007), 1185–1198.

[10] GOSWAMI, A., ORTIZ, L. E., AND DAS, S. R. Wigem: A learning-based approach for indoor localization. CoNEXT '11, ACM, pp. 3:1–3:12.

[11] GÜNTHER, A., AND HOENE, C. Measuring round trip times to determine the distance between wlan nodes. NETWORKING'05, Springer-Verlag, pp. 768–779.

[12] LI, X., PAHLAVAN, K., LATVA-AHO, M., AND YLIANTTILA, M. Comparison of indoor geolocation methods in dsss and ofdm wireless lan systems. In *IEEE Fall VTC 2000* (2000), vol. 6, pp. 3015–3020 vol.6.

[13] LIM, H., KUNG, L.-C., HOU, J., AND LUO, H. Zero-configuration, robust indoor localization: Theory and experimentation. In *INFOCOM 2006. 25th IEEE International Conference on Computer Communications. Proceedings* (April 2006), pp. 1–12.

[14] MARIAKAKIS, A. T., SEN, S., LEE, J., AND KIM, K.-H. Sail: Single access point-based indoor localization. In *Proceedings of the 12th Annual International Conference on Mobile Systems, Applications, and Services* (New York, NY, USA, 2014), MobiSys '14, ACM, pp. 315–328.

[15] MCCRADY, D., DOYLE, L., FORSTROM, H., DEMPSEY, T., AND MARTORANA, M. Mobile ranging using low-accuracy clocks. *Microwave Theory and Techniques, IEEE Transactions on 48*, 6 (2000), 951–958.

[16] YOUSSEF, M., AND AGRAWALA, A. The horus wlan location determination system. MobiSys '05, ACM, pp. 205–218.

Communication Networks of Visible Light Emitting Diodes with Intra-Frame Bidirectional Transmission

Qing Wang
IMDEA Networks Institute & UC3M
Madrid, Spain
qing.wang@imdea.org

Domenico Giustiniano
IMDEA Networks Institute
Madrid, Spain
domenico.giustiniano@imdea.org

ABSTRACT

Unlike traditional radio frequency communication of consumer devices, the "optical antenna" direction of Visible Light Communication (VLC), *i.e.*, the Field-Of-View (FOV), varies greatly from device to device. This encompasses wide FOVs of ambient infrastructure and directional FOVs of light emitted by low-end embedded devices. This variety of light wave propagation can severely affect the transmission reliability, despite "pointing" devices to each other may seem enough for a reliable link. In particular, the fact that FOVs are unknown makes traditional access protocols in VLC unreliable in presence of interference among nodes of different FOVs and exacerbates the hidden-node problem. In this paper, we propose a Carrier Sensing Multiple Access/Collision Detection&Hidden Avoidance (CSMA/CD-HA) Medium Access Control protocol for a network where each node solely uses one Light Emitting Diode (LED) to transmit and receive data. The CSMA/CD-HA can enable *in-band intra-frame* bidirectional transmission with just one optical antenna. The key idea is to exploit the intra-frame data symbols without emission of light to introduce an embedded communication channel. This approach enables the *transmission* of additional data *while receiving* in the same optical channel and it makes the communication robust to different types of FOVs. We build a software-defined embedded platform running on Linux operating system, implement the CSMA/CD-HA protocol, and evaluate its performance through experiments. Results show that collisions caused by hidden nodes can be reduced and our protocol can increase the saturation throughput by nearly up to 50% and 100% under the two-node and four-node scenarios, respectively.

Categories and Subject Descriptors

C.2.1 [**Computer-Communication Networks**]: Network Architecture and Design—*Wireless Communication*

CoNEXT'14, December 2–5, 2014, Sydney, Australia.

http://dx.doi.org/10.1145/2674005.2675000.

Keywords

Visible light communication networks; CSMA/CD-HA; Bidirectional transmission; Design; Implementation; Evaluation

1. INTRODUCTION

Visible Light Communication (VLC) is emerging as a complementary technology to mainstream research on Radio Frequency (RF) communication. VLC utilizes visible light from Light Emitting Diodes (LEDs) to convey digital information between devices. A network of visible LEDs could be enabled by connecting various devices such as ceiling bulbs, lamps, light emitters embedded into cars and mobile devices and perhaps, in the future, LED TVs. However, the directionality of the "optical antenna" of VLC, i.e., the Field Of View (FOV) of LEDs, varies greatly from device to device. An infrastructure, e.g., a light bulb on the ceiling, normally emits light with a wide-FOV. In contrast, mobile devices may have various FOVs, according to the space and power constraints.

This variety of light wave propagation calls for networking approaches that are robust to the specific optical antenna. The design opportunities can take advantage of two fundamental differences with respect to RF communication.

- First, VLC often adopts the On-Off Keying (OOK) modulation, thus a transmitter can be "idle" when transmitting an "OFF" signal. This implies that other communications could be established during these short times without light emission. These concurrent communications may improve the system performance, such as increasing the throughput and so on.
- Second, while photodiodes are normally used as receivers, a LED has been proved to work as a receiver in LED-to-LED communications [5, 6]. Thus, a network of LEDs would only require one LED as optical antenna at each transceiver. The challenge is then how to create a network of LEDs *with* different FOVs and *without* additional optical components.

As illustrated in Fig. 1, these differences *i*) bring opportunities to design new Medium Access Control (MAC) protocols to improve the network performance; *ii*) increase the hidden-node problem in some scenarios. In this paper, we propose a Carrier Sensing Multiple Access/Collision Detection&Hidden Avoidance (CSMA/CD-HA) Medium Access Control (MAC) protocol to enable intra-frame bidirectional VLC in a network of LEDs. Similarly to the emerging full-duplex of RF communications with a single antenna proposed by [3], CSMA/CD-HA only uses one "antenna" – a

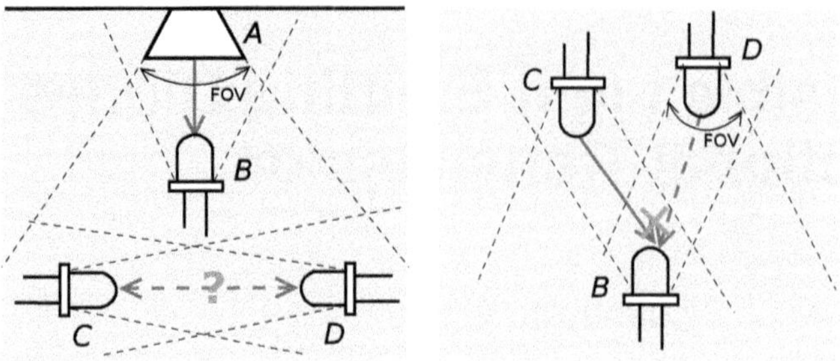

Figure 1: Motivation – various "optical antenna" directions of VLC nodes and OOK modulation: *left)* is in-band interference-free concurrent transmissions of $A \rightarrow B$ and $C \leftrightarrow D$ possible? *right)* exacerbate the hidden-node problem.

single LED to enable a secondary channel. In contrast to full-duplex research in RF domain, we target visible light spectrum and implement very simple techniques to enable the secondary channel with off-the-shelf embedded hardware that runs on credit-card-sized embedded board with a total unit cost of approximately 50 dollars. The proposed protocol can also alleviate the hidden-node problem without using the Request-To-Send/Clear-To-Send (RTS/CTS) method. To evaluate the performance of our protocol, we design a software-defined embedded platform for visible light communication networks, which runs Linux and implements CSMA/CD-HA as part of it. Experimental results show that CSMA/CD-HA can increase the saturation throughput by nearly up to 50% and 100% under the two-node and four-node scenarios, respectively, with respect to state-of-the-art MAC protocols.

2. SYSTEM DESIGN

We first briefly introduce background information on coding and decoding schemes employed in this work, and then present our method to enable intra-frame bidirectional transmission.

We use intensity modulation for data transmission, which is also adopted by the IEEE 802.15.7 standard [2] developed for short-range communication using visible light of wide-band light bulbs. Binary information is mapped to the presence (symbol HIGH) or absence (symbol LOW) of the visible light carrier. The main PHY layer of the IEEE 802.15.7 standard uses the OOK modulation with the Manchester Run-Length Limited (RLL) line code. RLL line codes are used to avoid long runs of light on and light off that could end up in flicker effects, as well as clock and data recovery detection problems. Therefore, bit 1 is mapped to symbol sequence LOW-HIGH, and bit 0 is mapped to HIGH-LOW. Demodulation is performed with direct detection. Based on the received signal's voltage, the receiving node detects the received signal as the sequence of symbols HIGH and LOW that are then converted to binary data.

2.1 Intra-Frame Bidirectional Transmission

The key enabler of intra-frame bidirectional transmission is that a node normally does not need to emit light when transmitting a symbol LOW. Therefore, the transmission of data is partially disentangled from the actual operation of the node, an essential difference from RF communication.

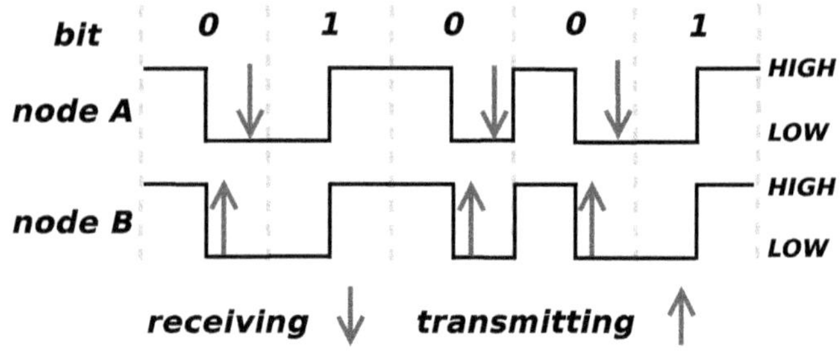

Figure 2: Key technique for intra-frame bidirectional transmission: node A can receive one symbol when transmitting the symbol LOW of bit "0" of the line code.

Let us consider two nodes, A and B. We assume that node A has gained access to the medium and it starts to transmit data to node B. *Since node A is "idle" when it transmits a symbol LOW, it can make use of this time to receive a data symbol.* To cooperate with this, node B can start itself to transmit a symbol if it can *predict* that it will receive a symbol LOW in the next symbol slot.

Under the assumption of Manchester RLL code, the prediction is based on: *i)* node B has received a HIGH symbol in current symbol slot; *ii)* the received HIGH symbol is the first part of a modulated bit (i.e., bit "0"). We illustrate an example in Fig. 2. Just with one LED, Node B is able to send data during the reception of a frame, while node A can receive data when it transmits a frame. This allows to enable intra-frame bidirectional transmission.

As shown in Fig. 2, node A should expect to receive a symbol only when it transmits the LOW symbol of bit "0". The reason is that node B can only predict the LOW symbol of bit "0", but it can not predict the LOW symbol of bit "1". In expectation, half of data from node A are with bit "1" and the other half with bit "0". Therefore, node B will transmit data for half of the payload of node A. This comes at the minor cost of not performing clock and data recovery for half of the data, which can be accepted for reasonable clock drift.

The approach can be extended to other RLL line codes. In more general terms, the intra-frame bidirectional transmission can be enabled for those symbols where there is a probability of one to jump to a state where node A transmits the LOW symbol.

2.2 The CSMA/CD-HA MAC Protocol

The Carrier Sensing Multiple Access / Collision Detection&Hidden Avoidance (CSMA/CD-HA) protocol is proposed to ensure fair channel access among all VLC nodes and reduce the impact of collisions and hidden nodes. We introduce our protocol, referring to the notations given in Table 1. When a frame is available for transmission, the MAC first senses the channel. The frame is transmitted immediately if the channel is sensed clear. If the channel is assessed busy, the MAC starts a backoff counter. The frame is transmitted when the counter reaches zero. The transmitting node and its corresponding receiver become a P-TX and a P-RX, respectively. Upon frame transmission, the P-TX switches to receiving mode when it transmits the LOW symbols of bit "0". The P-RX, similarly, switches to transmit a symbol when it finishes to receive a HIGH symbol of bit "0" (thus predicting that the next incoming symbol is LOW), to

Table 1: **Notations used in the CSMA/CD-HA MAC protocol.**

Primary TX (P-TX)	Node that has gained access to the medium with backoff protocol
Primary RX (P-RX)	Peer RX of a P-TX
Secondary TX (S-TX)	Node (not a P-RX) transmitting an in-band frame with a P-TX's transmission
Secondary RX (S-RX)	Peer RX of a S-TX
Primary frames	Frames sent by a P-TX to a P-RX
Embedded frames	Frames sent opportunistically by either a P-RX or a S-TX

perform the intra-frame bidirectional transmission, as presented in Sec. 2.1.

After the P-TX successfully receives the embedded frame, it appends an-octet ACK to the frame it is transmitting to acknowledge the reception of embedded data. The P-RX sends an ACK to the P-TX when it decodes a frame without error. The whole process is illustrated in Fig. 3 (with node A as the P-TX and B as the P-RX). If the P-TX has not received an ACK within the timeout, a retransmission occurs and the contention window is doubled unless it reaches the maximal contention window. The frame is dropped when a pre-defined number of retransmissions fail.

Hidden node avoidance As a result of intra-frame bidirectional transmission, the P-RX "always" sends signals when it is receiving a frame, and part of them are HIGH symbols. These HIGH symbols can be sensed by the nodes under its coverage, thus they will not send frames to the receiver during this period and the potential hidden-node problem is alleviated. The only part of the frame which is not protected to hidden nodes is before the embedded frames start to be transmitted, since during this time, a hidden node to the TX may judge the channel is clear. However, this duration is usually short compared to the whole frame transmission period and the influence tends to be very low. This is similar to the RTS/CTS handshake (which sends short frames to nodes under the TX and RX's coverage, to announce that the shared channel will be occupied for some time.) Sometimes the P-RX may have no data to transmit. Under this case, the P-RX can send dummy symbols to announce that the channel is busy while it is receiving a frame. To summarize, the embedded frames of the primary communication have twofold use: send additional in-band data and act as active acknowledgement of ongoing primary data reception.

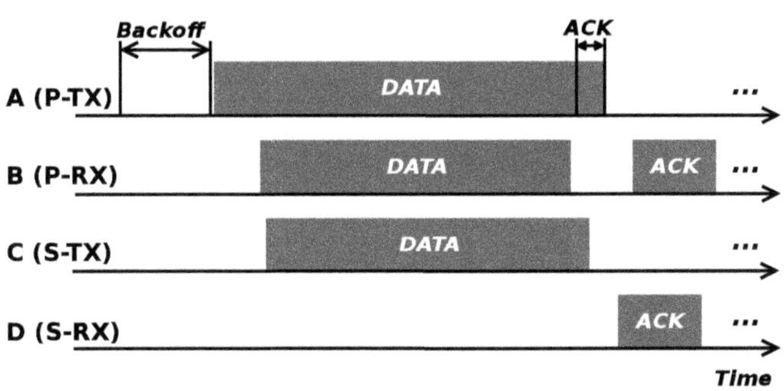

Figure 3: Proposed MAC protocol that supports intra-frame bidirectional transmission: an illustration for the left scenario of Fig. 1. ***(Note: the DATA/ACK frames shown here are transmitted by their corresponding nodes, not received.)***

Collision detection Traditional collisions caused by nodes reaching the backoff counter equal to zero are still possible. These collisions are immediately detected by the absence of embedded data during the payload, and thus the transmissions are stopped without waiting for the end of the payload.

Secondary intra-frame concurrent transmissions Further intra-frame concurrent transmissions can also be enabled, depending on the number of existing nodes, the FOVs of their LEDs and their positions. Take the left scenario in Fig. 1 as an example. The wide-FOV LEDs of node A make it possible to communicate with nodes B, C, and D, while the latter three have limited connectivity due to their narrow-FOV LEDs. We illustrate an example of the protocol in Fig. 3. Nodes C and D can receive A's signals, and C can detect that it is not (as well as D) the intended receiver of data from A. Node C then transmits embedded frames to D as node B transmits to A (C thus becomes a S-TX), while D can receive these frames following exactly A's receiving steps (D thus becomes a S-RX). After successfully decoding a frame from node C, D sends back an ACK without causing any interference to the communication between nodes A (the P-TX) and B (the P-RX).

2.3 Discussion

We continue to discuss some other important aspects of our MAC protocol.

Length of an embedded frame The length of an embedded frame heavily depends on the number of bit "0" containing in the primary frame body. This number can be calculated by the transmitter and appended to the MAC frame header.

When to send an embedded frame An embedded frame should be transmitted after a node receives the source address of the current primary frame. Only the intended receiver of the transmission can be declared as P-RX. Other nodes may act as S-TX, as long as they are not the intended receivers of P-RX. They start a secondary backoff process that follows the same rules as the primary one to decide the access to the medium.

Robustness of intra-frame concurrent transmissions The intra-frame current transmissions should be robust to expected or unexpected events, i.e., the secondary transmission should be disabled immediately if the primary transmission stops due to detections of collisions or hidden nodes or other unexpected errors. The CSMA/CD-HA protocol has this ability. For example, an underlying assumption of secondary transmissions is that the FOVs of nodes is such that the transmission of S-TX and S-RX does not interfere with the transmission of P-TX and P-RX. If this is not the case, the primary transmission is stopped due to detected collisions. As soon as P-TX stops its transmission because of a detected collision, the secondary transmission of S-TX and S-RX will be disabled for a while.

3. IMPLEMENTATION

We implement the proposed MAC protocol in our general-purpose software-defined open source platform OpenVLC for visible light communication networks [14]. The MAC protocol is implemented as a Linux driver – another network interface – that is able to communicate directly with the hardware and the Linux networking stack.

3.1 Hardware

The platform consists of a BeagleBone Black (BBB) board [1] and a front-end transceiver. The BBB board is equipped with the TI AM3359 CPU (1GHz), 512MB DDR3 RAM and 2GB on-board flash storage, and provides 4 timers and 65 General-Purpose Input/Output (GPIO) pins [1]. The front-end transceiver employs a single LED to both transmit and receive along with a few basic electronic components. This design has been proved to be resilient to ambient light interference without additional electronic processing [6] and we envision that it can be well suited to enable a communication network of consumer devices with LED front-end.

We rely on basic off-the-shelf electronic components and only use a very basic Physical Layer (PHY), though it can be scaled to use more advanced PHYs. The block diagram of the transceiver is shown in Fig. 4. It includes a TransConductance Amplifier (TCA) for transmission, a TransImpedance Amplifier (TIA) and an Analog-to-Digital Converter (ADC) for reception, a tristate-output buffer, and ancillary circuitry for transmission and reception.

A prerequisite to enable the intra-frame bidirectional transmission method is that nodes can switch between transmitting mode and receiving mode on a symbol basis. In our implementation, a software-defined TX/RX controller is used to switch the LED between TX and RX through the GPIO pins: *i*) in **TX mode**, encoded signals are amplified by the TCA and then fed to the forward-biased LED; *ii*) in **RX mode**, light signal is received by the reverse-biased LED and then the received small photocurrent is amplified by the TIA. Finally, an ADC converts the output analog signals to digital signals, which are then sent to the decoder through the Serial Peripheral Interface (SPI).

Through the TX/RX controller and the tri-state buffer, the LED can be switched between being TX mode and RX mode with low latency. This makes it possible to enable intra-frame bidirectional transmission as presented in Sec. 2.1.

3.2 Software

The Linux operating system running within the BBB board is the Angstrom Distribution with kernel version 3.8.13. Fig. 5 illustrates the software stack of the platform, where the MAC is built based on primitive functions we implement. These

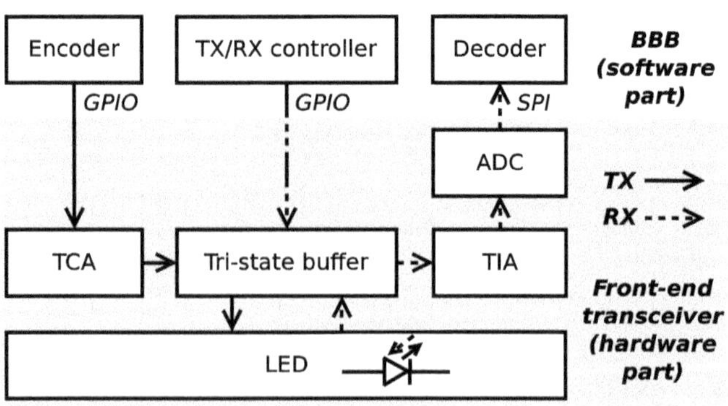

Figure 4: Diagram of the VLC platform.

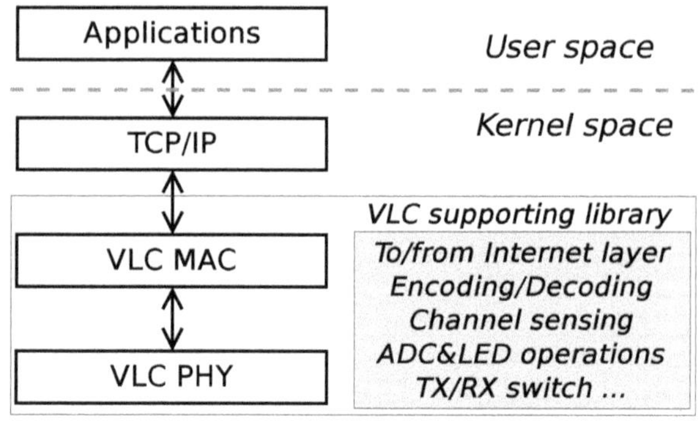

Figure 5: Implementation of the MAC protocol in embedded Linux operation system.

functions include writing a symbol to the LED, reading a symbol from ADC, coding/decoding, preamble detection, and so on. Furthermore, we implement functions to receive and send packets to the Internet layer. In this way, the MAC is connected with the TCP/IP layers of the Linux operating system and thus the MAC becomes transparent to various applications.

In our implementation, there are two types of frames in the MAC layer, DATA and Acknowledgement (ACK). The frame structure and octets each field occupies are shown in Fig. 6. Distinguishing DATA and ACK frames is through the length of frame body (payload): if the frame has no payload (i.e., "Length"= 0), it is an ACK. Otherwise, it is a DATA frame. Each DATA frame can carry a payload up to 255 bytes. The MAC destination and source addresses that follow the "Length" field each occupies 2 bytes. The 2-byte filed "Protocol" identifies the upper layer protocol encapsulated in the payload of current frame. The fields from "Length" to (upper layer) "Protocol" form the MAC frame header. A two-octet Cyclic Redundancy Check (CRC) over the frame header and frame body is appended to the end of each frame. A three-octet preamble is added to the beginning of each frame for frame synchronization.

In order to enable embedded communication, for simplicity we currently assume that the number of bit "0" is estimated by the receiver based on the length of primary frame body and the assumption that bits "0" and "1" are evenly distributed.

4. EVALUATION

In this section we evaluate the proposed CSMA/CD-HA protocol through experiments. The symbol slots of symbols LOW and HIGH are both set to 200 μs. An 8-symbol period is used for channel sensing, i.e., to determine whether the channel is clear or not. The minimum and maximum value of the contention window are set to 4 and 32, respectively. The maximal frame retransmission time is set to 4. Different to a primary frame, an embedded frame is coded with OOK modulation without the Manchester code (bit "0" is mapped

Preamble	SFD	Length	Dst	Src	Protocol	Payload	CRC
3 Bytes	1 B	1 B	2 B	2 B	2 B	0-255 B	2 B

Figure 6: Frame format of DATA and ACK: Length> 0 $\Longleftrightarrow$DATA; Length= 0 $\Longleftrightarrow$ACK.

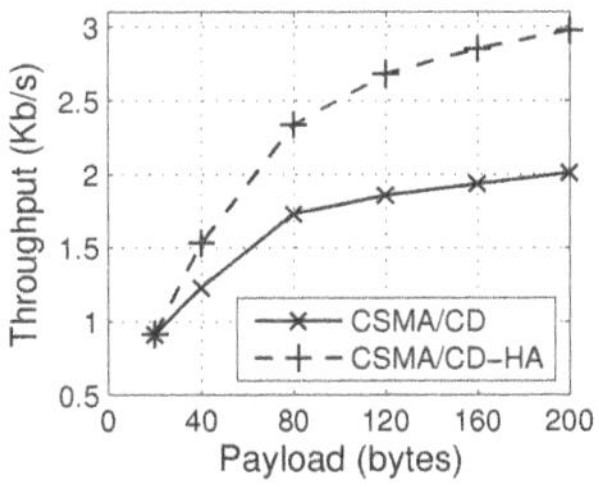

(a) Saturation throughput

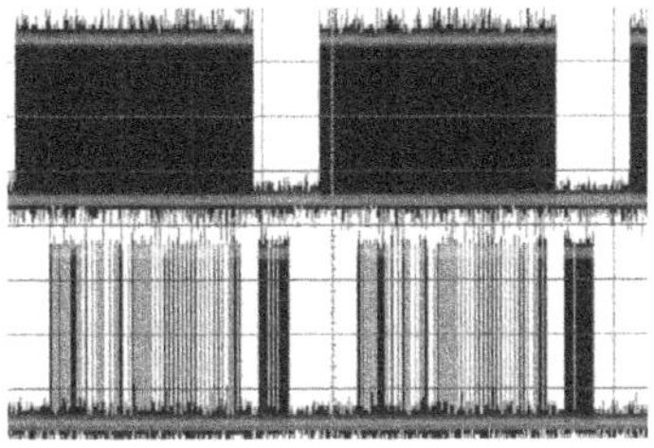

(b) Snapshot of CSMA/CD-HA

Figure 7: Evaluation results of a point-to-point link.

to symbol LOW and bit "1" to symbol HIGH.). Details of the electronic devices adopted in the testbeds can be found in [14]. Note that we use two narrow-FOV LEDs to emulate a wider-FOV LED when needed.

We compare CSMA/CD-HA with the CSMA/CD introduced in [6]. CSMA/CD uses the same backoff mechanism of the traditional Carrier Sensing Multiple Access/Collision Avoidance (CSMA/CA). While transmitting, a node adopting CSMA/CD senses the channel when it transmits a symbol LOW and stops the current transmission if the channel is declared busy. It has been shown in [6] that the CSMA/CD outperforms the CSMA/CA.

Point-to-point link We evaluate the MAC layer saturation throughput of a point-to-point link under the CSMA/CD-HA and CSMA/CD protocols, where two nodes are within the FOV of each other. The saturation throughput is achieved under the setting that both nodes always have data to transmit to each other. Throughput versus per-frame payload is shown in Fig. 7 (a), where the payload varies from 20 to 200 bytes. As expected, the throughputs under both protocols increase as the payload increases, e.g., under CSMA/CD, the saturation throughput is 1 kb/s when the payload is 20 bytes, while the throughput achieves a value of 2 kb/s when the payload increases to 200 bytes. Another observation from Fig. 7 (a) is that our proposed CSMA/CD-HA greatly outperforms CSMA/CD when the payload is long, e.g., when the payload is 200 bytes, the throughput under CSMA/CD-HA is about 150% of that under the CSMA/CD. This achievement comes from intra-frame bidirectional transmission in CSMA/CD-HA. The throughputs under the two MAC protocols are the same when the payload is 20 bytes. This is because the transmission of an embedded frame becomes impossible when the payload of a primary frame is too short. An oscilloscope snapshot of the protocol is shown in Fig. 7 (b), where we can see clearly the interaction of nodes and the transmission of embedded frames.

Three-node network without hidden nodes The performance of a three-node network without hidden nodes is evaluated, as shown in Fig. 8 (a). In this scenario, one node acts as a base station and keeps sending data alternately to the other two nodes (i.e, the base station uses the round-robin scheduling algorithm). For instance, this scenario may emulate a setup where the base station is the light bulb in the ceiling and most of the traffic is downlink. As expected, we observe from the figure that the throughputs at the two receivers are similar under various frame payloads. Another observation is that the throughput gain of CSMA/CD-HA over CSMA/CD increases with the frame payload. This gain achieves a value of 50% when the frame payload is 200 bytes.

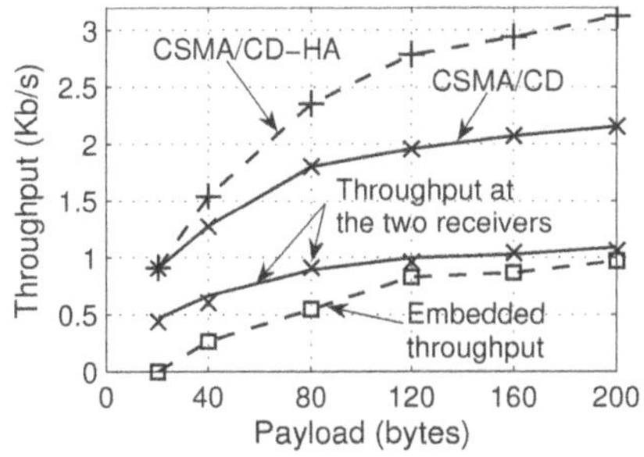

(a) Saturation throughput

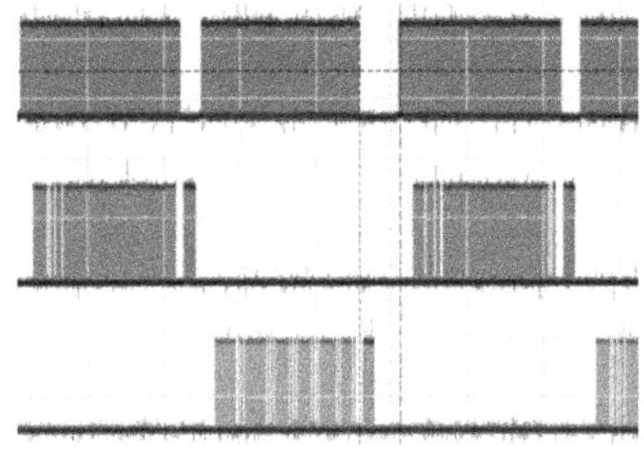

(b) Snapshot of CSMA/CD-HA

Figure 8: Evaluation results of the three-node network without hidden nodes.

The interactions between these three nodes are illustrated by the oscilloscope snapshot in Fig. 8 (b).

Three-node network with hidden nodes We also evaluate a three-node network with hidden nodes, similar to the illustration shown in the right sub-figure of Fig. 1. We compare the CSMA/CD-HA with the CSMA/CD without RTS/CTS. The position where a collision is detected within each collided frame is shown in Fig. 9. We can observe from Fig. 9 (a) that under CSMA/CD, most of the collisions happen at the beginning of frames. This is because the two TXs can not hear each other's transmission, thus causing a collision when both of them start transmitting. However, the collisions under CSMA/CD-HA occur either at the beginning or at the end of collided frames, as shown in Fig. 9 (b). This is because a RX starts sending an embedded frame after it receives the source address of the corresponding primary frame, and finishes sending the embedded frame before the whole primary frame is fully transmitted (as illustrated in Fig. 3). Although there are still collisions caused by the hidden node under CSMA/CD-HA, the number of collisions is actually reduced greatly. This is shown from Fig. 9 (c), where the saturation throughput versus frame payload is presented. We can observe that CSMA/CD-HA always outperforms CSMA/CD greatly independent of frame payloads, and the throughput improvement is up to 1000% when frame payload is set to 200 bytes.

Four-node network The performance of a four-node network is also evaluated. The setting of this scenario can be referred to the left sub-figure of Fig. 1. The four nodes act as a P-TX, P-RX, S-TX and S-RX, respectively. The oscilloscope snapshot of the interactions between these nodes is presented in Fig. 10 (a). We can see that three intra-frame concurrent transmissions are obtained. The corresponding saturation throughputs are presented in Fig. 10 (b). We observe that with the increase of frame payload, the throughputs under

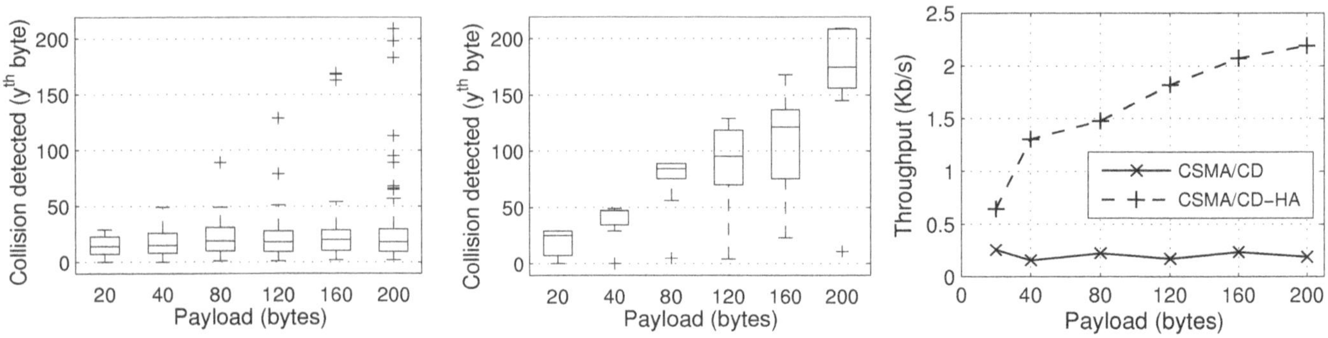

(a) Collision position of CSMA/CD (b) Collision position of CSMA/CD-HA (c) Saturation throughput

Figure 9: Evaluation results of the three-node network with hidden nodes.

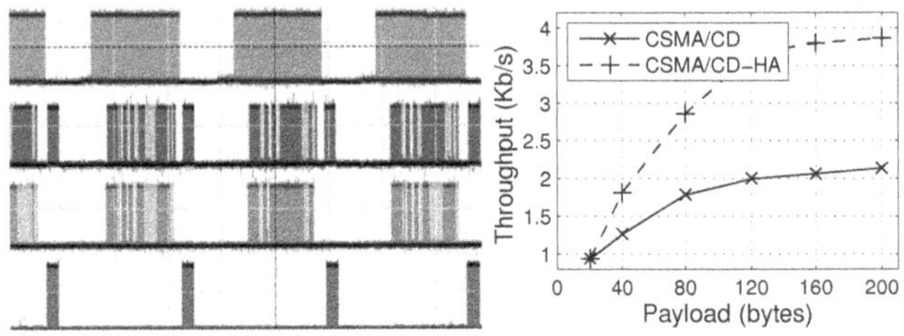

(a) Snapshot of CSMA/CD-HA (b) Saturation throughput

Figure 10: Evaluation results of a four-node network.

both protocols increase. The CSMA/CD-HA starts to outperform CSMA/CD after the payload is more than 20 bytes. The throughput gain under CSMA/CD-HA over CSMA/CD increases to around 100% when the payload is 200 bytes. This gain is twice as large as those under the scenarios of point-to-point link and three-node network without hidden nodes. The reason for this is in the four-node network, an additional intra-frame transmission is enabled between the S-TX and S-RX.

5. RELATED WORK

VLC has received strong attention from the designers of the next generation of cellular networks [13] and the point-to-point communication using smartphones [7, 8] and cars [11, 15]. The IEEE has also developed the 802.15.7 standard [2] for short-range communication using visible light.

Single antenna VLC communication While photodiodes are normally used as receivers, a reverse-biased LED instead of a photodiode is used in [5] as a receiver to implement a bidirectional communication network. This principle has been exploited by [6] to introduce a LED-to-LED communication network and is further developed in [12]. All these works operate on microcontrollers and are implemented as embedded software in the environment of non-operating system. Connecting these works with various networking protocols is not straightforward. In contrast, our implementation resides in the Linux operating system and appears as a normal network interface that can be easily extended to support different upper layer protocols.

Full-duplex RF/VLC communication In-band full-duplex RF communication was proposed in [4] and further implemented as a prototype in [9]. The key technique here is a device that uses the inverse of its transmitted signals to cancel the self-interference to its received signal. Compared to our proposed technique, both of them can achieve in-band bidirectional transmission. A different is that [4, 9] used two antennas for transmitting and receiving, respectively, while in our technique, the same LED is used for both transmitting and receiving purposes. Recently, a method combining analog and digital cancellation is proposed in [3]. This method enables the full duplex communication with a single antenna. To the best of our knowledge, there is yet no work on full-duplex (in-band) VLC, although some authors have proposed the use of visible light and infrared light or LEDs operating on different wavelengths for "full-duplex" communications, as in [10].

6. CONCLUSION

In this paper, we presented the design, implementation, and performance evaluation of the CSMA/CD-HA protocol for communication networks using visible light. By exploiting the OOK modulation used in VLC systems, we enabled intra-frame bidirectional transmission for networks of LEDs with heterogeneous FOVs. We implemented CSMA/CD-HA in an embedded platform and showed its superior performance for the detections of collision and hidden transmissions with respect to recent works in visible light communication networks. We expect that the next challenge to implement CSMA/CD-HA in real systems will be to study how well the protocol works at faster switching rate between symbols HIGH and LOW. For instance, this requires the design of novel synchronization schemes at system level, necessary for the transmission of data while receiving, and the understanding of the impact of the clock drift caused by not using half of the symbols of the line code for clock and data recovery.

7. REFERENCES

[1] BeagleBone Black. *http://beagleboard.org/Products/BeagleBone+Black.*

[2] IEEE standard for local and metropolitan area networks–part 15.7: Short-range wireless optical communication using visible light. *IEEE Std 802.15.7-2011* (Sept 2011), 1–309.

[3] Bharadia, D., McMilin, E., and Katti, S. Full duplex radios. In *Proceedings of the ACM SIGCOMM* (2013), pp. 375–386.

[4] Choi, J. I., Jain, M., Srinivasan, K., Levis, P., and Katti, S. Achieving single channel, full duplex

wireless communication. In *Proceedings of the ACM MobiCom* (2010), pp. 1–12.

[5] Dietz, P., Yerazunis, W., and Leigh, D. Very low-cost sensing and communication using bidirectional LEDs. In *TR2003-35* (2003).

[6] Giustiniano, D., Tippenhauer, N., and Mangold, S. Low-complexity visible light networking with LED-to-LED communication. In *Proceedings of the IFIP Wireless Days (WD)* (2012), pp. 1–8.

[7] Hao, T., Zhou, R., and Xing, G. Cobra: Color barcode streaming for smartphone systems. In *Proceedings of the ACM MobiSys* (2012), pp. 85–98.

[8] Hu, W., Gu, H., and Pu, Q. Lightsync: Unsynchronized visual communication over screen-camera links. In *Proceedings of the ACM MobiCom* (2013), pp. 15–26.

[9] Jain, M., Choi, J. I., Kim, T., Bharadia, D., Seth, S., Srinivasan, K., Levis, P., Katti, S., and Sinha, P. Practical, real-time, full duplex wireless. In *Proceedings of the ACM MobiCom* (2011), pp. 301–312.

[10] Lin, K., and Hirohashi, K. High-speed full-duplex multiaccess system for LEDs based wireless communications using visible light. In *Proceedings of the International Symposium on Optical Engineering and Photonic Technology (OEPT)* (2009), pp. 1–5.

[11] Liu, C. B., Sadeghi, B., and Knightly, E. W. Enabling vehicular visible light communication (V2LC) networks. In *Proceedings of the ACM VANET* (2011), pp. 41–50.

[12] Schmid, S., Corbellini, G., Mangold, S., and Gross, T. R. LED-to-LED visible light communication networks. In *Proceedings of the ACM MobiHoc* (2013), pp. 1–10.

[13] Tsonev, D., Videv, S., and Haas, H. Light Fidelity (Li-Fi): towards all-optical networking. vol. 9007, pp. 1–10.

[14] Wang, Q., Giustiniano, D., and Puccinelli, D. OpenVLC: Software-defined visible light embedded networks. In *1st ACM Workshop on Visible Light Communication Systems , in conjunction with MobiCom 2014* (September 2014), pp. 1 –6.

[15] Yu, S.-H., Shih, O., Tsai, H.-M., and Roberts, R. Smart automotive lighting for vehicle safety. *IEEE Communications Magazine 51*, 12 (2013), 50–59.

MIDAS: Empowering 802.11ac Networks with Multiple-Input Distributed Antenna Systems

Jie Xiong[†], Karthikeyan Sundaresan[‡], Kyle Jamieson[†], Mohammad A. Khojastepour[‡], Sampath Rangarajan[‡]
[†]Department of Computer Science, University College London, UK
‡NEC Laboratories America, NJ, USA
{j.xiong, k.jamieson}@cs.ucl.ac.uk[†],{karthiks, amir, sampath}@nec-labs.com[‡]

ABSTRACT

Next generation WLANs (802.11ac) are undergoing a major shift in their communication paradigm with the introduction of multi-user MIMO (MU-MIMO), transitioning from single-user to multi-user communications. We argue that the conventional AP deployment model of co-located antennas as well as their PHY and MAC mechanisms are not designed to realize the complete potential of MU-MIMO. We propose to leverage distributed antenna systems (DAS) to empower next generation 802.11ac networks. We highlight the multitude of benefits that DAS brings to MU-MIMO and 802.11ac in general. However, several challenges arise in the process of realizing these benefits in practice, where avoiding client modifications and making only minimal software modifications to APs is important to enable rapid adoption. Towards addressing these challenges, we present the design and implementation of *MIDAS*, the *Multiple-Input Distributed Antenna System*. MIDAS couples a DAS deployment of AP antennas with a suite of novel yet standards-compatible mechanisms at the PHY and MAC layers that best leverage the DAS deployment to maximize 802.11ac performance. Our WARP-based experimental evaluation demonstrates MIDAS's ability to significantly boost the performance of current 802.11ac design, demonstrating throughput gains over 802.11ac MU-MIMO for 100-200%, while remaining amenable to commercial adoption.

Categories and Subject Descriptors

C.2.1 [**Computer-Communication Networks**]: Network Architecture and Design—*Wireless communication*

Keywords

MIDAS; Distributed antenna system; DAS; Multi-user MIMO; MU-MIMO; 802.11ac; Multiple input

1. INTRODUCTION

Recently, wireless LAN (WLAN) designs are undergoing a paradigm shift, evolving from single-client to multi-client communication patterns with the introduction of the 802.11ac standard. One of the key reasons behind this move is a form factor of smart devices that limits

CoNEXT'14, December 2–5, 2014, Sydney, Australia.

ACM 978-1-4503-3279-8/14/12 ...$15.00.
http://dx.doi.org/10.1145/2674005.2675014.

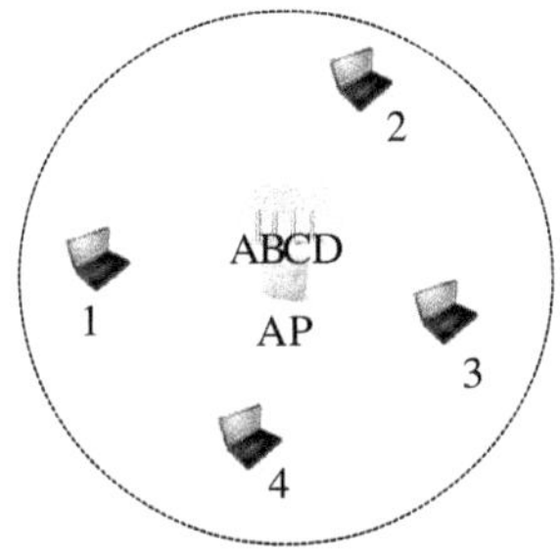

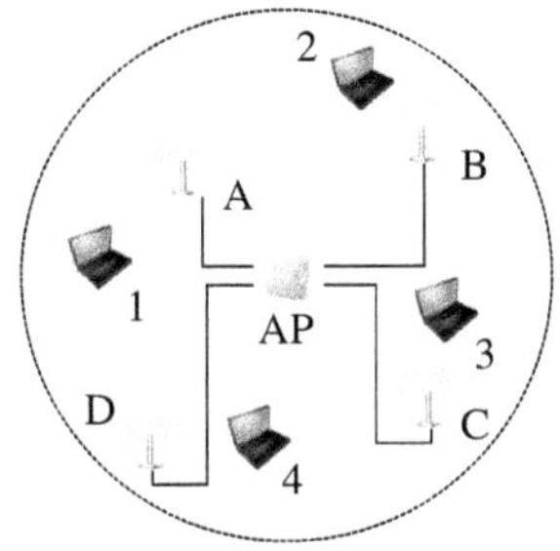

(a) A Co-located Antenna System (CAS) **(b)** A Distributed Antenna System (DAS)

Figure 1: CAS vs DAS deployment.

the number of antennas to one or two, with a consequent limit on the number of streams that the AP can send to a single client, even if the AP has many more antennas available. Multi-user MIMO allows the AP to use all its antennas to send multiple streams of data to different clients simultaneously. Clients measure the channel to the AP and feed this *channel state information* (CSI) back to the AP, which in turn sends different data streams on the downlink such that each client receives only the data stream it needs, while other unwanted (and otherwise interfering) data streams are suppressed (this process is called *precoding*). A popular and lightweight precoding scheme is called *zero-forcing beamforming* [27] (ZFBF), wherein undesired data streams are nulled (forced to zero) at a client. MU-MIMO thereby allows the AP to better leverage its spatial (antenna) resources and achieve multiplicative throughput increases: this is called *multiplexing gain*.

While the incorporation of MU-MIMO in 802.11ac is a welcome step towards utilizing the AP's radios and antennas effectively, the current WLAN deployment model is to co-locate all an AP's antennas within a few wavelengths of the carrier frequency, as shown in Figure 1(a); we refer to this as a co-located antenna system, or *CAS*. In this work we show that spatially separating the antennas of an 802.11ac AP via RF or optical cabling, and leveraging MU-MIMO through a *Distributed Antenna System* (DAS), as shown in Figure 1(b), is essential to getting the most out of MU-MIMO.

Specifically, a DAS design has the potential to improve WLAN performance by means of three distinct mechanisms:

1. Spatial Diversity. As illustrated in Figure 1, distributing the AP's antennas helps a client find an AP antenna closer to it on average compared to in a CAS. This reduces the path loss on average and hence improves link SNR and capacity.

2. Cell Capacity. In MU-MIMO, when data streams are sent to different clients simultaneously from the AP, they interfere with each

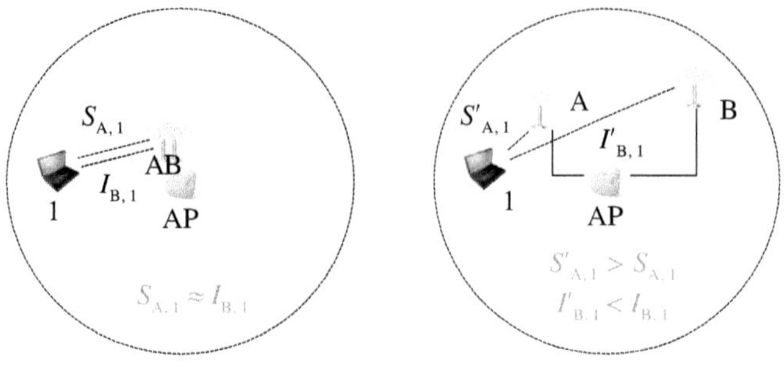

(a) CAS (b) DAS

Figure 2: DAS increases the signal strength but also decreases the interference cancellation burden on precoding.

other. This mutual interference is addressed through data encoding (precoding) at the AP. With DAS, a client will likely have a much stronger signal ($S'_{A,1}$) and weaker interference ($I'_{B,1}$) as shown in Figure 2(b). With carefully-chosen precoding, this better isolates desired and interfering streams compared to a CAS system, where path loss from different antennas is almost the same, as illustrated in Figure 2(a). The result is an improved effective SINR and hence better network throughput.

3. Network Capacity. In a DAS, the channel states (busy or idle) at different AP antennas can differ, unlike in an 802.11ac CAS. With each of the antennas having the ability to sense and decouple the channel states helps leverage spatial reuse with finer granularity. This not only allows for packing more concurrent transmissions in the network, resulting in improved network capacity, but also alleviates the hidden terminal issue (exacerbated with multi-client communication) and reduces the deadzones in the coverage area.

Challenges in realizing DAS. While DAS-based MU-MIMO systems might appear similar in effect to deploying multiple CAS APs (in place of distributed antennas), there are several performance and practical benefits to the former that directly cater to 802.11ac as we discuss in Section 2. To realize DAS, three practical, yet technically challenging issues arise:

Firstly, while a DAS's distributed antennas can emphasize the desired streams at closer clients more than the interfering streams, a conventional MU-MIMO precoding scheme such as zero-forcing beamforming (ZFBF) that splits the power equally across the streams neither meets practical 802.11ac per-antenna power constraints in a DAS nor leverages the inherent topology advantage of a DAS. On the other hand, precoding schemes for distributed MU-MIMO systems with a per-antenna power constraint are either too computationally complex to realize [11, 32] or require modifications to client receivers, hindering adoption.

Secondly, since it is designed for a CAS, 802.11ac's MAC keeps a single medium access channel state (idle or busy) for the entire AP, but a DAS' antennas are distributed, hence have different true channel states. This channel state coupling significantly limits the AP's ability to achieve fine-grained spatial reuse and alleviate hidden terminals in the network.

Finally, the MAC in a CAS treats all antennas alike, employing all during the downlink precoded transmission. But unlike in a CAS, in a DAS there is a large disparity across the channel gains from each antenna to a client. Hence, selecting clients intelligently based on the set of available idle antennas for MU-MIMO has a much larger impact in DAS and has to be carefully tailored.

MIDAS. In this paper we propose MIDAS (the *Multiple Input Distributed Antenna System*), a WLAN design that combines a DAS deployment of antennas with several software mechanisms at the PHY and MAC layer to leverage the full potential of MU-MIMO. MIDAS is standards-compliant in that it does not require any modifications to the PHY, requires minimal software modifications to the AP's MAC, while maintaining complete transparency to clients.

At the PHY layer, MIDAS's design includes a novel, lightweight, *power-balancing* mechanism for ZFBF-based precoding. It respects 802.11's per-antenna power constraint, while leveraging the inherent topology imbalance between desired and interfering data streams to appropriately assign power to the different streams. This enables MIDAS to deliver near-optimal precoding performance. Its lightweight nature is conducive for implementation especially for channels with small channel coherence time, and transparency to clients fosters easier deployment and adoption. Further, with topology imbalance being an inherent challenge for distributed MU-MIMO systems in general, our precoding scheme also improves upon those in the literature [19, 32].

At the MAC layer, MIDAS incorporates two novel mechanisms. First, it re-designs the carrier sensing mechanism to allow for *fine-grained carrier sensing* at each of the AP's antennas by maintaining multiple, independent medium occupancy states. With fine-grained carrier sensing enabled, MIDAS allows for improved spatial reuse and also alleviates hidden terminals. Second, it enables *virtual packet tagging*, where each packet (of a client) is tagged with a preferred list of antennas for transmission. The latter provides a means to perform client filtering for MU-MIMO transmissions that is tailored to the set of antennas available. This enhances MU-MIMO performance considerably, while allowing the MAC to leverage fine-grained spatial reuse opportunities.

We have implemented MIDAS on the Rice WARP [20] platform, and deployed DAS with RF cables in two different indoor office testbed environments. Experimental results demonstrate capacity gains of around 30% from MIDAS's precoding, 40% from DAS deployment and 65% from its MAC mechanisms, to result in a net gain of up to 200% over conventional 802.11ac MU-MIMO systems. These results show that it is possible to significantly boost the performance of MU-MIMO in next-generation WLANs while being amenable to practical realization with off-the-shelf clients.

The rest of this paper is structured as follows. Following a quick background on the most relevant technologies (§2), we present the design of MIDAS in §3, highlighting the above novel contributions and explaining how MIDAS addresses the above challenges. §4 describes our implementation of MIDAS. An experimental evaluation (§5) follows, investigating how overcoming the above challenges improves performance and why. §6 surveys the related work. §7 presents some additional discussion, and §8 concludes.

2. BACKGROUND

Conventional DAS. The distributed antennas of a DAS system merely radiate the received RF signal (from the AP) within the AP's contention domain. WLAN [7] and mobile cellular networks [4, 29] have long used conventional DASs to provide improved wireless coverage indoors, especially in larger venues, such as convention centers or stadiums. A conventional DAS simply broadcasts the *same* signal from all antennas with some designs even using "leaky feeder" coaxial cable that radiates RF energy continuously along the length of the cable [21]. Thus conventional DASs preclude the use of MU-MIMO and its associated spatial multiplexing gains. In contrast, MIDAS is a true MU-MIMO DAS that can send different RF signals to different antennas (i.e multiple input).

Multi-AP distributed MU-MIMO. Here transmitting antennas are located at different APs, which run a fine-grained synchronization protocol for phase-coherent transmissions. Considering the difference between MIDAS and a multi-AP distributed MU-MIMO system, there are several key differences. Distributed MIMO systems entail phase and time synchronizing all the APs and sharing all their data on the wired backhaul network to enable distributed MU-MIMO (*e.g.* MegaMIMO [19], AirSync [5]), which is a practical impediment to realization and deployment especially if different organizations or people administer different APs. Even if feasible, it would require a revamp of the 802.11ac protocol to allow multiple 802.11ac APs to share and jointly precode data to multiple clients. In MIDAS, each 802.11ac AP serves as the central processing node to realize MU-MIMO across its distributed antennas. Hence, phase and time synchronization comes for free, and incurs no backhaul overhead (RF signals are sent over DAS cables).

Deploy multiple conventional 802.11 CAS APs. Consider a Multi-AP approach, where a CAS AP is deployed in place of each of the antennas of a MIDAS deployment. Being logically similar, there are several key differences in both practical realization and performance between the two. Comparing MIDAS with Multi-AP, where each of the CAS APs is a *multiple* antenna AP, is unfair to MIDAS in terms of antenna and AP resources. However, even in this case, MIDAS has an advantage over Multi-AP. Note that the antennas of a MIDAS AP are distributed within the contention domain of the AP. Deploying multiple APs within one content domain is inefficient. The counterpart CAS APs in Multi-AP are still restricted to MU-MIMO transmissions from a single CAS AP since 802.11ac does not allow for cooperation across APs. On the other hand, an multiple stream transmission of higher aggregate rate is possible in MIDAS due to the potentially higher rank channel matrix (due to un-correlated channels) created by the distributed antennas. Further, when each CAS AP consists of a single antenna in Multi-AP (for a fair comparison), it would be restricted to a single stream within a contention domain unlike MIDAS that can support multiple streams.

In essence, it is better to distribute the antenna resources of an AP within a single contention domain for multi-user transmissions, and DAS provides a practical primitive to realize this. DAS confers the benefits of distributed MU-MIMO to a CAS-based MU-MIMO system, while remaining compatible with 802.11ac, thereby fostering easier adoption. However, it requires appropriate precoding and MAC mechanisms to deliver its gains, which in turn forms the objective for MIDAS.

3. DESIGN

In this section we describe the MIDAS design elements that complement the DAS model with a suite of PHY- and MAC-layer mechanisms capable of delivering the most benefits out of a multi-user communication system, while remaining standards-compliant. We begin by considering how to precode transmissions at the AP's distributed antennas while managing transmission power (§3.1). Next we discuss MIDAS's fine-grained channel sensing MAC (§3.2.2) and client selection algorithms (§3.2.4, §3.2.5) that are tailored for the DAS deployment. We put everything together in §3.2.1 and conclude with a discussion of how the above design elements fit readily into 802.11ac (§3.3), fostering easier adoption.

3.1 Pre-coding for MU-MIMO in MIDAS

To place MIDAS's precoding algorithm into context, we begin with a brief primer on conventional ZFBF, explaining the per-antenna power constraint that 802.11ac places on each of the AP's antennas and the reasons behind this constraint.

3.1.1 *Primer: Zero-forcing beamforming*

ZFBF maximizes the SNR of each desired stream subject to the constraint that the interference each causes to other clients be completely nulled. Such an approach is optimal for a total power constraint [28] and can be formulated as an optimization problem to choose precoding vectors $\vec{v}_j = \{v_{1j} \cdots v_{|\mathcal{T}|j}\}^\mathsf{T}$ for every client j in the set of chosen clients $\mathcal{C}$, where $\mathcal{T}$ is the set of transmit antennas.[1] The objective is to maximize the sum rate to the set of chosen clients $\mathcal{C}$:

$$\arg\max_{\vec{v}_j} \textstyle\sum_{j=1}^{|\mathcal{C}|} \log(1+\rho_j) \tag{1}$$

$$\text{where } \rho_j = \frac{|\sum_{k=1}^{|\mathcal{T}|} h_{jk} v_{kj}|^2}{N_o} \qquad (\forall j \in \mathcal{C})$$

subject to the following two constraints:

$$\sum_{k=1}^{|\mathcal{T}|}\sum_{j=1}^{|\mathcal{C}|} |v_{kj}|^2 \leq P_{tot} \qquad (\forall k \in \mathcal{T}) \tag{2a}$$

$$\sum_{k=1}^{|\mathcal{T}|} h_{ik} v_{kj} = 0 \qquad (j \in \mathcal{C}, i \neq j) \tag{2b}$$

where h_{jk} is the complex channel gain from antenna k to client j. Equation (2a) is the total power constraint, and (2b) is the precoding constraint, *i.e.*, precoded symbols should cancel each other at client i while arriving at a desired client j ($i \neq j$), resulting in an SINR of ρ_j from desired stream j. This optimization problem in fact has a closed-form solution: if the channel matrix is $\mathbf{H}$, the best precoder is the pseudoinverse of the channel matrix, $\mathbf{H}^\dagger$. Subsequently splitting power among all data streams keeps the power allocation process completely decoupled from precoding, making ZFBF a highly lightweight, yet efficient solution that is attractive for implementation.

The per-antenna power constraint. Since each antenna has its own power amplifier, 802.11ac specifies a per-antenna power constraint P to replace the total power constraint (2a):

$$\sum_{j=1}^{|\mathcal{C}|} |v_{kj}|^2 \leq P, \forall k \in \mathcal{T} \tag{3}$$

In the presence of this constraint, ZFBF may still distribute power equally across data streams, the sum power from all streams on one antenna might either exceed or fall short of the per-antenna power constraint, since each antenna serves a combination of all the data streams according to the precoding vectors $\{\vec{v}_j\}$. Furthermore, there is no closed-form solution to this challenging optimization problem [28], and employing numerical techniques incurs significant complexity without guaranteeing to converge to an optimal solution [11, 32]. Hence, the key challenge is to design a precoding solution that is as lightweight as ZFBF for implementation purposes but at the same time performs an intelligent power allocation across the data streams to leverage the available per-antenna power effectively and thus maximize performance.

Relating Precoding to SINR. Let $\mathbf{V} = [\vec{v}_1 \cdots \vec{v}_{|\mathcal{C}|}]$ be the precoding matrix applied at the AP and $\mathbf{S}$ be the matrix of resulting SINR values at the clients. Entry $s_{ij} \in \mathbf{S}$ measures the power from stream i received at client j, and so captures the interference power from stream i at client j when $i \neq j$. The SINR ρ_j for the desired stream at client j is

$$\rho_j = \frac{s_{jj}}{1+\sum_{i;i\neq j} s_{ij}} \quad \text{where } s_{ij} = \frac{|\sum_{k=1}^{|\mathcal{T}|} h_{jk} v_{ki}|^2}{N_o} \tag{4}$$

[1]The notation $(\cdot)^\mathsf{T}$ indicates transpose.

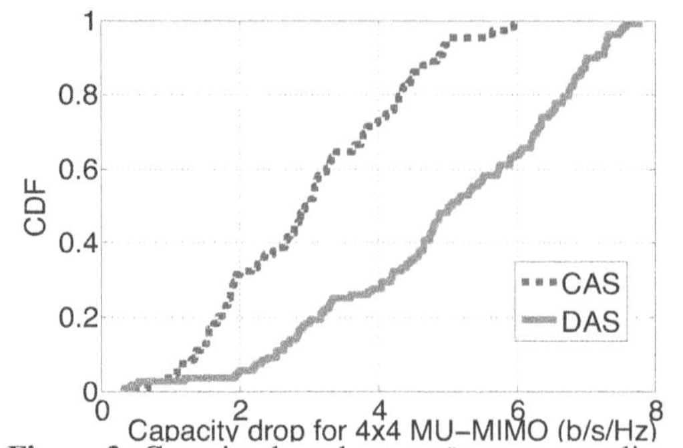

Figure 3: Capacity drop due to naïve power scaling.

$$\underbrace{\begin{bmatrix} w_1v_{11} & v_{12} & v_{13} & v_{14} \\ w_1v_{21} & v_{22} & v_{23} & v_{24} \\ w_1v_{31} & v_{32} & v_{33} & v_{34} \\ w_1v_{41} & v_{42} & v_{43} & v_{44} \end{bmatrix}}_{\text{Scaled precoding matrix } \mathbf{V}} \rightarrow \underbrace{\begin{bmatrix} w_1^2s_{11} & 0 & 0 & 0 \\ 0 & s_{22} & 0 & 0 \\ 0 & 0 & s_{33} & 0 \\ 0 & 0 & 0 & s_{44} \end{bmatrix}}_{\text{SINR matrix } \mathbf{S}}$$

Figure 4: SNR impact of scaling a client's precoding in **V**.

Since interference is completely nulled in the case of ZFBF, the SINR matrix reduces to a diagonal SNR matrix.

While ZFBF equally distributes total power among the streams it may not satisfy the per-antenna power constraint (3). One might wonder if a simple power reduction of individual streams on just the antennas that violate (3) would solve the problem. But note that under such a scaling, S becomes non-diagonal and inter-stream interference arises, significantly reducing performance.

Naïve power scaling. To preserve the ZFBF property, we might apply a "global" power reduction, scaling all streams on all antennas by the same value. This means that we would find the antenna k^* that violates (3) by the greatest amount:

$$k^* = \arg \max_{k:\sum_j |v_{kj}|^2 > P} \sum_j |v_{kj}|^2 \tag{5}$$

and then scale all streams on all antennas by a factor of $1/\sum_j |v_{kj}|^2$ so that (3) holds. Such an approach has the potential drawback that the available power on some of the antennas may be significantly underutilized in the process. While this may not be a big problem for CAS, the inherent imbalance in the topology of the antennas and clients in DAS results in a large deviation between the maximum and minimum power allocation to antennas. To illustrate this effect, Figure 3 shows the capacity drop with this naive extension of conventional ZFBF solution to meet the per-antenna power constraint. This trace-based simulation result (for details of testbed, see §5) is for a setup with single four-antenna AP and four single-antenna clients, and clearly indicates that the sub-optimality of a naive power allocation scheme is much more in DAS than in CAS.

3.1.2 Power-balanced precoding

The challenge in designing a lightweight yet efficient precoder for MIDAS is to address the tension between the need to provide interference-free streams and the need to deliver higher power to clients under the per-antenna power constraint. MIDAS balances both these needs to deliver improved MU-MIMO performance. Note that after ZFBF is applied, it is necessary to scale down certain rows of the precoding matrix (corresponding to antennas) that violate the per-antenna power constraint, but this raises the two following problems. Firstly, while different elements in the row may be scaled by different amounts, this must be carefully done as scaling each element of the row directly reduces the SNR and hence rate of one of the streams. Secondly, it is important to scale the elements in the same column (corresponding to a client) by the same factor in order to retain the interference-free property of ZFBF. Hence, the challenge is to pick *scaling weights* w_j $(0 < w_j \leq 1)$ for each client j to apply to the ZFBF precoding solution that will ensure all rows satisfy the per-antenna power constraint, while at the same time keeping the associated loss in power and hence in rate to a minimum. MIDAS realizes this through following novel, iterative, *power-balancing mechanism*:

- **Step 1:** Apply ZFBF to compute the precoding matrix **V**.
- **Step 2:** Normalize each of the columns (clients) of **V**, applying equal power to each stream.
- **Step 3:** Pick the row (AP antenna) k^* that violates the per-antenna power constraint by the most. Determine the appropriate scaling weight w_j $(0 < w_j \leq 1)$ for each element (client) in this row through reverse water-filling to correct the violation.
- **Step 4:** Apply the scaling weight (w_j) computed for each element (v_{k^*j}) of this row (k^*) to the *entire* column corresponding to that stream (*i.e.* $v_{kj} \leftarrow w_jv_{kj}$, $\forall k,j$), thereby retaining the interference-free property of ZFBF. With the updated precoding values, repeat steps 3 and 4 till all rows satisfy the per-antenna power constraint.

Restoring the per-antenna power constraint (Step 3). We now elaborate on the key and novel step of determining the right set of weights w_j to satisfy (3). The received SINR ρ_j in ZFBF is related to the precoded values through (4), where $\rho_j = s_{jj}$. Approximating $\sum_j \log_2(1+\rho_j) \approx \sum_j \log_2(\rho_j)$ for moderate to large ρ_j, we find that when we scale a column of **V** by w_j, the net rate decreases to

$$\sum_j \log_2 \left(\frac{|\sum_{k=1}^{|\mathcal{T}|} h_{jk}v_{kj}|^2}{N_o} \right) + \sum_j \log_2(w_j^2) \tag{6}$$

A 4×4 MU-MIMO precoding matrix scaling is shown in Figure 4. Note that while the rate reduction due to a scaling factor w_j is constant $(\log_2(w_j^2))$ and independent of the precoding value to which it was applied, the corresponding reduction in power allocated to different streams in the same antenna $(|w_jv_{kj}|^2)$ does depend on that precoding value. *Scaling larger precoding values thus contributes to a larger reduction in power, thereby helping meet the power constraint on the antenna with less loss in rate.* MIDAS leverages this key observation in its precoding power allocation algorithm.

When the same scaling factor is applied to all the elements of a row (antenna), this does not leverage the large variation in the precoding values of the row. Given that the latter is typical of a DAS deployment, this results in a large loss in rate. Hence, MIDAS determines a *separate* scaling factor for each of the elements in the row, taking into account their precoding values. It adopts an approach similar in principle to the classic technique of *waterfilling* [27], albeit tailored for our problem. In conventional waterfilling, given some power values in different bins and a remaining power budget, the goal is to find power allocations to the bins such that the aggregate rate is maximized. We have two requirements specifically for our problem: *(i)* we need to potentially re-allocate power in *all* the rows and zero power allocation to any of the streams is not allowed as it will eliminate the use of that stream all together, and *(ii)* when replacing existing power allocations in a row, we don't allow a stream to receive more power than its current allocation because this allocation increase will apply to the same stream in other rows as well, thereby resulting in potential power violations in other rows that were previously satisfied. This is particularly serious

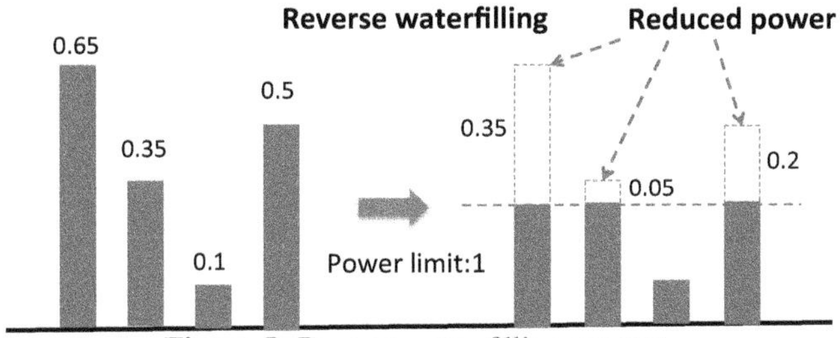

Figure 5: Reverse water-filling concept.

as it can result in oscillations and getting stuck in an infinite loop, preventing convergence to a solution.

Reverse Waterfilling. For these reasons, we address the reverse version of the waterfilling problem, wherein we compute the power *reductions* for each stream in the row so as to satisfy the corresponding antenna power constraint, while keeping the rate loss to a minimum. We refer to this problem as *reverse waterfilling*. Let k be the row in which power violation needs to be restored. The goal is to now maximize the net rate, while ensuring that the power reductions P_j (resulting from down-scaling the precoding values, i.e. $w_j v_{kj}$) restore the per-antenna power constraint.

$$\text{Maximize} \sum_j \log_2\left(1 + w_j^2 \rho_j\right)$$
$$\text{subject to, } \sum_j (|v_{kj}|^2 - P_j) \leq P \tag{7}$$

where $w_j^2 = 1 - \frac{P_j}{|v_{kj}|^2}$. The Lagrangian for the above problem with respect to the vector of power reductions $\mathbb{P}$ is

$$L(\mathbb{P}) = \sum_j \log_2\left(1 + (1 - \frac{P_j}{|v_{kj}|^2})\rho_j\right) - \lambda(\sum_j (|v_{kj}|^2 - P_j)) \tag{8}$$

Applying KKT conditions, one can obtain the power reductions as

$$P_j = \left[(1 + \frac{1}{\rho_j})|v_{kj}|^2 - \frac{1}{\lambda}\right]^+ \tag{9}$$

where $[x]^+ = \max\{x, 0\}$. We now compute λ by applying the $\{P_j\}$ in the power constraint in Eqn. 7. The resulting scaling weights are $w_j = \sqrt{\frac{1}{(|v_{kj}|^2 * \lambda)} - \frac{1}{\rho_j}}$. An illustration of our reverse waterfilling solution is shown in Figure 5. Note that by computing only positive power reductions, we ensure that prior rows for which power violations have been restored are not affected (thereby ensuring convergence). Zero power allocation is not allowed so none of the streams are removed from transmission.

Knowledge of the precoding values allows our solution to leverage the topology imbalance in DAS, while keeping the rate loss to a minimum. This results in a large improvement over applying conventional ZFBF-based MU-MIMO solutions for DAS (see Section 5). Further, computing the reverse waterfilling solution is a lightweight operation, can be done in closed form and needs to be run at most $|\mathcal{T}|$ times. This makes the proposed power-balanced precoding highly amenable to real-time implementation.

3.2 DAS-aware MAC for MU-MIMO

We first provide an overview of the joint MAC and PHY operations in MIDAS. Then, we discuss its various design elements that handle the MAC challenges unique to executing MU-MIMO over a DAS deployment in 802.11ac.

3.2.1 Overview

In MIDAS, each of the antennas at an AP competes for access to the channel independently. The sequence of MU-MIMO operations at each MIDAS AP is as follows:

Step 1: Opportunistic Antenna Selection - Once an antenna at an AP gains channel access, the AP checks the channel status (network allocation vector, NAV timers) of other antennas to see if more antennas can be opportunistically added (§3.2.2, §3.2.3).

Step 2: Virtual Packet Tagging - Each of the packets in the AP's queues are tagged with a subset of the DAS antenna IDs as their preferred antennas (based on channel strength) for transmission to the respective clients (§3.2.4).

Step 3: Client Selection - For each of the available antennas (say n antennas), the AP determines the packet (client) that needs to be scheduled based on both its tag as well as its fairness counter. The antennas are considered in order of their NAV timer expiration. Each antenna chooses a different client, resulting in n potential clients (§3.2.5) for MU-MIMO transmission.

Step 4: Channel Estimation - Once a subset of n clients are determined for MU-MIMO, the AP initiates the channel estimation procedure and obtains the channel state information necessary for precoding (§3.3).

Step 5: Power-balanced Precoding - The AP applies the power-balanced precoding solution to execute MU-MIMO from the available antennas to the selected clients (§3.1).

Step 6: Counter Updates: The fairness counters for all the clients serviced are updated and the procedure repeats.

3.2.2 Channel access at antenna granularity

Challenge: While the ability to sense the channels around the antennas independently allows for finer spatial reuse with DAS, the legacy MAC design in 802.11ac cannot leverage MIDAS's full potential for spatial reuse. This is because 802.11ac's MAC is still designed from the perspective of a CAS, allowing for a single channel state at the transmitter. The approximation of the channel states at multiple antennas with a single channel state parameter becomes highly sub-optimal in a DAS set-up, where the antennas could sense highly disparate channel states (some being idle while others are busy). Engaging all the DAS antennas using the single channel state conservatively (busy even if one antenna busy) would prevent us from leveraging the fine grained spatial reuse offered by DAS, while using it aggressively (idle even if one antenna idle) would exacerbate the hidden terminal problem in MU-MIMO. The key challenge here is to instrument 802.11ac's MAC to allow for independent channel sensing at each of the antennas and leverage it effectively to improve spatial reuse with DAS.

Virtual Carrier Sensing Per-antenna: In addition to physical carrier sensing at each of the antennas, MIDAS allows for independent virtual carrier sensing at each of the antennas by provisioning as many network allocation vector (NAV) timers as antennas. Each of these NAVs captures the duration for which the channel around an antenna is busy (based on overhead data or RTS/CTS headers), thereby indicating which antennas are actually available for a MU-MIMO transmission at any given instant. As we will discuss below in Section 3.3, none of the other MAC related parameters in 802.11ac such as contention window, backoff mechanisms, etc. need to change, making the modifications easier to effect.

3.2.3 Opportunistic antenna selection

Challenge: Since each distributed antenna can sense different channel states at the same time, it is possible that while one antenna is available for transmission, another antenna may not. However, the busy antenna may soon become available within a short duration in the future (based on its NAV timer). An important question arises here: *is it better to wait for additional antennas to become available for MU-MIMO transmission or go with current available antennas?* While waiting for more antennas to become available will increase the number of streams that can be multiplexed in MU-MIMO, thereby delivering better throughput, it could also waste precious air-time in waiting and hence lose throughput.

Opportunistic Selection: To strike a balance, MIDAS *opportunistically* picks antennas for MU-MIMO transmission. When one of the antennas gain access to the channel, the AP checks the NAV timers of the remaining antennas to see if any of them will expire within a DIFS duration. If so, it will wait for those particular antennas to become available and use them all towards MU-MIMO transmission. MIDAS selects the DIFS to be its short waiting period to accumulate antennas for MU-MIMO transmission for the following reasons: *(i)* DIFS is the basic time unit that every AP needs to check for an idle channel before proceeding with any transmission, *(ii)* it gives reasonable room to accumulate more antennas for MU-MIMO transmission, and *(iii)* is not too long to lose out channel access that has been gained.

3.2.4 Filtering clients based on available antennas

Challenge: Unlike CAS, the large disparity in the channel gains from different antennas to a client in a DAS, results in some antennas (with high gains) being naturally preferred for transmission to a client over other antennas. Further, when a antenna's channel state is busy, serving a client in its vicinity from another antenna that is free but farther away, is highly in-efficient. First, the channel gain and hence rate to the client from the farther antenna would be low. More importantly, the channel state of the antenna close to the client being busy should reflect the potential state of the client as well. Hence, making transmissions to such a client might not just be futile but might add to hidden terminals in the network.

Virtual Packet Tagging: Based on the average received signal strength from the different antennas at each client, the MIDAS AP orders the antennas in a decreasing order of preference with respect to each client. It then (virtually) tags each packet meant for a client with the two best antennas from the client's preference list. In other words, a packet for this client is considered for MU-MIMO transmission only if at least one of the two antennas it has been tagged to is available as illustrated in Figure 6. We can see that while A3 and A4 are busy, client 5 and 6 will not be tagged for transmission this round. This not only provides higher transmission rates but also leverages the independent channel sensing feature at antennas effectively to alleviate hidden terminals. Tagging only a single antenna per client can result in under-utilization in some scenarios (*e.g.* clustered user distribution), where some antennas, albeit available, are not leveraged since they have not been tagged by any packets in the AP's queue. Similarly, tagging all antennas per client can result in inefficient topologies as antennas will choose the client far away. With a medium client density, MIDAS tags *two* antennas per client to ensure efficient utilization of AP's antenna resources. This number can be adjusted accordingly with different client densities. Note that the goal of packet tagging is to aid client selection by filtering out clients that are inappropriate for communication from a given set of available antennas. Appropriate selection of clients leads to higher overall capacity.

3.2.5 Antenna-specific client selection

Challenges: An important challenge closely tied to the MAC design is the selection of clients for MU-MIMO transmissions. Once each antenna has been tagged with clients, we need to select a set of clients to receive packets. It is well known that the net rate of a

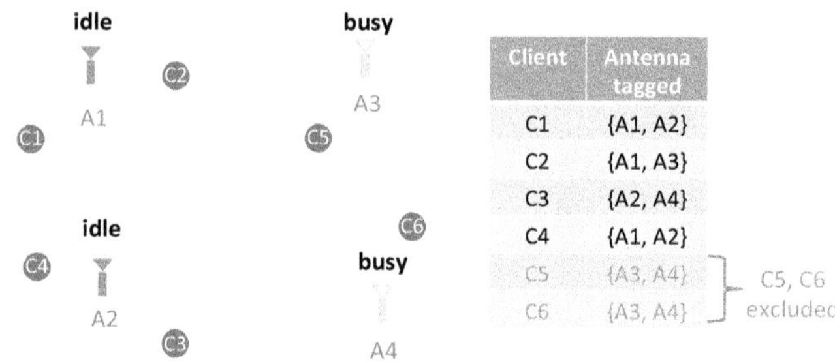

Figure 6: Virtual packet tagging enables more efficient precoding which leads to higher capacity.

MU-MIMO transmission depends on this set of clients chosen for the transmission. While client selection is important even for MU-MIMO in CAS, its significance is amplified in DAS. Due to the distributed topology of antennas, a large difference in the channel gains from different antennas to a client in DAS (unlike in CAS) can be leveraged to improve MU-MIMO performance. It can also hurt performance if clients are not properly chosen. Hence, picking the right set of clients for MU-MIMO has a much larger impact on MU-MIMO performance in DAS than in CAS. Further, client selection policies are implementation dependent and are typically a function of either just fairness or both fairness and instantaneous rate. Incorporating the latter for MU-MIMO is challenging because selecting the best set of clients for a given MU-MIMO transmission requires estimation and feedback of *all* clients' channels to make the decision. However, *measuring CSI from all clients involves not just the overhead of a CSI request (from AP) and response (from all clients), but also significant latency before being able to determine the best subset of clients.* The latter potentially making the estimates too stale to be useful in the first place due to small channel coherence time indoors. One might wonder if prior channel estimates can be used to perform client selection. For this to work, the prior estimates must still be within the coherence time of the clients' channels, which is in the order of tens of milliseconds for a day-time environment in enterprises, etc. [27].

Antenna-specific, Fairness-driven Selection: MIDAS leverages the DAS topology to select clients purely based on their antenna preference and fairness, thereby eliminating the associated channel estimation overhead. Based on opportunistic antenna selection, MIDAS orders the antennas according to their NAV expiry (earliest being first). It then picks the first antenna *(primary antenna)* that gained channel access and applies the scheduling policy only among those packets in the queue that have been tagged (preferred) to this antenna and picks a single packet. It then moves to the next antenna (*secondary antennas*) in the list of available antennas for MU-MIMO transmission and repeats this process to determine packets for all available antennas. Here, since a client's packet can tag two antennas, a client selected for a prior antenna is excluded from being re-considered for a later antenna. Once the set of clients is selected, MU-MIMO transmission is executed jointly from the available set of antennas using the precoding algorithm proposed. *Note that although one client is selected for each antenna, the data streams are transmitted from all the antennas to all the clients with precoding rather than each antenna transmitting to one client.*

Also note that in CAS, since all antennas are similar to each client, CSI estimation and scheduling are tightly coupled and all the clients needs to be considered for the best subset for MU-MIMO. However, due to the topology imbalance in DAS, *picking clients based on their antenna preference contributes to a large part of the client selection gain. This in turn allows MIDAS to decouple CSI estimation from scheduling without an appreciable loss in MU-MIMO performance.*

Scheduling Policy: In terms of the scheduling policy itself, one can employ any desired scheduling policy ranging from simple round-robin to more sophisticated weighted fair queuing schemes with delay guarantees in MIDAS. In particular, deficit round robin (DRR) is a type of weighted fair queuing that also incurs low complexity and is hence conducive for implementation. MIDAS employs DRR as its scheduling policy, albeit tailored for MU-MIMO, but can easily accommodate other scheduling policies as well. Briefly, a deficit counter is maintained for each client (in terms of number of time slots), indicating a measure of pending service for the client for fairness purposes. With each transmission opportunity (called TXOP in 802.11) spanning a contiguous set of time slots (few milliseconds, say T), once the primary antenna gains channel access, the client with the largest deficit counter among those tagged for that antenna is chosen for transmission. Similarly, clients for the other secondary antennas are also chosen based on their deficit counters. Then the deficit counters for all the chosen clients in MU-MIMO transmission are decremented by T, while those that had outstanding packets but did not get selected are incremented by $\frac{nT}{m}$ each, where n is the number of antennas participating in MU-MIMO transmission and m is the number of active clients not chosen for the transmission. In other words, the current service (nT) is distributed equally among the non-scheduled clients to guide the schedule towards a fair allocation.

3.3 Realizing MIDAS within 802.11 ac

MU-MIMO Precoding: 802.11ac provides the framework (channel estimation, precoding, etc.) to realize MU-MIMO. The determination of the specific precoder to apply is implementation dependent. However, since each antenna has its own power amplifier, the precoder needs to satisfy the per-antenna power constraint. Given that the power-balanced precoding in MIDAS is specifically designed to address the per-antenna power constraint and leverage the DAS deployment, it can be easily realized with 802.11ac.

MU-MIMO MAC: 802.11ac adopts a version of 802.11e's MAC and re-purposes it for MU-MIMO. 802.11e was introduced to provide quality of service (QoS) and service differentiation between different traffic classes. It employs four different transmission queues to account for four traffic classes, namely video, voice, best effort and background traffic. Different contention window and timing values are used for the different classes to explicitly prioritize between the classes in their access mechanism. Each of these traffic classes contend internally at the AP, while the AP contends externally with other APs. When the AP gains channel access, only one of the traffic classes gains access. 802.11ac re-purposes these four different queues to enable MU-MIMO transmissions. When one of the traffic classes gains channel access, it is made the primary access class. If sufficient clients (data) are not available in the primary class, clients from secondary traffic classes can be chosen.

MIDAS's MAC operations were explained with respect to a single traffic class. Being designed with 802.11ac in mind, it is easy to see it will readily fit in 802.11ac's MAC. The explicit priorities and channel access procedure for the traffic classes will determine the primary access class as before. Once the primary and secondary traffic classes are determined, MIDAS's client selection and scheduling procedure can be readily applied within each of the traffic classes.

Channel Estimation: Finally, 802.11ac provides complete and elaborate support for channel estimation (through a process called *sounding* with the help of null data packets) and feedback that are critical for MU-MIMO precoding. However, such estimation is invoked only after an AP gains channel access and hence *only CSI of those clients chosen for MU-MIMO transmission will be available to the AP*. Note that, MIDAS employs an antenna-specific, fairness-based client selection process that selects efficient client topologies for MU-MIMO without relying on CSI estimates. This makes it well-aligned with the support provided by 802.11ac.

4. IMPLEMENTATION

Testbed and Deployment: Our goal is to realize MIDAS with off-the-shelf 802.11ac APs and clients. However, the current 802.11ac APs do not implement MU-MIMO yet, which is expected to be a part of the next release, scheduled for the end of this year. Hence, we implement MIDAS on the WARP [20] platform using a representative version of the relevant PHY and MAC mechanisms in 802.11ac that we need for our purpose. Each WARP board can support up to four RF front-ends and is connected to a host PC. The host PC performs the (de-) construction and processing of baseband waveforms to and from the FPGA board with the RF front-ends. The WARP board along with the host PC serves as the AP itself, with its four RF boards connected with four antennas. Single antenna WARP boards are used for the clients. To realize a DAS set-up, the four antennas are distributed around the AP with the help of RF coaxial cables.

PHY/MAC Implementation: All the baseband processing happens on the main board. With the host PC processing the transmitted (received) data, our power-balanced precoding mechanism is implemented in the host PC and applied to the data streams that are transmitted through the RF front-ends. The precoding is performed while adhering to the constraints imposed by 802.11ac's PHY specification. With each of the RF front-ends having their own power amplifiers, this incorporates the per-antenna power constraint imposed by the 802.11ac specification. We significantly instrument the basic CSMA MAC in WARP to realize the DAS-aware MAC in MIDAS. We start with a basic implementation of 802.11g for WARP and then incorporate the relevant MAC features from 802.11ac that are needed for our purpose. Specifically, we provision individual MAC states, *i.e.* the virtual carrier sensing parameter (network allocation vector, NAV) and enable packet detection for each of the DAS antennas. We implement multiple NAV states, individual packet detection and opportunistic antenna selection along with the notion of virtual packet tagging. We also implement the deficit round robin policy for scheduling multiple clients tagged to an antenna. Because of the large delay of WARP platform, we are still not able to realize a close-loop MAC. Thus we implement the MAC schemes on top of the latest WARP 802.11 Reference Design with Xilinx XPS 13.4 and feed the MAC layer decision into the PHY layer implementation, in which we implement the channel estimation, power-balanced precoding and upto 4x4 MU-MIMO on WARPLab reference design.

5. EVALUATION

We break down our experimental evaluation of MIDAS into three parts: (i) PHY layer precoding, (ii) MAC layer features, and (iii) end-end PHY+MAC. We also evaluate MIDAS in larger topologies through simulations using channel traces.

5.1 Methodology, Baseline & Metrics

We deploy our testbed in both indoor enterprise and academic lab environments. We consider up to three APs, each with at most four antennas and capable of performing upto 4×4 MU-MIMO. APs are deployed with an inter-AP distance of around 15 m, while the WARP client boards are located in offices/rooms as well as in the corridor. The antennas are co-located at the AP in CAS with a half-wavelength distance in-between, while they are distributed around the AP in DAS with a distance of 5 -10 m from the AP. Each antenna has its own power amplifier in both CAS and DAS. We run our experiments by sending back to back packets for 10 seconds from the AP to clients and recording the results by averaging over multiple runs for each topology and over 50 to 100 different topologies.

We evaluate the benefits from MIDAS's precoding and MAC mechanism against several baselines. For precoding, we evaluate our power-balanced precoding against both the optimal precoding through the MATLAB numerical toolbox as well as a simple extension to conventional ZFBF precoding. The latter first splits power equally to all the streams, then scales the power of all the antennas by a common factor in order to satisfy the per-antenna power constraints. For MAC, we evaluate our proposed MAC against a CAS system with a conventional CSMA MAC.

We translate measured SINR for the data streams at different clients into network capacity using the Shannon capacity formula. Note that, unlike for open-loop MIMO schemes, where rate adaptation is needed, for closed-loop MIMO schemes like MU-MIMO, the CSI information is directly used to determine the appropriate rate (modulation and coding) that must be applied for a stream, eliminating the need for an explicit rate adaptation process. Hence, measured SINR from experiments would directly translate to capacity as well.

5.2 Power-balanced Precoding in MIDAS

5.2.1 Benchmarking link gain from DAS

The CDF curves of link layer SNR for CAS and DAS during SISO transmissions from a single AP are shown in Figure 7. The CAS antenna positions are fixed while DAS antennas and clients are randomly deployed in 60 different topologies. Each AP has four antennas attached. The SNR value is measured when only one antenna transmits to the client. Each client is mapped to one antenna in a greedy way: the client with the strongest signal is chosen and this mapped antenna-client pair is excluded for next round mapping. It can be seen that *the shorter DAS links to clients provide a median link gain of 5 dB with four antennas.* This gain keeps increasing with more clients and antennas.

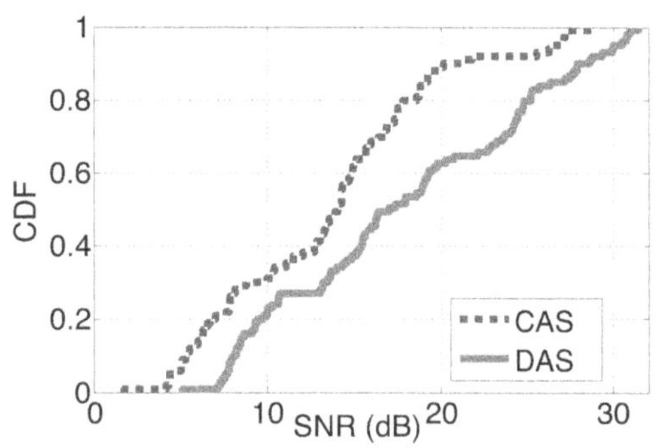

Figure 7: Distribution (across clients) of link layer SNR.

5.2.2 MU-MIMO capacity increase

In order to evaluate the MU-MIMO capacity increase, we fix the CAS antenna positions of a single AP and randomly deploy the clients and DAS antennas. We present the overall capacity (calculated from measured SINR) of MIDAS and CAS with 2x2 MU-MIMO and 4x4 MU-MIMO in Figure 8 and Figure 9. Here, while CAS employs the baseline precoding mechanism, MIDAS employs our power-balanced precoding. We carry out experiments in two different indoor office environments: an enterprise (Office A) and a graduate student lab (Office B), which is more crowded. We can see that *MIDAS has a median gain of 40-67% over CAS for two antennas, that increases to 45-80% with higher number (four) of antennas.* The gains are *contributed both by the link gain from DAS as well as the power-balanced precoding in MIDAS.*

5.2.3 Impact of power-balanced precoding

We isolate the impact of our smart, power-balanced precoding scheme in Figure 10 for the four antenna case (Office B). We compare the performance of DAS and CAS when applying our power-balanced precoding respectively. While our *smart precoding also helps CAS improve its median capacity by 12% (11.5 to 13 bits/s/Hz), the improvement is much greater for DAS (about 30%).* Thus, the benefits of the power-balanced precoding are more pronounced for DAS than for CAS. This also corroborates our intuition that a naive power allocation scheme (like the baseline), albeit fine for CAS, is not sufficient for DAS due to its inherent topology imbalance.

We also compare our smart precoding scheme and the optimal precoder obtained from solving the precoding optimization problem through the MATLAB numerical solver/toolbox in Figure 11. The evaluation is conducted on both the testbed as well as through traces. In trace-based simulations, we see that our *precoding in MIDAS performs efficiently within 99% of the optimal, while not incurring the complexity or processing latency of the latter.* In the experiments, interestingly, in a few of the topologies, the MIDAS precoding scheme even outperforms the optimal precoder. One possible reason for this is that it takes a couple of seconds for the optimization toolbox to calculate the optimal precoder. By the time the precoder is determined, the channel could have changed (even slightly), resulting in the precoder being no longer optimal. This also reinforces our claim that *a fast, light weight precoding algorithm is essential for MU-MIMO given the short coherence time of the wireless channel.*

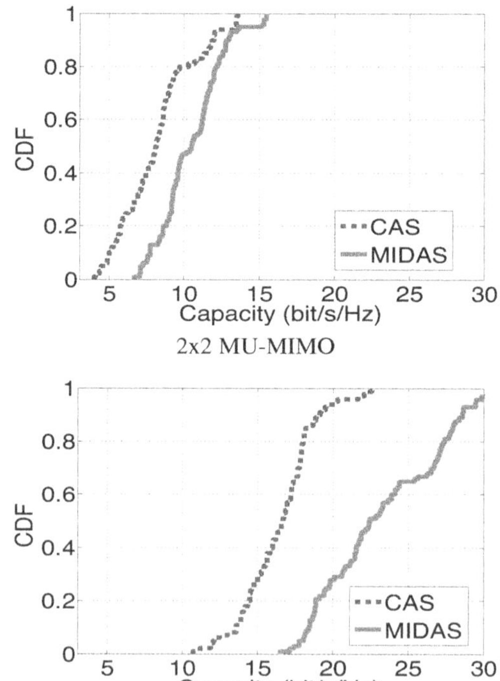

Figure 8: MIDAS capacity increase (Office A).

5.3 DAS-aware MAC in MIDAS

We evaluate in this section MIDAS' MAC described in §3.2.

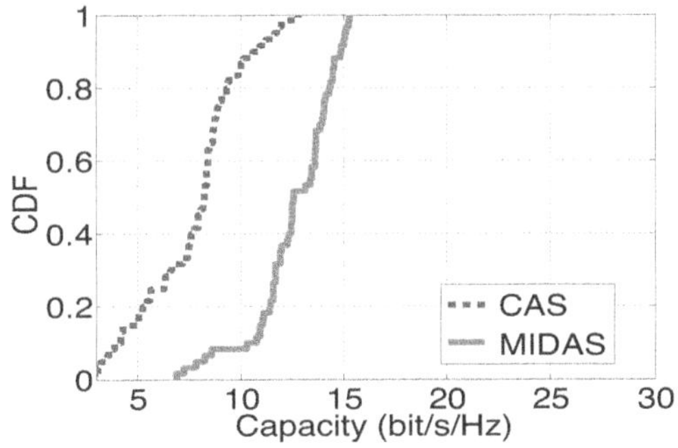

2x2 MU-MIMO

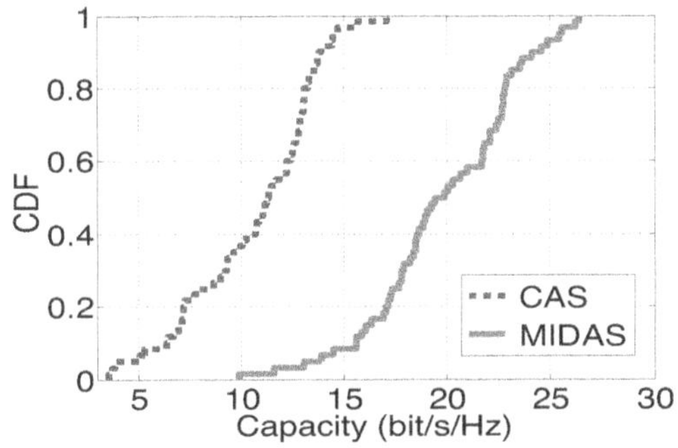

4x4 MU-MIMO

Figure 9: MIDAS capacity increase (Office B).

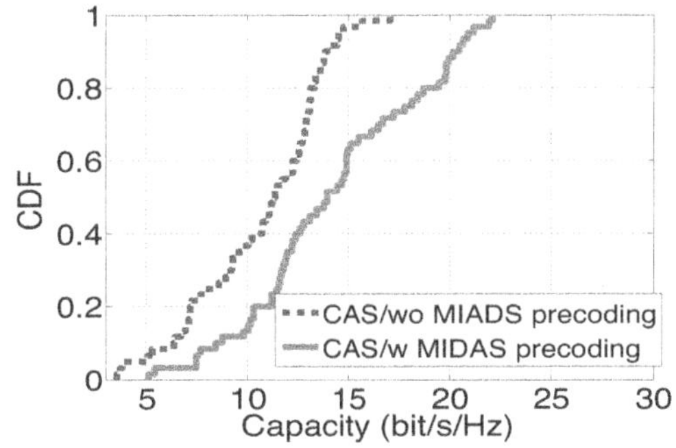

CAS improvement with MIDAS precoding

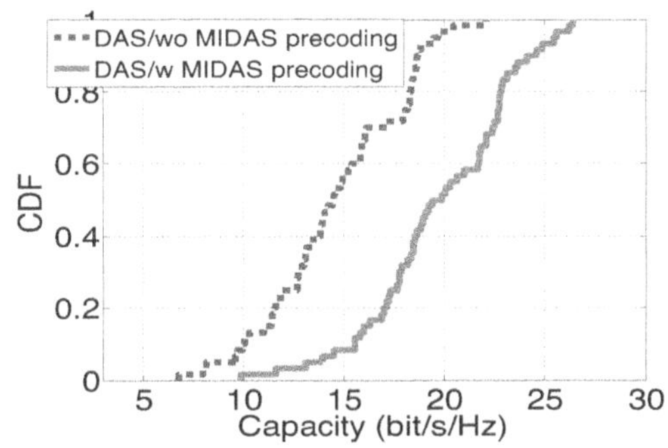

DAS improvement with MIDAS precoding

Figure 10: Impact of Smart Precoding in CAS and DAS.

5.3.1 Number of Simultaneous Transmissions

We first evaluate the total number of simultaneous transmissions (spatial reuse) that can be supported by the MAC. We deploy three APs that can overhear each other. For CAS setup, one AP can be activated at a time to support four simultaneous transmissions. As the antennas are distributed at different locations in MIDAS, the NAV values and channel sensing results are different at each DAS antenna. The channel is thus utilized more efficiently in a finer manner. To evaluate the number of simultaneous transmissions can be supported at the MIDAS APs, we randomly enable one to four transmissions at the first AP A and then check the number of transmissions can be supported simultaneously at the second AP B based on its NAVs and channel sensing results. Next, we enable all the transmissions supported at both A and B and similarly evaluate the number of transmissions that can be simultaneously supported at AP C. Note that more simultaneous transmissions does not necessarily mean higher overall capacity. The overall capacity also depends on the capacity of each transmission. We show the end-to-end capacity evaluation in Section 5.4. We run experiments for 30 topologies generated by random antenna deployments. In order to avoid bias in results, for each deployment, the following requirement is satisfied: any two antennas from the same AP cannot be deployed within a 60-degree sector measured with respect to the AP. This ensures that antennas are not clustered at the far end with respect to the other two APs to favor the results. Our testbed results in Figure 12 show that among all the 30 topologies, only two MIDAS deployments support less transmissions compared to CAS. *The median improvement in the total number of transmissions is around 50%, while 90% improvement can be achieved for some topologies. This can be directly attributed to the fine grained spatial reuse enabled in MIDAS to leverage the DAS deployment. Note that with the same number of transmissions in Section 5.2.2, MIDAS already outperforms CAS.*

5.3.2 Significance of virtual packet tagging

We consider a scenario where two antennas (out of four) at a MIDAS AP are available at the MAC layer, while there are a total of four clients to be selected for transmission. With virtual packet tagging, MIDAS chooses a more appropriate group of two clients. We also assume there are always packets for all the four clients in the queue. We present the results in Figure 14 and compare this scheme against a scheme that chooses two clients randomly. We can clearly observe a *50% increase in median capacity that results from picking clients intelligently to aid in better MU-MIMO transmissions.*

5.3.3 Deadzone reduction

We now show that a MIDAS deployment can help alleviate the problem of signal deadzones. We deploy the AP in both MIDAS and CAS modes, with the DAS antennas randomly deployed surrounding the AP. Then we carry out measurements within the coverage area for deadspots and one measurement is taken every 0.5 m. We show one typical MIDAS/CAS deadzone comparison map in Figure 13. The gray small squares indicate the deadspots identified. We can clearly see that deadzone spots are much fewer in MIDAS. On average of 10 different random antenna deployments, *DAS deployment helps provide more effective client coverage,resulting in a significant reduction of deadspots by about 91% compared to CAS.*

5.3.4 Alleviating hidden terminals

We setup two APs, AP1 and AP2. They are separated far enough that they cannot overhear each other but not too far to eliminate hidden terminals. We distribute the DAS antennas randomly around APs within a distance of 50%-75% of the CAS AP's transmission range from the original AP. We then measure the number of hidden terminal spots in the area with a distance of one meter between each measured spots in 10 random antenna deployment topologies. We found that, *on average DAS has 94% hidden terminal spots*

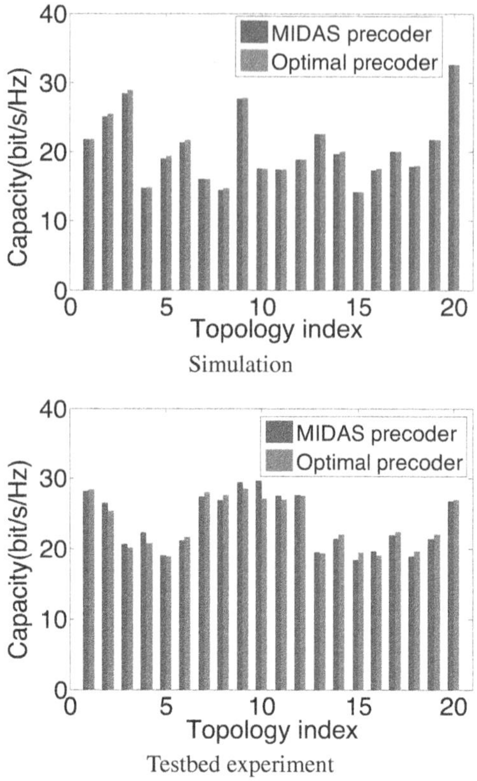

Figure 11: Comparing MIDAS vs optimal precoding.

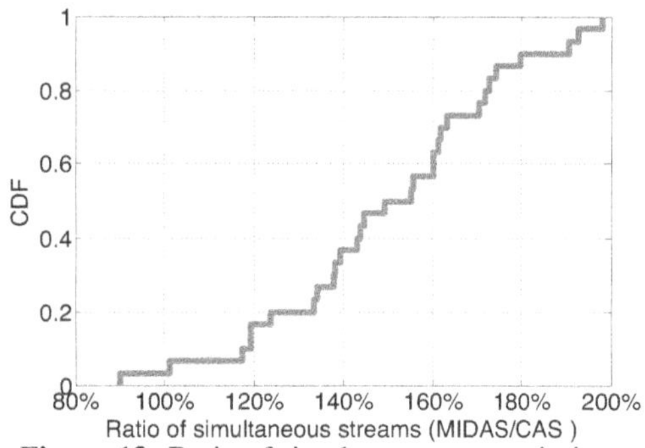

Figure 12: Ratio of simultaneous transmissions.

removed compared with CAS, thereby alleviating hidden terminals significantly. This can be attributed to two reasons: *(i)* distributed antennas in MIDAS are able to sense a larger region compared to collocated antennas in CAS, and *(ii)* while the transmission power is maximal at the AP and decreases with distance in CAS, it is more evenly distributed around the AP in DAS, allowing for better detection by other DAS/CAS APs.

5.4 End-End Evaluation of MIDAS

The setup consists of a three-AP network. Each of the APs is capable of up to 4 × 4 MU-MIMO transmissions. Each AP has four randomly deployed clients around it. The CAS APs employ the traditional CSMA MAC with the baseline precoding scheme while the MIDAS APs employ the DAS-aware MAC coupled with our power-balanced precoding described in Sections 3.2 and 3.1 respectively. The overall capacity performance between CAS and MIDAS is shown in Figure 15. The CDF is measured over 60 different topologies. *MIDAS achieves a significant improvement of*

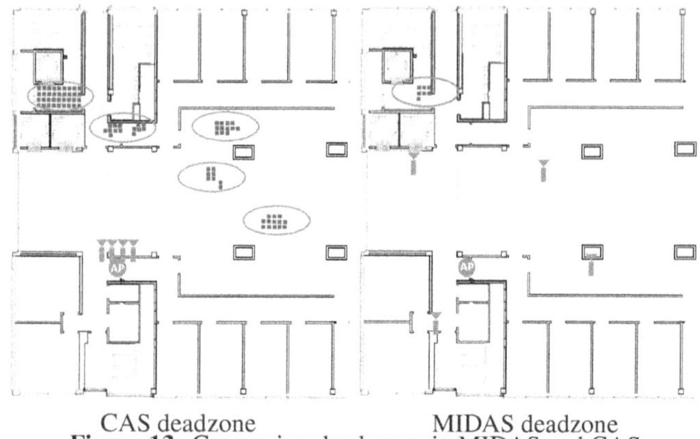

Figure 13: Comparing deadzones in MIDAS and CAS

200% in capacity gain over CAS. The substantial PHY+MAC gain in MIDAS is the culmination of three factors: *(i)* For the same number of streams, MIDAS outperforms CAS in MU-MIMO performance; *(ii)* For the same number of APs, more simultaneous streams are enabled in MIDAS due to its DAS-aware channel-sensing MAC; and *(iii)* Virtual packet tagging in MIDAS takes advantage of the DAS topology to further increase MU-MIMO performance through intelligent client selection.

5.5 Large Scale Trace-based Simulations

We carried out trace-based simulation to verify MIDAS end-to-end performance in a large scale setup. We randomly deploy eight APs in a 60 × 60 m region. All the APs are capable of performing up to 4 × 4 MU-MIMO transmission. We make sure none of the CAS APs can overhear more than three other APs for each deployment. For the DAS antenna deployment, none of the antennas can be deployed out of the original AP coverage area and no two antennas can be deployed within 5 m of distance. We measure the CSI and the interference level between AP antennas and clients and feedback the traces to the simulation. The overall result is shown in Figure 16. We can see that the large scale simulation result follows the trend we obtain in testbed: DAS outperforms CAS by more than 150%.

6. RELATED WORK

MIDAS makes contributions in the areas of MU-MIMO precoding power allocation and medium access control. In this section we survey the related work in each area and place MIDAS's contributions into context. We close with a review of other DAS systems and theoretical proposals.

MU-MIMO precoding. Several systems have taken multi-user MIMO [3, 26], interference alignment [8, 15] and distributed MU-MIMO [19, 5, 13, 30] from theory to practice. Falling under the multi-AP deployment model discussed in Section 2, their precoding solutions are neither designed to leverage the topology imbalance in DAS, nor satisfy the per-antenna power constraint imposed by 802.11ac in an lightweight manner. Other precoders specifically designed for DAS systems [14] are designed only for a sum-power constraint (§3.1) while [25] is designed for large number of users and high mobility users. On the other hand, prior precoders designed with the per-antenna power constraint in mind are unfortunately too complex to realize in practice [11, 18, 32] (and references therein). Waterfilling is a popular technique used to allocate a fixed power budget to orthogonal channels of varying gains, such as OFDM subcarriers. It has been extensively studied, both for Gaussian [27] as well as arbitrary input distributions for SISO and MIMO systems [17]. Prior work in power allocation for DAS systems either focus on

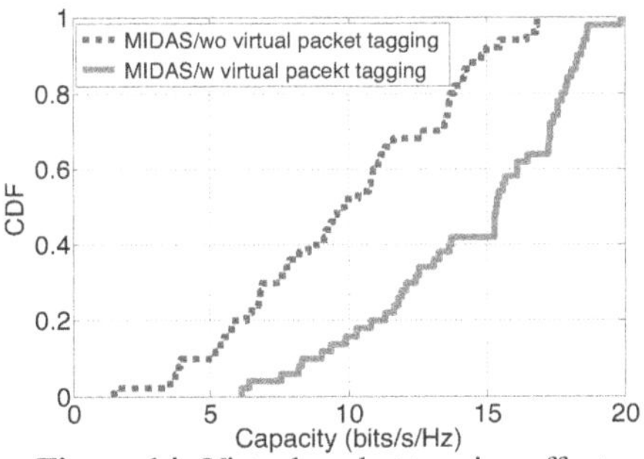

Figure 14: Virtual packet tagging effect

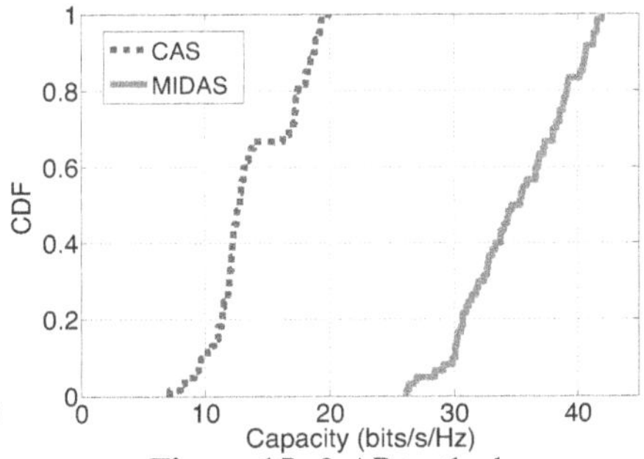

Figure 15: 3-AP testbed

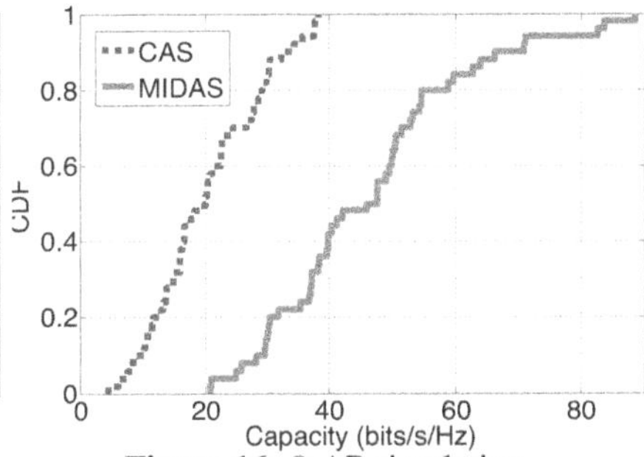

Figure 16: 8-AP simulation.

single-user communications [12, 31], or operates under a sum power constraint instead of a per-antenna power constraint [9]. The nature of the practical constraints to our MU-MIMO precoding problem over DAS prevents MIDAS from employing these solutions. Being specifically designed for the dual challenges of the per-antenna power constraint and a DAS deployment model, the lightweight precoder advances the state-of-the-art in this area.

Medium access control & rate adaptation. The MAC in MIDAS is also concerned with a virtual selection and tagging of antennas to aid client selection for MU-MIMO. This is different from conventional antenna selection [16], which arises because antennas used for communication are limited by the available RF chains. Recently, NEMOx [32] designed a random access MAC for distributed MU-MIMO systems. However, being designed from scratch, it does not directly lend itself to 802.11ac systems that in turn form our focus. Other work [24] focuses on rate adaption for MU-MIMO.

Other DAS systems. Serving as a simple broadcast medium, DAS has traditionally been used to provide coverage and handle mobility in WiFi and cellular systems [1, 2]. Recent proposals [33, 34] have combined DAS with frequency or spatial reuse to enable multi-user transmissions, albeit still operating under SISO. Other theoretical work [6, 23, 22, 10] has studied the benefits of applying MU-MIMO techniques over DAS, albeit using conventional MIMO precoding solutions that limit their potential to leverage DAS for reasons explained in §3.1.

7. DISCUSSION

Deployment. In most enterprises, APs are attached to walls/ceilings and wired over the ceilings for safety and aesthetics. A similar approach can be adopted in deploying the MIDAS antennas. The RF extension cables can be run over the ceiling, thereby incurring very little additional effort and expense. Deploying DAS antennas too close to the AP makes the system tend to a CAS, leading to reduced channel utilization. On the other hand, positioning too far from the AP may have an adverse impact on links and the MU-MIMO performance. From experience, a good distance is 50-75% of the AP's CAS coverage range. We leave the problem of optimizing placement of antennas open for future work.

Beamforming. While employing multiple antennas to send multiple streams to different clients would leverage multiplexing (MU-MIMO), using all them to alternatively send a single stream to a single client would leverage beamforming. However, beamforming (SNR) gain is logarithmic unlike the multiplexing gain (that is linear). Due to the decoupled nature of the antennas in MIDAS, when all antennas at an AP are leveraged for beamforming, this would not only come at the expense of multiplexing gain but would also silence other antennas (of other APs) in the neighborhood, thereby limiting the potential for improved spatial reuse from MIDAS. Hence, in low client densities, when an AP is restricted to beamforming to a single client, it is important to leverage only the antennas in the neighborhood of the client for beamforming in MIDAS, thereby not affecting spatial reuse by antennas of other nearby APs.

Co-located antennas in a DAS topology. In this work we deploy DAS antennas separately, but one might wonder whether it would be beneficial to co-locate more antennas, especially if clients have multiple antennas. We argue, however, that deploying non-co-located DAS antennas is still the right approach. If a client had more antennas (say m), and we also deploy m AP antennas at each location, which in turn would reduce the number of DAS deployment locations possible, degrading the DAS deployment advantage. Having more deployment locations (with a single antenna) and allowing them to cooperate still leverage all the multiplexing gain possible, while catering to more clients associated with the AP.

SVD precoding. SVD is employed as a precoding scheme in 802.11n, when multiple streams are sent to a single client with multiple antennas. However, due to the distributed nature of clients in 802.11ac, SVD is not suited because the clients do not share streams with each other in 802.11ac. Even with MIMO transmissions to a single client with multiple antennas in 802.11ac, SVD is still not a good candidate for MIDAS because of the imbalanced topology in DAS and the (equal) power allocation nature of SVD.

8. CONCLUSION

With next generation wireless local area networks moving to multi-user MIMO communication, we argue that the conventional co-located AP antenna topology is inefficient from both physical- and MAC-layer perspectives. Towards helping wireless service providers leverage the most out of 802.11ac APs, we have presented the design and implementation of MIDAS, a multiple input distributed antenna system, that migrates an 802.11ac AP to a DAS topology, supplementing it with a suite of novel PHY and MAC mechanisms to maximize network performance. We have shown that MIDAS's mechanisms are lightweight additions to an AP's software device driver, not requiring any changes to 802.11ac's hardware. We have described our WARP radio implementation and presented results from our experimental testbed that demonstrate MIDAS's techniques will significantly increase the capacity of tomorrow's 802.11ac networks.

9. ACKNOWLEDGEMENTS

The research leading to these results has received funding from the European Research Council under the EU's 7th Framework Programme (FP/2007-2013), ERC grant agreement number 279976. Jie Xiong is supported by a Google European Doctoral Fellowship in Wireless Networking and part of this work was done at NEC Labs America during his internship.

10. REFERENCES

[1] The hetnet forum. http://www.thedasforum.org.

[2] T. Alade, H. Zhu, and H. Osman. Spectral efficiency analysis of distributed antenna system for in-building wireless communication. In *Personal Indoor and Mobile Radio Communications*, 2011.

[3] E. Aryafar, N. Anand, T. Salonidis, and E. W. Knightly. Design and experimental evaluation of multi-user beamforming in wireless lans. In *MobiCom*, 2010.

[4] Distributed Antenna System: Keeping customers connected, wherever they are (AT&T). http://www.att.com/gen/press-room?pid=23351.

[5] H. V. Balan, R. Rogalin, A. Michaloliakos, K. Psounis, and G. Caire. Airsync: Enabling distributed multiuser mimo with full spatial multiplexing. *Networking, ACM Transactions on*, 21(6), 2013.

[6] B. Cho, S. Seo, and J. Kim. Practical scheme to enable MIMO communications in distributed antenna systems for efficient indoor coverage. In *International Symposium on Communications and Information Technology*, 2009.

[7] Positioning Statement on Cisco Wireless LAN over Distributed Antenna Systems (Cisco Corp.).

[8] S. Gollakota, S. D. Perli, and D. Katabi. Interference alignment and cancellation. In SIGCOMM, 2009.

[9] N. Hassan, C. Yuen, and Z. Zhang. Optimal power control and antenna selection for multi-user distributed antenna system with heterogeneous QoS constraints. In *Globecom Workshop*, 2012.

[10] R. Heath, T. Wu, Y. H. Kwon, and A. C. Soong. Multiuser mimo in distributed antenna systems. In *Signals, Systems and Computers (ASILOMAR), 2010 Conference Record of the Forty Fourth Asilomar Conference on*, pages 1202–1206. IEEE, 2010.

[11] S. Kaviani and W. Kryzmien. Optimal multiuser zero forcing with per-antenna power constraints for network mimo coordination. EURASIP *J on Wireless Comms. and Netw.*, 2011.

[12] H. Kim, S.-R. Lee, C. Song, and I. Lee. Optimal power allocation for energy efficiency maximization in distributed antenna systems. In ICC, 2013.

[13] S. Kumar, D. Cifuentes, S. Gollakota, and D. Katabi. Bringing cross-layer MIMO to today's wireless LANs. In *SIGCOMM*, 2013.

[14] Q. Li, X. Wang, and X. Feng. Design of linear pre-coders and equalizers for the uplink in multiuser distributed antenna system. In BMSB, 2013.

[15] K. Lin, S. Gollakota, and D. Katabi. Random access heterogeneous MIMO networks. In SIGCOMM, 2011.

[16] S. Mahboob, R. Ruby, and V. Leung. Transmit antenna selection for downlink transmission in a massively distributed antenna system using convex optimization. In BWCCA, 2012.

[17] F. P-Criz, , M. Rodrigues, and S. Verdu. Generlized mercury/waterfilling for multiple-input multiple-output channels. In *ACCC*, 2007.

[18] Z. Pi. Optimal mimo transmission with per-antenna power constraints. In *IEEE Globecom*, Dec 2012.

[19] H. Rahul, S. Kumar, and D. Katabi. MegaMIMO: Scaling Wireless Capacity with User Demands. In *ACM SIGCOMM 2012*, Helsinki, Finland, August 2012.

[20] Rice WARP Platform. http://warpproject.org.

[21] A. Saleh, A. Rustako, and R. Roman. Distributed antennas for indoor radio communications. IEEE *Trans. on Comms.*, COM-35(12):1245–51, 1987.

[22] S. Schwarz, R. W. Heath Jr, and M. Rupp. Single-user mimo versus multi-user mimo in distributed antenna systems with limited feedback. *EURASIP Journal on Advances in Signal Processing*, 2013(1), 2013.

[23] C. Shen, S. Zhou, and Y. Yao. Comparison of channel capacity for MIMO-DAS & MIMO-CAS. In APCC, 2003.

[24] W. Shen, Y. Tung, K. Lee, K. Lin, S. Gollakota, D. Katabi, and M. Chen. Rate adaptation for 802.11 multiuser mimo networks. In *MobiCom '12*.

[25] C. Shepard, N. Anand, and L. Zhong. Practical performance of mu-mimo precoding in many-antenna base stations. In *CellNet '13*.

[26] K. Tan, H. Liu, J. Fang, W. Wang, J. Zhang, M. Chen, and G. M. Voelker. SAM: Enabling practical spatial multiple access in wireless LAN. In *MobiCom*, 2009.

[27] D. Tse and P. Viswanath. *Fundamentals of Wireless Communication*. Cambridge University Press, 2005.

[28] A. Wiesel, Y. C. Eldar, and S. Shamai. Zero-forcing precoding and generalized inverses. *Signal Processing, IEEE Transactions on*, 56(9):4409–4418, 2008.

[29] H. Xia, A. Herrera, S. Kim, and F. Rico. A CDMA-distributed antenna system for in-building personal communications services. IEEE JSAC, 1996.

[30] Q. Yang, X. Li, H. Yao, J. Fang, K. Tan, W. Hu, Z. J, and Y. Zhang. Bigstation: Enabling scalable real-time signal processing in large mu-mimo systems. In *SIGCOMM'13*.

[31] X. Zhang, Y. Sun, X. Chen, S. Zhou, J. Wang, and N. Shroff. Distributed power allocation for coordinated multipoint transmissions in distributed antenna systems. IEEE *Trans. on Wireless Comms.*, 12(5), 2013.

[32] X. Zhang, K. Sundaresan, M. Khojastepour, S. Rangarajan, and K. Shin. NEMOx: Scalable network MIMO for wireless networks. In *MobiCom*, 2013.

[33] H. Zhu. On frequency reuse in distributed antenna systems. In VTC, 2011.

[34] H. Zhu and J. Wang. Radio resource allocation in multiuser distributed antenna systems. JSAC, 2013.

MoFA: Mobility-aware Frame Aggregation in Wi-Fi

Seongho Byeon, Kangjin Yoon
Okhwan Lee, Sunghyun Choi
Department of ECE and INMC
Seoul National Univeristy, Seoul, Korea
{shbyeon, kjyoon,
ohlee}@mwnl.snu.ac.kr
schoi@snu.ac.kr

Woonsun Cho, Seungseok Oh
CDD Team, Service Development Division
LG U+, Daejun, Korea
{vestsun, hanbawy}@lguplus.co.kr

ABSTRACT

IEEE 802.11n WLAN supports frame aggregation called aggregate MAC protocol data unit (A-MPDU) as a key MAC technology to achieve high throughput. While it has been generally accepted that aggregating more subframes results in higher throughput by reducing protocol overheads, our measurements reveal various situations where the use of long A-MPDU frames frequently leads to poor performance in time-varying environments. Especially, since mobility intensifies the time-varying nature of the wireless channel, the current method of channel estimation conducted only at the beginning of a frame reception is insufficient to ensure robust delivery of long A-MPDU frames. Based on extensive experiments, we develop MoFA, a standard-compliant mobility-aware A-MPDU length adaptation scheme with ease of implementation. Our prototype implementation in commercial 802.11n devices shows that MoFA achieves the throughput 1.8x higher than a fixed duration setting (i.e., 10 ms, the maximum frame duration according to IEEE 802.11n standard). To our best knowledge, this is the first effort to optimize the A-MPDU length for commercial 802.11n devices.

Categories and Subject Descriptors

C.2.1 [**Network Architecture and Design**]: Wireless communication

General Terms

Algorithms, Measurement, Performance

Keywords

IEEE 802.11 Wireless Local Area Network (WLAN); Frame Aggregation; Channel Estimation; Mobility

CoNEXT'14, December 2–5, 2014, Sydney, Australia.

ACM 978-1-4503-3279-8/14/12 ...$15.00.
http://dx.doi.org/10.1145/2674005.2674995.

1. INTRODUCTION

Wireless local area network (WLAN) technology has become an essential and indispensable part of our everyday life. Wi-Fi based on IEEE 802.11 WLAN standard has been one of the most successful wireless technologies supporting ever increasing demand of users. This tremendous success has led to significant growth of mobile WLAN data traffic volume primarily generated by pedestrian users. Accordingly, understanding the impact of mobility such as time-varying channel dynamics on the WLAN performance is becoming increasingly important.

IEEE 802.11 is evolving from 802.11a/b/g to 802.11n/ac in order to meet the much-needed high-throughput demand of smartphones, laptops, and tablet PCs [12]. To achieve high throughput, IEEE 802.11n defines two types of frame aggregation: MAC service data unit (MSDU) aggregation and MAC protocol data unit (MPDU) aggregation. In this paper, we deal with the latter, the aggregate MPDU (A-MPDU), which amortizes PHY protocol overhead over multiple frames by packing several MPDUs into a single A-MPDU. It is generally considered that A-MPDU is more efficient in error-prone environments thanks to the usage of block acknowledgements (BlockAcks) which allow each of the aggregated MPDUs (i.e., A-MPDU subframes) to be individually acknowledged and selectively retransmitted.

Understandingly, it has been believed that longer A-MPDU conveying more A-MPDU subframes always achieves higher throughput by reducing protocol overheads [8, 9, 11, 15]. All the existing studies have found the optimal length of MAC frames based on mathematical analysis and/or simulations, assuming a uniform distribution of errors across an entire A-MPDU.

However, our experimental results reveal strong evidence that the distribution of errors over the entire A-MPDU is not uniform, especially, for mobile users. For example, we observe that when long A-MPDU frames are used, the throughput is reduced by up to two thirds regardless of the channel condition at the receiver in time-varying channel environment, even if an appropriate PHY rate is selected. Furthermore, we find many scenarios where the performance actually degrades as the length of A-MPDU increases due to the limited channel compensation procedure executed by Wi-Fi devices. In such cases, the channel state information (CSI) measured using the physical layer convergence protocol (PLCP) preamble at the beginning of the A-MPDU may no longer be valid for subframes in the latter part of A-MPDU under the time-varying channel. Specifically, the

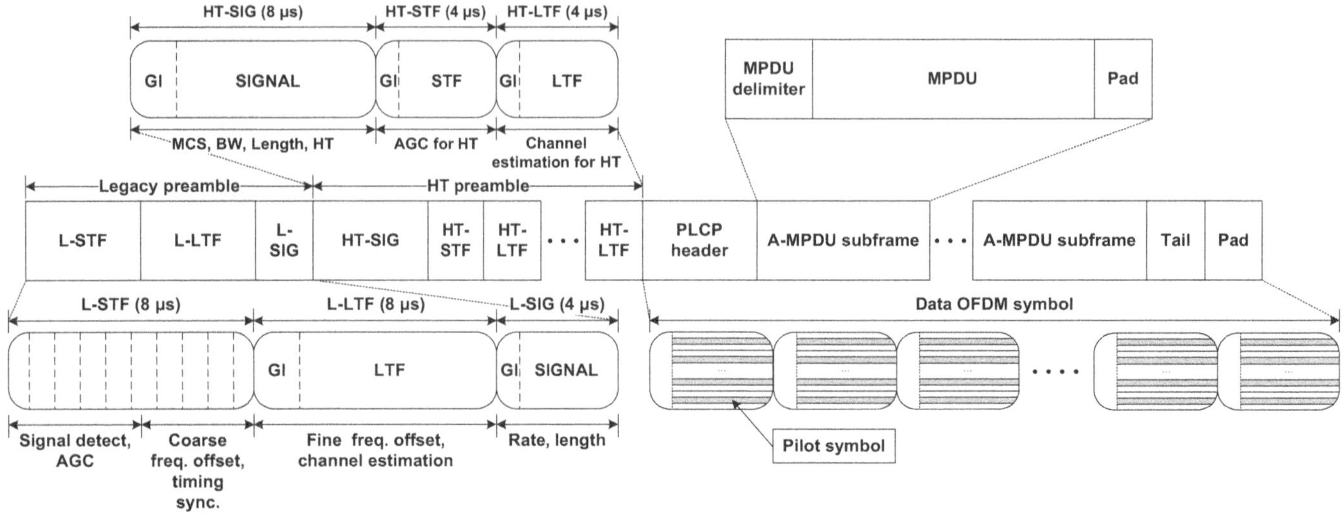

Figure 1: IEEE 802.11n MAC/PHY mixed-mode PPDU frame format of A-MPDU.

subframe error rate (SFER) may increase as the time gap between the preamble and subframe increases, since automatic gain control (AGC), timing acquisition, frequency acquisition, and channel estimation steps are conducted only during the PLCP preamble reception. It therefore leads to higher SFER in the latter part of A-MPDU than that in the beginning part when the channel condition substantially changes during the A-MPDU reception.

The primary contribution of this paper is a novel algorithm that dynamically adapts the length of A-MPDU that is robust against time-varying channels and without requiring any modification of the standard.

- We first analyze the wireless channel dynamics considering mobility in IEEE 802.11n WLAN through extensive measurements. From this, we reveal the fundamental problem of existing frame aggregation schemes manifested over a wide range of mobility and IEEE 802.11n PHY features.
- We then propose MoFA, a novel standard-compliant algorithm, which dynamically adapts the length of A-MPDU in real-time, by observing the mobility-caused channel dynamics in order to maximize the network performance.
- To demonstrate the effectiveness of MoFA, we conduct experiments using prototype implementation at the device driver of off-the-shelf 802.11n network interface cards (NICs).
- Finally, from the experimental results, the performance gain of our techniques over the standard 802.11n configuration is found to achieve up to 1.8x improvement.

To the best of our knowledge, this is the first work that develops mobility-aware adaptation of A-MPDU length that is robust against time-varying channels caused by mobility. We expect MoFA to enhance the performance of low error tolerant real-time applications such as online gaming and video streaming on a mobile device.

The rest of the paper is organized as follows. Section 2 introduces the background and describes our experimental setting. In Section 3, we empirically study the impact of mobility on IEEE 802.11n systems. Then, the detailed design of MoFA is presented in Section 4, and its implementation and our experimental results are presented in Section 5. Section 6 provides the related work, and finally, Section 7 concludes the paper.

2. PREREQUISITES

In this section, we first present a brief description of the channel estimation method defined in the 802.11n standard. It is then followed by the 802.11n High Throughput (HT) features, and finally the experimental setting used for our measurements is presented.

2.1 Channel Estimation and Compensation

A received signal through wireless channel is distorted by fading, shadowing, and noise, dramatically changing in mobile environments. For this reason, an 802.11 receiver estimates the channel conditions to obtain the CSI by using training symbols in the PLCP preamble, located at the beginning of a PHY layer Protocol Data Unit (PPDU). As shown in Figure 1, the 802.11n PLCP preamble is composed of the legacy preamble (from IEEE 802.11a) and the HT preamble. The legacy preamble includes legacy short training field (L-STF) and legacy long training field (L-LTF), which are followed by a signal field (L-SIG). The L-STF is used by a receiver for signal detection, AGC, timing synchronization, and coarse frequency offset estimation. On the other hand, the L-LTF provides a means for the receiver to estimate the channel and fine frequency offset. Then, the HT-LTFs as part of the HT preamble are used to measure the CSI of multiple-input multiple-output (MIMO) channel [12].

A received signal can also be distorted by the symbol time offset (STO), caused by the difference of the local oscillators in the transmitter and receiver. This clock mismatch results in a phase rotation linearly proportional to the subcarrier index in frequency domain, which causes loss of orthogonality between subcarriers, and hence, pilot subcarriers are embedded in each OFDM data symbol to assist channel com-

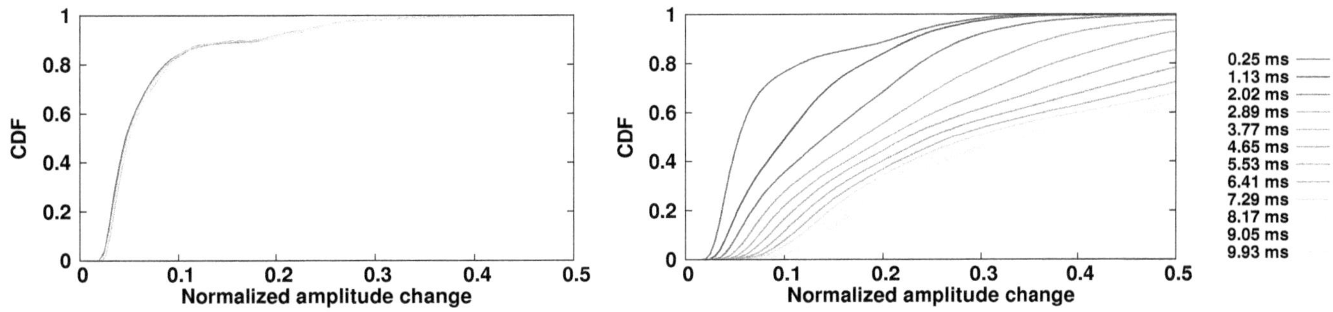

(a) Static trace. (b) Mobile trace.

Figure 2: CDF of the normalized amplitude changes with varying time gap, τ.

pensation during the frame reception. In the 802.11n, 4 out of 56 subcarriers are dedicated to pilot subcarriers, eliminating the channel distortion from STO. With the support of pilot subcarriers, the estimated channel using the CSI measured from LTFs is interpolated to enable the coherent detection [16].

In summary, the channel is estimated using the PLCP preamble at the beginning of a frame reception. The receiver then compensates the OFDM data symbols according to the measured CSI from LTF assisted by pilot subcarriers. However, if the channel is dynamically changing during a frame reception, the receiver has no way to catch up with the CSI variation. Accordingly, when the transmission time of a frame is long, the current channel estimation process of the 802.11 might not be sufficient to decode the latter part of the frame, especially, in mobile environments.

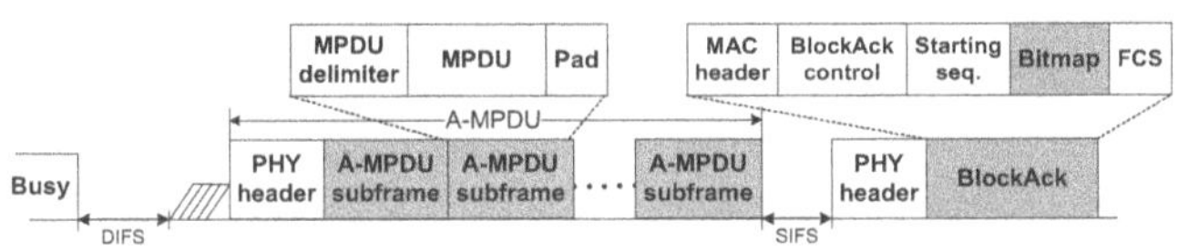

Figure 3: A-MPDU and BlockAck exchange.

2.2 IEEE 802.11n HT Features

2.2.1 *Frame aggregation*

Frame aggregation is a core feature of IEEE 802.11n to send multiple frames in a single transmission. Every data frame has a significant amount of overhead including PLCP preamble, MAC/PHY header, acknowledgement (ACK) transmission, and several Inter Frame Spaces (IFSs). These overheads often consume bandwidth comparable with the actual data payload, which results in much lower throughput compared with the underlying PHY data rate. To address this issue, the 802.11n defines two types of frame aggregation: MSDU and MPDU aggregation [12].

A-MSDU is literally the aggregation of MSDUs into a single frame at the upper MAC layer with the maximum size of 7,935 bytes. Since all aggregated MSDUs share a single MAC header and a single cyclic redundancy check (CRC) code, used for error detection by the receiver, the transmission of an A-MSDU fails as a whole even when just one of the aggregated MSDUs is corrupted.

On the other hand, A-MPDU, which is more commonly used in practice due to the merit explained below, combines multiple MPDUs into a single PPDU as shown in Figures 1 and 3. The maximum A-MPDU length is 65,535 bytes, and the A-MPDU transmission time should be smaller than the maximum PPDU duration, *aPPDUMaxTime*, defined as 10 ms [12]. Unlike A-MSDU, A-MPDU is more efficient in high error rate environment, because all individual subframes (or MPDUs conveyed in subframes) are positively/negatively acknowledged using BlockAcks as shown in Figure 3, and hence, can be individually retransmitted.

2.2.2 *MCSs*

Modulation and coding schemes (MCSs) are used to denote the combination of the number of spatial streams, modulation, and code rate. A higher order MCS index indicates a higher PHY data rate provided by higher order modulation and/or higher code rate. It is generally known that lower order MCS is more robust than higher order MCS, while higher order MCS can lead to higher throughput as long as the channel condition is good. IEEE 802.11n basically supports 32 MCSs from MCS 0 (one stream using BPSK and 1/2-rate code) to MCS 31 (four streams using 64-QAM and 5/6-rate code).

2.2.3 *MIMO, SM, STBC and channel bonding*

IEEE 802.11n supports MIMO operation which utilizes multiple antennas at both transmitter and receiver. There are two transmission techniques which use multiple antennas, namely spatial multiplexing (SM) and space-time block coding (STBC). SM transmits multiple data streams through multiple antennas to enhance the data rate. On the other hand, STBC transmits multiple coded copies of a data stream through multiple antennas to improve the reliability. The 802.11n also supports channel bonding which uses 40 MHz bandwidth by combining two 20 MHz channels. Apparently, such bandwidth expansion achieves higher data rate.

2.3 Experimental Setting

We have conducted our experiments in a controlled office environment, i.e., the basement of our building. Figure 4 illustrates the floor plan used for our experiments, and points P1 to P9 represent different locations where stations are located. IEEE 802.11n devices supporting A-MPDU, 3x3 MIMO (SM and STBC), and 40 MHz channel bonding are used. The operating channel number 44, i.e., 5,220 MHz center frequency, is used, where no external interference has been detected. We mainly use a programmable 802.11n device, Qualcomm Atheros AR9380 NIC, along with *hostAP* [5]

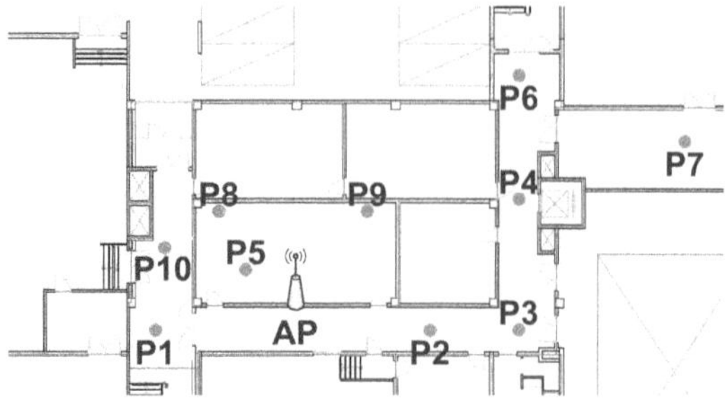

Figure 4: Experiment topology.

to build an AP on a *Ubuntu* 10.04 machine. Both AR9380 and IWL5300 (from Intel) NIC are utilized on the station side to consider various Wi-Fi devices [1]. We generate UDP downlink traffic from AP to stations using *Iperf* 2.0.5 to generate fixed length frames (of 1,534 bytes including MAC header) [3], and control the frame aggregation time bound by modifying the device drivers *ath9k* and *iwlwifi* for AR9380 and IWL5300, respectively [1, 2].

3. CASE STUDY

In this section, we first analyze the wireless channel dynamics based on the measurement results. Then, we investigate the impact of mobility on the performance of A-MPDU.

3.1 Temporal Selectivity

To illustrate our findings, we first present the temporal selectivity of the wireless channel by using CSI statistics in static and mobile environments. For the mobile scenario, the station comes and goes between P1 and P2 at an average speed of 1 m/s. We collect CSI traces from IWL5300 NIC using the modified device driver at the receiver side [4]. Specifically, the NIC reports measured 40,000 CSIs from HT-LTFs for 30 subcarrier groups in the form of 1×3 matrix [12]. We enable one antenna at a sender and three antennas at a receiver. The sender broadcasts a NULL data frame with MCS 0 using 15 dBm transmit power every 250 μs.

We employ the following metric representing the normalized amplitude changes to evaluate the temporal selectivity [7]:

$$\frac{\|A(t) - A(t+\tau)\|_2}{\|A(t+\tau)\|_2}, \tag{1}$$

where the vector $A(t)$ represents all the subcarriers' amplitudes of the frame received at t, and τ is the time gap. $\|\cdot\|_2$ is the l^2-norm, and τ varies from 250 μs to 10 ms, which is *aPPDUMaxTime*.

Figure 2 shows the cumulative distribution function (CDF) of the normalized amplitude changes between CSI of two frames with varying τ. As shown in Figure 2(a), the amplitude variation remains steady in the static scenario. More than 85% of samples show the amplitude changes under 10% even for $\tau = 10$ ms.

However, the amplitude variation increases with τ in the mobile scenario as shown in Figure 2(b). For $\tau = 10$ ms, the amplitude varies by more than 10% between two consecutive frames for over 95% of samples. Furthermore, for over 55% of samples, the amplitude changes by more than 30%.

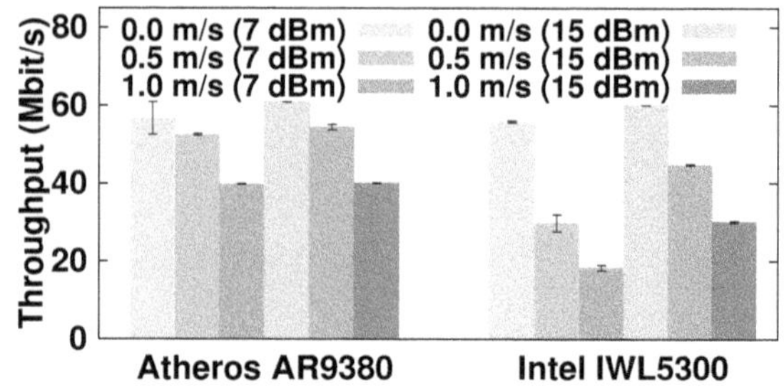

(a) Throughput results.

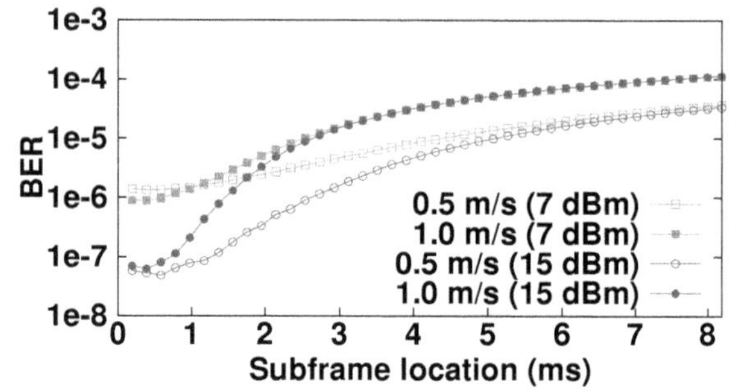

(b) BER of AR9380 NIC.

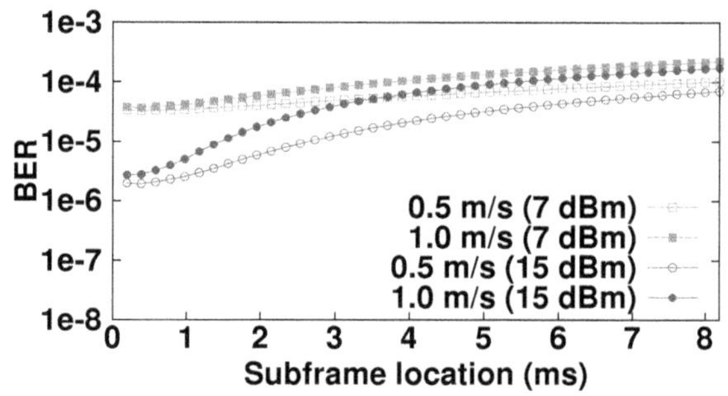

(c) BER of IWL5300 NIC.

Figure 5: Impact of mobility.

Consequently, the error rate of the latter part of A-MPDU is expected to increase because the channel estimation is performed only during the PLCP preamble reception as explained in Section 2.1.

The observation from Figure 2 is highly related to the channel coherence time, which represents the time duration over which the wireless channel does not seem to be varying. Mathematically, it is defined as the time range over which the correlation coefficient of signal amplitudes is less than a threshold, i.e., 0.9, between two different signals [17] as follows:

$$\frac{\langle a_t a_{t+\tau}\rangle - \langle a_t\rangle\langle a_{t+\tau}\rangle}{\sqrt{\left[\langle a_t{}^2\rangle - \langle a_t\rangle^2\right]\left[\langle a_{t+\tau}{}^2\rangle - \langle a_{t+\tau}\rangle^2\right]}} \geq 0.9, \tag{2}$$

where a_t and $a_{t+\tau}$ represent the amplitudes of signals at time t and $t+\tau$, respectively, and $\langle x\rangle$ denotes the ensemble average of x. Using the above traces and Equation (2), the measured coherence time for the scenario of 1 m/s average speed is about 3 ms, which is much shorter than *aPPDU-MaxTime*, i.e., 10 ms. It provides an important intuition

Table 1: Throughput with different time bounds

Time bound (μs)		0	1,024	2,048	4,096	6,144	8,192
Avg. # of aggregated frames		1	5	10	21	31	42
Throughput (Mbit/s)	0 m/s	31.19	50.95	56.47	59.62	60.50	60.90
	1 m/s	31.14	50.82	55.79	53.58	46.39	40.25
SFER (%)	1 m/s	0.05	0.13	1.10	10.01	23.33	34.00

that using A-MPDU without considering the wireless channel dynamics could severely deteriorate the throughput.

3.2 Impact of Mobility

We now examine how the limitation of the channel compensation procedure affects the reception of A-MPDU when mobility intensifies the time-varying nature of the wireless channel. As depicted in Section 2.3, we install a stationary AP equipped with AR9380, and use both AR9380 and IWL5300 on the station side. Saturated downlink traffic is sent from AP to a station which holds a position at P1 for the static scenario. For the mobile scenario, the station comes and goes between P1 and P2 at an average speed of 0.5 or 1 m/s. Frames are aggregated into A-MPDU frames, which are transmitted at the fixed MCS 7 (65 Mbit/s), employing 64-QAM and 5/6-rate code. The size of each subframe is set to 1,538 bytes including MPDU delimiter and padding bits, and hence, an A-MPDU can contain at most 42 subframes. Therefore, the actual transmission duration of a single A-MPDU is about 8 ms. The results are averaged over 5 runs, where each run lasts for 120 seconds.

We first investigate whether there exists significant performance degradation in mobile scenarios. As shown in Figure 5(a), we observe that the throughput decreases regardless of the NIC type and transmit power, as the degree of the mobility increases. Note that the wireless channel condition between AP and the station is pretty good in terms of signal-to-noise ratio (SNR). As an evidence, the results of the static case (0 m/s) achieve almost maximum throughput. However, in the case of the mobile scenario, the losses of throughput for AR9380 and IWL5300 are as high as one third and two thirds, respectively.

To investigate this further, we next analyze the bit error rate (BER) performance. Figure 5(b) shows the BER of A-MPDU subframes using AR9380 NIC on a logarithmic scale. The subframe location stands for the transmission starting instant of the corresponding subframe relative to the beginning of the PPDU over the air. We observe that subframes in the latter part of A-MPDU experience higher BER, and the curves show steep slope. The gradient of BER curves becomes higher as the average speed of the station increases. Additionally, BER curves converge depending on the mobility for both transmit powers (7 dBm and 15 dBm) regardless of the BER at the beginning of A-MPDU, since the mobility becomes the main cause of MPDU losses in the latter part of A-MPDU.

In other word, even if the appropriate PHY rate is used for transmission, this undesirable phenomenon can occur. Therefore, we can conclude that the adequate A-MPDU length selection is important to enhance the performance of A-MPDU. As shown in Figure 5(c), the result of IWL5300 shows a similar tendency even if RF circuit structure, antenna gain, and receiver sensitivity of these two NICs are different.

We calculate the optimal length of A-MPDU exhaustively based on the measured BER of AR9380 NIC with transmit

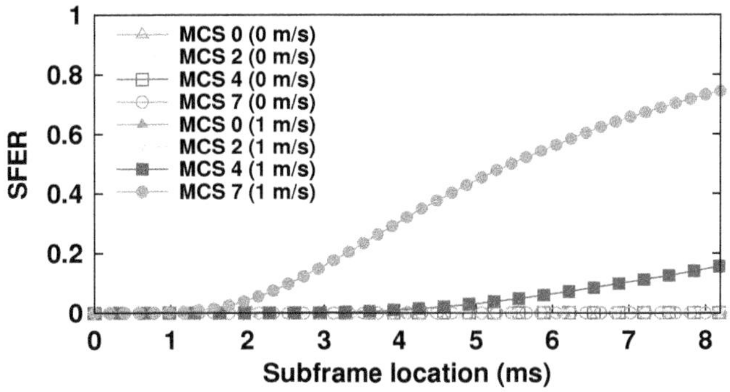

Figure 6: SFER for different MCSs.

power of 15 dBm.[1] When the station moves at an average speed of 1 m/s, the optimal length of the A-MPDU maximizing the throughput is 10 subframes (of 1,538 bytes), or equivalently the optimal A-MPDU transmission time equals about 2 ms. In addition, the optimal aggregation time for an average speed of 0.5 m/s is about 2.9 ms where an A-MPDU is composed of 15 subframes. Interestingly, the optimal aggregation time for the average speed of 1 m/s, i.e., 2 ms, is smaller than the coherence time, 3 ms, calculated in Section 3.1.

In order to delve into the aforementioned issues, we investigate the impact of A-MPDU length through additional experiments. For the remaining experiments, we use only AR9380 NIC since AR9380 has shown more stable MIMO performance and also is easier to play with.

3.3 Impact of A-MPDU Length

Table 1 summarizes the average throughput and SFER for varying aggregation time bound which determines the aggregation length of A-MPDU. The aggregation time of 0 μs represents the transmission of a single MPDU without aggregation. As the length of A-MPDU increases, the throughput of the static scenario (0 m/s) increases due to the overhead reduction, but for an average speed of 1 m/s, the maximum throughput is achieved at 2,048 μs aggregation time bound as calculated in Section 3.2. When the aggregation time bound is larger than 2,048 μs, the increased SFER induced by the mobility overwhelms the gain from the overhead reduction. Accordingly, the throughput decreases as the aggregation time bound increases.

Table 2: MCS information

	MCS 0	MCS 2	MCS 4	MCS 7
Modulation	BPSK	QPSK	16-QAM	64-QAM
Code rate	1/2	3/4	3/4	5/6
Data rate (Mbit/s)	6.5	19.5	39	65

3.4 Impact of MCSs

MCS is a critical factor determining the receiving performance as described in Section 2.2.2. Although higher order MCS achieves higher data rate, it is vulnerable not only to

[1]We translate BER into SFER according to the subframe location in Figure 5(b), and numerically calculate the achievable throughput employing A-MPDU for a given number of subframes.

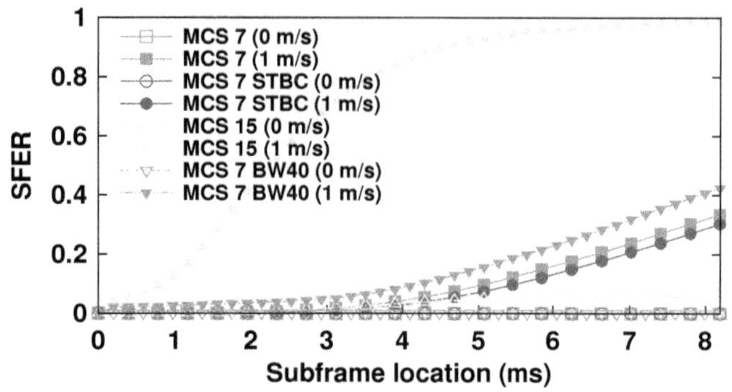

Figure 7: SFER with various 802.11n features.

the channel degradation but also to mobility, since constellation points are closer from each other and coding gain is generally smaller. To verify this, we conduct experiments by changing MCSs for a given mobility. Table 2 summarizes the detailed information of MCSs used in this measurement.

Figure 6 shows the SFER depending on the subframe location. Unlike the evaluation of previous sections, we plot SFER instead of BER for better intuition. When a station holds its position at P1, the SFER remains almost zero in all subframe locations regardless of the employed MCS, because the channel quality between AP and the station is considerably good. However, when the station moves at an average speed of 1 m/s, MCS 4 and MCS 7 employing both amplitude and phase modulation (i.e., 16-QAM and 64-QAM, respectively) show higher SFER in the latter part of A-MPDU, while MCS 0 and MCS 2 which use only phase modulation (i.e., BPSK and QPSK, respectively) achieve stable SFER across the entire subframe locations. That is, MCSs which use amplitude modulation are highly susceptible to mobility. An A-MPDU using high order MCS not only uses longer A-MPDU length for a given A-MPDU duration, but also suffers from higher SFER at the latter part of A-MPDU, especially, when the channel varies within the transmission time of A-MPDU. Therefore, the length of A-MPDU with high order MCS should be carefully determined.

3.5 IEEE 802.11n Features

We investigate the impact of IEEE 802.11n features, such as STBC, SM, and channel bonding, in order to verify whether these features alleviate or aggravate the observed problem. We narrow the moving range between P1 and P2 so that the transmitter can utilize double streams (i.e., MCS 15). Figure 7 shows SFER with various 802.11n features. We basically use the results of MCS 7 as a reference for the performance comparison.

First, STBC is well known for offering diversity gain, but we observe that the SFER is only slightly decreased by STBC. That is, STBC cannot suppress the increase of SFER in the latter part of A-MPDU.

With SM, which is denoted as MCS 15 (using two spatial streams with 64-QAM and 5/6-rate code), the SFER is further deteriorated. Even if the station does not move (i.e., MCS 15 with 0 m/s curve), the SFER grows as the subframe location number increases, since MIMO requires a more accurate channel compensation to eliminate the spatial interference. When the station moves, only a few subframes in the beginning part of A-MPDU can be successfully transmitted.

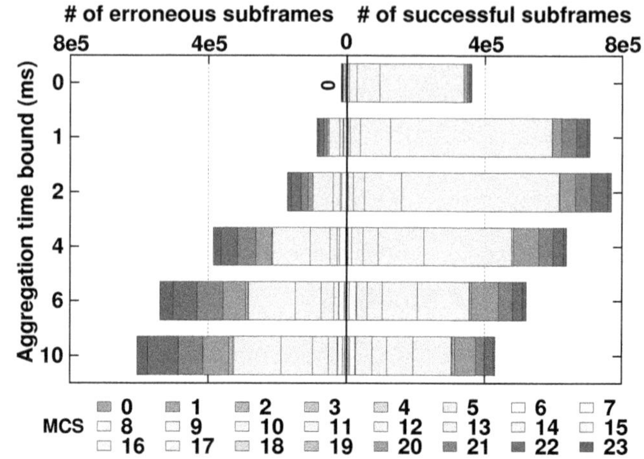

Figure 8: Rate distribution on *Minstrel*.

The result of 40 MHz bandwidth shows slightly higher SFER than that of 20 MHz bandwidth. That is because not only the power per bandwidth is decreased but also the channel compensation is more difficult than 20 MHz bandwidth due to the increased number of subcarriers.

In all the above cases, the 802.11n features do not solve the observed problem; SM and 40 MHz channel bonding are more severely affected by mobility. Moreover, STBC does not alleviate the performance degradation induced by mobility either.

Table 3: Throughput and SFER on *Minstrel*

Time bound (μs)	0	1,024	2,048	4,096	6,144	10,240
Throughput (Mbit/s)	37.54	73.12	79.83	66.38	53.64	44.24
SFER (%)	5.13	11.92	19.42	37.77	50.87	58.33

3.6 Rate Adaptation: *Minstrel*

Rate adaptation algorithm (RA) selects the most suitable MCS (or PHY rate) for a given channel condition. Every 802.11 device implements a RA to maximize the performance (e.g., to maximize the throughput) while these algorithms are implementation dependent. We use a measurement to investigate the impact of mobility when a RA runs. *Minstrel* is used in this experiment, since it is well known for achieving good performance in practical environments [19] and Linux wireless tool adopts it as the default embedded RA [6]. *Minstrel* is a window-based RA, which collects the wireless channel statistics by transmitting probing frames, i.e., data frames transmitted with a randomly selected PHY rate. The ratio of probing frames is generally 10% of the total traffic. Based on that, *Minstrel* calculates the best throughput rate within a time window, and adopts it as a basic rate for the next window.

Figure 8 illustrates the MCS distribution measured for a mobility scenario with varying aggregation time bound. Each stacked bar represents the number of subframes transmitted with a specific MCS, where left-side and right-side correspond to the numbers of erroneous and successful subframes, respectively. Probing frames are not counted in the statistics since they are not aggregated into A-MPDU. When

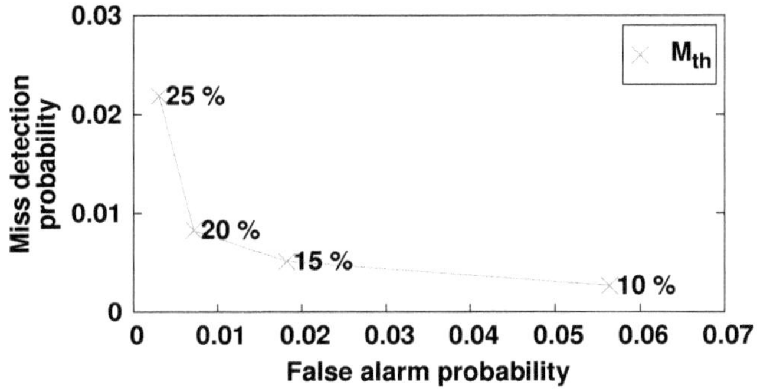

Figure 9: Accuracy of MD.

A-MPDU is not used, there are few frame errors. However, as the aggregation time bound increases, the SFER also increases, especially, it rises steeply between 2 ms and 4 ms. Consequently, the maximum throughput is achieved with 2 ms aggregation time bound, using mostly MCS 15.

We observe that *Minstrel* tries to use higher order MCSs over MCS 15 more often, when the aggregation time bound becomes larger than 2 ms. The reason of this bad MCS selection is caused by the fact that SFER using the current MCS increases, because subframes in the latter part of A-MPDU fail due to mobility. However, frame error rate (FER) of probing frames might be lower than that of the currently employed MCS, since probing frames are sent to the air without aggregation, even if the MCS used by probing frames is higher/lower and not suitable. Then, *Minstrel* decides to increase/decrease the PHY rate since the estimated throughput with the MCSs used for probing frames could be larger than that of the current one. As a result, the PHY rate is updated to one of the probed rates, which induces unnecessarily frequent PHY rate variation. Consequently, the throughput is further deteriorated when the RA runs in mobile environments.

More detailed information is summarized in Table 3. As expected, the maximum throughput is achieved with 2 ms aggregation time bound, which achieves the optimal tradeoff between the overhead reduction from aggregation and the SFER increment by mobility.

4. PROPOSED ALGORITHM DESIGN

Section 3 has demonstrated the inherent limitation of the 802.11n frame aggregation schemes. Motivated by this observation, we develop MoFA, a novel frame aggregation algorithm, composed of *mobility detection* (MD) and *A-MPDU length adaptation* in order to overcome the limitation. In addition, MoFA adopts an adaptive use of RTS/CTS to suppress the hidden collision which leads to an ill behavior of MoFA otherwise.

4.1 Mobility Detection

Mobility leads to SFER increase at subframes in the latter part of A-MPDU, while SFER caused by the poor channel (i.e., the channel in low SNR regime) is uniformly distributed irrespective of subframe location. Taking into account the different characteristics, we employ MD scheme into MoFA to determine the degree of the mobility. Let N be the number of aggregated subframes in an A-MPDU. $\overrightarrow{S} = \{s_1, s_2, \cdots, s_N\}$, updated after receiving a BlockAck, represents the transmission results of subframes, where s_i is equal to 1 or 0 depending on whether the corresponding ith subframe succeeds or fails, respectively. Then, the average SFERs of front and latter halves of an A-MPDU are respectively represented by:

$$\text{SFER}_f = \frac{\sum_{i=1}^{N_f} s_i}{N_f} \quad \text{and} \quad \text{SFER}_l = \frac{\sum_{i=N_f+1}^{N} s_i}{N - N_f}, \tag{3}$$

where $N_f = \lfloor N/2 \rfloor$.

We quantify the degree of the mobility, M, by using SFER_f and SFER_l, defined as follows:

$$M = \text{SFER}_l - \text{SFER}_f. \tag{4}$$

Therefore, if M is larger than the mobility detection threshold, M_{th}, MD scheme determines that the station is under a mobile environment.

To verify the accuracy of MD, we conduct experiments by assessing miss detection and false alarm probabilities. We use the same experiment settings as that described in Section 3.2, except that MD scheme is implemented in the AP. Figure 9 shows that as M_{th} increases, the false alarm probability decreases, while the miss detection probability increases. It is because high M_{th} effectively differentiates the loss caused by a poor channel from the loss caused by mobility, but it cannot detect mobility which causes relatively low M. Finding an appropriate M_{th} is important in order to achieve an accurate MD operation according to the degree of the mobility. Based on the measurement results, we observe that $M_{th} = 20\%$ results in suitable miss detection and false alarm probabilities. Therefore, we fix M_{th} to 20% throughout the rest of the paper.

4.2 A-MPDU Length Adaptation

We now propose an A-MPDU length adaptation algorithm to find an appropriate length with respect to the degree of the mobility.

4.2.1 A-MPDU length decrease

The length of A-MPDU should be decreased to maximize the throughput in a mobile environment. Given sufficient statistics, it is possible to find out the optimal aggregation time bound of A-MPDU. Assuming that the payload size is fixed, let N_t be the maximum number of possible aggregated subframes for a given aggregation time bound T_o. That is,

$$\begin{aligned} N_t &= \underset{n}{\text{argmax}}(n \cdot L/R + T_{oh}), \\ &\text{s.t. } n \cdot L/R + T_{oh} \leq T_o, \end{aligned} \tag{5}$$

where L is the subframe length including the overhead of A-MPDU delimiter and its padding bits. R represents the current PHY rate, and T_{oh} denotes the time overhead including DIFS, backoff, PLCP preamble, PLCP header, SIFS, and transmission time of a BlockAck.

$\overrightarrow{P} = \{p_1, p_2, \cdots, p_{N_t}\}$ represents the SFER statistics of each subframe, where p_i stands for the SFER of the ith subframe, which is calculated using an exponential weighted moving average (EWMA). $\overrightarrow{P}$ is updated at every BlockAck reception, and accordingly, each element is denoted by:

$$p_i := \begin{cases} (1-\beta)p_i + \beta, & \text{if fails,} \\ (1-\beta)p_i, & \text{if succeeds,} \end{cases} \tag{6}$$

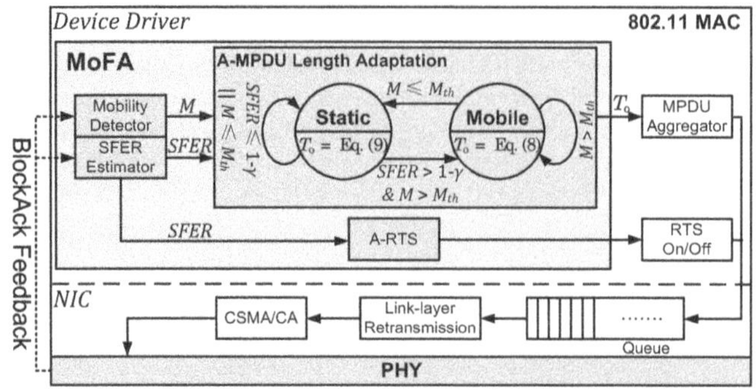

Figure 10: Operation of MoFA.

where β is a weighting factor, which implies that most recent sample carries β weight in the estimation. Throughout the rest of the paper, we set β in Equation (6) to 1/3, which implies the most recent transmission result carries 1/3 weight in the estimation. Meanwhile, using $\overrightarrow{P}$, the optimal length of A-MPDU, n_o, can be calculated as follows.

$$n_o = \underset{n \leq N_t}{\text{argmax}} \frac{\sum_{i=1}^{n} L(1-p_i)}{n \cdot L/R + T_{oh}}. \quad (7)$$

Then, N_t is updated to n_o, and finally, the aggregation time bound T_o is determined as follows:

$$T_o := n_o \cdot L/R + T_{oh}. \quad (8)$$

Note that the newly updated T_o is less than or equal to the previous value because $n_o \leq N_t$. By adjusting the aggregation time bound of A-MPDU based on the statistics, MoFA limits the number of aggregated subframes in order to achieve the optimal throughput.

4.2.2 A-MPDU length increase

Generally, longer A-MPDU improves the channel efficiency in static environments as shown in Section 3. Therefore, when $M \leq M_{th}$, the current channel is very likely ready to support a longer A-MPDU, and hence, the number of subframes should be increased.

In order to increase the length of A-MPDU, MoFA increases the aggregation time bound, T_o:

$$T_o := \min\left(T_o + n_p \cdot L/R, T_{max}\right), \quad (9)$$

where T_{max} is the maximum possible PPDU transmission time, 10 ms, and n_p is the number of additionally allowed subframes, which are referred to as probing subframes. The amount of increment varies according to the PHY data rate, since it is inversely proportional to the current PHY rate, R. To achieve rapid length adaptation of A-MPDU keeping up with the channel dynamics, n_p is determined by an exponential increment, i.e., $n_p = \varepsilon^{n_c}$, where ε is an exponential weighting factor, and n_c denotes the number of consecutive transmissions of A-MPDUs, satisfying that $M \leq M_{th}$. As ε becomes larger, A-MPDU length increase algorithm can operate faster by adapting to the wireless channel variation more rapidly. However, large ε can incur large unnecessary probing overhead once the A-MPDU length is properly determined. Here, we set ε to the minimum value, 2, conservatively in order to eliminate such overhead. For example, the numbers of probing frames are 2, 4, and 8 for 3 consecutive increases.

4.3 Adaptive Use of RTS/CTS

The performance of the 802.11 is severely deteriorated when there exist hidden stations. Since some error patterns induced by the hidden collision might not be clearly differentiated from the errors from mobility, i.e., both can induce relatively more errors in the latter part of A-MPDUs, the above schemes might not work properly in the presence of hidden stations. Therefore, to ameliorate such a hidden station problem, we employ an adaptive use of Request-To-Send (RTS) and Clear-To-Send (CTS) exchange. However, the use of RTS/CTS procedure without a prudent decision can degrade the performance of WLAN due to its overhead. Adaptive uses of RTS/CTS have been proposed recently [18, 13].

In this paper, we improve the concept of *adaptive RTS* (A-RTS) *filter* proposed in [18], which selectively turns on RTS transmission per data frame by adapting the dynamic collision level incurred by hidden stations. Different from the original A-RTS, which does not consider A-MPDU operation, MoFA decides when and how RTS should be turned on or off, according to the transmission result of an A-MPDU.

The key state of A-RTS in MoFA is *RTSwnd*, i.e., the window size of RTS, representing the number of consecutive A-MPDU frames that will use an RTS/CTS exchange before the transmission. *RTScnt*, which is set to *RTSwnd* whenever *RTSwnd* value is updated, keeps track of the remaining number of frames to be sent after an RTS/CTS exchange. That is, an RTS/CTS exchange is enabled before a data transmission as long as *RTScnt* > 0. *RTSwnd* is set to 0 initially, and adaptively increases whenever a collision is suspected. *RTSwnd* increases by one when the instantaneous SFER (*SFER*) of the last A-MPDU transmitted without RTS is larger than $1-\gamma$, where γ denotes SFER threshold. *RTSwnd* also employs multiplicative decrease to minimize the RTS/CTS exchange overhead; if $SFER > 1-\gamma$ with RTS or $SFER \leq 1-\gamma$ without RTS, *RTSwnd* becomes a half, since RTS/CTS exchange seems not useful.[2]

4.4 Operation of MoFA

In this section, we explain how the aforementioned three components of MoFA, i.e., MD, A-MPDU length adaptation, and A-RTS, interwork together. The detailed procedure of MoFA is best explained with a blueprint in Figure 10. The state transitions of A-MPDU length adaptation depend on two MoFA parameters, namely, (1) the degree of the mobility (*M*) and (2) the instantaneous SFER (*SFER*). Upon the reception of a BlockAck, MoFA estimates both M and *SFER* by using MD and SFER estimator, respectively.

A-MPDU length adaptation differentiates two states, namely, **static** and **mobile**. If the frame errors appear insignificant (i.e., $SFER \leq 1-\gamma$), or if the frame errors seem caused by poor channel (i.e., $M \leq M_{th}$), MoFA stays in the **static** state. In other words, MoFA decides not to decrease the

[2]After receiving a BlockAck, *SFER*, i.e., the number of transmission-failed subframes divided by the total number of subframes within the most recently transmitted A-MPDU, can be obtained. If BlockAck is not received after an A-MPDU transmission, $SFER := 1$.

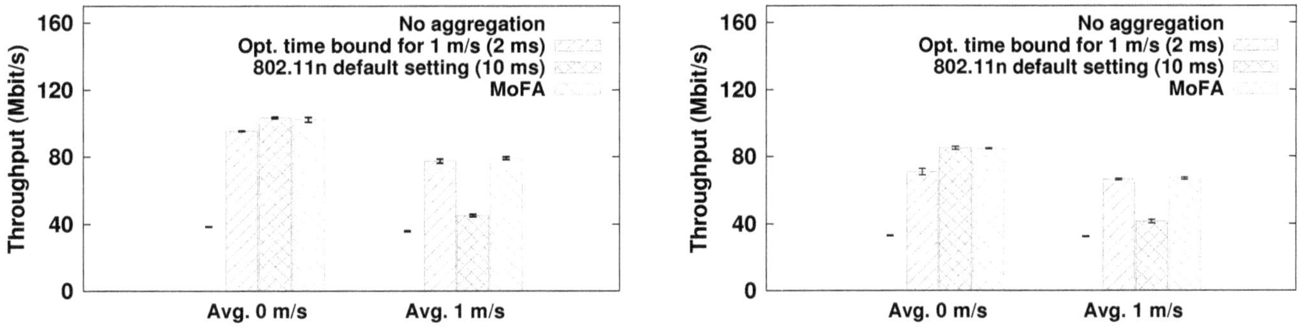

(a) Transmit power: 15 dBm.

(b) Transmit power: 7 dBm.

Figure 11: Throughput in one-to-one scenario.

aggregation time bound T_o, but tries to increase the bound according to Equation (9).

However, if $SFER > 1 - \gamma$ and MD detects that the loss caused by mobility (i.e., $M > M_{th}$), the state switches to the **mobile** state. In this state, MoFA decreases T_o according to Equation (8) until the reception of subframes in the latter part of A-MPDU is not affected by mobility (i.e., $M \leq M_{th}$). While obtaining the appropriate A-MPDU length, A-RTS operates independently and simultaneously to adapt the dynamic collision level as described in Section 4.3.

Considering both the overhead of RTS/CTS exchange and the trade-off between the loss induced by mobility and the benefit of amortizing the overhead using A-MPDU, selecting the appropriate γ is an open-problem, which remains as the future work. In the rest of the paper, we set SFER threshold, γ, to 0.9 as a rule of thumb, and hence, 10% subframe error in A-MPDU triggers A-MPDU length adaptation in mobile environments [20].

Note that MoFA works independently from RAs. Instead, it helps RAs not to be misled by the errors caused by mobility. Specifically, MoFA dynamically adjusts the length of A-MPDU according to the degree of the mobility and suppresses the mobility-induced excessive subframe errors, and hence, it can prevent malfunction of rate control algorithms.

5. EXPERIMENTAL EVALUATION

In this section, we comparatively evaluate the performance of MoFA measured under a wide range of scenarios. We have implemented MoFA on an off-the-shelf 802.11 NIC with AR9380 by modifying the *ath9k* device driver. Section 2.3 describes the details of the measurement setting for this evaluation. For each set of experiment scenarios, we average the results of 5 runs, where each lasts for 60 seconds.

5.1 One-to-One Scenario

For comparison, we apply the optimal fixed time bounds for both static and mobile stations, which we have verified in Section 3.3. The optimal fixed time bound of the static station is the maximum time bound, 10 ms, which is 802.11n default setting. On the other hand,the optimal fixed time bound is 2 ms for an average speed of 1 m/s.

5.1.1 *Static vs. mobile environments*

We evaluate the performance of MoFA in both static and mobile environments, where a single station stays or moves consistently during the experiment. Figure 11 shows the throughput for the given degree of the mobility, with error bars representing the standard deviation. We use 15 dBm and 7 dBm transmit powers in order to investigate the impact of the channel quality. We observe that if the aggregation is disabled, the throughput does not vary with the average speed since it is scarcely affected by the degree of the mobility. When the station does not move (i.e., average 0 m/s), 802.11n default setting shows the best throughput in both transmit powers as expected in Section 3. Using 15 dBm transmit power, the required transmission time of the longest A-MPDU is much lower than 10 ms.[3] Therefore, the achieved throughput of optimal fixed time bound for 1 m/s is 7.8% lower compared to the best throughput. However, when 7 dBm transmit power is used, it shows 17.7% lower throughput than that of 802.11n default setting as shown in Figure 11(b) because of the marginal overhead growth. MoFA tends to use the longest A-MPDU in stationary environment, and hence, achieves the maximum throughput for both transmit power cases.

On the other hand, when the station moves with an average speed of 1 m/s, the throughput of 802.11n default setting is deteriorated due to the limitation of the channel compensation. Interestingly, MoFA achieves the highest throughput, surpassing the optimal fixed time bound for 1 m/s, by adjusting the length of A-MPDU according to the degree of the mobility. Specifically, the degree of the mobility changes instantaneously, even though its average value does not vary. As a result, MoFA achieves 2.2% and 1.1% higher throughput than that of the optimal fixed time bound (= 2 ms) for 15 dBm and 7 dBm transmit power, respectively. Since 802.11n default setting sets longer length of A-MPDU as the optimal fixed time bound, it results in the increase of SFER at the latter part of A-MPDUs, which causes the throughput degradation. The gains of MoFA from 802.11n default setting are 75.6% and 62.4% for 15 dBm and 7 dBm transmit power, respectively. The reasons why the gain drops as the transmit power decreases, comes from the use of reliable modulation and code rate against the mobility.

5.1.2 *Time-varying mobile environment*

Here, we investigate the adaptability of MoFA, i.e., A-MPDU length adaptation capability as the degree of the

[3]Using high order MCS, A-MPDU length is limited not by the time bound but by the maximum A-MPDU length, 65,535 bytes.

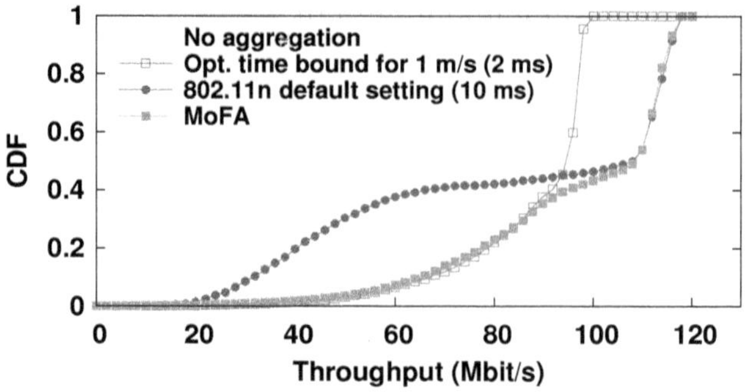

(a) CDF of instantaneous throughput.

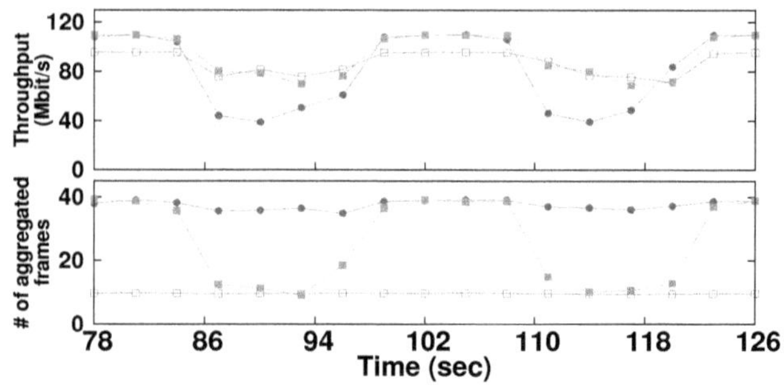

(b) Performance over time.

Figure 12: Performance of MoFA in time-varying mobile environment.

mobility changes over time. Figure 12(a) shows the empirical CDF of the instantaneous throughput for 200 ms. A station stays and moves half-and-half with a regular pattern. Therefore, 50% of the samples are exposed in mobile environments and the others are collected in static environments.

When frame aggregation is disabled, over 90% of the samples are in the range of 35 to 38 Mbit/s stably, since mobility does not affect the reception of a single non-aggregated frame. On the other hand, enabling A-MPDU, each curve is divided into two regions. Especially, the CDF from 0 to 0.5 corresponds to mobile environments, because the performance of A-MPDU is degraded in mobile environments as shown in Section 5.1.1. In this region, 802.11n default setting shows the worst performance where almost 40% of samples are below 60 Mbit/s. Meanwhile, the optimal fixed time bound for average speed of 1 m/s performs well by limiting the length of A-MPDU up to 2 ms. In the case of MoFA, its curve reaches up to the most outer curve which is obtained by the optimal fixed time bound for 1 m/s . Turning to the result of the static environment, the CDF from 0.5 to 1, 802.11n default setting shows the highest throughput apparently, and MoFA shows almost the same result, trying to use the longest A-MPDU.

Figure 12(b) demonstrates the trace of instantaneous throughput and number of aggregated frames over time. MoFA tries to use the maximum A-MPDU length in static environments while it strives to use short A-MPDUs, close to the optimal fixed time bound in mobile environments. Therefore, the instantaneous throughput of MoFA follows the upper-most curves. Interestingly, the number of aggregated subframes with 802.11n default setting slightly fluctuates in mobile environments. In fact, a BlockAck can acknowledge up to 64 consecutive MPDUs with a fixed-size bitmap. Accordingly, the difference between the sequence numbers of the first and the last MPDUs aggregated in a single A-MPDU frame should be less than 64. If the (re)transmissions of the first subframe continues to fail, then the maximum number of aggregated frames could decrease due to the constraint.

In summary, none of fixed time bound settings can achieve the best throughput all the time in time-varying mobile environment. However, MoFA, which adaptively changes the A-MPDU length according to the degree of the mobility, can approach the optimal throughput over the entire experiments. As an evidence, we have shown that the instantaneous throughput of MoFA follows the outer-most curves irrespective of the mobility level.

5.1.3 Hidden terminal environment

We now investigate how A-RTS in MoFA works in the presence of hidden terminals. Figure 13 presents the throughput for both static (with three kinds of hidden source rates) and mobile scenarios. A hidden AP is located at P7 and it sends downlink UDP traffic to a station located at P6. In the case of static scenario, a target station settled at P4 can carrier-sense both APs, but APs cannot detect the signal of each other. We compare MoFA against 802.11n default setting, 10 ms, since it is the optimal for static environments. For a fair comparison, we also use RTS/CTS exchange for the maximum time bound.[4]

In the absence of hidden traffic (i.e., 0 Mbit/s), the throughput of the optimal fixed time bound with RTS is slightly lower than the maximum throughput due to RTS/CTS overhead, but it shows the best performance as hidden source rate increases. Thanks to the A-RTS, MoFA achieves the high throughput close to the maximum throughput regardless of hidden source rate. MoFA enables RTS/CTS exchange before most A-MPDU transmissions when there exists hidden terminals, and vice versa.

We next investigate the performance of MoFA in the presence of both the hidden interference and the mobility. That is, a target station moves between P3 and P4 with an average speed of 1 m/s under the hidden interference from P7. We compare MoFA against the optimal fixed time bound for average speed of 1 m/s (2 ms), which shows the best performance for the mobile environments. Apparently, the optimal fixed time bound with RTS performs the best, because it aggregates average 10 subframes into a single A-MPDU scarcely affected by the mobility, and enables RTS/CTS exchange all the time to handle the hidden terminal problem effectively. The throughput of MoFA slightly decreases by 5.85% compared with the maximum throughput because of overlapping of both the miss detection/false alarm of MD and A-RTS.

5.2 Multiple Node Scenario

We finally evaluate the performance of MoFA in a multi-node environment. Five nodes and one AP are deployed with the floor plan as illustrated in Figure 4. The AP sends fully saturated downlink traffic to the each station. Three nodes (i.e., STA1, STA2, and STA3) move between P1 and P2,

[4]RTS/CTS exchange is always conducted before transmitting an A-MPDU. We refer to this as the 'optimal fixed time bound with RTS.'

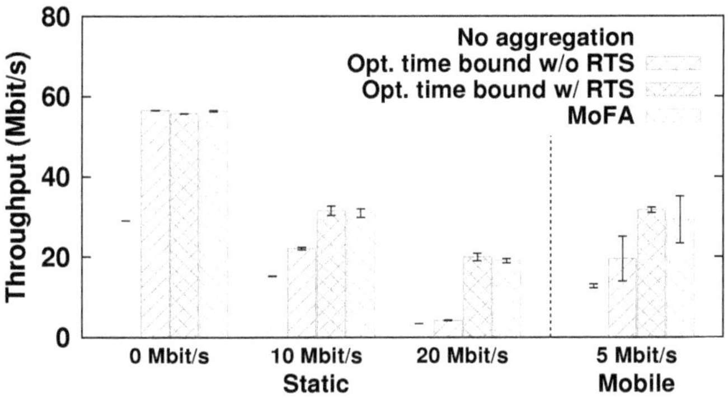

Figure 13: Throughput with hidden terminals.

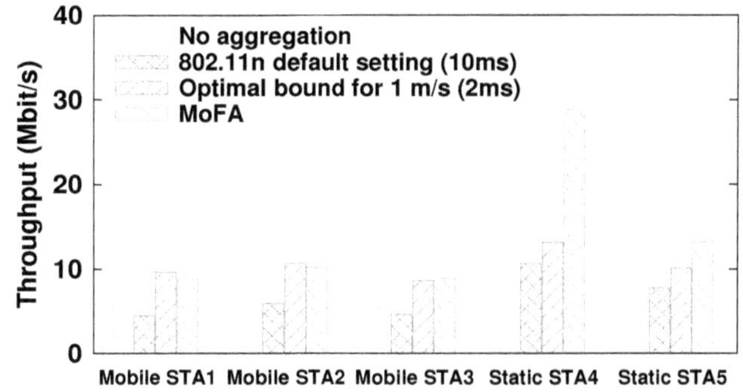

Figure 14: Throughput with multiple nodes.

P8 and P9, P3 and P4, respectively. STA4 and STA5 hold their positions at P5 and P10. We compare MoFA against no aggregation scheme, 802.11n default setting (= 10 ms), and the optimal fixed time bound for mobile scenarios.

Figure 14 shows the downlink throughput achieved by each station, with error bars representing the standard deviation. When frames are transmitted without aggregation, each station's achieved throughput is almost uniform because IEEE 802.11 MAC basically provides an equal opportunity for the channel access to all the contending stations in the long term. On the other hand, enabling A-MPDU provides different throughput for each station depending on the channel dynamics, since stations can transmit multiple MPDUs back-to-back without additional channel access procedures. Interestingly, the stationary STA4 achieves the biggest gain by using MoFA, which is counter intuitive. Main reason of this observation comes from the fact that stations share the wireless medium together. MoFA tends to use relatively short length of A-MPDUs for mobile stations by detecting mobility, which leads to low SFER, and hence, it prevents the waste of resource. All stations then share the additionally acquired resource, and especially, STA4 which is stationary and close to the AP, gets the biggest benefit thanks to the use of longer A-MPDUs. Overall, MoFA achieves 127%, 109%, and 35% higher network throughput than no aggregation, 802.11n default setting, and the optimal fixed length for mobile scenarios, respectively.

As we have observed so far, the overall performance of MoFA highly depends on the network topology and the degree of mobility of each station. We expect that the significant growth of Wi-Fi devices will lead to much higher degrees of mobility and hidden interferences, and hence, MoFA will highly benefit future large-scale Wi-Fi networks.

6. RELATED WORK

Numerous frame aggregation algorithms have been proposed to enhance the MAC efficiency, primarily based on numerical analysis and simulations (with unrealistic assumptions). Many papers have proposed the optimal frame length under error-prone channels. An analytic model for estimating the performance of A-MPDU and A-MSDU is presented in [9] to show that A-MSDU considerably degrades the performance as the aggregation length increases, while longer A-MPDU shows better performance over an erroneous channel. The optimal frame length adaptation algorithm for A-MSDU is proposed in [15], which provides a packet loss model, which includes collisions and channel fading.

The algorithms in [8, 11] use A-MPDU and A-MSDU simultaneously, and determine the A-MPDU subframe length in the same manner as the A-MSDU length optimization. In [11], He *et al.* find the optimal A-MPDU subframe length after rate selection. The proposed algorithm in this work utilizes the pre-designed mapping table which gives the optimal MPDU size according to BER input. Thanks to the mapping table, when the BER of the current wireless channel is given, the length of A-MPDU subframe is easily determined. The work in [8] also uses the mapping table, which provides the optimal MCS and MPDU size simultaneously, based on the SNR of the received signal. However, all these studies are based on the unrealistic assumption that all A-MPDU subframes experience the uniform SFER. Consequently, they are not concerned with finding the optimal A-MPDU length.

Robust channel estimation techniques for frames requiring long transmission time are proposed in [10, 14]. The former injects mid-amble which plays the same role as PLCP preamble, i.e., allowing the receiver to learn the channel, in the middle of A-MPDU reception while the latter develops scattered pilot technique which reorganizes the pilot pattern periodically. However, these approaches are not standard-compliant, thus making them costly and impractical for large-scale adoption by commercial products. In contrast, our approach fully complies with the current 802.11n standard which serves as a main advantage over others for wide deployment in the real world.

7. CONCLUDING REMARKS

In IEEE 802.11n WLAN, we reveal that using long A-MPDU frames cuts the throughput by up to two thirds regardless of the channel quality at the receiver in time-varying channel environments. Motivated by that observation, we develop MoFA, a novel standard-compliant algorithm, which dynamically adapts the length of the A-MPDU in run-time, by observing the mobility-caused channel dynamics in order to maximize the network performance. Our prototype implementation in commercial IEEE 802.11n Wi-Fi devices demonstrates that MoFA achieves throughput 1.8x higher than the default setting of 802.11n in mobile environments. To our best knowledge, this is the first effort to optimize the A-MPDU length for commercial IEEE 802.11n devices. Joint optimization of the length of A-MPDU and rate adaptation will be included in our future work.

Acknowledgment

This research was supported by LG U+ project, "Research on WLAN management and operation technologies for real-time service in condensed WLAN environments," and the Brain Korea 21 Plus Project in 2014.

8. REFERENCES

[1] Intel WiFi Link 5300. `http://www.intel.com/products/wireless/adapters/5000/`.

[2] Ath9k: Atheros Linux Wireless Driver. `http://wireless.kernel.org/en/users/Drivers/ath9k/`.

[3] Iperf: TCP/UDP Bandwidth Measurement Tool. `http://dast.nlanr.net/Projects/Iperf/`.

[4] Linux 802.11n CSI Tool. `http://dhalperi.github.io/linux-80211n-csitool/`.

[5] HostAP: IEEE 802.11 AP, IEEE 802.1X/WPA/WPA2/EAP/RADIUS Authenticator. `http://hostap.epitest.fi/hostapd/`.

[6] Linux Wireless Tools. `http://linuxwireless.org/`.

[7] Bhartia, A., Chen, Y. C., and Qiu, L. Harnessing Frequency Diversity in Wi-Fi Networks. In *Proc. ACM MobiCom'11* (Sept. 2011).

[8] Feng, K., Lin, P., and Liu, W. Frame-Aggregated Link Adaptation Protocol for Next Generation Wireless Local Area Networks. *EURASIP Journal on Wireless Communications and Networking* (2010).

[9] Ginzburg, B., and Kesselman, A. Performance Analysis of A-MPDU and A-MSDU Aggregation in IEEE 802.11n. In *Proc. IEEE Sarnoff Symposium* (May 2007).

[10] Grunheid, R., et al. Robust Channel Estimation in Wireless LANs for Mobile Environments. In *Proc. IEEE VTC'02 Fall* (Sept. 2002).

[11] He, X., Li, F. Y., and Lin, J. Link Adaptation with Combined Optimal Frame Size and Rate Selection in Error-Prone 802.11n Networks. In *Proc. IEEE ISWCS'08* (Oct. 2008).

[12] IEEE Std. *IEEE 802.11, Part 11: Wireless LAN Medium Access Control (MAC) and Physical Layer (PHY) Specifications*, Mar. 2012.

[13] Kim, J., Kim, S., Choi, S., and Qiao, D. CARA: Collision-Aware Rate Adaptation for IEEE 802.11 WLANs. In *Proc. IEEE INFOCOM'06* (Apr. 2006).

[14] Kim, S. I., Oh, H. S., and Choi, H. K. Mid-amble Aided OFDM Performance Analysis in High Mobility Vehicular Channel. In *Proc. IEEE IV'08* (June 2008).

[15] Lin, Y., and Wong, V. W. Frame Aggregation and Optimal Frame Size Adaptation for IEEE 802.11n WLANs. In *Proc. IEEE GLOBECOM'06* (Nov. 2006).

[16] Perahia, E. and Stacey, R. Next Generation Wireless LANs: Throughput, Robustness, and Reliability in 802.11n. Cambridge University Press, 2008.

[17] Steele, R. *Mobile Radio Communications*, first ed. IEEE Press, 1995.

[18] Wong, S. H. Y., et al. Robust Rate Adaptation for 802.11 Wireless Networks. In *Proc. ACM MobiCom'06* (Sept. 2006).

[19] Yin, W., Bialkowski, K., Indulska, J., and Hu, P. Evaluation of MadWifi MAC Layer Rate Control Mechanisms. In *Proc. IEEE IWQoS'10* (June 2010).

[20] Zhang, J., Tan, K., Zhao, J., Wu, H., and Zhang, Y. A Parctical SNR-Guided Rate Adaptation. In *Proc. IEEE INFOCOM'08* (June 2008).

Bringing Mobility-Awareness to WLANs using PHY Layer Information

Li Sun
University at Buffalo, SUNY
lsun3@buffalo.edu

Souvik Sen
HP Labs
souvik.sen@hp.com

Dimitrios Koutsonikolas
University at Buffalo, SUNY
dimitrio@buffalo.edu

ABSTRACT

With the proliferation of smartphones and tablets, mobile devices are soon becoming a preferred medium of Internet access in Wireless LANs (WLANs). Due to their smaller form factor, these truly mobile devices allow the users to access the wireless networks while undergoing different types of mobility, posing new challenges to wireless protocols. Current history-based protocols that maximize performance in static settings do not work well in mobile settings where wireless conditions change rapidly. Thus, today's WLANs need to be able to determine the type of the client's mobility and employ appropriate strategies in order to sustain high performance. While previous work tried to detect mobility using hints from sensors available in today's mobile devices, in this work, we demonstrate how different mobility modes can be distinguished by using physical layer information – Channel State Information (CSI) and Time-of-Flight (ToF) – available at commodity APs, with no modifications on the client side. In addition, we demonstrate how fine-grained mobility determination can be exploited to improve performance of client roaming, rate control, frame aggregation, and MIMO beamforming. Our testbed experiments show that our mobility classification algorithm achieves more than 92% accuracy in a variety of scenarios, and the combined throughput gain of all four mobility-aware protocols over their mobility-oblivious counterparts can be more than 100%.

Categories and Subject Descriptors

C.2.1 [**Network Architecture and Design**]: Wireless communication

Keywords

WLAN; Mobility; Channel State Information; Time-of-Flight; Client Roaming; Rate Adaptation; Frame Aggregation; Beamforming

CoNEXT'14, December 2–5, 2014, Sydney, Australia.
Copyright 2014 ACM 978-1-4503-3279-8/14/12 ... $15.00.
http://dx.doi.org/10.1145/2674005.2675017.

1. INTRODUCTION

Wireless LANs (WLANs) were previously dominated by static network users with devices such as laptops and notebooks. However, with the proliferation of smartphones, tablets, and the advent of the BYOD phenomenon, mobile devices are soon becoming the preferred medium of Internet access. Due to their smaller form factor, these truly mobile devices allow the users to access the wireless network while undergoing different forms of mobility. Thus, unlike previously when WLANs used to mainly serve static clients, today they need to be optimized for mobile clients as well.

Client mobility poses difficult problems to the WLAN protocols. In static scenarios, the wireless channel remains stable and hence wireless protocols can refer to the past transmission history, carefully adapting themselves to avoid any failures and optimize performance. In contrast, during mobility, wireless conditions may change frequently requiring protocols to be agile and apply different strategies. Designing such strategies is not trivial because they depend on the actual type of mobility demonstrated by the client. E.g., the length of past history that a wireless protocol can refer to depends on the intensity of the mobility of the client. If the client is walking *towards* her access point (AP), the wireless channel is likely to become better and hence transmission bit-rate control can be more aggressive. Whereas if the client is walking *away* from her AP, bit-rate control needs to be conservative. The WLAN should try to move the client to a better AP only when the client is moving away from her AP and should not consider roaming for static clients because it is unlikely that a better AP will be discovered. Likewise, mechanisms to obtain higher throughput in modern 802.11n/ac WLANs, such as frame aggregation, beamforming, multiuser-MIMO (MU-MIMO), require different optimizations based on the intensity of mobility of the client. Therefore, unless the WLAN protocols can somehow determine the type of the client's mobility and thereafter employ appropriate strategies, it is unlikely that they will be able to sustain high performance.

Today's WLAN protocols are unable to distinguish between different types of client mobility that a wireless client may undergo. They generally try to sustain performance by applying heuristics to reduce wireless errors. If the number of errors is high, current protocols try to improve performance by employing aggressive strategies. On the other hand, if the number of errors is low, they try to maintain reliability by being more conservative. Such a general framework is slow to adapt to client mobility.

Recognizing the difficulty to detect mobility using the client's RSSI values, recent work [1] tried to detect mobility using the accelerometer in a mobile phone. While this technique can broadly classify between stationary and mobile devices, it has a few disadvantages. First, the use of client's on-board sensor means that mobility detection can only be performed by the mobile client. This requires changes at both the client and the AP because, to benefit download traffic, the protocol is required to communicate the device's mobility state to the AP. Second, this technique can be implemented only on client devices that have an accelerometer, and it requires the sensor to be on consuming battery life. Rather than changing the client, which is a more difficult proposition, we demonstrate how different mobility modes can be distinguished by using physical (PHY) layer information available at commodity APs.

In our study we identify four broad categories of client mobility. If the client is stationary, it can be in the *static mobility mode* when there are no significant environmental changes affecting the channel between the AP and the client. A static client may also be in the *environmental mobility mode* when the channel changes due to external movements. Of course the wireless client itself may be moving – a mobility mode that we call *device mobility*. The wireless client may experience different speeds under device mobility. However, we identify two broad and dominant categories of device mobility in WLANs. First, the user may slowly move the device although she is stationary or her movement is confined within a small area. E.g., the user may be attending a VoIP call over WiFi and a little movement of her head may displace her smartphone. The user may be playing an online multi-user game where the game controls require her to shake the phone or tablet frequently. She may be roaming around within her office or cubicle while watching a streaming video or listening to streaming music. We define that the client is under *micro-mobility* if it is under device-mobility but its location is confined within a small area. On the other hand, device mobility may also cause the client to change its location as its user walks from one location to another. In such scenarios, we classify the client to be under *macro-mobility*.

We utilize Channel State Information (CSI) and Time-of-Flight (ToF) values available from off-the-shelf HP MSM APs to determine the client's mobility mode. CSI captures the fine-grained characteristics of the wireless channel. We show that the temporal changes in the CSI can discriminate between static, environmental, and device mobility. However the CSI value may change similarly for micro and macro mobility scenarios. To distinguish between these two device mobility modes, we find that the client's distance from the AP changes significantly under macro-mobility, whereas under micro-mobility her distance seldom changes. The ToF can reliably indicate the distance between the client and the AP because it captures the round trip propagation time between the two. The increasing vs. decreasing trend of the client's distance can further indicate her relative heading with respect to the AP, whether the client is *moving away* from or *moving towards* the AP.

In addition to mobility determination using PHY layer information, we make the following contributions:

- **Client roaming:** In section 3, we demonstrate how the knowledge of the mobile client's relative heading can be exploited to improve client roaming in WLANs. By encouraging the client to roam when it is moving away from its current AP, our protocol improves performance by up to 40% in our testbed experiments.

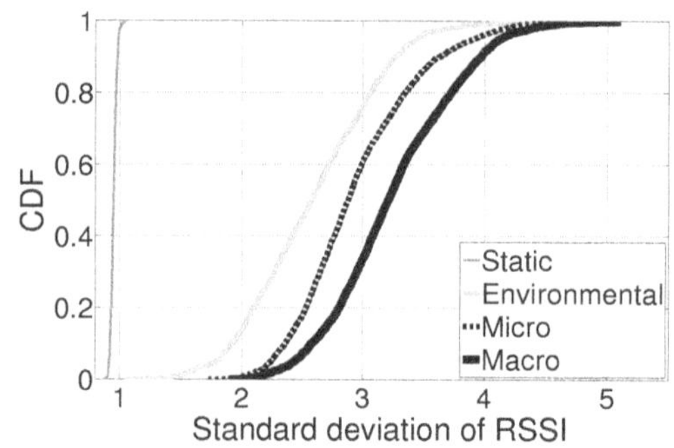

Figure 1: CDF of standard deviation of RSSI computed every 5 seconds, for various types of mobility.

- **Rate control:** In section 4, we show how mobility-awareness can further improve an existing frame-based rate control scheme. Mobility hints can help the rate control scheme determine when it can aggressively increase rate or whether past history should be accounted for while choosing the bit-rate. Testbed experiments show that mobility-aware rate control can improve performance by up to 30%.

- **Frame Aggregation:** In section 5, we demonstrate that the frame aggregation size needs to be adapted depending on the client's mobility mode. Our testbed experimentation shows that, when compared with schemes using default aggregation size, our adaptive scheme can improve throughput by up to 30%.

- **Beamforming and MU-MIMO:** Beamforming and MU-MIMO require frequent and expensive CSI feedback from the client. In section 6, we show that the frequency of CSI feedback depends on the mobility mode of the client. By adapting the CSI feedback frequency based on client's mobility, we demonstrate that performance can be improved by up to 70% in testbed experiments.

2. MOBILITY CLASSIFICATION

This section presents our design and algorithms for mobility classification using PHY layer information. We begin with a description of our experimental setting using commodity APs and smartphones.

2.1 Experimental Setup

We use HP MSM 460 APs with Atheros AR9390 chipset and Samsung Galaxy S5 smartphones in our experiments. We tuned the AP at 5.805GHz using a 40MHz channel width and the 802.11n protocol. The MSM AP is equipped with 3 transmit antennas while the Samsung smartphone has 2 antennas. We sent regular data packets from the AP and collected CSI, ToF, and Received Signal Strength Indicator (RSSI) information from the acknowledgment (ACK) sent by the client. We ran four different experiments to analyze different classes of mobility. First, we evaluated static mobility by placing the smartphone in our lab with several people present but not moving. Second, for environmental mobility, we experimented in a cafeteria during lunch hours where the smartphone was static on a table. Third, for micro-mobility, we picked up the phone and moved it around within a meter

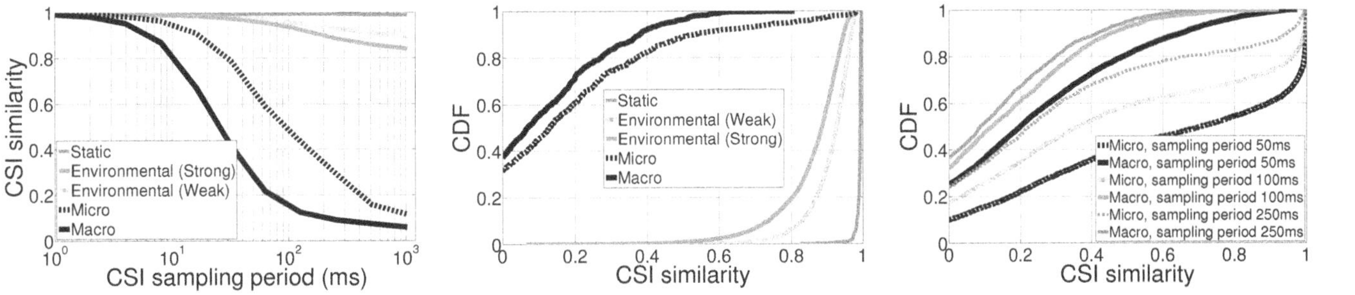

Figure 2: (a) Variation of CSI similarity values over time. CDF of CSI similarity values (b) for various mobility modes, (c) for device mobility at different CSI sampling frequencies.

of its location, using natural gestures. Lastly, for evaluating client macro-mobility, we walked naturally with the phone in our hand or inside the pocket. Our goal is to develop simple classification schemes that can distinguish among the above four scenarios.

2.2 Classifying Mobility using RSSI

We explore the possibility of classifying the mobility mode of the client solely by relying on the PHY layer information available from commodity WiFi APs. One possibility can be to utilize the RSSI of the client. In our experiments, we found that RSSI is quite stable in static scenarios in a quiet environment (Figure 1). However, RSSI is susceptible to any changes in the environment [1]. Often, the RSSI variation under environmental mobility is higher than the observed variation under device mobility (Figure 1). Therefore, we conclude that it is difficult to distinguish between environmental and device mobility solely based on RSSI. We will show next how CSI can conclusively classify these two types of mobility.

2.3 Classifying Mobility using CSI

Wireless is a broadcast medium. Any transmitted signal from the client undergoes reflections and arrives along multiple paths (multipath) at the AP. The wireless channel between the client and the AP is expected to vary under environmental or device mobility. This is because the fine-grained multipath structure may change if there are moving objects in the environment, or the device itself moves. These fine-grained variations of the wireless channel cannot be captured by RSSI because it only captures an aggregate indicator of all the multipath components. However, we found that the same variations can be reliably detected by CSI. CSI captures the fine-grained multipath characteristics between the client and the AP in the frequency domain. The Atheros 9390 chipset can export the CSI of a received packet. On a 20 MHz channel, CSI is reported as a matrix of complex numbers representing the channel gain for each of the 52 subcarriers and every transmit-receive antenna pair at the AP and the client. We track the change in the CSI values to detect any variations of the wireless channel. We define the *similarity* between CSI samples, csi_t and $csi_{t+\tau}$ collected at two different time instances t and $t+\tau$ as:

$$S(csi_t, csi_{t+\tau}) = \frac{\sum_{i=1}^{52}\left(|csi_t^i| - \overline{|csi_t|}\right)\left(|csi_{t+\tau}^i| - \overline{|csi_{t+\tau}|}\right)}{\sqrt{\sum_{i=1}^{52}\left(|csi_t^i| - \overline{|csi_t|}\right)^2}\sqrt{\sum_{i=1}^{52}\left(|csi_{t+\tau}^i| - \overline{|csi_{t+\tau}|}\right)^2}} \quad (1)$$

where τ is the time period between the two CSI samples, and $|csi_t^i|$, $|csi_{t+\tau}^i|$ represent the channel gain for the i-th subcarrier at times t and $t+\tau$, respectively. In static scenarios, for small values of τ, the similarity stays close to 1 because the CSI matches across time indicating a stable channel (Figure 2(a)). In contrast, the similarity value drops sharply under environmental or device mobility due to rapid changes in the wireless channel (Figure 2(a)). Furthermore, we found that the similarity drops faster for device mobility than environmental mobility. This happens because environmental mobility typically affects only a few multipath components, whereas if the client itself is moving, all the multipath components will be affected. Therefore, the wireless channel experiences faster variation under device mobility than under environmental mobility as evident by the larger change in CSI values.

Figure 2(b) shows the distribution of similarity of consecutive CSI samples collected at every 0.5 seconds. Clearly, the similarity distribution can be used to distinguish between static, environmental, and device-mobility scenarios. If the similarity of consecutive CSI samples is greater than $Thr_{sta} = 0.98$, we declare that the client is stationary with no environmental changes, whereas a similarity below $Thr_{env} = 0.7$ indicates device-mobility. However, from Figure 2(b), it appears that it is difficult to distinguish between device micro-mobility and macro-mobility using CSI. Figure 2(c) demonstrates that the gap between the micro and macro-mobility distribution increases if we sample the CSI more frequently. However, there are still large overlapping regions. We found that even if we sample the CSI every $50ms$, the probability of mis-classification between micro- and macro-mobility is higher than 50%. Therefore, we conclude that even if it is possible to use CSI to distinguish between device and environmental mobility, it cannot be reliably used to distinguish between different classes of device mobility.

2.4 Classifying Device Mobility using Time-of-Flight

To classify device mobility, we utilize the intuition that the distance between the client and the AP under macro-mobility changes more than that under micro-mobility. Client's distance can be estimated based on its RSSI [2] or CSI [3] measurements at the AP. However, previous work has shown that RSSI and CSI are unreliable indicators of distance [4]. In search of a better metric for distance, we find that a PHY layer metric called Time-of-Flight (ToF) can accurately capture the distance between the client and the AP [4, 5]. Due to space limitation, we provide here only a high-level overview of the

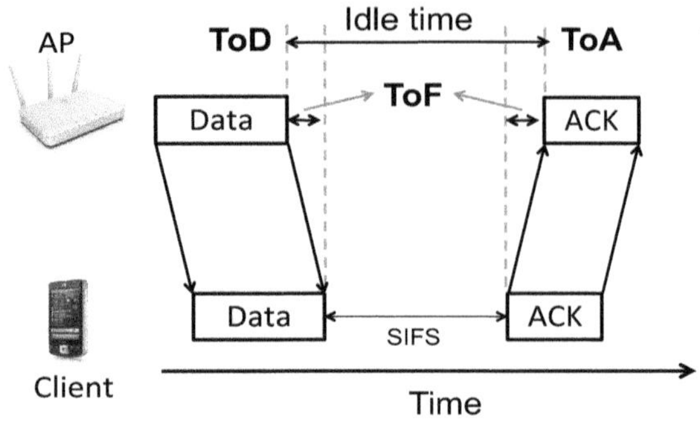

Figure 3: Computation of ToD and ToA in the PHY layer using data-ACK exchange.

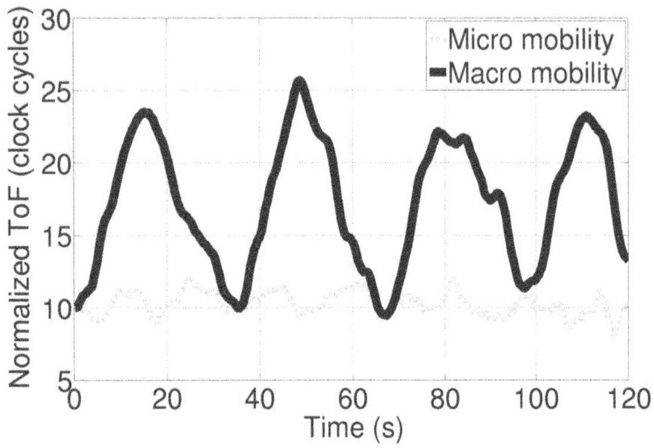

Figure 4: ToF values over time under device mobility. For the macro-mobility scenario the user walks towards and away from the AP periodically.

ToF estimation and refer the reader to [4] for details. ToF is defined as the round trip propagation time of a signal transmitted between the AP and the mobile device. The Atheros chipset can precisely compute the Time-of-Departure (ToD) of a data packet when it is sent out in the air at the PHY layer (Figure 3). On correct reception of the packet, the client waits for an SIFS duration (a fixed value in the 802.11 standard) and starts responding with an ACK packet. The chipset also reports an estimated Time-of-Arrival (ToA) of the ACK packet at the AP as shown in Figure 3. The difference between the ToA and ToD contains the ToF between the AP and the client. Since ToF is proportional to the distance between the client and the AP, it can be used to classify device-mobility.

Figure 4 plots the ToF values over time for two different device mobility scenarios. For the micro-mobility scenario, when the user naturally moves the device only within a small area, noisy ToF values can sometimes wrongly indicate changes in distance values. However, the change in noisy ToF values in the micro-mobility case is quite random, while for the macro-mobility scenario the ToF either steadily increases or decreases. This happens due to the fact that during macro-mobility a user typically walks a reasonable distance between two physical turns. Within a reasonable time interval a walking user may either approach or move away from the AP, without changing her orientation. Therefore, to detect macro-mobility, we maintain a moving window of ToF values. Only if all the ToF values in the moving window suggest an increasing or decreasing trend, we declare that the client is under macro-mobility, otherwise the client is under micro-mobility. The trend of the ToF values can also suggest the general direction of the client's motion – an increasing trend means that the client is moving away from the AP and vice versa. Later, we will demonstrate how the WLAN can optimize client roaming by exploiting the user's direction of motion.

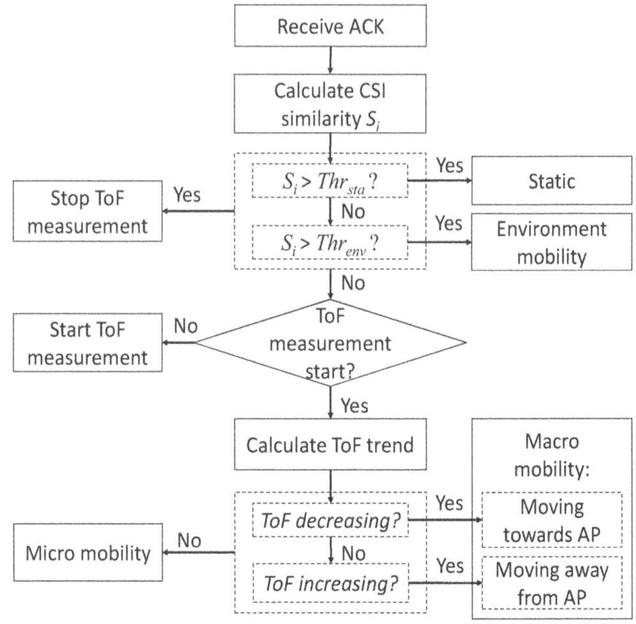

Figure 5: Mobility classification design

Ground truth	Detection result (%)			
	Static	Environmental	Micro	Macro
Static	99.7	0.3	0	0
Environmental	4.55	92.78	2.67	0
Micro-mobility	0	3.58	95.59	0.83
Macro-mobility	0	0	1.7	98.3

Table 1: Evaluation of mobility classification.

2.5 Evaluation of Mobility Classification

Figure 5 shows the overall design of mobility classification using CSI and ToF. We sample the CSI of the client periodically from existing data packet transmissions and maintain a moving average of the similarity between consecutive CSI values. We compare the CSI similarity values with empirically chosen thresholds (see Section 2.3) to distinguish between static, environmental and device mobility. If the CSI similarity indicates device mobility, we need to further consult the client's ToF values. To deal with measurement noise [4], we sample the client's ToF readings every $200ms$ and aggregate them every second using a median filter. In our implementation, if all ToF values within the past few seconds show an increasing or decreasing trend, we conclude that the client is under macro-mobility. Further, if all the ToF values show an increasing trend, we conclude that the client is moving away from the AP and vice versa.

We implemented our mobility classification algorithm using the HP MSM APs and evaluated its accuracy by performing experiments at more than 100 locations (different from those we used for learning the various thresholds and parameters of our scheme in Sections 2.3, 2.4) in two office buildings for over 24 hours. At each location we subject the client to different forms of mobility. Table 1 presents our overall performance results. We observe that the accuracy of our mobility

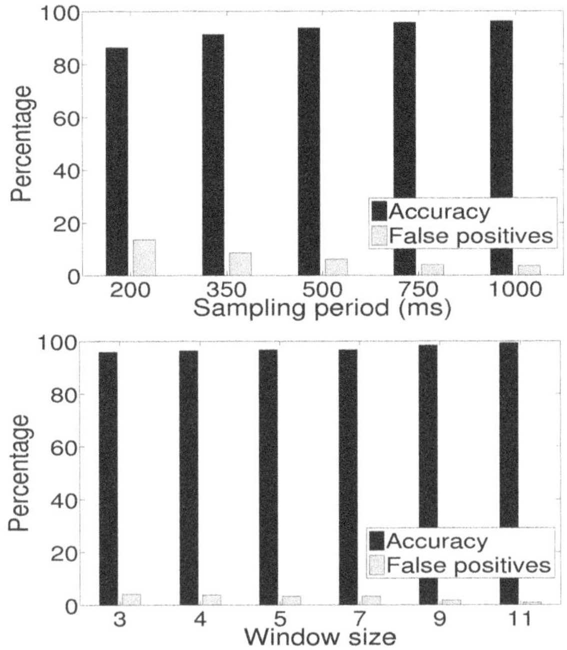

Figure 6: Accuracy and false positives of (a) CSI-based mobility detection for various CSI sampling intervals, (b) micro- and macro-mobility detection for various ToF detection window sizes.

classification is more than 92% in all scenarios.

We also found that the performance of distinguishing stationary vs. device mobility using CSI depends on the sampling period of the CSI (Figure 6(a)). The accuracy is low for short sampling period because the channel may not change very quickly even under device-mobility. We use a CSI sampling period of $500ms$ in the rest of our evaluation, yielding a median accuracy of 96%.

If the client is under device-mobility, we need to consider the ToF values within a detection window of a few seconds and determine if the ToF values have an increasing or decreasing trend. Of course, the larger the detection window, the greater will be the accuracy (Figure 6(b)), but large detection windows will delay the macro-mobility detection. Nonetheless, we find that a detection window of $4s$ yields a satisfactory accuracy of 98%, and hence we use the same in the rest of the paper.

In this work, we identify four broad categories of client mobility. One could suggest more fine-grained mobility classifications, e.g., distinguishing among different subcategories of macro-mobility based on the client's speed or among different types of micro-mobility based on whether the user is static or moves within a small area. However, we argue that in a WLAN environment categorizing client mobility in four broad categories is quite sufficient and yields simplicity in protocol design. In the following sections, we demonstrate that our broad mobility classification already offers substantial performance improvements to a number of wireless protocols.

3. MOBILITY-AWARE CLIENT ROAMING

Most wireless clients associate with the AP with the strongest RSSI value. When the RSSI falls below a predefined threshold, the client triggers a handoff, where it scans all the channels and associates with the AP with the strongest RSSI. The problem is that the client-based association control is agnostic of the user's mobility. A moving client may be close to a stronger AP, but it does not try to discover or associate with it, as long as the signal strength of the current AP is above a predefined threshold [6, 7]. Of course, if the client somehow knows that it is moving, it can scan aggressively to search for better APs [1]. But frequent scanning is time consuming and wastes energy (impacting battery life), consumes RF resources, and prevents the client from transmitting or receiving data (impacting throughput). Therefore, under mobility the client often remains wrongly connected to a far away AP, adversely affecting its own as well as the overall network performance. To address this issue, rather than designing a mobility-aware association scheme that requires changes at the client [1], we propose a controller-based protocol that moves the client to the appropriate AP whenever necessary.

3.1 Controller-based Roaming Protocol

Our roaming protocol is based on two main intuitions. First, when the client is stationary or under micro-mobility, it is less likely that a new, better AP will be discovered. Second, when the client is under macro-mobility, roaming is required only when the client moves away from the current AP. We validate these intuitions by performing more than 100 experiments at 50 different locations in our testbed. In each experiment, we subjected the client to different types of mobility and collected the RSSI values of different APs. We used the RSSI values to compute an expected throughput from different APs [8]. Figure 7(a) shows that in most mobility modes, roaming to another AP only marginally improves the performance of the client. Unless the client is walking away from the current AP, it need not roam to improve performance and can continue with the current AP. Environmental mobility can cause fluctuations of the channel between the client and the AP. However, these fluctuations are short term such that the AP with the strongest RSSI is likely to remain optimal over longer time-scales. Under micro-mobility, the client's overall physical location does not change significantly. WLAN deployments are typically well planned where each physical location is meant to be covered by a single strong AP. Therefore, roaming may be necessary only when the client's location changes significantly. But, even under macro-mobility, if the client is approaching her current AP, roaming is not necessary because the channel between the current AP and the client will only become better. On the other hand, if the client is moving away from the current AP, it may have a better channel quality to a neighboring AP. In such scenarios, the controller needs to act to move the client to the right AP.

Our controller-based protocol does not impose any changes in the client's association mechanism. The client initially connects with the strongest AP and thereafter scans if the current AP becomes weak. The current AP of the client continuously determines her mobility mode and shares it with the controller. If the current AP indicates that the client is moving away from it, the controller may have to explicitly encourage the client to roam to a better AP. To determine a candidate set of better APs, the controller instructs the neighboring APs to periodically transmit NULL data frames and compute the client's distance, RSSI and heading information towards themselves. If the client is moving towards another AP whose signal strength value is similar or higher than the current AP,

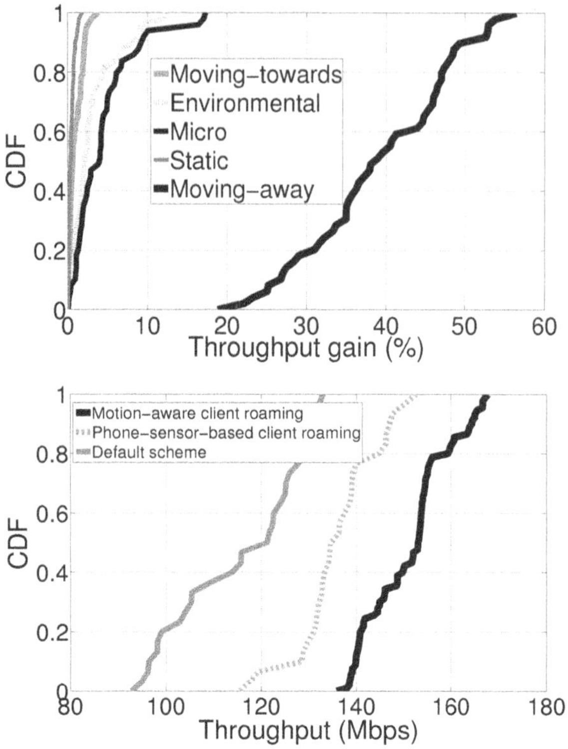

Figure 7: (a) Throughput gain by dynamically switching to the strongest AP vs. sticking to the current AP. (b) Comparison of proposed controller-based client roaming using mobility hints against existing protocols.

it is likely that the same AP will improve the client's long term performance. Note that there can be several such candidate APs which may be more appropriate (in terms of heading and signal strength) for the client. If the controller finds at least one such better AP, it instructs the current AP to disassociate the client and asks only the APs in the candidate set to respond to the client's probe request. Consequently, the client chooses an AP from the candidate set and roams to a better AP, ultimately improving performance.

3.2 Performance Evaluation

We implemented our mobility-aware client roaming protocol in our testbed of 6 HP APs (Figure 13(a)) and used a laptop connected to the APs over Ethernet as the controller. We walked naturally with the phone and injected UDP traffic from the controller to evaluate performance. We compared our scheme with the client's default roaming scheme as well as the client-based association control scheme described in [1] in which the client periodically scans for better APs if it is mobile. Figure 7(b) shows that the client's performance can be improved by assisting her to roam to a better AP when it is moving away from her current AP. Of course encouraging the client to roam requires forced disassociation from the current AP that triggers a scanning operation at the client. Scanning adds overhead. We find that the client typically completes association with a stronger AP within 200ms after being disassociated from the current AP. We believe this is reasonable because after association the client will probably use the new AP for a long duration. Nonetheless, even with the scanning overhead, our proposal improves median performance by nearly 30% over the default roaming scheme.

4. MOBILITY-AWARE BIT RATE ADAPTATION

Knowledge of client's mobility state can aid bit-rate adaptation because mobility affects wireless channel conditions. The higher the intensity of motion, the faster the channel may change and the quicker the optimal bit rate becomes stale. We investigate how the optimal bit-rate of the client changes under mobility. Figure 8(a) plots the time duration for which a particular bit-rate remains optimal for different mobility modes in our testbed. For this experiment we computed the optimal rate using trace-based emulation, similar to [9]. Clearly, the optimal bit-rate changes faster if the client is mobile than when it is static. It is possible to track the optimal bit-rate in static scenarios by maintaining long success/failure history. However, under mobility, the optimal bit-rate changes quickly and hence the rate control algorithm should rely only on the recent transmission history.

We further found that depending on the client's direction of motion, i.e., moving away from or moving towards the AP, the optimal rate typically changes either upwards or downwards (Figure 8(b)). Therefore, the client's direction of motion relative to the AP can be used as a hint by the rate control algorithm. Under environmental or micro-mobility, the rate change does not show any pattern (Figure 8(c)), but the optimal bit-rate stays within a small set of values. This happens because under environmental or micro-mobility, the frequency-selective nature of the channel may change but the overall path-loss between the AP and the client remains similar. These observations suggest that current rate control schemes can improve performance by adapting according to the client's mobility mode. We demonstrate how this may be feasible by incorporating mobility-awareness in the existing Atheros MIMO rate adaptation (RA) scheme.

4.1 Atheros MIMO Rate Adaptation

Atheros MIMO Rate Adaptation (RA) is the default RA in HP MSM 460 APs. It employs a transmitter-side frame-based adaptation approach and does not require any training or client feedback. The objective of the algorithm is to determine the bit-rate that maximizes the MAC layer throughput which is calculated as bit-rate * (1-PER) where PER is the packet error rate at the given bit-rate. After each frame transmission, the algorithm updates the PER at the current bit-rate based on the number of packet failures within the aggregated frame. It applies a low pass filter on the instantaneous PER PER_{new}, as calculated from the last transmitted frame, and maintains a weighted moving average of the PER value (PER_{avg}):

$$PER_{avg} = \alpha * PER_{new} + (1-\alpha) * PER_{avg} \qquad (2)$$

where α is called the *smoothing factor* and has a default value of 1/8 in the Atheros RA implementation. A larger α gives a smaller weight on the previous PER history. This operation smooths out the transients and takes into account past history. The algorithm further updates the PER of other bit-rates based on the PER of the current rate. This is done by assuming that the PER is a monotonically increasing function of rate [1].

[1]The Atheros RA skips the MCS $5-7$ for single stream and MCS $8-10$ for double stream to maintain PER monotonicity.

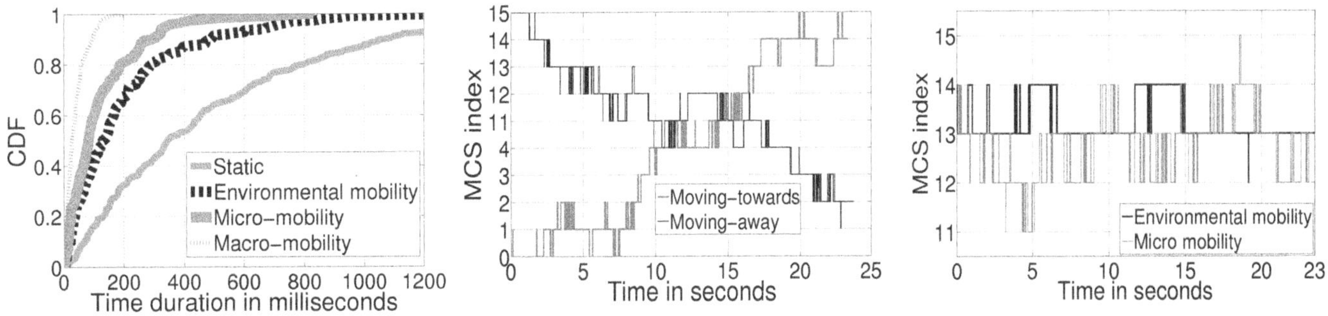

Figure 8: (a) CDF of time durations during which a current bit-rate remained optimal and no rate change was necessary. Optimal rate of a client over time when the client is under (b) macro-mobility, (c) environmental or micro-mobility.

The Atheros RA starts with the highest bit-rate and sends an aggregated frame containing several packets. If all the packets in a frame are lost such that it completely fails to get a link layer Block ACK, it often switches to the next lower rate. On the other hand, if the AP receives a Block ACK from the client, it updates the PER values and thereafter decides on a lower rate if the PER at the current rate is too high. The Atheros RA also tries to increase bit-rate whenever possible by sampling higher rates periodically. If the current rate has been successful for more than a predefined *probing interval*, the algorithm probes the next higher rate. Of course if the wireless channel is deteriorating, excessive probing may hurt performance. We show how Atheros RA can be improved using mobility hints.

4.2 Optimizing Atheros RA using Mobility Hints

Based on the observations from our measurements in the previous section (Figure 8), we make the following optimizations to the Atheros rate adaptation algorithm:

1. The Atheros RA often reduces the bit-rate if it fails to get a link layer Block ACK. This may be appropriate when the client is moving away from the AP because the wireless channel may be deteriorating. However, we note from Figures 8(b), 8(c) that if the client is moving towards the AP or if it is in any other mobility mode, this may be unnecessary because the optimal bit-rate either improves or fluctuates within a small band. In such scenarios, large errors can happen due to transient conditions such as fast fading or interference. We ignore such random effects by retrying at the current rate once or twice (Table 2) before reducing the rate, unless the client is moving away from the AP.

2. In static scenarios, we incorporate longer PER history by choosing a low value of the smoothing factor because bit-rate changes only occasionally if the client is static (Figure 8(a)). However, under mobility, the bit-rate may change quickly and thus the protocol should only account for recent packet successes and failures. Therefore, we choose a smoothing factor that is commensurate to the client's mobility mode.

3. We note that blindly probing higher rates may cause packet losses because the protocol may be already operating at the optimal rate. From Figure 8(b) we note that the optimal bit-rate of the client increases rapidly only when it is moving towards the AP. Otherwise, the optimal bit-rate seldom increases or improves only gradually. To avoid packet losses due to probing, we choose the probing interval based on the current mobility mode of the client. If the client is moving towards the AP, we use a short probing interval to quickly increase the rate whenever possible. In contrast, if the client is moving away from the AP, we remain conservative by choosing a long probing interval.

4.3 Rate Adaptation Evaluation

We study the benefit of augmenting mobility hints to Atheros RA in our testbed. We modified the rate control implementation in the Atheros driver to control multiple related parameters depending on the mobility mode of the client. We conducted more than 100 experiments on 30 different links with both UDP and TCP traffic. In each experiment, we subjected the client to different types of mobility and tried different values for the Atheros RA parameters. Our final chosen parameters are shown in Table 2. We then evaluated the throughput of download TCP traffic on 150 different links in two different office buildings. At each location we subjected the client to different forms of device mobility. Figure 9(a) shows that by augmenting mobility hints to Atheros RA, it is possible to improve its median performance by 23%.

We further compare the performance of our mobility-aware rate adaptation scheme with existing state-of-the art rate control schemes. To ascertain identical channel conditions we performed trace-based emulations using techniques similar to [9]. Specifically, we modified the wireless driver of a HP laptop containing Atheros 9390 chipset to extract the CSI information from any download packet from the AP. Thereafter, we walked with the laptop in random directions for 15 minutes each and collected CSI traces for 10 such walking experiments. Using the collected traces we evaluate the throughput of Atheros RA with and without mobility hints, RapidSample [1], SoftRate [10] and ESNR [9]. Figure 9(b) shows that the mobility-aware Atheros RA performs better than RapidSample which uses sensor hints to optimize rate control. Unlike our scheme, RapidSample is unable to discriminate between fine-grained device mobility modes, e.g. micro vs. macro mobility or moving towards vs. away, and thereafter is unable to apply specific optimizations. Both SoftRate and ESNR use PHY layer information at the client to calculate the bit-rate and report it back to the AP. We find that the mobility-aware Atheros RA achieves almost the same throughput as SoftRate. ESNR outperforms SoftRate because it can indicate the bit-rate of the channel using a single observation, while SoftRate can typically only indicate whether the rate should be increased, decreased, or unchanged [11]. Our scheme can achieve 90% of ESNR's performance but notably it does not require any modifications at the client or any

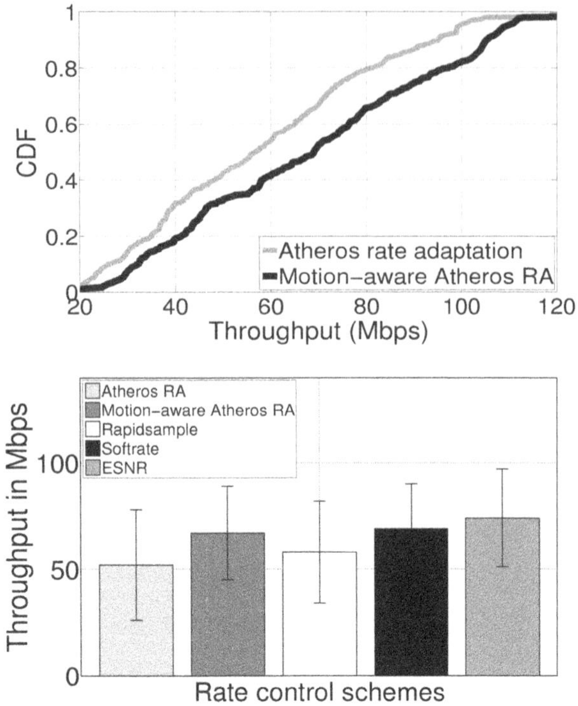

Figure 9: (a) Throughput gain by incorporating mobility-awareness in Atheros rate adaptation. (b) Comparison of mobility-aware Atheros RA against other state-of-the art schemes.

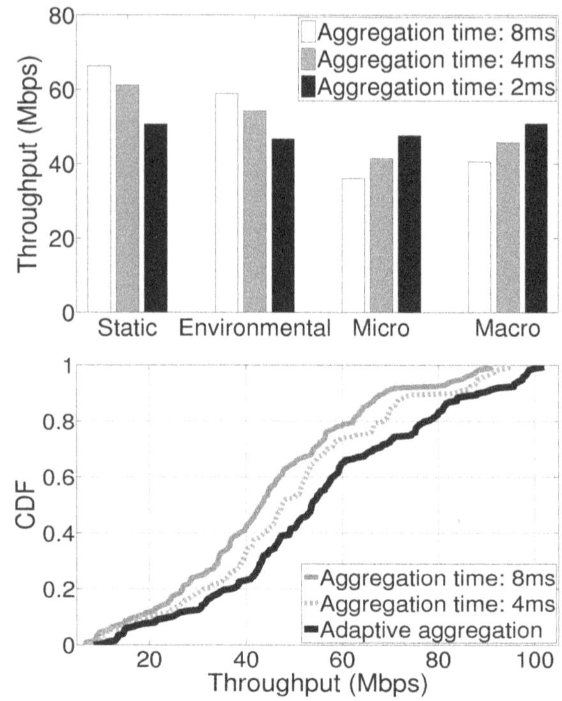

Figure 10: (a) Mean throughput vs. frame aggregation time in different mobility scenarios. (b) Comparison of the adaptive mobility-aware frame aggregation scheme against schemes that use a statically configured aggregation time.

per-client calibration to establish the ESNR vs. bit-rate relationship [9].

5. MOBILITY-AWARE FRAME AGGREGATION

To achieve high throughput, IEEE 802.11 allows the wireless transmitter to aggregate multiple packets in a single frame. Aggregation achieves higher throughput because the PHY protocol overhead over multiple packets can be amortized by packing them into a single frame. As the number of packets in a frame (often referred to as aggregation size) increases, the efficiency of the protocol improves resulting in greater performance. Thus, it is generally believed that choosing a larger aggregation size is beneficial. In fact, current implementations allow the transmitter to aggregate as many packets as it can within an aggregation time of 10ms [12]. However, choosing the highest aggregation size may hurt performance under mobility as the wireless channel may vary within an aggregated frame.

To understand the effect of channel variations on aggregation, we conducted a total of 60 experiments on 20 different links in our office building. We injected download traffic to the client while varying the aggregation size defined in the driver from $2ms$ to $8ms$ for each mobility mode. We found that in mobility scenarios, performance can actually decrease if a large aggregation size is used (Figure 10(a)). This happens because the channel equalization procedure employed by today's wireless radios estimates the channel only at the beginning of the frame. Under mobility, it is quite possible that the wireless channel changes by the end of frame resulting into packet losses.

5.1 Optimization and Performance Evaluation

To optimize the performance of frame aggregation, we note from Figure 10(a) that the optimal aggregation time varies across different classes of mobility. The higher the intensity of mobility, the lower is the channel coherence time and hence the lower is the optimal aggregation time. Therefore, we propose to tune the aggregation size at the AP based on the mobility state of the client. We modified the WiFi driver at the AP to vary the maximum allowed aggregation time based on the mobility mode of the client – 8ms for static and environmental mobility and 2ms for micro- and macro-mobility. The actual aggregation size depends on the bit-rate used to communicate to the client: Aggregation size = Maximum allowed aggregation time / Bit-rate.

We evaluated our modifications on 50 different links in two office buildings and subjected the client to various mobility modes, while injecting download TCP traffic from the AP. Figure 10(b) plots the performance of our aggregation scheme on 50 different links. By selecting the aggregation size based on mobility, it is possible to improve the median throughput performance by 15% over the default Atheros scheme which uses a statically configured $4ms$ maximum aggregation time.

6. MOBILITY-AWARE BEAMFORMING AND MU-MIMO

MIMO beamforming can improve the performance of a wireless link by exploiting multiple antennas at the transmitter. Single-user (SU) beamforming in 802.11n precodes a single packet across multiple antennas at the AP so that the signals

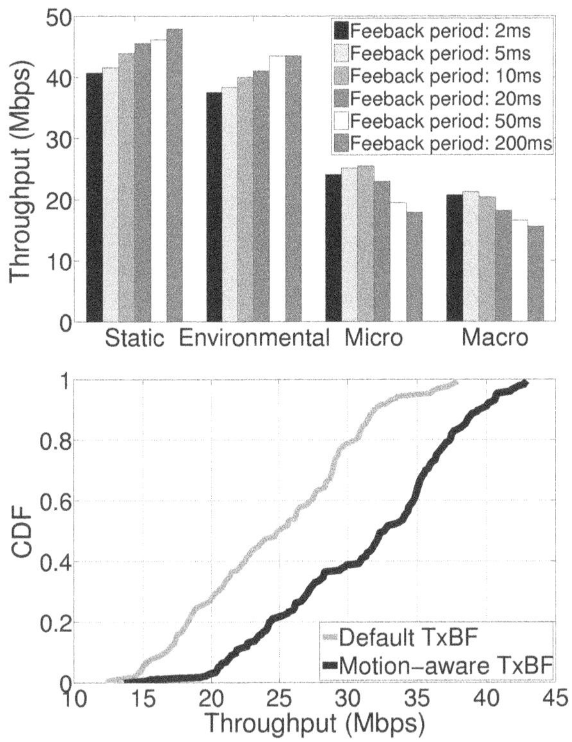

Figure 11: (a) Average throughput vs. CSI feedback period in different mobility scenarios using transmit beamforming. (b) CDF of throughput gain for 300 different links subjected to a variety of mobility modes.

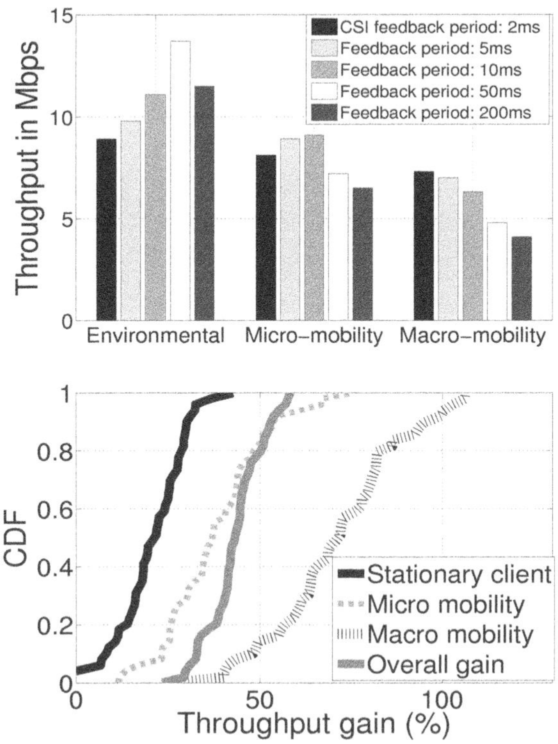

Figure 12: (a) Average throughput vs. CSI feedback period using MU-MIMO techniques to serve three different clients. (b) CDF of throughput gain for 200 emulation scenarios. Each scenario includes 3 clients, one each in environmental, micro-, and macro-mobility mode.

from different antennas combine coherently at the client, enhancing performance. Similarly, 802.11ac multi-user MIMO (MU-MIMO) precodes packets for different clients so that they can be transmitted simultaneously. The precoding operation combines the outgoing packets and carefully chooses the weights based on the CSI values between the AP (transmitter) and all the clients (receivers). Therefore, for effective beamforming, the AP must obtain timely CSI feedback from all the clients. The CSI feedback packet may consist of a real and imaginary value (quantized into up to 8 bits) for each subcarrier and transmit-receive antenna pair. Frequent CSI feedback may be harmful because the feedback packet is typically transmitted at the lowest bit-rate, consuming significant channel airtime. On the other hand, infrequent feedback may often result in stale CSI and consequently performance loss. Hence managing the CSI feedback period is critical to the performance of MIMO beamforming.

6.1 Effect of Mobility on SU-Beamforming

To understand the effect of CSI feedback period on SU-Beamforming, we conducted 150 experiments on more than 50 different links in our office building by allowing the AP to periodically initiate CSI feedback from the client and employ beamforming while transmitting the data packets. We found that none of the popular smartphones support explicit beamforming and hence we used an AP as the client in our beamforming experiments. Figure 11(a) shows that in static scenarios, a shorter CSI feedback period can actually hurt performance. This is because the wireless channel remains stable in static scenarios. Therefore, frequent feedback only adds to the overhead and does not always result in better CSI estimates. In contrast, if the client is mobile, the wireless channel can change quickly, requiring frequent CSI feedback. Thus, we need to adapt the CSI feedback period depending on the client's mobility mode.

6.2 Effect of Mobility on MU-MIMO

Our AP platform only supports 802.11a/b/g/n and hence is not amenable to MU-MIMO experiments. We resort to trace-based emulations to understand the effect of feedback period on MU-MIMO. We emulate a scenario where the AP has 3 antennas and employs MU-MIMO techniques to concurrently serve 3 clients – one each in environmental, micro- and macro-mobility scenarios. For the emulation, we simultaneously collected CSI traces at 3 locations using laptops containing Atheros 9390 chipset and a single receive antenna. We instrumented the Atheros driver used in the laptop to report the CSI values for every transmitter-receiver antenna pair for each data packet received from the AP. Thereafter we sent data packets from the AP to each laptop every 500us. We fed the series of CSI values to a MU-MIMO emulator written in C. The emulator simulates CBR traffic between the AP and the clients and reports the throughput for each client with and without MU-MIMO techniques.

Figure 12(a) shows that MU-MIMO is also sensitive to stale CSI values. Interestingly, mobility only affects the performance of the mobile client and does not impact the static clients noticeably. This happens because MU-MIMO precoding ensures that signals from all the transmit antennas combine coherently at each intended client, which is only re lated to the channel between the AP and the respective client Therefore it is possible to improve MU-MIMO performance b using different CSI feedback periods that are commensurat to the mobility modes of individual clients.

6.3 Performance Optimization & Evaluation

To optimize performance using SU-beamforming and MU-MI we note from figures 11(a) and 12(a) that the optimal CS feedback period varies across different classes of mobility. Th higher the intensity of mobility, the quicker the CSI become stale and hence the higher is the required frequency of the CS feedback. Therefore, we propose to tune the CSI feedback pe riod at the AP based on the mobility state of the client. W modified the WiFi driver at the AP to vary the feedback perio based on the mobility mode of the client – 200ms for static, 50ms for environmental mobility, 10ms for micro-, and 5ms for macro-mobility.

We evaluated SU-beamforming using adaptive CSI feedback on 300 different mobile links in two office buildings by injecting download TCP traffic from the AP. Figure 11(b) shows that by selecting the feedback period based on mobility, it is possible to improve the median throughput by 33% over the default Atheros scheme which uses a statically configured $200ms$ feedback period.

To evaluate the benefits of adaptive CSI feedback on MU-MIMO, we used the trace based emulation setup described in section 6.2. In total, we collected CSI traces from 50 uniformly chosen locations from a busy office environment. At each location, we kept the client stationary for approximately 5 minutes, followed by micro-mobility and macro-mobility experiments for the same interval. Apart from collecting the CSI trace at the client, we also recorded the CSI and ToF values from the data-ACK exchange at the AP. For each trace, we estimate the mobility mode of the client every second using our techniques described in section 2. Thereafter we randomly pick 3 client locations and feed the corresponding CSI traces and mobility estimates to our MU-MIMO emulator. To calculate the precoding vector, the MU-MIMO emulator samples the CSI traces every feedback period. For our scheme, the feedback period is chosen on a per client basis depending on her mobility state – 200ms for static, 50ms for environmental mobility, 10ms for micro-, and 2ms for macro-mobility, whereas the default scheme uses a 200ms CSI feedback period for all clients. The emulator uses Atheros RA for rate control and does not employ aggregation. We repeated the emulation 200 times, each time with a different set of 3 client locations. Figure 12(b) plots the throughput gain of MU-MIMO using adaptive CSI feedback over the static feedback period scheme. Performance gain is evident for all varieties of mobility, with the most gains for clients under macro-mobility. On average, our scheme improves MU-MIMO's network throughput by close to 40%.

7. OVERALL PROTOCOL PERFORMANCE

As explained in the preceding sections, we implement the client's mobility mode detection scheme at the AP. Further, depending on the client's mobility mode, at the AP and the WLAN controller, we implement several actions to improve rate control, client roaming, aggregation and beamforming

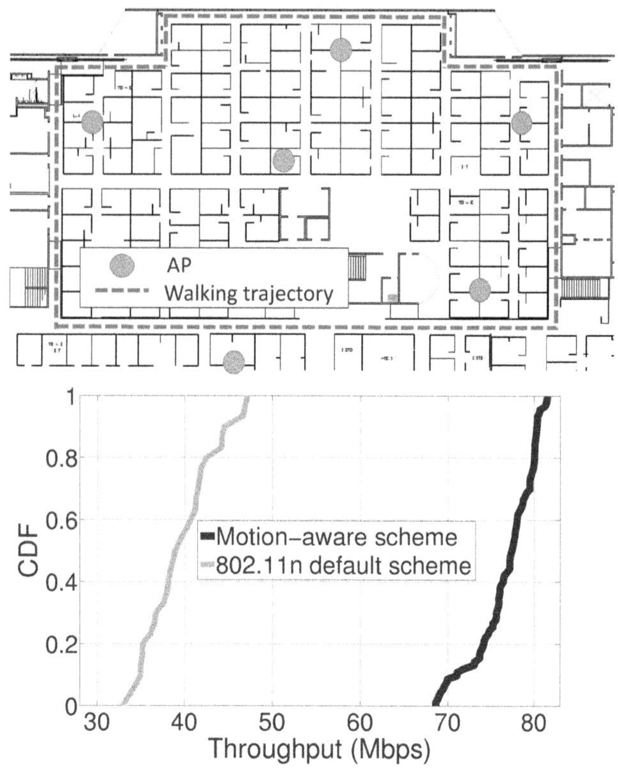

Figure 13: (a) Testbed setting for overall performance evaluation. (b) CDF of end-to-end throughput for 90 tests with and without mobility hints.

(Table 2)[2]. To evaluate the combined protocol performance for all such optimizations, we conducted iperf-based system throughput tests in our testbed using 6 APs (Figure 13(a)) with UDP traffic. We walked naturally with the client through different parts of the trajectory shown in Figure 13(a) and evaluated the performance of our system as well as the default system which does not distinguish client's mobility. As shown in Figure 13(b), the mobility-aware scheme outperformed the default system in all the 90 tests we conducted in our testbed. By taking appropriate actions based on the client's mobility mode, we improve overall protocol performance by almost 100%.

8. RELATED WORK

Sensor hint-based optimization: The work closest to ours is [1], which uses sensor hints (e.g., from GPS, accelerometers, gyroscopes) from mobile devices to augment wireless protocols. For example, the authors use mobility hints from the accelerometer to select between two rate adaptation algorithms; SampleRate [13] (in static environments) or RapidSample (in mobile environments). They further use accelerometer hints to implement a hint-aware roaming protocol. Our results in sections 3 and 4 demonstrate that due to our PHY-based fine-grained discrimination of mobility modes, we outperform both RapidSample and the client-based roaming protocol from [1]. Further, while [1] only considers legacy 802.11, we show how mobility hints can help high-throughput

[2]We could not implement our MU-MIMO optimizations in the testbed because of lack of 802.11ac support.

Protocol	Parameter	Mobility type				
		Static	Environment	Micro mobility	Macro mobility	
					Moving away	Moving towards
Client roaming	Roaming preparation	no	no	no	Encourage client to roam to better AP if available.	no
Rate adaptation	Probe interval	50ms	50ms	50ms	100ms	20ms
	PER smoothing factor	1/16	1/12	1/4	1/3	1/3
	Rate retries	1	1	1	0	2
Frame aggregation	Aggregation limit	8ms	8ms	2ms	2ms	2ms
Beamforming	CV update interval	200ms	50ms	10ms	5ms	5ms
MU-MIMO	CV update interval	200ms	50ms	10ms	2ms	2ms

Table 2: Summary of mobility-aware protocol actions.

mechanisms introduced in the 802.11n/ac standards, such as frame aggregation, beamforming and MU-MIMO. Trinity [14] also uses accelerometer-based mobility hints to optimize distributed antenna systems and network-MIMO. Mobisteer [15] uses location hints from GPS to find the best directional antenna orientation and the AP to associate with. Breadcrumbs [16] builds a mobility model based on GPS coordinates and uses it to predict the best AP to associate with. CARS [17] uses GPS readings to optimize rate control. In contrast to existing works, we exploit PHY layer information available from off-the-shelf APs to obtain the client's mobility information, without relying on any external sensor and without requiring any coordination with the client.

PHY-based mobility detection: Recently, there has been a lot of interest in developing device-free passive motion detection systems using radio signal dynamics. While most proposals require hardware modifications [18–20], [21–24] use RSSI, and FIMD [25] proposes CSI-based techniques. These systems can only identify environmental mobility and often have higher complexity than our system. For example, FIMD uses feature extraction and data fusion from multiple links to detect environmental mobility with 90% accuracy. We can classify among static, environmental, and device mobility by only calculating the similarity of the CSI values from a single link.

Rate control and client roaming: A large number of RA algorithms have been proposed in the past. They can be classified into frame-based [13, 26–31], SNR-based [9, 32–34], and PHY-layer based [9–11]. Frame-based algorithms are often used in practice due to their simplicity but they are slow to respond to rapidly changing channel conditions in mobile environments. SNR-based algorithms can adapt faster but they need "in-situ"training to overcome this sensitivity [35]. PHY-layer based approaches have been shown to outperform SNR-based algorithms but they cannot be implemented on commodity APs. ESNR [9] uses CSI from commodity cards to estimate the bit-rate, but it requires careful per-client calibration to obtain the ESNR vs. bit-rate relationship. Our mobility-aware modifications of the frame-based Atheros RA algorithm does not require any such calibration and achieves 90% of ESNR's performance on average. Like rate control, client roaming has been widely studied to improve wireless performance [36–39]. However, unlike our scheme, most proposals either require changes at the client [37, 38] or at both the AP and the client [39]. Like DenseAP [40], we manage the client's association from the controller with no modifications at the client. We further improve controller-based association control by incorporating mobility hints.

802.11n/ac enhancements: Impact of channel dynamics on 802.11n frame aggregation have been studied using simulation [41], modeling [42, 43] and testbed experiments [30]. [42] and [43] calculate the frame aggregation limit based on the bit error-rate (BER) and SNR respectively. While BER and SNR can be indirect indicators, we observe that mobility-hints can be a direct indicator of aggregation limit, improving wireless performance. CSI feedback remains a critical issue for high throughput 802.11n/ac mechanisms such as beamforming and MU-MIMO [44]. While there has been work towards experimental evaluation of MU-MIMO [45] and its variants [46], decreasing the overhead of CSI feedback is mostly limited to [44]. While [44] is limited to frequent CSI sampling, we show that by augmenting CSI with ToF, mobility hints can reduce the overhead due to the CSI feedback period.

9. DISCUSSION AND LIMITATIONS

Uplink traffic: In this work we focused on downlink traffic because download is still the dominant type of traffic in today's WLANs – often 20 times more than uplink traffic [47]. While some of our mobility-aware protocol modifications are mostly limited to the AP (e.g., controller-assisted roaming, beamforming, MU-MIMO), the others, such as bit-rate adaptation and frame aggregation can also be implemented on the client side as well to benefit uplink traffic.

Roaming for real time traffic: Our roaming protocol explicitly encourages the client to roam whenever it detects that the client is moving towards a better AP. While this approach improves throughput for bulk transfer applications, as we discussed in section 3, the 200 ms required for a handoff may increase both jitter and packet loss for real-time traffic. One solution to this problem will be to minimize the number of handoffs by choosing the farthest, yet reasonably strong, AP the client is moving towards. Alternatively, we note that fast BSS transition in 802.11r reduces the handoff overhead to only 40ms [48]; hence, clients such as Apple devices that support 802.11r [49] can immediately benefit from our roaming protocol without causing disruptions to real-time traffic.

Moving on a circle around the AP: If a client is moving on a circle around the AP, our system will wrongly classify the type of mobility as micro- instead of macro-mobility, as the ToF values will not be characterized by an increasing or decreasing trend. Although this is not a typical mobility pattern, in our future work, we plan to augment our system with Angle of Arrival (AoA) information [3, 50] to address this limitation.

Other benefits of mobility-awareness: Mobility-awareness could also guide the selection of channel width (a narrow 20 MHz channel may be more robust than the wider 40MHz,

80MHz, or 160 MHz channels, and hence, it may be preferred when the client is moving away from the AP) and the type of MIMO mode (spatial diversity may be preferred over spatial multiplexing when the client is moving away from the AP). However, our preliminary experiments did not show any significant gains for these two cases. We plan to investigate these in more detail in our future work. We also plan to study other protocols that could benefit from mobility-awareness, e.g., adapting the length of cyclic prefix based on the client speed, scheduling client traffic at an AP taking movement into account, network monitoring, as well as distributed MIMO techniques.

10. CONCLUSION

Today's WLANs have to be able to distinguish different types of client mobility and use adaptive, motion-aware protocols in order to sustain high performance. In this paper, we demonstrate how different client mobility modes can be distinguished by using physical layer information – Channel State Information (CSI) and Time-of-Flight (ToF) – available at commodity APs, with no modifications on the client side. Our testbed experiments show that our algorithm achieves more than 90% accuracy in a variety of scenarios. We also demonstrate how fine-grained motion determination can improve performance of client roaming, bit-rate control, frame aggregation, and MIMO beamforming in 802.11n/ac WLANs. Our extensive evaluation shows that motion-aware AP-side protocols outperform their motion-oblivious counterparts as well as prior mobility-aware client-side solutions. In particular, the combination of all four mobility-aware protocols improves throughput by almost 100% over the default AP implementation using motion-oblivious protocols.

11. ACKNOWLEDGMENTS

We thank our shepherd Sam Leffler and the anonymous CoNEXT reviewers for their insightful comments.

12. REFERENCES

[1] Hari Balakrishnan, Lenin Ravindranath, Calvin Newport, and Samuel Madden. Improving Wireless Network Performance Using Sensor Hints. In *Proc. of USENIX NSDI*, 2011.

[2] Krishna Chintalapudi, Anand Padmanabha Iyer, and Venkata N. Padmanabhan. Indoor localization without the pain. In *Proc. of ACM MobiCom*, 2010.

[3] Souvik Sen, Jeongkeun Lee, Kyu-Han Kim, and Paul Congdon. Avoiding multipath to revive inbuilding WiFi localization. In *Proc. of ACM MobiSys*, 2013.

[4] Alex Mariakakis, Souvik Sen, Jeongkeun Lee, and Kyu-Han Kim. Single access point based indoor localization. In *Proc. of ACM MobiSys*, 2014.

[5] Domenico Giustiniano and Stefan Mangold. Caesar: carrier sense-based ranging in off-the-shelf 802.11 wireless LAN. In *Proc. of ACM CoNEXT*, 2011.

[6] Ishwar Ramani and Stefan Savage. Syncscan: practical fast handoff for 802.11 infrastructure networks. In *Proc. of IEEE INFOCOM*, 2005.

[7] Minho Shin, Arunesh Mishra, and William A. Arbaugh. Improving the latency of 802.11 hand-offs using neighbor graphs. In *Proc. of ACM MobiSys*, 2004.

[8] Souvik Sen, Bozidar Radunovic, Jeongkeun Lee, and Kyu-Han Kim. Cspy: finding the best quality channel without probing. In *Proc. of ACM MobiCom*, 2013.

[9] Daniel Halperin, Wenjun Hu, Anmol Sheth, and David Wetherall. Predictable 802.11 packet delivery from wireless channel measurements. In *Proc. of ACM SIGCOMM*, 2010.

[10] Mythili Vutukuru, Hari Balakrishnan, and Kyle Jamieson. Cross-Layer Wireless Bit Rate Adaptation. In *Proc. of ACM SIGCOMM*, 2009.

[11] Souvik Sen, Naveen Santhapuri, Romit Roy Choudhury, and Srihari Nelakuditi. AccuRate: Constellation Based Rate Estimation in Wireless Networks. In *Proc. of USENIX NSDI*, 2010.

[12] Yang Xiao. IEEE 802.11n: enhancements for higher throughput in wireless LANs. *IEEE Wireless Communications*, 12(6):82–91, 2005.

[13] John C. Bicket. Bit-rate selection in wireless networks. Master's thesis, Massachusetts Institute of Technology, February 2005.

[14] Shailendra Singh, Karthikeyan Sundaresan, Amir Khojastepour, Sampath Rangarajan, and Srikanth V. Krishnamurthy. One strategy does not serve all: tailoring wireless transmission strategies to user profiles. In *Proc. of ACM HotNets*, 2012.

[15] Vishnu Navda, Anand Prabhu Subramanian, Kannan Dhanasekaran, Andreas Timm-Giel, and Samir R. Das. MobiSteer: Using Steerable Beam Directional Antenna for Vehicular Network Access. In *Proc. of ACM MobiSys*, 2007.

[16] Anthony J. Nicholson and Brian D. Noble. BreadCrumbs: Forecasting Mobile Connectivity. In *Proc. of ACM MobiCom*, 2008.

[17] Pravin Shankar, Tamer Nadeem, Justinian Rosca, and Liviu Iftode. CARS: Context-Aware Rate Selection for Vehicular Networks. In *Proc. of IEEE ICNP*, 2008.

[18] Qifan Pu, Sidhant Gupta, Shyamnath Gollakota, and Shwetak Patel. Whole-home gesture recognition using wireless signals. In *Proc. of ACM MobiCom*, 2013.

[19] Bryce Kellogg, Vamsi Talla, and Shyamnath Gollakota. Bringing gesture recognition to all devices. In *Proc. of USENIX NSDI*, 2014.

[20] Fadel Adib and Dina Katabi. See through walls with WiFi!. In *Proc. of ACM SIGCOMM*, 2013.

[21] Michael Wallbaum and Stefan Diepolder. A Motion Detection Scheme For Wireless LAN Stations. In *Proc. of IEEE ICMU*, 2006.

[22] Moustafa Youssef, Matthew Mah, and Ashok Agrawala. Challenges: Device-free Passive Localization for Wireless Environments. In *Proc. of ACM MobiCom*, 2007.

[23] Jie Yang, Yong Ge, Hui Xiong, Yingying Chen, and Hongbo Liu. Performing Joint Learning for Passive Intrusion Detection in Pervasive Wireless Environments. In *Proc. of IEEE INFOCOM*, 2010.

[24] Ahmed E. Kosba, Ahmed Saeed, and Moustafa Youssef. RASID: A Robust WLAN Device-free Passive Motion Detection System. In *Proc. of IEEE PerCom*, 2012.

[25] Jiang Xiao, Kaishun Wu, Youwen Yi, Lu Wang, and Lionel M. Ni. FIMD: Fine-grained Device-free Motion Detection. In *Proc. of IEEE ICPADS*, 2012.

[26] Ad Kamerman and Leo Monteban. WaveLAN-II: A High-Performance Wireless LAN for the Unlicensed Band. *Bell Labs Technical Journal*, 2(3):118–133, 1997.

[27] Gavin Holland, Nitin Vaidya, and Paramvir Bahl. A Rate-Adaptive MAC Protocol for Multi-Hop Wireless Networks. In *Proc. of ACM MobiCom*, 2001.

[28] Jongseok Kim, Seongkwan Kim, Sunghyun Choi, and Daji Qiao. CARA: Collision-Aware Rate Adaptation for IEEE 802.11 WLANs. In *Proc. of IEEE INFOCOM*, 2006.

[29] Starky H.W. Wong, Hao Yang, Songwu Lu, and Vaduvur Barghavan. Robust rate adaptation for 802.11 wireless networks. In *Proc. of ACM MobiCom*, 2006.

[30] Ioannis Pefkianakis, Yun Hu, Starsky H.Y. Wong, Hao Yang, and Songwu Lu. MIMO Rate Adaptation in 802.11n Wireless Networks. In *Proc. of ACM MobiCom*, 2010.

[31] Duy Nguyen and J.J. Garcia-Luna-Aceves. A practical approach to rate adaptation for multi-antenna systems. In *Proc. of IEEE ICNP*, 2011.

[32] Jiansong Zhang, Kun Tan, Jun Zhao, Haitao Wu, and Yongguang Zhang. A Practical SNR-Guided Rate Adaptation. In *Proc. of IEEE INFOCOM*, 2008.

[33] Glenn Judd, Xiaohui Wang, and Peter Steenkiste. Efficient Channel-aware Rate Adaptation in Dynamic Environments. In *Proc. of ACM MobiSys*, 2008.

[34] Lara Deek, Eduard Garcia-Villegas, Elizabeth Belding, Sung-Ju Lee, and Kevin Almeroth. Joint Rate and Channel Width Adaptation for 802.11 MIMO Wireless Networks. In *Proc. of IEEE SECON*, 2013.

[35] Joseph Camp and Edward Knightly. Modulation Rate Adaptation in Urban and Vehicular Environments: Cross-layer Implementation and Experimental Evaluation. In *Proc. of ACM MobiCom*, 2008.

[36] Minkyong Kim, Zhen Liu, Srinivasan Parthasarathy, Dimitrios Pendarakis, and Hao Yang. Association control in mobile wireless networks. In *Proc. of IEEE INFOCOM*, 2008

[37] Sudarshan Vasudevan, Konstantina Papagiannaki, Christophe Diot, Jim Kurose, and Don Towsley. Facilitating access point selection in IEEE 802.11 wireless networks. In *Proc. of ACM IMC*, 2005.

[38] George Athanasiou, Thanasis Korakis, Özgür Erçetin, and Leandros Tassiulas. Dynamic cross-layer association in 802.11-based mesh networks. In *Proc. of IEEE INFOCOM*, 2007.

[39] Yigal Bejerano, Seung-Jae Han, and Li Erran Li. Fairness and load balancing in wireless LANs using association control. In *Proc. of ACM MobiCom*, 2004.

[40] Rohan Murty, Jitendra Padhye, Ranveer Chandra, Alec Wolman, and Brian Zill. Designing high performance enterprise Wi-Fi networks. In *Proc. of USENIX NSDI*, 2008.

[41] Boris Ginzburg and Alex Kesselman. Performance analysis of A-MPDU and A-MSDU aggregation in IEEE 802.11n. In *Proc. of IEEE Sarnoff Symposium*, 2007.

[42] Xin He, Frank Y Li, and Jiaru Lin. Link adaptation with combined optimal frame size and rate selection in error-prone 802.11n networks. In *Proc. of IEEE ISWCS*, 2008.

[43] Feng Kai-Ten, Lin Po-Tai, and Liu Wen-Jiunn. Frame-aggregated link adaptation protocol for next generation wireless local area networks. *EURASIP Journal on Wireless Communications and Networking*, 2010:10:1–10:13, 2010.

[44] Xiufeng Xie, Xinyu Zhang, and Karthikeyan Sundaresan. Adaptive feedback compression for MIMO networks. In *Proc. of ACM MobiCom*, 2013.

[45] Hariharan Shankar Rahul, Swarun Kumar, and Dina Katabi. JMB: scaling wireless capacity with user demands. In *Proc. of the ACM SIGCOMM*, 2012.

[46] Horia Vlad Balan, Ryan Rogalin, Antonios Michaloliakos, Konstantinos Psounis, and Giuseppe Caire. Achieving high data rates in a distributed MIMO system. In *Proc. of ACM MobiCom*, 2012

[47] Ning Ding, Daniel Wagner, Xiaomeng Chen, Y. Charlie Hu, and Andrew Rice. Characterizing and modeling the impact of wireless signal strength on smartphone battery drain. In *Proc. of ACM SIGMETRICS*, 2013.

[48] Sangeetha Bangolae, Carol Bell, and Emily Qi. Performance study of fast BSS transition using IEEE 802.11r. In *Proc. of ACM MobiCom*, 2006.

[49] Deploying iPhone and iPad Wi-Fi. In *https://www.apple.com/kr/iphone/business/docs/ios_6_wifi_sep12.pdf*.

[50] Jie Xiong and Kyle Jamieson. Arraytrack: a fine-grained indoor location system. In *Proc. of USENIX NSDI*, 2013.

Measurement-Augmented Spectrum Databases for White Space Spectrum

Ayon Chakraborty and Samir R. Das
Computer Science Department
Stony Brook University
Stony Brook, NY 11747, USA
{aychakrabort, samir}@cs.stonybrook.edu

ABSTRACT

Spectrum databases used to estimate TV white space availability often provide inaccurate and largely conservative estimates as they are primarily based on empirical propagation models. This leads to 'loss' of white space spectrum that is critical in urban areas with large spectrum demand. While alternatives are possible in terms of incorporating direct spectrum measurements, the measurement locations must be judiciously chosen so that measurement effort is not prohibitive. Fundamentally, this boils down to addressing the estimation accuracy vs measurement effort question. We present a rigorous data driven analysis to address this using measurement data collected in parts of New York City metro area. We show that it is possible to develop models that estimate whether the current database estimates are reliable in a given location. Following this, we provide a recipe for developing a 'measurement-augmented' spectrum database that takes the help of measurements where needed and falls back on the current propagation model-based database technique in the rest of the areas. The final takeaway is that it is possible to improve database accuracy significantly with only modest amount of measurements.

Categories and Subject Descriptors

C.4 [**Performance of Systems**]: Design Studies, Measurement Techniques, Modeling techniques, Reliability, availability, and serviceability.

Keywords

TV Whitespace, Spectrum Databases, Propagation Model.

1. INTRODUCTION

According to the rules for white space (WS) spectrum access, 'secondary' (unlicensed or lightly licensed) use is allowed only when it does not adversely affect 'primary' (i.e., licensed incumbent) communications. To enable this, the recommended solution by the FCC in connection to TV band spectrum (so called TVWS) is to use one of the approved *spectrum databases* [9].[1] All secondary users are required to consult such a database prior to accessing any WS channels for communication. The database uses (i) detailed knowledge of TV transmitter characteristics and (ii) specific propagation models to estimate the TV signal power at any given location. This in turn provides the 'protection contours' for each TV channel – secondary operation is allowed only outside these contours.

Clearly, the accuracy of such databases is crucial for successful operation in the WS. 'False negative' estimates by the database mean that WS cannot be exploited even when it does not hurt primary communications. This leads to lost spectrum opportunities. 'False positive' estimates, on the other hand, mean that primaries are not protected leading to violation of regulations. Recent measurement studies have reported that the spectrum databases are prone to varying degrees of inaccurate estimates [22, 23, 24, 19]. The inaccuracy is somewhat biased towards generating more false negative errors as opposed to false positives. This is not entirely unexpected as the databases 1) rely entirely on empirically derived propagation models and 2) these models are tuned to provide more conservative estimates of protection regions due to legal issues pertaining to false positive estimates (more on this in Section 3). The actual database question aside, multiple measurement studies in the TV bands also independently point out limitations of propagation modeling approaches in estimating availability of TVWS channels for secondary use [11, 16, 22, 23, 24, 19].

Lost White Space: The database inaccuracies lead to a serious loss of spectrum opportunity in *urban* regions, specifically in large metro areas that are also population hotspots: 1) a large number of TV channels in these regions mean that fundamentally WS availability is poor [12] and 2) the spectrum demand is large due to dense populations. Losing spectrum opportunity precisely where more spectrum is needed does not bode well for the business case for TVWS. Our measurement study in parts of the New York City metro area [6] shows that roughly 40%–75% of available WS spectrum is lost (Section 2).

1.1 Measurement Augmentation

The problem can be easily remedied if the spectrum databases can use actual measurements [23, 24] instead of standard propagation models.[2] This is viable as the primary occupancy in the TV bands do not change often and thus the measurements do not need to repeat frequently in the same location. However, the challenge here is to limit the spatial extent of such measurements as

[1] There are several such database providers, e.g., Spectrum Bridge [7], Google [1], i-Connective [2], Keybridge [4], etc.

[2] We do not discuss regulatory issues that can arise here; we limit ourselves to technical issues only.

CoNEXT'14, December 2–5, 2014, Sydney, Australia.

http://dx.doi.org/10.1145/2674005.2675001.

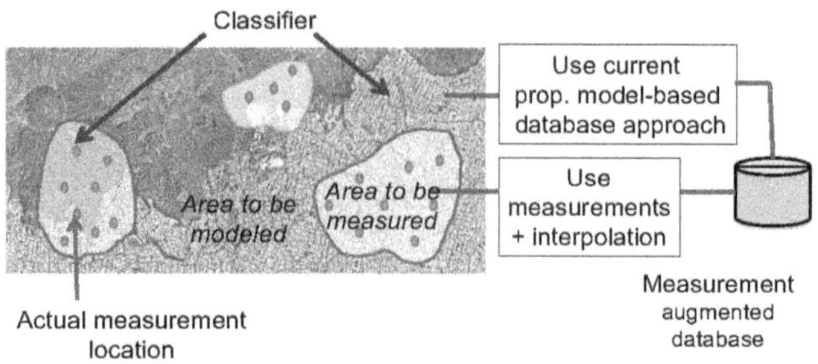

Figure 1: Overview of the proposed measurement-augmented spectrum database approach.

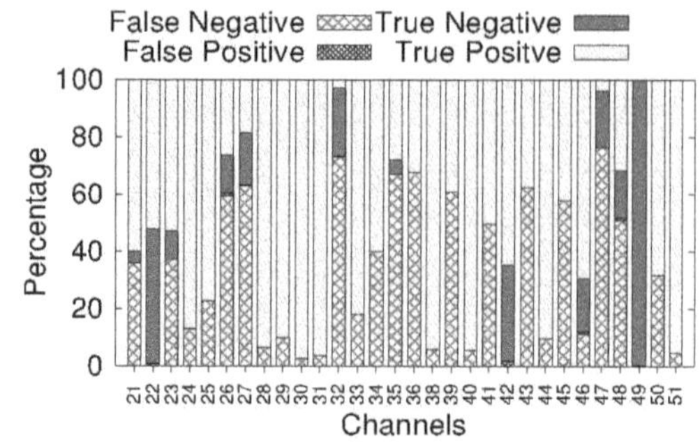

(a) New Jersey (NJ)

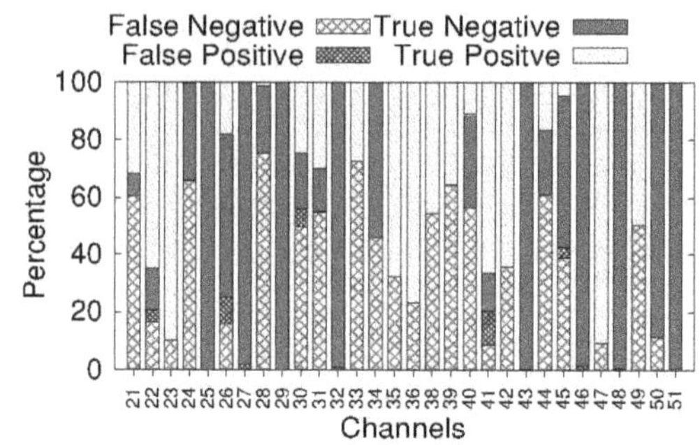

(b) Long Island (LI)

Figure 2: Database inaccuracies on a per-channel basis in the NJ and LI datasets. Note that false negatives are abundant, though false positives are rare.

measurements are expensive to the database operator.[3] Our goal in this work is thus to pose a fundamental question: *Can the spectrum database predictions be significantly improved with only a modest amount of measurements?*

We address this question with a data-driven analysis using spectrum measurements collected on 30 DTV channels at 5K+ locations in the NYC metro area - one of the major population hotspots in US (Section 2). Our specific contribution is a recipe to 'augment' current spectrum databases with actual measurement data. Unlike prior work that uses very extensive measurements to completely replace the current propagation model-based databases [23, 24], we propose a middle ground: measurements are used *strategically only in specific regions*; the rest of areas can still use the current database approach. This strikes a good balance between accuracy and cost in terms of measurement effort. Figure 1 provides a broad overview.

The centerpiece of the technique is a classifier model (Section 4) that predicts the accuracy of the current propagation model-based database estimates using factors that are poorly accounted for in these models (Section 3). This enables us to separate out the regions where the database accuracy could be poor. We use sparse measurements followed by standard interpolations in these regions, but stick to current database estimates in the rest of the areas (Section 5). Finally, we show that this approach as a whole *is able to recover a significant amount of lost white space with only modest measurement effort.*

2. MEASUREMENTS

We conducted measurements in two regions within New York City metro area [6] – 1) in the cities of Hoboken, Jersey City, Newark and Summit in New Jersey (NJ) and 2) parts of Suffolk and Nassau counties in Long Island (LI) in New York covering approximately 250 and 150 sq. kms, respectively. All these regions are urban with significant population and economic activities. The measurements are taken from the road with a vehicle mounted spectrum sensor (ThinkRF WSA4000 [8]). We scanned the UHF spectrum that includes the DTV channels 21 through 51 (512 MHz - 698 MHz except channel 37 which is used for astronomical purposes). The measurement yielded about 150 K+ data points in aggregate for 5K+ locations sampled. Each data point consists of a particular channel's FFT information tagged with corresponding GPS coordinates.

To set a stage for further analysis, we first determine the WS spectrum availability based on these measurements. Specifically, we use FCC's guidelines to determine whether WS channels are deemed available to *portable devices* hypothetically operating at the measurement locations [9]. For such devices, the FCC-mandated sensing threshold to detect a TV signal is quite low (-114 dBm). The noise in the spectrum sensor itself can make it challenging to detect weak TV signals. Even for the high-end spectrum sensor that we use, capturing a TV signal over a 6 MHz channel gives rise to overwhelmingly high noise floor compared to the required -114 dBm threshold. To address the high sensitivity needed, we leverage a salient feature of TV signals, viz., presence of a pilot signal at 309KHz offset above the lower edge of the 6MHz TV channel and the fact that the power of the pilot has a specific relationship to the channel's aggregate power.[4] We zoom into a very narrow band (first 488KHz of a TV channel) to detect the pilot's presence and power with a very low noise and use this to calculate the channel's aggregate power. A similar technique on the same sensor hardware was also used in [23, 24].

In Figure 2 we provide per-channel statistics of spectrum database inaccuracies assuming measurements as ground truth. Specifically, Spectrum Bridge [7] is used as the database provider.[5] In this figure, false positive (negative) indicates that the database predicts the channel to be available (not available) for secondary use, but the measurement detects presence (absence) of signal. True positive (negative) indicates that the database is correct in predicting the channel to be available (not available). The database is checked for each measurement location and the database esti-

[3]Various mechanisms are possible including deploying actual spectrum sensors [14], deploying sensors in public vehicles [23, 24] or drive tests like cellular operators, etc. All are expensive in terms of actual labor or cost.

[4]The pilot signal's power is less than the channel's aggregate power by approx. 11.3dB.

[5]Per FCC, all database providers should use the same modeling approach and thus should provide identical results.

mate for each channel is classified into one of the four categories – false/true positive/negative. The figure shows aggregated per-channel statistics. We make a couple of observations:

1. False negative predictions are frequent, averaging 35% and 32% for NJ and LI respectively. Also more than 70% of all measured locations show prediction error in atleast one channel. On the other hand, false positives are relatively rare (almost absent in NJ but present in a few channels in LI). This points to the general conservative nature of the database estimates leading to loss of WS. According to the measured data, the loss is staggering: *Approximately 75% and 40% of available WS is lost in NJ and LI respectively due to incorrect prediction by the database,* where the loss is measured as a fraction of channels inaccurately predicted to be unavailable, aggregated over all locations.

2. The observations in specific categories (false positive, etc.) are clustered and not randomly distributed.[6] This highlights the possibility that such regions can be identified in advance via an out-of-band modeling approach. This in turn provides the possibility of *advance partitioning of the entire area of interest into two types of regions –* $Area_{Measure}$ (current database approach is unreliable and measurements are preferred) and $Area_{Model}$ (database is reliable). See Figure 1. This forms the essential basis of the approach we present below.

3. ANALYZING PREDICTION ERRORS

We now follow up on the above observations by taking a deeper look at possible causes of the database inaccuracies. The first step is understanding what modeling approach is internally used in the spectrum databases and the second step is identifying factors responsible for erroneous estimates.

3.1 Modeling Approach in Databases

Per recommendation from FCC, the approved spectrum databases use a specific propagation modeling approach (called *F-curves* [20]) to identify the protection contours for TV channels. F-curves are statistical models derived from empirical measurements and are specified by operating band, effective radiated power (ERP), antenna height above average terrain (HAAT), antenna beam parameters, location and time percentage reliability requirements. For the latter, FCC specifies (50,90).[7] F-curves are used to estimate a contour boundary in each radial direction[8] such that the estimated field strength at the boundary point is 41dBu (this value is related to (50,90) above). These distances are again weighted by antenna patterns if they are not uniform.

One reason why F-curves overestimate the contour boundary is due to the use of 'average terrain' instead of fine-grained terrain information. However, in our experience more advanced approaches such as the Longley-Rice [13] that do use more granular terrain information do not appear to fare much better overall. We did an independent set of analysis to establish this. Figure 3 show scatter-plots for received power according to the Longley-Rice model and the measured power for two cases (channel available and not available). Note very poor correlation for the channel available case (TV signal absent), while some degree of correlation is indeed present when the channel is not available (TV signal detected).[9] Thus, Longley-Rice may not be very good in predicting white spaces.

[6]The analysis of spatial correlation in Section 5 demonstrates this.

[7]This means that the signal from the TV station is present at 50% of the locations for 90% of the times within the contour boundary.

[8]Radial HAAT is generally calculated every 1°azimuth.

[9]Not shown here, F-curves show poor correlation in both cases.

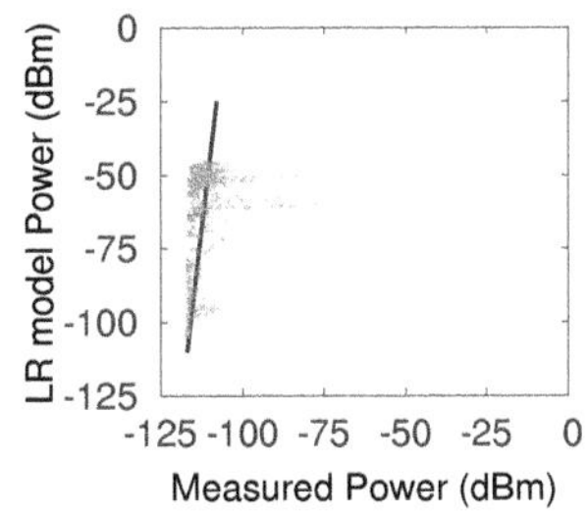

(a) Channel available.

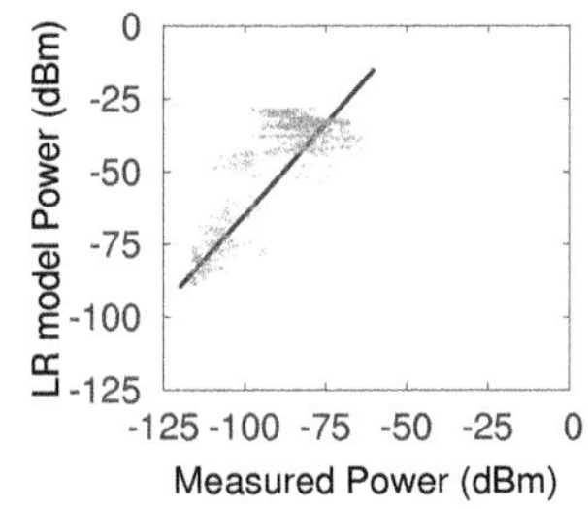

(b) Channel not available.

Figure 3: Modeled power according to Longley-Rice vs. Measured power. Note very poor correlation for the channel available case (TV signal absent).

3.2 Factor Analysis

With the above understanding, we hypothesize that certain propagation related parameters overwhelmingly influence the database accuracy. Our goal now is to explore this influence systematically. We identify three key parameters that have significant influence on the accuracy.[10]

Distance from Transmitter: For a given channel, this is the distance of the nearest TV transmitter operating in that channel. This parameter is important due to the fact that it is likely that the database will be able to predict accurately if the nearest transmitter is too close (channel not available) or too far (channel available) from the location.

Modeled Power: This represents the estimated received power for a channel as predicted by the FCC F-Curve Model. Just like above, too small or too large modeled power indicate that the database is likely accurate.

LOS Obstruction Length: This is the portion of the 'line-of-sight' from the closest TV transmitter at the specific channel that is 'obstructed' due to terrain irregularity. To understand this construct an imaginary straight line from the transmitter antenna to the location. Parts of this line could be 'obstructed' due to terrain elevations. We are interested in the total such obstruction length. To determine this, we use elevation profile from NASA's SRTM 1-arc-second terrain database (30m resolution) [5].

3.3 Types of Prediction Errors

Figure 4 shows the fraction of locations measured with respect to each of these parameters for specific accuracy categories (namely, false positive (FP), false negative (FN), true positive (TP) and true negative (TN)). NJ and LI data are presented separately for the purpose of illustration. To understand these plots, consider the database prediction – channel available or not available. These predictions can be correct or incorrect. Accordingly, channel available (not available) decisions contribute to FP and TN (FN and TP) categories. Thus, if the plot for FP is reasonably separate from that for TN, it is possible to 'learn' where the database is likely to make incorrect decisions for channel available. Similar is the case for channel not available. We do see that there is a separation between at least one of these pairs of plots for all three parameters and sometimes the separation is quite distinct. This indicates that these parameters could be effective in 'teasing apart' locations where the

[10]We explored several other factors like Antenna Height, ERP etc., but their influence seems lesser.

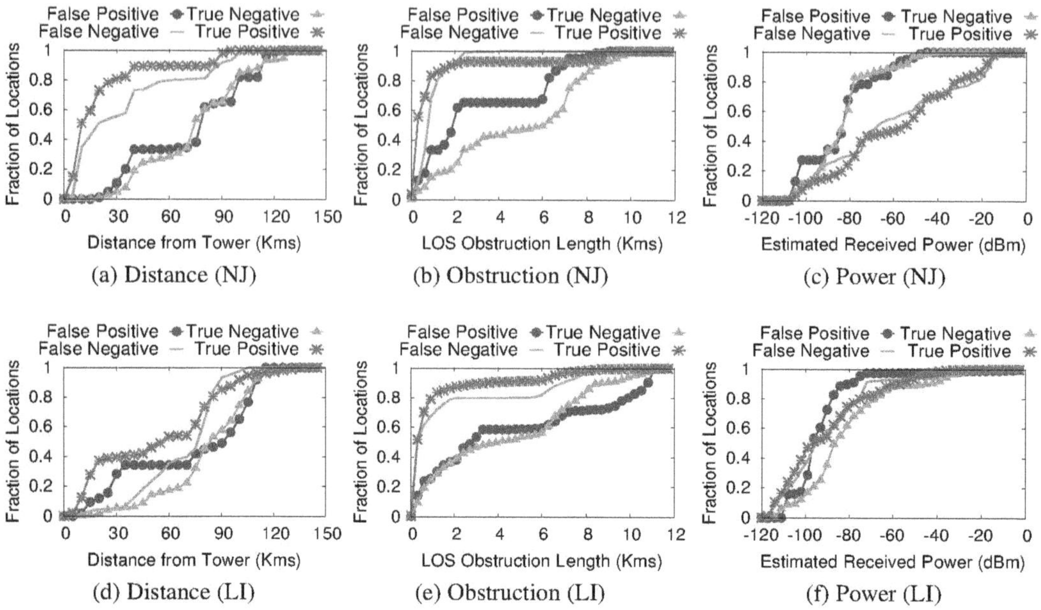

Figure 4: Influence of three factors, viz., Transmitter Distance, Line-of-Sight Obstruction lengths and Modeled Power on the prediction accuracies.

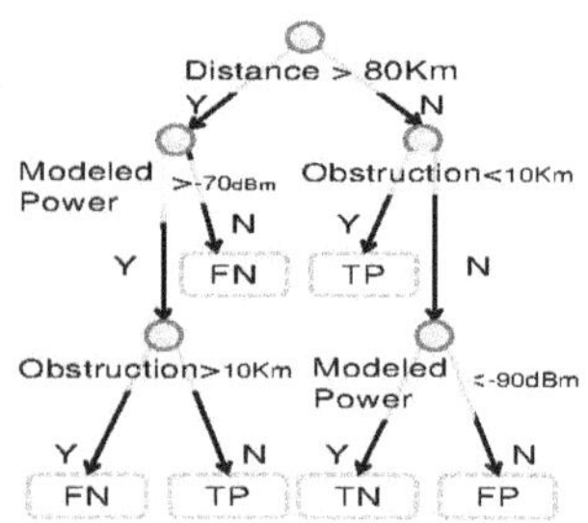

Figure 5: Example of a decision tree classifier.

database estimate is likely incorrect. Our general approach will be to use measurements in these locations as opposed to 'correcting' database estimates in some other way.

4. PREDICTING DATABASE INACCURACIES

We use the idea outlined in Section 3 to learn a classifier that takes the above three parameters as features[11] and produces a detection accuracy type (i.e., FP etc) as the output. While various approaches are possible, we use a Decision Tree Classifier (C4.5) as the decision boundaries are easily interpretable and thus manual corrections can be done more easily if necessary. A Decision Tree classifier produces *rule-like constructs*: by way of example, if the distance to the transmitter is more than, say, 100 km and the estimated received power is less than, say, -80 dBm, then it is highly likely the database is going to be inaccurate. See Figure 5 for an example.

Challenges: There are several challenges in building a useful classifier. First, we need to make a decision whether we should learn a separate classifier for each channel. While a separate classifier for each channel may handle frequency specific effects better than an aggregated classifier over all channels, the former is likely to be somewhat region specific. If in a different region, where TV channel occupancy is very different, channel specific classifier may not work well. We have investigated this aspect at length (not reported here for brevity) and finally settled on the aggregate classifier. It is only incrementally worse for the two regions we studied (NJ and LI), but is much superior (to channel-specific) when the model is learnt in one region and applied to the other. Second, even within a region, the amount of training data must be minimized to reduce measurement effort.

To analyze the above issues, we use a series of cross-validations. We use small contiguous portions (as opposed to random)[12] of the measurement data for training and run k-fold cross-validations where the folds are different contiguous partitions of the data set. We also run cross-validations across the two regions – NJ and LI. Figure 6 summarizes the results in terms of the expected classifier accuracy.[13]

Classifier Accuracy: There are two broad takeaways from Figure 6. 1) When the model is tested in the same region, the accuracy is very good with even with small amount of training. Just about 10% training data achieves about 85% accuracy. The cross validation results across regions (model learnt at NJ and applied to LI and vice versa) are also encouraging – roughly about 70% accuracy with about 20% data. Note that the straight line distance between these regions is roughly 150 km. Though more study from diverse geographic region is needed to prescribe a guideline for exactly how much to train, these results show a significant opportunity. In contrast, existing approaches require training per 100 m [23] thus requiring several orders of magnitude more effort.

[11]Note that these parameters come from independent data sets and do not require measurements.

[12] Contiguous data collection is much easier than random.

[13]Note that this is distinct from the database accuracy. This simply looks at whether the classifier is correctly classifying a test data in the four categories: FP, FN, TP, TN.

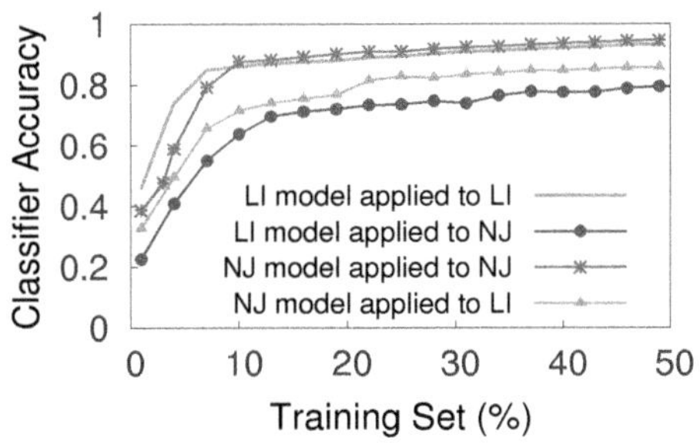

Figure 6: Decision tree classifier accuracy for predicting database errors.

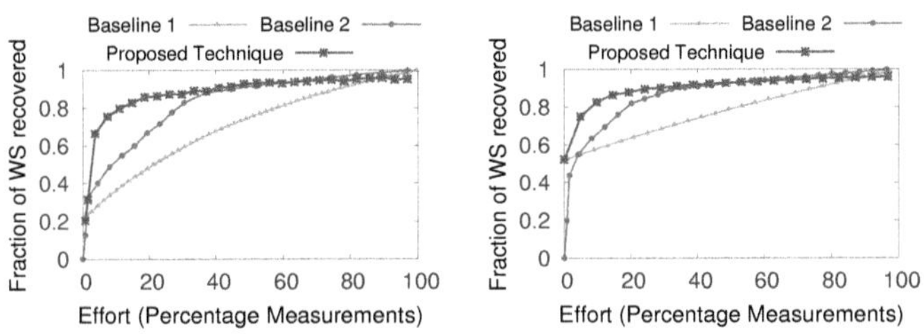

(a) New Jersey

(b) Long Island

Figure 7: Accuracy vs. measurement effort.

5. MEASUREMENT AUGMENTATION

We run the Decision Tree classifier trained with 10% of the measured data on the NJ and LI data sets to partition all locations into two subsets - $Area_{Model}$ and $Area_{Measure}$ (details in Algorithm 1). In subset $Area_{Model}$, the database accuracy is high (TP and TN). In subset $Area_{Measure}$ it is low (FN and FP) and thus predictions from these locations preferably should come from actual measurements. Further all locations in $Area_{Measure}$ do not need to be strictly measured – spatial subsampling followed by a suitable interpolation technique can be used to reduce the measurement effort (details in Algorithm 2). There is already a growing literature on this topic specifically targeting radio environment mapping [10, 18, 17].

Accuracy vs. Effort: Figure 7 shows overall accuracy vs effort for a couple of baseline mechanisms along with the proposed approach. Instead of showing the channel availability prediction accuracy (as in Figure 2) we show fraction of available channels correctly identified. The 'effort' in the plots here is measured in terms of number of locations that are actually measured (normalized as a fraction of all locations). The following cases are evaluated:

(i) *Baseline 1:* A random set of locations use measurements and rest use the current database for prediction.

(ii) *Baseline 2:* A random set of locations use measurements and the rest uses interpolation for prediction.[14]

(iii) *Proposed technique:* Briefly, for each channel the classifier is used first to partition the universe of locations into $Area_{Model}$ and $Area_{Measure}$. Then K locations are picked that belong to $Area_{Measure}$ for the most number of channels. These are actual measurement locations and K is indicative of measurement effort. Rest of the locations in $Area_{Measure}$ for each channel use interpolation using the available measurements as in (ii) above. All other locations (i.e., $Area_{Model}$) use standard propagation modeling as in current databases. Algorithms 1 and 2 have a more formal presentation.

[14]We use a simple linear interpolation technique called Inverse Distance Weighting or IDW [3]. [10] has shown linear interpolation techniques can achieve almost as good performance as more sophisticated geostatistical techniques such as Ordinary Kriging [18].

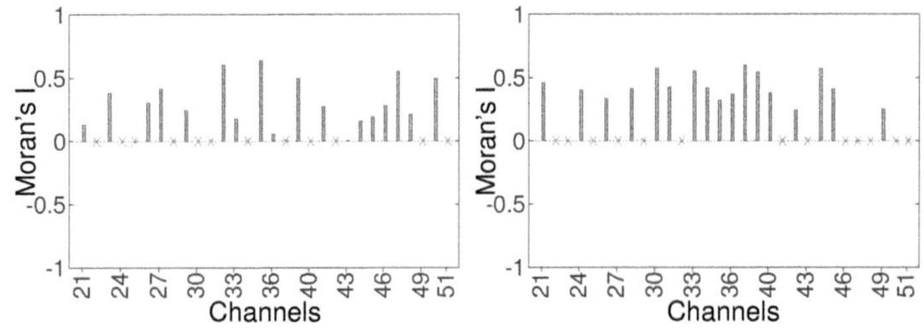

(a) New Jersey

(b) Long Island

Figure 8: Moran's-I statistic representing the spatial autocorrelation among the measurement locations shown in a per-channel basis. (The statistic is not calculated for channels lacking enough data points.)

Algorithm 1 Measurement area calculation for all channels

$L \leftarrow$ All discreet locations in *rasterized* area /*30m x 30m cells*/
$C \leftarrow$ All Channels under consideration /*21 through 51, except 37*/
for all $l \in L$ **do**
  for all $c \in C$ **do**
    $Feature_{l,c} \leftarrow < Distance_{l,c}, Obstruction_{l,c}, ModelPower_{l,c} >$
    $decision \leftarrow CLASSIFIER(Feature_{l,c})$ /*Decision Tree*/
    if $decision = TP$ or TN **then**
      Add location l to $Area_{Model,c}$
    else if $decision = FP$ or FN **then**
      Add location l to $Area_{Measure,c}$
    end if
  end for
  Add $Area_{Measure,c}$ to $Area_{Measure}$
end for

Algorithm 2 Channel occupancy decisions

$K \leftarrow EFFORT$ /*Number of measurement points*/
$M_K \leftarrow$ Most occurring K locations from $Area_{Measure}$
$Powers(M_K) \leftarrow$ Set of measured powers at all points in M_K
for all $l \in L$ **do**
  for all $c \in C$ **do**
    if $l \in M_K$ **then**
      $Power_l \leftarrow Measure(l)$ /*use actual measurements*/
    else if $l \in Area_{Measure,c}$ **then**
      $Power_l \leftarrow Interpolate_{IDW}(Powers(M_K))$ /*interpolate such a point from measured points*/
    else
      $Power_l \leftarrow PropagationModel(l, c)$ /*use existing spectrum database propagation model to estimate received power*/
    end if
    $decision_{l,c} \leftarrow Rules_{FCC}(Power_l)$ /*apply necessary rules to determine spectrum occupancy*/
  end for
end for

Figure 7 presents the accuracy vs effort of the three techniques above based on the measurement data. Note that with 0% effort (no measurement), the overall performance is the same as the current databases (roughly 25% (NJ) and 60% (LI) of available channels correctly predicted). The two baseline techniques show incremental improvement with more measurements. However, the proposed approach improves in accuracy quickly with more effort, reaching over 80% with only about 10% effort.

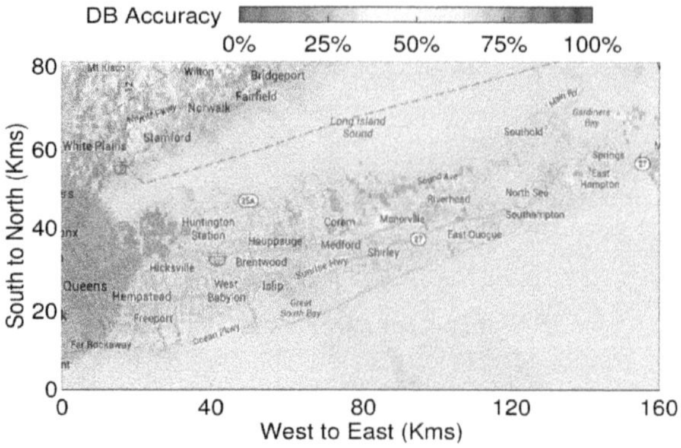

Figure 9: Heatmap showing estimated database accuracy in an extended region. The region shows eastern part of NYC, Long Island, parts of upstate NY and CT.

Spatial Clustering: Figure 7 does not show how clustered the actual measurement points are. In fact, it may appear that Baseline 2 does not do too poorly as it converges quickly as well - though at a lower rate than the proposed technique. However, in Baseline 2 the locations are random, while they are clustered in the proposed technique. This saves on actual measurement effort if drive tests are used. To demonstrate this, we show the spatial autocorrelation property of the measurement points in terms of 'Moran's I' in Figure 8. Moran's I [15] is a commonly used measure of spatial autocorrelation. A concept of distance is used to indicate proximity and is used as 'weights.' Moran's I is defined as:

$$I = \frac{N}{\sum_i \sum_j w_{ij}} \frac{\sum_i \sum_j w_{ij}(x_i - \overline{x})(x_j - \overline{x})}{\sum_i (x_i - \overline{x})^2}, \qquad (1)$$

where x is the random variable studied, $\overline{x}$ being the sample mean, x_i's are the observations. w_{ij} is the weight associated with each pair (x_i, x_j) and N is the number of observations. In our case, x_i is either 1 or 0 (depending on whether it is a measurement point), and w_{ij} is the distance between points x_i and x_j. We see that Moran's I is always > 0 and often substantial – between 0.3-0.6, demonstrating significant amount of spatial auto-correlation. On the other hand, in Baseline 2, Moran's I is 0 by definition.[15]

5.1 Scale-up Study

It will be interesting for the reader to understand what really happens if we scale up the area of study. To do this, we take a fairly large, 160 km × 80 km wide region covering part of the New York City metro area [6] and use the decision tree classifier (we use the LI based classifier as majority of the scale-up area lies in LI) to estimate the database accuracy for each channel throughout this region. Figure 9 shows the accuracy in the form of a heatmap. The accuracy numbers here indicate the percentage of all channels that the classifier predicts to be correctly estimated (TP or TN) by the database. Note the poor accuracy throughout NYC and immediately surrounding areas (large reddish patch on the left). Note also the general clustering of poor accuracy areas providing a guide where measurements should preferably be taken. Also, of note the large swaths of blueish high accuracy areas in most parts of Long Island and surrounding water. This primarily arises to a relatively flat terrain there relative to upstate NY and CT where a patchwork of low accuracy areas dot the map (see the northwest corner). An operator interested in providing augmented database service in this region will need to measure only the most red areas either according to a budget constraint, or using a heuristics. A simple heuristics could incrementally increase the measured area until the interpolation performance converges.

[15] Moran's I can range from -1 to +1; -1 indicates perfect disperson, 0 indicates random, +1 indicates perfect correlation.

6. RELATED WORKS

Several recent measurement papers study limitations of propagation modeling approaches in detecting channel availability in TVWS. For example, authors in [16] consider several models, viz.., Free-Space, Egli and Longley-Rice and show that while the former models perform poorly Longley-Rice is significantly better when used with terrain information. However, measurements reported in [11, 19] have poor experience with Longley-Rice much like our work. In [22], authors show that available TVWS in indoor vs outdoor locations could be significantly different demonstrating potential inability of current database systems to expose indoor WS.

Spatial interpolation techniques for radio environment mapping have been studied with a goal to adequately utilizing sparse spectrum sensing (e.g., [18, 10, 21]). Specifically, in [10] authors show that very few sample points may be adequate when coupled with an appropriate spatial interpolation technique. However, these points are not necessarily clustered and so drive tests to measure these locations can still incur a significant cost. The vScope system [23, 24] proposes leveraging public transport for spectrum measurements in TVWS. However, vScope is entirely opportunistic and measures all locations where the contracted public transport (with on-board sensor) travels. While the power of interpolation techniques has been demonstrated in [10, 21], neither [10, 21] nor [23, 24] give clear guidelines about the actual choice of measurement locations for doing an interpolation. Our approach remedies such shortcomings.

Finally, though not directly related to white space, SpecNet [14] developed a prototype to collect real time measurements from spectrum analyzers around the world put into a networked system. While such a system may be useful in connection to what we proposed here, the deployment must be strategic and much denser than proposed in the original paper.

7. CONCLUSIONS

If WS spectrum is to succeed commercially, inaccuracies in spectrum databases must be addressed. While previous work has recognized spectrum measurements as a way to address this issue, our work specifically develops mechanisms to reduce such measurement effort. The proposed approach relies on the current propagation model-driven databases where they are likely to be accurate and uses strategic measurements where they are not. The experimental results in parts of New York City metro area show that doing only modest amount of measurements – about 10% (25%) of the area studied that are also reasonably clustered – can recover above 80% (90%) of available WS.

Open issues do remain that we are pursuing in our ongoing work. They include 1) understanding how much data is needed to train the proposed classifier for a very large region, e.g., an entire state or country; 2) optimizing actual driving routes for measurements instead of number of locations as done in this paper.

8. ACKNOWLEDGMENTS

The authors acknowledge contributions of Sumit Roy, Milind Buddhikot, Chang Wook Kim, Luis Ortiz and Udit Kumar Gupta in various phases of this work. The work is partially supported by NSF grants CNS-1117719 and AST-1443951.

9. REFERENCES

[1] Google Spectrum Database. http://www.google.com/get/spectrumdatabase/.

[2] Iconectiv White Space Database. http://www.iconectiv.com/spectrum-mgmt/white-spaces/index.html.

[3] Inverse Distance Weighting. http://en.wikipedia.org/wiki/Inverse_distance_weighting.

[4] Keybridge White Space Database. https://keybridgeglobal.com/whitespace/.

[5] NASA SRTM Data,. lta.cr.usgs.gov/SRTM2.

[6] New York City Metro Area. http://en.wikipedia.org/wiki/New_York_metropolitan_area.

[7] Spectrum Bridge website. http://spectrumbridge.com.

[8] ThinkRF Spectrum Analyzer. thinkrf.com/.

[9] Second report and order and memorandum opinion and order in the matter of unlicensed operation in the TV broadcast bands. FCC ET Docket 08-260, Nov. 2008.

[10] A. Achtzehn, J. Riihijarvi, and P. Mahonen. Improving accuracy for TVWS geolocation databases: Results from measurement-driven estimation approaches. In *Proc. IEEE DySPAN*, 2014.

[11] A. Achtzehn, J. Riihijarvi, G. M. Vargas, M. Petrova, and P. Mahonen. Improving coverage prediction for primary multi-transmitter networks operating in the TV whitespaces. In *Proc. IEEE SECON Conference*, 2012.

[12] K. Harrison, S. M. Mishra, and A. Sahai. How much white-space capacity is there? In *Proc. IEEE DySPAN*, 2010.

[13] G. Hufford, A. Longley, and W. Kissick. A guide to the use of the Irregular Terrain Model in the area prediction mode. Technical report, NTIA, 1982.

[14] A. Iyer, K. K. Chintalapudi, V. Navda, R. Ramjee, V. Padmanabhan, and C. Murthy. SpecNet: Spectrum sensing sans frontieres. In *Proc. NSDI*, 2011.

[15] P. A. P. Moran. Notes on continuous stochastic phenomena. *Biometrika*, 37:1733, 1950.

[16] R. Murty, R. Chandra, T. Moscibroda, and P. Bahl. SenseLess: A Database-Driven White Spaces Network. *IEEE Transactions on Mobile Computing*, 11(2):189–203, Feb. 2012.

[17] C. Phillips. *Geostatistical Techniques for Practical Wireless Network Coverage Mapping*. PhD thesis, University of Colorado, 2012.

[18] C. Phillips, M. Ton, D. Sicker, and D. Grunwald. Practical radio environment mapping with geostatistics. In *Proc. IEEE DySPAN*, 2012.

[19] A. Saeed, K. A. Harras, and M. Youssef. Towards a characterization of white spaces databases errors: an empirical study. In *Proc. ACM WinTech*, 2014.

[20] White Space Database Administrator Group. Channel Calculations for White Spaces - Guidelines (1.29). http://spectrumbridge.com/wp-content/uploads/2014/08/Database-Calculation-Consistency-Specification.pdf, 2013. Date accessed: 2014-10-17.

[21] X. Ying, C.-W. Kim, and S. Roy. Revisiting TV coverage estimation with measurement-based statistical interpolation. http://www.dynamicspectrumalliance.org/assets/Revisiting_TV_Coverage_Estimation_with_Measurement-based_Statistical_Interpolation_08202014.pdf, 2014. Date accessed: 2014-10-17.

[22] X. Ying, J. Zhang, L. Yan, G. Zhang, M. Chenanant, and R. Chandra. Exploring indoor white spaces in metropolises. In *Proc. ACM MobiCom*, 2013.

[23] T. Zhang and S. Banerjee. Inaccurate spectrum databases?: Public transit to its rescue! In *Proc. ACM HotNets*, 2013.

[24] T. Zhang and S. Banerjee. A Vehicle-based Measurement Framework for Enhancing Whitespace Spectrum Databases. In *Proc. ACM MobiCom*, 2014.

Cuckoo Filter: Practically Better Than Bloom

Bin Fan, David G. Andersen, Michael Kaminsky[†], Michael D. Mitzenmacher[‡]
Carnegie Mellon University, [†]Intel Labs, [‡]Harvard University
{binfan,dga}@cs.cmu.edu, michael.e.kaminsky@intel.com, michaelm@eecs.harvard.edu

ABSTRACT

In many networking systems, Bloom filters are used for high-speed set membership tests. They permit a small fraction of false positive answers with very good space efficiency. However, they do not permit deletion of items from the set, and previous attempts to extend "standard" Bloom filters to support deletion all degrade either space or performance.

We propose a new data structure called the *cuckoo filter* that can replace Bloom filters for approximate set membership tests. Cuckoo filters support adding and removing items dynamically while achieving even higher performance than Bloom filters. For applications that store many items and target moderately low false positive rates, cuckoo filters have lower space overhead than space-optimized Bloom filters. Our experimental results also show that cuckoo filters outperform previous data structures that extend Bloom filters to support deletions substantially in both time and space.

Categories and Subject Descriptors

E.1 [**Data**]: Data Structures; E.4 [**Data**]: Data Compaction and Compression

Keywords

Cuckoo hashing; Bloom filters; compression

1. INTRODUCTION

Many databases, caches, routers, and storage systems use *approximate set membership* tests to decide if a given item is in a (usually large) set, with some small false positive probability. The most widely-used data structure for this test is the Bloom filter [ ], which has been studied extensively due to its memory efficiency. Bloom filters have been used to: reduce the space required in probabilistic routing tables [ ]; speed longest-prefix matching for IP addresses [ ]; improve network state management and monitoring [,]; and encode multicast forwarding information in packets [ ], among many other applications [ ].

CoNEXT'14, Dec 02-05 2014, Sydney, Australia
ACM 978-1-4503-3279-8/14/12.
http://dx.doi.org/10.1145/2674005.2674994

A limitation of standard Bloom filters is that one cannot remove existing items without rebuilding the entire filter (or possibly introducing generally less desirable false negatives). Several approaches extend standard Bloom filters to support deletion, but with significant space or performance overhead. *Counting Bloom filters* [ ] have been suggested for multiple applications [, ,], but they generally use 3–4× space to retain the same false positive rate as a space-optimized Bloom filter. Other variants include *d-left counting Bloom filters* [ ], which are still 1.5× larger, and *quotient filters* [ ], which provide significantly degraded lookup performance to yield comparable space overhead to Bloom filters.

This paper shows that supporting deletion in approximate set membership tests need not impose higher overhead in space or performance compared to standard Bloom filters. We propose the *cuckoo filter*, a practical data structure that provides four major advantages.

1. It supports adding and removing items dynamically;
2. It provides higher lookup performance than traditional Bloom filters, even when close to full (e.g., 95% space utilized);
3. It is easier to implement than alternatives such as the quotient filter; and
4. It uses less space than Bloom filters in many practical applications, if the target false positive rate ϵ is less than 3%.

A cuckoo filter is a compact variant of a cuckoo hash table [ ] that stores only *fingerprints*—a bit string derived from the item using a hash function—for each item inserted, instead of key-value pairs. The filter is densely filled with fingerprints (e.g., 95% entries occupied), which confers high space efficiency. A set membership query for item x simply searches the hash table for the fingerprint of x, and returns true if an identical fingerprint is found.

When constructing a cuckoo filter, its fingerprint size is determined by the target false positive rate ϵ. Smaller values of ϵ require longer fingerprints to reject more false queries. Interestingly, while we show that cuckoo filters are practically better than Bloom filters for many real workloads, they are asymptotically worse: the minimum fingerprint size used in the cuckoo filter grows logarithmically with the number of entries in the table (as we explain in Section 4). As a consequence, the per-item space overhead is higher for larger tables, but this use of extra space confers a lower false positive rate. For practical problems with a few billion items or fewer,

filter type	space cost	cache misses per lookup	deletion support
Bloom	1	k	no
blocked Bloom	1x	1	no
counting Bloom	3x ~ 4x	k	yes
d-left counting Bloom	1.5x ~ 2x	d	yes
quotient	1x ~ 1.2x	≥ 1	yes
cuckoo	$\leq$1x	2	yes

Table 1: Properties of Bloom filters and variants. Assume standard and counting Bloom filters use k hash functions, and d-left counting Bloom filters have d partitions.

a cuckoo filter uses less space *while supporting deletion* than a non-deletable, space-optimized Bloom filter when $\epsilon < 3\%$.

Cuckoo filters are substantially different from regular hash tables because only fingerprints are stored in the filter and the original key and value bits of each item are no longer retrievable. Because full keys are not stored, a cuckoo filter cannot even perform standard cuckoo hashing to insert new items, which involves moving existing keys based on their hash values. This difference means that the standard techniques, analyses, and optimizations that apply to cuckoo hashing do not necessarily carry over to cuckoo filters.

Technical contributions made by this paper include

- Applying partial-key cuckoo hashing—a variant of standard cuckoo hashing—to build cuckoo filters that support dynamic addition and deletion of items (Section 3).
- Exploring the reason why partial-key cuckoo hashing ensures high table occupancy for most real-world applications (Section 4).
- Optimizing cuckoo filters to outperform Bloom filters in space efficiency (Section 5).

2. BACKGROUND AND RELATED WORK

2.1 Bloom Filters and Variants

We compare standard Bloom filters and the variants that include support for deletion or better lookup performance, as summarized in Table 1. These data structures are evaluated empirically in Section 7. Cuckoo filters achieve higher space efficiency and performance than these data structures.

Standard Bloom filters [ ] provide a compact representation of a set of items that supports two operations: `Insert` and `Lookup`. A Bloom filter allows a tunable false positive rate ϵ so that a query returns either "definitely not" (with no error), or "probably yes" (with probability ϵ of being wrong). The lower ϵ is, the more space the filter requires.

A Bloom filter consists of k hash functions and a bit array with all bits initially set to "0". To insert an item, it hashes this item to k positions in the bit array by k hash functions, and then sets all k bits to "1". Lookup is processed similarly, except it reads k corresponding bits in the array: if all the bits are set, the query returns true; otherwise it returns false. Bloom filters do not support deletion.

Bloom filters can be very space-efficient, but are not optimal [ ]. For a false positive rate ϵ, a space-optimized Bloom filter uses $k = \log_2(1/\epsilon)$ hash functions. Such a Bloom filter can store each item using $1.44 \log_2(1/\epsilon)$ bits, which depends only on ϵ rather than the item size or the total number of items. The information-theoretic minimum requires $\log_2(1/\epsilon)$ bits per item, so a space-optimized Bloom filter imposes a 44% space overhead over the information-theoretic lower bound.

The information theoretic optimum is essentially achievable for a *static* set by using fingerprints (of length $\lceil 1/\epsilon \rceil$ bits) and a perfect hash table [ ]. To efficiently handle deletions, we replace a perfect hash function with a well-designed cuckoo hash table.

Counting Bloom filters [ ] extend Bloom filters to allow deletions. A counting Bloom filter uses an array of counters in place of an array of bits. An insert increments the value of k counters instead of simply setting k bits, and a lookup checks if each of the required counters is non-zero. The delete operation decrements the values of these k counters. To prevent *arithmetic overflow* (i.e., incrementing a counter that has the maximum possible value), each counter in the array must be sufficiently large in order to retain the Bloom filter's properties. In practice, the counter consists of four or more bits, and a counting Bloom filter therefore requires 4× more space than a standard Bloom filter. (One can construct counting Bloom filters to use less space by introducing a secondary hash table structure to manage overflowing counters, at the expense of additional complexity.)

Blocked Bloom filters [ ] do not support deletion, but provide better spatial locality on lookups. A blocked Bloom filter consists of an array of small Bloom filters, each fitting in one CPU cache line. Each item is stored in only one of these small Bloom filters determined by hash partitioning. As a result, every query causes at most one cache miss to load that Bloom filter, which significantly improves performance. A drawback is that the false positive rate becomes higher because of the imbalanced load across the array of small Bloom filters.

d-left Counting Bloom filters [ ] are similar to the approach we use here. Hash tables using *d-left hashing* [ ] store fingerprints for stored items. These filters delete items by removing their fingerprint. Compared to counting Bloom filters, they reduce the space cost by 50%, usually requiring 1.5 – 2× the space compared to a space-optimized non-deletable Bloom filter. Cuckoo filters achieve better space efficiency than d-left counting Bloom filters as we show, and have other advantages, including simplicity.

Quotient filters [ ] are also compact hash tables that store fingerprints to support deletion. Quotient filters uses a technique similar to linear probing to locate a fingerprint, and thus provide better spatial locality. However, they require additional meta-data to encode each entry, which requires 10 ~ 25% more space than a comparable standard Bloom

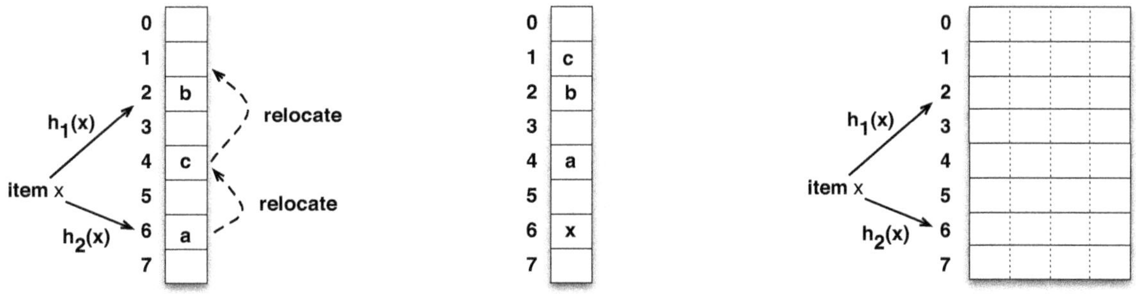

(a) before inserting item x (b) after item x inserted (c) A cuckoo filter, two hash per item and functions and four entries per bucket

Figure 1: Illustration of cuckoo hashing

filter. Moreover, all of its operations must decode a sequence of table entries before reaching the target item, and the more the hash table is filled, the longer these sequences become. As a result, its performance drops significantly when the occupancy of the hash table exceeds 75%.

Other Variants: Other variants have been proposed to improve Bloom filters, either in space and/or performance. Rank-Indexed Hashing [ ] builds linear chaining hash tables to store compressed fingerprints. Although similar to and somewhat more space efficient than d-left counting Bloom filters, updating the internal index that reduces the chaining cost is very expensive, making it less appealing in dynamic settings. Putze et al. proposed two variants of Bloom filters [ ]. One is the previously discussed *Blocked Bloom filter*; the other, called a *Golomb-Compressed Sequence* stores all items' fingerprints in a sorted list. Its space is near-optimal, but the data structure is static and requires non-constant lookup time to decode the encoded sequence. It is therefore not evaluated with other filters in this paper. Pagh et al. proposed an asymptotically space-optimal data structure [ ] based on Cleary [ ]. This data structure, however, is substantially more complex than its alternatives and does not appear amenable to a high performance implementation. In contrast, cuckoo filters are easy to implement.

2.2 Cuckoo Hash Tables

Cuckoo Hashing Basics: A basic cuckoo hash table [ ] consists of an array of buckets where each item has two candidate buckets determined by hash functions $h_1(x)$ and $h_2(x)$. The lookup procedure checks both buckets to see if either contains this item. Figure 1(a) shows the example of inserting a new item x in to a hash table of 8 buckets, where x can be placed in either buckets 2 or 6. If either of x's two buckets is empty, the algorithm inserts x to that free bucket and the insertion completes. If neither bucket has space, as is the case in this example, the item selects one of the candidate buckets (e.g., bucket 6), kicks out the existing item (in this case "a") and re-inserts this victim item to its own alternate location. In our example, displacing "a" triggers another relocation that kicks existing item "c" from bucket 4 to bucket 1. This procedure may repeat until a vacant bucket is found as illustrated in Figure 1(b), or until a maximum number of displacements is reached (e.g., 500 times in our implementation). If no vacant bucket is found, this hash table is considered too full to insert. Although cuckoo hashing may execute a sequence of displacements, its amortized insertion time is $O(1)$.

Cuckoo hashing ensures high space occupancy because it refines earlier item-placement decisions when inserting new items. Most practical implementations of cuckoo hashing extend the basic description above by using buckets that hold multiple items, as suggested in [ ]. The maximum possible load when using k hash functions and buckets of size b assuming all hash functions are perfectly random has been analyzed [ ]. With proper configuration of cuckoo hash table parameters (explored in Section 5), the table space can be 95% filled with high probability.

Using Cuckoo Hashing for Set-membership: Recently, standard cuckoo hash tables have been used to provide set membership information in a few applications. To support transactional memory, Sanchez et al. proposed to store the read/write set of memory addresses of each transaction in a cuckoo hash table, and to convert this table to Bloom filters when full [ ]. Their design used standard cuckoo hash tables, and thus required much more space than cuckoo filters. Our previous study in building high-speed and memory-efficient key-value stores [,] and software-based Ethernet switches [ ] all applied cuckoo hash tables as internal data structures. That work was motivated by and also focused on improving hash table performance by an optimization called *partial-key cuckoo hashing*. However, as we show in this paper, this technique also enabled a new approach to build a Bloom filter replacement which has not been studied before. As a result, this paper also applies partial-key cuckoo hashing, but more importantly it offers an in-depth analysis of using this technique specifically to serve set membership tests (rather than key-value queries) and further compares the performance of cuckoo filters with alternative set membership data structures.

Challenges in Cuckoo Filter: To make cuckoo filters highly space efficient, we use a multi-way associative cuckoo hash table to provide high-speed lookup and high table occupancy (e.g., 95% hash table slots filled); to further reduce the hash table size, each item is first hashed into a constant-sized fingerprint before inserted into this hash table. The challenge of applying this data structure is to redesign the insert process and carefully configure the hash table to minimize space usage per item:

- First, storing only fingerprints in the hash table prevents inserting items using the standard cuckoo hashing approach. Because in cuckoo hashing the insertion algorithm must be able to relocate existing fingerprints to their alternative locations. A space-inefficient but straightforward solution is to store each inserted item in its entirety (perhaps externally to the table); given the original item ("key"), calculating its alternate location is easy. In contrast, cuckoo filters use *partial-key cuckoo hashing* to find an item's alternate location based on only its fingerprint (Section 3).
- Second, cuckoo filter associates each item with multiple possible locations in the hash table. This flexibility in where to store an item improves table occupancy, but retaining the same false positive rate when probing more possible locations on each lookup requires more space for longer fingerprints. In Section 5, we present our analysis to optimize the balance between the table occupancy and its size to minimize the average space cost per item.

3. CUCKOO FILTER ALGORITHMS

In this paper, the basic unit of the cuckoo hash tables used for our cuckoo filters is called an *entry*. Each entry stores one fingerprint. The hash table consists of an array of *buckets*, where a bucket can have multiple entries.

This section describes how cuckoo filters perform `Insert`, `Lookup` and `Delete` operations. Section 3.1 presents *partial-key cuckoo hashing*, a variant of standard cuckoo hashing that enables cuckoo filters to insert new items *dynamically*. This technique was first introduced in previous work [ ], but there the context was improving the lookup and insert performance of regular cuckoo hash tables where full keys were stored. In contrast, this paper focuses on optimizing and analyzing the space efficiency when using partial-key cuckoo hashing with only fingerprints, to make cuckoo filters competitive with or even more compact than Bloom filters.

3.1 Insert

As previously stated, with standard cuckoo hashing, inserting new items to an existing hash table requires some means of accessing the original existing items in order to determine where to relocate them if needed to make room for the new ones (Section 2.2). Cuckoo filters, however, only store fingerprints and therefore there is no way to restore and rehash the original keys to find their alternate locations. To overcome this limitation, we utilize a technique called *partial-key cuckoo hashing* to derive an item's alternate location based on its fingerprint. For an item x, our hashing scheme calculates the indexes of the two candidate buckets as follows:

$$\begin{aligned} h_1(x) &= \text{hash}(x), \\ h_2(x) &= h_1(x) \oplus \text{hash}(x\text{'s fingerprint}). \end{aligned} \tag{1}$$

The xor operation in Eq. (1) ensures an important property: $h_1(x)$ can also be calculated from $h_2(x)$ and the fingerprint using the same formula. In other words, to displace a key originally in bucket i (no matter if i is $h_1(x)$ or $h_2(x)$), we directly calculate its alternate bucket j from the current bucket index i and the fingerprint stored in this bucket by

$$j = i \oplus \text{hash}(\text{fingerprint}). \tag{2}$$

Hence, an insertion only uses information in the table, and never has to retrieve the original item x.

In addition, the fingerprint is hashed before it is xor-ed with the index of its current bucket to help distribute the items uniformly in the table. If the alternate location were calculated by "$i \oplus$ fingerprint" without hashing the fingerprint, the items kicked out from nearby buckets would land close to each other in the table, if the size of the fingerprint is small compared to the table size. For example, using 8-bit fingerprints the items kicked out from bucket i will be placed to buckets that are at most 256 buckets away from bucket i, because the xor operation would alter the eight low order bits of the bucket index while the higher order bits would not change. Hashing the fingerprints ensures that these items can be relocated to buckets in an entirely different part of the hash table, hence reducing hash collisions and improving the table utilization.

Using partial-key cuckoo hashing, cuckoo filters add new items dynamically by the process shown in Algorithm 1. Because these fingerprints can be significantly shorter than the

Algorithm 1: `Insert(x)`

```
f = fingerprint(x);
i1 = hash(x);
i2 = i1 ⊕ hash(f);
if bucket[i1] or bucket[i2] has an empty entry then
    add f to that bucket;
    return Done;
// must relocate existing items;
i = randomly pick i1 or i2;
for n = 0; n < MaxNumKicks; n++ do
    randomly select an entry e from bucket[i];
    swap f and the fingerprint stored in entry e;
    i = i ⊕ hash(f);
    if bucket[i] has an empty entry then
        add f to bucket[i];
        return Done;
// Hashtable is considered full;
return Failure;
```

size of h_1 or h_2, there are two consequences. First, the total number of different possible choices of (h_1, h_2) as calculated by Eq. (1) can be much smaller than using a perfect hash to derive h_1 and h_2 as in standard cuckoo hashing. This may cause more collisions, and in particular previous analyses for cuckoo hashing (as in [,]) do not hold. A full analysis of partial-key cuckoo hashing remains open (and beyond this paper); in Section 4, we provide a detailed discussion of this issue and consider how to achieve high occupancy for practical workloads.

Second, inserting two different items x and y that have the same fingerprint is fine; it is possible to have the same fingerprint appear multiple times in a bucket. However, cuckoo filters are not suitable for applications that insert the same item more than $2b$ times (b is the bucket size), because the two buckets for this duplicated item will become overloaded. There are several solutions for such a scenario. First, if the table need not support deletion, then this issue does not arise, because only one copy of each fingerprint must be stored. Second, one could, at some space cost, associate counters with buckets, and increment/decrement them appropriately. Finally, if the original keys are stored somewhere (perhaps in slower external storage), one could consult that record to prevent duplicate insertion entirely, at the cost of slowing down insertion if the table already contains a (false positive) matching entry for the bucket and fingerprint. Similar requirements apply to traditional and d-left counting Bloom filters.

Algorithm 2: `Lookup(x)`

f = fingerprint(x);
i_1 = hash(x);
$i_2 = i_1 \oplus$ hash(f);
if bucket[i_1] or bucket[i_2] has f **then**
  return `True`;
return `False`;

3.2 Lookup

The lookup process of a cuckoo filter is simple, as shown in Algorithm 2. Given an item x, the algorithm first calculates x's fingerprint and two candidate buckets according to Eq. (1). Then these two buckets are read: if any existing fingerprint in either bucket matches, the cuckoo filter returns true, otherwise the filter returns false. Notice that this ensures no false negatives as long as bucket overflow never occurs.

Algorithm 3: `Delete(x)`

f = fingerprint(x);
i_1 = hash(x);
$i_2 = i_1 \oplus$ hash(f);
if bucket[i_1] or bucket[i_2] has f **then**
  remove a copy of f from this bucket;
  return `True`;
return `False`;

3.3 Delete

Standard Bloom filters cannot delete, thus removing a single item requires rebuilding the entire filter, while counting Bloom filters require significantly more space. Cuckoo filters are like counting Bloom filters that can delete inserted items by removing corresponding fingerprints from the hash tables on deletion. Other filters with similar deletion processes prove more complex than cuckoo filters. For example, d-left counting Bloom filters must use extra counters to prevent the "false deletion" problem on fingerprint collision[1], and quotient filters must shift a sequence of fingerprints to fill the "empty" entry after deletion and maintain their "bucket structure".[2]

The deletion process of cuckoo filters illustrated in Algorithm 3 is much simpler. It checks both candidate buckets for a given item; if any fingerprint matches in any bucket, one copy of that matched fingerprint is removed from that bucket.

Deletion does not have to clean the entry after deleting an item. It also avoids the "false deletion" problem when two items share one candidate bucket and also have the same fingerprint. For example, if both item x and y reside in bucket i_1 and collide on fingerprint f, partial-key cuckoo hashing ensures that they both can also reside in bucket i_2 because $i_2 = i_1 \oplus \text{hash}(f)$. When deleting x, it does not matter if the process removes the copy of f added when inserting x or y. After x is deleted, y is still perceived as a set member because there is a corresponding fingerprint left in either bucket i_1 and i_2. An important consequence of this is that the false-positive behavior of the filter is unchanged after deletion. (In the above example, y being in the table causes false positives for lookups of x, by definition: they share the same bucket and fingerprint.) This is the expected false-positive behavior of an approximate set membership data structure, and its probability remains bounded by ϵ.

Note that, to delete an item x safely, it must have been previously inserted. Otherwise, deleting a non-inserted item might unintentionally remove a real, different item that happens to share the same fingerprint. This requirement also holds true for all other deletion-supporting filters.

[1] A *naive implementation* of d-left counting Bloom filters has a "false deletion" problem. A d-left counting Bloom filter maps each item to d candidate buckets, each from a partition of the table, and stores the fingerprint in one of its d buckets. If two different items share one and only one bucket, and they have the same fingerprint (which is likely to happen when the fingerprints are small), directly deleting the fingerprint from this specific bucket may cause a wrong item to be removed. To address this issue, d-left counting Bloom filters use an additional counter in each table entry and additional indirections [ ].

[2] In quotient filters, all fingerprints having the same quotient (i.e., the q most significant bits) must be stored in contiguous entries according to their numerical order. Thus, removing one fingerprint from a cluster of fingerprints must shift all the fingerprints after the hole by one slot, and also modify their meta-data bits [ ].

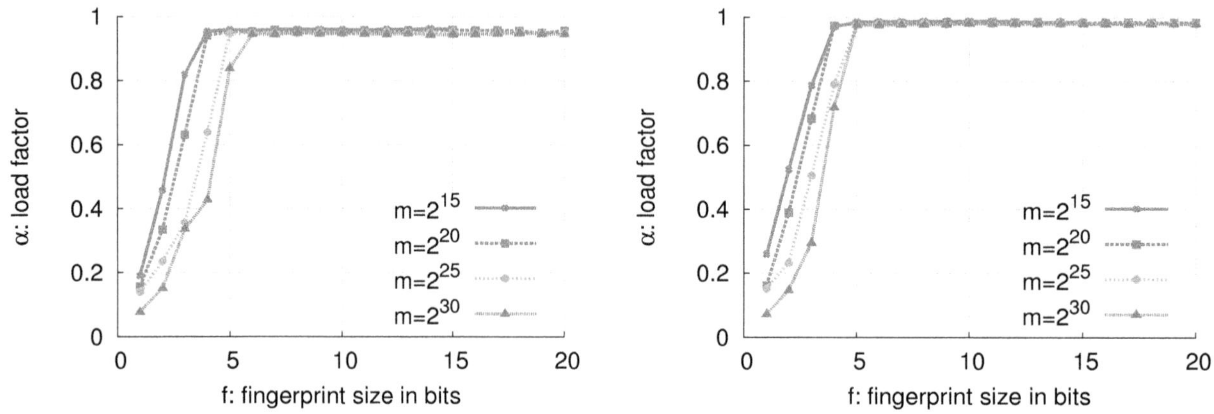

(a) bucket size $b = 4$

(b) bucket size $b = 8$

Figure 2: Load factor α achieved by using f-bit fingerprint using partial-key cuckoo hashing, in tables of different sizes ($m = 2^{15}, 2^{20}, 2^{25}$ and 2^{30} buckets). Short fingerprints suffice to approach the optimal load factor achieved by using two fully independent hash functions. $\alpha = 0$ means empty and 1 means completely full. Each point is the minimal load factor seen in 10 independent runs.

4. ASYMPTOTIC BEHAVIOR

Here we show that using partial-key cuckoo hashing to store fingerprints in a cuckoo filter to leads to a lower bound on fingerprint sizes that grows slowly with the filter size. This contrasts with other approaches (such as fingerprints and perfect hashing for a static Bloom filter, previously discussed) where the fingerprint size depended only on the desired false positive probability. While this might seem like a negative, in practice the effect seems unimportant. Empirically, a filter containing up to 4 billion items can effectively fill its hash table with loads of 95% when each bucket holds four fingerprints that are 6 bits or larger.

The notation used for our analysis in this and the next section is:

ϵ	target false positive rate
f	fingerprint length in bits
α	load factor ($0 \leq \alpha \leq 1$)
b	number of entries per bucket
m	number of buckets
n	number of items
C	average bits per item

Minimum Fingerprint Size: Our proposed partial-key cuckoo hashing derives the alternate bucket of a given item based on its current location and the fingerprint (Section 3). As a result, the candidate buckets for each item are not independent. For example, assume an item can be placed in bucket i_1 or i_2. According to Eq. (1), the number of possible values of i_2 is at most 2^f when using f-bit fingerprints. Using 1-byte fingerprints, given i_1 there are only up to $2^f = 256$ different possible values of i_2. For a table of m buckets, when $2^f < m$ (or equivalently $f < \log_2 m$ bits), the choice of i_2 is only a subset of all m buckets of the entire hash table.

Intuitively, if the fingerprints are sufficiently long, partial-key cuckoo hashing could still be a good approximation to standard cuckoo hashing; however, if the hash table is very large and stores relatively short fingerprints, the chance of insertion failures will increase due to hash collisions, which may reduce the table occupancy. This situation may arise when a cuckoo filter targets a large number of items but only a moderately low false positive rate. In the following, we determine analytically a lower bound of the probability of insertion failure.

Let us first derive the probability that a given set of q items collide in the same two buckets. Assume the first item x has its first bucket i_1 and a fingerprint t_x. If the other $q - 1$ items have the same two buckets as this item x, they must[3] (1) have the same fingerprint t_x, which occurs with probability $1/2^f$; and (2) have their first bucket either i_1 or $i_1 \oplus h(t_x)$, which occurs with probability $2/m$. Therefore the probability of such q items sharing the same two buckets is $\left(2/m \cdot 1/2^f\right)^{q-1}$.

Now consider a construction process that inserts n random items to an empty table of $m = cn$ buckets for a constant c and constant bucket size b. Whenever there are $q = 2b + 1$ items mapped into the same two buckets, the insertion fails. This probability provides a lower bound for failure (and, we believe, dominates the failure probability of this construction process, although we do not prove this and do not need to in order to obtain a lower bound). Since there are in total $\binom{n}{2b+1}$ different possible sets of $2b+1$ items out of n items, the expected number of groups of $2b + 1$ items colliding during

[3]Here we assume hashing the fingerprints (i.e., $t_x \rightarrow h(t_x)$) is collision-free, because in practice t_x is a few bits and $h(t_x)$ is much longer.

the construction process is

$$\binom{n}{2b+1}\left(\frac{2}{2^f \cdot m}\right)^{2b} = \binom{n}{2b+1}\left(\frac{2}{2^f \cdot cn}\right)^{2b} = \Omega\left(\frac{n}{4^{bf}}\right) \quad (3)$$

We conclude that 4^{bf} must be $\Omega(n)$ to avoid a non-trivial probability of failure, as otherwise this expectation is $\Omega(1)$. Therefore, the fingerprint size must be $f = \Omega(\log n/b)$ bits.

This result seems somewhat unfortunate, as the number of bits required for the fingerprint is $\Omega(\log n)$; recall that Bloom filters use a constant (approximately $\ln(1/\epsilon)$ bits) per item. We might therefore have concerns about the scalability of this approach. As we show next, however, practical applications of cuckoo filters are saved by the b factor in the denominator of the lower bound: as long as we use reasonably sized buckets, the fingerprint size can remain small.

Empirical Evaluation: Figure 2 shows the load factor achieved with partial-key cuckoo hashing as we vary the fingerprint size f, bucket size b, and number of buckets in the table m. For the experiments, we varied the fingerprint size f from 1 to 20 bits. Random 64-bit keys are inserted to an empty filter until a single insertion relocates existing fingerprints more than 500 times before finding an empty entry (our "full" condition), then we stop and measure achieved load factor α. We run this experiment ten times for filters with $m = 2^{15}$, 2^{20}, 2^{25}, and 2^{30} buckets, and measured their minimum load over the ten trials. We did not use larger tables due to the memory constraint of our testbed machine.

As shown in Figure 2, across different configurations, filters with $b = 4$ could be filled to 95% occupancy, and with $b = 8$ could be filled to 98%, with sufficiently long fingerprints. After that, increasing the fingerprint size has almost no return in term of improving the load factor (but of course it reduces the false positive rate). As suggested by the theory, the minimum f required to achieve close-to-optimal occupancy increases as the filter becomes larger. Also, comparing Figure 2(a) and Figure 2(b), the minimum f for high occupancy is reduced when bucket size b becomes larger, as the theory also suggests. Overall, short fingerprints appear to suffice for realistic sized sets of items. Even when $b = 4$ and $m = 2^{30}$, so the table could contain up to four billion items, once fingerprints exceed six bits, α approaches the "optimal load factor" that is obtained in experiments using two fully independent hash functions.

Insights: The lower bound of fingerprint size derived in Eq. (3), together with the empirical results shown in Figure 2, give important insights into the cuckoo filter. While in theory the space cost of cuckoo filters is "worse" than Bloom filters—$\Omega(\log n)$ versus a constant—the constant terms are very important in this setting. For a Bloom filter, achieving $\epsilon = 1\%$ requires roughly 10 bits per item, regardless of whether one thousand, one million, or billion items are stored. In contrast, cuckoo filters require longer fingerprints to retain the same high space efficiency of their hash tables, but lower false positive rates are achieved accordingly. The $\Omega(\log n)$ bits per fingerprint, as also predicted by the theory, grows slowly if the bucket size b is sufficiently large. We find that, for practical purposes, it can be treated as a reasonable-sized constant for implementation. Figure 2 shows that for cuckoo filters targeting a few billion items, 6-bit fingerprints are sufficient to ensure very high utilization of the hash table.

As a heuristic, partial-key cuckoo hashing is very efficient, as we show further in Section 7. Several theoretical questions regarding this technique, however, remain open for future study, including proving bounds on the cost of inserting a new item and studying how much independence is required of the hash functions.

5. SPACE OPTIMIZATIONS

The basic algorithms for cuckoo filter operations `Insert`, `Lookup`, and `Delete` presented in Section 3 are independent of the hash table configuration (e.g., how many entries each bucket has). However, choosing the right parameters for cuckoo filters can significantly affect space efficiency. This section focuses on optimizing the space efficiency of cuckoo filters, through parameter choices and additional mechanisms.

Space efficiency is measured by the average number of bits to represent each item in a full filter, derived by the table size divided by the total number of items that a filter can effectively store. Recall that, although each entry of the hash table stores one fingerprint, not all entries are occupied: there must be some slack in the table for the cuckoo filter or there will be failures when inserting items. As a result, each item effectively costs more to store than a fingerprint: if each fingerprint is f bits and the hash table has a load factor of α, then the amortized space cost C for each item is

$$C = \frac{\text{table size}}{\text{\# of items}} = \frac{f \cdot (\text{\# of entries})}{\alpha \cdot (\text{\# of entries})} = \frac{f}{\alpha} \quad \text{bits.} \quad (4)$$

As we will show, both f and α are related to the bucket size b. The following section studies how to (approximately) minimize Eq. (4) given a target false positive rate ϵ by choosing the optimal bucket size b.

5.1 Optimal Bucket Size

Keeping a cuckoo filter's total size constant but changing the bucket size leads to two consequences:

(1) Larger buckets improve table occupancy (i.e., higher $b \rightarrow$ higher α). With $k = 2$ hash functions, the load factor α is 50% when the bucket size $b = 1$ (i.e., the hash table is directly mapped), but increases to 84%, 95% or 98% respectively using bucket size $b = 2$, 4 or 8.

(2) Larger buckets require longer fingerprints to retain the same false positive rate (i.e., higher $b \rightarrow$ higher f). With larger buckets, each lookup checks more entries and thus has a higher chance to see fingerprint collisions. In the worst case of looking up a non-existent item, a query must probe two buckets where each bucket can have b entries. (While not all of these buckets may be filled, we analyze here

	bits per item	load factor α	avg. # memory references / lookup positive query	negative query
space-optimized Bloom filter	$1.44\log_2(1/\epsilon)$	–	$\log_2(1/\epsilon)$	2
cuckoo filter	$(\log_2(1/\epsilon)+3)/\alpha$	95.5%	2	2
cuckoo filter w/ semi-sort	$(\log_2(1/\epsilon)+2)/\alpha$	95.5%	2	2

Table 2: Space and lookup cost of Bloom filters and three cuckoo filters.

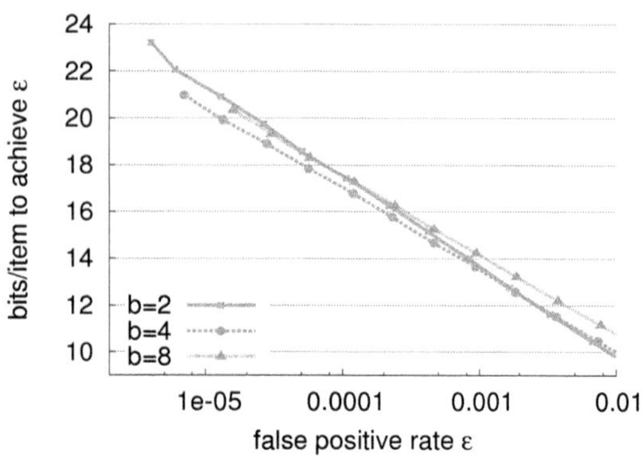

Figure 3: Amortized space cost per item vs. measured false positive rate, with different bucket size $b = 2, 4, 8$. Each point is the average of 10 runs

the worst case in which they are; this gives us a reasonably accurate estimate for a table that is 95% full.) In each entry, the probability that a query is matched against one stored fingerprint and returns a false-positive successful match is *at most* $1/2^f$. After making $2b$ such comparisons, the upper bound of the total probability of a false fingerprint hit is

$$1-(1-1/2^f)^{2b} \approx 2b/2^f, \qquad (5)$$

which is proportional to the bucket size b. To retain the target false positive rate ϵ, the filter ensures $2b/2^f \leq \epsilon$, thus the minimal fingerprint size required is approximately:

$$f \geq \lceil \log_2(2b/\epsilon) \rceil = \lceil \log_2(1/\epsilon) + \log_2(2b) \rceil \quad \text{bits.} \qquad (6)$$

Upper Bound of Space Cost As we have shown, both f and α depend on the bucket size b. The average space cost C by Eq. (4) is bound by:

$$C \leq \lceil \log_2(1/\epsilon) + \log_2(2b) \rceil / \alpha, \qquad (7)$$

where α increases with b. For example, when $b = 4$ so $1/\alpha \approx 1.05$, Eq. (7) shows cuckoo filters are asymptotically better (by a constant factor) than Bloom filters, which require $1.44\log_2(1/\epsilon)$ bits or more for each item.

Optimal bucket size b To compare the space efficiency by using different bucket sizes b, we run experiments that first construct cuckoo hash tables by partial-key cuckoo hashing with different fingerprint sizes, and measure the amortized space cost per item and their achieved false positive rates. As shown in Figure 3, the space-optimal bucket size depends on the target false positive rate ϵ: when $\epsilon > 0.002$, having two entries per bucket yields slightly better results than using four entries per bucket; when ϵ decreases to $0.00001 < \epsilon \leq 0.002$, four entries per bucket minimizes space.

In summary, we choose (2, 4)-cuckoo filter (i.e., each item has two candidate buckets and each bucket has up to four fingerprints) as the default configuration, because it achieves the best or close-to-best space efficiency for the false positive rates that most practical applications [ ] may be interested in. In the following, we present a technique that further saves space for cuckoo filters with $b = 4$ by encoding each bucket.

5.2 Semi-sorting Buckets to Save Space

This subsection describes a technique for cuckoo filters with $b = 4$ entries per bucket that saves one bit per item. This optimization is based on the fact that the order of fingerprints within a bucket does not affect the query results. Based on this observation, we can compress each bucket by first sorting its fingerprints and then encoding the sequence of sorted fingerprints. This scheme is similar to the "semi-sorting buckets" optimization used in [ ].

The following example illustrates how the compression saves space. Assume each bucket contains $b = 4$ fingerprints and each fingerprint is $f = 4$ bits (more general cases will be discussed later). An uncompressed bucket occupies $4\times4 = 16$ bits. However, if we sort all four 4-bit fingerprints stored in this bucket (empty entries are treated as storing fingerprints of value "0"), there are only 3876 possible outcomes in total (the number of unique combinations with replacement). If we precompute and store these 3876 possible bucket-values in an extra table, and replace the original bucket with an index into this precomputed table, then each original bucket can be represented by a 12-bit index ($2^{12} = 4096 > 3876$) rather than 16 bits, saving 1 bit per fingerprint.[4]

Note that this permutation-based encoding (i.e., indexing all possible outcomes) requires extra encoding/decoding tables and indirections on each lookup. Therefore, to achieve high lookup performance it is important to make the encoding/decoding table small enough to fit in cache. As a result, our "semi-sorting" optimization only apply this technique for tables with buckets of four entries. Also, when fingerprints are larger than four bits, only the four most significant bits of

[4]If the cuckoo filter does not need to support deletion, then it can ignore duplicate entries in the fingerprint list, creating the potential for saving an additional fraction of a bit per entry.

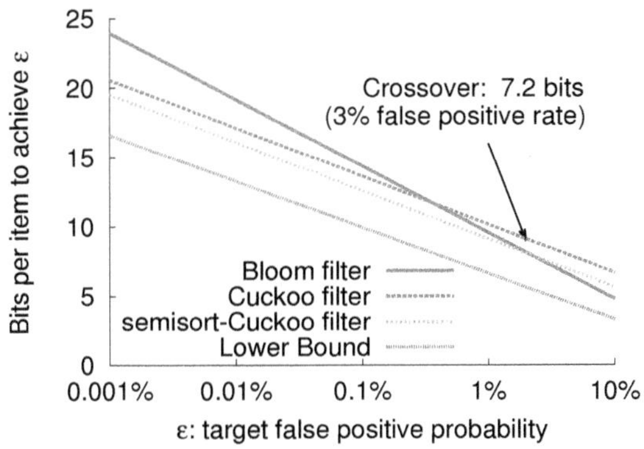

Figure 4: False positive rate vs. space cost per element. For low false positive rates (< 3%), cuckoo filters require fewer bits per element than the space-optimized Bloom filters. The load factors to calculate space cost of cuckoo filters are obtained empirically.

each fingerprint are encoded; the remainder are stored directly and separately.

6. COMPARISON WITH BLOOM FILTER

We compare Bloom filters and cuckoo filters using the metrics shown in Table 2 and several additional factors.

Space Efficiency: Table 2 compares space-optimized Bloom filters and cuckoo filters with and without semi-sorting. Figure 4 further shows the bits to represent one item required by these schemes, when ϵ varies from 0.001% to 10%. The information theoretical bound requires $\log_2(1/\epsilon)$ bits for each item, and an optimal Bloom filter uses $1.44 \log_2(1/\epsilon)$ bits per item, for a 44% overhead. Thus cuckoo filters with semi-sorting are more space efficient than Bloom filters when $\epsilon < 3\%$.

Number of Memory Accesses: For Bloom filters with k hash functions, a *positive query* must read k bits from the bit array. For space-optimized Bloom filters that require $k = \log_2(1/\epsilon)$, as ϵ gets smaller, positive queries must probe more bits and are likely to incur more cache line misses when reading each bit. For example, $k = 2$ when $\epsilon = 25\%$, but k is 7 when $\epsilon = 1\%$, which is more commonly seen in practice. A *negative query* to a space optimized Bloom filter reads two bits on average before it returns, because half of the bits are set. Any query to a cuckoo filter, positive or negative, always reads a fixed number of buckets, resulting in (at most) two cache line misses.

Value Association: Cuckoo filters can be extended to also return an associated value (stored external to the filter) for each matched fingerprint. This property of cuckoo filters provides an approximate table lookup mechanism, which returns $1 + \epsilon$ values on average for each existing item (as it can match more than one fingerprint due to false positive hits) and on average ϵ values for each non-existing item. Standard Bloom filters do not offer this functionality. Although variants like Bloomier filters can generalize Bloom filters to represent functions, these structures are more complex and require more space than cuckoo filters [ ].

Maximum Capacity: Cuckoo filters have a load threshold. After reaching the maximum feasible load factor, insertions are non-trivially and increasingly likely to fail, so the hash table must expand in order to store more items. In contrast, one can keep inserting new items into a Bloom filter, at the cost of an increasing false positive rate. To maintain the same target false positive rate, the Bloom filter must also expand.

Limited Duplicates: If the cuckoo filter supports deletion, it must store multiple copies of the same item. Inserting the same item $kb + 1$ times will cause the insertion to fail. This is similar to counting Bloom filters where duplicate insertion causes counter overflow. However, there is no effect from inserting identical items multiple times into Bloom filters, or a non-deletable cuckoo filter.

7. EVALUATION

Our implementation[5] consists of approximately 500 lines of C++ code for standard cuckoo filters, and 500 lines for the support of the "semi-sorting" optimization presented in Section 5.2. In the following, we denote a basic cuckoo filter as "CF", and a cuckoo filter with semi-sorting as "ss-CF". In addition to cuckoo filters, we implemented four other filters for comparison:

- Standard Bloom filter (BF) [ ]: We evaluated standard Bloom filters as the baseline. In all of our experiments, the number of hash functions k are configured to achieve the lowest false positive rate, based on the filter size and the total number of items. In addition, a performance optimization is applied to speed up lookups and inserts by doing less hashing [ ]. Each insert or lookup only requires two hash functions $h_1(x)$ and $h_2(x)$, and then uses these two hashes to simulate the additional $k - 2$ hash functions in the form of

$$g_i(x) = h_1(x) + i \cdot h_2(x).$$

- Blocked Bloom filter (blk-BF) [ ]: Each filter consists of an array of blocks and each block is a small Bloom filter. The size of each block is 64 bytes to match a CPU cache line in our testbed. For each small Bloom filter, we also apply the same optimization of simulating multiple hash functions as in standard Bloom filters.
- Quotient filter (QF) [ ]: We evaluated our own implementation of quotient filters[6]. This filter stores three extra bits for each item as the meta-data to help locate items. Because the performance of quotient filters degrades as they become more loaded, we set the maximum load factor to be 90% as evaluated in [ ].
- d-left counting Bloom filter (dl-CBF) [ ]: The filter is configured to have $d = 4$ hash tables. All hash tables

[5] https://github.com/efficient/cuckoofilter

[6] The source code from the original authors was not publicly available for comparison due to license issues.

metrics	CF	ss-CF	BF	blk-BF	QF	dl-CBF
# of items (million)	127.78	**128.04**	123.89	123.89	120.80	103.82
bits per item	12.60	**12.58**	13.00	13.00	13.33	15.51
false positive rate	0.19%	**0.09%**	0.19%	0.43%	0.18%	0.76%
constr. speed (million keys/sec)	5.00	3.13	3.91	**7.64**	1.91	4.78

Table 3: Space efficiency and construction speed. All filters are 192MB. Entries in bold are the best among the row.

have the same number of buckets; each bucket has four entries.

We emphasize that the standard and blocked Bloom filters do not support deletion, and thus are compared as a baseline.

Experiment Setup: All the items to insert are pre-generated 64-bit integers from random number generators. We did not eliminate duplicated items because the probability of duplicates is very small.

On each query, all filters first generate a 64-bit hash of the item using CityHash [ ]. Each filter then partitions these 64 bits in this hash as it needed. For example, Bloom filters treat the high 32 bits and low 32 bits as the first two independent hashes respectively, then use these two 32-bit values to calculate the other $k - 2$ hashes. The time to compute the 64-bit hash (about 20 ns per item in our testbed) is included in our measurement. All experiments use a machine with two Intel Xeon processors (L5640@2.27GHz, 12MB L3 cache) and 32 GB DRAM.

Metrics: To fully understand how different filters realize the trade-offs in function, space and performance, we compare above filters by the following metrics:

- *Space efficiency*: measured by the filter size in bits divided by the number of items a full filter contains.
- *Achieved false positive rate*: measured by querying a filter with non-existing items and counting the fraction of positive return values.
- *Construction rate*: measured by the number of items that a full filter contains divided by the time to construct this full filter from empty.
- *Lookup, Insert and Delete throughput*: measured by the average number of operations a filter can perform per second. The value can depend on the workload and the occupancy of the filter.

7.1 Achieved False Positive Rate

We first evaluate the space efficiency and false positive rates. In each run, all filters are configured to have the same size (192 MB). Bloom filters are configured to use nine hash functions, which minimizes the false positive rate with thirteen bits per item. For cuckoo filters, their hash tables have $m = 2^{25}$ buckets each consisting of four 12-bit entries. The d-left counting Bloom filter have the same number of hash table entries, but divided into $d = 4$ partitions. Quotient filter also has 2^{27} entries where each entry stores 3-bit meta-data and a 9-bit remainder.

Each filter is initially empty and items are placed until either the filter sees an insert failure (for CF, and dl-CBF), or it has reached the target capacity limit (for BF, blk-BF, and QF). The construction rate and false positive rate of different filters are shown in Table 3.

Among all filters, the ss-CF achieves the lowest false positive rate. Using about the same amount of space (12.60 bits/item), enabling semi-sorting can encode one more bit into each item's fingerprint and thus halve the false positive rate from 0.19% to 0.09%, On the other hand, semi-sorting requires encoding and decoding when accessing each bucket, and thus the construction rate is reduced from 5.00 to 3.13 million items per second.

The BF and blk-BF both use 13.00 bits per item with $k = 9$ hash functions, but the false positive rate of the blocked filter is 2× higher than the BF and 4× higher than the best CF. This difference is because the blk-BF assigns each item to a single block by hashing and an imbalanced mapping will create "hot" blocks that serve more items than average and "cold" blocks that are less utilized. Unfortunately, such an imbalanced assignment happens across blocks even when strong hash functions are used [ ], which increases the overall false positive rate. On the other hand, by operating in a single cache line for any query, the blk-BF achieves the highest construction rate.

The QF spends more bits per item than BFs and CFs, achieving the second best false positive rate. Due to the cost of encoding and decoding each bucket, its construction rate is the lowest.

Finally, the dl-CBF sees insert failures and stops construction when the entire table is about 78% full, thus storing many fewer items. Its achieved false positive rate is much worse than the other filters because each lookup must check 16 entries, hence having a higher chance of hash collisions.

7.2 Lookup Performance

Different Workloads We next benchmark lookup performance after the filters are filled. This section compares the lookup throughput and latency with varying workloads. The workload is characterized by the fraction of *positive queries* (i.e., items in the table) and *negative queries* (i.e., items not in the table), which can affect the lookup speed. We vary the fraction p of positive queries in the input workload from 0% (all queries are negative) to 100% (all queries are positive).

The benchmark result of lookup throughput is shown in Figure 5. Each filter occupies 192 MB, much larger than the L3 cache (20 MB) in our testbed.

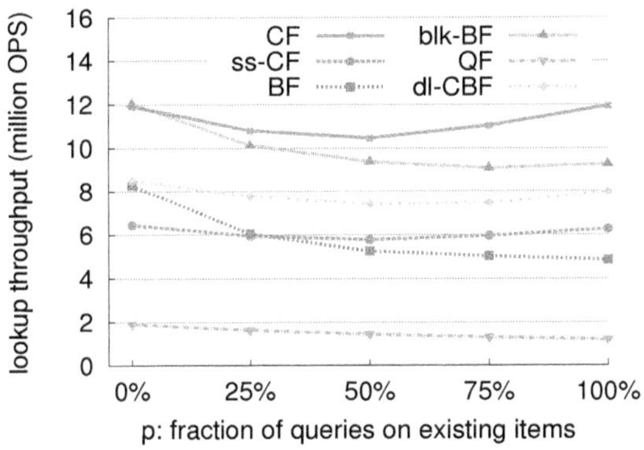

Figure 5: Lookup performance when a filter achieves its capacity. Each point is the average of 10 runs.

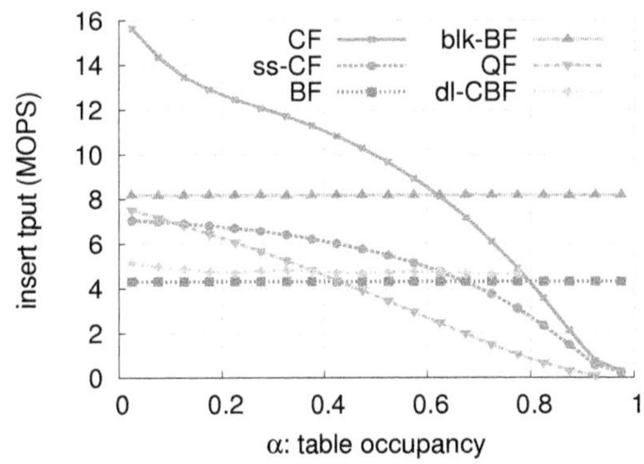

Figure 7: Insert throughput at different occupancy. Insert random keys in a large universe until each data structure achieves its designed capacity. Each point is the average of 10 runs.

The blk-BF performs well when all queries are negative, because each lookup can return immediately after fetching the first "0" bit. However, its performance declines when more queries are positive, because it must read additional bits as part of the lookup. The throughput of BF changes similarly when p increases, but is about 4 MOPS slower. This is because the BF may incur multiple cache misses to complete one lookup whereas the blocked version can always operate in one cache line and have at most one cache miss for each lookup.

In contrast, a CF always fetches two buckets[7], and thus achieves the same high performance when queries are 100% positive and 100% negative. The performance drops slightly when $p = 50\%$ because the CPU's branch prediction is least accurate (the probability of matching or not matching is exactly 1/2). With semi-sorting, the throughput of CF shows a similar trend when the fraction of positive queries increases, but it is lower due to the extra decoding overhead when reading each bucket. In return for the performance penalty, the semi-sorting version reduces the false positive rate by a factor of two compared to the standard cuckoo filter. However, the ss-CF still outperforms BFs when more than 25% of queries are positive.

The QF performs the worst among all filters. When a QF is 90% filled, a lookup must search a long chain of table entries and decode each of them for the target item.

The dl-CBF outperforms the ss-CF, but 30% slower than a BF. It also keeps about the same performance when serving all negative queries and all positive queries, because only a constant number of entries are searched on each lookup.

Different Occupancy In this experiment, we measure the lookup throughput when the these filters are filled at different levels of occupancy. We vary their load factor α of each filter from 0 (empty) to its maximum occupancy. Figure 6 shows the average instantaneous lookup throughput when all queries are negative (i.e., for non-existing items) and all queries are positive (i.e., for existing items).

[7] Instead of checking each item's two buckets one by one, our implementation applies a performance optimization that tries to issue two memory loads together to hide the latency of the second read.

The throughput of CF and ss-CF is mostly stable across different load factor levels on both negative and positive queries. This is because the total number of entries to read and compare remains constant even as more items are inserted.

In contrast, the throughput of QF decreases substantially when more loaded. This filter searches an increasingly long chain of entries for the target item as the load factor grows.

Both BF and blk-BF behave differently when serving negative and positive queries. For positive queries, they must always check in total k bits, no matter how many items have been inserted, thus providing constant lookup throughput; while for negative queries, when the filter is less loaded, fewer bits are set and a lookup can return earlier when seeing a "0".

The dl-CBF behaves differently from the BF. When all lookups are negative, it ensures constant throughput like the CF, because a total of 16 entries from four buckets must be searched, no matter how many items this filter contains. For positive queries, if there are fewer items inserted, the lookup may return earlier before all four buckets are checked; however, this difference becomes negligible after the dl-CBF is about 20% filled.

7.3 Insert Performance

The overall construction speed, measured based on the total number of items a full filter contains and the total time to insert these items, is shown in Table 3. We also study the instantaneous insert throughput across the construction process. Namely, we measure the insert throughput of different filters when they are at levels of load factors, as shown in Figure 7.

In contrast to the lookup throughput shown in Figure 6, both types of CF have decreasing insert throughput when they are more filled (though their overall construction speed is still high), while both BF and blk-BF ensure almost constant insert throughput. The CF may have to move a sequence of existing keys recursively before successfully inserting a new item, and this process becomes more expensive when the load factor grows higher. In contrast, both Bloom filters always

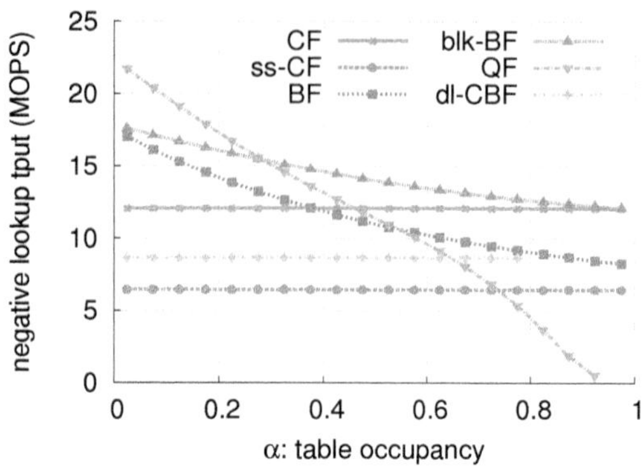

(a) Lookup random keys from a large universe

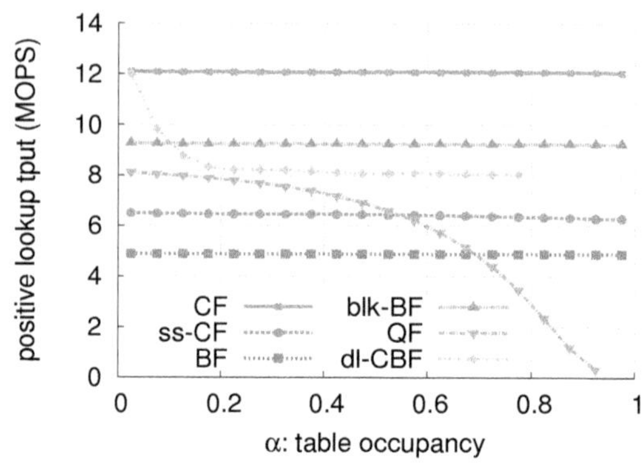

(b) Lookup random keys existing in the filter

Figure 6: Lookup throughput (MOPS) at different occupancy. Each point is the average of 10 runs.

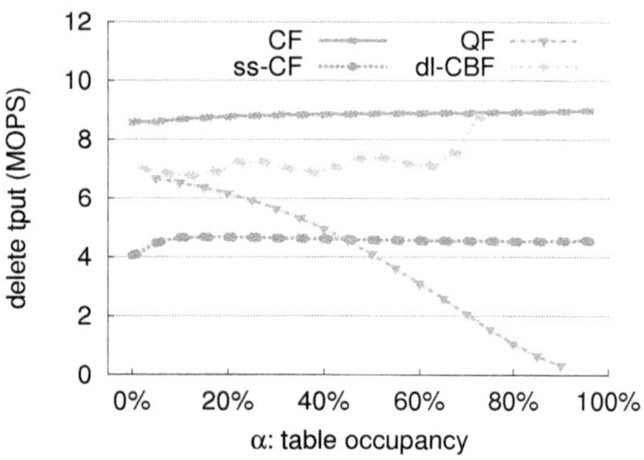

Figure 8: Delete-until-empty throughput (MOPS) at different occupancy. Each point is the average of 10 runs.

set k bits, regardless of the load factor.

The QF also has decreasing insert throughput, because it must shift a sequence of items before inserting a new item, and this sequence grows longer when the table is more filled.

The dl-CBF keeps constant throughput. For each insert, it must only find an empty entry in up to four buckets; if such an entry can not be found, the insert stops without relocating existing items as in cuckoo hashing. This is also why its maximum load factor is no more than 80%.

7.4 Delete Performance

Figure 8 compares the delete performance among filters supporting deletion. The experiment deletes keys from an initially full filter until it is empty. The CF achieves the highest throughput. Both CF and ss-CF provide stable performance through the entire process. The dl-CBF performs the second best among all filters. The QF is the slowest when close to full, but becomes faster than ss-CF when close to empty.

Evaluation Summary: The CF ensures high and stable lookup performance for different workloads and at different levels of occupancy. Its insert throughput declines as the filter is more filled, but the overall construction rate is still faster than other filters except the blk-BF. Enabling semi-sorting makes cuckoo filters more space-efficient than space-optimized BFs. It also makes lookups, inserts, and deletes slower, but still faster than conventional BFs.

8. CONCLUSION

Cuckoo filters are a new data structure for approximate set membership queries that can be used for many networking problems formerly solved using Bloom filters. Cuckoo filters improve upon Bloom filters in three ways: (1) support for deleting items dynamically; (2) better lookup performance; and (3) better space efficiency for applications requiring low false positive rates ($\epsilon < 3\%$). A cuckoo filter stores the fingerprints of a set of items based on cuckoo hashing, thus achieving high space occupancy. As a further key contribution, we have applied *partial-key cuckoo hashing*, which makes cuckoo filters significantly more efficient by allowing relocation based on only the stored fingerprint. Our configuration exploration suggests that the cuckoo filter, which uses buckets of size 4, will perform well for a wide range of applications, although appealingly cuckoo filter parameters can be easily varied for application-dependent tuning.

While we expect that further extensions and optimizations to cuckoo filters are possible and will further provide impetus for their use, the data structure as described is a fast and efficient building block already well-suited to the practical demands of networking and distributed systems.

9. ACKNOWLEDGMENTS

This work is supported by funding from Intel via the Intel Science and Technology Center for Cloud Computing (ISTC-CC), and National Science Foundation under awards CCF-0964474, CNS-1040801, CCF-1320231, CNS-1228598, and IIS-0964473. We gratefully acknowledge the CoNEXT reviewers for their feedback and suggestions; Rasmus Pagh for discussions on analyzing space usage of cuckoo filters that led to many of the insights about the asymptotic behavior; Hyeontaek Lim for code optimizations; and Iulian Moraru, Andrew Pavlo, Peter Steenkiste for comments on writing.

10. REFERENCES

[1] CityHash. https://code.google.com/p/cityhash/.

[2] M. A. Bender, M. Farach-Colton, R. Johnson, R. Kraner, B. C. Kuszmaul, D. Medjedovic, P. Montes, P. Shetty, R. P. Spillane, and E. Zadok. Don't thrash: How to cache your hash on flash. *PVLDB*, 5(11):1627–1637, 2012.

[3] B. H. Bloom. Space/time trade-offs in hash coding with allowable errors. *Communications of the ACM*, 13(7):422–426, 1970.

[4] F. Bonomi, M. Mitzenmacher, and R. Panigrahy. Beyond Bloom filters: From approximate membership checks to approximate state machines. In *Proc. ACM SIGCOMM*, Pisa, Italy, Aug. 2006.

[5] F. Bonomi, M. Mitzenmacher, R. Panigrahy, S. Singh, and G. Varghese. An improved construction for counting bloom filters. In *14th Annual European Symposium on Algorithms, LNCS 4168*, pages 684–695, 2006.

[6] A. Broder, M. Mitzenmacher, and A. Broder. Network Applications of Bloom Filters: A Survey. In *Internet Mathematics*, volume 1, pages 636–646, 2002.

[7] B. Chazelle, J. Kilian, R. Rubinfeld, A. Tal, and O. Boy. The Bloomier filter: An efficient data structure for static support lookup tables. In *Proceedings of SODA*, pages 30–39, 2004.

[8] J. G. Cleary. Compact Hash Tables Using Bidirectional Linear Probing. *IEEE Transactions on Computer*, C-33(9), Sept. 1984.

[9] S. Dharmapurikar, P. Krishnamurthy, and D. E. Taylor. Longest prefix matching using Bloom filters. In *Proc. ACM SIGCOMM*, Karlsruhe, Germany, Aug. 2003.

[10] M. Dietzfelbinger and C. Weidling. Balanced allocation and dictionaries with tightly packed constant size bins. *Theoretical Computer Science*, 380(1):47–68, 2007.

[11] B. Fan, D. G. Andersen, and M. Kaminsky. MemC3: Compact and concurrent memcache with dumber caching and smarter hashing. In *Proc. 10th USENIX NSDI*, Lombard, IL, Apr. 2013.

[12] L. Fan, P. Cao, J. Almeida, and A. Z. Broder. Summary cache: A scalable wide-area Web cache sharing protocol. In *Proc. ACM SIGCOMM*, Vancouver, BC, Canada, Sept. 1998.

[13] N. Fountoulakis, M. Khosla, and K. Panagiotou. The multiple-orientability thresholds for random hypergraphs. In *Proceedings of the Twenty-Second Annual ACM-SIAM Symposium on Discrete Algorithms*, pages 1222–1236. SIAM, 2011.

[14] N. Hua, H. C. Zhao, B. Lin, and J. J. Xu. Rank-Indexed Hashing: A Compact Construction of Bloom Filters and Variants. In *Proc. of IEEE Int'l Conf. on Network Protocols (ICNP) 2008*, Orlando, Florida, USA, Oct. 2008.

[15] P. Jokela, A. Zahemszky, C. Esteve Rothenberg, S. Arianfar, and P. Nikander. Lipsin: Line speed publish/subscribe internetworking. In *Proc. ACM SIGCOMM*, Barcelona, Spain, Aug. 2009.

[16] A. Kirsch and M. Mitzenmacher. Less hashing, same performance: Building a better Bloom filter. *Random Structures & Algorithms*, 33(2):187–218, 2008.

[17] H. Lim, B. Fan, D. G. Andersen, and M. Kaminsky. SILT: A memory-efficient, high-performance key-value store. In *Proc. 23rd ACM Symposium on Operating Systems Principles (SOSP)*, Cascais, Portugal, Oct. 2011.

[18] M. Mitzenmacher, A. W. Richa, and R. Sitaraman. The power of two random choices: A survey of techniques and results. In *Handbook of Randomized Computing*, pages 255–312. Kluwer, 2000.

[19] M. Mitzenmacher and B. Vocking. The asymptotics of selecting the shortest of two, improved. In *Proc. the Annual Allerton Conference on Communication Control and Computing*, volume 37, pages 326–327, 1999.

[20] A. Pagh, R. Pagh, and S. S. Rao. An optimal bloom filter replacement. In *Proc. ASM-SIAM Symposium on Discrete Algorithms, SODA*, 2005.

[21] R. Pagh and F. Rodler. Cuckoo hashing. *Journal of Algorithms*, 51(2):122–144, May 2004.

[22] F. Putze, P. Sanders, and S. Johannes. Cache-, hash- and space-efficient bloom filters. In *Experimental Algorithms*, pages 108–121. Springer Berlin / Heidelberg, 2007.

[23] D. Sanchez, L. Yen, M. D. Hill, and K. Sankaralingam. Implementing signatures for transactional memory. In *Proc. the 40th Annual IEEE/ACM International Symposium on Microarchitecture*, pages 123–133, Washington, DC, USA, 2007.

[24] H. Song, S. Dharmapurikar, J. Turner, and J. Lockwood. Fast hash table lookup using extended bloom filter: An aid to network processing. In *Proc. ACM SIGCOMM*, pages 181–192, Philadelphia, PA, Aug. 2005.

[25] M. Yu, A. Fabrikant, and J. Rexford. BUFFALO: Bloom filter forwarding architecture for large organizations. In *Proc. CoNEXT*, Dec. 2009.

[26] D. Zhou, B. Fan, H. Lim, D. G. Andersen, and M. Kaminsky. Scalable, High Performance Ethernet Forwarding with CuckooSwitch. In *Proc. 9th International Conference on emerging Networking EXperiments and Technologies (CoNEXT)*, Dec. 2013.

Sprinklers: a Randomized Variable-Size Striping Approach to Reordering-Free Load-Balanced Switching

Weijun Ding† Jun (Jim) Xu† Jim Dai‡ Yang Song* Bill Lin*
†Georgia Tech ‡Cornell University *UC San Diego

ABSTRACT

Internet traffic continues to grow exponentially, calling for switches that can scale well in both size and speed. While load-balanced switches can achieve such scalability, they suffer from a fundamental packet reordering problem. Existing proposals either suffer from poor worst-case packet delays or require sophisticated matching mechanisms. In this paper, we propose a new family of stable load-balanced switches called "Sprinklers" that has comparable implementation cost and performance as the baseline load-balanced switch, but yet can guarantee packet ordering. The main idea is to force all packets within the same virtual output queue (VOQ) to traverse the same "fat path" through the switch, so that packet reordering cannot occur. At the core of Sprinklers are two key innovations: a randomized way to determine the "fat path" for each VOQ, and a way to determine its "fatness" roughly in proportion to the rate of the VOQ. These innovations enable Sprinklers to achieve near-perfect load-balancing *under arbitrary admissible traffic*. Proving this property rigorously using novel worst-case large deviation techniques is another key contribution of this work.

Categories and Subject Descriptors

H.4 [**Information Systems Applications**]: Miscellaneous; D.2.8 [**Software Engineering**]: Metrics—*complexity measures, performance measures*

General Terms

Algorithm; Design; Performance

Keywords

Load-balanced switches; throughput guarantees

1. INTRODUCTION

Internet service providers need high-performance switch architectures that can scale well in both size and speed, provide throughput guarantees, achieve low latency, and maintain packet ordering. However, conventional crossbar-based switch architectures with centralized scheduling and arbitrary per-packet dynamic switch configurations are not scalable.

An alternative class of switch architecture is the load-balanced switch, first introduced by Chang et al. [2, 3], and later further developed by others (e.g. [9, 11, 13]). These architectures rely on two switching stages for routing packets. Fig. 1 shows a diagram of a generic two-stage load-balanced switch. The first switching stage connects the first stage of input ports to the center stage of intermediate ports, and the second switching stage connects the center stage of intermediate ports to the final stage of output ports. Both switching stages execute a deterministic connection pattern such that each input is connected to each output of a switching stage at $1/N$th of the time. This can be implemented for example using a deterministic round-robin switch (see Sec. 3). Alternatively, as shown in [11], the deterministic connection pattern can also be efficiently implemented using optics in which all inputs are connected to all outputs of a switching stage in parallel at a rate of $1/N$th the line rate. This class of architectures appears to be a practical way to scale high-performance switches to very high capacities and line rates.

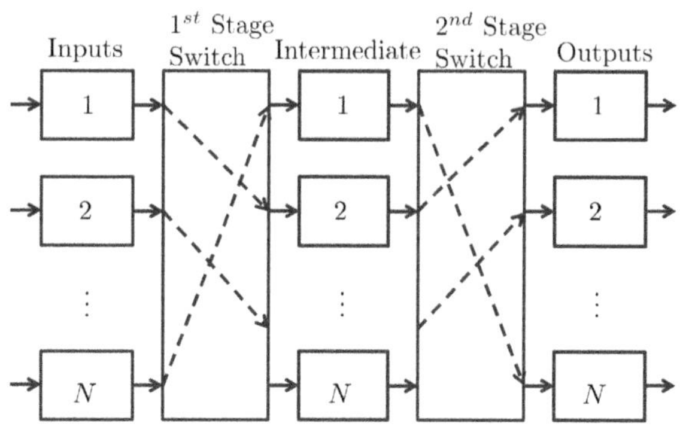

Figure 1: Generic load-balanced switch.

Although the baseline load-balanced switch originally proposed in [2] is capable of achieving throughput guarantees, it has the critical problem that packet departures can be badly out-of-order. In the baseline load-balanced switch, consecutive packets at an input port are spread to all N intermediate ports upon arrival. Packets going through dif-

CoNEXT'14, December 2–5, 2014, Sydney, Australia.

http://dx.doi.org/10.1145/2674005.2674986 .

ferent intermediate ports may encounter *different queueing delays*. Thus, some of these packets may arrive at their output ports out-of-order. This is detrimental to Internet traffic since the widely used TCP transport protocol falsely regards out-of-order packets as indications of congestion and packet loss. Therefore, a number of researchers have explored this packet ordering problem (e.g. [9, 11, 13]).

1.1 Our Approach

In this paper, we propose "Sprinklers," a new load-balanced switching solution that has comparable implementation cost and computational complexity, and similar performance guarantees as the baseline load-balanced switch, yet can guarantee packet ordering. The Sprinklers approach has a mild flavor of a simple, yet flawed solution called "TCP hashing"[1] [11]. The idea of TCP hashing is to force all packets at an input port that belong to the same application (TCP or UDP) flow to go through the same *randomly chosen* intermediate port by hashing on the packet's flow identifier. This approach ensures that all packets that belong to the same application flow will depart the switch in order because each port serves the packets in a FIFO manner. Although the TCP hashing scheme is simple and intuitive, it cannot guarantee stability because an intermediate port can easily be overloaded by having too many *large* flows randomly assigned to it.

Like the TCP hashing approach in which all packets within an application flow are forced to go through the same switching path, a Sprinklers switch requires all packets in a Virtual Output Queue (VOQ)[2] to go down the *same* "fat path" called a *stripe*. Specifically, for each VOQ, a Sprinklers switch stripes its packets across an interval of consecutive intermediate ports, which we call a *stripe interval*. The number of intermediate ports L in the stripe interval is referred to as its *size*. Different VOQs may have different sizes. In Sec. 2, we will show that by choosing a *largest stripe first* service policy at both input and intermediate ports, a Sprinklers switch guarantees that every stripe of packets departs from its input port and arrives at its output port both "in one burst" (i.e., in consecutive time slots). In other words, there is no interleaving between the servicing of two stripes in the same VOQ. This "no interleaving" service guarantee, combined with the FIFO order in which packets within a stripe and stripes within a VOQ are served, ensures that packet reordering cannot happen within any VOQ, and hence cannot happen within any application flow either.

A smaller L means less accumulation time of the stripe at the input ports. When every VOQ has L equal to the size of the switch N, the Sprinklers switch is reduced to the uniform frame spreading scheme in [11]. In the Sprinklers approach, the size L of the stripe interval is determined roughly in proportion to the traffic *rate* of the VOQ, and its placement is determined by means of *random permutation*. Therefore, the N^2 stripe intervals, corresponding to the N^2 VOQs at the N input ports, can be very different from one another in both size and placement. We will prove in Sec. 5 that the Sprinklers approach of combining random permutation with variable-size striping will ensure, with overwhelming probability, that none of the intermediate ports will be overloaded, under all admissible traffic workloads to the switch. This effectively solves the above-mentioned stability problem with the TCP hashing approach.

[1]TCP hashing is referred to as "Application Flow Based Routing" (AFBR) in [11].

[2]A VOQ refers to the set of packets arriving at an input port that are destined for the same output port.

1.2 Contributions

This paper makes the following major contributions:

- First, we introduce the design of a new load-balanced switch architecture based on randomized and variable-size striping that we call Sprinklers. Sprinklers is indeed scalable in that all its algorithmic aspects can be implemented in constant time at each input port and intermediate port in a fully distributed manner.
- Second, we develop novel large deviation techniques to prove that Sprinklers is stable under intensive arrival rates with overwhelming probability, while guaranteeing packet order.
- Third, to our knowledge, Sprinklers is the first load-balanced switch architecture based on randomization that can guarantee both stability and packet ordering, which we hope will become the catalyst to a rich family of solutions based on the simple principles of randomization and variable stripe sizing.

1.3 Outline

The rest of the paper is organized as follows. Sec. 2 introduces the structure of our switch and explains how it works. Sec. 3 discusses the scheduling policies at the input and intermediate ports of Sprinklers. Sec. 4 discuss how to determine the sizes and the placements of stripes. Sec. 5 provides a rigorous proof of stability based on the use of convex optimization theory and negative association theory to develop a Chernoff bound for the overload probability. This section also presents our worst-case large deviation results. Sec. 6 evaluates our proposed architecture. Sec. 7 provides a brief review of existing load-balanced switch solutions. Sec. 8 concludes the paper.

2. THE SPRINKLERS APPROACH

Sprinklers has the same architecture as the baseline load-balanced switch (see Fig. 1), but it differs in the way that it routes and schedules packets for service at the input and intermediate ports. In this section, we first provide an overview of how the Sprinklers switch operates. We then give some intuition behind the Sprinklers approach regarding why the stability can be achieved.

2.1 Operations of the Sprinklers Switch

As we explained in Introduction, the Sprinklers switch serves packets in units of stripes and the services of stripes do not intervene with each other. This "no interleaving" service guarantee, combined with the FIFO order in which packets within a stripe and stripes within a VOQ are served, ensures that packet reordering cannot happen within any VOQ. However, because the servicing of any two stripes cannot interleave in a Sprinklers switch (to ensure correct packet order), two stripes have to be serviced in two different frames (N time slots), if their stripe intervals have overlap. A rampant occurrence of such overlaps, which can happen if the stripe interval size of a VOQ is set strictly proportional to the rate of the VOQ (rounded to an integer), will result in gross waste of service capacity, and significantly reduce the maximum achievable throughput. Therefore, we would like any two stripe intervals to either "bear hug" (i.e., one contained entirely in the other) or does not touch (no overlap between the intervals) each other.

Our solution is a classical "computer science" one: making N a power of 2 (very reasonable in the modern switching literature) and every stripe interval a dyadic one (resulting from dividing the whole interval (0, N] into 2^k equal-sized subintervals for an integer $k \leq \log_2 N$).

As just explained, traffic inside each of the N^2 VOQs is switched through a dyadic interval of intermediate ports. The sizes of the corresponding N^2 stripe intervals are determined by the respective rates of the corresponding VOQs, and their placements to consecutive intermediate ports are performed using a randomized algorithm. Once generated, their placements remain fixed thereafter, while their sizes could change when their respective rates do.

Packets in each VOQ will be striped across its corresponding interval of intermediate ports as follows. Fix an arbitrary VOQ, and let its stripe size and interval be 2^k and $(\ell, \ell+2^k] \equiv \{\ell+1, \ell+2, \cdots, \ell+2^k\}$, respectively. (The integer ℓ must be divisible by 2^k for the interval to be dyadic, as discussed earlier. The precise algorithm to determine k and ℓ will be given in Sec. 4) Packets in this VOQ are divided, chronologically according to their arrival times, into groups of 2^k packets each and, with a slight abuse of the term, we refer to each such group also as a stripe. Such a stripe will eventually be switched through the set of intermediate ports $\{\ell+1, \ell+2, \cdots, \ell+2^k\}$ as follows. Assume this switching operation starts at time (slot) t, when the corresponding input port is connected to the intermediate port $\ell+1$ by the first switching fabric. Then, following the periodic connection sequence of the first switching fabric, the input port forwards the first packet in the stripe to the intermediate port $\ell+1$ at time t, the second packet to the intermediate port $\ell+2$ at time $t+1$, and so on, until it forwards the last packet in the stripe to the intermediate port $\ell+2^k$ at time $t+2^k-1$. That is, packets in this stripe go out of the input port to consecutive intermediate ports in consecutive time slots, as mentioned earlier. The same can be said about other stripes from this and other VOQs. This way, at each input port, the (switching) service is rendered by the first switching fabric in a stripe-by-stripe manner (i.e., finish serving one stripe before starting to serve another). The service at intermediate ports is also rendered in a stripe-by-stripe manner. In combination, these two service disciplines guarantee that every stripe of packets departs from its input port and arrives at its output port both "in one burst" (i.e., in consecutive time slots), as stated earlier.

2.2 Intuition behind the Sprinklers Approach

The Sprinklers approach is based on two techniques for balancing traffic evenly across all N intermediate ports: random permutation and variable-size striping. To provide some intuition as to why both techniques are necessary, we use an analogy from which the name Sprinklers is derived. Consider the task of watering a lawn consisting of N identically sized areas using N sprinklers with different pressure. The objective is to distribute an (ideally) identical amount of water to each area. This corresponds to evenly distributing traffic inside the N VOQs (sprinklers) entering a certain input port to the N intermediate ports (lawn areas) under the above-mentioned constraint that all traffic inside a VOQ must go through the same set of intermediate ports (i.e., the stripe interval) to which the VOQ is mapped.

An intuitive and sensible first step is to aim exactly one sprinkler at each lawn area, since aiming more than one sprinklers at one lawn area clearly could lead to it being flooded. In other words, the "aiming function," or "which sprinkler is aimed at which lawn area," is essentially a permutation over the set $\{1, 2, \cdots, N\}$. This permutation alone however cannot do the trick, because the water pressure (traffic rate) is different from one sprinkler to another, and the lawn area aimed at by a sprinkler with high water pressure will surely be flooded. To deal with such disparity in water pressures, we set the "spray angle range" of a sprinkler, which corresponds to the size (say L) of the stripe interval for the corresponding VOQ, proportional to its water pressure, and evenly distribute this water pressure across the L "streams" of water that go to the target lawn area and $L-1$ "neighboring" lawn areas.

However, such water pressure equalization (i.e., variable stripe sizing) alone does not prevent all scenarios of load-imbalance because it shuffles water around only "locally." For example, if a larger than average number of high pressure sprinklers are aimed at a cluster of lawn areas close to one another, some area within this cluster will be flooded. Hence, a simple yet powerful randomized algorithm is brought in to shuffle water around globally: we simply sample this permutation at uniform random from the set of all $N!$ permutations.

Besides load-balancing, there is another important reason for the size of a stripe interval to be set roughly proportional to the traffic rate of the corresponding VOQ. In some existing solutions to the packet reordering problem with load-balanced switches, each VOQ has to accumulate a full frame of N packets before the frame can depart from the input port. For a VOQ with low traffic rate, this buffering delay could be painfully long. By adopting rate-proportional stripe sizing, a Sprinklers switch significantly reduces the buffering delays experienced by the low-rate VOQs.

3. STRIPE SCHEDULING IN SPRINKLERS

At each input port, packets from the N VOQs originated from it contend for (the switching) service by the first switching fabric and hence must be arbitrated by a scheduler. For the same reason, scheduling is needed also at each intermediate port. In this section, we introduce this scheduling problem, and describe in details the Largest Stripe First (LSF) scheduling policy that is used at all input and intermediate ports.

3.1 Motivations for LSF

Since the (switching) service is rendered stripe-by-stripe by both switching fabrics, as explained above, the scheduling is really performed among the competing stripes. In general, two different scheduling policies are needed in a Sprinklers switch, one used at the input ports and the other at intermediate ports. Designing stripe scheduling policies that are well suited for a Sprinklers switch turns out to be a difficult undertaking because two tricky design requirements have to be met simultaneously.

The first requirement is that the resulting scheduling policies must facilitate a highly efficient utilization of the switching capacity of both switching fabrics. To see this, consider input port i and intermediate port ℓ. As explained in Sec. 1, these two ports are connected only once every N time slots, by the first switching fabric. Consider the set of packets at input port i that needs to be switched to the intermediate port ℓ. This set can be viewed and called a queue (a queueing-theoretic concept), because the stripe scheduling policy naturally induces a service order (and hence a service process) on this set of packets, and the arrival time of each packet is simply that of the stripe containing the packet. Clearly, the service rate of this queue is exactly $1/N$. Suppose this input port is heavily loaded, e.g., with a normalized arrival rate of 0.95. Then even with perfect load-balancing, the arrival rate to this queue is $0.95/N$, only slightly below the service rate $1/N$. Clearly, for this queue to be stable, there is no room for any waste of this service capacity. In other words, the scheduling policy must be throughput optimal.

The second requirement is exactly why we force all packets in a VOQ to go down the same fat path (i.e., stripe interval) through a Sprinklers switch, so as to guarantee that no packet reordering can happen. It is easy to verify that for packet order to be preserved within every stripe (and hence within every VOQ), it suffices to guarantee that packets in every stripe go into their destination output port from consecutive intermediate ports in consecutive time slots (i.e., continuously). However, it is much harder for a stripe of 2^k packets to arrive at an output port continuously (than to leave an input port), because these packets are physically located at a single input port when they leave the input port, but across 2^k different intermediate ports right before they leave for the output port.

After exploring the entire space of stripe-by-stripe scheduling policies, we ended up adopting the same stripe scheduling policy, namely Largest Stripe First (LSF), at both input ports and intermediate ports, but not for the same set of reasons. At input ports, LSF is used because it is throughput optimal. At intermediate ports, LSF is also used because it seems to be the only policy that makes every stripe of packets arrive at their destination output port continuously without incurring significant internal communication costs between the input and intermediate ports. In the rest of the section, we will describe the design and implementation of the LSF policy in details.

3.2 Largest Stripe First (LSF) Policy

Before we can describe the LSF policy, we need to first provide a brief description of the periodic sequences of connections executed at both switching fabrics shown in Fig. 1. The first switching fabric executes a periodic "increasing" sequence, that is, at any time slot t, each input port i is connected to the intermediate port $((i+t) \mod N)+1$. The second switching fabric, on the other hand, will execute a periodic "decreasing" sequence, that is, at any time slot t, each intermediate port ℓ is connected to the output port $((\ell - t) \mod N)+1$.

Algorithm 1 describes the Largest stripe first (LSF) policy used at input port i to make a decision as to, among multiple competing stripes, which one to serve next. Note that by the stripe-by-stripe nature of the scheduler, it is asked to make such a policy decision only when it completely finishes serving a stripe. The policy is simply to pick among the set of stripes whose dyadic interval starts at intermediate port ℓ – provided that the set is nonempty – the largest one (FIFO for tie-breaking) to start serving immediately.

Algorithm 1 LSF policy on "Who is next?"

```
l = (i + t mod N) + 1;
if No stripe is being served at time t then
    Let S be the set of stripes with interval (l − 1, ∗];
    if S is not empty then
        Start serving the largest stripe in S;
    end if
end if
```

The LSF policy is clearly throughput optimal because it is work-conserving in the sense whenever a connection is made between input port i and intermediate port ℓ, a packet will be served if there is at least one stripe at the input port whose interval contains ℓ. Using terms from queueing theory [12] we say this queue is served by a work-conserving server with service rate $1/N$.

3.3 LSF Scheduling at Input Ports

A stripe service schedule, which is the outcome of a scheduling policy acting on the stripe arrival process, is represented by a schedule grid, as shown in Fig. 2. There are N rows in the grid, each corresponding to an intermediate port. Each tiny square in the column represents a time slot. The shade in the square represents a packet scheduled to be transmitted in that slot and different shade patterns mean different VOQs. Hence, each "thin vertical bar" of squares with the same shade represents a stripe in the schedule. The time is progressing on the grid from right to left in the sense that packets put inside the rightmost column will be served in the first cycle (N time slots), the next column to the left in the second cycle, and so on. Within each column, time is progressing from up to down in the sense that packet put inside the uppermost cell will be switched to intermediate port 1 say at time slot t_0, packet put inside the cell immediately below it will be switched to intermediate port 2 at time slot t_0+1, and so on. Note this up-down sequence is consistent with the above-mentioned periodic connection pattern between the input port and the intermediate ports. Therefore, the scheduler is "peeling" the grid from right to left and from up to down.

For example, Fig. 2 corresponds to the statuses of the scheduling grid of a switch of size $N=8$ at time t_0 and t_0+8, where LSF is the scheduling policy. We can see that the rightmost column in the left part of Fig. 2, representing a single stripe of size 8, is served by the first switching fabric in the meantime, and hence disappears in the right part of the figure. The above-mentioned working conservation nature of the LSF server for any input port is also clearly illustrated in Fig. 2: There is no "hole" in any row.

While the scheduler always peels the grid from right to left and from up to down, the scheduler may insert a stripe ahead of other smaller stripes. In this case, the planned service time of all cells and bars to the left of the inserted vertical bar are shifted to the left by 1 column, meaning that their planned service time will be delayed by N time slots. For example, we can see from comparing the two parts of Fig. 2 that a stripe of size 4 (as circled in the figure) is inserted in the lower part of the 3rd column in the right part of Fig. 2, after two other stripes of size 4, but before some other stripes of smaller sizes.

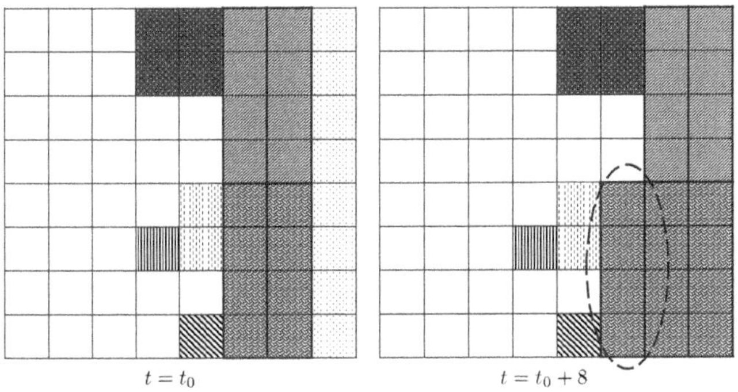

Figure 2: Statuses of the stripe scheduling at time t_0 (left) and $t_0 + 8$ (right), respectively.

3.3.1 Implementation of LSF at an Input Port

In this section, we describe data structures and algorithms for implementing the Longest Stripe First scheduling policy at an input port. Again we use input port 1 as an illustrative example. The LSF policy at input port 1 can be implemented using $N(\log_2 N + 1)$ FIFO queues as shown in Fig. 3. Conceptually, these FIFO queues are arranged into an array with N rows and $\log_2 N + 1$ columns. Row ℓ corresponds to FIFO queues that buffer packets to be sent to intermediate port ℓ. Each column of FIFO queues is used to buffer stripes of a certain size. The last column is for stripes of size N, the second last for stripes of size $N/2$, and so on. The very first column is for stripes of size 1. Therefore, the FIFO on the ℓth row and kth column is to queue packets going to intermediate port ℓ and from stripes of size 2^{k-1}.

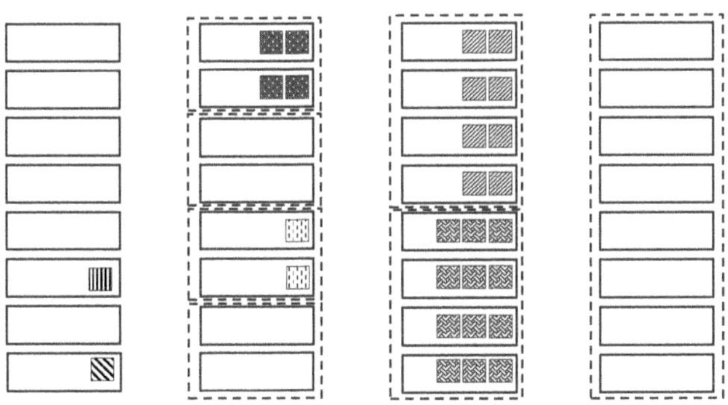

Figure 3: Data structure to implement LSF.

The implementation of LSF with this data structure is straightforward. Each VOQ will have a ready queue to buffer packets that have not filled up a stripe yet. Once a stripe is full, depending on the size of the stripe, it will be "plastered" into the corresponding interval in the corresponding column. At each column, stripes sent into the same interval will be queued in the FIFO order. For example, the contents of these FIFO queues at time $t_0 + 8$, that correspond to the scheduling grid shown as the right part of Fig. 2, are shown in Fig. 3.

During each time slot t, the scheduler either starts or is in the middle of serving the longest stripe that contain the intermediate port $t \mod N$. However, the scheduler does not need to be stripe-aware. At each time t, it only needs to scan the $(t \mod N)th$ row from right to left and serve the packet at the head of the first nonempty queue. If for each queue, we use a bit to encode whether it is empty, our problem boils down to looking for the "first one from right" in a bitmap $\log_2 N + 1$ bits long. This kind of function can be readily performed as a single operation by means of a hardware priority encoder in one to a few clock cycles on a modern processor or ASIC chip. Overall N such bitmaps are needed, one for each row (intermediate port). Thus, using an $N \times (\log_2 N + 1)$ 2D-bitmap to indicate the status of each queue (0 for empty, 1 for nonempty), the switch can identify the rightmost bit set in each row of the bitmap in constant time, which is used by LSF to identify the largest stripe to serve at each port.

Careful readers may note that it is unnecessary to maintain $N \log_2 N$ FIFO queues. Rather, we need only one FIFO queue for all stripes of size N, two for all stripes of size $N/2$, – namely one for the interval (0, N/2] and the other for $(N/2, N]$), – four for all stripes of size $N/4$, and so on. The total number of FIFO queues we need is indeed $1 + 2 + 4 + \cdots + N/2 + N = 2N - 1$. For example, in the above figure, we need only 15 queues: one FIFO queue for all stripes of size 8, two for all stripes of size 4, four for all stripes of size 2, and 8 for all stripes of size 1. We will indeed adopt such a simplified implementation for the input port. However, we still present the data structure in this "verbose" manner because this data structure will be modified for use at the intermediate ports, and there such a simplifying collapse is no longer possible, as will become clear next.

3.4 Stripe Scheduling at Intermediate Ports

The schedule grids at intermediate ports take a slightly different form. Every output port j is associated with a schedule grid also consisting of N rows. Row i of the grid corresponds to the tentative schedule in which packets destined for output port j at intermediate port i will follow. This schedule grid is really a virtual one, of which the N rows are physically distributed across N different intermediate ports, respectively. All stripes heading to output j show up on this grid. The LSF policy can be defined with respect to this virtual grid in almost the same way as in the previous case.

The data structure for implementing LSF at intermediate ports is the same as that at input ports, except the rows of the scheduling grid and the corresponding bitmaps are distributed across all N intermediate ports, thus requiring some coordination. This coordination however requires only that, for each packet switched over the first switching fabric, the input port inform the intermediate port of the size of the stripe to which the packet belongs. This information can be encoded in just $\log_2 \log_2 N$ bits, which is a tiny number (e.g., = 4 bits when N = 4096), and be included in the internal-use header of every packet transmitted across the first switching fabric.

4. GENERATING STRIPE INTERVALS

As we have already explained, the random permutation and the variable dyadic stripe sizing techniques are used to generate the stripe intervals for the N VOQs originated from a single input port, with the objective of balancing the traffic coming out of this input port very evenly across all N intermediate ports. In Sec. 4.1 and Sec. 4.2, we will specify this interval generating process precisely and provide detailed rationales for it. In Sec. 4.3, we will explain why and how the interval generating processes at N input ports should be carefully coordinated.

4.1 Stripe Interval Generation at a Single Input Port

Suppose we fix an input port and number the N VOQs originated from it as $1, 2, \cdots, N$, respectively. VOQ i is first mapped to a distinct *primary intermediate port* $\sigma(i)$, where σ is a permutation chosen uniformly randomly from the set of all permutations on the set $\{1, 2, \cdots, N\}$. Then the stripe interval for a VOQ i whose primary intermediate port is $\sigma(i)$ and whose interval size is $n = 2^k$ for some integer k is simply the unique dyadic interval of size n that contains $\sigma(i)$. A dyadic interval is one resulting from dividing the whole port number range $(0, N] \equiv \{1, 2, \cdots, N\}$ evenly by a power of 2, which takes the form $(2^{k_0}m, 2^{k_0}(m+1)]$ where k_0 and m are nonnegative integers.

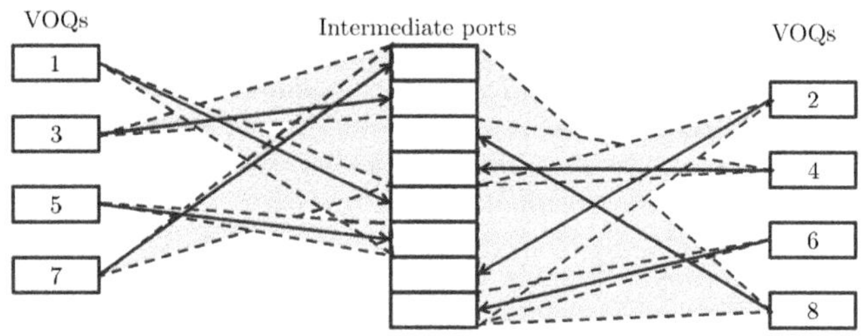

Figure 4: An example of VOQs being mapped to stripe intervals.

In Fig. 4, we show an example of mapping 8 VOQs at a single input port to their stripe intervals in an 8 by 8 switch. The middle column stands for the 8 intermediate ports and the columns on the left and on the right correspond to VOQs 1, 3, 5, 7 and VOQs 2, 4, 6, 8, respectively. Mapping a VOQ to its primary intermediate port is indicated by a solid arrow connecting the two. Its stripe interval is indicated by the "fanout" shadow that contains the solid line and is bounded at both ends by two dashed lines. For example, VOQ 7 (bottom one on the left) is mapped to the primary intermediate port 1 and its stripe size is 4. Therefore, its stripe interval is $(0, 4]$, the size-4 dyadic interval that contains intermediate port 1.

4.2 Stripe Size Determination

As mentioned in the "water pressure equalization" analogy, for a VOQ, the size of its stripe interval is roughly proportional to the (current) traffic rate of the VOQ. More precisely, the stripe interval size for a VOQ of traffic rate r, is determined by the following function:

$$F(r) = \min\left\{N, 2^{\lceil \log_2(rN^2)\rceil}\right\}. \quad (1)$$

The stripe size determination rule (1) tries to bring the amount of traffic each intermediate port within the stripe interval receives from this VOQ below $1/N^2$ while requiring that the stripe size be a power of 2. However, if the rate r is very high, say $> \frac{1}{N}$, then the stripe size $F(r)$ is simply N.

The initial sizing of the N^2 stripe intervals may be set based on historical switch-wide traffic matrix information, or to some default values. Afterwards, the size of a stripe interval will be adjusted based on the measured rate of the corresponding VOQ. To prevent the size of a stripe from "thrashing" between 2^k and 2^{k+1}, we can delay the halving and doubling of the stripe size. Although our later mathematical derivations assume the perfect adherence to the above stripe size determination rule, the change in the provable load-balancing guarantees is in fact negligible when a small number of stripe sizes are a bit too small (or too large) for the respective rates of their corresponding VOQs.

4.3 Coordination among Stripe Intervals

Like an input port, an output port is connected to each intermediate port also exactly once every N time slots, and hence needs to near-perfectly balance the traffic load coming into it. That is, roughly $\frac{1}{N}$ of that load should come from each intermediate port. In this section, we show how to achieve such load balancing at an output port, by a careful coordination among the (stripe-interval-generating) permutations σ_i, $i = 1, 2, \cdots, N$.

Now consider an arbitrary output port j. There are precisely N VOQs destined for it, one originated from each input port. Intuitively, they should ideally be mapped (permuted) to N distinct primary intermediate ports – for the same reason why the N VOQs originated from an input port are mapped (permuted) to N distinct primary intermediate ports – by the permutations σ_1, σ_2, $\cdots$, σ_N, respectively. We will show this property holds for every output port j if and only if the matrix representation of these permutations is an Orthogonal Latin Square (OLS).

Consider an $N \times N$ matrix $A = (a_{ij})$, $i, j = 1, 2, \cdots, N$, where $a_{ij} = \sigma_i(j)$. Consider the N VOQs originated at input port i, one destined for each output port. We simply number each VOQ by its corresponding output port. Clearly row i of the matrix A is the primary intermediate ports of these N VOQs. Now consider the above-mentioned N VOQs destined for output port j, one originated from each input port. It is easy see that the j_{th} column of matrix A, namely $\sigma_1(j)$, $\sigma_2(j)$, $\cdots$, $\sigma_N(j)$, is precisely the primary intermediate ports to which these N VOQs are mapped. As explained earlier, we would like these numbers also to be distinct, i.e., a permutation of the set $\{1, 2, \cdots, N\}$. Therefore, every row or column of the matrix A must be a permutation of $\{1, 2, \cdots, N\}$. Such a matrix is called an OLS in the combinatorics literature [4].

Our worst-case large deviation analysis in Sec. 5 requires the N VOQs at the same input port or destined to the same output port select their primary intermediate ports according to a uniform random permutation. Mathematically, we only require the marginal distribution of the permutation represented by each row or column of the OLS A to be uniform. The use of the word "marginal" here emphasizes that we do not assume any dependence structure, or the lack thereof, among the N random permutations represented by the N rows and among those represented by the N columns. We refer to such an OLS as being weakly uniform random, to distinguish it from an OLS sampled uniformly randomly from the space of all OLS' over the alphabet set $\{1, 2, \cdots, N\}$, which we refer to as being strongly uniform random. This distinction is extremely important for us, since whether there exists a polynomial time randomized algorithm for generating an OLS that is approximately strongly uniform random has been an open problem in theoretical computer science and combinatorics for several decades [6, 8]. A weakly uniform random OLS, on the other hand, can be generated in $O(N \log N)$ time, shown as following.

We first generate two uniform random permutations $\sigma^{(R)}$ and $\sigma^{(C)}$ over the set $\{1, 2, \cdots, N\}$ that are mutually independent, using a straightforward randomized algorithm [7]. This process, which involves generating $\log_2 N! = O(N \log N)$ random bits to "index" $\sigma^{(R)}$ and $\sigma^{(C)}$ each, has $O(N \log N)$ complexity in total. Then each matrix element $a(i,j)$ is simply set to $(\sigma^{(R)}(i) + \sigma^{(C)}(j) \mod N) + 1$. It is not hard to verify that each row or column is a uniform random permutation.

5. STABILITY ANALYSIS

As explained in Sec. 3, a queueing process can be defined on the set of packets at input port i that need to be switched to intermediate port ℓ. This (single) queue is served by a work-conserving server with a service rate $1/N$ under the LSF scheduling policy. It has been shown in [5] that such a queue is stable as long as the long-term average arrival rate is less than $1/N$. This entire section is devoted to proving a single mathematical result, that is, the arrival rate to this queue is less than $1/N$ with overwhelming probability, under all admissible traffic workloads to the input port i.

Between input ports $i = 1, 2, ..., N$ and intermediate ports $\ell = 1, 2, ..., N$, there are altogether N^2 such queues to analyze. It is not hard to verify, however, that the joint probability distributions of the random variables involved in – and hence the results from – their analyses are identical. We will present only the case for $i = 1$ and $\ell = 1$. Thus, the queue in the rest of the section specifically refers to the one serving packets from input port 1 to intermediate port 1. With this understanding, we will drop subscripts i and ℓ in the sequel for notational convenience.

There are another N^2 queues to analyze, namely, the queues of packets that need to be transmitted from intermediate ports $\ell = 1, 2, ..., N$ to output ports $j = 1, 2, ..., N$. Note each such queue is also served by a work-conserving server with service rate $1/N$, because the LSF scheduling policy is also used at the intermediate ports, as explained in Sec. 3.4. Therefore, we again need only to prove that the arrival rate to each such queue is statistically less than $1/N$. However, again the joint probability distributions of the random variables involved in – and hence the results from – their analyses are identical to that of the N^2 queues between the input ports and the intermediate ports, this time due to the statistical rotational symmetry of the above-mentioned weakly random OLS based on which the stripe intervals are generated. Therefore, no separate analysis is necessary for these N^2 queues.

5.1 Formal Statement of the Result

In this section, we precisely state the mathematical result. Let the N VOQs at input port 1 be numbered 1, 2, $\cdots$, N. Let their arrival rates be r_1, r_2, $\cdots$, and r_N, respectively, which we write also in the vector form $\vec{r}$. Let f_i be the stripe size of VOQ i, i.e., $f_i := F(r_i)$ for $i = 1, 2, \cdots, N$, where $F(\cdot)$ is defined in Equation 1. Let s_i be the load-per-share of VOQ i, i.e., $s_i := \frac{r_i}{F(r_i)}$ for $i = 1, 2, \cdots, N$. Let $|\vec{r}|$ be the sum of the arrival rates, i.e., $|\vec{r}| := r_1 + \cdots + r_N$.

Let $X(\vec{r}, \sigma)$ be the total traffic arrival rate to the queue when the N input VOQs have arrival rates given by $\vec{r}$ and the uniform random permutation used to map the N VOQs to their respective primary intermediate ports is σ. All N VOQs could contribute some traffic to this queue (of packets that need to be switched to intermediate port 1) and $X(\vec{r}, \sigma)$ is simply the sum of all these contributions. Clearly $X(\vec{r}, \sigma)$ is a random variable whose value depends on the VOQ rates $\vec{r}$ and how σ shuffles these VOQs around.

Consider the VOQ that selects intermediate port ℓ as its primary intermediate port. By the definition of σ, the index of this VOQ is $\sigma^{-1}(\ell)$. It is not hard to verify that this VOQ contributes one of its load shares to this queue, in the amount of $s_{\sigma^{-1}(\ell)}$, if and only if its stripe size is at least ℓ. Denote this contribution as $X_\ell(\vec{r}, \sigma)$. we have $X_\ell(\vec{r}, \sigma) = s_{\sigma^{-1}(\ell)} \mathbf{1}_{\{f_{\sigma^{-1}(\ell)} \geq \ell\}}$. Then:

$$X(\vec{r}, \sigma) = \sum_{\ell=1}^{N} X_\ell(\vec{r}, \sigma). \tag{2}$$

Note all the randomness of $X_\ell(\vec{r}, \sigma)$ and hence $X(\vec{r}, \sigma)$ comes from σ, as $\vec{r}$ is a set of constant parameters. The expectations of the functions of $X_\ell(\vec{r}, \sigma)$ and $X(\vec{r}, \sigma)$, such as their moment generating functions (MGF), are taken over σ. With this understanding, we will drop σ from $X_\ell(\vec{r}, \sigma)$ and $X(\vec{r}, \sigma)$ and simply write them as $X_\ell(\vec{r})$ and $X(\vec{r})$ in the sequel.

As explained earlier, the sole objective of this section is to prove that $\mathbb{P}(X(\vec{r}) \geq 1/N)$, the probability that the total arrival rate to this queue exceeds the service rate, is either 0 or extremely small. This probability, however, generally depends not only on $|\vec{r}|$, the total traffic load on input port 1, but also on how this total splits up (i.e., the actual rate vector $\vec{r}$).

Our result is composed of two theorems, namely, Theorems 1 and 2. Theorem 1 states that when this total load is no more than roughly 2/3, then this probability is strictly 0, regardless of how it is split up. When the total traffic load $|\vec{r}|$ exceeds that amount, however, this probability could become positive, and how large this probability is could hinge heavily on the actual $\vec{r}$ values. Theorem 2, together with the standard Chernoff bounding technique preceding it, provides a bound on the maximum value of this probability when the total load is no more than some constant ρ, but can be split up in arbitrary ways. More precisely, Theorem 2 helps establish an upper bound on $\sup_{\vec{r} \in V(\rho)} \mathbb{P}(X(\vec{r}) \geq 1/N)$, where $V(\rho) := \{\vec{r} \in \mathbb{R}_+^N : |\vec{r}| \leq \rho\}$. However, since $\mathbb{P}(X(\vec{r}) \geq 1/N)$, as a function of $\vec{r}$, is nondecreasing, this is equivalent to bounding $\sup_{\vec{r} \in U(\rho)} \mathbb{P}(X(\vec{r}) \geq 1/N)$, where $U(\rho) := \{\vec{r} \in \mathbb{R}_+^N : |\vec{r}| = \rho\}$. The same argument applies to $\mathbb{E}[\exp(\theta X(\vec{r}))]$, the MGF of $X(\vec{r})$. Therefore, we will use $U(\rho)$ instead of $V(\rho)$ in both cases in the sequel.

THEOREM 1. *$X(\vec{r}) < 1/N$ with probability 1 if $|\vec{r}| < \frac{2}{3} + \frac{1}{3N^2}$.*

The proof of Theorem 1 is postponed to the Appendix.

We now move on to describe the second theorem. By the standard Chernoff bounding technique, we have

$$\mathbb{P}(X(\vec{r}) \geq 1/N) \leq \inf_{\theta > 0} \exp(-\theta/N) \mathbb{E}[\exp(\theta X(\vec{r}))].$$

The above-mentioned worst-case probability can thus be upper-bounded as

$$\begin{aligned}
&\sup_{\vec{r}\in U(\rho)} \mathbb{P}(X(\vec{r}) \geq 1/N) \\
&\leq \sup_{\vec{r}\in U(\rho)} \inf_{\theta>0} \exp(-\theta/N)\mathbb{E}[\exp(\theta X(\vec{r}))] \\
&\leq \inf_{\theta>0} \sup_{\vec{r}\in U(\rho)} \exp(-\theta/N)\mathbb{E}[\exp(\theta X(\vec{r}))], \qquad (3)
\end{aligned}$$

where the interchange of the infimum and supremum follows from the max-min inequality [1].

Therefore, our problem boils down to upper-bounding the worst-case MGF of $X(\vec{r})$ as following:

$$\sup_{\vec{r}\in U(\rho)} \mathbb{E}[\exp(\theta X(\vec{r}))].$$

The upper bound is established in the following theorem.

THEOREM 2. *When* $\frac{2}{3} + \frac{1}{3N^2} \leq \rho < 1$, *we have*

$$\sup_{\vec{r}\in U(\rho)} \mathbb{E}[\exp(\theta X(\vec{r}))] \leq (h(p^*(\theta\alpha), \theta\alpha))^{N/2} \exp(\theta\rho/N),$$

where $h(p, a) = p\exp(a(1-p)) + (1-p)\exp(-ap)$, *and*

$$p^*(a) = \frac{\exp(a) - 1 - a}{\exp(a)a - a}$$

is the maximizer of $h(\cdot, a)$ *for a given* a.

For any given switch size N and a total load $\rho < 1$, Theorem 2 and the Chernoff bound (3) establish an upper bound on the above-mentioned worst-case probability. Table 1 provides the values of this probability under various settings of N and ρ. For example, when a Sprinklers switch has 2048 input and output ports (i.e., $N = 2048$) and is 93% loaded on input port 1, this upper bound is only 3.09×10^{-18}. Note however that it upper-bounds only the probability that a single queue, namely the set of packets at input port 1 that need to be switched to the intermediate ports 1, is overloaded. As mentioned earlier, there are altogether $2N^2$ such queues. Per the union bound, the probability that one or more such queues are overloaded across the entire 2048 × 2048 switch is simply $2N^2$ times that. In this example, the bound on the switch-wide overloading probability is 1.30×10^{-11}.

Table 1: Examples of overload probability bound

ρ	$N = 1024$	$N = 2048$	N = 4096
0.90	1.21×10^{-18}	1.14×10^{-29}	6.10×10^{-30}
0.91	3.06×10^{-15}	4.91×10^{-29}	7.10×10^{-30}
0.92	3.54×10^{-12}	1.26×10^{-23}	9.10×10^{-30}
0.93	1.76×10^{-9}	3.09×10^{-18}	1.58×10^{-29}
0.94	3.76×10^{-7}	1.42×10^{-13}	2.00×10^{-26}
0.95	3.50×10^{-5}	1.22×10^{-9}	1.48×10^{-18}
0.96	1.41×10^{-3}	1.99×10^{-6}	3.97×10^{-12}
0.97	2.50×10^{-2}	6.24×10^{-4}	3.90×10^{-7}

From these bounds, we can see that despite the use of the randomized and variable-size striping needed to prevent packet reordering and keep the packet buffering delay within a reasonable range, a Sprinklers switch can achieve very high throughputs (> 90%). In fact, the actual overload probabilities could be orders of magnitude smaller, due to unavoidable relaxations used to obtain such bounds. Another interesting phenomena reflected in Table 1 is that, given a certain traffic load, this bound decreases rapidly as the switch size N increases. In other words, the larger a Sprinklers switch is, the higher the throughput guarantees it can provide. This is certainly a desired property for a scalable switch.

If a certain traffic load condition sets in – that causes an overload situation at an input port – and persists, measures may need to be taken for the port to break away from the overload trap. Our solution is for the input port to double the stripe sizes for all N VOQs originating from it. It has minimal impact on the ongoing operation of the switch, because the placements of the stripe intervals – or the random permutation – at the input port remain unchanged. Some packets may be reordered during the transition, but this is a reasonable price to pay for avoiding the persistent overload situation. Our simulations show, with this approach, a Sprinklers switch can avoid being trapped into an overload condition, with overwhelming probabilities.

Symmetric to the above problem, this overload situation may also happen to one of the N above-mentioned queues between the intermediate ports and an output port. These N queues are fed in aggregate by the traffic inside N VOQs destined for the output port that originate from the N input ports, respectively. The solution is also symmetric, which is simply for the input ports to double the stripe size of all N VOQs.

5.2 Proof of Theorem 2

Recall $f_i = F(r_i)$ and $s_i = \frac{r_i}{f_i}$ for $i = 1, 2, \cdots, N$. For the convenience of our later derivations, we rewrite X as a function of $\vec{f}$ and $\vec{s}$ by defining $X(\vec{s}, \vec{f}) = X(\vec{s} \circ \vec{f})$, where $\vec{s} \circ \vec{f} = (f_1 \cdot s_1, f_2 \cdot s_2, \cdots, f_N \cdot s_N)$. With this rewriting, we can convert the optimization problem $\sup_{\vec{r}\in U(\rho)} \mathbb{E}[\exp(\theta X(\vec{r}))]$ in Theorem 2 to the following:

$$\sup_{\langle \vec{f}, \vec{s}\rangle \in A(\rho)} \mathbb{E}[\exp(\theta X(\vec{s}, \vec{f}))], \qquad (4)$$

where

$$\begin{aligned}
A(\rho) := \{\langle \vec{f}, \vec{s}\rangle | f_\ell &= 2^{k_\ell} \text{ for some integer } k_\ell, \forall \ell & (5)\\
s_\ell &\in [0, \alpha] \text{ if } f_\ell = 1, & (6)\\
s_\ell &\in (\alpha/2, \alpha] \text{ if } f_\ell = 2, 4, \cdots, N/2 & (7)\\
s_\ell &\in (\alpha/2, 1/N] \text{ if } f_\ell = N, & (8)\\
\sum_{\ell=1}^{N} s_\ell f_\ell &= \rho\}. & (9)
\end{aligned}$$

The rule for stripe size determination (1) induces the conditions (5) - (8) above.

We now replace the half-open intervals in conditions (7) and (8) by the closed ones, which is equivalent to replacing $A(\rho)$ with its closure $\bar{A}(\rho)$, because it is generally much easier to work with a closed set in an optimization problem. The resulting optimization problem is

$$\max_{\langle \vec{f}, \vec{s}\rangle \in \bar{A}(\rho)} \mathbb{E}_\sigma[\exp(\theta X(\vec{s}, \vec{f}))]. \qquad (10)$$

This replacement is logically correct because it will not decrease the optimal value of this optimization problem, and we are deriving an upper bound of it.

Our approach to Problem (10) is an exciting combination of convex optimization and the theory of negative associations in statistics [10], glued together by the Cauchy-Schwartz inequality. We first show that $\mathbb{E}[\exp(\theta X(\vec{s},\vec{f}))]$, viewed as a function of only $\vec{s}$ (i.e., with a fixed $\vec{f}$), achieves its maximum over $\bar{A}(\rho)$ when $\vec{s}$ satisfies certain extremal conditions, through convex optimization theory in Sec. 5.2.1. Then with $\vec{s}$ fixed at any such extreme point, we can decompose $X(\vec{s},\vec{f})$ into the sum of two sets of negatively associated (defined below) random variables. Using properties of negative association, we are able to derive a very tight upper bound on $\mathbb{E}[\exp(\theta X(\vec{s},\vec{f}))]$ in Sec. 5.2.2.

DEFINITION 1. *Random variables $X_1, X_2, \cdots, X_k$ are said to be negatively associated if for every pair of disjoint subsets A_1, A_2 of $\{1, 2, \cdots, k\}$,*

$$Cov\{g_1(X_i, i \in A_1), g_2(X_j, j \in A_2)\} \leq 0,$$

whenever g_1 and g_2 are nondecreasing functions.

In the proof below, we need to use the following properties of negative association [10].

LEMMA 1. *Let $g_1, g_2, \cdots, g_k$ be nondecreasing positive functions of one variable. Then $X_1, \cdots, X_k$ being negatively associated implies*

$$\mathbb{E}\left[\prod_{i=1}^{k} g_i(X_i)\right] \leq \prod_{i=1}^{k} \mathbb{E}\left[g_i(X_i)\right].$$

LEMMA 2. *Let $x = (x_1, \cdots, x_k)$ be a set of k real numbers. $X = (X_1, \cdots, X_k)$ is a random vector, taking values in the set of $k!$ permutations of x with equal probabilities. Then $X = (X_1, \cdots, X_k)$ is negatively associated.*

5.2.1 Extremal Property of $\vec{s}$ in An Optimal Solution

LEMMA 3. *Given $\frac{2}{3} + \frac{1}{3N^2} \leq \rho < 1$, for any $\theta > 0$, there is always an optimal solution $\langle \vec{f}^*, \vec{s}^* \rangle$ to Problem (10) that satisfies the following property:*

$$s_j^* = \begin{cases} 0 \text{ or } \alpha, & \text{if } f_j^* = 1; \\ \frac{\alpha}{2} \text{ or } \alpha, & \text{if } 2 \leq f_j^* \leq \frac{N}{2}. \end{cases} \tag{11}$$

PROOF. Suppose $\langle \vec{f}^*, \vec{s}^* \rangle$ is an optimal solution to Problem (10). We claim that at least one scalar in $\vec{f}^*$ is equal to N, since otherwise, the total arrival rate is at most $\frac{1}{N^2} \cdot \frac{N}{2} \cdot N = \frac{1}{2}$ by the stripe size determination rule (1), contradicting our assumption that $\rho \geq \frac{2}{3} + \frac{1}{3N^2} > \frac{1}{2}$. In addition, if more than one scalars in $\vec{f}^*$ are equal to N, we add up the values of all these scalars in $\vec{s}$, assign the total to one of them (say s_m), and zero out the rest. This aggregation operation will not change the total arrival rate to any intermediate port because an input VOQ with stripe size equal to N will spread its traffic evenly to all the intermediate ports anyway.

If the optimal solution $\langle \vec{f}^*, \vec{s}^* \rangle$ does not satisfy Property (11), we show that we can find another optimal solution satisfying Property (11) through the following optimization problem. Note that now with $\vec{f}^*$ fixed, $\mathbb{E}[\exp(\theta X(\vec{s},\vec{f}^*))]$ is a function of only $\vec{s}$.

$$\max_{\vec{s}} : \mathbb{E}[\exp(\theta X(\vec{s},\vec{f}^*))] \tag{12}$$

$$\text{s.t.:} 0 \leq s_j \leq \alpha, \forall j \text{ with } f_j^* = 1; \tag{13}$$

$$\frac{\alpha}{2} \leq s_j \leq \alpha, \forall j \text{ with } 2 \leq f_j^* \leq N/2; \tag{14}$$

$$\alpha/2 \leq s_m; \tag{15}$$

$$\sum_j s_j f_j^* = \rho. \tag{16}$$

$\mathbb{E}[\exp(\theta X(\vec{s},\vec{f}^*))] = \frac{1}{N!}\sum_\sigma \exp\left(\theta \sum_{j=1}^N s_j \mathbf{1}_{\{f_j^* \geq \sigma(j)\}}\right)$ where $\sigma(j)$ is the index of the intermediate port that VOQ j is mapped to. Given $\vec{f}^*$, the objective function $\mathbb{E}[\exp(\theta X(\vec{s},\vec{f}^*))]$ is clearly a convex function of $\vec{s}$.

The feasible region of $\vec{s}$ defined by (13) - (16) is a (convex) polytope. By the convex optimization theory [1], the (convex) objective function reaches its optimum at one of the extreme points of the polytope. The assumption $\rho \geq \frac{2}{3} + \frac{1}{3N^2}$ implies that Constraint (15) cannot be satisfied with equality. Thus, for any extreme point of the polytope, each of Constraint (13) and (14) must be satisfied with equality on one side. Thus there exists at least one optimal solution satisfying Property (11). This establishes the required result. □

5.2.2 Exploiting Negative Associations

Suppose the optimization objective $\mathbb{E}[\exp(\theta X(\vec{s},\vec{f}))]$ is maximized at $\vec{s}^*$, an extreme point of the above-mentioned polytope, and $\vec{f}^*$. Next, we prove that $\mathbb{E}[\exp(\theta X(\vec{s}^*,\vec{f}^*))]$ is upper-bounded by the right-hand side (RHS) of the inequality in Theorem 2, by exploiting the negative associations – induced by $\vec{s}^*$ being an extreme point – among the random variables that add up to $X(\vec{s}^*,\vec{f}^*)$. For notational convenience, we drop the asterisk from $\vec{s}^*$ and $\vec{f}^*$, and simply write them as $\vec{s}$ and $\vec{f}$.

Again for notational convenience, we further drop the terms $\vec{f}$ and $\vec{s}$ from $X(\vec{s},\vec{f})$, and simply write it as X. Such a dependency should be clear from the context. We now split X into two random variables X^L and X^U and a constant X^d, by splitting each s_ℓ into s_ℓ^L and s_ℓ^U, and each f_ℓ into f_ℓ^L and f_ℓ^U, as follows. If $f_\ell = N$, we let $s_\ell^L = s_\ell^U = 0$. Otherwise, we define $s_\ell^L = \min\{s_\ell, \alpha/2\}$ and $s_\ell^U = \max\{0, s_\ell - \alpha/2\}$. We then define $f_\ell^L = f_\ell \mathbf{1}_{\{s_\ell^L = \alpha/2\}}$ and $f_\ell^U = f_\ell \mathbf{1}_{\{s_\ell^U = \alpha/2\}}$. It is not hard to verify that $s_\ell^L + s_\ell^U = s_\ell$ and $f_\ell^L + f_\ell^U = f_\ell$, for $\forall \ell$ if $f_\ell \leq N/2$. We further define $X^L = \sum_{\ell=1}^N \alpha/2 \cdot \mathbf{1}_{\{f^L_{\sigma^{-1}(\ell)} \geq \ell\}}$ and $X^U = \sum_{\ell=1}^N \alpha/2 \cdot \mathbf{1}_{\{f^U_{\sigma^{-1}(\ell)} \geq \ell\}}$. Finally, we define $X^d = \sum_{\ell=1}^N s_\ell \mathbf{1}_{\{f_\ell = N\}}$. X^d is the total arrival rate from the (high-rate) VOQs that have stripe size N, which is a constant because how much traffic any of these VOQs sends to the queue is not affected by which primary intermediate port σ maps the VOQ to. It is not hard to verify that $X = X^d + X^U + X^L$.

By the Cauchy-Schwartz inequality, we have

$$\begin{aligned}\mathbb{E}[\exp(\theta X(\vec{r}))] &= \exp(\theta X^d(\vec{r}))\mathbb{E}[\exp(\theta X^U(\vec{r}))\exp(\theta X^L(\vec{r}))] \\ &\leq \exp(\theta X^d(\vec{r}))\left(\mathbb{E}[\exp(2\theta X^L(\vec{r}))]\right)^{1/2} \\ &\quad \cdot \left(\mathbb{E}[\exp(2\theta X^U(\vec{r}))]\right)^{1/2}. \end{aligned} \tag{17}$$

Let $p_\ell^L = \mathbb{P}(f^L_{\sigma^{-1}(\ell)} \geq \ell)$. We now upper bound the MGF of X^L as follows:

$$\begin{aligned}
\mathbb{E}[\exp(2\theta X^L)] &= \mathbb{E}\left[\exp\left(2\theta \cdot \alpha/2 \cdot \sum_{\ell=1}^{N} \mathbf{1}_{\{f^L_{\sigma^{-1}(\ell)} \geq \ell\}}\right)\right] \\
&= \mathbb{E}\left[\prod_{\ell=1}^{N} \exp\left(\theta\alpha \mathbf{1}_{\{f^L_{\sigma^{-1}(\ell)} \geq \ell\}}\right)\right] \\
&\leq \prod_{\ell=1}^{N} \mathbb{E}\left[\exp\left(\theta\alpha \mathbf{1}_{\{f^L_{\sigma^{-1}(\ell)} \geq \ell\}}\right)\right] \\
&= \prod_{\ell=1}^{N/2} \mathbb{E}\left[\exp\left(\theta\alpha \mathbf{1}_{\{f^L_{\sigma^{-1}(\ell)} \geq \ell\}}\right)\right] \\
&\leq \prod_{\ell=1}^{N/2} h(p^*(\theta\alpha), \theta\alpha) \exp(\theta\alpha p_\ell^L) \\
&= (h(p^*(\theta\alpha), \theta\alpha))^{N/2} \prod_{\ell=1}^{N/2} \exp(\theta\alpha p_\ell^L). \quad (18)
\end{aligned}$$

The first inequality holds due to Lemma 1 and the following two facts. First, $\{f^L_{\sigma^{-1}(1)}, f^L_{\sigma^{-1}(2)}, \cdots, f^L_{\sigma^{-1}(N)}\}$, as a uniform random permutation of $\{f_1^L, f_2^L, \cdots, f_N^L\}$, are negatively associated according to Lemma 2. Second, $\exp(\theta\alpha \mathbf{1}_{\{x \geq \ell\}})$ is a nondecreasing function of x for any given ℓ when $\theta > 0$. The third equality holds because with the way we define f^L above, $f^L_{\sigma^{-1}(\ell)} \leq N/2$ for any ℓ. The last inequality holds because each term in the product on the left-hand side, $\mathbb{E}[\exp(\theta\alpha \mathbf{1}_{\{f^L_{\sigma^{-1}(\ell)} \geq \ell\}})]$, is upper bounded by the corresponding product term on the RHS, $h(p^*(\theta\alpha), \theta\alpha)\exp(\theta\alpha p_\ell^L)$. It is not hard to verify because each $\mathbb{E}[\exp(\theta\alpha \mathbf{1}_{\{f^L_{\sigma^{-1}(\ell)} \geq \ell\}})]$ is the MGF of a Bernoulli random variable scaled by a constant factor $\theta\alpha$, and the function h reaches its maximum at p^* as defined in Theorem 2.

Letting $p_\ell^U = \mathbb{P}(f^U_{\sigma^{-1}(\ell)} \geq \ell)$, we can similarly bound $\mathbb{E}[\exp(2\theta X^U)]$ as follows:

$$\mathbb{E}[\exp(2\theta X^U)] \leq (h(p^*(\theta\alpha), \theta\alpha))^{N/2} \prod_{\ell=1}^{N/2} \exp(\theta\alpha p_\ell^U). \quad (19)$$

Combining (17), (18), and (19), we obtain

$$\begin{aligned}
\mathbb{E}[\exp(\theta X)] \leq & (h(p^*(\theta\alpha), \theta\alpha))^{N/2} \\
& \exp\left(\theta(X^d + \frac{\alpha}{2}\sum_{\ell=1}^{N/2}(p_\ell^L + p_\ell^U))\right) \\
= & (h(p^*(\theta\alpha), \theta\alpha))^{N/2} \exp(\theta\rho/N).
\end{aligned}$$

The final equality holds since $\rho/N = \mathbb{E}[X] = \mathbb{E}[X^d + X^L + X^U] = X^d + \frac{\alpha}{2}\sum_{\ell=1}^{N/2}(p_\ell^L + p_\ell^U))$. This concludes the proof of the theorem.

6. SIMULATION

In this section, we present the simulation results of our switching algorithm and other existing switching algorithms under different traffic scenarios. The switching algorithms studied in this section include the baseline load-balanced switch [2], the uniform frame spreading (UFS) switch [11], the full-ordered frame first (FOFF) switch [11], and the padded frame (PF) switch [9]. The baseline load-balanced switch does not guarantee packet ordering, but it provides the lower bound of the average delay that a load-balanced switch can achieve. UFS, FOFF, and PF are known to provide reasonably good performance and all of them guarantee packet ordering.

In our simulation experiments, we assume a Bernoulli arrival to each input port, i.e. in each time slot, there is a packet arrival with probability ρ. The ρ parameter will be varied to study the performance of the switches under different loads. We also use different ways to determine the output port of each arrival packet. The size of the switch in the simulation study is $N = 32$.

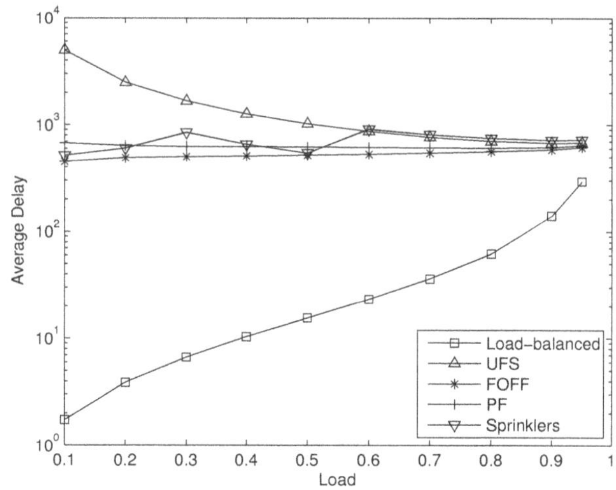

Figure 5: Average delay under uniform traffic

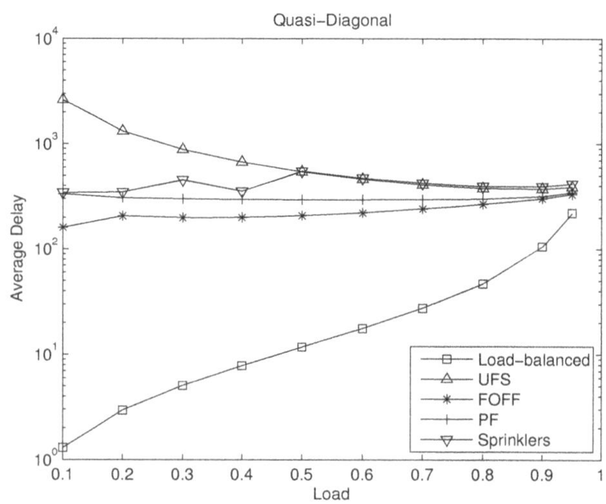

Figure 6: Average delay under diagonal traffic

Our first set of experiments assume uniform distribution of the destination port for the arrival packets, i.e. a new packet goes to output j with probability $\frac{1}{N}$. The simulation results are as shown in Fig. 5. The second set of experiments assume a diagonal distribution. A new packet arriving at input port i goes to output $j = i$ with probability $\frac{1}{2}$, and goes to any other output port with probability $\frac{1}{2(N-1)}$. The results are as shown in Fig. 6.

Our first observation of the comparison is that, under both the uniform and the diagonal traffic patterns, compared to UFS, our switch significantly reduces the average delay when the traffic load is low. This is understandable because the switch does not need to wait for additional packet to form a full frame. Secondly, like PF and FOFF, the average delay of our switching algorithm is quite stable under different traffic intensities. This property is quite preferable in practice. Finally, our switch has similar delay performance with PF and FOFF while the implementation of our switch is simpler than the other two switches.

7. RELATED WORKS

This section briefly reviews existing solutions to the packet reordering problem in load-balanced switches, grouped in accordance to their approach.

7.1 Hashing-Based

As discussed in Sec. 1, packets belonging to the same TCP flow can be guaranteed to depart from their output port in order if they are forced to go through the same intermediate port. The selection of intermediate port can be easily achieved by hashing on the packet header to obtain a value from 1 to N. Despite its simplicity, the main drawback of this TCP hashing approach is that stability cannot be guaranteed [11].

7.2 Aggregation-Based

An alternative class of algorithms to hashing is based on aggregation of packets into frames. One approach called Uniform Frame Spreading (UFS) [11] prevents reordering by requiring that each input first accumulates a full-frame of N packets, all going to the same output, before uniformly spreading the N packets to the N intermediate ports. Packets are accumulated in separate virtual output queues (VOQs) at each input for storing packets in accordance to their output. When a full-frame is available, the N packets are spread by placing one packet at each of the N intermediate ports. This ensures that the lengths of the queues of packets destined to the same output are the same at every intermediate port, which ensures every packet going to the same output experiences the same queuing delay independent of the path that it takes from input to output. Although it has been shown in [11] that UFS achieves 100% throughput for any admissible traffic pattern, the main drawback of UFS is that it suffers from long delays, $O(N^3)$ delay in the worst-case, due to the need to wait for a full-frame before transmission. The performance of UFS is particularly bad at light loads because slow packet arrivals lead to much longer accumulation times.

An alternative aggregation-based algorithm that avoids the need to wait for a full-frame is called Full Ordered Frames First (FOFF) [11]. As with UFS, FOFF maintains VOQs at each input. Whenever possible, FOFF will serve full-frames first. When there is no full-frame available, FOFF will serve the other queues in a round-robin manner. However, when incomplete frames are served, packets can arrive at the output out of order. It has been shown in [11] that the amount of reordering is always bounded by $O(N^2)$ with FOFF. Therefore, FOFF adds a reordering buffer of size $O(N^2)$ at each output to ensure that packets depart in order. It has been shown in [11] that FOFF achieves 100% throughput for any admissible traffic pattern, but the added reordering buffers lead to an $O(N^2)$ in packet delays.

Another aggregation-based algorithm called Padded Frames (PF) [9] was proposed to avoid the need to accumulate full-frames. Like FOFF, whenever possible, FOFF will serve full-frames first. When no full-frame is available, PF will search among its VOQ at each input to find the longest one. If the length of the longest queue exceeds some threshold T, PF will pad the frame with fake packets to create a full-frame. This full-frame of packets, including the fake packets, are uniformly spread across the N intermediate ports, just like UFS. It has been shown in [9] that PF achieves 100% throughput for any admissible traffic pattern, but its worst-case delay bound is still $O(N^3)$.

7.3 Matching-Based

Finally, packet ordering can be guaranteed in load-balanced switches via another approach called a Concurrent Matching Switch (CMS) [13]. Like hashing-based and aggregation-based load-balanced switch designs, CMS is also a fully distributed solution. However, instead of bounding the amount of packet reordering through the switch, or requiring packet aggregation, a CMS enforces packet ordering throughout the switch by using a fully distributed load-balanced scheduling approach. Instead of load-balancing packets, a CMS load-balances request tokens among intermediate ports, where each intermediate port concurrently solves a local matching problem based only on its local token count. Then, each intermediate port independently selects a VOQ from each input to serve, such that the packets selected can traverse the two load-balanced switch stages without conflicts. Packets from selected VOQs depart in order from the inputs, through the intermediate ports, and finally through the outputs. Each intermediate port has N time slots to perform each matching, so the complexity of existing matching algorithms can be amortized by a factor of N.

8. CONCLUSIONS

In this paper, we proposed Sprinklers, a simple load-balanced switch architecture based on the combination of randomization and variable-size striping. Sprinklers has comparable implementation cost and performance as the baseline load-balanced switch, but yet can guarantee packet ordering. We rigorously proved using worst-case large deviation techniques that Sprinklers can achieve near-perfect load-balancing under arbitrary admissible traffic. Finally, we believe that this work will serve as a catalyst to a rich family of solutions based on the simple principles of randomization and variable-size striping.

9. ACKNOWLEDGMENTS

This project is supported in part by an NSF INSPIRE project (1248117) and a collaborative NSF grant that includes awards CNS-1423182 and CNS-1422286.

10. REFERENCES

[1] S. P. Boyd and L. Vandenberghe. *Convex optimization.* Cambridge university press, 2004.

[2] C.-S. Chang, D.-S. Lee, and Y.-S. Jou. Load balanced birkhoff–von neumann switches, part i: one-stage

buffering. *Computer Communications*, 25(6):611–622, 2002.

[3] C.-S. Chang, D.-S. Lee, and C.-M. Lien. Load balanced birkhoff–von neumann switches, part ii: multi-stage buffering. *Computer Communications*, 25(6):623–634, 2002.

[4] C. J. Colbourn. *CRC handbook of combinatorial designs*. CRC press, 1996.

[5] J. Dai and B. Prabhakar. The throughput of data switches with and without speedup. In *INFOCOM 2000. Nineteenth Annual Joint Conference of the IEEE Computer and Communications Societies. Proceedings. IEEE*, volume 2, pages 556–564. IEEE, 2000.

[6] A. L. Drizen. Generating uniformly distributed random 2-designs with block size 3. *Journal of Combinatorial Designs*, 20(8):368–380, 2012.

[7] R. Durstenfeld. Algorithm 235: random permutation. *Communications of the ACM*, 7(7):420, 1964.

[8] M. T. Jacobson and P. Matthews. Generating uniformly distributed random latin squares. *Journal of Combinatorial Designs*, 4(6):405–437, 1996.

[9] J. J. Jaramillo, F. Milan, and R. Srikant. Padded frames: a novel algorithm for stable scheduling in load-balanced switches. *Networking, IEEE/ACM Transactions on Networking*, 16(5):1212–1225, 2008.

[10] K. Joag-Dev and F. Proschan. Negative association of random variables with applications. *The Annals of Statistics*, 11(1):286–295, 1983.

[11] I. Keslassy. *The load-balanced router*. PhD thesis, Stanford University, 2004.

[12] L. Kleinrock. Queueing systems. volume 1: Theory. 1975.

[13] B. Lin and I. Keslassy. The concurrent matching switch architecture. *Networking, IEEE/ACM Transactions on*, 18(4):1330–1343, 2010.

APPENDIX

A. PROOF OF THEOREM 1

Let r_ℓ be the arrival rate of the VOQ that selects intermediate port ℓ as primary port. The corresponding stripe size and load-per-share of r_ℓ is given by f_ℓ and s_ℓ. Given the vector $\vec{r} = (r_1, \cdots, r_N)$, the arrival rate the queue (at input port 1, serving packets going to intermediate port 1) receives is $X(\vec{r}) = \sum_{\ell=1}^{N} s_\ell \mathbf{1}_{\{f_\ell \geq \ell\}}$. We prove Theorem 1 by studying the following problem.

$$\min_r : \sum_{\ell=1}^{N} r_\ell \qquad (20)$$
$$s.t. \sum_{\ell=1}^{N} s_\ell \mathbf{1}_{\{f_\ell \geq \ell\}} \geq 1/N$$

LEMMA 4. *Suppose $r^* = (r_1^*, \cdots, r_N^*)$ is an optimal solution to Problem (20). Then $f_\ell^* = 2^{\lceil \log_2 \ell \rceil}$ if $r_\ell^* > 0$, for $\ell = 1, \cdots, N$.*

PROOF. We prove the lemma by contradiction.

1. Suppose there is $r_{\ell_0}^* > 0$ and $f_{\ell_0} < 2^{\lceil \log_2 \ell_0 \rceil}$, then $r_{\ell_0}^*$ does not contribute any arrival rate to the queue. Thus, we can reduce $r_{\ell_0}^*$ to zero without changing the total arrival rate to the queue. This contradicts the assumption that r^* is an optimal solution to Problem (20).
2. Suppose there is $r_{\ell_0}^* > 0$ and $f_{\ell_0}^* > 2^{\lceil \log_2 \ell_0 \rceil}$. According to stripe size rule (1), we know $s_{\ell_0}^* > 1/(2N^2)$.
   (a) If $s_{\ell_0}^* \leq 1/N^2$, we construct solution $r' = r^*$ except we set $r'_{\ell_0} = 2^{\lceil \log_2 \ell_0 \rceil}/N^2$. $f_{\ell_0}^* > 2^{\lceil \log_2 \ell_0 \rceil}$ implies $f_{\ell_0}^* \geq 2 \times 2^{\lceil \log_2 \ell_0 \rceil}$. Since $s_{\ell_0}^* > 1/(2N^2)$, we have that $r'_{\ell_0} < r_{\ell_0}^*$. It is easy to see that $X(r') > X(r^*)$, thus r' is also a feasible solution and has smaller total arrival rate than r^*. This contradicts the assumption that r^* is an optimal solution.
   (b) If $s_{\ell_0}^* > 1/N^2$, implying $f_{\ell_0}^* = N$, we suppose $r_{\ell_0}^* = 1/N + N\varepsilon$. Since $N = f_{\ell_0}^* > 2^{\lceil \log_2 \ell_0 \rceil}$, we have $\ell_0 \leq N/2$. Construct $r' = r^*$ except set $r'_{\ell_0} = 2^{\lceil \log_2 \ell_0 \rceil}/2N^2 + \delta$ and $r'_{N/2+1} = r^* N/2 + 1 + (1/(2N^2) + \varepsilon)N$ where $0 < \delta \ll \varepsilon$. Then $X(r') = X(r^*) + \delta/2^{\lceil \log_2 \ell_0 \rceil} > X(r^*)$ and the total arrival rate of r' is smaller than that of r^*. This contradicts the assumption that r^* is an optimal solution.

To conclude, we establish the property in the lemma. □

With the stripe size property in Lemma 4, if r^* is an optimal solution to Problem (20), then all r_1^* goes to the queue, 1/2 of r_2^* goes to the queue, 1/4 of r_3^* and r_4^* goes to the queue, and so on. To minimize the total arrival rate while have $X(r^*) \geq 1/N$, one should fill up r_ℓ^* that is closer to the queue first. Thus, $r_1^* = 1/N^2, r_2^* = 2/N^2, \cdots, r_{N/4+1}^* = \cdots = r_{N/2}^* = N/2 \cdot 1/N^2$. From these VOQs, the queue receives total arrival rate $N/2 \cdot 1/N^2 = 1/(2N)$. To achieve $X(r^*) = 1/N$, we set $r_{N/2+1}^* = N \cdot 1/(2N) = 1/2$ and all other $r_\ell^* = 0$. This optimal r^* results in total arrival rate $(1 + 2 + 4 + \cdots + N/4 \cdot N/2)/N^2 + 1/2 = 2/3 + 1/(3N^2)$.

Trees in the List: Accelerating List-based Packet Classification Through Controlled Rule Set Expansion

Sven Hager　　Stefan Selent　　Björn Scheuermann

Computer Engineering Group
Humboldt University of Berlin, Germany
{hagersve,scheuermann}@informatik.hu-berlin.de, stefan.selent@hu-berlin.de

ABSTRACT

Network packet classification is performed by a wide variety of network devices, like routers or firewalls. Accordingly, researchers have put great efforts in the development of fast packet classification algorithms. However, despite the fact that such approaches have been around for over a decade, most classification systems used in practice still rely on the slow linear search approach. In this work, we propose a methodology that enables linear search-based systems with jump semantics to take advantage of the superior matching performance of decision tree algorithms, without the need to touch the underlying system implementation. By performing source-to-source transformations on packet classification rule sets, we encode decision trees inside of the modified rule sets in order to guide and tweak the originally linear matching process. We implement this in a proof-of-concept tool which transforms Linux iptables firewall rule sets. Our evaluation demonstrates that throughput performance boosts of one order of magnitude and more are possible—without changing the semantics of the rule set, and without any modifications to the matching engine.

Categories and Subject Descriptors

C.2.0 [**Computer-Communication Networks**]: General—*security and protection*; C.2.3 [**Computer-Communication Networks**]: Network Operations—*network management*

General Terms

Algorithms, Performance, Security

Keywords

Packet classification; Rule set modification

1. INTRODUCTION

Network packet classification is a fundamental task that is performed by a multitude of networking devices, including, for instance, routers and firewalls. By matching information about network packets against a set of rules, traffic classes can be distinguished. This forms a key building block of important services such as firewalling, routing, QoS provisioning or traffic shaping.

However, it is well-known that packet classification at line speed in high-speed networks is notoriously difficult, because every single packet has to be matched against a potentially large number of rules [9]. Thus, packet processing devices tend to form performance bottlenecks. In fact, this major problem has attracted many researchers in the last two decades [5,6,8,13,19,22,24,25].

Yet, while many innovative and efficient algorithms were proposed, they have seldom been practically used—and if, this has mostly happened in high-end devices. The vast majority of devices performing complex packet processing in practice, though, are low-end, low-cost, software-based systems. Nevertheless, they are often used in performance-critical locations. Prominent examples are the widely used Linux netfilter/iptables subsystem [2], pf/pfctl in OpenBSD [3], FreeBSD's ipfw [1], and the OpenFlow reference switch [17].

These practically used packet classification systems are very rich in features and thus very complex. Their matching algorithms, though, are mostly trivial: they are most often based on basic linear search, scanning through the rule set one-by-one for each packet. In contrast, advanced classification algorithms barely support anything but stateless packet classification on certain header fields; they do this fast, but by itself it is not enough for what today's devices usually require. Changing the complex existing implementations at their heart to support more efficient matching is a huge undertaking—and apparently has not led to much over the past decade.[1] Moreover, there exists a huge basis of deployed network devices such as routers, NAT gateways, firewall appliances etc., where existing classification engines are deeply embedded. So, even if an implementation became available at some time in the future, a huge deployed basis of existing devices would not be able to benefit soon.

For these reasons, we take a somewhat different and indeed very pragmatic approach in this paper: we ask the question how we can boost the performance of linear-search classification engines *without the need to modify the implementations of the underlying matching algorithm.* We show that this is possible by building upon the jump ability that is present in many such classification engines.

We developed a proof-of-concept implementation called *HiTables*, which is publicly available at [10]. HiTables performs source-to-source transformations on Linux iptables rule sets without changing their semantics. It starts from the well-known HiCuts packet classification algorithm [8], but applies it in a very unconventional

[1] There have been projects with this aim, the most prominent one likely being nf-HiPAC (www.hipac.org) for Linux netfilter, but they have been abandoned long ago: nf-HiPAC development has ceased in 2005, and it is not compatible with today's kernels.

CoNEXT'14, December 2–5, 2014, Sydney, Australia.
Copyright 2014 ACM 978-1-4503-3279-8/14/12 ...$15.00.
http://dx.doi.org/10.1145/2674005.2675005.

way—not implementing it in the matching engine, but instead resembling it in the rule set structure. In essence, by re-arranging the rules and inserting jump rules with appropriate matching criteria, the linear search of the processing engine is tweaked into a search tree. In doing so, HiTables supports the full breadth of iptables features, because rules that are not amenable to re-structuring are transparently embedded into the transformed rule set.

In contrast to existing approaches in the domain of static rule set transformation [14–16], which are based on reducing the number of rules, we take the opposite approach and enlarge the rule set size during the transformation process. Nevertheless, our measurement results demonstrate that performance gains of more than one order of magnitude in terms of throughput are achievable, because the jump structure encoded into the rule set during HiTables processing leads to rule sets where only a small subset of the rules is actually used for each individual packet.

The remainder of this paper is structured as follows: Section 2 formally introduces the packet classification problem. Next, Section 3 describes related work in the field of packet classification. Section 4 explains the HiCuts algorithm, a major building block of the presented work. Subsequently, Section 5 presents in detail our proposed rule set transformation methodology, which is evaluated in Section 6. Finally, the paper is concluded by Section 7.

2. PACKET CLASSIFICATION

To pave the ground for our discussions throughout the rest of the paper, we first briefly recapitulate the standard terminology and notation of stateless packet classification as used here. Following [9], the problem can be formally defined as follows: Let $S_1,\dots,S_k$ be sets of non-negative integers representing the possible value ranges of packet header fields $1,\dots,k$, and let Act be a set of *actions*. Given a list of N rules (which is often referred to as the *classifier* or *rule set*)

$$C = \langle R_1,\dots,R_N \rangle$$

and a tuple of k non-negative integers (the packet header)

$$H = \langle h_1 \in S_1,\dots,h_k \in S_k \rangle,$$

find the smallest $i \in \{1,\dots,N\}$ such that H *matches* rule R_i. This assumes that rules with a smaller index (higher up in the list) have a higher priority if multiple rules apply to a packet. A rule R_i is defined by value ranges $D_{j,i}$ for each considered header field j and an associated action A_i:

$$R_i = \langle D_{1,i} \subseteq S_1,\dots,D_{k,i} \subseteq S_k, A_i \in Act \rangle.$$

H is said to match R_i if and only if all header fields lie within the respective value ranges, that is

$$\forall j \in \{1,\dots,k\} : h_j \in D_{j,i}.$$

According to previous works [6, 12, 13, 19, 21], it will be assumed for the rest of the paper that the field domains $D_{j,i}$ are (integer) intervals $[a,b]$. This holds for many practical applications, as firewall rules typically perform checks on IP subnets, port ranges, or single values such as protocol numbers, which can all be regarded as intervals. Moreover, any rule with checks on non-consecutive sets of integers can be transformed into a sequence of rules that consist only of interval-based checks. Typical actions include DROP or ACCEPT, meaning that the packet should either be rejected or accepted. Other actions are of course well conceivable (and exist in real packet classification systems).

Note that there exists a connection between the packet classification problem and computational geometry [9]: consider each rule R_i as a k-dimensional box $B(R_i) = D_{1,i} \times \cdots \times D_{k,i}$ within a k-dimensional universe $U = S_1 \times \cdots \times S_k$. Accordingly, a packet header H can be represented by a point $P(H)$ in U. Hence, finding the first matching rule R^* for H in the rule set is equivalent to locating the most highly prioritized box $B(R^*)$ containing $P(H)$.

This observation is important for two reasons: first, it served as inspiration for some of the most relevant classification algorithms. Second, it can be used to show that every algorithm that solves the packet classification problem for arbitrary k in $\mathcal{O}(\log N)$ time takes at least $\mathcal{O}(N^k)$ space, or needs at least $\mathcal{O}(\log^{k-1} N)$ time if it uses linear space [5, 9].

3. RELATED WORK

Packet classification has been the subject of intensive research in the last two decades and motivated a plethora of different approaches. Roughly, these approaches can be categorized into two partially overlapping domains: *rule set transformation* and *matching algorithms*.

3.1 Rule Set Transformation

One technique to improve the performance of packet classification engines is to analyze the characteristics of a specified rule set C_1 in order to compute another rule set C_2 that is equivalent to C_1, but hopefully finds matching rules faster. There exist online and offline variants of such rule set modification schemes. Online rule set modification observes the matching behavior at runtime, and continuously adjusts the data structures such that highly frequented rules can be found more quickly [4, 14].

Offline rule set modification typically aims to reduce the number of rules. This can happen either by detecting and removing redundant rules [15], or by decomposing, reordering, and merging rules [16]. Hence, offline rule set modification can be understood as a preprocessing step.

While the methodology proposed in this paper also performs offline preprocessing, it takes the opposite approach to existing techniques: instead of reducing the size of the rule set, we enlarge it in a controlled way in order to improve the matching performance.

3.2 Matching Algorithms

Classification algorithms which perform better than basic linear search build upon more advanced data structures, such as tries [5], hash maps [21], bit vectors [6, 13], or decision trees [8, 19, 24]. These data structures are precomputed from a given rule set and can be queried much faster than a linear list. However, they also require larger amounts of memory. Two particularly prominent classes of such algorithms are decomposition-based and decision tree-based approaches.

Decomposition-based approaches—like the Bit Vector [6, 13] or Crossproducting schemes [22]—reduce the k-dimensional search problem to k one-dimensional lookups, one for each relevant header field. The lookups can be performed efficiently and are amenable to parallelization. Subsequently, the one-dimensional outcomes are combined in order to obtain an overall match result.

Decision tree algorithms are inspired by the above discussed geometric view of packet classification [8, 19, 24]. During preprocessing, the universe U is decomposed into several areas which correspond to nodes in a tree structure. Subsequently, incoming packet headers are classified by traversing the decision tree. Prominent representative algorithms are HiCuts [8], HyperCuts [19], and EffiCuts [24].

Because the approach taken in this work is based on HiCuts and uses the algorithm in an unorthodox way, Section 4 will repeat the necessary essentials of HiCuts.

Rule	X range	Y range
1	[2,5]	[10,17]
2	[9,11]	[12,17]
3	[14,16]	[15,17]
4	[1,5]	[1,5]
5	[7,16]	[2,6]
6	[14,17]	[11,14]
7	[6,8]	[4,10]

(a) Example rule set.

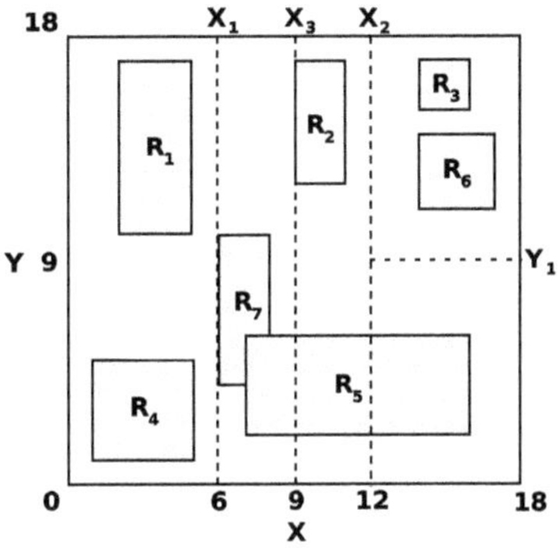

(b) Geometric view.

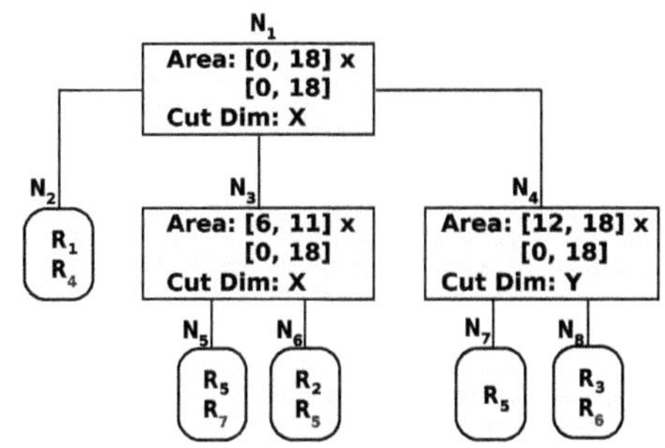

(c) Decision tree.

Figure 1: HiCuts example.

3.3 Practically Used Systems

Despite the existence of advanced matching algorithms like those described in the previous section, most practically used packet filters like iptables [2], pf [3], or ipfw [1] still perform a basic linear search in order to classify incoming network packets. Nevertheless, some of these systems provide a limited amount of optimizations. For instance, OpenBSD's pf offers a basic redundancy removal when loading rules. In addition, pf computes a database of so called *skip-steps*, which are used to skip rules in the list if they cannot match due to a failed check in a previous rule [11]. However, in order to be used efficiently, this technique typically requires a manual reordering of rules by the system administrator. FreeBSD's ipfw system provides the possibility to perform trie-based lookups on single fields in a rule. While this can surely speed up classification performance in specific scenarios, as for instance described in [7], it may be difficult to represent a large and complex rule set efficiently using this technique.

4. THE HICUTS ALGORITHM

The HiCuts algorithm was proposed by Gupta and McKeown in 1999 [8]. It is one of the most well-known packet classification approaches and has inspired many successive works that improved the original approach in matching performance, memory requirements, or preprocessing time [18, 19, 24]. However, the fundamental idea behind HiCuts persisted throughout these works and is sketched in this section.

In order to perform packet classification using HiCuts, a decision tree T is built from the rule set in a preprocessing step. This is done by recursively partitioning the universe U of all possible packet headers, which represents the root of T, hierarchically into nested smaller areas. These subareas correspond to the nodes in T, the tree resembles the nested structure of the areas. For an area A, the respective node in T will be denoted by $N(A)$ in the following.

The hierarchical area subdivision is done through so-called *cuts*. In one subdivision step, $l-1$ cuts ($l \geq 2$) are applied along one dimension (i. e., one header field). They partition an area A into l smaller areas $A_1, \dots, A_l$, resulting in l child nodes $N(A_1), \dots, N(A_l)$. Pointers to the newly created nodes $N(A_1), \dots, N(A_l)$ are stored in $N(A)$. Each of the newly created nodes $N(A_i)$ stores information about the area A_i as well as a pointer to every rule R_j that intersects with A_i. If the number of intersecting rules for a node $N(A_i)$ exceeds a predefined threshold called *binth*, then $N(A_i)$ is partitioned recursively (often with respect to a different header field). Otherwise, $N(A_i)$ represents a leaf in T. Hence, the binth parameter influences both the height of the generated tree as well as the time it takes to build the tree, because smaller binth values typically increase the number of cutting steps during tree construction.

In HiCuts, the partitioning cuts for each node are performed equidistantly along one dimension. The number l of cuts as well as the partitioning dimension are determined individually for each subdivision step by certain heuristics. Tweaks of these parameters and heuristics are a common theme of many HiCuts modifications and enhancements.

In the example shown in Figure 1, the rule set in Figure 1a is transformed into a decision tree depicted by Figure 1c, using a binth value of two. Figure 1b shows the geometric representation of the rules as labeled rectangles. It also shows the cuts that are performed, here indicated by dotted lines. First, the root node N_1 covering the area $[0,18] \times [0,18]$ is cut two times at points X_1 and X_2 along dimension X, which creates the child nodes N_2, N_3, and N_4, covering the areas $[0,5] \times [0,18]$, $[6,11] \times [0,18]$, $[12,18] \times [0,18]$, respectively. The area covered by node N_2 already intersects with only two rules R_1 and R_4, so it becomes a leaf. In contrast, the nodes N_3 and N_4 intersect with three rules each, so they are cut again at points X_3 and Y_1, respectively. The resulting four areas are covered by nodes N_5 to N_8. These nodes intersect with at most two rules each. Hence, the recursion terminates, and the decision tree is complete.

Note that during tree construction, rules can be duplicated when they are divided by cuts. In the example, rule R_5 was duplicated twice, as it was divided by cuts X_2 and X_3. Hence, nodes N_5, N_6, and N_7 each contain a pointer to R_5, as their areas intersect with the area spanned by R_5.

After the tree has been created, incoming packet headers can be matched against the rule set by traversing the decision tree, beginning at its root. Then, for each regarded node, it is first checked whether the node is a leaf or not. If yes, the rules pointed to by the leaf are searched linearly. This is fast, because the number of rules is limited by the binth parameter. If the node is not a leaf, the index of the child where the search continues must be computed. Because the cuts of each subdivision step are equidistant, this is doable in constant time with basic arithmetic operations. For further details on HiCuts, we refer the reader to [8].

HiCuts can accelerate packet matching significantly and is among the best-performing classification algorithms [5]. However, many common packet classification systems still lack an implementation of a sophisticated matching algorithm like HiCuts and rely on basic linear search. This can heavily reduce the maximum available network throughput, as we will demonstrate in Section 6.

5. JUMP-BASED TREE CONSTRUCTION

Even though HiCuts (and similar non-trivial packet matching algorithms) is not implemented in widespread software-based packet processing systems, we will now show how HiCuts-like matching can still be applied "on top" of existing linear search-based implementations, without changing their matching engines. To this end, we perform a source-to-source transformation on the input rule set using our proof-of-concept tool HiTables.

HiTables builds upon a widespread feature which allows to jump to different points in the rule set depending on intermediate match results. For instance, the likely by far most widespread packet classification engine in practice, Linux netfilter/iptables, includes the JUMP target for this purpose, which can be used to jump to a different so-called rule chain. Similarly, OpenFlow allows for GoTo instructions which are used to redirect the matching process to another flow table [17]. For the remainder of this section, our descriptions remain independent from a specific matching engine, but we assume that such JUMP semantics are supported.

Our proposed methodology consists of three basic steps: (1) parse the input rule set and decompose it into sub-lists that are either applicable for transformation or not, (2) build a decision tree for each sub-list that is marked as transformable, and (3) emit a new rule set that consists of those sub-lists that were marked as non-transformable as well as the decision trees which are encoded within the rule set.

5.1 Parsing and Decomposing the Rule Set

In the first step, each rule's semantics, such as its domain, its action, and its matching behavior, must be made accessible by parsing the input rule set. It can then be determined which of the input rules are amenable to transformation according to our approach. Although all practical real-world packet classification engines are able to discriminate packets based on their header fields, many of them support additional features like deep packet inspection or network connection tracking. For example, a rule could specify that it matches only on those TCP packets whose payload contains the sequence of characters "VIRUS", or that it depends on complex stateful filtering criteria. Rules using such features are present in almost every practically used rule set; however, they typically constitute only a small fraction of the rules, while the majority of rules performs stateless matching.

Decision tree algorithms are based on stateless classification as introduced in Section 2, and are not designed to handle complex matching schemes beyond stateless classification. Nevertheless, our proof-of-concept implementation is able to handle rules with arbitrary criteria: they are transparently taken over into the transformed rule set, while optimizations are performed "around" them, leaving the semantics fully intact. Rules which can be handled by a decision tree, namely those which match on the definition in Section 2, are called *transformable rules* in the following. Figure 2 sketches a rule set that consists of transformable rules as well as non-transformable rules.

5.2 Building the Decision Trees

Next, we construct HiCuts tree structures out of the transformable rules within the rule set. This is done separately for each consecutive sequence of transformable rules, interrupted by the non-transformable rules. In this step, the tree construction, in essence, follows the original HiCuts algorithm. The tree construction parameters, such as the binth parameter and the set of heuristics that guide the local cuts, can be specified when calling HiTables.

However, each decision tree introduces a certain amount of control overhead in the resulting rule set. Therefore, an additional

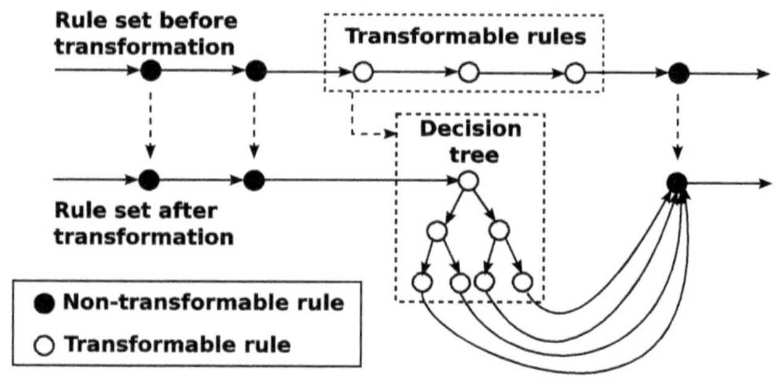

Figure 2: Rule set transformation.

parameter, the *minimum transformation length*, specifies the minimum number of consecutive transformable rules. If a consecutive group of transformable rules is shorter, it is taken over without transformation.

5.3 Emitting the Transformed Rule Set

In the key and final step of the transformation process, a new rule set is generated: the previously built decision trees are encoded in rules that are understandable by the used classification engine. During this step, the central idea of our approach comes into play: by exploiting the JUMP capabilities of the rule set semantics, we can encode the dispatch logic that is executed during the tree traversal in the rule set itself. Traversing the tree is then equivalent to a corresponding series of jumps in the linear list of rules.

Recall that the dispatch decisions at the tree nodes in the original HiCuts approach are performed by determining the respective child node, as discussed in Section 5. As explained above, this can be done in constant time by some basic arithmetic operations. Unfortunately, this necessitates the ability to *perform* such operations. Typical rule set semantics provide only one basic operation: checking whether a packet header matches a rule.

We take this hurdle by generating a sequence of rules that implements a binary search over the domains of the child nodes along the dimension which is used to perform the dispatch. As a simple example, Figure 3 sketches a node N_0 in a decision tree with five child nodes that performs a dispatch in dimension X. It is translated to the list of rules shown in Figure 4. First, a rule R_1 checks if the classification continues at child node N_3. Next, rule R_2 tests if the X packet header is located inside the bounding box of the child nodes N_1 and N_2, and dispatches to the left branch of the binary search. Rule R_3 specifies a wildcard match on the X header, which basically implements an unconditional jump into the right branch: Note that at this point the X header must lie inside of the interval $[5, 19]$, otherwise the HiCuts search would not have reached node N_0. Finally, rules R_4 to R_7 implement the left and right branches of the binary search.

In order to embed a decision tree for a sequence of transformable rules in the modified rule set, we traverse the tree and generate a binary search sequence of rules for each inner node. Once we visit a leaf node of the tree, the original rules pointed to by the leaf node are included in the order according to their priority in the input rule set. Therefore, we preserve the semantics of the original rule set in the modified rule set.

If the classification process enters a decision tree and does not find a matching rule in one of the leafs, the search must continue in the remaining part of the rule set in order to keep the semantics intact. Therefore, we add a last rule in each leaf which we call *exit rule*. If no other rule matches, the exit rule redirects the classification process to the subsequent (non-transformable) rule taken

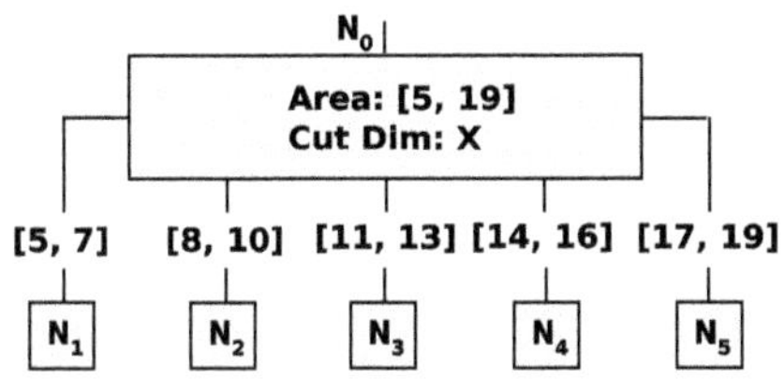

Figure 3: Node dispatch.

```
R1          <X ∈ [11,13], JUMP N3>
R2          <X ∈ [5,10], JUMP LEFT>
R3          <X ∈ *, JUMP RIGHT>
// left branch of binary search
R4 LEFT:    <X ∈ [5,7], JUMP N1>
R5          <X ∈ *, JUMP N2>
// right branch of binary search
R6 RIGHT: <X ∈ [14,16], JUMP N4>
R7          <X ∈ *, JUMP N5>
```

Figure 4: Rules implementing a binary search.

from the original rule set, as sketched in Figure 2. Thereby, the non-transformable rules from the original rule set are embedded. If further sequences of transformable rules follow further down in the original rule set, respective separate decision trees will be emitted.

6. EVALUATION

To demonstrate the feasibility of our approach, we performed measurements with our proof-of-concept implementation HiTables, which was used to transform Linux iptables rule sets. Our evaluation focuses on the achievable gain in classification performance in real and simulated environments with semantically equivalent transformed and non-transformed rule sets. In addition, we investigate the factor by which the size of the rule sets increases during transformation, the computation time required for the transformation itself, and the impact of non-transformable rules on classification performance. In our measurements, we used both self-generated synthetical rule sets as well as publicly available rule sets [20]. We varied the sizes of the self-generated rule sets from 100 to 3500 rules in steps of 200. Each generated rule specifies a random /24 IPv4 source subnet, a fixed destination address, and random source and destination UDP port ranges with a maximum range of 1000. In contrast, the public rule sets (`acl1_`N, `fw1_`N, `ipc1_`N, $N \in \{100, 1K, 5K, 10K\}$, where the suffix N indicates the different rule set size classes) vary widely in the sizes of the specified rule fields and contain a large number of wildcards. Furthermore, while the self-generated rule sets consisted only of transformable rules, the public rule sets also include non-transformable parts.

Path lengths. In our first experiment, we compared the number of rules that must be traversed in order to classify a trace of network packet headers in the original and the corresponding transformed rule sets. We did this by counting the number of traversed rules (the *path length*) for each header field specified by the traces in a simulated environment. Hereby, the size of the used traces was ten times as large as the number of rules in the original rule sets. The traces were generated by the ClassBench benchmark tool [23] in a way that they were uniformly distributed over the original rule sets and covered 100% of the rules. Figure 5a shows the speedup in terms of path length reduction for all public rule sets as well as the average speedup for ten self-generated rule sets of size 100, 1500, and 3500 (labeled `s_100`, `s_1500`, and `s_3500` in the figure), respectively. It can be seen that the performance gain grows with the size of the source rule sets, as the decision trees in the modified rule sets can be traversed significantly faster than the linear list in the source rule sets. In addition, Figure 5d illustrates the distribution of the path lengths for the transformed versions of the self-generated rule sets and the public rule sets `ipc1_1K`, `acl1_5K`, and `fw1_10K` in the same setting. While the transformed versions of the self-generated rule sets can classify every packet header from the used traces with less than 40 rules, the path lengths of the transformed public rule sets are more widely scattered, up to a maximum path length of 1939 rules. The reason for this is that the original public rule sets contain many non-transformable parts, which reduces the achievable gain of the transformation process. However, even in these cases, the path lengths of the transformed rule sets are still very small when compared to the sizes of the input rule sets.

Throughput. Next, we conducted a second experiment in order to evaluate the performance of our approach with real network traffic. Therefore, we configured the self-generated original rule sets on a resource-limited machine (Linux 3.14, 700 MHz ARM CPU, 512 MB RAM) which used the fixed destination address from the rule sets. A second, fast computer (Linux 3.13, 2.9 GHz Intel i7 CPU, 16 GB RAM) was used to send minimum-sized UDP packets for ten seconds as fast as possible, following a large ClassBench header trace corresponding to the currently installed rule set. In this setting, each action in each rule was ACCEPT, along with an ACCEPT default policy (which is applied when no rule matches). This is, of course, no sensible filter, but it is well suited for classification performance measurements: with such a configuration, the number of received UDP packets (determined with the netstat tool) corresponds to the number of packets that have been completely processed by the classification engine. We then computed the average processing time T_{orig} for the received packets. Subsequently, we repeated this process for the HiTables-transformed counterparts of the rule sets, using the same traffic traces as before, in order to compute the average processing time T_{mod} for the modified rule sets. We also determined the average packet processing time T_{IO} in the same setting for an empty rule set, which represents the I/O overhead of the packet processing. Finally, we computed the speedup factors with and without I/O overhead, i. e.,

$$\frac{T_{orig}}{T_{mod}} \quad \text{and} \quad \frac{T_{orig} - T_{IO}}{T_{mod} - T_{IO}}.$$

This benchmark was independently repeated ten times, and the average speedup factors as well as the standard deviations are shown in Figure 5b. It can be seen that the source rule sets can be processed faster for very small rule set sizes, which is due to the control overhead implemented by additional rules in the modified rule sets. However, Figure 5b also reveals that the transformation effort quickly pays off as the rule set size increases.

Non-transformable rules. In our third experiment, we examined the impact of non-transformable rules in the source rule sets on classification performance in the modified rule sets. We used synthetic source rule sets like above, each one consisting of 1000 rules. Then, we substituted an increasing number (zero to ten) of rules at equidistant positions with non-transformable ones. Thereby, we forced HiTables to emit $q+1$ decision trees instead of one when translating a source rule set with q non-transformable rules. We again ran this experiment in the real network setting and computed the same factors as above. As expected, Figure 5c shows that the performance of the transformed rule sets decreases. However, it also reveals that even in this sub-optimal setting, considerable per-

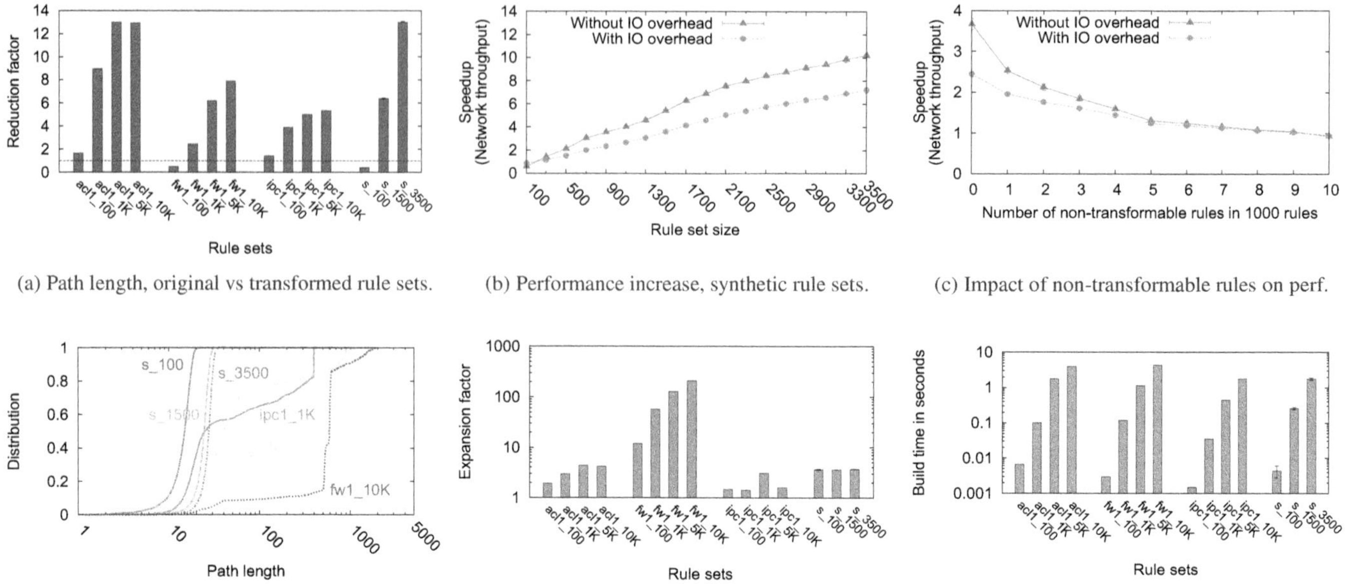

(a) Path length, original vs transformed rule sets.

(b) Performance increase, synthetic rule sets.

(c) Impact of non-transformable rules on perf.

(d) Cumulative distribution on path lengths.

(e) Rule set size increase.

(f) Transformation times.

Figure 5: Measurement results.

formance gains over the simple linear search are achieved if the number of separate decision trees does not become overly large.

Rule set size increase. Figure 5e illustrates the factors by which the transformed rule sets are increased. Again, we display these values for all used public rule sets as well as for the average values for synthetic rule sets of size 100, 1500, and 3500. Figure 5e reveals that the expansion factor does not directly depend on the size of the original rule sets, but instead is heavily influenced by the geometrical sizes and arrangements of the source rules. While the expansion factor of most rule sets is below ten, the transformed version of the `fw1_`*N* rule sets are very large (up to a factor of 208, in the case of `fw1_10K`). In fact, the `fw1_`*N* rule sets specify up to 38% more wildcarded fields in their rules than the other rule sets of the same size, which greatly favors rule duplications during the tree construction process.

Build time. Finally, Figure 5f displays the amount of time it took to compute the modified rule sets on our fast machine, which was in the order of seconds for all public and self-generated rule sets we used in the previous experiments. Hence, our approach is suitable for environments where the filtering rule sets do not change too frequently, as changes to the source rule set require a recomputation of the modified rule set in order to prevent a degeneration of the embedded decision trees. However, during our evaluation we encountered the problem that the transformation process for some very large rule sets (10K or more rules) or rule sets with many large rules (in a geometrical sense) took very long for a given binth parameter and cut heuristic. In such cases, it was often helpful to increase the binth parameter or to change the cut heuristic that guides the tree construction. For example, increasing the binth parameter from 8 to 20 reduced the transformation time for the `fw1_10K` rule set from 14.3 seconds to 4.3 seconds. Another way to mitigate this problem in the long term would be to apply one of HiCuts' successor algorithms, HyperCuts [19] or EffiCuts [24], which use more advanced techniques to reduce rule duplication during the tree construction process.

7. CONCLUSION

In this work we propose a technique to perform static transformations on rule sets of packet classification engines with JUMP semantics in order to increase their matching performance. In contrast to existing offline approaches for rule set optimization [15,16], which are based on reducing the number of rules, we take the opposite approach and enlarge the number of rules by encoding decision tree semantics within the rule sets themselves. That way, we can leverage the superior matching performance of an advanced classification algorithm without the need to change the implementation of the used classification engine. Our evaluation results reveal possible performance gains by over an order of magnitude when transforming rule sets with our proof-of-concept implementation.

Possible future work includes experimentation with more advanced decision tree algorithms like HyperCuts [19] of EffiCuts [24] in order to achieve even better matching performance at a smaller expansion factor.

Acknowledgments

Our sincere thanks go to the CoNEXT 2014 reviewers and, in particular, to Luigi Rizzo for very valuable feedback and discussions. This work was supported by a grant from the German Federal Ministry of Economic Affairs and Energy.

8. REFERENCES

[1] IPFW packet filter. https://www.freebsd.org/doc/en/books/handbook/firewalls-ipfw.html. Last accessed on September 28, 2014.

[2] The netfilter.org project. www.netfilter.org. Last accessed on June 14, 2014.

[3] OpenBSD packet filter. http://www.openbsd.org/faq/pf/. Last accessed on June 14, 2014.

[4] S. Acharya, M. Abliz, B. Mills, T. Znati, J. Wang, Z. Ge, and A. Greenberg. OPTWALL: A hierarchical traffic-aware firewall. In *NDSS '07: The 14th Annual Network and Distributed System Security Symposium*, Feb. 2007.

[5] F. Baboescu, S. Singh, and G. Varghese. Packet classification for core routers: Is there an alternative to CAMs? In *INFOCOM '03: Proceedings of the 22nd Annual Joint Conference of the IEEE Computer and Communications Societies*, pages 53–63, Mar. 2003.

[6] F. Baboescu and G. Varghese. Scalable packet classification. In *SIGCOMM '01: Proceedings of the 2001 Conference on Applications, Technologies, Architectures, and Protocols for Computer Communications*, pages 199–210, Aug. 2001.

[7] M. Carbone and L. Rizzo. An emulation tool for PlanetLab. *Computer Communications, Elsevier*, 34(16):1980–1990, Oct. 2011.

[8] P. Gupta and N. McKeown. Packet classification using hierarchical intelligent cuttings. In *HOTI '99: Proceedings of the 7th Symposium on High Performance Interconnects*, pages 34–41, Aug. 1999.

[9] P. Gupta and N. McKeown. Algorithms for packet classification. *IEEE Network: The Magazine of Global Internetworking*, 15(2):24–32, Mar. 2001.

[10] S. Hager. Hitables source code. https://github.com/shager/hitables.

[11] D. Hartmeier. Design and performance of the OpenBSD stateful packet filter (pf). In *Proceedings of the FREENIX Track: 2002 USENIX Annual Technical Conference*, pages 171–180, Berkeley, CA, USA, June 2002.

[12] K. Kogan, S. Nikolenko, O. Rottenstreich, W. Culhane, and P. Eugster. SAX-PAC (scalable and expressive packet classification). In *SIGCOMM '14: Proceedings of the 2014 Conference on Applications, Technologies, Architectures, and Protocols for Computer Communications*, pages 15–26, Aug. 2014.

[13] T. V. Lakshman and D. Stiliadis. High-speed policy-based packet forwarding using efficient multi-dimensional range matching. In *SIGCOMM '98: Proceedings of the 1998 Conference on Applications, Technologies, Architectures, and Protocols for Computer Communications*, pages 203–214, Aug. 1998.

[14] H. Lam, D. Wang, and H. Chao. A traffic-aware top-n firewall approximation algorithm. In *INFOCOM WKSHPS '11: 2011 IEEE Conference on Computer Communications Workshops*, pages 1036–1041, Apr. 2011.

[15] A. Liu and M. Gouda. Removing redundancy from packet classifiers. In *SIGCOMM '04: Proceedings of the 2004 Conference on Applications, Technologies, Architectures, and Protocols for Computer Communications*, Sept. 2004.

[16] A. Liu, E. Torng, and C. Meiners. Firewall compressor: An algorithm for minimizing firewall policies. In *INFOCOM '08: Proceedings of the 27th Annual Joint Conference of the IEEE Computer and Communications Societies*, pages 176–180, Apr. 2008.

[17] A. Nygren et al. OpenFlow switch specification. Technical report, Open Networking Foundation, Oct. 2013.

[18] Y. Qi, L. Xu, B. Yang, Y. Xue, and J. Li. Packet classification algorithms: From theory to practice. In *INFOCOM '09: Proceedings of the 28th Annual Joint Conference of the IEEE Computer and Communications Societies*, pages 648–656, Apr. 2009.

[19] S. Singh, F. Baboescu, G. Varghese, and J. Wang. Packet classification using multidimensional cutting. In *SIGCOMM '03: Proceedings of the 2003 Conference on Applications, Technologies, Architectures, and Protocols for Computer Communications*, pages 213–224, Aug. 2003.

[20] H. Song. Evaluation of packet classification algorithms. http://www.arl.wustl.edu/~hs1/PClassEval.html. website includes publicly available rulesets, last access: October 3, 2014.

[21] V. Srinivasan, S. Suri, and G. Varghese. Packet classification using tuple space search. In *SIGCOMM '99: Proceedings of the 1999 Conference on Applications, Technologies, Architectures, and Protocols for Computer Communications*, pages 135–146, Aug. 1999.

[22] V. Srinivasan, G. Varghese, S. Suri, and M. Waldvogel. Fast and scalable layer four switching. In *SIGCOMM '98: Proceedings of the 1998 Conference on Applications, Technologies, Architectures, and Protocols for Computer Communications*, Aug. 1998.

[23] D. Taylor and J. Turner. Classbench: a packet classification benchmark. *IEEE/ACM Transactions on Networking*, 15(3), June 2007.

[24] B. Vamanan, G. Voskuilen, and T. N. Vijaykumar. Efficuts: Optimizing packet classification for memory and throughput. In *SIGCOMM '10: Proceedings of the 2010 Conference on Applications, Technologies, Architectures, and Protocols for Computer Communications*, pages 207–218, Aug. 2010.

[25] T. Woo. A modular approach to packet classification: Algorithms and results. In *INFOCOM '00: Proceedings of the 19th Annual Joint Conference of the IEEE Computer and Communications Societies*, pages 1213–1222, Mar. 2000.

Multi-Layer Packet Classification with Graphics Processing Units

Matteo Varvello[†]*, Rafael Laufer[◇], Feixiong Zhang[□], T.V. Lakshman[◇]

[†]Telefonica Research, matteo.varvello@telefonica.com
[◇]Bell Labs, {firstname.lastname}@alcatel-lucent.com
[□]Rutgers University, feixiong@winlab.rutgers.edu

ABSTRACT

The rapid growth of server virtualization has ignited a wide adoption of software-based virtual switches, with significant interest in speeding up their performance. In a similar trend, software-defined networking (SDN), with its strong reliance on rule-based flow classification, has also created renewed interest in multi-dimensional packet classification. However, despite these recent advances, the performance of current software-based packet classifiers is still limited, mostly by the low parallelism of general-purpose CPUs. In this paper, we explore how to accelerate packet classification using the high parallelism and latency-hiding capabilities of graphic processing units (GPUs). We implement GPU-accelerated versions for both linear and tuple search, currently deployed in virtual switches, and also introduce a novel algorithm called *Bloom search*. These algorithms are integrated with high-speed packet I/O to build *GSwitch*, a GPU-accelerated software switch. Our experimental evaluation shows that GSwitch is at least 7x faster than an equally-priced CPU classifier and is able to reach 10 Gbps with minimum-sized packets and a rule set containing 128K OpenFlow entries with 512 different wildcard patterns.

Categories and Subject Descriptors

C.2.1 [**Network Architecture and Designs**]: Network communications; C.2.6 [**Internetworking**]: Routers; D.2.8 [**Software Engineering**]: Metrics—*complexity measures, performance measures*

General Terms

Algorithms, Design

Keywords

Packet classification; Software-defined networking; OpenFlow; Software switch; GPU; CUDA

*Work done while at Bell Labs.

CoNEXT'14, December 2–5, 2014, Sydney, Australia.

http://dx.doi.org/10.1145/2674005.2674990.

1. INTRODUCTION

Recent trends in virtualization are stimulating the wide adoption of *virtual switches*, *i.e.*, software programs that run within the hypervisor to enable the communication among virtual machines. Commercial virtual switches, such as Open vSwitch [1] and Cisco Nexus 1000V [4], are already deployed in datacenters, mostly because of the tight integration they provide with virtualization software suites.

For high performance, virtual switches must sustain rates of at least 10 Gbps without incurring much overhead at the server. This is a major challenge, because it requires not only high-speed packet I/O, but also efficient packet classification algorithms. Recent advances in software-based packet I/O have shown that wire speed is achieved with optimizations in the data path [7, 10, 20]. The same, however, cannot be said about packet classification. In fact, the recent emergence of software defined networking (SDN) and OpenFlow [17], with its large rule tables and long multi-dimensional tuples, have been imposing unforeseen challenges to current packet classifiers [6, 18]. As a result, new directions to accelerate software-based switching are required in order to support the ever-increasing throughput demands.

Due to their high parallelism, graphics processing units (GPUs) have been recently proposed to accelerate several software functions, such as IP lookup [10, 14, 26], pattern matching [3, 13, 25], and packet classification [10, 11]. However, the performance evaluation of recent GPU-based packet classifiers [10, 11] shows that they still cannot sustain high packet I/O rates as the size and dimension of forwarding tables grow, e.g., the case of SDN. Exploiting the full potential of GPUs is particularly challenging because of their unique parallel programming model, which demands in-depth knowledge of the underlying hardware architecture to support high speeds. Consequently, existing software-based packet classification schemes designed for sequential general-purpose CPUs model cannot directly exploit the GPU parallelism.

In this paper, we show that much faster packet classifiers are attainable with a careful design aimed at GPU hardware architectures. In particular, our design incorporates several GPU-specific features, including (1) memory accesses are always coalesced to significantly reduce latency to off-chip memory; (2) on-chip SRAM memory is heavily utilized and shared among threads to speed up rule matching; and (3) all available GPU cores are exploited to their full extent, *i.e.*, 100% occupancy is guaranteed. Using these directives, we introduce highly efficient GPU implementations for three packet classification algorithms: linear and tuple search, currently deployed in virtual switches, and *Bloom search*, an optimization of tuple search that takes advantage of Bloom filters to avoid expensive table lookups. The three proposed algorithms are integrated with high-speed packet I/O to build *GSwitch*, a GPU-accelerated software switch.

GSwitch is evaluated using both synthetic and real rule sets [24]. We provide an experimental evaluation of each packet classification algorithm, considering only its GPU performance at first to fully understand its tradeoffs. The analysis is composed of several GPU microbenchmarks, an in-depth comparison between GPU and CPU performance using OpenCL, and a study on the classification throughput for different rule sets. Experiments with high-speed packet I/O are also performed to evaluate the forwarding throughput and packet latency of GSwitch under different scenarios.

The major outcome of this work is that a single GPU, if exploited correctly, is capable of attaining high enough throughput to shift the performance bottleneck in the data path from packet classification back to packet I/O once again. Additional outcomes of this work are summarized in the following:

- Depending on the algorithm, packet classification in our GPU is up to 7x (linear search), 11x (tuple search), and 12x (Bloom search) faster than an OpenCL implementation in an equally-priced 8-core CPU;
- Bloom search is our fastest and most scalable algorithm, supporting up to 10 Gbps with minimum-sized 64-byte Ethernet frames and a large table with 128K OpenFlow rules and 512 different wildcard patterns;
- Under a real rule set [24], GSwitch is able to forward 64-byte frames at 30 Gbps and a maximum per-packet latency of 500 μs, and achieves higher throughputs with more relaxed delay requirements.

The remainder of this paper is organized as follows. We present the related work in Section 2, and provide a brief overview of the GPU architecture in Section 3. Section 4 describes the design and implementation of the linear, tuple, and Bloom search algorithms for GPU. In Section 5 we introduce GSwitch, a GPU-accelerated software switch with high-speed packet I/O. Section 6 describes our experimental evaluation, whose results are discussed in Section 7. Finally, Section 8 concludes the paper.

2. RELATED WORK

Graphics processing units (GPUs) have been applied to several computation-intensive applications, such as IP lookup [10, 14, 26] and pattern matching [3, 13, 25]. More recently, GPUs have also been adopted to improve the performance of general packet classifiers [10, 11].

Han *et al.* [10] introduce a GPU-accelerated software router, PacketShader, where GPUs are used for packet classification and provide major performance gains. The system focus is mostly on improving packet I/O performance at the operating system level as well as efficiently offloading packet batches to GPU. To classify packets, the authors adopt an implementation of linear search. Performance results show that PacketShader is able to classify incoming packets at 7 Gbps with two GPUs, assuming a rule set of 1M exact matching rules and 1K wildcard matching rules[1].

Comparing our work with [10] is challenging due to the following reasons. First, our GPU has 32 additional cores than the GPU used in [10]. Second, the results in [10] are derived assuming two GPUs working in parallel. Third, it was not possible for the authors of [10] to open source the GPU code of PacketShader. Nevertheless, for the same scenario of 1K wildcard rules, our linear search implementation achieves 20 Gbps, cf. Figure 6(c). Assuming that the bottleneck in [10] is the wildcard matching algorithm, this indicates a 2.8x throughput gain despite we only rely on a single GPU, or 512 cores versus 960 cores. This throughput improvement is due to (1) our careful implementation that fully exploits the GPU parallelism and enforces memory coalescing, and (2) the heavy utilization of fast on-chip SRAM memory for speeding up rule matching.

[1]PacketShader implements the full OpenFlow matching algorithm, *i.e.*, exact matching plus wildcard matching in case of a miss.

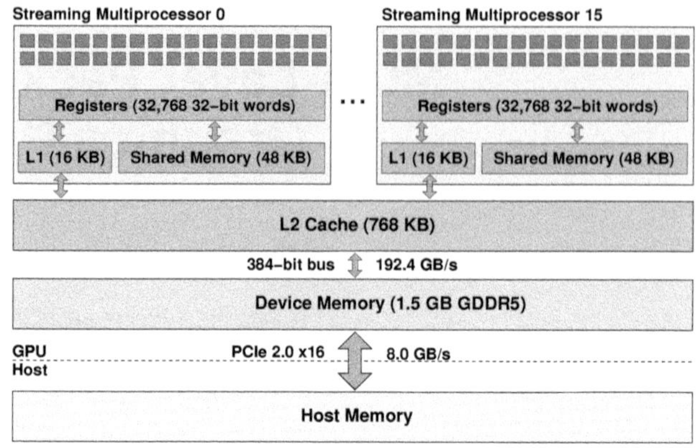

Figure 1: Architecture of the NVIDIA GTX 580 GPU.

Kang *et al.* [11] explore *metaprogramming*, *i.e.*, generating source or executable code dynamically from a more abstract program, to implement linear search in GPUs. Under this premise, rules are embedded in the code as compilation-time constants, which are locally stored in a read-only cache.

Compared to [11], our linear search implementation provides comparable performance figures. In fact their metaprogramming approach is likely to achieve caching of classifiers in SRAM memory, similarly to our design rationale. Nonetheless, linear search is our slowest solution; both tuple and Bloom search are able to classify packets up to 7x faster.

3. GPU BACKGROUND

This section reviews the architecture and operation of a graphics processing unit (GPU) as well as few metrics used to measure its performance.

Figure 1 shows the architecture of the NVIDIA GTX 580 GPU used in this work. It has a total of 16 streaming multiprocessors (SMs), each with 32 stream processors (SPs) running at 1544 MHz. Memory is hierarchically organized with higher positions reflecting faster response times as well as lower storage capacities. At the bottom of the hierarchy, the device memory (1.5 GB) and the L2 cache (768 KB) are shared among the SMs and are off-chip. In contrast, the small L1 cache (16 KB) and the shared memory (48 KB) are on-chip and guarantee low latency and high bandwidth. Finally, at the top of the hierarchy, registers (32K per SM) provide the fastest access speed, but limited storage space.

All threads in the GPU execute the same function, called *kernel*. A kernel execution consists of three steps: (1) copying the input dataset from the host CPU memory to the GPU device memory; (2) kernel execution; and (3) copying the results back from device to host memory. Although significant, the overhead of these data transfers can be amortized by pipelining via concurrent copy and execution [21]. As a result, kernel execution is usually the bottleneck and must be optimized for high performance (cf. Section 4).

The degree of parallelism of a kernel is controlled by two parameters, namely, the number of *blocks* and the number of *threads per block*. Blocks are sets of concurrently executing threads that collaborate with each other using shared memory and barrier synchronization primitives. At run-time, each block is assigned to a SM that first allocates the resources for the block, such as registers and shared memory (both known at compile-time), and then activates it for execution.

During execution, each SM follows the single instruction multiple thread (SIMT) parallel programming model, with all 32 SPs executing the same instruction in lockstep for a *warp* (*i.e.,* a set of 32 threads). Threads in a warp use unique identifiers to access different memory addresses, and thus perform the same task for a large dataset in parallel.

After activating a block for execution, the SM partitions it into 32-thread warps, that are independently scheduled by a dual-warp scheduler. The scheduler selects two warps at a time and issues one instruction from each. The block resources remain allocated in the SM for as long as the block is active, resulting in zero context-switch overhead for the scheduler. If a warp stalls on an instruction fetch, a synchronization barrier, or a data dependency (e.g., memory reads), other eligible warps are immediately scheduled in an attempt to hide latency.

There are several metrics to evaluate the performance of a kernel. We now describe the two most important metrics which motivate our design of packet classification in GPU. A full description of other GPU metrics can be found in [15].

Load efficiency: Cache lines in the NVIDIA GTX 580 GPU have a 128-byte granularity, which incurs a high loading overhead if threads only require a handful of these bytes. However, if all threads in a warp are instructed to read/write memory addresses within the same cache line, then the GPU efficiently maps these reads/writes into a single transaction from device memory. This memory access pattern is called *coalesced*. The load efficiency is a metric to measure the amount of coalesced memory accesses, and it is defined as the ratio between the number of requested bytes and the total number of bytes fetched from device memory.

Occupancy: The occupancy is defined as the fraction of time that the threads in the SMs are actually working, and it is limited by two factors. First, SMs have a hard limit on the number of blocks and threads concurrently executing. As a result, kernels must be carefully dimensioned to respect these limitations. Second, registers and shared memory must be available in the SM for each block before (and during) its execution. Therefore, the required per-block resources should be low to allow more blocks to run in parallel.

In the NVIDIA GTX 580, a maximum of 8 blocks and 48 warps (1536 threads) can be concurrently allocated and executing within each SM. In addition, no block is allowed to have more than 1024 threads. It follows that only a few ⟨blocks per SM, threads per block⟩ configurations are able to achieve 100% occupancy, namely $\langle 8, 192\rangle$, $\langle 6, 256\rangle$, $\langle 4, 384\rangle$, $\langle 3, 512\rangle$, and $\langle 2, 768\rangle$. In addition, each thread must not use more than $\lfloor 32\text{K}/1536 \rfloor = 21$ registers and more than 48 KB/1536 = 32 bytes of shared memory[2] to have all 1536 threads concurrently running.

4. DESIGN AND IMPLEMENTATION

This section introduces the design and implementation of linear, tuple, and Bloom search for GPUs. Before doing so, we briefly summarize the adopted terminology.

A *tuple* is defined as the set of header fields used for packet classification. A *rule* is the ensemble of a value, a mask, an action, and a priority [9]. The rule value specifies the bits required in the header of an incoming packet to have a match, with wildcards allowed. The mask specifies the position of the wildcarded fields within the rule value. The action is the operation to perform on a packet whose tuple matches the corresponding rule. Finally, the priority defines the importance of a rule and it is used to handle the case of overlapping rules, *i.e.,* multiple rules that match the same tuple. We call a collection of rules a *rule set*.

Packet classification consists of identifying the highest-priority rule that matches the tuple of an incoming packet. After classification, the action of the matching rule is then applied to the packet.

4.1 Linear Search

Linear search consists of checking the tuple of an incoming packet against all entries in the rule set. For each rule, the tuple is first masked using the wildcard bits from the rule mask and then compared with the rule value.

Algorithm 1 shows our linear search kernel. As input, it requires the arrays R and T that contain the rules and tuples to be looked up, respectively. The kernel computes the index of the matching rule for each tuple $t \in T$ and stores them in the index array I, which is later used by the CPU to find the proper action for the packet. This design choice of storing only the rule value, mask, and priority in GPU while keeping the rule action in CPU allows us to avoid dealing with variable-sized actions, and to more efficiently exploit the memory space in GPU. The R, T, and I arrays reside in the GPU device memory. Each block also keeps a copy of n rules that are loaded at run-time to the R' array in shared memory to improve the matching speed. In GPU programming, a few variables are available to threads at run-time: blockIdx and threadIdx, corresponding to the block and the thread indexes, respectively, as well as blocks and threads, corresponding to the number of blocks and threads per block, respectively.

The kernel is designed to maximize parallelism by splitting the rule set among the several blocks, such that each block is responsible for checking the incoming tuples only against part of the set. Accordingly, line 1 computes the maximum number of rules per block, respecting the shared memory limit of n rules, and line 2 calculates the offset of the block within the rule set.

Lines 3–24 are the core of linear search. In each iteration, at most n rules are copied to shared memory and then compared to all tuples in T. The while loop in line 3 runs until the current offset exceeds the number of rules $|R|$. Line 4 computes the actual number of rules to copy. Line 5 performs coalesced memory accesses to load the subset of rules to shared memory. The READAOS call is showed in Algorithm 2, where each thread copies a 32-bit word at a time from an array of structures (AoS). Threads with consecutive indexes access consecutive addresses, guaranteeing coalesced memory accesses. The SYNCTHREADS() call in line 6 imposes a synchronization barrier to ensure that all threads in the block have finished copying after this line.

After loading rules to shared memory (lines 5-6), matching is then performed (lines 8–20). Each thread uses its threadIdx (line 7) to read a tuple t from the array T using the READSOA() call showed in Algorithm 3. In this case, the array T is organized as a structure of arrays (SoA) with 32-bit granularity, *i.e.,* the first 32-bit word of each tuple is stored sequentially in memory, then the second word of each tuple, and so on. The SoA format allows each thread to load a unique tuple while still ensuring that memory accesses are coalesced. In lines 12–18, the tuple t is checked against all rules in shared memory. If, after proper masking, t matches a rule with higher priority than any previous rule, then the priority (line 15) and global index (line 18) of this rule are saved. In case of a match,

[2]Shared memory is allocated per block, hence the limit is in practice $32 \times T$ bytes, where T is the number of threads per block.

Algorithm 1: Linear search kernel

Input: rules R, tuples T
Output: rule indexes I for each tuple $t \in T$
Data: rules $R'[n]$ in shared memory

```
1  rulesPerBlock ← MIN(⌈|R|/blocks⌉, n)
2  rulesOffset ← rulesPerBlock × blockIdx
3  while rulesOffset < |R| do
4      rules ← MIN(|R| − rulesOffset, rulesPerBlock)
5      R' ← READAOS(R, rulesOffset, rules)
6      SYNCTHREADS()
7      tid ← threadIdx
8      while tid < |T| do
9          t ←READSOA(T, tid)                    // Get a tuple
10         rIdx ← NIL
11         rPri ← NIL
12         for i ← 0 to rules − 1 do             // Look for a match
13             val ←GETVALUE(R'[i])
14             mask ←GETMASK(R'[i])
15             pri ←GETPRIORITY(R'[i])
16             if (t & mask) = val and pri > rPri then
17                 rPri ← pri
18                 rIdx ← rulesOffset + i
19         if rIdx ≠ NIL then                    // Write to memory
20             ATOMICMAX(I[tid], (rPri ≪ 24) | rIdx)
21         tid ← tid+ threads
22     SYNCTHREADS()
23     rulesOffset ←rulesOffset + rulesPerBlock×blocks
```

Algorithm 2: Read from an array of structs (READAOS)

Input: array A, offset o, entries n
Output: array A' containing entries $A[o, \ldots, o+n-1]$
Data: pointer B to access A as an array of 32-bit words
pointer B' to access A' as an array of 32-bit words

```
size ← WORDSPERENTRY()
tid ← threadIdx
while tid < n × size do
    B'[tid] ← B[o × size + tid]
    tid ← tid+ threads
```

lines 19–20 write the index of the matching rule with highest priority to device memory. In line 19, the ATOMICMAX(u, v) call stores the value of v into u only if v is higher than the value of u. This call is atomic to prevent potential racing conditions across all SMs. The rule priority is an 8-bit integer stored in the most significant bits to ensure that a higher-priority rule has precedence regardless of its index value.

Finally, SYNCTHREADS() is called in line 22 to ensure that all threads have finished with the current rule subset in shared memory before moving on to the next. The rule offset is then increased in line 23 and matching is performed on the next rule subset.

Algorithm 3: Read from a struct of arrays (READSOA)

Input: array A, entry index $eIdx$
Output: entry e containing entry $A[eIdx]$
Data: pointer B to access A as an array of 32-bit words
pointer B' to access e as an array of 32-bit words

```
size ← WORDSPERENTRY()
for i = 0 to size − 1 do
    B'[i] ← B[eIdx + i × |A|]
```

4.2 Tuple Search

Although simple, linear search takes $O(RT)$ time and does not scale well as the number of rules increases. Therefore, we now introduce a GPU-accelerated algorithm for tuple space search [23], which is more efficient for large rule sets. Tuple search is the packet classification algorithm adopted by Open vSwitch [1].

Tuple search uses the notion of a *class* or a set of rules with the same mask, *i.e.,* wildcards in the same header bits. Rules belonging to a class are stored in the same *class table*, which is typically implemented as a hash table for efficient lookup. In this case, the rule value is the key being hashed and the rule, represented by the set ⟨value, action, priority⟩, is stored in the table. Each class has a *class mask* which is the same for all rules. Matching in tuple search consists of, for each class, masking the tuple using the class mask and looking the result up in the class table. The rule with the highest priority among rules of all classes is the final match.

We implement class tables using cuckoo hashing [19], which provides constant lookup time and is provably more efficient than chaining. In cuckoo hashing, the table is composed of s equally-sized subtables, each with d slots. Let $R = \{r_1, r_2, \ldots, r_n\}$, with $n \leq s \times d$, be the set of rules to be inserted into the class table. To insert a rule r_i, the values $h_1(r_i), h_2(r_i), \ldots, h_s(r_i)$ are computed from a set of independent and uniform hash functions $\{h_j \mid j = 1, \ldots, s\}$ and used as indexes in each of the corresponding subtables. If one of these slots is empty, then rule r_i is stored at this slot and the insertion terminates. Otherwise, a subtable q must be selected and the rule r_j, stored at the required slot $h_q(r_i) = h_q(r_j)$, is evicted to make space for r_i. The same procedure is then repeated to reinsert r_j back into the table. If, during this procedure, a given number of tries is reached, then a new set of hash functions is selected and all rules are reinserted. Rehashes, however, are very rare if the tables are well dimensioned. The lookup of a tuple t consists of two steps. First, the class mask is applied to the tuple t, deriving the masked tuple u. Then, the slots $h_1(u), h_2(u), \ldots, h_s(u)$ in each of the corresponding subtables are checked, which is done in $O(s)$ in the worst case.

For hashing, we implement and analyze the GPU computation performance of three non-cryptographic hash functions: universal, MurmurHash3, and SuperFastHash. Due to their simplicity, universal hash functions provide by far the highest computation throughput and are chosen for our kernel. The universal hash functions used are defined as $h_i(x) = [(a_i\, x + b_i) \bmod p] \bmod d$, where p is a large prime and both a_i and b_i are randomly selected integers modulo p with $a_i \neq 0$. The parameters a_i and b_i are loaded to constant memory at the GPU initialization and stored at a read-only cache during the kernel execution for faster computations.

Algorithm 4 shows our tuple search kernel. As input, it requires arrays H, M, and T that contain the cuckoo hash tables, class masks, and tuples to be looked up, respectively. As before, the kernel returns the indexes of the highest priority rule for each tu-

Algorithm 4: Tuple search kernel

Input: cuckoo hash tables H, class masks M, tuples T
Output: rule indexes I for each tuple $t \in T$
Data: cuckoo hash table $H'[s, d]$ in shared memory
class mask M' in shared memory

```
1  H' ← READAOS(H, blockIdx, 1)
2  M' ← READAOS(M, blockIdx, 1)
3  SYNCTHREADS()
4  tid ← threadIdx
5  while tid < |T| do
6      t ←READSOA(T, tid)                  // Get a tuple
7      u ← t & M'                          // Get masked tuple
8      x ←TUPLEHASH(u)                     // Compute tuple hash
9      rIdx ← NIL
10     rPri ← NIL
11     for subtable i ← 0 to s − 1 do
12         j ← h_i(x)                      // Get subtable slot
13         if u = H'[i, j] then
14             rPri ← GETPRIORITY(H'[i, j])
15             rIdx ← blockIdx × s × d + i × d + j
16             break
17     if rIdx ≠ NIL then                  // Write to memory
18         ATOMICMAX(I[tid], (rPri ≪ 24) | rIdx)
19     tid ← tid+ threads
```

ple $t \in T$ in array I. In this design, each block is responsible for matching all tuples against a single class. For improved matching performance, each block keeps a copy of the class table and mask in H' and M', which are loaded at run-time to shared memory.

Lines 1–2 load the class table and mask to shared memory using coalesced accesses. Note that, since each block is responsible for a class, we use blockIdx as the offset in both cases. A SYNCTHREADS() call is then used to ensure that threads in the block have finished copying after this line. Lines 5–16 perform the table lookup. In line 6, each thread loads a tuple $t \in T$ and a bitwise AND with the class mask is performed in line 7, deriving u. Then, line 8 computes the 32-bit tuple hash x to speed up the slot computations in line 12. The for loop (line 11) goes over each subtable, computes the candidate slot for u based on x (line 12), compares it with the rule value in that slot (line 13). If so, the priority and the global index of this rule are saved (lines 14–15) for later writing them to memory (lines 17–18). The tuple index is then increased in line 19 to load the next tuple.

4.3 Bloom Search

Tuple search requires checking a tuple against each class table, which translates to a large number of table lookups in the case of many classes. We therefore propose to use Bloom filters as a compact representation of the class tables to quick identify the matching classes and perform table lookups only when there is a filter match. This technique is similar to solutions proposed for high-speed IP lookup in SRAM [8, 22], but not yet explored in GPUs.

A Bloom filter [2] is a space-efficient data structure that consists of an array with m bits and k independent hash functions $g_1, g_2, \ldots, g_k$ whose outputs are uniformly distributed over the discrete range $\{0, 1, \ldots, m-1\}$. We use a Bloom filter to represent

Algorithm 5: Bloom search kernel

Input: Bloom filters B, tables H, masks M, tuples T
Output: rule indexes I for each tuple $t \in T$
Data: Bloom filter B' in shared memory
cuckoo hash table $H'[s, d]$ in shared memory
class mask M' in shared memory

```
1  B' ← READAOS(B, blockIdx, 1)
2  H' ← READAOS(H, blockIdx, 1)
3  M' ← READAOS(M, blockIdx, 1)
4  SYNCTHREADS()
5  tid ← threadIdx
6  while tid < |T| do
7      t ←READSOA(T, tid)                  // Get a tuple
8      u ← t & M'                          // Get masked tuple
9      x ←TUPLEHASH(u)                     // Compute tuple hash
10     match ← TRUE
11     for i ← 0 to k − 1 do               // Check BF bits
12         j ← g_i(x)
13         if B'[j] =FALSE then
14             match ← FALSE
15             break
16     if match = TRUE then                // Find matching rule
17         rIdx ← NIL
18         rPri ← NIL
19         for subtable i ← 0 to s − 1 do
20             j ← h_i(x)                  // Get subtable slot
21             if u = H'[i, j] then
22                 rPri ← GETPRIORITY(H'[i, j])
23                 rIdx ← blockIdx(s × d) + (i × d) + j
24                 break
25         if rIdx ≠ NIL then              // Write to memory
26             ATOMICMAX(I[tid], (rPri ≪ 24) | rIdx)
27     tid ← tid+ threads
```

the set $R = \{r_1, r_2, \ldots, r_n\}$ of n rules within a class. Initially, all bits in the filter are set to 0. Then, for each rule $r_i \in R$, the bits of positions $g_1(r_i), g_2(r_i), \ldots, g_k(r_i)$ are set to 1. The lookup for a tuple t in a class C works as follows. First, we mask t with the class mask and derive u, then we check whether the bits of positions $g_1(u), g_2(u), \ldots, g_k(u)$ are set to 1. If at least one bit is 0, then no rule $r_i \in R$ applies to t. Otherwise, a matching rule exists in C with high probability and, with a low probability $(1 - e^{-kn/m})^k$, this is a false positive. This probability can be maintained low in practice by properly choosing parameters k and m for a given number n of rules. After a match is found in the filter, for each candidate matching class, we check the corresponding tables to either rule out eventual false positives or to retrieve the rule priority.

Algorithm 5 shows our Bloom search kernel. This kernel is similar to the tuple search kernel (cf. Algorithm 4). The main differences between the two kernels are that Bloom filters also need to be loaded to shared memory at run-time (line 1) and its bits must be checked for every incoming tuple (lines 10-14). Also, the table lookup is only performed if a rule is found by the filter (line 15). For the filter hash functions, we use universal hash functions defined as

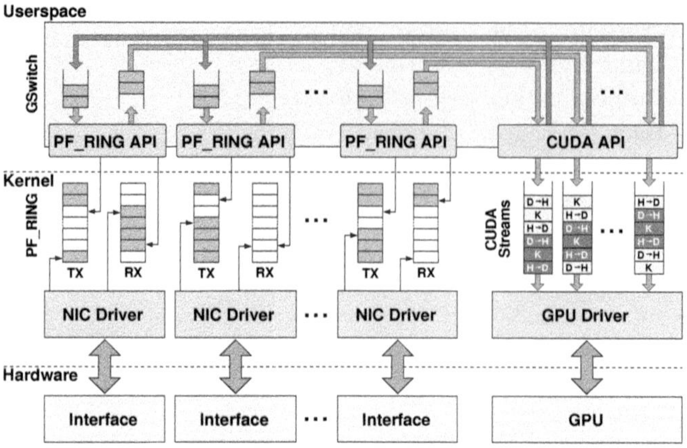

Figure 2: The software architecture of GSwitch.

$h_i(x) = (a_i x + b_i) \gg (32 - \log_2 m)$, where the filter size m is a power of two to avoid modular operations on a per-packet basis. The lookup in the cuckoo hash table is only performed if a match is found in the filter.

5. GSWITCH

We now integrate the previous algorithms with high-speed packet I/O. GSwitch is a multi-threaded application running in userspace and capable of classifying packets from multiple 10GbE ports simultaneously. It is built on top of publicly available APIs and composed of roughly 7K lines of C++ code. High-speed packet I/O is realized using PF_RING [7], a network socket optimized for capturing minimum 64-byte packets at wire speed. PF_RING directly exposes the NIC ring buffer to applications in userspace, thus reducing the high overhead of the OS network stack. Compared to alternative packet I/O acceleration engines, such as netmap [20] and PacketShader [10], PF_RING provides higher configuration flexibility and the same high-speed performance. For interfacing with the GPU, GSwitch uses the compute unified device architecture (CUDA) API provided by NVIDIA.

Figure 2 shows the software architecture of GSwitch. At the bottom, the NIC driver interfaces with the TX/RX ring buffers of PF_RING, and manages the hardware. When the incoming traffic rate is low, packets are received via direct memory access (DMA) initiated by regular interrupt calls. As the rate grows, packet I/O interrupts are disabled to avoid receive livelock, and periodic device polling is used for efficient interrupt coalescing. Similarly, packet transmissions are initiated by DMA requests when the number of enqueued packets in the TX ring buffer is above a minimum threshold of 128 packets.

PF_RING modifies the NIC driver to enable the NIC to share its circular buffer with an application such as GSwitch. When a packet is received at the NIC, the driver advances the writer pointer forward in the RX ring buffer; GSwitch then reads the packet and advances the reader pointer. Transmissions are performed using the TX ring buffer, with GSwitch having the role of the writer and the driver as the reader. Since each ring only has a single reader/writer, I/O operations are lock-free in the OS kernel.

GSwitch assigns a separate thread to each TX/RX ring buffer; these threads are hard-affinitized to a CPU core to eliminate processing bottlenecks and migration costs. Packets are read from the RX ring buffer either when the buffer contains enough packet to form a batch or when a timeout occurs (cf. Section 7).

GSwitch takes advantage of CUDA *streams*, which are FIFO task queues that allow threads to asynchronously send jobs to the GPU in a guaranteed execution order. Each thread has its own stream, to which it issues a sequence of commands to (1) copy a batch of tuples (header fields) from host to device memory, (2) run the packet classification kernel in GPU, (3) copy the results from device to host memory, and (4) register the batch completion using a CUDA *event*. Streams allow the CPU and GPU to overlap in time, with the CPU receiving packets of the next batch while the GPU classifies the packets of the current batch. Streams also improve overall GPU utilization with concurrent copy and execution, *i.e.,* while a kernel from one stream is running, a data copy from another stream may occur in parallel.

After dispatching a batch to the GPU, the RX thread inserts the batch information (e.g., memory address and length) into a buffer shared with the TX thread of the same NIC. The TX thread then uses a synchronous call to wait for the corresponding CUDA event indicating the batch completion. Once the GPU is finished with the batch, its packets are forwarded to the selected output TX queues. To prevent race conditions, each TX queue has a read-write lock which must be acquired before the queue can be updated.

6. EXPERIMENTAL METHODOLOGY

We perform an experimental evaluation of packet classification in GPU and GSwitch. In this paper, we assume that classifiers are statically stored in the device memory of GPU, *i.e.,* classifiers are already in the GPU before the packets arrive. Experiments are conducted both with and without packet I/O in order to isolate performance bottlenecks in the packet classification and in the packet I/O. When packet I/O is turned off, the batch of incoming packets is generated at 10 Gbps per interface directly at the switch. When packet I/O is active, the software switch is connected to a software-based traffic generator based on PF_RING, which acts both as packet source and sink.

GSwitch runs on a server equipped with two Intel Nehalem quad-core Xeon X5550 2.66 GHz processors, a Super Micro X8DAH+F motherboard, 12 GB DDR3 memory, and a NVIDIA GTX580 GPU [16] (cf. Section 3). We choose this configuration since it only includes inexpensive commodity hardware, as the whole system costs about $2,000. Additionally, this configuration allows us to make a fair comparison between the GPU and CPU performance, since the total cost of the two Intel Nehalem quad-core Xeon X5550 2.66 GHz processors is about $400, which is approximately the same price of the NVIDIA GTX 580 GPU. The traffic generator runs on a machine equipped with an 8-core AMD FX-8350 processor and 16 GB DDR3 memory. Each machine is further equipped with two Intel X520-DA2 dual-port 10GbE NICs for a theoretical aggregate rate of 40 Gbps.

Each experiment consists of 1,000 runs for which we report average and standard deviation by mean of error bars. To quantify the speed of each classification algorithm when packet I/O is turned off, we measure the number of tuples per second classified by the GPU and then derive the throughput in gigabits per second (Gbps) assuming, unless otherwise stated, 84-byte Ethernet frames, *i.e.,* the minimum 64-byte payload size plus 20-byte Ethernet overhead. With packet I/O enabled, we experiment with several different packet sizes (cf. Section 7.4) and measure the throughput as the rate at which GSwitch is able to forward the received packets.

Rule sets and incoming tuples are sampled from both real and synthetic traces. We consider two scenarios:

Realistic scenario: This scenario quantifies the performance gains of GPU acceleration for packet classification in a real setting (Sec-

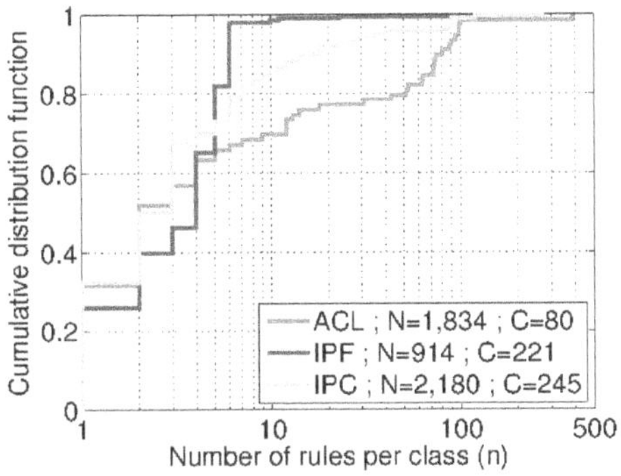

Figure 3: The cumulative distribution function (CDF) of the number of rules per class for ACL, IPF, and IPC.

tion 7.2 and 7.4). We use real rule sets from ClassBench [24], a publicly available tool for benchmarking packet classification algorithms. ClassBench comes with three real rule sets: Access control list (ACL), containing 1834 rules and 80 classes; IP forwarding (IPF), with 914 rules and 221 classes; and IP chaining (IPC), with 2180 rules and 245 classes. Each set only contains classic 5-tuple rules[3]. Figure 3 plots the cumulative distribution function (CDF) of the number of rules per class for the ACL, IPF, and IPC rule sets, respectively. Overall, the distribution of rules per class is skewed; the three sets exhibit a high number of classes (about 25-30%) with a single rule, and only few classes (about 1-2%) with more than 100 rules. The largest class is found in the ACL rule set and contains 384 rules. The trace containing the packets to be classified are also provided by ClassBench along with each rule set.

Synthetic scenario: This scenario explores the impact of system parameters and rule set characteristics on each classification algorithm (Sections 7.1 and 7.3). For this purpose, we generate synthetic rule sets varying features like the number of rules and classes. Rule generation is done by mean of a simple tool we wrote that takes a tuple with f fields as input and generates a rule set composed of N rules, each with f fields, organized as C classes. The tool uses the input tuple to generate C masks by replacing its fields with unique combinations of wildcards. Rules in a class are created by randomly varying the non-wildcarded fields. The input tuples to be classified are derived from the synthetic rule set by randomly setting masked fields.

7. EVALUATION

This section experimentally evaluates our packet classification algorithms in GPU. Section 7.1 presents the results from a series of microbenchmarks conducted to properly set system parameters. Section 7.2 then compares the throughput achieved by the GPU and our multi-core CPU. Next, Section 7.3 analyzes the impact of system parameters and rule set characteristics on the throughput achieved by each classification algorithm. Finally, Section 7.4 analyzes the performance of GSwitch focusing on throughput and delay.

7.1 GPU Microbenchmarks

Batch size: Data transfers between host and device memory occur before and after each kernel execution, and may incur a significant overhead. We are interested in determining if these transfers could affect the classification throughput.

[3]To our knowledge, there are no public OpenFlow rule sets.

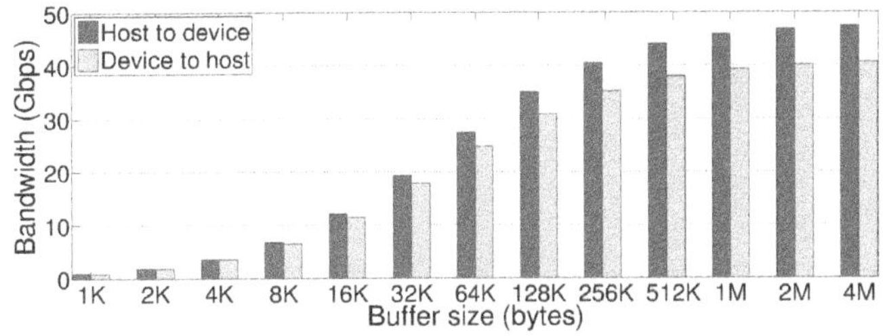

Figure 4: Data transfer rates between host and device.

Figure 4 plots the bandwidth measured for a 1-GB transfer from host to device, CPU to GPU, and vice-versa, using different buffer sizes. The buffer size determines the amount of data transferred in each transaction. Although host and device memory are connected via PCIe 2.0 x16 (64 Gbps), we measure a maximum of 48 Gbps from host to device, and 40 Gbps in the opposite direction, assuming buffer sizes of few MB. This bandwidth difference compared to the theoretical 64 Gbps is due to system call, DMA, and PCIe overheads. The asymmetry between the bandwidth measured in the two directions is expected as detailed in [10]. The figure also shows that for buffers of 1 MB or less, these overheads are even higher, which further reduces the bandwidth. Nonetheless, a 10-Gbps link carries a maximum of 14.8 million 64-byte packets; assuming the largest tuple size, *i.e.,* a 288-bit OpenFlow tuple per packet, a bandwidth of only 4.3 Gbps is required between host and device memory. Figure 4 shows that this bandwidth can be achieved with buffers of at least 8 KB, or equivalently, a batch of at least $\lfloor 8\ \text{KB}*8/288 \rfloor = 227$ packets.

In addition to significantly reducing the data transfer overhead, batches also impose an interesting tradeoff. On the one hand, the transfer time should be lower than the kernel execution time in order for the data transfer to overlap with a previous kernel execution (cf. Section 3). On the other hand, we aim to offload enough tuples to the GPU in order to fully exploit its parallelism. Figure 5(a) and 5(b) analyze this tradeoff by plotting, respectively, the kernel execution time versus the data transfer time, and the throughput of each classification algorithm for different batch sizes P. We use a synthetic rule set with 1K rules equally distributed among 128 classes, which is representative of a realistic trace (cf. Figure 3).

Figure 5(a) shows that, for $P \leq 1$K, the transfer time is longer than each kernel time, indicating that it cannot be effectively hidden by a concurrent kernel execution. Conversely, when $P > 1$K, the transfer time is shorter than the execution time of even the fastest kernel, e.g., Bloom search requires 170 μs for $P = 8$K whereas the transfer time takes only 100 μs. However, Figure 5(b) shows that, independent from the algorithm, the batch must contain at least 8K tuples to maximize throughput, and $P > 8$K provides only a marginal throughput increase. As a result, in the remainder of the evaluation we set $P = 8$K.

Blocks and threads per block: The number of blocks and threads also have to be properly chosen in order to maximize GPU occupancy. Table 1 shows the configurations that achieve 100% occu-

Blocks per SM (B)	2	3	4	6	8
Total number of blocks	32	48	64	96	128
Threads per block	768	512	384	256	192
Shared memory per block	24 KB	16 KB	12 KB	8 KB	6 KB

Table 1: Kernel configurations with 100% occupancy.

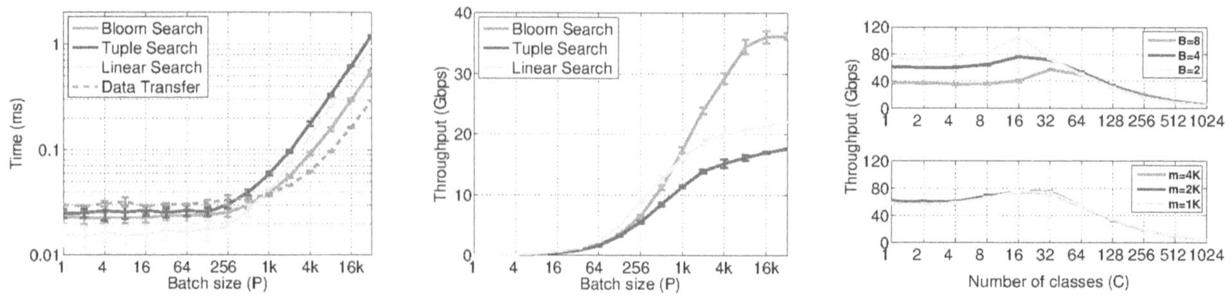

(a) $N = 1\text{K}, C = 128$. (b) $N = 1\text{K}, C = 128$. (c) Variable rules per class, see Table 2.

Figure 5: Microbenchmarks to evaluate (a) the kernel execution time versus the data transfer time, (b) the throughput as a function of the batch size, and (c) the throughput of Bloom search as a function of the number C of classes.

pancy for each possible number B of blocks per SM (cf. Section 3). We now investigate the impact of B on the proposed classification algorithms.

In linear search, each block compares all tuples against the rules in its shared memory (cf. Section 4.1). Since shared memory is equally partitioned among the B blocks, a smaller B results in a larger shared memory size per block. In this case, each block is responsible for a larger subset of rules and, due to the smaller B, tuples are read less often from device memory, significantly increasing throughput. Hence, for linear search, we set $B = 2$, as this is the best setting. We confirm this with experiments (omitted here due to space).

For tuple and Bloom search, each block handles one class at a time (cf. Sections 4.2 and 4.3), and performance depends on the number of classes in the rule set. Figure 5(c) (top plot) shows the throughput of Bloom search for different numbers C of classes assuming that (1) B equals either 2, 4, or 8; (2) the Bloom filter size is 1/6th of the available shared memory per block; and (3) each class holds the maximum number of rules (cf. Table 2). We only evaluate Bloom search as the tradeoffs are the same as those of tuple search.

Figure 5(c) shows that for $C < 64$, $B = 8$ blocks per SM provides the lowest throughput. This occurs because several blocks remain idle as there are not enough classes to occupy all blocks. As the number of classes increases, there are no idle blocks regardless of the value of B and the performance gap between the three curves is reduced. Despite being hard to see, four and eight blocks per SM guarantees the highest throughput for $50 \leq C < 200$ and $C \geq 200$ classes, respectively.

Blocks per SM	2			**4**			8		
Shared memory per block (KB)	24			**12**			6		
Tuple search									
Cuckoo hash subtables	3			**3**			3		
Slots per subtable	56			**113**			227		
Max. rules per class	168			**339**			681		
Bloom search									
Cuckoo hash subtables	3			**3**			3		
Bloom filter hash functions	2			**2**			2		
Bloom filter size (KB)	0.5	1	2	1	**2**	4	2	4	8
Slots per subtable	51	47	37	103	**94**	75	208	189	151
Max. rules per class	153	141	111	309	**282**	225	624	567	453
False positive rate	6e-3	1e-3	1e-4	6e-3	**1e-3**	1e-4	6e-3	1e-3	1e-4

Table 2: Partition of the shared memory per block.

Data structures dimensioning: Table 2 shows how shared memory is partitioned in tuple and Bloom search. In both cases, we use three subtables per cuckoo hash table, which provides a low worst-case lookup time and a theoretical load factor of 90%. Each slot in the table stores a 288-bit OpenFlow tuple and the priority used for matching. The number of slots per subtable changes according to the available shared memory and the classification algorithm.

In Bloom search, we use $k = 2$ hash functions per Bloom filter in order to keep the per-tuple computation low, and consider three values for the filter size m, namely 1/3rd, 1/6th, and 1/12th of the available shared memory per block. We choose these ratios to ensure that m is a power of two, which accelerates the modulo operations in the hash computations (cf. Section 4.2). Table 2 shows that as m decreases, the maximum number of rules per class increases, since more shared memory space is available for the hash table. However, smaller filters also result in slightly higher false positive rates. These rates are relatively low and remain constant as B varies, since the ratio between the number of rules and the filter size is practically unchanged.

Figure 5(c) (bottom plot) shows the impact of different filter sizes (1, 2, and 4 KB) on Bloom search throughput; we use the same rule set of the top plot and set $B = 4$. Clearly, a similar throughput is measured for the different filter sizes, e.g., less than a 5% throughput decrease as m reduces from 4 to 1 KB. This indicates that the few extra table lookups due to the slightly higher false positive rate do not critically impact the classification throughput. A similar behavior was also observed for $B = 2$ and $B = 8$ (not showed).

In summary, the choice of the Bloom filter size m and the number B of blocks per SM largely depends on the rule set. We thus use the information derived from real rule sets (cf. Figure 3) to set m and B for the performance evaluation. Since the number of classes ranges between 80 and 245, we set $B = 4$ and, since the maximum number of rules per class ranges between 100 and 400 rules, we set $m = 2$ KB. The chosen configuration is shown in Table 2 in boldface.

With $B = 4$ and $m = 2$ KB, each class can store up to 282 and 339 rules for Bloom and tuple search, respectively. However, we set the maximum number of rules per class n to 256 for both algorithms in order to (1) not overload the table, leaving the load factor at 90%, and (2) simplify the evaluation in Section 7.3, since the performance is the same for different numbers of rules per class. Classes with $n > 256$ are logically organized in multiple classes with the same mask, e.g., a class with 1K rules is split into four classes, each with 256 rules.

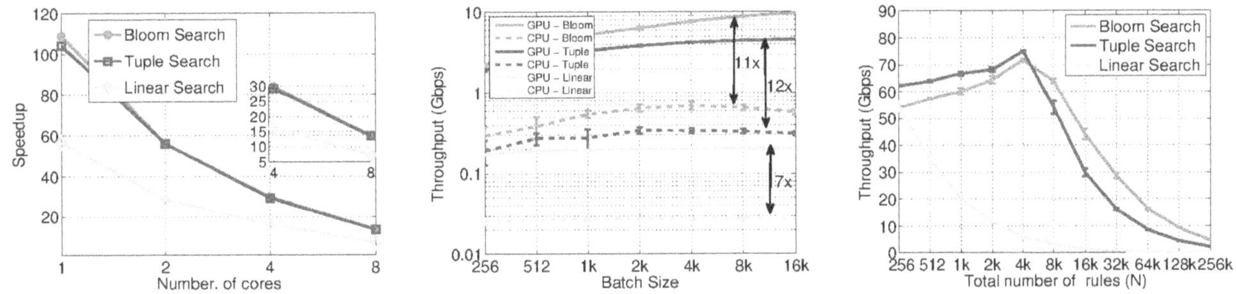

(a) $N = 128\text{K}, C = 512$. (b) $N = 128\text{K}, C = 512$. (c) $N = 256C$.

Figure 6: (a) The speedup of GPU over CPU as a function of the number of cores, (b) throughput of both GPU and CPU as a function of the batch size, and (c) throughput of GPU as a function of the total number N of rules.

GPU metrics: We measure our implementation of linear, tuple, and Bloom search using the GPU performance metrics discussed in Section 3. Each algorithm was implemented to reuse as many registers as possible; in total, the per-thread register count is 19 for both Bloom and tuple search, and 20 for linear search. The number of blocks and threads per blocks are chosen as discussed above, which coupled with the low register count and the proper shared memory partition guarantees 100% occupancy. Load efficiency is also 100%, as expected (cf. Algorithms 2 and 3).

7.2 GPU versus CPU

In this section, we compare the performance of packet classification in GPU and CPU. The two Intel Nehalem quad-core Xeon X5550 2.66 GHz used in our comparison is about $400 and is equivalent to the price of our NVIDIA GTX 580 GPU. For the comparison, we port the CUDA code for each algorithm to OpenCL, the open standard for parallel programming of heterogeneous systems [12]. OpenCL is a library that allows us to run packet classification in CPU in a parallel fashion. Next, we call *speedup* the ratio between the throughput measured in GPU and the throughput measured in CPU for a given experiment.

For these experiments, we assume a synthetic rule set composed by $N = 128$K OpenFlow rules equally distributed among $C = 512$ classes. These parameters are chosen to represent a challenging rule set composed of a large number of rules and classes. We first assume a batch of 8K tuples is offloaded to GPU and later we vary the batch size from 256 up to 16K tuples.

Figure 6(a) plots the speedup of each packet classification algorithm as a function of the number of used CPU cores. In general, the speedup decreases as the number of cores increases; however, even when the maximum of 8 CPU cores are used, the GPU guarantees 7x speedup (linear search), 11x speedup (tuple search), and 12x speed (Bloom search). Figure 6(a) also shows an overall higher speedup for both tuple and bloom search compared to linear search; this happens because linear search in CPU takes better advantage of caching due to its serial nature.

Figure 6(b) plots the throughput achieved by each packet classification algorithm in both CPU (8 cores) and GPU as a function of the batch size. We see that the speedup is largely independent of the batch size. This occurs because our implementations are designed to maximize CPU/GPU utilization even if the number of input packets is low. That is, we still use a large number of threads by having each thread match the same packet on a different fraction of the rule set. Nevertheless, increasing the batch size is beneficial since the same thread can work on multiple packets absorbing the cost of loading rules to shared memory (GPU) or cache (CPU). Figure 6(b) shows another important result: tuple and Bloom search in CPU outperform linear search in GPU, which highlights the algorithmic benefits of these packet classification strategies. At its peak, Bloom search achieves about 0.7 Gbps in CPU, which is remarkably fast considering the rule set contains 128K rules.

7.3 Throughput Analysis

Rule set size: In this section, we first evaluate the throughput achieved by linear, tuple, and Bloom search as a function of the total number of rules in a set. We use synthetic rules sets composed by OpenFlow rules [5, 17], *i.e.,* 288-bit tuples with 12 fields from L2 to L4. We generate several synthetic traces where C grows exponentially from 1 to 1K classes, with each class containing the maximum number of rules (*i.e.,* $n = 256$ rules). In this case, the total number N of rules grows exponentially from 256 to 256K.

Figure 6(c) plots the throughput measured for each algorithm, as the total number of rules (and classes) increases. When $N = 256$ rules, the three algorithms have similar performance: tuple search achieves the highest throughput of 62 Gbps, whereas Bloom and linear search achieve about 55 Gbps. As N increases, the throughput of linear search drops and diverges from both Bloom and tuple search. However, our implementation of linear search still guarantees more than 20 Gbps with a set of 1K rules. When the number of classes is low ($C \leq 16$), tuple search achieves a throughput 10% higher than Bloom search. This indicates that the additional complexity required by Bloom search to load and check Bloom filters is not amortized by the gain of avoiding multiple hash table lookups, as required by tuple search. For $C > 16$, Bloom search outperforms tuple search guaranteeing about a 50% throughput increase, e.g., 45 Gbps versus 30 Gbps with 16K rules ($C = 64$). The figure also shows that Bloom search supports a 10-Gbps link with minimum packet size assuming 128K rules and 512 different classes.

Figure 6(c) also shows a counterintuitive result. As N grows from 256 to 4K rules (1 to 16 classes), the throughput measured for both Bloom and tuple search increases. This occurs because in both implementation a block is responsible for at least a class. Hence, when the number of classes is lower than the number of SMs in the GPU (16 SMs in GTX580), some blocks are idle and waste resources, as previously discussed. It follows that increasing the number of rules, and thus classes, generates a higher throughput.

Number of classes: We now evaluate the throughput of each algorithm as the number of classes C increases, but the total number of rules N remains fixed. Figure 7(a) plots the throughput achieved by linear, tuple, and Bloom search as a function of C when $N = 32$K rules. Since each class contains 256 rules at maximum, at least $N/256$ classes are required, *i.e.,* 128 classes.

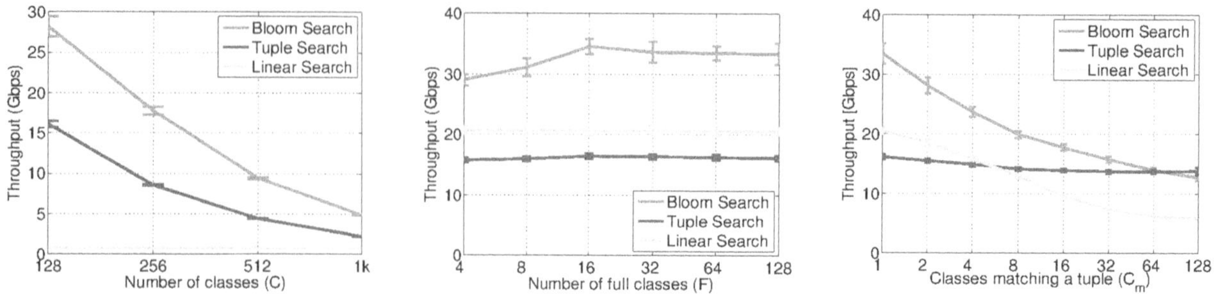

(a) $N = 32$K. (b) $N = 1$K, $C = 128$. (c) $N = 1$K, $C = F = 128$.

Figure 7: Throughput as a function of (a) the number of classes C, (b) the number of full classes F, and (c) the number of classes matching a tuple C_m.

Overall, Bloom search is the fastest packet classification algorithm, reaching more than 10 Gbps when rules are organized in less than 512 classes. In comparison, tuple search achieves about half the throughput of Bloom search, e.g., 5 Gbps versus 10 Gbps when $C = 512$ classes. Linear search is the slowest packet classification algorithm, reaching only 1 Gbps regardless of the value of C, since it does not take advantage of the presence of classes.

Rule distribution: We now evaluate the throughput of each algorithm assuming that not all classes have the same number of rules. First, we introduce a parameter that expresses how rules are distributed among classes. By definition, a class exists only if it contains at least one rule. We define F as the number of *full* classes, *i.e.,* the number of classes that contain $[N - (C - F)]/F$ rules, whereas the remaining $(C - F)$ classes contain a single rule. This allows us to express the rule distribution as skewed, *i.e.,* $F = 1$ and thus a single class contains most of rules whereas the remaining classes contain a single rule, to uniform, *i.e.,* $F = C$ and thus each class contains the same number of rules.

We set $N = 1$K and $C = 128$ to generate several synthetic traces where the distribution of rules among classes varies from skewed ($F = 4$) to uniform ($F = 128$). Figure 7(b) shows the throughput of linear, tuple, and Bloom search as F grows. Overall, the figure shows that both linear and tuple search do not depend on F, whereas a lower throughput is measured for Bloom search in presence of a skewed distribution ($F \leq 16$). For linear search, this is intuitive, since there is no notion of classes. For tuple search, this confirms that the number of classes, and not the number of rules per class, is key to predicting performance. For Bloom search, we notice a 20% throughput increase as F grows from 4 to 16 classes. This is due to the presence of idle blocks for small values of F (cf. Section 7.1). Despite each block works on two classes (*i.e.,* 128 classes divided by 64 blocks), the load distribution is uneven. In fact, the probability of finding a match in one of the classes with a single entry is very low, which means that blocks responsible for such classes only perform Bloom filter lookups, whereas F blocks perform both Bloom filter and hash table lookups.

Overlapping rules: We now evaluate the throughput of each algorithm in the presence of overlapping rules, where an incoming tuple matches several rules at once. By definition, overlapping rules must belong to different classes; we thus define C_m as the number of classes that match an incoming tuple. For this experiment, we set $N = 1$K and $C = F = 128$, *i.e.,* uniform rule distribution and 8 rules per class, and generate several synthetic traces where C_m grows exponentially from 1 to 128 classes.

Figure 7(c) shows the throughput of each algorithm in this scenario. The throughput of linear search reduces from 20 to only 6 Gbps as C_m grows from 1 to 128 classes. This throughput decrease is due to the higher contention caused by atomic operations (ATOMICMAX, line 20 in Algorithm 1). A similar effect is noticeable for tuple search, though less evident due to the higher complexity of the tuple search kernel compared to linear search. The throughput of Bloom search largely decreases as C_m increases. The main reason of such reduction is the increase in the number of hash table accesses to solve conflicts. In the worst case, when $C_m = 128$ classes, tuple search becomes faster than Bloom search, which is intuitive since, when all classes match each incoming tuple, the lookup in the Bloom filter does not provide any benefits, but instead only introduces additional work.

5-tuple rules: We have assumed so far 288-bit OpenFlow rules composed of 12 fields. We now experiment with sets with 128-bit rules composed of 5 tuples, as commonly used by firewalls. We set $N = 1$K and $C = F = 128$, *i.e.,* uniform rules distribution and 8 rules per class, and $C_m = 1$, *i.e.,* no overlapping rules, to generate synthetic traces where rules are composed by 5 and 12 fields.

Figure 8 compares the throughput of our algorithms when the tuple size is 5 and 12 fields. The results for 12 fields are the same as Figure 7(c) for the case of $C_m = 1$. Overall, reducing the tuple size guarantees a higher throughput, e.g., the throughput achieved by Bloom search grows from 35 to 50 Gbps. Tuple search shows

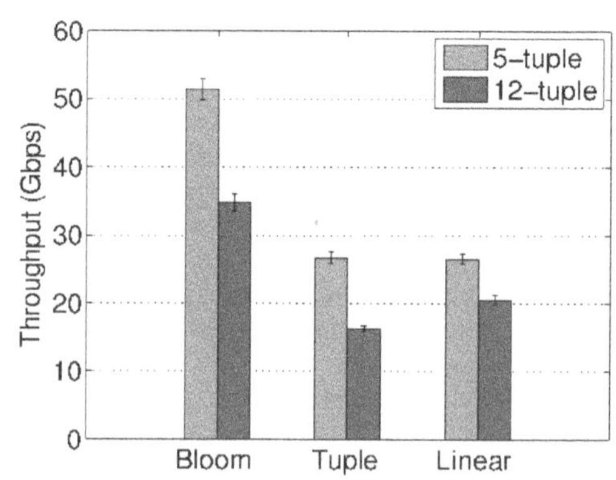

Figure 8: Throughput as a function of the number of fields in a tuple f ; N=1K, C=F=128, C_m=1.

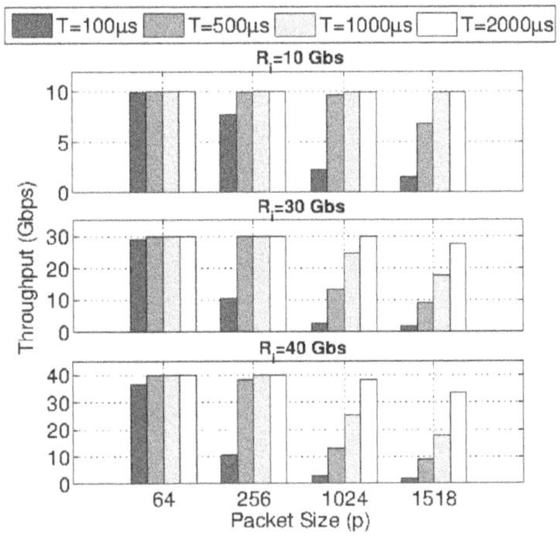

Figure 9: Bloom search throughput as a function of packet size p and maximum latency T.

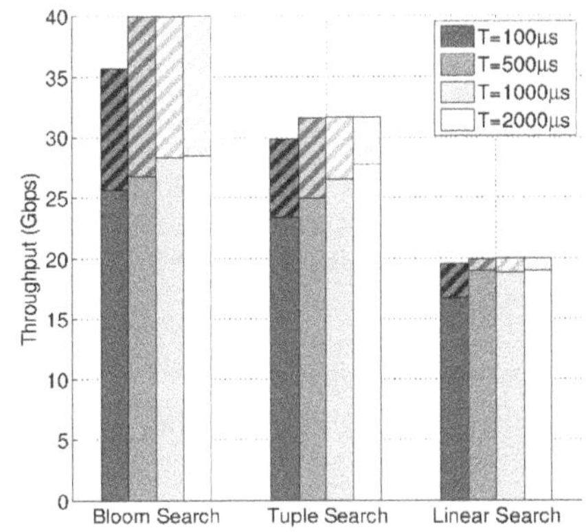

Figure 10: Forwarding throughput as a function of T.

the highest percentage increase, a 63% increase from 16 to 26 Gbps versus 43% and 25% for Bloom and linear search, respectively.

7.4 Delay Assessment

Packet processing in GPU requires large batches to maximize throughput (cf. Figure 5). However, large batches may sometimes come at the expense of additional delay. As an example, a batch of a thousand 64-byte packets requires only 67 μs to arrive in a 10 GbE link. For 1518-byte packets, however, the same thousand packets take 1.2 ms.

So far, a fixed batch size of P = 8K packets was assumed in order to maximize GPU performance. In a real switch with delay constraints, however, dynamic batching is required to offload packets to the GPU as either the batch is complete or a timeout occurs. In the previous example, in order to guarantee a maximum delay of 67 μs per packet when the source is transmitting at 5 Gbps, the batch size must drop to a maximum of 500 packets. We implement a mechanism in GSwitch (cf. Section 5) to allow an operator to manually specify the maximum per-packet buffering delay. The switch then configures a timeout interval to guarantee that this delay is not exceeded.

We now assess the impact of imposing a maximum tolerable packet delay on the throughput of GSwitch, considering different packet sizes and input rates. We initially focus on Bloom search, our fastest packet classification algorithm, assuming no packet I/O. The analysis is then generalized to other classification algorithms, and packet I/O is also turned on to analyze its effect on the forwarding throughput. For both experiments, the realistic scenario with the ACL trace is used.

Figure 9 shows the throughput of Bloom search as a function of the packet size, as the maximum delay T grows from 100 μs up to 2 ms. For a maximum packet size p, we consider the worst-case scenario, where traffic is composed only by packets of that size. Each subplot refers to an input rate R_i of 10, 30, and 40 Gbps, respectively. Each combination of $\langle$input rate, packet size, delay$\rangle$ imposes a maximum batch size supported by GSwitch. Figure 9 shows that, for minimum-sized 64-byte packets, the GPU forwards traffic at almost 40 Gbps with a delay as low as 100 μs. As the packet size increases to 256 bytes, GSwitch incurs a maximum delay of 500 μs to accumulate enough packets in a batch and sustain the maximum throughput. The delay must increase to 1 ms for 1 KB packets, but even 2 ms is not enough for 1518-byte packets. In this case, however, since the packet size is large, the maximum rate is only 812 Kpps per interface, which could be easily handled by the CPU. In fact, for the combination $\langle$40 Gbps, 1518 bytes, 2 ms$\rangle$ the batch size is equal to 6K packets; for this batch size, Bloom search in CPU reaches 0.7 Gbps or about 1 Mpps with 64-byte packets, cf. Figure 6(b).

We now enable packet I/O at GSwitch and show the performance of all packet classification algorithms in Figure 10. We assume 64-byte packets in order to stress the network I/O and packet classification modules. Hardware flow control is active at the NICs to slow down the traffic generator when GSwitch cannot forward packets fast enough. This occurs due to a limitation either in the packet I/O or in the packet classification algorithm. In order to isolate these effects, we plot as stacked bars the additional throughput achieved by GSwitch assuming no real packet I/O, but with batches of incoming packets being generated directly at the switch.

Overall, Figure 10 shows that, with packet I/O enabled, GSwitch achieves a maximum forwarding throughput of 27 Gbps using both tuple and Bloom search. With locally generated traffic, however, the GPU supports the maximum aggregate traffic of 40 Gbps using Bloom search when the maximum delay is larger than 100 μs. Tuple and linear search, on the other hand, are still limited by the packet classification at the GPU, and are not able to achieve 40 Gbps, even if not limited by packet I/O.

8. CONCLUSION

In this work, we investigate the benefits of using GPUs for packet classification in software-based switches such as Open vSwitch. We first propose efficient GPU-accelerated implementations for linear search, a baseline packet classification algorithm, for tuple search, the algorithm currently implemented by Open vSwitch, and for Bloom search, a proposed extension of tuple search that uses Bloom filters to prefilter table lookups. We then build *GSwitch*, a GPU-accelerated software switch with high-speed packet I/O. We show by experimental evaluation that, under a realistic scenario, GSwitch is capable of attaining attaining a much higher throughput than current software-based packet I/O engines.

Acknowledgments

We would like to thank our shepherd, Robert Ricci, and the anonymous reviewers for their constructive comments.

9. REFERENCES

[1] Open vswitch. http://openvswitch.org/.

[2] BLOOM, B. H. Space/Time Trade-offs in Hash Coding with Allowable Errors. *Communications of the ACM 7*, 13 (July 1970), 442–426.

[3] CASCARANO, N., ROLANDO, P., RISSO, F., AND SISTO, R. iNFAnt: NFA pattern matching on GPGPU devices. *SIGCOMM Comput. Commun. Rev.* (2010), 20–26.

[4] CISCO. Nexus1000v. http://cisco.com/.

[5] CONSORTIUM, O. S. Openflow switch specification. Tech. Rep. Version 1.1.0, Feb. 2011.

[6] CURTIS, A. R., MOGUL, J. C., TOURRILHES, J., YALAGANDULA, P., SHARMA, P., AND BANERJEE, S. DevoFlow: Scaling Flow Management for High-Performance Networks. In *Proc. ACM SIGCOMM* (Toronto, Canada, Aug. 2011).

[7] DERI, L. Improving Passive Packet Capture: Beyond Device Polling. In *Proc. SANE* (Amsterdam, The Netherlands, Sept. 2004).

[8] DHARMAPURIKAR, S., KRISHNAMURTHY, P., AND TAYLOR, D. E. Longest Prefix Matching Using Bloom Filters. In *Proc. ACM SIGCOMM* (Karlsruhe, Germany, Aug. 2003).

[9] FOSTER, N., HARRISON, R., FREEDMAN, M. J., MONSANTO, C., REXFORD, J., STORY, A., AND WALKER, D. Frenetic: a network programming language. *SIGPLAN Not. 46* (2011), 279–291.

[10] HAN, S., JANG, K., PARK, K., AND MOON, S. PacketShader: A GPU-Accelerated Software Router. In *Proc. ACM SIGCOMM* (New Dehli, India, Aug. 2010).

[11] KANG, K., AND YANGDONG, D. Scalable packet classification via GPU metaprogramming. In *DATE* (Grenoble, France, Mar. 2011).

[12] KHRONOS OPENCL WORKING GROUP. The opencl specification. http://khronos.org/.

[13] LIN, C.-H., TSAI, S.-Y., LIU, C.-H., CHANG, S.-C., AND SHYU, J.-M. Accelerating String Matching Using Multi-threaded Algorithm on GPU. In *Proc. GLOBECOM* (Miami, FL, USA, Dec. 2010).

[14] MU, S., ZHANG, X., ZHANG, N., LU, J., DENG, Y. S., AND ZHANG, S. IP routing processing with graphic processors. In *Proc. DATE* (Dresden, Germany, Mar. 2010).

[15] NVIDIA. Profiler User's Guide – CUDA Toolkit Documentation. http://docs.nvidia.com/cuda/profiler-users-guide/index.html/.

[16] NVIDIA. GTX 580. http://geforce.com/hardware/desktop-gpus/geforce-gtx-580/.

[17] OPENFLOW. Switching reference system. http://www.openflow.org/wp/downloads/.

[18] OVERMARS, M. H., AND VAN DER STAPPEN, A. F. Range searching and point location among fat objects. *Journal of Algorithms 21* (1996), 629–656.

[19] PAGH, R., AND RODLER, F. F. Cuckoo Hashing. *Journal of Algorithms 51*, 2 (May 2004), 122–144.

[20] RIZZO, L. Netmap: a novel framework for fast packet I/O. In *Proc. USENIX* (Boston, MA, June 2012).

[21] SANDERS, J., AND KANDROT, E. *CUDA by Example: An Introduction to General-Purpose GPU Programming*, 1 ed. Addison-Wesley Professional, July 2010.

[22] SONG, H., HAO, F., KODIALAM, M., AND LAKSHMAN, T. IPv6 Lookups using Distributed and Load Balanced Bloom Filters for 100Gbps Core Router Line Cards. In *Proc. IEEE INFOCOM* (Rio de Janeiro, Brazil, Apr. 2009).

[23] SRINIVASAN, V., SURI, S., AND VARGHESE, G. Packet Classification Using Tuple Space Search. In *Proc. ACM SIGCOMM* (Cambridge, USA, Aug. 1999).

[24] TAYLOR, D. E., AND TURNER, J. S. ClassBench: A Packet Classification Benchmark. In *Proc. IEEE INFOCOM* (Hong Kong, China, Mar. 2004).

[25] WANG, Y., ZU, Y., ZHANG, T., PENG, K., DONG, Q., LIU, B., MENG, W., DAI, H., TIAN, X., XU, Z., WU, H., AND YANG, D. Wire speed name lookup: a GPU-based approach. In *Proc. NSDI* (Lombard, IL, Apr. 2013).

[26] ZHAO, J., ZHANG, X., WANG, X., AND XUE, X. Achieving O(1) IP lookup on GPU-based software routers. In *Proc. ACM SIGCOMM* (New Delhi, India, Aug. 2010).

From Cells to Streets: Estimating Mobile Paths with Cellular-Side Data

Ilias Leontiadis
Telefonica Research
ilias@tid.es

Antonio Lima
University of Birmingham
a.lima@cs.bham.ac.uk

Haewoon Kwak
Qatar Computing Research Institute *
hkwak@qf.org.qa

Rade Stanojevic
Telefonica Research
rade@tid.es

David Wetherall
University of Washington
djw@cs.washington.edu

Konstantina Papagiannaki
Telefonica Research
dina@tid.es

ABSTRACT

Through their normal operation, cellular networks are a repository of continuous location information from their subscribed devices. Such information, however, comes at a coarse granularity both in terms of space, as well as time. For otherwise inactive devices, location information can be obtained at the granularity of the associated cellular sector, and at infrequent points in time, that are sensitive to the structure of the network itself, and the level of mobility of the device. In this paper, we are asking the question of whether such sparse information can help to identify the paths followed by mobile connected devices throughout the day. If such a task is possible, then we would not only enable continuous mobility path estimation for smartphones, but also for the millions of future connected "things".

The challenge we face is that cellular data has one to two orders of magnitude less spatial and temporal resolution than typical GPS traces. Our contribution is to devise path segmentation, de-noising, and inference procedures to estimate the device stationary location, as well as its mobility path between stationary positions. We call our technique *Cell**. We complement the lack of spatio-temporal granularity with information on the cellular network topology, and GIS (Geographic Information System).

We collect more than 3,000 mobility trajectories over 8 months and show that *Cell** achieves a median error of $230m$ for the stationary location estimation, while mobility paths are estimated with a median accuracy of $70m$. We show that mobility path accuracy improves with its length and speed, and counter to our intuition, accuracy appears to improve in suburban areas. *Cell** is the first technology, we are aware of, that allows location services for the new generation of connected mobile devices, that may feature no GPS, due to cost, size, or battery constraints.

*This work has been completed while the author was working at Telefonica Research

CoNEXT'14, December 2–5, 2014, Sydney, Australia.

ACM 978-1-4503-3279-8/14/12 ...$15.00.
http://dx.doi.org/10.1145/2674005.2674982 .

Categories and Subject Descriptors

C2.1 [**COMPUTER-COMMUNICATION NETWORKS**]: Wireless communication—*Mobility*; C2.3 [**COMPUTER-COMMUNICATION NETWORKS**]: Network monitoring

General Terms

Algorithms

Keywords

Mobility Modeling, CDRs, Network Events, Trajectory Estimation, Localization, Cellular Networks, Street Routing

1. INTRODUCTION

Mobile devices are increasingly being seen as a unique sensor to individuals and humanity as a whole. Pocket-sized devices tend to follow us throughout our lives, capturing our day to day routines and providing us with valuable services, that exploit our context and preferences. A significant amount of research has gone into developing technologies that allow such devices to enable novel computing interactions, based on an increasingly greater number of sensors on board. The fundamental obstacle that needs to then be overcome is that of limited battery power. During the past 5-10 years, the research community has focused on ways to improve battery consumption for smartphones and define techniques for energy efficient location acquisition, through sophisticated energy efficient sensor hubs, WiFi, or the careful duty cycling of GPS; see [17] and references therein.

While smartphones are reaching nearly ubiquitous penetration in developed regions, a whole new array of connected devices emerges and is projected to reach billions by the year 2020. These devices tend to be connected to the cellular network (through 2G/3G or 4G), and are oftentimes mobile (see sim-watch.com or the array of devices supporting fleet management). However, due to cost, size or battery constraints, rarely do such devices feature GPS capabilities or sophisticated sensor architectures. The question we are addressing with this work is whether there is a way of enabling this whole new set of devices with precise location path information by utilizing the fact that these devices are continuously connected to the cellular network.

Mobility management is a fundamental function of the cellular infrastructure. However, unlike recent public belief, *in normal op-*

eration a cellular network is not in a position to accurately localize every single subscriber in space. In most cellular infrastructures today, mobile subscribers leave a trace of their associated tower, only when making/receiving calls, sending/receiving SMS, crossing Location Area Codes (LACs) or are routinely polled by the network due to stale information that exceeds a preconfigured duration (on the order of a few hours). Full handover information [1] is further accessible through RNC-level monitoring. In this paper we approach the problem of localizing subscribers from such sparse and noisy data available to the cellular operator.

We develop *Cell**, an algorithm that is able to parse the continuous sector observations and identify the segments corresponding to a stationary position, and the segments corresponding to actual mobility. We use the stationary segments, that typically feature multiple sector observations, to derive more accurate estimations for the stationary position. Using those enhanced locations that go beyond the sector coverage area, we develop an algorithm that is able to extract mobility paths between stationary points. Our path estimation algorithm uses cellular topology information to identify the areas on the map that are consistent with the observed sector associations, and weighs them according to the likelihood for a mobile subscriber to have connected with a tower from different locations within the respective sector coverage area. It then biases the route selection to pass through high probability areas while respecting the underlying road network.

To understand the accuracy and the limitations of *Cell** we study continuous mobility patterns for more than 30 individuals, while recording their ground truth GPS locations, and their associated cellular sectors (for every single handover). Our measurements cover more than 3000 unique trajectories in a European country.

*Cell** is able to identify the stationary position of the connected device with a median error of 230 meters which is comparable to the GSM triangulation technologies that actively probe the subscribers' signal strength [22]. In case of mobile paths, *Cell** has even lower median error of 70 meters due to the de-noising and GIS information that enrich the path inference. Somewhat intuitively, we show that the accuracy of our algorithm improves with the speed of the connected device and its length. Counter to our intuition, we further see that estimating mobility paths in suburban areas is more accurate. We speculate that this is due to the fact that sparser cellular network deployments occur in areas with sparser road infrastructure, thus limiting the number of possible roads that could have been taken by the connected device. In summary, we find *Cell** able to provide sufficient accuracy in path estimation for the billions of connected mobile devices that will be seen in the future.

The remainder of this work is structured as follows: we first present the problem formulation and an overview of our methodology that is composed of five steps. In Section 3, we present the details concerning each of these steps. In the following section ((§ 4)), we describe the probe that we implemented and the datasets that we collected whereas in Section 5 we evaluate the quality of the paths that are produced by *Cell**. A detailed discussion about the implications of *Cell** is given at Section 6. Finally, in Section 7 we compare with existing related work.

2. PROBLEM AND APPROACH

We begin with a definition of the problem we explore and an overview of the proposed solution.

[1]Notice that handovers are typically associated with an active communication. In our case we loosely use the term to indicate that the user switched between two sectors.

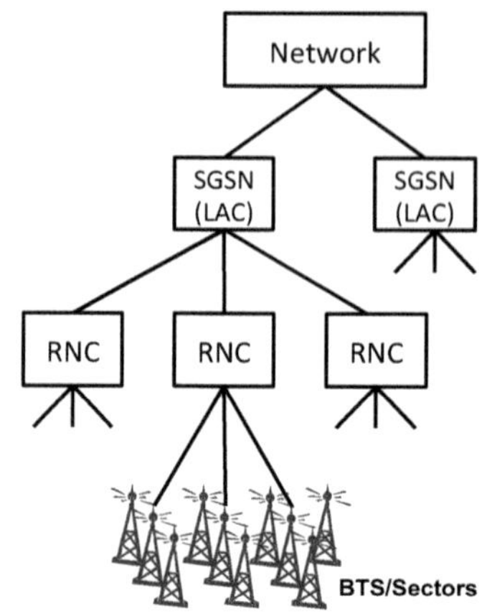

Figure 1: Overview of GSM hierarchy.

2.1 Formulation

We formulate the problem of estimating mobile paths from operational cellular data as follows. For each mobile device m or subscriber in the network, we have a sequence of time-stamped sector associations:

$$C_m = [(t_m[0], S_m[0]), (t_m[1], S_m[1]), \ldots] \quad (1)$$

Each element $S_m[i]$ is the sector the mobile m is associated with at the time $t_m[i]$. A graphical representation of such a sequence of observed sectors is shown on Figure 2a. This sequence represents what can be collected from the cellular infrastructure at the BSC/RNC as part of normal operation. We note that cellular networks do not presently log data at this granularity because of its significant volume over time and the network overhead that might be imposed. Information may only be kept when a device switches across different RNCs or even LACs (Figure 1). However, it is technically and economically feasible to keep information at the BTS level if it proves useful.

The sequence C_m is a proxy for the true location of the mobile m over time, which we call the ground truth. Ideal ground truth is continuous and accurate. However, to collect or evaluate it in practice, ground truth must be sampled at discrete times by using another localization method. Thus we model ground truth in the form we will use it in our experiments as:

$$L_m = [(t_m[0], l_m[0]), (t_m[1], l_m[1]), \ldots] \quad (2)$$

where $l_m[i]$ is the location of the mobile device m at the time $t_m[i]$. Later, we will collect ground truth location using GPS as it is the most accurate sensor that is available to us.

Our goal is *to use the cellular observations C_m for each subscriber m to construct an estimate of the path of the mobile device $\hat{P}_m$ that is close to its actual path represented by L_m.* Observe that we have simplified our formulation for convenience. Both C_m and L_m are discrete trajectories that give a sequence of mobile positions at given times. We estimate the continous path $\hat{P}_m$ of the subscriber that gives its range of positions but *not the exact times* at which it progressed along the path.

This subtle change from trajectories to paths both meets our needs, since often we simply care about the street-level path, and makes it more straightforward to assess whether our estimates are close to the ground truth. We formally define what it means for estimated paths to be "close" to ground truth later on.

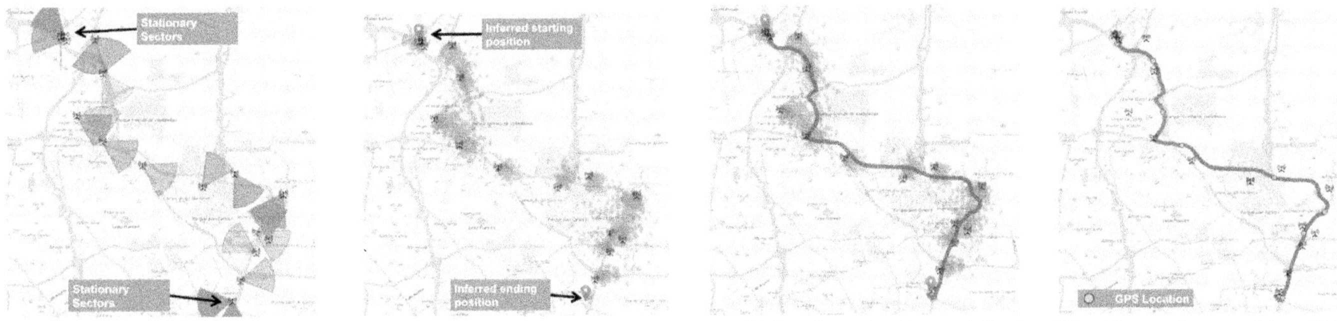

(a) Sequence of observed sectors. (b) Extracting start/end points and intermediate street probabilities (c) Cell* through the weighted streets (d) Comparison with GPS ground-truth

Figure 2: Cell* Steps [Best viewed in Color].

2.2 Challenges

There is much work on localization, yet the problem we explore is significantly more difficult than traditional formulations because the input data is much more limited.

Firstly, The spatial granularity of the location information is at best that of a sector/BTS (Figure 1), which is often quite large (especially in rural areas). Most significantly, there is no information on the set of cell sectors that are within range of a subscriber and there is no measurement of the signal strength (i.e., RSSI) with which a mobile can hear its associated cell sector or vice versa. While some of this information does reach the BSC/RNC when there is an active communication (i.e., data exchange), logging it would be a major departure from current operational practices such that we do not consider it a possibility in this paper. Given these restrictions, we cannot use popular localization methods that use WiFi signal fingerprinting or cell tower signal attenuation models.

Furthermore, the sequence of associations is logged at a lower granularity. Firstly, the mobile terminals may switch between BTSs of the same RNC without even notifying the network (Figure 1), making this an undetectable operation by the network. While modern smartphones frequently exchange frames with the associated towers (e.g., periodic e-mail checking), in practice, in most cellular deployments it is only viable to log information at the SGCN level: tower associations may only be recorded when a user is making/receiving calls, sending/receiving SMS, crossing Location Area Codes (LACs) or when polled by the network (usually every 2-3 hours).

Finally, even if the associated BTS is known, deriving the exact location of the mobile terminal is still challenging. Often, to balance load the BSC/RNCs may not associate mobiles to the nearest sector. Moreover, a mobile terminal itself may not necessarily switch to the nearest sector, even when it would provide a better signal, as long as it maintains a good connection with the previously associated tower. Therefore, the associated sector is partly a function of the connection history, as well as the current load, the topology and the availability of certain technologies in the area (2G/3G/4G).

As a consequence, our problem is significantly more challenging, due to the inherent sparse nature of the data under consideration.

2.3 Solution Overview

We divide our mobile path estimation procedure into five steps. We briefly explain the goal of each step and why it is appropriate. The next sections describe the methodology of each step in more detail.

- **STEP 1: Model the coverage area of the sectors.**
  To interpret mobile associations with cell sectors, we first need to model where a subscriber is likely to be while associated. That is, we need to understand the coverage of the cell sectors. For each sector, we build a model for the expected coverage based on the information that is available to the network operator. This information includes the sector location, orientation, beam width, and the intended spatial extent of the installation (i.e., macro, micro, or femto cell). A visualization of these characteristics (location, beam width, orientation and power) for an observed set of sectors C_m is shown in Figure 2a. The coverage models can be combined to identify *the overlap* between two sectors S_i and S_j to understand likely handover locations.
- **STEP 2: Identify stationary and mobile segments.**
  We model mobile subscribers as alternating between stationary and mobile states. Since different estimation procedures are appropriate for the different states, we split the cellular observations C_m into *stationary* and *mobile* sub-sequences. A stationary sequence is defined as the sequence of cell sectors S a mobile device sees while in the same logical location (e.g., building) for more than τ=15 minutes. A mobile sequence is defined as the sequence between two stationary sequences (Figure 2b).

  Separating stationary and mobile segments is not trivial because devices may typically connect to multiple towers even when they are stationary. By using the coverage maps, we can understand when handovers are consistent with a single underlying location and when handovers imply significant motion as the more likely behavior.
- **STEP 3: Estimate location for a stationary sequence.**
  To generate a path $\hat{P}_m$ we need to identify the two end-point locations. During each stationary sequence (derived from step 2), a number of sectors may be observed: the median is four unique sectors. Therefore, we can use the whole set of observed sectors over time to derive a more accurate estimate of the device's fixed location than using the whole coverage area of a single sector. Our procedure uses the coverage area of each tower (step 1) plus the duration the mobile was associated with each sector. Figure 2b shows this estimated location for the two endpoints (stationary periods) of a path. In this example, at each endpoint 3 unique sectors where used to approximate the device's stationary location.

- **STEP 4: Identify high-probability areas of the path.** For each mobile sequence (given from step 2), a number of intermediate sectors are observed (median is 12 unique sectors) between the stationary sequences that serve as endpoints (Figure 2a). The coverage of the observed sectors indicates the areas that the mobile device traveled through with high probability. An illustration of these inferred coverage areas of the intermediate sectors is shown in Figure 2b. We find that these areas typically constrain the path of the mobile subscriber, as shown in Figure 2c. Note that there are tradeoffs between accuracy and completeness. We find it more useful to estimate incomplete but high-probability areas such as handovers at the intersection between adjacent sectors rather than estimate complete but lower-probability areas such as the entire coverage area of all associated cell sectors.
- **STEP 5: Estimate the path with map information.** The previous steps give us estimates of the starting and ending locations of the path of a mobile subscriber (step 3), plus high-probability intermediate areas (step 4). We also know that humans typically move on streets or public transport routes and take fairly direct trips. Thus we use the high-probability areas to bias route search over mapping (GIS) information. More specifically, we apply the A* [16] street-routing algorithm over a map where the streets have adjusted weights based on the inferred coverage (Figure 2b). Figure 2c shows the inferred path through these high probability areas. The combination tends to work well. People typically take short paths but frequently do not take the *exact* shortest path, so a straightforward map lookup does not work well. Using the high-probability area as a bias factor captures the idiosyncratic deviations that people make from shortest paths. Figure 2d shows an example where the user did not take the shortest path.

Notice that in the above process there is no use of the timestamp $t_m[i]$ information. These can be potentially used to estimate the average speed of the device (e.g., to differentiate between highways and secondary roads) and the means of transport (e.g., walking v.s. driving). This information may be provided to the A* algorithm to improve its accuracy. However, the way that the associations are logged exhibits significant temporal noise, especially for shorter trips. More specifically, we cannot be certain about the exact time that the user departed and arrived to a certain destination: this can be only detected when there is network activity and it can happen minutes or even hours before the departure or after the arrival. Furthermore, given the large coverage area of a tower we do not know the exact location where an association took place and, therefore, calculating an average speed between events is challenging. As such, *Cell** is not making use of timestamp information.

3. SOLUTION DETAILS

We present our solution by detailing each of the five steps (§3) in turn.

3.1 Model the coverage of sectors

We build a coverage map to estimate the likelihood that a mobile subscriber m is at a particular position given the fact that it is associated with sector S. It is convenient to use a polar coordinate model for positions. The likelihood is then a function of three parameters: the power P of the sector; the distance d between the mobile and the cell tower; and the angle factor ϕ of the mobile relative to the sector. The angle factor is defined as the ratio of the polar angle of the mobile relative to the major axis of the sector and the beam-width of the sector. Thus $\phi = 0$ represents the major

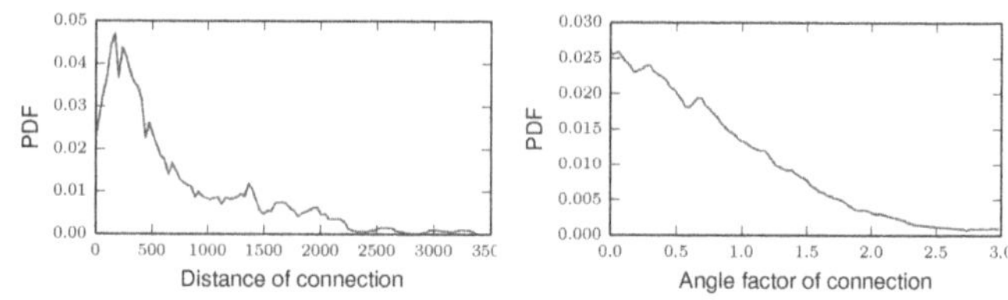

Figure 3: Projections of the coverage PDF for a macro-sectored tower on (a) distance of connection and (b) angle factor of connection.

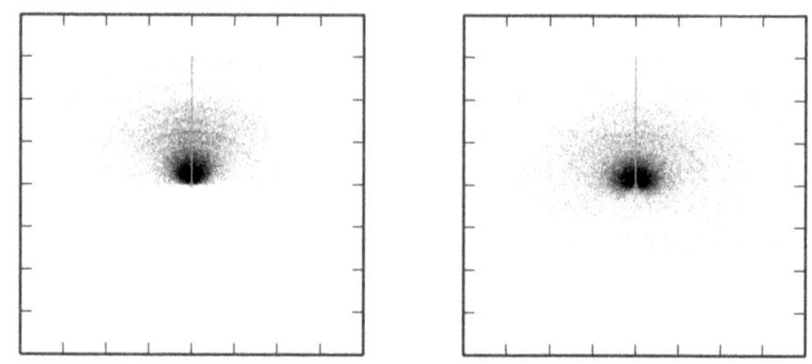

Figure 4: Coverage PDF for sectors having beam width of 60 degrees (left) and 120 degrees (right).

axis of the sector while $\phi = 1$ represents the nominal extent of the antenna beam.

Rather than compute the coverage map analytically, we use ground truth data of associations at different locations to approximate it empirically. We find this to be simple and effective. (We describe how this data was collected and cleaned in §4.) The result is the coverage probabilities as a PDF that we denote by $W_P(d, \phi)$, using the same notation for parameters as explained above.

To get a sense of coverage, the projection of $W_P(d, \phi)$ on both dimensions for a macro-sectored tower is shown in Figure 3. It shows how the association probability falls off roughly exponentially with distance d (left side) and more linearly with angle factor ϕ (right side). We treat the coverage map as fixed even though the probability of associating to a particular sector changes with RF conditions, as this works sufficiently well in practice[2].

Figure 4 shows the coverage PDF directly for sectors with beamwidths of 60 and 120 degrees. For the efficient computation, we discretize space into 15m $\times$ 15m grid squares over the entire map. For every square g in the grid we derive the probability of connecting to the sector S by integrating the coverage PDF $W_P(d, \phi)$ over all points x in the square g.

$$Q(g, S) = \int_{x \in g} W_P(d_x, \phi_x)$$

We call $Q(g, S)$ the *probability grid*. In the steps that follow, we work with these squares as the most convenient form of the coverage map.

Recall that we have as input a discrete trajectory in the form of a sequence of time-stamped cell sector associations. We want to split this sequence into stationary and mobile segments. To do so, we build on the coverage PDF in the form of the probability grid $Q(g, S)$.

[2] For example, weather condition changes will affect the probability of attachment of the mobile to different sectors.

3.2 Identification of stationary and mobile segments

We call two sectors S_1 and S_2 *adjacent* if there is a square g in the grid such that $Q(g, S_1) > 0$ and $Q(g, S_2) > 0$. That is, a mobile can connect to both sectors without moving. We say a sequence of sectors $S_1, \ldots, S_n$ is *stationary* if every two sectors are adjacent and the duration of the sequence as determined by its timestamps is greater than τ. That is, the mobile can connect to all sectors without moving and this situation persists for long enough that non-adjacent handovers would likely have occured if it was actually moving.

Finally, we extend stationary periods as far along the sequence as possible. Then we define the sequence of sectors between two stationary periods (which cannot itself be stationary) to be a *mobile* period. In our data (see §4), we find that many subscribers connect to a single sector for long periods of time in a stationary period. The median number of connected sectors in a stationary period is 4. In contrast, in mobile periods the subscriber tends to associate to multiple non-adjacent sectors with frequent handovers. The median is 12 sectors per mobile period.

3.3 Finding the location while stationary

We use all information in the stationary period to estimate the stationary location because an accurate endpoint is instrumental in inferring an accurate route for the mobile segment.

If a stationary segment consists of only one sector S, the most likely position is simply the square g that maximizes $Q(g, S)$. There is little we can do to improve the accuracy of the estimate. However, when the stationary period contains several sectors $S_1, \ldots, S_n$ then we can use all of the sectors to refine our location estimate. To do so, we find the point g that maximizes the sum of probabilities $Q(g, S_i)$ over the sectors weighted by the amount of time τ_i the subscriber was connected to the sector S_i. That is:

$$g^* = \arg\max_g \sum_{i=1}^{n} Q(g, S_i)\tau_i.$$

For a complete path consisting of a starting stationary period, mobile period, and ending stationary period, this procedure gives us an estimated location for the start and end points. We note that the end point for one path forms the start period for the next path with no discontinuities because they share the same stationary period.

3.4 Likelihood of crossing a square in the grid

While we have an estimate for the stationary locations, we have not yet used the information in the mobile period. As a final input to our path estimation procedure, we mine the mobile sequence for locations that the subscriber passes through with high-probability. In the next step, we will bias our estimated path to follow the high-probability locations.

Recall that for a square g, $Q(g, S)$ is the probability that a subscriber in g is connected to S. For each square g we denote the *score* $\rho(g)$ of the mobile segment $S_1, \ldots, S_n$ as:

$$\rho(g) = \sum_{i=1}^{n} Q(g, S_i). \qquad (3)$$

That is, we compute the union of the coverage PDF for all sectors in the mobile segment. This score is no longer a probability, but the higher the score for a square g the more likely that the path of the subscriber passed through that square. Observe that summing the coverage PDFs also increases the weight on locations that overlap between sectors by "double counting" them. These are precisely the most likely handover locations.

3.5 From mobile segment to a path

Our early efforts at path estimation showed us that purely geometric approaches based on cell tower locations were unlikely to yield good accuracy. (We evaluate this in §5.) The location problem is simply too under-constrained. To improve accuracy, we observe that real paths are consistent with the underlying road infrastructure. We can use the road network to constrain the path between the stationary endpoints.

An obvious question is whether, given the use of GIS maps, we need to use the mobile segment at all – we do not if people simply follow the shortest (or fastest) path on the road network between two locations. Zhu and Levinson [23] demonstrate that humans do tend to follow short paths when traveling between two locations, but with variations on the shortest route owing to many attributes such as how they value their time, willingness to pay tolls and fuel, time budgets, behavioral preferences, habituation, and experience of a given route. They show that 60% of the users take the exact shortest path as their route, and in almost 90% of cases people choose routes that have small deviations, of at most 5 minutes away from the optimal one.

Our approach is to use the scores of the squares $\rho(g)$ to bias routing on the road network. By using the scores, we preferentially search for a route in the "corridor" formed by the coverage areas of all sectors in the mobile segment. High scores close to the shortest path represent likely deviations.

Our implementation uses OpenStreetMaps (OSM) [10], a community-driven repository that contains data about roads, POIs, railway connections, etc. OSM is designed to be used for navigation purposes as it includes information for routing by many modes including car, foot and bicycle. The OSM data can be thought of as a graph $G = (\mathcal{V}, E)$ of the road network. Nodes $\mathcal{V}$ represent the geographical locations of intersections or points along curved road segments, while each edge represents a directional road-segment between two nodes. In the rest of the paper, we use the car OSM mode, and leave the problem of also inferring the mode of transport for future work. We proceed as follows.

Initial edge weights: For each edge $e \in E$ an initial weight, $\mathcal{W}(e) \in \mathbb{R}$ is assigned that represents the *expected time* that is required to traverse it. This weight depends on: i) the length of the road segment; ii) the type of the road segment (e.g., motorway, primary, secondary, footpath); and iii) the mode of transport (e.g., walking, driving). The required information and the default values of these weights for each mode of transport are calculated based on the OSM recommendations [10]. Notice that for some means of transport certain roads might be restricted (e.g., motorways cannot be used for walking routes).

Modifying the weights based on mobile segment sectors $S_1, \ldots, S_m$: After calculating the default weights for every road segment, we adjust them based on the scores of squares in the grid. Each road segment e crosses several square grids $g_1, \ldots, g_l$. We want to up-weigh roads with high scores and down-weigh roads with low scores to prefer locations that the subscriber crossed with high probability. We adjust the weight of the segment e heuristically as:

$$\bar{\mathcal{W}}(e) = \frac{\mathcal{W}(e)}{\frac{1}{l}\sum_{i=1}^{l} \rho(g_i) + \epsilon \max \rho(g)}$$

The use of ϵ allows the route to gracefully handle gaps in coverage due to low (zero) scores rather than require a major diversion. It basically allows to balance the tradeoff between the short/best routes and the routes that are close to the observed sectors. We experiment with various ϵ values and observe that as long as $\epsilon \leq 0.1$ the expected errors reported in the evaluation section are insensitive of the choice of ϵ.

Routing: After adjusting the weights, we use the standard A* algorithm to search the graph for a shortest weighted path between the start and end points. We use A* for pathfinding because running Dijkstra on the entire network graph is computationally expensive; A* is much faster and performs well in our setting. The resulting path in the graph is our final estimate for the path taken by the mobile subscriber, i.e $\hat{P}_m$. An example is shown in Figure 2d.

4. EXPERIMENTAL DATASET

To evaluate *Cell**, we need a dataset that contains cellular-side observations and the corresponding ground truth for the paths taken by mobile subscribers. While our algorithm is designed to work solely with cellular-side data, we find it expedient to collect matching trajectories for cellular data and location ground truth using a smartphone. We describe the collection method and dataset in this section.

4.1 Probe Application

We implemented a probe application for Android and used mobile phones to collect a dataset for evaluation. The probe runs as a background service collecting either event-driven or periodic measurements. Measured samples are stored locally at the device as a collection of geographically-annotated, time-stamped GeoJSON objects. They are periodically uploaded to our servers. The most important types of measurements are summarized below.

Location: A location sample is generated whenever there is any change to the *network-based* (WiFi or GSM trilateration) location of the device as reported by the Android API. In addition, we *periodically collect GPS samples.* To avoid depleting the user's battery, *one GPS sample per minute* is collected and the GPS sampling is paused while the user is connected to a WiFi network and associated to the same cell (e.g., when stationary at work/home).

Cellular Information: A sample is generated every time there is a handover from one sector to another. The collected information includes the IDs of the sector, RNC, and LAC (see §2). This information can be used to identify the tower in the database of the cellular operator. Notice that additional information, such as periodic collection of the full lists of received towers and the RSSI to each one of them, is also collected by the probe, but it is not used for this study because this information cannot readily be logged by the cellular operator. Finally, any connectivity changes or switches between types of connectivity (2G/3G/4G) are also logged.

Wi-Fi Information: Events concerning the Wi-Fi connectivity changes (e.g., connections and disconnections) are logged. This information can help us to further geo-locate the mobile in post-processing when the accuracy reported by Android is not adequate (e.g., due to a lack of connectivity to query Google servers) and to understand if the user was in the same indoor location.

4.2 Dataset and Cleaning

The probe was installed by 30 users and used over a period of 8 months[3]. All users live within a single country but multiple cities are covered. To increase diversity we selected users that cover a variety of age groups (20-60), who live in both urban and suburban areas, and who exhibit different commute patterns (bus, walking, cycling, driving, underground). In total, we logged more than 4.6 million samples over 19,000 hours of collection. A break-down of these samples is shown in Table 1.

[3]Some users did not run the probe for the full duration of the experiment.

Type	Number
Total number of Cell samples	1,718,504
Total number of Hand-overs	433,031
Number of Distinct Sectors observed	15,455
Sectors in the operator's database	> 100,000
Number of Location samples (Netw. and GPS)	673,468
Number of GPS samples	259,032
Total time logged (all devices)	19,438 hours
Total time stationary	18,335 hours
Total time moving	1,102 hours
Number of trajectories (trips)	3,216
Total distance traveled	19,840 km

Table 1: The collected dataset. Each sample is a record of a sector association, handover, GPS/network location update, etc.

Before using the dataset for experiments, we had to clean it to remove outliers. We proceeded as follows.

Inaccurate GPS: GPS or network-based location is used as the ground truth in our study but it does have its own accuracy errors. Android reports location information along with an estimate of its error L_{error}. In our samples, we observe a 90th-percentile error of 86 meters for GPS (median is 19 meters). This compares to 142 meters for indoor network-based locations (median is 65 meters). To limit problems, we discard any location measurements with reported error $L_{error} \geq 100$ meters. These inaccurate samples make up 8% of the 673,468 location samples.

Stale sector database: We have access to a database for all the sectors of a major cellular operator that contains the exact location, orientation, beam-width, power characteristics and type of installation of more than 100,000 sectors within a country. The database is updated continually. For instance, we notice that more than 100 sectors are re-located monthly whereas more than 3000 cells are added or removed. To protect against stale data, we remove any associations to sectors that have moved or are obviously misplaced (e.g., more than 20km away from the GPS location of the user). This cleaning process removed only 0.06% of the 433,031 observed associations.

Gaps in collection: Gaps in data collection may happen occasionally because smartphones might run out of battery or terminate the probe application. The difficulty with gaps is that they can lead to unrealistic trajectories without a normal start or end. We mark these gaps so that we can filter out any trajectory that includes them.

Subway usage: In the country that we collected the data, metro (underground) stations have cellular coverage through a *radiating cable* that runs along the whole metro line. This means that while a user is traveling within a single metro line, she is always associated to the same sector. Thus different methods are required for estimating trajectories that include metro usage. Since the metro is not our focus, we identify and remove any sectors that cover metro lines.

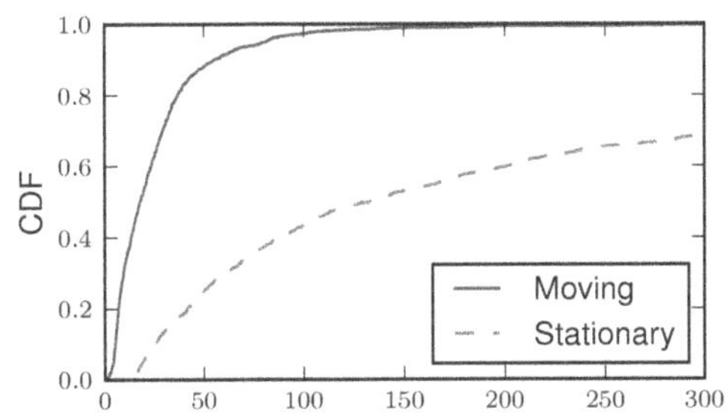

(a) CDF of interval duration.

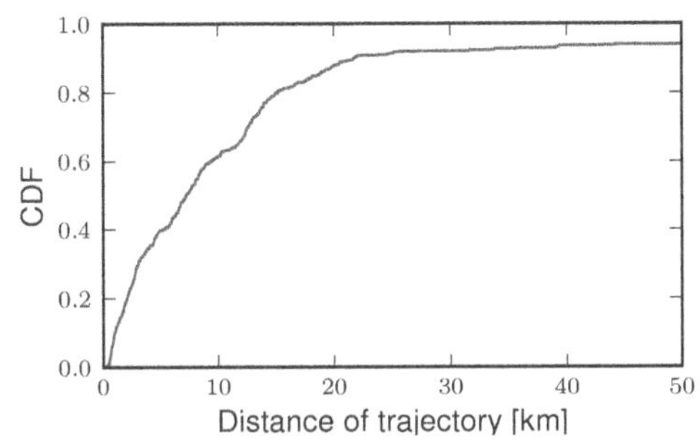

(b) Distance of a trajectory.

Figure 5: Ground-truth statistic.

4.3 Ground-Truth Trajectories

We need ground-truth trajectories to evaluate how well *Cell** estimates the paths. Notice that even when a user is stationary, the reported GPS or network (WiFi-based) locations can exhibit small variations over time. An example is given in Figure 6. Therefore, to identify when the user is stationary and to find the actual fixed location we follow the *Leader-based Clustering* methodology described in [14]. In essence we merge nearby location samples: for every location sample, we determine if it belongs to any of the already generated clusters by computing its distance to the cluster leader's location. If this radius is below a threshold $R_{cluster}$ the point is added to the cluster and the most central point (median) is the new leader. At the end of this process each cluster contains all the location samples that are within $R_{cluster}$ of the center of the cluster.

To determine the threshold (the cluster radius) we used the WiFi connectivity and the distribution of L_{error}. We considered a user stationary when they stayed connected to a specific WiFi BSSID (e.g., at home or work). We determined that $R_{cluster} = 100m$ produced clusters that correctly contain such intervals. This value is also consistent with the L_{error} that we used for GPS data-cleaning.

To find trajectories, we consider the user in a stationary period, that represents an endpoint, if the time that the user stayed in the cluster is larger than τ. For consistency, we use the same $\tau = 15$ minutes as with *Cell**. Users are in mobile periods between stationary periods. This procedure identifies 3,216 distinct trajectories from our dataset.

Figure 5a shows the distribution of the time that a user was in stationary and mobile states using the ground-truth. Mobile trajectories are much shorter in duration than stationary periods. The median duration for a mobility segment is 23 minutes, and the majority of all recorded trajectories do not exceed one hour. In Figure 5b we observe that most mobile trajectories are shorter than 10 kilometers. On the other hand, stationary periods have a median duration of 132 minutes, while 22% of them last for more than 8 hours. Such a result is expected because most stationary segments correspond to the user being at work during the day or at home during the night.

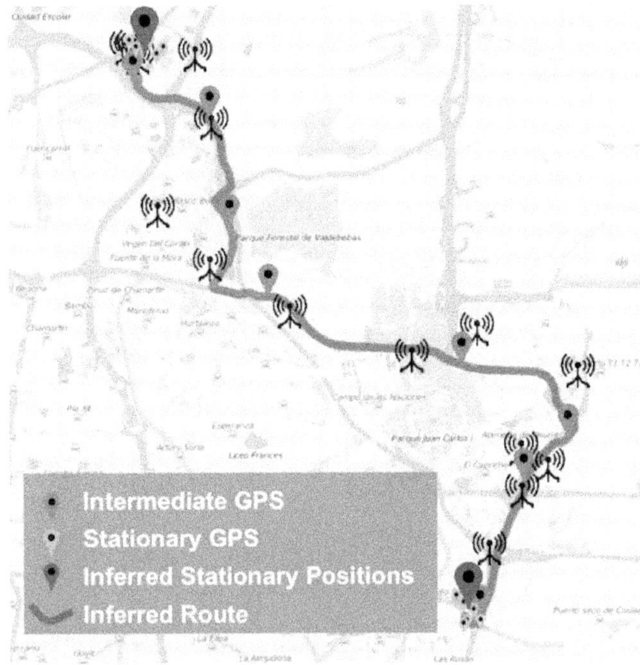

Figure 6: GPS ground-truth locations and estimated path

5. EVALUATION

In this section, we use our experimental dataset to evaluate the quality of the paths that are produced by *Cell**.

5.1 Methodology

We want to know how closely the paths $\hat{P}_m$, output by *Cell**, match the true paths of mobile subscribers. Recall our situation as shown for an example trajectory in Figure 6.

The subscriber follows a true path that is not shown in the figure or known to us. What is known is the measured GPS trajectory L_m. The GPS samples of this trajectory are shown in green (near the ends) for stationary periods and red (in the middle) for mobile periods. We use L_m as ground truth for our evaluation since it is the best estimate of the true path that we can gather.

However, note that the GPS samples are not true locations. They have an accuracy of L_{error} meters that is collected as part of GPS sampling. Even if the user is stationary the recorded location may slightly vary over time (especially when the user is indoors). The median reported accuracy is 19 m. This implies that, even if *Cell** estimates the mobile path perfectly, a comparison with GPS-based ground truth will show a residual inaccuracy.

The cellular trajectory C_m is denoted in the figure by the cell towers used for each handover. *Cell** uses these observations to produce the estimated path of the subscriber $\hat{P}_m$ that is shown as the solid blue line. While there are many ways that we might measure the accuracy of estimated paths, we use a simple method that we found to be sufficient. For each GPS sample, we can compute the shortest distance between the GPS location and the estimated path. We denote this error sample e_i. It represents how close the

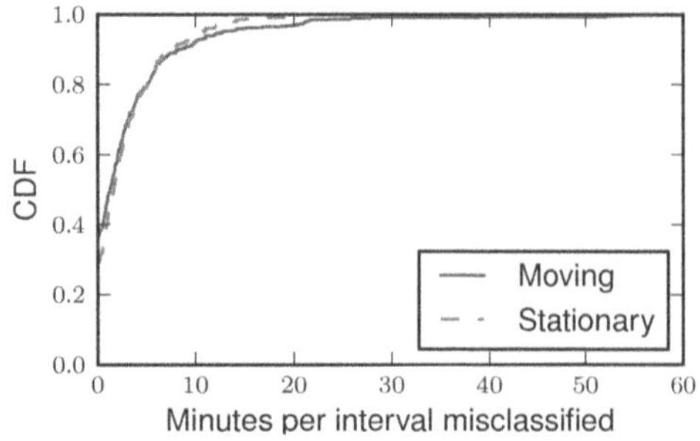

(a) CDF of time that was misclassified per period.

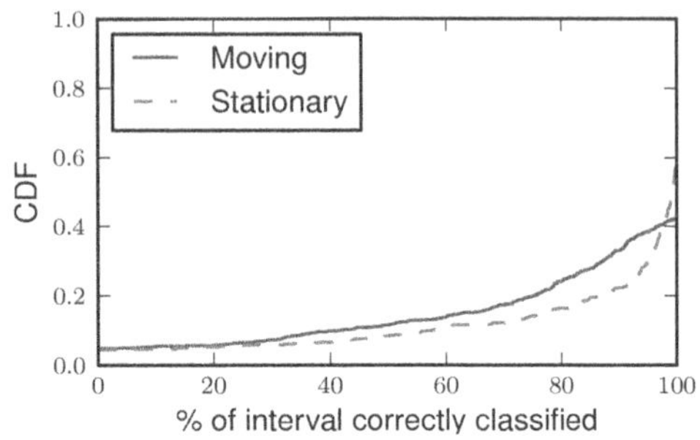

(b) Percentage of a period that was correctly classified.

Figure 7: Accuracy of detecting stationary/mobile periods.

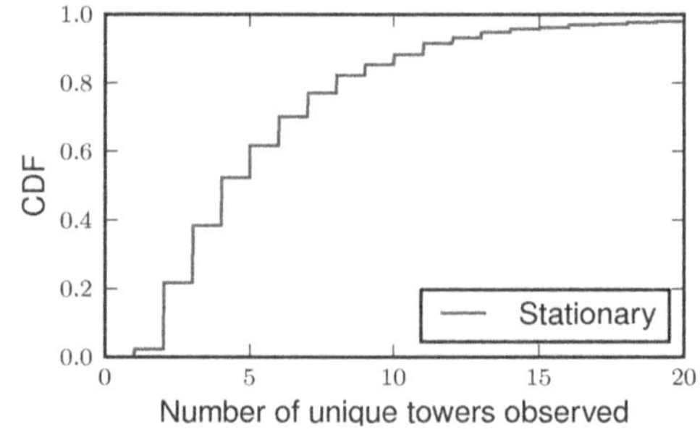

(a) # of unique sectors observed.

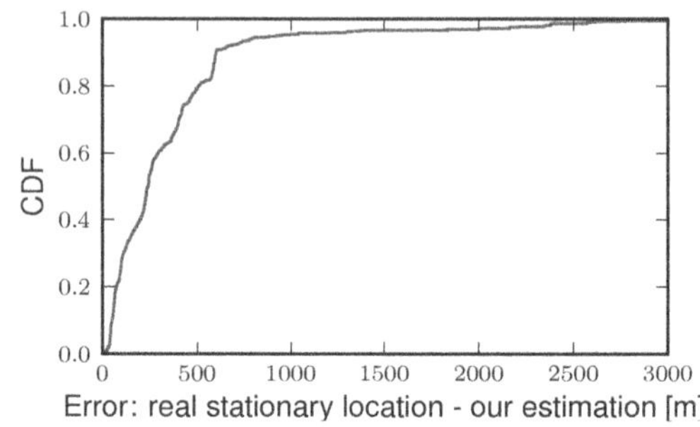

(b) Error of estimated stationary location.

Figure 8: Accuracy of estimating stationary location.

path goes to the GPS location, and we look at the distribution of error samples across all estimated paths. We also compute the error samples for a complete estimated path so that we can look at accuracy at the level of individual paths. We denote this sequence of error samples for an estimated path E_m.

In the next subsections, we evaluate the steps of our procedure. We begin by seeing how well *Cell** identifies the stationary and mobile segments of the trajectories (§3.2). Then we compute the accuracy of the stationary locations compared to GPS locations (§ 3.3). Finally, we look at the accuracy of the estimated paths (§5.5).

To help understand why the steps in our procedure lead to high accuracy, we contrast *Cell** with two methods that estimate paths with less information: a method that incorporates the most likely location of the mobile while associated with the recorded sectors, but that does not use any GIS information (just connects the points); and a pure map method that finds a route between the endpoints while ignoring all intermediate sector information. These comparisons indicate that a combination of methods is needed. Finally, we characterize the conditions under which *Cell** operates well.

5.2 Accuracy of static and mobile segments

In §3.2, we separate the sequence of sector observations into stationary and mobile periods to form trajectories. We use the ground-truth GPS trajectories L_m to evaluate the accuracy of this process. We use three measures: i) the time that is misclassified; ii) the percentage of a ground-truth stationary/mobile period that is misclassified; and iii) the number of trajectories that could not be identified.

Figure 7a shows the distribution of time (in minutes) that is misclassified per ground-truth stationary/mobile period. The median error is 2 minutes and the 80th-percentile of errors is less than 5 minutes. These results are quite good given that we are limited by coarse-grained cellular-side data that only captures user movement when a handover occurs. As we will see later, most of these errors occur during the beginning and the end of a mobile period when the user is still connected to the same sectors as in the stationary periods.

In Figure 7b we plot the distribution of the percentage of the ground-truth period that was correctly identified. We observe that we accurately identify a large percentage of the stationary and mobile periods. For each of 80% of static periods and 70% of mobile ones, we achieve more than 90% of accuracy.

Finally, only 3.1% of the mobile trajectories are not identified at all by using cellular-side data. Further investigation showed that these are short trips within the same coverage area; we cannot identify trajectories without handovers.

5.3 Accuracy of stationary locations

Next, we evaluate the accuracy with which we estimate the stationary location of a subscriber. These locations are important because they form the endpoints of the estimated path. In §3.3, we describe how we exploit multiple sector observations to narrow down our estimate of the stationary position of the subscriber. Figure 8 shows the distribution of number of unique towers observed during a stationary period. In most of the cases (98%) a user is associated to 2 or more sectors while the median is 4 sectors. This confirms that we do stand to improve accuracy by combining multiple cellular observations for the stationary location.

We define the error in stationary location as the geodesic distance between the *Cell** estimated location and the median of GPS locations during a stationary period. The CDF of errors is plotted in Figure 8b. About 50% of estimated locations have an error smaller than $230m$, and 80% of the estimated locations have an error less than $500m$. These results are significantly more accurate than the median distance of $480m$ at which a mobile subscriber is associated to a tower.

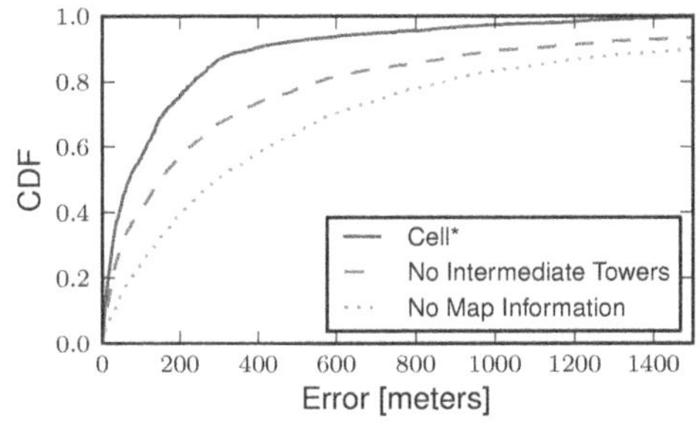

Figure 9: Error between GPS locations and estimated paths.

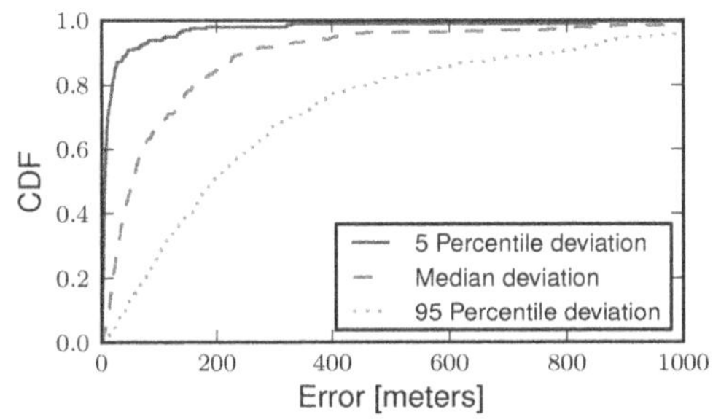

Figure 10: Per-path error statistics.

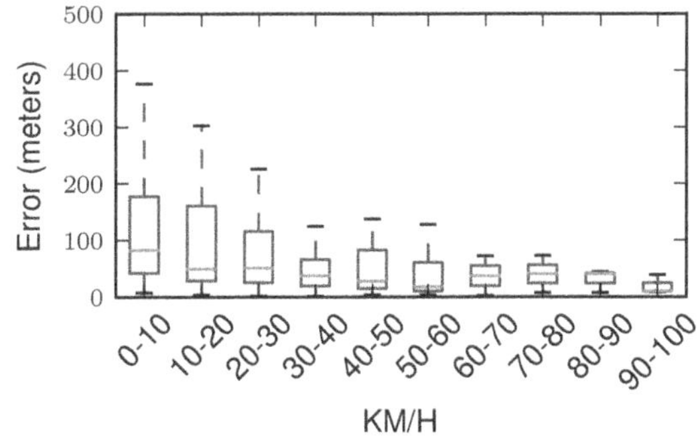

(a) Path median error vs its Speed.

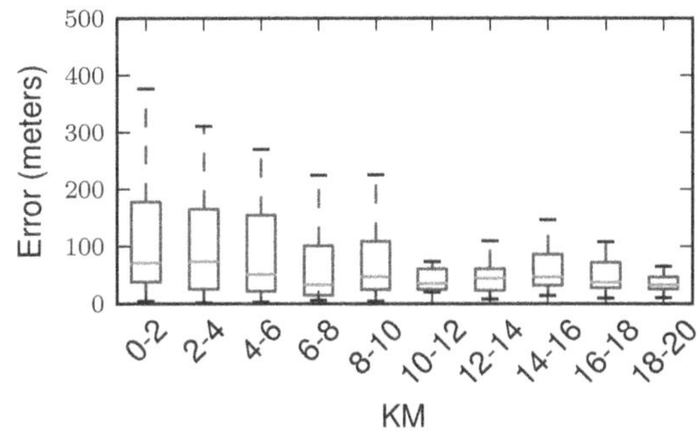

(b) Path median error vs its Distance.

Figure 11: Median error per route.

5.4 Accuracy of estimated paths

Now we evaluate the quality of complete paths produced by *Cell**. To get an overall sense of accuracy, we compute the error samples e_i that are the shortest geodesic distance from each GPS location associated with a trajectory to the estimated path. Figure 9 shows the distribution of the error samples across all trajectories. We observe that 75% of the errors fall below $180m$, and the median error is only $70m$. This positive result shows that *Cell** can accurately estimate paths given only the set of cellular handovers and without the assistance of GPS. For comparison, the median GPS accuracy for the same data is $19m$.

To understand how the different steps of our method contribute to the accuracy of paths, we make two comparisons. First, we run the street-routing algorithm on the road network between the stationary endpoints with basic weights of the roads according to their types. This process is equivalent to asking directions on Google maps or any other navigation system; no intermediate points due to handovers are considered. As we observe in Figure 9, while the median error is doubled to $150m$, many of the errors are reasonably low. This implies that street-routing provides valuable semantic information for finding real paths. However, 10% of the errors have large deviations of more than 1km. Street-routing is not sufficient by itself – it can go very wrong which is why it is important to use intermediate handovers.

Second, to see the value of using the intermediate handovers alone, we compare *Cell** paths to a path that simply connects the observed trajectory sectors with a straight line. The errors for this simple path are also shown in Figure 9. We see that they are significantly larger than *Cell** or even street-routing. The median error is 298 meters and in 10% of the cases we find deviations of more than 2.5km. We conclude that street-routing is essential.

We can also look at error samples on a per path basis. For each estimated path, we compute the 5th, median, and 95th percentile of the sequence of errors for the path E_m. In Figure 10 we see that 50% of the estimated paths have a median error of just $54m$, and a 95th percentile error of $200m$. If we consider that the average block size of a city is approximately 200 meters, we are able to estimate paths plus or minus one block 95% of the time.

5.5 Accuracy by Type of Path

Finally, we look into path properties that may make their estimation easier or harder. One such property could be the speed. High speed paths are likely to generate a larger number of handovers, and be constrained in a smaller area of the road network like arterial roads. Another related factor is distance, since longer paths generate a larger number of handovers.

Figure 11a shows the distribution of median errors per path when the paths are clustered according to their average speed. We observe it is harder to infer low-speed paths, as these are typically more chaotic walking routes in dense, urban environments. (They may also require the use of a different mode of OSM). For instance, some of these routes do not have specific destinations as they are random city walks, searching to shop etc. In contrast, we can accurately estimate high-speed paths as these typically include highway segments that are easier to predict.

Much the same behavior is observed when we look into how distance affects the error (Figure 11b). We are less accurate to estimate short paths as these include very few sector handovers, and the selection of route may deviate even farther from the absolute shortest path.

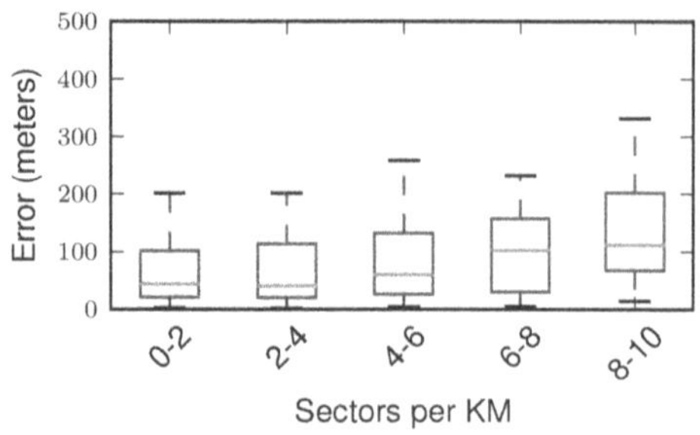

(a) Path median error vs Density of deployment.

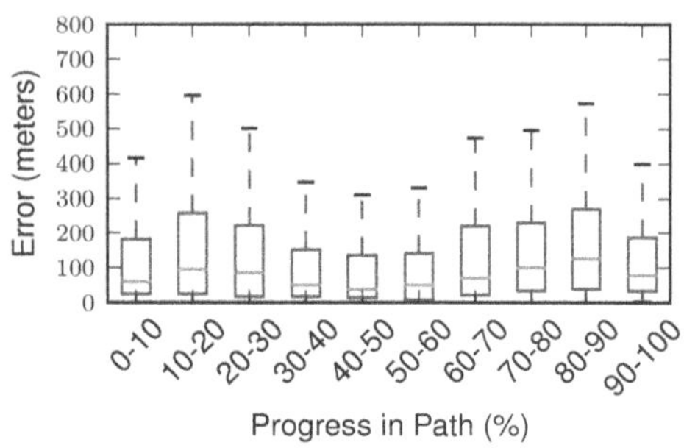

(b) Path median error vs Stage within the route.

Figure 12: Median error per path (meters).

It is also evident to us that the errors in path estimation are impacted by the density of the cellular deployment in the vicinity of travel. For example, suburban areas are expected to be covered with far fewer sectors than densely populated urban areas, and to cover a far greater distance with one sector. Indeed, the highest errors in our static location estimation come from suburban areas. To see density effects for the whole path, we define sector density for a path as the number of sectors available throughout the path divided by the path length.

Figure 12a shows the relationship between the path median error and its sector density. Contrary to our original intuition, we have more accurate path estimates in less dense tower installations (e.g., suburban areas with less than 0-2 towers per km). We conjecture that this happens because suburban areas tend to have sparser road networks as well, and their inhabitants tend to use cars more than in urban areas. We leave an exploration of the correlation between road density and cell infrastructure density for future work.

Finally, in Figure 12b we plot the accuracy of the estimated path as a function of the normalized elapsed time from the beginning of the path. Interestingly, *Cell** is more accurate during the initial and final 10% of the route. This happens due to the fact that we have a good estimation for the start and ending points. Furthermore, the accuracy is also good for the middle part of the trip as most people use primary roads (e.g., highways). It is slightly worse transitioning between these situations, likely due to less predictable secondary roads.

6. DISCUSSION

*Cell** enables mobility path estimation for connected devices that feature no GPS nor WiFi due to size, cost, or energy constraints. It can further be used on anomymized cellular network data in order to get information about the mobility patterns of the millions of subscribed devices, that could span both the "things" of the future,

Figure 13: Path estimation can sometimes be one block off from actual taken path

but also smartphone users. One possible implementation could be through a network API, that given the IMEI could return the estimated path for a predefined period of time.

Our results demonstrate a median accuracy of less than 70 meters, that falls within an average size city block, i.e. in 50% of the cases, our path estimation may take the road parallel to the one actually taken by the device. Figure 13 shows an example of such a case in our evaluation data - a part of the estimated path deviates from the actual path by one single block. As a result, *Cell** could enable a number of novel services for mobile connected devices, but may not be able to estimate the exact path taken under all conditions.

We find that the applications of mobility paths with such a level of accuracy could still be numerous. Examples could span city transportation planning, traffic monitoring at the macro level, or fleet management tracking in a computation and energy free fashion through an opt-in service, where the cellular network acts as a repository of mobility information.

Despite the fact that mobility path accuracy is not always to the exact street level, we find that higher order metrics computed on the extracted trajectories could still allow different operations with sufficient accuracy. For instance, we have computed the total length of the extracted mobility paths and compared it with the ground truth, as computed from GPS data. We find that despite the slight deviations in the derived paths, the total distance is just within 4.1% of the actual path on average. One could envision services where the estimation of the total distance may be more important than the precise path taken (for instance within a car insurance context, where the insurance company assigns risk based on the total distance driven).

Another point of discussion has to do with the granularity of data considered. While collection of handover events from all mobile subscribers is technically feasible today, in practice it comes at a cost with respect to the required network infrastructure (although with the adoption of LTE, logging information at high granularity might become economically viable). Our data captures device GPS location, along with BTS/RNC/LAC cellular information. In what follows we quantify the loss in accuracy in *Cell** if it is provided with even sparser data, that may be accessible at the RNC level or at the LAC (Figure 1). To do that we sub-sample the location infor-

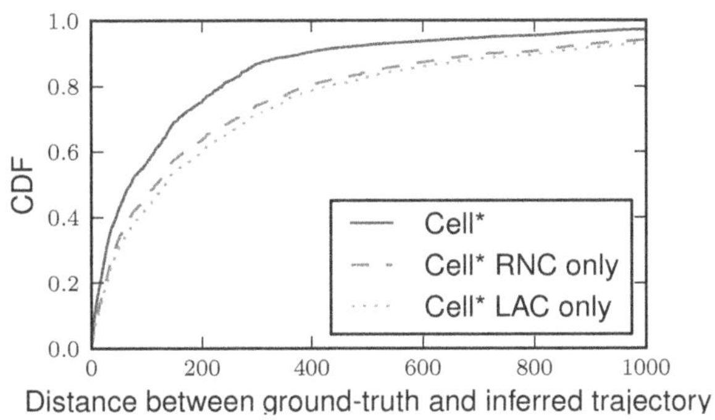

Figure 14: Path accuracy as a function of the cellular layer where location information is collected.

mation collected by our Android probe to only include handovers that are visible at the i) RNC or ii) LAC level [4]. We find that sparser observations for the mobile device lead to increased inaccuracy of 129 meters in the median case (up from 69.7 meters), while the 75th percentile error is now 340 meters (up from 200 meters). The entire distribution of errors for cellular location information collected at the different layers of the cellular infrastructure is shown in Figure 14. We were actually quite surprised that *Cell** still behaves well under such loss of information. We intend to look deeper into this in future work.

Finally, we note that the results presented in this paper capture the properties of the studied cellular provider network and the road network of the studied city. As mentioned previously, we speculate that geographic areas with dense road networks are very likely candidates for denser cellular network deployments. The tendency in the telecommunications area is that of reducing the radius of cell towers, going to micro- or femto-cell deployments. A decrease in the coverage area of cell towers and sectors will only improve the accuracy of *Cell**.

7. RELATED WORK

Along with the advance of tools to monitor fine-grained human mobility through mobile devices, our understanding on human mobility has been expanded in recent years. Researchers have found not only a basic law of governing human mobility [7] but also a limitation of predictability [21] based on the unprecedented volume of mobility traces. One of the important discoveries is a high degree of spatial and temporal regularities of human mobility [7]. It offers a strong foundation for a wide range of research challenges, such as important places identification [11], next location prediction [5] and frequent trajectory extraction [6].

Research on human mobility becomes important for urban planning, land use identification, population movement monitoring, traffic forecasting, transportation system management, travel demand prediction, and even infection control. Among many data sources for those studies, Call Detail Records (CDRs) play a prominent role due to their scalability. CDRs inherently have low spatial and temporal resolution, but a tremendous advantage - that of observing the mobility patterns of millions of cellular subscribers with no support required on the cellular device. Given the sparsity of data, most approaches working on route or location mining on CDRs are based on probabilistic approaches. Görnerup proposes a scalable probabilistic method based on locality-sensitive hashing and graph clustering for inferring common routes from sequences of sectors [8]. Saravanan et al. propose to aggregate CDRs to find people's daily routes by constructing a Gaussian model that explains the probability of people being around specific towers [19]. Also, Isaacman et al. present how to model people's movements in metropolitan-scale areas using spatial and temporal probability distributions extracted from CDRs [12]. All such approaches do not consider the geographic information but take the resolution of cell towers. By contrast, *Cell** enables to estimate the street-level path by incorporating the geographic information.

Building origin-destination (OD) matrices, which usually estimate the number of vehicles commuting between residence and workplace, is one of the popular applications [11]. In contrast to conventional methods to acquire OD matrices mainly depending on household surveys or road monitoring, using a GSM network is much more cost-effective [3, 4]. It shows the potential of huge volume of CDRs for urban planning and transportation engineering. Beyond OD matrices, that reveal endpoints of trajectories, there have been a few studies to infer a street-level path by using cellular-side information. Becker et al. use cellular hand-off patterns to identify commuting routes [1]. They generate a collection of hand-off patterns, as observed through fingerprinting by previously test driving the target area. The proposed method achieves high accuracy but the dictionary of hand-off patterns for every route is essential in advance, limiting the areas where such an approach can help.

Looking at client-side solutions, Paek et al. propose a lightweight positioning system using a mapping between GPS locations and associated cells for regular and relatively long routes [17]. In their system, each device records GPS locations and associated towers regularly. Then, a sequence of passed cells and the elapsed time can refine the current locations based on history. As this system essentially requires GPS readings as input, it does not directly compare to *Cell**.

Schlaich et al. propose a method to generate all the possible routes by using a multi-path route generation algorithm based on cellular-side location-area update messages [20]. They propose heuristics, such as taking road type into account, to restrict the selection of routes, but they do not have well defined criteria to choose the most probable route among many candidates. *Cell** neither collects specific data for each road, historical data, nor proposes all possible options. It suggests the most probable path by combining sector characteristics and GIS information.

With the near ubiquity of GPS-enabled devices, map matching becomes a core component of a wide range of applications, such as car navigation, route prediction, and activity recognition. Quddus et al. [18] conduct a comprehensive review of the map matching algorithms, from simple point-to-point mapping [2], to topological analysis of the spatial map [9], probabilistic approaches dealing with error regions [15], and sophisticated fuzzy modeling ones [13]. Cellular-side data is coarse-grained at the resolution of sectors. Thus, there are clear analogies between inferring a trajectory based on such low-resolution observations and identifying the most relevant road segment based on inaccurate GPS positioning data, although errors in distance can be quite different. *Cell** uses the probabilistic approach to refine locations and paths.

[4]Given space constraints we omit the details for cellular network infrastructure.

8. SUMMARY

Through their normal operation, cellular networks are a repository of continuous location information from its subscribed devices. Such information, however, comes at a coarse granularity both in terms of space, as well as time. For otherwise inactive devices location information can be obtained at the granularity of a BTS, and at infrequent points in time, that are sensitive to the structure of the network itself, and the level of mobility of the device. *Cell** enables the extraction of mobility paths from sparse spatio-temporal cellular location information. Using more than 3,000 mobility trajectories, we show that we are able to estimate the stationary locations with a median accuracy of 230 meters. When the device is mobile, we can estimate its mobility path with a median error of 70 meters. To achieve such accuracy, we are taking into account the cellular network topology, as well as geographic information. We show that mobility path accuracy improves with its length and speed, and counter to our intuition, accuracy appears to improve in suburban areas. *Cell** is the first technology, we are aware of, that allows location services for the new generation of connected mobile devices, that may feature no GPS, due to cost, size, or battery constraints.

Acknowledgments:
The research leading to these results has received funding from the European Union under the FP7 Grant Agreement n. 318627 (Integrated Project "mPlane"). We would also like to thank Yan Grunenburger, Enrique Garcia Illera, Hosung Park and Andreu Urrela Planas for their support and comments on this work.

9. REFERENCES

[1] R. A. Becker, R. Caceres, K. Hanson, J. M. Loh, S. Urbanek, A. Varshavsky, and C. Volinsky. Route classification using cellular handoff patterns. In *Proceedings of the 13th international conference on Ubiquitous computing*, UbiComp '11, 2011.

[2] D. Bernstein and A. Kornhauser. An introduction to map matching for personal navigation assistants. 1998.

[3] N. Caceres, J. Wideberg, and F. Benitez. Deriving origin destination data from a mobile phone network. *Intelligent Transport Systems, IET*, 1(1):15–26, 2007.

[4] F. Calabrese, G. Di Lorenzo, L. Liu, and C. Ratti. Estimating origin-destination flows using mobile phone location data. *IEEE Pervasive Computing*, 10(4):36–44, 2011.

[5] S. Gambs, M.-O. Killijian, and M. N. del Prado Cortez. Next place prediction using mobility markov chains. In *Proceedings of the First Workshop on Measurement, Privacy, and Mobility*, page 3. ACM, 2012.

[6] F. Giannotti, M. Nanni, F. Pinelli, and D. Pedreschi. Trajectory pattern mining. In *Proceedings of the 13th ACM SIGKDD international conference on Knowledge discovery and data mining*, pages 330–339. ACM, 2007.

[7] M. C. Gonzalez, C. A. Hidalgo, and A.-L. Barabasi. Understanding individual human mobility patterns. *Nature*, 453(7196):779–782, 2008.

[8] O. Görnerup. Scalable mining of common routes in mobile communication network traffic data. In *Proceedings of the 10th international conference on Pervasive Computing*, Pervasive'12, pages 99–106, 2012.

[9] J. S. Greenfeld. Matching gps observations to locations on a digital map. In *National Research Council (US). Transportation Research Board. Meeting (81st: 2002: Washington, DC). Preprint CD-ROM*, 2002.

[10] M. Haklay and P. Weber. Openstreetmap: User-generated street maps. *Pervasive Computing, IEEE*, 7(4):12–18, 2008.

[11] S. Isaacman, R. Becker, R. Cáceres, S. Kobourov, M. Martonosi, J. Rowland, and A. Varshavsky. Identifying important places in peopleâĂŹs lives from cellular network data. In *Pervasive Computing*, pages 133–151. Springer, 2011.

[12] S. Isaacman, R. Becker, R. Cáceres, M. Martonosi, J. Rowland, A. Varshavsky, and W. Willinger. Human mobility modeling at metropolitan scales. In *Proceedings of the 10th international conference on Mobile systems, applications, and services*, MobiSys '12, pages 239–252, 2012.

[13] S. Kim and J.-H. Kim. Adaptive fuzzy-network-based c-measure map-matching algorithm for car navigation system. *Industrial Electronics, IEEE Transactions on*, 48(2):432–441, 2001.

[14] A. Kirmse, T. Udeshi, P. Bellver, and J. Shuma. Extracting patterns from location history. In *Proceedings of the 19th ACM SIGSPATIAL International Conference on Advances in Geographic Information Systems*, GIS '11, pages 397–400, New York, NY, USA, 2011. ACM.

[15] W. Y. Ochieng, M. Quddus, and R. B. Noland. Map-matching in complex urban road networks. *Revista Brasileira de Cartografia*, 2(55), 2004.

[16] N. J. N. P. E. Hart and B. Raphael. A formal basis for the heuristic determination of minimum cost paths. *IEEE Transactions on Systems, Science, and Cybernetics*, SSC-4(2):100–107, 1968.

[17] J. Paek, K.-H. Kim, J. P. Singh, and R. Govindan. Energy-efficient positioning for smartphones using cell-id sequence matching. In *Proceedings of the 9th international conference on Mobile systems, applications, and services*, pages 293–306. ACM, 2011.

[18] M. A. Quddus, W. Y. Ochieng, and R. B. Noland. Current map-matching algorithms for transport applications: State-of-the art and future research directions. *Transportation Research Part C: Emerging Technologies*, 15(5):312–328, 2007.

[19] M. Saravanan, S. Pravinth, and P. Holla. Route detection and mobility based clustering. In *Proceedings of IEEE 5th International Conference on Internet Multimedia Systems Architecture and Application (IMSAA)*, pages 1–7, 2011.

[20] J. Schlaich, T. Otterstätter, and M. Friedrich. Generating trajectories from mobile phone data. In *Proceedings of the 89th Annual Meeting Compendium of Papers, Transportation Research Board of the National Academies*, 2010.

[21] C. Song, Z. Qu, N. Blumm, and A.-L. Barabási. Limits of predictability in human mobility. *Science*, 327(5968):1018–1021, 2010.

[22] A. Varshavsky et al. Are gsm phones the solution for localization? In *Mobile Computing Systems and Applications, 2006. WMCSA'06. Proceedings. 7th IEEE Workshop on*, pages 34–42. IEEE, 2005.

[23] S. Zhu and D. Levinson. Do people use the shortest path? an empirical test of wardropâĂŹs first principle. In *91th annual meeting of the Transportation Research Board, Washington*, volume 8, 2010.

The Cost of the “S” in HTTPS

David Naylor*, Alessandro Finamore†, Ilias Leontiadis‡, Yan Grunenberger‡,
Marco Mellia†, Maurizio Munafò†, Konstantina Papagiannaki‡, and Peter Steenkiste*

*Carnegie Mellon University †Politecnico di Torino ‡Telefónica Research

{dnaylor, prs}@cs.cmu.edu {finamore, mellia, munafo}@tlc.polito.it
{ilias, yan, dina}@tid.es

ABSTRACT

Increased user concern over security and privacy on the Internet has led to widespread adoption of HTTPS, the secure version of HTTP. HTTPS authenticates the communicating end points and provides confidentiality for the ensuing communication. However, as with any security solution, it does not come for free. HTTPS may introduce overhead in terms of infrastructure costs, communication latency, data usage, and energy consumption. Moreover, given the opaqueness of the encrypted communication, any in-network value added services requiring visibility into application layer content, such as caches and virus scanners, become ineffective.

This paper attempts to shed some light on these costs. First, taking advantage of datasets collected from large ISPs, we examine the accelerating adoption of HTTPS over the last three years. Second, we quantify the direct and indirect costs of this evolution. Our results show that, indeed, security does not come for free. This work thus aims to stimulate discussion on technologies that can mitigate the costs of HTTPS while still protecting the user's privacy.

Categories and Subject Descriptors

C.2.2 [**Computer-Communication Networks**]: Network Protocols

Keywords

HTTP 2.0; HTTPS; TLS; privacy; security; Web proxies

1. INTRODUCTION

The HyperText Transfer Protocol (HTTP) was first introduced in the early '90s. Since then, the Internet has changed significantly, becoming a vital infrastructure for communication, commerce, education, and information access. HTTPS, the secure version of HTTP, runs HTTP on top of SSL/TLS[1]. While originally geared toward services that require data confidentiality or authentication between client and server, like online banking or e-commerce, the increasing personalization of the web has led to a number of other services adopting HTTPS, such as GMail, Facebook, and even YouTube. Furthermore, HTTP is on the verge of a new milestone: the standardization of HTTP 2.0 [10] is slated for the end of 2014. Some discussions assume TLS will be used for *all* connections, mirroring a fundamental design decision of SPDY [14], which was used as the starting point for HTTP 2.0.

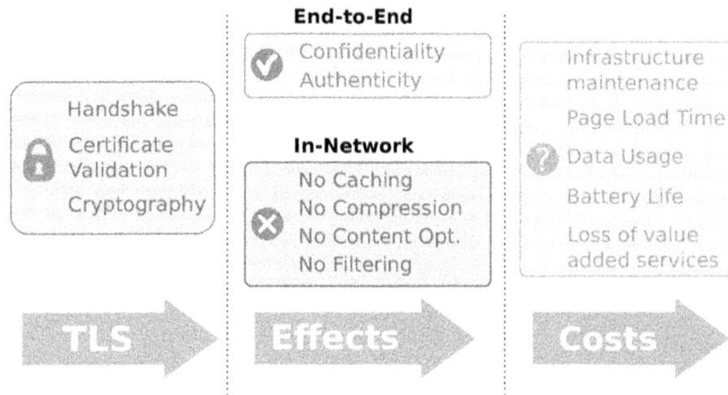

Figure 1: The HTTPS adoption impact chain.

Given users' growing concerns about security and privacy on the Internet, adopting encryption by default in all HTTP communication sounds like a good idea. However, security always comes at a cost, and HTTPS is no different (graphically depicted in Fig. 1). In this paper, we aim to categorize and quantify the cost of the “S” in HTTPS.

First, we look at the way HTTPS adoption has evolved over the past three years. Such an analysis is important because, besides quantifying trends, it sheds light on the cost of deploying HTTPS for web services, a cost that seems to be diminishing: 50% of web traffic flows today are secure, including, for the first time, large content (e.g., 50% of YouTube streaming flows are over HTTPS).

Second, we study how TLS impacts latency, data consumption, and battery life for clients. HTTPS requires an additional handshake between the client and the server in addition to the added computational cost of cryptographic operations. We study how significant these costs are for fiber, Wi-Fi, and 3G connections.

Lastly, while encryption provides a clear value to the end user in terms of confidentiality and authentication, it could have implications that are harder to assess. Over the past 15 years, an increasing number of network functionalities have been performed by transparent and explicit middleboxes, aiming to reduce the amount of backbone traffic, compress content before transmission on expensive wireless links, fil-

CoNEXT '14, December 02–05, 2014, Sydney, Australia.
Copyright 2014 ACM 978-1-4503-3279-8/14/12 ...$15.00.
http://dx.doi.org/10.1145/2674005.2674991.

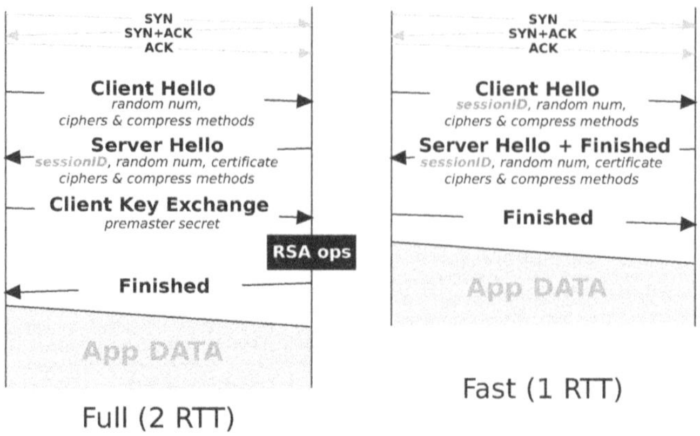

Figure 2: SSL/TLS negotiation.

ter inappropriate/undesired content, and protect users and organizations from security threats. These boxes suddenly become blind in the presence of encryption. We show that there are clear cases where losing such functionality may not only harm network efficiency, but also increase latency by more than 50% and consume up to 30% more energy for 3G mobile devices.

Using three different datasets, captured in residential and cellular networks, as well as controlled experiments, our work shows that: (i) HTTPS usage is increasing despite potential deployment costs, (ii) HTTPS has a perceptible impact on clients in terms of latency, (iii) its data overhead seems to be limited, (iv) it could lead to significantly increased battery consumption for large objects.

This creates a complex tradeoff that depends on many factors, including context and personal preference. While specific workloads will always be served through HTTPS (e.g., financial transactions), there are a number of applications where encryption could be optional or the service could be assisted by *trusted proxies*, which bring back the benefits of value-added services, as described in a recent IETF proposal [9]. How to best manage this tradeoff is an open question that challenges the research community. We hope this paper stimulates discussion in that direction.

2. HTTPS OVERVIEW

SSL/TLS is the standard protocol for providing authenticity and confidentiality on top of TCP connections. Today, it is used to provide a secure version of traditional protocols (e.g., IMAP, SMTP, XMPP, etc.); in particular, the usage of HTTP over TLS is commonly known as HTTPS.

Each TLS connection begins with a *handshake* between the server and the client. In this handshake, the Public Key Infrastructure (PKI) suite is used to authenticate the server (and sometimes the client) and to generate cryptographic keys to create a secure channel for data transmission.

Fig. 2 (left) sketches the steps in a *full* TLS negotiation. In this scenario, the client and the server incur different costs. On the server side, the primary cost is computing the session key. This involves complex public key cryptography operations (typically RSA), limiting the number of connections per second the server can support [2, 3, 4]. For clients, the major cost is latency. This depends on (i) server performance, (ii) the distance between client and server since a *full* negotiation requires 2 RTTs (3 including the TCP handshake), and (iii) the latency to verify the server's certificate with the PKI (e.g., an OSCP/CRL check).

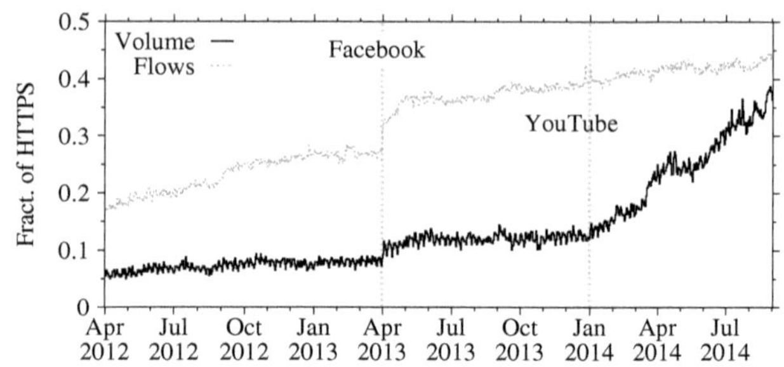

Figure 3: Evolution of HTTPS volume and flow shares over 2.5 years. Results from Res-ISP dataset. Vertical lines show the transition to HTTPS for Facebook and YouTube.

Unsurprisingly, a few optimizations have been proposed to reduce handshake costs. Hardware accelerators, GPU architectures [12], or "rebalancing" the RSA computations [3] can easily boost server performance by a factor of 10. Also, the TLS standard provides a *fast* negotiation mechanism, shown in Fig. 2 (right). In this case a `SessionID` is used to retrieve a previously negotiated session key, (i) avoiding the cost of creating a new session key and (ii) reducing the handshake to 1 RTT (2 including the TCP handshake). Note that the adoption of fast negotiation is controlled by the server; as we see in Sec. 4, only some services deploy it.

3. HTTPS USAGE TRENDS

A common belief is that deploying HTTPS increases infrastructure costs (to accommodate the resulting computational, memory, and network overhead) in addition to the cost of certificates (up to $1,999/year each[1]). Thus, one would expect services to carefully deploy HTTPS only when needed. To test this, we examine recent HTTPS usage trends. We collected per-flow logs from a vantage point monitoring the traffic of about 25,000 residential ADSL customers of a major European residential ISP ("Res-ISP"). The vantage point runs Tstat [7], which implements a classifier supporting both HTTP and TLS identification. For TLS traffic, Tstat parses the `ClientHello` and `ServerHello` TLS handshake messages to extract (i) Server Name Indication (SNI), i.e., the hostname to which the client is attempting to connect, and (ii) Subject Common Name (SCN) carried in the server certificate, i.e., the name the server itself presents. Tstat is also able to identify the presence of SPDY in the TLS connections. In the following, we use this rich ISP dataset to characterize the evolution of HTTPS usage. At the time of writing, HTTPS and HTTP combined represent 75% of all TCP traffic (by volume) in Res-ISP.

Fig. 3 reports the evolution of the HTTPS traffic share from April 2012 to September 2014. Both volume and flow shares are shown. The growth of HTTPS adoption is striking, with the HTTPS flow share more than doubling in two years. In September 2014, 44.3% of web connections already use HTTPS.[2] The sharp bump in April 2013 is due to Facebook enabling HTTPS by default for all users [13].

[1]https://www.symantec.com/page.jsp?id=compare-ssl-certificates

[2]Curiously, only 5.5% of flows successfully negotiated SPDY, despite 55% of clients offering the option. This highlights

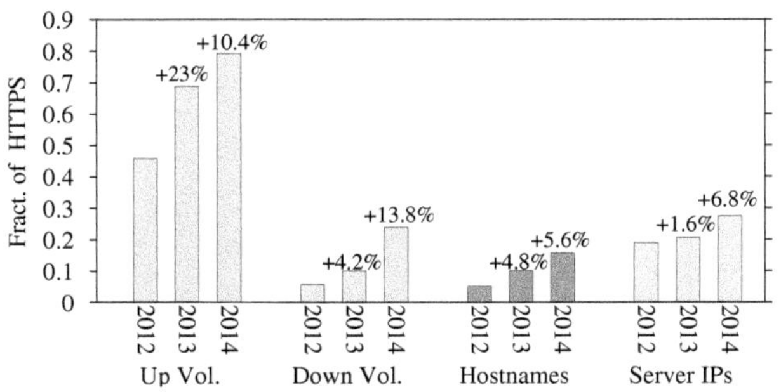

Figure 4: Comparing HTTPS shares over three one-week periods in the Res-ISP dataset. Percentages highlight year-to-year growth.

Looking at volume, we see a much slower growth. Intuitively, one would expect that most HTTPS flows carry small, privacy-sensitive objects. We see this until January 2014 when YouTube began delivering video content over HTTPS, clearly increasing the HTTPS volume share. As of September 2014, as much as 50% of YouTube's aggregate traffic volume is carried over HTTPS.

Fig. 4 further details HTTPS trends with respect to upload volume, download volume, number of hostnames, and number of server IP addresses. We compare the first week of April in 2012, 2013 and 2014 (results are consistent for other weeks). Percentages show the year-to-year increase. The growth of HTTPS is again evident. For instance, HTTPS accounts for 80% of the upload volume in 2014; it was only 45.7% in 2012. This reflects the fact privacy-sensitive information tends to be uploaded using HTTPS more and more. Interestingly, the fraction of data downloaded using HTTPS is smaller than the fraction uploaded. However, YouTube's shift to HTTPS in 2014 dramatically changed the landscape: HTTPS download volume more than doubled compared to 2013. Fig. 4 also highlights a constant year-by-year increase for both the fraction of hostnames and server IP addresses accessed using TLS. Interestingly, 72% of the TLS hostnames are accessed exclusively over TLS in 2014.

These results clearly show that, despite the perceived costs, services are rapidly deploying HTTPS. This shift is undoubtedly related to the recent attention toward guaranteeing end-users privacy. However, this may also be an indication of increasingly manageable infrastructural costs. This is consistent with the report from the GMail team after their switch to HTTPS: "On our production frontend machines, SSL/TLS accounts for less than 1% of the CPU load, less than 10KB of memory per connection and less than 2% of network overhead."[3] Reports from Facebook are similar.[4]

Takeaway: *HTTPS accounts for 50% of all HTTP connections and is no longer used solely for small objects, suggesting that the cost of deployment is justifiable and manageable for many services.*

that SPDY is only supported by a handful of (popular) services, namely Google and Facebook.

[3]https://www.imperialviolet.org/2010/06/25/overclocking-ssl.html

[4]http://lists.w3.org/Archives/Public/ietf-http-wg/2012JulSep/0251.html

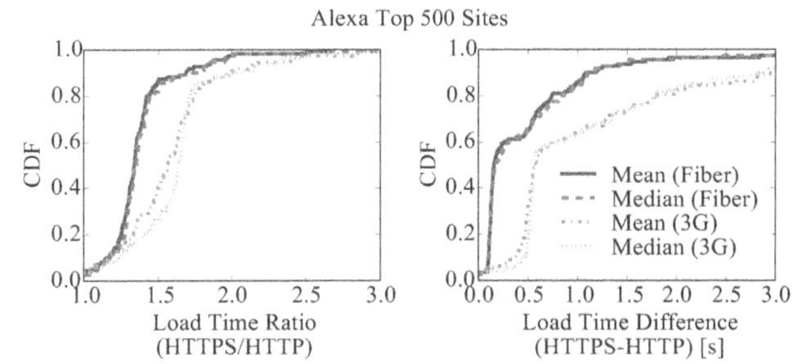

Figure 5: Webpage load time inflation for the Alexa top 500.

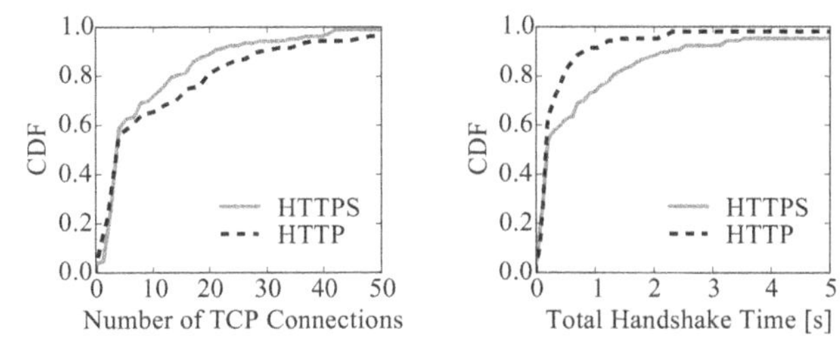

Figure 6: Number of TCP handshakes (left) and total handshake time (right) for the Alexa top 500 (fiber).

4. WEBPAGE LOAD TIME

We now investigate how much HTTPS affects load time, an important quality-of-experience metric for web browsing.

Overall Page Load Time: First we quantify the HTTPS page load time overhead through active experiments. We load each of the top 500 Alexa sites 20 times, first using HTTP and then using HTTPS. For the download, we use PhantomJS[5], a fully-fledged headless browser running on a Linux PC. From each run, we extract the average and median load times. The test PC is connected first using a 3G USB modem and then via fiber, two typical real-world environments. The local cache is cleared between page loads.

Results are reported in Fig. 5. Plots show the Cumulative Distribution Function (CDF) of the ratio of HTTPS to HTTP page load time (left) and the absolute difference (right). The benchmark shows that using HTTPS significantly increases load time. This is especially evident on 3G, where the extra latency is larger than 500 ms for about 90% of websites, and 25% of the pages suffer an increase of at least 1.2 s (i.e., an inflation factor larger than 1.5x). On fiber, the extra latency is smaller; still, for 40% of the pages, HTTPS adds more than 500 ms (1.3x).

We also captured an HTTP Archive (HAR) for each page, which contains statistics about the individual connections used to load the page. Fig. 6 (left) shows 40% of the sites open fewer TCP connections when loaded over HTTPS compared to HTTP. Even so, Fig. 6 (right) shows nearly half of the sites spend *more time* establishing those connections; the increased time per handshake is caused primarily by TLS negotiation overhead (see below). By examining the HARs, we see that many of the sites using fewer connections serve fewer objects (1–3 fewer on average, but in some cases upwards of 100 fewer) and do so from fewer hosts (typically 1–2 fewer, but in some cases up to 40 fewer). We suspect these are intentional changes to the HTTPS version of the site designed to avoid costly TLS handshakes.

[5]http://phantomjs.org/

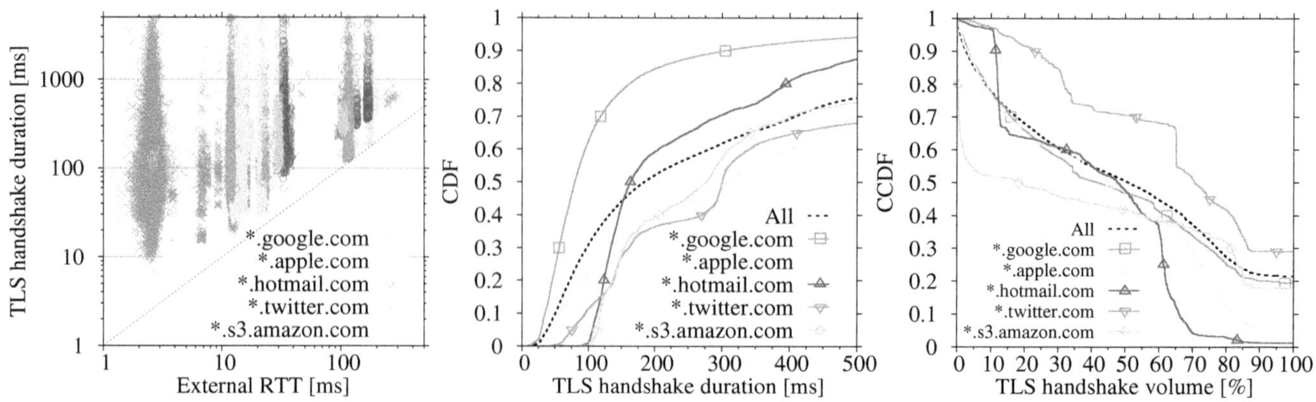

Figure 7: Quantifying TLS handshake costs. Scatter plot of the TLS handshake duration with respect to server distance (left). TLS handshake duration CDF (center). Ratio of TLS handshake bytes with respect to total TCP connection bytes CCDF (right).

TLS Handshake delay cost: Webpage load time has been an active area of research [8, 5, 6, 15, 11]; understanding the exact cause(s) of the inflation noted above is quite complex and out of scope for this work. However, it is still interesting to understand whether the overall page latency is primarily affected by network latency or by protocol overhead. To better understand this, we modified Tstat to extract the (i) duration and (ii) number of bytes of each TLS handshake from a one-hour pcap trace collected on April 3rd 2014 from Res-ISP. About 1 million TLS flows are present.

Fig. 7 (left) shows a scatter plot of the TLS handshake duration with respect to the minimum external RTT (i.e., the RTT between the vantage point and the remote server[6]). The external RTT is reasonably representative of the distance to the remote server. For this analysis we selected popular services as representative cases (we classify based on the Server Name Indication in the `ClientHello`).

First, all services exhibit vertical clusters of points, which likely reflect the different data centers offering that service. For instance, when the external RTT is larger than 100 ms, the server is outside Europe. More interestingly, no matter how close the servers are, all clusters contain samples with very high TLS handshake duration, i.e., up to several seconds. To better capture this effect, Fig. 7 (center) reports the CDF of the TLS handshake duration for individual services and for the traffic aggregate (black dotted line). Google services (which are also the closest) exhibit the smallest TLS negotiation delay, though 10% of measurements are more than 300 ms. Since a full TLS handshake requires at least 2 RTT (1 RTT in case of `SessionID` reuse), services handled by U.S. servers (e.g., Hotmail, Twitter, Amazon S3) experience huge extra costs. For instance, for Twitter, negotiation takes over 300 ms for more than 50% of the HTTPS connections. In general, 5% of requests experience a handshake at least 10 times longer than the RTT. This might be due to client or server overhead, network congestion, or a slow OCSP check.

Looking closer, we find that 4% of clients experience at least one connection with a TLS handshake duration higher than 300 ms. For such connections, 50% (75%) have an internal RTT (i.e., the RTT between the vantage point and the end-user device) of 51 ms (97 ms). The same holds true with less conservative thresholds (e.g., 1 second). This demonstrates that even clients with good network connectivity can still significantly suffer from TLS handshake overhead. TLS fast negotiation can help to reduce the handshake latency, but we find this being used in only 30% of the connections. We speculate this represents a lower bound, but, unfortunately, based on available data, we cannot assess the achievable upper bound obtained from a wider adoption of TLS fast negotiation.

Takeaway: *The extra latency introduced by HTTPS is not negligible, especially in a world where one second could cost 1.6 billion in sales.*[7]

5. DATA USAGE

HTTPS also impacts the volume of data consumed due to (i) the size TLS handshake and (ii) the inability to utilize in-network caches and compression proxies.

TLS Handshake Data Cost: The impact of the TLS handshake overhead depends on how much use the connection sees; the more data transferred, the lower the relative cost of the negotiation packets. Fig. 7 (right) reports the Complementary Cumulative Distribution Function (CCDF) of the ratio between TLS handshake size and total bytes carried in the TCP connection. Results refer to a peak hour in April 2014 for the Res-ISP dataset and are consistent with other time periods. We see that many TLS connections are not heavily used. In fact, for 50% of them, the handshake represents more than 42% of the total data exchanged. However, some services, like those running on Amazon S3, do actually use connections efficiently, reducing the impact of the negotiation cost. Some services also try to mask negotiation latency by "pre-opening" connections before they actually need to send data. In this case, the negotiation overhead is 100% if the connection is never used. This is captured in the rightmost part of Fig. 7 (right), which also highlights how this optimization is heavily used by Google, Amazon S3, and Twitter, but is not by Hotmail and Apple

[6]Tstat extracts RTT per-flow statistics monitoring the time elapsed between TCP data segments and the corresponding TCP ACK.

[7]http://www.fastcompany.com/1825005/how-one-second-could-cost-amazon-16-billion-sales

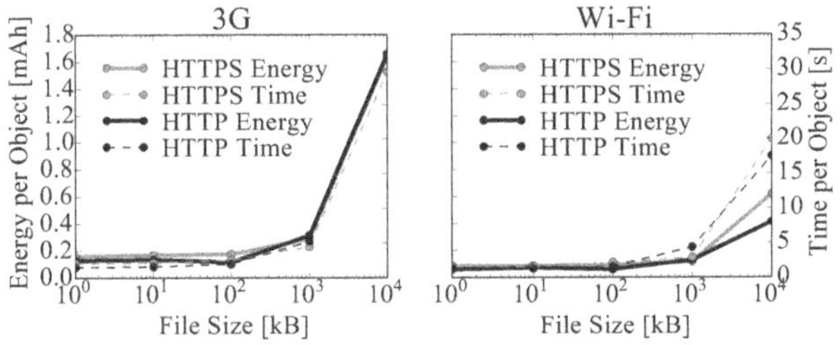

Figure 8: Energy consumption on 3G (left) & Wi-Fi (right).

services. Despite all this variability, the average TLS negotiation overhead amounts to 5% of the total volume in this dataset.

In-Network Proxies: HTTPS prevents in-network content optimizations, like proxies that perform compression and caching. To evaluate the impact of this loss, we analyze logs from two production HTTP proxies for mobile networks: Transp-Proxy and OptIn-Proxy. Transp-Proxy refers to a transparent proxy in a major European mobile carrier serving more than 20 million subscribers. OptIn-Proxy, on the other hand, is an explicit proxy serving 2000 mobile subscribers daily in a major European country. For Transp-Proxy, we analyze the past two years of traffic and for OptIn-Proxy we consider a week-long trace from May 2014.

Caching (ISP Savings): An ISP can save upstream bandwidth by serving static content from its own transparent cache. In the Transp-Proxy dataset, the average cache hit ratio over the past two years was 14.9% (15.6% of the total data volume), amounting to savings of 2 TB per day for a single proxy instance serving 3 million subscribers. For OptIn-Proxy, we see daily savings of 1.3 GB, which, if scaled up to the Transp-Proxy population, matches the observed Transp-Proxy savings.

We also witnessed a decrease in cache efficiency: the cache hit ratio of Transp-Proxy dropped from 16.8% two years ago to 13.2% in June 2014. Based on our analysis, it is not easy to conclude how much of the decreasing effectiveness of caching is related to the adoption of HTTPS and how much is caused by the increased personalization of web traffic. Either way, savings of this size can be still be significant to network operators; such savings will be totally eliminated if content delivery moves entirely to HTTPS.

Compression (Users Savings): Before returning content to users, web proxies typically apply lossless (e.g., gzip) compression to objects and, in more aggressive settings, even scale or re-encode images. This functionality is particularly helpful in cellular networks where the capacity is limited and where users often have restrictive data allowances. The Transp-Proxy trace shows a compression ratio of 28.5% (i.e., the last-mile of the network and the users save one-third of the original data size). In terms of average volume, this amounts to only 2.1 MB per user per day (on average a mobile user downloads less than 10 MB per day). For heavy users, though, this may translate to significant savings (e.g., more than 300 MB per month).

Takeaway: *Most users are unlikely to notice significant jumps in data usage due to loss of compression, but ISPs stand to see a large increase in upstream traffic due to loss of caching.*

	Total Energy (mAh)		Avg. Current (mA)	
	3G	*Wi-Fi*	*3G*	*Wi-Fi*
HTTP	210.8	175.7	633	520
HTTPS	217.7	178.0	653	531

Table 1: Energy consumed loading CNN homepage.

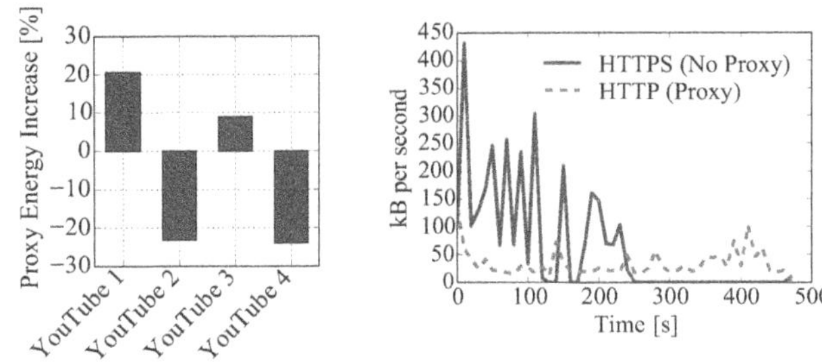

Figure 9: Comparing YouTube video playback over HTTP (with proxy) and HTTPS (without proxy): energy consumption increase when using HTTP+proxy (left) and download rate over time for one video (right). Results for 3G.

6. BATTERY LIFE

HTTPS has the potential to negatively impact battery life (particularly on mobile devices) due to (i) the extra CPU time required for the cryptographic operations and (ii) increased radio uptime due to longer downloads.

Synthetic Content: To measure the raw energy overhead of HTTPS, we instrumented a Galaxy S II with a power meter that samples the current drawn by the phone every 200 μs. We used the test phone to download synthetic objects over 3G and Wi-Fi (i.e., an access point connected to a fiber link). Objects range in size from 1 kB to 1 MB and are hosted on a web server under our control. Objects are downloaded 100 times each over HTTP and HTTPS using `curl` (compiled for Android). We configured the server to deliver traffic avoiding any proxy cache along the path.[8] During our tests, the screen was on at its minimum brightness.

Fig. 8 shows both average time (right y-axis) and energy (left y-axis) to complete each download. It is immediately clear that energy consumption is strongly correlated to download time; this is not surprising, as leaving the radio powered up is costly. (We also see a slight overhead for large objects over HTTPS on Wi-Fi but not on 3G, but we were unable to precisely determine the cause. The difference is less than one standard deviation.) The key takeaway here is, download time aside, we do not see a noticeable overhead due to cryptographic operations.

Real Content: We complement the previous analysis by loading real content. We mirror the CNN homepage on our controlled webserver and download it 50 times using Chrome for Android over HTTP and HTTPS (enforcing 20 seconds of wait between consecutive downloads). Results are listed in Table 1 (numbers presented are cumulative for all 50 loads). As in the previous benchmark, HTTPS tests do not show an appreciable increase in energy costs.

In a second experiment, we play four 5- to 12-minute YouTube videos. Since the YouTube app does not deliver

[8]The 3G carrier used in the experiment runs transparent proxies acting on traffic to port 80. By configuring the webserver to listen on a different port, we bypass the cache.

video content over HTTPS for mobile devices (nor does the YouTube mobile site), we first force the phone to load the desktop version of the YouTube portal. Over Wi-Fi, there was no difference; on 3G, on the other hand, our network's Web proxy significantly impacted the HTTP results. For two videos, playback over HTTP (with proxy) consumes nearly 25% less energy than over HTTPS (without proxy); for the other two, 10%–20% more (Fig. 9 left).

The differences are caused by two distinct proxy behaviors. First, the proxy throttles the download rate (Fig. 9 right) to reduce congestion and avoid wasting bandwidth if the user abandons the video. Without the proxy (HTTPS), the whole video loads immediately and the radio sleeps while it plays. With the proxy (HTTP), the download is slow and steady, lasting the duration of the video. Without the opportunity to sleep, playback over HTTP consumes more energy. Second, the proxy injects javascript into the pages it returns, which, among other things, rewrites the URLs sent to YouTube to request encodings and qualities more appropriate for mobile devices. For YouTube 2 and YouTube 4, the player requests the content in the `webm` format, for which our phone does not have hardware decoding support; the proxy changes `webm` to `mp4`, which our phone can decode in hardware. The benefit of hardware decoding outweighed the cost of radio uptime.

Of course, these numbers should be taken with a grain of salt, since using the desktop version of YouTube on a phone is unrealistic (but they are still relevant to PC users connecting via USB modem or tethering). We played the same four videos with YouTube's mobile portal in addition to two new videos from Vimeo's mobile site and verified that the mobile players request `mp4` from the start, so the proxy does not help decrease decoding costs. The mobile video was still throttled.

Stepping back, we see these results as concrete examples of a proxy helping and a proxy hurting end users, suggesting that (1) operators should think carefully about how they configure middleboxes and (2) the community should think carefully about shutting them out by switching to HTTPS by default.

Takeaway: *HTTPS' cryptographic operations have almost no impact on energy costs, but the loss of proxies can significantly impact battery life (positively and negatively).*

7. LOSS OF VALUE-ADDED SERVICES

From the previous experiments it becomes evident that the most significant HTTPS overheads on client performance are increased latency and the inability to utilize "useful" middleboxes that may bring content closer to the client or reduce its size through network-aware compression. There are a number of other in-network services that would also be affected by ubiquitous adoption of HTTPS, but the effects of these losses are more difficult to quantify.

For example, ubiquitous encryption will render all deep packet inspection (DPI) boxes ineffective. The advantage that in-network DPIs have is the ability to observe the traffic of multiple clients at the same time to draw inferences, while access to application layer content allows them to block threats by searching for pre-defined signatures (e.g., a known malware binary). Unsophisticated DDoS attacks may still be detectable through statistical analysis of the HTTPS traffic, but application layer fingerprinting will have to be pushed to the client.

Simpler URL filtering will also become ineffective. For instance, a number of telecommunications providers today provide parental filtering through the use of explicit blacklists, such as the Internet Watch Foundation[9] list. Through direct communication with IWF, we found out that only 5% of their current blacklist is pure domains or sub-domains that could still be blocked in the presence of HTTPS. To maintain full functionality, the IWF list would have to again be moved to the client, where one can still observe the complete URL being accessed.

Other opt-in services offered by some providers are similarly affected, like content prioritization (e.g., postponing ad delivery) or blocking tracking cookies. (Interestingly, losing the ability to block tracking cookies hurts privacy, which is one of the goals of using TLS to begin with.)

Takeaway: *Though difficult to quantify, the loss of in-network services is potentially substantial; some of that functionality could be equally well performed on the client, while some may require a total rethink, like DPI-based Intrusion Prevention Systems (IPSes).*

8. CONCLUSION

Motivated by increased awareness of online privacy, the use of HTTPS has increased in recent years. Our measurements reveal a striking ongoing technology shift, indirectly suggesting that the infrastructural cost of HTTPS is decreasing. However, HTTPS can add direct and noticeable protocol-related performance costs, e.g., significantly increasing latency, critical in mobile networks.

More interesting, though more difficult to fully understand, are the *indirect* consequences of the HTTPS: most in-network services simply cannot function on encrypted data. For example, we see that the loss of caching could cost providers an extra 2 TB of upstream data per day and could mean increases in energy consumption upwards of 30% for end users in certain cases. Moreover, many other value-added services, like parental controls or virus scanning, are similarly affected, though the extent of the impact of these "lost opportunities" is not clear.

What *is* clear is this: the "S" is here to stay, and the network community needs to work to mitigate the negative repercussions of ubiquitous encryption. To this end, we see two parallel avenues of future work: first, low-level protocol enhancements to shrink the performance gap, like Google's ongoing efforts to achieve "0-RTT" handshakes.[10] Second, to restore in-network middlebox functionality to HTTPS sessions, we expect to see trusted proxies [9] become an important part of the Internet ecosystem.

Acknowledgements

The research leading to these results has received funding from the European Union under the FP7 Grant Agreement n. 318627 (Integrated Project "mPlane"), from NSF under award number CNS-1040801, and from DoD, Air Force Office of Scientific Research, National Defense Science and Engineering Graduate (NDSEG) Fellowship, 32 CFR 168a.

[9]https://www.iwf.org.uk

[10]http://blog.chromium.org/2013/06/experimenting-with-quic.html

9. REFERENCES

[1] The Transport Layer Security (TLS) Protocol — RFC 5246.

[2] G. Apostolopoulos, V. Peris, and D. Saha. Transport layer security: How Much Does It Really Cost? In *INFOCOM 1999*.

[3] C. Castelluccia. Improving Secure Server Performance by Rebalancing SSL/TLS Handshakes. In *USENIX Security Symposium*, 2005.

[4] C. Coarfa, P. Druschel, and D. S. Wallach. Performance Analysis of TLS Web Servers. *ACM Trans. Comput. Syst.*, 24(1):39–69, Feb. 2006.

[5] Y. El-khatib, G. Tyson, and M. Welzl. Can SPDY Really Make the Web Faster? In *IFIP Networking 2014*.

[6] J. Erman, V. Gopalakrishnan, R. Jana, and K. K. Ramakrishnan. Towards a SPDY'Ier Mobile Web? In *CoNEXT '13*.

[7] A. Finamore, M. Mellia, M. Meo, M. M. Munafò, and D. Rossi. Experiences of Internet Traffic Monitoring with Tstat. *IEEE Network*, 25(3), 2011.

[8] P. Guy. Not as SPDY as You Thought. `http://goo.gl/RQkTwx`, June 2012.

[9] HTTPBis Working Group. Explicit Trusted Proxy in HTTP/2.0. `http://goo.gl/BUxQ22`, February 2014.

[10] IETF HTTPbis Working Group. Http/2. `http://http2.github.io/`.

[11] S. Ihm and V. S. Pai. Towards Understanding Modern Web Traffic. In *IMC 2011*.

[12] K. Jang, S. Han, S. Han, S. Moon, and K. Park. SSLShader: Cheap SSL Acceleration with Commodity Processors. In *NSDI 2011*.

[13] S. Renfro. Secure browsing by default. `http://goo.gl/B7U3jv`, July 2013.

[14] The Chromium Projects. Spdy. `http://www.chromium.org/spdy`.

[15] X. S. Wang, A. Balasubramanian, A. Krishnamurthy, and D. Wetherall. Demystifying Page Load Performance with WProf. In *NSDI 2013*.

A Tangled Mass: The Android Root Certificate Stores

Narseo Vallina-Rodriguez
ICSI
Berkeley, CA, USA
narseo@icsi.berkeley.edu

Johanna Amann
ICSI
Berkeley, CA, USA
johanna@icir.org

Christian Kreibich
ICSI / Lastline
Berkeley, CA, USA
christian@icir.org

Nicholas Weaver
ICSI / UC Berkeley
Berkeley, CA, USA
nweaver@icsi.berkeley.edu

Vern Paxson
ICSI / UC Berkeley
Berkeley, CA, USA
vern@icir.org

ABSTRACT

The security of today's Web rests in part on the set of X.509 certificate authorities trusted by each user's browser. Users generally do not themselves configure their browser's *root store* but instead rely upon decisions made by the suppliers of either the browsers or the devices upon which they run. In this work we explore the nature and implications of these trust decisions for Android users. Drawing upon datasets collected by Netalyzr for Android and ICSI's Certificate Notary, we characterize the certificate root store population present in mobile devices in the wild. Motivated by concerns that bloated root stores increase the attack surface of mobile users, we report on the interplay of certificate sets deployed by the device manufacturers, mobile operators, and the Android OS. We identify certificates installed exclusively by apps on rooted devices, thus breaking the audited and supervised root store model, and also discover use of TLS interception via HTTPS proxies employed by a market research company.

Categories and Subject Descriptors

C.2.3 [**Computer-communication networks**]: Network Operations; D.4.6 [**Operating Systems**]: Security and Protection; E.3 [**Data Encryption**]: Public Key Cryptosystems

Keywords

Mobile; TLS; HTTPS; man-in-the-middle; Root Store; Android; public-key infrastructure; X.509; certificates; security; measurement

1. INTRODUCTION

While most mobile device users realize that handset vendors and mobile network operators may customize their devices' firmware, UI, and pre-loaded apps, the effect of these alterations on the device's basic security posture are not widely recognized. The X.509 certificate root store population of a device defines the trust relationships that secure its network communications. Bloated or compromised root stores significantly increase the attack surface of the device, with potentially serious consequences for the user. In this paper, we draw upon on datasets collected by Netalyzr for Android as well as the ICSI Certificate Notary to characterize and evaluate the root stores of thousands of mobile devices in the wild. We make three contributions:

1. Using data from thousands of handsets in active use around the world, we describe vendor and operator-specific additions to the official Android Open Source Project (AOSP) root store populated by Google. Using the ICSI Certificate Notary, we evaluate the extent to which we see these certificates in use in large networks around the world.
2. We identify and describe how third-party apps executed on rooted handsets break the existing model of supervised and audited root stores. Any malicious app can add and remove certificates in the root store without any user awareness, making mobile users more vulnerable to MITM attacks.
3. We report on a case of TLS interception on proxied mobile devices for the purpose of user profiling and marketing, and analyze the mobile apps and domains it affects.

As reported in previous studies [26, 29], removing unnecessary certificates from the root store and tightly controlling certificate additions improves HTTPS security. Any of the certificate authorities (CAs) in the system can lead to violations of the apps' trusted communication channels.

2. BACKGROUND

As a key component of today's Internet security, the Transport Layer Security (TLS) protocol provides endpoint authentication using the X.509 certificate infrastructure. Trusted certificate authorities (CAs) sign server certificates. Clients can verify these certificates using a list of trusted root CA certificates shipping with their browser or operating system. As CAs can sign certificates for *any* site on the Internet, they form one of the weakest links of the global trust hierarchy. When a CA suffers compromise, the attacker (or the entity compelling it) can obtain certificates which enable TLS interception attacks on any target domain [27].

More technically, X.509 certificates contain a public key, a subject string that identifies them, information about the issuer of the certificate, as well as a signature by that issuer.[1] Tampering with the

[1]According to RFC 5280 [23], signature computation involves taking the hash of the names of the subject and issuer, a public key associated with the subject (RSA Key modulus), a validity period, version number and a serial number, signing it with a signature algorithm specified in the certificate and the private key of the certificate.

CoNEXT'14, December 2–5, 2014, Sydney, Australia.
Copyright 2014 ACM 978-1-4503-3279-8/14/12 ...$15.00.
http://dx.doi.org/10.1145/2674005.2675015.

	Android version					
Operating system	4.1	4.2	4.3	4.4	iOS7	Mozilla
No. certificates	139	140	146	150	227	153

Table 1: Number of certificates in different root stores.

Device model	No. sessions	Manufacturer	No. sessions
Samsung Galaxy SIV	2,762	Samsung	7,709
Samsung Galaxy SIII	2,108	LG	2,908
LG Nexus 4	1,331	ASUS	1,876
LG Nexus 5	1,010	HTC	963
Asus Nexus 7	832	Motorola	837

Table 2: Top 5 mobile devices and manufacturers in our Android dataset.

certificate will invalidate the signature. Server certificate validation requires following a chain of signatures from the server certificate to a trusted CA certificate contained in the root-store, potentially crossing several intermediate CA certificates.

Before Android 4.0, each app had to maintain its own root store if it wanted to validate certificates. In later versions, Android incorporates a system-wide read-only root store[2] and an API that regulates application access to it. Nevertheless, apps can still maintain their own root store [20, 21].

Table 1 shows the number of root certificates included in Android's official AOSP distribution as supported by Google. Apps automatically consider these certificates secure and trustworthy despite the fact that some of the CAs included, such as Comodo and Türktrust, got compromised in the past [16]. Certificates which do not chain to any of these root certificates can evoke a visual warning message in apps implementing techniques like cert pinning such as Twitter and Facebook apps when encountered [20]. The AOSP root store has increased in size in each consecutive release but currently still weighs in below the corresponding Mozilla and iOS7 root stores. The AOSP root store currently contains one certificate, by *Autoridad de Certificacion Firmaprofesional*, which expired in Oct. 2013. In fact, 117 of AOSP 4.4's 150 certificates also exist in Mozilla's root store. In addition, hardware vendors and mobile operators can (and do) add their own trusted certificates to the root store in the firmware they ship on their own Android handsets.

Any Android user can manually add, disable or delete any certificate in the root store through system settings. While the root store by default only provides read access (i.e., only applications and services with system permissions can modify it) a rooted operating system still allow alterations. Any application with root permissions (either because they are executed on rooted handsets by the users or because they perform root exploits [22]) can add new certificates and delete or modify existing ones. This notably increases the attack surface for such Android users. Despite the fact that a mobile app can protect itself from fraudulently issued certificates using techniques such as certificate pinning and customary X.509 checks, the fact that SSL library developers delegate the responsibility to implement such techniques to application developers [12, 15, 21] means that apps frequently do not employ those checks correctly. Android 4.4 detects and prevents the use of fraudulent Google certificates used in secure SSL/TLS communications. Unfortunately, as opposed to Mozilla's root store, Android does not support specifying trust levels for different CA certificates: they can be used for any operation from TLS server verification to code signing [26].

3. RELATED WORK

To our knowledge, to date there has been no in-depth analysis of the root stores of active Android devices or the root certificates added by hardware vendors. Previous work by Perl et al. [26] compared the root stores of several operating systems to Android, but did not examine differences between devices. They concluded that a large number of certificates can be removed from most root-stores as they are not used for HTTPS traffic. Our analysis confirms this result. Fahl et al. [20] and Georgiev et al. [21] examined security issues of Android applications validating certificates by performing MITM attacks and detailed app-oriented tests (they do not examine the root store of devices). They argued that one of the main problems in mobile security is that users still need to see and interpret the warning messages correctly. Amrutkar et al. [18] measured the display of security indicators in mobile browsers, but they did not evaluate differences in root stores. Huang et al. [24] analyzed MITM attacks on Facebook using forged certificates to intercept encrypted traffic Via embedded Flash they obtained copies of the presented certificates, finding a low number of potential exploit attempts (mainly generated by anti-virus software and corporate-scale content filters). In our work, we instead examine the presumed-trustworthy certificates installed on Android devices.

4. DATASET AND METHODOLOGY

To study the root stores of a large number of providers and handset models, we require a distributed platform enabling the measurement of mobile device information at a global scale. To this end, we use two tools implemented and maintained by ICSI: *(1)* Netalyzr for Android [9, 10] to measure *(i)* the root certificates installed on Android devices, *(ii)* the full trust chain for a collection of popular domains and mobile-services, and *(iii)* a broad spectrum of connectivity aspects; *(2)* the ICSI SSL Notary [13, 17] to *(iv)* validate and classify the observed certificates, *(v)* examine how often Internet services (on any port, not only HTTPS) use the certificates present in Android root stores, and *(vi)* the number of TLS certificates that each root certificate collected by Netalyzr can validate.

4.1 Netalyzr

We collected information about 2.3 million root certificates in 15,970 Netalyzr executions between November 2013 and April 2014. Only 314 root certificates are unique based on the certificate signature. In order to preserve user privacy, we do not collect information that could identify a device or a user uniquely such as the IMEI. We use tuples of recorded WiFi and cellular networks, public IP addresses, handset model, and OS version as a proxy for device identity. Based on the number of unique tuples, we estimate that the Netalyzr session set covers at least 3,835 different handsets and 435 device models. Most of the models belong to a small number of handset manufacturers, as shown in Table 2.

We inspected Google's official Android source code repository to obtain the root certificates maintained by Google. With that information in hand, we grouped the certificates Netalyzr encountered by manufacturer, mobile operator, and handset. We then established certificate identity based on unique fields (RSA key modulus and signature string) and compared each certificate to its equivalent AOSP version root store. Since different Android versions format certificate information differently, we had to inspect the subject and issuer fields manually. If none or more than one value is identified, we crosscheck the signature with Mozilla's root store or in the certificate authority's website to obtain a single value. We analyzed rooted handsets separately from operator and manufacturer root stores to

[2] Android root certificates reside in `/system/etc/security/cacerts/`.

avoid any bias, as users and third-party apps have permissions to modify the root store. We report on them separately in Section 6.

4.2 The ICSI Certificate Notary

As opposed to related efforts such as Convergence [4] and the EFF's SSL observatory [5], ICSI's Certificate Notary collects certificates passively from live upstream traffic to any port at 8 research and university networks [16], aggregating them into a central database. The certificates collected reflect the activity of about 300K active users, including any traffic originating from mobile devices connected to the network over WiFi. We started the data collection in February 2012. Currently the Notary contains more than 1.9 million unique certificates. Out of these, one million have not expired. The Notary also contains information about more than 66 billion SSL sessions as well as the certificates included in Android, iOS7, and Mozilla official root stores.

We again use the RSA key modulus and the signature of the certificates as collected by Netalyzr to compare them with the Notary's entries for validation. When comparing certificates in different root stores, one needs to note that even though root certificates are not byte-equivalent they can still be "equivalent" if their subject and RSA key modulus are identical (i.e., when they can validate the same child-certificates). In most cases, only the expiration date change.

5. ANDROID ROOT STORES IN THE WILD

The scatter plot shown in Figure 1 details the distribution of Netalyzr devices depending on the number of AOSP certificates (x-axis) and non-AOSP certificates (y-axis, in square-root scale to bring out the differences in lower values) grouped by manufacturer and OS version. The dashed vertical lines indicate the number of certificates present in the official AOSP distribution, as distributed by Google. Despite the fact that most devices have the same number of certificates in their root stores as in their equivalent AOSP distribution, 39% of sessions also have additional certificates. Only 5 handsets were missing some certificates present in their respective AOSP distributions.

The number of additional certificates varies depending on handset manufacturer and OS version. More than 10% of Android 4.1 and 4.2 devices—mainly HTC, Motorola (4.1 and 4.2), LG (4.1 and 4.2) and Samsung 4.4 devices—expand the AOSP certificate set by more than 40 additional certificates. On the other hand, Motorola (4.3 and 4.4 versions), Huawei, Sony, and Asus devices have a similar root store to their equivalent AOSP distribution, with fewer than 10 additions. In the case of some Sony 4.1 devices, we identified a certificate was added which is also present in newer AOSP versions.

5.1 Manufacturer and vendor-specific certificates

This section explains the role played by mobile operators and hardware manufacturers for the 39% of handsets with extended root stores. Figure 2 maps the additional certificates issued per Android version for the most popular manufacturers and mobile operators in our dataset. We omit handset manufacturers and operators with fewer than 10 sessions exhibiting modified root stores. The size of the marker represents the ratio of sessions in which Netalyzr identified a given certificate to the total number of sessions with modified root stores for a given manufacturer or operator. The shape represents whether the Notary identified the certificate as part of iOS7 and Mozilla root stores simultaneously (6.7%), iOS7 root store exclusively (16.2%), Android-specific (37.1%), or if the Notary has

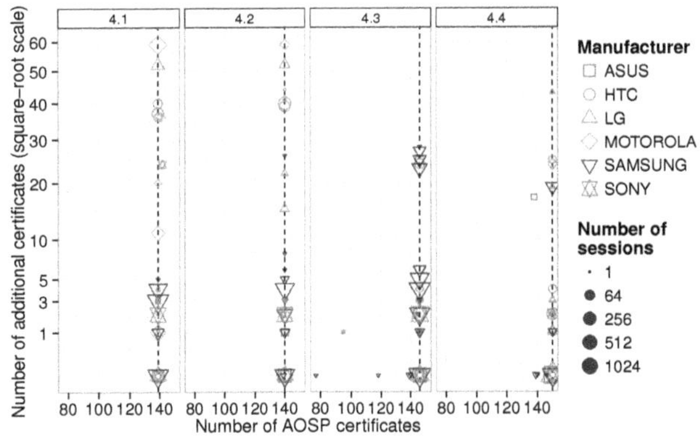

Figure 1: Scatter plot showing the number of devices (size of the symbol in $log2$ scale) with a given number of AOSP certificates (x-axis) and extra root certificates (y-axis, square-root scale) per OS version and manufacturer. The vertical line shows the number of root certificates present in Google's official AOSP distribution.

no record of the certificate at all (40.0%). The latter group contains certificates that may serve uncommon or offline operations such as code signing or firmware updates that the Notary never encounters in network traffic.

Non-AOSP certificates can be issued by well-known CAs such as Verisign, government bodies, or hardware manufacturers. Small variations can arise due to certificates added by the users through the system settings or by apps after requesting user permission. Mobile manufacturers such as HTC and Samsung[3] have alike additional certificates on their root store (e.g., *AddTrust*, *Deutsche Telekom*, *Sonera* and *U.S. Department of Defense*[4]) independently of the mobile operator, as shown in Figure 2. In this case, it is possible that hardware vendors add these certificates to the firmware images they build for their handsets. On the other hand, we find some roots, such as *CertiSign* and *ptt-post.nl*[5] exclusively on 60 to 70% of Motorola 4.1 devices, all of them subscribed to Verizon Wireless. Given that mobile operators have the ability to modify the firmware they ship on their subsidized handsets, Verizon Wireless may be the agent responsible for these certificates' presence. Similarly, we identified potential AT&T-specific inclusions on Motorola handsets, such as a *Microsoft Secure Server* certificate.

Certain handset-specific certificates are not used for TLS operations, such as the *GeoTrust CA for UTI* certificate (installed on Samsung 4.2 and 4.3 devices) or Motorola's certificates for FOTA (Firmware over-the-air) and SUPL (Secure User Plane Location). UTI (Unified Testing Initiative) is a non-profit group led by hardware vendors and mobile operators to improve the quality of mobile apps [2]. GeoTrust restricts the use of the certificate to members of the Java Verified Program [8]. The FOTA and SUPL certificates secure firmware updates and location-sensor assistance [28], respectively. Given the privacy-sensitive information transmitted over SUPL (including neighboring WiFi APs and cellular base stations)

[3] Note that Samsung 4.1 and 4.2 devices have similar root stores, but different to 4.3 and 4.4 ones, which are extended.

[4] The subject and issuer for this certificate is: *CN=DoD CLASS 3 Root CA,OU=PKI,OU=DoD,O=U.S. Government,C=US*. iOS7 also contains this certificate by default. It is not a WebTrust audited CA, so Mozilla considers it as an Intranet CA [25].

[5] Issued by the Dutch Postal Services, and also present in the Windows root store.

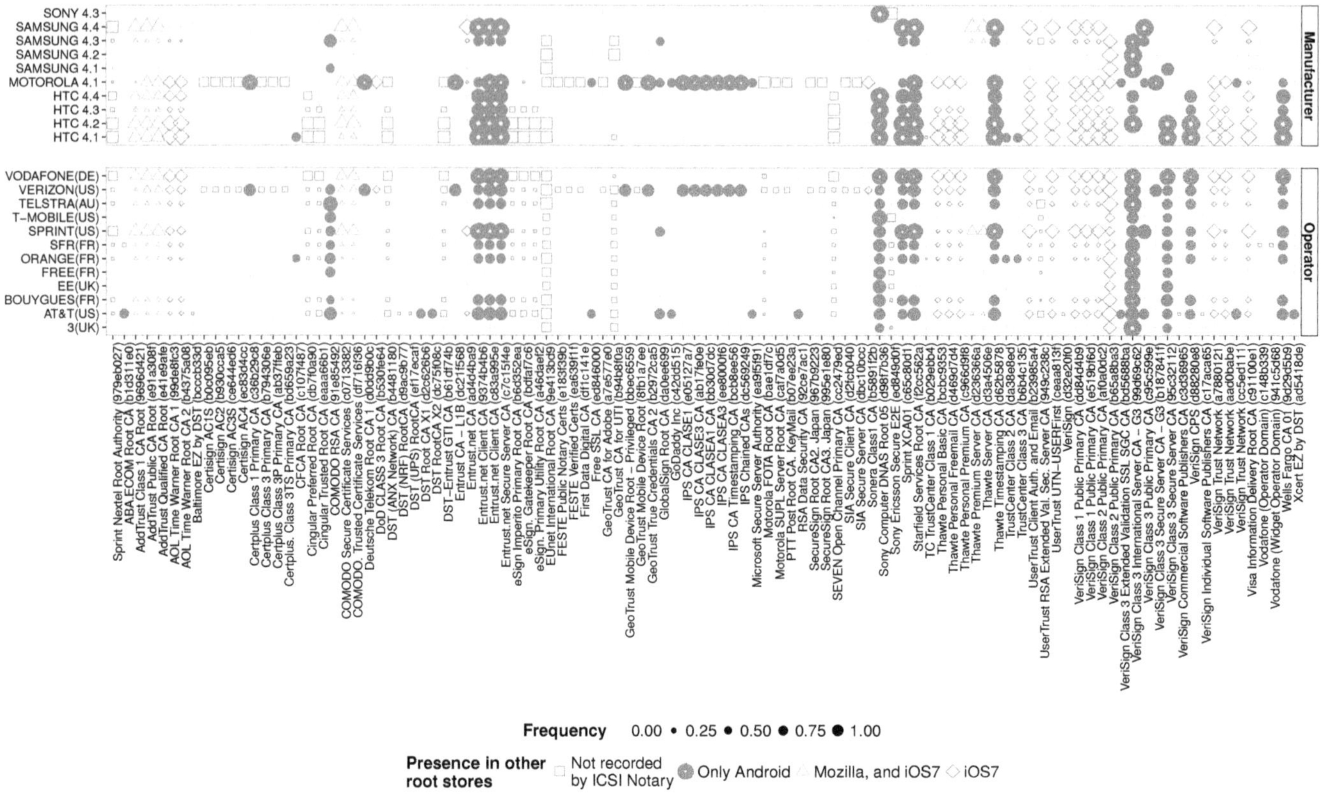

Figure 2: Scatterplot showing the ratio of sessions (size) with a given root certificate (x-axis) relative to the total number of sessions for a given operator or manufacturer (y-axis). The value in brackets shows the first 32 bits of the certificate subject.

and the security implications of software updates, these operations require a secure channel. Google, as well as mobile operators, Assisted GPS (A-GPS) chipset and handset vendors can also provide SUPL and FOTA services. Consequently, it is plausible that some of the root certificates included by other vendors may be used for similar purposes.

5.2 Additional observations

We observed several unusual root certificates for which we could not definitively establish their origin. These certificates, issued by 15 CAs, can be found in a wide range of handsets, mobile operators and countries. Here we group them into three categories and speculate regarding their possible origin:

- Certificates added manually by users for general connectivity management (VPN). We identified a number of self-signed certificates, each recorded exclusively on a single device.
- Certificates added by mobile operators for custom services and APIs such as location services, widgets, email or messaging. For these we observer *Vodafone Group* certificates, a *Verizon Wireless* certificate found on three Verizon Pantech[6] 4.1 devices, likely associated with the Verizon Network API [14]; *Meditel* certificates (a Moroccan ISP) recorded in several Samsung 4.1 devices in Bermuda; and two root certificates issued by *Telefonica* and recorded in Motorola 4.1 devices. These devices were connected to Telefonica/Movistar and Claro networks in Argentina, Colombia, Mexico and Peru. Presumably, the appearance of a root certificate issued by an operator different than the operator providing the network access suggests a user roaming or traveling abroad.
- Certificates issued by government agencies. These certificates are presumably legitimately installed by applications using Android APIs or directly by handset manufacturers. Two examples are the certificates issued by *Venezuelan National CA*—recorded in Compal devices in Taiwan—and the four certificates issued by the Chinese Finance CA (CFCA) found in HTC, Motorola and Lenovo devices from a number of countries such as Albania, Argentina, Belarus, Brazil, Bulgaria, China, Colombia, India, Mexico and Russia. The addition of CFCA certificates to Mozilla's root store program has spurred discussion [3].

These certificates did not manifest in the ICSI Notary data.

5.3 Root store validation with ICSI's Notary

Table 3 shows the total number of TLS certificates known to the Notary validated by each AOSP version and Mozilla root store. The results indicate that there few practical differences between them. The small variations mostly arise due to the fact some government-issued CA certificates (e.g., the U.S. DoD) do not appear in all root stores. However, not all certificates contribute equally to these numbers. Figure 3 shows the ECDF of the number of certificates (out of the more than 1 million non-expired certificates recorded by the Notary) that each root certificate can validate, grouped by different categories. We include the iOS7 and Mozilla root stores for comparison. The figure shows that the subset of AOSP certificates that are also included on Mozilla root store can validate most TLS

[6]Pantech manufactures phones for AT&T and Verizon in the USA.

Root store	No. validated certificates
Mozilla	744,069
iOS 7	745,736
AOSP 4.1	744,350
AOSP 4.2	744,350
AOSP 4.3	744,384
AOSP 4.4	744,398

Table 3: Number of certificates validated by Mozilla and AOSP root stores.

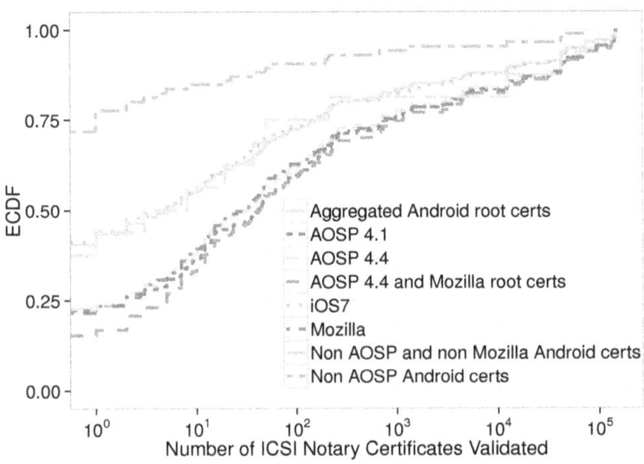

Figure 3: ECDF of the number of TLS certificates recorded by ICSI's Notary that each root store can progressively validate as we cumulatively consider each of its certificates (starting with the certificates that can validate the most additional certs).

sessions, while the superset of all Android root certificates collected by Netalyzr has a similar behavior as the iOS7 root store (the largest one).

An interesting observation concerns the y-axis offset in Figure 3 for each category. The offset indicates the percentage of certificates for a given group that did not validate any of the certificates recorded by the Notary for common operations such as HTTPS connections or TLS-secured email delivery. In particular, 23% of AOSP 4.4 root certificates did not validate any of the Notary TLS certificates, as opposed to 72% of the extra Android certificates that appear in neither the official AOSP 4.4 root store nor in Mozilla's. One could seemingly disable these certificates with little negative effect on the user experience or TLS functionality, though the Notary's does not provide a comprehensive enough perspective for us to state this definitively.

6. ROOTING ANDROID HANDSETS

In Section 2, we explained how rooting mobile handsets allows malicious mobile apps to add, delete and modify certificates on the root store. 24% of our Netalyzr sessions ran on rooted handsets. We identified certificates that appear exclusively in rooted handsets in 6% of those (so about 1.5% of all sessions).

Table 5 reports the set of root certificates more frequently appearing on rooted rather than non-rooted devices. None of these occurred in Notary traffic. Generally, the issuers of these certificates are the users themselves or small corporations looking to employ other means of secure communication such as VPNs. This is the case for the certificates signed by USER_X[7] and Mind Overflow

[7]Anonymized.

Root store category	Total root certs	Root certs that do not validate Notary certs
Non AOSP and Non Mozilla root certs	85	72%
Non AOSP root certs found on Mozilla's	16	38%
AOSP 4.4 and Mozilla root certs	130	15%
AOSP 4.1 certs	139	22%
AOSP 4.4 certs	150	23%
Aggregated Android root certs	235	40%
Mozilla root store certs	153	22%
iOS 7 root store certs	227	41%

Table 4: Number of root certificates found in ICSI's Notary per category, and how many of them did not validate any of the certificates stored on ICSI's Notary.

Certificate authority	Total devices
CRAZY HOUSE	70
MIND OVERFLOW	1
USER_X	1
CDA/EMAILADDRESS	1
CIRRUS, PRIVATE	1

Table 5: List of CAs and user self-signed certificates found more frequently on rooted devices.

(we could not identify any application or real CA with this name), both collected from the same device. Likewise, *CDA (Chaine de Distribution Alimentaire) Senegal* certificate was identified on a rooted Nexus 7 device connected from a Senegalese WiFi AP.

The certificate issued by Madkit-Crazy House (Ukraine) recorded in 70 different handsets illustrates the sort of security hazard that can result on rooted Android handsets. The ICSI Certificate Notary has no record of this certificate. After checking the applications running in the background on the affected handsets, we verified that this certificate is installed by the Freedom app [7], which enables free in-app purchases on the Google Play Store. This app requires root permissions (so it can modify the root store) and compels the user to accept egregious permissions such as accessing the Google accounts set up on the device, reading phone status and identity, and modifying system settings.

7. TLS INTERCEPTION

Netalyzr for Android checks the full trust chain of TLS connections to the domains of popular websites and mobile apps. We use the ICSI Notary to assess each of the observed certificates. Out of the 15K sessions, we identified a case of TLS interception for one user running a Nexus 7 device on Android 4.4, communicating with an HTTPS-proxied WiFi access point. In this case, a British marketing research provider called Reality Mine [11] signed the root certificates.

Looking deeper at the connectivity results reported by Netalyzr, we observe that this user's traffic flows via a `tun` interface that tunnels all traffic to a proxy controlled by Reality Mine (`v-us-49.analyzeme.me.uk`). The proxy name matches the name a Reality Mine app on Google Play [1]. In fact, all Android applications published by Reality Mine in Google Play (ConsumerInput Mobile, USA TouchPoints, MediaTrack, and AnalyzeMe) require (as of Oct. 2014) the user to accept both a permission for

Intercepted domains	Whitelisted domains [6]
gmail.com:443	google-analytics.com:443
mail.google.com:443	maps.google.com:443
mail.yahoo.com:443	orcart.facebook.com:8883
orcart.facebook.com:443	play.google.com:443
www.bankofamerica.com:443	supl.google.com:7275
www.chase.com:443	www.facebook.com:443
www.hsbc.com:443	www.google.com:443
www.icsi.berkeley.edu:443	www.google.co.uk:443
www.outlook.com:443	www.twitter.com:443
www.skype.com:443	
www.viber.com:443	
www.yahoo.com:443	

Table 6: Domains being intercepted and whitelisted by Reality Mine HTTPS proxy.

changing handset network configuration and one to intercept user traffic. The latter permission, requested by any app behaving as a VPN client, allows the application to create a virtual `tun` interface with which it associates a raw read socket. In this case, we cannot identify whether TLS interception takes place on the local host versus the remote server, since the app could employ either approach.

In addition to network and traffic interception permissions, the application requires access to protected storage and the ability to read contacts, calendar, location, text messages, device ID, call information, Web bookmarks and history, and sensitive log data. The application requires an invitation from Reality Mine to run and does not require including any certificate in the root store.

The proxy listens on ports 80 and 443, intercepting and regenerating both root and intermediate certificates on-the-fly for specific domains. The proxy whitelists Google's SUPL service (7275) and Facebook chat (8883), as well as popular apps implementing mechanisms like certificate pinning for security [19, 21]: Facebook, Twitter, and most Google services. Table 6 summarizes this observation. We contacted Reality Mine to verify whether their TLS interception occurs with user consent. According to their statements, they recruit participants and all data is cleaned and anonymized in line with the best practices defined by Esomar association [6]. As of this writing, we have not received a response we requested from Reality Mine regarding the terms of use and the privacy considerations of app users.

8. RECOMMENDATIONS

Given that Android does not differentiate the use and scope of certificates installed in the root store, and does not protect the root store from malicious apps with root permissions, a bloated root store increases the attack surface for malicious apps. Such design decisions make mobile users more vulnerable to TLS interception attacks. In order to improve mobile user security, we recommend enforcing an audited and more strict root store for Android, per the approaches adopted by Mozilla and iOS. If operators wish to install additional certificates, they should do so via this auditing process.

We question whether users have sufficient awareness of the consequences of their actions on their own security and privacy. Our results highlight how rooting an Android device can seriously undermine user protections. As widely reported in previous work, users must exercise prudence and caution when granting rights to applications during initial installation and subsequent updates. App developers can mask malicious intentions behind seemingly helpful permission requests such as traffic interception to enable VPNs, which, if granted, provide access to a user's entire traffic. In effect, abusing such app permissions breaks the app sandboxing model implemented in Android to protect users' privacy.

9. SUMMARY

It is generally recognized that certificate root stores represent a significant potential weak link in TLS security. X.509 certificates found in the root store are automatically considered secure and trustworthy: users will trust any CA that their mobile device and its apps trusts. In this work we used data from Netalyzr for Android and the ICSI Certificate Notary to characterize the root stores of thousands of Android phones in the wild. Our analysis highlights three concerns. First, we demonstrate how mobile operators and hardware manufacturers modify and extend Google's official Android root store. Second, we report on how rooted Android handsets can lead to undermining the model of audited and supervised root stores, allowing malicious apps to modify the store without user awareness. Third, we illustrate the use of TLS interception for marketing research. We show how apps can request overreaching permissions to exploit the lack of security mechanisms such as certificate pinning. These observations lead us to highlight the need for an audited and strictly controlled root store for Android, and efforts towards improving user awareness of the implications of their actions when granting permissions.

10. ACKNOWLEDGMENTS

We are deeply grateful to *Netalyzr*'s many users for making this study possible, and also for their helpful feedback. We would like to thank the anonymous reviewers for their valuable comments. This work was supported by the National Science Foundation under grants NSF-0831535, NSF-1213157, and NSF-1237265, and by the DHS Directorate of Science and Technology under grant N66001-12-C-0128. We also wish to thank Amazon, Comcast, and Google for their generous support.

11. REFERENCES

[1] AnalyzeMe App. https://play.google.com/store/apps/details?id=com.apadmi.analyzeme.android.

[2] App Quality Alliance. http://www.appqualityalliance.org.

[3] Bugzilla @ Mozilla. CFCA root CA. https://bugzilla.mozilla.org/show_bug.cgi?id=926029.

[4] Convergence. http://convergence.io.

[5] EFF Observatory. https://www.eff.org/observatory.

[6] Esomar. http://www.esomar.org.

[7] Freedom App. http://system.in-appstore.com/freedom.

[8] Geotrust Unified Testing Initiative (UTI) Root Key Certificate. https://www.geotrust.com/resources/root-certificates/root12_terms.html.

[9] Netalyzr. http://netalyzr.icsi.berkeley.edu.

[10] Netalyzr for Android. Google Play. https://play.google.com/store/apps/details?id=edu.berkeley.icsi.netalyzr.android.

[11] Reality Mine. http://www.realitymine.com.

[12] Security with HTTPS and SSL. http://developer.android.com/training/articles/security-ssl.html.

[13] The ICSI Certificate Notary. http://notary.icsi.berkeley.edu.

[14] Verizon Network API. http://developer.verizon.com/content/vdc/en/verizon-tools-apis/verizon_apis/network-api.html.

[15] X509TrustManager Android API. http://developer.android.com/reference/javax/net/ssl/X509TrustManager.html.

[16] B. Amann, R. Sommer, M. Vallentin, and S. Hall. No Attack Necessary: The Surprising Dynamics of SSL Trust Relationships. In *Proc. of ACM ACSAC*, 2013.

[17] B. Amann, M. Vallentin, S. Hall, and R. Sommer. Extracting Certificates from Live Traffic: A Near Real-Time SSL Notary Service. Technical Report TR-12-014, ICSI, November 2012.

[18] C. Amrutkar, P. Traynor, and P. C. van Oorschot. Measuring SSL Indicators on Mobile Browsers: Extended Life, or End of the Road? In *Proc. Inf. Sec. Conf.*, 2012.

[19] Facebook. Secure browsing by default. https://www.facebook.com/notes/facebook-engineering/secure-browsing-by-default/10151590414803920.

[20] S. Fahl, M. Harbach, T. Muders, L. Baumgärtner, B. Freisleben, and M. Smith. Why Eve and Mallory Love Android: An Analysis of Android SSL (in)Security. In *ACM CCS*, 2012.

[21] M. Georgiev, S. Iyengar, S. Jana, R. Anubhai, D. Boneh, and V. Shmatikov. The Most Dangerous Code in the World: Validating SSL Certificates in Non-browser Software. In *Proc. ACM CCS*, 2012.

[22] T. Ho, D. Dean, X. Gu, and W. Enck. Prec: practical root exploit containment for android devices. In *Proc. ACM CODASPY*, 2014.

[23] R. Housley, W. Ford, W Polk, and D. Solo. Rfc 5280: Internet X. 509 Public Key Infrastructure Certificate and CRL profile, 2008.

[24] L. Huang, A. Rice, E. Ellingsen, and C. Jackson. Analyzing Forged SSL Certificates in the Wild. In *Proc. IEEE Symposium on Security and Privacy*, 2014.

[25] Mozilla Foundation. Bug 208323 - Add DoD root CA. https://bugzilla.mozilla.org/show_bug.cgi?id=208323.

[26] H. Perl, S. Fahl, and M. Smith. You Won't Be Needing These Any More: On Removing Unused Certificates From Trust Stores. In *Financial Cryptography and Data Security*, 2014.

[27] B. Schneier. New NSA Leak Shows MITM Attacks Against Major Internet Services. https://www.schneier.com/blog/archives/2013/09/new_nsa_leak_sh.html, 2014.

[28] N. Vallina-Rodriguez, J. Crowcroft, A. Finamore, Y. Grunenberger, and K. Papagiannaki. When Assistance Becomes Dependence: Characterizing the Costs and Inefficiencies of A-GPS. *ACM SIGMOBILE Mob. Comput. Commun. Rev.*, 2013.

[29] D. Wendlandt, D. Andersen, and A. Perrig. Perspectives: Improving SSH-style Host Authentication with Multi-Path Probing. In *USENIX Annual Technical Conference*, 2008.

FlowBender: Flow-level Adaptive Routing for Improved Latency and Throughput in Datacenter Networks

Abdul Kabbani
Google Inc.
Mountain View, CA, USA
akabbani@google.com

Balajee Vamanan
Purdue University
West Lafayette, IN, USA
bvamanan@ecn.purdue.edu

Jahangir Hasan
Google Inc.
Mountain View, CA, USA
jahangir@google.com

Fabien Duchene
Universite catholique de Louvain
Louvain-La-Neuve, Belgium
fabien.duchene@uclouvain.be

ABSTRACT

Datacenter networks provide high path diversity for traffic between machines. Load balancing traffic across these paths is important for both, latency- and throughput-sensitive applications. The standard load balancing techniques used today obliviously hash a flow to a random path. When long flows collide on the same path, this might lead to long lasting congestion while other paths could be underutilized, degrading performance of other flows as well. Recent proposals to address this shortcoming incur significant implementation complexity at the host that would actually slow down short flows (MPTCP), depend on relatively slow centralized controllers for rerouting large congesting flows (Hedera), or require custom switch hardware, hindering near-term deployment (DeTail).

We propose FlowBender, a novel technique that: (1) Load balances distributively at the granularity of flows instead of packets, avoiding excessive packet reordering. (2) Uses end-host-driven rehashing to trigger dynamic flow-to-path assignment. (3) Recovers from link failures within a Retransmit Timeout (RTO). (4) Amounts to less than 50 lines of critical kernel code and is readily deployable in commodity data centers today. (5) Is very robust and simple to tune. We evaluate FlowBender using both simulations and a real testbed implementation, and show that it improves average and tail latencies significantly compared to state of the art techniques without incurring the significant overhead and complexity of other load balancing schemes.

Categories and Subject Descriptors

C.2.2 [**Computer Communication Networks**]: Network Protocols

CoNEXT'14, December 2–5, 2014, Sydney, Australia.
ACM 978-1-4503-3279-8/14/12.
http://dx.doi.org/10.1145/2674005.2674985.

General Terms

Algorithms, Design, Performance

Keywords

Data Centers; ECMP; Load Balancing; TCP

1. INTRODUCTION

Datacenter networks are typically based on multistage fat-tree topologies which provide high bisection bandwidth via a large number of paths between any pair of hosts [5, 15]. Efficient utilization of these paths is critical to the performance of datacenter applications. If traffic distribution across paths is uneven, some paths may congest unnecessarily while others go underutilized, adversely affecting the throughput and tail latency of network flows. The impact of long tail latencies on datacenter applications is well understood and has been the subject of recent work [7, 21, 23]. In particular, large-scale online services such as Web search, retail, and advertising run under soft real-time requirements for improved user experience and revenue. Because a user-facing response is constructed by aggregating the results from thousands of servers, the tail latency of the individual flows directly affects response time and quality.

Equal Cost Multiple Path (ECMP) forwarding is the standard mechanism used today for spreading traffic across multiple paths in datacenter networks. ECMP randomly maps a given flow to one of the paths by hashing some fields in the packet headers. The fields for hashing are chosen such that all packets of a given flow follow the same path (i.e., flow to path mapping is static). ECMP works well in balancing the aggregate load across all paths when there are a large number of flows with sufficient entropy across the headers. However, in reality, datacenter traffic is often heavy tailed with a small number of long flows contributing a significant fraction of all traffic [8]. These few long flows may not have enough entropy to uniformly distribute the load. Therefore, a handful of long flows could collide on some path to create a long-lasting congestion while other paths go underutilized. Despite its shortcomings, ECMP has widespread adoption because it is supported by commodity off-the-shelf switches and works out of the box with standard unmodified TCP/IP stacks.

The solution space for load balancing traffic in datacenter networks can be classified along two independent dimensions: (1) whether the solution is static, or whether it dynamically reacts to current network conditions; and (2) the extent of out-of-order delivery of packets in a given flow. For example, ECMP is a static scheme with strict packet ordering. We argue that the most desirable design point in this space would be a solution that is dynamic and has very little to no re-ordering within a flow. Being dynamic makes the scheme robust by freeing it from assumptions about traffic properties (e.g., ECMP requires entropy), and a small degree of packet re-ordering keeps the end host implementation simple and close to stock TCP/IP stacks. Though a number of recent proposals have attempted to address the shortcomings of ECMP, none of them fall under the desirable design point we have described. Switch-driven schemes like *DeTail* [23] are dynamic but incur significant packet re-ordering and additionally require hardware changes to switch silicon which incur high cost and hinder incremental deployment. End-host-driven schemes like MPTCP [17] are dynamic but have significant end host complexity to manage their packet re-ordering. Random Packet Scatter (RPS) [13] is static and also incurs high degree of packet re-ordering.

We propose *FlowBender*, an end-host-driven load balancing scheme that is dynamic but incurs little to no packet re-ordering. FlowBender offers *both* simplicity and high-performance. Our central idea addresses the fundamental problem with ECMP: the flow-to-path assignment is *static*; there is no consideration for re-routing if it turns out that the current path is oversubscribed or even broken. Our solution is to transmit each flow as a single stream, through the same commodity ECMP-based network, until the flow is congested or disconnected, at which point the flow is *selectively re-routed.* We base FlowBender's design on the *key* observation that a handful of long flows account for a large fraction of network load (bytes) [8], and that addressing the load imbalance caused by ECMP's non-uniform hashing amounts *mainly* to re-balancing the long flows. Because long flows tend to span several Round-Trip Times (RTTs), the problem naturally lends itself to an end-to-end design, obviating the need to make hardware changes to switches. Also, because we change a flow's path (route) *selectively* and *only* in response to congestion, we drastically reduce out-of-order packet delivery, thereby nearly *eliminating* packet re-ordering effort.

FlowBender requires two components: (1) a mechanism to detect congestion or link failures at the host, and (2) a means for the end host to reroute a specific flow. For congestion and link failure detection, we improvise on Explicit Congestion Notification (ECN) which is commonly used in today's datacenters, in addition to standard TCP Timeouts. With ECN, senders monitor the fraction of marked packets to decide whether a flow needs to be re-routed. We chose end-to-end signals such as ECN and Timeouts as opposed to link-level, hop-by-hop signals such as Priority Flow Control (PFC) or queue lengths so that we can react to congestion and route failures at any hop within the route while preventing congestion spreading episodes such as Tree Saturation [11, 20, 12].

For re-routing a flow, we configure the hash function in the switches to compute its output based on an additional *flexible* field in the packet header such as Time-To-Live (TTL), in addition to the other fields the switch is already hashing upon. This flexible field would have its value updated independently for a flow *only* when re-routing is desired. The updated value would then be used for all the future packets in that flow (hence arriving in order) until the flow gets rerouted again. Therefore, the flexible field acts conceptually as a path ID for the flow, and changing it causes the flow to explore a new path through the network. Thus, while other competing schemes [23, 17, 13] might end up routing *each* packet differently, we choose to reroute a flow to a different path *selectively* and *only* during congestion or route failures, thereby avoiding the cost of excessive packet re-ordering.

To summarize, the key strengths of FlowBender's design are that it:

- Requires no changes to switch hardware (silicon).
- Amounts to *only* 50 lines of kernel code change.
- Requires simple re-configuration to ECMP hash functions (a handful of commands).
- Substantially outperforms ECMP and matches the performance of other more complex schemes.
- Incorporates robust end-to-end congestion notifications (ECN) and failure signals (Timeouts).
- Reroutes at the Round-trip Time (RTT) granularity and recovers from link failures essentially within an RTO.

We evaluate FlowBender using simulations and a real implementation. With our real implementation we show that FlowBender reduces the tail latency over ECMP by more than 40% on average for large flows. With our at-scale ns-3 [4] simulations with workloads representative of datacenter applications, we show that FlowBender reduces the mean and tail latency of all-to-all workloads by 73% and 93% respectively as compared to ECMP, while staying within 2% of other expensive schemes like DeTail and RPS. With storage-type workloads which generate incast, FlowBender still helps jobs complete in half to quarter the time relative to ECMP (i.e. in terms of the Avg. time for the last flow of an incast job to finish), while also closely matching the performance of other expensive schemes like DeTail and RPS (within 2% of their completion times on average and in terms of the tail). Thus, FlowBender makes a strong case for a non-intrusive, end-host- and flow-level load balancing using the classic end-to-end principle [19].

The remainder of the paper is organized as follows. In Section 2 we discuss related work on improving datacenter load balancing. Section 3 describes our FlowBender proposal in detail. We present our experimental methodology and results in Section 4 followed by several suggestions for further design and performance optimizations in Section 5, and we conclude in Section 6.

2. RELATED WORK

There is a plethora of work that focus on load balancing. While it is beyond the scope of this paper to cover all of them in detail, we present a brief summary of recent work in this area.

Equal Cost Multiple Path (ECMP) forwarding is the standard mechanism used in today's datacenters for load balancing traffic across multiple paths. The switch computes a hash function on the various fields of the packet header that identify a flow, and uses the resulting hash value to pick a port from the set of eligible ports to forward the packet along. Such static flow-to-path assignment can work well

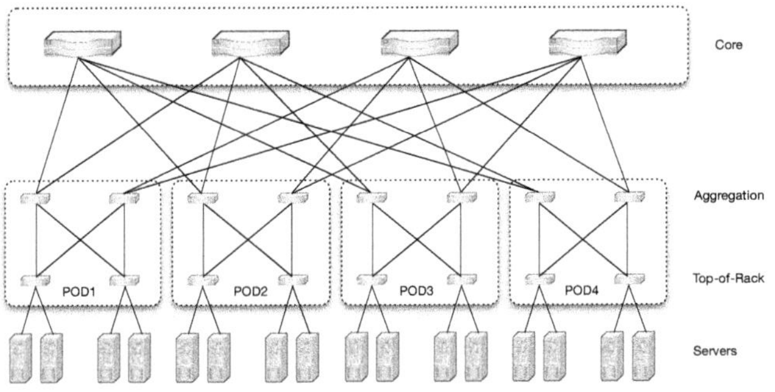

Figure 1: Fat-tree Datacenter Network Topology

when the flows are plentiful and short-lived. However, when there are relatively few long flows present and their hash values happen to collide, these flows suffer long-lasting congestion even though other eligible paths go under-utilized. The key problem with ECMP is that *the flow-to-path assignment is static; there is no opportunity for rerouting if it turns out that the current path is oversubscribed.*

MPTCP [17] addresses the problem by splitting a TCP flow into multiple subflows with different port numbers. The different port numbers, being part of the input to the ECMP hashing function, cause the subflows to hash to different paths through the network. The sender splits the original data stream across the subflows and monitors the RTT, throughput, and packet loss along the various subflows[22] to prioritize those with good performance. The receiver requires additional logic to stitch the arriving data back into the original data stream. While MPTCP shows improvements over ECMP for flows larger than 70KB, it incurs significant implementation complexity because of the more complex sender-side congestion control algorithm and the receiver-side data reassembly logic (more than 10,000 lines of kernel code), rendering its performance worse than ECMP's for smaller flows [18]. Moreover, MPTCP suffers from high CPU overhead, shooting up to around 40% on every client and 10% on every server [17], which is considered to be too costly for datacenters.

SPAIN [16], another host-based load balancing scheme, suggests pre-computing a set of paths spanning the entire network and mapping them to different VLANs. In order to achieve higher throughput and better fault-tolerance, a sender dynamically changes its VLAN if a route associated with the current VLAN fails or at constant intervals in order to shift a long-lived flow to another path to avoid load imbalance. In constrast, FlowBender incurs less overhead as it changes routes selectively and only if a flow is congested. Moreover, if a route has a lower capacity than another between two hosts, FlowBender has the natural tendency to send less traffic on the lower-capacity route (Section 4), whereas SPAIN obliviously uses both paths equally. Unlike SPAIN, FlowBender does not require any routing pre-computations and its potential usage of VLANs is merely for adding hashing entropy. We elaborate on FlowBender's usage of VLANs in Section 3.

In contrast to MPTCP and SPAIN, Random Packet Spraying (RPS) [13] and DeTail [23] place the burden of load balancing the traffic upon the switches themselves at the packet level, requiring hardware changes at the switches. With RPS, a switch *randomly* selects an output port from a set of eligible outports *independently* for *every* packet. While RPS works well for symmetric topologies such as fat-trees (aside from the out-of-order packet delivery issues mentioned below), when asymmetries arise in a network due to incremental deployments or link failures, RPS causes severe throughput inefficiencies [23].

DeTail overcomes RPS's limitations by combining two distinct techniques that work synergistically to improve the tail latency and utilization of the network. First, DeTail employs Priority Flow Control (PFC) [1] which guarantees lossless packet-forwarding in the network, but is fraught with the risks of network deadlock and intra-priority head-of-line (HOL) blocking issues [11, 20, 12]. Second, DeTail load balances via a flavor of packet-level adaptive routing [14]. When a packet arrives at the switch, it chooses the less congested eligible port to send on. However, such adaptive routing design has a number of shortcomings. First, it requires custom switching silicon for monitoring queue length changes at line rates and for switching packets based on this information. Custom hardware incurs high cost and long turn-around time that hinders rapid deployment. Second, because DeTail performs load balancing on a per-packet granularity, it causes frequent out-of-order delivery of TCP segments. Accordingly, DeTail entirely disables fast retransmit in the TCP stack. However, a TCP stack with such modification will not operate well when the remote end of the connection is a legacy TCP stack (as could be the case with external or VM-based traffic) or when the intervening network lacks end-to-end PFC or has a large RTT. Furthermore, link-level schemes like DeTail cannot handle link failures that occur on the deterministic part of a path (i.e. when there is a single downlink towards the destination). In contrast, FlowBender, being end-to-end and host-based, can re-route around broken paths within an RTO (section 3).

Centralized approaches [6, 9, 10] have also been proposed to address ECMP's shortcomings and are motivated by the observation that efficiently load balancing datacenter traffic flows entails load balancing the relatively fewer larger ones (given the heavy-tailed nature of datacenter flow size distributions [8]). While software-based switch controllers could be leveraged to globally allocate long flows to non-congested paths, they are not as prompt at handling sudden traffic changes compared to our RTT-based load balancing schemes as we discuss in the next section.

Next we describe FlowBender in details and highlight the major features that distinguish it from the schemes we have just summarized.

3. FLOWBENDER

We now explain the details of FlowBender, beginning with the insight that informs its design.

3.1 Flow versus Packet-level Load Balancing

FlowBender operates in between the extreme of statically sending a flow on one path (ECMP) and that of spreading its packets across multiple paths simultaneously (e.g. RPS, DeTail, and MPTCP). Efficient load balancing does not necessarily mean that we have to simultaneously spread a flow across several paths and then stitch it back together at the receiver, especially when there is no congestion to start with. Instead, we target the simpler mechanism of shifting (rerouting) the entire flow to a different path only once it is congested or disconnected, thus avoiding sustained out of order packet delivery and any hardware updates to existing datacenter infrastructures.

3.2 Flow Control: Link versus Transport Layer

Link and transport-level congestion signals are important for realizing better rate control mechanisms, but they could be also leveraged for guiding our load balancing decisions as will be explained next. The question we are trying to answer now is: which congestion signals should we leverage?

Link-level notification mechanisms such as PFC have faster reaction times compared to RTT-based ones such as Explicit Congestion Notification (ECN), especially when the congestion point is close to the traffic source itself. When the congestion point is far away from the traffic source, however, such link-level schemes can notoriously result in congestion spreading trees [11, 20, 12]. Rather than worrying about this phenomenon and adding complexity into our switches for load balancing based on PFC signals, our argument is that something simple like ECN has been already demonstrated to be prompt enough in propagating congestion information back to the sources. Of course, relying on ECN end-to-end signals means that we are targeting those longer flows that take several roundtrips to finish, which happen to be those flows carrying most of the network traffic anyway [8]. Otherwise, in the hypothetical scenario where most of the traffic is generated by very small flows only, ECMP should perform quite well handling such traffic given the much higher hashing entropy involved.

Another important reason supporting our transport-layer choice is that, unlike link-level ones, algorithms such as TCP can quickly detect link failures end-to-end, which can influence FlowBender to promptly avoid broken paths as will be discussed in the next section.

With the clear motivation to pursue flow-level and RTT-based load balancing only once congestion occurs, we now proceed to discuss the details of FlowBender.

3.3 The Design of FlowBender

In designing FlowBender we resist any temptations to pursue complex optimization and aim for an ultra-simple approach that can work with today's commodity datacenter switches. We are strictly interested in an approach that avoids all of the following: added switch hardware complexity, sustained out of order packet delivery, high overhead due to complicated multi-pathing techniques, and very coarse load balancing timescales as is typically the case with centralized schemes. All of these issues can be avoided by an approach that *transmits a flow on a single path, through an ECMP-based network, and reroutes that individual flow only once it is congested.* The two questions that naturally follow this last sentence are (1) how is a flow perceived as congested, and (2) how is rerouting initiated in a simple ECMP-based network? We address these questions next.

3.3.1 Sensing Congestion

ECN is a standard congestion notification scheme supported in today's switches. Our FlowBender approach is not strictly tied to one way of triggering and handling this feedback vs another, but we chose to demonstrate it using state of the art DCTCP-style marking, where *a congested switch marks every packet exceeding a desired queue size threshold, and the TCP[1] sender keeps track of the fraction of ECN-marked ACKs every RTT.* If this fraction is larger than a certain threshold for any flow, this means that this flow is congested and should be rerouted as discussed next.

3.3.2 Rerouting Flows

The ECMP engines in switches are typically set to compute a hash function based on the packet header fields that uniquely identify a connection. However, the hash engines can be also normally configured to hash upon other fields in the packet as well (e.g. the VLAN ID field from the Ethernet header [2, 3]), and there are actually some already existing commercial platforms today that allow hashing based on programmable header offsets such as hashing based on the TTL value of a packet [2]. Per FlowBender, each TCP socket independently keeps track of the value V it should consistently insert into such a "flexible" hashing field (for every outgoing packet), and the socket updates V only once a flow is congested, thus effectively triggering sender-initiated rerouting then.

Note that from our FlowBender perspective, we are interested in "hacking" only one such flexible field that (i) does not require any pre-negotiations between the sender and the receiver for setting the value of (i.e. in contrast to MPTCP's port numbers) and (ii) does not cause packet delivery failures at the receiver or within the fabric if changed. An example of such a value is the TTL field (as long as its value V is large enough for a data center environment): whether it is set to say 90 or 163, a packet will have no issues getting routed and received properly but would probably traverse a different path in each case. The VLAN ID is another hashing input that is also easy to leverage as a flexible field, even when conventional VLANs are setup.[2]

To recap, each TCP socket sender (i.e. flow) independently keeps track of its value V and the per-RTT fraction of marked ACKs F. Once F exceeds a set threshold T, the current path is considered to be potentially congested and the packets of the corresponding flow are rerouted by changing the value V of the flexible field.

Before we move to discussing low-level details and optimizations, there is one more extremely important aspect of FlowBender that is yet to be emphasized: A packet could be at an advanced stage in its route where the only way for reaching the destination happens to be broken. In such a case, link-level schemes like DeTail or PacketScatter would be stuck unable to reroute around the broken path until the routing tables are updated (which is normally O(seconds) in a large-scale datacenter). In the case of our end-to-end FlowBender approach, however, rerouting can be also triggered once an RTO takes place, bringing the failure recovery time several orders of magnitude smaller! Of course, it is not guaranteed that the new value V would necessarily avoid broken routes from the first attempt. Actually the same could be said in the case of congestion-triggered rerouting, where the new route could be even more congested than the

[1]Datacenter operators have the option of running the transport layer they desire, and the vast majority of flows in a Datacenter are TCP flows anyway [7].

[2]Having a wide range for selecting the value V from usually means that there are more options for rerouting. We experimented with a wide range of values and have unsurprisingly found that even when we restricted each flow to 2 options only, FlowBender was extremely effective. We have empirically chosen a range of 8 options for V in our experiments.

previous one. The catch, however, is that as long as there is a statistical drift to avoid broken or congested routes, they will be avoided, even if this takes a couple of attempts before things are straightened out.

3.4 Recommended Parameter Settings and Simple Optimizations

FlowBender is very simple to tune. In its simplest form, the main parameter to configure is the T congestion threshold, which should be chosen to be small enough in order to alleviate congestion at its early onset. The smaller it is, the sooner we could be avoiding severe congestion episodes, but the more rerouting false alarms we might be getting. We have empirically varied T, the threshold for the percentage of marked ACKs, between 1% and 10% for our experiments and found FlowBender to be very effective across this range.[3] The reason FlowBender continued to be very effective at very low T thresholds is that it would not switch to a new route until at least one RTT has elapsed, thus causing packet reordering only among those packets transmitted around the rerouting instance (i.e. relatively few compared to the extent of reordering in the case of DeTail or RPS). In other words, false alarms, potentially due to bursty marking, would not be that expensive after all.

3.4.1 Even Less Reordering?

If an argument is made for a specific scenario or application where very little packet reordering instances could be tolerated, FlowBender could be readjusted to reroute only after a flow is consistently congested (T is exceeded) for N consecutive RTTs.[4] The pseudocode for the basic FlowBender algorithm together with this addition is shown below. We ran another instance of the experiments described in the next section with such an optimization, where N was set equal to 2, and saw very similar performance compared to the basic version described earlier.

```
for every RTT do
  F ← num_marked_pkts/total_pkts
  if F > T then
    num_congested_rtts + +
    if num_congested_rtts >= N then
      num_congested_rtts ← 0
      Change V
    end if
  else
    num_congested_rtts ← 0
  end if
end for
```

As is clear from its pseudo code and description, FlowBender's design is simple enough that its complete implementation requires only about 50 lines of kernel code on the hosts, and 5 lines of configuration code on the switches. Such simplicity is in stark contrast to the software complexity of schemes like MPTCP and the hardware complexity of DeTail.

[3] All of this while maintaining the default tcp_reordering threshold of 3 and confirming that the CPU overhead does not increase due to FlowBender.

[4] One might even want to exponentially average F across those N RTTs for a smoother reaction, but we don't think such optimizations are necessary at this stage.

3.4.2 Desynchronizing Flows

When a link is congested, it could be that two or more long flows would be triggered to reroute at the same time, and it's important to ensure that we are avoiding the situation where multiple simultaneous rerouting events would cascade into a rerouting wave in the fabric. Reacting at a very early congestion onset and having the RTT epochs for calculating F naturally jittered seems to be already quite helpful desynchronizing these events per the results discussed in the next section. Another design option for fortifying these jitters further is by avoiding that all flows reroute after exactly N consecutively congested RTTs, and randomly choosing the number to be something like N, $N+1$, or $N-1$ instead.

3.4.3 FlowBender beyond TCP

Even though our discussion in this paper has been focused on illustrating FlowBender's potential on top of TCP, the same load balancing principles could be easily applied to other transport protocols that sense congestion (whether CE-based, drop-based, RTT-based, etc). Moreover, for unreliable transport protocol flows such as UDP, one can argue that packet or burst-level "spraying," by changing the V value at the desired pace, would be extremely helpful for load-balancing the network traffic more effectively, especially given that applications that use UDP are usually robust or oblivious to packet reordering (of course, Weighted instead of Equal Cost Multi-pathing is required anyway to handle non-uniform link capacities and topological asymmetries).

3.4.4 Other Optimizations?

We clearly don't claim that FlowBender provides the absolutely best performance or would always lead to an optimal performance in theory. There are several optimizations that can be applied for improving FlowBender, as discussed in Section 5. However, at this stage, we are more interested in illustrating how this simplest version can still drastically improve datacenters performance!

4. EVALUATION

We evaluate FlowBender against existing schemes (i.e., ECMP, RPS, and DeTail) using both simulations and a real implementation. DeTail requires custom silicon modification so we rely on simulations to perform at-scale evaluations. We simulate production-like workloads in a typical datacenter-like topology. We also evaluate FlowBender on real testbed implementation as a proof-of-concept and to capture the effect of real system limitations and side-effects (e.g., Large Segment Offload (LSO)).

4.1 A Note on MPTCP

In our evaluations, we were not able to compare to MPTCP for the following reasons: (1) There is a lack of a reliable NS simulation package that we could leverage. (2) The latest publicly available MPTCP Linux release suffers from performance issues due to several implementation artifacts. These issues impact small flows drastically (similar to those reported in [13]), to the extent that the performance of MPTCP can be lower than a well-tuned ECMP network. Because the performance numbers capture the effect of implementation artifacts instead of the technical idea itself, such a comparison would be unfair to MPTCP and we opt

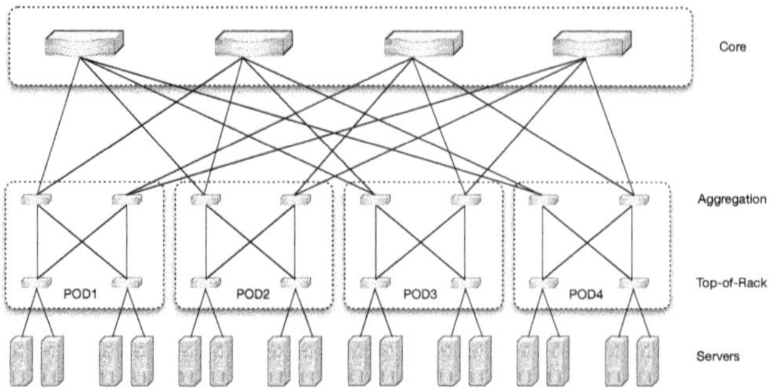

Figure 2: Fat-tree Datacenter Network Topology

to omit such a comparison. That said, even if those artifacts were to be adjusted appropriately, MPTCP's improvement relative to FlowBender's, if any, would be marginal because both DeTail and FlowBender closely match the performance of RPS (Section 4.2.3 and Section 4.2.5), which is optimal for the symmetric fat-tree datacenter topologies we evaluate.

In addition to quantitative performance, MPTCP possesses certain qualitatively undesirable design issues. For example, MPTCP has complex implementation, and because it pre-negotiates multiple routes for every connection it unnecessarily incurs higher overhead for very short flows.

4.2 Simulation

4.2.1 *Methodology*

Topology: We use ns-3 [4] simulations to evaluate FlowBender on production-like workloads. We model the network topology and the traffic after typical production deployments. We simulate a fat-tree network [15] analogous to that depicted in Figure 2. The network has 128 servers, organized into four pods, each having four Top of the Rack (ToR) and four aggregation switches, with eight core switches interconnecting the pods (overall oversubscription factor of four from servers to core switches). Because 10 Gbps ethernet is typical in today's datacenters, we use 10 Gbps point-to-point ethernet links across our entire network. All our switches use combined input-output queuing in order to better suit DeTail's requirements (the switch architecture does not impact ECMP, FlowBender or RPS). We configure the host delay to be 20 μs and the switch delay to be 1 μs, and we obtain a *baremetal RTT* of $2 \times 5 \times 1 + 4 \times 20 = 90\mu s$ between two servers on different pods, which is realistic per today's datacenters RTTs.

ECMP: Because DCTCP provides faster congestion response and helps eliminate costly timeouts, we chose DCTCP as the base TCP stack upon which we build all the other schemes. We start with ns-3's TCP New Reno protocol, and implement DCTCP [7] on top of it, faithfully capturing all its optimizations. We set the parameters of DCTCP to match those in [7]: (1) g, the factor for exponential weighted averaging, is set to $\frac{1}{16}$; and (2) K, the buffer occupancy threshold for setting the CE-bit, is set to 90 KB (typical for 10 Gbps links). So, our base case (ECMP) is DCTCP running over a commodity datacenter network with ECMP-enabled switches.

FlowBender: We implement FlowBender on top of DCTCP. We set T, the congestion threshold, to 5%, and N, the number of RTTs a sender must be congested before switching paths, to 1. Both DCTCP and FlowBender use an RTO_{min} of $10ms$.

DeTail: We use the same implementation from [23] in conjunction with DCTCP instead of the standard DropTail TCP. We set the pause and unpause thresholds to 20 KB and 10KB on the ingress queues respectively, per the guidelines in [1]. As suggested by the DeTail paper, we also disable TCP's fast retransmit to handle out-of-order packet delivery. The DeTail paper uses two thresholds of 16 KB and 64 KB to reduce the implementation complexity of determining the least congested output port at the switches, at the cost of a small performance loss (due to inaccuracy in the determination of the least congested output port). To abstract away the effect of this trade-off, we *generously* do a full comparison across all output port counters in DeTail to *always* find the minimally congested path without introducing *any* additional latency/throughput overhead due to this optimization. Thus, we compare FlowBender to the best-possible implementation of DeTail.

RPS: Our implementation of RPS consists of DCTCP running over switches that support RPS i.e., switches uniformly randomly choose a random output port from a set of eligible ports.

4.2.2 *Functionality Verification*

We start by evaluating FlowBender's efficiency in load balancing large flows to validate its functionality. In this experiment, we simultaneously initiate a small number of 250 MB flows from hosts on one ToR in a specific pod transmitting to hosts on another specific ToR in a different pod. We compare the average and worst completion times of the flows with FlowBender to that under ECMP. Because all flows are of equal size, as load balancing *improves*, both the mean and the maximum flow completion times improve. Furthermore, with better load balancing, we expect a *tighter* distribution of flow completion times i.e., the mean and the tail are close. Therefore, we can think of the ratio between the mean and the tail as a quantitative measure for quality of load balancing.

Table 1: FlowBender's flow completion times relative to ECMP's

Flows	ECMP (ms)		FlowBender (ms)	
	Mean	Max	Mean	Max
8	588	1950	294	367
16	1468	5220	580	740
24	2515	9238	897	1144

In this experiment, we vary the number of flows as 8, 16 and 24 flows, which translates to an average number of 1, 2 and 3 flows per route respectively. Consequently, we expect the best flow completion times to be roughly 200, 400, and 600 milliseconds respectively (modulo the round-trip time delay and assuming instantaneous rate convergence to the fair share with no slow-start delays). Table 1 shows the mean and maximum flow completion times. As expected, we see that FlowBender improves ECMP's mean by 2x and maximum flow completion times by 5-8x respectively. Also, the ratio of the maximum flow completion time to the mean flow completion time is more than 3.3 with ECMP, while with FlowBender the ratio reduces to less than 1.3 implying a tighter latency distribution with lower variance.

4.2.3 All-to-All Workloads

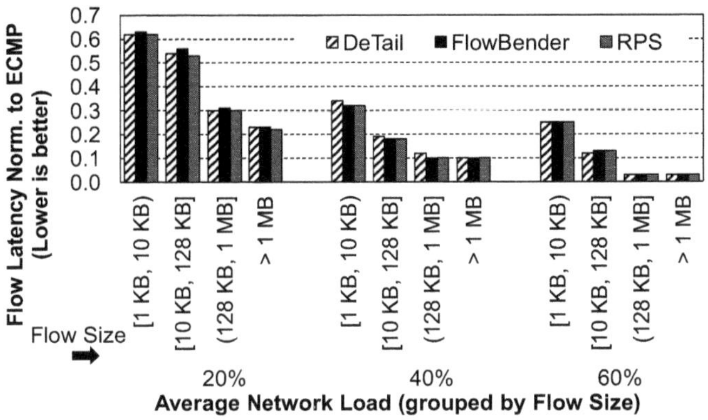

Figure 3: All-to-All workloads: Mean Latency Norm. to ECMP

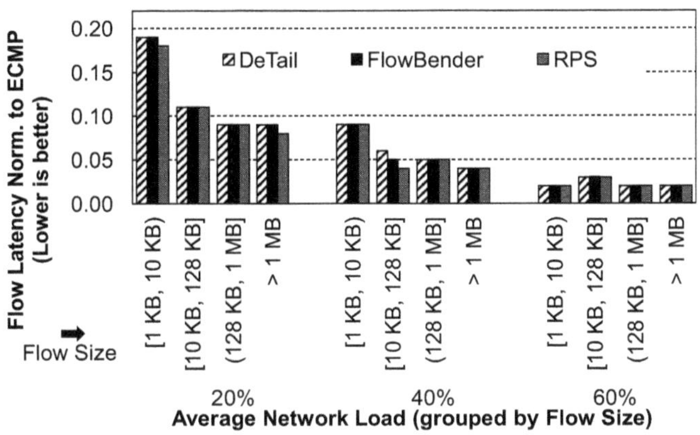

Figure 4: All-to-All workloads: Tail Latency Norm. to ECMP

We compare ECMP, RPS, DeTail, and FlowBender with traffic patterns typical of large-scale online services such as Web search. Our flow size distribution is heavy-tailed and is modeled based on the data from [8]. Every server randomly picks another server in the network to send data to, and flows arrive at the sender as a poisson process with the mean adjusted to produce the desired load. We vary the load (reported relative to the bisectional bandwidth), and compare the different schemes in terms of the mean and the 99th*percentile* latency.

We show the means in Figure 3 and the 99th percentile latencies in Figure 4, with each being binned across flow sizes: (a) less than or equal to 10KB, (b) greater than 10KB but less than or equal to 128KB, (c) greater than 128KB but less than or equal to 1MB, and (d) greater than 1MB. The load is plotted along the X-axis, and we plot the latency of RPS, DeTail, and FlowBender normalized to that of ECMP along the Y-axis. Across all of these loads, we see that all the three schemes i.e., DeTail, FlowBender and RPS *substantially* outperform ECMP. The high level takeaway from our experiments here is that though DeTail, RPS, and FlowBender achieve similar performance in general, FlowBender does not require *any* hardware change at the switches *and* is not strictly predesigned to operate in symmetric topologies, unlike DeTail and RPS.

4.2.4 Out-of-order Packet Delivery

FlowBender incurs *negligble* out-of-order packets relative to what DeTail and RPS incur. In fact, we monitored the number of out-of-order packets in all simulations and found that with FlowBender, the probability of a packet arriving out of order was about 0.006% higher than ECMP's. Compared to FlowBender's performance, DeTail had more than 97.9% the number of out-of-order packet delivery that RPS experienced.

Furthermore, DeTail suffers from the Tree Saturation problem due to its reliance on link-level PFC signals [11, 20, 12], and RPS cannot cope with asymmetric topologies and link failures [23].

4.2.5 Partition Aggregate Workloads

In this experiment, we evaluate FlowBender's ability in reducing tail latency under synchronized Partition-Aggregate traffic patterns typical of datacenter applications like Web search. We use the same heavy-tailed flow size distribution here that is used in the previous all-to-all experiment. We initiate Partition-Aggregate jobs as a Poisson arrival process with mean such that the total utilization of the bisectional bandwidth is equal to 40%. Each Partition-Aggregate job corresponds to a 1MB transaction broken evenly across n workers that are spread randomly in the fabric with all workers responding simultaneously together with their data but essentially finishing at different times. In Figure 5, we vary n between 4 and 32 along the X-axis and plot the average job completion time normalized to ECMP's i.e., the average of flow completion times of flows that finish last in each job, along the Y-axis. As expected, FlowBender performs better with smaller fan-in degrees (larger flow sizes) than with larger fan-in degrees (smaller flow sizes). FlowBender's performance, like that of RPS and DeTail, suffers with a larger fan-in degree due to synchronized packet arrivals to the destination ToR with the receiver's last hop being *the* bottleneck i.e., multipathing does not help in principle. Overall, across different fan-in degrees, FlowBender achieves a reduction in the average job completion time by a factor of *four* in the best case (fan-in degree of 4), and by a factor of two in the worst case (fan-in degree of 32), and closely matches the performance of other expensive schemes such as DeTail and RPS.

4.2.6 Sensitivity Analysis

In this section, we perform sensitivity analysis of FlowBender, by varying two of its primary knobs: N, the number of RTTs a sender must be congested for before switching paths, and T, the congestion threshold.

In Figure 6, we vary N along the X-axis and show the mean latency across different flow sizes normalized to the default setting i.e., $N = 1$. As expected, as N increases, FlowBender's performance suffers as its response slows down with higher values of N. Nevertheless, the performance variation to N is *marginal*, and FlowBender exhibits robust performance across a broad range of values.

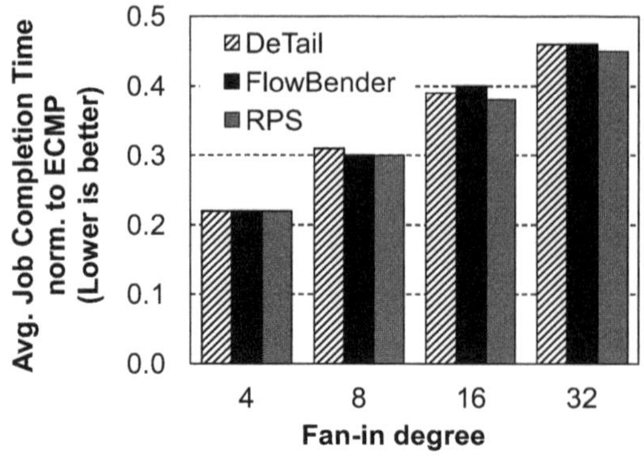

Figure 5: Partition Aggregate Workloads: Avg. Job Completion Time

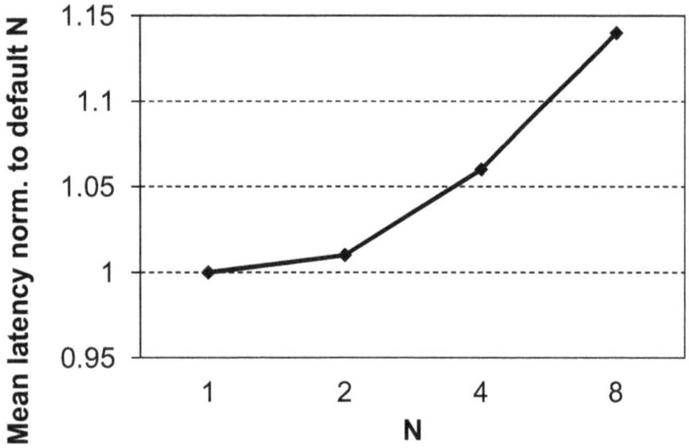

Figure 6: Sensitivity to N

In Figure 7, we vary T, the congestion threshold, along X-axis, and show the mean latency across different flow sizes normalized to the its default setting i.e., $T = 5\%$. For small values of T i.e., $T = 1\%$, FlowBender suffers marginal performance degradation as it responds to bursty spikes in the fraction of marked packets. We attain the best performance for $T = 5\%$. Increasing T beyond 5% slows down FlowBender's response, causing marginal performance degradation. Overall, similar to N, we see that FlowBender's performance is relatively robust across a wide range of T values.

4.3 Testbed Implementation

Our real implementation (testbed) has 15 ToR switches with 12 to 16 servers each. The servers are connected to the ToRs via $10Gbps$ links, and the ToRs are interconnected via 4 aggregation switches with one $10Gbps$ link to each of the 4 switches. In other words, each server has 4 distinct paths to reach any other server on the other ToR. Servers are running with Linux 3.0, including the aforementioned FlowBender changes (less than 50 lines of code added to the kernel) and the DCTCP implementation, and have their RTO set to $10msec$. We use standard ECMP-capable switches with a shared buffer space of $2MB$. The switches are configured with the CE marking threshold set to $90KB$.

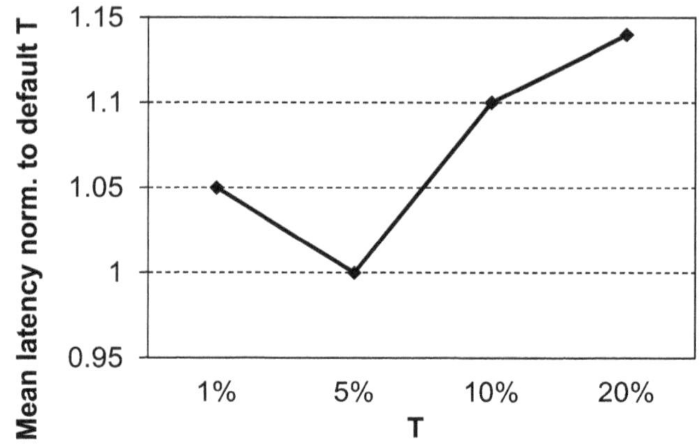

Figure 7: Sensitivity to T

4.3.1 All-to-All Traffic

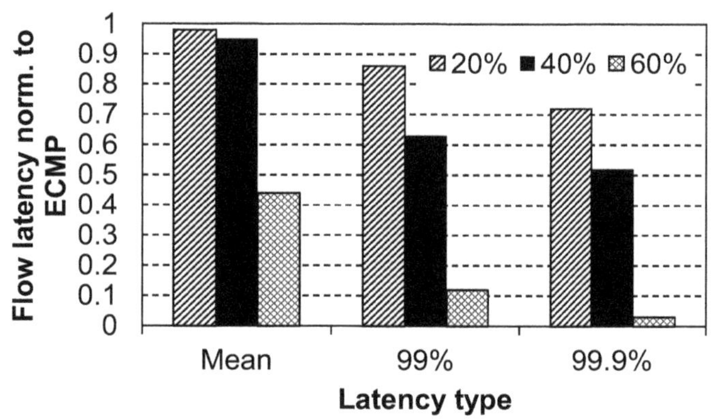

Figure 8: FlowBender's Latency Reduction at 20, 40, and 60% load (Bisectional)

In this experiment servers on one ToR initiate 1 MB flows randomly to any other server in the network with exponential inter-arrival times at a rate that cumulatively amounts to 20%, 40%, or 60% average utilization across the bisectional links. We initiate a total of 1.2 million flows, and wait for all flows to finish. We use the default TCP re-ordering threshold of 3, and monitor the out-of-order delivery numbers to ensure that FlowBender does not introduce *undesired CPU (processing) overhead.* To reconfirm that FlowBender does not lead to any abnormal packet re-ordering activity, we re-ran our experiments with a TCP re-ordering threshold of 30, and we didn't see any noticeable difference in performance.

In Figure 8, we show the *mean*, the 99th percentile, and the 99.9^{th} percentile latencies along the X-axis, and FlowBender's completion time normalized to that of ECMP along the Y-axis. We use default parameter settings for FlowBender i.e., $N = 1$ and $T = 5\%$. FlowBender improves the 99th and 99.9^{th} percentiles by $15 - 26\%$ and $34 - 45\%$ respectively, in comparison to ECMP. At 60% load, FlowBender's flows finish more than *twice* as fast as ECMP on average, and $87 - 96\%$ faster at the tail end.

A real implementation has a number of performance-affecting system-level details (e.g., application-level delays, kernel latencies, offload inefficiencies, CPU power-saving modes, etc.) which are typically absent in simulations. Accordingly we see that the testbed results are not quantitatively equal to that of simulations. However the qualitative results are similar and support the claim that FlowBender offers drastic improvement over static schemes like ECMP.

4.3.2 Decongesting HotSpots

We now evaluate FlowBender's ability to decongest flows by re-routing them around hotspots. We simplify our traffic matrix in this case and initiate an all-to-all random shuffle of $1MB$ TCP flows from one ToR to another (all in the same direction). The aggregate TCP traffic generates $14Gbps$ from the sending ToR (arbitrarily spread across the 4 $10Gbps$ links). We also initiate 1 UDP flow between the same pair of ToRs, in the same direction as the TCP traffic, and rate limit it to $6Gbps$. The purpose of the UDP flow is to create a static (asymmetric) hot spot along one of the four paths given that this flow will not be re-routed or load balanced by FlowBender. We denote the path which this UDP flow hashes on by U.

Note that the aggregate TCP and UDP traffic on the four routes between the sending and the receiving ToRs amounts to 20Gbps. Hence, in an ideal setting, one would wish that the $14Gbps$ would have been equally split across the three paths other than U given that $14/3Gbps$ is still less than UDP's $6Gbps$ that was already routed on U. With ECMP, on one hand, U was unsurprisingly getting around quarter of the TCP traffic ($14/4 = 3.5Gbps$) obliviously mapped to it, thus ending up with around $9.5Gbps$ on average in total, driving that link practically unstable. FlowBender, on the other hand, succeeded in load balancing the traffic to a great extent with only around $1.5Gbps$ of the $14Gbps$ going on U. This experiment confirms FlowBender's ability to adaptively re-route around congestive hotspots in the network, and to respond to congestion created by non-TCP traffic.

The above experiment is also interesting from a Weighted Cost Multipathing (WCMP) perspective (as opposed to ECMP) in the context of asymmetric topologies, where in order to reach a certain destination group, the viable ports at a switch are configured with different forwarding weights so as not to prematurely oversubscribe those paths with lower capacities. One of the challenges with WCMP is to be able to reflect the different weights of the forwarding ports accurately, which is highly dependent on how many entries the forwarding table can accommodate as per current ECMP implementations (i.e. larger tables can represent the different weights with higher granularity). The significance of this experiment is in how even if the forwarding weights suffer some inaccuracy because of the forwarding table being constrained to have few entries only (as is the case with our testbed and most of the commodity switches), FlowBender is able to dynamically re-adjust the traffic on the different available paths such that those with lower capacities are not severely congested (i.e. more robustness to forwarding weight misconfigurations or chip limitations).

4.3.3 Topological Dependencies

Our simulation and testbed results above are based on a topology with 8 and 4 different paths between any pair of pods or ToRs respectively. A question that commonly arises here is: how helpful would FlowBender be when the path diversity between any pair of pods increases? In other words, what role does FlowBender play if the port density of each switch is, say, doubled, together with the number of servers per ToR, while keeping the over-subscriptions ratios the same (i.e. the path diversity quadruples)? The extent to which FlowBender helps clearly depends on the number of the available paths P, but it also depends on the number of those larger flows L that we're trying to spread out on those paths. More precisely, and particularly true in the limits, the performance improvement depends on the ratio $R = L/P$ of the two numbers as we show next, which is typically expected to remain constant given that as the bisectional capacity (i.e. P) is scaled up, the load, and hence, L would be also scaled up proportionally to maintain the same utilization.

Considering the micro benchmark basic validation results discussed earlier, where FlowBender is shown to do a good job in evenly spreading the flows across the different paths, FlowBender's performance improvement amounts to how bad ECMP's flow distribution performance was in the first place. Given the oblivious nature of ECMP, the distribution of the number of large flows per each route is, in steady state, a very straightforward binomial distribution with a mean R and a variance $R(1 - 1/P)$, which is therefore not that different for a reasonably large P. For example, varying P from 8 to 32 would increase the variance by less than 11% only and hence would have a negligible effect in practice. In fact, we reran our All-to-All experiments with a different fan-out degree, and the performance improvement due to FlowBender was almost the same.

5. FURTHER OPTIMIZATIONS AND FUTURE WORK

Our paper presents one of the most basic versions of FlowBender. As discussed earlier, we have intentionally resisted any temptations to optimize FlowBender in the interest of demonstrating how effective this simple idea is, and our evaluation results confirm our position for all the practical cases that we have discussed. Looking forward, however, FlowBender might be desired to operate in more challenging environments, potentially outside datacenters, and could benefit from some of the suggestions summarized below.

5.1 Stability

FlowBender does not monitor the load on all available paths before taking a rerouting decision. Instead, it randomly chooses a new path when it detects that the current path is congested. Therefore, the new path it reroutes to may be also congested. If that happens to be the case because say of an incast episode or because the network is highly congested in general, FlowBender will trigger yet another path change, and the rerouting process may repeat. In some pathological cases, such a design could continuously thrash from one path to the other if no further measures for preventing this are taken. Because every rerouting instance carries the potential of out-of-order delivery of packets to the receiver, such thrashing is undesirable.[5] Accordingly, FlowBender can be extended to limit the number of path

[5]Even though such artifacts are more likely to occur in an incast situation, the extent to which they occurred in our simulations was negligible as is evident from the improvement ratios discussed earlier. We do bring up the feature suggested herein, however, so as to add more confidence around FlowBender's ability to handle some of those quite

changes that could occur when the network is severely congested. More specifically, FlowBender can be constrained to switch paths for a maximum of S consecutive times before it goes into a *locked* state. In the locked state, it will pick one path out of the last S paths that had the lowest value of F, the fraction of ECN-marked ACKs, and will lock in to that path for the next U RTTs. At the end of the locked phase, FlowBender resumes business as usual, tracking F and switching paths if it exceeds T for N consecutive RTTs. Note that if we were to choose S and U as 5 and 10, respectively, with an N of 2 (which gives almost the same performance as the default $N = 1$ configuration), then we would be limiting the rerouting events to a maximum of 5 times in every $5 \times 2 + 10 = 20$ RTTs, thus significantly limiting the number of out-of-order packets that could be triggered by FlowBender.

5.2 Gradual Rerouting

Instead of shifting the traffic of a congested flow all at once from one route to another, the rerouting process can be attempted gradually. Of course, this is assuming the transport layer is adjusted to tolerate out-of-order packe delivery. For example, we can start by initially transmitting 10% of the traffic of a congested flow on a new path[6] while monitoring whether this has any effect on alleviating congestion. If congestion has been already mitigated by partially migrating to the new path, then this could be an indication that more traffic should be routed on the new path (e.g. go up to transmitting 20% of the traffic on the new path and so on). Otherwise, it could be that the desire to send on a different, uncongested path was not really met (potentially because of partially or fully overlapping with the existing path at one or more congested links), so the flow would attempt to send on a different new path instead (i.e. abandon the intermediate one).

The above discussion has focused on the case of load balancing across 2 subflows, which might be sufficient for most practical purposes, but the same approach can be extended to load balancing across more than two paths simultaneously.

5.3 Selective Rehashing

In our current implementation, we change the value of V for the flexible hashing input field obliviously once congestion occurs. Changing the value of V, however, does not always mean that the route will change as this really depends on the hashing function. That said, given sufficient knowledge about the hashing functions in the fabric, one can avoid this artifact by having each flow precompute a number of potential values for V that would result in hashing to different paths. The process for precomputing such values might be very challenging and time consuming to perform for general hashing functions, but if the network operators choose their hashing functions in a way such that flipping one of the hashing inputs bits would result in a different hashing output (e.g. XOR hash functions), then this process would become much easier to perform. Alternatively, flows can correlate the different RTT estimates or values for F corresponding to different V's in order to infer, with a high probability, how these V's map to different paths and avoid choosing a redundant value for rerouting.

5.4 Proactive Probing and Route Caching

We have demonstrated the reactive version of FlowBender, where a flow is rerouted only once congestion has been detected. Of course, one might argue that FlowBender is already quite prompt in rerouting when congestion arises, given its low congestion detection threshold T, but the load balancing performance could be still further improved by allowing a flow to proactively probe across the different paths. By probing we mean that a flow can periodically send a few of its packets with different V values, keeping track of their sequence numbers ranges, and check once they have been acked which of them have experienced congestion. One of those V's corresponding to probe packets which did not seem to be congested at all could be proactively selected as the basic V once F has exceeded a threshold T' smaller than T. Alternatively, a flow may attempt to keep track of some of those *better* V's to hash upon once congestion occurs, instead of choosing V obliviously, or might simply blacklist those highly congested V's and avoid revisiting them until sufficient time has elapsed.

5.5 Rerouting and Flow Control

Rerouting, in the load balancing sense, and flow control, in the congestion control sense, are two ways for handling congestion in multipath environments. When both mechanisms rely on the same congestion signal (e.g. ECN driving both, FlowBender and DCTCP), it becomes useful to decide on which of the two mechanisms should be triggered based on the nature of the congestion event. For example, if congestion is occuring at the receiving ToR (e.g. an incast event), then it is unlikely that rerouting the individual congested responses will help (though rerouting still did not have a noticeable negative impact on the overall performance per our simulation results). Alternatively, if a flow is mainly bottlenecked at a core switch while other core switches are lightly loaded, then slowing down the rate of this flow would be rather harmful when it could have been rerouted instead. In our evaluation for FlowBender, we did not attempt any optimizations along these lines given that DCTCP would not have kicked in aggressively yet once the very low threshold T would have been just exceeded. In the future, however, FlowBender and other congestion control and load balancing mechanisms could significantly benefit from more informative congestion control signals that can somehow distinguish whether congestion is occuring at the edge of the fabric and/or somewhere else.

6. CONCLUSION

In this paper, we proposed a new load balancing mechanism called FlowBender. The main motivation for introducing FlowBender is to overcome the limitations of oblivious hashing schemes such as ECMP, prominent in today's datacenters, without suffering from high packet re-ordering or requiring custom hardware changes and complicated host mechanisms that could offset any potential benefits. FlowBender is a host-based, congestion-driven scheme that distributively re-routes individual flows around congested hotspots only once congestion is experienced, end-to-end, or when link failures occur. FlowBender relies on ECN and ECMP

unlikely pathological scenarios that our evaluations did not cover.

[6]This can be done in a periodic manner to avoid CPU-intensive computations for generating random numbers (e.g. every 10th pkt is sent on a new path).

switch support, which is typical in today's datacenters, and implements the load-balancing logic at the end-hosts via a very straightforward kernel patch. In contrast to centralized flow scheduling schemes, FlowBender recovers from link failures after an RTO occurs and reroutes congested flows at the RTT granularity, several orders of magnitude faster than state of the art routing management schemes.

Our ns-3 [4] simulations, with workloads representative of datacenter applications, show that FlowBender *substantially* reduces the mean and tail latency compared to ECMP, while achieving performance very similar to that of other expensive or undesirable schemes like DeTail and RPS. In particular, our tail latencies are reduced by more than 5x to 20x relative to ECMP's, and our partition-aggregate jobs are about 2x to 4x faster on average. We have also evaluated FlowBender using a real implentation and found that it cuts the flow completion tail latencies by around 40% relative to ECMP's for large flows.

7. REFERENCES

[1] 802.1Qbb - priority-based flow control. `http://www.ieee802.org/1/pages/802.1bb.html`.

[2] Avoiding network polarization and increasing visibility in cloud networks using broadcom smart hash technology. `http://www.broadcom.com/collateral/wp/StrataXGS_SmartSwitch-WP200-R.pdf`.

[3] Cisco cli command reference. `http://www.cisco.com/en/US/docs/wireless/asr_901/Command/Reference/Cmdref_asr901.html`.

[4] NS-3 network simulator. `http://www.nsnam.org/`.

[5] M. Al-Fares, A. Loukissas, and A. Vahdat. A scalable, commodity data center network architecture. In *Proceedings of the ACM SIGCOMM 2008 conference on Data communication*, SIGCOMM '08, pages 63–74, New York, NY, USA, 2008. ACM.

[6] M. Al-Fares, S. Radhakrishnan, B. Raghavan, N. Huang, and A. Vahdat. Hedera: dynamic flow scheduling for data center networks. In *Proceedings of the 7th USENIX conference on Networked systems design and implementation*, NSDI'10, pages 19–19, Berkeley, CA, USA, 2010. USENIX Association.

[7] M. Alizadeh, A. Greenberg, D. A. Maltz, J. Padhye, P. Patel, B. Prabhakar, S. Sengupta, and M. Sridharan. Data center tcp (dctcp). In *Proceedings of the ACM SIGCOMM 2010 conference*, SIGCOMM '10, pages 63–74, New York, NY, USA, 2010. ACM.

[8] T. Benson, A. Akella, and D. A. Maltz. Network traffic characteristics of data centers in the wild. In *Proceedings of the 10th ACM SIGCOMM conference on Internet measurement*, IMC '10, pages 267–280, New York, NY, USA, 2010. ACM.

[9] A. R. Curtis, W. Kim, and P. Yalagandula. Mahout: Low-overhead datacenter traffic management using end-host-based elephant detection. In *INFOCOM*, pages 1629–1637. IEEE.

[10] A. R. Curtis, J. C. Mogul, J. Tourrilhes, P. Yalagandula, P. Sharma, and S. Banerjee. Devoflow: scaling flow management for high-performance networks. In *Proceedings of the ACM SIGCOMM 2011 conference*, SIGCOMM '11, pages 254–265, New York, NY, USA, 2011. ACM.

[11] W. J. Dally. Virtual-channel flow control. *IEEE Trans. Parallel Distrib. Syst.*, 3(2):194–205, Mar. 1992.

[12] D. M. Dias and M. Kumar. Preventing congestion in multistage networks in the presence of hotspots. In *ICPP (1)'89*, pages 9–13, 1989.

[13] A. Dixit, P. Prakash, Y. Hu, and R. Kompella. On the impact of packet spraying in data center networks. In *INFOCOM, 2013 Proceedings IEEE*, pages 2130–2138, 2013.

[14] J. Kim, W. J. Dally, and D. Abts. Adaptive routing in high-radix clos network. In *Proceedings of the 2006 ACM/IEEE conference on Supercomputing*, SC '06, New York, NY, USA, 2006. ACM.

[15] C. E. Leiserson. Fat-trees: universal networks for hardware-efficient supercomputing. *IEEE Trans. Comput.*, 34(10):892–901, Oct. 1985.

[16] J. Mudigonda, P. Yalagandula, M. Al-Fares, and J. C. Mogul. Spain: Cots data-center ethernet for multipathing over arbitrary topologies. In *Proceedings of the 7th USENIX Conference on Networked Systems Design and Implementation*, NSDI'10, 2010.

[17] C. Raiciu, S. Barre, C. Pluntke, A. Greenhalgh, D. Wischik, and M. Handley. Improving datacenter performance and robustness with multipath tcp. In *Proceedings of the ACM SIGCOMM 2011 conference*, SIGCOMM '11, pages 266–277, New York, NY, USA, 2011. ACM.

[18] C. Raiciu, C. Paasch, S. BarrÈ, A. Ford, M. Honda, F. Duchene, O. Bonaventure, and M. Handley. How hard can it be? designing and implementing a deployable multipath tcp. In *USENIX Symposium of Networked Systems Design and Implementation (NSDI'12), San Jose (CA)*, 2012.

[19] J. H. Saltzer, D. P. Reed, and D. D. Clark. End-to-end arguments in system design. *ACM Trans. Comput. Syst.*, pages 277–288, 1984.

[20] J. R. Santos, Y. Turner, and G. (john Janakiraman. End-to-end congestion control for infiniband. In *In proceedings of Infocom03*, 2003.

[21] B. Vamanan, J. Hasan, and T. Vijaykumar. Deadline-aware datacenter tcp (d2tcp). In *Proceedings of the ACM SIGCOMM 2012 Conference on Applications, Technologies, Architectures, and Protocols for Computer Communication*, SIGCOMM '12, 2012.

[22] D. Wischik, C. Raiciu, A. Greenhalgh, and M. Handley. Design, implementation and evaluation of congestion control for multipath tcp. In *Proceedings of the 8th USENIX conference on Networked systems design and implementation*, NSDI'11, pages 8–8, Berkeley, CA, USA, 2011. USENIX Association.

[23] D. Zats, T. Das, P. Mohan, D. Borthakur, and R. Katz. Detail: reducing the flow completion time tail in datacenter networks. In *Proceedings of the ACM SIGCOMM 2012 conference on Applications, technologies, architectures, and protocols for computer communication*, SIGCOMM '12, pages 139–150, New York, NY, USA, 2012. ACM.

Distributed Route Aggregation on the Global Network

www.route-aggregation.net

João Luís Sobrinho
Instituto de Telecomunicações
Instituto Superior Técnico
Universidade de Lisboa
joao.sobrinho@lx.it.pt

Laurent Vanbever
Princeton University
vanbever@cs.princeton.edu

Franck Le
IBM T. J. Watson Research
fle@us.ibm.com

Jennifer Rexford
Princeton University
jrex@cs.princeton.edu

ABSTRACT

The Internet routing system faces serious scalability challenges, due to the growing number of IP prefixes it needs to propagate throughout the network. For example, the Internet suffered significant outages in August 2014 when the number of globally routable prefixes went past 512K, the default size of the forwarding tables in many older routers. Although IP prefixes are assigned hierarchically, and roughly align with geographic regions, today's Border Gateway Protocol (BGP) and operational practices do not exploit opportunities to aggregate routes. We present a distributed route-aggregation technique (called DRAGON) where nodes analyze BGP routes across different prefixes to determine which of them can be filtered while respecting the routing policies for forwarding data-packets. DRAGON works with BGP, can be deployed incrementally, and offers incentives for ASs to upgrade their router software. We present a theoretical model of route-aggregation, and the design and analysis of DRAGON. Our experiments with realistic assignments of IP prefixes, network topologies, and routing policies show that DRAGON reduces the number of prefixes in each AS by about 80% and significantly curtails the number of routes exchanged during transient periods of convergence.

Categories and Subject Descriptors

C.2.2 [**Network Protocols**]: Routing Protocols; C.2.3 [**Network Operations**]: Network management; C.2.6 [**Internetworking**]: Routers

General Terms

Algorithms; Management; Performance; Theory

Keywords

Inter-domain Routing; Route Aggregation; Scalability; BGP

CoNEXT'14, December 2–5, 2014, Sydney, Australia.
Copyright 2014 ACM 978-1-4503-3279-8/14/12 ...$15.00.
http://dx.doi.org/10.1145/2674005.2674999.

1. INTRODUCTION

Ideally, a global routing system should scale by having each node maintain detailed information about nearby destinations and only coarse-grained information about far-away destinations [18, 34, 19]. Such a scalable system would be possible under careful, centralized planning of the network topology, address assignment, and route computation. However, the Internet is anything but centralized, and its growth has been anything but orderly. Each Autonomous System (AS) makes its own decisions about where to connect, how to acquire address space, and what routes to select and make available to others. Increasingly, even ASs at the perimeter of the Internet are multi-homed, making it necessary to propagate their routing information beyond their providers. As a result, more than half a million IP prefixes are distributed by the global routing system [1].

The growing number of globally routable IP prefixes has serious consequences for the Internet. The number of prefixes determines the size of *forwarding-tables* (or, Forwarding Information Base, or FIB) stored in expensive high-speed memory on the routers, as well as that of *routing-tables* (or, Routing Information Base, or RIB). Many older routers devote a default size of 512K entries to the IPv4 forwarding table, which lead to the Internet outages of August 12, 2014, when the number of prefixes crossed this threshold [10, 22]. The number of prefixes also affects the message overhead and convergence time of the Border Gateway Protocol (BGP), and the time required to bring up a single BGP session [15, 37]. BGP's scalability challenges also hinder the deployment of security enhancements like S-BGP, since the substantial computational overhead for signing and verifying BGP routes grows with the number of prefixes.

Fortunately, the underlying structure of the global routing system makes better route aggregation possible. The assignment of IP prefixes is mostly aligned with the AS-level topology and business relationships, since blocks of IP addresses are allocated hierarchically by Regional Internet Registries (RIRs) to Internet Service Providers (ISPs) who, in turn, assign sub-blocks to their customers. Some ASs acquire Provider-Independent (PI) prefixes directly from the RIRs. Nonetheless, these prefixes still align roughly with geographic regions. Likewise, despite the prevalence of multi-homing, most ASs connect to multiple providers in the same geographic area, leaving potential for far-away ASs to route based on coarser-grained routing information.

Existing routing protocol implementations and operational practices do *not* exploit these opportunities for route aggregation. According to best current practices, an ISP configures its routers to filter BGP routes from single-homed customers with IP addresses allocated out of the ISP's address space, but not from customers who are multi-homed or have PI addresses. The reason is simple: network operators cannot reason about how more aggressive filters would affect how other parts of the Internet reach their customers. In the face of uncertainty, ISPs are understandably conservative in applying route filters. Worse yet, some ISPs do not filter at all, out of ignorance, sloppy operational practices, or legitimate concerns that a previously single-homed customer might later become multi-homed.

In this paper, we introduce DRAGON (Distributed Route Aggregation on the Global Network), a route-aggregation solution for inter-domain routing. DRAGON operates with today's BGP protocol and any routing policies that ensure correct operation of BGP. We show that by comparing routes for different prefixes, an AS can determine which prefixes can be filtered locally without worsening the type of route used to forward data-packets. DRAGON can be deployed incrementally and has built-in incentives for ASs to participate. Our experiments with realistic AS-level topologies, IP prefix assignments, and routing policies show that DRAGON dispenses with about 80% of the IP prefixes in each AS.

Inter-domain routing policies are neither arbitrary nor random. They reflect business goals and are constrained by BGP's configuration mechanisms. Seen in this light, it is not surprising that many routing policies end-up satisfying properties which leave a distinctive mark on the global routing system. One such property is isotonicity [8, 32], enjoyed by the Gao-Rexford (GR) routing policies [13] among others [31, 23]. In loose terms, isotonicity means that if an AS prefers one route over another, a neighbor AS does not have the opposite preference after its local processing of the two routes. We show that, in the face of isotone routing policies, DRAGON attains an optimal aggregated state that preserves the global routes traversed by data-packets on their way to the destinations.

The fundamentals of DRAGON are valid for any prefix-based routing system substantiated on a routing vector-protocol. We honor that generality in the way we present DRAGON even if our examples and experiments pertain to inter-domain routing. The paper has three main parts: the design of DRAGON, illustrated with examples, Section 3; the theoretical justification for DRAGON, Section 4; and experiments quantifying the scalability benefits of DRAGON, Section 5. The next section establishes the routing model. There is also a section on related work, Section 6, and a concluding section, Section 7.

2. ROUTING AND FORWARDING MODEL

A network is composed of nodes joined by links. Addresses are strings of bits of fixed length. A prefix is a string of bits of length shorter than that of the addresses, representing all the addresses whose first bits coincide with those of the prefix. Prefixes are assigned to nodes and made known to all other nodes in the network through a routing vector-protocol, in accordance with the routing policies configured at the various nodes. In inter-domain routing, nodes are ASs, prefixes are IP prefixes, the routing vector-protocol is BGP, and there is a two-way link between two ASs if at least two border routers, one on each AS, established a BGP-session between them.

A route is an association between a prefix and an attribute.[1] Attributes are totally ordered by preference. A route pertaining to prefix p is called a p-route. A standard vector-protocol instantiates a distinct computation process for every prefix. The node to which p has been assigned is the origin of p. This node attaches an attribute to p thus forming a p-route that it announces to its neighbors. Each node stores in its routing-table, for each one of its neighbors, a candidate p-route that extends the last of the p-routes announced by the neighbor that was received by the node. The node elects the candidate p-route with the most preferred attribute and, in turn, announces the elected p-route to its neighbors. Every time a node elects a p-route, it makes an entry in its forwarding-table associating p to the forwarding neighbors for p, those being the neighbor nodes for which the candidate p-route coincides with the elected p-route. Allowing for multi-path routing, a prefix may be associated with more than one forwarding neighbor. Routing policies specify the relative preference among attributes and how the attribute of an elected route at one node is extended to the attribute of a candidate route at a neighbor node.

The prototypical inter-domain routing policies are the Gao-Rexford (GR) routing policies [13], which postulate that neighbor nodes establish either a customer-provider or a peer-peer relationship. The policies are supported on just the three attributes "learned from a customer," "learned from a peer," and "learned from a provider." Following standard terminology, we use the term "customer route" as shorthand for "route with attribute 'learned from customer'," and similarly for the terms "peer route" and "provider route," and talk about the preference among routes signifying the preference among their attributes. A customer route is preferred to a peer route which is preferred to a provider route.[2] Customer routes are exported to all neighbors, all routes are exported to customers, and these are the only exportations allowed. A route originated by a node can be assumed to have attribute "learned from a customer," since it is subjected to the same treatment as if it were learned from a customer, namely, the route is exported to all of the node's neighbors.

A vector-protocol is correct in a network if it terminates in a stable state that guides data-packets to their destinations. Reference [32] gives a condition on the cycles of a network that guarantees correctness. In the case of the GR routing policies, that condition stipulates the absence of cycles where each node is a customer of the next around the cycle.

Figure 1 shows a network operating according to the GR routing policies. Solid lines join a provider and a customer, with the provider drawn higher than the customer, and a dashed line joins two peers. For instance, u_2 is a provider of both u_3 and u_4, and a peer of u_1. Node u_6 is multi-homed to two providers, u_3 and u_4. Prefix p was assigned to node u_4 which originates a p-route that it exports to all its neighbors. Once the vector-protocol terminates, u_2 elects a customer p-route, learned from u_4, which becomes u_2's forwarding neighbor for p; u_1 elects a peer p-route, learned from u_2; and u_5 elects a provider p-route, learned both from u_1 and u_3.

A prefix q is *more specific* than a prefix p if it is longer than p and its first bits coincide with those of p. Delegation of prefixes from providers to customers combined with operational practices, such as those related to multi-homing and traffic engineering, cause prefixes at different levels of specificity to be propagated throughout the network and maintained in the routing- and forwarding-tables of nodes. The longest prefix match rule [12] prescribes that data-packets are forwarded at a node according to the elected route of the most specific of the prefixes that contains the destination address of the data-packet. In Figure 1, prefix q, assigned to u_6, is more specific than prefix p. Node u_3 elects a customer q-route, learned from u_6, and a provider p-route, learned from u_2. Data-packets arriving

[1]Our use of the term "attribute" is generic and not meant to single out the parameters of BGP, such as LOCAL-PREF and AS-PATH.

[2]Peer routes do not have to be preferred to provider routes [13]. We make this extra assumption because it seems to be valid in practice and it simplifies the exposition.

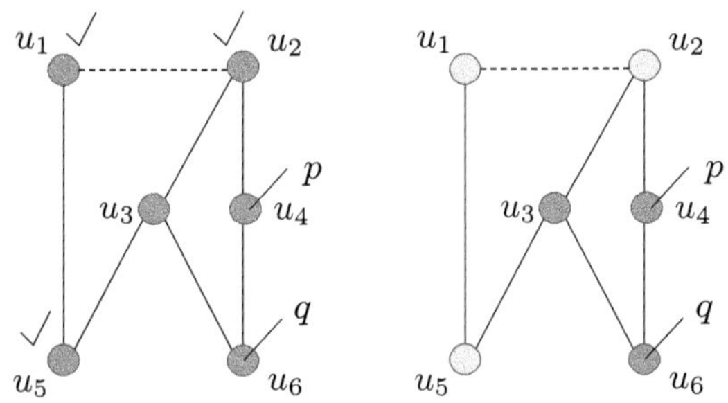

Figure 1: Providers are drawn above customers and joined with solid lines. Peers are joined with dashed lines. Node u_6 is multi-homed to u_3 and u_4. Node u_4 is assigned p and delegates q to its customer u_6, with q more specific than p. Left. Standard stable state. Checks mark nodes that satisfy the condition for filtering q. Right. Stable state after all nodes execute code **CR** in whatever order, with light-shaded nodes forgoing q.

at u_3 with destination in q are forwarded to u_6, whereas those arriving with destination in p but *not* in q are forwarded to u_2.

3. MECHANISMS OF DRAGON

DRAGON relies on standard routing messages of a vector-protocol and augments local routing decisions with filtering of prefixes and generation of aggregation prefixes. Section 3.1 presents basic filtering code for DRAGON and Section 3.2 presents a rule for originating routes that ensures that the filtering code does not cause black holes. Section 3.3 introduces a property of routing policies known as isotonicity and shows that, in their presence, DRAGON attains optimally filtered routing states. Section 3.4 deals with partial deployment. Section 3.5 discusses alternative filtering codes. Section 3.6 concerns multiple levels of prefixes and Section 3.7 presents aggregation prefixes. Section 3.8 discusses the reaction of DRAGON to network events, such as link failures. Last, Section 3.9 shows how DRAGON accommodates prefix de-aggregation for the purposes of traffic engineering.

3.1 Filtering code

The goal of DRAGON is for many nodes to dispense with routes pertaining to more specific prefixes with little or no change in the properties of paths traversed by data-packets. Towards this goal, some nodes filter some prefixes. Filtering of a prefix means that no entry for the prefix is installed in the forwarding-table of the node and the prefix is not announced to neighbor nodes. Routes pertaining to the prefix are still kept in the routing-table of the node for a prompt reaction to network events (Section 3.8).

Let q be more specific than p. We investigate the following code to filter q, to be executed autonomously at every node.

Code CR: If the node is not the origin of p and the attribute of the elected q-route equals or is less preferred than the attribute of the elected p-route, then filter q. Otherwise, do not filter q.

This code is intuitively reasonable as it maintains or improves the attribute of the route according to which data-packets are forwarded at a node. Certainly, the origin of p should not filter q-routes. Otherwise, data-packets arriving there with destination in q would have nowhere to go and would have to be dropped. For a node other than the origin of p, if the attribute of the elected q-route equals that of the elected p-route, then the node filters q. On filtering, the node saves on forwarding state while it still forwards data-packets with destination in q according to an elected route—that for p—whose attribute is the same as that of the elected q-route without filtering. Last, if the attribute of the elected q-route is less preferred than the attribute of the elected p-route, then all the more reason for the node to filter q. On filtering, the node saves on forwarding state and improves the attribute of the route according to which it forwards data-packets with destination in q.

Throughout the paper, we will study the global effect of local code **CR**. For now, we exemplify that effect with Figure 1 assuming the GR routing policies. Node u_6 acquired its address space from its provider u_4. The acquired address space is represented by prefix q which is more specific than prefix p. Despite this acquisition, u_6 wants to send and receive data-packets to and from both providers u_4 and u_3. Thus, both p and q are propagated by the vector-protocol throughout the network. The stable state is depicted on the left-hand side of the figure and described next alongside the possibility of filtering q upon execution of code **CR**.

- Node u_4 is the origin of p. Thus, u_4 cannot filter q.
- Node u_6, which is the origin of q, elects a customer q-route (originated by itself) and a provider p-route. Thus, u_6 cannot filter q-routes.
- Node u_3 elects a customer q-route, learned from u_6, and a provider p-route, learned from u_2. Thus, it cannot filter q-routes.
- Node u_2 elects both a customer q-route, learned from u_3 and u_4, and a customer p-route, learned from u_4. Thus, it can filter q-routes.
- Node u_1 elects both a peer q-route and a peer p-route, both routes learned from u_2. Thus, it can filter q-routes.
- Node u_5 elects both a provider q-route and provider p-route, both routes learned from u_1 and u_3. Thus, it can filter q-routes.

Suppose that u_2 executes **CR**, thereby filtering q. Despite the absence of a q-route, u_2 still forwards data-packets with destination in q according to a customer route, that elected for p. Because u_2 filters q, u_1 no longer receives a q-route from u_2 and, hence, does not elect any q-route. It forwards data-packets with destination in q according to the elected p-route which was also learned from u_2. Since u_1 does not elect a q-route, it exports none to its customer u_5. Node u_5 still elects a provider q-route learned from u_3. In this state, suppose that u_5 executes **CR**. It, too, filters q and starts forwarding data-packets with destination in q according to the elected provider p-route, learned from u_3 and u_1. In summary, if u_2 then u_5 execute **CR**, then we arrive at the routing state depicted in the right-hand side of Figure 1 and commented upon next.

- Nodes u_2 and u_5 filter q while u_1 is oblivious of q. We say that a node *forgoes* q if either it filters q or is oblivious of q. In real topologies, most nodes will forgo q. Of these, a few will filter q, while the majority will be oblivious of q. Routing state pertaining to q only needs to be kept in some small vicinity of the node originating q.
- Data-packets are delivered to the destinations, there being no route oscillations, forwarding loops, or black holes. When this happens, we say that DRAGON is *correct* (Section 3.2).
- Data-packets are forwarded at each node according to an elected route whose attribute equals that of the elected route used to forward them when there was no filtering. Such a

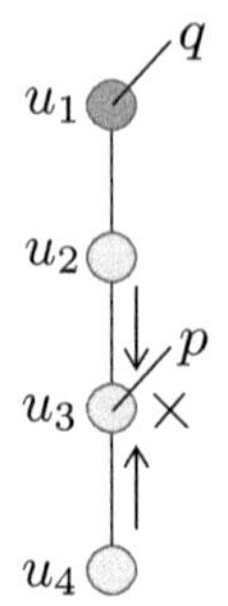

Figure 2: Prefix q is more specific than p. Node u_1 originates q, and u_3 originates p by sending a p-route to all its neighbors. Node u_2 executes **CR**, in the process creating a black hole at u_3. Arrows indicate the expedition of data-packets with destination in q.

desirable global state is called *route consistent*. A route-consistent state is *optimal* if the set of nodes forgoing q is maximal (Section 3.3). The routing state depicted in the right-hand side of Figure 1 is optimal and can be arrived at by executing **CR** once at each node in whatever order.

3.2 Announcement rule and correctness

Through code **CR**, DRAGON subordinates the computation of q-routes to the computation of p-routes. Therefore, even if the vector-protocol is correct for p and q, taken individually as two unrelated prefixes, it is legitimate to ask whether DRAGON is correct, always delivering data-packets to their destinations. The main concern is that filtering of q by some nodes may create black holes for data-packets with destination in q. In Section 4.2, we prove that the following rule for originating prefixes guarantees correctness of DRAGON.

Rule RA: The origin of p announces p with a route whose attribute is equal or less preferred than the attribute of the elected q-route.

The necessity of rule **RA** can be appreciated with the example of Figure 2. Node u_1 is the origin of q and u_3—which a customer of a customer of u_1—is the origin of p. Node u_3 elects a provider q-route. Suppose that it originates p with a customer route, thus violating rule **RA**: the attribute of the p-route with which u_3 originates p ("learned from a customer") is preferred to the attribute of the elected q-route ("learned from a provider"). Node u_2 elects a provider q-route and a customer p-route. On executing **CR**, u_2 filters q. As a consequence, no q-route arrives at u_3 and u_4. Data-packets arriving at u_2 and u_4 with destination in q are forwarded to u_3 by the elected p-route to be dropped there. Node u_3 becomes a black hole for q. In order to satisfy rule **RA**, u_3 can originate p only with a provider route, meaning that it can export p-routes only to its customers; in this case, to node u_4. If u_3 does export a p-route to u_4, then u_4 elects both a provider q-route and a provider p-route. Node u_4 may filter q-routes that data-packets with destination in q will be delivered to u_1.

It must be noted that the assignment of prefixes in Figure 2 is unlikely to be found in the Internet where blocks of IP addresses are delegated from providers to customers rather than the other way round.

3.3 Isotonicity and optimal route-consistency

Routing policies are isotone [8, 32] whenever the relative preference among attributes of elected routes is respected among the attributes of the candidate routes derived from them. Let u and v be two neighbor nodes and α and β be any two attributes such that α is preferred to β. Suppose that elected routes with attributes α and β at v are extended to candidate routes with attributes α' and β' at u, respectively. The combined routing policies of u and v are isotone if α' equals β' or α' is preferred to β'.

The GR routing policies are isotone. For instance, suppose that u is a customer of v. All of a customer route, a peer route, and a provider route at v are exported by v to u, and all become provider routes at u. Thus, isotonicity holds. Suppose, instead, that u is a provider of v. A customer route is preferred to both a peer route and a provider route at v. The customer route is exported by v to u where it becomes a customer route too, whereas the peer route and the provider route are not exported by v to u. Clearly, the customer route at u is preferred to no route. Isotonicity holds as well. A similar argument can be made if u is a peer of v. Many other practical routing policies are isotone. For example, the next-hop routing policies proposed in [31] for inter-domain routing generalize the GR routing policies and are isotone as well. So are the routing policies that incorporate siblings in the landscape of Internet business relationships [23].

A global routing state attained by DRAGON is *route consistent* if it is stable and always forwards data-packets according to an elected route whose attribute is the same as that of the elected route used to forward them without DRAGON. A route-consistent routing state is *optimal* if the set of nodes that forgoes q is maximal. Ideally, DRAGON would lead to optimal route-consistent states and this is exactly what happens if routing policies are isotone and all nodes execute code **CR** once in whatever order. A proof of this result is given in Section 4.3. The intuition is the following. With isotonicity, if the attribute of the elected q-route is the same or less preferred than the attribute of the elected p-route at a node v—as in the premise of code **CR**—then, at a neighbor u of v, the attribute of the q-route learned from v is also the same or less preferred than the attribute of the p-route learned from v. Therefore, the filtering of q at v is consistent with the filtering decision that would be made at u based on routes learned from v.

If routing policies are not isotone, then code **CR** may not conduce to route-consistent states. Consider the network of Figure 3 where the GR routing policies are used with two important exceptions.

- Node u_5 prefers routes learned from provider u_3 to routes learned from provider u_1.
- Node u_3 exports provider routes to its customer u_5, but it does not export customer routes to u_5. Thus, the combined routing policies of u_3 and u_5 are *not* isotone. A customer route is preferred to a provider route at u_3, but the former is not exported to u_5 whereas the latter is.

Node u_3 elects a customer q-route and a provider p-route. It exports a p-route to u_5, but it does not export a q-route to u_5. Thus, u_5 elects a p-route learned from its *most preferred* provider, u_3, but a q-route learned from its *least preferred* provider, u_1. The longest prefix match rule directs data-packets arriving at u_5 with destination in q exclusively to u_5's least preferred provider, u_1. Suppose that u_1 executes **CR**. In this case, u_5 is oblivious of q. It starts forwarding data-packets with destination in q according to the elected p-route which is the one learned from its most preferred provider, u_3. DRAGON changed the attribute of the route according to which data-packets with destination in q are forwarded at u_5, from "learned from least preferred provider" to "learned from most preferred provider." It can be argued that the preference of the route according to which u_5 forwards data-packets with destination

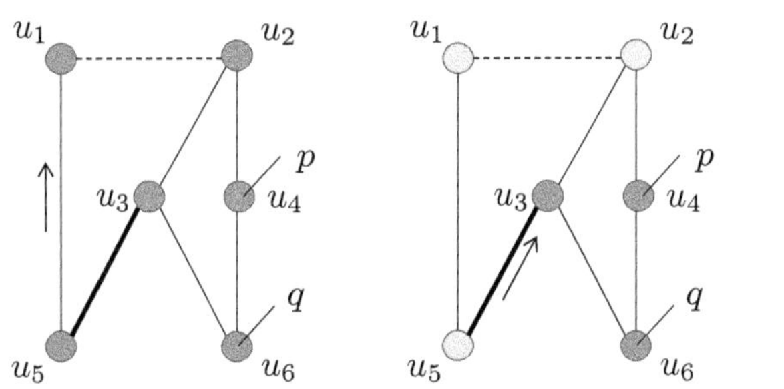

Figure 3: The thicker line means that u_5 prefers provider u_3 to provider u_1. Node u_3 exports only provider routes to u_5. Left. Standard stable state. Right. State after all nodes execute $\mathbf{CR}$. Arrows indicate the expedition of data-packets at u_5 with destination in q. Route consistency is not satisfied.

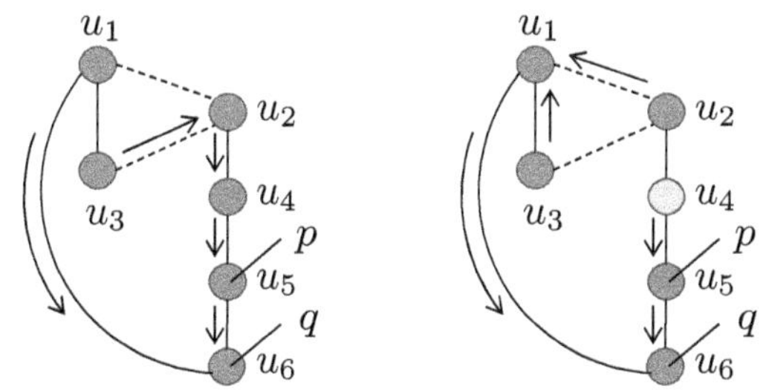

Figure 4: Arrows indicate the expedition of data-packets with destination in q. Left. Initial, standard stable state. Deployment of DRAGON first by u_3, then by u_2, and last by u_4 guarantees route-consistent states at all stages. Right. Filtering of q by u_4 alone decreases the preference of the elected q-routes at u_2 and u_3. This decrease in preference reinforces u_2's and u_3's readiness to filter q.

in q has improved. That is one more counter-intuitive behavior of vector-protocols when routing policies are not isotone [36]. However, the point we are making here is that DRAGON did not lead to a route-consistent state (maybe u_3 agreed with u_5 to forward u_5's data-packets further *except* for those with destination in q).

The following comments summarize the significance of isotonicity for DRAGON.

- The incentive for an individual node to deploy DRAGON is embodied in code $\mathbf{CR}$ and does *not* depend on isotonicity.
- The correctness of DRAGON derives from the correctness of a standard vector-protocol and rule $\mathbf{RA}$, and does *not* depend on isotonicity.
- Isotonicity guarantees an optimal route-consistent state if all nodes adopt DRAGON, by executing code $\mathbf{CR}$, but it does say if that state is *efficient*, in the sense of having many nodes forgoing q. For example, the routing policies that substantiate shortest-path routing are isotone, while it is well-known that we cannot compact routing and forwarding state without stretching distances, in general [19]. In inter-domain routing, the efficiency of DRAGON stems from the hierarchy established by the provider-customer relationships and the alignment, even if imperfect, between this hierarchy and prefix assignment (Section 5).
- Isotonicity guarantees that there is an order for adoption of DRAGON among all nodes that is route-consistent at all stages. This is shown in the next section.

3.4 Partial deployment

DRAGON can be deployed progressively, one node at a time. With isotone routing policies, it is always possible to sequence the adoption of DRAGON so that route-consistency is ensured at all stages of deployment. In the particular case of the GR routing policies, all sequences of adoptions obeying the following general condition ensure route-consistency.

Condition $\mathbf{PD}$: First, execute $\mathbf{CR}$ at nodes that elect either a peer or a provider q-route, *in whatever order*. Next, execute $\mathbf{CR}$ at nodes that elect a customer q-route top-down in the provider-customer hierarchy, that is, only execute $\mathbf{CR}$ at a node that elects a customer q-route after the code has been executed at its providers.

If condition $\mathbf{PD}$ is violated, then there may exist stages of deployment that are not route-consistent. However, these stages entail incentives for nodes to adopt DRAGON. Pursuing these incentives, nodes settle quickly in route-consistent states.

We illustrate with Figure 4. Node u_5 is the origin of p and u_6 is the origin of q. Node u_1 is a provider of both u_3 and u_6. Node u_2 is a peer of both u_1 and u_3. The left-hand side of the figure shows the initial stage, where DRAGON is not deployed at all. At this stage, only u_2, u_3, and u_4 will be able to filter q on executing $\mathbf{CR}$. Node u_3 elects a peer p-route and a peer q-route, whereas u_2 and u_4 both elect a customer p-route and a customer q-route. In order to satisfy condition $\mathbf{PD}$, u_3 is first in adopting DRAGON, executing $\mathbf{CR}$ and filtering q. On doing so, it continues to forward data-packets with destination in q to its peer u_2. Next, u_2 must execute $\mathbf{CR}$ before u_4 because it is a provider of u_4. On executing $\mathbf{CR}$, u_2 filters q while still forwarding data-packets with destination in q to its customer u_4. Last, u_4 executes $\mathbf{CR}$, filters q, and forwards data-packets with destination in q to u_5, the same as without DRAGON. All intermediate stages of deployment are route-consistent.

Back to the initial stage, suppose that u_4, rather than u_3, is first in adopting DRAGON. The resulting state is depicted in the right-hand side of Figure 4. Node u_4 forwards data-packets with destination in q to u_5, as before, but it stops exporting a q-route to u_2. As a consequence, u_2 elects a peer q-route, learned from u_1. It no longer exports a q-route to u_3 whose reaction is to elect a provider q-route, learned as well from u_1. The routing state after u_4 alone adopts DRAGON is not route-consistent. On the other hand, both u_2 and u_3 now have strong incentives to deploy DRAGON because, by doing so, they improve the attribute of the route used to forward data-packets. On executing $\mathbf{CR}$, u_2 forwards data-packets with destination in q to its customer u_4 rather than to its peer u_1; on executing $\mathbf{CR}$, u_3 forwards data-packets with destination in q to its peer u_2 rather than to its provider u_1. In addition, on executing $\mathbf{CR}$, both u_2 and u_3 save on forwarding state.

3.5 Alternative filtering codes

Preserving forwarding neighbors. Code $\mathbf{CR}$ may reduce the multi-path potential of a vector-protocol. For example, in the right-hand side of Figure 1, after all nodes execute $\mathbf{CR}$, u_2 loses u_3 as a neighbor to which it can forward data-packets with destination in q, since u_3 is a forwarding neighbor for q that is not a forwarding neighbor for p. It is possible to tighten code $\mathbf{CR}$ so that it preserves or improves, not only route attributes, but also the sets of forwarding neighbors. Reference [33] outlines such a code for the especial case of the GR routing policies.

Notwithstanding, application of $\mathbf{CR}$ at the router-level, with router-level attributes, provides a multi-path effect at the AS-level which may be sufficient in practice. For example, suppose that nodes in Figure 1 represent ASs containing several routers. On executing **CR** at the routers, it likely happens that u_2's border routers connected to u_3 do not filter q whereas those connected to u_4 do filter it. At the AS-level, it is as if data-packets arriving at u_2 with destination in q were forwarded to both u_3 and u_4.

Relaxing AS-paths. Attributes of BGP routes (our use of the term "attributes") can be seen as composed of two component-attributes: those implemented with BGP's parameter LOCAL-PREF, which we will call L-attributes in the remainder of this section; and AS-paths, which exactly correspond to BGP's parameter AS-PATH. L-attributes typically reflect the business relationships between neighbor ASs and take precedence in route election, with the lengths of AS-paths serving as tie-breakers among routes having the same L-attributes.

For filtering, code **CR** requires the whole attribute of the elected q-route to equal or be less preferred than the whole attribute of the elected p-route. However, attempting to preserve or improve the lengths of AS-paths does not lead to significant savings in routing state, in general. On the other hand, since AS-paths only play a secondary role to L-attributes in route election and, additionally, they are not even good indicators of network performance [31], we may specialize code **CR** to allow for some slack in the lengths of AS-paths. A node other than the origin of p will filter q if and only if: the L-attribute of the elected q-route is less preferred than that of the elected p-route; or the L-attribute of the elected q-route equals that of the elected p-route and the AS-path of the elected q-route is not shorter than that of the elected p-route by more than X links, where $X \geq 0$ becomes a parameter of the filtering strategy. The limiting case of $X = +\infty$ amounts to code **CR** applied exclusively to L-attributes.

3.6 Multiple levels of prefixes

A very large number of prefixes at different levels of specificity is announced in the network. We define the *parent* of a prefix q in a set of prefixes as the most specific of the prefixes that are less specific than q in the set. DRAGON operates by having every node contrast each prefix q against its parent prefix in the set of prefixes learned from the vector-protocol, in the same way that q is contrasted against p in code **CR**.

We can impose that every node executes code **CR** on the list of prefixes it learns from the vector-protocol, from the least to the most specific ones. However, the executions of code **CR** at different nodes are not correlated in time and may depend on route dynamics outside the control of network operators. Thus, the parent of a prefix may vary from node to node at any given time, and throughout time. Despite the asynchrony, DRAGON remains correct for the same routing policies that make the vector-protocol correct. In addition, if routing policies are isotone, then DRAGON leads to an optimal route-consistent state.

3.7 Aggregation prefixes

Provider-independent (PI) prefixes are those acquired by nodes directly from registrars. These prefixes do not have a parent in the routing system and, as it stands, cannot be filtered. DRAGON promotes the generation of a few aggregation prefixes to allow filtering of many of the PI prefixes. Each node determines autonomously which aggregation prefixes it originates, if any. The specification for an aggregation prefix requires it to be as short as possible without introducing new address space and to be announced with an attribute that respects rule **RA**. This specification can be realized with a quick algorithm that traverses twice the binary tree of prefixes that has the empty prefix for root and the prefixes without parent for leaves, as they are known locally at a node.

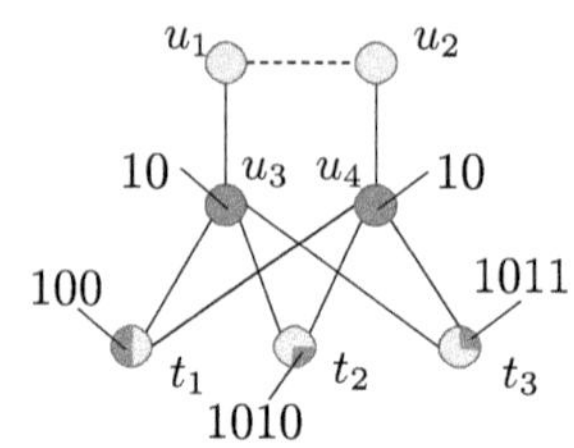

Figure 5: Both u_3 and u_4 originate prefix 10. Both u_1 and u_2 filter prefixes 100, 1010, and 1011.

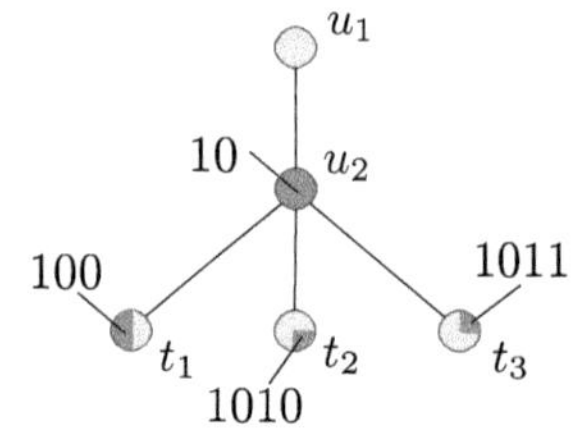

Figure 6: The announcement of 10 by u_2 subsumes that by u_1, and allows u_1 to filter prefixes 100, 1010, and 1011.

DRAGON self-organizes when more than one node originates the same aggregation prefix. We illustrate two distinct aspects of this self-organization. In Figure 5, nodes t_1, t_2, and t_3 were assigned PI prefixes 100, 1010, and 1011, respectively. Both u_3 and u_4 elect customer routes for each of these prefixes. Independently of each other and possibly at different moments in time, both u_3 and u_4 originate aggregation prefix 10. Then, the vector-protocol anycasts to 10 with both u_3 and u_4 knowing how to further data-packets with destination in 10. There is an advantage in having both u_3 and u_4 originate 10. This way, both u_1 and u_2 can filter the PI prefixes. If, say, u_3 alone originated 10, then u_2 would elect a peer 10-route, but customer routes for 100, 1010, and 1011. Node u_2 would not be able to filter any of the PI prefixes.

In Figure 6, nodes t_1, t_2, and t_3 were again allocated PI prefixes 100, 1010, and 1011, respectively. Suppose that u_1 originates aggregation prefix 10 while u_2 does not. Therefore, u_2 elects a provider 10-route, learned from u_1, but customer routes for all the PI prefixes. Node u_2 cannot filter any of the latter. However, it, too, can originate 10. Suppose it does originate 10. As a consequence, u_1 learns a customer 10-route from u_2, elects that route, and stops originating 10. Because u_1 also elects a customer route for each of the PI prefixes, it may filter them. Any data-packet arriving at u_1 with destination in 10 is forwarded to u_2 which delivers it to the appropriate customer.

3.8 Network dynamics

DRAGON reacts automatically to network events, such as link failures or additions. We illustrate that reaction calling again upon the network of Figure 1 and starting from the route-consistent state depicted on its right-hand side. The failure of a link that does not affect the election of a customer q-route at the origin of p, u_4, is handled solely by code **CR**. For instance, suppose that two-way link $\{u_3, u_6\}$ fails. Consequently, the elected q-route at u_3 changes from customer to provider, the latter route learned from u_2. Since u_3 also elects a provider p-route, it now filters q on executing **CR**.

Suppose, instead, that two-way link $\{u_4, u_6\}$ fails. Node u_4 no longer elects a customer q-route. Hence, it cannot announce p

with a customer route as such an action would violate rule **RA**. Rather, u_4 de-aggregates p into longer prefixes that can be announced with customer routes. For instance, suppose that $p = 10$ and $q = 10000$. Node u_4 withdraws p and announces the three prefixes 10001, 1001, and 101, which together with the missing prefix $q = 10000$ partition the address space of p. Node u_2 elects customer routes for 10001, 1001, and 101, learned from u_4. Through u_3, it also elects a customer 10000-route. Therefore, u_2 no longer filters q, but rather pieces together the prefixes 10001, 1001, 101, and $q = 10000$ to originate aggregation prefix $p = 10$. In global terms, the failure of $\{u_4, u_6\}$ moved the origin of p upwards in the provider-customer hierarchy, from u_4 to its provider u_2. Node u_1 elects a peer p-route and a peer q-route, filtering q on executing **CR**. Similarly, u_5 elects a provider p-route and a provider q-route, filtering q on executing **CR**.

In practice, if u_4 assigned q to u_6 and two-way link $\{u_4, u_6\}$ fails, then u_4 would likely wait some time for two-way link $\{u_4, u_6\}$ to be repaired before de-aggregating p.

3.9 Traffic engineering

Customers connected to multiple providers sometimes perform in-bound traffic engineering by de-aggregating their assigned prefixes and announcing different sub-prefixes to different providers [9]. DRAGON allows for route consistent filtering of the sub-prefixes.

We illustrate with Figure 7. Node u_7 is a customer of both u_4 and u_5. It was assigned prefix p. In order to balance its incoming traffic between its two providers, u_7 de-aggregates prefix p into sub-prefixes $p0$ and $p1$. It announces p and $p0$ to u_4, while it announces p and $p1$ to u_5. All data-packets with destination in $p0$ arrive at u_7 via its provider u_4, and all data-packets with destination in $p1$ arrive at u_7 via its provider u_5. The left-hand side of the figure shows the flow of data-packets with destination in $p0$. Note that u_5 forwards data-packets with destination in $p0$ to its own providers u_1 and u_2, although the block of addresses represented by $p0$ belongs to its customer u_7 (!). Node u_5 could just thwart the intention of its customer u_7 by filtering $p0$-routes, so that all data-packets arriving at u_5 with destination in $p0$ would be forwarded directly to u_7.

Thus, we assume that the traffic engineering intention of u_7 is respected by its providers. Specifically:

- If a provider of u_7 elects both a $p0$-route and a $p1$-route, then it announces p according to rule **RA**.

- If a provider of u_7 learns a p-route from a neighbor other than u_7, then it refrains from electing the customer p-route learned from u_7.

Node u_4 elects a customer $p0$-route and a provider $p1$-route. Hence, in order to obey rule **RA**, u_4 announces p with a provider route, exporting a p-route only to its customers; in this case, to u_6. Node u_6 elects both a provider $p0$-route and a provider p-route. Executing **CR** on $p0$, u_6 filters $p0$. The situation at u_5 is analogous. It originates a provider p-route that it exports to its customer u_8. Node u_8 elects both a provider $p0$-route and a provider p-route. Executing **CR** on $p0$, u_8 filters $p0$.

If nothing else were done, only u_6 and u_8 would be able to filter $p0$. However, note that u_1 elects both a customer $p0$-route and a customer $p1$-route. Therefore, u_1 can originate aggregation prefix p with a customer p-route, announcing p to all its neighbors. Suppose it does so. Node u_3 now elects both a provider $p0$-route and a provider p-route. It filters $p0$ after executing **CR** on $p0$. Node u_2 elects a peer $p0$-route and a peer p-route. It, too, filters $p0$ after executing **CR** on $p0$. Node u_5 learns a p-route from u_1 and

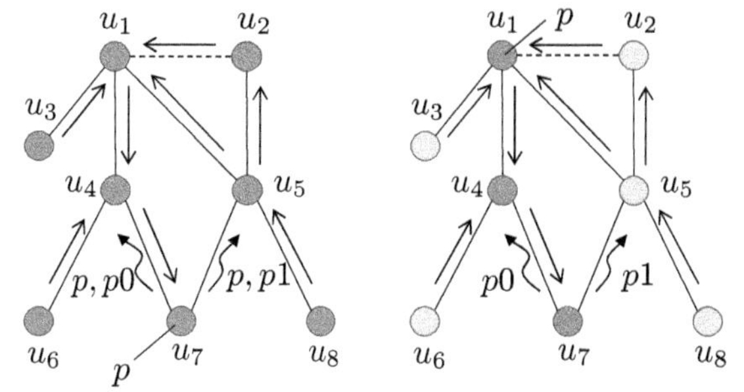

Figure 7: Node u_7 is a multi-homed to u_4 and u_5. It is assigned prefix p which it de-aggregates into prefixes $p0$ and $p1$. Node u_7 announces p and $p0$ to u_4, and p and $p1$ to u_5. Wiggled arrows indicate prefix announcements and straight arrows indicate the expedition of data-packets with destination in $p0$. Left. Standard stable state for $p0$. Right. Route consistent state for $p0$ with u_1 originating p and light-shaded nodes forgoing $p0$.

u_2, thereby electing a provider p-route. If u_5 now executes **CR** on $p0$, it filters $p0$, because it elects both a provider $p0$-route and a provider p-route. The resulting routing state for prefix $p0$ is shown at the right-hand side of Figure 7. The routes used to forward data-packets with destination in $p0$ are the same as without DRAGON. Route-consistency is satisfied.

If two-way link $\{u_4, u_7\}$ fails, then $p0$ is eliminated from the network, u_1 no longer originates p, and the only p-route that u_5 learns is the one from u_7. Thus, u_5 elects a customer p-route, learned from u_7, announcing p to all its neighbors. All data-packets with destination in $p0$ are guided by elected p-routes, ending up in u_7 via u_5.

4. THEORY OF DRAGON

In Section 4.1, we briefly review the algebraic framework of [32] which allows us to reason with generality about vector-protocols and about DRAGON. Based on this framework, we sketch the proof of correctness of DRAGON in Section 4.2, and the proof of optimality of DRAGON under isotonicity in Section 4.3.

4.1 Correctness of vector-protocols

The set of attributes is denoted by Σ and their order by $\preceq$. For $\alpha, \beta \in \Sigma$, the inequality $\alpha \prec \beta$—equivalently, $\beta \succ \alpha$—means that α is preferred to β. The especial attribute $\bullet$ denotes unreachability, being the least preferred of all attributes. For simplicity, we assumed that routing policies do not depend on prefixes. The transformations of attributes as routes propagate in a network are modeled by maps on Σ. A map L on Σ such that $L(\bullet) = \bullet$ is called a *label*. Links point in the direction of traffic flow. Each link uv is associated with a label $L[uv]$ telling how the attribute α of a route elected at v extends into the attribute $L[uv](\alpha)$ of a candidate route at u. The label of a walk $P = u_n u_{n-1} \cdots u_1 u_0$, denoted by $L[P]$, is obtained through composition of the labels of its constituent links: $L[P] = L[u_n u_{n-1}] \cdots L[u_1 u_0]$.

Cycle $C = u_0 u_{n-1} \cdots u_0$ is *strictly absorbent* if

$$\forall_{\alpha_0 \prec \bullet, \ldots, \alpha_{n-1} \prec \bullet} \; \exists_{0 \leq i < n} \; \alpha_{i+1} \prec L[u_{i+1} u_i](\alpha_i), \qquad (1)$$

with subscripts interpreted modulus n. Intuitively, C is strictly absorbent if whatever the attributes of routes learned by each node *externally* to C at least one of the nodes prefers the attribute of that route to the attribute of the route it learns from its neighbor around C. This suggests that the propagation of routes around C eventually subsides and that once a stable state is reached C does not contain a forwarding loop. Indeed, the following theorem is proven in [32].

Theorem 1 *If all cycles in a network are strictly absorbent, then a vector-protocol is correct in that network.*

We assume that all cycles in every network are strictly absorbent. The origin of p is denoted by t^p. It announces a p-route with an attribute denoted by $R^*[t^p; p]$. Let $R[u;p]$ be the attribute of the p-route elected at u in the stable state ($R[u;p] = \bullet$ if u does not elect a p-route). Node t^p elects the p-route it announced, $R[t^p;p] = R^*[t^p;p]$, and every node u other than t^p elects the candidate p-route with the most preferred attribute. If v is a forwarding neighbor of u for p, then $R[u;p] = L[uv](R[v;p])$; otherwise, if v is a neighbor of u, but not a forwarding neighbor of u for p, then $R[u;p] \prec L[uv](R[v;p])$. A forwarding path for p is a path ending at t^p that joins every node, other than t^p, to one of the node's forwarding neighbors for p.

4.2 Correctness of DRAGON

Given cycle C and two distinct nodes of the cycle, u and v, uCv denotes the unique path in C from u to v. The next lemma states an easy, but useful, implication of strict-cycle-absorbency. The proof is omitted.

Lemma 1 *Suppose cycle C is strictly absorbent. Let u and v be two distinct nodes of C and $\alpha_u \prec \bullet$ and $\alpha_v \prec \bullet$ be two attributes. Then, either $\alpha_u \prec L[uCv](\alpha_v)$ or $\alpha_v \prec L[vCu](\alpha_u)$ (or both).*

We consider two prefixes p and q such that q is less specific than p.

Theorem 2 *If all cycles in a network are strictly absorbent, then DRAGON is correct in that network whatever the set of nodes executing* **CR**.

PROOF. We divide the proof into three claims.

Claim 1: *DRAGON terminates.* The vector-protocol terminates for prefix p, Theorem 1. Some nodes execute **CR** which may lead them to filter q. Filtering does not compromise termination for prefix q.

Claim 2: *DRAGON does not yield forwarding loops.* The stable states for p and q do not contain forwarding loops, Theorem 1. A data-packet with destination in q may be forwarded from a node that *does not* elect a q-route to one that does, but never back. Once a data-packet reaches a node that elects a q-route, it is guided all the way along a forwarding path for q.

Claim 3: *DRAGON does not yield black holes.* A black hole could only exist at t^p, and only if t^p did not elect a q-route. We will show that every node on a forwarding path for q starting at t^p, other than t^p itself, elects a q-route whose attribute is *preferred* to that of the elected p-route. Hence, even if the node executes **CR**, it does not filter q. Rather, it keeps announcing q-routes according to the rules of the vector-protocol, so that t^p always elects a q-route.

In order to arrive at a contradiction, assume that there is a node in a forwarding path P for q starting at t^p such that the attribute of the elected q-route equals or is less preferred than the attribute of the elected p-route. Let u be the first such node along P. Hence, by hypothesis, we have

$$R[u;q] \succeq R[u;p]. \tag{2}$$

Let Q be a forwarding path for p starting at u and let v be the first node along Q that meets P. We distinguish two cases. If $v = t^p$, then, from rule **RA**, we obtain $R^*[v;p] = R[v;p] \succeq R[v;q]$. Otherwise, if $v \neq t^p$, then since u is the first node along P such that $R[u;q] \succeq R[u;p]$, we must have $R[v;q] \prec R[v;p]$. In both cases,

$$R[v;p] \succeq R[v;q]. \tag{3}$$

Path vPu is the sub-path of P running from v to u and uQv is the sub-path of Q running from u to v. The union of vPu and uQv is a cycle, denoted by $uQvPu$. Because P is a forwarding path for q, we write $R[v;q] = L[vPu](R[u;q])$; because Q is a forwarding path for p, we write $R[u;p] = L[uQv](R[v;p])$. With $\alpha_u = R[u;q]$ and $\alpha_v = R[v;p]$, Inequalities (2) and (3) become $\alpha_u \succeq L[uQv](\alpha_v)$ and $\alpha_v \succeq L[vPu](\alpha_u)$, respectively. From Lemma 1, we conclude that $uQvPu$ is not strictly absorbent, contradicting the premise of the theorem. Thus, the attribute of the elected q-route is preferred to the attribute of the elected p-route at any node along a forwarding path for q starting at t^p. □

4.3 Optimal route-consistency

A label L is isotone if $\alpha \preceq \beta$ implies $L(\alpha) \preceq L(\beta)$ for all attributes α and β. A link, or a walk, is isotone if its label is isotone. A walk all links of which are isotone is itself isotone. Isotonicity confers optimality to the attributes of routes elected at the various nodes. The next theorem is proven in [32].

Theorem 3 *If all links in a network are isotone, then the attribute of an elected route at a node equals or is preferred to the attribute of any route propagated to the node from its origin along a walk in that network.*

In symbols, the previous theorem states that, for all nodes u, all prefixes p, and all walks P from u to t^p, we have

$$R[u;p] \preceq L[P](R^*[t^p;p]). \tag{4}$$

Theorem 4 *Suppose that all links in a network are isotone. Then, DRAGON attains the optimal route-consistency state once all nodes execute* **CR** *in whatever order.*

PROOF. We divide the proof into four claims, the first two of which assert properties of the stable state previous to the execution of DRAGON.

Claim 1: *At any node u, the attribute of the elected q-route is the same or preferred to the attribute of the elected p-route.*

In symbols, we need to show that $R[u;q] \preceq R[u;p]$, for all nodes u and prefixes p. Let P be a forwarding path for q starting at u; Q be a forwarding path for p starting at u; and T be a forwarding path for q starting at t^p. Denote by Qt^pT the walk composed of path Q followed by path T. From rule **RA**, we have

$$L[T](R^*[t^q;q]) = R[t^p;q] \preceq R^*[t^p;p].$$

Applying label $L[Q]$ to the previous inequality yields, due to isotonicity,

$$L[Qt^pT](R^*[t^q;q]) \preceq L[Q](R^*[t^p;p]) = R[u;p]. \tag{5}$$

Hence,

$$\begin{aligned} R[u;q] &\preceq L[Qt^pT](R^*[t^q;q]) && \text{(from Theorem 3)} \\ &= R[u;p]. && \text{(from (5))} \end{aligned}$$

Claim 2: *Let E be the set of nodes, not containing t^p, for which the attribute of the elected q-route equals that of the elected p-route. If u does not belong to E neither does any of its forwarding neighbors for q.*

We prove the contrapositive statement. Let v be a forwarding neighbor of u for q, $R[u;q] = L[uv](R[v;q])$, and assume that v belongs to E, $R[v;q] = R[v;p]$. Thus,

$$R[u;p] \preceq L[uv](R[v;p]) = L[uv](R[v;q]) = R[u;q].$$

From Claim 1, we know that $R[u;q] \preceq R[u;p]$. Thus, $R[u;q] = R[u;p]$, meaning that u belongs to E as well.

Claim 3: *Set E is the optimal set of nodes that can forgo q while maintaining route-consistency.*

Nodes in E, and only those, can forgo q while preserving the attribute of the route according to which they forward data-packets with destination in q. Moreover, from Claim 2, filtering of q by nodes in any subset of E does not affect the elected q-routes of nodes *not* in E.

Claim 4: *Suppose that an arbitrary subset of nodes of E filter q and let S be the subset of nodes of E that do not forgo q. Any node u in S will filter q on executing* **CR**.

A node that filters q is a node that can be removed from the network as far as the computation of elected q-routes for all other nodes is concerned. Removal of nodes reduces the set of paths in the network. Invoking Theorem 3, we conclude that the attribute of the elected q-route at any node either remains the same or becomes less preferred. Hence, the premise of **CR** remains valid at any node in S. □

5. EVALUATION

We evaluate the scalability benefits brought to inter-domain routing when all ASs deploy DRAGON. Section 5.1 describes the network topologies, prefix assignments, and routing policies we used. The savings in routing and forwarding state achieved by DRAGON are presented in Section 5.2, and the impact on convergence is discussed in Section 5.3.

5.1 Methodology and datasets

We ran DRAGON on inferred Internet topologies provided by UCLA [2] and lists of IP prefixes originated by each AS collected by CAIDA [3]. In the inferred topologies, each link is labeled as provider-to-customer, customer-to-provider, or peer-to-peer. Accordingly, we assumed the GR routing policies. We used data from November 2012 and September 2013, but only consider the 2013 results in the following as the findings are almost identical in the two cases.

Fixing inaccuracies in the datasets. We first fixed inaccuracies usually found in the data [30]. Regarding the Internet topology, we broke every customer-provider cycle and ensured that the topology is policy-connected [33] —meaning that there is a valid path from every AS to every other—by removing ASs that prevented this from happening. From 46,455 ASs and 184,024 links, we ended up with 39,193 ASs (keeping 84% of them) and 165,235 links (keeping 90% of them). Most of these ASs (84% of them) are at the perimeter of the provider-customer hierarchy having no customers. These ASs are called stubs. Regarding the prefixes, we removed any prefixes originated by multiple ASs and those whose parent prefix is not originated by a direct or indirect provider. From 491,936 prefixes, we ended up with 433,244 prefixes (keeping 88% of them). The median number of prefixes originated by an AS is 2, with a 95-th percentile of 33 prefixes and a 99-th percentile of 159 prefixes.

Accounting for missing peering links. Inferred Internet topologies typically underestimate the number of peering links [5]. In order to compensate this distortion, we experimented introducing peering links between ASs connected at common Internet Exchange

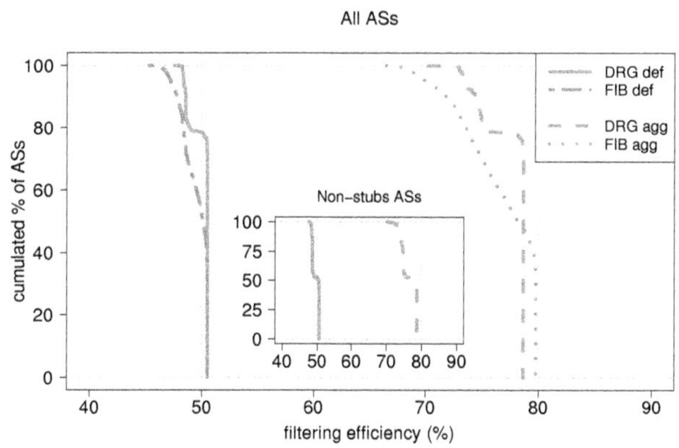

Figure 8: CCDF of filtering efficiency. Around 80% of the ASs reach the maximum filtering efficiencies of 50% (without aggregation prefixes, `DRG def`) and 79% (with aggregation prefixes, `DRG agg`). Inset. CCDF of filtering efficiency of non-stubs only, exhibiting a similar behavior.

Points, following the approach used in [24]. We found that the performance of DRAGON was only marginally affected with median values within less than 1% of the original ones. In hindsight, this is reasonable. The performance of DRAGON mostly results from the alignment between the provider-customer hierarchy and the assignment of prefixes, and, therefore, it is not significantly impacted by peering links.

Introducing aggregation prefixes. Half of the prefixes in our dataset are PI prefixes that do not have a parent prefix in the routing system. In order to subject these prefixes to filtering, we introduced around 45,000 aggregation prefixes subject to the conditions specified in Section 3.7, increasing the total number of prefixes by ~11%. Among all ASs, 8% originate at least one aggregation prefix, with a median value of 3 prefixes, a 95th (resp. 99th) percentile of 66 (resp. 306) prefixes.

5.2 Filtering efficiency

We define *filtering efficiency* as the normalized difference between the number of entries in the forwarding-table of an AS before and after DRAGON is deployed on all ASs.[3] The results for routing-tables mimic those for forwarding-tables and are not referred to explicitly. Without aggregation prefixes, the maximum possible filtering efficiency is 50% as half of the prefixes do not have a parent. With aggregation prefixes, the maximum filtering efficiency rises to 79%.

Figure 8 plots the filtering efficiency according to whether or not aggregation prefixes are introduced (`DRG` curves). Results are presented as Complementary Cumulative Distribution Functions (CCDFs). A point (x, y) of a curve means that $y\%$ of the ASs have a filtering efficiency of more than $x\%$. The main plot depicts the filtering efficiency for *all* ASs, whereas the inset focuses on *non-stubs*.

DRAGON enables near-maximum filtering results for each AS. We first consider the case without aggregation prefixes. Every AS forgoes more than 47.5% of the prefixes. This is partially justified by the fact that for a large number of prefixes having a parent (83% of them), the prefix and its parent have the same origin AS [9, 4].

[3]Equivalently, it is the difference between the number of prefixes forgone and the number of aggregation prefixes introduced divided by the number prefixes in the original routing system.

Thus, these prefixes are immediately filtered by the neighbors of those common ASs and become oblivious to the rest of the Internet. Note, however, that DRAGON finds filtering opportunities for all prefixes whatever their origin.

Moreover, DRAGON enables close to 80% of the ASs to realize the maximum possible filtering efficiency of 50%. This is not surprising since the topology is policy-connected and the majority of ASs are stubs. When the topology is policy-connected, stubs *without peers* retain only the parent prefixes. Interestingly, the subplot in Figure 8 asserts the good performance of DRAGON *even* for non-stubs, where around 50% of them still attain the maximum possible filtering efficiency.

As expected, aggregation prefixes improve performance. With aggregation prefixes, every AS has a filtering efficiency of more than 70% with close to 80% of the ASs attaining the maximum filtering efficiency of 79%. It is rarely the case that the origin AS of an aggregation prefix coincides with the origin ASs of the prefixes it covers, that is, of the prefixes that have the aggregation prefix for parent. On the other hand, the algorithm to generate aggregation prefixes ensures that their origin ASs are as close as possible, in terms of the provider-customer hierarchy, to the origin ASs of the covered prefixes. Consequently, although the covered prefixes are not necessarily filtered by the neighbors of their origin ASs, they are filtered along a small vicinity of those ASs, justifying the good performance of DRAGON.

DRAGON performs better than traditional FIB compression techniques for the majority of the ASs. FIB compression refers to algorithms run locally at each AS with the purpose of reducing the size of forwarding-tables without change in the forwarding of data-packets [38, 35, 29]. FIB compression does not affect routing-tables or the dynamics of BGP. Next to the curves for DRAGON, Figure 8 plots the filtering efficiency obtained when running a typical FIB compression algorithm [38] on our dataset (`FIB` curves), using the code provided by the authors.

Like DRAGON, FIB compression allows aggregation prefixes to be introduced. Without aggregation prefixes, DRAGON *performs better* than FIB compression on the majority of the ASs, and at least as good on all of them. This is because DRAGON is more relaxed on its filtering assumptions. DRAGON keeps only the attributes of routes used to forward data-packets whereas FIB compression preserves the exact forwarding neighbors, ties broken by the length of AS-PATH.

With aggregation prefixes, FIB compression can perform slightly better than DRAGON ($\sim$1% better). This is because the introduction of aggregation prefixes is not optimized in DRAGON. An AS originates an aggregation prefix only if it elects customer routes for all covered prefixes. There are PI prefixes whose address space could be aggregated except that no AS elects a customer route for all of them. Hence, no AS originates an aggregation prefix for those PI prefixes, preventing them from being subject to filtering. In contrast, FIB compression does not care about elected routes when it aggregates prefixes. It is possible to optimize the introduction of aggregation prefixes in DRAGON in order to match the filtering efficiency of FIB compression. An AS could originate an aggregation prefix covering prefixes for which it elects a peer or a provider route as long as the aggregation prefix is announced with a provider route, meaning that it is announced only to the customers of the AS, so as to satisfy rule **RA**.

5.3 Convergence upon link failures

We implemented a DRAGON simulator on top of SimBGP [28], an event-driven simulator for BGP. Using our simulator, we compare the transient behavior of DRAGON against that of standard BGP upon link failures. We focus on link failures as they are more demanding on the routing system than link additions [20]. For simplicity, we do not consider the case where new aggregation prefixes are introduced.

We run our simulations on *prefix-trees*. A prefix-tree is a subset of the prefixes of the routing system composed of a prefix without a parent and all less specific prefixes. The dynamics of DRAGON is independent from one prefix-tree to another. The majority of the prefix-trees are trivial, containing a single prefix. For them, DRAGON and BGP share the same convergence behavior as filtering is impossible. Since we are interested in understanding the difference between DRAGON and BGP, we only consider non-trivial prefix-trees. There are 25,266 of them having a median of 5 prefixes. We present results for 250 randomly selected non-trivial prefix-trees.

For each non-trivial prefix-tree, we distinguish between link failures that trigger de-aggregation of the root of the prefix-tree and those that do not (see Section 3.8). The probability of a link failure triggering de-aggregation is small. In the worst case, only 0.03% of all link failures can cause the root of the prefix-tree to be de-aggregated. For each prefix-tree, we *exhaustively* fail all links that can cause de-aggregation. For the rest of the links, we run 4,000 independent trials, each trial corresponding to a link failure selected randomly. In both cases, we measure the total number of routes (advertisements and withdrawals) exchanged network-wide after the failure until a new stable state is reached. We used the default Minimum Route Advertisement Interval (MRAI) value of 30 seconds.

Figure 9 plots the results. On the left, we show the CCDF of the number of routes exchanged network-wide for link failures that do not cause de-aggregation. On the right, we show the CCDF for those link failures that cause de-aggregation.

DRAGON exchanges fewer routes than BGP upon link failures. For non-trivial prefix-trees, DRAGON exchanges less routes than BGP in 95% of the cases and less than half those exchanged with BGP in more than 50% of the cases.

When de-aggregation is not required (99.97% of the failures), a link failure in DRAGON produces, at worst, a network-wide effect for the prefix at the root of the prefix-tree and only a local effect for each of the other prefixes. In contrast, in BGP, all prefixes in the prefix-tree are prone to network-wide effects. The left plot in Figure 9 corroborates this. DRAGON generates more than 100 routes for only 5% of the cases whereas BGP generates more than 100 routes for more than 15% of the cases. Furthermore, DRAGON does not generate *any* route for 40% of the link failures, while BGP generates routes for more than 98% of the link failures.

When a link failure causes de-aggregation (0.03% of the failures), DRAGON can generate more routes than BGP. The right plot in Figure 9 shows that DRAGON announces more routes in 60% of the cases. The number of de-aggregated prefixes originated by an AS for a given prefix-tree is bounded by the difference in length between the most and the least specific prefixes in that prefix-tree. Consistent with this observation, the plot shows that the number of routes exchanged by DRAGON never exceeds that exchanged by BGP by more than one order of magnitude. While the results are already good, we believe that they can be improved further by ensuring that the combination of de-aggregates into an aggregation prefix at a different AS (see Section 3.8) occurs before the de-aggregates are propagated network-wide.

6. RELATED WORK

Scalability limits of routing. The study of the scalability limits of routing has a long and rich history [18, 34, 19]. However,

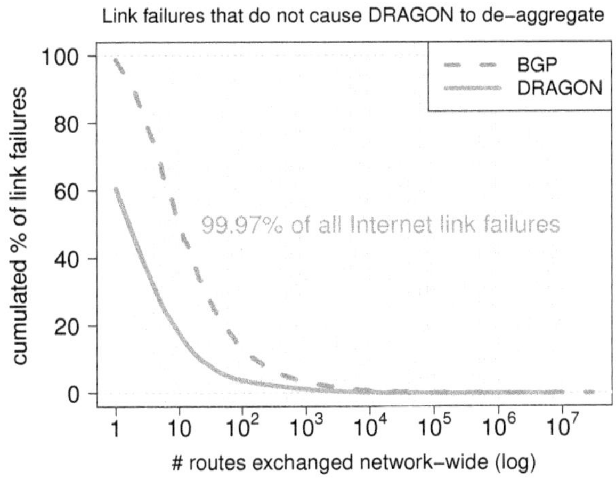

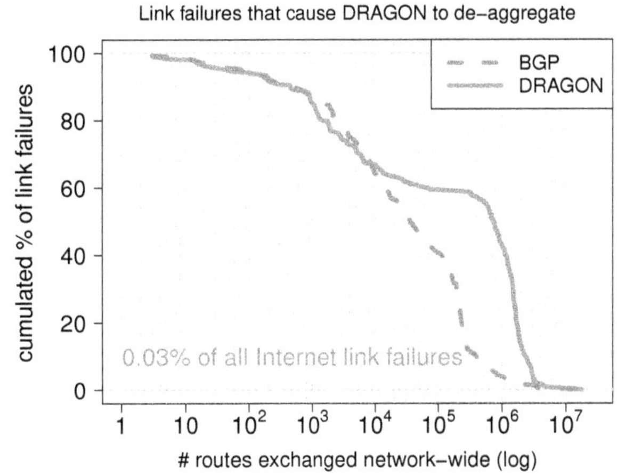

Figure 9: In 95% of the cases, BGP exchanges more routes than DRAGON for non-trivial prefix-trees. When a failure does not cause de-aggregation (99.97% of the cases), DRAGON (resp., BGP) sends more than 100 routes for 5% (resp. 15%) of the cases (left plot). When a failure causes de-aggregation (0.03% of the cases), DRAGON can generate more routes than BGP, but never more than one order of magnitude (right plot).

almost all of the scalability work is premised on shortest-path routing, showing a fundamental trade-off between the sizes of forwarding tables and the stretch in the lengths of paths followed by data-packets in relation to distances. A recent paper embarks on the scalability limits of policy-based routing [14], suggesting that the export rules of the GR routing policies lead to efficient routing, a result that is consistent with our findings. In contrast to the routing strategies of [14], DRAGON is a distributed algorithm proposed for the Internet's existing IP addressing scheme and has been framed for arbitrary routing policies.

Characterizing growth of the routing system. Measurement studies track the growth in the number of IP prefixes and BGP update messages over time [1, 16], and identify the *causes* of growth such as multi-homing, traffic engineering, and address-allocation policies [26, 7, 25, 11]. DRAGON *reduces* the number of prefixes and update messages.

Reducing forwarding-table size. As the number of IP prefixes grew, researchers explored ways to compress the *forwarding-tables* by aggregating related entries [38, 35, 29] or directing some traffic to routers with room for larger tables [6]. These optimization techniques do not reduce the size of *routing-tables* or the number of BGP update messages, and require re-optimization when forwarding decisions change.

Reducing routing-table size. Best current practices for reducing the size of routing-tables rely on the diligence of network operators to apply static filters to BGP routes learned from each neighbor. However, these techniques cannot aggregate routes originating several hops away, and can sometimes lead to black holes and loops [21]. Other techniques for reducing the size of routing-tables [17] work only within a single AS, missing opportunities for global scalability gains.

Inter-domain route aggregation. Our recent short paper [33] presented filtering strategies to scale the Internet routing system, assuming the GR routing policies and only one parent prefix. One of these strategies applies exclusively to nodes that elect provider routes whereas the other requires changes to both the control- and data-planes. In the present paper, the filtering strategy and accompanying announcement rule are valid for general routing policies and arbitrary levels of prefixes, apply to all nodes, and operate exclusively at the control-plane. In addition, in the present paper, we build the filtering strategy into the design of DRAGON, addressing route-consistency, aggregation prefixes, partial deployment, traffic engineering, and network dynamics.

Clean-slate architectures. Many "clean-slate" routing architectures have been proposed (see [27] for a survey) that route on AS numbers or loose source routes. However, these architectures require a major overhaul of Internet routing, whereas DRAGON works with today's BGP.

7. CONCLUSIONS

DRAGON is a distributed route-aggregation algorithm that operates with standard routes of a vector-protocol. It comprises a filtering code and an announcement rule that together allow nodes to forgo prefixes while avoiding black holes. DRAGON applies to any routing policies, but if these policies are isotone, then DRAGON leads to an optimal route-consistent state, reachable through intermediate stages of deployment all of which are route-consistent.

In inter-domain routing, DRAGON harnesses the existing alignment between prefix allocation and the provider-customer Internet hierarchy to produce a very efficient routing system. Evaluation of DRAGON on inferred topologies of the Internet show reductions in the amount of forwarding and routing state on the order of 80% and a parallel decrease in the route activity needed to deal with network events.

8. ACKNOWLEDGMENTS

We would like to thank Sharon Goldberg, Michael Schapira, Stefano Vissicchio, Lucca Cittadini, and José Brázio for their feedback on this work. João's research was supported in part by Fundação para a Ciência e a Tecnologia (FCT), Portugal, under project PEst-OE/EEI/LA0008/2013. Franck's research was sponsored by the U.S. Army Research Laboratory and the U.K. Ministry of Defence and was accomplished under Agreement Number W911NF-06-3-0001. The views and conclusions contained in this document are those of the author and should not be interpreted as representing the official policies, either expressed or implied, of the U.S. Army Research Laboratory, the U.S. Government, the U.K. Ministry of Defence or the U.K. Laurent's and Jennifer's research was supported in part by the National Science Foundation under grant CNS-1409056.

9. REFERENCES

[1] BGP routing table analysis reports. bgp.potaroo.net.

[2] Internet AS-level Topology Archive. irl.cs.ucla.edu/topology.

[3] Routeviews Prefix to AS mappings Dataset. www.caida.org/data/routing/routeviews-prefix2as.xml.

[4] CIDR report, 2014. www.cidr-report.org/as2.0.

[5] B. Ager, N. Chatzis, A. Feldmann, N. Sarrar, S. Uhlig, and W. Willinger. Anatomy of a large European IXP. In *ACM SIGCOMM*, pages 163–174, August 2012.

[6] H. Ballani, P. Francis, T. Cao, and J. Wang. Making routers last longer with ViAggre. In *USENIX NSDI*, pages 453–466, April 2009.

[7] T. Bu, L. Gao, and D. Towsley. On characterizing BGP routing table growth. *Computer Networks*, 45(1):45–54, May 2004.

[8] B. Carré. *Graphs and Networks*. Clarendon Press, Oxford, UK, 1979.

[9] L. Cittadini, W. Muhlbauer, S. Uhlig, R. Bush, P. Francois, and O. Maennel. Evolution of Internet address space deaggregation: Myths and reality. *IEEE Journal on Selected Areas in Communications*, 28(8):1238–1249, October 2010.

[10] C. Edwards. Internet routing failures bring architecture change back to the table. *ACM News*, September 2014.

[11] A. Elmokashfi, A. Kvalbein, and C. Dovrolis. On the scalability of BGP: The role of topology growth. *IEEE Journal on Selected Areas in Communications*, 28(8):1250–1261, October 2010.

[12] V. Fuller and T. Li. Classless inter-domain routing (CIDR): The Internet address assignment and aggregation plan. RFC 4632, August 2006.

[13] L. Gao and J. Rexford. Stable Internet routing without global coordination. *IEEE/ACM Transactions on Networking*, 9(6):681–692, December 2001.

[14] A. Gulyas, G. Retvari, Z. Heszberger, and R. Agarwal. On the scalability of routing with policies. *IEEE/ACM Transactions on Networking*, 2014. Early access through IEEE Xplore.

[15] Z. B. Houidi, M. Meulle, and R. Teixeira. Understanding slow BGP routing table transfers. In *Internet Measurement Conference*, pages 350–355, November 2009.

[16] G. Huston. Analyzing the Internet's BGP routing table. *The Internet Protocol Journal*, 4(1), March 2001.

[17] E. Karpilovsky, M. Caesar, J. Rexford, A. Shaikh, and J. van der Merwe. Practical network-wide compression of IP routing tables. *IEEE Transactions on Network and Service Management*, 9(4):446–458, December 2012.

[18] L. Kleinrock and F. Kamoun. Hierarchical routing for large networks: Performance evaluation and optimization. *Computer Networks*, 1:155–170, January 1977.

[19] D. Krioukov, kc claffy, K. Fall, and A. Brady. On compact routing for the Internet. *ACM SIGCOMM Computer Communications Review*, 37(3):41–52, July 2007.

[20] C. Labovitz, A. Ahuja, A. Bose, and F. Jahanian. Delayed internet routing convergence. In *ACM SIGCOMM*, pages 175–187, August 2000.

[21] F. Le, G. G. Xie, and H. Zhang. On route aggregation. In *ACM CoNEXT*, December 2011.

[22] R. Lemos. Internet routers hitting 512K limit, some become unreliable, August 2014. ArsTechnica, ars.to/1r9AbxJ.

[23] Y. Liao, L. Gao, R. Guérin, and Z.-L. Zhang. Safe interdomain routing under diverse commercial agreements. *IEEE/ACM Transactions on Networking*, 18(6):1829–1840, December 2010.

[24] R. Lychev, S. Goldberg, and M. Schapira. BGP security in partial deployment: Is the juice worth the squeeze? In *ACM SIGCOMM*, pages 171–182, August 2013.

[25] X. Meng, Z. Xu, B. Zhang, G. Huston, S. Lu, and L. Zhang. IPv4 address allocation and the BGP routing table evolution. *ACM SIGCOMM Computer Communications Review*, 35(1):71–80, January 2005.

[26] H. Narayan, R. Govindan, and G. Varghese. The impact of address allocation and routing on the structure and implementation of routing tables. In *ACM SIGCOMM*, pages 125–136, August 2003.

[27] J. Pan, S. Paul, and R. Jain. A survey of the research on future Internet architectures. *IEEE Communications Magazine*, 49(7):26–36, July 2011.

[28] J. Qiu. SimBGP: Python Event-driven BGP simulator. www.bgpvista.com/simbgp.php.

[29] G. Retvari, J. Tapolcai, A. Korosi, A. Majdan, and Z. Heszberger. Compressing IP forwarding tables: Towards entropy bounds and beyond. In *ACM SIGCOMM*, pages 111–122, August 2013.

[30] M. Roughan, W. Willinger, O. Maennel, D. Perouli, and R. Bush. 10 lessons from 10 years of measuring and modeling the Internet's autonomous systems. *IEEE Journal on Selected Areas in Communications*, 29(9):1810–1821, October 2011.

[31] M. Schapira, Y. Zhu, and J. Rexford. Putting BGP on the right path: A case for next-hop routing. In *ACM SIGCOMM Workshop on Hot Topics in Networks*, pages 3:1–3:6, October 2010.

[32] J. L. Sobrinho. An algebraic theory of dynamic network routing. *IEEE/ACM Transactions on Networking*, 13(5):1160–1173, October 2005.

[33] J. L. Sobrinho and F. Le. A fresh look at inter-domain route aggregation. In *IEEE INFOCOM Mini-Conference*, pages 2556–2560, April 2012.

[34] P. F. Tsuchiya. The Landmark hierarchy: A new hierarchy for routing in very large networks. In *ACM SIGCOMM*, pages 35–42, August 1988.

[35] Z. Uzmi, M. Nebel, A. Tariq, S. Jawad, R. Chen, A. Shaikh, J. Wang, and P. Francis. SMALTA: Practical and near-optimal FIB aggregation. In *ACM CoNEXT*, 2011.

[36] S. Vissicchio, L. Cittadini, L. Vanbever, and O. Bonaventure. iBGP deceptions: More sessions, fewer routes. In *IEEE INFOCOM*, pages 2122–2130, April 2012.

[37] L. Wang, M. Saranu, J. Gottlieb, and D. Pei. Understanding BGP session failures in a large ISP. In *IEEE INFOCOM*, pages 350–355, May 2007.

[38] X. Zhao, Y. Liu, L. Wang, and B. Zhang. On the aggregatability of router forwarding tables. In *IEEE INFOCOM*, pages 848–856, March 2010.

COLD: PoP-level Network Topology Synthesis

Rhys Bowden
University of Adelaide
Adelaide, Australia
rhysbowden@gmail.com

Matthew Roughan
University of Adelaide
Adelaide, Australia
matthew.roughan@adelaide.edu.au

Nigel Bean
University of Adelaide
Adelaide, Australia
nigel.bean@adelaide.edu.au

ABSTRACT

Network topology synthesis seeks methods to generate large numbers of example network topologies primarily for use in simulation. It is a topic that has received much attention over the years, underlying which is a conflict between randomness and design. Random graphs are appealing because they are simple and avoid the messy details that plague real networks. However real networks *are* messy, because network operators design their networks in the context of complex technological constraints, costs, and goals. When random models have been used they often produce patently unrealistic networks that only match a few artificial connectivity statistics of real networks: the features that make the network useful and interesting are ignored. At best a network divorced from context is a purely mathematical object with no meaning or utility. At worst it can be completely misleading. However, design alone cannot generate an ensemble of networks with the variability needed in simulation. We need to balance design and randomness in a way that generates reasonable networks with given characteristics and predictable variability. This paper presents such a method, Combined Optimization and Layered Design (COLD), incorporating randomness and design principles to create ensembles of PoP-level synthetic networks.

Categories and Subject Descriptors

C.2.1 [**Computer Communication Networks**]: Network Architecture and Design—*Network Topology*; C.2.5 [**Computer Communication Networks**]: Local and Wide-Area Networks

General Terms

Design,Theory

Keywords

Topology generation, Heuristically Optimal Topologies

CoNEXT'14, December 2–5, 2014, Sydney, Australia.

http://dx.doi.org/10.1145/2674005.2675012.

1. INTRODUCTION

> Everything should be made as simple as it can be — but not simpler.
>
> – *Attributed to A. Einstein*

The core problem of network synthesis is: *take one or more network topologies, and produce a larger set of topologies that is similar in some fundamental way.* The resultant topologies have most commonly been used in network simulation and emulation in order to test new networking algorithms and protocols whose properties and performance often depend on the structure of the underlying network.

The problem imposes requirements, with most attention historically aimed at "similarity", because it is difficult to universally define for all types of network. It may mean something completely different when considering virtual networks (*e.g.,* the Facebook Social graph) or physical networks (*e.g.,* data networks). For instance, a virtual network need not be connected, whereas a disconnected data network is broken. This paper is concerned with data-communications networks.

Our approach is motivated by Li *et al.* [1] who note that the criteria for measuring similarity must originate with network operators. Their goals, constraints and decisions result in a network, and any method that ignores this in favor of overly simplified abstract synthesis risks generating unreasonable networks. We extend this idea from HOT router-level synthesis described in [1] to multi-layered networks, where it takes a different form. Large data networks are not designed by a pure router-level optimization, they use hierarchy and templated design to simplify the design process [2–4]. The most common form of hierarchy being the division into PoPs (Points of Presence). Our approach, COLD (Combined Optimized Layered Design), is aimed at mirroring this design process.

In this paper we focus on the synthesis of the PoP-level, as the first step of a layered approach to generating a more detailed router-level network. We focus on the PoP-level because:

- this is the level at which many of the interesting problems lie (the generation of the router-level network from the PoP level can be easily accomplished using either existing probabilistic methods [5], or structural methods [6]);
- networks change less frequently at the PoP level than at the router level [7]; and
- the PoP level is the more interesting level for many activities [7], because it is less dependent on the details of

protocol implementations, router vendor and model, and other technological details.

The last point is subtle but important. When using a network as part of a simulation, one would like to have a network that is *invariant* to the method being tested. If a network designer might change his/her network in response to a new protocol, say a routing or traffic engineering algorithm, then the test will be ambiguous. PoP-level networks are less sensitive to these details than router-level networks, because routers impose physical and technological constraints that are almost completely dependent on the details of the router vendor, model and even the version of software running on the router.

PoP-level optimization is substantially different from the router-level optimization considered in [1]. At the PoP level, we have different constraints – we are no longer limited by technological issue such as port numbers – and the optimization objectives are different, so a considerable part of this paper is concerned with framing, and then solving, this problem (see Sections 3-7).

There are additional challenges to be met:

1. Simulation requires us to generate a potentially large number of network topologies that are "similar", but varied enough to perform statistical analysis of results, *e.g.*, generating confidence intervals for performance estimates [8,9].
2. A network's form is driven by real costs and technical constraints. For instance, it must be able to carry a given volume of traffic. If this is ignored, then the resulting network could be unreasonably expensive, or even impossible to construct [1].
3. Model parameters must be operationally meaningful. Parameters with only abstract meaning (*e.g.*, n^{th} degree distribution) are much harder to use in practice. For instance, it is often hard to scale abstract parameters correctly if one wishes to consider the effect of network growth. Parameters such as costs allow one to test network protocols given different tradeoff decisions by network engineers.
4. The approach should be *tunable*: it should be possible to control the output to see what effect the type of network has on a protocol or algorithm. For instance, one may wish to see the effect of a network becoming more highly connected or more clustered.
5. The model should generate a "network", not just an abstract graph. Simulations often need details such as link capacity, distances, and routing. Ideally these should be generated as part of the model. If these details are generated after the topology synthesis then that additional process should be taken into account when considering the complexity of the method.
6. The model should be "as simple as it can be – but not simpler". Simplicity has many virtues: it improves our intuitive understanding, reduces the complexity of parameter estimation, and prevents over fitting. There is a tension between "realism" and "simplicity" – determining the correct tradeoff between these is perhaps the most difficult of these challenges.

COLD satisfies these requirements. The key is choosing a synthesis process that parallels the real network design used by many network engineers, *i.e.*, heuristic optimization of economic and demographic objectives and constraints, followed by templated design to implement physical router-level structures within PoPs (see [6] for example), mimicking the highly structured and pattern-based methods recommended in basic texts on network management [2–4]. Likewise, simple heuristics can be used to create interdomain connectivity between networks if such is needed. Although this paper focusses on the PoP-level construction, our Matlab code available at [10] implements both the PoP-level algorithms described here, along with extensions to create router-level, and inter-AS level networks, and these will be described more fully in subsequent work.

The generation process is deterministic. For any given context, the resulting network would be fixed. To generate the *stochastic variety* necessary for simulation, we randomize the *context* in which the network is generated, most notably the location of PoPs and the traffic matrix the network must carry.

The result is a conceptually-simple intuitive method for generating "designed" networks. The parameters are meaningful – they are costs, allowing them to be tuned to control the type of network generated. For instance, a newly formed network servicing a burgeoning market in a developing country wishes primarily to provide connectivity as quickly and as cheaply as possible. As the market matures there is an incentive to increase the level of service by providing higher bandwidth, lower latency, or more reliability. Our process can take these differing economic incentives or *planning variety* into account through *tuning* the input parameters.

We can generate a large number of different networks by randomizing the network context. The resulting networks come with all the details needed for simulation (*e.g.*, link capacities), and satisfy a range of simple standard network-engineering constraints. The model is easily extensible where needed.

2. BACKGROUND AND COMPARISONS

In this section we evaluate and compare previous methods to the list of goals outlined in the Introduction. Table 1 compares several different methods of network synthesis: Erdös-Rényi graphs, Waxman graphs, Power-law random graphs (PLRGs), Li *et al.*'s HOT graphs and Mahadevan *et al.*'s dK-series graphs against these criteria. While in many cases it is clear how these models perform against the criteria, some evaluations require further explanation.

Erdös-Rényi and Waxman graphs have a very simple model with few parameters. They are both simple and succeed in generating statistically varied graphs when given the same input. They also partially succeed in providing a mechanism to tune the output, though it is limited to controlling node degree for Erdös-Rényi graphs, and an additional notion of geographical distance dependence for Waxman graphs. Unfortunately, the parameters are of questionable physical meaning, and without modification these graphs don't even meet simple technical constraints like connectivity. Further, these graphs do not come with any additional details such as link capacities.

Power-Law Random Graphs (PLRGs) [11] address the observed power-law node degree distribution of networks in measurement studies (at router- or AS-level). The method is simple, involves few parameters, and the general class of such methods allows tuning of the average degree and the degree-distribution, but has limited control of properties

	ER	Waxman	PLRG	HOT	dK-series	COLD
1. statistical variation	✓	✓	✓	✓	×	✓
2. meets constraints	×	×	×	✓	*P*	✓
3. meaningful parameters	×	×	×	*P*	×	✓
4. tunable	*P*	*P*	*P*	*P*	×	✓
5. generates network	×	×	×	✓	×	✓
6. simple model	✓	✓	✓	✓	×	✓

Table 1: Table of comparisons between six synthesis methods against the criteria outlined in the introduction (in order). *P* refers to partially satisfying the requirement, for instance the dK-series can satisfy some constraints (*e.g.,* port numbers), but not others such as capacity constraints. Most of the models are only partially tunable because they can control one particular aspect of the network, *e.g.,* node degree, but not others.

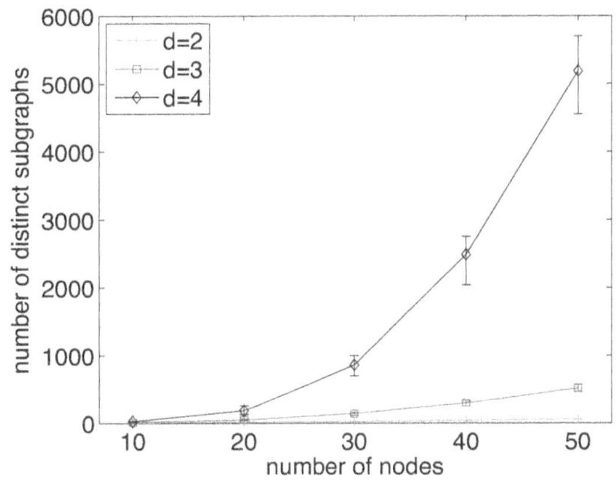

Figure 1: An example of how the number of parameters for dK-series grows rapidly both with the size of the graph and with d.

such as assortativity. Furthermore, these models have come under criticism [1,12,13] at the router level for violating technical constraints. At a deeper level, the model (preferential attachment) used to generate these networks has parameters that are, perhaps, meaningful for certain graph generation problems, but which certainly *aren't* meaningful for generating the types of networks considered here. PoPs do not "attach" to other PoPs according to a probability based on degree!

Li *et al.* [1] provide an outline of problems in previous topology synthesis techniques. They articulate engineering constraints that a real network must satisfy to function efficiently, and use these constraints to suggest a heuristic structure for real router-level networks. To aid their demonstration they introduce the entropy function for a graph (related to the assortativity) to clearly demonstrate the flaws of PLRG techniques. Their method has many appealing features, but the parameters and constraints of the model only represent a partial set of those that network engineers care about, and the design framework used does not mirror that used for the design of larger networks, though it may be reasonable for small networks.

Degree-series-based methods tackle the problem by attempting to extend the random graph methods to address the problems noted in places such as [1]. In the foremost examples of this approach, Mahadevan *et al.* [14,15] provide a general and extremely powerful framework for characterizing graphs, dK-series. When defining a dK-series, each node of a connected graph G is labeled with its node degree. The dK-distribution of G is the number of occurrences of each possible labeled connected subgraph of G of size d, where subgraphs are considered isomorphic if their labels and edges match.

The 0K distribution for a graph is simply its average node degree, and the 1K distribution is the node-degree distribution, both commonly studied when synthesising topologies. The 2K-distribution is used to replicate the commonly seen *assortativity* statistic, as well as the entropy statistic used in [1]. The 3K-distribution determines the *clustering* of a graph. A dK-series for a graph G with n nodes is this sequence of dK-distributions for $d = 0, ..., n$. As d increases, the dK-distribution becomes more and more specific, increasingly restricting the graphs that match it; the set of graphs matching G in 1K-distribution is a subset of those that match the 0K-distribution, the set of graphs matching the 2K-distribution is in turn a subset of those that match the 1K-distribution, *etc.*

The dK-series are an elegant generalisation of the concepts of degree distribution to allow for increased fidelity with respect to an observed graph. It becomes very difficult to synthesize random dK graphs for $d > 3$, but a much more serious problem is that the dK-series hides an incredibly detailed characterisation of a graph G. A dK distribution isn't just a single statistic, it is a huge list of the number of occurrences of each labeled subgraph. Thus, although conceptually simple, the dK-series is very far from simple in practical terms, such as measurement of the large number of parameters involved. Figure 1 illustrates the rapid growth in the number of parameters with both d and the number of nodes n. Note that even for $d = 3$, we quickly approach the point where there are more parameters than nodes n, or possible edges in the graph. That is, the dK sequence is a longer specification than just listing the edges of the graph.

Moreover, though some of the parameters have meaning to graph theorists, they have little meaning to network engineers. Others have little meaning to anyone.

Finally, there is a more subtle problem. The dK-series can so overconstrain the problem that there is only one possible graph that can be generated. This problem is hidden by the graph isomorphism problem – it is difficult to determine if two graphs are isomorphic (*i.e.,* effectively identical). Design-based approaches avoid this problem by providing nodes with meaningful labels (*ex post facto* addition of labels doesn't solve the problem because such labels are not associated with network properties such as capacities, and if these are added as well, the resulting generation techniques lose any shred of simplicity).

The issue is illustrated in Figure 2, which shows a simple input graph, along with some Erdös-Rényi graphs with the same number of links, and 3K-series graphs generated to match it. Upon careful consideration it should be clear that the only possible 3K graph that can match the input is isomorphic to the input itself, though this might not be so obvious if the outputs were not aligned as in the figure.

This problem is far from a trivial issue. There are many examples where a given input graph completely determines

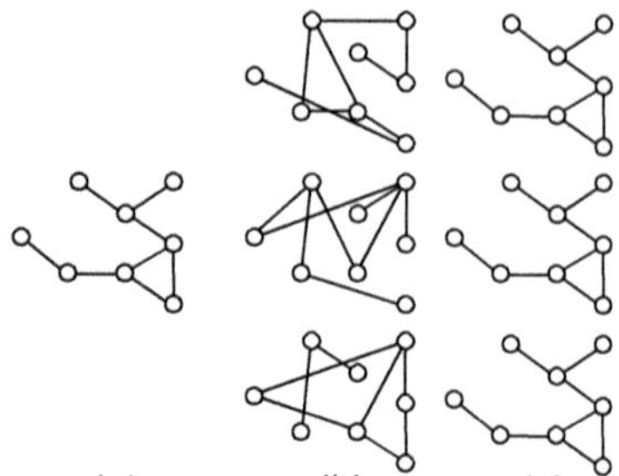

Figure 2: (a) A small example network. (b) Erdös-Rényi graphs based on that network - they all have the same number of links but in random places. One graph is not even connected and the others have very long shortest paths between some pairs of nodes. (c) graphs with the same 3K-distribution as in (a).

the output, *e.g.,* both cliques and rings. Moreover, it is not just a question of the outputs all being isomorphic – even if this is not strictly true, it is possible to have outputs that have a large isomorphic subnetwork and hence only trivial differences. These are even harder to test for.

COLD satisfies the criteria listed above:

1. The networks are distinct by construction. We also present results showing the degree of variation through confidence intervals on observed statistics.
2. COLD uses techniques motivated directly by operator practice. While it may not be exactly what one specific operator does, there is always a tradeoff between verisimilitude and simplicity.
3. The parameters are costs, which are intrinsically meaningful.
4. It is tunable, at least within the observed PoP-level networks of [16].
5. COLD generates more than just a series of connected nodes. It generates link capacities and distances along with routing.
6. The PoP-level model has only four parameters, and we show why at least this many are needed. In particular, the hub cost is needed to create networks that could match observed instances.

The last point raises one additional feature: extensibility. The optimization algorithm facilitates extension because it is generally easy to add additional costs or constraints to the model. For example, COLD could naturally be extended to multiple ASes. Imagine the PoPs are in fact cities, in which different networks may have presence. PoP interconnects in same cities could then be assigned a cost, and we could run the optimization with respect to this additional cost.

Obviously, there are many other network synthesis approaches available, and we don't attempt to survey them all here. However, the examples above provide a sufficient cross-section to understand the limitations of the vast majority of synthesis techniques.

3. POP-LEVEL SYNTHESIS

We focus here on synthesizing a single network, such as a network run by a single Internet Service Provider (ISP). In an individual network a single set of design rules have the most influence, because the network is under the control of a small group of designers all following a common process. Inter-AS design is impacted by decisions of multiple organizations and has aspects of game theory.

Most of the optimization steps in network design concern the PoP-level. The internal design of PoPs is almost completely determined by simple templates [2–4], since the cost of internal links is much lower than inter-PoP links. Here we focus on the PoP-level.

We use optimization to create our networks, but it is important to realize that few network designers are mathematicians or trained to use formal optimization tools. Moreover, the actual design problem for a large network is very complex, and costs depend on long-term business relationships with vendors. And networks are rarely designed from scratch – they evolve. Operators and managers try to optimize (by reducing costs, or improving performance) but usually do so heuristically, and we cannot hope to mimic all of the details of every type of heuristic used through the history of networking.

Hence, the guiding principles of the optimization are:

1. We must mirror the real-life process of designing a network, though acknowledging that it is mirrored in goals and constraints, not the exact detail.
2. The process needs to be *tunable.* As previously mentioned, real networks come in a wide variety [16], determined by different underlying cost/benefit tradeoffs. We aim to be able to tune the input parameters of our process to replicate this wide range.
3. The optimization cost function and constraints must be as *simple* as possible; most notably they should have few parameters. The more detailed and complicated a cost function is, the less general and adaptable it is. If it becomes too complicated, it is hard to develop an understanding of the relationship between the input parameters and output networks, and hard to estimate parameters when needed.
4. The optimization cost function should be *meaningful,* and related to the criteria that are important to network engineers. Fabrikant *et al.* [17] show that it is possible to generate a wide variety of topologies by tuning an optimization process, but their cost function did not have a strong analogue to real-life costs. The meaning of the cost function also makes several tasks easier, such as extrapolating a network to examine what it might look like as it grows [9, 15].

There are several parts to an optimization scheme:

1. The input or *context* of the optimization problem: the PoP locations and the traffic matrix. The generation of these is described in §3.1.
2. The optimization problem itself. This includes the variables, the constraints and the optimization objective function. We minimize the cost of the network with the constraint that it can carry all of the expected traffic. We discuss this in detail in §3.2.
3. The algorithm for choosing an optimal network topology, which we describe in §3.3.

3.1 Context

It is not strictly correct to divide the area of network synthesis into *random* and *designed* graphs as all the interesting models synthesize a random ensemble of graphs. The distinction lies in the way randomness is introduced: random graphs are typically constructed by repeated application of simple random rules, but designed approaches can introduce randomness through the inputs to the design process, *i.e.,* the context. In our problem the context consists of:

- the spatial locations of the nodes or PoPs; and
- the traffic matrix, giving traffic demands between each pair of PoPs.

We generate these randomly, so that each time we synthesize a new network we generate different PoP locations and traffic matrices. Thus, the generated networks are guaranteed to be different. It would certainly be possible to choose PoPs according to real-life city locations, but providing the desired variety in context would then further thought.

PoP-locations are chosen according to a 2D point process on some region. We started by testing a number of alternatives:

- different region shapes, for instance rectangles with different aspect ratios; and
- different distributions of PoP locations, for instance, we experimented with making the locations of PoPs correlated so as to make them more or less bursty.

Our experiments found, suprisingly, that these details had comparitively small affects on the resulting networks (see §7 for details). A region had to be quite long and thin before it changed the resulting networks significantly, and likewise, even highly bursty PoP locations only changed the statistics of the resulting networks slightly.

In keeping with the underlying philosophy of this work – keep the model as simple as possible – the model presented here selects n PoP locations independently, and uniformly at random on the unit square. The result is a 2D Poisson process conditional on the number of PoPs. The behavior of such a process is mathematically tractable and very well understood. However, our code is designed to be modular, so that users can use our bursty model for PoP locations, or other region shapes. In fact, it is easy to write your own module for this component, or use real PoP locations if required.

Our traffic matrix is created using a *gravity model,* proposed in [18–20], and tested [21] as a model for synthesizing traffic matrices. It suffers from identifiable flaws [20], but matches the distribution of real traffic matrices well [21]. Moreover, it is the maximum entropy model for traffic matrices under the circumstances described here [22]. The gravity model is created by choosing a random population for each PoP. We tested two types of population model, the exponential model (populations were independent, identically distributed exponentials with mean 30), and the Pareto with shape parameters 10/9 and 1.5 (and the same mean), in order to test the impact of varying degrees of heavy tail on the results. Surprisingly, the effect on the inter-PoP topology was small (see §7 for details).

By default we choose the simpler exponential model in most of the subsequent work, though once again it is trivial to alter this, and our tool provides this option.

It may seem counter-intuitive that the selection of context provides the randomness in our synthesis model, but that the results are not sensitive to the actual model chosen. However, note that we are not saying that the PoP locations, and the traffic don't matter. We are saying that the ensemble of networks generated is statistically similar for different context models. The individual networks generated by different instantiations of contexts are still quite different.

The statistical insensitivity of the resulting networks to the context model is interesting, but note that it only applies at the PoP-level. When we consider, for instance, the router-level network, then it is far more dependent on the traffic matrix model. A Pareto model will generate a wider spread of traffic volumes per PoP, and as a result PoPs will have a wider spread in the numbers of routers needed than in the exponential model. This insensitivity is another example of the advantage of starting synthesis at the PoP level.

3.2 Formulation of the optimization problem

Each candidate PoP-level topology is represented by an undirected graph $\mathcal{G}(N, E)$ with nodes N (the PoPs) and edges, E (the links between PoPs). The variables in our optimization are thus the locations of the links and their capacities w_i. The main constraint in the problem is that the capacities of the network are sufficient to carry the inter-PoP traffic which implicitly requires the network to be connected. We do not include redundancy, port numbers or other complex constraints at this level.

Our cost function represents the cost of building the network and was chosen to be as simple as possible yet still able to approximate real-life objectives and produce a wide range of behavior. Its two components are link- and node-based costs, each described below.

3.2.1 Link cost

The cost for a link depends on many factors including the economic and geographical environment, existing infrastructure and networks, and other technical limitations. If these are modeled in too much detail we risk overfitting the model to one particular setting, reducing its generality, and making it less applicable to, for instance, future networks.

As a result, we use a linear cost model, which is as simple and general as possible, while allowing it to be tuned to produce a wide variety of networks. The cost for link $i \in E$ is given by $C_i = k_0 + k_1 \ell_i + k_2 \ell_i w_i$, where ℓ_i is the length of link i and w_i is the bandwidth required on link i to carry the traffic routed across this link, and k_0, k_1 and k_2 are constants giving

0. k_0: The cost for existence of the link.
1. $k_1 \ell_i$: The cost for the physical length of a link; for instance, the cost of digging a trench for cabling or renting space in a conduit.
2. $k_2 \ell_i w_i$: The bandwidth cost, representing the cost of a given capacity over the length of the link. This term includes operating expenses, as well as initial expenditure on fiber/copper, repeaters, *etc.* [23].

Real costs have discontinuities and non-linearities (*e.g.,* a discount on the per-unit-length cost when buying longer links), but these make the model more complex, and the resulting optimization harder.

The linear cost model also has the advantage that we can rewrite the bandwidth component of cost

$$\sum_{i \in E} k_2 \ell_i w_i = O k_2 \sum_{r \in R} t_r L_r, \qquad (1)$$

where R denotes the set of routes, L_r is the length of route $r \in R$, and t_r is the traffic along the route. The constant O

is the factor by which the capacity will exceed the required bandwidth, constant across all links for the sake of simplicity. This does not feature in the optimization formulation (2) since the same factor will be used regardless of which topology is chosen.

As a result, we will make the natural choice of shortest-path routing in the model, which will minimize the length of routes, and hence the bandwidth dependent component of cost. This speeds up the calculation of the required capacity, w_i, for each link, which is the dominant computational cost in the optimization process. It also means that the synthesis process provides routes as well as link locations and bandwidths. Shortest path routing is also at the core of what ISPs actually do, with tweaks to length values or to allow load balancing, *etc.*

3.2.2 Node Cost

The number of nodes n is fixed, so typically in optimization this would result in a constant node cost. However, we found that we needed a cost to differentiate types of PoPs.

Real networks show tremendous variability [16]. Some are meshy, and others resemble a hub-and-spoke network. Optimization of link costs alone tends to produce meshy networks – for instance, when the k_2 cost is dominant, it results in cliques. We found we could not get hub-and-spoke networks purely through optimizing against link costs (see Section 7).

Further examination of the networks in [16] also shows that they often have two classes of PoPs: *leaf* and *core*. Typically leaf PoPs had only one link[1] connecting them to the network (*i.e.,* they had node degree 1), and core PoPs had two or more links. Obviously, hub-and-spoke networks have more leaves than meshy networks.

The simplest and cleanest way of inducing leaf nodes in our optimization-based networks was to add a cost for *non-leaf* nodes. So each node j with degree$(j) > 1$ incurs a cost of k_3. This represents a *complexity cost*; a PoP with multiple connections to the outside world is more complicated to implement and maintain than one with only one connection. Complexity has a cost in real networks [24]. Managing a small PoP with only a single router, and/or single link is much simpler than a multi-router, multi-link PoP.

3.2.3 Optimization Problem

The optimization problem is therefore:

$$\min_{G(N,E)} \sum_{i \in E} (k_0 + k_1 \ell_i + k_2 \ell_i w_i) + \sum_{j \in N_C} k_3, \qquad (2)$$

where G is the set of graphs on n nodes that have sufficient capacity to carry the traffic, and $N_C = \{j \in N \mid \text{degree}(j) > 1\}$ is the set of core nodes.

The costs k_0, k_1, k_2 and k_3 allow the process to be *tuned* to produce different types of topologies, by changing the relative importance of each part of the cost. To understand how this trade-off works, we consider the impact of each component of the cost separately.

- *k_0-cost*: This cost depends on the number of links. Networks must be connected, so if this cost dominates, the *spanning trees* are optimal solutions.
- *k_1-cost*: This is a cost for the total length of all links. If this cost dominates, then the optimum solution is a *minimum spanning tree*.
- *k_2-cost*: The k_2 cost can be interpreted as a cost for the length of the routes, see (1). Hence, when k_2 dominates the routes will be as short as possible, *i.e.,* the result will be a *clique*.
- *k_3-cost*: If this cost is dominant, the optimal network will have only one node with degree greater than one, *i.e.,* it will be *hub-and-spoke* network.

Typically more than one cost will contribute, and so we will get a network that is a mixture of these.

Note that costs are all relative, and so there are really only three degrees of freedom in the above model. Hence, in the following we fix $k_1 = 1$, and only need set the other three costs.

[1]Note that a *link* in a PoP-level network may actually correspond to multiple links between multiple routers. Hence, a degree 1 node in the PoP-level graph is not necessarily an indication of lack of redundancy.

3.3 Optimization Algorithm

The components of the objective functions are simple in themselves, and optimizing against any one is not difficult. However, the mixed optimization is not so simple. There are too many potential solutions for a complete enumeration for even moderate values of n. Moreover, the problem does not decompose into smaller problems, and the relaxation of the integer problem to the reals is not useful. Hence we solve it heuristically.

Guarantees that our solution is truly optimal are not necessary. This paper is not about perfect optimization, *per se*, but rather about an attempt to replicate the process of network engineering. Given the uncertainties in inputs such as the traffic matrix and cost model, network engineers are typically looking for a good solution, not the optimal, and they do so using their own heuristics. So we have no need to find the very best possible network; only a set of good networks.

Hence we use a heuristic search algorithm, in this case a *Genetic Algorithm* (GA). It works by evaluating the objective function on a population of candidate topologies. The topologies with lower costs are more likely to be chosen to pass on their *genes* to subsequent generations of candidate topologies through crossover, mutation and direct selection. The process is repeated for many generations, with fitter topologies more likely to survive as the overall population improves until the topologies are well-adapted to the environment and the population reaches an almost-stable state.

The trick is to describe a topology in a form suitable for *genetic transcription*, and to create mutation and cross-over procedures that, for instance, preserve connectivity. Details of our solutions to these problems are given in §4 and Matlab code implementing the algorithm is available at [10].

However, it is worth noting that the choice of a GA over the alternative heuristics was motivated by the fact that they are:

1. *Flexibile*: GAs only require small adaptations to cope with changes to the objective function.
2. *Competitive:* We do not need to find the true optimal solution, but we do need to find a good solution. One way to ensure this is to require that the GA's solution is at least as good as competitors. A key advantage of GAs is that we can include alternative solutions in the initial population, and thereby guarantee the result will be at least as good as these.

3. *Non-exclusive:* For a given optimization problem, one run of a GA generates a population of solutions. The variation between these solutions can give a better idea of which characteristics are important in optimizing these topologies, and which are irrelevant. It also allows us to create multiple networks with the same context, potentially providing additional support for simulation where one wants a fixed context, but multiple topologies.

Of these, the first property has been most important here as it has allowed us to test multiple possible objectives in our search for a simple but realistic set (the results of which are given in §3.2.3).

4. DETAILS OF THE GENETIC ALGORITHM

In this section we provide some of the details of the Genetic Algorithm.

Inputs

- Matrix containing the coordinates and population of each *Point of Presence* (PoP).
- The optimization parameters: $k_0, \ldots, k_3$.
- The genetic algorithm settings, including the number of chromosomes in a generation and the number of generations. More settings appear below, in italics.

Outputs

- Adjacency matrix of the best topology found by the Genetic Algorithm.
- The routing matrix for the best topology found by the Genetic Algorithm.
- Link capacities for the best topology found by the Genetic Algorithm
- (Optionally) Adjacency matrices, routing matrices and link capacities of the whole population in the final generation.
- Costs of the candidate topologies in the final generation.

State

- Each candidate topology in the current generation is stored as an n by n adjacency matrix.
- The costs for each topology are also stored.

4.1 Algorithm

1. Determine the first generation of topologies
    - One starting topology is the minimum spanning tree (using the physical distances determined by the PoP-positions in the input).
    - One starting topology is the fully connected topology (every PoP is linked directly to every other PoP).
    - Topologies can be provided directly as input, typically from other optimization methods.
    - The remaining topologies are generated randomly using Erdos-Renyi graphs with a chosen probability for each link. This probability p can be fixed over all these topologies, or be different for each topology as desired. We use a value of p such that $p\binom{n}{2}$ is approximately equal to the expected number of links in the optimal topology; approximations to the optimal number of links can be obtained through previous runs of the algorithm. This aids convergence speed of the genetic algorithm but is otherwise unnecessary.
2. Evaluate the cost of each of the topologies in the current generation.
3. Create the next generation of topologies. These consist of:
    - The best *num_saved_topologies* topologies from the previous generation.
    - *num_crossover_topologies* topologies resulting from crossover (breeding).
    - *num_mutation_topologies* topologies resulting from mutation.
4. Repeat from Step 2 until there have been T generations.
5. Output the topology with the lowest cost.

For a Genetic Algorithm to be effective, it must be possible to efficiently generate "better" topologies by breeding and mutating "good" topologies. Consequently, the key challenge in designing a Genetic Algorithm is designing the crossover and mutation steps so that they work quickly and have a reasonable likelihood of producing good topologies.

4.1.1 Crossover

Crossover involves choosing several topologies ("parents") from the current generation to combine and create a new topology of the next generation. COLD picks b topologies uniformly at random as candidates to become parents, then chooses the best a of them as parents for a crossover. This process occurs once for each new topology created by crossover. We typically chose $a = 2$ and $b = 10$. Choosing parents this way ensures that the worst topologies will not become parents, and it induces a strong bias towards the better topologies as parents. We chose $a = 2$ and $b = 10$ to produce a good tradeoff between convergence speed (number of generations until the best cost was not changing very often) and reliability (that is, finding similarly costed topologies over several runs of the GA). If smaller values of b and larger values of a were used, this would allow more variety to be kept at each generation, at the expense of the average cost of topologies across that generation.

Once the parents of the new topology are chosen, it simply remains to generate the new topology from them. Since each topology is a graph with n nodes, there are $\binom{n}{2}$ possible links in the new topology. For each of these possible links, we choose one of the a parents at random and copy whether the link exists or not from that parent. When choosing the parents at random, they are chosen with probability inversely proportional to their cost. This crossover step occurs once for each of the new chromosomes created by crossover. We also tested other methods of crossover, but more complicated versions proved no more effective in efficiently finding low-cost topologies.

4.1.2 Mutation

To create a mutated topology, one of the topologies from the previous generation is selected at random, with probabilities inversely proportional to cost. Then one of two types of mutation occurs:

- *Link mutation*: A pair (m_+, m_-) is determined using a random function *mutate_fn()*. m_+ links that exist in the chromosome are removed, and m_- of the links that do not exist are added to the chromosome. We choose mutate_fn() so that m_+ and m_- are both geometric random variables with parameter 0.5, giving an average of two link changes each time a mutation occurs.

- *Node mutation*: One of the non-leaf nodes is chosen uniformly at random and made into a leaf node, with its only link now running to the closest non-leaf node.

4.1.3 Connectedness

The mutation and crossover steps can produce a network that is disconnected. If this occurs, COLD finds all the connected components and the shortest link between each pair of connected components. COLD then finds a minimum spanning tree (minimum in terms of physical link distance) to connect these components. This ensures that the resulting networks are always connected. It is used rarely. However, when the costs induce topologies with low numbers of links, this step becomes more frequent, although it is still rare to be forced to add more than one or two links to ensure connectedness.

5. PERFORMANCE OF THE GA

The first issue to resolve is the choice of settings for the GA to produce near-optimal topologies while managing its run-time. These settings include the number of generations T, the number of networks in each generation M, and the extent of mutation and crossover.

We choose the settings by running many examples with a fixed input (context), and testing a wide range of values. The goal is to choose values that produce topologies that are near optimal with minimal run-time. However, testing optimality is non-trivial, for the same reasons we are using a heuristic in the first place.

We start by comparing our results to the results of brute-force enumeration. This is infeasable for even moderately sized networks as the number of possible graphs is super-exponential in the number of nodes, but we at least ensure that for networks of up to 8 PoPs that the GA always finds the real optimal solution. This allowed us to obtain lower-bounds on settings such as the population size, and number of generations.

The other approach we use to test the GA is to compare its results to various heuristics. The heuristics were chosen so that they would work well for particular cost structures. For instance, we know that when the cost k_1 dominates, the optimal networks are minimum spanning trees, and so we use this to ensure that the GA can perform well for these parameter values.

We use a number of more complicated heuristics, primarily based on greedy approaches, described below. Each test algorithm starts with one hub node, and every other node a leaf node connected to it. Leaf nodes are converted to hub nodes one at a time, in such a way that the cost of the network reduces with each new hub (the way in which the hubs connect to each other varies). At every step the remaining leaf nodes are reconnected to the new closest hub node. If a hub can not be added without increasing the cost of the network, the algorithm terminates. The alternate methods for adding hubs are as follows:

- *Random Greedy*: A random permutation of all the nodes is chosen. The algorithm then iterates over the PoPs in this order. For each PoP it decides whether changing it to a hub reduces the cost of the network, and if so, the node made a hub. New hubs are linked to the existing hubs greedily: picking the lowest cost connecting link, etc., until there are no more cost reductions. Once all the PoPs in the permutation have been evaluated, the process repeats for many different random permutations of the PoPs.
- *Complete*: All the PoPs are tested as a possible hub and the best one is taken. This repeats until none of the remaining nodes will reduce the cost when added as a hub. Each new hub is connected to all the existing hubs, thus making a network where the hubs form a completely connected graph or clique.
- *MST*: Just like complete, but the hubs are connected in a minimum spanning tree.
- *Greedy attachment*: Like complete and MST, but inter-hub connections are chosen greedily for each new hub (as in Random Greedy).

We compared the GA to each of the greedy algorithms by generating a set of contexts and running each algorithm on each context. We then compared the costs of the best solutions found by each algorithm. The relative cost of the optimal solution found by each algorithm is plotted against k_2 in Figure 3, and we have similar plots against the other cost parameters. It is clear from the figure that different algorithms perform better in different circumstances (with different values of k_2, k_3).

Though specific greedy algorithms outperform the GA for some parameter values, the GA performs well over a range of parameters when $k_3 = 0$ (left), but is not as effective when k_3 (the hub cost) is larger. However, a significant advantage of the GA is that it can take, as part of its initial population, the output of other algorithms. When we include the output of our heuristics as inputs to the GA – the *initialized GA* results – we see that the approach outperforms all of its competitors over all parameter ranges tested. The greedy algorithms are relatively fast in many cases, thus running them before the GA is not a significant cost.

As a result of these comparisons, we determined reasonable settings for the GA, most notably we chose to fix T and M at 100 each. These values provide a reasonable tradeoff between performance and speed. The GA was tested for sensitivity to increases in M and T, and despite quadrupling the number of topologies and the number of generations, the GA showed at most 10% decrease in costs for all values of (k_0, k_1, k_2, k_3) tested. We could also choose to stop the GA once the relative rate of change of best cost was sufficiently low, but a choice of $T = 100$ proved to function similarly.

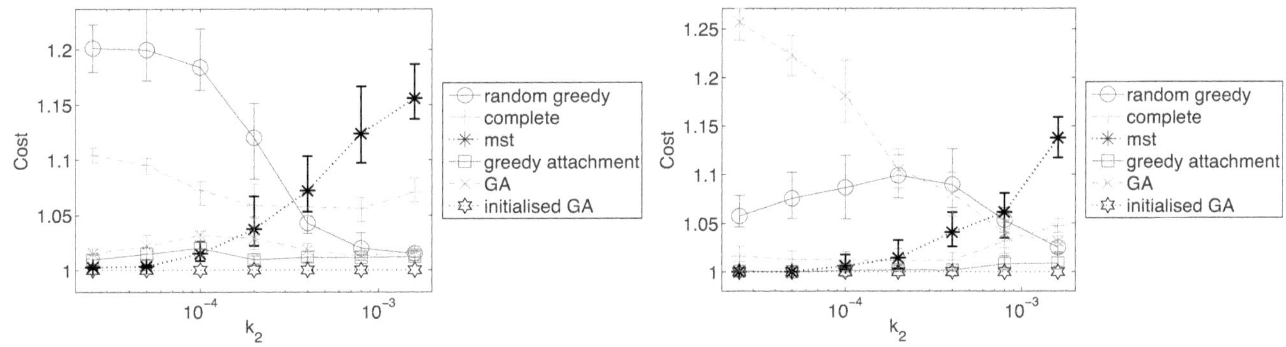

Figure 3: Cost of best solution versus k_2, normalized by initialised GA result, $n = 30$. Error bars denote 95% bootstrap confidence intervals for the mean of the results, 20 trials for each set of parameters. $k_3 = 0$ *(left)* and $k_3 = 10$ *(right)*. In both figures, $k_0 = 10, k_1 = 1$.

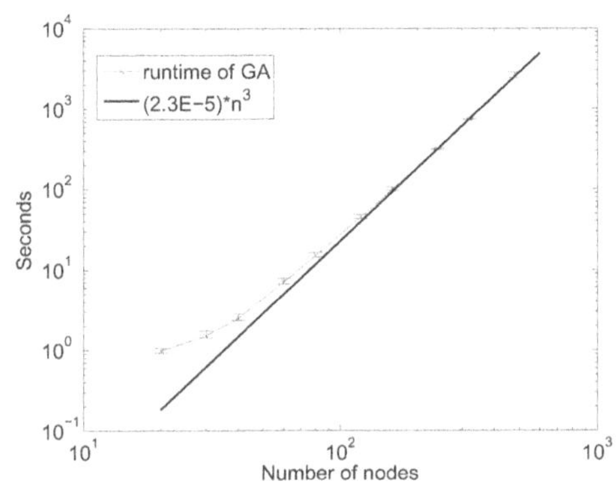

Figure 4: The run time of the genetic algorithm grows cubically in the number of nodes, with $T = M = 100$.

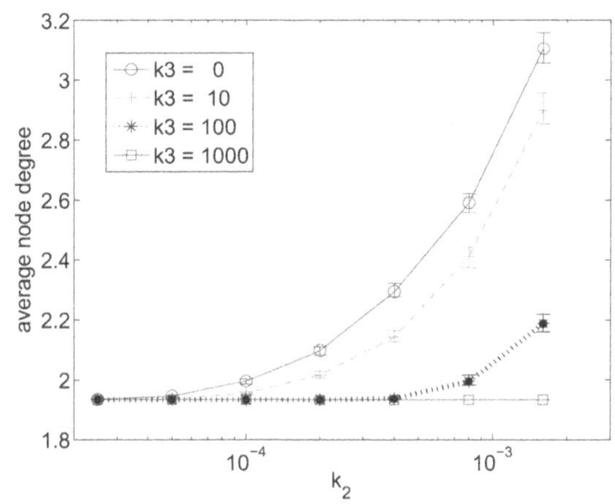

Figure 5: The average node degree versus the cost k_2, for various values of k_3, with $k_0 = 10$, $k_1 = 1$, and $n = 30$. 95% confidence intervals based on 200 simulations per data point are shown by horizontal bars.

Figure 4 shows the runtime of the GA, which grows as $O(n^3MT)$, where n is the number of PoPs, T is the number of generations and M is the number of topologies in each generation. Linearity of the GA with respect to M and T is obvious, and the n^3 term arises in evaluating the all-pairs shortest paths routing calculation for each topology.

$O(n^3)$ might seem less than ideal as an order of scaling for the run time of the GA, but given current hardware it was quite feasible to generate networks with hundreds of PoPs. This is another advantage of generating a PoP-level network: a large ISP can have thousands of routers, but it is rare to see a network with more than a 100 PoPs [7, 16]. It would be much more difficult to implement this type of optimization across all of the routers in a network.

6. TUNABILITY

One of our goals is that the output of the optimization process be tunable, as expressed in the introduction. Knight *et al.* [16] present a large set of PoP-level network maps created from data presented by network operators themselves. As a base-line, we are able to tune the output of our synthesis to produce a range of networks like those seen in this dataset. Note that we are not asserting that our networks are the same as the networks in this dataset. That is a much stronger claim that is, in point of fact, not possible to justify based on any small set of statistics (despite many claims otherwise). Rather we aim to show we can control the output of our generated networks so as to allow experimenters to test the impact of particular features of topologies on their experiments. As such, our goal is to show that for commonly studied features, we can reproduce a representative range of these features.

We illustrate here tunability with respect to average node degree, network diameter, clustering coefficient and the coefficient of variation of node degree. These encompass many of the features that have drawn research interest in the past, but we make no assertion that it is a complete set, and we have examined other features: for instance assortivity, average shortest-path lengths, and average node and link betweenness. However, the results are all of a similar nature, and the additional graphs add little additional insight.

COLD has four control parameters k_0, k_1, k_2 and k_3, but they are only unique up to a constant factor, so we can fix one (say k_1). Additionally, we found that costs k_0 and k_1 have a similar impact on the resultant networks, and so in these experiments we fix the ratio between these two by setting $k_0 = 10$ and $k_1 = 1$.

The average node degree is an important and frequently examined statistic. The higher the node degree, the more "meshy" the graph is. Intuitively, the number of links should increase as k_2 increases since it becomes more cost-efficient to have direct links between PoPs. Consequently, we expect average degree to increase with k_2. Likewise, as the cost k_3 increases, there should be fewer core PoPs, and hence fewer links, and so average degree should decrease. Figure

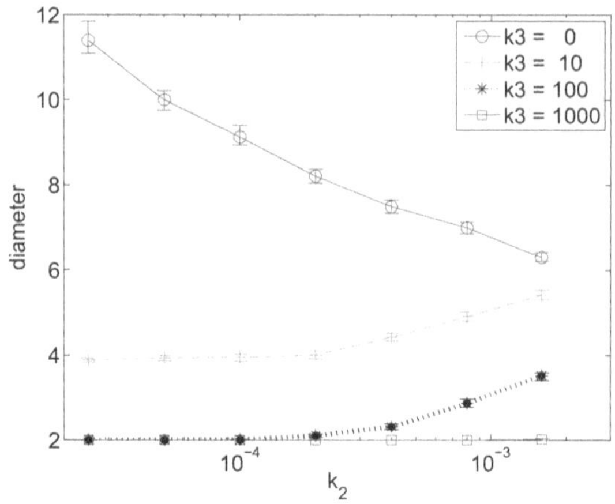

Figure 6: Network diameters for differing values of k_2 and k_3, with the same parameters as Figure 5.

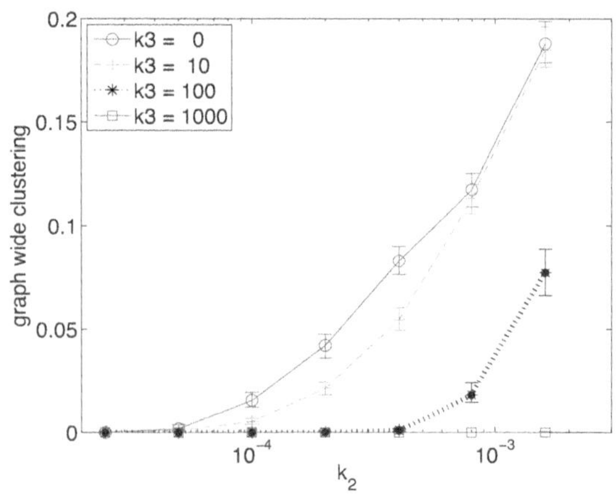

Figure 7: Global clustering coefficient for differing values of k_2 and k_3, with the same parameters as Figure 5.

5 shows exactly this behaviour. Moreover, the achievable degrees range from the minimum possible (for a tree the average degree is $2 - \frac{2}{n}$), up to the maximum (the curves continue to increase for larger values of k_2, and when k_2 dominates the optimal network is a clique).

Also of importance is the fact that the curves are smooth and monotonic, and the confidence intervals are tight around each curve, which makes it easier to generate a set of networks with well-controlled features.

The diameter of a graph is another frequently used statistic [9]. It denotes the maximum number of hops between pairs of nodes in the graph, and is important for network properties such as latency. Graphs with small diameter relative to their size and node degree demonstrate the "small-world" property, which has been of some interest in the research literature. Figure 6 shows the diameter of generated graphs with respect to k_2 and k_3. A high hub cost k_3 results in centralized networks that have low diameter. A high bandwidth cost k_2 results in meshy networks that also have low diameter. When neither cost dominates, we see higher diameters – for instance, networks with a few hubs, or networks that have too few links (especially long links) to have low diameters. Once again we can see a smooth, well-controlled progression of values, with a range that encompasses those seen in networks of comparable size in [16].

Clustering coefficients are a way of measuring locality, a principle commonly referred to in network design. The global clustering coefficient (GCC) measures the number of triangles present in the graph compared to the maximum number of triangles possible. In [16] 90% of the GCCs are below 0.25, and all of the higher GCCs belong to networks with very few nodes. Varying the value of k_2 causes the GA to move from producing trees (with a GCC of 0) to producing fully connected graphs (with a GCC of 1), importantly the GCC is controlled finely and reliably by k_2 and k_3, allowing the degree of locality present in the synthetic graphs to be finely tuned across all reasonable values as shown in Figure 7. However, note also that while GCC increases with k_2, the diameter can decrease with k_2, resulting in "small-world" networks.

We have examined a much larger set of network features, and different values of the ratio of k_0 and k_1, and different network sizes ($n = 50$ and $n = 80$), and uniformly we observe the same controlled variation in the statistics of the resulting networks over the observed range in real networks, or wider.

However, in our original experiments there was one statistic where the range of values observed in [16] was difficult to match, and it was this that lead us to include k_3, the hub cost, and we discuss this in more detail in the following section.

7. NODE-BASED COST

In this section we show that while it is possible to generate reasonable networks just using link costs $\sum_{i \in E}(k_0 + k_1 \ell_i + k_2 \ell_i w_i)$, a node-based cost $\sum_{j \in N_C} k_3$ is required to encompass all the variety we see in networks [16].

Without a node-based cost, we can vary k_2 to control the statistics mentioned above over the range seen in [16]. However, some networks in [16] have mainly PoPs of degree 1 (leaf PoPs), and few higher degree PoPs (core or hub PoPs). This "hubbiness" was measured in [16] using the coefficient of variation of node degree (CVND), which is the standard deviation of the node degree divided by the mean. Some networks in [16] have a CVND of nearly 2 (Figure 8a).

Figure 8b shows that for small k_3 (*i.e.,* the case where we don't include a hub-based cost) the synthetic networks have a CVND significantly less than one. Likewise, Figure 9 shows that the number of hub nodes is large when the hub cost is insignificant.

We need a means to induce some PoPs to be leafs. It may seem that this could be accomplished through changes in the context, *e.g.,* by making the traffic mode heavy-tailed. As noted earlier, we tried several models for PoP location generation with varying degrees of correlation, and we also considered Pareto-distributed, heavy tailed traffic models. In the later case, we trialled Pareto distributions with shape parameter $\alpha = 1.5$ and 1.1, corresponding to the infinite variance case.

All of these approaches had an effect on the generated networks. They did induce additional leaf nodes, but the effect was small. Even in the most extreme cases (bursty PoP location, and Pareto distributed traffic with $\alpha = 1.1$) the CVND was not sufficiently increased to represent the full gamut from [16].

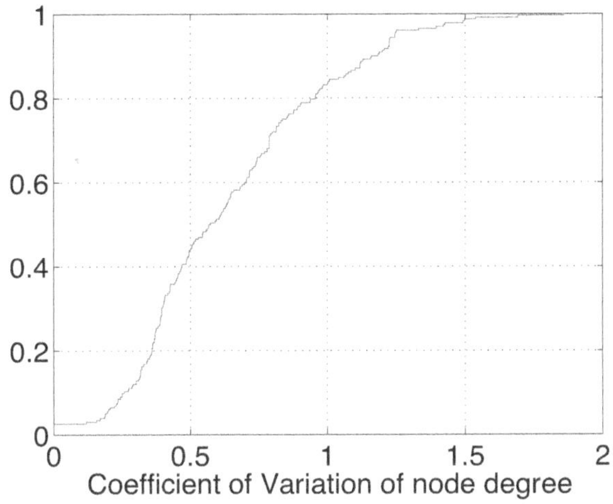

(a) Distribution of CVND degree for networks in [16]. About 15% of the networks have a CVND over 1, a value unattainable without a node-based cost.

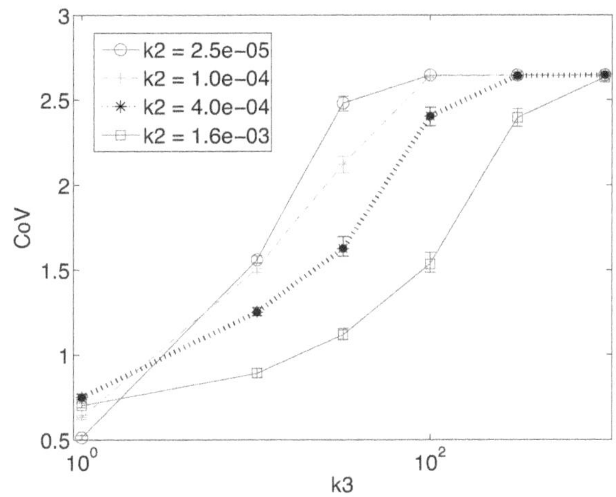

(b) Coefficient of variation of node degree versus k_3. Note that for small k_3, CVND is well below 1 for all cases.

Figure 8: Measured and simulated CVND, using the same parameters as Figure 5.

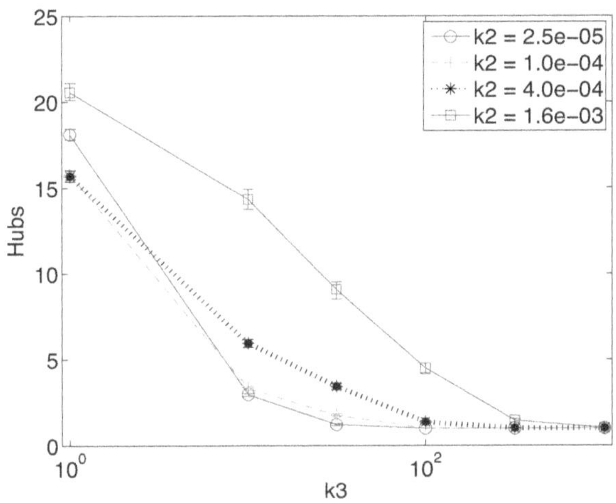

Figure 9: Number of core PoPs, for networks with 30 nodes. Again note that for small k_3 the number is always large.

The only method we found that did increase the CVND sufficiently was to include an explicit cost for non-leaf nodes. Once a hub cost is incorporated, it is possible to control both the CVND and the number of hubs, as is shown in Figures 8b and 9.

8. CONCLUSION

This paper presents COLD, an algorithm for generating synthetic data-network topologies motivated by real-world design approaches. It is as simple as possible, yet tuning the input parameters allows a wide variety of topologies to be produced mirroring those of real-world networks.

The benefits of this type of approach include that it allows for intuitive and sensible scaling. If small networks can be generated, so can larger networks, including networks with more nodes, spanning a larger area, carrying more traffic or some combination of these.

COLD is a conceptually simple model for synthesizing networks. It relies on a complex algorithm (optimization and graph products); but we provide an open implementation written in Matlab [10]. This paper has focussed on the PoP-level component of this approach, we explore the other components in later work.

In the future we aim to explain in more detail how the PoP-level design rules can be exploited to perform router-level network generation and AS-level network generation. The former requires a structured approach mimicking the design rules used by network engineers, which can be expressed through graph products [25]. The latter requires elements of geography and traffic optimisation as expressed in COLD, but routing policy is also more complicated than the shortest-path routing used here.

We also plan to use statistical estimation techniques, most notably ABC (Approximate Bayesian Computation) to map real networks to parameters k_i, to assist experimenters in determining appropriate values for these parameters in specific contexts.

9. ACKNOWLEDGMENTS

This work was supported by an Australian Postgraduate Award, the Australian Research Council Centre of Excellence CE140100049 and the Australian Research Council's Discovery Projects funding scheme (# DP120102834).

10. REFERENCES

[1] L. Li, D. Alderson, W. Willinger, and J. Doyle, "A first-principles approach to understanding the Internet's router-level topology," in *ACM SIGCOMM*, New York, NY, USA, 2004, pp. 3–14.

[2] Cisco, "ISP network design," 2005. [Online]. Available: ws.edu.isoc.org/data/2005/41363436042fc2b563533b/d1-6up.pdf

[3] V. Gill, "Analysis of design decisions in a 10G backbone." [Online]. Available: {www.nanog.org/meetings/nanog34/presentations/gill.pdf}

[4] M. Morris, "Network design templates," www.networkworld.com/community/blog/network-design-templates, July 18 2007.

[5] E. W. Zegura, K. L. Calvert, and M. J. Donahoo, "A quantitative comparison of graph-based models for Internet topology," *IEEE/ACM Trans. Netw.*, vol. 5, pp. 770–783, December 1997.

[6] E. Parsonage, H. X. Nguyen, R. Bowden, S. Knight, N. J. Falkner, and M. Roughan, "Generalized graph products for network design and analysis," in *Proc. of the 19th IEEE ICNP*, Vancouver, CA, October 2011.

[7] Y. Shavitt and N. Zilberman, "A structural approach for PoP geo-location," in *IEEE INFOCOM*, 2010.

[8] H. Ringberg, M. Roughan, and J. Rexford, "The need for simulation in evaluating anomaly detectors," *ACM SIGCOMM CCR*, vol. 38, no. 1, pp. 55–59, January 2008.

[9] J. Leskovec, D. Chakrabarti, J. Kleinberg, C. Faloutsos, and Z. Ghahramani, "Kronecker graphs: An approach to modeling networks," *J. Mach. Learn. Res.*, vol. 11, pp. 985–1042, March 2010.

[10] R. Bowden. (2012) COLD: A method for synthesising data network topologies. [Online]. Available: https://github.com/rhysbowden/COLD

[11] W. Aiello, F. Chung, and L. Lu, "A random graph model for power law graphs," *Experimental Mathematics*, vol. 10, no. 1, pp. 53–66, 2001.

[12] W. Willinger, D. Alderson, J. C. Doyle, and L. Li, "More "normal" than normal: scaling distributions and complex systems," in *Proceedings of the 36th conference on Winter simulation*, ser. WSC '04. Winter Simulation Conference, 2004, pp. 130–141.

[13] D. Alderson, L. Li, W. Willinger, and J. Doyle, "Understanding Internet topology: principles, models, and validation," *IEEE/ACM Transactions on Networking*, vol. 13, pp. 1205–1218, 2005.

[14] P. Mahadevan, D. Krioukov, K. Fall, and A. Vahdat, "Systematic topology analysis and generation using degree correlations," in *Proceedings of the ACM SIGCOMM '06*. New York, NY, USA: ACM, 2006, pp. 135–146.

[15] P. Mahadevan, C. Hubble, D. Krioukov, B. Huffaker, and A. Vahdat, "Orbis: rescaling degree correlations to generate annotated Internet topologies," in *ACM SIGCOMM*, 2007, pp. 325–336.

[16] S. Knight, H. Nguyen, N. Falkner, R. Bowden, and M. Roughan, "The Internet Topology Zoo," in *IEEE Journal on selected areas in communications*, vol. VOL. 29, NO. 9, October 2011.

[17] A. Fabrikant, E. Koutsoupias, and C. Papadimitriou, "Heuristically optimized trade-offs: A new paradigm for power laws in the Internet," in *Automata, Languages and Programming*, ser. Lecture Notes in Computer Science. Springer Berlin / Heidelberg, 2002, vol. 2380, pp. 781–781.

[18] P. Pöyhönen, "A tentative model for the volume of trade between countries," *Weltwirtschaftliches Archive*, vol. 90, pp. 93–100, 1963.

[19] J. Kowalski and B. Warfield, "Modeling traffic demand between nodes in a telecommunications network," in *ATNAC'95*, 1995.

[20] Y. Zhang, M. Roughan, C. Lund, and D. Donoho, "An information-theoretic approach to traffic matrix estimation," in *ACM SIGCOMM*, Karlsruhe, Germany, August 2003, pp. 301–312.

[21] D. Alderson, H. Chang, M. Roughan, S. Uhlig, and W. Willinger, "The many facets of Internet topology and traffic," *Networks and Heterogeneous Media*, vol. 1, no. 4, pp. 569–600, December 2006.

[22] K. N. Oikonomou, "Analytic forms for most likely matrices derived from incomplete information," *Int. J. Systems Science*, vol. 43, no. 3, pp. 443–458, Sept. 2010.

[23] K. E. Lindqvist and B. Woodcock, "Ip network architecture: Lessons learned over time." [Online]. Available: http://www.sanog.org/resources/sanog6/lindquvist-woodcock-network-architecture.pdf

[24] T. Benson, A. Akella, and D. Maltz, "Unraveling the complexity of network management," *Proc. NSDI*, 2009.

[25] E. Parsonage, H. X. Nguyen, R. B. andSimon Knight, N. Falkner, and M. Roughan, "Generalized graph products for network design and analysis," in *19th IEEE International Conference on Network Protocols*, 2011.

Remote Peering: More Peering without Internet Flattening

Ignacio Castro [§†*] Juan Camilo Cardona [§‡*] Sergey Gorinsky [§] Pierre Francois [§]

[§] IMDEA Networks Institute [†] Open University of Catalonia [‡] Carlos III University of Madrid

ABSTRACT

The trend toward more peering between networks is commonly conflated with the trend of Internet flattening, i.e., reduction in the number of intermediary organizations on Internet paths. Indeed, direct peering interconnections bypass layer-3 transit providers and make the Internet flatter. This paper studies an emerging phenomenon that separates the two trends: we present the first systematic study of remote peering, an interconnection where remote networks peer via a layer-2 provider. Our measurements reveal significant presence of remote peering at IXPs (Internet eXchange Points) worldwide. Based on ground truth traffic, we also show that remote peering has a substantial potential to offload transit traffic. Generalizing the empirical results, we analytically derive conditions for economic viability of remote peering versus transit and direct peering. Because remote-peering services are provided on layer 2, our results challenge the traditional reliance on layer-3 topologies in modeling the Internet economic structure. We also discuss broader implications of remote peering for reliability, security, accountability, and other aspects of Internet research.

Categories and Subject Descriptors

C.2.1 [**Computer-Communications Networks**]: Network Architecture and Design—*Network topology*

General Terms

Measurements

Keywords

Internet; interconnection economics; evolution; transit; peering; remote peering

* Both authors contributed equally to this paper.

CoNEXT'14, December 2–5, 2014, Sydney, Australia.

ACM 978-1-4503-3279-8/14/12 ...$15.00.
http://dx.doi.org/10.1145/2674005.2675013.

1. INTRODUCTION

The Internet economic structure is important for reliability, security, and other aspects of Internet design and operation. In spite of its importance, the economic structure remains poorly understood. It is typically modeled on layer 3 of Internet protocols because economic relationships can be inferred from BGP (Border Gateway Protocol) [55] and IP (Internet Protocol) [53] measurements. In particular, BGP identifies ASes (Autonomous Systems) on announced paths, enabling inference of layer-3 structures where ASes act as economic entities interconnected by transit or peering relationships [30]. ASes are imperfect proxies of organizations, e.g., multiple ASes can be owned by a single organization and act as a single unit. Nevertheless, AS-level topologies [19, 64] have proved themselves useful for reasoning about Internet connectivity, routing, and traffic delivery. While being useful, layer-3 models struggle to detect and correctly classify a significant portion of all economic relationships in the dynamic Internet.

Validated evolutionary changes in the economic structure include a trend toward more peering. The proliferation of peering relationships is caused partly by their cost advantages over transit. IXPs (Internet eXchange Points) are layer-2 switching facilities where peering commonly takes place [1, 8]. IXPs keep growing in the number of their members and amount of peering traffic [15].

Internet flattening refers to a reduction in the number of intermediary organizations on Internet paths [13, 24, 31]. For example, the Internet becomes flatter when a major content provider expands its own network to bypass transit providers and connect directly with eyeball networks, which primarily serve residential users. Internet flattening is routinely conflated with the trend towards more peering. Indeed, peering relationships are commonly established to bypass transit providers and thus reduce the number of organizations on end-to-end paths.

This paper presents the first empirical and analytical study on an emerging phenomenon of remote peering. Remote peering is an interconnection where a remote network reaches and peers with other networks via a layer-2 intermediary called a remote-peering provider. Remote-peering providers include not only new companies, such as IX Reach [37] and Atrato IP Networks [6], but also traditional transit providers that leverage their traffic-delivery expertise to act as remote-peering intermediaries. By buying a remote-peering service, networks can peer without extending their own infrastructures to a shared location.

Remote peering separates the trends of increasing peering and Internet flattening. On layer 3, remote peering is not distinguishable from direct peering. When a network buys a remote-peering service to establish new paths around a transit provider, the Internet becomes flatter on layer 3 because the new paths bypass the layer-3 transit provider. However, the layer-3 perspective is misleading because the new paths replace the transit provider with the layer-2 remote-peering provider. When one broadens the layer-3 perspective to include the organizations that provide layer-2 services, remote peering does not necessarily reduce the number of intermediary organizations on Internet paths in spite of the enabled additional peering relationships. Hence, remote peering means more peering without Internet flattening.

Our paper reports two measurement studies and a mathematical model that generalizes the empirical findings. First, we develop a ping-based method that conservatively estimates the spread of remote peering. We apply the method in 22 IXPs worldwide and detect remote peers in more than 90% of the studied IXPs, with remote peering by up to 20% of the members at an IXP. Our second study evaluates how remote peering can affect traffic patterns. Based on ground truth from a research and education network, we estimate the amount of transit-provider traffic that this network might offload via remote peering when the number of reached IXPs varies from 1 to 65. The results show a significant offload potential around 25% of the traffic in some scenarios. While the measurements reveal diminishing marginal utility of reaching an extra IXP, we generalize this property in the mathematical model and derive conditions for economic viability of remote peering.

By demonstrating the wide spread and significant traffic offload potential of remote peering, our results challenge the research community's reliance on layer-3 topologies in representing the Internet economic structure. Due to the failure to include the organizations that provide layer-2 remote-peering services, layer-3 models substantially distort the economic structure and can lead to incorrect conclusions about its properties, e.g., by conflating the trends of increasing peering and Internet flattening. Our findings call for new topological models to represent the prominent role of layer-2 organizations in the Internet economic structure.

The wide spread of remote peering also has broader implications for Internet research. When a provider offers transit and remote peering, buying both might not yield reliable multihoming. The presence of intermediaries that are invisible to layer-3 protocols adds to existing security concerns, e.g., the invisible layer-2 intermediaries can monitor traffic or deliver it through undesired geographies. For Internet accountability, it is a challenge to associate an action with the responsible invisible entity. As a new economic option, remote peering opens a whole new ballgame for connectivity, routing, and traffic distribution, e.g., via newly enabled IXPs [44]. To sum up, our paper makes the following main contributions:

- The paper reports the first systematic study of remote peering. The work illuminates the emerging phenomenon that many in the research community are unaware of. Even those who already know about remote peering benefit from our quantification of its wide spread and significant traffic offload potential.
- Our work reveals separation between the trends of increasing peering and Internet flattening. While enabling additional peering relationships, remote peering does not necessarily decrease the number of intermediary organizations on Internet paths.
- The results call for a rethink of modeling the Internet economic structure as layer-3 topologies. There is a need for new models to represent the increasing role of layer-2 entities in the Internet structure.
- The demonstrated prominence of remote peering also has broader implications for reliability, security, accountability, economics, and other aspects of Internet research.

The rest of the paper is organized as follows. Section 2 provides background on Internet economic interconnections. Section 3 empirically studies the spread of remote peering. Section 4 estimates a network's potential to offload transit traffic to remote peering. Section 5 analyzes economic viability of remote peering versus transit and direct peering. Section 6 discusses broader implications of our findings. Section 7 presents related work. Finally, section 8 sums up the paper.

2. INTERCONNECTION LANDSCAPE

We start by providing relevant background on economic relationships between networks in the Internet.

2.1 Transit

Transit refers to a bilateral interconnection where the customer pays the provider for connectivity to the global Internet. In a common setting, transit traffic is metered at 5-minute intervals and billed on a monthly basis, with the charge computed by multiplying a per-Mbps price and the 95th percentile of the 5-minute traffic rates [25, 62]. In the early commercial Internet, traffic flowed mostly through a hierarchy of transit relationships, with a handful of tier-1 networks at the top of the hierarchy.

2.2 Peering

Peering is an arrangement where two networks exchange traffic directly, rather than through a transit provider, and thereby reduce their transit costs. The exchange is commonly limited to the traffic belonging to the peering networks and their customer cones, i.e., their direct and indirect transit customers. To reduce costs further, peering is typically done at IXPs.

Networks differ in their policies for recognizing another network as a potential peer. The peering policies are typically classified as open, selective, and restrictive [45, 52]. An open policy allows the network to peer with every network. A network with a selective policy peers only if certain conditions are met. A restrictive policy has stringent terms that are difficult to satisfy.

Costs of peering and transit have different structures. Peering involves a number of traffic-independent costs, e.g., IXP membership fees and equipment maintenance expenses at the IXP. Peering also has traffic-dependent costs, e.g., IXP ports for higher traffic rates are more expensive. Over the years, peering relationships have proven themselves as cost-effective alternatives to transit.

Partly due to the lower costs, peering has spread widely, with the IXPs growing into major hubs for Internet traffic. Peering relationships bypass layer-3 transit providers and thus make the Internet flatter, at least on layer 3.

In this paper, *direct peering* at an IXP refers to peering by a network that has IP presence in the IXP location. If a network is not co-located with the IXP already, the network can establish its IP presence at the IXP by contracting an IP transport service or extending its own IP infrastructure to reach the IXP location.

2.3 Remote peering

Remote peering constitutes an emerging type of interconnection where an IP network reaches and peers at a distant IXP via a layer-2 provider [12]. The remote-peering provider delivers traffic between the layer-2 switching infrastructure of the IXP and remote interface of the customer. On the customer's behalf, the remote-peering provider also maintains networking equipment at the IXP to enable the remote network to peer with other IXP members. Figure 1 depicts a typical setting for the remote-peering relationship.

Remote peering provides a smaller connectivity scope than transit. Instead of global Internet access, this service limits the connectivity to the reached IXP members and their customer cones. Technologically, remote peering can be implemented with standard methods, such as those used in layer-2 MPLS (MultiProtocol Label Switching) VPNs (Virtual Private Networks). The main innovation of remote peering lies in its economics.

Remote peering has both traffic-dependent and traffic-independent costs. In comparison to direct peering, the traffic-independent cost is lower, and the traffic-dependent cost is higher: the remote-peering provider has multiple customers and reduces its per-unit costs due to traffic aggregation and acquisition of IXP resources in bulk. Compared to transit, remote peering has lower traffic-dependent costs. Thus, from the cost perspective, remote peering represents a trade-off between direct peering and transit.

IXPs and remote peering are highly symbiotic. IXPs benefit from remote peering because the latter brings extra traffic to IXPs, enriches geographical diversity of IXP memberships, and strengthens the position of IXPs in the Internet economic structure. To promote remote peering, AMS-IX (Amsterdam Internet Exchange), DE-CIX (German Commercial Internet Exchange), LINX (London Internet Exchange), and many other IXPs establish partnership programs that incentivize distant networks to peer remotely at the IXP. For example, some IXPs reduce membership fees for remotely peering networks. AMS-IX started its partnership program around year 2003. According to our personal communications with AMS-IX staff, about one fifth of the AMS-IX members were remote peers at the time of our study.

Implications of remote peering for transit providers are mixed. On the one hand, remote peering gives transit customers alternative means for reaching distant networks. On the other hand, remote peering is a new business niche where transit providers can leverage their traffic-delivery expertise.

According to anecdotal evidence, remote peering successfully gains ground and satisfies diverse needs in the Internet ecosystem. In this paper, we focus on usages where remote peering at IXPs is purchased by distant networks or other IXPs. For example, AMS-IX Hong Kong and AMS-IX interconnect their infrastructures via remote peering to create additional peering opportunities for their members [60]. We do not consider an alternative usage where remote peering at an IXP is bought by a local network to benefit from cost reductions that remote peering provides even over short distances [21].

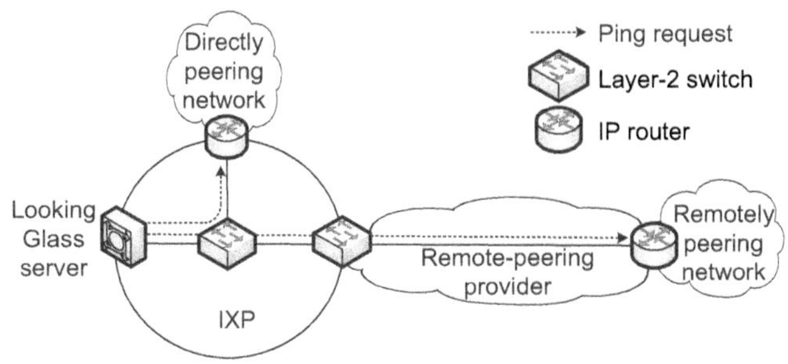

Figure 1: Directly and remotely peering networks, and probing of their IP interfaces from an LG server

3. SPREAD OF REMOTE PEERING

In this section, we report measurements that conservatively estimate the spread of remote peering in the Internet.

3.1 Measurement methodology

Because remote peering is provided on layer 2, conventional layer-3 methods for Internet topology inference are unsuitable for the detection of remote peering. For instance, traceroute and BGP data do not reveal IP addresses or ASNs (AS Numbers) of remote-peering providers.

The basic idea of our methodology for detecting a remotely peering network at an IXP is to measure propagation delay between the network and IXP. Specifically, we use the ping utility to estimate the minimum RTT (Round-Trip Time) between the IXP location and the IP interface of the network in the IXP subnet. If the minimum RTT estimate exceeds a threshold, we classify the network as remotely peering at the IXP.

While our ping-based method is intuitive, the main challenges lie in its careful implementation and include: identification of probed interfaces, selection of vantage points, adherence to straight routes, sensitivity to traffic conditions, identification of networks, choice of IXPs, threshold for remoteness, IXPs with multiple locations, impact of blackholing, and measurement overhead. We discuss these challenges below.

Identification of probed interfaces: The targets of our ping probes are the IP interfaces of the IXP members in the IXP subnet. IXP members do not typically announce the IP addresses of these interfaces via BGP. To determine the IP addresses of the targeted interfaces, we look up the addresses on the websites of PeeringDB [52], PCH (Packet Clearing House) [51], and IXP itself.

Selection of vantage points: The ping requests need be launched into the IXP subnet from within the IXP location so that the requests take the direct route from the IXP location to the probed interface. We send the ping requests from LG servers that PCH and RIPE NCC (Réseaux IP Européens Network Coordination Centre) [57] maintain at IXP locations. Figure 1 depicts our probing of IP network interfaces from an LG server at an IXP.

Adherence to straight routes: With our choice of the vantage points, the ping requests and ping replies are expected to stay within the IXP subnet. It is important to keep the probe routes straight because otherwise the RTT mea-

IXP acronym	IXP name	Location		Peak traffic (Tbps)	Number of members	Number of analyzed interfaces
		City	Country			
AMS-IX	Amsterdam Internet Exchange	Amsterdam	Netherlands	5.48	638	665
DE-CIX	German Commercial Internet Exchange	Frankfurt	Germany	3.21	463	535
LINX	London Internet Exchange	London	UK	2.60	497	521
HKIX	Hong Kong Internet Exchange	Hong Kong	China	0.48	213	278
NYIIX	New York International Internet Exchange	New York	USA	0.46	132	239
MSK-IX	Moscow Internet eXchange	Moscow	Russia	1.32	367	218
PLIX	Polish Internet Exchange	Warsaw	Poland	0.63	235	207
France-IX	France-IX	Paris	France	0.23	230	201
PTT	PTTMetro São Paolo	São Paolo	Brazil	0.30	482	180
SIX	Seattle Internet Exchange	Seattle	USA	0.53	177	175
LoNAP	London Network Access Point	London	UK	0.10	142	166
JPIX	Japan Internet Exchange	Tokyo	Japan	0.43	131	163
TorIX	Toronto Internet Exchange	Toronto	Canada	0.28	177	161
VIX	Vienna Internet Exchange	Vienna	Austria	0.19	121	134
MIX	Milan Internet Exchange	Milan	Italy	0.16	133	131
TOP-IX	Torino Piemonte Internet Exchange	Turin	Italy	0.05	80	91
Netnod	Netnod Internet Exchange	Stockholm	Sweden	1.34	89	71
KINX	Korea Internet Neutral Exchange	Seoul	South Korea	0.15	46	71
CABASE	Argentine Chamber of Internet	Buenos Aires	Argentina	0.02	101	68
INEX	Internet Neutral Exchange	Dublin	Ireland	0.13	63	66
DIX-IE	Distributed Internet Exchange in Edo	Tokyo	Japan	N/A	36	56
TIE	Telx Internet Exchange	New York	USA	0.02	149	54

Table 1: Properties of the 22 IXPs in our measurement study on the spread of remote peering

surements might be high even for a directly peering network. Potential dangers include an unexpected situation where the device of a probed IP interface replies from one of its other IP interfaces and thereby sends the ping reply through an indirect route with multiple IP hops. A more realistic danger is that some of our targeted IP addresses are actually not in the IXP subnet because the respective website information is incorrect. To protect our method from such dangers, we examine the TTL (Time To Live) field in the received ping replies. When ping replies stay within the layer-2 subnet, their TTL values stay at the maximum set by the replying interface [66]. When the path of a ping reply includes an extra IP hop, the TTL value in the reply decreases. Therefore, we discard the ping replies with different TTL values than an expected maximum. We refer to this discard rule as a *TTL-match filter*. For the expected maximum TTL, our experiments accept two typical values of 64 and 255 hops. Although ping software might set the maximum TTL to other values (e.g., 32 or 128 hops), these alternative settings are relatively infrequent, and ignoring them does not significantly increase the number of discarded ping replies in our experiments. Also, different ping replies from the same interface might arrive with different TTL values, e.g., because the replying interface changes its maximum TTL. Whereas we are interested in a conservative estimate for the extent of remote peering, we discard all replies from an IP interface if their TTL value changes during the measurement period. We call this rule a *TTL-switch filter*.

Sensitivity to traffic conditions: Even if a probe stays within the IXP subnet, RTT might be high due to congestion. To deal with transient congestion, we repeat the measurements at different times of the day and different days of the week for each probed IP interface, and record the minimum RTT observed for the interface during the measurement period. This minimum RTT serves as a basis for deciding whether the interface is remote. Again to be on the conservative side, we exclude an IP interface from further consideration if we do not get at least 8 TTL-accepted ping replies from this interface for each probing LG server. We call this rule a *sample-size filter*. The limit of 8 replies and other parameter values in our study are empirically chosen to obtain reliable results while keeping the measurement overhead low. If less than 4 of the collected ping replies have RTT values within the maximum of 5 ms and 10% of the minimum RTT, i.e., below $\text{RTT}_{min} + \max\{5 \text{ ms}, 0.1 \cdot \text{RTT}_{min}\}$, we apply an *RTT-consistent filter* to disregard the interface. For an IXP that has both PCH and RIPE NCC servers, we probe each IP interface from both LG servers and exclude the interface from further consideration if the larger of the two respective minimum RTTs is not within the maximum of 5 ms and 10% of the smaller one. We refer to this rule as an *LG-consistent filter*.

Identification of networks: To identify the network that owns a probed IP interface, we use the network's ASN. We map the IP addresses to ASNs through a combination of looking up PeeringDB, using the IXPs' websites and LG servers, and issuing reverse DNS (Domain Name System) queries. If the ASN of an IP interface changes during the measurement period, we exclude the IP interface from further consideration. This exclusion rule is called an *ASN-change filter*.

Choice of IXPs: In choosing IXPs, we strive for a global scope surpassing the regional focuses of prior IXP studies. Our choice is constrained to those IXPs that have at least one LG server. Under the above constraints, we select and experiment at 22 IXPs in the following 4 continents: Asia, Europe, North America, and South America. After manually crawling the websites of the IXPs in January 2014, we collect data on their location, peak traffic, and number of members. Table 1 sums up these data. While informa-

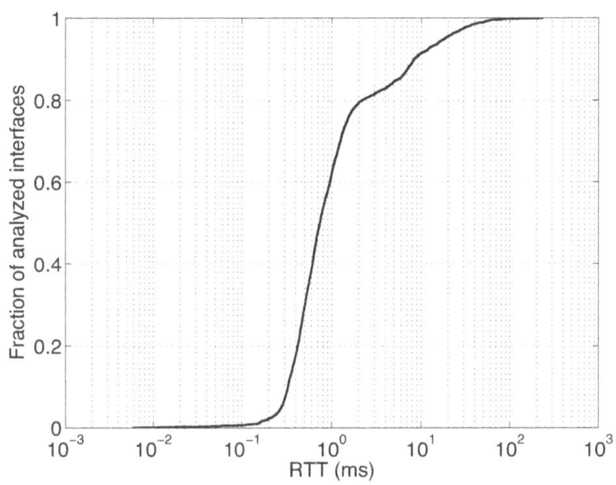

Figure 2: Cumulative distribution of the minimum RTTs for all the analyzed interfaces

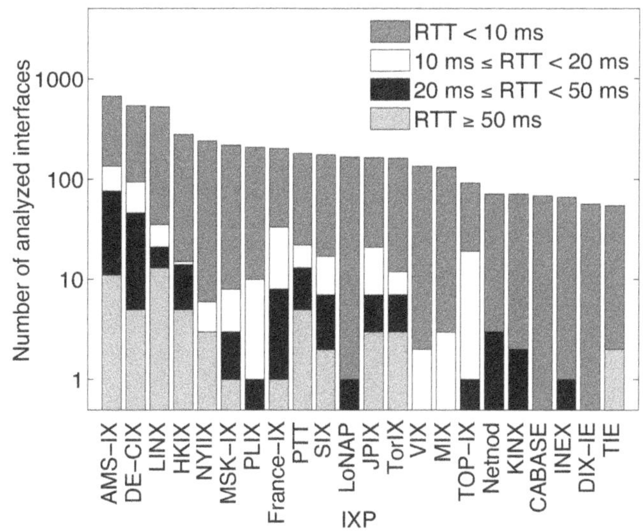

Figure 3: Classification of the analyzed interfaces with respect to 4 ranges of minimum RTTs

tion at IXP websites is often incomplete, out of date, or inconsistent in presenting a property (e.g., peak traffic), our measurement method does not rely on these data. We report this information just to give the reader a rough idea about the geography and size of the studied IXPs. For each studied IXP, table 1 also includes the *number of analyzed interfaces*, i.e., interfaces that stay in our analyzed dataset after applying all 6 aforementioned filters. Across all the 22 IXPs, we apply the filters in the following order: sample-size, TTL-switch, TTL-match, RTT-consistent, LG-consistent, and ASN-change. After the filters discard 20, 82, 20, 100, 28, and 5 interfaces respectively, we have a total of 4,451 analyzed interfaces. The high count of TTL-switch discards is likely due to operating system changes during our measurements.

Threshold for remoteness: We classify a network as remotely peering at an IXP if the minimum RTT observed for its IP interface at the IXP exceeds a threshold. Despite the redundancy of our RTT measurements, the minimum RTT might still include non-propagation delays, e.g., due to persistent congestion of the IXP subnet or probe processing in the network devices. To minimize the possibility that such extra delays trigger an erroneous classification of a directly peering network as remote, the threshold should be sufficiently high. Figure 2 plots the cumulative distribution of the minimum RTTs for all the 4,451 analyzed interfaces. A majority of the analyzed interfaces have minimum RTTs distributed almost uniformly between 0.3 and 2 ms. This is a pattern expected for directly peering networks. The likelihood of a network being a direct peer declines as the minimum RTT increases. Our manual checks do not detect any directly peering network with the minimum RTT exceeding 10 ms. Thus, we set the remoteness threshold in our study to 10 ms. While this relatively high threshold value comes with a failure to recognize some remotely peering networks as remote peers, the false negatives do not constitute a significant concern because we mostly strive to avoid false positives in estimating the spread of remote peering conservatively.

IXPs with multiple locations: If an IXP operates interconnected switches in multiple locations, probes from an LG server at one location to an IP interface at another location might have a large RTT. The chosen remoteness threshold of 10 ms is sufficiently high to avoid false positives in cases where all locations of the IXP are in the same metropolitan area. False positives are possible if the geographic footprint of the IXP is significantly larger, e.g., spans multiple countries. We do not observe such situations in our experiments. In a more common scenario, two partner IXPs from different regions, e.g., AMS-IX Hong Kong and AMS-IX, interconnect by buying layer-2 connectivity from a third party. Our methodology correctly classifies such scenarios as remote peering.

Impact of blackholing: If a probed interface intentionally blackholes or accidentally fails to respond to ping requests, the IP interface might be excluded from our analyzed data due to a low number of ping replies for the interface, as discussed above. In a hypothetical (not observed in our experiments) scenario where the probed interface forwards the probe to another machine that sends a ping reply on the interface's behalf, the ping reply is discarded by our TTL-match filter and does not affect accuracy of our RTT measurements.

Measurement overhead: While our method relies on probing from public LG servers, it is important to keep the measurement overhead low. The probes are launched through HTML (HyperText Markup Language) queries to the servers. The LG servers belonging to RIPE NCC and PCH react to an HTML query by issuing respectively 3 and 5 ping requests. For any LG server, we submit at most one HTML query per minute and generally spread the measurements over 4 months. The maximum number of ping replies received from any probed IP interface is 21 and 54 for respectively RIPE NCC and PCH servers.

We conducted the measurements during the 4 months from October 2013 to January 2014. The measurement data are available at [56].

3.2 Experimental results

Figure 3 classifies all the 4,451 analyzed interfaces across the 22 IXPs according to the minimum RTT measured for

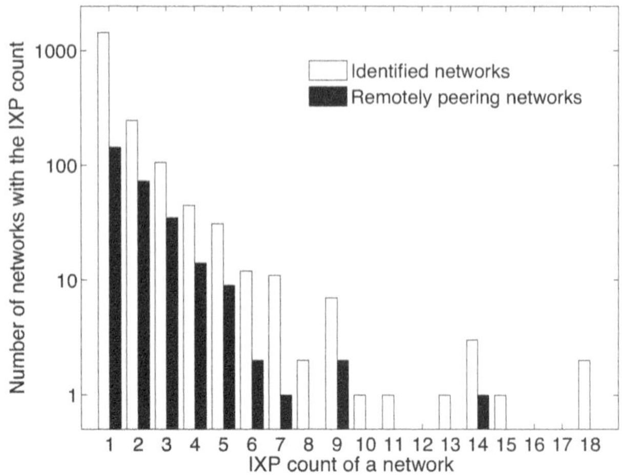

(a) Distributions of the IXP counts

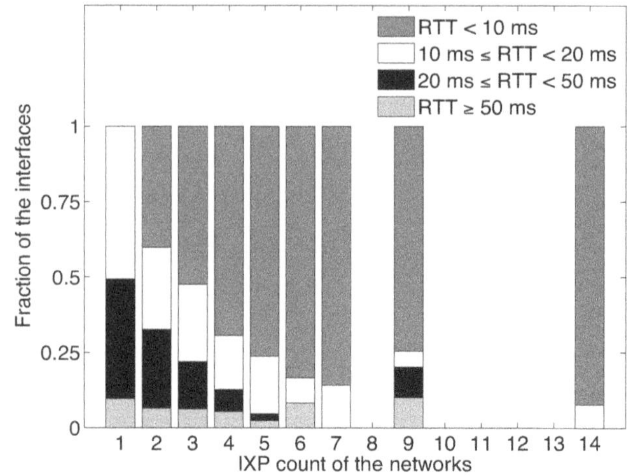

(b) Interfaces of all the 285 remotely peering networks

Figure 4: IXP-count distributions and interface classifications for identified networks

each interface. Our conservative estimate finds remote peering in 91% of the studied IXPs. While the numbers of remote interfaces are large in the 3 biggest IXPs (AMS-IX, DE-CIX, and LINX), these numbers are also large at smaller IXPs such as France-IX in France, PTT in Brazil, JPIX in Japan, and TOP-IX in Italy. Despite using the high remoteness threshold of 10 ms, the classification does not reveal remote interfaces in only two IXPs (DIX-IE and CABASE). Hence, our method independently confirms wide presence of remote peering in the Internet economic structure.

The classification in figure 3 looks at the remote interfaces in greater detail by considering the following 3 ranges for the minimum RTT: [10 ms; 20 ms), [20 ms; 50 ms), and [50 ms; ∞) which roughly correspond to intercity, intercountry, and intercontinental distances respectively. We detect the intercontinental-range peering at 12 IXPs, i.e., a majority of the studied IXPs. For example, Italian network E4A remotely peers at both TIE and TorIX, based in the USA and Canada respectively. Brazilian networks comprise most of the remote peers at PTT, the largest among the 21 IXPs of the PTTMetro project in Brazil. The high fraction of remote interfaces at the Turin-based TOP-IX likely results from the IXP's interconnections with VSIX and LyonIX, two other Southern European IXPs located in Padua and Lyon respectively.

Switching the perspective from the interfaces to the networks that own them, we apply our network identification method (described in section 3.1) to determine ASNs for 3,242 out of the 4,451 analyzed interfaces. While a network might have interfaces at multiple IXPs, we identify a total of 1,904 networks. We refer to the number of the studied IXPs where a network peers as an *IXP count* of the network. Figure 4a presents the distribution of the IXP counts for all the 1,904 identified networks. While a majority of the networks connect to only one IXP, some networks peer at as many as eighteen IXPs.

285 of the identified networks have a remote interface at a studied IXP. Business services offered by the remotely peering networks are diverse and include transit (e.g., Türk Telecom), access (e.g., E4A and Invitel), and hosting (e.g., Trunk Networks). Figure 4a also plots the distribution of the IXP counts for all the 285 remotely peering networks. Both distributions in figure 4a are qualitatively similar, suggesting that the choice of IXPs for a network to peer is relatively independent of whether the network peers directly or remotely.

We also examine the remotely peering networks with respect to the minimum RTTs of their analyzed interfaces. For each IXP count, we consider all the analyzed interfaces of the remotely peering networks with this IXP count and classify the interfaces in regard to the following 4 ranges of minimum RTTs: [0 ms; 10 ms), [10 ms; 20 ms), [20 ms; 50 ms), and [50 ms; ∞). Figure 4b depicts the fractions of these 4 categories. While our study sets the remoteness threshold to 10 ms, the remotely peering networks with the IXP count of 1 have no interfaces with the minimum RTT below 10 ms. As the IXP count increases, the fraction of the remote interfaces tends to decline because some interfaces of the remotely peering networks are used for direct peering. E4A exemplifies networks with a large number of remote interfaces: 6 of its 9 analyzed interfaces are classified as remote.

3.3 Method validation

While our methodology employs a series of filters and high remoteness threshold of 10 ms to avoid false positives, this section reports how we validate the method and its conservative estimates of remote peering.

First, we use ground truth from TorIX, an IXP located in Toronto. TorIX staff confirmed that their members classified as remotely peering networks in our study are indeed remote peers. In one case, the TorIX staff initially thought that a network identified as a remote peer by our method was rather a local member with a direct peering connection. Nevertheless, a closer examination showed that throughout our measurement period this local member conducted maintenance of its Toronto PoP (Point of Presence) and connected to TorIX from its remote PoP via a contracted layer-2 facility.

Then, we take a network-centric perspective and focus on E4A and Invitel. Both networks specialize in providing Internet access. Based on the measurements, our method classifies the E4A interfaces at DE-CIX, France-IX, LoNAP, TorIX, and TIE as remote. Using public information on IXP websites [3, 43] and insights from private conversations, we confirm that E4A indeed peers remotely at these 6 IXPs.

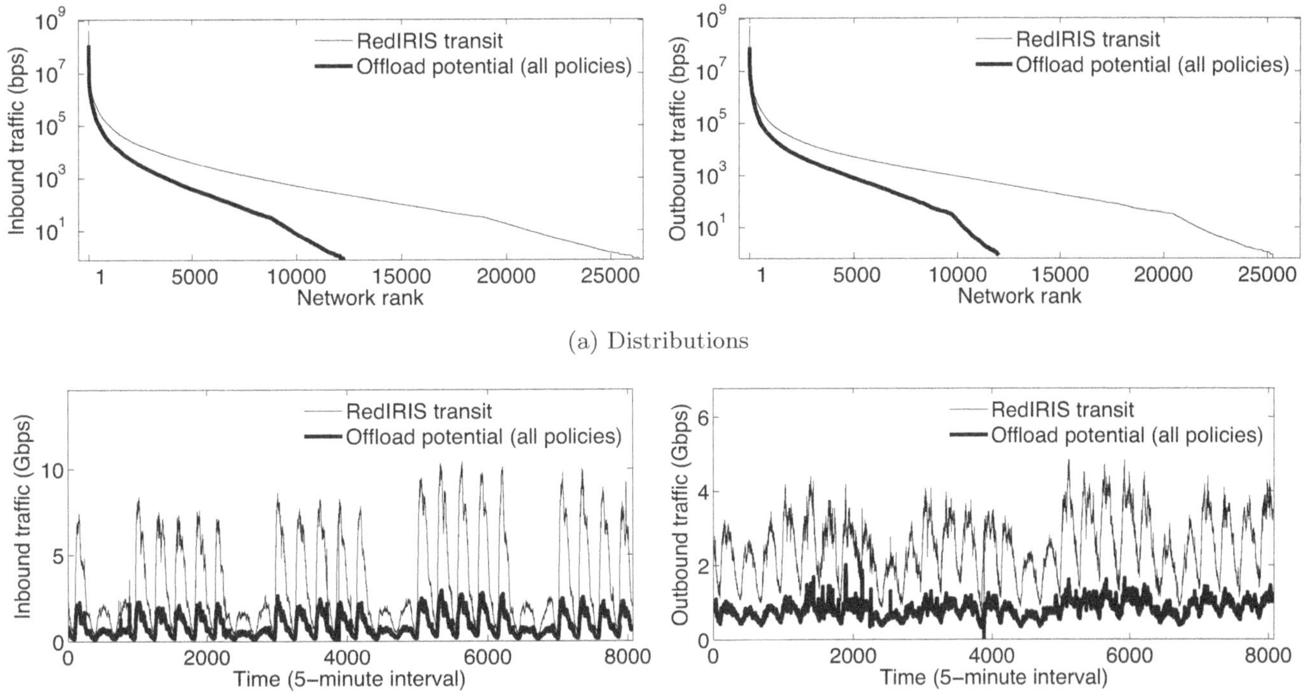

(a) Distributions

(b) Time series

Figure 5: Network contributions to the transit-provider traffic and offload potential with peer group 4

Our method also identifies Invitel as a remote peer at AMS-IX and DE-CIX, with the minimum RTTs of 22 and 18 ms respectively. Our private inquiries indicate that Invitel uses remote-peering services of Atrato IP Networks to reach and peer at AMS-IX and DE-CIX.

Finally, we receive an independent confirmation that our RTT measurement methodology is accurate. On our request, the TorIX staff measured minimum RTTs between the TorIX route server and member interfaces. Their results for our analyzed interfaces closely match our RTT measurements from the local PCH LG server. The mean and variance of the differences are respectively 0.3 and 1.6 ms.

4. TRAFFIC OFFLOAD POTENTIAL

While section 3 demonstrates that remote peering is common, we now estimate the *traffic offload potential* of a network, i.e., the transit-provider traffic that the network might be able to offload via remote peering. Based on ground truth from a research and education network, we also examine sensitivity of the offload potential to the number of reached IXPs and choice of peers at the reached IXPs.

4.1 Traffic data

We collect and use traffic data from RedIRIS, the NREN (National Research and Education Network) in Spain. This network interconnects with GÉANT (backbone for European NRENs), buys transit from two tier-1 providers, peers with major CDNs (Content Delivery Networks), and has memberships in two IXPs: CATNIX in Barcelona and ESpanix in Madrid. In February 2013, we used NetFlow to collect one month of traffic data at the 5-minute granularity in the ASBRs (Autonomous System Border Routers) of RedIRIS.

Utilizing the BGP routing tables in the ASBRs, we determine the AS-level path and traffic rate for each of the traffic flows. While a network can be associated with a traffic flow in the role of a traffic origin, destination, or intermediary, we classify the traffic flows associated with a network as its:

(a) *origin traffic*, i.e., originated in the network;

(b) *destination traffic*, i.e., terminated in the network;

(c) *transient traffic*, i.e., passing through the network.

Among all the inter-domain traffic, only the traffic between RedIRIS and its transit providers might contribute to the offload potential. Depending on whether RedIRIS receives the traffic from its transit providers or sends the traffic to them, we respectively classify the transit-provider traffic as *inbound* or *outbound*. The collected dataset identifies networks by their ASNs and contains records for 29,570 networks that are origins of the inbound traffic or destinations of the outbound traffic.

To illustrate the contributions of the 29,570 networks to the transit-provider traffic of RedIRIS, we report how much traffic each individual network contributes as an origin of the inbound traffic and destination of the outbound traffic. Figure 5a plots the average traffic rates for the respective inbound and outbound contributions by the individual networks during the measurement period. The figure ranks the networks in the decreasing order of the contributions. While a few networks make huge contributions close to the Gbps mark, most networks contribute little. In the range where the networks are ranked about 20,000 and contribute average traffic rates around 100 bps, the distributions of the inbound and outbound traffic exhibit a similar change in the qualitative profile of the decreasing individual contributions: a bend toward a faster decline. While the raw data exhibit

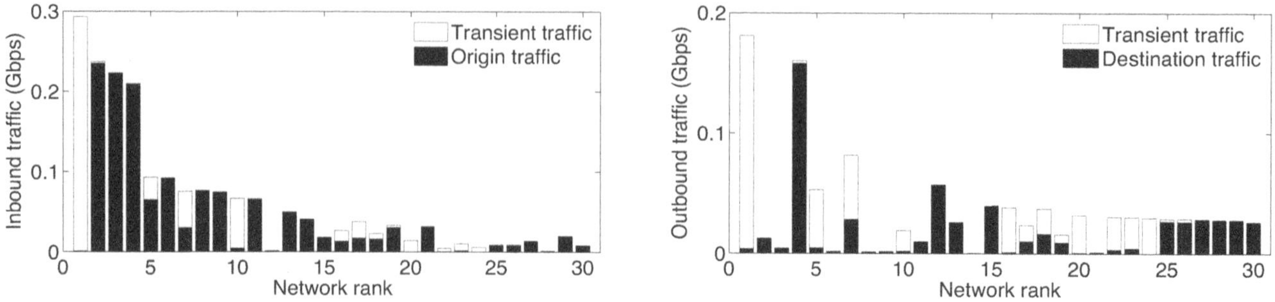

Figure 6: Origin and destination traffic vs. transient traffic for top contributors to the offload potential

the bend as well, reasons for the bend constitute an interesting topic for future work. Figure 5b reveals daily and weekly fluctuations in the transit-provider traffic of RedIRIS, with the periodic fluctuations being clearly pronounced for the inbound traffic.

4.2 Offload scenarios

RedIRIS cannot offload all of its transit-provider traffic. The offload potential depends on the set of IXPs that the network is able to reach via remote peering. Also, the memberships of the reached IXPs do not include all the networks that contribute to the transit-provider traffic of RedIRIS. Finally, not all the members of the reached IXPs are likely to peer with RedIRIS.

For the set of IXPs that RedIRIS might be able to reach, we consider the Euro-IX association formed, as of February 2013, by 65 IXPs from all the continents [28]. The considered 65 IXPs are a superset of the 22 IXPs studied in section 3, with the set enlargement made feasible by removing the constraint of having LG servers in the IXPs. Based on Euro-IX data from February 2013, we limit potential peers of RedIRIS to the members of these 65 IXPs.

We further trim the group of potential peers by excluding the networks that are highly unlikely to peer with RedIRIS. First, we do not consider the transit providers of RedIRIS as its potential peers because transit providers typically do not peer with their customers. It is worth noting that no network sells transit to these two tier-1 providers, and thus no such network needs to be excluded due to its transitive transit relation with RedIRIS. Second, since RedIRIS already has memberships in CATNIX and ESpanix, the other members of these two IXPs are disregarded as candidates for remote peering with RedIRIS. In particular, we exclude all the other tier-1 networks because they have memberships in ESpanix. Third, due to the cost-effective interconnectivity that comes with the GÉANT membership, we do not consider the other GÉANT members as potential peers of RedIRIS. After applying the above three rules, the group of potential remote peers of RedIRIS reduces to 2,192 networks. Even after eliminating the highly unlikely peers, there remains a significant uncertainty as to which of the 2,192 networks might actually peer with RedIRIS.

To deal with the remaining uncertainty about potential peers, we examine a range of *peer groups*, i.e., groups of networks that might peer with RedIRIS. Using PeeringDB which reports peering policies of IXP members [45, 52], we compose the following 4 peer groups so that the peering policies of their members comprise:

[peer group 1] *all open policies*;

[peer group 2] *all open and top 10 selective policies*, which adds to peer group 1 the 10 networks that have the largest offload potentials among the networks with selective policies;

[peer group 3] *all open and selective policies*;

[peer group 4] *all policies*, i.e., all open, selective, and restrictive policies.

Peer group 4 constitutes our upper bound on the likely peers of RedIRIS. When RedIRIS reaches all the 65 IXPs, this peer group 4 includes all the aforementioned 2,192 networks. Peer group 1 represents a lower bound on the networks that might actually peer with RedIRIS. It is common for such open-policy networks to automatically peer with any interested IXP member via the IXP route server [58].

For each peer group, we determine the offload potential of RedIRIS by fully shifting to remote peering the traffic that the networks of this peer group and their customer cones contribute to the transit-provider traffic of RedIRIS. While RedIRIS is in control of its outbound transit traffic, we assume that the networks of the peer group shift the inbound transit traffic of RedIRIS to remote peering as well.

In addition to studying sensitivity of the offload potential to the peer groups, we also evaluate its sensitivity to the choice of reached IXPs. Specifically, our evaluation varies the set of reached IXPs from a single IXP to all the 65 IXPs in the Euro-IX data.

4.3 Offload evaluation results

We start by estimating the maximal offload potential with peer group 4 (all policies) when RedIRIS reaches all the 65 IXPs. In this scenario, RedIRIS offloads traffic of 12,238 networks including the 2,192 members of the peer group. Figure 5a shows how much traffic these 12,238 networks contribute to the offload potential in the inbound and outbound directions. The plot ranks the networks in the decreasing order of their traffic contributions. The results suggest that the maximal offload potential is substantial: RedIRIS offloads around 27% and 33% of its transit-provider traffic in the inbound and outbound directions respectively. While the inbound traffic dominates the outbound traffic, figure 5b reveals that the peaks of the transit-provider traffic and offload potential of RedIRIS consistently coincide, implying that the traffic offload can reduce transit bills, which are typically determined by traffic peaks.

Figure 6 zooms in on the top 30 contributors to the maximal offload potential. These 30 networks make the largest traffic contributions to the combined inbound and outbound

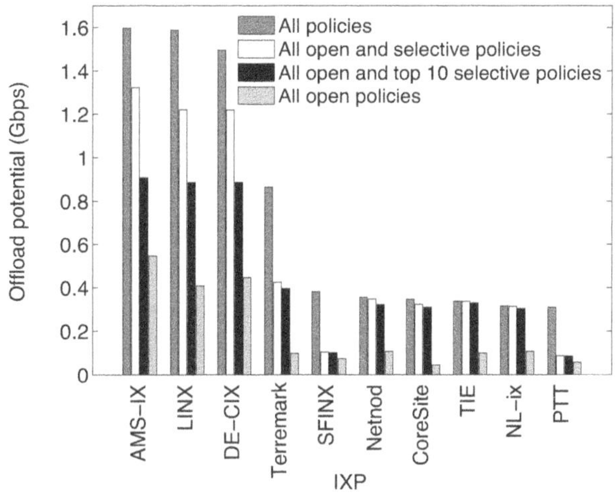

Figure 7: Offload potential at a single IXP

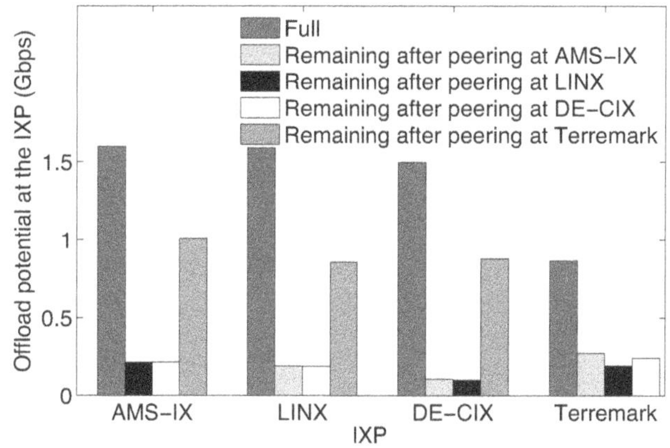

Figure 8: Additional value of reaching a second IXP after realizing the offload potential at a single IXP

offload potential. The top contributors include Microsoft, Yahoo, and CDNs (Content Delivery Networks), suggesting that content-eyeball traffic features heavily in the offload potential. For a majority of the top contributors, the origin and destination traffic dominates the transient traffic.

Switching to the sensitivity analyses, we first evaluate the offload potential for the 4 peer groups when RedIRIS reaches a single IXP. This single IXP is chosen among the 10 IXPs where RedIRIS has the largest offload potential. Figure 7 reports the offload potential of RedIRIS at each of the 10 IXPs. The top 4 of the IXPs include the big European trio (AMS-IX, LINX, and DE-CIX) and Terremark from Miami, USA. For any of the 4 peer groups, the offload potential is similar across the 3 largest European IXPs because these IXPs have many common members. On the other hand, the offload potential at Terremark is significantly different due to its different membership: numerous members of Terremark from South and Central America [49] contribute significantly to the transit-provider traffic of RedIRIS and are not present in Europe.

We now assess the additional value of reaching a second IXP after RedIRIS fully realizes its offload potential at a single IXP. When the two reached IXPs have common members that contribute to the transit-provider traffic of RedIRIS, realizing the offload potential at the first IXP reduces the amount of traffic that RedIRIS can offload at the second IXP. For peer group 4 (all policies), figure 8 illustrates this effect when AMS-IX, LINX, DE-CIX, and Terremark act as either first or second IXP. When LINX and AMS-IX act as the first and second IXPs respectively, the offload potential remaining at AMS-IX after fully realizing the offload potential at LINX is 0.2 Gbps, which is much lower than the full potential of 1.6 Gbps at AMS-IX. When Terremark acts as the second IXP, the decrease in its offload potential is less pronounced because Terremark shares only about 50 of its 267 members with either of the 3 largest European IXPs.

Generalizing the above, we examine the additional value for RedIRIS to reach an extra IXP. We iteratively expand the set of reached IXPs by adding the IXP with the largest remaining offload potential. For peer group 4, the first 4 reached IXPs are added in the following order: AMS-IX, Terremark, DE-CIX, and CoreSite. For all the 4 peer groups, figure 9 plots the remaining transit-provider traffic of RedIRIS as the number of reached IXPs increases. The overall reduction in transit-provider traffic of RedIRIS varies from 8% for peer group 1 (all open policies) to 25% for peer group 4 (all policies). Figure 9 shows that the marginal utility of reaching an extra IXP diminishes exponentially and that reaching only 5 IXPs enables RedIRIS to realize most of its overall offload potential.

While the previous results are specific to RedIRIS, we now present evidence that the property of diminishing marginal utility of reaching an extra IXP holds in general. These additional experiments change the metric from transit-provider traffic to the number of IP interfaces reachable only through transit providers. By adding the IXP that reduces this metric the most, we iteratively expand the set of reached IXPs. Figure 10 plots the number of IP interfaces reachable only through transit providers as the number of reached IXPs increases. Without reaching any IXP, around 2.6 billion IP interfaces are reachable through the transit hierarchy. For peer group 4 (all policies), the number of IP interfaces reachable only through transit providers decreases to about 1 billion after reaching the first IXP. The marginal utility of reaching an extra IXP declines with any of the 4 peer groups. Figures 9 and 10 show that this decline is qualitatively consistent with the exponentially diminishing pattern in the above RedIRIS traffic study. Note that the generalized result for the metric of reachable IP interfaces does not depend on particulars of RedIRIS or another network.

5. ECONOMIC VIABILITY

While section 4 exposes the significant offload potential of remote peering and diminishing marginal utility of reaching an extra IXP, we now generalize the empirical results in the mathematical model and derive conditions for economic viability of remote peering versus transit and direct peering.

5.1 Model

In our model, a network delivers its global traffic via 3 options: (1) transit, (2) expansion of its own infrastructure for direct peering at n IXPs, and (3) remote peering at m IXPs. The respective traffic fractions are denoted as t, d, and r:

$$t + d + r = 1. \tag{1}$$

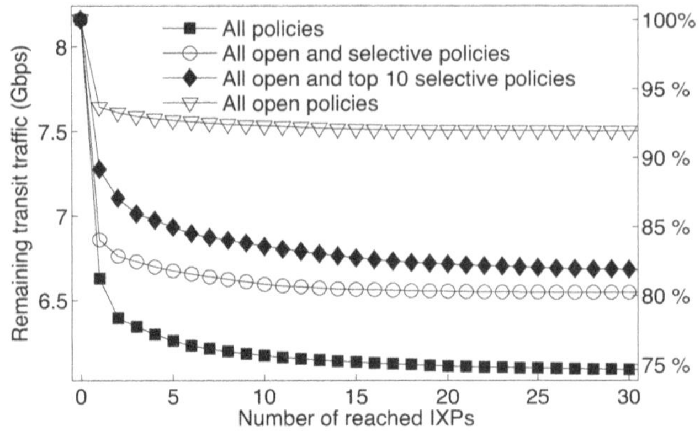

Figure 9: Additional value for RedIRIS to reach an extra IXP

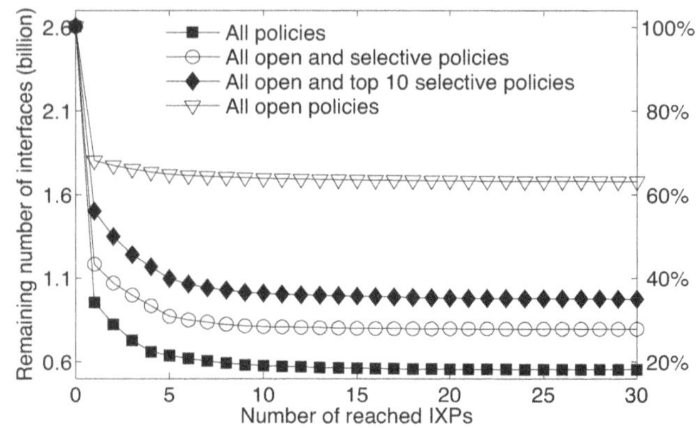

Figure 10: Generalized additional value of reaching an extra IXP

Total cost C of the traffic delivery consists of transit, direct-peering, and remote-peering components C_t, C_d, and C_r:

$$C = C_t + C_d + C_r. \tag{2}$$

While section 4.3 shows diminishing marginal utility of reaching one more IXP, we fit the RedIRIS data to exponential decay and model the transit traffic fraction as the following function of the number of IXPs where the network peers either directly or remotely:

$$t = e^{-b\cdot(n+m)}. \tag{3}$$

Equality 3 generalizes our empirical results via parameter b that controls how quickly the transit traffic fraction declines. While $b = 0$ represents networks that cannot reduce its transit traffic by peering at distant IXPs, $b = \infty$ enables offload of all transit traffic by reaching a single IXP. Low values of b are characteristic for networks with mostly global traffic, e.g., Google and other networks with highly distributed traffic. The results in figure 4a suggest that networks with high b values are more common. With parameter p denoting the normalized transit price, we model the transit cost as

$$C_t = p \cdot t = p \cdot e^{-b\cdot(n+m)}. \tag{4}$$

The direct-peering cost depends on both the number of reached IXPs and traffic delivered through them:

$$C_d = g \cdot n + u \cdot d. \tag{5}$$

While parameter g accounts for membership fees and other traffic-independent costs of the network in the distant IXPs, parameter u reflects traffic-dependent costs.

The remote-peering cost has a similar structure with traffic-independent parameter h and traffic-dependent parameter v:

$$C_r = h \cdot m + v \cdot r. \tag{6}$$

According to section 2, the per-IXP traffic-independent cost for remote peering is lower than for direct peering:

$$h < g, \tag{7}$$

and the per-unit traffic-dependent cost for remote peering is larger than for direct peering but smaller than for transit:

$$u < v < p. \tag{8}$$

Combining equalities 2, 4, 5, and 6, we express the total traffic-delivery cost of the network as

$$C = p \cdot e^{-b\cdot(n+m)} + g \cdot n + u \cdot d + h \cdot m + v \cdot r. \tag{9}$$

5.2 Analysis

Seeking to minimize its total cost, the network might first consider only transit and direct peering at distant IXPs without purchase of remote peering, i.e., $m = 0$ and $r = 0$. Under this strategy, the total cost is

$$C = (p - u) \cdot e^{-b\cdot n} + u + g \cdot n, \tag{10}$$

and the network minimizes the cost by reaching $\tilde{n}$ IXPs to offload traffic fraction $\tilde{d}$ via direct peering:

$$\tilde{n} = \frac{\log\left(\frac{b\cdot(p-u)}{g}\right)}{b} \text{ and } \tilde{d} = 1 - e^{-b\cdot\tilde{n}}. \tag{11}$$

Continuing from the above solution, the network might widen its strategy to include remote peering, with the total cost becoming

$$C = (p - v) \cdot e^{-b\cdot(\tilde{n}+m)} + (v - u) \cdot e^{-b\cdot\tilde{n}} + g \cdot \tilde{n} + u + h \cdot m. \tag{12}$$

The network minimizes the cost in equality 12 by remote peering at $\tilde{m}$ extra IXPs:

$$\tilde{m} = \frac{\log\left(\frac{g\cdot(p-v)}{h\cdot(p-u)}\right)}{b}, \tag{13}$$

Inequality $\tilde{m} \geq 1$ means that remote peering at one or more IXPs reduces the total cost. Thus, we establish the following condition for economic viability of remote peering:

$$\frac{g \cdot (p - v)}{h \cdot (p - u)} \geq e^b. \tag{14}$$

The economic viability condition in inequality 14 implies that remote peering is more viable for networks with lower b values, i.e., networks with global traffic. Google, major content providers, and other networks with large volumes of global traffic can afford extending their own infrastructures to peer directly at distant IXPs. By realizing this potential for direct peering, the networks with large-volume global traffic contribute to Internet flattening. For such networks, remote peering is just an extra option for bypassing their transit providers. On the other hand, there are also networks with global traffic that is too small in volume to justify the costs of extending their own infrastructures. Invitel and E4A are examples of such networks. For networks with small-volume global traffic, remote peering constitutes the only economically viable opportunity to reach and peer at distant IXPs. By taking the opportunity to buy the services of remote-peering providers, the networks with small volumes of global traffic increase the extent of peering in the Internet without necessarily making the Internet flatter.

The economic viability condition contains g/h, i.e., the ratio of the per-IXP traffic-independent costs for direct and remote peering. In regions such as Africa, h tends to be much smaller than g because local IXPs offer little opportunities to offload traffic, and transit is expensive [33]. Thus, our analytical model explains why remote peering is economically attractive for African networks. A comprehensive validation of the economic viability model and its implications represents an interesting topic for future work.

6. DISCUSSION

The trends toward more peering and Internet flattening are typically conflated because direct peering interconnections bypass transit providers and thereby reduce the number of intermediary organizations on Internet paths. Complementing direct peering, remote peering enables additional peering as well. However, this increase in peering involves a remote-peering provider that acts as a middleman. Furthermore, the intermediary that sells the remote-peering service can be the same company that provided the bypassed transit services. Hence, remote peering increases peering without necessarily flattening the Internet economic structure.

The observed separation of the two trends questions the usage of AS-level topologies for representing the Internet economic structure. With remote-peering services provided on layer 2, layer-3 modeling of the Internet structure fails to distinguish remote peering from direct peering and ignores the intermediary presence of remote-peering providers. Below, we elaborate on various dangers posed by this omission of the intermediary economic entities.

Layer-3 topologies can make the Internet structure look more reliable than it is. When a company employs the same physical infrastructure to provide transit and remote-peering services, buying both might not translate the redundancy into higher reliability for the multihomed customers.

The emergence of remote peering makes AS-level paths even less representative of the underlying physical paths. The hidden presence of layer-2 remote-peering infrastructures in layer-3 paths creates an additional reason why a path with the smallest number of ASes does not necessary provide the shortest delay of data delivery.

While it is common to use AS-level models for reasoning about Internet security, the hidden presence of layer-2 intermediaries adds to existing security concerns. The invisible intermediaries might be unwanted entities, e.g., those associated with problematic governments. The risks include monitoring or modification of traffic by the intermediaries and exposure of traffic to other parties, e.g., by delivering it through undesired geographies.

The reliance on layer-3 models also compromises accountability. Whereas a layer-2 intermediary might delay or discard traffic, attribution of responsibility for such performance disruptions is complicated because the middleman is invisible on layer 3.

Because remote peering has different economics than transit and direct peering, the omission of the layer-2 intermediaries from layer-3 models weakens economic understanding of the Internet. In developing markets such as Africa, remote peering becomes a cost-effective alternative for reaching well-connected areas in Europe and North America [33]. Since remote peering has a smaller connectivity scope than transit, adoption of remote peering necessitates new strategies for traffic distribution. IXPs greatly benefit from remote peering: existing IXPs gain members, and new IXPs are enabled by bringing together a critical mass of traffic [44]. Ignoring the remote-peering providers distorts substantially the Internet economic landscape.

Thus, our results call for alternative models of the Internet structure that explicitly represent layer-2 entities. The relevant additions include not only remote-peering providers but also other layer-2 economic entities such as IXPs. With the growing prominence of IXPs and remote-peering connectivity to them, integrated modeling of the Internet structure on layers 2 and 3 becomes increasingly important for understanding the Internet. The refined mapping of the Internet economic structure will likely require novel methods for inference of economic entities and their relationships [27].

7. RELATED WORK

The Internet structure is highly important for network accountability [4], multihoming [2], routing security [32], traffic delivery economics [10,11], and various problems in content delivery via overlay systems [14,26,36,38,40,47,50,63,67]. By clarifying the Internet structure, our study of remote peering enables further advances in these and other significant practical domains.

Because network operators do not publicly disclose connectivity of their networks, the research community relies on measurements and inference to characterize the Internet structure [34]. A prominent means for the topology discovery is the traceroute tool that exposes routers on IP delivery paths [19,22]. For example, iPlane [48] and Hubble [39] use traceroute to generate and maintain annotated Internet maps. Paris traceroute enhances traceroute with the ability to discover multiple paths [7]. A complementary approach is to utilize BGP traces [5,30,35,61,64]. Our work employs active probing in the data plane to understand the role of remote peering in the Internet structure.

Delay measurements are common in Internet studies, e.g., to understand evolution of Internet delay properties [42] or Internet penetration into developing regions [33]. Our paper uses delay measurements to investigate how geography affects peering of networks.

While previous research studies only mention remote peering [1,21,33,54,60], our paper is the first to closely examine this emerging type of network interconnection. Our results show wide spread, significant traffic offload potential, and conditions for economic viability of remote peering.

The Internet structural evolution [46] changes the dominant sources of traffic [23] and diversifies network types and their interconnection arrangements [17,18,29]. For example, partial transit [65] and paid peering [24] complement the dominant relationships of transit and peering. Our study of remote peering confirms the trend toward diversification of interconnection types.

The arguments that the Internet structure becomes flatter are multifaceted [24, 31, 41], with the continued growth of IXPs [1, 16, 60] cited in support of this trend. Our work reveals separation between the trends of increasing peering and Internet flattening. Also, while analyses of interconnection options are typically restricted to networks that share a location [20, 59], our work exhibits remote peering as a cost-effective solution that enables distant networks to peer over a layer-2 intermediary.

With our results showing the increasing opaqueness of the Internet structure from layer-3 perspectives, the opaqueness is likely to increase further with adoption of software-defined networking [9]. Our paper calls for new approaches to mapping the Internet economic structure on both layers 2 and 3.

8. CONCLUSION

The paper presented the first empirical and analytical study on remote peering. Using careful measurements of RTTs at 22 IXPs worldwide, our ping-based method exposed wide spread of remote peering, with remote peering in more than 90% of the examined IXPs and peering on the intercontinental scale in a majority of them. Based on ground truth from RedIRIS, we also estimated how much transit-provider traffic the network can offload via remote peering when the number of reached IXPs varies from 1 to 65. The assessment showed a significant traffic offload potential around 25% in some cases. While the results exhibited diminishing marginal utility of reaching an extra IXP, reaching only 5 IXPs realized most of the overall offload potential. After generalizing the diminishing marginal utility in the mathematical model, we derived conditions for economic viability of remote peering versus transit and direct peering.

While important in itself as an emerging factor in the Internet ecosystem, remote peering was argued to have broader implications for Internet research. Remote peering revealed separation between the commonly conflated trends of increasing peering and Internet flattening. With remote peering provided on layer 2, we discussed why the omission of remote-peering providers from traditional layer-3 representations of the Internet topology compromised research on Internet reliability, security, accountability, and economics. Finally, we called for refined modeling of the Internet economic structure on both layers 2 and 3.

9. ACKNOWLEDGMENTS

We are grateful to RedIRIS for the access to its traffic data. We also thank TorIX and Jon Nistor for their help in validating our RTT measurements. This research was financially supported in part by the European Commission (FP7-ICT 288021, EINS), Spanish Ministry of Science and Innovation (RYC-2009-04660), and Cisco Systems (CG 573362).

10. REFERENCES

[1] B. Ager, N. Chatzis, A. Feldmann, N. Sarrar, S. Uhlig, and W. Willinger. Anatomy of a Large European IXP. In *Proc. SIGCOMM*, 2012.

[2] A. Akella, B. Maggs, S. Seshan, A. Shaikh, and R. Sitaraman. A Measurement-based Analysis of Multihoming. In *Proc. SIGCOMM*, 2003.

[3] Amsterdam Internet Exchange (AMS-IX). `https://www.ams-ix.net`.

[4] D. G. Andersen, H. Balakrishnan, N. Feamster, T. Koponen, D. Moon, and S. Shenker. Accountable Internet Protocol (AIP). In *Proc. SIGCOMM*, 2008.

[5] D. G. Andersen, N. Feamster, S. Bauer, and H. Balakrishnan. Topology Inference from BGP Routing Dynamics. In *Proc. IMC*, 2002.

[6] Atrato IP Networks. `https://www.atrato.com`.

[7] B. Augustin, X. Cuvellier, B. Orgogozo, F. Viger, T. Friedman, M. Latapy, C. Magnien, and R. Teixeira. Avoiding Traceroute Anomalies with Paris Traceroute. In *Proc. SIGCOMM*, 2006.

[8] B. Augustin, B. Krishnamurthy, and W. Willinger. IXPs: Mapped? In *Proc. SIGCOMM*, 2009.

[9] J. Bailey, R. Clark, N. Feamster, D. Levin, J. Rexford, and S. Shenker. SDX: A Software Defined Internet Exchange. In *Proc. SIGCOMM*, 2014.

[10] P. Bangera and S. Gorinsky. Impact of Prefix Hijacking on Payments of Providers. In *Proc. COMSNETS*, 2011.

[11] P. Bangera and S. Gorinsky. Economics of Traffic Attraction by Transit Providers. In *Proc. Networking*, 2014.

[12] S. Biernacki. Remote Peering at IXPs. EURONOG 1 presentation, 2011.

[13] M. Calder, X. Fan, Z. Hu, E. Katz-Bassett, J. Heidemann, and R. Govindan. Mapping the Expansion of Google's Serving Infrastructure. In *Proc. IMC*, 2013.

[14] F. Cantin, B. Gueye, D. Kaafar, and G. Leduc. Overlay Routing Using Coordinate Systems. In *Proc. CoNEXT*, 2008.

[15] J. C. Cardona and R. Stanojevic. A History of an Internet eXchange Point. *CCR*, 2012.

[16] J. C. Cardona and R. Stanojevic. IXP Traffic: A Macroscopic View. In *Proc. LANC*, 2012.

[17] I. Castro and S. Gorinsky. T4P: Hybrid Interconnection for Cost Reduction. In *Proc. NetEcon*, 2012.

[18] I. Castro, R. Stanojevic, and S. Gorinsky. Using Tuangou to Reduce IP Transit Costs. *ToN*, in press, 2014.

[19] H. Chang, S. Jamin, and W. Willinger. Inferring AS-level Internet Topology from Router-Level Path Traces. In *Proc. ITCOM*, 2001.

[20] H. Chang, S. Jamin, and W. Willinger. To Peer or Not to Peer: Modeling the Evolution of the Internet AS-level Topology. In *Proc. INFOCOM*, 2006.

[21] N. Chatzis, G. Smaragdakis, A. Feldmann, and W. Willinger. There Is More to IXPs than Meets the Eye. *CCR*, 2013.

[22] K. Chen, D. R. Choffnes, R. Potharaju, Y. Chen, F. E. Bustamante, D. Pei, and Y. Zhao. Where the Sidewalk Ends: Extending the Internet AS Graph Using Traceroutes from P2P Users. In *Proc. CoNEXT*, 2009.

[23] K. Cho, K. Fukuda, H. Esaki, and A. Kato. Observing Slow Crustal Movement in Residential User Traffic. In *Proc. CoNEXT*, 2008.

[24] A. Dhamdhere and C. Dovrolis. The Internet is Flat: Modeling the Transition from a Transit Hierarchy to a Peering Mesh. In *Proc. CoNEXT*, 2010.

[25] X. Dimitropoulos, P. Hurley, A. Kind, and M. Stoecklin. On the 95-percentile Billing Method. In *Proc. PAM*, 2009.

[26] Z. Duan, Z.-L. Zhang, and Y. T. Hou. Service Overlay Networks: SLAs, QoS, and Bandwidth Provisioning. *ToN*, 2003.

[27] R. Durairajan, J. Sommers, and P. Barford. Layer 1-Informed Internet Topology Measurement. In *Proc. IMC*, 2014.

[28] Euro-IX. `https://www.euro-ix.net`.

[29] P. Faratin, D. Clark, P. Gilmore, S. Bauer, A. Berger, and W. Lehr. Complexity of Internet Interconnections: Technology, Incentives and Implications for Policy. In *Proc. TPRC*, 2007.

[30] L. Gao. On Inferring Autonomous System Relationships in the Internet. *ToN*, 2001.

[31] P. Gill, M. Arlitt, Z. Li, and A. Mahanti. The Flattening Internet Topology: Natural Evolution, Unsightly Barnacles or Contrived Collapse? In *Proc. PAM*, 2008.

[32] P. Gill, M. Schapira, and S. Goldberg. Let the Market Drive Deployment: A Strategy for Transitioning to BGP Security. In *Proc. SIGCOMM*, 2011.

[33] A. Gupta, M. Calder, N. Feamster, M. Chetty, E. Calandro, and E. Katz-Bassett. Peering at the Internet's Frontier: A First Look at ISP Interconnectivity in Africa. In *Proc. PAM*, 2014.

[34] H. Haddadi, M. Rio, G. Iannaccone, A. Moore, and R. Mortier. Network Topologies: Inference, Modeling, and Generation. *Communications Surveys & Tutorials*, 2008.

[35] S. Hasan and S. Gorinsky. Obscure Giants: Detecting the Provider-free ASes. In *Proc. Networking*, 2012.

[36] S. Hasan, S. Gorinsky, C. Dovrolis, and R. Sitaraman. Trade-offs in Optimizing the Cache Deployments of CDNs. In *Proc. INFOCOM*, 2014.

[37] IX Reach. `http://www.ixreach.com`.

[38] W. Jiang, S. Ioannidis, L. Massoulié, and F. Picconi. Orchestrating Massively Distributed CDNs. In *Proc. CoNEXT*, 2012.

[39] E. Katz-Bassett, H. V. Madhyastha, J. P. John, A. Krishnamurthy, D. Wetherall, and T. E. Anderson. Studying Black Holes in the Internet with Hubble. In *Proc. NSDI*, 2008.

[40] R. Keralapura, N. Taft, C.-N. Chuah, and G. Iannaccone. Can ISPs Take the Heat from Overlay Networks. In *Proc. HotNets*, 2004.

[41] C. Labovitz, S. Iekel-Johnson, D. McPherson, J. Oberheide, and F. Jahanian. Internet Inter-domain Traffic. In *Proc. SIGCOMM*, 2010.

[42] D. Lee, K. Cho, G. Iannaccone, and S. Moon. Has Internet Delay Gotten Better or Worse? In *Proc. CFI*, 2010.

[43] London Internet Exchange (LINX). `https://www.linx.net`.

[44] LINX NoVA. `https://www.linx.net/service/publicpeering/nova`.

[45] A. Lodhi, N. Larson, A. Dhamdhere, C. Dovrolis, and K. Claffy. Using PeeringDB to Understand the Peering Ecosystem. *CCR*, 2014.

[46] R. Ma, J. Lui, and V. Misra. On the Evolution of the Internet Economic Ecosystem. In *Proc. WWW*, 2013.

[47] H. V. Madhyastha, T. Anderson, A. Krishnamurthy, N. Spring, and A. Venkataramani. A Structural Approach to Latency Prediction. In *Proc. IMC*, 2006.

[48] H. V. Madhyastha, T. Isdal, M. Piatek, C. Dixon, T. Anderson, A. Krishnamurthy, and A. Venkataramani. iPlane: An Information Plane for Distributed Services. In *Proc. OSDI*, 2006.

[49] D. Madory. "Crecimiento" in Latin America. Renesys Blog, 2013.

[50] V. Misra, S. Ioannidis, A. Chaintreau, and L. Massoulié. Incentivizing Peer-Assisted Services: a Fluid Shapley Value Approach. In *Proc. SIGMETRICS*, 2010.

[51] Packet Clearing House. `https://www.pch.net`.

[52] Peering Database. `https://www.peeringdb.com`.

[53] J. Postel. Internet Protocol DARPA Internet Program Protocol Specification. RFC 791, 1981.

[54] A. H. Rasti, N. Magharei, R. Rejaie, and W. Willinger. Eyeball ASes: from Geography to Connectivity. In *Proc. IMC*, 2010.

[55] Y. Rekhter and T. Li. A Border Gateway Protocol 4 (BGP-4). RFC 1771, 1995.

[56] Remote Peering Data. `https://svnext.networks.imdea.org/repos/RemotePeering`.

[57] Réseaux IP Europèns Network Coordination Centre (RIPE NCC). `http://www.ris.ripe.net/cgi-bin/lg/index.cgi`.

[58] P. Richter, G. Smaragdakis, A. Feldmann, N. Chatzis, J. Boettger, and W. Willinger. Peering at Peerings: On the Role of IXP Route Servers. In *Proc. IMC*, 2014.

[59] S. Shakkottai and R. Srikant. Economics of Network Pricing with Multiple ISPs. *ToN*, 2006.

[60] J. H. Sowell. Empirical Studies of Bottom-Up Internet Governance. In *Proc. TPRC*, 2012.

[61] N. Spring, R. Mahajan, D. Wetherall, and T. Anderson. Measuring ISP Topologies with Rocketfuel. *ToN*, 2004.

[62] R. Stanojevic, N. Laoutaris, and P. Rodriguez. On Economic Heavy Hitters: Shapley Value Analysis of 95th-percentile Pricing. In *Proc. IMC*, 2010.

[63] A.-J. Su, D. R. Choffnes, A. Kuzmanovic, and F. E. Bustamante. Drafting Behind Akamai: Inferring Network Conditions Based on CDN Redirections. *ToN*, 2009.

[64] L. Subramanian, S. Agarwal, J. Rexford, and R. Katz. Characterizing the Internet Hierarchy from Multiple Vantage Points. In *Proc. INFOCOM*, 2002.

[65] V. Valancius, C. Lumezanu, N. Feamster, R. Johari, and V. Vazirani. How Many Tiers? Pricing in the Internet Transit Market. In *Proc. SIGCOMM*, 2011.

[66] H. Wang, C. Jin, and K. G. Shin. Defense Against Spoofed IP Traffic Using Hop-count Filtering. *ToN*, 2007.

[67] M. Yu, W. Jiang, H. Li, and I. Stoica. Tradeoffs in CDN Designs for Throughput Oriented Traffic. In *Proc. of CoNEXT*, 2012.

Tango: Simplifying SDN Control with Automatic Switch Property Inference, Abstraction, and Optimization

Aggelos Lazaris[+] Daniel Tahara[×]
Xin Huang[⋆] Li Erran Li[†] Andreas Voellmy[×] Y. Richard Yang[•×] Minlan Yu[+]
[†]Bell Labs, Alcatel-Lucent [⋆]Cyan Inc. [+]USC [•]Tongji University [×]Yale University

ABSTRACT

A major benefit of software-defined networking (SDN) over traditional networking is simpler and easier control of network devices. The diversity of SDN switch implementation properties, which include both diverse switch hardware capabilities and diverse control-plane software behaviors, however, can make it difficult to understand and/or to control the switches in an SDN network. In this paper, we present Tango, a novel framework to explore the issues of understanding and optimization of SDN control, in the presence of switch diversity. The basic idea of Tango is novel, simple, and yet quite powerful. In particular, different from all previous SDN control systems, which either ignore switch diversity or depend on that switches can and will report diverse switch implementation properties, Tango introduces a novel, proactive probing engine that infers key switch capabilities and behaviors, according to a well-structured set of Tango patterns, where a Tango pattern consists of a sequence of standard OpenFlow commands and a corresponding data traffic pattern. Utilizing the inference results from Tango patterns and additional application API hints, Tango conducts automatic switch control optimization, despite diverse switch capabilities and behaviors. Evaluating Tango on both hardware switches and emulated software switches, we show that Tango can infer flow table sizes, which are key switch implementation properties, within less than 5% of actual values, despite diverse switch caching algorithms, using a probing algorithm that is asymptotically optimal in terms of probing overhead. We demonstrate cases where routing and scheduling optimizations based on Tango improves the rule installation time by up to 70% in our hardware switch testbed.

Categories and Subject Descriptors

C.2.1 [**Computer-Communication Networks**]: Network Architecture and Design—*Packet switching networks*; C.2.3 [**Computer-Communication Networks**]: Network Operations—*Network Management*

Keywords

Software-defined Networking; OpenFlow; Switch Diversity

CoNEXT'14, December 2–5, 2014, Sydney, Australia.
Copyright 2014 ACM 978-1-4503-3279-8/14/12 ...$15.00.
http://dx.doi.org/10.1145/2674005.2675011 .

1. INTRODUCTION

A major benefit of software-defined networking (SDN) over traditional networking is simpler and easier control of network switches. In particular, OpenFlow [11] has provided a standard, centralized mechanism for a network controller to install forwarding rules at the forwarding engines (called flow tables) of a heterogeneous set of network switches, substantially reducing controller-switch dependency, and hence control programming complexity.

One key issue that such a standard controller-switch protocol cannot resolve, however, is the diversity of switch implementation properties, which we define to include both hardware capabilities and control software behaviors. In particular, the hardware of switches can have significant differences in their physical structures such as TCAM size, which significantly affects forwarding throughput over large sets of rules; the software implementing the control of switches can differ substantially as well, such as in their TCAM management algorithms and flow installation efficiency. Since such diversity reflects many factors, including real-life, random, idiosyncratic designs as well as systematic switch vendor engineering exploration (which can be essential to foster switch vendor innovation), it is inconceivable that all switches will have the same hardware capabilities and software behaviors.

The presence of SDN switch diversity can pose significant challenges in the control of SDN switches. In particular, we identify two challenges. First, diversity creates an understanding challenge. Although newer versions of OpenFlow [16] allow switches to report configurations and capabilities (called features), the reports can be inaccurate. For example, the maximum number of flow entries that can be inserted is approximate and depends on the matching fields (*e.g.*, IPv4 vs. IPv6). Furthermore, many important configurations and behaviors are not reported, for example, whether a switch uses a software flow table and the caching policy that determines when a rule should be in the software flow table or TCAM.

Second, diversity can create a substantial utilization challenge, which can lead to control programming complexity. For example, consider two switches with the same TCAM size, but one adds a software flow table on top. Then, insertion of the same sequence of rules may result in a rejection in one switch (TCAM full), but unexpected low throughput in the other (ended up in the software flow table). Now consider that the two switches have the same TCAM and software flow table sizes, but they introduce different cache replacement algorithms on TCAM: one uses FIFO while the other is traffic dependent. Then, insertion of the same sequence of rules may again produce different configurations of flow tables entries: which rules will be in the TCAM will be switch dependent. Whether a rule is in TCAM, however, can have a significant impact on its throughput, and therefore quality of service (QoS).

In this paper, we design Tango, a novel approach to explore the issues of SDN control in the presence of switch implementation diversity. Tango addresses both the understanding challenge and the utilization challenge.

The basic idea of Tango is novel, simple, and yet quite powerful. In particular, different from all previous SDN programming systems, which ignore switch diversity or at most simply receive reports of switch features (in newer version of OpenFlow), Tango is designed with the observation that instead of depending on switch reports, one can use real measurements to achieve better understanding of switch diversity. Based on this observation, Tango introduces a novel, proactive probing engine that measures key properties of each switch according to a well-structured set of *Tango patterns*. Each Tango pattern consists of a sequence of standard OpenFlow flow modification commands and a corresponding data traffic pattern, based on the general knowledge of the switch architecture. For example, a Tango switch TCAM capacity discovery pattern sends data packets matching the inserted rules. If Tango detects larger delay of the packets for newly installed rules, Tango has detected the TCAM size.

Utilizing the measurement results from the Tango patterns, Tango derives switch capabilities as well as the costs of a set of equivalent operations that can be utilized, through *expression rewriting*, to optimize networks with diverse capabilities and behaviors. For example, the Tango priority pattern inserts a sequence of rules in ascending priority and descending priority in two separate tests. In the hardware switch we tested, Tango records that the descending pattern has a substantially longer latency than that of the ascending pattern. The difference is about 6 fold if Tango priority pattern has 5,000 rules. The Tango scheduling algorithm automatically exploits these Tango patterns. Therefore, if Tango has 5,000 rules to install on the hardware switch, it will write the sequence in the ascending order to achieve low rule installation latency. Second, comparing across switches, Tango records that insertion into the flow table of the hardware switch is substantially slower than into that of the software switch. Hence, when Tango needs to install a low-bandwidth flow where start up latency is more important, Tango will put the flow at the software switch, instead of the hardware switch.

We use both experiments on three types of hardware switches and simulations with Open vSwitch (OVS) to evaluate Tango. Tango inference engine is highly accurate. In particular, our inference accuracy of flow table size is with 5% of actual value. For a real switch, Tango can reduce rule installation time by a factor of 12.

We emphasize that despite the progress made by Tango, its scope is still limited, focusing mainly on performance. Additional switch diversities, such as ability to provide different functionalities, remain to be explored.

The remainder of this paper is organized as follows: Section 3 motivates our work by first examining standard switch architecture and then proceeding to explore the diversity of their implementation. Section 4, 5, and 6 provide a concrete specification for the Tango system, the inference process used by the Tango controller to understand the switch diversity, and an example Tango scheduler. We provide evaluations of our inference algorithms and performance optimizations in Section 7, explore related work in Section 8, and conclude in Section 9.

2. BACKGROUND: TYPICAL SWITCH ARCHITECTURE

We start with some background on a typical architecture of switches that implement the OpenFlow specification, which is the key SDN controller-switch protocol. The OpenFlow specification only defines an interface between a controller and a switch supporting OpenFlow. It leaves switch vendors the freedom to implement the internals in their convenient ways and perform optimizations, as long as the rule matching and traffic processing semantics are preserved. As a result, switches can have diverse implementations in their software layers and on how much they leverage the hardware interfaces. Such diversity leads to varying switch behavior and performance, both on the control plane and the data plane. In this paper, we use three proprietary switches from three vendors as both examples and evaluation targets. We refer to these three vendors as Vendor #1, Vendor #2, and Vendor #3; their switches as Switch #1, Switch #2, and Switch #3 respectively.

Figure 1 illustrates the architecture of an OpenFlow enabled hardware switch. It usually includes three key components:

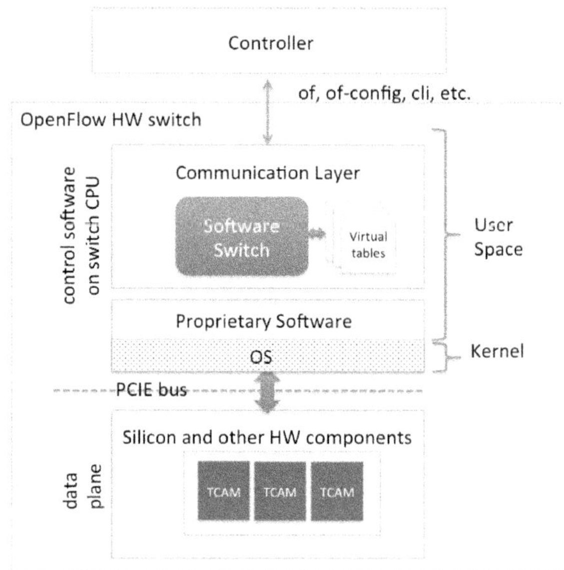

Figure 1: OpenFlow switch software stack architecture.

Communication Layer: This layer is responsible for the communication between the switch and remote controllers. It consists of software agents supporting standard network programming and management protocols such as OpenFlow, OF-CONFIG, and SNMP. Most vendors use the OVS (Open vSwitch [17]) userspace code as the OpenFlow agent, and then perform vendor-specific extensions to better match OVS to their platform design. This is where interesting things happen and we will get back to this topic in details at the end of this section.

Proprietary Layer: Below the communication layer is the proprietary layer, in which a vendor provides its own software to translate from the platform independent model (*e.g.*, OpenFlow model) to platform specific commands and configurations. This layer includes components such as line card manager, driver, and vendor SDK. The proprietary layer obtains access to the switch hardware via switch OS. Similar to a computer system, switch OS is responsible for managing switch hardware resources (*e.g.*, switching ASIC, TCAM, and Bus) as well as the communications among software layers and modules (*e.g.*, between OVS and proprietary software).

Although there are proposals on developing and open sourcing generic an OpenFlow hardware abstraction layer (HAL) across heterogeneous switching platforms [22], these projects are still at very early stage. Today, the proprietary software is still mainly developed and maintained by individual switch vendors.

TCAM and Switch Hardware: Modern switch silicon consists of multiple physical tables (*e.g.*, L2 MAC table, L3 LPM table, and TCAM) that are shared among multiple pipeline stages along the fast path packet processing. Although potentially all these tables could be used as OpenFlow flow tables, so far most switch vendors appear to have leveraged only TCAM. Even for switches (*e.g.*, Switch 1 in this paper) that support OpenFlow 1.1 and higher, the multiple tables in OpenFlow pipelines are mostly implemented in switch software. Only entries belong to a single table are eligible to be chosen and pushed into TCAM.

As described above, vendor-specific implementations usually happen at the communication layer or the proprietary layer. For example, Switch 1 maintains multiple virtual tables in user space and uses a certain algorithm to figure out which entries should be pushed down to TCAM and when. Both tables could be used for packet forwarding. TCAM facilitates fast path packet forwarding and virtual tables are used for slow path packet forwarding. Only packets that hit neither of the tables will be sent to the controller. Switch 2 chooses to have the TCAM table as the only flow table. That is, packets that are able to match TCAM entries will be forwarded in the fast path. All other packets will be forwarded to the controller. Switch 1 can afford more rules than the number of entries that can be held in TCAM, but traffic processed in slow path will suffer from longer delay and less throughput. As a contrast, the number of entries that can be supported on Switch 2 is limited by the on-board TCAM but all matching packets will be guaranteed to go through fast path and be forwarded in line rate.

At the proprietary layer, vendors often have different switch software stack designs (*e.g.*, multi-threaded vs. single-threaded processing, synchronous vs. asynchronous message passing, memory hierarchy and management, data sharing mechanism). All these design and implementation details could potentially impact OpenFlow control channel performance (e.g., OpenFlow packet generation and processing rate) or the slow path packet-processing rate. At the same time, vendors are also left with the freedom to perform optimization for OpenFlow (*e.g.*, putting user space virtual tables into the kernel, taking advantage of DMA to remove switch CPU from critical packet processing pipeline).

All these variations contribute to the varying performance and behavior of the OpenFlow hardware switches. We will take a closer look at a few key performance and behavior differences in the next section using real experimental results.

3. SWITCH DIVERSITY: EXAMPLES

Despite the fact that many switches use the typical architecture presented in the preceding section, their details differ substantially, and such differences can have large impacts.

Diverse flow installation behaviors: For OpenFlow switches that maintain more than one table, switch vendors must implement algorithms to manage the assignment of flow entries to different flow tables, and maintain certain mapping between the tables. This is totally vendor dependent.

For example, OVS based software switch makes decision based on data plane traffic. Whenever a flow entry is pushed down to the switch, it first gets installed in the user space software table. Only when data plane traffic matches this entry, an exact match entry will be pushed to the kernel table [17]. This explains the three-tier delay in Figure 2(a). In this experiment, we first install 80 non-overlapping OpenFlow entries. Then, we start generating 160 data plane flows, with 2 packets per flow, and measure the delay. Among

Switch	**user space software tables**		**TCAM/kernel tables**	
	L2/L3	L2+L3	L2/L3	L2+L3
OVS	$< \infty$	$< \infty$	$< \infty$	$< \infty$
Switch #1	$< \infty$	$< \infty$	4K	2K
Switch #2	None	None	2560	2560
Switch #3	None	None	767	369

Table 1: Diversity of tables and table sizes.

the 160 flows, the first 80 match the existing entries, while the rest do not. Since the entries are installed in user space table only, the first packet of any flow will not match any kernel table entry, and thus will be forwarded one level up, to the user space table (i.e., slow path). It will then match an entry in the user space table, get processed and forwarded to the right output port. At the same time, an exact match entry will be installed in kernel so that the following packets belongs to the same flow (i.e., the second packet) will be processed in the fast path. Flows that do not match any existing entries will be forwarded and processed by the controller. Thus, three levels of delay are shown in the plot: fast path and slow path for the first 80 flows, and control path for rest of the flows. OVS uses this simple 1-to-N mapping (i.e., one user space entry could map to multiple kernel space entries) between the two tables. There are more complex caching algorithms proposed [7].

In contrast, the software table in Switch #1 works as a FIFO buffer for TCAM. That is, the oldest entry in the software table will be pushed into TCAM whenever an empty slot is available. This is observed in Figure 2(b). In this experiment, we first install 3500 non-overlapping flow entries. Then we generate a total more than 5000 data plane flows (again, two packets per flow) and make the first 3500 flows match installed entries. Again, we observe three-tier delays, but there is no delay difference between the first packet and the second packet of a particular flow. This indicates that unlike the OVS case, flow entry allocation here is independent of the traffic. The first 2047 flows have much shorter delay than rest of the flows. This means the first 2047 entries (there is an default route pre-installed when switches get connected with controllers) are installed in TCAM and the corresponding flows are forwarded through fast path. The rest entries reside in user-space software table(s), and thus the corresponding flows are forwarded through slow path. When a flow does not match any of the existing flow entries, it will be forwarded to controller and get processed there. Although FIFO is simple, it may lead to policy violation problem [7] when there are overlapping entries in both tables and the higher priority ones are in software tables.

Switch #2 only has one table (TCAM). It corresponds to the two-tier delay in Figure 2(c) . Flows matching TCAM entries are forwarded in fast path, while flows matching no TCAM entries will be forwarded and processed by controller at control path.

Diverse flow tables and table sizes: Although all switches must expose flow tables as their forwarding engine model to the controller, per OpenFlow specifications, different switches may map this model to different tables. In particular, we can identify three types of tables: user space software table, kernel software table, and TCAM hardware table. Table 1 shows the types of flow tables of four OpenFlow switches, including an OVS based software switch and three HW switches from different vendors that cover a variety of switch implementations.

As shown in Table 1, OVS maintains software tables in both user space and kernel space. Switch #1 has both a hardware table implemented in TCAM, and can support 256 virtual tables in the user space. In contrast, switches 2 and 3 have only TCAM tables, but no software tables.

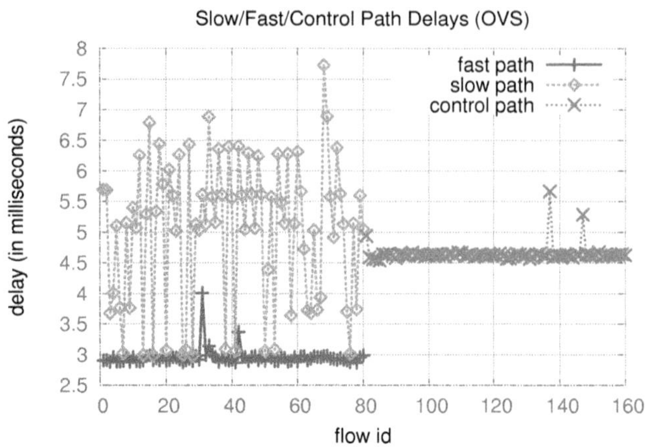

(a) Three tier delay in OVS.

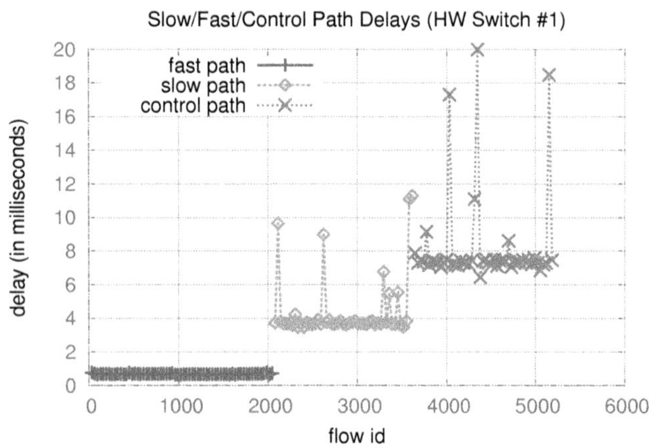

(b) Three tier delay in Switch #1.

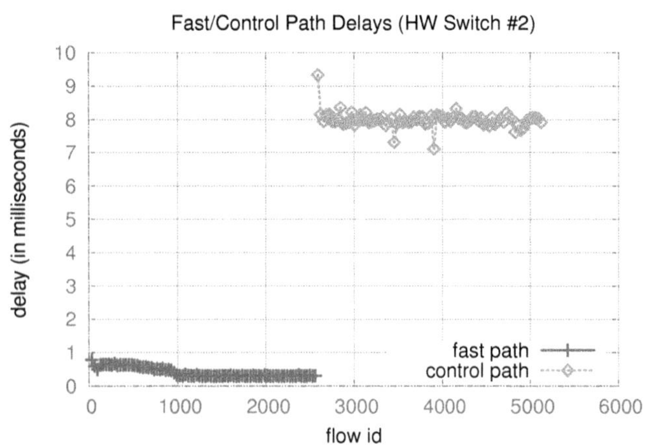

(c) Two tier delay in Switch #2.

Figure 2: Various edge detection algorithms.

Even if two switches have the same type of tables, their tables may have different number of entries. Although we could assume software tables have virtually unlimited size, this does not apply to TCAM tables. TCAMs are expensive and power hungry, thus TCAM size on a switch is quite limited and varies from one model to another. Moreover, the number of entries that can be stored in a fix-sized TCAM depends on: 1) entry type, and 2) operation mode. For example, in single-wide mode, entries can match only L2 headers or only L3 headers, while in double-wide mode, entries can match both L2 and L3 headers. When configured in the double-wide mode, TCAM can only hold half as many entries as in the single-wide mode.

It is interesting to see how this would impact the flow table size on different switches. Switch #1 allows the user to configure the TCAM mode. If being configured in L2 only or L3 only mode, it could have 4k L2 or L3 only flows. However, if we want to match on both L2 and L3, we can only get 2K entries installed in TCAM. Switch #2 and #3 does not allow user to customize TCAM mode. However, the experiment results in Table 1 reveal that the TCAM in Switch #2 has been configured as double-wide mode, since we can only install 2560 flow entries no matter whether the entries are L2 only, L3 only, or a mix of L2 and L3. This obviously is not an efficient design under the scenario that most of the flow entries are either L2 only or L3 only. Switch #3 is a better design in this aspect, since it could automatically adjust the table size according to entry type. When all flow entries are L2 only or L3 only, it could hold 767 flow entries comparing with only 369 L2 and L3 entries.

Unlike TCAM (or other hardware tables), software tables in either user space or kernel space can support virtually unlimited number of entries, but their matching and forwarding performance will be limited by CPU capability and the type of rules we install [13].

Diverse delay with different orders of rule operations: We measure the installation latency of various numbers of rules in various orders using Switch #1, Switch #2, and OVS. For Switch #1, and OVS, we preinstall 1000 rules in random priority, and for Switch #2 we preinstall 500 rules (in order not to exceed the TCAM capacity of the hardware switches). Then, we measure the speed to perform a set of flow addition, deletion and modification operations with different permutations with the same start and end sets of rules. Specifically, we implement all the six possible permutations of 200 flow additions, 200 deletions, and 200 modifications. We repeat the experiment 10 times and we present the average over the 10 experiments. The result for the hardware Switch #1 is shown in Figure 3(a).

Diverse delay using different flow tables: from above description, it is easy to understand that packets match different flow tables encounter different forwarding delays. In general, we expect fast path delay to be much smaller than slow path delay. Control path delay should be the longest since packets need to traverse between separate boxes.

As shown in Figure 2(a), OVS based software switch has three-tier delays: a constant fast path delay of 3 ms, a varying slow path delay of 4.5 ms on average, and a control path delay of 4.65 ms. This numbers do not differ much. The varying slow path delay was resulted from the variation of switch CPU utilization to install the micro-flow at the kernel space. Similarly, Figure 2(b) has three-tier delays. The fast path delay is consistent around 0.665 ms, which is much faster than the slow path delay (typically 3.7 ms) and control path delay (7.5 ms on average). Here the fast path could process and forward packets in line rate. Figure 2(c) shows that the fast path performance and the control path performance of Switch #2

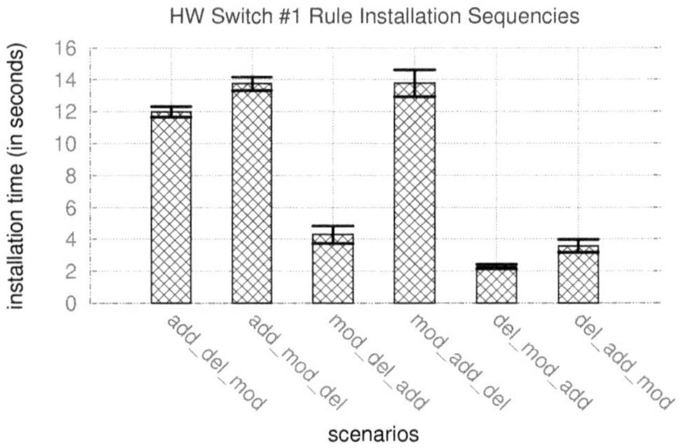

(a) Total flow installation time for the case of 200 adds, 200 mods, and 200 dels for HW Switch #1.

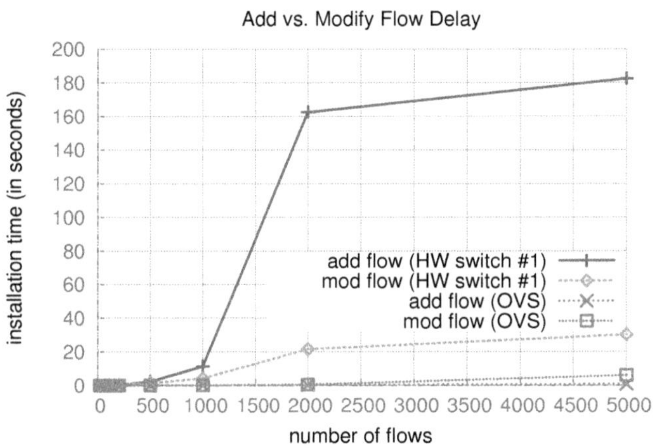

(b) Performance of mod vs. add for an OF HW Switch.

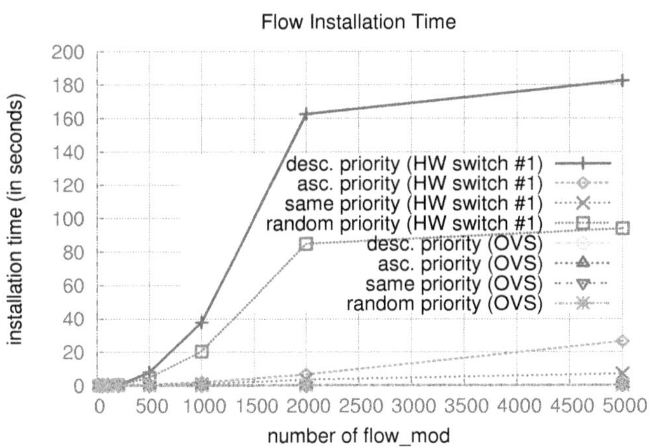

(c) Flow installation time for different priority patterns in OVS and a OF HW Switch. (The four curves for OVS overlap with each other.)

Figure 3: Rule installation time under different scenarios.

are comparable with Switch #1, with a data path delay of 0.4 ms on average and a control path delay of 8 ms on average.

Diverse controller-switch channel performance: The controller - switch interactions are also diverse in key aspects. First, different rule operations (e.g., add new entries or modify existing entries) have different performance. This is especially true for hardware OpenFlow switches that use TCAM in fast path forwarding. Figure 3(b) shows how long it takes to either install n new entries or update n existing entries, where n varies from 20 to 5000. In order to support the priority concept defined in OpenFlow specification, entries in TCAM need to be sorted, with higher priority entries on top. When a packet comes, it will be processed according to the first TCAM entry it hits. In this case, adding a new entry may lead to shifting multiple existing TCAM entries. This is not needed when modifying an existing entry. From Figure 3(b), we observe that modifying 5000 entries could be six times faster than adding new flows under our setup.

Second, different rule priorities have different performance, especially for hardware switches. Inserting the same number of new flows with exactly the same priority takes the least amount of time. This is because increasing priority avoids shifting existing TCAM entries to make room for new entries. Figure 2(c) shows that it takes significant less time to insert 5000 new flow entries in ascending priority order than in descending priority order. So far, we have observed 46X performance boosting by comparing the descending with constant priority ordering in the case of 2000 entries. Even by comparing random with ascending priority ordering, we can get 12X performance boosting to install 2000 non-overlapping entries. In addition, Figure 2(c) shows the results from the same experiment in OVS where we observed that priority has no impact on the rule installation delay.

The above observations have significant importance even in the cases where proactive rule installation is used (e.g. failover rules), since there are applications like traffic engineering that still requires a very fast rule update in order to adapt to the new network conditions.

4. TANGO ARCHITECTURE

Overview: The real measurement results in the preceding section provide both motivations and inspiration for the design of Tango. In other words, real measurements can give insights on the diversity of switches, and hence can form a foundation of understanding and handling SDN switch diversity. Measurement based programming is not new. For example, many programming systems first run test scripts to test the capability and availability of features of a platform, to handle platform diversity. The key novelty of Tango is that we apply this methodology in the context of handling SDN switch diversity, which poses its own unique challenges: (1) What are the measurements to reveal switch capabilities and behaviors? (2) How to hide, as much as possible, switch diversity?

Components: Figure 4 shows the basic components and information flow of Tango. The key component is the central Tango Score and Pattern Databases (TangoDB), where each Tango pattern is defined as a sequence of OpenFlow flow mod commands and a corresponding data traffic pattern. As an extensible architecture, Tango allows new Tango Patterns to be continuously added to the database.

Given a Tango Pattern and a switch, the Probing Engine applies the pattern to the switch, and collects measurement results. The collection of switch measurements can be either offline testing of the switch before it is plugged in the network, but online testing when the switch is running. The measurement results are stored into a central Tango Score Database, to allow sharing of results across components. All components in Tango can send requests to the Probing Engine to apply Tango Patterns on switches. One particular basic component is the Switch Inference Engine, which

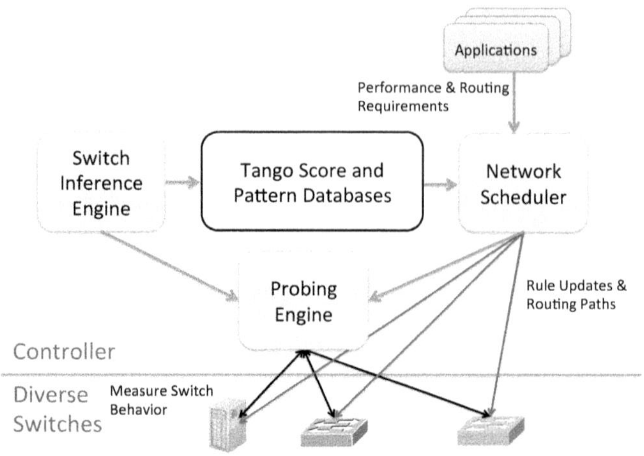

Figure 4: Tango architecture components.

derives switch capabilities and behaviors (e.g., TCAM size, processing throughput, and cache replacement algorithm). The Switch Inference Engine generates Tango Patterns that it may need and stores them in the Tango Pattern Database. It then sends requests to the Probing Engine to apply the patterns. In Section 5, we will define two sets of Tango Patterns which the Switch Inference Engine will use.

Another component that may utilize the Probing Engine and Tango Patterns is Network Schedulers. Our goal is that different Network Schedulers may utilize Tango derived information to achieve its own goals. In Section 6, we will give more details on an example Network Scheduler, which uses Tango derived information to schedule flow priorities and installation sequence, using a technique that is similar to expression rewriting in compiler optimization.

5. HARDWARE INFERENCE PATTERNS

In this section, we design Tango patterns to infer switch sizes and cache replacement algorithms. In particular, we will present two patterns to infer the size and the cache replacement algorithm respectively. The key challenge of designing the two Tango patterns is to handle the challenge that the probing traffic itself can change the cache state. For example, OpenFlow switches keep traffic counters and usage timers that are updated each time the switch receives a packet matching a given flow, so probing a flow that was not initially cached might cause some other flow to be evicted.

5.1 Switch Model

Before explaining our inference algorithms, we first present a conceptual model of an OpenFlow switch that guides our designs. Hardware-based OpenFlow switches (as opposed to Open vSwitch) generally comprise of a flow table that can be partitioned into multiple levels of hardware-backed (TCAM tables) and software-backed (*i.e.*, kernel and user space tables) rules. Since the latency of forwarding using different tables can differ significantly (for instance, hardware forwarding has significantly lower latency than software forwarding), we can view the flow table organization as a multilevel cache for the entire set of forwarding rules in the switch. Analogously, then, the switch policy for deciding how to populate a flow table layer can be viewed as a cache policy. Thus, the flow table layer size, hit rate, and relative performance of hardware and software forwarding of a switch can be used to characterize its performance in the same way as caches in an operating system.

Specifically, consider a cache's managing policy. We formalize such a policy as defining a relation that creates an ordering among all memory elements and removes the element that comes last in this ordering. The cache policy examines some set of attributes of the memory elements (such as usage time or frequency) and then selects the element with the lowest "score" to be evicted (this may be the new element, in which case the cache state does not change). The evicted element may be saved in the next cache, but we focus on one cache at a time. Although many cache policies exist that deviate somewhat from a total ordering (*e.g.*, by introducing randomness), an approximation using a total ordering gives statistically similar results.

Thus, we formalize a switch cache policy as follows:

1. [ATTRIB] The algorithm operates on a subset of the following attributes that OpenFlow switches maintain on a per-flow basis: time since insertion, time since last use, traffic count, and rule priority[1].
2. [MONOTONE] A comparison function between two values of a given attribute is monotonic. The function can be either increasing or decreasing.
3. [LEX] A total ordering on the flows is created by sorting them lexicographically under some permutation of the attributes[2].

We can make a few observations based on these assumptions. First, ATTRIB minimizes the search space of possible cache policies, but in a way that does not affect the generality of the overall probing pattern since both MONOTONE and LEX can apply to arbitrary numbers of attributes. Second, MONOTONE implies that we do not care about the magnitude of the difference between two given values, only the sign. This means that we do not need to worry about the effect of, for example, a single packet on traffic count, provided that the difference between the two flows under comparison was sufficiently large (*i.e.*, greater than 2). Third, LEX is simply a natural extension of single element sort, and is sufficiently general because cache algorithms that do not obey LEX, such as second chance and clock, require hardware support that is not present and unlikely to be built into OpenFlow switches.

Our probing patterns are motivated by the previously mentioned observation that the different flow table layers have significantly different latency. In a two level model of a TCAM-based hardware table and software table, the TCAM-based hardware forwarding has significantly lower latency than software forwarding, so a cached flow entry will have a significantly lower round trip time than one that is not cached. These round trip times will fall into two clusters, with the faster round trip times corresponding to cached entries. Switches with multiple levels of caching (*e.g.*, division of software tables into kernel space and userspace) will have a number of clusters equal to the number of cache layers. This situation is demonstrated in Figure 5, which has three layers. Our algorithm handles the general case of multiple levels of caching.

[1]Note that match layer is likely to be a filter on the cache-eligible flows rather than an ordering constraint.

[2]For example, assume the attributes are permuted in order of traffic count, priority, use time, and finally insertion time. A flow with traffic = 20 would precede one with traffic = 10, and a flow with traffic = 20 and priority = 4 would precede one with traffic = 20 and priority = 2 (the orders are reversed if lower priority or traffic is better).

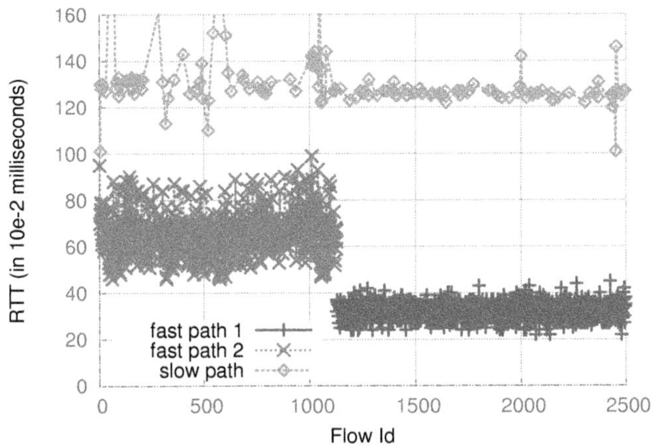

Figure 5: Round trip times for flows installed in HW Switch #2.

5.2 Flow-table Sizes

Our size-probing algorithm (Algorithm 1, Size Probing Algorithm) uses a statistical approach to estimate the flow table sizes of a given switch, relying on the previously described switch model along with the observation that for any possible cache state, a cache hit does not change that state. Thus, we design our algorithm with three stages, as follows. In stage 1 (lines 4-12), as long as we have not overflown the cache (we explain this condition in detail below), we insert a batch of rules (lines 7-10). Stage 2 starts after inserting these rules. In this stage (lines 14-21), we send packets corresponding to the inserted flow rules and measure the RTTs. We cluster the RTT to determine the number of flow table layers– each cluster corresponds to one layer. In stage 3 (lines 23-42), we perform a sampling experiment (let m be the number of rules inserted, and let $n_1, n_2, \ldots, n_N$ be the cache size of levels $1 \ldots N, n = \Sigma n_i$):

1. Select one of the m rules at random (line 27/31)
2. Record the RTT for a packet matching that rule (line 28/32)
3. Repeat the previous two steps as long as the rules are in the same cache layer and we have sent fewer than m packets (line 29)

Since a cache hit does not affect the cache state, this process will terminate if and only if there is a cache miss. Assuming we have $m > n$, therefore, if we record the result of this experiment over multiple trials for a given m, we get an approximation of the expected value of the number of consecutive cache hits. If we perform k trials, the total number of packets sent corresponds to the random variable $X \sim NB(1, n_i/m)$, where $NB(r,p)$ is the Negative Binomial distribution for r negative results sampling with probability p for a cache hit. We can infer the value of p using maximum likelihood estimation over the results of k samples, which yields the expression: $\hat{p} = \frac{\sum_{i=0}^{k} X_i}{k + \sum_{i=0}^{k} X_i}$. Setting $\hat{p} = \hat{n}_i/m$, we get:

$$\hat{n}_i = m * \hat{p} = m * \frac{\sum_{i=0}^{k} X_i}{k + \sum_{i=0}^{k} X_i}.$$

The only remaining question is how we can determine when m has exceeded the total cache size n. By installing flows and sending traffic for each flow upon insertion (before performing the sampling), our switch model guarantees that there are no wasted slots in the cache; that is, there are only empty cache entries if there are fewer flows than slots in the cache. We continue installing new flows until the OpenFlow API rejects the call, which indicates that we have exceeded the total cache size.

Our algorithm is asymptotically optimal in the number of rule installations and probing traffic sent. By doubling the number of rules installed until rule installation fails, and then halving the number of rules and installing, we install n rules $O(n)$ in $2 * \log_2 n$ batches, so we can take advantage of batching effects that switches may have for rule installation. Moreover, each rule installed requires 1 packet to be sent. Furthermore, in the experiment phase of the algorithm, we send $O(n)$ packets (we impose a cap on the number of consecutive packets to be m in case n_i is very close to m). Since we are trying to measure the size of the cache layers, we need to install at least n rules and send at least n packets of traffic, so this algorithm being linear with respect to total cache layers' size in both number of rule installations and packets sent is asymptotically optimal.

Algorithm 1 Size Probing Algorithm

```
1: k ← NUM_TRIALS_PER_ITERATION
2:
3: function PROBE_SIZE(switch)
4:     cache_full ← FALSE; x ← 1
5:     while !cache_full do
6:         for all i ∈ [0, x), i ∉ switch.flows do
7:             f ← INSERT_FLOW(switch, i)
8:             if rejected then cache_full ← TRUE; break
9:             SEND_PROBE_PACKET(switch, f)
10:        end for
11:        x ← x * 2
12:    end while
13:
14:    g ← ∅
15:    for all i ∈ [0, x) do
16:        f ← SELECT_RANDOM(switch)
17:        rtt ← MEASURE_RTT(switch, f)
18:        APPEND_RTT(g, rtt)
19:    end for
20:
21:    clusters, n_clusters ← COMPUTE_CLUSTERS(g)
22:
23:    for all level ∈ [1, n_clusters) do
24:        a ← 0
25:        for all i ∈ [0, k) do
26:            j ← 0
27:            f ← SELECT_RANDOM(switch)
28:            rtt ← MEASURE_RTT(switch, f)
29:            while WITHIN_CLUSTER(switch, rtt, clusters, level) AND j < m do
30:                j ← j + 1
31:                f ← SELECT_RANDOM(switch.flows)
32:                rtt ← MEASURE_RTT(switch, f)
33:            end while
34:
35:            if j = m then
36:                break
37:            else
38:                a ← a + j
39:            end if
40:        end for
41:        sizes[i] ← m * a/(k + a)
42:    end for
43:    return sizes
44: end function
```

5.3 Cache Algorithm

We leverage MONOTONE and LEX in order to generate patterns that successfully observe cache state without violating the relative ordering of the inserted flows. LEX suggests a clear structure for

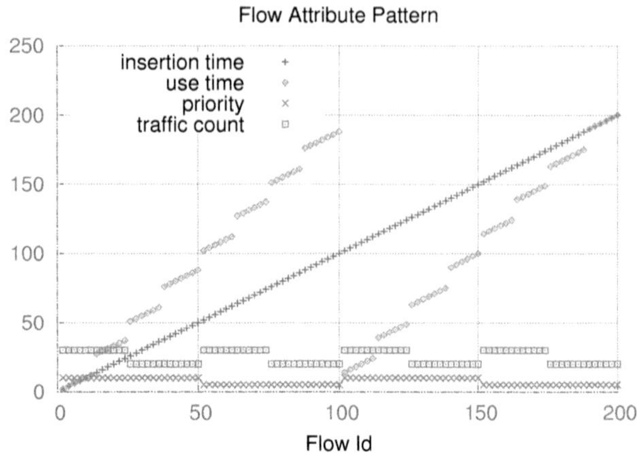

Figure 6: Visualization of Cache Algorithm Pattern for Cache Size = 100.

our probing. If we first identify the primary sorting attribute, we can then hold it constant to recursively identify the next sorting attribute, and continue until we have determined the correct permutation of the attributes. We identify the primary sorting attribute by ensuring, for each attribute for a given flow, the corresponding value is either less than or greater than the values of half (n = cache size) of the other flows. If we ensure that there is no subset of flows for which this condition holds for more than one attribute at a time, we can fairly easily identify the sorting attribute by seeing which correlates most strongly (positive or negative) with the caching decisions.

Algorithm 2 presents the details of policy patterns. We first insert $2 * cache\_size$ flows (line 4) and initialize them subject to the constraints explained in the paragraph above (lines 5-7). The traffic generation pattern in line 9 ensures that our probing does not affect the flow's relative position in an ordering on any attribute. Considering each attribute in turn, priority and insertion time are unaffected by probing, whereas traffic count could be affected by probing if two flows had counts that differed by only one, but the algorithm initializes the values to be far apart (10 in our specific implementation). We maintain invariant relative use times by querying in order of reverse use time (line 9). For example, by the time we send traffic for what was initialized as fifth most recently used rules, only the four rules that had succeeded it have been queried again, so the ordering is left unchanged.

Similarly to the size probing patterns, the policy patterns examine the round trip times to determine which elements are cached (based on the data collected during size probing). LEX guarantees that the cached flows should have some attribute for which they all have the highest values or all have the lowest ('highest' and 'lowest' meaning greater than or less than the values for at least n other flows). We identify this variable by statistical correlation (line 24), and then recur to find subsequent sort attributes if necessary (lines 27-30).

As an example, consider probing the cache replacement algorithm for a cache of size 100. The post-initialization state of each of the flows is shown in Figure 6. If the replacement algorithm is LRU, we will see that packets matching the flow entries with $use\_time > 100$ will have round trip times near the mean cache processing time computed as part of the size inference process. Since use time values are unique, the flow entries can be arranged in a strict total order on the basis of just use time, and the algorithm would terminate.

Algorithm 2 Policy Probing Algorithm

1: $ATTRIBUTES \leftarrow \{insertion, usage\_time, traffic, priority\}$
2: $SERIAL\_ATTRIBUTES \leftarrow \{insertion, usage\_time\}$
3:
4: **function** PROBE_POLICY($switch, policy$)
5: $attributes \leftarrow ATTRIBUTES \setminus policy$
6: $s \leftarrow 2 * switch.cache\_size$
7:
8: **for all** $i \in [0, s)$ **do**
9: $f \leftarrow$ INSERT_FLOW(switch, i)
10: **for all** $a \in attributes$ **do**
11: INITIALIZE_FLOW_ATTRIBUTE($switch, f, a$)
12: **end for**
13: **end for**
14:
15: $rtts \leftarrow \{\}$
16: **for all** $f \in$ SORT_BY_MRU(switch.flows) **do**
17: $rtts[f] \leftarrow$ MEASURE_RTT(switch, f)
18: **end for**
19:
20: $correlations \leftarrow \{\}$
21: **for all** $o \in ATTRIBUTES \times \{incr, decr\}$ **do**
22: $correlations[o] \leftarrow$ CORRELATE(o, rtts)
23: **end for**
24: $a \leftarrow$ ARGMAX(correlations)
25: $policy$.APPEND(a)
26:
27: **if** $a \in SERIAL\_ATTRIBUTES$ **then**
28: **return** $policy$
29: **else**
30: **return** PROBE_POLICY($switch, policy$)
31: **end if**
32: **end function**

6. TANGO SCHEDULER

The hardware table inference patterns provide basic information about individual switches and their performance. Rewriting patterns provide information to allow a scheduler to identify effective operational patterns. In this section, we demonstrate the benefits of using Tango pattern in scheduling and optimization of flow installation. We emphasize that the algorithm depends on the available patterns, and designers should continue to add new patterns to guide scheduling and optimizations.

Application requests: The design intention of Tango is that it can be integrated with a wide range of SDN controllers, and different SDN controllers may offer different APIs for applications to submit requests. Hence, application requests can range from simple static flow pusher style requests (*e.g.*, [20]), where the whole path is given in each request, to declarative-level requests such that the match condition is given but the path is not given (*e.g.*, ACL style spec) in each request [14], to algorithmic policies such that even the match condition will be extracted (*e.g.*, [23]).

Switch request DAG: Given application requests and/or other events (*e.g.*, link status changes), a compiler or run time at the central SDN controller will generate operations, which we call switch requests, to individual switches to update the rules in their flow tables. Using a general format, we consider that each request has the following format:

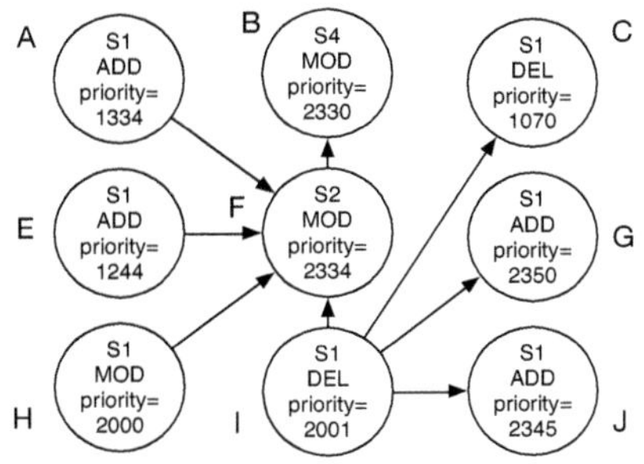

Figure 7: An example DAG of switch requests.

```
req_elem = {
    'location': switch_id,
    'type' : add | del | mod,
    'priority': priority number or none
    'rule parameters' : match, action
    'install_by': ms or best effort}
```

Each switch request has a location field, which specifies the switch at which the operation should be installed. A switch request also has other common fields such as the operation type, the priority of the new flow table rule, and other parameters such as match fields and actions. Priority is needed, since that TCAM match conditions cannot include negation, and hence one must introduce higher-priority barrier rules [23] for such cases. A switch request may have a deadline by which the request should be installed (*e.g.*, derived from aforementioned application requests). A switch request may leave the deadline field empty for best efforts.

Switch requests may not be independent. For example, to achieve consistent updating, a controller may specify that the requests are finished in a given order (*e.g.*, from the destination switch back to the source switch, for the path of a new flow). The aforementioned case of using priority to implement logic negation may also require that some rules are installed before the other, to avoid transient breaches. Using a graph G where each node represents a switch request, if a switch request A must be completed before another request B, we say that there is a direct edge from A to B in the graph. Our Tango scheduler assumes that the graph G is a directed-acyclic graph (DAG). If the dependency forms a loop, the upper layer must break the loop to make G a DAG. Figure 7 shows an example DAG that indicates multi-switch requests, and their dependencies. At any instance of time, we say that the controller has a current switch-request DAG.

Basic Tango scheduler: The basic Tango scheduler algorithm, shown in Algorithm 3, processes the switch requests in the current switch-request DAG. To understand Algorithm 3, first consider the scheduling of switch requests without Tango measurements. Given the current DAG, it is intuitive that one schedules the requests starting from those with no dependencies, such as the Dionysus [6] algorithm. In particular, the algorithm identifies those requests without dependencies, which we refer to as independent requests, and schedules the independent request that belongs to the longest path first.

A major issue of this approach, however, is that a typical DAG can have a large number of independent requests with the same longest-path length. For example, consider Figure 7. The three requests on the left (i.e., requests A, E, H) and the one on the lower middle (i.e., request I) have no dependency and have the same longest path length. Hence, a key issue is how one schedules these four requests. This is where Tango patterns may provide substantial guidelines. Specifically, at line 3, the scheduler extracts the current independent set of switch requests (*e.g.*, during the first round, the requests A, E, H, I), and uses the Tango Score and Pattern Database for a suggested ordering of the switch requests in the set. Applying pattern 1 (deletions followed by modifications followed by additions in ascending priority order) at line 12, the algorithm computes a score of -91 ($= -(10 \times 1 + 1 \times 1 + 20 \times 2^2)$, where the first 1 means one DEL, the second 1 means one MOD in the set of requests, and 2 for the 2 ADD requests, and 10, 1, and 20 are the weights for DEL, MOD, and ADD, respectively). Applying pattern 2 gives a lower score of -171. Hence, the scheduler picks the first scheduling pattern and issues the requests in the suggested order.

Algorithm 3 BasicTangoScheduler

1: **function** BASICTANGOSCHEDULER(G)
2: **while** true **do**
3: $G_i \leftarrow independent\ set\ in\ G$
4: $Git \leftarrow orderingTangoOracle(G_i)$
5: issue requests in Git
6: remove finished requests in Git
7: **end while**
8: **end function**
9: **function** $orderignTangoOracle(G_i)$
10: $maxScore \leftarrow NEGATIVE\_INFINITY$
11: **for all** $pattern \in TangoPatterns$ **do**
12: $score \leftarrow computePatternScore(G_i, pattern)$
13: **if** (score > maxScore) **then**
14: $maxScore \leftarrow score$
15: $maxPattern \leftarrow applyPattern(Gi, pattern)$
16: **end if**
17: **end for**
18: **return** maxPattern
19: **end function**
20: $TangoPatterns \leftarrow [$
21: $\{pattern: ``DEL\ MOD\ ASCEND\_ADD",$
22: $score: -(10 \times \{DEL\} + 1 \times \{MOD\} + 20 \times \{ADD^2\})\},$
23: $\{pattern: ``DEL\ MOD\ DESCEND\_ADD",$
24: $score: -(10 \times \{DEL\} + 1 \times \{MOD\} + 40 \times \{ADD^2\})\},$
25: ...
26:]

Extensions: The basic scheduling algorithm uses greedy batching of independent requests. For example, the basic algorithm schedules all four requests (A, E, H, I) in one batch, in the order of I, H, E, A. One extension that may improve the basic algorithm is to consider non-greedy batching. Specifically, after computing the ordering I, H, E, A, the scheduler evaluates different prefixes to determine if there is a better ordering, by considering issuing the prefix, and then the batch enabled by the completion of the prefix. Consider the prefix I, its completion will produce a new independent set (A, E, H, C, G, J). The scheduler computes the total score of schedule (1): batch 1 with I, and batch 2 with C, H, E, A, J, G, vs that of schedule (2): batch 1 with I, H, E, A and then batch 2 with C, F, J, G. This process leads to a scheduling tree of possibilities and the scheduler picks the schedule with the best overall score.

Another extension of the basic algorithm is to schedule dependent switch requests concurrently. Specifically, Tango probing engine can provide measurement results to guide the scheduling of concurrent requests. Specifically, in case of a dependency S_1 ADD$\rightarrow$ S_2 ADD (between switches S_1 and S_2), the scheduler does not have to wait for the first command to finish if we can estimate (using the Tango latency curves) that the second command is much slower than the first (e.g. if the switch is overloaded, or it has a

Flow Files	Topological Priorities	R Priorities	Flows Installed
Classbench1	64	829	829
Classbench2	38	989	989
Classbench3	33	972	972

Table 2: Number of flows per Classbench file and their associated priorities.

slower CPU). On the contrary, we can push both rules such that the estimated (using the Tango latency curves) finishing time of the operation S_1 ADD precedes the estimated finishing time of the rule S_2 ADD by a "guard" time interval. This is suitable for senarios with weak consistency requirement.

7. EVALUATIONS

In this section, we present the results from the evaluation of Tango and demonstrate that using Tango patterns, we can achieve substantially better SDN programming efficiency both in a per-switch and network-wide basis.

7.1 Single Switch Evaluation

With basic switch properties inferred from the preceding section and additional rewriting patterns, Tango scheduler optimizes the assignment and installation of flow table rules. We evaluate how much gain that Tango can achieve compared with approaches that are oblivious of switch diversity. For this, we test four algorithms that combine different priority assignments and installation order to the rules and measure their performance.

Methodology: In order to find the optimal scheduling policy that can minimize flow installation time, we use three sets of rules from Classbench [21] access control lists to generate flow rules with dependencies. We then process the dependency graph with the algorithm taken from [23] in order to generate a) the minimum set of priorities needed to install the rules while satisfying the dependency constraints, and b) a set of priorities that are mapped 1-1 to the flow rules but they still satisfy the dependency constraints of the rules.

We denote the first set of priorities *Topological Priorities* (we use topological sorting to obtain the rule schedule and then use the same priority number for rules that have no dependencies with each other), and the second R Priorities. The next step is to measure the installation time using Tango pattern under the following scheduling scenarios: 1) topological priority assignment and the optimal rule installation order taken from our probing engine, 2) topological priority assignment and random rule installation order, 3) 1-1 priority assignment that satisfies the dependency constraints and the optimal installation order taken from our probing engine, and 4) 1-1 priority assignment that satisfies the dependency constraints and random installation order. We repeat the above experiment three times using three different Classbench files. The number of flows per Classbench file as well as the number of Topological and R priorities generated are shown in Table 2.

Per Switch Evaluation: For each Classbench file, and for the four scheduling scenarios shown above, we measure the installation time in OVS and HW Switch #1, as shown in Figures 8(a)-9(c). We can observe that the topological priority assignment combined with the optimal policy taken from our probing engine achieved the best performance in terms of flow installation time in five out of the six scenarios under study. For example, in Figure 8(a)-8(c), we can observe that the decrease in the installation time is 10%, 9%, and 8%, respectively. In addition, in the case of the hardware switch (Figure 9(a)-9(c)), the decrease in the installation time is 87%, 80%, and 89%, respectively. The improvement in the case of OVS is lower since OVS is very fast for a relatively small number of rules (i.e., <1000).

The only exception was the case of Classbench 1 for HW Switch #1, where the installation time is slightly more than the one using priority assignment of type R and the rules are installed in ascending priority.

To further analyze the behavior of real hardware switches, we repeated the experiment using descending priority installation order, instead of ascending. As expected, the installation time was up to 12 times higher compared to the one using ascending priority (we do not show these results here due to space limitations).

7.2 Network-Wide Evaluation

To further evaluate the performance of Tango, we conduct experiments on both a hardware testbed and a virtual network emulator (Mininet [24]), that represent the following real-life scenarios: (a) *Link Failure (LF):* one or more links from the physical topology fails causing existing flows to be rerouted; and (b) *Traffic Engineering (TE):* a traffic matrix change causes a number of flows to be added, removed, or modified. In both scenarios, we ensure that the flow updates are conducted in reverse order across the source-destination paths to ensure update consistency [18].

We compare the performance of Basic Tango Scheduler with Dionysus [6], a network update scheduler for SDN. The core of Dionysus uses a critical path scheduling algorithm that constantly calculates the critical path on the scheduling DAG (that represents the rules to be pushed to each switch and their dependencies), and pushes the rules to the switches that belong to the critical path, first. However, unlike Tango, Dionysus does not take into account the diversity in the latency of each rule type, as well as the diversity of the switch implementations (e.g., caching algorithm).

Evaluation on hardware testbed: First, we conduct experiments on a small testbed consisting of three hardware switches, denoted as s_1, s_2, and s_3. Switch s_1 and s_2 are from Vendor #1, and s_3 is from Vendor #3. Initially these switches are fully connected forming a triangle. We use this testbed to implement both LF and TE scenarios, as follows. In the LF case, the link between s_1 and s_2 got disconnected causing 400 existing flows to be rerouted from s_1 to s_2 via s_3. In the TF case, a traffic matrix change at s_1 causes a number of flows to be added, removed, or modified. We have implemented two TE scenarios (denoted as TE 1 and TE 2) with different distributions on the number of rules of each type required (i.e., ADD, MOD, DEL) in order to transition from the initial state to the target state. In the TE1 scenario, we randomly generate 800 flow requests with twice as many additions as deletions or modifications, while in TE2, these three types of requests are equally distributed. We assume explicitly specifies priorities for their rules, Tango can optimize the rules with priority pattern (called *Priority sorting*).

Figure 10 shows the results of LF, TE1, and TE2 scenarios. By applying only a rule-type optimal pattern, Tango gets 0%[3], 20%, and 26% improvement compared to Dionysus, respectively. In addition, by applying both rule-type pattern optimization and priority pattern optimization, Tango could further reduce the flow installation time by 70%, 33% and 28%, respectively.

Figure 11 explores two settings about priorities: The first is *priority sorting* as described above. The second is *priority enforcement*. When applications do not specify the flow priorities (as men-

[3]This is because in LF scenario, there are only rule additions on s_1 and rule modifications on s_2. Thus, there is no room for rule-type optimization.

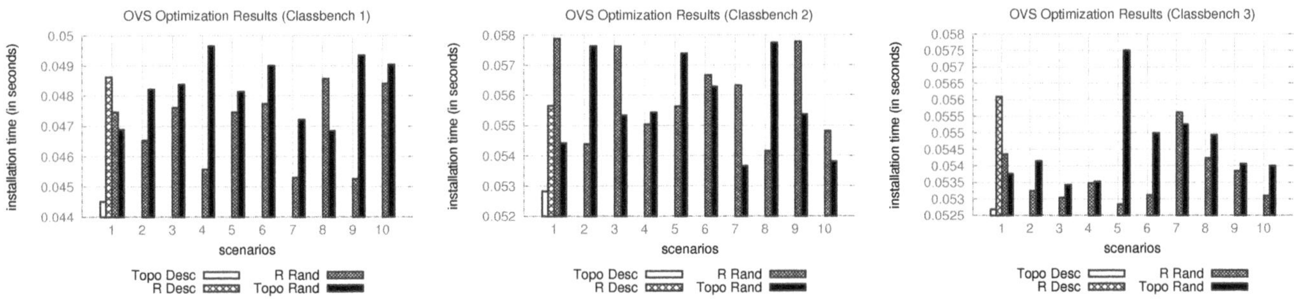

(a) Classbench 1 (b) Classbench 2 (c) Classbench 3

Figure 8: Installation time for various priority assignments and installation order in OVS.

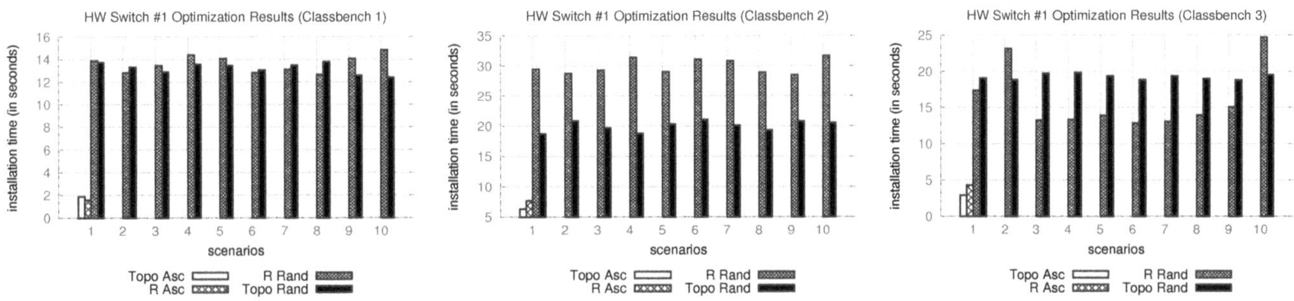

(a) Classbench 1 (b) Classbench 2 (c) Classbench 3

Figure 9: Installation time for various priority assignments and installation orders in HW switch #1.

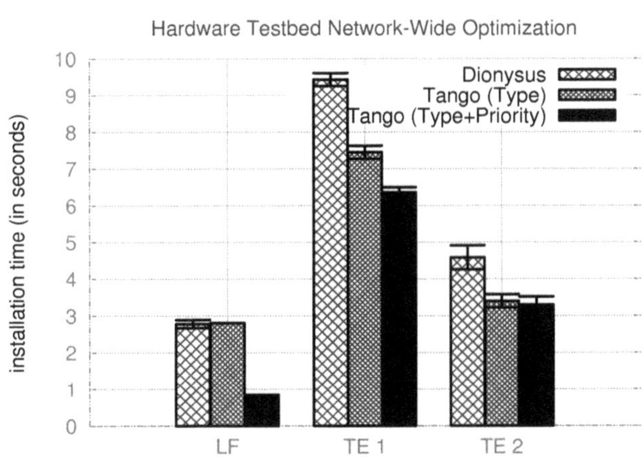

Figure 10: Hardware testbed Link Failure and Traffic Engineering Scenarios.

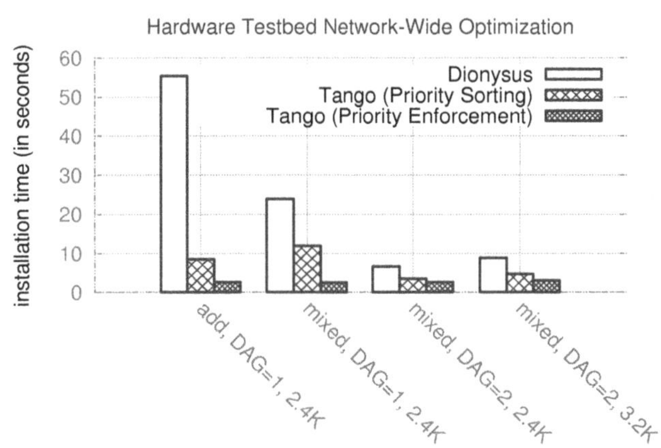

Figure 11: Hardware testbed measurements.

tioned in Sec. 6), Tango can optimize the assignment of priorities based on the dependency constraints. We evaluate four scenarios, each with a different type of rules pushed in the network (i.e., ADD only, or mix of ADD, MOD, DEL), a different number of levels in the dependency graph, and a different total number of rules. In general, Tango outperforms Dionysus in all cases with a maximum improvement of 85% and 95% via priority sorting and priority enforcement, respectively. This happens once the request only consists of flow additions. In the last two scenarios, we explore the situation where the DAG has more than one levels, under the same number of rules as before. In these cases, the performance benefit of Tango is smaller, since each level has less independent rules, and thus less optimization options.

Network emulation on OVS: To evaluate Tango in larger networks, we evaluate Tango scheduler on Google's backbone network topology [5] using Mininet [24]. In the TE case, we implement a traffic matrix change in the B4 topology that triggers a sequence of rule additions, modifications, and deletions, based on the max-min fair allocation algorithm used in [5]. The results are shown in Figure 12. We observe 8% flow installation improvement compared with Dionysus results, for a total of 2200 end-to-end flow requests. Similar improvements are observed in the LF case. This improvements come from rule-type pattern. This is smaller than the improvements on hardware testbed, because OVS has smaller performance differences betwen rule type patterns. We also note that priority optimization does not help in the case of OVS. This is priority has little impact on OVS rule installation performance.

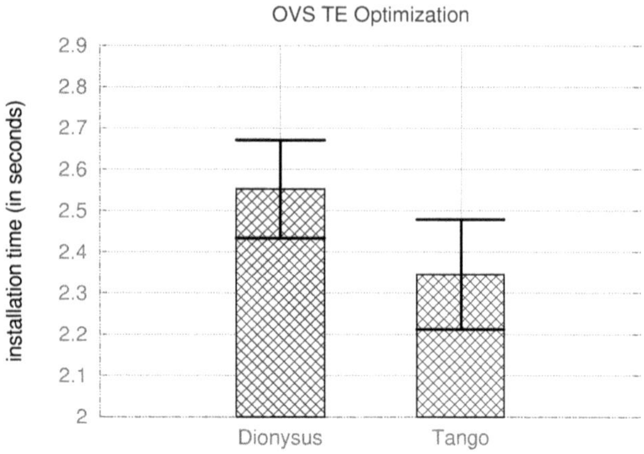

Figure 12: Mininet TE Scenario.

8. RELATED WORK

Managing switch diversity: Discussions on OpenFlow 2.0 (*e.g.*, [1]) highlight the difficulties of handling switch diversity. OF-config [15] provides a management protocol for the controller to understand and control switch-specific configurations. However, these protocols do not fully capture switch diversity and do not provide mechanisms to quantify the diversity. For example, they do not specify a mechanism to query the caching policy, and quantify switch update latencies. In [4], the authors explore the diversity of different switch implementations using manual inspection. We propose algorithms to automatically infer switch parameters and Tango patterns. Oflops [19] provides a standalone controller to benchmark OpenFlow switch performance. Tango builds on Oflops but designs smart probing algorithms to infer Tango patterns.

High level abstractions: Existing SDN controllers and languages (e.g., Frenetic [12], Onix [8], Maple [23]) provides a high-level abstraction of network elements (e.g., switches, hosts, ports) to reduce the complexity of programming SDN, and leverage compilers and runtime systems to optimize the application performance independent of diverse switches. In Tango, we optimizes application performance by leveraging switch-specific opportunities (i.e., Tango patterns). One can view Tango as a "backend" compiler optimizer which none of the existing compilers [3, 23] provide. It is possible to integrate Tango with Frenetic and Maple. We leave that to future work.

Switch level optimizations: Previous work has proposed optimizations at both software and hardware switches to improve performance. For example, DevoFlow [2] introduces rule cloning to reduce the use of TCAM entries. CacheFlow [7] proposes new caching solutions for overlapping rules between software and hardware switches. However, it is challenging for applications to leverage these optimizations without knowing their design details. With Tango, these optimizations are just new Tango patterns for applications.

There have also been active research on optimize rule updates to ensure consistency [18, 10] and reducing transient congestions during updates [9, 6]. Complementary to these works, we focus on how to reorder or modify rule updates based on diverse switch capabilities to improve performance. One can view Tango as a mechanism to optimize per-switch rule updates. The consistent update mechanisms can use Tango to minimize their overall rule setup completion time.

9. CONCLUSION AND FUTURE WORK

Our measurement studies show that SDN switches have diverse implementations, capabilities and behaviors. Current controller implementations ignore the diversity. This leads to inefficient usage of switch resources. Most importantly, ignoring switch diversity can adversely impact application performance, e.g. packets end up in switch slow path. To simplify SDN programming, we present Tango, the first systematic design. Tango automatically infers switch behavior using a well-structured set of Tango patterns, where a Tango pattern consists of a sequence of standard OpenFlow commands and a corresponding data traffic pattern. Tango presents a simple API for controller applications to specify their requirements. Tango optimizes network performance exploiting the cost of a set of equivalent operations through expression rewriting. Our evaluation shows the effectiveness of Tango. For our future work, we would like to expand the set of Tango patterns to infer other switch capabilities such as multiple tables and their priorities.

Acknowledgments

We thank Haibin Song for providing examples of specific switches; James Aspnes and Shenil Dodhia for extensive discussions on the inference algorithms; and CoNEXT reviewers for their suggestions. Daniel Tahara is partially supported by a gift from Futurewei. Andreas Voellmy and Y. Richard Yang are supported by a gift from Futurewei and NSF CNS-1218457. Minlan Yu is supported in part by NSF CNS-1423505.

10. REFERENCES

[1] P. Bosshart, D. Daly, G. Gibb, M. Izzard, N. McKeown, J. Rexford, C. Schlesinger, D. Talayco, A. Vahdat, G. Varghese, and D. Walker. P4: Programming protocol-independent packet processors. *SIGCOMM Computer Communications Review*, 2013.

[2] A. R. Curtis, J. C. Mogul, J. Tourrilhes, P. Yalagandula, P. Sharma, and S. Banerjee. DevoFlow: Scaling flow management for high-performance networks. In *Proceedings of ACM SIGCOMM*, August 2011.

[3] N. Foster, R. Harrison, M. J. Freedman, C. Monsanto, J. Rexford, A. Story, and D. Walker. Frenetic: A network programming language. In *Proceedings of the 16th ACM SIGPLAN International Conference on Functional Programming (ICFP)*, September 2011.

[4] D. Y. Huang, K. Yocum, and A. C. Snoeren. High-fidelity switch models for software-defined network emulation. In *Proceedings of the Second ACM SIGCOMM Workshop on Hot Topics in Software Defined Networking (HotSDN)*, August 2013.

[5] S. Jain, A. Kumar, S. Mandal, J. Ong, L. Poutievski, A. Singh, S. Venkata, J. Wanderer, J. Zhou, M. Zhu, J. Zolla, U. Hölzle, S. Stuart, and A. Vahdat. B4: Experience with a globally-deployed software defined WAN. In *Proceedings of ACM SIGCOMM*, August 2013.

[6] X. Jin, H. H. Liu, R. Gandhi, S. Kandula, R. Mahajan, J. Rexford, R. Wattenhofer, and M. Zhang. Dionysus: Dynamic scheduling of network updates. In *Proceedings of ACM SIGCOMM*, August 2014.

[7] N. Katta, J. Rexford, and D. Walker. Infinite CacheFlow in software-defined networks. *Princeton Computer Science Technical Report TR-966-13*, 2013.

[8] T. Koponen, M. Casado, N. Gude, J. Stribling, L. Poutievski, M. Zhu, R. Ramanathan, Y. Iwata, H. Inoue, T. Hama, and S. Shenker. Onix: A distributed control platform for large-scale production networks. In *Proceedings of the 9th USENIX Conference on Operating Systems Design and Implementation (OSDI)*, October 2010.

[9] H. H. Liu, X. Wu, M. Zhang, L. Yuan, R. Wattenhofer, and D. Maltz. zUpdate: Updating data center networks with zero loss. In *Proceedings of the ACM SIGCOMM*, August 2013.

[10] R. Mahajan and R. Wattenhofer. On consistent updates in software defined networks. In *Proceedings of the 12th ACM Workshop on Hot Topics in Networks (HotNets-XII)*, November 2013.

[11] N. McKeown, T. Anderson, H. Balakrishnan, G. Parulkar, L. Peterson, J. Rexford, S. Shenker, and J. Turner. OpenFlow: Enabling innovation in campus networks. *SIGCOMM Computer Communications Review*, 2008.

[12] C. Monsanto, J. Reich, N. Foster, J. Rexford, and D. Walker. Composing software-defined networks. In *Proceedings of the 10th USENIX Conference on Networked Systems Design and Implementation (NSDI)*, April 2013.

[13] M. Moshref, M. Yu, A. Sharma, and R. Govindan. Scalable rule management for data centers. In *Proceedings of the 10th USENIX Symposium on Networked Systems Design and Implementation (NSDI)*, April 2013.

[14] T. Nelson, A. D. Ferguson, M. J. Scheer, and S. Krishnamurthi. Tierless programming and reasoning for software-defined networks. In *Proceedings of the 11th USENIX Symposium on Networked Systems Design and Implementation (NSDI)*, April 2014.

[15] OF-config: `https://github.com/AndreasVoellmy/data-driven-sdn-paper`.

[16] OpenFlow switch specification 1.4.0: `https://www.opennetworking.org/images/stories/downloads/sdn-resources/onf-specifications/openflow/openflow-spec-v1.4.0.pdf`.

[17] Openvswitch: `http://openvswitch.org/`.

[18] M. Reitblatt, N. Foster, J. Rexford, and D. Walker. Consistent updates for software-defined networks: Change you can believe in! In *Proceedings of the 10th ACM Workshop on Hot Topics in Networks (HotNets-X)*, November 2011.

[19] C. Rotsos, N. Sarrar, S. Uhlig, R. Sherwood, and A. W. Moore. Oflops: An open framework for OpenFlow switch evaluation. In *Proceedings of the 13th International Conference on Passive and Active Measurement*, March 2012.

[20] Ryu SDN controller: `http://osrg.github.io/ryu/`.

[21] D. E. Taylor and J. S. Turner. Classbench: a packet classification benchmark. *IEEE/ACM Transactions on Networking*, pages 499–511, 2007.

[22] The eXtensible DataPath Daemon (xdpd): `https://www.codebasin.net/redmine/projects/xdpd/wiki`.

[23] A. Voellmy, J. Wang, Y. R. Yang, B. Ford, and P. Hudak. Maple: Simplifying SDN programming using algorithmic policies. In *Proceedings of the ACM SIGCOMM*, August 2013.

[24] Mininet: An Instant Virtual Network on your Laptop. `http://mininet.org`.

Merlin: A Language for Provisioning Network Resources

Robert Soulé* Shrutarshi Basu† Parisa Jalili Marandi* Fernando Pedone*
Robert Kleinberg† Emin Gün Sirer† Nate Foster†
*University of Lugano †Cornell University

ABSTRACT

This paper presents Merlin, a new framework for managing resources in software-defined networks. With Merlin, administrators express high-level policies using programs in a declarative language. The language includes logical predicates to identify sets of packets, regular expressions to encode forwarding paths, and arithmetic formulas to specify bandwidth constraints. The Merlin compiler maps these policies into a constraint problem that determines bandwidth allocations using parameterizable heuristics. It then generates code that can be executed on the network elements to enforce the policies. To allow network tenants to dynamically adapt policies to their needs, Merlin provides mechanisms for delegating control of sub-policies and for verifying that modifications made to sub-policies do not violate global constraints. Experiments demonstrate the expressiveness and effectiveness of Merlin on real-world topologies and applications. Overall, Merlin simplifies network administration by providing high-level abstractions for specifying network policies that provision network resources.

Categories and Subject Descriptors

C.2.4 [**Distributed Systems**]: Network operating systems
; D.3.2 [**Language Classifications**]: Specialized application languages

Keywords

Software-defined networking; resource management; delegation; verification; Merlin.

1. INTRODUCTION

Network operators today must deal with a wide range of management challenges from increasingly complex policies to a proliferation of heterogeneous devices to ever-growing traffic demands. Software-defined networking (SDN) provides tools that could be used to address these challenges, but existing APIs for SDN programming are either too low-level or too limited in functionality to enable effective implementation of rich network-wide policies. As a result, there is widespread interest in academia and industry in higher-level programming languages and "northbound" (i.e., application-facing) APIs that provide convenient control over the full set of resources available in a network.

Unfortunately, despite several notable advances, there is still a wide gap between the capabilities of existing SDN APIs and the realities of network management. Current programming languages focus mostly on packet forwarding and largely ignore functionality such as bandwidth and packet-processing functions that can only be implemented on middleboxes, end hosts, or with custom hardware [20, 46, 65, 3, 50]. Network orchestration frameworks provide powerful mechanisms that handle a larger set of concerns including middlebox placement and bandwidth [22, 34, 55, 58], but they either fail to provide a programmable API to those mechanisms, or expose APIs that are extremely simple (e.g., sequences of middleboxes). Overall, the challenges of managing real-world networks using existing SDN APIs remain unmet.

This paper presents a new SDN programming language designed to fill this gap. This language, called Merlin, provides a collection of high-level programming constructs for (i) classifying packets; (ii) controlling forwarding paths; (iii) specifying packet-processing functions; and (iv) provisioning bandwidth in terms of maximum limits and minimum guarantees. These features go far beyond what can be realized just using SDN switches or with existing languages like Frenetic [20], Pyretic [47], and Maple [65]. As a result, implementing Merlin is non-trivial because it involves determining allocations of network-wide resources such as bandwidth—the simple compositional translations used in existing SDN compilers cannot be readily extended to handle the new features provided in Merlin.

The Merlin compiler uses a variety of techniques to determine forwarding paths, map packet-processing functions to network elements, and allocate bandwidth. These techniques are based on a unified logical representation of the network that encodes the constraints of the physical topology as well as the constraints expressed by the policy. For traffic with bandwidth constraints, the compiler uses a mixed-integer program formulation to solve a variant of the multi-commodity flow optimization problem. For traffic without bandwidth constraints, Merlin leverages properties of regular expressions and finite automata to efficiently generate forwarding trees that respect the path constraints encoded in the logical topology. Handling these two types of traffic separately allows the compiler to provide a uniform interface to programmers while reducing the size and number of expensive constraint problems it must solve. The compiler also generates configurations for a variety of network elements including switches, middleboxes, and end hosts.

Although the configurations emitted by the Merlin compiler are static, the system also incorporates mechanisms for handling dynamically changing policies. Run-time components called *negotia-*

CoNEXT'14, December 2–5, 2014, Sydney, Australia.

ACM 978-1-4503-3279-8/14/12 ...$15.00.
http://dx.doi.org/10.1145/2674005.2674989.

$loc \in$ *Locations*
$t \in$ *Packet-processing functions*
$h \in$ *Packet headers*
$f \in$ *Header fields*
$v \in$ *Header field values*
$id \in$ *Identifiers*
$n \in \mathbb{N}$

$pol ::= [s_1; \ldots; s_n], \phi$	Policies
$s ::= id : p \rightarrow r$	Statements
$\phi ::= \mathsf{max}(e, n) \mid \mathsf{min}(e, n)$	Presburger Formulas
$\quad \mid \phi_1 \;\mathsf{and}\; \phi_2 \mid \phi_1 \;\mathsf{or}\; \phi_2 \mid !\, \phi_1$	
$e ::= n \mid id \mid e + e$	Bandwidth Terms
$a ::= . \mid c \mid a\, a \mid a \mid a \mid a^* \mid !\, a$	Path Expression
$p ::= p_1 \;\mathsf{and}\; p_2 \mid p_1 \;\mathsf{or}\; p_2 \mid !\, p_1$	Predicates
$\quad \mid h.f = v \mid \mathsf{true} \mid \mathsf{false}$	
$c ::= loc \mid t$	Path Element

Figure 1: Merlin abstract syntax.

tors communicate among themselves to dynamically adjust bandwidth allocations and *verify* that the modifications made by other negotiators do not lead to policy violations. Again, the design of Merlin's policy language plays a crucial role. The same core language constructs used by the compiler for mapping policies into a constraint problem provide a concrete basis for analyzing, processing, and verifying policies modified dynamically by negotators.

We have built a working prototype of Merlin, and used it to implement a variety of practical policies that demonstrate the expressiveness of the language. These examples demonstrate that Merlin supports a wide range of network functionality including simple forwarding policies, richer packet-processing functions such as deep-packet inspection that are usually implemented on middleboxes, and policies that include bandwidth constraints. We have also implemented negotiators that realize max-min fair sharing and additive-increase multiplicative-decrease dynamic adaptation schemes. Our experimental evaluation shows that the Merlin compiler can provision and configure real-world datacenter and enterprise networks, and that Merlin can be used to obtain better application performance for data analytics and replication systems.

Overall, this paper makes the following contributions:

- It presents the design of high-level network management abstractions realized in an expressive policy language that models packet classification, forwarding, and bandwidth.
- It describes a novel compilation algorithm that selects forwarding paths and allocates bandwidth using a mixed-integer program formulation and constraint solver.
- It develops techniques for dynamically adapting policies using negotiators and accompanying verification techniques, made possible by the language design.

The rest of this paper describes the design of the Merlin language (§2), compiler (§3), and runtime transformations (§4). It then describes the implementation (§5) and presents the results from our performance evaluation (§6).

2. LANGUAGE DESIGN

The Merlin policy language gives programmers a collection of constructs that allow them to specify the intended behavior of the network at a high level of abstraction. As an example, suppose that we want to place a bandwidth cap on FTP control and data transfer traffic, while providing a bandwidth guarantee to HTTP traffic. The program below realizes this specification using a sequence of Merlin policy statements, followed by a logical formula. Each statement contains a variable that tracks the amount of bandwidth used by packets processed with that statement, a predicate on packet headers that identifies a set of packets, and a regular expression that describes a set of forwarding paths through the network:

```
[ x : (ip.src = 192.168.1.1 and
       ip.dst = 192.168.1.2 and
       tcp.dst = 20) -> .* dpi .* ;
  y : (ip.src = 192.168.1.1 and
       ip.dst = 192.168.1.2 and
       tcp.dst = 21) -> .* ;
 [z : (ip.src = 192.168.1.1 and
       ip.dst = 192.168.1.2 and
       tcp.dst = 80) -> .* dpi *. nat .* ],
  max(x + y,50MB/s) and min(z,100MB/s)
```

The statement on the first line asserts that FTP traffic from the host at IP address `192.168.1.1` to the host at address `192.168.1.2` must travel along a path that includes a packet-processing function that performs deep-packet inspection (`dpi`). The next two statements identify and constrain FTP control and HTTP traffic between the same hosts respectively. The statement for FTP control traffic does not include any constraints on its forwarding path, while the HTTP statement includes both a deep-packet inspection (`dpi`) and a network address translation (`nat`) constraint. The formula on the last line declares a bandwidth cap (`max`) on the FTP traffic, and a bandwidth guarantee (`min`) for the HTTP traffic.

Note that packet-processing functions may modify packet headers. In this example policy, the `nat` function will re-write the packet IP addresses. To allow such functions to coexist with predicates on packet headers that identify sets of traffic, Merlin uses a tag-based routing scheme that will be explained in Section 3.4. The rest of this section describes the constructs used in this policy in detail.

2.1 Syntax and semantics

The syntax of the Merlin policy language is defined by the grammar in Figure 1. A policy is a set of *statements*, each of which specifies the handling of a subset of traffic, together with a *logical formula* that expresses a global bandwidth constraint. For simplicity, we require that the statements have disjoint predicates and together match all packets. In our implementation, these requirements are enforced using a simple policy pre-processor.

Statements. Each policy statement comprises several components: an *identifier*, a *logical predicate*, and a *regular expression*. The identifier provides a way to identify the set of packets matching the predicate, while the regular expression specifies the forwarding paths and packet-processing functions that should be applied to matching packets. Together, these abstractions facilitate thinking of the entire network as a single switch that forwards traffic between its external ports (i.e., a "big switch" [35]), while enabling programmers to retain precise control over forwarding paths and bandwidth usage.

Logical predicates. Merlin supports a predicate language for classifying packets. Atomic predicates of the form $h.f = v$ denote the set of packets whose header field $h.f$ is equal to v. For instance, in the example policy above, statement `z` contains the predicate that matches packets with `ip` source address `192.168.1.1`, destination address `192.168.1.2`, and `tcp` port `80`. Merlin provides atomic predicates for a number of standard protocols including Ethernet, IP, TCP, and UDP, and a special predicate for matching packet payloads. Predicates can also be combined using conjunction (`and`), disjunction (`or`), and negation (`!`).

Regular expressions. Merlin allows programmers to specify the set of allowed forwarding paths through the network using regular expressions—a natural and well-studied formalism for describing paths through a graph (such as a finite state automaton or a network topology). However, rather than matching strings of characters, as with ordinary regular expressions, Merlin regular expressions match sequences of network locations, including names of packet-processing functions, as described below. The compiler is free to select any matching path for forwarding traffic as long as the other constraints expressed by the policy are satisfied. We assume that the set of network locations is finite. As with POSIX regular expressions, the dot symbol (`.`) matches any single location.

Packet-processing functions. Merlin regular expressions may also contain names of packet-processing functions that may transform the headers and contents of packets. Such functions can be used to implement a variety of useful operations including deep packet inspection, network address translation, wide-area optimizers, caches, proxies, traffic shapers, and others. The compiler determines the location where each function is enforced, using a mapping from function names to possible locations supplied as a parameter. The only requirements on these functions are that they must take a single packet as input and generate zero or more packets as output, and they must only access local state. In particular, the restriction to local state allows the compiler to freely place functions without having to worry about maintaining global state.

Bandwidth constraints. Merlin policies use logical formulas to specify constraints that either limit (`max`) or guarantee (`min`) bandwidth. In addition to conjunction (`and`), disjunction (`or`), and negation (`!`), Merlin supports an addition operator. The addition operator can be used to specify an aggregate cap on traffic, such as in the `max(x + y, 50MB/s)` term from the running example. By convention, policies without a rate clause are unconstrained—policies that lack a minimum rate are not guaranteed any bandwidth, and policies that lack a maximum rate may send traffic at rates up to line speed. Bandwidth constraints are expressed formally using first-order logic with addition—a system known as Presburger arithmetic. Note that other operators such as subtraction and division do not make as much sense in the context of bandwidth and that excluding multiplication ensures decidability.

Intuitively, a formula specifies the rate at which sources of various types of traffic may emit packets. Assume the universe of rates is `[0, MAX]` where `MAX` is given by physical constraints. Then `max(x, 100Mbps)` says the rate of `x` traffic must be in the interval `[0, 100Mbps)`, whereas `min(x, 100Mbps)` says the rate of `x` traffic must be in `[100Mbps, MAX]`, assuming the source is attempting to push that much data. Negation inverts the set of rates allowed, so that `!max(x,100Mbps)` is in fact `min(x, 100Mbps)`.

Bandwidth constraints differ from packet-processing functions in one important aspect: they represent an explicit allocation of global network resources. Hence, additional care is needed in compiling them.

Syntactic sugar. Merlin also supports several forms of syntactic sugar that simplify the expression of complex policies including set literals and several functions on sets. For example, the following policy,

```
srcs := {192.168.1.1}
dsts := {192.168.1.2}
foreach (s,d) in cross(srcs,dsts):
  tcp.dst = 80 ->
  ( .* dpi .* nat .*) at min(100MB/s)
```

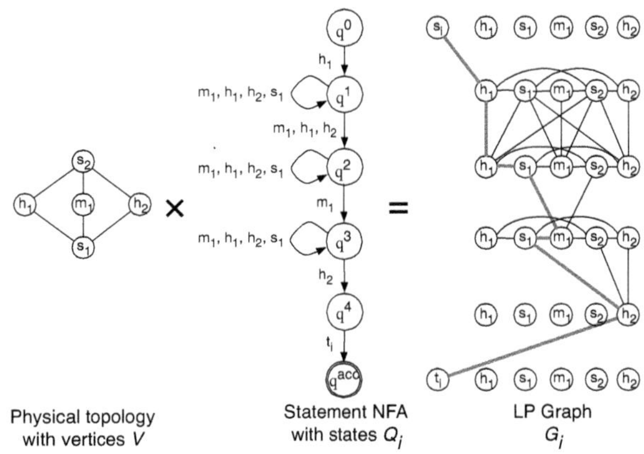

Figure 2: Logical topology for the example policy. The thick, red path illustrates a solution.

is equivalent to statement `z` from the example. The sets `srcs` and `dsts` refer to singleton sets of hosts. The `cross` operator takes the cross product of these sets. The `foreach` statement iterates over the resulting set, creating a predicate from the source `s`, destination `d`, and term `tcp.dst = 80`.

Summary. Overall, Merlin's policy language enables direct expression of high-level network policies. Programmers write policies as though they were centralized programs executed on a single network device. In reality, each policy consists of several components that run on a variety of devices distributed throughout the network. Collectively, these component constructs enforce the global policy. The subsequent sections present these distribution and enforcement mechanisms in detail.

3. COMPILER

The Merlin compiler performs three essential tasks: (i) it translates global policies into locally-enforceable policies; (ii) it determines the paths used to carry traffic across the network, places packet-processing functions on middleboxes and end hosts, and allocates bandwidth to individual flows; and (iii) it generates low-level configuration instructions for network devices and end hosts.

To do this, the compiler takes as inputs the Merlin policy, a representation of the physical topology, and a mapping from processing functions to possible placements, and builds a logical topology that incorporates the structure of the physical topology as well as the constraints encoded in the policy. It then analyzes the logical topology to determine allocations of resources and emits low-level configurations for switches, middleboxes, and end hosts.

3.1 Localization

Merlin's Presburger arithmetic formulas are an expressive way to declare bandwidth constraints, but actually implementing them leads to several challenges: aggregate guarantees can be enforced using shared quality-of-service queues on switches, but aggregate bandwidth limits are more difficult, since they require distributed state in general. To solve this problem, Merlin adopts a pragmatic approach. The compiler first rewrites the formula so that the bandwidth constraints apply to packets at a single location. Given a formula with one term over n identifiers, the compiler produces a new formula of n local terms that collectively imply the original. By default, the compiler divides bandwidth equally among the local terms, although other schemes are permissible. For example, the running example would be localized to:

```
[ x : (ip.src = 192.168.1.1 and
       ip.dst = 192.168.1.2 and
       tcp.dst = 20) -> .* dpi .* ;
  y : (ip.src = 192.168.1.1 and
       ip.dst = 192.168.1.2 and
       tcp.dst = 21) -> .* ;
 [z : (ip.src = 192.168.1.1 and
       ip.dst = 192.168.1.2 and
       tcp.dst = 80) -> .* dpi *. nat .* ],
  max(x,25MB/s) and
  max(y,25MB/s) and
  min(z,100MB/s)
```

Rewriting policies in this way involves an inherent tradeoff: localized enforcement increases scalability, but risks underutilizing resources if the static allocations do not reflect actual usage. In Section 4, we describe how Merlin navigates this tradeoff via a run-time mechanism, called *negotiators*, that can dynamically adjust allocations.

3.2 Provisioning for Guaranteed Rates

The most challenging aspect of the Merlin compilation process is provisioning bandwidth for traffic with guarantees. To do this, the compiler encodes the input policy and the network topology into a constraint problem whose solution, if it exists, can be used to determine the configuration of each network device.

Logical topology. Recall that a statement in the Merlin language contains a regular expression, which constrains the set of forwarding paths and packet-processing functions that may be used to satisfy the statement. To facilitate computing a set of paths that satisfy these constraints, the compiler constructs an internal representation with a directed graph $\mathcal{G}$ in which each path corresponds to a physical path that respects the constraints expressed in a single policy statement. The overall graph $\mathcal{G}$ for the policy is a union of disjoint components $\mathcal{G}_i$, one for each statement i.

The regular expression a_i in statement i is over the set of locations and packet-processing functions. The first step in the construction of $\mathcal{G}_i$ is to map a_i into a regular expression $\bar{a}_i$ over the set of locations using a simple substition: for every occurrence of a packet processor, we substitute the union of all locations associated with that function. (Recall that the compiler takes an auxiliary input specifying this mapping from functions to locations.) For example, if `h1`, `h2`, and `m1` are the three locations capable of running deep packet inspection, then the regular expression `.* dpi .*` would be transformed into `.* (h1|h2|m1) .*`. The next step is to transform the regular expression $\bar{a}_i$ into a nondeterministic finite automaton (NFA), denoted $\mathcal{M}_i$, that accepts the set of strings in the regular language given by $\bar{a}_i$.

Letting L denote the set of locations in the physical network and $\mathcal{Q}_i$ denote the state set of $\mathcal{M}_i$, the vertex set of $\mathcal{G}_i$ is the Cartesian product $L \times \mathcal{Q}_i$ together with two special vertices $\{s_i, t_i\}$ that serve as a universal source and sink for paths representing statement i respectively. The graph $\mathcal{G}_i$ has an edge from (u, q) to (v, q') if and only if: **(i)** $u = v$ or (u, v) is an edge of the physical network, and **(ii)** (q, q') is a valid state transition of $\mathcal{M}_i$ when processing v. Likewise, there is an edge from s_i to (v, q') if and only if (q^0, q') is a valid state transition of $\mathcal{M}_i$ when processing v, where q^0 denotes the start state of $\mathcal{M}_i$. Finally, there is an edge from (u, q) to t_i if and only if q is an accepting state of $\mathcal{M}_i$. Paths in $\mathcal{G}_i$ correspond to paths in the physical network that satisfy the path constraints of statement i, as captured in the following lemma.

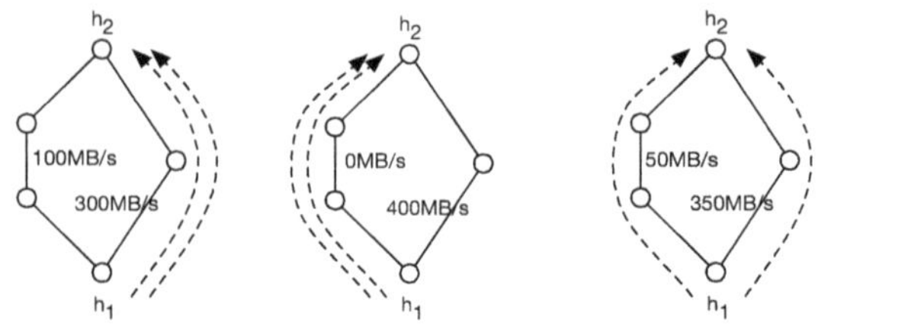

(a) Shortest-Path (b) Min-Max Ratio (c) Min-Max Reserved

Figure 3: Path selection heuristics. The edge labels in the graphs indicate the remaining capacities after path selection.

LEMMA 1. *A sequence of locations $u_1, u_2, \ldots, u_k$ satisfies the constraint described by regular expression $\bar{a}_i$ if and only if $\mathcal{G}_i$ contains a path of the form $s_i, (u_1, q_1), (u_2, q_2), \ldots, (u_k, q_k), t_i$ for some state sequence $q_1, \ldots, q_k$. A path in $\mathcal{G}_i$ of this form will be called a lifting of $u_1, u_2, \ldots, u_k$ henceforth.*

PROOF. The construction of $\mathcal{G}_i$ ensures that

$$s_i, (u_1, q_1), (u_2, q_2), \ldots, (u_k, q_k), t_i$$

is a path in the graph if and only if **(i)** the sequence $u_1, \ldots, u_k$ represents a path in the physical network (possibly with vertices of the path repeated more than once consecutively in the sequence), and **(ii)** the automaton $\mathcal{M}_i$ has an accepting computation path for $u_1, \ldots, u_k$ with state sequence $q^0, q^1, \ldots, q^k$. The lemma follows from the fact that a string belongs to the regular language defined by $\bar{a}_i$ if and only if $\mathcal{M}_i$ has a computation path that accepts that string. □

Figure 2 illustrates the construction of the graph $\mathcal{G}_i$ for a statement with path expression `h1 .* dpi .* nat .* h2`, on a small example network. We assume that deep packet inspection (`dpi`) can be performed at `h1`, `h2`, or `m1`, whereas network address translation (`nat`) can only be performed at `m1`. Paths matching the regular expression can be "lifted" to paths in $\mathcal{G}_i$; the thick, red path in the figure illustrates one such lifting. Notice that the physical network also contains other paths such as `h1`, `s1`, `h2` that do not match the regular expression. These paths do not lift to any path in $\mathcal{G}_i$. For instance, focusing attention on the rows of nodes corresponding to states q^2 and q^3 of the NFA, one sees that all edges between these two rows lead into node (m_1, q^3). This, in turn, means that any path that avoids `m1` in the physical network cannot be lifted to an s_i-t_i path in the graph $\mathcal{G}_i$.

Path selection. Next, the compiler determines a satisfying assignment of paths that respect the bandwidth constraints encoded in the policy. The problem bears a similarity to the well-known *multi-commodity flow problem* [1], with two additional types of constraints: (i) *integrality constraints* demand that only one path may be selected for each statement, and (ii) *path constraints* are specified by regular expressions, as discussed above. To incorporate path constraints, we formulate the problem in the graph $\mathcal{G} = \bigcup_i \mathcal{G}_i$ described above, rather than in the physical network itself. Incorporating integrality constraints into multi-commodity flow problems renders them NP-complete in the worst case, but a number of practical approaches have been developed over the years, ranging from approximation algorithms [9, 11, 15, 37, 39], to specialized algorithms for topologies such as expanders [7, 21, 36] and planar graphs [52], to the use of mixed-integer programming [6]. Our current implementation adopts the latter technique.

Our mixed-integer program (MIP) has a $\{0,1\}$-valued decision variable x_e for each edge e of $\mathcal{G}$; selecting a route for each statement corresponds to selecting a path from s_i to t_i for each i and setting $x_e = 1$ on the edges of those paths, $x_e = 0$ on all other edges of $\mathcal{G}$. These variables are required to satisfy the flow conservation equations

$$\forall v \in \mathcal{G} \sum_{e \in \delta^+(v)} x_e - \sum_{e \in \delta^-(v)} x_e = \begin{cases} 1 & \text{if } v = s_i \\ -1 & \text{if } v = t_i \\ 0 & \text{otherwise} \end{cases} \quad (1)$$

where $\delta^+(v)$, $\delta^-(v)$ denote the sets of edges exiting and entering v, respectively. For bookkeeping purposes the MIP also has real-valued variables r_{uv} for each physical network link (u, v), representing what fraction of the link's capacity is reserved for statements whose assigned path traverses (u, v). Finally, there are variables $r_{\max}$ and $R_{\max}$ representing the maximum fraction of any link's capacity devoted to reserved bandwidth, and the maximum net amount of reserved bandwidth on any link, respectively. The equations and inequalities pertaining to these additional variables can be written as follows. For any statement i, let $r^i_{\min}$ denote the minimum amount of bandwidth guaranteed in the rate clause of statement i. ($r^i_{\min} = 0$ if the statement contains no bandwidth guarantee.) For any physical link (u, v), let c_{uv} denote its capacity and let $E_i(u, v)$ denote the set of all edges of the form $((u, q), (v, q'))$ or $((v, q), (u, q'))$ in $\mathcal{G}_i$.

$$\forall (u,v) \;\; r_{uv} c_{uv} = \sum_i \sum_{e \in E_i(u,v)} r^i_{\min} x_e \quad (2)$$

$$\forall (u,v) \;\; r_{\max} \geq r_{uv} \quad (3)$$

$$\forall (u,v) \;\; R_{\max} \geq r_{uv} c_{uv} \quad (4)$$

$$r_{\max} \leq 1 \quad (5)$$

Constraint 2 defines r_{uv} to be the fraction of capacity on link (u, v) reserved for bandwidth guarantees. Constraints 3 and 4 ensure that $r_{\max}$ (respectively, $R_{\max}$) is at least the maximum fraction of capacity reserved on any link (respectively, the maximum net amount of bandwidth reserved on any link). Constraint 5 ensures that the path assignment will not exceed the capacity of any link, by asserting that the fraction of reserved capacity does not exceed 1.

Path selection heuristics. In general, there may be multiple assignments that satisfy the path and bandwidth constraints. To indicate the preferred assignment, programmers can invoke Merlin with one of three optimization criteria:

- *Weighted shortest path:* minimizes the total number of hops in assigned paths, weighted by bandwidth guarantees: $\min \sum_i \sum_{u \neq v} \sum_{e \in E_i(u,v)} r^i_{\min} x_e$. This criterion is appropriate when the goal is to minimize latency as longer paths tend to experience increased latency.

- *Min-max ratio:* minimizes the maximum fraction of capacity reserved on any link (i.e., $r_{\max}$). This criterion is appropriate when the goal is to balance load across the network links.

- *Min-max reserved:* minimizes the maximum amount of bandwidth reserved on any link (i.e., $R_{\max}$). This criterion is appropriate when the goal is to guard against failures, since it limits the maximum amount of traffic that may disrupted by a single link failure.

The differences between these heuristics are illustrated in Figure 3 which depicts a simple network with hosts `h1` and `h2` connected by a pair of disjoint paths. The left path comprises three edges of capacity 400MB/s. The right path comprises two edges of capacity 100MB/s. The figure shows the paths selected for two statements each requesting a bandwidth guarantee of 50MB/s. Depending on the heuristic, the MIP solver will either select two-hop paths (weighted shortest path), reserve no more than 25% of capacity on any link (min-max ratio), or reserve no more than 50MB/s on any link (min-max reserved).

The Merlin compiler finds solutions that use a single path for each traffic class. While there exist approaches to multi-commodity flow that take advantage of multiple paths, certain protocols (e.g. TCP congestion control) assume that all packets in a given connection going from one host to another will traverse the same path.

3.3 Provisioning for Best-Effort Rates

For traffic requiring only best-effort rates, Merlin does not need to solve a constraint problem. Instead, the compiler only needs to compute sink-trees that obey the path constraints expressed in the policy. A sink-tree for a particular network node forwards traffic from elsewhere on the network to that node. Merlin does this by computing the cross product of the regular expression NFA and the network topology representation, as just described, and then performing a breadth-first search over the resulting graph. To further improve scalability, the compiler uses a small optimization: it uses a topology that only includes switches, and computes a sink tree for each egress switch. The compiler adds instructions to forward traffic from the egress switches to the hosts during code generation. This allows the BFS to be computed in $O(|V||E|)$, where $|V|$ is the number of switches rather than the number of hosts.

3.4 Code Generation

Next, the Merlin compiler generates code to enforce the policy. To do this, Merlin applies a form of *program partitioning*. Programmers write the high-level Merlin policy without regard to how the policy is implemented on the devices distributed throughout the network. The compiler partitions the policy into separate programs, instructions, or configuration files that are deployed on the various devices. The actual code is determined both by the requested functionality and the type of target device.

- *Switches.* For basic forwarding, Merlin generates instructions for OpenFlow [45] enabled switches. For bandwidth guarantees, Merlin generates device-specific port queue configuration scripts. To install the OpenFlow instructions, Merlin generates the code for a network controller written using Frenetic's OCaml OpenFlow libraries [19].

- *Middleboxes.* For functionality such as deep packet inspection, load balancing, or intrusion detection, Merlin generates Click [38] configuration scripts to declare what packet-processing functions to apply, and the order in which to apply them. Other approaches are possible—e.g., Merlin could generate Puppet [54] scripts to declare and manage virtual machines that implement the specified functions.

- *End hosts.* Traffic filtering and rate limiting are implemented using the standard Linux utilities `iptables` and `tc`.

Merlin can provide greater flexibility and expressiveness by directly generating packet-processing code, which can be executed by an interpreter running on end hosts or on middleboxes. We have also built a prototype that runs as a Linux kernel module and uses the `netfilter` callback functions to access packets on the network stack. The interpreter accepts and enforces programs that can filter or rate limit traffic using a richer set of predicates than those offered by `iptables`. It is designed to have minimal dependencies on operating system services in order to make it portable across different systems. The current implementation requires only about a dozen system calls to be exported from the operating system to the interpreter. In on-going work, we are exploring additional functionality, with the goal or providing a general runtime as the target for the Merlin compiler. However, using end hosts assumes a trusted deployment in which all host machines are under administrative control. An interesting, but orthogonal, problem is to deploy Merlin in an untrusted environment. Several techniques have been proposed to verify that an untrusted machine is running certain software. Notable examples include proof carrying code [49], and TPM-based attestations [16, 61].

Tag-based routing. Because Merlin controls forwarding paths but also supports packet-processing functions that may modify headers (such as NAT boxes), the compiler needs to use a forwarding mechanism that is robust to changes in packet headers. Our current implementation uses VLAN tags to encode paths to destination switches, one tag per sink tree. All packets destined for that tree's sink are tagged with a tag when they enter the network. Subsequent switches simply examine the tag to determine the next hop. At the egress switch, the tag is stripped off and a unique host identifier (e.g., the MAC address) is used to forward traffic to the appropriate host. This approach is similar to the technique used in other systems designed to combine programmable switches and middleboxes such as FlowTags [17].

To sum up, the Merlin compiler is designed with flexibility in mind and can be easily extended with additional backends that capitalize on the capabilities of the various devices available in the network. Although the expressiveness of policies is bounded by the capabilities of the devices, Merlin provides a unified interface for programming them.

4. DYNAMIC ADAPTATION

The Merlin compiler described in the preceding section translates policies into static configurations. Of course, these static configurations may under-utilize resources, depending on how traffic demands evolve over time. Moreover, in a shared environment, network tenants may wish to customize global policies to suit their own needs—e.g., to add additional security constraints.

To allow for the dynamic modification of policies, Merlin uses small run-time components called *negotiators*. Negotiators are policy transformers and verifiers—they allow policies to be delegated to tenants for modification and they provide a mechanism for verifying that modifications made by tenants do not lead to violations of the original global policy. Negotiators depend critically on Merlin's language-based approach. The same abstractions that allow policies to be mapped to constraint problems (i.e., predicates, regular expressions, and explicit bandwidth reservations), make it easy to support *verifiable* policy transformations.

Negotiators are distributed throughout the network in a tree, forming a hierarchical overlay over network elements. Each negotiator is responsible for the network elements in the subtree for which it is the root. Parent negotiators impose policies on their children. Children may refine their own policies, as long as the refinement implies the parent policy. Likewise, siblings may renegotiate resource assignments cooperatively, as long as they do not violate parent policies. Negotiators communicate amongst themselves to dynamically adjust bandwidth allocations to fit particular deployments and traffic demands.

4.1 Transformations

With negotiators, tenants can transform global network policies by *refining* the delegated policies to suit their own demands. Tenants may modify policies in three ways: (i) policies may be refined with respect to packet classification; (ii) forwarding paths may be further constrained; and (iii) bandwidth allocations may be revised.

Refining policies. Merlin policies classify packets into sets using predicates that combine matches on header fields using logical operators. These sets can be refined by introducing additional constraints to the original predicate. For example, a predicate for matching all TCP traffic:

```
ip.proto = tcp
```

can be partitioned into ones that match HTTP traffic and all other traffic:

```
ip.proto = tcp and tcp.dst = 80
ip.proto = tcp and tcp.dst != 80
```

The partitioning must be total—all packets identified by the original policy must be identified by the set of new policies.

Constraining paths. Merlin programmers declare path constraints using regular expressions that match sequences of network locations or packet processing functions. Tenants can refine a policy by adding addition constraints to the regular expression. For example, an expression that says all packets must go through a traffic logger (LOG) function:

```
.* log .*
```

can be modified to say that the traffic must additionally pass through a DPI function:

```
.* log .* dpi .*
```

The requirement for a transformation that involves changing regular expressions to be valid is that the set of paths denoted by the new expression must be a subset of the paths denoted by the original.

Re-allocating bandwidth. Merlin's limits (`max`) and guarantees (`min`) constrain allocations of network bandwidth. After a policy has been refined, these constraints can be redistributed to improve utilization. The requirement for a transformation that involves changing bandwidth constraints to be valid is that the sum of the new allocations must not exceed the original allocation.

Example. As an example that illustrates the use of all three transformations, consider the following policy, which caps all traffic between two hosts at 700MB/s:

```
[x : (ip.src = 192.168.1.1 and
      ip.dst = 192.168.1.2) -> .*],
max(x, 700MB/s)
```

This policy could be modified as follows:

```
[ x : (ip.src = 192.168.1.1 and
       ip.dst = 192.168.1.2 and
       tcp.dst = 80) -> .* log .* ;
  y : (ip.src = 192.168.1.1 and
       ip.dst = 192.168.1.2 and
       tcp.dst = 22) -> .* ;
  z : (ip.src = 192.168.1.1 and
       ip.dst = 192.168.1.2 and
       !(tcp.dst=22|tcp.dst=80)) -> .* dpi .* ],
max(x, 500MB/s)
and max(y, 100MB/s)
and max(z, 100MB/s)
```

It gives 500MB/s to HTTP traffic, which must flow through a `log` box that monitors requests; it gives 100MB/s to SSH traffic, and it gives 100MB/s to the remaining traffic, which must flow through a `dpi` box.

4.2 Verification

Allowing tenants to make arbitrary modifications to policies would not be safe. For example, a tenant could lift restrictions on forwarding paths, eliminate transformations, or allocate more bandwidth to their own traffic—all violations of the global policy set down by the administrator. Fortunately, Merlin negotiators can leverage the policy language representation to check policy inclusion, which can be used to establish the correctness of policy transformations implemented by untrusted tenants.

Intuitively, a valid refinement of a policy is one that makes it only more restrictive. To verify that a policy modified by a tenant is a valid refinement of the original, the negotiator simply has to check that for every statement in the original policy, the set of paths allowed for matching packets in the refined policy is included in the set of paths in the original, and the bandwidth constraints in the refined policy imply the bandwidth constraints in the original. These conditions can be decided using a simple algorithm that performs a pair-wise comparison of all statements in the original and modified policies, (i) checking for language inclusion [28] between the regular expressions in statements with overlapping predicates, and (ii) checking that the sum of the bandwidth constraints in all overlapping predicates implies the original constraint.

4.3 Adaptation

Bandwidth re-allocation does not require recompilation of the global policy, and can thus happen quite rapidly. As a proof-of-concept, we implemented negotiators that can provide both min-max fair sharing and additive-increase, multiplicative decrease allocation schemes. These negotiators allow traffic policies to change with dynamic workloads, while still obeying the overall static global policies. Changes in path constraints require global recompilation and updating forwarding rules on the switches, so they incur a greater overhead. However, we believe these changes are likely to occur less frequently than changes to bandwidth allocations.

5. IMPLEMENTATION

We have implemented a full working prototype of the Merlin system in OCaml and C. Our implementation uses the Gurobi Optimizer [25] to solve constraints, the Frenetic controller [19] to install forwarding rules on OpenFlow switches, the Click router [38] to manage software middleboxes, and the `ipfilters` and `tc` utilities on Linux end hosts. Note that the design of Merlin does not depend on these specific systems. It would be easy to instantiate our design with other systems, and our implementation provides a clean interface for incorporating additional backends.

Our implementation of Merlin negotiator and verification mechanisms leverages standard algorithms for transforming and analyzing predicates and regular expressions. To delegate a policy, Merlin simply intersects the predicates and regular expressions in each statement the original policy to project out the policy for the sub-network. To verify implications between policies, Merlin uses the Z3 SMT solver [48] to check predicate disjointness, and the Dprle library [27] to check inclusions between regular expressions.

6. EVALUATION

To evaluate Merlin, we investigated three main issues: (i) the expressiveness of the Merlin policy language, (ii) the ability of Merlin to improve end-to-end performance for applications, and (iii) the scalability of the compiler and negotiator components with respect to network and policy size. We used two testbeds in our evaluation. Most experiments were run on a cluster of Dell r720 PowerEdge servers with two 8-core 2.7GHz Intel Xeon processors, 32GB RAM, and four 1GB NICs. The Ring Paxos experiment (§6.2) was conducted on a cluster of eight HP SE1102 servers equipped with two quad-core Intel Xeon L5420 processors running at 2.5 GHz, with 8 GB of RAM and two 1GB NICs. Both clusters used a Pica8 Pronto 3290 switch to connect the machines. To test the scalability we ran the compiler and negotiator frameworks on various topologies and policies.

Overall, our experiments show that Merlin can effectively provision and configure real-world datacenter and enterprise networks, that Merlin can be used to obtain better performance for big-data processing applications and replication systems, and that Merlin enables succinctly expressing rich network policies.

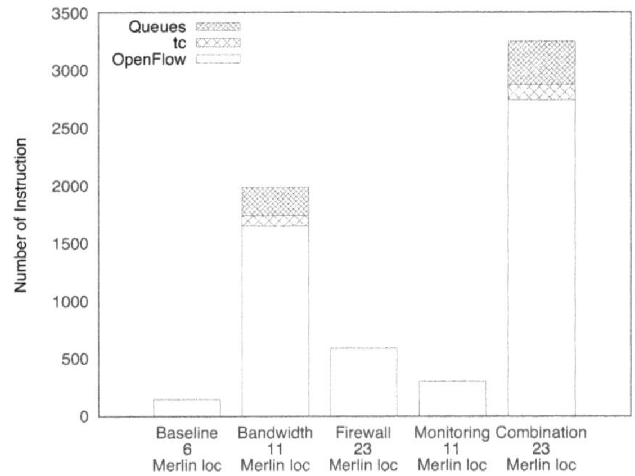

Figure 4: Merlin expressiveness, measured using policies for the Stanford campus network topology.

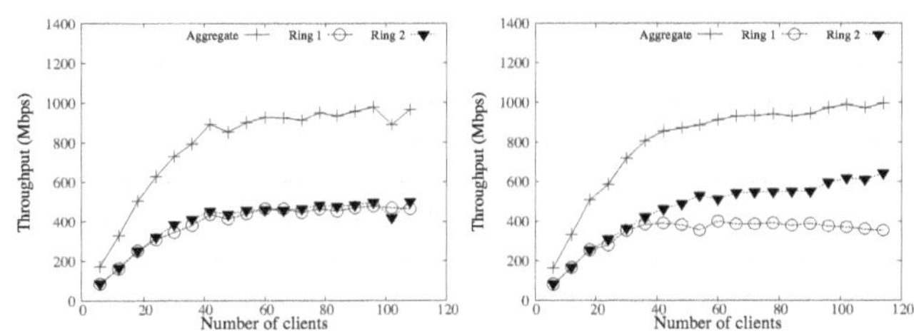

(a) (b)

Figure 5: Ring-Paxos (a) without and (b) with Merlin.

6.1 Expressiveness.

To explore the expressiveness of the Merlin policy languages, we built several network policies for the 16-switch Stanford core campus network topology [4]. We added 24 hosts to each of the 12 edge switches in the topology and identified each pair-wise exchange of traffic between hosts as a separate traffic class. Hence, there are $(24 * 12)^2 - (24 * 12) = 82,656$ total traffic classes. We then implemented a series of policies in Merlin, and compared the sizes of the Merlin source policies and the outputs generated by the compiler. This comparison measures the degree to which Merlin is able to abstract away from hardware-level details and provide effective constructs for managing a real-world network.

The Merlin policies we implemented are as follows:

1. *All-pairs connectivity.* This policy creates pair-wise forwarding rules for all hosts in the network. The policy is restricted to only forwarding, and does not specify packet-processing functions or provide bandwidth caps and guarantees. It therefore provides a baseline measurement of the number of low-level instructions that would be needed in almost any non-trivial application. The Merlin policy is only 6 lines long and compiles to 145 OpenFlow rules.
2. *Bandwidth caps and guarantee.* This policy augments the basic connectivity by providing 10% of traffic classes a bandwidth guarantee of 1Mbps and a cap of 1Gbps. Such a guarantee would be useful, for example, to prioritize emergency messages sent to students. This policy required 11 lines of Merlin code, but generates over 1600 OpenFlow rules, 90 TC rules and 248 queue configurations. The number of OpenFlow rules increased dramatically due to the presence of the bandwidth guarantees which required provisioning separate forwarding paths for a large collection of traffic classes.
3. *Firewall.* This policy assumes the presence of a middlebox that filters incoming web traffic connected to the network ingress switches. The baseline policy is altered to forward all packets matching a particular pattern (e.g., `tcp.dst = 80`) through the middlebox. This policy requires 23 lines of Merlin code, but generates over 500 OpenFlow instructions.
4. *Monitoring middlebox.* This policy attaches middleboxes to two switches and partitions the hosts into two sets of roughly equal size. Hosts connected to switches in the same set may send traffic to each other directly, but traffic flowing between sets must be passed through a middlebox. This policy is useful for filtering traffic from untrusted sources, such as student dorms. This policy required 11 lines of Merlin code but generates 300 OpenFlow rules, roughly double the baseline.
5. *Combination.* This policy augments the basic connectivity with a filter for web traffic, a bandwidth guarantee for certain traffic classes and an inspection policy for a certain class of hosts. This policy requires 23 lines of Merlin code, but generates over 3000 low-level instructions.

The results of this experiment are depicted in Figure 4. Overall, it shows that using Merlin significantly reduces the effort, in terms of lines of code, required to provision and configure network devices for a variety of real-world management tasks.

6.2 Application Performance

Our second set of experiments explore Merlin's ability to express policies that are beneficial for real-world applications. As one would expect, they show that bandwidth provisioning improves the performance of data center applications. However, the experiments are provide a proof-of-concept that Merlin policies can be used to effectively manage data center traffic.

Hadoop. Hadoop is a popular open-source MapReduce [13] implementation, and is widely-used for data analytics. A Hadoop computation proceeds in three stages: the system (i) applies a *map* operator to each data item to produce a large set of key-value pairs; (ii) *shuffles* all data with a given key to a single node; and (iii) applies the *reduce* operator to values with the same key. The many-to-many communication pattern used in the shuffle phase often results in heavy network load, making Hadoop jobs especially sensitive to background traffic. In practice, this background traffic can come from a variety of sources. For example, some applications use UDP-based gossip protocols to update state, such as system monitoring tools [64, 63], network overlay management [32], and even distributed storage systems [64, 14]. A sensible network policy would be to provide guaranteed bandwidth to Hadoop so jobs finish quickly, and give the UDP traffic only best-effort guarantees.

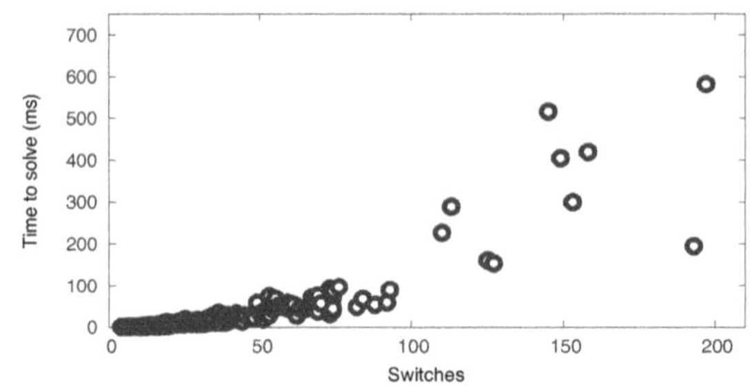

Figure 6: Compilation times for Internet Topology Zoo.

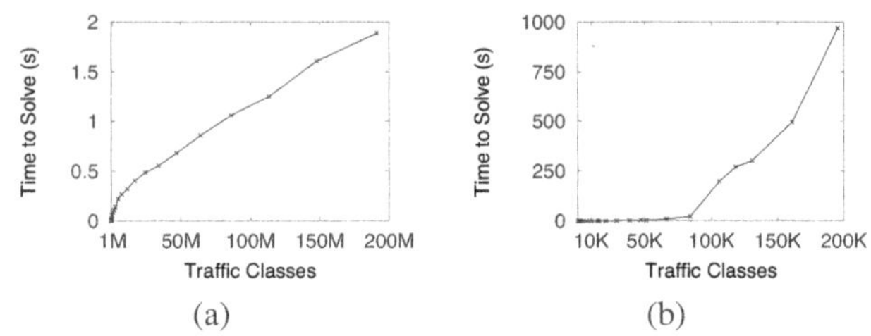

Figure 7: Compilation times for an increasing number of traffic classes in a balanced tree topology for (a) all pairs connectivity, (b) 5% of the traffic with guaranteed priority.

With Merlin, we implemented this policy using just three statements. To show the impact of the policy, we ran a Hadoop job that sorts 10GB of data, and measured the time to complete it on a cluster of four servers, under three different configurations:

1. *Baseline.* Hadoop had exclusive access to the network.
2. *Interference.* We used the `iperf` tool to inject UDP packets, simulating background traffic.
3. *Guarantees.* We again injected background traffic, but guaranteed 90 percent of the capacity for Hadoop.

The measurements demonstrate the expected results. With exclusive network access, the Hadoop job finished in 466 seconds. With background traffic causing network congestion, the job finished in 558 seconds, a roughly 20% slow down. With the Merlin policy providing bandwidth guarantees, the job finished in 500 seconds, corresponding to the 90% allocation of bandwidth.

Ring-Paxos. State-machine replication (SMR) is a fundamental approach to designing fault-tolerant services [41, 57] that is used at the core of many current systems (e.g., Google's Chubby [8], Scatter [23], Spanner [12]). State machine replication provides clients with the abstraction of a highly available service by replicating the servers and regulating how commands are propagated to and executed by the replicas: (i) every nonfaulty replica must receive all commands in the same order; and (ii) the execution of commands must be deterministic.

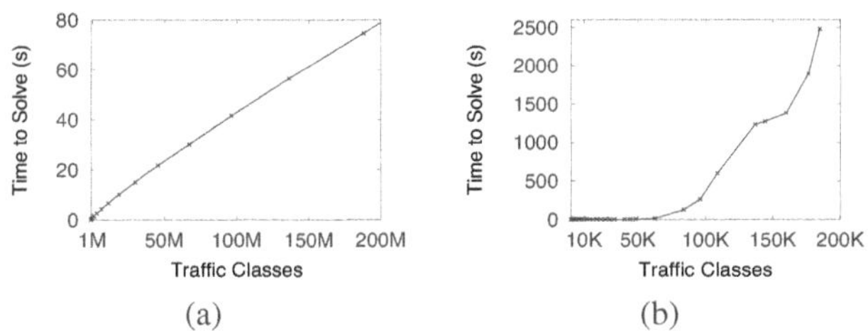

Figure 8: Compilation times for an increasing number of traffic classes in a fat tree topology for (a) all pairs connectivity, (b) 5% of the traffic with guaranteed priority.

Because ordering commands in a distributed setting is a non-negligible operation, the performance of a replicated service is often determined by the number of commands that can be ordered per time unit. To achieve high performance, the service state can be partitioned and each partition replicated individually (e.g., by separating data from meta-data), but the partitions will compete for shared resources (e.g., common nodes and network links).

We assessed the performance of a key-value store service replicated with state-machine replication. Commands are ordered using an open-source implementation of Ring Paxos [44], a highly efficient implementation of the Paxos protocol [42]. We deployed two instances of the service, each one using four processes. One process in each service is co-located on the same machine and all other processes run on different machines. Clients are distributed across six different machines and submit their requests to one of the services and receive responses from the replicas.

Figure 5 (a) depicts the throughput of the two services; the aggregate throughput shows the accumulated performance of the two services. Since both services compete for resources on the common machine, each service has a similar share of the network, the bottlenecked resource at the common machine. In Figure 5 (b), we specified a guarantee of 60 percent of the capacity for Service 2. Note that this guarantee does not come at the expense of utilization. If Service 2 stops sending traffic, Service 1 is free to use the available bandwidth.

Summary. Overall, these experiments show that Merlin policies can concisely express real-world policies, and that the Merlin system is able to generate code that achieves the desired outcomes for applications on real hardware.

6.3 Compilation and Verification

The scalability of the Merlin compiler and verification framework depend on both the size of the network topology and the number of traffic classes. Our third set of experiment evaluate the scalability of Merlin under a variety of scenarios.

Compiler. The measured the compilation time of the Merlin compiler on three different sets of network topologies.

1. *Topology Zoo.* The Internet Topology Zoo [29] dataset contains 262 topologies that represent a large diversity of network structures. We treated each node in the Topology Zoo graph as a switch, and attached one host to each switch. The topologies have an average size of 40 switches, with a standard deviation of 30 switches. We measured the compilation time needed by Merlin to determine pair-wise forwarding rules for all hosts in each topology. In other words, the policy provides basic connectivity for all hosts in the network. The results are shown in Figure 6.
2. *Balanced Trees.* We used the NetworkX Python software package [51] to generate balanced tree topologies. In a balanced tree, each node has n children, except the leaves. We treated internal node as switches, and leaf nodes as hosts. We varied the depth of the tree from 2 to 3, and the fanout (i.e., number of children) over a range of 2 to 24, to give us trees with varying numbers of hosts and switches. We identified each pair-wise exchange of traffic between hosts as a separate traffic class. We measured the compilation time for two different policies for an increasing number of traffic classes. Figure 7 (a) shows the time to provide pair-wise connectivity with no guarantees, and Figure 7 (b) shows the time to provide connectivity when 5% of the traffic classes receive bandwidth guarantees.
3. *Fat Trees.* Finally, we used the NetworkX to generate fat tree topologies [2]. A fat tree contains a set of *pods*. Each pod of size n has two layers of $n/2$ switches. To each switch in a lower layer, we attached two hosts. Each pair-wise exchange of traffic between hosts is a separate traffic class. We increased the pod size n to create larger numbers of traffic classes. Figure 8 (a) shows the compilation time to provide pair-wise connectivity with no guarantees, and Figure 8 (b) shows the time to provide connectivity when 5% of the traffic classes receive bandwidth guarantees. To provide more detail for fat tree topologies, Figure 9 shows a sample of topology sizes and solution times for various traffic classes, along with a finer-grained accounting of compiler time.

The results in Figure 6 show that for providing basic connectivity, Merlin scales well on a diverse set of topologies. The compiler finished in less than 50ms for the majority of topologies, and less than 600ms for all but one of the topologies. To improve the readability of the graph, we elided the largest topology, which has 754 switches and took Merlin 4 seconds to compile. In practice, we expect that this task could be computed offline. To put the results in context, a similar experiment was used to evaluate VMware's NSX, which reports approximately 30 minutes to achieve 100% connectivity from a cold boot [40].

Figures 7 and 8 show the impact of bandwidth guarantees on compilation time. As expected, the guarantees add significant overhead. The worst case scenario that we measured, shown in Figure 8 (b), was a network with 184,470 total traffic classes, with 9,224 of those classes receiving bandwidth guarantees. Merlin took around 41 minutes to find a solution. To put that number in perspective, B4 [31] only distinguishes 13 traffic classes. Merlin finds solutions for 100 traffic classes with guarantees in a network with 125 switches in less than 5 seconds.

Figure 9 shows more detail about where the compiler time is spent. The LP construction column measures how long it takes to create the LP problem. Our prototype implementation writes the problem to a file on disk before invoking the solver in a separate process. So, much of this time is attributed to string allocations and file I/O. The LP solution column measures how long it takes the solver to find a solution to the LP problem. As expected, this is where most of the time is spent as we increase the problem size. The Best-Effort solution column measures how long it takes to find paths with best-effort guarantees for the remaining traffic. The compiler spends little time finding paths that do not provide guaranteed rates.

These experiments show that Merlin can provide connectivity for large networks quickly and our mixed-integer programming ap-

Traffic Classes	Hosts	Switches	LP construction (ms)	LP solution (ms)	Best-Effort solution (ms)
870	30	45	25	22	33
8010	90	80	214	160	36
28730	170	125	364	252	106
39800	200	125	1465	1485	91
95790	310	180	13287	248779	222
136530	370	180	27646	1200912	215
159600	400	180	29701	1351865	212
229920	480	245	86678	10476008	451

Figure 9: Number of traffic classes, topology sizes, and details of compilation time for fat tree topologies with 5% of the traffic classes with guaranteed bandwidth.

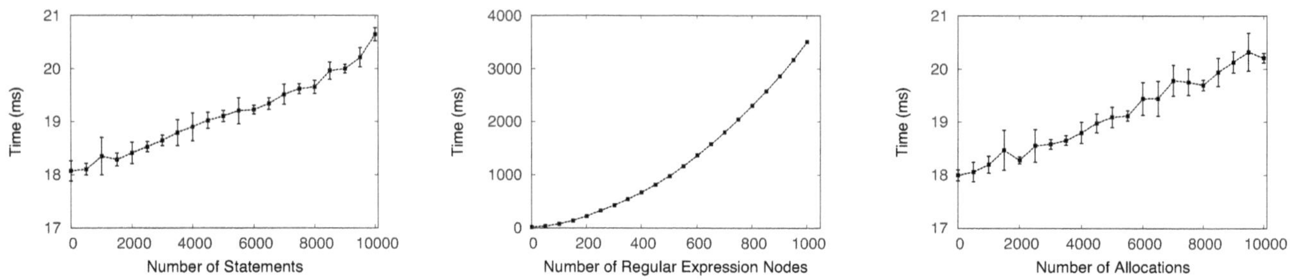

Figure 10: Time taken to verify a delegated policy for an increasing number of delegated predicates, increasingly complex regular expressions, and an increasing number of bandwidth allocations.

proach used for guaranteeing bandwidth scales to large networks with reasonable overhead.

Verifying negotiators. Delegated Merlin policies can be modified by negotiators in three ways: by changing the predicates, the regular expressions, or the bandwidth allocations. We ran three experiments to benchmark our negotiator verification runtime for these cases. First, we increased the number of additional predicates generated in the delegated policy. Second, we increased the complexity of the regular expressions in the delegated policy. The number of nodes in the regular expression's abstract syntax tree is used as a measure of its complexity. Finally, we increased the number of bandwidth allocations in the delegated policy. For all three experiments, we measured the time needed for negotiators to verify a delegated policy against the original policy. We report the mean and standard deviation over ten runs.

The results, shown in Figure 10, demonstrate that policy verification is extremely fast for increasing predicates and allocations. Both scale linearly up to tens of thousands of allocations and statements and complete in milliseconds. This shows that Merlin negotiators can be used to rapidly adjust to changing traffic loads. Verification of regular expressions has higher overhead. It scales quadratically, and takes about 3.5 seconds for an expression with a thousand nodes in its parse tree. However, since regular expressions denote paths through the network, it is unlikely that we will encounter regular expressions with thousands of nodes in realistic deployments. Moreover, we expect path constraints to change relatively infrequently compared to bandwidth constraints.

Dynamic adaptation. Merlin negotiators support a wide range of resource management schemes. We implemented two common approaches: *additive-increase, multiplicative decrease* (AIMD), and *max-min fair-sharing* (MMFS). Both implementations required two components: a negotiator which ran on the same machine as the SDN controller, and end-host software, which monitors per-host bandwidth usage, and sends requests to the negotiator.

With AIMD, the end-host components send requests to the negotiator to incrementally increase their bandwidth allocation. The negotiator maintains a mapping of hosts to their current bandwidth limits. When the negotiator receives a new request, it attempts to satisfy the demand. If, however, satisfying the demand violates the global policy, it then exponentially reduces the allocation for the host. After computing the new allocations, the negotiator generates the updated Merlin policies, which are processed by the compiler to generate new `tc` commands that are installed on the end-hosts.

With MMFS, the end-host components declare resource requirements ahead of time by sending demands to the negotiator. The negotiator maintains a mapping of hosts to their demands. When the negotiator receives a new demand, it re-allocates bandwidth for all hosts. It does this by attempting to satisfy all demands starting with the smallest. When there is not enough bandwidth available to satisfy any further demands, the left-over bandwidth is distributed equally among the remaining tenants. Once the new allocations are computed, the negotiator generates a new policy that reflects those allocations. The new policy is processed by the compiler to generate new queue configurations for switches, and `tc` commands for end hosts. The queues configurations ensure that satisfied demands are respected, and the `tc` commands ensure that the remaining traffic does not exceed the allocation specified by the original policy.

Figure 11 (a) shows the bandwidth usage over time for two hosts using the AIMD strategy. Figure 11 (b) shows the bandwidth usage over time for four hosts using the MMFS negotiators. Host `h1` communicates with `h2`, and `h3` communicates with `h4`. Both graphs were generated on our hardware testbed. Overall, negotiators allow the network to quickly adapt to changing resource demands, while respecting the global constraints imposed by the policy.

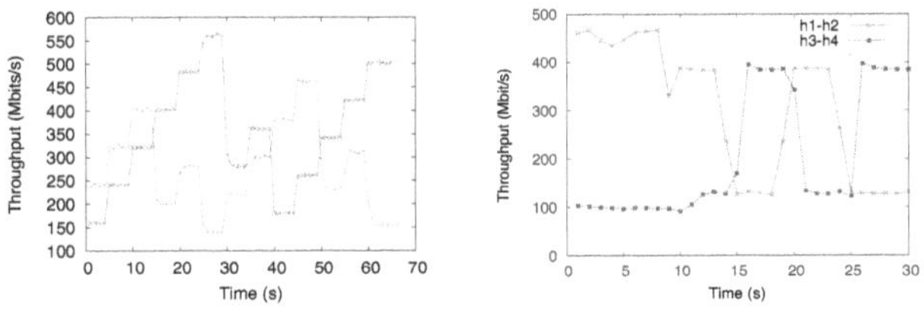

(a) (b)

Figure 11: (a) AIMD and (b) MMFS dynamic adaptation.

7. RELATED WORK

An earlier workshop paper presented a preliminary design for Merlin including sketching the encoding of path selection as a constraint problem, and presenting ideas for language-based delegation and verification [62]. This paper expands our earlier work with a complete description of Merlin's design and implementation, and an experimental evaluation.

A number of systems in recent years have investigated mechanisms for providing bandwidth caps and guarantees [5, 60, 53, 33], implementing traffic filters [30, 56], or specifying forwarding policies at different points in the network [20, 24, 47, 26]. Merlin builds on these approaches by providing a unified interface and central point of control for switches, middleboxes, and end hosts.

SIMPLE [55] is a framework for controlling middleboxes. SIMPLE attempts to load balance the network with respect to TCAM and CPU usage. Like Merlin, it solves an optimization problem, but it does not specify the programming interface to the framework, or how policies are represented and analyzed.

The APLOMB [59] system allows network operators to specify middlebox processing services that should be applied to classes of traffic. The actual processing of packets is handled by virtual machines deployed in a cloud-based architecture. Merlin is similar, in that policies allow users to specify packet-processing functions. However, Merlin does not directly target cloud-services. Moreover, Merlin allocates paths with respect to bandwidth constraints while APLOMB does not.

Many different programming languages have been proposed in recent years including Frenetic [20], Pyretic [46], and Maple [65]. These languages typically offer abstractions for programming OpenFlow networks. However, these languages are limited in that they do not allow programmers to specify middlebox functionality, allocate bandwidth, or delegate policies. An exception is the PANE [18] system, which allows end hosts to make explicit requests for network resources like bandwidth. Unlike Merlin, PANE does not provide mechanisms for partitioning functionality across a variety of devices and delegation is supported at the level of individual network flows, rather than entire policies.

The Merlin compiler implements a form of program partitioning. This idea has been previously explored in a variety of other domains including secure web applications [10], and distributed computing and storage [43].

8. CONCLUSION

The success of programmable network platforms has demonstrated the benefits of high-level languages for managing networks. Merlin complements these approaches by further raising the level of abstraction. Merlin allows administrators to specify the functionality of an entire network, leaving the low-level configuration of individual components to the compiler. At the same time, Merlin provides tenants with the freedom to tailor policies to their particular needs, while assuring administrators that the global constraints are correctly enforced. Overall, this approach significantly simplifies network administration, and lays a solid foundation for a wide variety of future research on network programmability.

Acknowledgements

The authors wish to thank Ricardo Padilha for his help with setting up experiments. This work is partially funded by the following grants: NSF CNS-1111698, CNS-1413972, SHF-1422046, CCF-1253165, ONR N00014-12-1-0757, AFOSR 9550-09-1-0100, and a gift from Fujitsu.

9. REFERENCES

[1] R. K. Ahuja, T. L. Magnanti, and J. B. Orlin. *Network Flows: Theory, Algorithms, and Applications*. Prentice-Hall, Inc., 1993.

[2] M. Al-Fares, A. Loukissas, and A. Vahdat. A Scalable, Commodity Data Center Network Architecture. In *Conference on Applications, Technologies, Architectures, and Protocols for Computer Communication*, pages 63–74, Aug. 2008.

[3] C. J. Anderson, N. Foster, A. Guha, J.-B. Jeannin, D. Kozen, C. Schlesinger, and D. Walker. NetKAT: Semantic Foundations for Networks. In *Symposium on Principles of Programming Languages*, pages 113–126, Jan. 2014.

[4] Automatic test packet generation. https://github.com/eastzone/atpg.

[5] H. Ballani, P. Costa, T. Karagiannis, and A. Rowstron. Towards Predictable Datacenter Networks. In *Conference on Applications, Technologies, Architectures, and Protocols for Computer Communication*, pages 242–253, Aug. 2011.

[6] C. Barnhart, C. A. Hane, and P. H. Vance. Using Branch-and-Price-and-Cut to Solve Origin-Destination Integer Multicommodity Flow Problems. *Operations Research*, 48(2):318–326, Mar. 2000.

[7] A. Z. Broder, A. M. Frieze, and E. Upfal. Static and Dynamic Path Selection on Expander Graphs: A Random Walk Approach. In *Symposium on Theory of Computing*, pages 531–539, May 1997.

[8] M. Burrows. The Chubby Lock Service for Loosely-coupled Distributed Systems. In *Symposium on Operating Systems Design and Implementation*, pages 335–350, Nov. 2006.

[9] A. Chakrabarti, C. Chekuri, A. Gupta, and A. Kumar. Approximation Algorithms for the Unsplittable Flow Problem. In *International Workshop on Approximation Algorithms for Combinatorial Optimization*, pages 51–66, Sept. 2002.

[10] S. Chong, J. Liu, A. C. Myers, X. Qi, K. Vikram, L. Zheng, and X. Zheng. Secure Web Applications via Automatic Partitioning. In *Symposium on Operating Systems Principles*, pages 31–44, Oct. 2007.

[11] J. Chuzhoy and S. Li. A Polylogarithmic Approximation Algorithm for Edge-Disjoint Paths with Congestion 2. In *IEEE Symposium on Foundations of Computer Science*, pages 233–242, Oct. 2012.

[12] J. C. Corbett, J. Dean, M. Epstein, A. Fikes, C. Frost, J. J. Furman, S. Ghemawat, A. Gubarev, C. Heiser, P. Hochschild, W. Hsieh, S. Kanthak, E. Kogan, H. Li, A. Lloyd, S. Melnik, D. Mwaura, D. Nagle, S. Quinlan, R. Rao, L. Rolig, Y. Saito, M. Szymaniak, C. Taylor, R. Wang, and D. Woodford. Spanner: Google's Globally-distributed Database. In *Symposium on Operating Systems Design and Implementation*, pages 251–264, Oct. 2012.

[13] J. Dean and S. Ghemawat. MapReduce: Simplified Data Processing on Large Clusters. In *Symposium on Operating Systems Design and Implementation*, pages 137–150, Dec. 2004.

[14] G. DeCandia, D. Hastorun, M. Jampani, G. Kakulapati, A. Lakshman, A. Pilchin, S. Sivasubramanian, P. Vosshall, and W. Vogels. Dynamo: Amazon's Highly Available Key-Value Store. In *Symposium on Operating Systems Principles*, pages 205–220, Oct. 2007.

[15] Y. Dinitz, N. Garg, and M. X. Goemans. On the Single-Source Unsplittable Flow Problem. *Combinatorica*, 19(1):17–41, Jan. 1999.

[16] C. Dixon, H. Uppal, V. Brajkovic, D. Brandon, T. Anderson, and A. Krishnamurthy. ETTM: A Scalable Fault Tolerant Network Manager. In *Symposium on Networked Systems Design and Implementation*, pages 7–21, Mar. 2011.

[17] S. K. Fayazbakhsh, L. Chiang, V. Sekar, M. Yu, and J. C. Mogul. Enforcing Network-wide Policies in the Presence of Dynamic Middlebox Actions Using Flowtags. In *Symposium on Networked Systems Design and Implementation*, pages 533–546, Apr. 2014.

[18] A. Ferguson, A. Guha, C. Liang, R. Fonseca, and S. Krishnamurthi. Participatory Networking: An API for Application Control of SDNs. In *Conference on Applications, Technologies, Architectures, and Protocols for Computer Communication*, pages 327–338, Aug. 2013.

[19] N. Foster, A. Guha, et al. The Frenetic Network Controller. In *The OCaml Users and Developers Workshop*, Sept. 2013.

[20] N. Foster, R. Harrison, M. J. Freedman, C. Monsanto, J. Rexford, A. Story, and D. Walker. Frenetic: A Network Programming Language. In *International Conference on Functional Programming*, pages 279–291, Sept. 2011.

[21] A. M. Frieze. Disjoint Paths in Expander Graphs via Random Walks: A Short Survey. In *Workshop on Randomization and Approximation Techniques in Computer Science*, pages 1–14, Oct. 1998.

[22] A. Gember, P. Prabhu, Z. Ghadiyali, and A. Akella. Toward Software-Defined Middlebox Networking. In *Workshop on Hot Topics in Networks*, pages 7–12, Oct. 2012.

[23] L. Glendenning, I. Beschastnikh, A. Krishnamurthy, and T. Anderson. Scalable Consistency in Scatter. In *Symposium on Operating Systems Principles*, pages 15–28, Oct. 2011.

[24] P. B. Godfrey, I. Ganichev, S. Shenker, and I. Stoica. Pathlet Routing. *SIGCOMM Computer Communication Review*, 39(4):111–122, Aug. 2009.

[25] Gurobi Optimization Inc. The Gurobi optimizer. `http://www.gurobi.com`.

[26] T. Hinrichs, N. Gude, M. Casado, J. Mitchell, and S. Shenker. Practical Declarative Network Management. In *Workshop: Research on Enterprise Networking*, pages 1–10, 2009.

[27] P. Hooimeijer. Dprle decision procedure library. `http://www.cs.virginia.edu/~ph4u/dprle/`.

[28] J. Hopcroft and J. Ullman. *Introduction to Automata Theory, Languages, and Computation*. Addison-Wesley, 1979.

[29] The Internet Topology Zoo. `http://www.topology-zoo.org`.

[30] S. Ioannidis, A. D. Keromytis, S. M. Bellovin, and J. M. Smith. Implementing a Distributed Firewall. In *Conference on Computer and Communications Security*, pages 190–199, Nov. 2000.

[31] S. Jain, A. Kumar, S. Mandal, J. Ong, L. Poutievski, A. Singh, S. Venkata, J. Wanderer, J. Zhou, M. Zhu, J. Zolla, U. Hölzle, S. Stuart, and A. Vahdat. B4: Experience with a Globally Deployed Software Defined WAN. In *Conference on Applications, Technologies, Architectures, and Protocols for Computer Communication*, pages 3–14, Aug. 2013.

[32] M. Jelasity, A. Montresor, and Ö. Babaoglu. T-Man: Gossip-based Fast Overlay Topology Construction. *Computer Networks*, 53(13):2321–2339, Jan. 2009.

[33] V. Jeyakumar, M. Alizadeh, D. Mazières, B. Prabhakar, A. Greenberg, and C. Kim. EyeQ: Practical Network Performance Isolation at the Edge. In *Symposium on Networked Systems Design and Implementation*, pages 297–312, Apr. 2013.

[34] D. A. Joseph, A. Tavakoli, I. Stoica, D. Joseph, A. Tavakoli, and I. Stoica. A Policy-aware Switching Layer for Data Centers. In *Conference on Applications, Technologies, Architectures, and Protocols for Computer Communication*, pages 51–62, Aug. 2008.

[35] N. Kang, Z. Liu, J. Rexford, and D. Walker. Optimizing the "One Big Switch" Abstraction in Software-defined Networks. In *International Conference on Emerging Networking Experiments and Technologies*, pages 13–24, Dec. 2013.

[36] J. Kleinberg and R. Rubinfeld. Short Paths in Expander Graphs. In *IEEE Symposium on Foundations of Computer Science*, pages 86–95, Oct. 1996.

[37] J. M. Kleinberg. Single-Source Unsplittable Flow. In *IEEE Symposium on Foundations of Computer Science*, pages 68–77, Oct. 1996.

[38] E. Kohler, R. Morris, B. Chen, J. Jannotti, and M. F. Kaashoek. The Click Modular Router. *Transactions on Computer Systems*, 18(3):263–297, Aug. 2000.

[39] S. G. Kolliopoulos and C. Stein. Approximation Algorithms for Single-Source Unsplittable Flow. *SIAM Journal on Computing*, 31(3):919–946, June 2001.

[40] T. Koponen, K. Amidon, P. Balland, M. Casado, A. Chanda, B. Fulton, I. Ganichev, J. Gross, P. Ingram, E. Jackson, A. Lambeth, R. Lenglet, S.-H. Li, A. Padmanabhan, J. Pettit, B. Pfaff, R. Ramanathan, S. Shenker, A. Shieh, J. Stribling, P. Thakkar, D. Wendlandt, A. Yip, and R. Zhang. Network Virtualization in Multi-tenant Datacenters. In *Symposium on Networked Systems Design and Implementation*, pages 203–216, Apr. 2014.

[41] L. Lamport. Time, Clocks, and the Ordering of Events in a Distributed System. *Communications of the ACM*, 21(7):558–565, July 1978.

[42] L. Lamport. The Part-Time Parliament. *Transactions on Computer Systems*, 16(2):133–169, May 1998.

[43] J. Liu, M. D. George, K. Vikram, X. Qi, L. Waye, and A. C. Myers. Fabric: A Platform for Secure Sistributed Computation and Storage. In *ACM SIGOPS European Workshop*, pages 321–334, Oct. 2009.

[44] P. Marandi et al. Ring Paxos: A high-throughput atomic broadcast protocol. In *International Conference on Dependable Systems and Networks*, pages 527 –536, May 2010.

[45] N. McKeown, T. Anderson, H. Balakrishnan, G. Parulkar, L. Peterson, J. Rexford, S. Shenker, and J. Turner. OpenFlow: Enabling Innovation in Campus Networks. *SIGCOMM Computer Communication Review*, 38(2):69–74, Mar. 2008.

[46] C. Monsanto et al. Composing Software-Defined Networks. In *Symposium on Networked Systems Design and Implementation*, pages 1–13, Apr. 2013.

[47] C. Monsanto, N. Foster, R. Harrison, and D. Walker. A Compiler and Run-time System for Network Programming Languages. In *Symposium on Principles of Programming Languages*, pages 217–230, Jan. 2012.

[48] L. D. Moura and N. Bjørner. Z3: An Efficient SMT Solver. In *International Conference on Tools and Algorithms for the Construction and Analysis of Systems*, pages 337–340, 2008.

[49] G. C. Necula. Proof-Carrying Code. In *Symposium on Principles of Programming Languages*, pages 106–119, Jan. 1997.

[50] T. Nelson, M. Scheer, A. D. Ferguson, and S. Krishnamurthi. Tierless Programming and Reasoning for Software-Defined Networks. In *Symposium on Networked Systems Design and Implementation*, Apr. 2014.

[51] NetworkX. `https://networkx.github.io`.

[52] H. Okamura and P. D. Seymour. Multicommodity Flows in Planar Graphs. *Journal of Combinatorial Theory, Series B*, 31(1):75–81, 1981.

[53] L. Popa, G. Kumar, M. Chowdhury, A. Krishnamurthy, S. Ratnasamy, and I. Stoica. FairCloud: Sharing the Network in Cloud Computing. In *Conference on Applications, Technologies, Architectures, and Protocols for Computer Communication*, pages 187–198, Aug. 2012.

[54] Puppet. `http://puppetlabs.com`.

[55] Z. A. Qazi, C.-C. Tu, L. Chiang, R. Miao, V. Sekar, and M. Yu. SIMPLE-fying Middlebox Policy Enforcement Using SDN. In *Conference on Applications, Technologies, Architectures, and Protocols for Computer Communication*, pages 27–38, Aug. 2013.

[56] M. Roesch. Snort—Lightweight Intrusion Detection for Networks. In *Conference on System Administration*, pages 229–238, Nov. 1999.

[57] F. B. Schneider. Implementing Fault-Tolerant Services Using the State Machine Approach: A Tutorial. *Computing Surveys*, 22(4):299–319, Dec. 1990.

[58] V. Sekar, N. Egi, S. Ratnasamy, M. K. Reiter, and G. Shi. Design and Implementation of a Consolidated Middlebox Architecture. In *Symposium on Networked Systems Design and Implementation*, pages 24–38, Apr. 2012.

[59] J. Sherry, S. Hasan, C. Scott, A. Krishnamurthy, S. Ratnasamy, and V. Sekar. Making Middleboxes Someone Else's Problem: Network Processing as a Cloud Service. In *Conference on Applications, Technologies, Architectures, and Protocols for Computer Communication*, pages 13–24, Aug. 2012.

[60] A. Shieh, S. Kandula, A. Greenberg, and C. Kim. Seawall: Performance Isolation for Cloud Datacenter Networks. In *Workshop on Hot Topics in Cloud Computing*, pages 1–8, June 2010.

[61] E. G. Sirer, W. de Bruijn, P. Reynolds, A. Shieh, K. Walsh, D. Williams, and F. B. Schneider. Logical Attestation: An Authorization Architecture for Trustworthy Computing. In *Symposium on Operating Systems Principles*, pages 249–264, Oct. 2011.

[62] R. Soulé, S. Basu, R. Kleinberg, E. G. Sirer, and N. Foster. Managing the Network with Merlin. In *Workshop on Hot Topics in Networks*, Nov. 2013.

[63] R. Subramaniyan, P. Raman, A. D. George, M. A. Radlinski, and M. A. Radlinski. GEMS: Gossip-Enabled Monitoring Service for Scalable Heterogeneous Distributed Systems. *Cluster Computing*, 9(1):101–120, Jan. 2006.

[64] R. Van Renesse, K. P. Birman, and W. Vogels. Astrolabe: A Robust and Scalable Technology for Distributed System Monitoring, Management, and Data Mining. *Transactions on Computer Systems*, 21(2):164–206, Feb. 2003.

[65] A. Voellmy, J. Wang, Y. R. Yang, B. Ford, and P. Hudak. Maple: Simplifying SDN Programming Using Algorithmic Policies. In *Conference on Applications, Technologies, Architectures, and Protocols for Computer Communication*, pages 87–98, Aug. 2013.

Controller-agnostic SDN Debugging

Ramakrishnan Durairajan
University of Wisconsin-Madison
rkrish@cs.wisc.edu

Joel Sommers
Colgate University
jsommers@colgate.edu

Paul Barford
University of Wisconsin-Madison
pb@cs.wisc.edu

ABSTRACT

Complexity in software-defined network (SDN) applications calls for methods and tools that can facilitate comprehensive debugging and analysis. A key challenge in this regard is that SDN configurations interact with network devices that can behave in unexpected ways, depending on factors such as traffic and application mix. In this paper, we describe *OFf*, a debugging and test environment for SDN developers. *OFf* is built on top of the *fs-sdn* simulator, which was developed to offer simple-to-use, accurate and scalable evaluation of OpenFlow-based SDN configurations. *OFf* offers standard debugging features for controller applications such as stepping, breakpoints, and watch variables. It also offers features that provide visibility into network behavior including packet tracing, packet replay and visualization features, and alerts that are triggered when, *e.g.*, configurations change. *OFf* is accessed through a text interface and is designed to interoperate with any standard SDN controller platform. We demonstrate the capabilities of *OFf* through three test scenarios that illustrate its utility and modest performance impact on running applications. Specifically, we show how *OFf* can be used to analyze and fix bugs in a traffic engineering application, and to detect and repair a security vulnerability due to multiple application interaction and unexpected rule expiration.

Categories and Subject Descriptors

C.2.3 [**Network Operations**]: Network management; D.2.5 [**Testing and Debugging**]: Testing tools; I.6.3 [**Simulation and Modeling**]: Applications

General Terms

Design, Measurement, Performance, Reliability

Keywords

Debugging; OpenFlow; Simulation; Software-Defined Networks

CoNEXT'14, December 2–5, 2014, Sydney, Australia.

http://dx.doi.org/10.1145/2674005.2674993.

1. INTRODUCTION

Like other software systems, the development of complex SDN configurations requires tools that facilitate debugging. Standard capabilities of debuggers include step-by-step execution, pausing execution, and tracking variables to enable the details of controller applications to be examined. However, the fact that a particular SDN configuration "runs as designed" may be insufficient to ensure that it behaves in a robust and predictable fashion when deployed in a live environment.

SDN deployments must cope with potentially a wide range of operating conditions that include the possibility of unanticipated traffic behavior or interactions between deployed applications. Such conditions can have a range of consequences including degradation of performance, exposure of security vulnerabilities or application failures. The potential severity of these unexpected behaviors calls for robust testing capability that goes beyond standard debugging and includes the ability to assess configurations across a wide range of operating conditions.

In this paper, we describe *OFf* [1], a debugging and test environment for SDN developers. *OFf* is designed for debugging controller applications developed within *any* standard controller environment, such as POX [1], OpenDaylight [2], Ryu [3], Trema [4] and Floodlight [5]. It supports standard debugging capabilities such as stepping, breakpoints, and watch variables through a simple command-line interface. More importantly, it is designed to support comprehensive testing of SDN applications in a representative, controlled and repeatable fashion by providing visibility into network behavior. Key capabilities for testing include packet tracing, packet replay and visualization features, and alerts. *OFf*s unique capability to simultaneously trace program execution and network state enables unwanted behavior in the network to be tied directly to the control program.

OFf is built on top of *fs-sdn* [6], a simulation environment for SDN that offers the unique capability to accurately assess configurations that might be deployed in large-scale environments such as those found in typical datacenters. *fs-sdn* achieves scalability by using a core abstraction that captures details of *network flows* while avoiding fine-grained packet-level concerns. *OFf* can accommodate any controller platform through a proxy component which has a design similar in spirit to FlowVisor [7], and is situated between a controller under test and the simulated network over which

[1]Source code for *OFf* is openly available to the community and can be found at: `https://github.com/52-41-4d/fs-generic`

the developer has complete control. The proxy translates messages between the controller and the simulated network, and vice versa, and starts a controller in a runtime cradle that masks other differences between the simulated and non-simulated worlds, *e.g.*, simulation time versus wall-clock time. *OFf*'s support for fine-grained source code debugging is enabled by simply including a library when coding the application and does not affect program execution unless specifically directed by the developer.

We illustrate the capabilities of *OFf* through three test scenarios. The experiments are designed to highlight how *OFf* can be used to find bugs that might otherwise lead to inconsistent network state or expose security vulnerabilities. Specifically, our examples show how *OFf* can be used to find and fix *(i) race conditions* and *inconsistent ordering* of rule updates in a traffic engineering application, *(ii)* a *security vulnerability* in a multiple application interaction environment, and *(iii)* a security issue due to *rule expiration* and *rule shadowing*.

2. BACKGROUND

In this section we give a brief overview of the *fs-sdn* tool on which *OFf* is built, and describe prior studies that influence and inform the design and implementation of *OFf*.

2.1 *fs-sdn* overview

fs-sdn [6] is a simulation-based tool that is designed to facilitate prototyping and evaluating new SDN applications. It is based on the *fs* [8] tool that was designed to efficiently generate realistic network measurements such as flow records and SNMP-like counters for use in different types of networking studies. *fs*, and by extension *fs-sdn*, use discrete event simulation techniques to generate network measurements and simulate network conditions. Unlike other simulation-based systems, its core abstractions are based on network flows and as a result it achieves significantly better performance than packet-based simulators. *fs-sdn* extended the *fs* engine by transparently incorporating the POX [1] OpenFlow controller framework and API, including switch components that can be controlled and configured through the OpenFlow control protocol. In this work, we significantly extend *fs-sdn* in order to accommodate *any* standard SDN controller platform.

2.2 Related work

Debugging in an SDN world inherits many of the same challenges of debugging complex software. While "`printf`" debugging is, for better or worse, a common practice, there are more effective techniques for development and testing, including using debuggers such as gdb [9] to trace and modify the state of running programs, techniques such as test-driven development (TDD) [10], and the use of assertions to test invariants. *OFf* is most closely related to work on tools for exposing and tracing program and network state in SDN. In particular, ndb [11] and its successor NetSight [12] offer some similar features as *OFf*. A key difference, however, is that *OFf* offers capabilities not only to trace network state, but also to trace controller program execution state, thus tying together observed network behavior with the control program that induced that behavior. *OFf* is also related to the OFRewind [13] system that enables replaying packets collected in an SDN setting in order to understand the effect of different control programs on traffic flows. Also related is the work by Scott *et al.* to associate "minimal causal sequences" of trace data from tests to an observed bug in order to narrow the focus for debugging source code [14]. Somewhat more distantly related to *OFf* are efforts to verify that certain invariants hold. In particular, the works by Kazemian *et al.* on header space analysis [15, 16], the Anteater system [17], Veriflow [18], and NICE [19] each seek to verify that certain network properties are never violated.

3. SYSTEM DESIGN

In this section we describe the design, implementation, and features provided by *OFf*.

3.1 OFf Overview

OFf is a comprehensive source-level debugger for SDN applications. *OFf* does not require any special effort from the developer before debugging an application: the library can simply be included when coding the application like any other standard library. *OFf* also does not require any additional hardware and does not affect the program execution unless the developer issues a debugging command. Therefore, *OFf* can be used spontaneously and only when needed during the application development.

OFf provides both generic debugging commands as well as features that are specifically designed to meet the needs of SDN application developers. The commands and features are described in more detail later in this section. All commands are source-level em i.e., they operate on symbols defined in the source code of the program.

3.2 OFf Architecture

OFf consists of two parts: the *OFf proxy* and *OFf controller/debugger runtime interfaces* that connect to the *fs-sdn* simulator and the SDN controller platforms. The overall architecture is illustrated in Figure 1, and we describe each part below.

3.2.1 OFf Proxy

The proxy unit provides a bridge between the simulated network in *fs-sdn*, and real controller platforms. Openflow switches in *fs-sdn* are configured with one or more controllers, which communicate with proxy components. The proxy component translates simulated messages from switches to control plane packets to a real controller platform, and vice versa. In response to a switch initiating a control plane connection, the proxy creates a real network connection to the configured controller. One proxy may act on behalf of any number of switches, and thus has complete visibility of network control plane interactions.

To enable *fs-sdn* interoperability with multiple controllers, we modified the controller class in *fs-sdn* to behave instead as a proxy, leaving the switch implementation in *fs-sdn* unmodified. We also modified a class in *fs-sdn* that is used to abstract individual connections from the controller to switches. The original class used *fs-sdn*'s API to deliver and receive messages to a fake controller; the new class instead handles connections to real controllers and overrides the *fs-sdn* connection APIs.

Besides its core "bridging" functionality, the proxy is composed of four components. First, a *UI wrapper* provides a text-based interface that dispatches commands from the developer to one of the three other units and prints any output to a display. Second, the *Debugger* component provides an abstract interface to a language-level debugger in order to associate controller application source code with control plane activity. The debugger component contains separate modules (with enhanced features as described later in the section) to deal with all specialized *OFf* commands such as enable and disable watch points, tracking variables, etc., that are not recognized by language-specific debuggers such as Python's PDB. From an application developer's perspective, simulators producing mere text outputs are less preferred than simulators producing visual output [20]. To that end, we developed the third component—*Trace Replay*—that has the ability to reproduce network activity that has been captured in a trace and replay it later. Finally, the *Diff Report Generator* component helps detect changes in topology, mutations in rules/actions across switches, and performance variations from previous runs (or across configuration changes) of *fs-sdn*, then generates a report to help assess implications of configuration changes.

There are several advantages to our proxy-based approach. First, it completely eliminates the issue of controller compatibility with the simulation environment. That is, the controllers are entirely unmodified and can be used off-the-shelf. Second, the *OFf* proxy acts as a simulation-oriented equivalent of FlowVisor [7], *i.e.*, it acts as a proxy between a real controller and the switches in the network. Instead of the proxy communicating with real switches, however, it communicates via *fs* API calls to simulated switches. This makes the prototyping and debugging generalizable to real networks. Finally, this approach is entirely language and platform agnostic, and opens up interesting avenues for debugging. For instance, since the proxy sees *all* Openflow control messages, it can be used to trace the effects of various high-level operations from the controller code. We also have complete control over the switches, and could augment our current simulated switch implementation to facilitate debugging operations such as tracing packets, observing which rules match (and which one eventually fires) when packets arrive, detect configuration changes, etc.

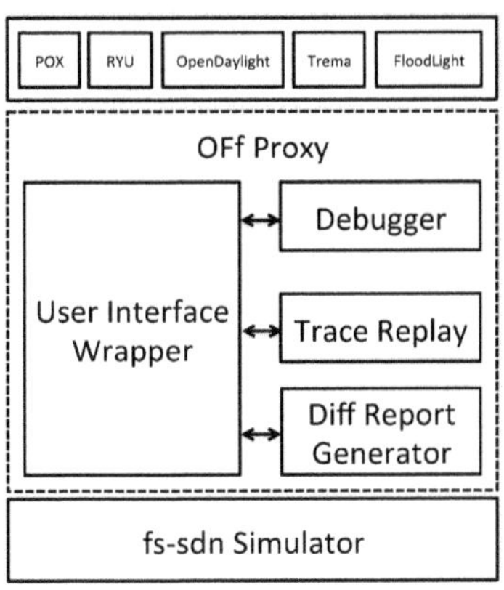

Figure 1: The architecture of OFf.

3.2.2 OFf Controller/Debugger Runtime Interfaces

The *OFf* Proxy described above can be linked to a specific controller platform and language-level debugging environment through an *OFf* runtime interface component. This component handles starting a controller using a library interposition agent [21] that ensures that any time-related calls by the controller will return *fs-sdn* simulation time instead of wall-clock time. This component also provides a translation layer between the generic *OFf* proxy debugging component, and a specific source code debugging environment and command set.

While we have used *OFf* with the OpenDaylight [2], Ryu [3], Floodlight [5], and Trema [4] controllers (shipped as part of [22]), the source-level debugging runtime interface is currently limited to PDB and thus the Python-based controllers. In our ongoing work, we are expanding the debugging runtime interface to accommodate GDB [9], which will enable support of additional controller application source code languages. This effort is primarily one of creating translations between the command set provided in *OFf* (described next) and the equivalent commands available in GDB.

3.3 OFf Commands

Commands in *OFf* are entered through a command-line interface similar to PDB, GDB, and other debuggers. *OFf* supports both basic commands provided by these debuggers, and new features to enhance the SDN application development and debugging experience.

3.3.1 Basic Commands

OFf directly exports the most commonly used commands that are provided by PDB including the ability to pause, continue, and step through execution. It also adds many features to the basic PDB command set by providing the ability to *(i)* longlist and shortlist source code during debugging, *(ii)* pretty print expressions, *(iii)* hide and unhide hidden code frames during debugging, *(iv)* interact (via interpreter) with all variables in scope, *(v)* track, watch, or unwatch variables, *(vi)* edit source files during debugging, *(vii)* enable or disable break points on the fly, and *(viii)* sticky mode visualize code during debugging session.

3.3.2 Additional Features

OFf provides the following additional new features to enhance the SDN application development experience. In what follows, we give a general overview of these additional features, but omit many details due to space constraints.

- **Trace packet through the network.** *fs-sdn* provides the ability to model Openflow switches and controllers. *OFf* can interact directly with these components, providing the ability to trace *fs-sdn flowlets* as they pass through switches and cause Openflow events to be generated (*e.g.*, PacketIn) and controller components and code to be invoked. As a result *OFf* enables a *holistic* view of every network flow, how flows and controller code interact, and provides opportunities to comprehensively trace network events with no additional hardware support needed for data collection and processing (*e.g.*, as in [12]).
- **Packet replay.** Motivated by OFRewind [13], *OFf* includes a light-weight packet replay feature that enables network administrators to reproduce and locate software errors in network configuration. Features in *OFf* differ from OFRewind in the following way: *(a)* there is no explicit record component that *intercepts* all the messages from controller, and the traces are generated in such a way to balance efficiency and accuracy, and *(b)* no additional Openflow protocol-level support is needed

to enable network event tracing and capture of device state (*e.g.*, flow table dump) or to reset network devices to known states (*i.e.*, to clear previously installed rules that led to incorrect behavior). Since *OFf* has an oracular view of the (simulated) network, it does not need any special protocol or hardware support in devices.

- **Detect configuration changes.** Debugging SDN programs is complicated by the fact that program behavior is affected by controller program state, switch state, and network traffic patterns. To combat this complexity, we believe that one way to improve the experience of debugging SDN programs is to provide capabilities for detecting configuration and network changes across multiple executions of a controller program. To that end, *OFf* contains a novel capability via the *Diff Report Generator* to produce an account of differences across several runs of the same control program and network traffic scenario. In particular, it highlights changes in network topology, differences in rules and actions across network switches, and performance variations, and displays these differences to developer in a meaningful way.

4. OFf IN ACTION

In this section, we demonstrate how *OFf* can be used to find logical bugs in the source code that can lead to poor performance or transient outages, and eventually to inconsistent network state or security vulnerabilities. We developed three test scenarios based on ideas from existing literature like [23, 24]. Our approach is to run a series of identical topological simulations in *fs-sdn* with and without *OFf* and identify those bugs that lead to transient outages and losses.

4.1 Scenario 1: Incorrect Ordering of Updates

A testing process with *OFf* can include careful evaluation of traffic before and after rule installation. In this scenario, we used a simple traffic engineering application in the network topology shown in Figure 2. The scenario premise is that a developer has coded an application to install rules in switches in the following order: switch B and C are updated simultaneously (*barrier* messages are not used), then switch A is updated. The developer has not considered latency differences between the controller and switches, leading to a potential race condition. Specifically, rules may be installed at switches C and A, and data packets may start flowing before the appropriate rules are installed at switch B. This inconsistent state will lead to poor performance for traffic flows until switch B is updated, and could result in *e.g.*, initial discontinuity in a VoIP call or high jitter at the start of a video stream.

To resolve this problem, the rules must be installed in the order of switch C, switch B, then switch A. For example, *barrier* messages could be introduced to ensure a sequential ordering of updates and consistent network state.

To identify this bug, the developer could initiate *OFf*s packet replay feature and find that packets are dropped at switch B because of rules not being correctly preinstalled. The developer might set a *break point* at the rule installation logic and restart the simulation in *sticky mode*. On *stepping* through the execution and *watching* flow table entries and relevant variables at switch B, the developer might observe that there is an *ordering problem* because of the race

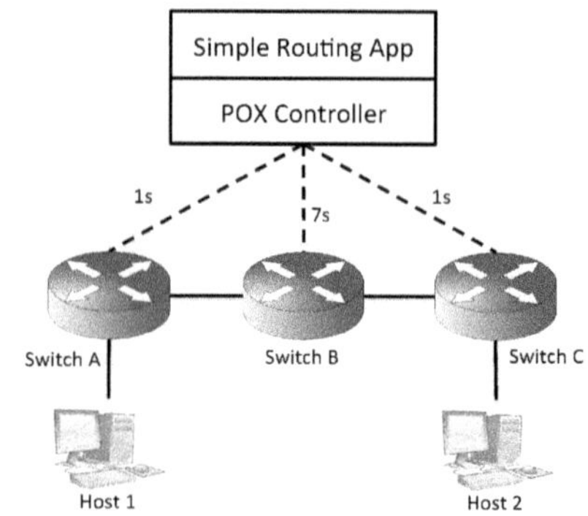

Figure 2: Topology used to evaluate incorrect ordering of updates scenario.

condition between switches B and C. After fixing the bug, the developer could invoke *OFf*s *trace replay* and *diff report* capabilities to analyze if the expected rules fired in the expected order.

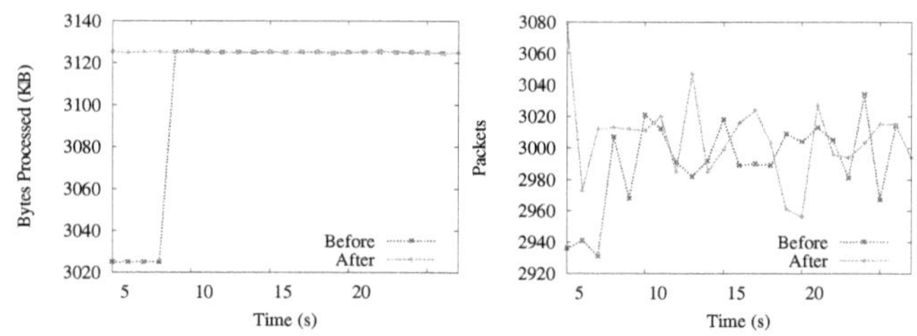

Figure 3: (left) Bytes processed and (right) Packets processed at switch C before and after fixing the bug in scenario 1.

Figure 3 shows the number of packets and bytes processed at switch C before and after the bug is fixed, and generated via *OFf* diff report. In the first few seconds of the connection, before the bug is fixed, there is reduction in the number of packet and bytes processed. Once the bug is fixed (at around 8 sec), there is a noticeable increase in both the number of packets and bytes processed over that same time span.

4.2 Scenario 2: Bad Multi-app Interaction

SDN controllers typically permit multiple, logically separate control programs to be run simultaneously, each of which can receive network events and modify switch state. It is well known that inconsistent network state can arise when SDN programs are not *composed* correctly. We call this problem *Multi-app Interaction Inconsistency* (MAII).

To evaluate this test scenario, we used the topology in Figure 4 (from the *dynamic-flow tunneling* example in [24]). A firewall written by developer 1 installs a rule to block traffic from an external host (10.0.0.1) to an internal web server (10.0.0.4). At the same time, a routing application written by developer 2 is deployed, and at a certain time implements three rules within the controller application. The first rule changes the source IP address of a packet to 10.0.0.2 if the packet is delivered from 10.0.0.1. The second rule changes the destination IP address of a packet to 10.0.0.4 if the packet is destined to 10.0.0.3. The final rule simply allows packet forwarding from 10.0.0.2 to 10.0.0.3. Unfortunately, now any packet arriving from 10.0.0.1 destined to 10.0.0.3 can bypass the firewall and reach the web server.

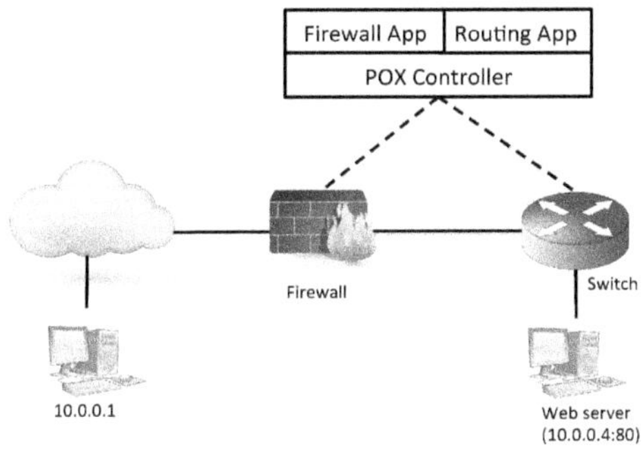

Figure 4: Topology used to evaluate bad multi-app interaction scenario.

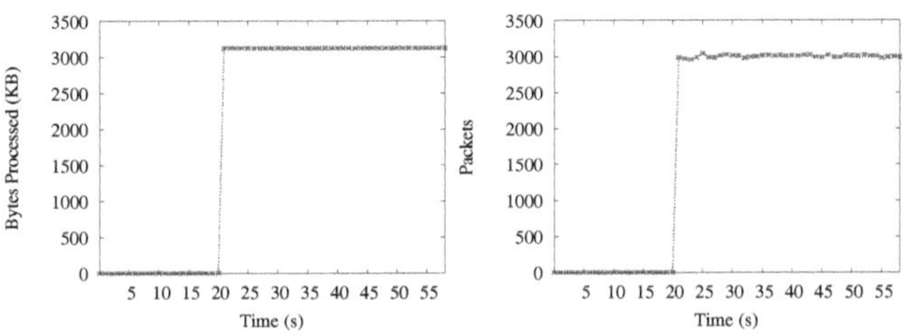

Figure 5: (left) Bytes processed and (right) Packets processed at switch before the Multi-app Interaction Inconsistency bug is fixed in scenario 2.

The MAII problem can be addressed with *OFf* as follows. First, before deploying the routing application, developer 2 can prototype the application and collect network traces using *fs-sdn*. Figure 5 shows the number of packets and bytes seen at the switch after the routing application is prototyped (and before MAII is identified). Once deployed in an environment with the firewall application, network traces can be collected again. At this point, the problem can be easily resolved using *OFf*'s *diff reports* as it can report changes across configurations and alert the developer that the routing rule set conflicts with the existing firewall rule set. To verify if the bug is fixed, the developer can then invoke *trace replay* and *diff reports* to analyze if the firewall invariants are maintained. These capabilities of *OFf* highlight its potential to act as a *proactive invariant generator* for tools like VeriFlow [18], which we intend to investigate in future work.

4.3 Scenario 3: Unexpected Rule Expiration

It is well known that unexpected interactions can occur when wildcarded rules overlap, or specific *microflow* rules are shadowed by wildcard rules. If the actions associated with the rules differ, unexpected behavior can occur if the more specific rule is removed while traffic is still flowing.

In this scenario, we extended the topology from scenario 2 to include an additional switch (switch D, attached to switch B), as depicted in Figure 6. Assume for this scenario that switch B sees two types of flows: *trusted* traffic, which is forwarded to switch D, and *untrusted* traffic, which is forwarded to switch C. A wildcarded rule (*e.g.*, for 10.0.0.0/8) is installed at switch B for untrusted traffic, and a separate rule for 10.5.0.0/16 exists for forwarding trusted traffic. Note that the trusted rule is *shadowed* by the untrusted rule (*i.e.*, the untrusted rule is more general). Lastly, assume that the rule for trusted traffic expires due to a hard timeout (at t=30 sec), causing all trusted traffic to erroneously be forwarded to switch C and exposing a potential security vulnerability.

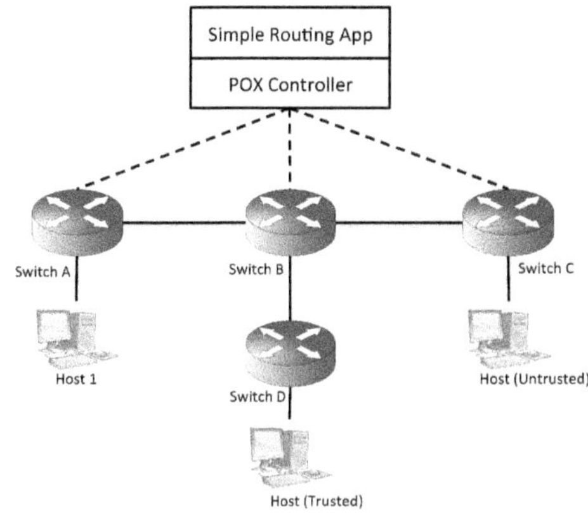

Figure 6: Topology used to evaluate unexpected rule expiration scenario.

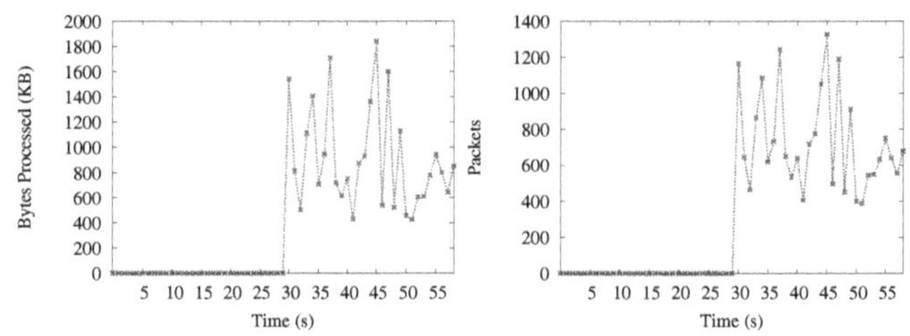

Figure 7: (left) Bytes processed and (right) Packets processed at switch C before rule expiration bug in scenario 3 is fixed.

A developer might use *OFf* in the following way to evaluate and debug this problem. First, after prototyping the application in *fs-sdn*, flows are captured and replayed using *OFf*'s *trace replay* facilities and the problematic leak of flows to switch C is identified. Figure 7 shows the number of packets and bytes processed at switch C; observe that no traffic is seen prior to t=30 when the more specific rule expires and the wrong forwarding rule is applied. At this point, the developer could trace the flows and the specific rules that are applied to observe that the wrong rule is triggered. The developer could then change the timeout behavior of the rule for forwarding trusted traffic, or use some other approach for fixing the problem. Once fixed, the developer could invoke *trace replay* and *diff reports* to verify that trusted traffic is never forwarded to switch C.

4.4 Performance Impact of OFf

For the tests described above, we examined the performance impact of *OFf* by enabling between 1 and 3 breakpoints, and between 1 and 3 *watch* variables and comparing with an *OFf*-less simulation. Table 1 shows execution times for scenarios consisting of either 60 or 180 simulated seconds. We see from the table that breakpoints have a relatively small impact on runtime compared with watched variables, especially for shorter simulations. We also observe that overheads of *OFf* are amortized for longer simulations and that performance impacts are, overall, modest.

Table 1: Wall-clock execution times for an SDN simulation scenario with and without *OFf* capabilities enabled.

	60 simulated seconds		180 simulated seconds	
	w/o *OFf*	with *OFf*	w/o *OFf*	with *OFf*
Break 1	2.254	3.419	6.568	7.411
Break 2	2.254	3.765	6.568	7.700
Break 3	2.254	4.005	6.568	7.942
Watch 1	2.254	8.261	6.568	10.883
Watch 2	2.254	8.843	6.568	11.010
Watch 3	2.254	9.677	6.568	11.318

5. SUMMARY AND FUTURE WORK

Ensuring that SDN configurations behave as expected is predicated on careful and comprehensive debugging and testing. In this paper, we describe *OFf*, a controller-agnostic SDN debugging and testing tool that provides standard debugging capabilities such as stepping and watch variables, as well as SDN-specific capabilities to assess details of network interactions and changes over iterations of the same program. *OFf* is built on top of *fs-sdn*, which provides accurate and scalable simulation of OpenFlow-based SDN configurations. We highlight the capabilities of *OFf* through three test scenarios, and demonstrate the tool's utility and modest performance impact on running applications. We show that *OFf* can be used to identify and eliminate bugs in a traffic engineering application, and to identify and remove a security vulnerability that is exposed by the interaction of multiple applications, and unexpected rule expiration. *OFf* is openly available to the community and development of additional features and capabilities is ongoing.

In future work, we plan to focus on the following extensions and applications of *OFf*:

- **Application-level consistency.** We intend to evaluate several applications for which the source code is available by running failure scenarios across configurations to identify consistency issues. In particular, we plan to select applications based on problems identified in prior work, and where a tool like *OFf* would be helpful. For instance, a key finding in [25] is that middleboxes experience a variety of misconfigurations and that failover between middlebox replicas can be ineffective due to configuration bugs. As another example, OF.CPP [26] presents two classes of bugs related to consistency issues, and we believe that capabilities in *OFf* may provide ways to completely avoid such bugs. We also plan to investigate the potential for *OFf* to generate *invariants* for efforts like SIMPLE [27], HotSwap [28], and PyResonance [29].
- **Switch implementation models.** The work by Huang *et al.* [30] argues that vendor-specific emulation of SDN switches are required, and describes a method to record the switch behavior of various vendors. The *OFf* proxy component is a natural place for implementing such fingerprinting methods and could be used to evaluate such models by comparing multiple switch models simultaneously. To that end, we intend to add a benchmarking capability in *OFf* to record various vendor-specific switch implementation models and establish ideal switch models for a wide variety of configurations.
- **Distributed controller simulations.** To provide reliability and scalability, SDN controllers should be logically centralized and physically distributed. A natural requirement for such distributed controllers (*e.g.*, [31]) is correct and consistent behavior across distributed configurations. Since multiple controllers are supported by *fs-sdn*, *OFf* could be used as an orchestration layer to test distributed controllers and ensure correctness by identifying errors across distributed configurations.

6. ACKNOWLEDGMENTS

We thank the reviewers for their invaluable feedback. This material is based upon work supported by the National Science Foundation under grants CNS-1054985, CNS-0905186, ARL grant W911NF1110227, DHS BAA 11-01 and AFRL grant FA8750-12-2-0328. Any opinions, findings, and conclusions or recommendations expressed in this material are those of the author and do not necessarily reflect the views of the NSF, ARL, DHS or AFRL.

7. REFERENCES

[1] POX, Python-based OpenFlow Controller. `http://www.noxrepo.org/pox/about-pox/`.

[2] The OpenDaylight Controller. `http://www.opendaylight.org`.

[3] The Ryu Framework. `http://osrg.github.io/ryu/`.

[4] The Trema Controller. `http://trema.github.io/trema/`.

[5] The Floodlight Controller. `http://www.projectfloodlight.org/floodlight/`.

[6] M. Gupta, J. Sommers, and P. Barford. Fast, Accurate Simulation for SDN Prototyping. In *Proceedings of ACM HotSDN*, 2013.

[7] R. Sherwood, G. Gibb, K. K. Yap, G. Appenzeller, M. Casado, N. McKeown, and G. Parulkar. Can the production network be the testbed? In *Proceedings of OSDI*, 2010.

[8] J. Sommers, R. Bowden, B. Eriksson, P. Barford, M. Roughan, and N. Duffield. Efficient network-wide flow record generation. In *Proceedings of INFOCOM*, 2011.

[9] GDB: The GNU Project Debugger. `http://www.gnu.org/software/gdb/`.

[10] S. Vissicchio D. Lebrun and O. Bonaventure. Towards test-driven software defined networking. In *Proceedings of IEEE NOMS*, May 2014.

[11] N. Handigol, B. Heller, V. Jeyakumar, D. Maziéres, and N. McKeown. Where is the Debugger for My Software-defined Network? In *Proceedings of ACM HotSDN*, 2012.

[12] N. Handigol, B. Heller, V. Jeyakumar, D. Mazières, and N. McKeown. I Know What Your Packet Did Last Hop: Using Packet Histories to Troubleshoot Networks. In *Proceedings of the 11th USENIX Symposium on Networked Systems Design and Implementation*, 2014.

[13] A. Wundsam, D. Levin, S. Seetharaman, and A. Feldmann. OFRewind: Enabling Record and Replay Troubleshooting for Networks. In *Proceedings of the 2011 USENIX Annual Technical Conference*, 2011.

[14] C. Scott, A. Wundsam, B. Raghavan, A. Or, J. Lai, E. Huang, Z. Liu, A. El-Hassany, S. Whitlock, H. B. Acharya, K. Zarifis, and S. Shenker. Troubleshooting SDN Control Software with Minimal Causal Sequences. In *Proceedings of the ACM SIGCOMM*, 2014.

[15] P. Kazemian, G. Varghese, and N. McKeown. Header Space Analysis: Static Checking for Networks. In *Proceedings of the 9th USENIX Conference on Networked Systems Design and Implementation*, 2012.

[16] P. Kazemian, M. Chang, H. Zeng, G. Varghese, N. McKeown, and S. Whyte. Real Time Network Policy Checking Using Header Space Analysis. In *Proceedings of the 10th USENIX Conference on Networked Systems Design and Implementation*, 2013.

[17] H. Mai, A. Khurshid, R. Agarwal, M. Caesar, P. B. Godfrey, and S. T. King. Debugging the Data Plane with Anteater. In *Proceedings of the ACM SIGCOMM 2011 Conference*, 2011.

[18] A. Khurshid, X. Zou, W. Zhou, M. Caesar, and P. B. Godfrey. VeriFlow: Verifying Network-wide Invariants in Real Time. In *Proceedings of the 10th USENIX Conference on Networked Systems Design and Implementation*, 2013.

[19] M. Canini, D. Venzano, P. Perešíni, D. Kostić, and J. Rexford. A NICE Way to Test Openflow Applications. In *Proceedings of the 9th USENIX Conference on Networked Systems Design and Implementation*, 2012.

[20] E. Tufte. The Visual Display of Quantitative Information.

[21] Timothy W. Curry and Sun Microsystems Inc. Profiling and tracing dynamic library usage via interposition. In *Proc. of the USENIX Summer 1994 Technical Conf*, pages 267–278, 1994.

[22] All-in-one SDN App Development Starter VM. `http://sdnhub.org/tutorials/sdn-tutorial-vm-64-bit/`.

[23] M. Reitblatt, N. Foster, J. Rexford, and D. Walker. Consistent Updates for Software-defined Networks: Change You Can Believe in! In *Proceedings of the ACM HotNets*, 2011.

[24] P. Porras, S. Shin, V. Yegneswaran, M. Fong, M. Tyson, and G. Gu. A Security Enforcement Kernel for OpenFlow Networks. In *Proceedings of the ACM HotSDN*, 2012.

[25] R. Potharaju and N. Jain. Demystifying the Dark Side of the Middle: A Field Study of Middlebox Failures in Datacenters. In *Proceedings of the ACM Internet Measurement Conference*, 2013.

[26] P. Perešíni, M. Kuzniar, N. Vasić, M. Canini, and D. Kostiū. OF.CPP: Consistent Packet Processing for Openflow. In *Proceedings of ACM HotSDN*, 2013.

[27] Z. A. Qazi, C. Tu, L. Chiang, R. Miao, V. Sekar, and M. Yu. SIMPLE-fying Middlebox Policy Enforcement Using SDN. In *Proceedings of the ACM SIGCOMM*, 2013.

[28] L. Vanbever, J. Reich, T. Benson, N. Foster, and J. Rexford. HotSwap: Correct and Efficient Controller Upgrades for Software-defined Networks. In *Proceedings of ACM HotSDN*, 2013.

[29] A. K. Nayak, A. Reimers, N. Feamster, and R. Clark. Resonance: Dynamic Access Control for Enterprise Networks. In *Proceedings of the ACM Workshop on Research on Enterprise Networking*, 2009.

[30] D. Y. Huang, K. Yocum, and A. C. Snoeren. High-fidelity switch models for software-defined network emulation. In *Proceedings of ACM HotSDN*, 2013.

[31] T. Koponen, M. Casado, N. Gude, J. Stribling, L. Poutievski, M. Zhu, R. Ramanathan, Y. Iwata, H. Inoue, T. Hama, and S. Shenker. Onix: A distributed control platform for large-scale production networks. In *Proceedings of USENIX OSDI*, 2010.

On the Fairness-Efficiency Tradeoff for Packet Processing with Multiple Resources

Wei Wang, Chen Feng, Baochun Li, and Ben Liang
Department of Electrical and Computer Engineering, University of Toronto
{weiwang, cfeng, bli, liang}@ece.utoronto.ca

ABSTRACT

Middleboxes are widely deployed in today's networks. They apply a variety of complex network functions to transform, filter, and optimize incoming traffic based on the payload of packets. These functions require the support of multiple types of resources, such as CPU and link bandwidth, for processing incoming packets. Hence, a multi-resource packet scheduling algorithm is needed to allow flows to share these resources fairly and efficiently. However, unlike traditional fair queueing where bandwidth is the only concern, we show in this paper that fairness and efficiency are conflicting objectives that cannot be achieved simultaneously in the presence of multiple resources. Ideally, a scheduling algorithm should allow network operators to flexibly specify their fairness and efficiency requirements, so as to meet the Quality of Service demands while keeping the system at a high utilization level. Yet, existing multi-resource scheduling algorithms focus on fairness only, and may lead to poor resource utilization. In this paper, we propose a new scheduling algorithm to achieve a flexible tradeoff between fairness and efficiency for packet processing, consuming both CPU and link bandwidth. Experimental results based on both real-world implementation and trace-driven simulation suggest that trading off a modest level of fairness can potentially improve the efficiency to the point where the system capacity is almost saturated.

Categories and Subject Descriptors

C.2.6 [**Computer-Communication Networks**]: Internetworking

General Terms

Scheduling Theory

Keywords

Fair Queueing; Middleboxes; Fairness-Efficiency Tradeoff

1. INTRODUCTION

Queueing algorithms determine the order in which packets in various independent flows are processed, and serve as a fundamental mechanism for allocating resources in a network appliance. Traditional queueing algorithms [1, 9, 21, 28] make scheduling decisions in network switches that simply forward packets to their next hops, and link bandwidth is the only resource being allocated.

In modern network appliances, *e.g.*, *middleboxes* [25, 27], link bandwidth is no longer the only resource shared by flows. In addition to packet forwarding, middleboxes perform a variety of critical network functions that require deep packet inspection based on the payload of packets, such as IP security encryption, WAN optimization, and intrusion detection. Performing these complex network functions requires the support of multiple types of resources, and may bottleneck on either CPU or link bandwidth [10, 13]. For example, flows that require basic forwarding may congest the link bandwidth [13], while those that require IP security encryption need more CPU processing time [10]. A queueing algorithm specifically designed for multiple resources is therefore needed for sharing these resources *fairly* and *efficiently*.

Fairness offers predictable service isolation among flows. It ensures that the service a flow receives (*i.e.*, number of packets processed per second) in an n-flow system is at least $1/n$ of that it achieves when the flow monopolizes all resources, independent of the behavior of other rogue flows. The notion of Dominant Resource Fairness (DRF) [14, 22] embodies this isolation property, with which each flow receives approximately the same processing time on its *dominant resource*, defined as the one that requires the most packet processing time [13].

Efficiency serves as another important metric measuring the resource utilization achieved by a queueing algorithm. High resource utilization naturally translates into high traffic throughput. This is of particular importance to enterprise networks, given the surging volume of traffic passing through middleboxes [27, 36].

Both fairness and efficiency can be achieved at the same time in traditional single-resource fair queueing, where bandwidth is the only concern. As long as the schedule is *work conserving* [39], bandwidth utilization is 100% given a non-empty system. That leaves fairness as an independent objective to optimize.

However, in the presence of multiple resources, fairness is often a *conflicting objective* against efficiency. To see this, consider two schedules shown in Fig. 1 with two flows whose packets need CPU processing before transmission. Packets that finishes CPU processing are placed into a buffer in front of the output link. Each packet in Flow 1 has a *processing time vector* $\langle 2, 3\rangle$, meaning that it requires 2 time units for CPU processing and 3 time units for transmission; each packet in Flow 2 has a processing time vector $\langle 9, 1\rangle$. The dominant resource of Flow 1 is link bandwidth, as it takes more time to transmit a packet than processing it using CPU; similarly, the dominant resource of Flow 2 is CPU. To achieve DRF, the transmission time Flow 1 receives should be ap-

CoNEXT'14, December 2–5, 2014, Sydney, Australia.
Copyright 2014 ACM 978-1-4503-3279-8/14/12 ...$15.00.
http://dx.doi.org/10.1145/2674005.2675010.

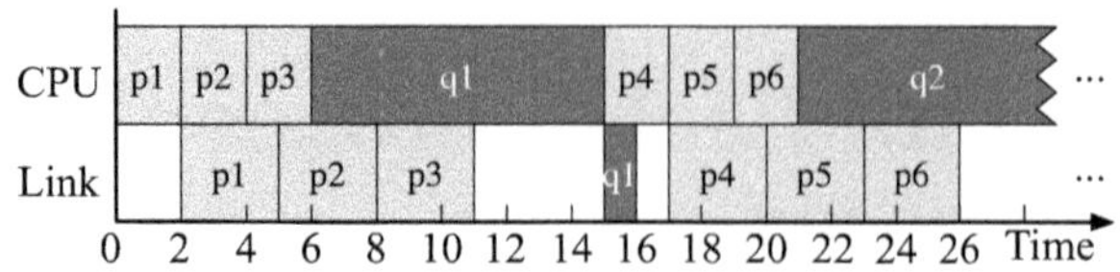

(a) A packet schedule that is fair but inefficient.

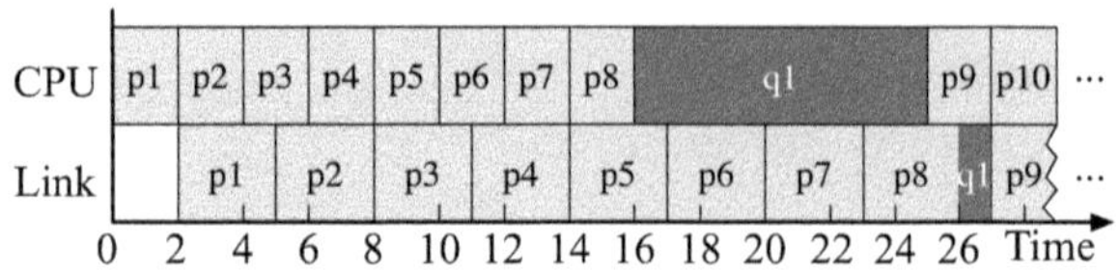

(b) A packet schedule that is efficient but violates DRF.

Figure 1: An example showing the tradeoff between fairness and efficiency for multi-resource packet scheduling. Packets that finishes CPU processing are placed into a buffer in front of the output link. Flow 1 sends packets p1, p2, ..., each having a processing time vector $\langle 2,3 \rangle$; Flow 2 sends packets q1, q2, ..., each having a processing time vector $\langle 9,1 \rangle$. Schedule (a) achieves DRF but is inefficient; Schedule (b) is efficient but unfair.

proximately equal to the CPU processing time Flow 2 receives. In this sense, Flow 1 should schedule three packets whenever Flow 2 schedules one, so that each flow receives 9 time units to process its dominant resource, as shown in Fig. 1a. This schedule, though fair, leads to poor bandwidth utilization—the link is idle for 1/3 of the time. On the other hand, Fig. 1b shows a schedule that achieves 100% CPU and bandwidth utilization by serving eight packets of Flow 1 and one packet of Flow 2 alternately. The schedule, though efficient, violates DRF. While Flow 1 receives 24/25 of the link bandwidth, Flow 2 receives only $9/25$ of the CPU time.

The fairness-efficiency tradeoff shown in the example above generally exists for multi-resource packet scheduling, but it has received little attention before. Existing multi-resource queueing algorithms focus solely on fairness [13, 32, 35]. However, for applications having a loose fairness requirement, trading off a modest degree of fairness for higher efficiency and higher throughput is well justified. In general, depending on the underlying applications, a network operator may weigh fairness and efficiency differently. Ideally, a multi-resource queueing algorithm should allow network operators to flexibly specify their tradeoff preference and implement the specified tradeoff by determining the "right" packet scheduling order.

However, designing such a queueing algorithm is non-trivial. It remains to be seen how *efficiency* can be quantitatively defined. Further, it remains open how the tradeoff requirement should be appropriately specified. But most importantly, given a specific tradeoff requirement, how can the scheduling decision be correctly made to implement it?

This paper represents the first attempt to address these challenges. We clarify the efficiency measure as the *schedule makespan*, which is the completion time of the last flow. We show that achieving a flexible tradeoff between fairness and efficiency is generally NP-hard. We hence limit our discussion to a typical scenario where CPU and link bandwidth are the two types of resources required for packet processing, which is usually the case in middleboxes. We show that the fairness-efficiency tradeoff can be strictly enforced by a GPS-like (Generalized Processor Sharing [9, 21]) fluid model, where packets are served in arbitrarily small increments on both resources. To implement the idealized fluid in the real world, we design a packet-by-packet tracking algorithm, using an approach similar to the virtual time implementation of Weighted Fair Queueing (WFQ) [9, 16, 21]. We have prototyped our tradeoff algorithm in the *Click* modular router [19]. Both our prototype implementation and trace-driven simulation show that a $15\% \sim 20\%$ fairness tradeoff is sufficient to achieve the optimal efficiency, leading to a nearly 20% improvement in bandwidth throughput with a significantly higher resource utilization.

2. FAIRNESS AND EFFICIENCY

Before discussing the tradeoff between fairness and efficiency, we shall first clarify how the notion of fairness is to be defined, and how efficiency is to be measured quantitatively. We model packet processing as going through a resource pipeline, where the first resource is consumed to process the packet first, followed by the second, and so on. A packet is not available for the downstream resource until the processing on the upstream resource finishes. For example, a packet cannot be transmitted (which consumes link bandwidth) before it has been processed by CPU.

2.1 Dominant Resource Fairness

Fairness is one of the primary design objectives for a queueing algorithm. A fair schedule offers service isolation among flows by allowing each flow to receive the throughput at least at the level when every resource is evenly allocated. The notion of Dominant Resource Fairness (DRF) embodies this isolation property by achieving the max-min fairness on the *dominant resources* of packets in their respective flows [13]. The dominant resource of a packet is defined as the one that requires the maximum packet processing time. In particular, let $\tau_r(p)$ be the time required to process packet p on resource r. The dominant resource of packet p is $r_p = \arg\max_r \tau_r(p)$. Given a packet schedule, let $D_i(t_1, t_2)$ be the time flow i receives to process the dominant resources of its packets in a backlogged period (t_1, t_2). The function $D_i(t_1, t_2)$ is referred to as the *dominant service* flow i receives in (t_1, t_2). A schedule is said to *strictly* implement DRF if for all flows i and j, and for any period (t_1, t_2) they backlog, we have

$$D_i(t_1, t_2) = D_j(t_1, t_2). \tag{1}$$

In other words, a strict DRF schedule allows each flow to receive the same dominant service in any backlogged period.

However, because packets are scheduled as separate entities and are transmitted in sequence, strictly implementing DRF at all times may not be possible in practice. For this reason, a practical fair schedule only requires flows to receive *approximately the same* dominant services over time [13, 32, 35], as shown in the previous example of Fig. 1a.

2.2 The Efficiency Measure

In addition to fairness, efficiency is another important concern for a multi-resource scheduling algorithm, but has received no significant attention before. Even the definition of efficiency needs clarification.

Perhaps the most widely adopted efficiency measure is system throughput, whose conventional definition is the *rate of completions* [17], computed as the processed workload divided by the elapsed time (*e.g.*, bits per second). While this performance metric is well defined for single-resource systems, extending its definition to multiple types of resources leads to a *throughput vector*, where each component is the throughput of one type of resource (*e.g.*, 10 CPU instruction completions per second and 5 bits transmitted through the output link per second), and different throughput vectors may not be comparable.

Another possible efficiency measure is *resource utilization given non- empty system*, or simply *resource utilization* in the remainder of this paper.[1] However, in a middlebox, different resources may see different levels of utilization. The question is: how should the "system utilization" be properly defined? One possible definition is to add up the utilization rates of all resources. This definition implicitly assumes *exchangeable resources*, say, 1% CPU usage is equivalent to 1% bandwidth consumption, which may not be well justified in many circumstance, especially when one type of resource is scarce in the system and is valued more than the other.

In this paper, we measure efficiency with the *schedule makespan*. Given input flows with a finite number of packets, the makespan of a schedule is defined as the time elapsed from the arrival of the first packet to the time when all packets finish processing on all resources. One can also view makespan as the completion time of the last flow. Intuitively, given a finite traffic input, the shorter the makespan is, the faster the input traffic is processed, and the more efficient the schedule is.[2]

2.3 Tradeoff between Fairness and Efficiency

With the precise measure of efficiency, we are curious to know how much efficiency is sacrificed for fair queueing. To answer this question, we first generalize the definition of work conserving schedules from traditional single-resource fair queueing to multiple resources. In particular, we say a schedule is *work conserving* if at least one resource is fully utilized for packet processing when there is a backlogged flow. In other words, a work conserving schedule does not allow resources to be wasted in idle if they can be used to process a backlogged packet. Existing multi-resource fair queueing algorithms [13, 32, 35] use the goal of achieving work conservation as an indication of efficiency. However, in the theorem below, we observe that such an approach is ineffective.

Theorem 1. *Let m be the number of resource types concerned. Given any traffic input I, let $T^\sigma(I)$ be the makespan of a work conserving schedule σ, and $T^*(I)$ the minimum makespan of an optimal schedule. We have*

$$T^\sigma(I) \leq mT^*(I). \tag{2}$$

PROOF. Given a traffic input I, let the work conserving schedule σ consist of n_b *busy period*. A busy period is a time interval during which at least one type of resource is used for packet processing. When the system is empty and a new packet arrives, a new busy period starts. The busy period ends when the system becomes empty again. We consider the following two cases.

Case 1: $n_b = 1$. Let traffic input I consist of N packets, ordered based on their arrival times, where packet 1 arrives first. For packet i, let $\tau_r^{(i)}$ be its packet processing time on resource r. It is easy to check that the following inequality holds for the optimal schedule with the minimum makespan:

$$T^*(I) \geq \max_r \sum_{i=1}^{N} \tau_r^{(i)}. \tag{3}$$

On the other hand, for work conserving schedule σ, its makespan reaches the maximum when packet processing does not overlap in time, across all resources, *i.e.*,

$$T^\sigma(I) \leq \sum_{i=1}^{N}\sum_{r=1}^{m} \tau_r^{(i)} \tag{4}$$

This leads to the following inequalities:

$$T^\sigma(I) \leq \sum_{i=1}^{N}\sum_{r=1}^{m} \tau_r^{(i)} \leq \sum_{i=1}^{N} m \max_r \tau_r^{(i)} \leq mT^*(I). \tag{5}$$

Case 2: $n_b > 1$. Given traffic input I, let $I(t^+)$ be the packets that arrive on or after time t. For schedule σ, let t_0 be the time when its second last busy period ($n_b - 1$) ends, and t_1 the time when the last busy period (n_b) starts. Because schedule σ is work conserving, no packet arrives between t_0 and t_1. We have

$$T^\sigma(I) = t_1 + T^\sigma(I(t_1^+)), \tag{6}$$

and

$$T^*(I) = t_1 + T^*(I(t_1^+)). \tag{7}$$

Note that given traffic input $I(t_1^+)$, schedule σ consists of only one busy period. By the discussion of Case 1, we have

$$\begin{aligned} T^\sigma(I) &= t_1 + T^\sigma(I(t_1^+)) \\ &\leq t_1 + mT^*(I(t_1^+)) \\ &\leq mT^*(I), \end{aligned} \tag{8}$$

where the last inequality is derived from (7). □

We make the following three observations from Theorem 1. First, the tradeoff between fairness and efficiency is a *unique* challenge facing multi-resource scheduling. When the system consists of only one type of resource (*i.e.*, $m = 1$), work conservation is sufficient to achieve the minimum makespan, leaving fairness as the only concern. For this reason, efficiency has never been a problem for traditional single-resource fair queueing. Second, while work conservation also provides some efficiency guarantee for multi-resource scheduling, the more types of resources, the weaker the guarantee. Third, even with a small number of resource types, the efficiency loss could be quite significant. Since bandwidth throughput is inversely proportional to the schedule makespan, Theorem 1 implies that solely relying on work conservation may incur up to 50% loss of bandwidth throughput when there are two types of resources. While this is based on the worst case, as we shall see later in §6, our experiments confirm that a throughput loss of as much as 20% is introduced by the existing fair queueing algorithms. Trading off some degree of fairness for higher efficiency is therefore well justified, especially for applications with loose fairness requirements.

2.4 Challenges

Unfortunately, striking a desired balance between fairness and efficiency in a multi-resource system is technically non-trivial. Even minimizing the makespan without regard to fairness—a special case of fairness-efficiency tradeoff—is NP-hard. In particular, we note that minimizing the makespan of a packet schedule can be modeled as a *multi-stage flow shop* problem [6, 20, 23] studied in operations research, where the equivalent of a packet is a job, and the equivalent of a type of resource is a machine. However, flow shop scheduling is a notoriously hard problem, even in its *offline setting* where the entire input is known beforehand. Specifically, when all jobs (packets) are available at the very beginning, finding the mini-

[1]This definition is different from that of queueing theory, where the utilization is defined as the fraction of time a device is busy [17]. Under this definition, high utilization usually means a high congestion level with a large queue backlog and long delays [37], and is usually not desired.

[2]In general, makespan is not the only efficiency measure that one can define. For example, we can also measure efficiency with the average flow completion time. We choose makespan as the efficiency measure in this paper because it leads to tractable analysis. More importantly, makespan closely relates to "system utilization" and is conceptually easy to understand. The discussion of other possible efficiency measures is out of the scope of this paper.

mum makespan is strongly NP-hard when the number of machines (resources) is greater than two [12].

Given the hardness results above, in this paper, we limit our discussion to two types of resources, CPU and link bandwidth, as these are the two most concerned middlebox resources [13,25]. We note that even with two types of resources, minimizing the schedule makespan remains a hard problem. Because packets arrive dynamically over time, the problem resembles a 2-machine *online flow shop scheduling* problem where jobs (packets) do not reveal their information until they arrive. For this problem, only a limited amount of *negative* results is known [6,20,23,26,30]. Specifically, no online algorithm can ensure a makespan within a factor of 1.349 of the optimum *in all cases* [24]. We also notice that no existing work gives a concrete solution, even a heuristic algorithm, that jointly considers both makespan and fairness.

3. FAIRNESS, EFFICIENCY, AND THEIR TRADEOFF IN THE FLUID MODEL

The difficulty of makespan minimization is mainly introduced by the combinatorial nature of multi-resource scheduling. One approach to circumvent this problem is to consider a *fluid relaxation*, where packets are served in arbitrarily small increments on all resources. For each packet, this is equivalent to processing it *simultaneously* on all resources with the *same* progress, and head-of-line packets of backlogged flows can also be served *in parallel*, at (potentially) different processing rates. Such a parallel processing fluid model eliminates the need for discussing the scheduling orders of flows. Instead, it allows us to focus on the resource shares allocated to flows, hence relaxing a combinatorial optimization problem to a simpler dynamic resource allocation problem. While in general, optimally solving such a dynamic problem requires knowing future packet arrivals, we show in this section that, under some practical assumptions, a greedy algorithm gives an optimal *online* schedule with the minimum makespan. We can then strike a balance between efficiency and fairness by imposing some fairness constraints to the fluid schedule. We shall discuss later in §4 and §5 how this fluid schedule is implemented in practice with a packet-by-packet tracking algorithm at acceptable complexity.

3.1 Fluid Relaxation

In the fluid model, a flow is relaxed to a fluid where each of its packets is served simultaneously on all resources with the same progress. Packets of different flows are also served in parallel. The schedule needs to decide, at each time, the resource share allocated to each backlogged flow. In particular, let $\mathcal{B}^t$ be the set of flows that are backlogged at time t. Let $a_{i,r}^t$ be the fraction (share) of resource r allocated to flow i at time t. The fluid schedule determines, at each time t, the resource allocation $a_{i,r}^t$ for each backlogged flow i and each resource r.

Two constraints must be satisfied when making resource allocation decisions. First, we must ensure that no resource is allocated more than its total availability:

$$\sum_{i\in\mathcal{B}^t} a_{i,r}^t \le 1, \quad r = 1, 2. \tag{9}$$

The second constraint ensures that a packet is processed at a *consistent* rate across resources. In particular, for a backlogged flow i and its head-of-line packet at time t, let $\tau_{i,r}^t$ be its packet processing time on resource r, and

$$r_i = \arg\max_r \tau_{i,r}^t \tag{10}$$

Table 1: Main notations used in the fluid model. The superscript t is dropped when time can be clearly inferred from the context.

Notation	Explanation
n	maximum number of flows that are concurrently backlogged
α	fairness knob specified by the network operator
$\mathcal{B}$ (or $\mathcal{B}^t$)	set of flows that are currently backlogged (at time t)
d_i (or d_i^t)	dominant share allocated to flow i (at time t)
$\bar{d}$ (or $\bar{d}^t$)	fair dominant share (at time t), given by (16)
$\tau_{i,r}$ (or $\tau_{i,r}^t$)	packet processing time on resource r required by the head-of-line packet of flow i (at time t)
$\bar{\tau}_{i,r}$ (or $\bar{\tau}_{i,r}^t$)	normalized $\tau_{i,r}$ (or $\bar{\tau}_{i,r}^t$), defined by (12)

be its dominant resource. The processing rate that this packet receives on resource r is computed as the ratio between the resource share allocated and the processing time required: $a_{i,r}^t/\tau_{i,r}^t$. To ensure a consistent processing rate, we have

$$a_{i,r}^t/\tau_{i,r}^t = a_{i,r'}^t/\tau_{i,r'}^t, \quad \text{for all } r \text{ and } r'.$$

Substituting r_i into r' above, we see a *linear relation* between the allocation share of resource r and that of the dominant resource:

$$a_{i,r}^t - \frac{\tau_{i,r}^t}{\tau_{i,r_i}^t} a_{i,r_i}^t = \bar{\tau}_{i,r}^t d_i^t, \tag{11}$$

where

$$\bar{\tau}_{i,r}^t = \tau_{i,r}^t/\tau_{i,r_i}^t \tag{12}$$

is the *normalized packet processing time* on resource r, and

$$d_i^t = a_{i,r_i}^t \tag{13}$$

is the *dominant share* allocated to flow i at time t. Plugging (11) into (9), we combine the two constraints into one *feasibility constraint* of a fluid schedule:

$$\sum_{i\in\mathcal{B}^t} \bar{\tau}_{i,r}^t d_i^t \le 1, \quad r = 1, 2. \tag{14}$$

Before we discuss the tradeoff between fairness and efficiency, we first consider two special cases, where either fairness or efficiency is the only objective to optimize in the fluid model. For ease of presentation, we drop the superscript t when time can be clearly inferred from the context. Table 1 summarizes the main notations used in the fluid model.

3.2 Fluid Schedule with Perfect Fairness

We first consider the fairness objective. To achieve perfect DRF, the fluid schedule enforces strict max-min fairness on flows' dominant shares, under the feasibility constraint. Specifically, the fluid schedule solves the following *DRF allocation problem* [14, 22] at each time t:

$$\begin{aligned} \max_{d_i} \quad & \min_{i\in\mathcal{B}} d_i \\ \text{s.t.} \quad & \sum_{i\in\mathcal{B}} \bar{\tau}_{i,r} d_i \le 1, \quad r = 1, 2. \end{aligned} \tag{15}$$

Let n be the number of backlogged flows. The optimal solution, denoted by $\bar{\mathbf{d}} = (\bar{d}_1, \ldots, \bar{d}_n)$, allocates each backlogged flow the same dominant share, *i.e.*,

$$\bar{d}_i = \bar{d} = 1/\max\left\{\sum_i \bar{\tau}_{i,1}, \sum_i \bar{\tau}_{i,2}\right\}. \tag{16}$$

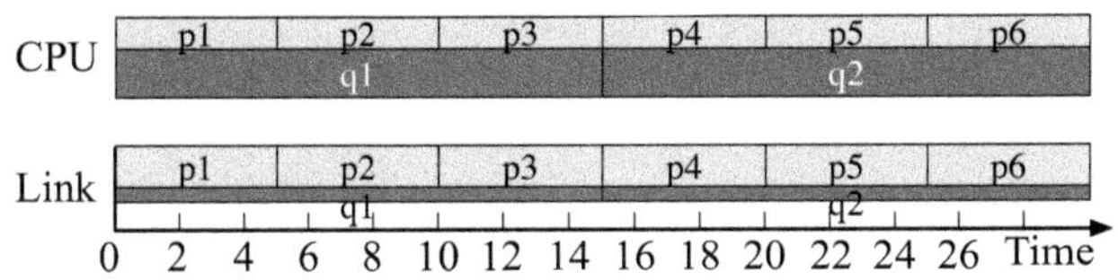

Figure 2: The DRGPS fluid that implements the perfect fairness in the example of Fig. 1. Flow 1 sends packets p1, p2, ..., and receives $\langle 3/5$ CPU, $1/15$ bandwidth$\rangle$; Flow 2 sends packets q1, q2, ..., and receives $\langle 3/5$ CPU, $1/15$ bandwidth$\rangle$. Only 2/3 of the link bandwidth is utilized.

In any backlogged periods, because flows are allocated the same dominant shares, they receive the same dominant services, achieving strict DRF at all times. The resulting fluid schedule is also known as DRGPS [33], a multi-resource generalization to the well-known GPS [9,21].

Any discrete fair schedule is essentially a packet-by-packet approximation to DRGPS. For instance, applying DRGPS to the example of Fig. 1 leads to a fluid schedule shown in Fig. 2, where the normalized packet processing times of Flow 1 and Flow 2 are $\langle \bar{\tau}_{1,1}, \bar{\tau}_{1,2} \rangle = \langle 2/3, 1 \rangle$ and $\langle \bar{\tau}_{2,1}, \bar{\tau}_{2,2} \rangle = \langle 1, 1/9 \rangle$, respectively. By (16), both flows are allocated the same dominant share $\bar{d} = 3/5$. Specifically, Flow 1 receives $\langle 2/5$ CPU, $3/5$ bandwidth$\rangle$; Flow 2 receives $\langle 3/5$ CPU, $1/15$ bandwidth$\rangle$. In total, only 2/3 of the bandwidth is utilized, the same as the discrete fair schedule shown in Fig. 1a.

3.3 Fluid Schedule with Optimal Efficiency

We next discuss the efficiency objective. While there are some schedules proposed in the operations research literature that can achieve the minimum makspan for a flow shop problem, none of them applies in the context of packet scheduling: they either assume no packet arrivals (*e.g.*, [29]) or require full knowledge of future information (*e.g.*, [5]). We propose a simple *greedy* fluid schedule as follows.

For a given time instant, we define the system's *instantaneous dominant throughput* as the sum of the dominant share allocated, *i.e.*, $\sum_{i\in\mathcal{B}} d_i$. Intuitively, by maximizing $\sum_{i\in\mathcal{B}} d_i$ at all times, one would expect a high *average dominant throughput* $\sum_{i\in\mathcal{B}} D_i/T$, where T is the schedule makespan and D_i is the total dominant services (processing time) required by flow i. Given dominant workload $\sum_{i\in\mathcal{B}} D_i$, maximizing the average dominant throughput is equivalent to minimizing the schedule makespan T. Following this intuition, we propose a greedy fluid schedule that solves the following resource allocation problem to maximize the instantaneous dominant throughput at every time:

$$\begin{aligned} \max_{d_i \geq 0} \quad & \sum_{i\in\mathcal{B}} d_i \\ \text{s.t.} \quad & \sum_{i\in\mathcal{B}} \bar{\tau}_{i,r} d_i \leq 1, \quad r = 1, 2. \end{aligned} \tag{17}$$

In case that the optimal solution, denoted $\mathbf{d}^* = (d_1^*, \ldots, d_n^*)$, is not unique, the schedule chooses the one with the maximum overall utilization:

$$\max_{d_i^*} \sum_r \sum_{i\in\mathcal{B}} \bar{\tau}_{i,r} d_i^* . \tag{18}$$

In the example of Fig. 1, solving (17) allocates Flow 1 the dominant share $d_1^* = 9/25$ and Flow 2 the dominant share $d_2^* = 24/25$. It is easy to check that both CPU and link bandwidth are fully utilized.

Compared to those schedules proposed in the operations research literature, the greedy schedule defined by (17) is particularly attractive for packet scheduling due to the following three properties. First, it is an online algorithm without any *a priori* knowledge of future packet arrivals. Further, among all packets that are backlogged, only the information regarding head-of-line packets is required. This suggests that the schedule only needs to maintain a very simple per-flow state. Most importantly, the greedy schedule is more than a simple heuristic. Below we show that under some practical assumptions, greedily maximizing the dominant throughput gives the minimum makespan. Our analysis requires the following lemma, where we show that the schedule will not waste any resource in idle, unless all flows bottleneck on the same resource, in which case the other resource cannot be fully utilized anyway. The proof is deferred to our technical report [31] due to space constraint.

Lemma 1. *The fluid schedule defined by* (17) *fully utilizes both resources if there are two head-of-line packets with different dominant resource,* i.e., *there exist two flows j and l, such that $\bar{\tau}_{j,1} = 1 > \bar{\tau}_{j,2}$ and $\bar{\tau}_{l,1} < \bar{\tau}_{l,2} = 1$.*

With Lemma 1, we analyze the makespan of the fluid schedule defined by (17). Following [13], we say a flow is *dominant-resource monotonic* if it does not change its dominant resource during backlogged periods. To make the analysis tractable, we assume that flows are dominant-resource monotonic. This is often true in practice as packets in the same flow usually undergo the same processing, and hence have the same dominant resource. The following lemma,whose proof can be found in [31], states the optimality of the fluid schedule in a static scenario without dynamic packet arrivals.

Lemma 2. *For dominant-resource monotonic flows, the fluid schedule defined by* (17) *gives the minimum makespan if all packets are available at the beginning.*

We now extend the results of Lemma 2 to an online case where packets dynamically arrive over time. The following theorem gives the optimality condition of the fluid schedule. The proof is deferred to [31].

Theorem 2. *For dominant-resource monotonic flows, the fluid schedule defined by* (17) *gives the minimum makespan among all schedules, if after the system has two flows with different dominant resources, whenever a new flow arrives, there exist two backlogged flows with different dominant resources.*

The optimality conditions required by Theorem 2 can be easily met in practice. Because the number of backlogged flows is usually large, it is almost true that we can always find two flows with different dominant resources. In fact, even in a very unfortunate case where all flows bottleneck on the same resource, the greedy fluid schedule does not deviate far away from the optimum: no matter what fluid schedule is used, the bottleneck resource is always fully utilized when the system is non-empty and hence has the same backlog, which is a dominant factor in determining the schedule makespan.

The significance of Theorem 2 is that it connects makespan, a measure defined in the *time domain*, to the instantaneous dominant throughput, a measure defined in the *space domain*. More importantly, it shows that minimizing the former is, in a practical sense, equivalent to maximizing the latter at all times, without the need to know future packet arrivals. We shall use this intuition to strike a balance between fairness and efficiency in the next subsection.

3.4 Tradeoff between Fairness and Efficiency

When both fairness and efficiency are considered, we express the tradeoff between the two conflicting objectives as a constrained optimization problem—minimizing makespan under some specified fairness requirements. Recall that when perfect fairness is enforced, all flows receive the same dominant share $\bar{d}$ computed by (16), *i.e.*, $d_i = \bar{d}$ for all i. When fairness is not a strict requirement, we introduce a *fairness knob* $\alpha \in [0, 1]$ to specify the fairness degradation. In particular, an allocation $\mathbf{d}$ is called *α-portion fair* if $d_i \geq \alpha\bar{d}$ for all backlogged flow i. In other words, each flow receives at least an α-portion of its fair dominant share $\bar{d}$. A fluid schedule is called α-portion fair if it achieves the α-portion fair allocation at all times.

By choosing different values for α, a network operator can precisely control the fairness degradation. As two extreme cases, setting $\alpha = 0$ means that fairness is not considered at all; setting $\alpha = 1$ means that perfect fairness must be enforced at all times.

Given the specified fairness knob α, the fluid schedule tries to minimize makespan under the corresponding α-portion fairness constraints. Since minimizing makespan is, in a practical sense, equivalent to maximizing the system's dominant throughput, we obtain a simple tradeoff heuristic that maximizes the dominant throughput, subject to the required α-portion fairness at every time t:

$$\begin{aligned} \max_{d_i} \quad & \sum_{i \in \mathcal{B}} d_i \\ \text{s.t.} \quad & \sum_{i \in \mathcal{B}} \bar{\tau}_{i,r} d_i \leq 1, \quad r = 1, 2, \\ & d_i \geq \alpha\bar{d}, \quad \forall i \in \mathcal{B}, \end{aligned} \tag{19}$$

where the fair share $\bar{d}$ is given by (16). We see that the fluid schedule captures both DRGPS and the greedy schedule defined by (17) as special cases with $\alpha = 1$ and 0, respectively.

Special Solution Structure. The tradeoff problem (19) has a *closed-form* solution, based on which the tradeoff schedule can be easily computed. We first allocate each flow its guaranteed portion of dominant share $\alpha\bar{d}$. We then denote

$$\tilde{d}_i = d_i - \alpha\bar{d} \tag{20}$$

as the *bonus dominant share* allocated to flow i. Substituting (20) into (19), we equivalently rewrite (19) as a problem of determining the bonus dominant share received by each flow:

$$\begin{aligned} \max_{\tilde{d}_i \geq 0} \quad & \sum_{i \in \mathcal{B}} \tilde{d}_i + |\mathcal{B}|\alpha\bar{d} \\ \text{s.t.} \quad & \sum_{i \in \mathcal{B}} \bar{\tau}_{i,r} \tilde{d}_i \leq \mu_r \quad r = 1, 2, \end{aligned} \tag{21}$$

where

$$\mu_r = 1 - \alpha\bar{d} \sum_{i \in \mathcal{B}} \bar{\tau}_{i,r}, \quad r = 1, 2, \tag{22}$$

and is the *remaining share* of resource r after each flow receives its guaranteed dominant share $\alpha\bar{d}$. Without loss of generality, we sort all the backlogged flows based on the processing demands on the two types of resources required by their head-of-line packets as follows:

$$\bar{\tau}_{1,1}/\bar{\tau}_{1,2} \geq \cdots \geq \bar{\tau}_{n,1}/\bar{\tau}_{n,2}. \tag{23}$$

The following theorem shows that at most two flows are awarded the bonus share at a time. Its proof is deferred to our technical report [31].

Theorem 3. *There exists an optimal solution $\tilde{\mathbf{d}}^*$ to (21) where $\tilde{d}_i^* = 0$ for all $2 \leq i \leq n-1$. In particular, $\tilde{\mathbf{d}}^*$ is given in the following three cases:*

Case 1: $\mu_1/\mu_2 < \bar{\tau}_{n,1}/\bar{\tau}_{n,2}$. *In this case, resource 1 is fully utilized, with $\tilde{d}_n^* = \mu_1/\bar{\tau}_{n,1}$ and $\tilde{d}_i^* = 0$ for all $i < n$.*

Case 2: $\mu_1/\mu_2 > \bar{\tau}_{1,1}/\bar{\tau}_{1,2}$. *In this case, resource 2 is fully utilized, with $\tilde{d}_1^* = \mu_2/\bar{\tau}_{1,2}$ and $\tilde{d}_i^* = 0$ for all $i > 1$.*

Case 3: $\bar{\tau}_{n,1}/\bar{\tau}_{n,2} \leq \mu_1/\mu_2 \leq \bar{\tau}_{1,1}/\bar{\tau}_{1,2}$. *In this case, both resources are fully utilized, and we have*

$$\tilde{d}_i^* = \begin{cases} (\mu_1\bar{\tau}_{n,2} - \mu_2\bar{\tau}_{n,1})/(\bar{\tau}_{1,1}\bar{\tau}_{n,2} - \bar{\tau}_{1,2}\bar{\tau}_{n,1}), & i = 1; \\ (\mu_2\bar{\tau}_{1,1} - \mu_1\bar{\tau}_{1,2})/(\bar{\tau}_{1,1}\bar{\tau}_{n,2} - \bar{\tau}_{1,2}\bar{\tau}_{n,1}), & i = n; \\ 0, & o.w. \end{cases}$$

Once the optimal bonus dominant share has been determined as shown above, the optimal solution $\mathbf{d}^*$ to (19), which is the dominant share allocated to each flow, can be easily computed as the sum of the bonus share and the guaranteed share:

$$d_i^* = \tilde{d}_i^* + \alpha\bar{d}, \quad \text{for all } i. \tag{24}$$

We give an intuitive explanation of Theorem 3 as follows. The first two cases of Theorem 3 correspond to the scenario where after each flow receives its guaranteed share, the remaining amounts of the two types of resources are *unbalanced* and cannot be fully utilized simultaneously. In this case, the schedule awards the bonus share to the flow (either Flow 1 or Flow n) whose processing demands can better utilize the remaining resources. The third case covers the scenario where the remaining amounts of the two types of resources are *balanced*, and can be fully utilized when the system is non-empty. In this case, they are allocated to two flows (Flow 1 and Flow n) with *complementary* resource demands as their bonus shares.

Theorem 3 reveals an important structure, that *at most two* flows are allocated more dominant shares than others. We refer to these flows as the *favored flows* and all the others as the *regular flows*. We shall show in §5 that this structure leads to an efficient $O(\log n)$ implementation of the fluid schedule.

4. PACKET-BY-PACKET TRACKING

So far, all our discussions are based on an idealized fluid model. In practice, however, packets are processed as separate entities. In this section, we present a discrete tracking algorithm that implements the fluid schedule as a packet-by-packet schedule in practice. We show that the discrete schedule is asymptotically close to the fluid schedule, in terms of both fairness and efficiency. We start with a comparison between two typical tracking approaches.

4.1 Start-Time Tracking vs. Finish-Time Tracking

Two common tracking algorithms may be used to implement a fluid schedule in practice, *start-time tracking* and *finish-time tracking*. The former tracks the order of packet start times—among all packets that have already started in the fluid schedule, the one that starts the earliest is scheduled first. Finish-time tracking, on the other hand, assigns the highest scheduling priority to the packet that completes service the earliest in the fluid schedule. In traditional single-resource fair queueing, FQS [16] uses the former approach to track GPS, while WFQ [1,9,21] adopts the latter approach.

While both algorithms closely track the fluid schedule of fair queueing, only start-time tracking is well defined for the tradeoff schedule given by (19). This is due to the fact that, in the tradeoff schedule, future traffic arrivals may lead to a different allocation of packet processing rates and may subsequently change the packet finish times of current packets. As a result, determining the order of finish times requires future traffic arrival information and hence is unrealistic.[3] Start-time tracking avoids this problem as packets are scheduled only *after* they start in the fluid schedule.

For this reason, we use start-time tracking to implement the fluid schedule. We say a discrete schedule and a fluid schedule *correspond* to each other if the former tracks the latter by the packet start time. Specifically, we maintain the fluid schedule in the background. Whenever there is a scheduling opportunity, among all head-of-line packets that have already started in the fluid schedule, the one that starts the earliest is chosen. Below we show that this discrete schedule is *asymptotically close* to its corresponding fluid schedule.

4.2 Performance Analysis

To analyze the performance of start-time tracking, we introduce the following notations. Let $\tau^{\max}$ be the maximum packet processing time required by any packet on any resource. Let n be the maximum number of flows that are *concurrently* backlogged. Let T^{F} be the makespan of the fluid schedule, and T^{D} the makespan of its corresponding discrete schedule.Due to space constraints, all proofs are deferred to our technical report [31].

The following theorem bounds the difference between the makespan of the fluid schedule and its corresponding discrete schedule.

Theorem 4. *For the fluid schedule with $\alpha > 0$ and its corresponding discrete schedule, we have*

$$T^{\mathrm{D}} \leq T^{\mathrm{F}} + n\tau^{\max}. \tag{25}$$

The error bound $n\tau^{\max}$ can be intuitively explained as the total packet processing time required by all n concurrent flows, each sending only one packet. In practice, the number of packets a flow sends is usually significantly larger than one. As a result, the traffic makespan is significantly larger than the error bound, *i.e.*, $T^{\mathrm{F}} \gg n\tau^{\max}$. Theorem 4 essentially indicates that in terms of makespan, the two schedules are asymptotically close to each other.

We next analyze the fairness performance of the discrete schedule by comparing the dominant services a flow receives under both schedules. In particular, let $D_i^{\mathrm{F}}(0,t)$ be the dominant services flow i receives in $(0,t)$ under the fluid schedule, and $D_i^{\mathrm{D}}(0,t)$ the dominant services flow i receives in $(0,t)$ under the corresponding discrete schedule. The following theorem shows that flows receive approximately the same dominant services under both schedules.

Theorem 5. *For the fluid schedule with $\alpha > 0$ and its corresponding discrete schedule, the following inequality holds for any flow i and any time t:*

$$D_i^{\mathrm{F}}(0,t) - 2(n-1)\tau^{\max} \leq D_i^{\mathrm{D}}(0,t) \leq D_i^{\mathrm{F}}(0,t) + \tau^{\max}. \tag{26}$$

In other words, the difference between the dominant services a flow receives under the two corresponding schedules is bounded by a constant amount, irrespective of the time t. Over the long run, the discrete schedule achieves the same α-portion fairness as its corresponding fluid schedule. To summarize, start-time tracking retains both the efficiency and fairness properties of its corresponding fluid schedule in the asymptotic regime.

5. AN $O(\log n)$ IMPLEMENTATION

To implement the aforementioned start-time tracking algorithm, two modules are required: packet profiling and fluid scheduling. The former estimates the packet processing time on both CPU and link bandwidth; the latter maintains the fluid schedule as a reference system based on the packet profiling results. We show in this section that packet profiling can be quickly accomplished in $O(1)$ time using a simple approach proposed in [13]. The main challenge comes from the complexity of maintaining the fluid schedule, where direct implementation requires $O(n)$ time. Here, n is the number of backlogged flows. We give an $O(\log n)$ implementation based on an approach similar to virtual time. We shall show in §6 that the implementation can be easily prototyped in the Click modular router [19].

5.1 Packet Profiling

As pointed out by Ghodsi *et al.* [13], any multi-resource fair queueing algorithm, including our fluid schedule, requires knowledge of the packet processing time on each resource. Fortunately, as shown in [13], CPU processing time can be accurately estimated as a linear function of packet size. Specifically, for a packet of size l, the CPU processing time is estimated as $al+b$, where a and b are the coefficients depending on the type of packet processing (*e.g.*, IPsec). We have validated this linear model through an upfront experiment using Click [19]. For each type of packet processing, we measure the exact CPU processing time required by packets of different sizes. This allows us to determine the coefficients a and b. We fit such a linear model to the scheduler and use it to estimate the CPU processing time required by a packet. As for the packet transmission time, the estimation is simply the packet size divided by the outgoing bandwidth, which is known *a priori*.

5.2 Direct Implementation of Fluid Scheduling

Based on the packet profiling results, the fluid schedule is constructed and is maintained by the fluid scheduler. In particular, we need to determine the next packet that starts in the fluid schedule. This requires tracking the work progress of all n flows. Below we give a direct implementation that will be used later in our virtual time implementation.

For each flow i, we record d_i^*, which is the dominant share the flow receives in the fluid schedule at the current time and is computed by (24). We also record R_i, the *remaining dominant processing time* required by the head-of-line packet of the flow at the current time.

For flow i, its head-of-line packet will finish in R_i/d_i^* time if no event occurs then. An *event* is either a *packet departure* or a packet being the *new head-of-line* in the fluid schedule. Either of them may change the head-of-line packet of a flow, leading to different coefficients of the tradeoff problem (19). With d_i^* and R_i, we can accurately track the work progress of flow i in an *event-driven* basis. Specifically, upon the occurrence of an event, let Δt be the time elapsed since the last update. If $\Delta t < R_i/d_i^*$, meaning that the event occurs *before* the head-of-line packet finishes, we update $R_i \leftarrow R_i - d_i^*\Delta t$. If $\Delta t = R_i/d_i^*$, meaning that the event occurs *at the time* when the head-of-line packet finishes, we check if flow i has a next packet p to process. If it does, then packet p becomes the new head-of-line and should start in the fluid schedule. We update R_i as the dominant processing time required by p. Otherwise, we reset $R_i \leftarrow 0$, and flow i leaves the fluid system. We also recompute d_i^* after R_i is updated. (Note that it is impossible to have $\Delta t > R_i/d_i^*$.)

However, purely relying on the approach above to track the work progress of all n flows is highly inefficient. Whenever an event

[3]This is not a problem of single-resource fair queueing as different flows are allocated the same processing rate, so that future traffic arrivals will not affect the order of finish times of current packets.

occurs, each flow must be updated individually, which requires at least $O(n)$ time per event and is too expensive. We next introduce a more efficient implementation that requires the above procedure for at most two flows.

5.3 Virtual Time Implementation of Fluid Scheduling

To avoid the high complexity required by the direct implementation above, we have noted, by Theorem 3, that *at most two* flows are favored and are allocated more dominant shares than others. Therefore, it suffices to maintain *at most three* dominant shares at a time—two for the favored flows and one for the other regular flows. For regular flows, we track their work progress using an approach similar to the *virtual time* implementation of GPS [9, 21]. Our intuition is that, by Theorem 3, all the regular flows are allocated the *same* dominant share, and their scheduling *resembles fair queueing*. For favored flows, since there are at most two of them, we track their work progress directly, using the direct implementation above. Our approach is detailed below.

5.3.1 Identifying Favored and Regular Flows

We first discuss how favored and regular flows can be quickly identified upon the occurrence of an event. By Theorem 3, it suffices to sort flows in order (23) and examine the three cases. Flows that receive the bonus share (*i.e.*, $\tilde{d}_i^* > 0$) are favored. Note that the entire computation requires only information regarding the head-of-line packet of the first and the last flow in order (23) ($\bar{\tau}_{1,r}$ and $\bar{\tau}_{n,r}$, the normalized dominant processing time). We store all the head-of-line packets in a double-ended priority queue maintained by a *min-max heap* for fast retrieval, where the packet order is defined by (23). This allows us to apply Theorem 3 and identify the favored and regular flows in $O(\log n)$ time.

5.3.2 Tracking Favored Flows

For favored flows, because there are at most two of them, we track their work progress using the direct implementation mentioned in §5.2, where we record d_i^* and R_i for each favored flow i. It is easy to see that the update complexity is dominated by the computation of d_i^*. As mentioned in the previous discussion, this can be done in $O(\log n)$ time by Theorem 3. Also, since there are at most two favored flows, the overall tracking complexity remains $O(\log n)$ per event.

5.3.3 Tracking Regular Flows

For regular flows, since they receive the same dominant share, their scheduling resembles fair queueing. We hence track their work progress using *virtual time* [1, 9, 21]. Specifically, we define virtual time $V(t)$ as a function of real time t evolving as follows:

$$\begin{aligned} V(0) &= 0, \\ V'(t) &= \alpha \bar{d}^t, \quad t > 0. \end{aligned} \tag{27}$$

Here, $\bar{d}^t$ is the fair dominant share computed by (16) at time t, and is fixed between two consecutive events; $\alpha \bar{d}^t$ is the dominant share each regular flow receives.[4] Thus, V can be interpreted as increasing at the marginal rate at which regular flows receive dominant services. Each regular flow i also maintains *virtual finish time* F_i, indicating the virtual time at which its head-of-line packet finishes in the fluid schedule. The virtual finish time F_i is updated as follows when flow i has a new head-of-line packet p at time t:

$$F_i = V(t) + \tau^*(p), \tag{28}$$

[4]We restore the superscript t here to emphasize that the fair dominant share computed by (16) may change over time.

where $\tau^*(p)$ is the dominant packet processing time required by p. Among all the regular flows, the one with the smallest F_i has its head-of-line packet finishing first in the fluid schedule. Unless some event occurs in between, at time t, the next packet departure for the regular flows would be in $t_N = (\min_i F_i - V(t))/\alpha\bar{d}$ time.

Using virtual time defined by (27), we can accurately track the work progress of regular flows in an event-driven basis. Specifically, upon the occurrence of an event at time t, let t_0 be the time of the last update, and $\Delta t = t - t_0$ the time elapsed since the last update. If $\Delta t < t_N$, meaning that the event occurs before the next packet departure of regular flows, we simply update the virtual time following (27):

$$V(t) = V(t_0) + \alpha \bar{d} \Delta t. \tag{29}$$

If $\Delta t = t_N$, then the event occurs at the time when a packet of a regular flow, say flow i, finishes in the fluid schedule. In addition to updating the virtual time, we check to see if flow i has a next packet p to process. If it does, meaning that the packet p should start in the fluid schedule, we update its virtual finish time F_i following (28). Otherwise, flow i departs the system. We also recompute $\bar{d}$ by (16).

The tracking complexity is dominated by the computation of the minimum virtual finish time, *i.e.*, $\min_i F_i$. By storing F_i's in a priority queue maintained by a heap, we see that the tracking complexity is $O(\log n)$ per event.

5.3.4 Handling Identity Switching

We note that the identity of a flow is not fixed: upon the occurrence of an event, a favored flow may switch to a regular flow, and vice versa. We show that such identity switching can also be easily handled in $O(\log n)$ time.

We first consider a favored flow i switching to a regular one at time t, which requires the computation of the virtual finish time F_i. Recall that we have recorded R_i, the remaining dominant processing time required by the head-of-line packet, for flow i as it is previously favored. By definition, the virtual finish time F_i can be simply computed as

$$F_i = V(t) + R_i. \tag{30}$$

Adding F_i to the heap takes at most $O(\log n)$ time.

We next consider a regular flow i switching to a favored one at time t, which requires the computation of R_i. Recall that we have recorded the virtual finish time F_i for flow i. By definition, the remaining dominant processing time required by its head-of-line packet is simply

$$R_i = F_i - V(t), \tag{31}$$

which is a dual of (30).

We also need to remove the virtual finish time, F_i, from the heap. To do so, we maintain an index for each regular flow, recording the location of its virtual finish time stored in the heap. Following this index, we can easily locate the position of F_i and delete it from the heap, followed by some standard "trickle-down" operations to preserve the heap property in $O(\log n)$ time.

To summarize, our approach maintains the fluid schedule by identifying favored and regular flows, tracking their work progress, and handling the potential identity switching. We show that any of these operations can be accomplished in $O(\log n)$ time. As a result, maintaining the fluid schedule takes $O(\log n)$ time per event.

5.4 Start-Time Tracking and Complexity

With the fluid schedule maintained as a reference system, the implementation of start-time tracking is straightforward. Whenever a packet starts in the fluid schedule, it is added to a FIFO queue.

Upon a scheduling opportunity, the scheduler polls the queue and retrieves a packet to schedule. This ensures that packets are scheduled in order of their start times in the fluid schedule. To minimize the update frequency, the scheduler lazily updates the fluid schedule only when the FIFO queue is empty.

We now analyze the scheduling complexity of the aforementioned implementation. The scheduling decisions are made by updating the fluid schedule in an event-driven basis. For each event, the update takes $O(\log n)$ time, where n is the number of backlogged flows. Note that there are only two types of events in the fluid schedule, new head-of-line and packet departure. Because a packet served in the fluid schedule triggers exactly these two events over the entire scheduling period, scheduling N packets triggers $2N$ updates in the fluid schedule, with the overall complexity $O(2N \log n)$. On average, the scheduling decision is made in $O(2 \log n)$ time per packet, the same order as that of DRFQ [13].

6. EVALUATION

We evaluate the tradeoff algorithm via both our prototype implementation and trace-driven simulation. We use a prototype implementation to investigate the detailed functioning of the algorithm, in a microscopic view. We then take a macroscopic view to evaluate the algorithm using trace-driven simulation, where flows dynamically join and depart the system.

6.1 Experimental Results

We have prototyped our tradeoff algorithm as a new scheduler in the Click modular router [19], based on the $O(\log n)$ implementation given in the previous section. The scheduler classifies packets to flows (based on the IP prefix and port number) and identifies the types of packet processing based on the port number specified by a *flow class table*. The scheduler also exposes an interface that allows the operator to dynamically configure the fairness knob α. Our implementation consists of roughly 1,000 lines of C++ code.

We run our Click implementation in user mode on a Dell PowerEdge server with an Intel Xeon 3.0 GHz processor and 1 Gbps Ethernet interface. To make fairness relevant, we throttle the outgoing bandwidth to 200 Mbps while keeping the inbound bandwidth as is. We also throttle the Click module to use only 20% CPU so that CPU could also be a bottleneck. We configure three packet processing modules in Click to emulate a multi-functioning middlebox: packet checking, statistical monitoring, and IPsec. The former two modules are bandwidth-bound, though statistical monitoring requires more CPU processing time than packet checking does. The IPsec module encrypts packets using AES (128-bit key length) and is CPU-bound. We configure another server as a traffic source, initiating 60 UDP flows each sending 2000 800-byte packets per second to the Click router. The first 20 flows pass through the packet checking module; the next 20 flows pass through the statistical monitoring module; and the last 20 flows pass through the IPsec module.

6.1.1 *Fairness-Efficiency Tradeoff*

We first evaluate the achieved tradeoff between schedule fairness and makespan. To fairly compare the makespan at different fairness levels, it is critical to ensure the same traffic input when running the algorithm with different values of fairness knob α. Therefore, we initially consider an idealized scenario where each flow queue has *infinite* capacity and never drops packets. Table 2 lists the observed makespans with various fairness requirements, in an experiment where each flow keeps sending packets for 10 seconds. We see that, as expected, trading off some level of fairness leads to a shorter makespan and higher efficiency. Furthermore, the marginal improvement of efficiency is decreasing. This suggests that one does not need to compromise too much fairness in order to achieve high efficiency. In our experiment, trading off 15% of fairness shortens the makespan by 15.3% from the strictly fair schedule ($\alpha = 1$), which is equivalent to a 18.1% bandwidth throughput enhancement and is near-optimal as seen in Table 2. Fig. 3 gives a detailed look into the achieved resource utilization over time, at four fairness levels. We see that strictly fair queueing ($\alpha = 1$) wastes 30% of CPU cycles, leaving the bandwidth as the bottleneck at the beginning. This situation remains until bandwidth-bound flows finish, at which time the bottleneck shifts to CPU. By relaxing fairness, CPU-bound flows receive more services, leading to a steady increase of CPU utilization up to 100%. Meanwhile, bandwidth-bound flows experience slightly longer completion times due to the fairness tradeoff.

Table 2: Schedule makespan observed in Click at different fairness levels. The queue capacity is infinite.

Fairness knob α	**Makespan (s)**	**Normalized Makespan**
1.00	55.68	100.00%
0.95	52.50	94.28%
0.90	48.97	87.95%
0.85	47.17	84.72%
0.70	47.13	84.64%
0.60	47.07	84.54%
0.50	47.07	84.54%

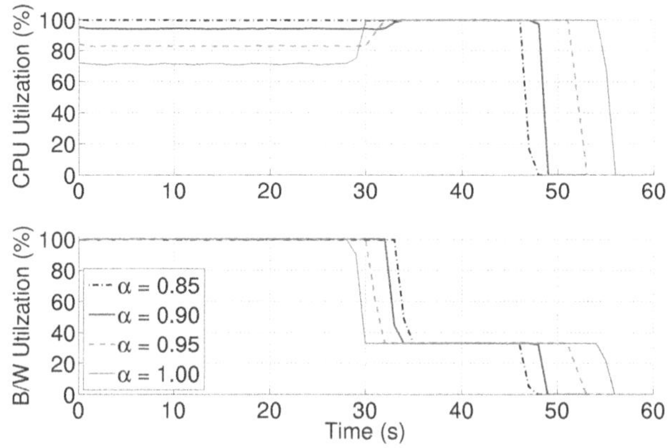

Figure 3: Overall resource utilization observed in Click. No packet drops.

We now verify the fairness guarantee. We run the scheduler at various fairness levels. At each level, for each flow, we measure its received dominant share *every second* for the first 20 seconds, during which all flows are backlogged. Fig. 4 shows the results, where each cross ("x") corresponds to the dominant share of a flow measured in one second. As expected, under strict fairness ($\alpha = 1$), all flows receive the same dominant share (around 2%). As α decreases, the fairness requirement relaxes. Some flows are hence favored and are allocated more dominant share, while others receive less. However, the minimum dominant share a flow receives is lower bounded by the α-portion of the fair share, shown as the solid line in Fig. 4. This shows that the algorithm is correctly operating at the desired fairness level.

We next extend the experiment to a more practical setup, where each flow queue has a limited capacity and drops packets when it is full. We set the queue size to 200 packets for each flow and repeat the previous experiments. In this case, comparing makespan

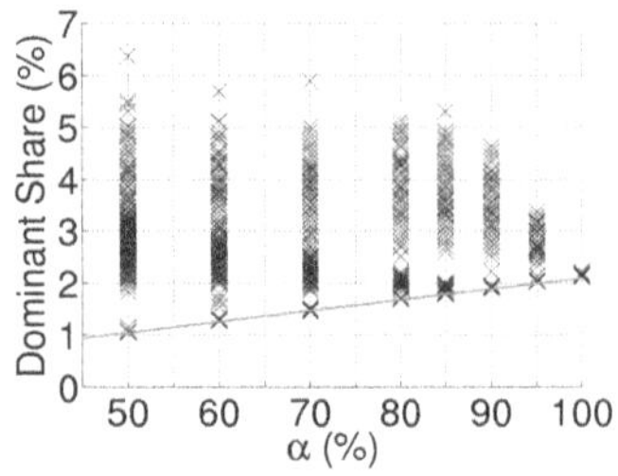

Figure 4: Dominant share each flow receives per second in Click. No packet drops. The strict fair share is 2%.

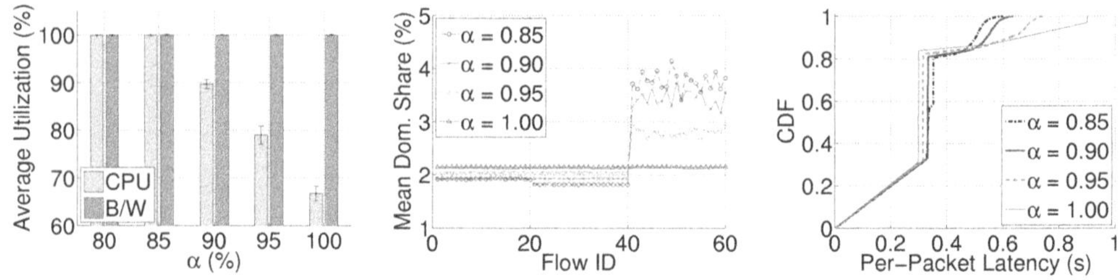

(a) Resource utilization. (b) Dominant share. (c) Per-packet latency

Figure 5: Average resource utilization and dominant share each flow receives in Click at different fairness levels. The queue capacity is 200 packets. The measurement of resource utilization and dominant share is conducted every second over the entire schedule.

is inappropriate as the scheduler may drop different packets when running at different fairness level. We instead measure the resource utilization achieved *every second* over the entire scheduling period. Fig. 5a illustrates the average utilization of both CPU and bandwidth, where the error bar shows one standard deviation. Similar to the previous experiments, a fairness degradation of 15% is sufficient to achieve the optimal efficiency, enhancing the CPU utilization from 71% to 100%. Further trading off fairness is not well justified. As shown in Fig. 5b, the increased CPU throughput is mainly used to process those CPU-bound flows (Flows 41 to 60), doubling their dominant shares. Meanwhile, the dominant share received by all the other flows is at least 85% of the fair share, as promised by the algorithm. We also depict the per-packet latency CDF in Fig. 5c. We see that trading off fairness for efficiency significantly improves the tail latency, usually caused by flows that finish the last. On the other hand, flows whose shares have been traded off see slightly longer delays of their packets. Fortunately, these latency penalties are strictly bounded—thanks to the fairness guarantee—and are compensated by the significant latency improvement of favored flows.

We have also measured the scheduling overhead in the experiments. In particular, we configure the tradeoff scheduler for strict fair queueing by setting $\alpha = 1$. We then compare the incurred CPU overhead with that of MR^3 [32], a low complexity fair scheduler. Our measurement shows that the tradeoff scheduler introduces 1% CPU overhead compared with MR^3.

6.1.2 *Service Isolation*

We next examine the impact of fairness tradeoff on service isolation. We initiate 6 UDP flows sending 800-byte packets. Flows 1 to 3 are *elephant flows*, each sending 20,000 packets per second, and undergo the checking, monitoring, and IPsec modules, respectively. Flows 4 to 6 are *mice flows*, each sending 2 packets per second, and undergo the checking, monitoring, and IPsec modules, respectively. The queue capacity is set to 200 packets. Fig. 6 shows the per-packet latency of each flow at different fairness levels. We see that the tradeoff mainly affects those high-rate flows. For mice flows, even if they may receive less resource share when $\alpha < 1$, the guaranteed share is sufficient to accommodate their low-rate traffic. As a result, their packets are scheduled almost immediately upon arrival, with two orders of magnitude lower latency than the elephant flows.

We also compare our tradeoff scheduler against other fair queueing algorithms. In particular, we have implemented MR^3 [32] and GMR^3 [35] as two other round-robin $O(1)$ schedulers in Click, and conducted the same experiments mentioned above. We find that they achieve almost the same makespan and resource utilization as that of the tradeoff scheduler running with the strict fairness requirement ($\alpha = 1$). This should come with no surprises, as all the existing multi-resource fair queueing algorithms are essentially different approximations to the fluid schedule with perfect DRF. These results are omitted to avoid redundancy.

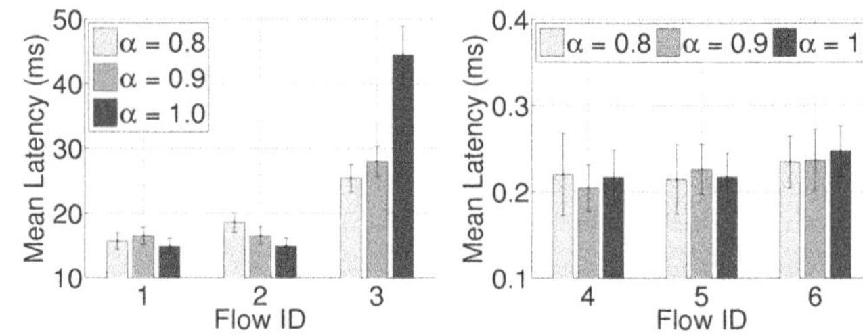

(a) Elephant flows. (b) Mice flows.

Figure 6: Mean per-packet latency of elephant (sending 20,000 pkts/s) and mice flows (sending 2 pkts/s) in Click. The error bar shows the standard deviation.

6.2 Trace-Driven Simulation

Next, we use trace-driven simulation to further evaluate the proposed algorithm from a macroscopic perspective. We have written a packet-level simulator consisting of 3,000 lines of C++ code and fed it with real-world traces [2] captured in a university switch. The traces are dominated by UDP packets. Based on the IP prefix and port number, we classify packets in the traces into nearly 3,000 flows and synthesize the input traffic by randomly assigning each flow to one of three middlebox modules: basic forwarding, statistical monitoring, and IPsec. The CPU processing time of each module follows a linear model based on the measurement results of [13]. The flow queue size is set to 200 packets, and the outgoing bandwidth is set to 200 Mbps. We linearly scale up the traffic by 5× to simulate a heavy load. Depending on the total resource consumption, the synthesized traffic is classified into the following three patterns: *CPU-bound* traffic where the CPU processing time exceeds 1.2× the transmission time, *bandwidth-bound* traffic where the transmission time exceeds 1.2× the CPU time, and *balanced* traffic otherwise.

Fig. 7 shows the mean utilization achieved at various fairness levels, where each data point is averaged over 10 runs under the corresponding traffic pattern. The error bar shows one standard deviation. We observe similar trends in all three patterns, that trading off fairness leads to higher utilization on both resources. Similar to our Click implementation results, we see that the marginal

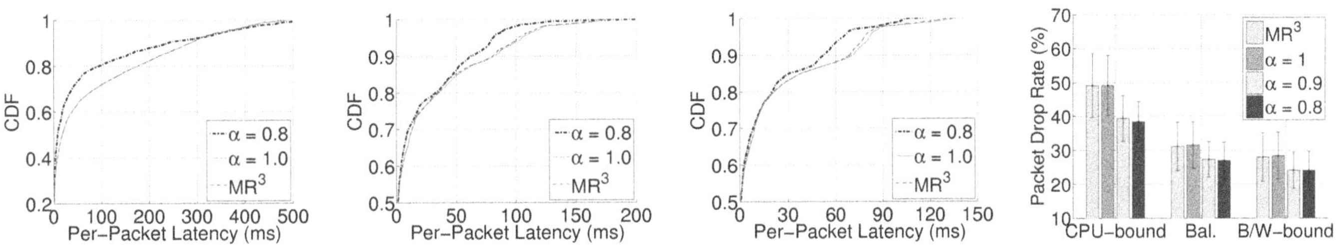

(a) CPU-Bound. (b) Balanced. (c) Bandwidth-Bound. (d) Packet drop rate.

Figure 8: The improvement of per-packet latency and packet drop rate due to the fairness tradeoff.

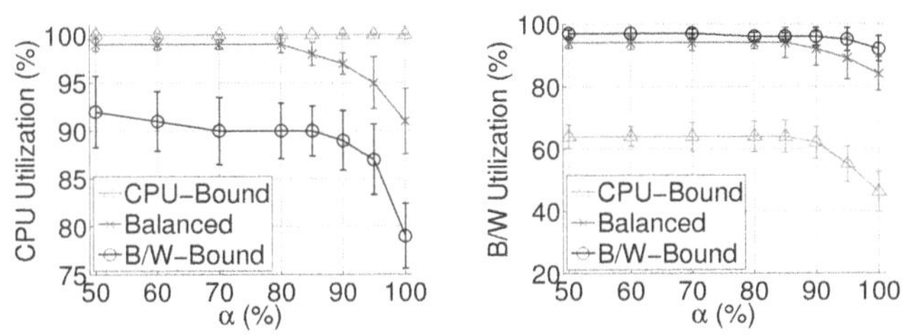

(a) CPU utilization. (b) Bandwidth utilization.

Figure 7: Resource utilization achieved at different fairness levels in the simulation, averaged over 10 runs.

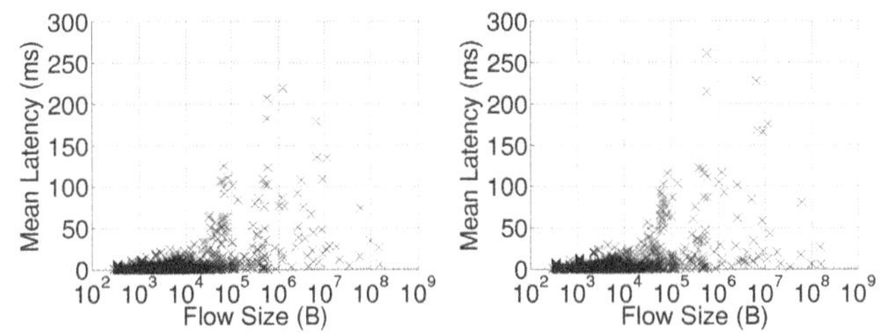

(a) $\alpha = 1$. (b) $\alpha = 0.8$.

Figure 9: Per-packet latency against flow sizes in the first 20s of simulation, feeding CPU-bound traffic, with and without the fairness tradeoff.

improvement in utilization is decreasing, with the optimal utilization achieved by trading off more than 15% of fairness. Among all three patterns, traffic with balanced resource consumption has the least incentive to trade off fairness, as flows have complementary resource demands and can *dove-tail* one another [13]. In this case, fair queueing is sufficient to realize high efficiency. We have also simulated the other two multi-resource fair queueing algorithms, DRFQ [13] and MR^3 [32], and observed almost the same performance as that of the strictly fair queueing ($\alpha = 1$). We omit these results to avoid redundancy.

We examine in Fig. 8 the tradeoff impact on other measures relevant to efficiency. Specifically, we depict the per-packet latency CDF of three scheduling algorithms—tradeoff with $\alpha = 0.8$, complete fairness ($\alpha = 1.0$), and another round-robin fair scheduler called MR^3 [32]—in Figs. 8a, 8b, and 8c, for each of the three traffic patterns. In general, the enhanced resource utilization due to the fairness tradeoff translates into shorter latencies in all three traffic patterns. The improvements are mainly attributed to the shortened packet latency of favored flows. Furthermore, the packet drop rates are compared in Fig. 8d. We observe an average of 15% to 20% decrease in the packet drop rate under all three traffic patterns, suggesting that higher bandwidth throughput is achieved.

Finally, we investigate the tradeoff impact on service isolation in a dynamic environment. Ideally, we would like to see that compromising a small percentage of fairness will not affect the per-packet latency of mice flows as their guaranteed resource share, even when traded off, is sufficient to support their low packet rate. Fig. 9 confirms this isolation property with CPU-bound traffic, where we depict the mean packet latency for each flow in the first 20 seconds of the simulation, running with complete fairness and 80% of fairness, respectively. We see that compared to strictly fair queueing, trading off fairness has no impact on the latency of small flows, but it affects those medium and large ones: Some see shorter latency while others experience longer delay, depending on if they are favored flows or not. We have similar observations in the other two traffic patterns.

7. RELATED WORK

Ghodsi *et al.* [13] identified the need of multi-resource fair queueing for deep packet inspection in middleboxes. They compared a set of queueing alternatives and proposed DRFQ, the first multi-resource fair queueing algorithm, that implements DRF in the time domain. Two follow-up queueing algorithms [32, 35] have also been proposed with lower scheduling complexity and bounded scheduling delay. All these works focus solely on fairness, and use the goal of achieving work conservation as the only indication of efficiency, similar to traditional single-resource fair queueing [9,21].

However, as we have shown in this paper, unlike single-resource scheduling, there is a general tradeoff between fairness and efficiency when packet processing requires multiple types of resources. We have briefly mentioned this problem in our previous position paper [34], where we shared our visions on several possible directions that may lead to a concrete solution. We have materialized some of our visions in this paper by formally characterizing the tradeoff problem and proposing an implementable queueing algorithm to achieve a flexible balance between fairness and efficiency in the two-resource setting.

While the tradeoff problem has received little attention in the fair queueing literature, striking a balance between allocation fairness and efficiency has been a focus of many recent works in both networking and operations research. Specifically, Danna *et al.* [8] have presented an efficient bandwidth allocation algorithm to achieve a flexible tradeoff between fairness and throughput for traffic engineering. Joe-Wong *et al.* [18] have proposed a unifying framework with fairness and efficiency requirements specified by two parameters for a given multi-resource allocation problem. Discussions on the tradeoff between fairness and performance have also been given in the context of P2P networks [11, 38]. In the literature of operations research, Bertsimas *et al.* [3] have derived a tight bound to characterize the efficiency loss under proportional fairness and max-min fairness, respectively. They have later developed a more general framework to characterize the fairness-efficiency tradeoff in a family of "α-fair" welfare functions [4]. All these works focus on one-shot resource allocation in the space domain. In contrast, our focus in this paper is a packet scheduling problem where resources are shared in the time domain.

As explained in §2.4, our tradeoff problem captures the flow shop problem [5–7, 12, 15, 20, 23, 24, 30] as a special case when efficiency is the only concern. Our approach borrows the idea of WFQ [1, 9, 21], in relaxing a discrete packet flow to an idealized fluid and tracking the fluid schedule based on virtual time. However, for single-resource fair queueing, the main challenge is to design a packet-by-packet tracking algorithm, because the fluid schedule, GPS [1, 9, 21], is fairly straightforward and easy to compute. Our problem is more complex, requiring more careful modeling of the fluid schedule, packet-by-packet tracking with multiple resources, and tradeoff analysis.

8. CONCLUSION AND FUTURE WORK

Middleboxes perform complex network functions whose packet processing requires the support of multiple types of hardware resources. A multi-resource packet scheduling algorithm is therefore needed. Unlike traditional single-resource fair queueing, where bandwidth is the only concern, there exists a general tradeoff between fairness and efficiency in the presence of multiple resources. Ideally, we would like to achieve flexible tradeoff to meet QoS requirements while maintaining the system at a high resource utilization level. We show the difficulty of the general problem and limit our discussion to a common scenario where CPU and link bandwidth are the two resources required for packet processing. We propose an efficient scheduling algorithm by tracking an idealized fluid schedule. We show through both our Click implementation and trace-driven simulation that our algorithm achieves a flexible tradeoff between fairness and efficiency in various scenarios.

Despite the initial progress made by this paper, many challenges remain open. First, while optimized, the current implementation requires $O(\log n)$ time per packet scheduling, which may be a concern given a large number of flows. A simpler scheduler with lower complexity may be desired. Given the extensive techniques developed for low-complexity scheduler in the fair queueing literature, it would be interesting to see if and how these techniques extend to the multi-resource setting. Also, as shown by Theorem 1, in general, the more types of resources a system has, the more salient the fairness-efficiency tradeoff would be. For a system with more than two types of resources, we believe the intuition and technique developed in this paper may still be applied. We could define a similar fluid schedule that maximizes the dominant throughput under the specified fairness constraint, and use start-time tracking to implement it in practice.

9. ACKNOWLEDGEMENT

We thank our shepherd, Daniel Menasche, and the anonymous reviewers for their invaluable feedback. This work was partially funded by the Natural Sciences and Engineering Research Council (NSERC) of Canada.

10. REFERENCES

[1] J. Bennett and H. Zhang. WF^{2}Q: Worst-case fair weighted fair queueing. In *Proc. IEEE INFOCOM*, 1996.

[2] T. Benson. Data set for IMC 2010 data center measurement. `http://pages.cs.wisc.edu/~tbenson/IMC_DATA/univ2_trace.tgz`, 2010.

[3] D. Bertsimas, V. F. Farias, and N. Trichakis. The price of fairness. *Oper. Res.*, 59(1):17–31, 2011.

[4] D. Bertsimas, V. F. Farias, and N. Trichakis. On the efficiency-fairness trade-off. *Management Sci.*, 58(12):2234–2250, 2012.

[5] D. Bertsimas and J. Sethuraman. From fluid relaxations to practical algorithms for job shop scheduling: the makespan objective. *Math. Program.*, 92(1):61–102, 2002.

[6] B. Chen, C. N. Potts, and G. J. Woeginger. A review of machine scheduling: Complexity, algorithms and approximability. In D.-Z. Du and P. M. Pardalos, editors, *Handbook of Combinatorial Optimization*, pages 1493–1641. Springer, 1999.

[7] J. G. Dai and G. Weiss. A fluid heuristic for minimizing makespan in job shops. *Oper. Res.*, 50(4):692–707, 2002.

[8] E. Danna, S. Mandal, and A. Singh. A practical algorithm for balancing the max-min fairness and throughput objectives in traffic engineering. In *Proc. IEEE INFOCOM*, 2012.

[9] A. Demers, S. Keshav, and S. Shenker. Analysis and simulation of a fair queueing algorithm. In *Proc. ACM SIGCOMM*, 1989.

[10] H. Dreger, A. Feldmann, V. Paxson, and R. Sommer. Predicting the resource consumption of network intrusion detection systems. In *RAID*, 2008.

[11] B. Fan, D.-M. Chiu, and J. C. Lui. The delicate tradeoffs in bittorrent-like file sharing protocol design. In *Proc. IEEE ICNP*, 2006.

[12] M. R. Garey, D. S. Johnson, and R. Sethi. The complexity of flowshop and jobshop scheduling. *Math. Oper. Res.*, 1(2):117–129, 1976.

[13] A. Ghodsi, V. Sekar, M. Zaharia, and I. Stoica. Multi-resource fair queueing for packet processing. In *Proc. ACM SIGCOMM*, 2012.

[14] A. Ghodsi, M. Zaharia, B. Hindman, A. Konwinski, S. Shenker, and I. Stoica. Dominant resource fairness: Fair allocation of multiple resource types. In *Proc. USENIX NSDI*, 2011.

[15] T. Gonzalez and S. Sahni. Flowshop and jobshop schedules: Complexity and approximation. *Oper. Res.*, 26(1):26–52, 1978.

[16] A. Greenberg and N. Madras. How fair is fair queuing. *J. ACM*, 39(3):568–598, 1992.

[17] M. Harchol-Balter. *Performance Modeling and Design of Computer Systems: Queueing Theory in Action*. Cambridge University Press, 2013.

[18] C. Joe-Wong, S. Sen, T. Lan, and M. Chiang. Multi-resource allocation: Fairness-efficiency tradeoffs in a unifying framework. In *Proc. IEEE INFOCOM*, 2012.

[19] E. Kohler, R. Morris, B. Chen, J. Jannotti, and M. F. Kaashoek. The Click modular router. *ACM Trans. Comput. Sys.*, 18(3):263–297, 2000.

[20] J. Y. Leung. *Handbook of Scheduling: Algorithms, Models, and Performance Analysis*. CRC Press, 2004.

[21] A. Parekh and R. Gallager. A generalized processor sharing approach to flow control in integrated services networks: The single-node case. *IEEE/ACM Trans. Netw.*, 1(3):344–357, 1993.

[22] D. Parkes, A. Procaccia, and N. Shah. Beyond dominant resource fairness: Extensions, limitations, and indivisibilities. In *Proc. ACM EC*, 2012.

[23] M. L. Pinedo. *Scheduling: Theory, Algorithms, and Systems.* Springer, 2012.

[24] S. S. Seiden. A guessing game and randomized online algorithms. In *Proc. ACM STOC*, 2000.

[25] V. Sekar, N. Egi, S. Ratnasamy, M. Reiter, and G. Shi. Design and implementation of a consolidated middlebox architecture. In *Proc. USENIX NSDI*, 2012.

[26] J. Sgall. On-line scheduling. In A. Fiat and G. J. Woeginger, editors, *Online Algorithms*. Springer, 1998.

[27] J. Sherry, S. Hasan, C. Scott, A. Krishnamurthy, S. Ratnasamy, and V. Sekar. Making middleboxes someone else's problem: Network processing as a cloud service. In *Proc. ACM SIGCOMM*, 2012.

[28] M. Shreedhar and G. Varghese. Efficient fair queuing using deficit round-robin. *IEEE/ACM Trans. Netw.*, 4(3):375–385, 1996.

[29] J. B. Sidney. The two-machine maximum flow time problem with series parallel precedence relations. *Oper. Res.*, 27(4):782–791, 1979.

[30] A. P. A. Vestjens. *On-line Machine Scheduling*. PhD thesis, Technische Universiteit Eindhoven, 1997.

[31] W. Wang, C. Feng, B. Li, and B. Liang. On the fairness-efficiency tradeoff for packet processing with multiple resources. Technical report, University of Toronto, 2014. `http://iqua.ece.toronto.edu/~bli/papers/tradeoff.pdf`.

[32] W. Wang, B. Li, and B. Liang. Multi-resource round robin: A low complexity packet scheduler with dominant resource fairness. In *Proc. IEEE ICNP*, 2013.

[33] W. Wang, B. Liang, and B. Li. Multi-resource generalized processor sharing for packet processing. In *Proc. ACM/IEEE IWQoS*, 2013.

[34] W. Wang, B. Liang, and B. Li. On fairness-efficiency tradeoffs for multi-resource packet processing. In *Proc. IEEE ICDCS Workshop on Data Center Performance (DCPerf)*, 2013.

[35] W. Wang, B. Liang, and B. Li. Low complexity multi-resource fair queueing with bounded delay. In *Proc. IEEE INFOCOM*, 2014.

[36] Z. Wang, Z. Qian, Q. Xu, Z. Mao, and M. Zhang. An untold story of middleboxes in cellular networks. In *Proc. SIGCOMM*, 2011.

[37] W. Whitt. Understanding the efficiency of multi-server service systems. *Management Sci.*, 38(5):708–723, 1992.

[38] B. Zhang, S. C. Borst, and M. I. Reiman. Optimal server scheduling in hybrid P2P networks. *Perform. Eval.*, 67(11), 2010.

[39] H. Zhang. Service disciplines for guaranteed performance service in packet-switching networks. *Proc. IEEE*, 83(10):1374–1396, 1995.

NetAgg: Using Middleboxes for Application-specific On-path Aggregation in Data Centres

Luo Mai† Lukas Rupprecht† Abdul Alim†
Paolo Costa‡ Matteo Migliavacca* Peter Pietzuch† Alexander L. Wolf†
†Imperial College London ‡Microsoft Research *University of Kent

Abstract

Data centre applications for batch processing (e.g. map/reduce frameworks) and online services (e.g. search engines) scale by distributing data and computation across many servers. They typically follow a *partition/aggregation* pattern: tasks are first partitioned across servers that process data locally, and then those partial results are aggregated. This data aggregation step, however, shifts the performance bottleneck to the network, which typically struggles to support many-to-few, high-bandwidth traffic between servers.

Instead of performing data aggregation at edge servers, we show that it can be done more efficiently along network paths. We describe NETAGG, a software platform that supports *on-path aggregation* for network-bound partition/aggregation applications. NETAGG exploits a middlebox-like design, in which dedicated servers (*agg boxes*) are connected by high-bandwidth links to network switches. Agg boxes execute aggregation functions provided by applications, which alleviates network hotspots because only a fraction of the incoming traffic is forwarded at each hop. NETAGG requires only minimal application changes: it uses *shim layers* on edge servers to redirect application traffic transparently to the agg boxes. Our experimental results show that NETAGG improves substantially the throughput of two sample applications, the Solr distributed search engine and the Hadoop batch processing framework. Its design allows for incremental deployment in existing data centres and incurs only a modest investment cost.

Categories and Subject Descriptors: C.2.1 [Network Architecture and Design]: Network communications; Distributed Networks

General Terms: Design, Performance.

Keywords: Data Centres, Middleboxes, In-network Processing, On-path Aggregation.

1. INTRODUCTION

Many applications in data centres (DCs) achieve horizontal scalability by adopting a *partition/aggregation* pattern [4]. These include search [36] and query processing [44], dataflow computing [17, 25], graph [42] and stream processing [16, 54], and deep learning frameworks [24]. In the partition step, a job or request is divided into independent subtasks, which are executed in parallel by different work servers ("workers"). Each worker operates on a subset of the data and locally generates partial results. In the aggregation step, partial results are collected and aggregated to obtain a final result.

These applications are challenging from a network perspective because they rely on an aggregation step in which a large number of workers cause *many-to-few* traffic patterns among servers. For example, traces from Facebook's DCs show that 46% of the overall network traffic is generated in the aggregation phase [19]. This creates network bottlenecks for the following two reasons: (i) the *scarce inbound bandwidth* available at the edge servers (e.g. 1 Gbps or 10 Gbps) caps the maximum transfer rate; and (ii) DC networks typically exhibit some degree of *bandwidth over-subscription* [13, 29], limiting available inter-rack bandwidth.

As a result, the network is often cited as one of the main performance bottlenecks for partition/aggregation applications [4, 20, 36]. Interactive applications such as search are significantly impacted by network activity: the network, on average, contributes 12% of latency in Microsoft's Bing search engine, accounting for 34% of outliers and 21% of timeouts [36]. In Facebook map/reduce jobs, network transfers on average are responsible for 33% of the execution time of the jobs with a reduce phase, and in 16% of these jobs network transfers account for more than 70% of the execution time [20]; in Microsoft Scope jobs, the network is responsible for a 62% median increase in the reduce and shuffle time [8].

Existing approaches attempt to counter this problem by overprovisioning DC networks using full-bisection bandwidth topologies [2, 29, 30, 53], using specialised network technologies [31, 47, 61], or carefully scheduling data movements to avoid network hotspots [3, 20]. Fundamentally, however, all these approaches do not reduce the network traffic and, hence, ultimately their performance is limited by the scarce bandwidth at the end hosts. While many DCs are in the process of upgrading to 10 Gbps networks, cost-effective 40 Gbps networks without an increased oversubscription ratio are still years away.

In contrast, we propose to reduce network traffic by aggregating data along the network paths in a distributed fashion. We describe **NETAGG**, a **software middlebox platform** that provides an **on-path aggregation service**. Middleboxes have been used extensively in DCs to enhance network functionality [37, 48]. A middlebox is a network appliance attached to a switch that provides services such as firewalls, web proxies, SSL offloading, and load balancing [51]. To maximise performance, middleboxes are often implemented in hardware [45], and adopt a vertically integrated architecture focusing on a narrow function, e.g. processing standard packet headers or performing relatively simple payload inspection.

CoNEXT'14, December 02-05 2014, Sydney, Australia
Copyright 2014 ACM 978-1-4503-3279-8/14/12 ...$15.00
http://dx.doi.org/10.1145/2674005.2674996.

The need to reduce costs, shorten update cycles, and allow more rapid innovation have instead motivated several proposals for *software* middlebox platforms [9, 14, 50, 52], typically based on commodity server hardware. Advances in leveraging multi-core parallelism and kernel engineering allow such middlebox platforms to run competitively at or near line rate [43].

We leverage this trend by using middleboxes to execute *application-specific* aggregation functions at each hop. This exploits the observation that often the aggregation phase exhibits high data reduction [18,25]. By virtue of this aggregation performed by middleboxes, the amount of network traffic is reduced at each hop, thereby loosening network bottlenecks and, ultimately, increasing application performance. This differs from traditional approaches for traffic redundancy elimination [6], which operate only at the network level and have only limited visibility (if any) into application semantics.

To process data at the highest possible rate, NETAGG aggregation middleboxes (or *agg boxes*) decompose aggregation computation into cooperatively scheduled aggregation tasks, which are executed in parallel across many CPU cores. Multiple agg boxes can exist in a topology to cooperatively form an *aggregation tree*. NETAGG uses *shim layers* at edge servers to intercept application traffic and redirect it transparently to agg boxes. This minimises the changes required to existing applications for benefitting from on-path aggregation.

Multiple applications with different requirements can share a NETAGG deployment because agg boxes manage the scheduling of aggregation tasks: e.g. they can give priority to aggregation computation on behalf of latency-sensitive online applications over throughput-oriented batch applications.

We evaluate NETAGG both at scale, using simulation, and on a 34-server testbed with two deployed applications: Apache Solr [11], a distributed search engine, and the Apache Hadoop map/reduce framework [10]. In simulation, we show that NETAGG reduces the flow completion time up to 88% compared to existing solutions. We also show that our NETAGG deployment improves the performance of Solr search queries by up to 9.3× and Hadoop jobs by up to 5.2×.

2. DISTRIBUTED DATA AGGREGATION

We now describe how application performance can become network-bound due to a partition/aggregation communication pattern in DCs (§2.1) and discuss previous attempts to solve this problem (§2.2). We then sketch how we make use of middleboxes to perform on-path aggregation (§2.3) and present the results of a simulation-based feasibility study that supports our claim of the effectiveness of the approach, both in terms of performance and cost (§2.4).

2.1 Partition/aggregation applications

The partition/aggregation pattern is at the core of many distributed DC applications. A partition/aggregation application has a set of *worker nodes* ("workers"), deployed on edge servers. In the *partition* step, a request or job is divided into independent subtasks, which are executed in parallel by different workers. Each worker operates on a subset of the data and locally generates partial results. In the *aggregation* step, partial results are collected by a *master node*, such as a frontend server, and aggregated into the final result.

For example, online search queries are sent to multiple index servers in parallel, each hosting a small portion of the web index. Each index server processes the query locally and returns the top k results best matching the query. These partial results are aggregated to select the final set of results returned to the user.

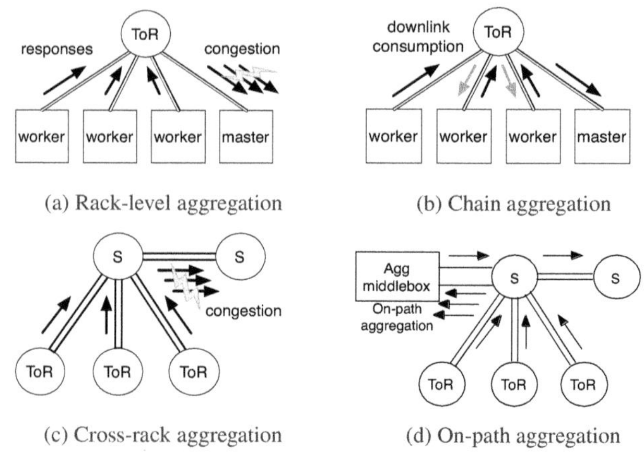

Figure 1: Distributed data aggregation strategies

Similarly, in map/reduce, the input data is partitioned into small chunks (with a typical size of 64–128 MB) and processed by a number of parallel map tasks (the *map* phase). The intermediate results are then sent to one or many reduce tasks (the *shuffle* phase), which perform the final step of aggregation (the *reduce* phase). Other frameworks, such as graph [42] or stream processing systems [16], adopt a similar approach for scaling.

Typically, the aggregation functions used in these applications exhibit two properties. First, they are *associative* and *commutative* [59], which implies that the aggregation step can be performed through a sequence of *partial* aggregations without affecting the correctness of the final result. Examples of aggregation functions exhibiting this property include `max`, `sum` and `top-k`. While there are some functions that do not satisfy this property, e.g. `median`, it does hold for many aggregations, especially those used for analytic queries [44] and graph processing [59].

Second, in most cases, the size of the aggregated results is a small fraction of the intermediate data generated. For example, the average final output data size in Google jobs is 40% of the intermediate data sizes [25]. In Facebook and Yahoo jobs, the reduction in size is even more pronounced: in 82% of the Facebook jobs with a reduce phase, the final output size is only 5% of the intermediate size, while for Yahoo jobs the number is 8% in 91% of the jobs [18]. Similar trends also hold for traces collected in Microsoft Scope, which show a reduction factor of up to two orders of magnitude between the intermediate and final data [12].

These two properties are important because they show that, by performing partial aggregation on-path, it is possible to reduce the traffic at each hop significantly, thus alleviating network bottlenecks as described below.

2.2 Edge-based aggregation

We are not the first to notice the benefits of partial aggregation of intermediate data to reduce network traffic. Prior work on interactive services [44] and dataflow frameworks [40, 59] proposes strategies to reduce inter-rack traffic through *rack-level aggregation*: one server per rack acts as an *aggregator* and receives all intermediate data from the workers in the same rack. The chosen server aggregates the data and sends it to another server for final aggregation (e.g. a map/reduce reducer).

The main drawback of rack-level aggregation is that its performance is limited by the inbound bandwidth of the aggregator (Figure 1a). For example, assuming 40 servers per rack and 1 Gbps edge network links, the maximum transmission rate per worker is only approximately 25 Mbps.

Rack-level aggregation can be extended to generalised *edge-based aggregation* by forming a d-ary tree of servers that aggregate data within a rack first and then progressively across racks. Intuitively, a lower d (including the degenerate case of $d=1$, when the tree becomes a *chain*), leads to a higher maximum transmission rate per worker.

While d-ary trees eliminate some of the shortcomings of rack-level aggregation, they introduce new challenges: (i) small values of d increase the depth of the tree, affecting the performance of latency-sensitive applications; (ii) small values of d also increase intra-rack bandwidth usage because the incoming links of workers, as opposed to only outgoing links, are used to move data (Figure 1b). As we show in §4, this can drastically reduce the performance of other flows in the network that cannot be aggregated. For example, in a map/reduce job, only the shuffle flows can be aggregated, while other flows, e.g. used to read from the distributed file system, cannot. By using more links, the bandwidth available to these other flows is reduced.

More generally, a fundamental drawback of any edge-based aggregation approach is that it only applies to *intra-rack* traffic and not traffic in the core of the network. As shown in Figure 1c, if aggregation computation spans multiple racks, the links between aggregation switches can become a bottleneck, especially in the presence of over-subscription.

2.3 On-path aggregation with middleboxes

In contrast to edge-based aggregation approaches, we propose to use software middleboxes ("agg boxes") to perform aggregation along the network path. This allows us to minimise edge server bandwidth usage as well as congestion in the core of the network. While aggregation has been shown to increase efficiency in wireless sensor networks [41] and in overlay networks [15, 35, 58], its potential to improve the performance of partition/aggregation applications in DC networks remains unexplored. Existing work on data aggregation has either focused on per-packet aggregation, as in sensor networks, which is not appropriate for application-layer data flows in DCs, or on scalability issues for Internet system monitoring rather than on throughput requirements.

We assume a set-up similar to the one depicted in Figure 1d, in which middleboxes are directly attached to network switches and perform on-path aggregation. We create a spanning tree (hereafter referred to as the *aggregation tree*), in which the root is the final master node, the leaves are the workers and the internal nodes are the agg boxes. Each agg box aggregates the data coming from its children and sends it downstream. To fully exploit the path diversity available in most DC topologies, we use *multiple* aggregation trees that balance the traffic between them. We detail the design of our NetAgg middlebox platform in §3.

Due to its compatibility with existing middlebox deployments in DCs, our approach based on application-specific middleboxes can be deployed with low effort. It also allows for an incremental roll-out in which the agg boxes are attached to only a subset of the switches.

2.4 Feasibility study

A potential issue in using middleboxes based on commodity servers for on-path aggregation is the lower processing rate that they can achieve as compared to custom hardware solutions. To understand the feasibility of a software-only approach, we conduct a number of simulation experiments to understand (i) the minimum processing rate R of an agg box required to achieve noticeable benefits and (ii) the performance/cost trade-off involved. We describe the simulation set-up and the full set of results in §4.1. Here we highlight the main results, which led to the NetAgg design described in the next section.

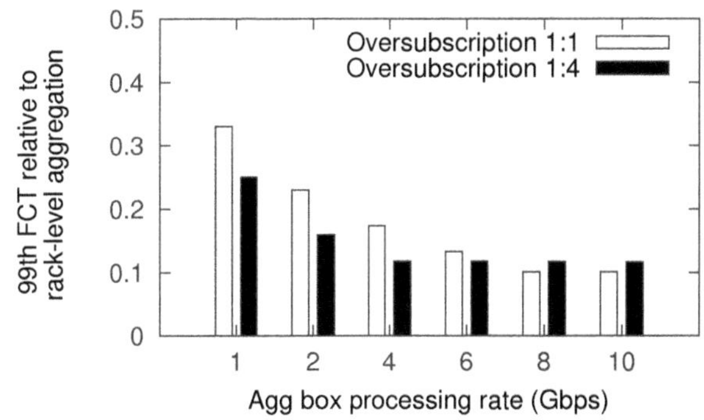

Figure 2: Flow Completion Time (FCT) for different aggregation processing rates R

Simulation set-up. We consider a three-tier, multi-rooted network topology, modelled after recently proposed scalable DC architectures [2, 29]. Each server is connected through a 1 Gbps link to a top-of-the-rack (ToR) switch. In this experiment, we assume an over-subscription ratio of 1:4, which is consistent with values reported in the literature [29]. We also show the results for the non-oversubscribed case. We consider a mid-sized DC with 1,024 servers and a synthetic workload modelled after Facebook network traces [19], in which 46% of traffic is aggregatable (see §4.1 for more details).

Performance requirements. As our baseline, we consider rack-level aggregation, as described above, and we assume ECMP [32] as the routing protocol. We use *flow completion time* (FCT), i.e. the time elapsed between the start and the end of a flow, as our metric [27] and vary the maximum processing rate that can be sustained by the agg boxes.

Figure 2 shows that relatively modest processing rates are sufficient to achieve significant benefits. Interestingly, even a rate of 1 Gbps per agg box reduces the total completion time by more than 74% for the 1:4 oversubscribed scenario and 63% for the non-oversubscribed one (88% and 90% for the rate of 8 Gbps, respectively). This shows that, although the bandwidth per agg box is identical to the one used by the rack-level aggregator, performing aggregation at all network tiers (as opposed to just within a rack) reduces the pressure placed on the over-subscribed network core. Note that these results include *all* flows, not just the aggregation flows, which means that even flows that cannot be aggregated benefit from more efficient bandwidth usage.

In §4.2, we show that an agg box in our NetAgg prototype is able to aggregate data at a rate of 9.2 Gbps. Based on the results presented here, this is sufficient to obtain a significant reduction in flow completion time.

Cost analysis. Next we perform a simple cost analysis to understand the trade-off between deploying agg boxes versus increasing the network bandwidth. We consider three alternative options to NetAgg: a full-bisection network topology with 1 Gbps edge links (FullBisec-1G); a 1:4 over-subscribed network with 10 Gbps edge links (Oversub-10G); and a full-bisection network topology with 10 Gbps edge links (FullBisec-10G).

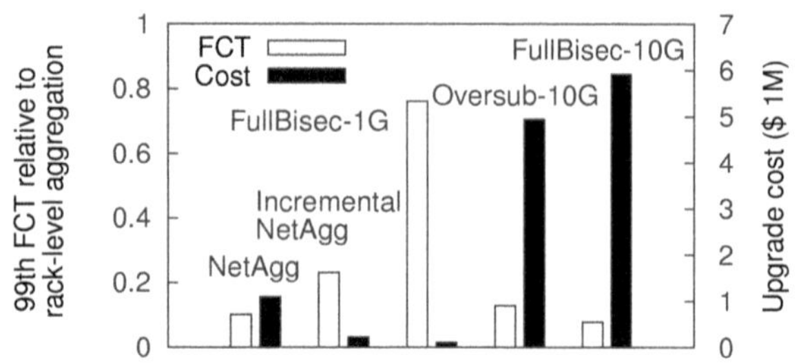

Figure 3: Performance and cost of different DC configurations

We compare the performance and cost when using rack-level aggregation in the three configurations above to deploying agg boxes using our approach in the base set-up (1:4 over-subscription and 1 Gbps network). We use the same workload as in the previous experiment, and we conservatively assume a configuration with a processing rate R=9.2 Gbps because this is similar to the rate achieved by our NETAGG prototype (§4.2). For NETAGG, we consider two deployment options: NetAgg, in which we assume that each switch is connected to an agg box, and Incremental-NetAgg, in which only the middle tier of switches (corresponding to 20% of all switches) is connected to agg boxes. We adopt the prices for network equipment from a recently published study [46]. We assume hardware specifications for servers and agg boxes as used in our evaluation testbed (see §4.2).

Figure 3 shows the performance improvement and upgrade costs with respect to the base set-up. As expected, upgrading to a 10 Gbps full-bisection network (FullBisec-10G) provides the largest benefit (92% reduction of FCT), but it also incurs the highest upgrade cost. FullBisec-1G has a much lower deployment cost but does not result in the same benefit (only 24% reduction).

In contrast, deploying NetAgg achieves almost the same performance improvement (88%) as FullBisec-10G and outperforms Oversub-10G (87%), with only a fraction of the cost (18% and 22%, respectively). Incremental-NetAgg is also a practical deployment option: it only incurs 4% of the cost of Oversub-10G but reduces FCT by 75%.

Discussion. While we compare the performance of on-path agg boxes against the performance of an upgraded network infrastructure, our solution remains complementary: even with more available network bandwidth, on-path aggregation can reduce bandwidth consumption and provide more bandwidth to other, non-partition/aggregation traffic flows.

In an upgraded network infrastructure (e.g. with 10 Gbps edge links), however, the performance of agg boxes should increase accordingly. As we describe in the next section, the aggregation on agg boxes is embarrassingly parallelisable, which means that agg boxes can exploit increasing numbers of CPU cores for higher performance. In addition, given the nature of aggregation, it is possible to *scale out* agg boxes by deploying multiple agg boxes connected to one network switch. We evaluate the performance implications of scaling out agg boxes in §4.

3. DESIGN AND IMPLEMENTATION

Next we describe the design of the NETAGG middlebox platform. We explain how it performs aggregation (§3.1), and give details on the implementation of aggregation boxes and shim layers (§3.2). We also report on two application case studies (§3.3).

3.1 Overview

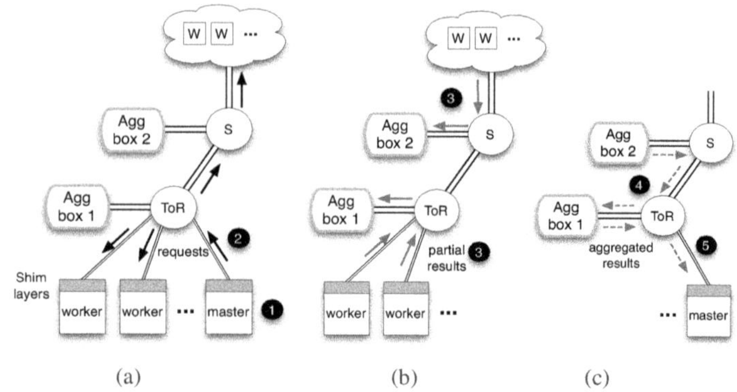

Figure 4: NETAGG middlebox deployment with sample workflow (numbers correspond to steps in workflow)

As shown in Figure 4, a deployment of NETAGG in a DC consists of two main components, *agg boxes* and *shim layers*: (i) agg boxes are connected to a subset of the switches in the DC via high-bandwidth network links. They perform the on-path aggregation of application data according to aggregation functions; (ii) edge servers in the DC are fitted with shim layers that intercept request and result data flows, interacting with the agg boxes.

The agg boxes cooperate to establish an on-path *aggregation tree* that aggregates partial results from worker nodes before sending the final result to the master node. As discussed in §2, an aggregation tree permits NETAGG to exploit the larger core network bandwidth for data aggregation. Its construction relies on the associativity and commutativity of aggregation functions.

The workflow between agg boxes and shim layers for on-path aggregation follows the steps shown in Figs. 4a–4c:

1. A client submits a request to a master node, which partitions it into multiple sub-requests (Figure 4a).
2. The master node sends the sub-requests, which pass through the shim layer of the master node without modification, to a set of worker nodes.
3. The partial results generated by the workers are intercepted by the shim layers of the worker nodes. The shim layers redirect the data to the first agg box along the network path from the worker to the master node (Figure 4b). For example, agg box 2, connected to an aggregation switch, aggregates partial results from workers in other parts of the DC.
4. Each agg box aggregates the partial results according to the aggregation function (Figure 4c). It sends its partially aggregated results to the next agg box that is along the network path to the master node.
5. The agg box nearest to the master node (i.e. agg box 1 in the example) sends the fully aggregated results to the master node. The shim layer of the master node passes the results to the application.

Multiple applications. Multiple applications may be executing aggregation trees concurrently on agg boxes. Based on the knowledge of its child and parent nodes, an agg box therefore always forwards partial results to a chosen next-hop towards the master node along a given aggregation tree belonging to that application. The next agg box on-path is determined by hashing an application/request identifier. This ensures that partial data for a given application request traverses the same agg boxes.

Multiple aggregation trees per application. With a single per-application aggregation tree, it is not possible to exploit DC network topologies that support multiple routing paths and thus have higher core network bandwidth (see §2.3). NETAGG therefore supports multiple aggregation trees that are used concurrently for a given application, partitioning the aggregation load among the trees. Each aggregation tree uses a disjoint set of agg boxes (except for the agg box that is in the same rack as the master and the workers), exploiting different routing paths in a multi-path topology.

With multiple aggregation trees per application, the shim layers at the worker nodes partition partial results across the trees. Typically this can be achieved by hashing request identifiers (as in the case of online services) or keys in the data (as in the case of batch processing applications). When an application has multiple aggregation trees, the master node must perform a final aggregation step of the data returned by the roots of the trees.

Multiple agg boxes per switch. To increase the throughput of an agg box connected to a switch, it is possible to scale out processing by load-balancing aggregation computation across multiple agg boxes connected to the same switch. In this case, aggregation trees are assigned to agg boxes in a way that balances the load between them.

Handling failures. The NETAGG design uses a lightweight failure detection service, running at both the agg boxes and the master shim layer, that monitors the status of downstream agg boxes in the distributed aggregation tree. When a node N (either an agg box or the master node) detects that a downstream agg box F has failed, it contacts the child nodes (either agg boxes or the worker nodes) of F and instructs them to redirect future partial results to N.

To avoid duplicate results, when N contacts the downstream nodes of F, it also sends the last result that has been correctly processed, e.g. the last partial result received, so that already-processed results are not resent.

Handling stragglers. NETAGG is designed to be compatible with existing mechanisms used by applications to handle straggling worker nodes. For example, Hadoop uses speculative execution of backup tasks and reducers can start fetching data from completed mappers while waiting for stragglers or backup tasks to finish [25]. In this case, the agg box just aggregates available results, while the rest is sent directly to the reducer.

Since an aggregation tree involves multiple agg boxes, each agg box itself can potentially become a straggler, delaying the computation of the final result. To handle this scenario, NETAGG uses a similar mechanism to the one for failures: if a node detects that the downstream agg box S is too slow (based on an application-specific threshold), it contacts the downstream nodes of S to redirect future results. The difference with the failure protocol is that the redirection is only applied to results of the same request because the cause of straggling may be specific to it. However, if low performance is observed repeatedly across different requests, the agg box is considered permanently failed, and the failure recovery procedure described above is employed.

3.2 Implementation

We implement a prototype version of NETAGG in Java, which permits the agg boxes to execute unmodified aggregation functions of partition/aggregation applications written in Java. Agg boxes can host aggregation functions of multiple applications.

An important goal is for agg boxes to use available hardware resources efficiently in order to process data with high throughput. Their implementation is therefore data-parallel: they decompose aggregation functions and parallelise their execution across CPU cores using *cooperative scheduling*. In addition, we minimise the application-specific functions that agg boxes execute: they only receive and process data traffic and do not participate in control interactions of applications.

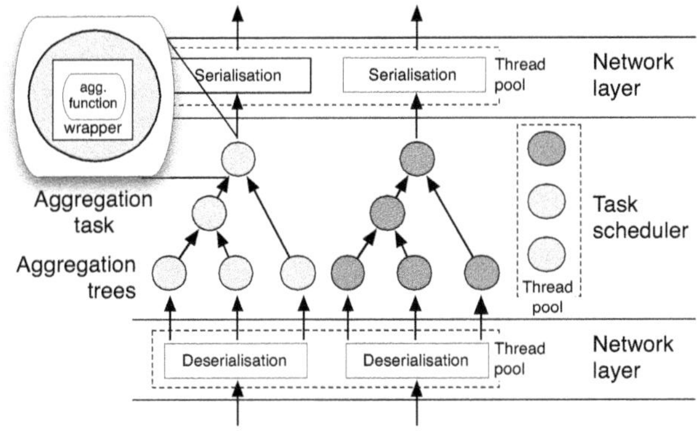

Figure 5: Architecture of a NETAGG agg box with two deployed applications (shading represents different aggregation functions)

For multiple applications to share a NETAGG deployment, it is necessary to schedule access to the limited CPU and bandwidth resources of agg boxes. Agg boxes implement prioritised access for certain classes of applications, such as latency-sensitive ones. They schedule the execution of aggregation computation belonging to different applications using *adaptive weighted fair scheduling*, taking different priorities into account.

To make it easy for applications to benefit from on-path aggregation, NETAGG transparently *intercepts* data flows and redirects them to agg boxes. Traffic is intercepted at the level of Java network sockets due to its well-defined interface across applications.

3.2.1 Agg boxes

We show the architecture of an agg box in Figure 5: (i) it executes *aggregation tasks* that wrap the applications' aggregation computations; (ii) the tasks are organised into a *local aggregation tree* that parallelises the aggregation function; (iii) tasks are scheduled cooperatively across CPU cores by a *task scheduler*; and (iv) a *network layer* serialises and deserialises data.

Aggregation tasks. An agg box represents computation as aggregation tasks, which are fine-grained compute units that can be scheduled in parallel on CPU cores.

Different applications require different interfaces for aggregation functions. An aggregation task therefore wraps aggregation computation using an *aggregation wrapper*. For example, a Hadoop aggregation wrapper exposes the standard interface of combiner functions, `Combiner.reduce(Key k, List<Value> v)`, which enables agg boxes to run such functions without modification.

Local aggregation trees. Similar to how aggregation computation is decomposed across multiple agg boxes, the computation within a single agg box forms a *local* aggregation tree of tasks. Local aggregation trees have a large fan-in and are executed in a pipelined fashion by streaming data across the aggregation tasks. This allows for efficient and scalable aggregation, as aggregation executes in parallel and little data is buffered.

As shown in Figure 5, the intermediate tree nodes are aggregation tasks, acting as producers and consumer of data. Leaf nodes receive partial results from worker nodes or downstream agg boxes and send them to their parent aggregation tasks. Tasks are scheduled by the task scheduler (see below) when new input data is available and there is sufficient buffer space at the parent task. They execute the aggregation function on the data from their child nodes. Partially aggregated results propagate up the tree until the root node obtains the final result for that tree. If the computation in the local aggregation tree is not fast enough to sustain the rate at which data arrives from the network, a back-pressure mechanism ensures that the workers reduce the rate at which they produce partial results.

Task scheduler. To reduce the overhead of thread synchronisation, aggregation tasks are executed by a task scheduler using *cooperative scheduling*: when aggregation is possible, a task is submitted to a task queue and waits to be scheduled. The scheduler assigns tasks to threads from a fixed-sized thread pool and runs the tasks to completion. We assume that aggregation functions are well-behaved and terminate—we leave mechanisms for isolating faulty or malicious aggregation tasks to future work.

If there are multiple applications using an agg box, resources must be shared to achieve acceptable processing times for aggregation computation. For this purpose, an agg box maintains a separate task queue for each application and adopts a *weighted fair queuing* policy over these queues. This enforces weighted fair shares among applications, similar to other cluster schedulers [60]. When a thread becomes available, the scheduler offers that thread to a task of application i with probability $w_i / \sum_{i=1}^{n} w_i$ that is proportional to its target allocation, where w_i is application i's weight and n is the number of applications on the agg box.

Resource sharing must take the heterogeneity of aggregation tasks into account: the computation and bandwidth requirements of tasks vary depending on the application. To handle this, the scheduler periodically adapts the weights of application i according to the task execution time $\bar{t_i}$ measured at runtime. The intuition is that if an application usually spends twice the time finishing tasks compared to another, the scheduler needs to halve the weight of that application to achieve the targeted proportional share. More formally, given a target resource share s_i for application i, w_i is set to $\frac{s_i}{\bar{t_i}} / \sum_{i=1}^{n} \frac{s_i}{\bar{t_i}}$. Our implementation uses a moving average to represent the measured task execution time—the experiments in §4 show that this is sufficient in practice.

Network layer. Instead of relying on a potentially wasteful application-specific network protocol, such as HTTP or XML, agg boxes transfer data with an efficient binary network protocol using KryoNet [39], an NIO-based network communication and serialisation library for Java. The shim layers also maintain persistent TCP connections to the agg box and parallelise deserialisation using a thread pool.

Since the network data must be deserialised before the aggregation wrapper can call the aggregation function, the network layer of the agg box includes a serialiser/deserialiser taken from the application. For example, to support the aggregation of Hadoop key/value pairs, the agg box uses Hadoop's `SequenceFile` reader and writer classes for serialisation/deserialisation.

3.2.2 Shim layers

The shim layers control the redirection of application data and manage the collection of partial results.

Network interception. A shim layer intercepts network traffic at the level of network sockets by wrapping the actual Java network socket class in a NETAGG socket. By using Java's ability to change the default socket implementation via the `SocketImplFactory`, applications transparently generate an instance of the custom NETAGG socket class when a new socket is created.

Partial result collection. A challenge is that agg boxes must know when all partial results were received before executing the aggregation function but, for many applications including Apache Solr, it is not known ahead of time how many partial results will be returned by the worker nodes. We solve this problem by having the shim layer of the master node maintain state about ongoing requests. After intercepting an incoming request, the shim layer records information about the request, typically found in headers, such as the number of partial results, and sends this information to agg boxes.

App.-specific NETAGG *code*	*Solr*	*Hadoop*
Agg box (serialisation)	8	93
Agg box (aggregation wrapper)	156	142
Shim layer	449	528
Total	613	763
Relative to NETAGG *code base*	13%	16%
Relative to application code base	0.19%	0.03%

Table 1: Lines of application-specific code in NETAGG

Empty partial results. The master node expects to receive partial results from all worker nodes, but with NETAGG this is no longer the case: since the partial results have already been aggregated, only a single fully aggregated result is returned. This means that the shim layer at the master node must emulate empty results from all but one worker, which will include the fully aggregated results. The aggregation logic in the master node is not be affected by the empty results because we assume that aggregation functions are commutative and associative.

3.3 Application deployments

To demonstrate the generality of NETAGG, we describe its deployment with two partition/aggregation applications: Apache Solr, a distributed full-text search engine [11], and Apache Hadoop [10], a data-parallel map/reduce processing framework. NETAGG can support both applications after providing application-specific serialiser/deserialiser, aggregation wrapper and shim layer code. The required implementation effort is summarised in Table 1.

Apache Solr performs full-text search across multiple *backend* server nodes, acting as workers. Clients send small requests to a *frontend* node, i.e. the master node, which dispatches sub-requests to the backend nodes. The backends return partial search results to the frontend node, which combines them into a ranked result using an aggregation function.

To support Solr, NETAGG requires around 600 lines of code. The aggregation wrapper wraps the custom `QueryComponent` class, which allows user-defined aggregation of the result data. The deserialiser buffers all partial results before invoking the local aggregation tree: this is feasible because results are only of the order of hundreds of kilobytes.

Apache Hadoop uses worker nodes to execute mappers, which produce partial results for partitions of the input data. Partial results are aggregated by reducers.

There are fewer than 800 lines of code needed to support Hadoop. The aggregation wrapper implements the Hadoop interface for combiner functions. The deserialiser for Hadoop is slightly more complex than for Solr: as chunks of key/value pairs are processed by agg boxes in a streaming fashion, the deserialiser must account for incomplete pairs at the end of each received chunk.

4. EVALUATION

We begin our evaluation by extending the simulation study from §2.4. In §4.2, we show the experimental results obtained by deploy-

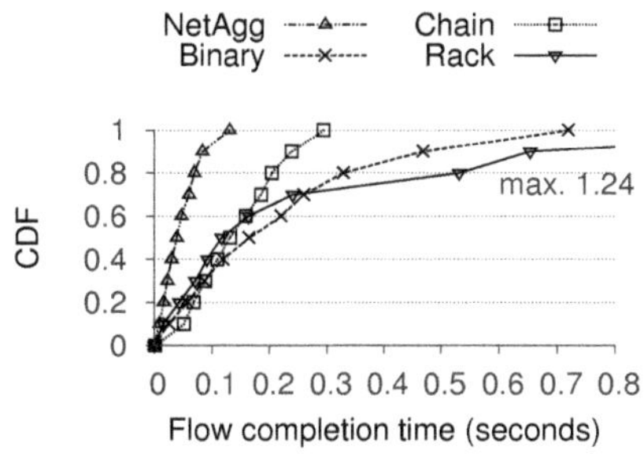

Figure 6: CDF of flow completion time of all traffic

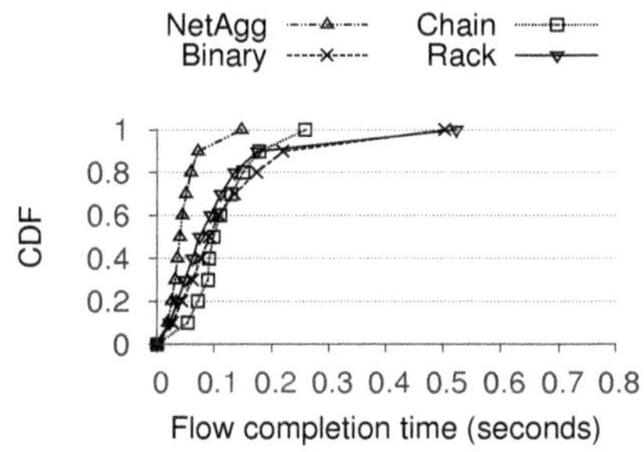

Figure 7: CDF of flow completion time of non-aggregatable traffic

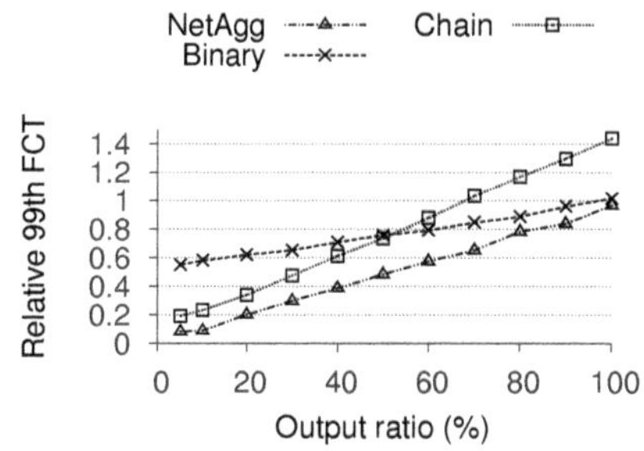

Figure 8: Flow completion time relative to baseline with varying output ratio α

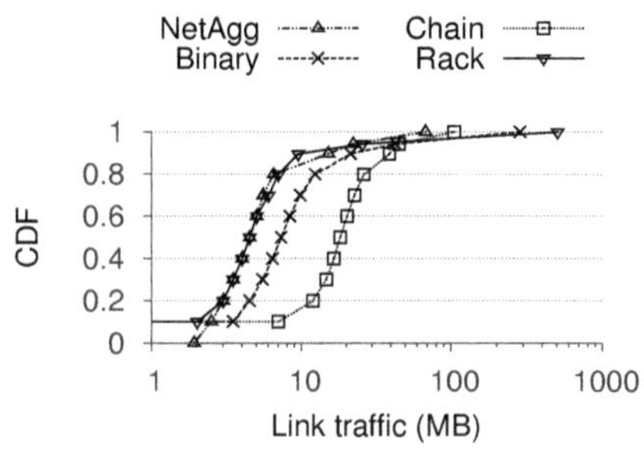

Figure 9: CDF of link traffic ($\alpha = 10\%$)

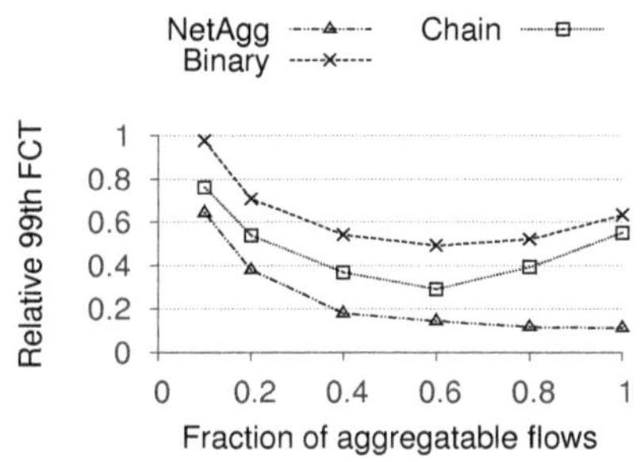

Figure 10: Flow completion time relative to baseline with varying fraction of aggregatable traffic

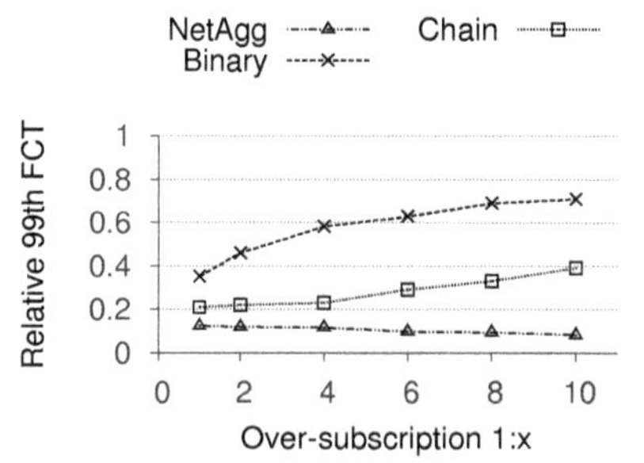

Figure 11: Flow completion time relative to baseline with different over-subscription ($\alpha = 10\%$)

ing our NETAGG middlebox prototype with different applications on a 34-server testbed.

4.1 Simulation results

We simulate a three-tier, multi-rooted network topology based on recently proposed scalable DC architectures [2, 29]. The network consists of 320 20-port switches that connect 1,024 servers using 1 Gbps links, unless noted otherwise. As a default, we assume a 1:4 over-subscription ratio at the ToR tier, varying it from 1:1 to 1:10 in one of the experiments. We use a packet-level simulator (OMNeT++), which implements TCP max-min flow fairness and uses standard Equal Cost Multi Path (ECMP) for routing.

Unless noted otherwise, we assume that each agg box is connected to a switch through a 10 Gbps link, and we assume that it can process network flows at 9.2 Gbps. As we show in §4.2, this is representative of the performance of our current NETAGG prototype implementation.

We use a synthetic traffic workload, modelled after published network traces from a cluster running large data mining jobs [29]. The sizes of flows follow a Pareto distribution with a mean of 100 KB and a shape parameter of 1.05. The number of flows is chosen so that the load at the edge links is 15% [5]. Except when simulating straggler nodes, all flows start at the same time, which is a worst case for network contention. We also ran experiments using dynamic workloads with various arrival patterns, obtaining comparable results (between 1%–4% of the reported FCT values).

A typical partition/aggregation application generates a mix of flows, of which only a fraction can be aggregated. For example, some of the network flows in Hadoop contain HDFS data, which cannot be aggregated. To account for this, we generate a mixed workload in which only 46% of flows are aggregatable, while the rest constitutes non-aggregatable background traffic. This split is consistent with evidence reported by Facebook [19].

The number of workers generating flows follows a power-law distribution where 61% of requests or jobs have fewer than 10 workers, consistent with a recent study on Microsoft and Facebook production clusters [7]. Workers are deployed using a locality-aware allocation algorithm that greedily assigns workers to servers as close to each other as possible. Unless stated otherwise, we use an aggregation output ratio α, defined as the ratio between the output and the input data sizes, of 0.1 (in line with the workloads presented in §2.1).

Baselines. We use the *flow completion time* (FCT) as our evaluation metric because our goal is to improve network performance. Since our focus is on network bottlenecks that increase FCTs for individual flows, we report the 99th percentile of FCT, unless stated otherwise. We compare the performance of NETAGG against the aggregation strategies described in §2.2: rack-level aggregation (rack), a binary aggregation tree ($d=2$; binary) and chain aggregation ($d=1$; chain). Unless reporting absolute FCTs, we normalise the performance of the other strategies against rack.

Distribution of flow completion times. We report the CDF of the absolute FCTs for *all* flows in Figure 6. As explained in §2.2, binary and chain increase link utilisation, which in turn reduces the bandwidth available for other flows. This explains why they reduce the FCT tail but worsen the median. In contrast, NETAGG improves the performance for all flows by reducing the traffic of the aggregatable flows.

Interestingly, NETAGG also improves the performance of non-aggregatable flows, as shown in Figure 7. The reason is that by reducing the traffic of aggregatable flows, more bandwidth becomes available for other flows.

Aggregation output ratio. In Figure 8, we show the impact of the output ratio α. We vary α from 0.05 (i.e. high data reduction that emulates n-to-1 aggregation patterns such as top-k, max or count)

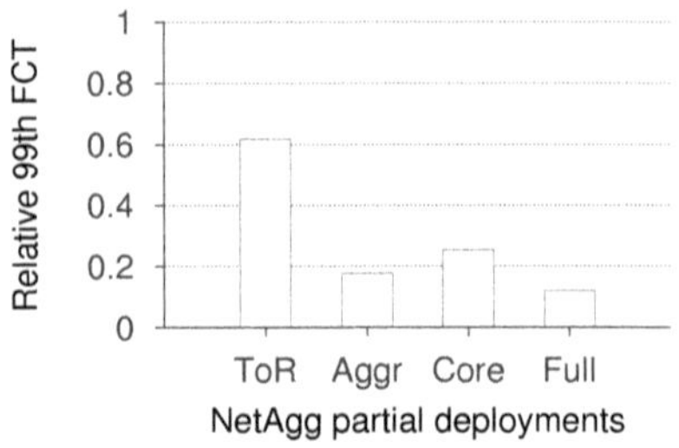

Figure 12: Flow completion time relative to baseline with different partial NETAGG deployments

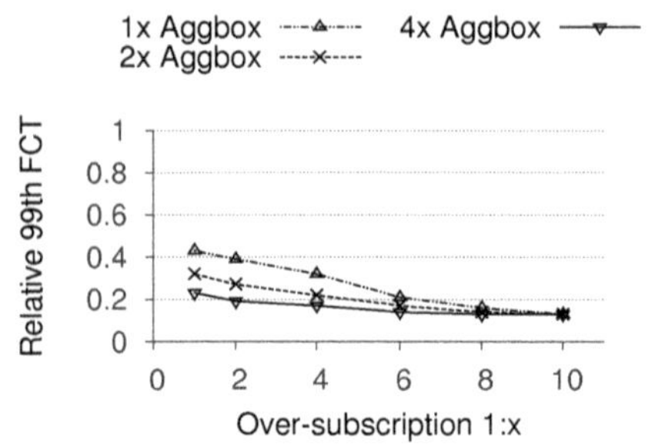

Figure 13: Flow completion time relative to baseline in 10 Gbps network with varying over-subscription

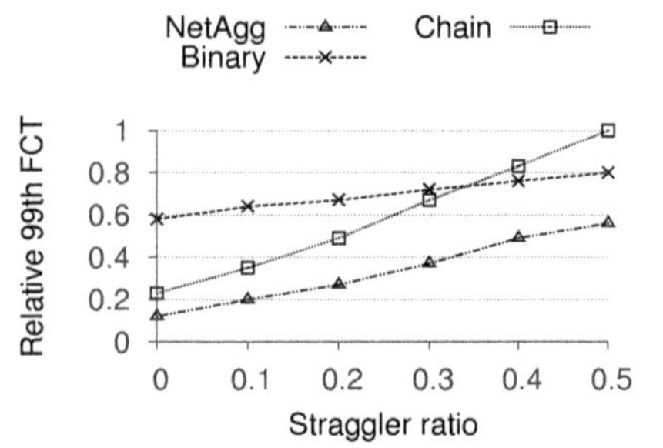

Figure 14: Flow completion time relative to baseline with varying stragglers

to 1 (i.e. no aggregation is possible). As expected, the benefits of NETAGG decrease for high values of α. When α is small, NETAGG significantly reduces the FCT: for $\alpha = 10\%$, NETAGG reduces the 99th FCT compared to rack by 88% (by 80% and 52% for binary and chain, respectively).

For very high values of α, the performance of NETAGG is only marginally better than rack. The reason is that, when there is little or no aggregation, the use of NETAGG penalises throughput because it forces the cross-rack traffic still to be processed by the agg box (at a maximum rate of 9.2 Gbps in our experiments), which constraints the overall throughput, without providing a benefit in terms of data reduction. However, since production traces show that most applications exhibit an output ratio lower than 10% [12, 18], a small α is representative of typical workloads, and we adopt $\alpha = 10\%$ in the rest of the experiments.

It is also worthwhile to analyse why chain is always outperformed by rack for $\alpha > 70\%$. The reason of this counter-intuitive behaviour is that, as explained in §2.2, chain utilises more link bandwidth compared to rack. As shown in Figure 9, with $\alpha = 10\%$, the median link traffic for chain is 4× higher than for rack (2.5× for binary, respectively). When the network is highly loaded and α is large, this aspect dominates, thus lowering throughput.

Fraction of aggregatable flows. As described in §2.4, a typical DC traffic workload contains a mix of flows, of which only a fraction can be aggregated. We conduct a sensitivity analysis in which we vary the fraction of aggregatable flows from 0.1 to 1 (i.e. all flows can be aggregated).

Figure 10 shows the 99th percentile of FCT relative to rack. With more aggregatable flows, the benefit of all three aggregation strategies increases. With more than 60% of aggregatable flows, however, the effectiveness of binary and chain starts to decrease again because their more wasteful usage of network bandwidth introduces network bottlenecks. In contrast, NETAGG maintains the lowest FCTs, all the way to a fully-aggregatable workload.

Over-subscription. We quantify the performance impact of the bisection bandwidth on NETAGG and our baselines in Figure 11. We vary over-subscription from 1:1 (i.e. full-bisection bandwidth) to 1:10. As expected, NETAGG performs best when over-subscription is high. By aggregating flows along the network paths, it reduces congestion in the core, alleviating network bottlenecks.

However, the use of NETAGG is beneficial even for networks with full-bisection bandwidth. In a full-bisection network, the inbound bandwidth of the rack and the master becomes the bottleneck. By aggregating the traffic along the network path, NETAGG reduces the congestion at the master, thus decreasing the completion time.

Partial deployment. One important question is whether it would be possible to achieve a performance close to NETAGG by simply deploying a 10 Gbps server in each rack and use it for rack-level aggregation. More generally, we want to understand what should be the best deployment configuration if we had only a limited number of agg boxes.

In Figure 12, we compare the performance of a full NETAGG deployment against three configurations: (i) agg boxes only at the ToR switches; (ii) only at the aggregation switches; and (iii) only at the core switches. The results show that the biggest improvement is achieved with agg boxes at the aggregation or core network tiers—deploying them at the rack tier provides limited benefits, improving the FCT by 38% against 83% and 75%, respectively.

This comparison, however, does not take into account that in a DC topology the number of switches at each tier varies significantly. For example, in our simulated topology, we have 128 ToR switches, 128 aggregation and 64 core switches. Therefore, we fix the number of agg boxes to 64, and we measure the performance when deploying them (i) at the core tier only; (ii) uniformly distributed at the aggregation tier; and (iii) uniformly distributed at the two tiers.

Interestingly, the first configuration achieves the largest improvements (75%) while the other two achieve 29% and 43%, respectively. The reason is that the core tier has the best opportunity for aggregating data because it intercepts more flows originating from the workers. This result is important because it shows the benefit of aggregating in the network and not just at the edge. Furthermore it also demonstrates that NETAGG can be deployed incrementally while still yielding most of the benefits.

Upgrading to a 10 Gbps network. In our next simulation experiment, we explore the performance of NETAGG when deployed in a 10 Gbps network. We use the same topology and workload as before but with 10 Gbps links connecting servers to ToR switches.

In Figure 13, we vary the over-subscription from 1:1 to 1:10. For large over-subscription values, NETAGG provides significant benefits compared to rack. Although edge servers have the same bandwidth as agg boxes, the over-subscription creates high contention in the core, which limits the throughput of rack. This shows the benefits of aggregating flows at each network hop as opposed to the edge servers only.

For smaller over-subscription values, the agg box processing rate becomes the bottleneck, reducing benefit. To further increase performance, we explore a *scale out* configuration in which we attach 2 or 4 agg boxes to each switch. We use a strategy similar to ECMP to assign flows of the same application to the same set of agg boxes. As the results show, two agg boxes are sufficient to reduce the FCTs by up to 85% compared to rack. This demonstrates

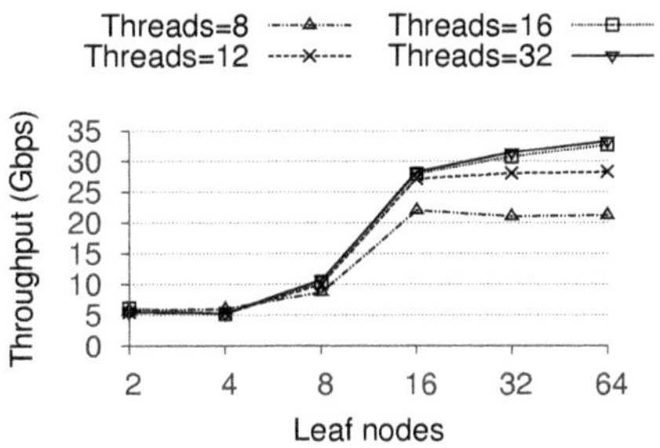

Figure 15: Processing rate of an in-memory local aggregation tree on a 16-core server

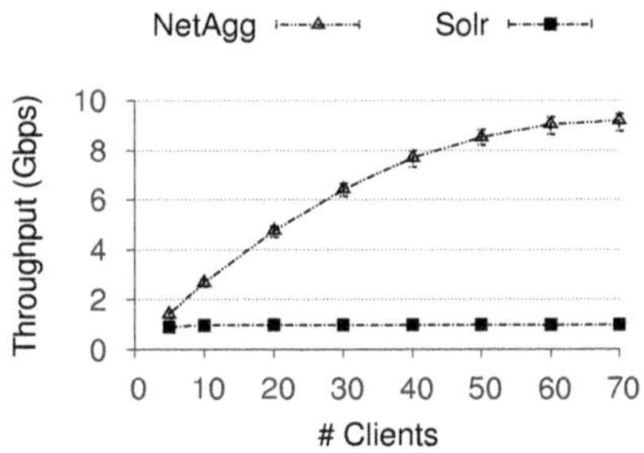

Figure 16: Network throughput against number of clients (Solr)

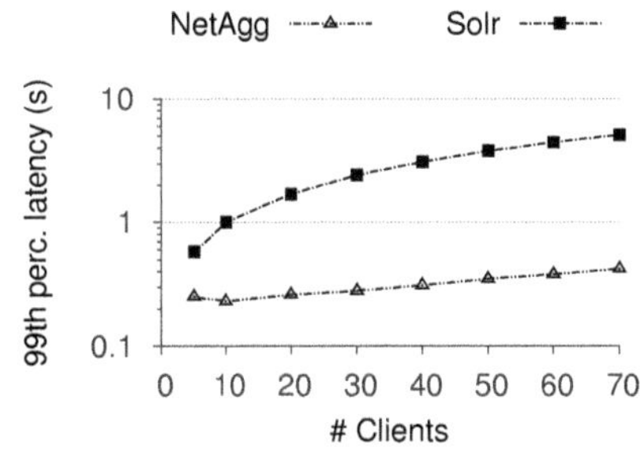

Figure 17: Response latency against number of clients (Solr)

the value of scaling out, making NETAGG compatible with future network upgrades.

Stragglers. To quantify the impact of straggling workers on our solution, we run an experiment in which we artificially delay the starting time of some of the flows of a given request or job, following the distribution reported in the literature [8]. The results in Figure 14 show that for reasonable ratios of stragglers, NETAGG can still provide significant traffic reduction. As expected, however, with a higher number of stragglers, the benefits of NETAGG decrease as there are fewer opportunities to aggregate data.

4.2 Testbed results

Next we describe the results of our testbed experiments designed to evaluate the effectiveness of our NETAGG middlebox prototype. To demonstrate the flexibility of NETAGG, we experiment with an online application, the Apache Solr distributed text search engine [11], and a batch-processing application, the Apache Hadoop map/reduce framework [10]. The two applications set different objectives for NETAGG, namely increased request throughput (Solr) and reduced job completion time (Hadoop).

We first evaluate the applications in isolation (§4.2.1 and §4.2.2) and then, to demonstrate NETAGG's ability to host multiple applications, run them simultaneously (§4.2.3).

Testbed set-up. The experiments are performed using a prototype NETAGG implementation deployed on a 34-server testbed across two racks. Each rack contains one 16-core 2.9 Ghz Intel Xeon server with 32 GB of RAM, acting as a master node, and ten 4-core 3.3 Ghz Intel Xeon servers with 8 GB of RAM, acting as the workers. In addition, each rack has five 4-core 1.8 Ghz AMD Opteron servers, generating the client queries in the Solr experiments. All servers have 1 Gbps network links to their ToR switches. Agg boxes have the same hardware as the master nodes and are attached to the ToR switches via 10 Gbps links.

Performance of local aggregation tree. We first conduct a micro-benchmark that evaluates the processing performance of differently-sized in-memory local aggregation trees. The experiments use a 16-core 2.9 Ghz Intel Xeon server with 32 GB of RAM. For an n-input binary tree, n worker threads feed deserialised data to the tree. We use the Hadoop WordCount workload (see below) with an output ratio of $\alpha = 10\%$.

Figure 15 shows the processing throughput for different thread pool sizes when varying the number of leaves in a tree (L). We only consider binary trees and, hence, the number of internal nodes, i.e. the aggregation tasks, is equal to $L-1$. We observe that 8 leaves are sufficient to saturate a 10 Gbps link. When the number of leaves increases, more aggregation tasks can be executed concurrently, and the throughput increases accordingly.

4.2.1 Apache Solr

We begin our testbed evaluation with Apache Solr in a single-rack scenario with 1 frontend, 10 backend and 5 client servers. We load the Wikipedia dataset, a snapshot of all Wikipedia pages in XML format from June 2012 [57], into the backends, and each client continuously submits a query for three random words. To generate different workloads, we vary the number of concurrent clients generating requests. Unless stated differently, error bars indicate the 5th and 95th percentiles.

We use two aggregation functions with different computational costs, representing extremes for functions commonly used in search engines. The first function, sample, has low computational cost: it returns a randomly chosen subset of the documents to the user according to a specified output ratio α, which therefore controls the amount of data reduction: a lower value of α means more aggregation, i.e. less data is returned to the clients.

The second function, categorise, is CPU-intensive: it classifies Wikipedia documents according to their *base categories* [56] and returns the top-k results per category. Each base category contains several sub-categories, and categorisation is performed by parsing the document content for category strings and determining the base category for the majority of strings.

Throughput. Figure 16 shows the median throughput with an increasing number of clients for Solr deployed on NETAGG. To test the capability of NETAGG to process at line rate, we use the sample function for aggregation with a fixed output ratio of $\alpha = 5\%$ to prevent the link to the frontend from becoming a bottleneck. For comparison, we also show the throughput of plain Solr.

For plain Solr, the throughput with 5 clients is limited by the client workload. As the number of clients increases, the throughput also increases until saturation. For 10 clients, packets from the backends start to queue on the 1 Gbps link to the frontend until the system completely saturates for 30 clients (processing at a maximum rate of 987 Mbps). After that, adding clients results in queuing at the frontend without improving the throughput.

With NETAGG, the throughput grows steadily up to 50 clients and then starts to saturate, reaching a median throughput of 9.2 Gbps for 70 clients. This corresponds to a 9.3× increase compared to Solr. After this, the throughput is bottlenecked by the incoming link bandwidth of the agg box.

Latency. Besides improving the throughput, NETAGG also reduces the request latency. Figure 17 shows the 99th percentile of the response times when varying the number of clients. For Solr, as the throughput of the frontend is limited to 1 Gbps, response times rise significantly when the workload increases. NETAGG can serve a higher load with low response times: with 70 clients, the response time for Solr is 5.1 s, while it only increases to 0.4 s for NETAGG.

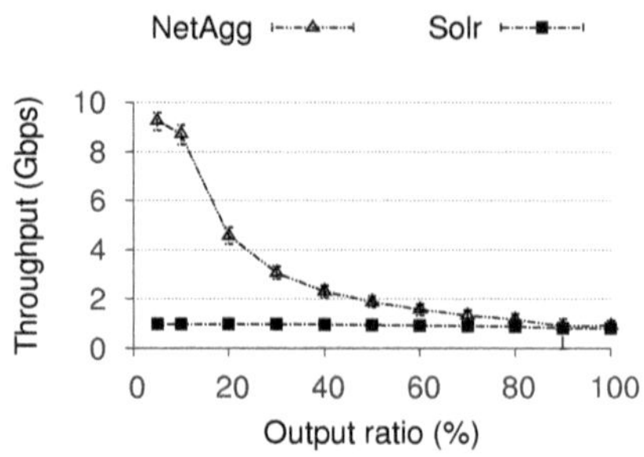

Figure 18: Network throughput against outgoing ratio (Solr)

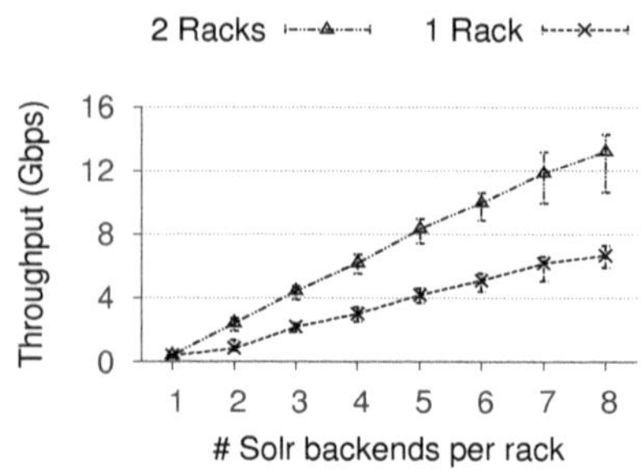

Figure 19: Throughput against number of backend servers per rack (Solr)

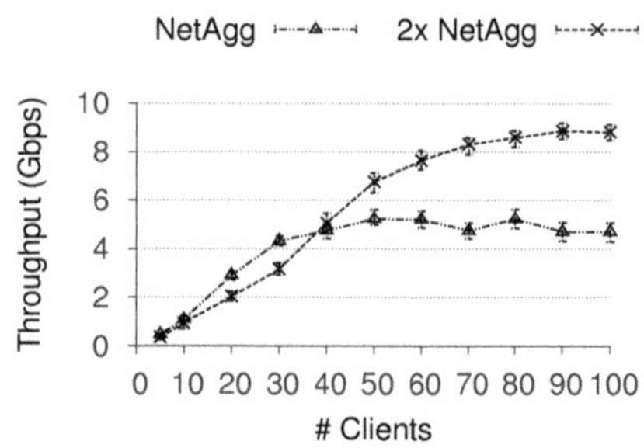

Figure 20: Agg box scale out for CPU-intensive aggregation (Solr)

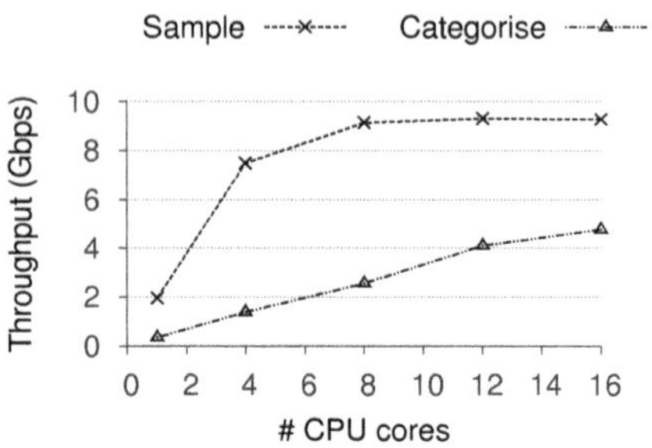

Figure 21: Throughput against number of CPU cores (Solr)

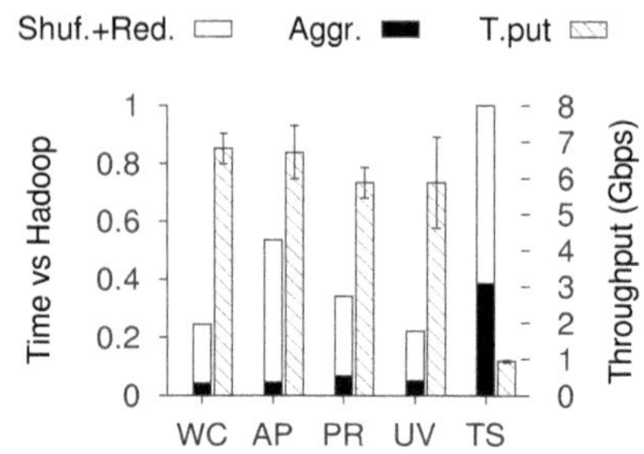

Figure 22: Performance of Hadoop benchmarks

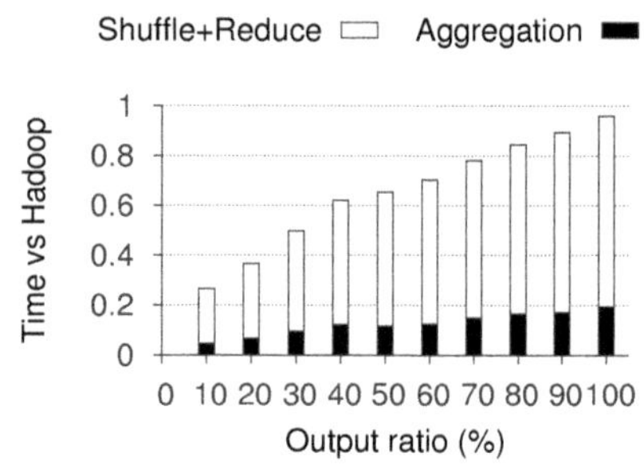

Figure 23: Shuffle and reduce time against output ratio (Hadoop)

This shows that NETAGG achieves low response times because it removes congestion from the network link to the frontend.

Output ratio. Next we vary the output ratio α of Solr requests with the sample aggregation for a fixed client population of 70. Figure 18 shows the throughput for Solr and NETAGG. Since the performance of Solr is network-bound, the throughput does not depend on the output ratio. For NETAGG, a higher output ratio also increases the utilisation of the network path between the agg box and the frontend, which remains limited to 1 Gbps. Therefore the effectiveness of NETAGG decreases. As described in §2.1, output ratios in production environments typically range from 5% to at most 40%, in which case NETAGG can offer significant benefit.

Two-rack deployment. To investigate the performance of NETAGG with multiple agg boxes, we extend our set-up to two racks, each with one agg box. We also add a second Solr deployment to generate a higher request load. We vary the number of backends per Solr deployment, which are divided equally between the racks to generate cross-rack traffic.

Figure 19 compares the throughput of a single agg box in one rack to the aggregate throughput of two agg boxes in two racks. For both configurations, throughput scales linearly with the number of backends. With two racks, the agg boxes serve twice as many backends compared to one rack, and hence their aggregate throughput doubles. This shows the ability of NETAGG to operate in larger deployments.

Scale out. To show the feasibility of increasing the performance of NETAGG by connecting multiple agg boxes to a single switch, we conduct an experiment in which we compare the performance of a single agg box with two agg boxes attached to the same switch. Requests are split equally between the agg boxes by hashing request identifiers. We use the computationally-expensive categorise aggregation function to ensure that the agg box is the bottleneck.

The results in Figure 20 confirm our expectation: they show that, by adding a second agg box, the throughput increases until the agg boxes become network-bound.

Scale up. To demonstrate the effectiveness of data-parallel processing on agg boxes, we increase the number of active CPU cores on a single agg box from 1 to 16 for both of our aggregation functions. The results in Figure 21 show that, while the performance of the computationally-inexpensive sample function is network bound, the performance for the categorise function increases linearly with more CPU cores due to increased parallelism.

4.2.2 *Apache Hadoop*

Next we investigate the performance of NETAGG when used with a batch processing application (Apache Hadoop). We deploy Hadoop in one rack with 8 mappers and 1 reducer, with a single aggregation tree. The workload consists of a set of benchmarks: (i) WordCount (WC), counting unique words in text; (ii) AdPredictor (AP), a machine learning job for generating click-through predictions from search engine web logs [28,38]; (iii) PageRank (PR), an implementation of the PageRank algorithm [33]; (iv) UserVisits (UV), a job for computing ad revenue per source IP address from web logs [12]; and (v) TeraSort (TS), a sorting benchmark with an identity reduce function [33].

Job completion time. We deploy each benchmark job on plain Hadoop and on Hadoop with NETAGG. For each job, we measure (i) the total shuffle and reduce time (SRT) relative to Hadoop, which includes the time spent at the agg box (AGG) and at the reducer; and (ii) the corresponding processing throughput at the agg box. We ignore the map phase because it is not affected by NETAGG.

Figure 22 shows the shuffle and reduce times (normalised with respect to plain Hadoop) and the agg box processing rate. NETAGG reduces SRT up to 4.5× compared to plain Hadoop. Only

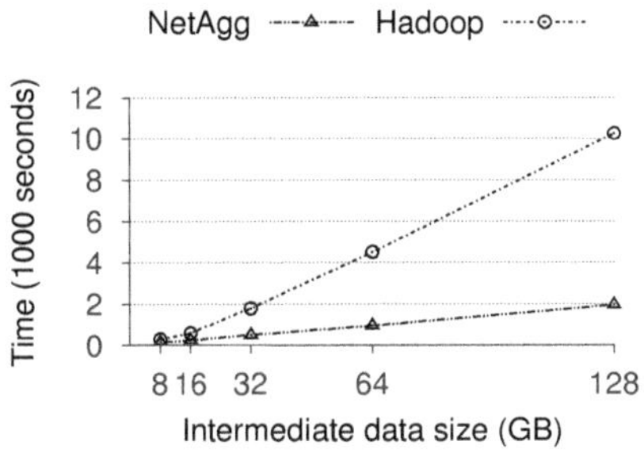

Figure 24: Shuffle and reduce time against intermediate data sizes (Hadoop)

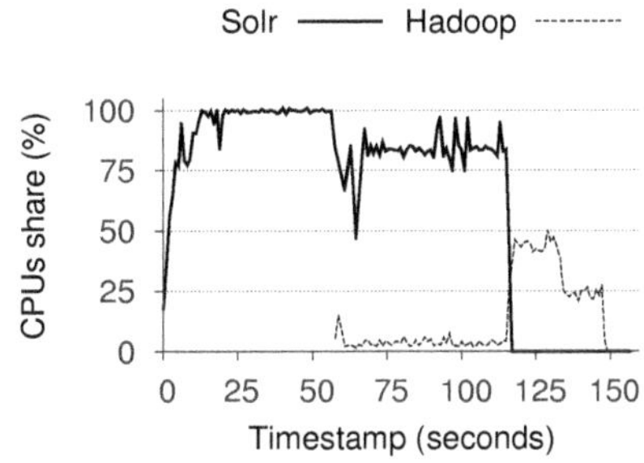

Figure 25: CPU resource fair sharing on NETAGG (Solr and Hadoop) achieved by a no-adaptive scheduler.

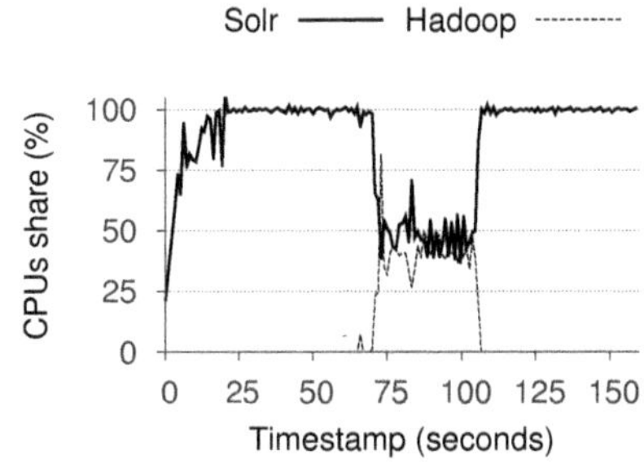

Figure 26: CPU resource fair sharing on NETAGG (Solr and Hadoop) achieved by an adaptive scheduler

for TS, there is no benefit because sorting does not reduce data. AP exhibits a speed-up of only 1.9× because the benchmark is compute-intensive.

Notably, in all cases, the time spent at the agg box (AGG) is a small fraction of the total SRT. This is due to the fact that the reducer is unaware that the results received from the agg box are already final and, regardless, reads them again. This is a conscious design decision because it makes agg boxes transparent to applications—with more invasive modifications of the application, the end-to-end SRT can be reduced to be closer to the AGG time.

The figure also shows that the agg box processes traffic at around 6 Gbps for almost all jobs—the processing rate for TS is lower due to a bottleneck at the reducer.

Output ratio. Next we compare the performance of Hadoop and Hadoop deployed with NETAGG for different output ratios α, obtained by varying the repetition of words in the input for the WC job. The size of the input data is 8 GB, and we measure SRT.

Figure 23 shows that relative SRT increases with higher output ratios. This is due to the fact that, with higher ratios, there are more results that are written to disk. A decrease in the output ratio, however, does not alleviate the network bottleneck at the reducer, which has to receive data from all the mappers over a 1 Gbps link.

For all output ratios, NETAGG improves performance over plain Hadoop, up to a factor of 3.7× for $\alpha = 10\%$. The improvement is highest for low output ratios for the same reason as in the case of Solr: performance eventually becomes restricted by the limited edge bandwidth.

Data size. We explore how the performance benefit of NETAGG is affected by the amount of data processed by the reducer. For this experiment, we fix the output ratio at 10%. Figure 24 shows the absolute shuffle and reduce times for different intermediate data sizes, ranging from 8 GB to 128 GB.

As we increase the amount of intermediate data, the effect of the shuffle phase on the overall job completion time becomes more pronounced because more data is sent across the network. Hence, the benefit of NETAGG increases with more intermediate data, up to a factor of 5.2× for 128 GB. In addition, the reducer receives only a small fraction of the already reduced intermediate data. This reduces processing time as well as CPU cycles and disk I/O.

4.2.3 Multiple applications

In our final experiment, we evaluate the behaviour of NETAGG in the presence of multiple deployed applications, focusing on the fairness that the adaptive task scheduler of an agg box can achieve (§3.2.1). For this, we execute a Hadoop job on NETAGG while running a Solr deployment at the same time. We route all aggregation traffic through a single agg box and measure the CPU share of each application. As the resource consumption of a single Solr task is significantly higher than that of a Hadoop one, the task scheduler must be able to account for this heterogeneity.

Figure 25 shows the CPU usage of the two applications when the task scheduler uses regular weighted fair queuing with fixed weights, which are set according to application priorities (see §3.2.1). Although each application is assigned a desired utilisation of 50%, this is not reflected in the achieved CPU usage: a Solr task takes, on average, 34 ms to run on the CPU, while a Hadoop task runs only for 2 ms. Fixed weights therefore lead to a starvation of the Hadoop tasks, which exhibit low performance.

In contrast, Figure 26 shows the same set-up using our adaptive task scheduler, which adjusts weights based on the actual CPU consumption by applications. As a result, CPU usage is split fairly between the processing of aggregation tasks for Solr and Hadoop.

5. RELATED WORK

Middleboxes. Researchers have proposed efficient software middlebox platforms to process network flows using commodity hardware [50, 52]. ClickOS [43], for example, improves the network performance of Xen using netmap [49]. In contrast to NETAGG, these platforms operate at the packet level, which makes them unsuitable to aggregate payload data in application flows.

A flow-based middlebox platform is provided by xOMB [9], which can process application protocols such as HTTP. Yet its focus remains on a small set of network-level services, whereas NETAGG can host a number of application-specific aggregation functions on middleboxes to improve application performance. FlowOS [14] runs in kernel space and provides zero-copy flow construction for multiple, independent flows. However, FlowOS does not support aggregation across multiple, dependent flows, as in NETAGG.

Recently, SDN-based techniques were used to manage the traffic to and from middleboxes [48]. As part of NETAGG, we could use a similar approach to relay traffic to agg boxes instead of employing shim layers. However, shim layers selectively redirect traffic, not only based on packet headers, but also depending on application data semantics, which requires deserialising the application data.

Data aggregation. In map/reduce [25], aggregation of single map tasks through combiner functions is a common technique to help reduce network load and job execution time. To reduce the traffic at the network core, additional aggregation steps at one of the rack servers can be performed [40, 44, 59]. At scale, however, rack-level aggregation provides only limited opportunities for data reduction and is often bottlenecked by the lower edge bandwidth available at the servers (see §2).

Tyson et al. [21] describe Hadoop Online, an extension to map/reduce that allows reducers to start reducing intermediate results as soon as they become available. While this is orthogonal to the goals of NETAGG, our agg boxes use a similar technique to aggregate partial results with a streaming aggregation tree.

Camdoop [22] proposes an extreme solution to improve the performance of map/reduce by adopting a direct-connect DC topology. All traffic is forwarded between servers without switches, which can therefore aggregate the traffic. This approach, however, requires a custom network topology and redeveloped DC applications. In contrast, NETAGG is compatible with today's DCs and supports existing applications.

Aggregation was successfully applied in other domains, including wireless sensor networks and Internet systems. In sensor networks, packet-based aggregation is used to improve the efficiency of data-collection protocols, primarily targeting energy savings [34, 41]. Internet-scale aggregation systems use overlay networks to collect data in a scalable fashion [15, 35, 58]. Neither use of aggregation requires high throughput, a key design requirement of NETAGG. For example, the design proposed by Yalagandula and Dahlin [58] uses a DHT overlay in a WAN, which is a structure optimised for scale and churn, not throughput.

Multi-point flow scheduling. Recent work considered how to schedule multi-point flows efficiently in DCs [19, 20]. While we show an approach that improves network performance when the flows can be aggregated (*many-to-one*), we also note that application-specific middleboxes can implement efficient versions of multicast or broadcast protocols (*one-to-many*). This would enable further performance improvement of iterative applications with a distributed broadcast phase, such as graph processing or logistic regression [20].

Traffic compression. There are a variety of techniques that have been proposed to compress in-network traffic, mainly for the purposes of reducing bandwidth usage: network coding [1], traffic redundancy elimination [6], and even multicast [26, 55] are prime examples. These techniques are therefore complementary to our work, but do not address NETAGG's goal of supporting application-specific aggregation functions.

6. CONCLUSIONS

Many applications in today's DCs operate in a partition/aggregation fashion. We observe that in typical workloads, the aggregation functions are associative and commutative, and exhibit high data reduction. This motivates us to explore a novel point in the network design space in which data are aggregated on the network path before reaching the end hosts.

We describe the design and implementation of NETAGG, an on-path aggregation service that transparently intercepts aggregation flows at edge servers using shim layers and redirects them to aggregation nodes (agg boxes). NETAGG is designed to aggregate data of multiple applications at high rate by decomposing aggregation computation within and across agg boxes to exploit parallelism. We evaluate the effectiveness of NETAGG using a combined approach of simulations and a prototype implementation deployed with real-world applications. Our results show that NETAGG outperforms typical DC set-ups while incurring little extra deployment cost.

This work is part of a larger effort aimed at bridging the gap between networking and applications by enabling application-specific in-network processing [23]. Our ultimate goal is to provide novel expressive high-level abstractions coupled with efficient low-level mechanisms that allow users to deploy application-specific code within the network in a safe and efficient way.

Acknowledgements

The authors wish to thank the anonymous reviewers and our shepherd, Christian Kreibich, who provided valuable feedback and advice. This work was supported by grant EP/K032968 ("NaaS: Network-as-a-Service in the Cloud") from the UK Engineering and Physical Sciences Research Council (EPSRC). Luo Mai is supported by a 2012 Google European Doctoral Fellowship in Cloud Computing.

7. REFERENCES

[1] R. Ahlswede, N. Cai, S.-Y. Li, and R. W. Yeung. Network Information Flow. *IEEE Transactions on Information Theory*, 46(4), 2000.

[2] M. Al-Fares, A. Loukissas, and A. Vahdat. A Scalable, Commodity Data Center Network Architecture. In *SIGCOMM*, 2008.

[3] M. Al-Fares, S. Radhakrishnan, B. Raghavan, N. Huang, and A. Vahdat. Hedera: Dynamic Flow Scheduling for Data Center Networks. In *NSDI*, 2010.

[4] M. Alizadeh, A. Greenberg, D. A. Maltz, J. Padhye, P. Patel, B. Prabhakar, S. Sengupta, and M. Sridharan. Data Center TCP (DCTCP). In *SIGCOMM*, 2010.

[5] M. Alizadeh, A. Kabbani, T. Edsall, B. Prabhakar, A. Vahdat, and M. Yasuda. Less is More: Trading a Little Bandwidth for Ultra-low Latency in the Data Center. In *NSDI*, 2012.

[6] A. Anand, V. Sekar, and A. Akella. SmartRE: An Architecture for Coordinated Network-Wide Redundancy Elimination. In *SIGCOMM*, 2009.

[7] G. Ananthanarayanan, A. Ghodsi, S. Shenker, and I. Stoica. Effective Straggler Mitigation: Attack of the Clones. In *NSDI*, 2013.

[8] G. Ananthanarayanan, S. Kandula, A. G. Greenberg, I. Stoica, Y. Lu, B. Saha, and E. Harris. Reining in the Outliers in Map-Reduce Clusters Using Mantri. In *OSDI*, 2010.

[9] J. W. Anderson, R. Braud, R. Kapoor, G. Porter, and A. Vahdat. xOMB: Extensible Open Middleboxes with Commodity Servers. In *ANCS*, 2012.

[10] Apache Hadoop. `http://hadoop.apache.org`.

[11] Apache Solr. `http://lucene.apache.org/solr`.

[12] R. Appuswamy, C. Gkantsidis, D. Narayanan, O. Hodson, and A. Rowstron. Scale-up vs Scale-out for Hadoop: Time to rethink? In *SOCC*, 2013.

[13] T. Benson, A. Akella, and D. A. Maltz. Network Traffic Characteristics of Data Centers in the Wild. In *IMC*, 2010.

[14] M. Bezahaf, A. Alim, and L. Mathy. FlowOS: A Flow-based Platform for Middleboxes. In *HotMiddlebox*, 2013.

[15] J. Cappos and J. H. Hartman. San Fermın: Aggregating Large Data Sets Using a Binomial Swap Forest. In *NSDI*, 2008.

[16] R. Castro Fernandez, M. Migliavacca, E. Kalyvianaki, and P. Pietzuch. Integrating Scale Out and Fault Tolerance in Stream Processing Using Operator State Management. In *SIGMOD*, 2013.

[17] R. Chaiken, B. Jenkins, P.-A. Larson, B. Ramsey, D. Shakib, S. Weaver, and J. Zhou. SCOPE: Easy and Efficient Parallel Processing of Massive Data Sets. In *VLDB*, 2008.

[18] Y. Chen, A. Ganapathi, R.Griffith, and R. Katz. The Case for Evaluating MapReduce Performance Using Workload Suites. In *MASCOTS*, 2011.

[19] M. Chowdhury, S. Kandula, and I. Stoica. Leveraging Endpoint Flexibility in Data-Intensive Clusters. In *SIGCOMM*, 2013.

[20] M. Chowdhury, M. Zaharia, J. Ma, M. I. Jordan, and I. Stoica. Managing Data Transfers in Computer Clusters with Orchestra. In *SIGCOMM*, 2011.

[21] T. Condie, N. Conway, P. Alvaro, J. M. Hellerstein, K. Elmeleegy, and R. Sears. MapReduce Online. In *NSDI*, 2010.

[22] P. Costa, A. Donnelly, A. Rowstron, and G. O'Shea. Camdoop: Exploiting In-network Aggregation for Big Data Applications. In *NSDI*, 2012.

[23] P. Costa, M. Migliavacca, P. Pietzuch, and A. L. Wolf. NaaS: Network-as-a-Service in the Cloud. In *Hot-ICE*, 2012.

[24] J. Dean, G. S. Corrado, R. Monga, K. Chen, M. Devin, Q. V. Le, M. Z. Mao, M. Ranzato, A. Senior, P. Tucker, K. Yang, and A. Y. Ng. Large Scale Distributed Deep Networks. In *NIPS*, 2012.

[25] J. Dean and S. Ghemawat. MapReduce: Simplified Data Processing on Large Clusters. In *OSDI*, 2004.

[26] C. Diot, W. Dabbous, and J. Crowcroft. Multipoint Communication: A Survey of Protocols, Functions, and Mechanisms. *J-SAC*, 15(3), 1997.

[27] N. Dukkipati and N. McKeown. Why Flow-Completion Time is the Right Metric for Congestion Control. *CCR*, 36(1), 2006.

[28] T. Graepel, J. Q. Candela, T. Borchert, and R. Herbrich. Web-scale Bayesian Click-through Rate Prediction for Sponsored Search Advertising in Microsoft's Bing Search Engine. In *ICML*, 2010.

[29] A. Greenberg, J. R. Hamilton, N. Jain, S. Kandula, C. Kim, P. Lahiri, D. A. Maltz, P. Patel, and S. Sengupta. VL2: A Scalable and Flexible Data Center Network. In *SIGCOMM*, 2009.

[30] C. Guo, G. Lu, D. Li, H. Wu, X. Zhang, Y. Shi, C. Tian, Y. Zhang, and S. Lu. BCube: A High Performance, Server-centric Network Architecture for Modular Data Centers. In *SIGCOMM*, 2009.

[31] D. Halperin, S. Kandula, J. Padhye, P. Bahl, and D. Wetherall. Augmenting Data Center Networks with Multi-Gigabit Wireless Links. In *SIGCOMM*, 2011.

[32] C. Hopps. Analysis of an Equal-Cost Multi-Path Algorithm, 2000. IETF RFC 2992.

[33] S. Huang, J. Huang, J. Dai, T. Xie, and B. Huang. The HiBench Benchmark Suite: Characterization of the MapReduce-Based Data Analysis. In *ICDE Workshops*, 2010.

[34] C. Intanagonwiwat, R. Govindan, D. Estrin, J. Heidemann, and F. Silva. Directed Diffusion for Wireless Sensor Networking. *ToN*, 11(1), 2003.

[35] N. Jain, D. Kit, P. Mahajan, P. Yalagandula, M. Dahlin, and Y. Zhang. STAR: Self-tuning Aggregation for Scalable Monitoring. In *VLDB*, 2007.

[36] V. Jalaparti, P. Bodik, S. Kandula, I. Menache, M. Rybalkin, and C. Yan. Speeding up Distributed Request-Response Workflows. In *SIGCOMM*, 2013.

[37] D. A. Joseph, A. Tavakoli, and I. Stoica. A Policy-aware Switching Layer for Data Centers. In *SIGCOMM*, 2008.

[38] KDD Cup 2012. `http://www.kddcup2012.org/`.

[39] Kryo library. `http://code.google.com/p/kryonet/`.

[40] D. Logothetis, C. Trezzo, K. C. Webb, and K. Yocum. In-situ MapReduce for Log Processing. In *USENIX ATC*, 2011.

[41] S. Madden, M. J. Franklin, J. M. Hellerstein, and W. Hong. TAG: A Tiny Aggregation Service for Ad-hoc Sensor Networks. *OSR*, 36(SI), 2002.

[42] G. Malewicz, M. H. Austern, A. J. Bik, J. C. Dehnert, I. Horn, N. Leiser, and G. Czajkowski. Pregel: A System for Large-Scale Graph Processing. In *SIGMOD*, 2010.

[43] J. Martins, M. Ahmed, C. Raiciu, V. Olteanu, M. Honda, R. Bifulco, and F. Huici. ClickOS and the Art of Network Function Virtualization. In *NSDI*, 2014.

[44] S. Melnik, A. Gubarev, J. J. Long, G. Romer, S. Shivakumar, M. Tolton, and T. Vassilakis. Dremel: Interactive Analysis of Web-scale Datasets. In *VLDB*, 2010.

[45] Palo Alto Networks. `http://www.paloaltonetworks.com`.

[46] L. Popa, S. Ratnasamy, G. Iannaccone, A. Krishnamurthy, and I. Stoica. A Cost Comparison of Data Center Network Architectures. In *CoNEXT*, 2010.

[47] G. Porter, R. Strong, N. Farrington, A. Forencich, P. Chen-Sun, T. Rosing, Y. Fainman, G. Papen, and A. Vahdat. Integrating Microsecond Circuit Switching into the Data Center. In *SIGCOMM*, 2013.

[48] Z. A. Qazi, C.-C. Tu, L. Chiang, R. Miao, V. Sekar, and M. Yu. SIMPLE-fying Middlebox Policy Enforcement Using SDN. In *SIGCOMM*, 2013.

[49] L. Rizzo. Netmap: A Novel Framework for Fast Packet I/O. In *USENIX ATC*, 2012.

[50] V. Sekar, N. Egi, S. Ratnasamy, M. K. Reiter, and G. Shi. Design and Implementation of a Consolidated Middlebox Architecture. In *NSDI*, 2012.

[51] J. Sherry, S. Hasan, C. Scott, A. Krishnamurthy, S. Ratnasamy, and V. Sekar. Making Middleboxes Someone Else's Problem. In *SIGCOMM*, 2012.

[52] A. Shieh, S. Kandula, and E. G. Sirer. SideCar: Building Programmable Datacenter Networks without Programmable Switches. In *HotNets*, 2010.

[53] A. Singla, C.-Y. Hong, L. Popa, and P. B. Godfrey. Jellyfish: Networking Data Centers Randomly. In *NSDI*, 2012.

[54] Twitter Storm. `http://goo.gl/Y1AcL`.

[55] Y. Vigfusson, H. Abu-Libdeh, M. Balakrishnan, K. Birman, R. Burgess, G. Chockler, H. Li, and Y. Tock. Dr. Multicast: Rx for Data Center Communication Scalability. In *EuroSys*, 2010.

[56] Wikipedia Categories. `http://goo.gl/n60jg1`.

[57] Wikimedia Downloads, June 2012. `http://goo.gl/DQFJk`.

[58] P. Yalagandula and M. Dahlin. A Scalable Distributed Information Management System. In *SIGCOMM*, 2004.

[59] Y. Yu, P. K. Gunda, and M. Isard. Distributed Aggregation for Data-Parallel Computing: Interfaces and Implementations. In *SOSP*, 2009.

[60] M. Zaharia, D. Borthakur, J. Sen Sarma, K. Elmeleegy, S. Shenker, and I. Stoica. Delay Scheduling: A Simple Technique for Achieving Locality and Fairness in Cluster Scheduling. In *EuroSys*, 2010.

[61] X. Zhou, Z. Zhang, Y. Zhu, Y. Li, S. Kumar, A. Vahdat, B. Y. Zhao, and H. Zheng. Mirror Mirror on the Ceiling: Flexible Wireless Links for Data Centers. In *SIGCOMM*, 2012.

MSPlayer: Multi-Source and multi-Path LeverAged YoutubER

Yung-Chih Chen
UMass Amherst
yungchih@cs.umass.edu

Don Towsley
UMass Amherst
towsley@cs.umass.edu

Ramin Khalili
T-labs/TU-Berlin
ramin@inet.tu-berlin.de

ABSTRACT

Online video streaming through mobile devices has become extremely popular nowadays. YouTube, for example, reported that the percentage of its traffic streaming to mobile devices has soared from 6% to more than 40% over the past two years. Moreover, people are constantly seeking to stream high quality video for better experience while often suffering from limited bandwidth. Thanks to the rapid deployment of content delivery networks (CDNs), popular videos are now replicated at different sites, and users can stream videos from close-by locations with low latencies. As mobile devices nowadays are equipped with multiple wireless interfaces (e.g., WiFi and 3G/4G), aggregating bandwidth for high definition video streaming has become possible.

We propose a client-based video streaming solution, MSPlayer, that takes advantage of multiple video sources as well as multiple network paths through different interfaces. MSPlayer reduces start-up latency and provides high quality video streaming and robust data transport in mobile scenarios. We experimentally demonstrate our solution on a testbed and through the YouTube video service.

Categories and Subject Descriptors

C.2 [**Computer-communication Networks**]: Network Protocols; C.2.1 [**Network Architecture and Design**]: Wireless communication; C.4 [**Performance of System**]: Design studies

Keywords

Video Streaming; HTTP; MPTCP; CDN; LTE

1. INTRODUCTION

With the high demand for online video streaming, video content providers are offering better technology to satisfy customers' desires for streaming high quality videos. However, streaming video to a user nowadays still encounters the following issues. First, people from time to time experience insufficient bandwidth. Research has shown that viewers are not patient enough to wait for a start-up delay longer than a few seconds [20] and video quality has a huge impact on user engagement [9]. Also, connections to a particular network can break down temporarily due to mobility and re-establishing a connection introduces additional delays. Last, as network bandwidth is highly variable, the commercial video players have experimented with video rate adaption, which in turn results in performance issues such as variable video quality, unfairness to other players, and low bandwidth utilization [5,6,18,19,21].

As mobile devices are now equipped with multiple wireless interfaces connected to different networks (WiFi or cellular 3G/4G), one possible solution is to use multi-path TCP (MPTCP) [11]. However, since MPTCP requires kernel modifications at both the client and server sides [22], and many network operators do not allow MPTCP traffic to pass their middleboxes [15,16], it has been slow to deploy MPTCP globally. Furthermore, although MPTCP provides a means for balancing loads over different paths to a single server, it does not utilize source diversity in the networks in order to facilitate content delivery. Therefore, it is urgent and necessary to develop a solution to stream high quality videos to end users without overloading the video servers. Thus, we ask the following question: *Is it possible to leverage both path diversity and source diversity to provide robust video delivery and to reduce video start-up latency?*

In this paper, we take a first step to answering this question. We show that one can utilize both of the available WiFi and 4G interfaces simultaneously to aggregate bandwidth for higher quality video streaming. The video streaming solution does not require modifications in the kernel stacks and is not hindered by network middleboxes. We then instantiate these designs in our YouTube player, MSPlayer. By investigating the YouTube service architecture and its streaming mechanisms, we further demonstrate how to leverage the existence of multiple video sources in different networks at the same time. We then experimentally evaluate the performance of different MSPlayer schedulers as well as the performance of MSPlayer through the YouTube service.

The remainder of this paper is organized as follows: Sec. 2 introduces the design principles of MSPlayer. We overview the architecture of MSPlayer in Sec. 3. Implementation details of MSPlayer are described in Sec. 4 and we evaluate MSPlayer's performance in our testbed and over YouTube infrastructure in Sec. 5 and 6. We discuss future work and conclude this paper in Sec. 7.

CoNEXT'14, December 2–5, 2014, Sydney, Australia.

http://dx.doi.org/10.1145/2674005.2675007.

2. DESIGN PRINCIPLES

In this paper, we present MSPlayer, a client-based approach for video streaming that requires no changes in either the server or the client's kernel stacks. It leverages diversity in the network and performs load balancing at the client side. MSPlayer also supports user mobility and provides robust data transport. In order to be fair to other TCP users, MSPlayer limits the number of paths to two (one over WiFi and one over 3G/4G) and leverages HTTP range requests to stream videos. It has the following design features.

Just-in-time with High Quality: Since viewers often prematurely stop watching videos [10, 20], streaming the entire video to a viewer at once can result in waste of bandwidth and network resources. This, along with the rise of adaptive streaming over HTTP [24], has drawn attention to *just-in-time* video delivery, which has been exploited by most large scale video streaming services such as YouTube, Netflix, and Hulu. A video is partitioned into many small file segments called *video chunks.* The video server maintains multiple profiles of the same video for different bitrates and video quality levels. Clients then *periodically* request video chunks and adapt video bitrates.

Just-in-time video delivery avoids a waste of resources if a user drops the video during its playback. Dynamically adapting video bitrates, however, results in performance problems such as low link utilization [5], unfairness to other TCP users [5, 18], and unstable video quality [6, 21]. In our design, we share the same just-in-time concept for video delivery. However, we do not investigate rate adaption and focus on how to stream videos to users with a *fixed bitrate* by exploiting *network diversity.*

Robust Data Transport: When a mobile user streams a video, his connection (mostly WiFi) can break and the downloaded video will thus be abandoned. In order to resume the video, the user then needs to switch to another available interface with connectivity to another network, establish a new TCP connection, and move/skip to the break point. In the worst case, one will have to wait until reaching the next WiFi hotspot and repeat the entire process mentioned above.

One possible solution is to use Multi-Path TCP (MPTCP) [11], which has been standardized by the IETF, aimed at providing robust data transport. However, MPTCP still faces several deployment challenges: First, MPTCP requires kernel modifications at *both* the server and client sides [22]. Second, it relies on the TCP option field to exchange path and interface information. In the later case, research has shown that MPTCP suffers significantly from network middleboxes as they very often strip away unknown options [15, 16], forcing MPTCP connections to fall back to legacy single-path TCP. In our measurements, two out of three major US cellular carriers do not allow MPTCP traffic to pass through the default HTTP 80 port, which is a potential problem for video streaming to popular sites such as YouTube or Netflix.

We design a client-based multi-path solution to provide robust data transport for high quality video streaming. Furthermore, each path runs legacy TCP and is therefore guaranteed to successfully pass network middleboxes.

Content Source Diversity: Current MPTCP design [11] and other similar approaches such as [7], only allow flows or paths to be established between a client and *a single server.* If the current YouTube infrastructure were to support MPTCP, users streaming videos from one server with high aggregate bandwidth through multiple paths could quickly incur server demand surges. This high demand, particularly for high quality videos, can overload the server and congest shared bottleneck links. The outcome of this can directly or implicitly affect other viewers' experience.

As popular content is now replicated at multiple locations or data centers, content delivery networks (CDNs) are responsible for handling video replicas and delivering videos across different data centers for large scale video streaming services such as YouTube, Netflix, and Hulu [1, 2]. As part of our design is to provide robustness, MSPlayer, at the initial phase, collects a list of YouTube servers' addresses in each network exploited. If a server in a network fails or is overloaded, MSPlayer switches to another server in that network and resumes video streaming. Other proposals, such as [14], aim to emulate the use of multiple paths in a controlled environment by setting up multiple connections to the servers connected by a switch with only one *single interface.* Although this approach can potentially distribute the load among the connected servers, having multiple connections over one interface could quickly saturate the bottleneck link.

As wireless interfaces are associated with different networks, MSPlayer requests partial content from *video servers in all networks* simultaneously to avoid overwhelming particular video servers and to balance the load across the servers. In this work, we use Google's public DNS service to resolve the IP addresses of YouTube servers.

Chunk Scheduler: MSPlayer relies on range requests to retrieve video chunks over different paths. As making a range request incurs additional overhead (packets start to arrive one RTT after the request is sent) and different paths usually exhibit diverse latencies [8], how to schedule chunks over different paths efficiently is challenging. Therefore, it is desirable to have a good scheduler that estimates path quality over time and efficiently assigns chunks to each path.

To satisfy just-in-time video delivery, the scheduler pauses chunk retrieval when the playout buffer is full and resumes chunk requesting when the amount of buffered video falls below a certain level (that is referred to as periodic downloading or ON/OFF cycles [23]). To reduce memory usage of out-of-order chunks from different paths, the MSPlayer scheduler attempts to complete the transfer of a chunk over each path at the same time, and allows *at most one* out-of-order chunk to be stored.

3. MSPLAYER OVERVIEW

We now overview the MSPlayer architecture. We first describe how YouTube video streaming works and the just-in-time video delivery, followed by descriptions of the MSPlayer's design components: multi-source, multi-path, and chuck scheduler.

3.1 YouTube Video Streaming

People usually go to the YouTube website and choose a video to watch, or just click on an URL of the following form `http://www.youtube.com/watch?v=qjT4T2gU9sM` on a web

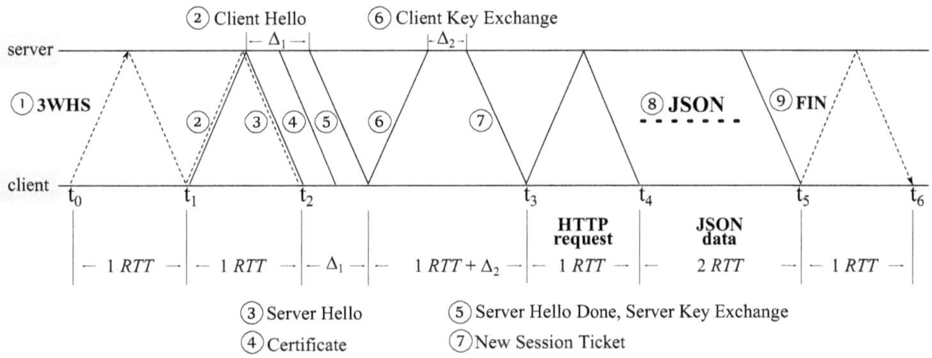

Figure 1: HTTPS connection to YouTube web server: retrieving JSON objects of video information.

page. Users can then watch the video through their browsers using a built-in Adobe Flash player [4]. Each YouTube video is identified by an 11-literal video ID after `watch?v=` in the URL [2].

With this URL, the video player (e.g., Adobe Flash) first performs a DNS lookup to resolve the IP address of the domain name `www.youtube.com` and the user's video request is then directed to one of YouTube's web proxy servers. The YouTube web proxy server processes the request and returns the related video information and a new URL to the user in JavaScript Object Notation (JSON) format, indicating where the associated and available YouTube video servers are. The player then establishes another connection to one of the dedicated video servers and starts to stream the YouTube video using HTTP range requests.

The streaming process starts with a *pre-buffering phase* followed by a periodic *re-buffering phase* [23]. The pre-buffering phase takes place at the beginning of the streaming, aimed at retrieving enough video data in the playout buffer. When the amount of video content in the playout buffer falls below a certain level, the player enters the re-buffering phase, making new requests to refill the playout buffer. This periodic re-buffering repeats until the video is completely watched or dropped.

3.2 Multi-Source and Multi-Path

Before describing our scheme with multiple sources and multiple paths, we first describe how each path establishes a connection to the YouTube web proxy server and the associated video server. Fig. 1 illustrates a flow diagram when a user contacts YouTube's web proxy server to retrieve video information. The connection starts with a TCP 3-way handshake (3WHS). Afterwards, the client initiates a secure connection handshake message at time t_1. It takes the server timesΔ_1 andΔ_2 to verify the key and complete the key exchange process. The first HTTP request is made at time t_3, and the first JSON packet from the web proxy server arrives at t_4. Note that these JSON packets are delivered within two round trips (slightly less than 20 packets)[1], and the secure connection ends at t_5 followed by a TCP FIN.

If we denote by R_1 and R_2 the RTTs of the first and the second paths, and by $\theta = R_2/R_1$ the RTT ratio (assuming $R_1 \leq R_2$, i.e., the first path is a fast path), it takes time $\eta_i = 4R_i + \Delta_1 + \Delta_2$ to establish a secure HTTP connection over path i, and time $\psi_i = 6R_i + \Delta_1 + \Delta_2$ to receive complete video information before contacting the video server. If the YouTube's web proxy server is close to the video server, and both servers have similar capability of key verification, it takes approximately time $\pi_i \approx \psi_i + \eta_i$ for path i to receive the first video packet from the video server. As part of chunk scheduling in MSPlayer, the first path is designed to contact its video server as soon as its IP address is decoded, without waiting for the second path to finish its decoding process. Chunks are scheduled over the first path before the second path becomes available. Therefore, before the second path starts to retrieve video packets from its associated video server, the first path will have received video packets for a duration of $\pi_2 - \pi_1 \approx 10 \cdot (R_2 - R_1) = 10 \cdot (\theta - 1)R_1$.

In MSPlayer, the processes of fetching video chunks over each path are executed by independent threads, which are under the management of the chunk scheduler (described in the next section).

3.3 Chunk Scheduler

In order to reduce out-of-order delay for video streaming, and to reduce memory usage to store out-of-order chunks, our design is to schedule chunks (of different sizes) over both paths so that chunk transfers *complete* at roughly the same time.

To optimize video streaming performance with MSPlayer, chunk size selection for each path is critical and should be adapted over time in response to network dynamics. A previous measurement study shows that YouTube players, such as Adobe Flash or HTML5, use 64 KB and 256 KB as their default chunk sizes, while Netflix player (silverlight) uses larger chunk sizes that range from 2 MB to 4 MB [23]. Since different mobile devices have pre-buffering periods of different lengths (ranging from 20 seconds to 1 minute) [22], we also investigate the performance of different schedulers when applying different chunk sizes and pre-buffering periods.

We denote by $S_i(t)$ the chunk size of path i at time t, by B the base chunk size, and by T_i the time required to download chunk $S_i(t)$. The estimated throughput to download $S_i(t)$ is denoted by $w_i(t) = S_i(t)/T_i$.

We first showcase a baseline scheduler called *Ratio* and then propose two different chunk size schedulers that adjust chunk sizes according to network bandwidth changes, namely the exponential weighted moving average (*EWMA*) and *Harmonic*. MSPlayer's chunk size selection should adapt

[1]As of July 2014, YouTube has applied algorithms to encode copyrighted video signatures. Since these signatures are needed to contact the video servers, for copyrighted videos, an additional operation is required to fetch the video web page containing a decoder to decipher the video signature.

Algorithm 1 Dynamic chunk size adjustment

procedure DCSA($i, \hat{w}_0, \hat{w}_1, w_i, \delta, B$) ▷ $i = 0{,}1$
  if $\hat{w}_i$ not available **then**
    $S_i \leftarrow B$ ▷ initial chunk size
  else if $\hat{w}_i < \hat{w}_{1-i}$ **then** ▷ slow path
    if $w_i > (1+\delta)\hat{w}_i$ **then**
      $S_i \leftarrow 2 \cdot S_i$
    else if $w_i < (1-\delta)\hat{w}_i$ **then**
      $S_i \leftarrow \max\{\lceil S_i/2 \rceil, \mathit{16KB}\}$
    else
      S_i unchanged
    end if
  else ▷ fast path
    $\gamma = \lceil \hat{w}_i / \hat{w}_{1-i} \rceil$
    $S_i \leftarrow \gamma \cdot S_{1-i}$
  end if
  return S_i ▷ final chunk size
end procedure

to path quality variations over time, and the bandwidth estimator of MSPlayer thus plays a critical role in the chunk size selection process. In this paper, we label the chunk scheduler according to the bandwidth estimator used. We compare and evaluate the performance of these three schedulers in our testbed.

Baseline Scheduler: Suppose $w_i(t) \leq w_{1-i}(t)$, the baseline *Ratio* scheduler assigns a fixed chunk size to the path with lower throughput such that $S_i(t+1) = B$ and adjusts the chunk size of the path with higher throughput based on throughput ratio (i.e., $S_{1-i}(t+1) = w_{1-i}(t)/w_i(t) \cdot B$ and $i = 0, 1$ labels the first and the second path).

Dynamic Chunk Adjustment Scheduler: When path bandwidth estimates are available, the chunk size of each path is adjusted according to Alg. 1. We denote by δ the throughput variation parameter in Alg. 1. If the current bandwidth measurement of the slow path is $(1+\delta)$ times larger than the estimated value, the chunk size is doubled. Similarly, if the current value is $(1-\delta)$ times worse than the estimated value, the chunk size is halved. The chunk size of the fast path is adjusted based on the throughput ratio.

Here we focus on two bandwidth estimators: exponential weighted moving average (*EWMA*) and harmonic mean (*Harmonic*). The weighted moving average is defined as:

$$\hat{w}_i(t+1) = \alpha \cdot \hat{w}_i(t) + (1-\alpha) \cdot w_i(t). \tag{1}$$

Due to the space constraint, in this paper we only report the results of $\alpha = 0.9$ (details see next section).

As network bandwidth can vary quickly, extreme measurement values can bias our estimated results, following we introduce another bandwidth estimator called harmonic mean. The benefit to estimating path bandwidth by harmonic mean is that it tends to mitigate the impact of large outliers due to network variation [19].

Given a series of bandwidth measurements, $w_i(t)$, where $t = 0, 1, 2, \cdots, n-1$ and $w_i(t) > 0$, the harmonic mean is $\hat{w}_i(n) = n / \sum_{t=0}^{n-1} \frac{1}{w_i(t)}$. A key factor of computing harmonic mean is to maintain a number of past measurements [19]. However, to reduce memory usage and computational cost, one can compute the current harmonic mean without maintaining all previous states. Statistics from the past can be recovered simply by recording an additional parameter, n, the total number of past measurements. The harmonic mean can be updated with the most recent measurement of path i, $w_i(n)$, and the previous harmonic mean $\hat{w}_i(n)$. That is,

$$\hat{w}_i(n+1) = \frac{n+1}{\sum_{t=0}^{n} \frac{1}{w_i(t)}} = \frac{n+1}{\frac{n}{\hat{w}_i(n)} + \frac{1}{w_i(n+1)}}. \tag{2}$$

In the following sections, we describe MSPlayer implementation details and evaluate MSPlayer's performance.

4. MSPLAYER IMPLEMENTATION

In order to exploit both available wireless interfaces simultaneously, we pass additional interface information to the socket API to bind each interface to an IP address and packets can thus be scheduled to a desired interface. Moreover, we configure an independent routing table for each interface so that when a source IP address is specified, instead of using the default interface and gateway, the desired interface and gateway are used. Since video players can access YouTube videos through Google's Data APIs [13], MSPlayer is developed to leverage source and path diversity in the network for YouTube video streaming by interacting with Google APIs.[2]

First, when the desired video object is chosen, the player contacts the web proxy server with the URL containing the 11-literal video ID. The web proxy server then authenticates the user (player type and/or the user account) with `OAuth 2.0` and verifies the video operations requested by the user [13]. When the requested operations are granted, the web proxy server resolves the user's public IP address and check to see which video server is suitable and available to this user based on YouTube's server selection mechanism [3]. Afterwards, the web proxy server generates an access token (valid for an hour) that matches the video server's IP address as well as the operations requested.

The web proxy server then encodes the token, together with the user's public IP address and the video's information (i.e., available video formats and quality, title, author, file size, video server domain names, ... , etc) in JavaScript Object Notation (JSON) format and returns these objects to the user through the requested interface. MSPlayer then decodes the JSON objects received on each interface and synthesizes a new URL (with the required information, video server address, and a valid token) to contact the corresponding video server in the associated network. Video content is then retrieved by making HTTP range requests to different video servers with *persistent connections* through both interfaces. Note that YouTube has been gradually replacing insecure HTTP connections with secure ones. To be compatible to the current and future YouTube's data service, we follow YouTube's latest HTTPS connection policy with both web proxy servers and video servers.

As part of the *just-in-time* video delivery principle, MSPlayer uses the following streaming strategy similar to commercial YouTube players such as Adobe Flash player or HTML5: a pre-buffering phase followed by a steady-state re-buffering phase [23]. MSPlayer leaves the pre-buffering phase when more than 40-second video data is received. It then consumes the video data until the playout buffer contains less than 10-second video. MSPlayer resumes requesting chunks from both YouTube servers and refills the playout buffer until 20 seconds of video data are retrieved.

[2]As YouTube's client libraries are mostly in web languages, MSPlayer, however is programmed in python rather than JavaScript or PHP.

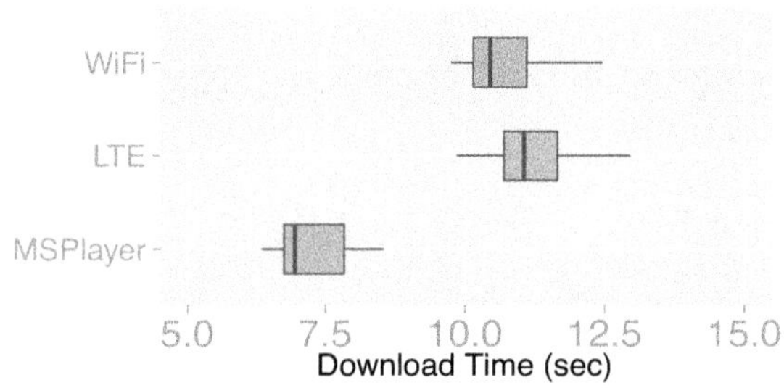

Figure 2: Comparison of MSPlayer with WiFi and LTE for 40-sec pre-buffering (emulated).

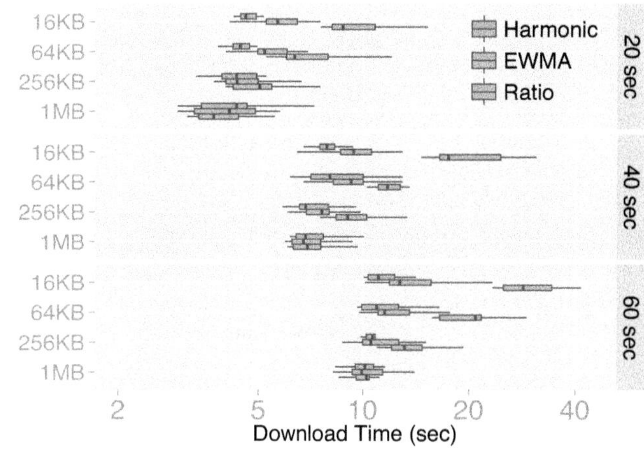

Figure 3: Download times of three schedulers: Harmonic/EWMA/Ratio (top to down order) for different pre-buffering periods (right Y-axis) and initial unit chunk sizes (left Y-axis).

5. TESTBED EXPERIMENTATION

We first evaluate the performance of each design component of MSPlayer on a testbed in a controlled environment that emulates YouTube's video streaming mechanisms. The final performance evaluation is carried out on the YouTube infrastructure and service (see Sec. 6). Two types of servers are emulated in our testbed: web proxy servers (responsible for authentication and video object information delivery) and video servers. Both types of servers use the standard Linux 3.5 kernel with `CUBIC` congestion control [12] with Apache service. Each type of server is hosted in two different UMass subnets for source diversity.

The client running MSPlayer for video streaming is a Lenovo X220 laptop equipped with a built-in 802.11 a/b/g/n WiFi interface connecting to a home WiFi network and an LTE dongle connecting to one of the major US cellular carriers. Video requests are sent over both interfaces simultaneously to two different YouTube video web proxy servers. Upon receiving packets from the web server, MSPlayer decodes the associated JSON objects (with a pre-loaded video server's IP address in our testbed) and fetches video chunks from the video servers. In our testbed, the videos are predownloaded in the servers from YouTube with MP4 format of HD (720p) video quality and 44,100 Hz audio quality.

5.1 Multi-Source and Multi-Path

Fig. 2 demonstrates the initial video pre-buffering download time using single-path WiFi, single-path LTE, and MSPlayer for HD videos in our emulated testbed. Note that a 40-sec pre-buffering period is presented here as this is YouTube servers' default pre-buffering size for Flash videos [23]. The median download time of MSPlayer is 6.9 seconds while that of the best single-path over WiFi is 10.9 seconds, a 37% delay time reduction in the pre-buffering phase.

As MSPlayer leverages multiple video sources and interfaces/paths, how packets are scheduled through each path to each server can significantly affect the performance. The MSPlayer results in Fig. 2 are based on the Ratio scheduler with initial chunk size 1 MB. Next, we will investigate different MSPlayer schedulers and evaluate their performance.

5.2 Chunk Scheduler

We examine the performance of the following three schedulers: *Harmonic*, *EWMA*, and *Ratio* (the baseline). We first examine the download time for different pre-buffering durations (for 20/40/60 seconds). For each pre-buffering duration, we further inspect each scheduler's performance with respect to different initial chunk sizes (from 16 KB to 1 MB). Throughout the experiments, we randomize the order in which the configurations are tested and repeat this 20 times over the course of 12 hours. Note that the throughput variation parameter $\delta = 5\%$ and the *EWMA* weight $\alpha = 0.9$.

As shown in Fig. 3, for each pre-buffering duration, download time decreases as chunk size increases. For small chunk sizes, MSPlayer requires more range requests to accumulate the same amount of video in the pre-buffering phase. For larger chunk sizes, fewer requests are made and less overhead is included in the download time.

The baseline scheduler does not perform well and exhibits higher variability as it fails to respond to bandwidth changes quickly. Dynamic chunk size adjustment schedulers (*EWMA* and *Harmonic*), on the other hand, vary path chunk sizes according to estimated bandwidth and exhibit better performance. More specifically, the scheduler using the harmonic mean estimator outperforms the others in most cases as this estimator is designed to mitigate large outliers such as large bursts. In our experiments, we use harmonic mean estimator as the default estimator in our scheduler. Since the performance of the harmonic mean scheduler is similar for chunk sizes 256 KB and 1 MB, we use a default initial chunk size of 256 KB as smaller chunk sizes are preferable to reduce network bursts [12].

6. EVALUATION ON YOUTUBE SERVICE

We evaluate MSPlayer performance over the YouTube video infrastructure by comparing the download time of MSPlayer and the streaming schemes of the commercial YouTube players in both the *pre-buffering phase* and the *re-buffering phase*. We first look at the pre-buffering phase (where commercial players accumulate video data of a specified amount as one large chunk) and check to see how MSPlayer can reduce the start-up latency. Fig. 4 shows that MSPlayer outperforms both single-path TCP over WiFi and LTE for different specified amounts of pre-buffered video data. In comparison to the best single-path technology used, MSPlayer reduces start-up delay by 12%, 21%, 28% for 20, 40, 60 second pre-buffering durations, respectively.

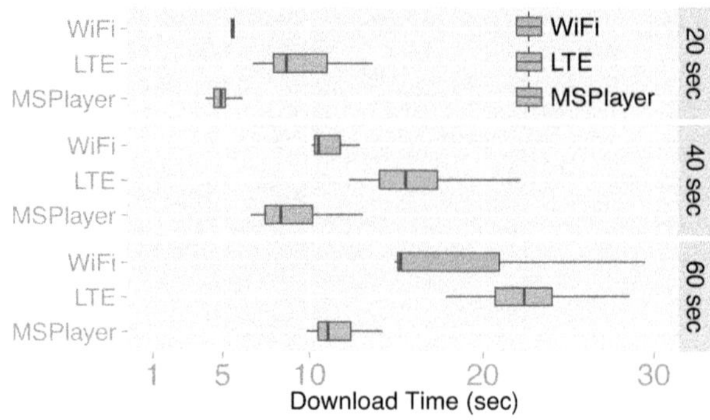

Figure 4: Pre-buffering 20/40/60 second video for single-path WiFi, LTE, and MSPlayer on YouTube.

When MSPlayer enters the periodic re-buffering phase, we investigate how quickly it refills the playout buffer and compare its performance to that of other commercial players with HTTP range requests using default chunk sizes of 64 KB (Adobe Flash) and of 256 KB (HTML5) over single path WiFi and LTE [23]. Similarly, we also look at different re-buffering sizes for 20/40/60 seconds.

Fig. 5 presents the performance when streaming YouTube videos over single-path WiFi/LTE with HTTP byte ranges of sizes 64 KB and 256 KB for different re-buffering sizes. All of the players refill the playout buffer quickly when using larger chunks. This is because more requests are required for smaller chunks and introduces more overhead. MSPlayer, on the other hand, efficiently estimates network bandwidth and adjusts the chunk size accordingly. It outperforms all the single-path schemes and can significantly reduce the time to refill the playout buffer.

Table 1: Fraction of Traffic over WiFi (mean ±std)

	Pre-buffering	Re-buffering
20 sec	64·1±9.3%	61·8±7.1%
40 sec	60·1±15.0%	61·7±11.5%
60 sec	63·7±12.6%	56·5±11.6%

In order to understand how the MSPlayer chunk scheduler distributes traffic over paths, we investigate the fraction of traffic carried by each path. Table 1 lists the fraction of traffic carried by WiFi for both pre-buffering and re-buffering phases with initial chunk size 256 KB. We observe that the WiFi path on average carries more than 60% of traffic in the pre-buffering phase. This is mainly due to the fact that our design allows the fast path to start fetching video chunks as soon as it decodes necessary information from YouTube's web proxy server (as discussed in Sec. 3.2). In our experiments, the RTTs of the LTE network are two to three times larger than those of the WiFi network, and hence the WiFi path starts the streaming process earlier than the LTE path.

During the re-buffering phase, the WiFi path slightly dominates packet delivery. This is because each path needs to wait for one RTT before receiving the first packet from the associated video source for each range request. As WiFi exhibits much smaller RTT values in our experiments, the WiFi path saves a time of length $R_2 - R_1$ for each range request and introduces less overhead when compared with the LTE path in the re-buffering phase.

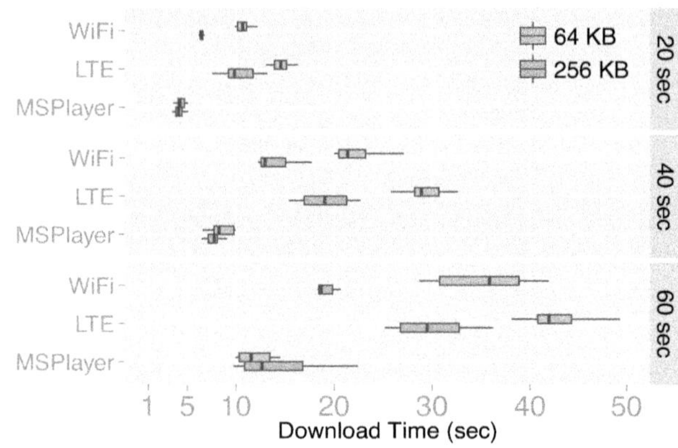

Figure 5: Re-buffering 20/40/60 second video with HTTP byte range of sizes 64/256 KB for single-path WiFi, LTE, and MSPlayer over YouTube service.

7. CONCLUSION AND FUTURE WORK

We propose a client-based video streaming solution, MSPlayer, that streams videos from multiple YouTube video servers via two interfaces (WiFi and LTE) simultaneously. MSPlayer manages to reduce video start-up delay and can quickly refill the video playout buffer for just-in-time high quality video delivery. It does not require kernel modifications at either the server or the client side. Moreover, it provides robust data transport and does not suffer from middleboxes in the networks as does MPTCP. Due to space constraint, we do not report the results on how MSPlayer provides robustness for video delivery in mobile scenarios.

As for future work, our scheduler currently does not take into account energy constraints when leveraging multiple interfaces on mobile devices [17]. Also, we use a simple periodic downloading mechanism for playout re-buffering. A more careful investigation of periodic downloading and ON/OFF mechanisms will be explored. Last, as we have taken an initial step to demonstrate the possibility of leveraging multiple video sources with different interfaces/paths in a real video service network, we only focus on using a constant video bit-rate. As dynamic adaptive streaming over HTTP (DASH) [24] is now widely used, exploring how rate adaption can be integrated with MSPlayer and how MSPlayer can be used for other streaming services are also our future works.

Acknowledgements

We are grateful to the anonymous reviewers and our shepherd, Anirban Mahanti, for their valuable comments and suggestions. This research was partially sponsored by US Army Research Laboratory and the UK Ministry of Defense under Agreement Number W911NF-06-3-0001. This material is also based upon work supported by the National Science Foundation under Grant No. CNS-1040781.

8. REFERENCES

[1] V. K. Adhikari, Y. Guo, F. Hao, M. Varvello, V. Hilt, M. Steiner, and Z.-L. Zhang. Unreeling netflix: Understanding and improving multi-cdn movie delivery. In *IEEE INFOCOM*, 2012.

[2] V. K. Adhikari, S. Jain, Y. Chen, and Z.-L. Zhang. Vivisecting youtube: An active measurement study. In *IEEE INFOCOM*, 2012.

[3] V. K. Adhikari, S. Jain, and Z.-L. Zhang. Where do you" tube"? uncovering youtube server selection strategy. In *IEEE International Conference Computer Communications and Networks (ICCCN)*, 2011.

[4] Adobe HTTP dynamic streaming. www.adobe.com/products/hds-dynamic-streaming.html.

[5] S. Akhshabi, L. Anantakrishnan, A. C. Begen, and C. Dovrolis. What happens when http adaptive streaming players compete for bandwidth? In *ACM NOSSDAV*, 2012.

[6] S. Akhshabi, A. C. Begen, and C. Dovrolis. An experimental evaluation of rate-adaptation algorithms in adaptive streaming over http. In *ACM Multimedia Systems*, 2011.

[7] D. H. Bui, K. Lee, S. Oh, I. Shin, H. Shin, H. Woo, and D. Ban. Greenbag: Energy-efficient bandwidth aggregation for real-time streaming in heterogeneous mobile wireless networks. In *IEEE Real-Time Systems Symposium (RTSS)*, 2013.

[8] Y.-C. Chen, Y.-s. Lim, R. J. Gibbens, E. M. Nahum, R. Khalili, and D. Towsley. A measurement-based study of multipath TCP performance over wireless networks. In *ACM IMC*, 2013.

[9] F. Dobrian, V. Sekar, A. Awan, I. Stoica, D. Joseph, A. Ganjam, J. Zhan, and H. Zhang. Understanding the impact of video quality on user engagement. *ACM SIGCOMM Computer Communication Review*, 41(4):362–373, 2011.

[10] A. Finamore, M. Mellia, M. M. Munafò, R. Torres, and S. G. Rao. Youtube everywhere: Impact of device and infrastructure synergies on user experience. In *ACM IMC*, 2011.

[11] A. Ford, C. Raiciu, M. Handley, and O. Bonaventure. RFC 6824: TCP Extensions for Multipath Operation with Multiple Addresses.

[12] M. Ghobadi, Y. Cheng, A. Jain, and M. Mathis. Trickle: Rate limiting youtube video streaming. In *USENIX ATC*, 2012.

[13] Google APIs Client Library. https://developers.google.com/api-client-library/.

[14] S. Gouache, G. Bichot, A. Bsila, and C. Howson. Distributed & adaptive http streaming. In *IEEE International Conference on Multimedia and Expo (ICME)*, 2011.

[15] B. Hesmans, F. Duchene, C. Paasch, G. Detal, and O. Bonaventure. Are TCP extensions middlebox-proof? In *ACM SIGCOMM workshop on Hot topics in middleboxes and network function virtualization*, 2013.

[16] M. Honda, Y. Nishida, C. Raiciu, A. Greenhalgh, M. Handley, and H. Tokuda. Is it still possible to extend TCP? In *ACM IMC*, 2011.

[17] J. Huang, F. Qian, Y. Guo, Y. Zhou, Q. Xu, Z. M. Mao, S. Sen, and O. Spatscheck. An in-depth study of lte: Effect of network protocol and application behavior on performance. In *ACM SIGCOMM*, 2013.

[18] T.-Y. Huang, N. Handigol, B. Heller, N. McKeown, and R. Johari. Confused, timid, and unstable: picking a video streaming rate is hard. In *ACM IMC*, 2012.

[19] J. Jiang, V. Sekar, and H. Zhang. Improving fairness, efficiency, and stability in http-based adaptive video streaming with festive. In *ACM CoNEXT*, 2012.

[20] S. S. Krishnan and R. K. Sitaraman. Video stream quality impacts viewer behavior: inferring causality using quasi-experimental designs. In *ACM IMC*, 2012.

[21] R. K. Mok, X. Luo, E. W. Chan, and R. K. Chang. Qdash: a qoe-aware dash system. In *ACM Multimedia Systems*, 2012.

[22] C. Raiciu, C. Paasch, S. Barre, A. Ford, M. Honda, F. Duchene, O. Bonaventure, and M. Handley. How hard can it be? Designing and implementing a deployable multipath TCP. In *USENIX NSDI*, 2012.

[23] A. Rao, A. Legout, Y.-s. Lim, D. Towsley, C. Barakat, and W. Dabbous. Network characteristics of video streaming traffic. In *ACM CoNEXT*, 2011.

[24] T. Stockhammer. Dynamic adaptive streaming over http–: standards and design principles. In *ACM Multimedia Systems*, 2011.

Deep Packet Inspection as a Service

Anat Bremler-Barr
School of Computer Science
The Interdisciplinary Center
Herzliya, Israel
bremler@idc.ac.il

Yotam Harchol
School of Computer Science and Engineering
The Hebrew University
Jerusalem, Israel
yotamhc@cs.huji.ac.il

David Hay
School of Computer Science and Engineering
The Hebrew University
Jerusalem, Israel
dhay@cs.huji.ac.il

Yaron Koral
School of Computer Science and Engineering
The Hebrew University
Jerusalem, Israel
ykoral@princeton.edu

ABSTRACT

Middleboxes play a major role in contemporary networks, as forwarding packets is often not enough to meet operator demands, and other functionalities (such as security, QoS/QoE provisioning, and load balancing) are required. Traffic is usually routed through a sequence of such middleboxes, which either reside across the network or in a single, consolidated location. Although middleboxes provide a vast range of different capabilities, there are components that are shared among many of them.

A task common to almost all middleboxes that deal with L7 protocols is Deep Packet Inspection (DPI). Today, traffic is inspected from scratch by all the middleboxes on its route. In this paper, we propose to treat DPI as a service to the middleboxes, implying that traffic should be scanned only once, but against the data of all middleboxes that use the service. The DPI service then passes the scan results to the appropriate middleboxes. Having DPI as a service has significant advantages in performance, scalability, robustness, and as a catalyst for innovation in the middlebox domain. Moreover, technologies and solutions for current Software Defined Networks (SDN) (e.g., SIMPLE [41]) make it feasible to implement such a service and route traffic to and from its instances.

1. INTRODUCTION

Inspired by current suggestions for *Network Function Virtualization (NFV)* and the flexible routing capabilities of *Software Defined Networks (SDN)*, this paper calls for finding common tasks among middleboxes and offering these tasks as services.

Specifically, we focus on *Deep Packet Inspection (DPI)*, where the payload of packets is inspected against a set of patterns. DPI is a common task in many middleboxes. A partial list is shown in Table 1. In many of these devices, DPI is the most time-consuming task and it may take most of the middlebox processing time.[1] Thus, great effort was invested over the years in optimizing it.

CoNEXT'14, December 02-05, 2014, Sydney, Australia.

http://dx.doi.org/10.1145/2674005.2674984.

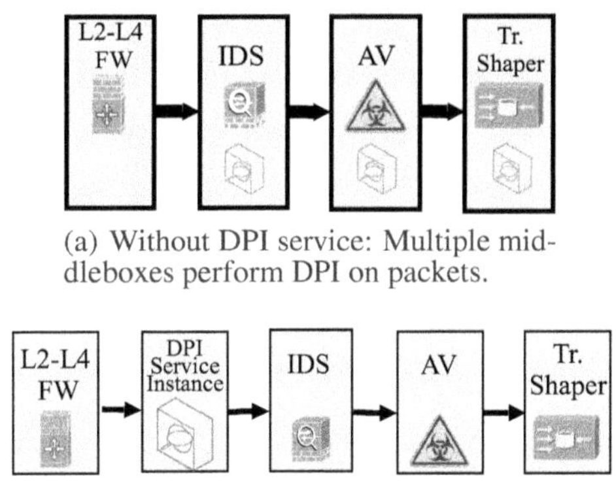

(a) Without DPI service: Multiple middleboxes perform DPI on packets.

(b) With DPI service: Packets go through DPI once.

Figure 1: Examples of the chain of middleboxes (a.k.a. policy chains [41]) with and without DPI as a service.

As detailed in [41], and referenced therein, traffic nowadays goes through a chain of middleboxes before reaching its destination. This implies that traffic is scanned over and over again by middleboxes with a DPI component [39] (see Figure 1(a)). Alternatively, an opposite trend is to consolidate middleboxes in a single location (or even a hardware device) [4,45]. However, the different components of this consolidated middlebox perform DPI separately, from scratch.

Our proposed framework extracts the DPI engine from the different middleboxes and provides it as a service for various middleboxes in the network. This service is provided by deploying one or more *service instances* around the network, all controlled by a logically-centralized *DPI Controller*. Thus, a packet in such network would go through a single DPI service instance and then

[1]In an experiment we conducted on Snort IDS [48], DPI slows packet processing by a factor of at least 2.9.

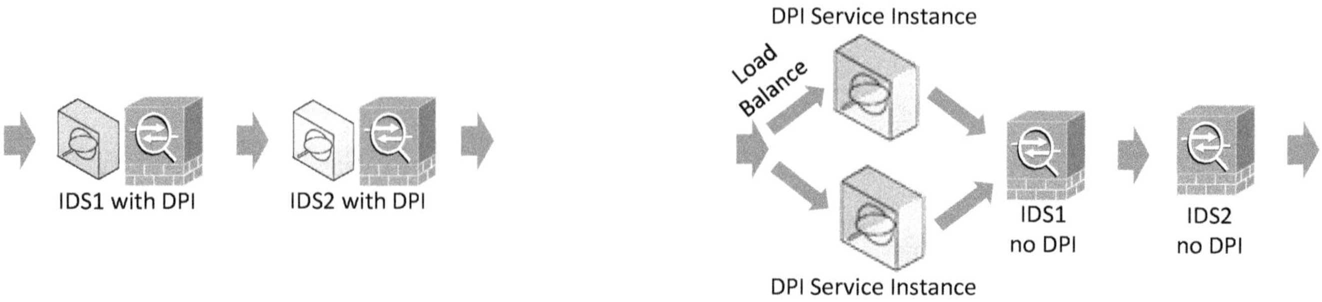

(a) Without a DPI Service (b) With a DPI Service

Figure 2: Pipelined middlebox scenario. With DPI Service, resources are used for running multiple instances of the service while middleboxes do not have to re-scan the packets.

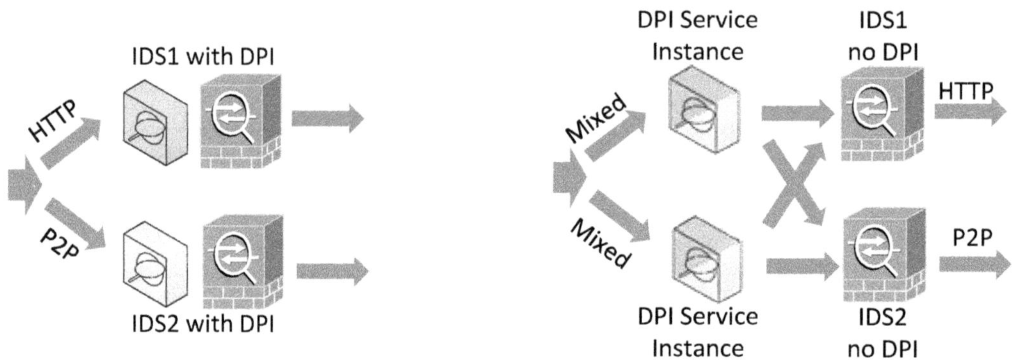

(a) Without a DPI Service (b) With a DPI Service

Figure 3: An example of multiple service chains scenario. With DPI Service, flows are multiplexed to multiple DPI Service instances. This allows dynamic load balancing on the DPI engines without adding middleboxes.

Middlebox	DPI patterns	Examples
Intrusion Detection System	Malicious activity	SNORT [48], BRO [10]
AntiVirus/SPAM	Malicious activity	ClamAV [12]
L7 Firewall	Malicious activity	Linux L7-filter, ModSecurity [34]
L7 Load Balancing	Apps/URLs	F5 [37], A10 [35]
Leakage Prevention System	Leakage activity	Check Point DLP [11]
Network Analytic	Protocol IDs	Qosmos [13]
Traffic Shaper	Applications	Blue Coat PacketShapper [8]

Table 1: DPI in different types of middleboxes.

visit middleboxes according to its policy chain.[2] Its payload would not have to be scanned again as the results of the scan are provided along with the original packet (or instead without the original packet if the latter is not needed anymore).[3] Upon receiving the results from the DPI Service, each middlebox applies the rules corresponding to the matched patterns according to its internal logic. Figures 2 and 3 show two configurations for using DPI as a service. We elaborate on these scenarios and provide their corresponding experimental results in Section 6.4.

It is important to note that while fields in a packet header might be modified along the path of the packet, the payload is usually not changed, and thus, the DPI service may be used even in policy chains that contain NATs and other middleboxes that modify header fields.

Our approach is shown to provide superior performance and also reduces the memory footprint of the DPI engine data-structures. The framework also allows dynamic resource sharing as the hardware used for DPI is decoupled from the specific middlebox, as shown in Section 6.4. Since DPI is performed once, the effect of decompression or decryption, which usually takes place prior to the DPI phase, may be reduced significantly, as these heavy processes are executed only once for each packet.

[2] We assume that patterns are either not proprietary or can be disclosed to our service over a secure channel.

[3] Section 4.2 discusses this mechanism in detail.

We believe that having DPI and other shared functionalities as network services also creates necessary room for innovation in the middlebox domain, which is usually closed and proprietary. For example, when consolidating DPI to a single piece of software, one might find it beneficial to implement more advanced DPI functionalities, such as decryption and decompression, or use special hardware accelerators.

Moreover, as a central component, security devices, and specifically their DPI engines, are a preferred target for denial-of-service attacks [50]. Recent works show that DPI components within the NIDS (such as Snort [48] and Bro [10]) expose the entire system to attacks that may knock down the device [1]. Having DPI as a service is especially appealing in this case, since a developer is now focused on strengthening the DPI only at a single implementation, rather than tailoring the security solution for each middlebox that uses DPI. Furthermore, as most DPI solutions nowadays use software, one can easily deploy more and more instances of the DPI to servers across the network, and thus mitigate attacks and unintentional failures.

Our contribution in this paper is two-fold. First, we detail a framework in which DPI is deployed as a service, including an algorithm that combines DPI patterns from different sources. Second, we implemented in Mininet over OpenFlow an SDN system that enables deploying DPI as a service. This includes both the DPI service itself and the control components required for the service to work correctly. We show via experiments that our framework provides performance improvements of 67% and more.

This paper is organized as follows: In Section 2 we discuss related work. Section 3 provides the necessary background on middlebox design and DPI. Our proposed system overview is described in Section 4, and algorithmic aspects of how to perform DPI simultaneously for multiple middleboxes are discussed in Section 5. Experimental results are presented in Section 6. Finally, we conclude in Section 7.

2. RELATED WORK

2.1 Middlebox Design

Over the last few years, much effort was invested in redesigning middlebox architecture. In this section, we go over some new directions in this field, highlight the deficiencies they intended to solve, and compare them with our work.

Forwarding traffic through policy chains: In traditional networks, middleboxes are placed at strategic places along the traffic path, determined by the network topology; traffic goes through the middleboxes as dictated by the regular routing mechanism. SDN makes it possible to perform *traffic steering*, where routing through a chain of middleboxes is determined using middlebox-specific routing considerations that might differ significantly from traditional routing schemes. Our paper uses this flexibility, as was shown in [41], to route traffic to a DPI service when needed.

Virtualizing network functionalities: Recently, telecommunication vendors launched the *Network Functions Virtualization (NFV)* initiative [16] that aims to virtualize network appliances at the operator. The main objective of NFV is to reduce the operational costs of these appliances (which are traditionally implemented in middleboxes) by obtaining the same functionality in software that runs on commodity servers. NFV provides easier management and maintenance by eliminating the need to deal with multiple hardware types and vendors; moreover, as NFV is implemented in software, it promotes innovation in this domain. DPI is a significant example of an appliance or functionality that may be virtualized [16].

There are several pioneer works on middlebox virtualization. Rajagopalan et al. [44] present a mechanism to place a middlebox, such as the Bro NIDS, in a virtual environment, where the VM might migrate between different machines. Gember et al. [23] deal with standardization of unified control to middleboxes, inspired by the SDN paradigm. Nevertheless, virtualizing middleboxes raises several issues that should be carefully dealt with, such as efficient fault tolerance [26], availability [43], and management [22]. Our work mostly addresses algorithmic aspects of virtualized DPI, which are orthogonal to these works.

Middlebox consolidation and programmability: A different approach to tackle the problem raised by managing multiple middleboxes is to offer a consolidated solution [4,14,25,45] consisting of a single hardware, possibly programmable, that consolidates multiple logical middleboxes. DPI as a service may complement such consolidated architectures to improve the overall performance, either by extracting the DPI engine from these boxes to a virtual service, or by using our algorithm to merge multiple DPI engines and utilize shared hardware better. Note that in such a case, several parts of our framework (such as message passing and routing between middleboxes) may be eliminated.

Outsourcing middlebox functionality: To reduce the high equipment and operating costs of middleboxes, several works proposed outsourcing middlebox functionalities [24,47] as a service [17] provided by an entity outside the network. Note that our suggestion is that the DPI, as a critical building block, will be a service for the middleboxes but would be placed in the same network.

2.2 Deep Packet Inspection

The classical algorithms for exact multiple string matching used for DPI are those of Aho-Corasick [2] and Wu-Manber [51]. For regular expression matching, two common solutions are using Deterministic Finite Automata (DFA) or Nondeterministic Finite Automata (NFA) [6,28]. Efficient regular expression matching is still an active area of research [7,19,28,29,52].

There is extensive research on accelerating the DPI process, both in hardware [5, 15, 33] and in software [19, 28]. Most software-based solutions [19,28] accelerate the DPI process by optimizing its underlying data structure (namely, its DFA). To the best of our knowledge, no specific design for accelerating DPI in a virtual, consolidated, or NFV environment has been proposed. The only exception is an industrial product of QOSMOS [13], which specializes in protocol classification and does not deal with the general DPI problem. Moreover, no details are disclosed on its implementation. DPI optimization and acceleration are orthogonal to this work, as they may be applied as a part of the DPI service, for further acceleration. Multicore optimization may also benefit from having DPI as a service, as instead of splitting the work between cores, it may be split among instances running over different machines.

We are not aware of any work directly performed on combining the data of several middleboxes' DPI to a single service. However, a similar concept was studied in the context of virtual IP-lookup, where trie-based data structures are considered [21, 31, 49]. This research is not applicable to DPI as the underlying algorithms are significantly different.

3. BACKGROUND

DPI lies at the core of many middlebox applications (see Table 1), and is based on *pattern matching*, in which the payload of the packet is compared against a predetermined set of *patterns* (with either strings or regular expressions).

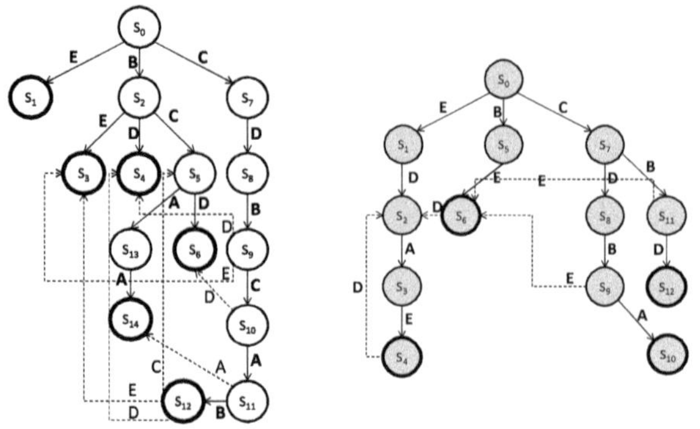

Figure 4: The Aho-Corasick Automata corresponding to the pattern sets $\{E,BE,BD,BCD,BCAA,CDBCAB\}$ and $\{EDAE,BE,CDBA,CBD\}$. Solid edges are forward transitions while dashed edges are other transitions. Non-forward transitions to DFA depths 0 and 1 are omitted for brevity.

String matching is an essential building block of most contemporary DPI engines. In many implementations (such as Snort [48] and our own implementation, discussed in Section 5), even if most patterns are regular expressions, string matching is performed first (namely, as a pre-filter) and constitutes most of the work performed by the engine. Specifically, Snort extracts the strings that appeared in the regular expressions (called anchors). Then, string matching is performed over these anchors, and if all anchors originating from a specific regular expression are matched, then a regular expression matching of the corresponding expression is performed (e.g., using PCRE [38]).

This is a common procedure since regular expression engines work inefficiently on a large number of expressions. The aforementioned DFA solutions suffer from memory explosion especially when combining a few expressions into a single data structure, while the NFA solutions suffer from lower performance due to multiple active state computation for each state transition. Efficient regular expression matching is still an active area of research. Any future novel regular expression matching algorithm may easily be incorporated into our system.

The Aho-Corasick (AC) algorithm [2] is the de-facto standard for contemporary network intrusion detection systems (NIDS). It matches multiple strings simultaneously by first constructing a DFA that represents the pattern set (also known as signature set); then, with this DFA at its disposal, the algorithm scans the text in a single pass.

The DFA construction is done in two phases. First, a tree of the strings is built, where strings are added one by one from the root as chains (each node in the tree corresponds to a DFA state). When patterns share a common prefix, they also share the corresponding set of states in the tree. The edges of the first phase are called *forward transitions*. In the second phase, additional edges deal with situations where, given an input symbol b and a state s, there is no forward transition from s using b. Let the *label* of a state s, denoted by $L(s)$, be the concatenation of symbols along the path (of forward transition) from the root to s. Furthermore, let the depth of a state s be the length of the label $L(s)$. The transition from s given symbol b is to a state s', whose label $L(s')$ is the longest suffix of $L(s)b$ among all other DFA states. For example, Figure 4 depicts two DFAs that were constructed for pattern sets $\{E,BE,BD,BCD,BCAA,CDBCAB\}$ and $\{EDAE,BE,CDBA,CBD\}$.

The DFA is traversed starting from the root. Traversing to an *accepting state* indicates that some patterns are a suffix of the input; one of these patterns always corresponds to the label of the accepting state.

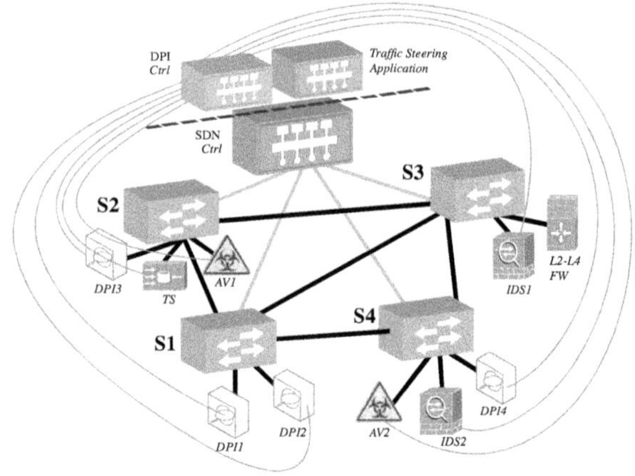

	Policy Chain	Middlebox Chain	Physical Sequence
1.	L2L4_FW-DPI-IDS	L2L4_FW-DPI3-IDS1	S1 S3 **L2L4_FW** S3 S2 **DPI3** S2 S3 **IDS1** S3 S4
2.	DPI-IDS-AV-TS	DPI3-IDS2-AV1-TS	S1 S2 **DPI3** S2 S4 **IDS2** S4 S2 **AV1** S2 **TS** S2 S4

Figure 5: System Illustration. The DPI controller abstracts the DPI process to other network elements and controls DPI service instances across the network. Packets flow through the network as dictated by policy chains.

4. SYSTEM OVERVIEW

This section details the underlying architecture that supports DPI as a service. The main idea is to insert the DPI service in the middlebox chain prior to any middlebox that requires DPI. The DPI service scans the packet and logs all detected patterns as meta-data to the packet. As the packet is forwarded, each middlebox on its route retrieves the DPI scan results instead of performing the costly DPI task. We assume an SDN environment with a *Traffic Steering Application (TSA)* (e.g., SIMPLE [41]) that attaches policy chains to packets and routes the packets appropriately across the network. Naturally, our solution will negotiate with the TSA, so that policy chains are changed to include DPI as a service (see Figure 1).

4.1 The DPI Controller

DPI service scalability is important since DPI is considered a bottleneck for many types of middleboxes. Therefore, we envision that DPI service instances will be deployed across the network. The *DPI controller* is a logically centralized entity whose role is to manage the DPI process across the network and to communicate both with the SDN controller and the TSA to realize the appropriate data plane actions. Logically, the DPI controller resides at the SDN application layer on top of the SDN controller as in Figure 5.

Two kinds of procedures take place between the DPI Controller and the middleboxes, namely: registration and pattern set management. The first task of the DPI controller is to register middleboxes that use its service. Communication between the DPI Controller and middleboxes is performed using JSON messages sent over a direct (possibly secure) communication channel. Specifically, a middlebox registers itself to the DPI service using a registration message . The DPI Controller address and the middlebox's unique ID and name are preconfigured (we have not deployed any bootstrap procedures at the current stage). A middlebox may inherit the pattern set of an already registered middlebox. A middlebox may state that the DPI service it requires should maintain their state across the packet boundaries of a flow, or that it operates in a read-only mode, in which it performs no actions at the packet itself and it therefore requires receiving only pattern matching results and may avoid unnecessary routing of the packet itself. An IDS is an example of a read-only middlebox as opposed to an IPS, which performs actions over the packets.

Abstractly, middleboxes operate by *rules* that contain *actions*, and *conditions* that should be satisfied to activate the actions. Some of the conditions are based on *patterns* in the packet's content. The DPI service responsibility is only to indicate appearances of *patterns*, while resolving the logic behind a condition and performing the action itself is the middlebox's responsibility. Patterns are added to and removed from the DPI controller using dedicated messages from middleboxes to the controller. The DPI Controller maintains a global pattern set with its own internal IDs. If two middleboxes register the same pattern (since each one of them has a rule that depends on this pattern), it keeps track of each of the rule IDs reported by each middlebox and associates them with its internal ID. For that reason, when a pattern removal request is received, the DPI Controller removes the middlebox reference to the corresponding pattern. Only if there are no other middleboxes referrals to that pattern, is it removed.

One concern is the traffic incurred by transmitting the pattern sets. However, as opposed to DPI DFAs, which are large, the pattern sets themselves are compact: Recent versions of pattern sets such as Bro or L7-Filter are 12KB and 14KB, respectively. Larger pattern sets such as Snort or ClamAV are 2MB and 5MB, respectively. Still, if the patterns are compressed, their size is no more than two megabytes (55KB and 2MB, respectively). The construction of the data structure that represents the patterns is the responsibility of the DPI instance, and therefore does not involve communication over the network.

The DPI controller also receives from the TSA the relevant policy chains (namely, all the sequences of middlebox types a packet should traverse). It assigns each policy chain a unique identifier that is used later by the DPI service instances to indicate which pattern matching should be performed. Usually, the TSA pushes some VLAN or MPLS tag in front of the packet to easily steer it over the network ([41]). DPI service instances can then read these tags in order to identify the set of patterns a packet should be matched against. In case this tag is not available, the DPI controller can push such a tag, for example using an OpenFlow directive.

Finally, the DPI controller is also responsible for initializing DPI service instances (see Section 5.1), deployment of different DPI service instances across the network (see Section 4.3), and advance features that require a network-wide view (e.g., as described in Section 4.3.1).

4.2 Passing Pattern Matching Results

Passing the pattern matches results to the middleboxes should take into account the following three considerations: First, it should be oblivious to the switches and not interfere with forwarding the packet through the chain of middleboxes and then to its destination. Second, the meta-data is of a variable size as the number of matches varies and is not known in advance. Third, the process should be oblivious to the middleboxes (and hosts) that are not aware of the DPI service. Having these considerations in mind, we suggest three solutions that may suit different network conditions:

- Adding match result information as an additional layer of information prior to the packet's payload. This allows maximal flexibility and the best performance. Publicly available frameworks such as Network Service Header (NSH) [42] and Cisco's vPath [46] may be used to encapsulate match data, also in an SDN setting [27]. Several commercial vendors support this method in service chain scenarios (e.g. Qosmos [13]). The downside of this approach is that middleboxes that refer to the payload on the service chain should be aware of this additional layer of information. However, if all middleboxes that use the DPI service are grouped and placed right after the DPI service instance in the service chain, the last middlebox can simply remove this layer and forward the original packet.

- An option that does not require reordering of service chains relies on using some flexible pushing and pulling of tags (e.g., MPLS labels, VLAN tags, PBB tags). This method is supported in current OpenFlow-based SDN networks [20]. A similar alternative is to use the FlowTags mechanism [18]. The downside of the tagging option is that it might be messy as each matching result may require several such tags, which in turn must not collide with other tags used in the system.

- When middleboxes on the service chain are all in *read-only* mode, where the middlebox requires only the DPI results rather than the packet itself, it may be appealing to send only the match results using a dedicated packet without the packet itself. As most packets do not contain matches at all, this option may dramatically reduce traffic load over the middlebox service chain. For example, in Big Switch Networks' Big Tap [36] fabric, the traffic is tapped from production networks to a separate monitoring network, where monitoring is done while the original packet is forwarded at the production network regardless of the monitoring results.

In all three options one may use a single bit in the header to mark whether patterns were matched. Specifically, a packet with no matches is always forwarded as is without any modification.

As our experimental environment is based on Mininet over OpenFlow 1.0, which supports neither NSH nor MPLS, in our implementation we passed the matching results using dedicated packets.

4.3 Deployment of DPI Service Instances

The DPI controller abstracts the DPI service for the TSA, SDN controller, and the middleboxes. Hence, one of its most important tasks is to deploy the DPI instances across the network. There might be many considerations for such deployment and in this section we discuss only a few.

First, we emphasize that not all DPI instances need to be the same. Thus, a common deployment choice is to group together similar policy chains and to deploy instances that support only one group and not all the policy chains in the system. The DPI controller will then instruct the TSA to send the traffic to the right instance. Alternatively, one might group the middlebox types by the traffic they inspect. For example, sets of patterns that correspond to HTTP traffic may be allocated to some DPI service instances, while a set of patterns that corresponds to FTP is allocated to other DPI service instances.

Additionally, the DPI controller should manage the DPI instance resources, so that an instance is not overwhelmed by traffic, and therefore, performs poorly. Thus, the DPI controller should collect performance metrics from the working DPI instances and may decide to allocate more instances, to remove service instances, or to migrate flows between instances. This should be done exactly in the same manner as suggested in [44]. Notice that, in general, performing operations on the DPI service instances rather than the middleboxes themselves is easier as most of the flow's state is typically kept within the middlebox, while the DPI instance keeps only the current DFA state and an offset within the packet.[4] Finally, we note that allocation, de-allocation, and migration affect the way packets are forwarded in the network. Thus, the DPI controller should collaborate with the TSA (and the SDN controller) to realize the changes and take into account other network considerations (such as bandwidth and delay).

The ability to dynamically control the DPI service instances and to scale out provides the DPI controller great flexibility, which can be used for powerful operations. Section 4.3.1 shows how this ability is used to enhance the robustness of the DPI service and its performance.

4.3.1 Enhancing Robustness and Security

DPI engines, as a core building block of many security appliances, are known to be the target of attacks [1, 32]. A recently-suggested architecture, called MCA^2 [1], mitigates such attacks by deploying several copies of DPI engines over multiple cores of the same machine. The key operation of MCA^2 is to detect and isolate the *heavy* packets that cause the degraded performance, and divert them to a dedicated set of cores. Moreover, the dedicated cores may run a different AC implementation (other than the full-table AC described in Section 3) that is more suitable for handling this kind of traffic (see [1, 9] for more details).

MCA^2 can be implemented as-is in each DPI service instance, provided it runs on a multi-core machine. In addition, our architecture may implement MCA^2, while scaling out to many DPI service instances. As in the original MCA^2 design, each DPI service instance should perform ongoing monitoring and export telemetries that might indicate attack attempts. In the MCA^2 design, these telemetries are sent to a central *stress monitor* entity. Here, the *DPI controller*, described in Section 4.1, takes over this role. This is illustrated in Figure 6: Under normal traffic, all DPI service instances work regularly. Whenever the *DPI controller* detects an attack on one of the instances, it sets some of the instances as 'dedicated', and *migrates* the heavy flows, which are suspected to be malicious, to those dedicated DPI instances (these instances might also use a different DPI algorithm that is tailored for heavy traffic). Flow migration is performed as described in Section 4.3, and requires close cooperation with the traffic steering application. Moreover, dedicated DPI instances can be dynamically allocated as an attack becomes more intense, or deallocated as its significance decreases.

5. DPI SERVICE INSTANCE IMPLEMENTATION

This section describes the implementation of a DPI service instance. At the core of the implementation, we present a *virtual DPI algorithm* that handles multiple pattern sets. We first focus on *string matching* and then extend it to handle *regular expressions*.

5.1 Initialization

We first show how to combine multiple pattern sets, originating

[4]Notice that flow migration might require some packet buffering at the source instance, until the process is completed.

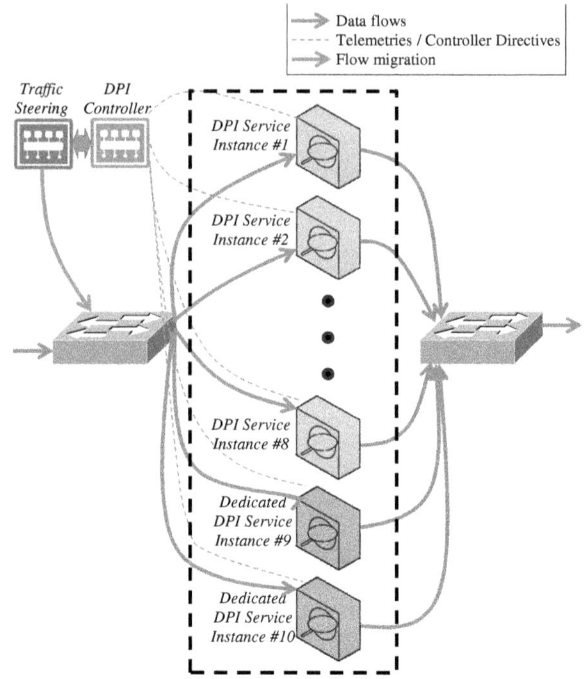

Figure 6: MCA^2 system design for virtual DPI environment.

from different middleboxes such that each packet is scanned only once.

Each middlebox type has a unique identifier and it registers its own pattern set with the DPI controller (see details in Section 4). As the DPI controller is a logically-centralized entity that allocates the identifiers, we may assume identifiers are sequential numbers in $\{1,\ldots,n\}$, where n is the number of middlebox types registered to the DPI service. Let P_i be the pattern set of middlebox type i.

Upon instantiation, the DPI controller passes to the DPI instance the pattern sets and the corresponding middlebox identifiers. Along with these sets, the DPI controller may pass additional information, such as a stopping condition for each middlebox (namely, how deep into L7 payload the DPI instance should look[5]), or whether the middlebox is stateless (scans each packet separately) or stateful (considers the entire flow, and therefore, should carry the state of the scan between successive packets). Moreover, the DPI controller passes the mapping between policy chain identifiers and the corresponding middlebox identifiers in the chain.

Our simple algorithm works in two steps. First, we construct the AC automaton as if the pattern set was $\bigcup_i P_i$. Note that the number of accepting states in the resulting DFA, denoted by f, is $|\bigcup_i P_i|$, as there is an accepting state for each pattern, no matter whether it originates in one or more middlebox. Further note that the state identifier in the DFA is meaningless; we use this degree of freedom and map the identifiers of the accepting states to the range $\{0,\ldots,f\}$; this will make the resolution stage for matched patterns more efficient in terms of time and space.

The second step is to determine, for each accepting state, which middleboxes have registered the pattern and what the identifier of the pattern is within the middlebox pattern set. This is done by storing a pre-computed direct-access array `match` of f entries such

[5]The stopping condition is useful, for example, when middleboxes only care about specific application-layer headers with a fixed or bounded length.

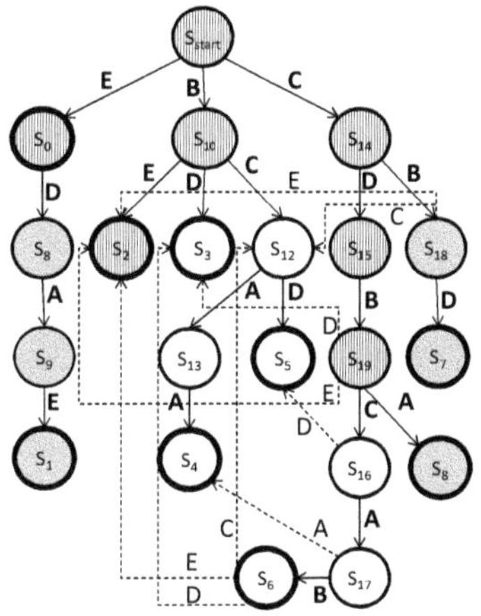

match table

0	$\langle 0, E \rangle$
1	$\langle 0, E \rangle, \langle 1, EDAE \rangle$
2	$\langle 0, E \rangle, \langle 0, BE \rangle, \langle 1, BE \rangle$
3	$\langle 0, BD \rangle$
4	$\langle 0, BEAA \rangle$
5	$\langle 0, BCD \rangle$
6	$\langle 0, CDBCAB \rangle$
7	$\langle 0, BD \rangle, \langle 1, CBD \rangle$
8	$\langle 1, CDBA \rangle$

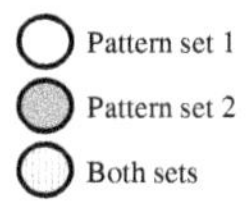

Figure 7: The DFA and `match` table for $P_0 = \{E, BE, BD, BCD, BCAA, CDBCAB\}$ and $P_1 = \{EDAE, BE, CDBA, CBD\}$ (as in Figure 4). States common to both sets are marked in gray. White accepting states are marked with bitmap 10, gray accepting states with bitmap 01, and striped accepting states with bitmap 11. Non-forward transitions to s_{start}, s_0, s_9, and s_{13} are omitted for brevity.

that its ith entry holds the information corresponding to the pattern of accepting state i, as a sorted list of ⟨middlebox id, pattern id⟩ pairs. It is important to note that if we have a pattern i (e.g., DEF) that is a suffix of another pattern j (e.g., ABCDEF), we should add all the pairs corresponding to pattern i also to the jth entry.

Furthermore, traditional DFA implementations mark accepting state using one bit; when n is relatively small, it is beneficial to mark the accepting state by a bitmap of the middlebox identifiers in its corresponding list; in such a case, a simple bitwise-AND operation can indicate if we need to check the table at all, or may continue scanning the packets, since the matching pattern is not relevant to the packet. In our implementation, it is also possible to check whether the state ID is less than a predefined constant whose value is the number of accepting states in the automaton.

An example of the resulting DFA and the `match` table is depicted in Figure 7.

We also store in a separate table the mapping between a policy chain identifier and the corresponding middlebox identifiers. Another table holds the mapping between a middlebox identifier and its properties (namely, its stopping condition and whether it is stateless or stateful). Finally, if at least one of the middleboxes is stateful, we will initialize an empty data structure of active flows,[6] which will hold the state and offset of scans done on that flow up until now.

5.2 Packet Inspection

Packets should be compared with several (but, in general, not all) pattern sets. The relevant identifiers for pattern set selection are marked at the packet header (as explained in Section 4.1), and the DPI service uses them to determine which pattern sets apply to each packet. Hence, upon packet arrival, the DPI service first resolves (using the mapping saved in the initialization phase) what the relevant middlebox identifiers are (we shall call them the *active* middleboxes for the packet). Moreover, the stopping condition for the packet is determined as the most conservative condition among all active middleboxes and an empty match-list for each active middlebox is initialized, as well as a global counter variable `cnt` (which counts the number of bytes scanned so far). When n is sufficiently small, a bitmap of size n is constructed such that the ith bit is set if and only if middlebox i is active.

Finally, if the packet is part of a flow that has already been scanned, its DFA state is restored. The offset of the packet within the flow is stored in another variable, called `offset` (in case of stateless scan, `offset=0`).

Then, the packet is scanned against the combined DFA, while maintaining the value of `cnt`. When reaching an accepting state j, the bitmap of the packet is compared against the bitmap stored at the state; if a match is found then all pattern identifiers corresponding to active middleboxes in `match[j]` are added to the corresponding match-lists, along with the value of `cnt`. In the end of the scan, irrelevant matches are deleted from the match-lists: For stateful active middleboxes, a match is deleted if the value of `cnt+offset` exceeds the stopping condition of the specific middlebox. For stateless middleboxes, in which the packet scan should have started at s_{start} but instead started at the restored state for the stateful middleboxes, we delete patterns whose length is smaller than their value of `cnt`, [7] as well as patterns whose stopping condition is smaller than the value of `cnt`.

After the packet scan is finished, the match-lists are sent to the corresponding active middleboxes as described in Section 4; along with the pattern identifier, we pass the value of either `cnt` (for stateless middleboxes) or `cnt+offset` (for stateful middleboxes). If at least one active middlebox is stateful, the state of the DFA in the end of the scan is recorded and `offset` is incremented by `cnt`.

5.3 Dealing with Regular Expressions

As explained in Section 3, we take an approach similar to the one implemented in Snort NIDS and use a string matching process as pre-filtering for regular expression matching. Specifically, for each regular expression, we first extract sufficiently long strings (which we call *anchors*) from each regular expression. These anchors must be matched for the entire regular expression to be matched. Short strings of length less than 4 characters are not extracted. For example, in the regular expression "`regular\s*expression\s*\d+`", the anchors "`regular`" and "`expression`" are extracted. We add the anchors extracted from the regular expressions of middlebox i to pattern set P_i. In addition, we hold a mapping between the regular expression and its anchors. The packet is scanned as before (with the DFA obtained by the new pattern set). Upon completion, we check if there are regular expressions of an active middlebox for which all anchors were found. If there are, an off-the-shelf regular expression engine (e.g., PCRE [38]) is invoked on these regular expressions (one by one). Otherwise, no further operation is needed. Note that ideally, if a regular expression can be matched by only relying on its anchors, it is recommended to add it as an exact string matching rule rather than as a regular expression. In Snort, for example, 57% of the rules are regular expression rules, 99.7% of which invoke PCRE only if all of its underlying anchors were matched. The remaining 0.3% rules could have been written as exact string matching rules at the first place.

Finally, we note that sometimes there are middleboxes whose regular expressions contain almost no anchors (or, alternatively, very short anchors). In such a case, we use a regular expression

[6] The set of active flows is maintained in the same manner as for stateful middleboxes today, and is outside the scope of this paper.

[7] This implies that the pattern has started in the previous packet, and therefore should be ignored in a stateless DPI

matching algorithm (e.g., as suggested in [28] and references therein), and run it in parallel to our string matching algorithm.

6. EXPERIMENTAL RESULTS

In this section we evaluate the feasibility and performance of our virtual DPI algorithm.

6.1 Implementation

We implemented a complete system with a simple controller and tested it inside a Mininet [30] virtual machine. The code is available at `https://github.com/DeepnessLab/moly`. Our basic experimental topology includes two user hosts, two middlebox hosts, and a DPI service instance host that can utilize multiple cores. All hosts are connected through a single switch and the TSA, implemented as a POX [40] module, steering traffic from one user host to the other according to the defined policy chains.

Our experimental DPI service instance receives match rules in JSON format and builds an AC DFA as described in Section 5. If a packet matches one or more rules, the DPI service instance marks it so that middleboxes will know it has matches (we use the IP ECN field for this purpose) and constructs a result packet that is sent right after the marked data packet.

We decided to send match information in our experiments as a separate packet since POX only implements OpenFlow version 1.0, which does not support the other methods suggested in Section 4.2. We also find it easier to debug and trace.

In addition, we implemented a sample virtual middlebox application that receives traffic from the DPI service instance and if necessary, buffers packets until their corresponding results or data packet arrives. This sample implementation only counts the total number of rules that were reported to it.

We compare our design to a system where middleboxes perform DPI and counting of rules (and possibly much more). To do so, we also implement an application that does both and use it as a baseline for comparison.

In the URL above we also provide a prototype implementation for a Snort 2.9.6.2 plugin that parses DPI Service results instead of scanning the packets using Snort's traditional pattern matching engines. The plugin itself requires less than 100 lines of code and in order to use it, *only six lines of code were added* to existing Snort code files, in addition to our plugin files. A similar plugin can be written for other software middleboxes with the appropriate adaptations for the internals of each middlebox's DPI module.

6.2 Experimental Environment

Experiments were performed on a machine with Intel Sandybridge Core i7 2600 CPU, quad-core, each core having two hardware threads, 32 KB L1 data cache (per core), 256 KB L2 cache (per core), and 8 MB L3 cache (shared among cores). The system runs Linux Ubuntu 11.10, on which we run one or more instances of a Linux Ubuntu virtual machine using VMWare Player. We use exact-match patterns of length eight characters or more from Snort [48] (up to 4,356 patterns) and Clam-AV [12] (31,827 patterns). As input traffic we used two traces: a campus wireless network tapped trace of about 9GB, and a 170MB HTTP traffic trace crawled from most popular websites [3][8]. Our code provided comparable results on both traces and thus, unless specifically noted, results shown are of the second trace.

Note that we did not use Mininet for performance testing as it incurs major overheads and we found the variance between results to be too high. We verified our solution in Mininet and then tested each component by feeding it with the appropriate traffic and measuring its performance.

[8]This trace contains various website data such as HTML, JavaScript, images, etc. In some cases we repeated the trace to create a longer experiment.

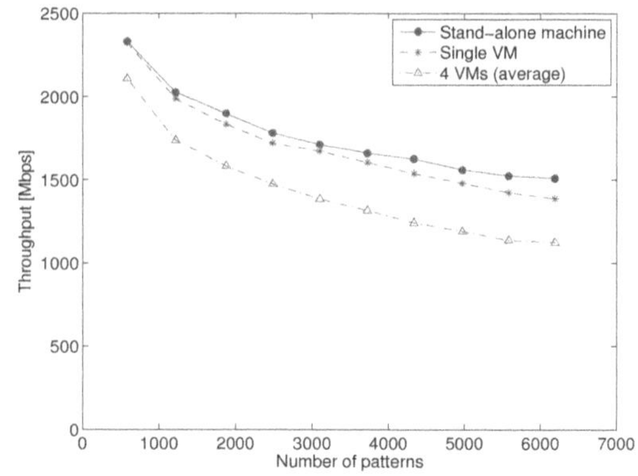

Figure 8: The effect of virtualization and number of patterns on the throughput of the AC algorithm.

Sets	Patterns	Space	Throughput
Snort1	2169	36.73 MB	981 Mbps
Snort2	2187	37.69 MB	931 Mbps
Snort1+Snort2	**4356**	**71.18 MB**	**768 Mbps**

Table 2: Comparing the performance of two middleboxes, one running on pattern sets of *Snort1* and the other on pattern sets of *Snort2*, to one virtual DPI instance with the combined pattern sets of *Snort1* and *Snort2*.

6.3 Virtual DPI Performance

As a first step, we evaluate the impact of the virtualization environment on DPI in order to ensure that DPI is suitable to run as a VM. This test is done on the original AC algorithm (and not our virtual DPI algorithm). We run three different scenarios: first, when the DPI runs on a stand-alone machine; second, when the DPI runs on a VM while the other cores are idle; third, when four instances of the DPI are running, each of them on a separate VM that uses a separate core (such that they occupy all cores of the machine), and throughput is calculated as the average throughput of the four cores. The tests were done for different numbers of patterns. Figure 8 shows that virtualization has a minor impact on DFA throughput. The number of patterns has a major impact. From here on, we will focus on running our virtual DPI algorithm as an instance, where the instance runs on a VM in all our experiments.

In addition to the virtual DPI instance, we always have one or more instances of a virtual middlebox application that receives the results from the DPI instances, counts and reports them. In our experiments, these applications operate much faster than the virtual DPI instances and thus are not a bottleneck in the system. For this reason, the overhead of buffering and reordering packets in these applications do not impose significant delays or any throughput degradation.

6.4 Comparison to Different Middlebox Configurations

Next, we check and evaluate the benefit of our algorithm. In order to evaluate the savings of our mechanism, we took the patterns of Snort and randomly divided them into two sets, *Snort1*

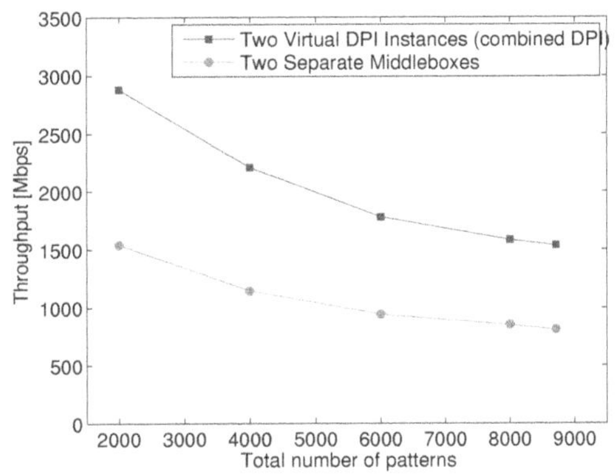

(a) *Snort1* and *Snort2*

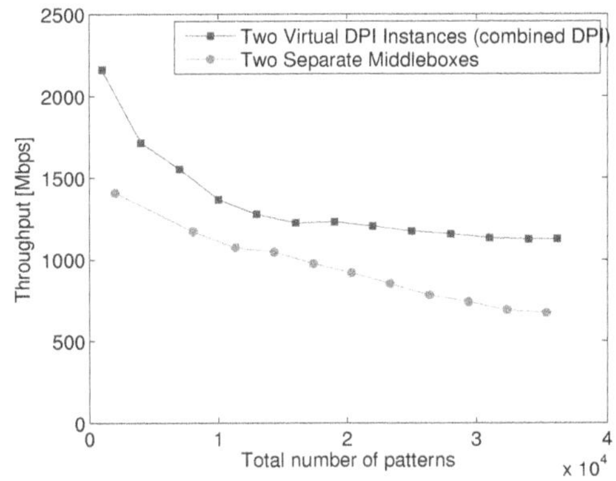

(b) Full Snort and ClamAV

Figure 9: Comparing the throughput that can be handled by two pipelined middleboxes, and by our Virtual DPI.

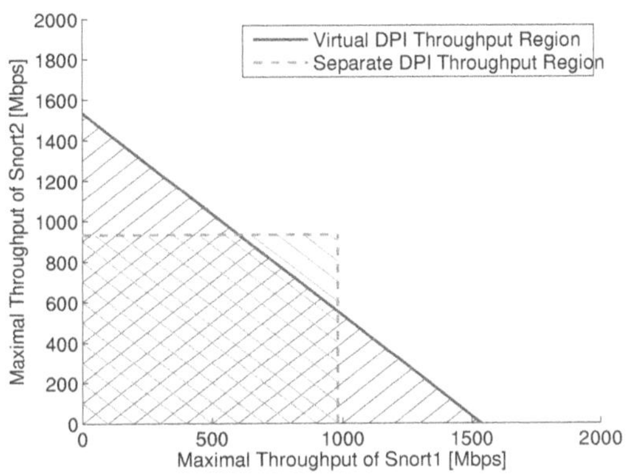

(a) *Snort1* and *Snort2*

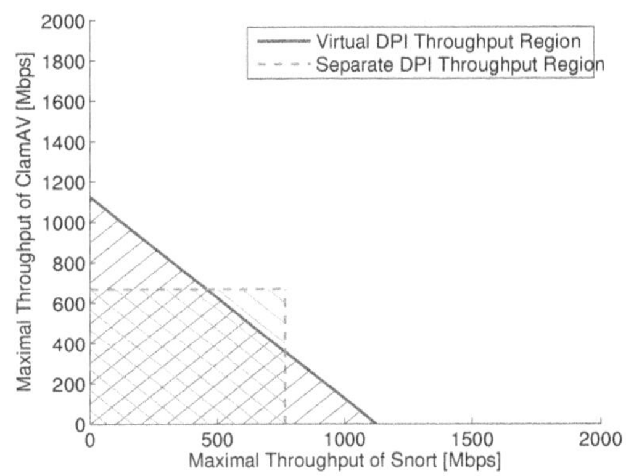

(b) Full Snort and ClamAV

Figure 10: Actual achievable throughput for two separate middleboxes that handle different traffic (see red, dashed rectangle), compared to the theoretical achievable throughput of our combined instances of virtual DPI (see blue, solid triangle).

and *Snort2*, simulating a configuration where we have two stand-alone middleboxes, *Snort1* and *Snort2*. Table 2 shows the space requirement and throughput of each of the middleboxes when using a regular DPI process, compared with a single virtual DPI that runs the DPI for the combined set of patterns *Snort1* and *Snort2*. The throughput of the combined machine is just 12% less than that of each separate machine. As we previously showed, this is mainly due to the impact of the number of patterns.

To understand the gain from the virtual DPI, we simulate two scenarios: in the first scenario, shown in Figure 2, traffic should go through a pipeline of two middleboxes, one with pattern set *A* and the other with pattern set *B* (for example, *Snort1* and *Snort2*, or full Snort and ClamAV). In the second scenario, shown in Figure 3 there are two service chains, for example for two types of traffic: one should be handled by a middlebox with pattern set *A* and the other by a middlebox with pattern set *B*. In both cases we compare the naïve solution of two instances, where each instance runs the DPI with different sets of patterns (*A* or *B*), to the case of using two instances of our virtual DPI solution.

Figure 9 shows the throughput in the first scenario and compares it to a setup of two virtual DPI instances that run on both machines simultaneously, where the load is equally distributed between them. It is clear that our virtual DPI solution is at least 86% faster in the first case, and *more than 67% faster* in the second case.

Figure 10 evaluates the savings in the second scenario. The dashed rectangle is the actual achieved throughput region of traffic that the naïve DPI solution can handle, given that each pattern set is handled by a single middlebox. The triangle is the theoretical achievable throughput region that our virtual DPI solution can handle, given that both machines run our virtual DPI, based on the actual achieved throughput in our experiments.

Consider two such middleboxes as appear in Figure 10(a). The motivation to use virtual DPI in this scenario is that most of the time not all middleboxes handle full load, and thus combined virtual DPI machines could make use of free resources from one middlebox to provide higher capacity for another middlebox. This can be seen in the figure as the areas inside the triangle but outside the rectangle. For example, in Figure 10(b), if Snort is under-utilized and Clam-AV faces high load, Clam-AV could actually exceed 100% of its original capacity without adding more resources (see blue triangular area above the red rectangle), and the same is true for the opposite situation where Clam-AV is under-utilized and Snort is over-utilized.

Since the DPI is now a service, additional throughput can be gained by deploying additional virtual DPI instances. This can be

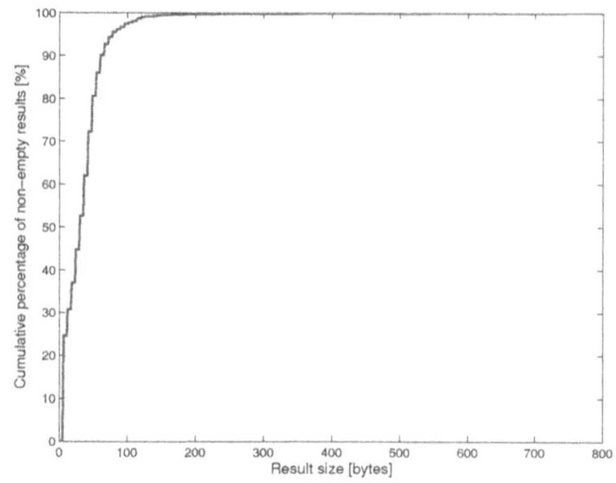

Figure 11: Cumulative distribution of non-empty match report size per packet.

done dynamically as it only requires starting another virtual machine and steering some of the traffic to it. Moreover, DPI service instances can be quickly migrated to specific points in the network to handle transient loads in specific areas.

6.5 Analysis of Match Report Size

A single match can be reported with up to 4 bytes. Occasionally, when a pattern consists of the same character one or more times, and this character appears in a packet multiple times sequentially, multiple matches of the same pattern (or set of patterns) should be reported. For these cases we also allow reporting ranges of matches, with a given starting position and length. Such ranges can be reported with up to 6 bytes.

Figure 11 shows the cumulative distribution of non-empty match reports in the campus network trace, when using 6 bytes per match report (to allow faster encoding and decoding of both regular and range reports). Note that in both traces we used, more than 90% of the packets have no matches, but the figure refers only to packets that do have matches. The average report size is 34 bytes, while most of the packets are smaller than that, and only 1% of the reports are above 120 bytes.

7. CONCLUSIONS

Middleboxes and monitoring tools have been known as closed, expensive and hard-to-manage boxes, though very widely deployed in all kinds of networks due to their important roles.

Virtualization, NFV, and SDN promise a revolution in the way middleboxes and monitoring tools are designed and managed. Many monitoring applications share a wide range of common tasks. We believe that these tasks should be provided as services, managed by a logically-centralized control, to allow enhanced performance, lower costs, flexible and scalable design, and easy innovation for monitoring applications.

This paper focuses on Deep Packet Inspection, which is one of the heaviest tasks of contemporary middleboxes. We design a framework for making DPI a service: each packet that requires a DPI by any of the middleboxes on its policy chain is forwarded to the DPI service, where it is inspected only once. Then, the inspection results (namely, the patterns that were matched) are communicated to the corresponding middleboxes, either on the same packet (e.g., using NSH) or on a different packet. Our framework relies heavily on virtualization and therefore includes both a *virtual* DPI service, which is instantiated across the network, and a DPI controller, whose role is to orchestrate the different DPI service instances. Making DPI a service has implications not only for the architecture and the system design of a middlebox that uses DPI, but also for the algorithmic aspects of the DPI engine (which is implemented by the virtual DPI service) itself. Specifically, this work presents one such tailor-made algorithm that benefits from the flexibility of a virtual environment.

Finally, we provide an SDN implementation for our framework and experiments to show that these ideas are realized into performance improvements and much more flexible and scalable design. In future work, we plan to investigate the possibility of also turning other common tasks, such as flow tagging and session reconstruction, into services.

Acknowledgements

This work was supported by the European Research Council under the European Union's Seventh Framework Programme (FP7/2007-2013)/ERC Grant agreement no 259085, and by the Chief Scientist Office of the Israeli Ministry of Industry, Trade and Labor within the "Neptune" consortium.

8. REFERENCES

[1] Yehuda Afek, Anat Bremler-Barr, Yotam Harchol, David Hay, and Yaron Koral. MCA^2: multi-core architecture for mitigating complexity attacks. In *ANCS*, pages 235–246, 2012.

[2] Alfred V. Aho and Margaret J. Corasick. Efficient string matching: An aid to bibliographic search. *Commun. of the ACM*, 18(6):333–340, 1975.

[3] Alexa: The web information company, 2013. http://www.alexa.com/topsites.

[4] James W. Anderson, Ryan Braud, Rishi Kapoor, George Porter, and Amin Vahdat. xOMB: extensible open middleboxes with commodity servers. In *ANCS*, pages 49–60, 2012.

[5] Zachary K. Baker and Viktor K. Prasanna. Time and area efficient pattern matching on FPGAs. In *FPGA*, pages 223–232, 2004.

[6] Michela Becchi and Patrick Crowley. A hybrid finite automaton for practical deep packet inspection. In *CoNEXT*, page 1, 2007.

[7] Michela Becchi and Patrick Crowley. An improved algorithm to accelerate regular expression evaluation. In *ANCS*, pages 145–154, 2007.

[8] Blue coat packet shapper. http://www.bluecoat.com/products/packetshaper.

[9] Anat Bremler-Barr, Yotam Harchol, and David Hay. Space-time tradeoffs in software-based deep packet inspection. In *HPSR*, pages 1–8, 2011.

[10] The Bro Network Security Monitor. http://bro-ids.org.

[11] CheckPoint. Check Point DLP software blade. http://www.checkpoint.com/products/dlp-software-blade/.

[12] Clam AntiVirus. http://www.clamav.net.

[13] Intel Corp. Service-aware network architecture based on SDN, NFV, and network intelligence, 2014. http://www.qosmos.com/wp-content/uploads/2014/01/Intel_Qosmos_SDN_NFV_329290-002US-secured.pdf.

[14] Crossbeam. Virtualized security: The next generation of consolidation, 2012. http://www.computerlinks.ch/FMS/14322.virtualized_security_en_.pdf.

[15] Sarang Dharmapurikar, John Lockwood, and Member Ieee. Fast and scalable pattern matching for network intrusion detection systems. *IEEE Journal on Selected Areas in Communications*, 24:2006, 2006.

[16] ETSI. Network functions virtualisation - introductory white paper, 2012. `http://portal.etsi.org/NFV/NFV_White_Paper.pdf`.

[17] Seyed Kaveh Fayazbakhsh, Michael K Reiter, and Vyas Sekar. Verifiable network function outsourcing: requirements, challenges, and roadmap. In *HotMiddlebox*, pages 25–30, 2013.

[18] Seyed Kaveh Fayazbakhsh, Vyas Sekar, Minlan Yu, and Jeffrey C. Mogul. FlowTags: enforcing network-wide policies in the presence of dynamic middlebox actions. In *HotSDN*, pages 19–24, 2013.

[19] Domenico Ficara, Stefano Giordano, Gregorio Procissi, Fabio Vitucci, Gianni Antichi, and Andrea Di Pietro. An improved DFA for fast regular expression matching. *Computer Communication Review*, 38(5):29–40, 2008.

[20] Open Networking Foundation. Openflow switch specification version 1.4.0, October 2013. `https://www.opennetworking.org/images/stories/downloads/sdn-resources/onf-specifications/openflow/openflow-spec-v1.4.0.pdf`.

[21] Jing Fu and Jennifer Rexford. Efficient IP-address lookup with a shared forwarding table for multiple virtual routers. In *CoNEXT*, page 21, 2008.

[22] Aaron Gember, Anand Krishnamurthy, Saul St. John, Robert Grandl, Xiaoyang Gao, Ashok Anand, Theophilus Benson, Aditya Akella, and Vyas Sekar. Stratos: A network-aware orchestration layer for middleboxes in the cloud. *CoRR*, abs/1305.0209, 2013.

[23] Aaron Gember, Prathmesh Prabhu, Zainab Ghadiyali, and Aditya Akella. Toward software-defined middlebox networking. In *HotNets*, pages 7–12, 2012.

[24] Glen Gibb, Hongyi Zeng, and Nick Mckeown. Outsourcing network functionality. In *HotSDN*, pages 73–78, 2012.

[25] Lukas Kekely, Viktor Pus, and Jan Korenek. Software defined monitoring of application protocols. In *INFOCOM*, pages 1725–1733, 2014.

[26] Junaid Khalid and Josh Slauson. Fault tolerant middleboxes. Technical report, University of Wisconsin - Madison, 2012.

[27] Pritesh Kothari. Network Service Header support for OVS. OVS Code Patch, September 2013. `http://openvswitch.org/pipermail/dev/2013-September/032036.html`.

[28] Sailesh Kumar, Sarang Dharmapurikar, Fang Yu, Patrick Crowley, and Jonathan Turner. Algorithms to accelerate multiple regular expressions matching for deep packet inspection. In *SIGCOMM*, pages 339–350, 2006.

[29] Sailesh Kumar, Jonathan Turner, and John Williams. Advanced algorithms for fast and scalable deep packet inspection. In *ANCS*, pages 81–92, 2006.

[30] Bob Lantz, Brandon Heller, and Nick McKeown. A network in a laptop: Rapid prototyping for software-defined networks. In *Hotnets-IX*, pages 19:1–19:6, 2010.

[31] Hoang Le, Thilan Ganegedara, and Viktor K Prasanna. Memory-efficient and scalable virtual routers using FPGA. In *FPGA*, pages 257–266, 2011.

[32] Wenke Lee, João B. D. Cabrera, Ashley Thomas, Niranjan Balwalli, Sunmeet Saluja, and Yi Zhang. Performance adaptation in real-time intrusion detection systems. In *RAID*, pages 252–273, 2002.

[33] Chad R. Meiners, Jignesh Patel, Eric Norige, Eric Torng, and Alex X. Liu. Fast regular expression matching using small TCAMs for network intrusion detection and prevention systems. In *USENIX Security*, pages 8–8, 2010.

[34] ModSecurity. `http://www.modsecurity.org`.

[35] A10 Networks. aFleX advanced scripting for layer 4-7 traffic management. `http://www.a10networks.com/products/axseries-aflex_advanced_scripting.php`.

[36] Big Switch Networks. Big tap monitoring fabric, 2014. `http://www.bigswitch.com/products/big-tap-monitoring-fabric`.

[37] F5 Networks. Local traffic manager. `https://f5.com/products/modules/local-traffic-manager`.

[38] PCRE - Perl Compatible Regular Expressions. `http://www.pcre.org/`.

[39] Personal communication with several networking and security companies.

[40] Pox controller, 2013. `http://www.noxrepo.org/pox/about-pox`.

[41] Zafar Ayyub Qazi, Cheng-Chun Tu, Luis Chiang, Rui Miao, Vyas Sekar, and Minlan Yu. SIMPLE-fying middlebox policy enforcement using SDN. In *SIGCOMM*, pages 27–38, 2013.

[42] Paul Quinn, Puneet Agarwal, Rajeev Manur, Rex Fernando, Jim Guichard, Surendra Kumar, Abhishek Chauhan, Michael Smith, Navindra Yadav, and Brad McConnell. Network service header. IETF Internet-Draft, February 2014. `https://datatracker.ietf.org/doc/draft-quinn-sfc-nsh`.

[43] Shriram Rajagopalan, Dan Williams, and Hani Jamjoom. Pico replication: a high availability framework for middleboxes. In *SoCC*, pages 1:1–1:15, 2013.

[44] Shriram Rajagopalan, Dan Williams, Hani Jamjoom, and Andrew Warfield. Split/merge: System support for elastic execution in virtual middleboxes. In *NSDI*, pages 227–240, 2013.

[45] Vyas Sekar, Norbert Egi, Sylvia Ratnasamy, Michael K Reiter, and Guangyu Shi. Design and implementation of a consolidated middlebox architecture. In *NSDI*, pages 24–38, 2012.

[46] Nisarg Shah. Cisco vPath technology enabling best-in-class cloud network services, August 2013. `http://blogs.cisco.com/datacenter/cisco-vpath-technology-enabling-best-in-class-cloud-network-services/`.

[47] Justine Sherry, Shaddi Hasan, Colin Scott, Arvind Krishnamurthy, Sylvia Ratnasamy, and Vyas Sekar. Making middleboxes someone else's problem: network processing as a cloud service. In *SIGCOMM*, pages 13–24, 2012.

[48] Snort. `http://www.snort.org`.

[49] Haoyu Song, Murali Kodialam, Fang Hao, and TV Lakshman. Building scalable virtual routers with trie braiding. In *INFOCOM*, pages 1–9, 2010.

[50] Sony Ericsson Latest Victim of SQL Injection Attack, 2011. `http://www.eweek.com/c/a/Security/Sony-Data-Breach-Was-Camouflaged-by-Anonymous-DDoS-Attack-807651`.

[51] Sun Wu and Udi Manber. A fast algorithm for multi-pattern

searching. Technical report, Chung-Cheng University, University of Arizona, 1994.

[52] Fang Yu, Zhifeng Chen, Yanlei Diao, T. V. Lakshman, and Randy H. Katz. Fast and memory-efficient regular expression matching for deep packet inspection. In *ANCS*, pages 93–102, 2006.

Subsidization Competition: Vitalizing the Neutral Internet

Richard T. B. Ma
National University of Singapore
and Advanced Digital Science Center
tbma@comp.nus.edu.sg

ABSTRACT

Unlike telephone operators, which pay *termination fees* to reach the users of another network, Internet Content Providers (CPs) do not pay the Internet Service Providers (ISPs) of users they reach. While the consequent cross subsidization to CPs has nurtured content innovations at the edge of the Internet, it reduces the investment incentives for the access ISPs to expand capacity. As potential charges for terminating CPs' traffic are criticized under the net neutrality debate, we propose to allow CPs to voluntarily subsidize the usage-based fees induced by their content traffic for end-users. We model the regulated subsidization competition among CPs under a neutral network and show how deregulation of subsidization could increase an access ISP's utilization and revenue, strengthening its investment incentives. Although the competition might reduce the throughput of certain CPs, we find that the main cause comes from high access prices rather than the existence of subsidization. Our results suggest that subsidization competition will increase the competitiveness and welfare of the Internet content market; however, regulators might need to regulate access prices if the access ISP market is not competitive enough. We envision that subsidization competition could become a viable model for the future Internet.

Keywords

Internet Economics; Subsidization Competition; Net Neutrality

1. INTRODUCTION

Driven by bandwidth-intensive video applications and pervasive Internet access via mobile devices, Internet inter-domain traffic has been growing more than 50% per annum [24] and is expected to grow more than 100% per annum for mobile networks [38]. To sustain such rapid traffic growth, Internet Service Providers (ISPs), especially the mobile access ISPs, need to upgrade their network infrastructures and expand capacities. However, revenues from online services are growing more than twice as fast as those from Internet access [38], whose market capitalizations have stagnated as investors weigh high capital requirements against continued margin pressure. This raises serious challenges regarding the viability

CoNEXT '14, December 02 - 05 2014, Sydney, Australia

http://dx.doi.org/10.1145/2674005.2674987.

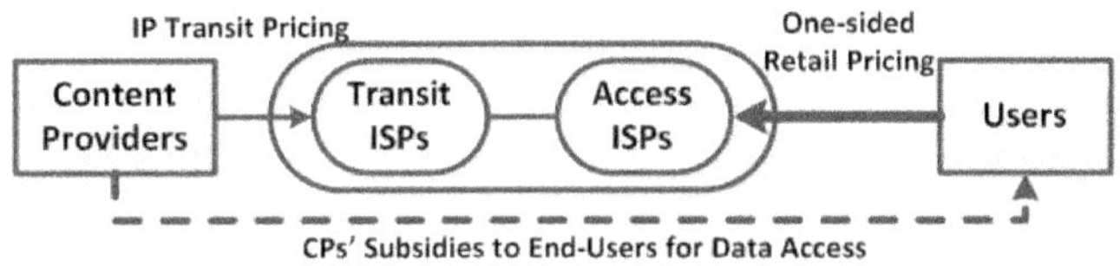

Figure 1: Subsidization in a two-sided Internet market.

of the current Internet model in the future. The fundamental problem lies in the two-sided market structure [8, 41] of the Internet, where the ISPs provide a platform connecting end-users to the Internet Content Providers (CPs). The CP-side transit ISPs are often the backbone ISPs that provide IP transit services. Due to market competition, recent years have witnessed a constant decrease in IP transit prices [36]. The more serious problem lies in the last-mile connections toward the end-users, which are often the bottlenecks of the Internet [13]. For these last-mile access ISPs, including the mobile providers, the main source of revenue is from their end-users. Traditionally, they also need to pay transit ISPs for transit services, although settlement-free peering is common in practice. Existing proposals to resolve this issue include: 1) allowing ISPs to impose termination fees [9] on CPs' traffic towards their end-users, and 2) allowing ISPs to prioritize traffic, differentiate services and thus charge users non-uniformly. However, both proposals have triggered a heated debate over network neutrality [49, 14], whose advocates argue that *zero-pricing* [26] and the neutrality of physical networks are needed to protect and encourage content innovations of the Internet. After all, the limited capacities and rising access costs will dampen user demand, if CPs cannot return the created value to ISPs.

Traditionally, wireline access ISPs charge flat-rate prices and implicitly subsidize CPs for content delivery; however, usage-based pricing is commonly used by wireless providers. The FCC chairman has recently backed usage-based pricing for broadband to penalize heavy Internet users [22, 42] and major U.S. broadband and cable providers, e.g., Verizon [43] and AT&T [47], have adopted tiered schemes where charges are imposed to the metered usage above a predefined data cap. We assume the adoption of usage-based pricing by access ISPs, under which heavy users share the burden of subsidizing CPs. Our goal is to realign the created value and stimulate the needed investment in the Internet value chain and our high-level idea is illustrated in Figure 1, where we propose to allow CPs to voluntarily subsidize the usage-based access costs caused by their content traffic, partially or fully, for the end-users. Our solution modularizes the issue along the tussle boundary such that the physical network is kept neutral while innovative competition among CPs is enabled at higher service layers so as to incentivize ISP investments. As a special case of full subsidization, AT&T's recent *sponsored data* [1] plan will likely be available by the end of 2014. Nevertheless, it raised concerns over anti-competitive practices, and the FCC says that they will be monitoring and prepared to intervene if necessary [34].

To understand and demonstrate the potential impact of subsidization, we take an analytical approach as no market data is available for an empirical study yet. We develop a macroscopic Internet model and study the status quo one-sided pricing of the access ISPs in Section 3. Building upon this framework, we model the policy that regulates subsidization and analyze the competition game among CPs in Section 4. We evaluate the policy implications on the ISP's revenue and system welfare in Section 5 and discuss the regulatory and implementation issues, as well as the limitations of our model in Section 6. Our analytical results include:

- We characterize the impact of capacity, user population (Theorem 1) and one-sided ISP pricing (Theorem 2) on the system utilization and the CPs' throughput.
- We analyze the CPs' subsidization competition game and characterize the Nash equilibrium (Theorem 3), its uniqueness and its dynamics (Theorem 4 and 6).
- We characterize the impact of subsidization policy on the CPs' throughput, user population, and the system's utilization (Theorem 8) and welfare (Corollary 2).

Through our theoretical results and qualitative evaluations, we also identify important policy implications as follows.

- If allowed, profitable CPs tend to subsidize users more (Theorem 5) and achieve higher throughput (Lemma 3), leading to higher system welfare (Corollary 2).
- For fixed ISP pricing, deregulation of subsidization will increase the utilization and revenue of the access ISPs (Corollary 1), strengthening their investment incentives.
- Certain CPs' throughput might decrease due to the ISP's high price (Theorem 8), which could be triggered by the deregulation of subsidization. Thus, access prices might need to be regulated if the access ISP market is not competitive enough.

In short, subsidization provides a feedback channel for the highly profitable CPs to repay their users and indirectly transfer value to the access ISPs. It helps the access ISPs attract investment for capacity expansion while keeping their physical networks neutral. Our results suggest that regulators should promote this subsidization competition; however, they might need to regulate the ISP's pricing if the access market is not competitive enough. We envision that subsidization competition could become a viable model for the future Internet so as to accommodate the growing demand for data traffic.

2. RELATED WORK

A report from A.T. Kearney [38] studied the performance, economic and policy pressures of the Internet and identified four models for the future Internet: 1) modification of retail pricing schemes, 2) traffic-dependent charges, 3) enhanced-quality services over the public Internet, and 4) bilateral service agreements. Subsidization competition is a new regulatory model that preserves the neutrality of the physical networks. We discuss the above existing models and their relationships with our subsidization competition model.

2.1 Modification of Retail Pricing Schemes

Historically, the Internet adopted flat-rate prices [37, 44] for simplicity. Economists [30] and computer scientists [12, 21, 23] advocated usage-based pricing, which was shown to provide congestion control [21], quality of service [23] and economic efficiency [12], and is adopted by mobile providers [32]. Subsidization competition assumes the adoption of usage-based pricing by access ISPs, under which consumers' usage charges could be subsidized by the CPs.

2.2 Imposition of Termination Fees on CPs

One core question under the net neutrality debate [49] is whether ISPs should be allowed to use two-sided pricing and charge CPs for terminating their content traffic. Prior work [10, 33, 35] studied the investment incentives in Internet-like two-sided markets and drew different conclusions. Njoroge et al. [35] found that through CP-side pricing, ISPs could extract higher surplus and maintain higher investment levels. However, Choi et al. [10] found that expending capacity will decrease the CP-side sale price. Musacchio et al. [33] found that although the returns on investment under one-sided or two-sided pricings are comparable, the size of investment and profit depend on the advertising rates and users' price sensitivity. From an economic efficiency point of view, [35] concluded that two-sided pricing results in higher social welfare; however, Lee and Wu [26] argued that the *zero pricing* at the CP-side could be optimal in theory [8, 41]. Also, [10] found that the short-run welfare is higher under one-sided neutral regulation. Our subsidization mechanism does not impose charges on the CPs by the ISPs, but provides an indirect mechanism for them to voluntarily return the *zero-pricing subsidy* back to the ISPs via their end-users.

2.3 Differentiated Services over the Internet

Another core debate under net neutrality is whether ISPs should be allowed to differentiate services and prices. Wu [49] surveyed the discriminatory practices of broadband operators and proposed solutions to manage bandwidth and police ISPs. Sidak [46] focused on consumer utility and argued that differential pricing is essential to maximize utility. Shetty et al. [45] considered a two-class service model and studied capacity planning, regulation, as well as differentiated pricing to consumers. Economides et al. [16] compared various regulations for quality of service and price discrimination, and drew conclusions about desirable regulation regimes. As net neutrality is undergoing heated debate, regulation of desirable differentiation is a rich area for further study. Under our solution, ISPs do not make any physical or economic differentiation and CPs' subsidies are made voluntarily. Subsidization serves as a policy mechanism that encourages competition and provides investment incentives and economic efficiency for the Internet ecosystem.

2.4 Bilateral Settlements for Valued Services

A fundamental cause of investment shortage is the misalignment between the value created and the revenue obtained in the Internet value chain. Clark et al. [11] discussed various economic tussles among the ISPs, CPs and users. Ma et al. [28] advocated the use of the Shapley profit-sharing mechanism for multi-lateral ISP settlements and studied bilateral implementations [29]. Laskowski [25] identified that the network's lack of accountability is an obstacle to implement desirable contracting systems for the Internet. Because accounting of traffic towards the end-users is feasible for access ISPs, our subsidization mechanism can be regarded as a contracting system between the CPs and access ISPs, even through they might not be directly connected to each other. Through the feedback channel from CPs to end-users, subsidization provide a new avenue for the Internet ecosystem to realign the profit distribution among different stakeholders.

3. MACROSCOPIC INTERNET MODEL

To understand the implications of policy on the Internet, we start with a macroscopic model that captures the physical and business dynamics in the status quo Internet among an access ISP, its users and the CPs used by these consumers.

3.1 Basic Physical System Model

We denote μ as the capacity of an access ISP serving the users of a certain geographical region and $\mathcal{N}$ as the set of CPs used by the ISP's consumers. For each CP $i \in \mathcal{N}$, we denote m_i as its user population and define $\theta_i \triangleq m_i\lambda_i$ as its total throughput, where λ_i denotes the CP's average per user throughput. We define $\theta \triangleq \sum_{k\in\mathcal{N}} \theta_k$ as the aggregate system throughput. Under any fixed capacity μ and aggregate throughput θ, we define $\phi \triangleq \Phi(\theta,\mu)$ as the system utilization, a function of θ and μ. We assume the average user throughput is a function of the utilization, i.e., $\lambda_i \triangleq \lambda_i(\phi)$.

Assumption 1. *$\Phi(\theta,\mu)$ and any $\lambda_i(\phi)$ are differentiable. $\Phi(\theta,\mu)$ is strictly decreasing in μ, strictly increasing in θ and satisfies $\lim_{\theta\to 0}\Phi(\theta,\mu) = 0$ for all $\mu > 0$. $\lambda_i(\phi)$ is strictly decreasing in ϕ and satisfies $\lim_{\phi\to\infty}\lambda_i(\phi) = 0$.*

Assumption 1 captures the physics of capacity utilization: utilization increases when the system accommodates higher throughput or has less capacity, and vice-versa. Because the system utilization and congestion are two sides of the same coin (congestion happens when the system is over-utilized), it also captures the physics of user throughput: users achieve higher throughput when the system is less congested.

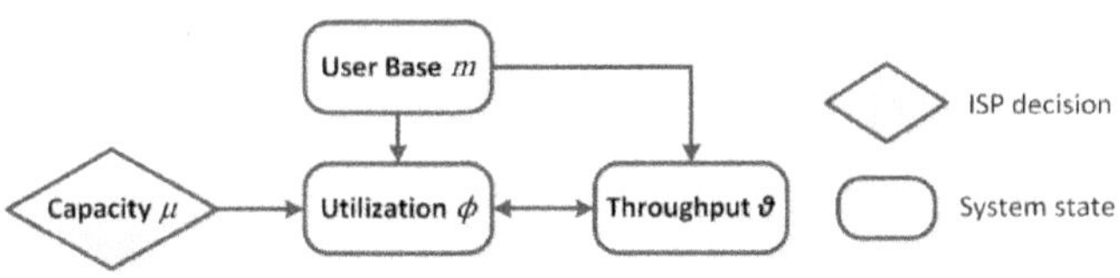

Figure 2: The basic system model $(\mathbf{m},\mu)$.

We denote $\mathbf{m}$ as the vector of user populations of the CPs. Figure 2 illustrates our basic model $(\mathbf{m},\mu)$, where the user populations $\mathbf{m}$ and system capacity μ collectively determine the system utilization ϕ and each CP i's throughput θ_i. Because utilization increases with the accommodated throughput, which decreases with the utilization (congestion), the resulting system utilization should be in an equilibrium.

Definition 1 (UTILIZATION). *ϕ is the utilization of a system $(\mathbf{m},\mu)$ if it satisfies the following condition:*

$$\phi = \Phi\left(\sum_{k\in\mathcal{N}} m_k\lambda_k(\phi), \mu\right). \tag{1}$$

Definition 1 states that the utilization ϕ should induce the aggregate system throughput $\theta = \sum_{k\in\mathcal{N}} m_k\lambda_k(\phi)$ such that it leads to exactly the same level of utilization $\phi = \Phi(\theta,\mu)$.

We define $\Theta(\phi,\mu) \triangleq \Phi^{-1}(\phi,\mu)$ as the inverse function of $\Phi(\theta,\mu)$ with respect to ϕ. $\Theta(\phi,\mu)$ can be interpreted as the implied amount of throughput that induces a utilization level ϕ for a system with capacity μ. By Assumption 1, $\Theta(\phi,\mu)$ is strictly increasing in both ϕ and μ. To characterize the utilization of a system $(\mathbf{m},\mu)$, we define a *gap* function $g(\phi)$ between the supply and demand of throughput under a fixed level of utilization ϕ as $g(\phi) \triangleq \Theta(\phi,\mu) - \sum_{k\in\mathcal{N}} m_k\lambda_k(\phi)$.

Lemma 1. [1]*Given fixed capacity μ and user populations $\mathbf{m}$, $g(\phi)$ is strictly increasing in ϕ. The system operates at a unique level of utilization ϕ, which solves $g(\phi) = 0$.*

Lemma 1 characterizes the uniqueness of the system utilization ϕ under which the throughput supply $\Theta(\phi,\mu)$ equals the aggregate throughput demand $\sum_{k\in\mathcal{N}} m_k\lambda_k(\phi)$. Based on Lemma 1, for any system $(\mathbf{m},\mu)$, we denote $\phi(\mathbf{m},\mu)$ as its unique system utilization and $\theta_i(\mathbf{m},\mu)$ as CP i's corresponding throughput, i.e., $\theta_i(\mathbf{m},\mu) \triangleq m_i\lambda_i(\phi(\mathbf{m},\mu))$.

We define the marginal change of the *throughput gap* $g(\phi)$ due to the marginal change in the system utilization ϕ as

$$\frac{dg}{d\phi} \triangleq \frac{\partial\Theta(\phi,\mu)}{\partial\phi} - \sum_{k\in\mathcal{N}} m_k \frac{d\lambda_k(\phi)}{d\phi} > 0, \tag{2}$$

where the first term (second summation) captures the change of throughput in supply (total demand). We characterize the impact of user population m_i and capacity μ on the utilization ϕ and throughput θ_i, as a function of $dg/d\phi$ as follows.

Theorem 1 (CAPACITY AND USER EFFECT). *The system utilization ϕ decreases if the capacity μ increases or any user population m_i decreases. In particular, we have*

$$\frac{\partial\phi}{\partial\mu} = -\left(\frac{dg}{d\phi}\right)^{-1}\frac{\partial\Theta(\phi,\mu)}{\partial\mu} < 0, \tag{3}$$

$$\text{and} \quad \frac{\partial\phi}{\partial m_i} = \left(\frac{dg}{d\phi}\right)^{-1}\lambda_i > 0, \quad \forall i \in \mathcal{N}. \tag{4}$$

Any CP i's throughput θ_i increases with capacity μ and its user population m_i; however, the increase in m_i reduces the throughput θ_j of all other CPs $j \neq i$. In particular,

$$\frac{\partial\theta_i}{\partial\mu} = m_i\frac{d\lambda_i}{d\phi}\frac{\partial\phi}{\partial m_i} > 0, \qquad \frac{\partial\theta_i}{\partial m_i} = \lambda_i + m_i\frac{d\lambda_i}{d\phi}\frac{\partial\phi}{\partial m_i} > 0$$

$$\text{and} \quad \frac{\partial\theta_j}{\partial m_i} = m_j\frac{d\lambda_j}{d\phi}\frac{\partial\phi}{\partial m_i} < 0, \quad \forall j \neq i.$$

Theorem 1 intuitively states that 1) when the system capacity becomes more abundant, the throughput of any CP increases and the system utilization decreases, and 2) when more users of a CP join the system, the system utilization and the throughput of that CP increase, while that of any other CP decreases. Equation (3) explicitly shows that the capacity effect on the system utilization can be expressed as its impact on the feasible system throughput $\partial\Theta(\phi,\mu)/\partial\mu$, normalized by $dg/d\phi$, which re-balances the supply and demand of throughput so as to fill the *throughput gap* $g(\cdot)$ under the new system utilization. Similarly in Equation (4), λ_i can be interpreted as the marginal increase in throughput when a new user of CP i joins the system. It also implies that the user impact on the utilization is proportional to the per user throughput, i.e., $\partial\phi/\partial m_i : \partial\phi/\partial m_j = \lambda_i : \lambda_j$.

CPs' throughput depends on whether their users are sensitive to congestion. This can be characterized by *utilization-elasticity of throughput* or *ϕ-elasticity of λ_i*, defined as $\epsilon_\phi^{\lambda_i}$.

[1]Due to space limit, we include the proofs of selected results in appendix. Complete proofs of all results can be found in technical report [27].

Definition 2 (ELASTICITY). *The elasticity of y with respect to x, or x-elasticity of y, ϵ_x^y is defined as* $\epsilon_x^y \triangleq \frac{\partial y}{\partial x}\frac{x}{y}$.

Elasticity is often expressed as $\epsilon_x^y = (\partial y/y)/(\partial x/x)$ and interpreted as the percentage change in y (the numerator) in respond to the percentage change in x (the denominator). In particular, $\epsilon_\phi^{\lambda_i}$ captures the percentage change in λ_i in respond to the percentage change in the system utilization ϕ.

Lemma 2. *If CP i is replaced by a new CP j which satisfies that $m_j\lambda_j(0) = m_i\lambda_i(0)$ and $\epsilon_\phi^{\lambda_j}(\phi) = \epsilon_\phi^{\lambda_i}(\phi)$ for all $\phi > 0$, then the system utilization does not change.*

Lemma 2 characterizes CPs' throughput by ϕ-elasticity. Mathematically, by keeping the same elasticity $\epsilon_\phi^{\lambda_i}$, we could scale up the maximum throughput $\lambda_i(0)$ by $\tilde{\lambda}_i(0) = \kappa\lambda_i(0)$ and scale down m_i by $\tilde{m}_i = \kappa^{-1}m_i$ for some constant $\kappa > 0$ without affecting the system utilization ϕ and the throughput of all other CPs. Operationally, it implies that we could treat the traffic of a CP i as if it has a single big user, i.e., $\tilde{m}_i = 1$, with the maximum throughput $\tilde{\lambda}_i(0) = m_i\lambda_i(0)$. It also implies that for multiple CPs, e.g., a set $\mathcal{S} \subset \mathcal{N}$, with the same ϕ-elasticity of throughput, we could conceptually aggregate them as a single CP k with parameters m_k and $\lambda_k(0)$ that satisfy $m_k\lambda_k(0) = \sum_{i\in\mathcal{S}} m_i\lambda_i(0)$. By this result, we will use a single CP to model a group of CPs that have similar traffic characteristics in our later numerical evaluations.

3.2 One-Sided ISP Pricing

In the current Internet, most access ISPs only charge their end-users. We denote t_i as the per-unit usage charge for the data traffic of CP i. We assume that CP i's user population m_i is a function of its per-unit charge t_i, i.e., $m_i = m_i(t_i)$.

Assumption 2. *$m_i(t_i)$ is continuously differentiable and decreasing with $\lim_{t_i\to\infty} m_i(t_i) = 0$.*

Assumption 2 states that the user demand decreases with the per-unit charge on the content traffic. This model is quite general and coincides with existing models [8, 41] where the heterogeneity of users are modeled by the distribution of their valuations on data traffic and only the users whose valuations are higher than t_i consume data traffic from CP i.

Because traffic from different CPs should not be differentiated under net neutrality, ISPs often impose a uniform charge. We denote p as this uniform charge for all types of traffic. When CPs do not provide subsidies, we have $t_i = p$ for any $i \in \mathcal{N}$. We define the ISP's revenue as $R \triangleq p\theta = p\sum_{i\in\mathcal{N}} m_i\lambda_i$ and each CP i's utility as $U_i = v_i\theta_i$, where v_i denotes CP i's average per-unit traffic profit. Because the price p affects the user demand $\mathbf{m}$, we extend our basic system model to capture the one-sided ISP pricing as follows.

Figure 3 shows that the user populations $\mathbf{m}$ are influenced by the price p, and that the utilization ϕ affects the ISP's revenue $R = p\sum_{i\in\mathcal{N}} m_i\lambda_i(\phi)$. ISPs can use revenue as feedback to guide their pricing and capacity decisions; however, CPs' utilities are determined by throughput, which they have no means to influence in the one-sided pricing model.

Because $t_i = p$ for any CP i, by Assumption 2, we express the user populations as a function of price as $\mathbf{m} = \mathbf{m}(p)$. For a fixed capacity μ, we define $\phi(p) \triangleq \phi(\mathbf{m}(p), \mu)$ as the utilization of system $(\mathbf{m}(p), \mu)$ and $\theta_i(p) \triangleq m_i(p)\lambda_i(\phi(p))$ as the corresponding throughput of CP i under price p. By Assumption 1 and 2, both $\phi(p)$ and $\theta_i(p)$ are differentiable functions of p. We characterize the impact of price p on the system utilization ϕ and each CP i's throughput θ_i in the following theorem. The price's impact on U_i is simply its impact on θ_i scaled by v_i and we will study its impact on the revenue R under a more general setting in Section 5.

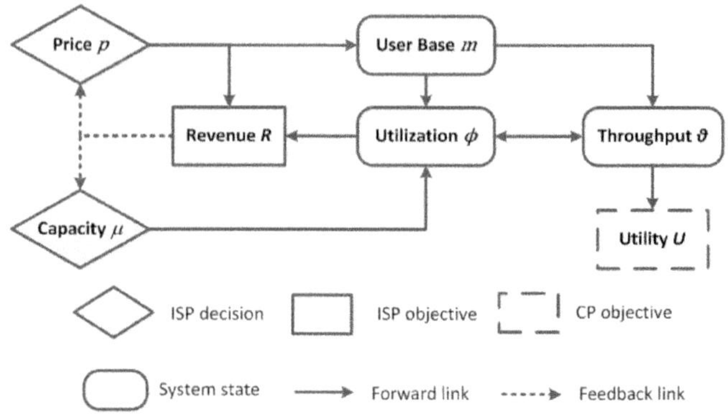

Figure 3: The system model with one-sided ISP pricing.

Theorem 2 (PRICE EFFECT). *The system utilization ϕ decreases with the price p. In particular, we have*

$$\frac{\partial\phi}{\partial p} = \left(\frac{dg}{d\phi}\right)^{-1} \sum_{k\in\mathcal{N}} \frac{dm_k}{dp}\lambda_k \le 0. \tag{5}$$

The aggregate throughput θ decreases with the price p,

$$\frac{\partial\theta}{\partial p} = \frac{\partial\Theta}{\partial\phi}\left(\frac{\partial\Theta}{\partial\phi} - \sum_{i\in\mathcal{N}} m_i\frac{d\lambda_i}{d\phi}\right)^{-1} \sum_{i\in\mathcal{N}} \frac{dm_i}{dp}\lambda_i \le 0, \tag{6}$$

and any CP i's throughput θ_i increases with p if and only if

$$\epsilon_p^{m_i}/\epsilon_\phi^{\lambda_i} < -\epsilon_p^\phi. \tag{7}$$

Theorem 2 states that when the price increases, due to its direct impact on decreasing the user demand, the system utilization decreases, which implies that the aggregate throughput of all the CPs also decreases. Similar to (3) and (4), the price effect on the system utilization can be expressed as its impact on the aggregate throughput $d\theta/dp$, normalized by $dg/d\phi$ in Equation (5). However, a CP i's throughput might increase or decrease, depending on its utilization elasticity of (per user) throughput $\epsilon_\phi^{\lambda_i}$ and price elasticity of user demand $\epsilon_p^{m_i}$, i.e., the percentage change in the population m_i in response to the percentage change in price p. In particular, θ_i increases with p if its users are less price-sensitive and more congestion-sensitive, i.e., $|\epsilon_p^{m_i}|$ is small and $|\epsilon_\phi^{\lambda_i}|$ is large. Notice that the right hand side of (7) measures the overall impact of price on the system utilization.

To understand the price effect more intuitively, we illustrate a numerical example as follows. We consider a utilization function $\Phi(\theta, \mu) = \theta/\mu$, which uses *per capacity throughput* as the metric for system utilization. We consider the forms of throughput $\lambda_i(\phi) = e^{-\beta_i\phi}$ and user demand $m_i(t_i) = e^{-\alpha_i t_i}$ that satisfy Assumption 1 and 2. Under these exponential forms, the ϕ-elasticity of throughput $\epsilon_\phi^{\lambda_i}$ equals $-\beta_i\phi$ and the p-elasticity of user population $\epsilon_p^{m_i}$ equals $-\alpha_i p$. Based on the above setting, we can express a CP i's throughput as $\theta_i = e^{-(\alpha_i p + \beta_i\phi)}$, where α_i and β_i neatly characterize θ_i's sensitivity to price and congestion, respectively. We obtain $dg/d\phi = \mu + \sum_{i\in\mathcal{N}} \beta_i\theta_i$ and

$$\frac{\partial\phi}{\partial p} = \left(\frac{dg}{d\phi}\right)^{-1}\left(\sum_{i\in\mathcal{N}} \frac{dm_i}{dp}\lambda_i\right) = -\frac{\sum_{i\in\mathcal{N}} \alpha_i\theta_i}{\mu + \sum_{i\in\mathcal{N}} \beta_i\theta_i}.$$

By Theorem 2, throughput θ_i increases at price p if

$$\frac{\alpha_i p}{\beta_i \phi} < \frac{\sum_{j\in\mathcal{N}} \alpha_j \theta_j}{\mu + \sum_{k\in\mathcal{N}} \beta_k \theta_k}. \tag{8}$$

We set the system capacity to be $\mu = 1$ and consider a set of 9 types of CPs with values of (α_i, β_i) chosen from $\{1, 3, 5\}$.

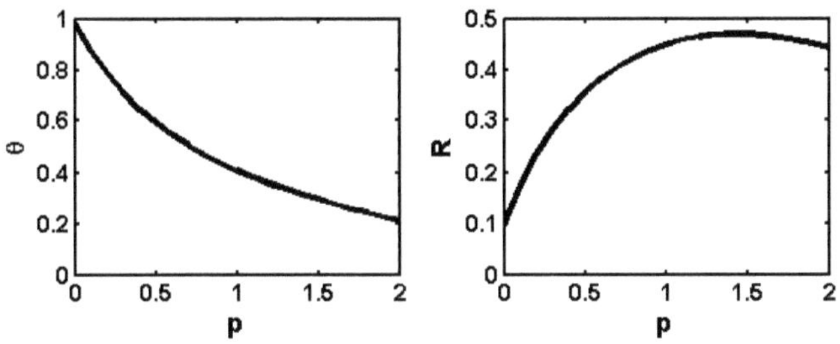

Figure 4: Aggregate throughput θ and ISP's revenue R.

Figure 4 plots the aggregate throughput θ (left) and the ISP's revenue R (right) as a function of price p that varies along the x-axis. We observe that the aggregate throughput decreases with the price as indicated by Theorem 2; however, the revenue $R = p\theta$ depends on both the price and aggregate throughput and shows a single-peak pattern.

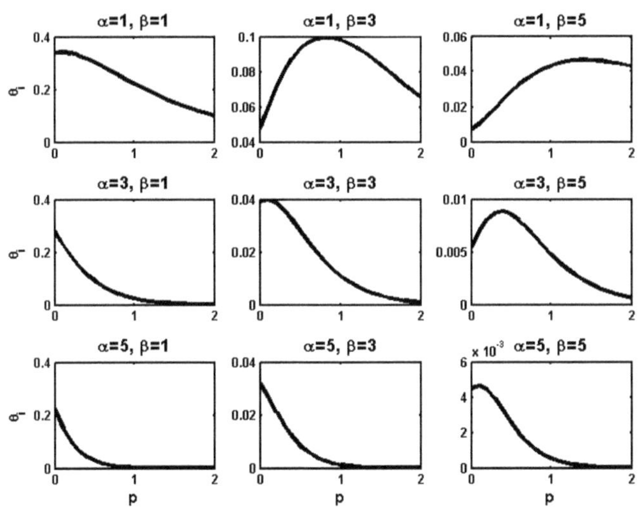

Figure 5: Throughput θ_i of different CPs.

Figure 5 shows the throughput θ_i of the 9 individual CPs as a function of the price p in each sub-figure, respectively. In general, the throughput is low with large values of α_i and β_i (the lower and right sub-figures), because the user population is more sensitive to price and the per user throughput is more sensitive to congestion. By Theorem 2, when p increases, ϕ decreases, and therefore $(\alpha_i/\beta_i)(p/\phi)$ increases. As indicated by condition (8), each θ_i decreases with p eventually; however, when p is small, we observe that the CPs with a small ratio of α_i/β_i (the upper and right sub-figures) demonstrate an increasing trend in throughput. Intuitively, for these CPs, the increase in the per user throughput λ_i is much higher than the decrease in the user population m_i so that the aggregate throughput θ_i could still increase.

Regulatory Implications: Under the existing one-sided pricing, an increase in the access ISP's price reduces the user demand (by Assumption 2), and consequently reduces the system utilization and the total system throughput (by Theorem 2). Regulators might want to regulate the price of an access ISP if its high price induces low utilization and drives the total system throughput too low (shown in Figure 4). However, as the existing wireless capacities of many carriers are often under-provisioned and highly-loaded, and regulations will further limit the ISPs' profit margin, we do not see the need for price regulation under the status quo.

4. SUBSIDIZATION COMPETITION

As the access ISPs can neither differentiate services nor charge CPs in the one-sided pricing model in Figure 3, the limited profit margin does not provide enough investment incentive for them to expand capacities. Neither do the CPs have any means to express preferences and improve their utilities. In this section, we propose to create a feedback channel for the CPs to influence the system by allowing them to voluntarily subsidize the usage-based fees for their users.

4.1 The Subsidization Competition Model

We denote $q \geq 0$ as a subsidization policy that limits the maximum subsidy allowed. We denote $s_i \in [0, q]$ as the per-unit usage subsidy provided by CP i for its content traffic for users. We denote $\mathbf{s}$ as the vector of subsidies of the CPs. We extend the definition of CP i's utility as $U_i \triangleq (v_i - s_i)\theta_i$.

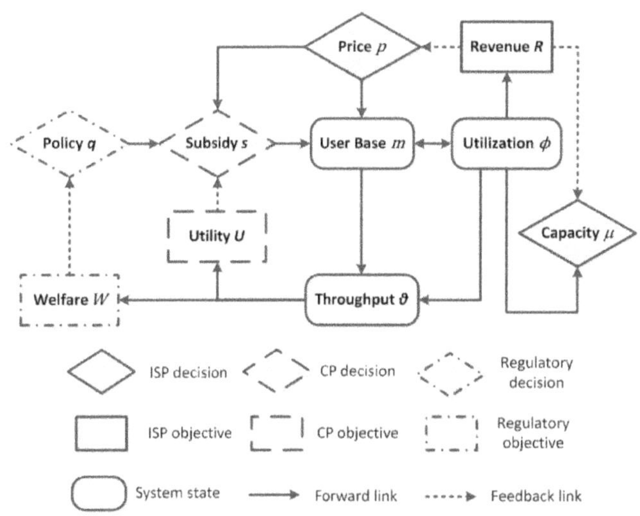

Figure 6: One-sided ISP pricing with CP subsidization.

Figure 6 illustrates the extended model where subsidization from CPs is allowed. In this model, each CP i could strategically choose its subsidy s_i to influence its throughput θ_i via its user population m_i so as to optimize its utility U_i. Regulators can also use any welfare metric W to determine the desirable upper-bound q of subsidization for the industry.

Under price p and subsidies $\mathbf{s}$, user population m_i satisfies $m_i(t_i) = m_i(p - s_i)$. Given any fixed ISP decision (p, μ), we denote $\phi(\mathbf{s}) \triangleq \phi(\mathbf{m}(p, \mathbf{s}), \mu)$ as the system utilization and define $\theta_i(\mathbf{s}) = m_i(p - s_i)\lambda_i(\phi(\mathbf{s}))$ as CP i's throughput.

Lemma 3. *For any $s_i' > s_i$, let $\mathbf{s}' = (s_i', \mathbf{s}_{-i})$ and $\mathbf{s} = (s_i, \mathbf{s}_{-i})$ for some fixed strategy profile $\mathbf{s}_{-i}$. For any price p, $\phi(\mathbf{s}') \geq \phi(\mathbf{s})$, $\theta_i(\mathbf{s}') \geq \theta_i(\mathbf{s})$ and $\theta_j(\mathbf{s}') \leq \theta_j(\mathbf{s})$, $\forall j \neq i$.*

Lemma 3 states that if a CP i unilaterally increases its subsidy s_i, its throughput θ_i and the system utilization ϕ might increase; however, the throughput of any other CP cannot increase. It shows that the subsidization mechanism creates a competitive game among the CPs, where each CP i could use subsidy s_i to maximize its utility U_i. Notice that besides the policy constraint q, each CP's optimal subsidy strategy depends on all other CPs' strategies as well as the ISP's price p. In this section, we study the policy implications of subsidization and therefore, we often assume a fixed price p for the access ISP. This setting corresponds to a competitive access market where the ISPs cannot easily manipulate prices, or a case where the ISP's price is regulated. We will study an ISP's pricing strategy, its revenue and the policy implication on the system welfare in the next section.

Definition 3 (NASH EQUILIBRIUM). *Given any fixed ISP price p and policy q, a strategy profile $\mathbf{s}$ is a* Nash equilibrium *if each s_i solves CP i's utility maximization problem:*

$$\begin{aligned} \max \quad & U_i(s_i;\mathbf{s}_{-i}) = (v_i - s_i)\theta_i(\mathbf{s}) \\ \text{subject to} \quad & 0 \le s_i \le q. \end{aligned}$$

We characterize the Nash equilibrium of the subsidization competition game in the following theorem.

Theorem 3 (CHARACTERIZATION). *For any fixed p and q, a strategy profile $\mathbf{s}$ is a Nash equilibrium only if*

$$s_i = \min\{\tau_i(\mathbf{s}), q\}, \quad \forall\, i \in \mathcal{N},$$

where each τ_i denotes a threshold for CP i, defined by

$$\tau_i(\mathbf{s}) \triangleq (v_i - s_i)\, \epsilon_{s_i}^{m_i} \left(1 + \epsilon_{\phi}^{\lambda_i} \epsilon_{m_i}^{\phi}\right). \tag{9}$$

In particular, $v_i \le (\partial\theta_i/\partial s_i)^{-1}\theta_i$ holds if $s_i = 0$. Moreover, if $U_i(\mathbf{s}) = U_i(s_i, \mathbf{s}_{-i})$ is concave in s_i for all $i \in \mathcal{N}$, then the above conditions are also sufficient.

Theorem 3 characterizes the Nash equilibrium in two ways. First, it indicates that any CP i does not subsidize if its profitability v_i is lower than $(\partial\theta_i/\partial s_i)^{-1}\theta_i$. Second, if the policy constraint is not tight, i.e., $s_i < q$, the equilibrium subsidy s_i can be characterized by its profit margin $v_i - s_i$ and the elasticity metrics $\epsilon_{s_i}^{m_i}$, $\epsilon_{\phi}^{\lambda_i}$ and $\epsilon_{m_i}^{\phi}$. Equation (9) can also be written as $\tau_i(\mathbf{s}) = (v_i - s_i)\epsilon_{s_i}^{\theta_i} = (v_i - s_i)\epsilon_{s_i}^{m_i}\left(1 + \epsilon_{m_i}^{\lambda_i}\right)$. This characterization also implies that a CP would subsidize its users more if 1) its traffic profitability v_i (and therefore its profit margin $v_i - s_i$) increases, or 2) its throughput elasticity $\epsilon_{s_i}^{\theta_i}$ or user demand elasticity of subsidy $\epsilon_{s_i}^{m_i}$ increases.

By Assumption 1 and 2, each $U_i(\mathbf{s})$ is differentiable in $\mathbf{s}$. For any strategy profile $\mathbf{s}$, we define $\mathbf{u}(\mathbf{s}) = \{u_i(\mathbf{s}) : i \in \mathcal{N}\}$ as the vector of marginal utilities, where each $u_i(\mathbf{s})$ denotes the marginal utility of CP i, defined as $u_i(\mathbf{s}) \triangleq \partial U_i(\mathbf{s})/\partial s_i$. Next, we characterize the uniqueness of Nash equilibrium based on a condition on the marginal utilities $\mathbf{u}(\mathbf{s})$.

Theorem 4 (UNIQUENESS). *For any fixed price p and policy q, if for any distinct pair of feasible strategy profiles $\mathbf{s}' \ne \mathbf{s}$, there always exist a CP $i \in \mathcal{N}$ such that*

$$(s_i' - s_i)\left(u_i(\mathbf{s}') - u_i(\mathbf{s})\right) < 0, \tag{10}$$

then there always exists a unique Nash equilibrium.

Technically, the above sufficient condition for uniqueness requires $-\mathbf{u}$ to be a *P-function* [31]. Notice that this uniqueness property holds for any subset $\mathcal{Q} \subset [0, q]^{|\mathcal{N}|}$ of the strategy space if condition (10) holds in the domain $\mathcal{Q}$.

4.2 Dynamics of Subsidies in Equilibrium

Since a Nash equilibrium is defined under a fixed price p and policy q by Definition (3), we use $\mathbf{s} = \mathbf{s}(p, q)$ to indicate a Nash equilibrium under p and q. Equation (9) in Theorem 3 hinted that a CP with higher profitability subsidizes users more in an equilibrium. We formally show this as follows.

Theorem 5 (PROFITABILITY EFFECT ON SUBSIDY). *If a CP i's profitability increases from v_i to $\hat{v}_i$ unilaterally, and under the condition (10) of Theorem 4, $\mathbf{s}$ and $\hat{\mathbf{s}}$ are the corresponding Nash equilibria, then we must have $\hat{s}_i \ge s_i$.*

If a CP's profitability increases, Theorem 5 tells that it will increase its subsidy in equilibrium, and hints that its throughput will increase by Lemma 3. Through subsidization, CPs can respond to their profitability and influence throughput.

After analyzing the impact of CPs' profitability, we study how an equilibrium $\mathbf{s}(p, q)$ is influenced by the price p and policy q. We define $\mathcal{N}_-$ and $\mathcal{N}_+$ as the set of CPs whose subsidies are 0 and q, respectively, and $\widetilde{\mathcal{N}} = \mathcal{N} \backslash (\mathcal{N}_- \cup \mathcal{N}_+)$ as the remaining set of CPs whose subsidies are strictly positive and less than q. We define $\tilde{\mathbf{s}}$ and $\tilde{\mathbf{u}}$ as the subsidies and marginal utilities of the set $\widetilde{\mathcal{N}}$ of CPs.

Theorem 6 (EQUILIBRIUM DYNAMICS). *If a Nash equilibrium $\mathbf{s}$ satisfies 1) $i \in \widetilde{\mathcal{N}}$ if $u_i(\mathbf{s}) = 0$, and 2) the condition (10) for a neighborhood of $\mathbb{R}^{|\mathcal{N}|}$ centered at $\mathbf{s}$ in the strategy space, then in a neighborhood of (p, q), a unique Nash equilibrium is a differentiable function $\mathbf{s}(p, q)$, satisfying*

$$\frac{\partial s_i}{\partial q} = \begin{cases} 0 & \text{if } i \in \mathcal{N}_-; \\ 1 & \text{if } i \in \mathcal{N}_+; \\ -\displaystyle\sum_{k \in \widetilde{\mathcal{N}}} \psi_{ik} \sum_{j \in \mathcal{N}_+} \frac{\partial u_k}{\partial s_j}, & \text{if } i \in \widetilde{\mathcal{N}}, \end{cases} \tag{11}$$

$$\text{and} \quad \frac{\partial s_i}{\partial p} = \begin{cases} 0 & \text{if } i \notin \widetilde{\mathcal{N}}; \\ -\displaystyle\sum_{k \in \widetilde{\mathcal{N}}} \psi_{ik} \frac{\partial u_k}{\partial p}, & \text{if } i \in \widetilde{\mathcal{N}}, \end{cases} \tag{12}$$

where $\Psi = \{\psi_{ij}\} \triangleq (\nabla_{\tilde{\mathbf{s}}}\tilde{\mathbf{u}})^{-1}$, i.e., ψ_{ij} is at the ith row and jth column of the inverse of the Jacobian matrix $\nabla_{\tilde{\mathbf{s}}}\tilde{\mathbf{u}}$.

Theorem 6 states that a marginal change in the ISP's price or the regulatory policy will not affect the behavior of the set $\mathcal{N}_-$ and $\mathcal{N}_+$ of CPs: the CPs who do not subsidize remain the same and the CPs who subsidize the amount q keep subsidizing at the maximum level as q increases. When p changes, the set $\widetilde{\mathcal{N}}$ of CPs readjust subsidies among themselves in a new equilibrium such that their marginal utilities remain zero in (12); when q changes, since the set $\mathcal{N}_+$ of CPs increase subsidies accordingly, their impacts have to be counted in the new equilibrium in (11). By applying the KKT condition to Definition 3, we know $u_i(\mathbf{s}) = 0$ for all $i \in \widetilde{\mathcal{N}}$, and the first condition of Theorem 6 is a bit stronger which guarantees that the equilibrium $\mathbf{s}$ is *regular*, i.e., locally differentiable. The second condition only assumes (10) locally, which guarantees the local uniqueness of equilibrium in a neighborhood centered at $\mathbf{s}$ by Theorem 4.

Corollary 1 (DEREGULATION). *Under a fixed ISP price p and the conditions of Theorem 6, in a neighborhood of q, we can express $\phi(q)$ and $R(q)$ as the system utilization and the ISP's revenue under the Nash equilibrium $\mathbf{s}(q)$. If $\mathbf{u}$ is off-diagonally monotone, i.e., $\partial u_i(\mathbf{s})/\partial s_j \ge 0$ for all $i \ne j$,*

$$\frac{\partial \phi}{\partial q} \ge 0, \quad \frac{\partial R}{\partial q} \ge 0 \quad \text{and} \quad \frac{\partial s_i}{\partial q} \ge 0, \quad \forall i \in \mathcal{N}.$$

The off-diagonally monotone property makes $-\mathbf{u}$ to be a Leontief type [18] of P-matrix, which guarantees the stability of a macroeconomic system due to Wassily Leontief [20]. Intuitively, it assumes although the utility of a CP i decreases when other CPs increase their subsidies, its marginal benefit of subsidizing its own users, i.e., u_i, increases. Corollary 1 states that under this stability condition, when allowed to subsidize more, CPs will increase subsidies, which will lead to an increase in the system utilization and the ISP's revenue.

Regulatory Implications: Under a competitive or price regulated access market, deregulation of subsidization encourages CPs to subsidize users (by Theorem 5 and 6), and consequently increases the system utilization and the ISPs' revenue (by Corollary 1). CPs' user populations $\mathbf{m}$ increase because the usage charges become cheaper after subsidization (by Assumption 2), but the induced higher utilization (by Theorem 1) might cause congestion. The total system throughput also increases (implied by Corollary 1 as ϕ increases), while the throughput of certain CPs might decrease. However, this is caused by the negative network externality, i.e., the physics of congestion of shared capacity. Although it might be unfavorable for the CPs whose traffic is more congestion sensitive in the short term, as the ISPs improve profit margins from higher utilization, they will have more incentives to expand capacities so as to accommodate more traffic and relieve congestion in the long term.

5. ISP REVENUE AND SYSTEM WELFARE

Although the policy q, the price p and the subsidies $\mathbf{s}$ all impact the system, these decisions are not made simultaneously and independently. The system is fundamentally driven by a regulatory policy q, under which the ISP determines its price $p(q)$ and then the CPs respond with strategies $\mathbf{s}(p,q)$. Theorem 6 characterizes the dynamics of $\mathbf{s}(p,q)$ and Corollary 1 characterizes the impact of policy q when p is fixed. In practice, ISPs often use price to optimize revenue, and by Theorem 6 the subsidies $\mathbf{s}$ are also influenced by p. In this section, we study the impact of the ISP's price on its revenue and the impact of policy on the system welfare when the response of ISP's pricing is taken into account.

5.1 Impact of ISP's Pricing on Its Revenue

Under a fixed policy q, by Theorem 6, we can write $\mathbf{s}(p)$ as the induced subsidies under price p. Thus, the induced system utilization is $\phi(\mathbf{s}(p))$ and the ISP's induced revenue is $R(p) = p\sum_{i\in\mathcal{N}}\theta_i(p) = p\sum_{i\in\mathcal{N}} m_i(p-s_i(p))\lambda_i(\phi(\mathbf{s}(p)))$.

Theorem 7 (MARGINAL REVENUE). *If the ISP's revenue is differentiable at p, then its marginal revenue is*

$$\frac{dR(p)}{dp} = \sum_{i\in\mathcal{N}}\theta_i + \Upsilon\sum_{i\in\mathcal{N}}\epsilon_p^{m_i}\theta_i, \tag{13}$$

where Υ and the m_i-elasticity of price p satisfy

$$\Upsilon = 1 + \sum_{j\in\mathcal{N}}\epsilon_{m_j}^{\lambda_j} \quad and \quad \epsilon_p^{m_i} = \frac{p}{m_i}\frac{dm_i}{dt_i}\left(1-\frac{\partial s_i}{\partial p}\right).$$

Theorem 7 characterizes the change in revenue as the price varies and isolates the effect of subsidization into the elasticities $\epsilon_p^{m_i}$, where $\partial s_i/\partial p$ plays a role. It also generalizes the case of one-sided pricing, i.e., $\partial s_i/\partial p = 0$ for all $i\in\mathcal{N}$. The second term in (13) measures the price's impact on the aggregate throughput, i.e., $p(\partial\theta/\partial p)$, which can be factorized by Υ, a parameter determined by the physical model in Figure 2, because $\epsilon_{m_j}^{\lambda_j}$ can be decomposed as $\epsilon_{m_j}^{\phi}\epsilon_{\phi}^{\lambda_j}$ and

$$\epsilon_{m_j}^{\phi}\epsilon_{\phi}^{\lambda_j} = \frac{m_j}{\lambda_j}\frac{d\lambda_j}{d\phi}\frac{\partial\phi}{\partial m_j} = m_j\frac{d\lambda_j}{d\phi}\left(\frac{dg}{d\phi}\right)^{-1}. \tag{14}$$

5.2 Impact of Regulatory Policy on Welfare

By Theorem 7, we understand how the ISP's pricing affects its revenue. We assume that the ISP would adapt its price p as a function of a given policy q. The next theorem captures the impact of the policy q on the system states, i.e., ϕ, m_i and θ_i, where the responses of both the ISP's price $p(q)$ and the CPs' subsidies $\mathbf{s}(p,q)$ are taken into account.

Theorem 8 (POLICY EFFECT). *If the ISP's price is a differentiable function $p(q)$ of policy q and $\mathbf{s}$ is a Nash equilibrium of $p(q)$ and q, under the conditions of Theorem 6, in a neighborhood of q, we can express the Nash equilibrium as $\mathbf{s}(q)\triangleq\mathbf{s}(p(q),q)$. The corresponding system utilization $\phi(q)$, user population $m_i(q)$ and throughput $\lambda_i(q)$ satisfy*

$$\frac{dm_i}{dq} = \frac{dm_i}{dt_i}\frac{dt_i}{dq} = \frac{dm_i}{dt_i}\left(\left(1-\frac{\partial s_i}{\partial p}\right)\frac{dp}{dq} - \frac{\partial s_i}{\partial q}\right), \tag{15}$$

$$\frac{d\phi}{dq} = \left(\frac{dg}{d\phi}\right)^{-1}\sum_{i\in\mathcal{N}}\frac{dm_i}{dq}\lambda_i \quad and \quad \frac{d\lambda_i}{dq} = \frac{d\lambda_i}{d\phi}\frac{d\phi}{dq}. \tag{16}$$

Any CP i's throughput θ_i increases with q if and only if

$$\epsilon_{t_i}^{m_i}\epsilon_q^{t_i}/\epsilon_\phi^{\lambda_i} < -\epsilon_q^{\phi}. \tag{17}$$

Theorem 8 shows that the policy effect on utilization $d\phi/dq$ in (16) and the condition (17) for throughput θ_i have similar forms as the price effect $d\phi/dp$ in (5) and the condition (7). This is because the policy effect is carried out by its impact on the user populations, i.e., $\epsilon_q^{m_i} = \epsilon_{t_i}^{m_i}\epsilon_q^{t_i}$, via its impact on the price and subsidies. By Assumption 1 and 2, both $\epsilon_\phi^{\lambda_i}$ and $\epsilon_{t_i}^{m_i}$ are negative. Inequality (17) tells that a CP's throughput decreases if any only if $(-\epsilon_{t_i}^{m_i})(-\epsilon_q^{t_i}) < -\epsilon_\phi^{\lambda_i}\epsilon_q^{\phi}$, which implies that the subsidy could help increase throughput via $(-\epsilon_q^{t_i})$; however, $(-\epsilon_{t_i}^{m_i})$ could be decreased due to the ISP's increasing price, which will reduce the CP's throughput.

Corollary 2 (POLICY IMPACT ON WELFARE). *Under the conditions of Theorem 8, let $W(q)\triangleq\sum_{i\in\mathcal{N}}\theta_i(q)v_i$ define the system welfare. Suppose $d\phi/dq$ in (16) is positive, then the marginal welfare dW/dq is positive if and only if*

$$\sum_{i\in\mathcal{N}}\frac{w_i}{\sum_{k\in\mathcal{N}}w_k}v_i > \sum_{i\in\mathcal{N}}-\epsilon_{m_i}^{\lambda_i}v_i, \quad where \quad w_i\triangleq\lambda_i\frac{dm_i}{dq}.$$

We measure the welfare by $W=\sum_{i\in\mathcal{N}}\theta_i v_i$ for two reasons. First, it internalizes the subsidy transfer from CPs to ISP. Second, because CP profits are often positively correlated to their values to users, it also serves an estimate for user welfare. In Corollary 2, $w_i v_i$ can be interpreted as the increase in welfare due to the policy's impact on the user population m_i, and therefore, the left side of the inequality represents the normalized increase in welfare due to the changes in the user populations. The right side of the inequality represents the normalized decrease in welfare due to the policy's impact on each average throughput λ_i via m_i. Corollary 2 states that the welfare increases if and only if the increasing component is larger than the decreasing component. Notice that the decreasing component only depends on the physical characteristics (14) of the

CPs, while the weight $w_i / \sum_{j \in \mathcal{N}} w_j$ for each v_i tends to be large if v_i is large, because profitable CPs will have stronger tendencies to subsidize their users so as to attract a larger population m_i.

To understand the policy effect more intuitively, we perform a numerical evaluation as follows. We use the same setting $m_i(t_i) = e^{-\alpha_i t_i}$, $\lambda_i(\phi) = e^{-\beta_i \phi}$ and $\Phi(\theta, \mu) = \theta/\mu$ as in Section 3. We model 8 types of CPs with $\alpha_i, \beta_i \in \{2, 5\}$ and $v_i \in \{0.5, 1\}$. By Lemma 2, each CP represents the aggregation of a group of CPs with similar characteristics of traffic and user demand. In each of the following figures, we vary the policy q at 5 levels from 0 to 2.0 and vary the ISP's price p from 0 to 2 along the x-axis. When $q = 0$, the figures show the baseline case where subsidization is not allowed.

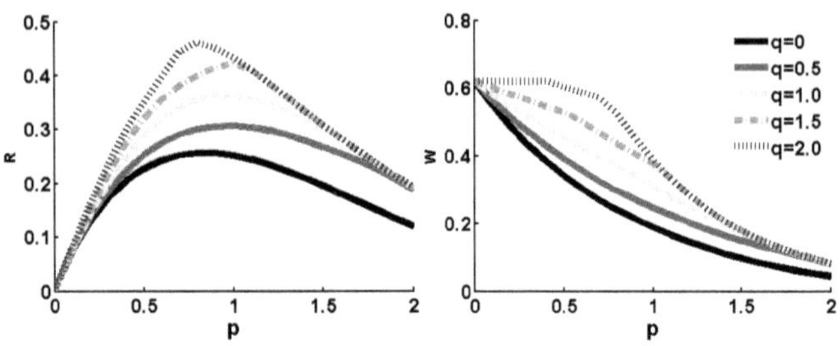

Figure 7: ISP's Revenue R and System Welfare W.

Figure 7 plots the ISP's revenue R (left) and the system welfare W (right) when the price p varies along the x-axis. We observe that under any fixed price p, both the ISP's revenue and the system welfare are higher when the CPs' subsidization is less regulated, i.e., q is large. However, if the deregulation of subsidization will trigger a higher ISP price, it also shows that the system welfare will decrease with the price p under any fixed policy q.

Figures 8 and 9 plot the individual subsidy s_i and throughput θ_i of the 8 types of CPs under equilibrium, respectively[2]. In Figure 8, we observe that the CPs that have a higher profitability, i.e., $v_i = 1$ in the lower 4 sub-figures, or a higher demand elasticity, i.e., $\alpha_i = 5$ in the right 4 sub-figures, provide much higher subsidies compared to their counterparts. We also observe that when the price p is small, except for the two CPs with $\alpha_i = 2$ and $v_i = 0.5$, most CPs want to subsidize at the maximum level q constrained by the policy; however, when p increases, subsidies may stay flat and then decrease due to the decrease in profit margin. By comparing Figure 8 with Figure 7, we observe that when $q = 2$, the ISP maximizes its revenue by setting p a bit less than 1, where the subsidies from the CPs are kept at a high level. In Figure 9, we observe that the CPs with higher profitability, i.e., $v_i = 1$, or lower congestion elasticity, i.e., $\beta_i = 2$, achieve higher throughput compared to their counterparts. When comparing the throughput with that of the baseline, i.e., $q = 0$, we observe that the CPs with high profitability achieve higher throughput, with the only exception for the case $(\alpha_i, \beta_i, v_i) = (2, 5, 1)$ when p is small. As p is small, the system attracts large user demand and is relatively congested. Because this CP is more congestion sensitive, i.e., β_i is large, and by Corollary 1, subsidization will further increase the system utilization, its throughput will be reduced. By comparing Figure 9 with Figure 7, we observe that with higher throughput for the CPs of higher profitability, the system welfare increases when the policy q is relaxed.

Regulatory Implications: In a deregulated market where CPs are allowed to subsidize their users, highly profitable CPs will provide greater subsidies (by Theorem 5) and obtain more users (by Assumption 2), achieving higher throughput (by Theorem 1) and leading to a higher system welfare (by Corollary 2). However, deregulation of subsidization might trigger an increase in the ISP's price, leading to a decrease in the system welfare (shown in Figure 7). High ISP prices also discourage user demand (by Assumption 2) and consequently decrease their throughput (shown in Figure 9). Our results suggest that the subsidization competition will increase the ISP's revenue and system welfare (by Corollary 1); however, price regulations might be needed if the access market is not competitive and the ISP's price is set too high.

[2]Figures of population m_i and utility U_i can also be found in [27].

6. DISCUSSIONS

In this section, we discuss related issues of subsidization, its connections to other recent developments in the Internet industry and comment on some limitations of our proposed model.

6.1 Implementation and Regulatory Issues

Subsidization works with the usage-based pricing schemes of the access ISPs. For mobile providers, implementing data caps and accounting for data traffic consumptions are common in practice. Broadband providers in countries like India and Australia have been using usage-based pricing, and major U.S. ISPs like Verizon [43] and AT&T [47] have also adopted usage-based pricing after gaining support from the FCC [42, 22]. To differentiate content and enable subsidization from different CPs, platforms such as FreeBand [3] have been developed to provide data traffic statistics to mobile carriers so as to lower the bills of consumers, based on the type of applications. AT&T's recent sponsored data [1] plan allows CPs to fully subsidize their users, and Syntonic Wireless [7] provides the corresponding *Sponsored Content Store* for end-users to use sponsored applications. Our model allows partial subsidization and the implementation would be easy if the CP has a direct financial relationship with its end-users, e.g., a shopping site. Otherwise, ISPs could implement accounting mechanisms to realize the subsidization as an intermediary; however, they would be preferred not to be involved in the payment transfer if net neutrality is concerned.

Deregulation of subsidization might reduce the throughput of certain CPs, e.g., the upper-left ones in Figure 9. These CPs either do not have incentives to subsidize, because their users are not price-sensitive, i.e., the elasticity $\epsilon_{s_i}^{m_i}$ is small, or they cannot afford to subsidize, because their profitability v_i is low. In the former case, the decrease in throughput is mainly due to a higher utilization of the system, which will be relieved in the long term when the ISPs expand capacities. Startup companies with low profits are of the latter case. The decrease in throughput is mainly due to the ISP's high price that limits the user demand, and therefore, regulators might want to regulate ISP's monopolistic pricing or introduce competition, e.g., municipal infrastructures. However, if they are promising, we also expect that venture capital would provide the funding source for them to subsidize their users and achieve their potential high profitability. After all, we believe in a transparent and competitive market where users can choose CPs based on quality and prices, and the businesses drive the evolution of the Internet ecosystem.

Although our analyses imply that a deregulation of subsidization will provide CPs more freedom to subsidize and increase the competitiveness of the content market, regulators might still want to impose policies that prevent discriminatory subsidization of the access ISPs. For example, Comcast's Xbox XFinity [2] service enables its users to access on-demand content on their Xbox devices, which does not count against their 250GB data cap. By implicitly subsidizing their users, this service favors the ISP's vertically integrated business over other content competitors, e.g., Netflix. Some

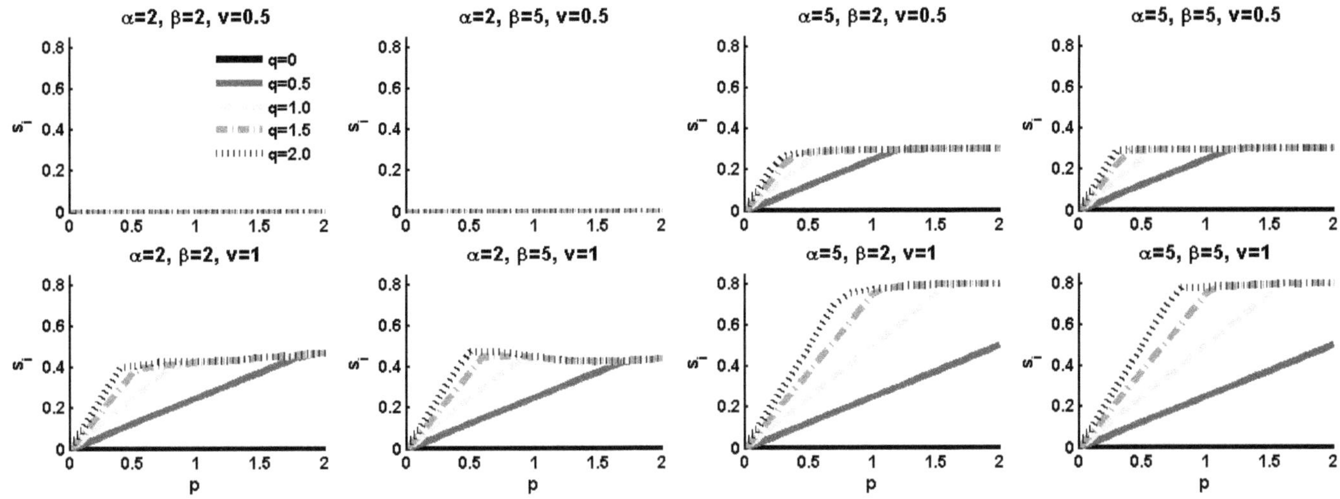

Figure 8: The subsidies s_i of the 8 types of CPs under equilibrium.

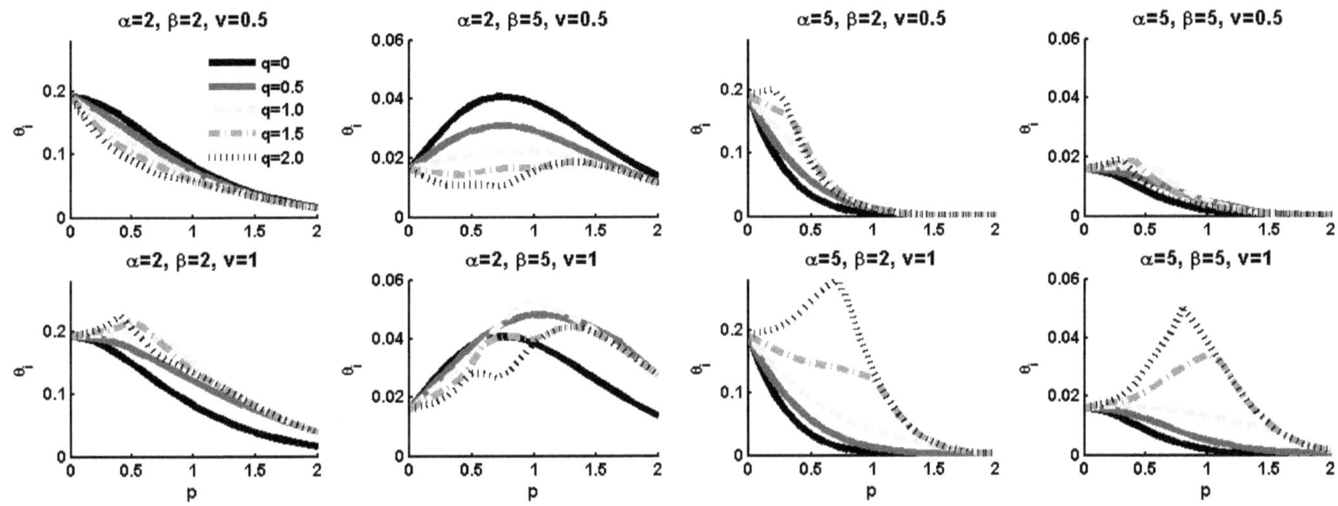

Figure 9: The throughput θ_i of the 8 types of CPs under equilibrium.

CPs work with access ISPs to provide better services and cheaper prices for their users, e.g., Google Apps for Verizon [4]; however, this might also inversely affect the competitors of those favored CPs. We believe that the subsidization option should be identical, and should be given to all CPs equally. Through this, the access ISPs would treat CPs more neutrally and the subsidization would create a transparent and uniform platform for the CPs to compete.

6.2 Connections to Industrial Developments

Our proposed subsidization framework is mostly close to AT&T's sponsored data [47], under which CPs could pay the access ISP so as to fully subsidize their users. However, there are two major differences. First, our framework is more flexible such that partial subsidization is allowed and determined by CPs. Second, our framework is more fair and transparent, i.e., the usage-based pricing for users are the same for all CPs and the subsidizations paid by CPs are equally treated. Much efforts have been made by CPs to provide better services for their users, e.g., Netflix's OpenConnect [6] and Google Global Cache (GGC) [5]. These efforts make the Internet transit more efficient and competitive. Nevertheless, to support quality of service for content delivery, more severe issues are related to the monopolistic position of the last-mile broadband providers and the scarce capacity of the wireless providers. This is why Netflix has agreed to pay access ISPs like Comcast [40] and Verizon [19] via paid-peering agreements for better content delivery. Although paid-peering provides higher revenue for the access ISPs and some CPs do have incentives to pay for it, access ISPs need to actively manage their network capacity and differentiate CPs' traffic, in other words, maintaining a non-neutral physical network. Our proposed subsidization framework, on the other hand, is a pricing mechanism, which preserves the neutrality of the physical network.

6.3 Model Limitations

Our analytical framework is based on a macroscopic equilibrium model that captures the interactions among an access ISP, a set of CPs and end-users via the CPs' subsidization and the ISP's capacity and pricing decisions. Our theoretical results are mostly qualitative, which provides understanding and predictions of the changes in the system states when some of the driving factors change. The limitation is that it might not be able to capture short-term off-equilibrium types of system dynamics, where players' decisions are not rational or optimal. Our numerical evaluations are limited to a styled model of CPs to capture qualitative trends; however, more detailed experiments and validations could be challenging, because market data are needed so as to obtain the characteristics of the CPs, e.g., their profitability and elasticities, and an ISP needs to execute such a plan in the market. With the emerging sponsored data plan from AT&T, we expect this type of market data could be available for regulatory authorities as well as research communities. This study focuses on a single access ISP; however, we believe that competition between ISPs will also incentivize them to adopt subsidization schemes, through which users can obtain subsidized services. Finally, our result shows that under the subsidization mechanism, the access ISP could increase utilization and revenue. Because ISPs care about their profit, which is a function of both utilization and revenue, the increase in profit will further provide investment incentives for them to expand capacity. We do not have sufficient space to study the ISP's capacity planning decision in detail, which is a direction of our future work.

7. CONCLUSIONS

The Internet is facing a dilemma of increasing traffic demand and decreasing incentives for the access ISPs to expand capacity, because service prioritization and two-sided pricing are still under debate in terms of their implications for net neutrality. We propose to allow CPs to voluntarily subsidize the data usage costs incurred at the access ISPs for their end-users. Our solution modularizes the issue along the tussle boundary such that the physical network is kept neutral. Through modeling and analyses, we show that a deregulated subsidization policy will incentivize profitable CPs to subsidize users and increase the system welfare and the revenue of the access ISPs. With the improved profit margins, the access ISPs would obtain more investment incentives under subsidization. However, the deregulation of subsidization might trigger an ISP to increase price, which would decrease the system welfare as well as the throughput of certain CPs. We suggest that price regulation might be needed if the access market is not competitive enough and the price is too high. Because subsidization creates a feedback channel for CPs to return value to the access ISPs and realign the created value and investment in the value chain, we believe that subsidization competition could vitalize neutral Internet for the future.

8. ACKNOWLEDGMENTS

The author would like to thank the shepherd of this paper, Matthew Andrews, for useful advices on revising this work. The author would also like to thank Vishal Misra for discussions and suggestions, and the anonymous reviewers for their insightful comments.

This study is supported by Ministry of Education of Singapore AcRF grant R-252-000-526-112 and the research grant for the Human Sixth Sense Programme at the Advanced Digital Sciences Center from Singapore's Agency for Science, Technology and Research (A*STAR).

APPENDIX

A. PROOFS OF SELECTED RESULTS

Proof of Lemma 1: By Assumption 1, we know $\Theta(\phi,\mu)$ is strictly increasing in ϕ and $\lambda_i(\phi)$ is strictly decreasing in ϕ; therefore, $g(\phi) = \Theta(\phi,\mu) - \sum_{i\in\mathcal{N}} m_i\lambda_i(\phi)$ is strictly increasing in ϕ. Because $\lim_{\phi\to 0}\Theta(\phi,\mu) = 0$ and $\lambda_i(0) > 0$ for all $i \in \mathcal{N}$, $lim_{\phi\to 0}g(\phi) < 0$; because $\lim_{\phi\to\infty}\lambda_i(\phi) = 0$ for all $i \in \mathcal{N}$, $lim_{\phi\to\infty}g(\phi) = \lim_{\phi\to\infty}\Theta(\phi,\mu) > 0$. As a result, $g(\phi) = 0$ must have a unique solution.

Finally, when $g(\phi) = 0$, $\Theta(\phi,\mu) = \sum_{i\in\mathcal{N}} m_i\lambda_i(\phi)$, which is equivalent to Equation (1) of Definition 1. ∎

Proof of Theorem 1: Because $g(\phi)$ is strictly increasing in ϕ by Lemma 1 and by Equation (2), we have

$$\frac{dg}{d\phi} = \frac{\partial\Theta}{\partial\phi} - \sum_{k\in\mathcal{N}} m_k\frac{d\lambda_k}{d\phi} > 0.$$

When considering the capacity effect, we write the system utilization $\phi(\mu)$ as a function of the system capacity. By Lemma 1, $g(\phi(\mu)) = \Theta(\phi(\mu),\mu) - \sum_{k\in\mathcal{N}} m_k\lambda_k(\phi(\mu)) = 0$. By taking derivative of μ on both sides, we obtain

$$\frac{\partial\Theta}{\partial\phi}\frac{\partial\phi}{\partial\mu} + \frac{\partial\Theta}{\partial\mu} - \sum_{k\in\mathcal{N}} m_k\frac{d\lambda_k}{d\phi}\frac{\partial\phi}{\partial\mu} = 0,$$

which is equivalent to

$$\left(\frac{\partial\Theta}{\partial\phi} - \sum_{k\in\mathcal{N}} m_k\frac{d\lambda_k}{d\phi}\right)\frac{\partial\phi}{\partial\mu} = -\frac{\partial\Theta}{\partial\mu} \quad\text{or}\quad \frac{dg}{d\phi}\frac{\partial\phi}{\partial\mu} = -\frac{\partial\Theta}{\partial\mu}.$$

Since $\Theta(\phi,\mu)$ is increasing in μ, $\partial\Theta/\partial\mu > 0$, which implies

$$\frac{\partial\phi}{\partial\mu} = -\left(\frac{dg}{d\phi}\right)^{-1}\frac{\partial\Theta}{\partial\mu} < 0.$$

When considering the user effect, we write the system utilization $\phi(\mathbf{m})$ as a function of the user populations. By Lemma 1, $g(\phi(\mathbf{m})) = \Theta(\phi(\mathbf{m}),\mu) - \sum_{k\in\mathcal{N}} m_k\lambda_k(\phi(\mathbf{m})) = 0$. By taking derivative of m_i on both sides, we obtain

$$\frac{\partial\Theta}{\partial\phi}\frac{\partial\phi}{\partial m_i} - \sum_{k\in\mathcal{N}} m_k\frac{d\lambda_k}{d\phi}\frac{\partial\phi}{\partial m_i} - \lambda_i = 0,$$

which is equivalent to

$$\left(\frac{\partial\Theta}{\partial\phi} - \sum_{k\in\mathcal{N}} m_k\frac{d\lambda_k}{d\phi}\right)\frac{\partial\phi}{\partial m_i} = \lambda_i \quad\text{or}\quad \frac{dg}{d\phi}\frac{\partial\phi}{\partial m_i} = \lambda_i.$$

Since $\frac{dg}{d\phi} > 0$, the above implies $\frac{\partial\phi}{\partial m_i} = \left(\frac{dg}{d\phi}\right)^{-1}\lambda_i > 0$. Finally, the results for $\partial\theta_i/\partial\mu$, $\partial\theta_i/\partial m_i$ and $\partial\theta_j/\partial m_i$ can be derived by using $\theta_i(\phi) = m_i\lambda_i(\phi)$ and chain rules, and applying the above results for $\partial\phi/\partial\mu$ and $\partial\phi/\partial m_i$. ∎

Proof of Lemma 3: Because $s_i' > s_i$, $t_i' = p - s_i' < p - s_i = t_i$ and by Assumption 2, $m_i' = m_i(t_i') \geq m_i(t_i) = m_i$.

By Theorem 1, we know that $\partial\phi/\partial m_i > 0$, and therefore, $\phi(\mathbf{s}') \geq \phi(\mathbf{s})$. Also by Theorem 1, we know that $\partial\theta_i/\partial m_i > 0$ and $\partial\theta_j/\partial m_i < 0$ for all $j \neq i$. As a result, $\theta_i(\mathbf{s}') \geq \theta_i(\mathbf{s})$ and $\theta_j(\mathbf{s}') \leq \theta_j(\mathbf{s})$ for all $j \neq i$, which implies $U_j(\mathbf{s}') = v_j\theta_j(\mathbf{s}') \leq v_j\theta_j(\mathbf{s}) = U_j(\mathbf{s})$ for all $j \neq i$. ∎

Proof of Theorem 3: If $\mathbf{s}$ is a Nash equilibrium, each $s_i \in [0,q]$ maximizes $U_i(s_i;\mathbf{s}_{-i}) = (v_i - s_i)m_i(p - s_i)\lambda_i(\phi(\mathbf{s}))$. By Karush-Kuhn-Tucker condition, we can derive that

$$\frac{\partial U_i}{\partial s_i}\begin{cases} \leq 0 & \text{if } s_i = 0; \\ \geq 0 & \text{if } s_i = q; \\ = 0 & \text{if } 0 < s_i < q; \end{cases} \qquad \forall\, i \in \mathcal{N}. \tag{18}$$

For CP i with $s_i = 0$, the above condition tells that

$$\frac{\partial U_i}{\partial s_i} = (v_i - s_i)\frac{\partial\theta_i}{\partial s_i} - \theta_i = v_i\frac{\partial\theta_i}{\partial s_i} - \theta_i \leq 0.$$

By Lemma 3, we know $\partial\theta_i/\partial s_i > 0$ and the above implies $v_i \leq (\partial\theta_i/\partial s_i)^{-1}\theta_i$. By taking partial derivatives of s_i on $U_i = (v_i - s_i)m_i\lambda_i$, we deduce that

$$\frac{\partial U_i}{\partial s_i} = (v_i - s_i)\left(m_i\frac{\partial \lambda_i}{\partial s_i} + \lambda_i\frac{\partial m_i}{\partial s_i}\right) - m_i\lambda_i.$$

Dividing $m_i\lambda_i$ on both sides of (18), we have

$$(v_i - s_i)\left(\frac{1}{\lambda_i}\frac{\partial \lambda_i}{\partial s_i} + \frac{1}{m_i}\frac{\partial m_i}{\partial s_i}\right)\begin{cases} \leq 1 & \text{if } s_i = 0; \\ \geq 1 & \text{if } s_i = q; \\ = 1 & \text{if } 0 < s_i < q; \end{cases}$$

When we multiply s_i on both sides of the above, the left hand side becomes

$$(v_i - s_i)\left(\epsilon_{s_i}^{m_i} + \epsilon_{s_i}^{\lambda_i}\right) = (v_i - s_i)\left(\epsilon_{s_i}^{m_i} + \epsilon_{\phi}^{\lambda_i}\epsilon_{m_i}^{\phi}\epsilon_{s_i}^{m_i}\right) = \tau_i(\mathbf{s}).$$

When $s_i = 0$, $\tau_i(\mathbf{s}) = 0 = s_i$, and therefore, we have

$$\tau_i(\mathbf{s})\begin{cases} \geq s_i & \text{if } s_i = q; \\ = s_i & \text{if } 0 \leq s_i < q, \end{cases} \quad or \quad s_i = \min\{\tau_i(\mathbf{s}), q\}.$$

Finally, if $U_i(\mathbf{s})$ is concave in s_i for all $i \in \mathcal{N}$, local optimality also guarantees the global optimality and therefore, the above first order necessary conditions become sufficient condition for $\mathbf{s}$ being a Nash equilibrium. ∎

Proof of Theorem 4: The condition (10) implies that $U_i(s_i;\mathbf{s}_{-i})$ is concave in s_i for any $\mathbf{s}_{-i}$. Because the strategy space $[0,q]$ is compact, it guarantees the existence of Nash equilibrium. Suppose there exists two distinct Nash equilibria $\hat{\mathbf{s}}$ and $\tilde{\mathbf{s}}$. By concavity of $U_i(s_i;\mathbf{s}_{-i})$ in s_i and the maximum principle, for any $i \in \mathcal{N}$ and any $x_i \in [0,q]$, $(x_i - \hat{s}_i)u_i(\hat{\mathbf{s}}) \leq 0$ and $(x_i - \tilde{s}_i)u_i(\tilde{\mathbf{s}}) \leq 0$. By substituting $\mathbf{x} = \tilde{\mathbf{s}}$ in the first inequality and $\mathbf{x} = \hat{\mathbf{s}}$ in the second inequality, we deduce for any $i \in \mathcal{N}$, $(\tilde{s}_i - \hat{s}_i)u_i(\hat{\mathbf{s}}) \leq 0$, and $(\hat{s}_i - \tilde{s}_i)u_i(\tilde{\mathbf{s}}) \leq 0$. By adding the above inequalities, we further deduce that $(\tilde{s}_i - \hat{s}_i)(u_i(\hat{\mathbf{s}}) - u_i(\tilde{\mathbf{s}})) \leq 0, \quad \forall i \in \mathcal{N}$. The above is equivalent to $(\tilde{s}_i - \hat{s}_i)(u_i(\tilde{\mathbf{s}}) - u_i(\hat{\mathbf{s}})) \geq 0$ for all $i \in \mathcal{N}$, which contradicts the condition (10). ∎

Proof of Theorem 5: For any CP $j \in \mathcal{N}\backslash\{i\}$, we show that $(\hat{s}_j - s_j)(u_j(\hat{\mathbf{s}}) - u_j(\mathbf{s})) \geq 0$. Without loss of generality, we consider the cases of $s_j \leq \hat{s}_j$. By the KKT condition of (18), we have 4 cases. 1) $s_j = \hat{s}_j$: we have $(\hat{s}_j - s_j)(u_j(\hat{\mathbf{s}}) - u_j(\mathbf{s})) = 0$. 2) $s_j = 0$ and $\hat{s}_j \in (0,q)$: $u_j(\mathbf{s}) < 0$ and $u_j(\hat{\mathbf{s}}) = 0$; and therefore, the above becomes $\hat{s}_j(-u_j(\mathbf{s})) \geq 0$. 3) $s_j = 0$ and $\hat{s}_j = q$: $u_j(\mathbf{s}) < 0$ and $u_j(\hat{\mathbf{s}}) > 0$; and therefore, we have $q(u_j(\hat{\mathbf{s}}) - u_j(\mathbf{s})) \geq 0$. 4) $s_j \in (0,q)$ and $\hat{s}_j = q$: $u_j(\mathbf{s}) = 0$ and $u_j(\hat{\mathbf{s}}) > 0$; and therefore, the above becomes $(q - s_j)u_j(\hat{\mathbf{s}}) \geq 0$.

By the condition (10), we have $(\hat{s}_i - s_i)(u_i(\hat{\mathbf{s}}) - u_i(\mathbf{s})) < 0$. Suppose $\hat{s}_i < s_i$, the above implies that $u_i(\hat{\mathbf{s}}) > u_i(\mathbf{s})$. However, if $\hat{s}_i < s_i$, we must have $s_i > 0$ and by the KKT condition of (18), we have $u_i(\mathbf{s}) \geq 0$, which further implies that $u_i(\hat{\mathbf{s}}) > u_i(\mathbf{s}) \geq 0$. Again by the KKT condition of (18), $u_i(\hat{\mathbf{s}}) > 0$ implies $\hat{s} = q$ which contradicts with the assumption $\hat{s}_i < s_i$. Consequently, we have $\hat{s}_i \geq s_i$. ∎

Proof of Theorem 6: The condition (10) of Theorem 4 implies the local concavity of the utility functions. By Proposition 1.4.2 of [17], the Nash equilibrium $\mathbf{s}$ can be equivalently characterized as the solution of a variational inequality, denoted as $VI(F,K)$, where $F \triangleq -\mathbf{u}$ and $K \triangleq [0,q]^{|\mathcal{N}|}$. $\mathbf{s} \in \mathcal{K}$ is a solution of $VI(F,K)$ if $(\mathbf{x} - \mathbf{s})^T F(\mathbf{s}) \geq 0$ for all $\mathbf{x} \in K$. We apply the sensitivity analysis [48, 15] of variational inequalities to obtain the dynamics of the Nash equilibrium $\mathbf{s}(p,q)$ as the price p or the policy q changes.

For each CP i, the constraint $s_i \in [0,q]$ can be written as two linear constraints $g_i^-(\mathbf{s}) \triangleq s_i \geq 0$ and $g_i^+(\mathbf{s}) \triangleq q - s_i \geq 0$. For any $\mathbf{s}$, the set of binding constraints are

$$\mathcal{G} = \{g_i^-(\mathbf{s}) : i \in \mathcal{N}_-\} \cup \{g_i^+(\mathbf{s}) : i \in \mathcal{N}_+\}. \quad (19)$$

Because $\mathcal{N}_- \cap \mathcal{N}_+ = \emptyset$, the gradients of the binding constraints are linearly independent. Because $u_i(\mathbf{s}) = 0$ implies $s_i \in \widetilde{\mathcal{N}}$ for all $i \in \mathcal{N}$, by the KKT condition of (18), we know that the strict complementary slackness condition of Theorem 3.1 of [48] holds. By Theorem 4, the Nash equilibrium is locally unique, and therefore, by Theorem 3.1 of [48], in a neighborhood of (p,q), the Nash equilibrium can be written as a differentiable function $\mathbf{s}(p,q)$.

Let $m \triangleq |\mathcal{N}_-| + |\mathcal{N}_+|$ be the number of binding constraints. We define G as a $m \times n$ matrix, whose ith row is the gradient of the ith binding constraint with respect to $\mathbf{s}$. We define E_p and E_q as $m \times 1$ vectors, whose ith component are the partial derivatives of the ith binding constraint with respect to p and q, respectively. Following [15], we define $Q = G^T(GG^T)^{-1}G$ and M to be an $n \times m$ matrix satisfying $MG = Q$ and $QM = M$. Given the set $\mathcal{G}$ of linear constraints in (19), $Q = \{q_{ij}\}$ is a diagonal matrix satisfying $q_{ii} = 1$ if $i \notin \widetilde{\mathcal{N}}$ and $q_{ii} = 0$ otherwise, and $M = G^T$.

When q is the sensitivity parameter, $E_q = \{e_j\}$ satisfies that $e_j = 1$ if the jth constraint is a type of $g_i^+(\mathbf{s}) = q - s_i$ constraint and $e_j = 0$ otherwise. Because the constraints $\mathcal{G}$ are linear, Theorem 3.1 of [15] implies that $Q\nabla_q\mathbf{s}(q) = -ME_q$ and $(I - Q)(\nabla_\mathbf{s}F\nabla_q\mathbf{s}(q) + \nabla_q F) = \mathbf{0}$. Because when multiplying $\nabla_q\mathbf{s}(q)$ by Q, the values associated with the non-binding strategies vanish, the first equation implies

$$\partial s_i/\partial q = 0, \ \forall i \in \mathcal{N}_- \text{ and } \partial s_i/\partial q = 1, \ \forall i \in \mathcal{N}_+. \quad (20)$$

Because $F \triangleq -\mathbf{u}$ and $\mathbf{u}$ does not depend on q, the second equation can be written as $(I - Q)\nabla_\mathbf{s}\mathbf{u}\nabla_q\mathbf{s} = \mathbf{0}$. Because when multiplied by $I - Q$, the components associated with the binding strategies vanish, by substituting (20) into the above, we obtain $\nabla_{\tilde{\mathbf{s}}}\tilde{\mathbf{u}}\nabla_q\tilde{\mathbf{s}} + \nabla_\mathbf{s}\tilde{\mathbf{u}}E_q = \mathbf{0}$. By the condition (10) of Theorem 4, we deduce that $F \triangleq -\mathbf{u}$ is a *P-function* [31]. If we restrict to the CPs in $\widetilde{\mathcal{N}}$, we know that the Jacobian $\nabla_{\tilde{\mathbf{s}}}(-\tilde{\mathbf{u}})$ is a *P-matrix* [31], which is always non-singular. Therefore, we deduce $\nabla_q\tilde{\mathbf{s}} = -(\nabla_{\tilde{\mathbf{s}}}\tilde{\mathbf{u}})^{-1}\nabla_\mathbf{s}\tilde{\mathbf{u}}E_q = -\Psi\nabla_\mathbf{s}\tilde{\mathbf{u}}E_q$, the same as the third case of (11).

When taking p as the sensitivity parameter and applying Theorem 3.1 of [15], we can obtain $Q\nabla_p\mathbf{s}(p) = -ME_p$ and $(I - Q)(\nabla_\mathbf{s}F\nabla_p\mathbf{s}(p) + \nabla_p F) = \mathbf{0}$. Because the constraints in $\mathcal{G}$ do not depend on p, E_p is a zero vector, therefore, the first equation implies that $\partial s_i/\partial p = 0$ for all $i \notin \widetilde{\mathcal{N}}$. By substituting $F \triangleq -\mathbf{u}$ into the second equation, we have $(I - Q)(\nabla_\mathbf{s}\mathbf{u}\nabla_p\mathbf{s} + \nabla_p\mathbf{u}) = \mathbf{0}$. Similarly, by substituting $\partial s_i/\partial p = 0$ for all $i \notin \widetilde{\mathcal{N}}$ into the above, we obtain $\nabla_{\tilde{\mathbf{s}}}\tilde{\mathbf{u}}\nabla_p\tilde{\mathbf{s}} + \nabla_p\tilde{\mathbf{u}} = \mathbf{0}$. Because $\nabla_{\tilde{\mathbf{s}}}(-\tilde{\mathbf{u}})$ is non-singular, it is equivalent to the second case of (12) in a matrix form as

$$\nabla_p\tilde{\mathbf{s}} = -(\nabla_{\tilde{\mathbf{s}}}\tilde{\mathbf{u}})^{-1}\nabla_p\tilde{\mathbf{u}} = -\Psi\nabla_p\tilde{\mathbf{u}}. \quad ∎$$

Proof of Corollary 1: By (11) of Theorem 6, $\partial s_i/\partial q \geq 0$ is immediate for $i \notin \widetilde{\mathcal{N}}$. For the CPs in $\widetilde{\mathcal{N}}$, by Theorem 6, we have $\nabla_q\tilde{\mathbf{s}} = -(\nabla_{\tilde{\mathbf{s}}}\tilde{\mathbf{u}})^{-1}\nabla_\mathbf{s}\tilde{\mathbf{u}}E_q = -\Psi\nabla_\mathbf{s}\tilde{\mathbf{u}}E_q$. Because $\mathbf{u}$ is off-diagonally monotone, we know that $\nabla_{\tilde{\mathbf{s}}}(-\tilde{\mathbf{u}})$ is a P-matrix with non-positive off-diagonal entries or an M-matrix [39], which implies that all the entries of $-\Psi$ are nonnegative. By Theorem 6, we know that $\nabla_\mathbf{s}\tilde{\mathbf{u}}E_q$ is a vector of $\{\partial u_i/\partial s_j : i \in \widetilde{\mathcal{N}}, j \in \mathcal{N}_+\}$. Because $\mathbf{u}$ is off-diagonally monotone, the components of $\nabla_\mathbf{s}\tilde{\mathbf{u}}E_q$ are all non-negative, and therefore, $\nabla_q\tilde{\mathbf{s}} = -\Psi\nabla_\mathbf{s}\tilde{\mathbf{u}}E_q \geq \mathbf{0}$.

Now we have shown that $\partial s_i/\partial q \geq 0$ for all $i \in \mathcal{N}$. Since all the subsidies are monotonic, by Lemma 3, we deduce that $\partial\phi/\partial q \geq 0$. Finally, because the ISP's revenue can be written as $R = p\Theta(\phi,\mu)$

and $\partial\Theta(\phi,\mu)/\partial\phi \geq 0$, we have

$$\frac{\partial R}{\partial q} = \frac{\partial R}{\partial \phi}\frac{\partial \phi}{\partial q} = p\frac{\partial\Theta(\phi,\mu)}{\partial \phi}\frac{\partial \phi}{\partial q} \geq 0. \qquad \blacksquare$$

B. REFERENCES

[1] AT&T Sponsored Data. http://www.att.com/att/sponsoreddata/.

[2] Comcast Xbox Xfinity. http://xbox.comcast.net/.

[3] Freeband Technologies, Inc. http://www.freebandtechnologies.com.

[4] Google Apps for Verizon. http://www.verizon.com/smallbusiness/products/business-apps/google-apps/.

[5] Google global cache.

[6] Netflix's openconnect.

[7] Syntonic Wireless. http://www.syntonic.com/.

[8] M. Armstrong. Competition in two-sided markets. *RAND Journal of Economics*, 37(3):668–691, 2006.

[9] M. Campbell and J. Browning. Apple, Google asked to pay up as mobile operators face data flood. *Bloomberg News*, December 7 2010.

[10] J. P. Choi and B.-C. Kim. Net neutrality and investment incentives. *The Rand Journal of Economics*, 41(3):446–471, Autumn 2010.

[11] D. D. Clark, J. Wroclawski, K. R. Sollins, and R. Braden. Tussle in cyberspace: defining tomorrow's Internet. *IEEE/ACM Transactions on Networking*, 13(3), June 2005.

[12] C. Courcoubetis, F. Kelly, V. Siris, and R. Weber. A study of simple usage-based charging schemes for broadband networks. *Telecommunication Systems*, 15:323–343, 2000.

[13] C. Courcoubetis and R. Weber. *Pricing Communication Networks: Economics, Technology and Modelling*. John Wiley & Sons Ltd., 2003.

[14] J. Crowcroft. Net neutrality: the technical side of the debate: a white paper. *ACM SIGCOMM Computer Communication Review*, 37(1), January 2007.

[15] S. Dafermos. Sensitivity analysis in variational inequalities. *Mathematics of Operations Research*, 13(3):421–434, August 1988.

[16] N. Economides and J. Tag. Network neutrality and network management regulation: Quality of service, price discrimination, and exclusive contracts. *Research Handbook on Governance of the Internet. Ed. Ian Brown. London: Edward Elgar*, 2012.

[17] F. Facchinei and J.-S. Pang. *Finite-Dimensional Variational Ineqaulities and Complementarity Problems*. Springer-Verlag New York, Inc, 2003.

[18] D. Gale and H. Nikaido. The Jacobian matrix and global univalence of mappings. *Mathematische Annalen*, 159(2):81–93, 1965.

[19] S. Gustin. Netflix pays verizon in streaming deal, following comcast pact. *Time Magazine*, Apr. 28 2014.

[20] D. Hawkins and H. A. Simon. Note: Some conditions of macroeconomic stability. *Econometrica*, 17(3/4), 1949.

[21] M. L. Honig and K. Steiglitz. Usage-based pricing of packet data generated by a heterogeneous user population. *Proceedings of IEEE INFOCOM*, 1995.

[22] T. Johnson. FCC chairman supports net neutrality rules but not limits on usage-based pricing. *Variety.com*, (December 2nd), 2013.

[23] G. Kesidis, A. Das, and G. de Veciana. On flat-rate and usage-based pricing for tiered commodity internet services. *Proceedings of the 42nd Annual Conference on Information Sciences and Systems (CISS)*, 2008.

[24] C. Labovitz, D. McPherson, S. Iekel-Johnson, J. Oberheide, and F. Jahanian. Internet inter-domain traffic. In *Proceedings of the ACM SigComm*, New Delhi, India, 2010.

[25] P. Laskowski and J. Chuang. Network monitors and contracting systems: competition and innovation. In *Proceedings of the ACM SigComm*, Pisa, Italy, 2006.

[26] R. S. Lee and T. Wu. Subsidizing creativity through network design: Zero-pricing and net neutrality. *Journal of Economic Perspectives*, 23(3):61–76, 2009.

[27] R. T. B. Ma. Subsidization competition: Vitalizing the neutral Internet. http://arxiv.org/pdf/1406.2516v1.pdf.

[28] R. T. B. Ma, D. Chiu, J. C. Lui, V. Misra, and D. Rubenstein. Internet Economics: The use of Shapley value for ISP settlement. *IEEE/ACM Transactions on Networking*, 18(3), June 2010.

[29] R. T. B. Ma, D. Chiu, J. C. Lui, V. Misra, and D. Rubenstein. On cooperative settlement between content, transit and eyeball Internet service providers. *IEEE/ACM Transactions on Networking*, 19(3), 2011.

[30] J. K. MacKie-Mason and H. R. Varian. Some FAQs about usage-based pricing. *Computer Networks and ISDN Systems*, 28:257–265, 1995.

[31] J. Moré and W. Rheinboldt. On P- and S-functions and related classes of n-dimensional nonlinear mappings. *Linear Algebra and its Applications*, 6:45–68, 1973.

[32] M. Morgan. Pricing schemes key in LTE future. *Telecomasia.net, September 12*, 2011.

[33] J. Musacchio, G. Schwartz, and J. Walrand. A two-sided market analysis of provider investment incentives. *Review of Network Economics*, 8(1):22–39, March 2009.

[34] G. Nagesh. FCC says 'ready to intervene' over AT&T data plan. *The Wall Street Journal, January 8*, 2014.

[35] P. Njoroge, A. E. Ozdaglar, N. E. Stier-Moses, and G. Y. Weintraub. Investment in two sided markets and the net neutrality debate. *Columbia Business School DRO Working Paper No. 2010-05.*, 2010.

[36] W. Norton. The Internet peering playbook: connecting to the core of the Internet. *DrPeering Press*, 2011.

[37] A. Odlyzko. Internet pricing and the history of communications. *Computer Networks*, 36(5):493–517, 2001.

[38] M. Page, L. Rossi, and C. Rand. A viable future model for the Internet. *A. T. Kearney Paper*, December 2010.

[39] G. Poole and T. Boullion. A survey on m-matrices. *SIAM Review*, 16(4):419–427, 1974.

[40] S. Ramachandran. Netflix to pay Comcast for smoother streaming. *The Wall Street Journal*, Feb. 23 2014.

[41] J.-C. Rochet and J. Tirole. Platform competition in two-sided markets. *Journal of the European Economic Association*, 1(4):990–1029, 2003.

[42] A. Schatz and S. E. Ante. FCC chief backs usage-based broadband pricing. *Wall Street Journal*, (December 2), 2010.

[43] L. Segall. Verizon ends unlimited data plan. *CNN Money, July 6*, 2011.

[44] S. Shakkottai, R. Srikant, A. Ozdaglar, and D. Acemoglu. The price of simplicity. *IEEE Journal on Selected Areas of Communications*, 26(7), September 2008.

[45] N. Shetty, G. Schwartz, and J. Walrand. Internet QoS and regulations. *IEEE/ACM Transactions on Networking*, 18(6), December 2010.

[46] J. G. Sidak. A consumer-welfare approach to network neutrality regulation of the Internet. *Journal of Competition Law and Economics*, 2(3):349–474, September 2006.

[47] P. Taylor. AT&T imposes usage caps on fixed-line broadband. *Financial Times, March 14*, 2011.

[48] R. L. Tobin. Sensitivity analysis for variational inequalities. *Journal of Optimization Theory and Applications*, 48(1):191–204, 1986.

[49] T. Wu. Network neutrality, broadband discrimination. *Journal of Telecommunications and High Technology Law*, 2:141–179, 2003.

Pricing The Last Mile: Data Capping For Residential Broadband

Konstantinos Poularakis
ECE Dept.
University of Thessaly
Volos, Greece

Ioannis Pefkianakis
Technicolor Labs
Paris, France

Jaideep Chandrashekar
Technicolor Labs
Paris, France

Leandros Tassiulas
Electrical Eng. Dept. &
Institute of Network Science
Yale University
New Haven CT 06520

ABSTRACT

In recent years, ISPs in mature residential broadband markets have been moving away from flat-rate pricing schemes to ones that involve usage limits (or "data caps"). These changes have led to a lively debate about the merits of data capping. While previous work has studied the theoretical benefits of data capped pricing models, there is relatively little work that provides insights into exactly how to design data capped tariffs, and their impact on the parties involved, i.e., ISPs and their broadband subscribers. In this paper, we formulate the problem of selecting optimal data capped tariffs based on a simple, extensible model of ISP costs and revenues, and a novel model that captures how users evaluate a set of offered tariffs. We show that the problem is NP-Hard and describe two heuristics that provide reasonable solutions. We also describe an approximation algorithm that yields bounded solutions. We apply this framework on a novel broadband usage dataset collected from real-users and examine the cost-benefit impact of data capping for various cost regimes that reflect different regional markets around the world. We find that in highly competitive markets with relatively high traffic costs, data capping can indeed help the ISP to manage costs while resulting in a more equitable per unit data cost across the users. However, in the absence of meaningful competition or when traffic costs are low, data capping largely benefits the ISP and is to the detriment of subscribers.

Categories and Subject Descriptors

C.2.3 [**Computer Communication Networks**]: Network Operations; C.4 [**Performance of Systems**]: Measurement Techniques, Modeling Techniques

CoNEXT'14, December 2–5, 2014, Sydney, Australia.
Copyright 2014 ACM 978-1-4503-3279-8/14/12 ...$15.00.
http://dx.doi.org/10.1145/2674005.2675008.

Keywords

Broadband Access Networks; Usage-based Pricing; Data Caps

1. INTRODUCTION

Flat rate models, where subscribers pay a fixed monthly price independent of actual usage, have traditionally been the dominant pricing model in many residential broadband markets and this by virtue of appealing to both providers and subscribers. Subscribers find the predictability of a fixed monthly bill compelling and easy to understand. At the same time, service providers benefit by doing away with complicated accounting systems. However, in recent years, a significant number of ISPs are moving away from such models towards those that involve usage limits or "data caps". Here, a subscription plan is associated with a data usage (traffic volume) cap over a time interval (typically the billing period). When the data cap is exceeded, the provider applies an overage policy to the subscriber and this can range from lowering or degrading the service levels, charging block price increments, or even interrupting the service. While usage limits have long existed in certain regions with poor network connectivity (e.g., S.E. Asia, Africa), their adoption in highly connected, mature markets is a recent trend. Some notable examples include Verizon and Comcast in the US, Belgacom and Deutsche Telekom in Europe. The rationalization offered by providers while introducing such pricing plans largely centers around managing increases in bandwidth costs, caused by increasing traffic demands on their networks from online video streaming [1] or BitTorrent traffic. However, these pricing changes have led to a consumer outcry against the practice of data capping [2, 3], arguing that the practice is unfair [1] and hinders new innovative services.

While both sides present valid arguments, the actual merits of data capping, or the lack thereof, depend on a host of factors that vary by region – broadband competition, subscriber behavior, transit and capacity prices, and so on. Despite the fact that there has been considerable work applying economic theory to the issue of data caps, the investigations have either focused on examining the theoretical benefits of data capping [4–7], or quantitatively evaluated the benefits for a pre-specified set of data capping tariffs [8, 9]. There has been relatively less work in understanding exactly how

[1]Some service providers often exclude their own bandwidth intensive Video-on-Demand service from the data caps.

a provider should design a data capped pricing structure, and how the provider (and subscribers) will fare as these behaviors and costs change over time (or from region to region). Such an investigation is critical to cutting through the rhetoric that exists today and informing the current debate on exactly who benefits from the practice of data capping. To carry this out, we need a valid mechanism to identify a set of feasible tariffs, which takes into account the ISP's cost structure the motivation and behavior of subscribers; however, identifying such a mechanism is challenging for the following reasons. First, ISP cost structures are typically confidential and not (easily) available to the research community. Second, subscribers may be unpredictable (or even irrational), which makes modeling behavior difficult at a high level. Lastly, the tariffs must be evaluated on a realistic and sufficiently fine-grained dataset of broadband usage in the context of various regional cost scenarios.

In this paper, we present an initial attempt to tackle these challenges. To address the first, we design the *Tariff Formulation Problem* that marries a simple, extensible model of ISP costs and revenues to a model that captures user utility in a framework that can select a set of optimal tariffs. We show this problem to be NP-Hard. Subsequently, we identify two heuristics and an approximation algorithm that yields bounded solutions. The TFP framework enables a quantitative analysis of the impact of introducing data capping on both providers and subscribers. To overcome the last challenge, we leverage a dataset of detailed traffic usage data obtained from 260 subscribers of a large European ISP. Collating traffic pricing information from several sources, we synthesize a variety of regional markets and investigate the impact of data capping in each. Our work in this paper combines strong theoretical contributions with a careful empirical data analysis from real ISP subscribers. The results we present provide valuable insights in the current data capping debate and clearly differentiate situations in which data capping can indeed help users, and those in which the imposition of data caps largely benefits the ISPs bottom line at the cost of subscribers. The main contributions of this paper are summarized as follows.

1) We analyze a dataset of 260 ISP subscribers and investigate the merits of data capping (which limits data volume) as a mechanism to reduce traffic rates (which affect network traffic costs). We find that aggregate data usage of subscribers is proportional to their contribution to the ISP's peak rates (and costs). This establishes that under certain conditions, moving to a data capped regime can lead to transit and capacity cost reductions for the ISP (§4).

2) We study the problem of determining optimal tariffs (price, speed, data cap) for an ISP. Using simple and intuitive models of user behavior and ISP costs & revenue, we formulate the *Tariff Formation Problem* (TFP) and show that it is NP-Hard. We present a set of three algorithms, one of which is an approximation algorithm that yields solutions with bounded performance (§5).

3) We examine various cost scenarios reflecting various regional markets around the world and, evaluate the impact of moving from flat-rate pricing to a data capped model. We find that ISPs are able to use data capping to indirectly reduce network costs only in markets with relatively high transit and capacity prices. In the best case scenario – with traffic prices near $1€/\mathrm{Mbps}$, and with 8 tariffs – an ISP can improve their bottom line by 23% by instituting caps, and with a small net change in subscription revenues (less than 5%). In competitive markets where traffic prices are low, ISPs gain relatively little from instituting data caps (they have more to lose from customers departing). On the other hand, a lack of competition reduces the probability of subscribers departing, which allows the ISP more freedom in instituting caps – even when traffic prices are low (§6).

2. RELATED WORK

There is a large body of existing work that has investigated usage-based pricing – data-capped models are a specific instance – from the perspective of economic theory [4–7, 10–13]. The general consensus across these works is that, in theory, data caps are overall beneficial to both service providers and subscribers: they can raise the ISP's revenue, alleviate cross-subsidization across services, and potentially reduce network congestion. In our work, we take these benefits as theoretical possibilities and seek to assess, quantitatively, how the ISP is affected by adopting data caps and by exploring a number of cost scenarios that reflect markets worldwide. In order to do so, we first construct a framework to actually determine the appropriate data caps for a set of cost structures (and a subscriber population). Our work is also novel in that we perform an empirical evaluation using a fine-grained broadband usage dataset from real ISP subscribers.

There have been a few efforts related to ours that provide an empirical analysis of data capped pricing plans in residential broadband markets [8, 9, 14]. However, our own work is different in the several respects. The work in [8, 9] evaluates the effect of a given set of data caps that are taken as inputs; in contrast, one of the main contributions of our work is a mechanism to design *optimal* data capped tariffs, which we then evaluate on a number of different market conditions. In contrast to the datasets presented in [8, 9], the dataset used in this paper spans different access technologies and speed tiers, allowing us to contrast behavior across these populations. Finally in [14], the authors propose a scheme where access-*rates* are capped at certain times, rather than aggregate data usage. While such an approach is potentially interesting, it has not yet been adopted by any ISPs to date.

While data capped pricing plans have recently become popular in mature markets, they are the most common offerings of almost all mobile cellular providers today [6], possibly due to spectrum scarcity, and very high costs of deploying new infrastructure. In [15], it is shown that usage limits on SMS, voice and data can inflate the difference between revenues and costs by a factor of 2 without a significant erosion of the subscriber base. A more recent work has also shown that a wireless provider obtains a higher revenue with usage-based (or flat-rate) time-dependent scheme if the capacity is insufficient (or sufficient) [16]. Finally, previous work has looked at the issue of pricing in Internet transit markets [17]. In our own work, apart from the focus on a different market (residential broadband), we go beyond setting tariff prices and extract tariff sets which requires an optimal distribution of data caps across speed tiers in conjunction with fixing the price.

3. BACKGROUND

In this section, we first provide a very brief overview of the residential broadband market and the popular pricing models seen today. Subsequently, we describe the broadband usage dataset of real users that we leverage to understand the impact of data caps.

3.1 Pricing in Residential Broadband

There are three dominant access technologies for residential broadband available today – ADSL2, Cable and Fiber. ADSL and its variants reuse legacy twisted pair copper wire meant for fixed line telephony. The latest ADSL2+ deployments offer capacity up to 24/1Mbps (downstream/upstream), but the speeds degrade quickly with increasing distance from the and performance is adversely impacted by distance from the local point of presence. Newer variants, e.g., VDSL offer significantly higher capacity ($\sim$100 Mbps) by shortening the local loop (and using alternative technologies for back haul). Cable broadband networks deliver data over the coax cable TV infrastructure (the access network is shared by subscribers behind a cable *head end*), offering download speeds of up to 42.88 Mbps, with emerging standards promising rates upwards of 100 Mbps. Finally, residential Fiber Internet service covers a range of technologies that transmit data over fiber optic cables at speeds that exceed the other technologies.

Independent of the access technology, there are two dominant pricing models in existence. With **flat-rate** pricing, the ISP charges a fixed, typically monthly price, allowing for *unlimited* use by the subscriber. Such flat-rate models have so far been predominant in residential markets (particularly in the western hemisphere). In contrast, **data capped** pricing models associate a subscription price with a usage limit (the data-cap), and apply an overage policy when this limit is exceeded. To illustrate one such policy, AT&T, Comcast and MediaCom charge increments of $10 (for each 50GB of data used above the cap). Data caps are typically specified monthly; however, some ISPs (e.g., CableOne) are even experimenting with daily usage limits. In both models, it is common for providers to offer several *speed tier* offerings (downstream/upstream *speed* limits) at different prices. Often, ISPs offer several data cap choices for a given speed tier (with suitable price differentiation). Finally, additional services – VoIP, Television, Home Automation, etc. – are often *bundled* together with the basic broadband connectivity service. Subscribers enjoy a small cost benefit from the bundling and in return, increase their affinity to the ISP (which benefits the latter).

3.2 Dataset Description

The broadband usage dataset used in this paper was collected from 260 residential gateways over six months of normal operation (Oct. 2013 - Mar. 2014). Each subscriber gateway[2] corresponds to a single billing address, and thus a single home network. The 260 subscribers in our dataset were all enrolled in triple-play service offerings (i.e., Broadband, IPTV + VoIP), but vary in the access technology and speed tier. The subscribers in our dataset were part of a voluntary trial deployment wherein an additional software module was added to the ISP provided home gateway. This module extracted a set of low level traffic usage counters that were timestamped and sent to a back end server approximately every minute where it was recorded into a database. Among other things, most relevant to this paper, the counters recorded the number of incoming (and outgoing) bytes and packets seen at the home gateway to WAN interface.

While the subscribers in our dataset were enrolled in triple-play packages, our empirical analysis only focuses on the Internet broadband service, so the prices we consider are based on what the unbundled service would have cost a subscriber. Table 1 presents a summary of the subscriber population in our dataset, across the different service tiers; the adjusted monthly monthly subscription price is indicated with each tier. Our dataset has the following salient properties: (i) it is temporally fine-grained (1 minute samples), which allows us to understand traffic demand – *individually and in the aggregate* – over short time scales, (ii) by extending to six-months, it is unlikely to be biased by any short term variations in subscriber behavior (vacations, seasonal effects, etc.), (iii) it includes subscribers from different tariffs and access technologies, allowing us to contrast behavior across these populations. While our dataset captures behavior from a relatively small population (the actual ISP has in excess of a million users), we do see a great deal of variability in data usage across subscribers (even within the same tier). Furthermore, we compare our dataset against a much

[2]We use "subscriber", "home", "gateway" and "user" interchangeably.

Access	Speed Tier(r_t) Mbps	Monthly Price(p_t) €	% Subscribers
ADSL	24/1	21.94	34.8
Fiber	30/3	25.20	5.3
Fiber	100/10	33.33	59.9

Table 1: Tariff plans for all the subscribers in our dataset. The ISP currently only offers flat-rate tariffs.

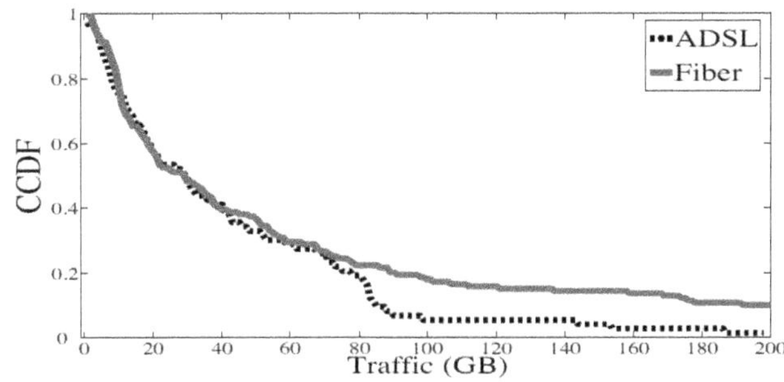

Figure 1: Tail Distribution of Monthly Data Usage for Dec. 2013.

larger dataset, which has been made available by FCC Measuring Broadband America program [18]. In Figure 1, we plot the tail distribution of monthly data usage (in gigabytes) seen across the 260 subscribers for one particular month (we observed similar statistics for the remaining months). The shape of the distribution closely resembles the one presented in the FCC study (cf. chart 24 in [18]). Overall, the FCC statistics indicate that the data usage is slightly higher than observed in our dataset; we believe this can be explained by the penetration of online video streaming services in the US (Netflix, Hulu, etc.), which did not exist in Europe at the time of this study.

4. DO DATA CAPS WORK?

Putting aside some of the arguments about why data capping is finding favor with ISPs, does it even work as a mechanism? That is, can an ISP reduce traffic costs by imposing data caps on users. At first glance, it does not appear to be the case. On the one hand, traffic costs, particularly at transit and peering links are generally tied to *rates*. For example, transit (traffic) payments are based on the 95%-ile of rates, computed over 5 min. intervals, seen over a month (we denote this P_{95}). Capacity upgrades are often triggered by sustained, upward shifts in the peak traffic, i.e. the 100%-ile of the traffic rates in the ISP's network. On the other hand, data caps have the effect of limiting the aggregate traffic volume of the ISP over a *long period* (usually a month). Thus, instituting data caps may not necessarily lower the transit and capacity cost. Moreover, it may not target the right users. Consider two subscribers with the same monthly data usage, but very different behaviors. One of them may create traffic *only* in the peak times and thus bears a higher traffic cost than the other. Data caps penalize them both!

To understand the prevalence of such cases, we examined the correlation between a subscriber's monthly data usage and its impact on the traffic costs of the ISP. The latter metric is computed as follows: we first aggregate traffic across all the users and compute the P_{95} statistic for each month. Then, we identify all the 5 min. intervals where the aggregate traffic rate exceeds P_{95}. We call these the *peak traffic* windows and the peak traffic volume is the volume of traffic across these windows. Each subscriber's traffic cost contribution is simply the ratio of the traffic volume that she generates (in the peak traffic windows) to the peak traffic volume of the ISP.

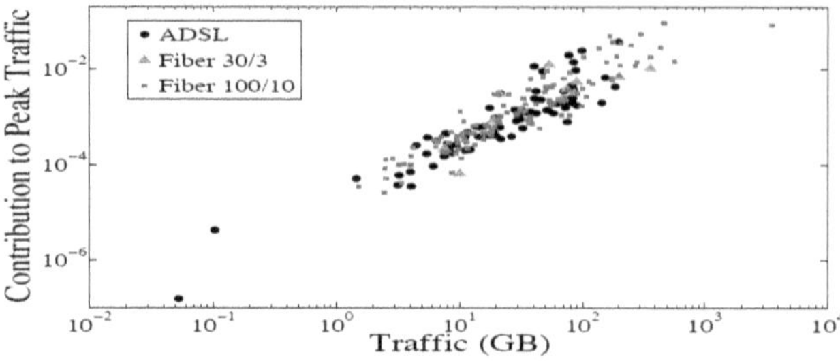

Figure 2: Relationship between subscriber's (monthly) data usage and contribution to ISP peak traffic (and costs).

Figure 2 is a scatter plot across the subscribers in our dataset which shows the subscriber monthly data usage (on x-axis) against their traffic cost contribution for the month of Dec. 2013 (on y-axis). Surprisingly, we find a strong linear relationship that extends several orders of magnitude, and across *all* the different service offerings. We obtained similar results in all the other months and we omit these due to a lack of space. As captured in Fig. 2, the more data a subscriber consumes over the month, the higher his contribution to the traffic cost becomes. This relationship may be explained by the fact that most subscribers (typically) tend to use their devices at particular times of the day (evenings, nights and weekends) and these periods coincide with the peak traffic windows. While this relationship might not hold for some kinds of application usage (for e.g., heavy bit-torrent users), it is likely to apply for typical application usage. Importantly, video streaming – which drives much of the traffic demand today – requires user engagement with the device, and this can happen only at given periods in a day. The takeaway from this analysis is that imposing data caps would on average limit the monthly data usage of a subscriber, and consequently, his contribution to the traffic cost. Thus, under certain circumstances, implementing data caps could possibly reduce the traffic cost burden of an ISP (this can be a significant cost).

Figure 2 also comments on the *unfairness* inherent in flat-rate pricing. The monthly data usage spans two orders of magnitude across subscribers. Importantly, this holds inside each service class, particularly in Fiber/100/10 and ADSL/24/1, which are the dominant populations. This wide disparity in usage, even as all users in a service class pay the same monthly price (with flat-rate), implies that subscribers bear different "costs" for the ISP; typically, heavy users cost the ISP more than light users. In order not to suffer from having to service the heavy users, the ISP has two choices: (i) increase the costs uniformly so that no subscriber leads to a negative gain for the ISP, or (ii) spread the higher cost from heavy users across the lightweight users. The former approach risks losing customers while the latter is inherently unfair. Clearly, flat rate pricing cannot lead to a scheme that is fair and satisfactory to all parties. In contrast, a pricing model with differentiated data caps, i.e., where subscribers with a type of service are offered multiple data caps (at different prices), reduces the inequity across subscribers.

Summarizing, in circumstances that cover most kinds of subscriber application usage, data caps can be a feasible mechanism to reduce the traffic volume, and also the traffic rates needed to be supported by the ISP. However, the overall *cost* benefit is likely to depend on a number of factors – subscriber behavior, bandwidth unit costs, ISP competition, and so on. In the next section, we introduce a model and a tariff computation framework that allows us to understand the cost impact of imposing data caps over a range of traffic pricing scenarios.

5. DETERMINING DATA CAPS

We formulate the *Tariff Formation Problem* (TFP), which takes as input (i) a set of subscribers with their current tariff prices, (ii) a set of cost parameters and (iii) a *target* number of tariffs and which returns a *set* of tariffs, each defined as a triple (speed tier, data cap, price). We show that TFP is NP-Hard and describe two heuristics and an approximation algorithm. The solutions obtained reflect viable choices for an ISP trying to balance subscription revenue with network costs. However, in real life, an ISP may have to balance a number of other considerations – some very long term – when selecting tariff offerings and so we consider the tariff solutions we obtain to establish a lower bound.

5.1 The ISP Model

We model an ISP that has a set of subscribers, $\mathcal{N}$. Each subscriber $n \in \mathcal{N}$ selects a particular tariff t from a set of tariffs, $\mathcal{T}$, where $T = |\mathcal{T}|$. Each tariff t represents a triple (p_t, r_t, x_t), where p_t is the monthly subscription price (Table 1, column 3), r_t is the speed tier (Table 1, column 2), and x_t is the associated data cap. The speed tier r_t is selected from a *finite* set of tiers, $\mathcal{L}$. Finally, x_t is selected from a finite, possibly large set $\mathcal{X}$. We make two simplifying assumptions: (i) subscribers do not exceed the data caps associated with the tariff selected (this allows us to ignore the effect of ISP overage policies); (ii) a subscriber can select any one of the offered tariffs, even though in practice all the offerings may not be available to them (e.g., fiber access may not be available in rural areas).

The (network) cost of serving traffic in a residential broadband network has two main components: (i) *capacity* and infrastructure costs, which includes all costs related to networking equipment, last mile access, power, etc., and (ii) *transit* costs, paid for the fraction of traffic going through upstream transit providers. In general, there are a number of other considerations that may come into play – sunk costs relating to last mile infrastructure upgrades, building and personnel costs, and so on. However, we expect these costs to be less dynamic and managed on far slow(er) timescales (over years). On the other hand, the transit and capacity costs are affected each month by the behavior of subscribers. Our model mainly focuses on these, noting that the sunk costs can be captured by an additional constant factor (when amortized over a long enough period of time).

We then define the residual (or balance) of an ISP, denoted J, as the net difference between incoming subscriber revenue and the outgoing costs associated with serving the subscribers.

$$J = \sum_{t \in \mathcal{T}} (p_t \cdot D_t) - C(\mathbf{D}) - G(\mathbf{D}) \tag{1}$$

D_t is the number of subscribers that choose $t \in \mathcal{T}$ at a price p_t. Thus, $p_t \cdot D_t$ represents revenue from the single tariff t. We denote the demand vector across tariffs as $\mathbf{D} = (D_t)$. The functions $C(\mathbf{D})$ and $G(\mathbf{D})$ capture the capacity and transit costs, respectively. In the following, we first discuss a way to model the demand vector $\mathbf{D}$ and subsequently describe the cost functions for transit and capacity.

5.1.1 Subscriber Demand

Previous efforts at modeling subscriber utility have considered speed tier and data caps *individually*. For example, the work in [19, 20] considers subscriber utility to be logarithmically related to the speed tier and this is based on the principle of diminishing returns. Users that stream movies regularly are able to watch higher quality videos with higher access speeds, but only up to a point (the video bit rate is bounded); after this point, the utility increases very

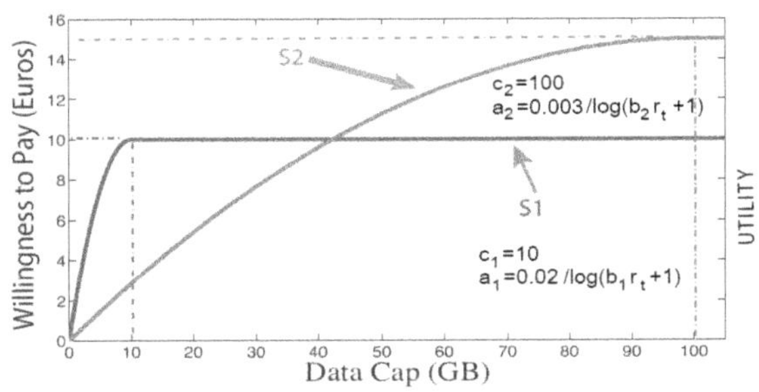

Figure 3: Utility function for two users (S1, S2) realized for a single speed tier r_t.

slowly or not at all. Furthermore, users that carry out very different activities (e.g., video streaming and web browsing) are like to value high speed tiers very differently (web browsing quality is not improved with higher access speeds). Considering data caps, the work in [9, 21] considers utility to be quadratically related to them until a certain saturation point. Intuitively, each subscriber typically has a finite (possibly large) set of activities that she may wish to carry out over a period of time – watch movies or videos, stream music, video chat with friends and family, and so on. These activities, which are limited by the time available to the subscriber, and can be associated with a certain data need. Having data caps that are significantly larger than this *need*, is not likely to be more valuable to the user. In our work, we combine these two factors, speed tier and data caps, and construct a utility function governed by three user parameters: (i) a scaling parameter a_n that captures how different people evaluate a fixed amount of resource, (ii) a parameter b_n that specifies the slope of the logarithmic function for the speed, and (iii) a parameter c_n that determines the saturation point for data usage.

Based on these, we define the utility of user n for tariff t as:

$$U_n(t) = \begin{cases} a_n \cdot \log(b_n \cdot r_t + 1) \cdot (c_n \cdot x_t - \frac{x_t^2}{2}) & : 0 \leq x_t \leq c_n \\ a_n \cdot \log(b_n \cdot r_t + 1) \cdot (\frac{c_n^2}{2}) & : x_t > c_n \end{cases} \tag{2}$$

For a fixed speed tier r_t, utility increases with the data cap x_t, until $x_t = c_n$, and flattens out beyond this value. Moreover, $U_n(t) = 0$ if $r_t = 0$, since all users need *some* bandwidth (even if small). Similarly, for a given cap x_t, utility increases as r_t increases and where the shape of this increase is controlled by the parameter b_n. To illustrate this, we depict the utility functions for two subscribers S1 and S2 (for a single speed tier, r_t) in Figure 3. Here, S1 and S2 have identical values for b_n and only differ in the parameters a_n and c_n. Here, based on their respective utility functions, S1 is willing to pay at most 10€ for a 10GB cap while S2 is willing to pay at most 15€ for a 100GB cap. If the ISP were to impose a data cap less than 10GB (for S1) and 100GB (for S2), their individual utilities would decrease. In order to assess demand for a particular tariff, users are assigned to particular tariffs, and we consider two distinct families of demand functions, *deterministic* and stochastic *logit*, that allow D_t to be reconstructed for every $t \in \mathcal{T}$.

Deterministic demand model: In this model, a subscriber $n \in \mathcal{N}$ is interested purely in maximizing his *surplus*, defined as $U_n(t) - p_t$. The surplus is the gap between how much a certain tariff is worth to the user and how much the ISP charges for it. Thus, subscriber n will pick tariff t as $\arg\max_{t \in \mathcal{T}}(U_n(t) - p_t)$.

If the surplus is negative over all offered tariffs, i.e., the price of every offered tariff is higher than the subscriber's willingness to pay, then the subscriber leaves the ISP. To simplify the notation when dealing with a large set of subscribers $\mathcal{N}$, we define the binary decision $q_{n,t}$, such that $q_{n,t} = 1$ if subscriber n selects tariff t, and 0 otherwise. Then, $\mathbf{q} = (q_{n,t} : n \in \mathcal{N}, t \in \mathcal{T})$ is the tariff selection vector.

There are two shortcomings with the deterministic demand model. First, it assumes that subscribers always are rational and driven by self-interest which may not be the case in real life. For e.g., a subscriber may desire to stay with a higher priced tariff even if equally suitable, cheaper tariffs are available [4], or else may choose to stay with the ISP even if there is no tariff with positive surplus because the cost of switching ISPs is high [22]. Second, the deterministic model does not capture ISP competition. In non-monopoly markets, a subscriber may depart for a competitor if the price or convenience is better than the status quo. The *logit* model, widely used in econometric demand estimation [23] and also applied previously towards modeling Internet transit pricing [17], can model such uncertainties.

Logit demand model: This stochastic model defines a probability distribution over the set of offered tariffs, where the probabilities depend on the individual utility functions. Thus, the probability that subscriber n selects the tariff t is given as:

$$s_{n,t} = \frac{e^{u_n(t) - p_t}}{\sum_{t' \in \mathcal{T}} (e^{u_n(t') - p_{t'}}) + c} \tag{3}$$

Note that unlike in the deterministic model, a subscriber could have a non zero probability associated with more than one tariff. In Eq. 3, c is non-negative constant that incorporates the notion of competition in the ISP market. In a monopoly market, $c = 0$ and $\sum_{t \in \mathcal{T}} s_{n,t} = 1, \forall n$, and each subscriber will pick one of the offered tariffs. However, when ISPs compete, $c > 0$ and $\sum_{t \in \mathcal{T}} s_{n,t} < 1$, the probability that the subscriber n will leave the ISP is given by $1 - \sum_{t \in \mathcal{T}} s_{n,t}$. It should be pointed out that c does not count the number of competing entities, but simply captures the level of competition. In general, higher c is associated with a larger risk of a subscriber departing to a competitor. Finally, with the *logit* model, we describe demand for tariff t simply as the sum of probabilities over subscribers: $D_t = \sum_{n \in \mathcal{N}} s_{n,t}$.

5.1.2 ISP Network Costs

We now describe how we model and estimate the actual cost functions for transit and capacity. Note that in each case, we take the unit price(s) as parameters; we elaborate on this further in Section 6.

Transit Cost: Of the total traffic generated by the subscribers of a residential ISP, a fraction $0 \leq f \leq 1$, goes from the ISP network towards one of its transit providers; these essentially sell connectivity to the rest of the Internet. The particular value of f depends on several factors such as ISP size, geographic area, user demographics, and so on. For example, f is around 0.3 in the case of some Japanese ISPs, while it can be as large as 0.8 in parts of Africa [24]. Transit providers charge their customers on the P_{95} rate and with a unit price of t_p €/Mbps that is negotiated between the parties. Stanojevic et al. observed an increase in P_{95} with measured total data usage up to a saturation point [24]. This may be explained by noting that increased cumulative traffic usage is likely to be distributed in time, and contribute marginally less to P_{95} which depends on volumes during peak periods. With this insight, we can model the transit cost as a concave function of the total data usage of subscribers. Given that the total traffic volume of the ISP is bounded by the sum over all subscriber caps, we consider that transit traffic is a concave function of the data caps. One such function is the following:

$$P_{95} = f \cdot d \cdot log(\sum_{t \in \mathcal{T}} D_t \cdot x_t) \quad (4)$$

Here, d is a positive (scaling) constant that relates volume to rates. We estimate this term by extracting the summation term in Eq. 4 for each month of data in our dataset, and fitting this to the values of P_{95} which is also extracted from the data. Finally, the network transit cost function is:

$$G(\mathbf{D}) = t_p{\cdot}P_{95} \quad (5)$$

Network Capacity Costs: ISPs typically provision core network capacity to satisfy peak demand (with a small over-provision factor) to ensure that utilization stays under a threshold. Based on anecdotal evidence and informal discussions with some providers, we believe this threshold to be between $50-70\%$. As traffic demand shifts upwards over time, the utilization starts to approach the threshold which forces the ISP to carry out capacity upgrades and network expansion in the core. Note that this is quite different from last mile upgrades, which tend to be expensive and are planned a long time in advance. We denote the average utilization as v, and the unit cost to carry traffic as c_p. Note that this is pegged to the peak traffic level [13, 25]. Since the total network traffic is bounded by the cumulative data caps, the capacity cost is likely to scale proportionally with the latter:

$$C(\mathbf{D}) = \frac{c_p}{v} \cdot g \cdot \sum_{t \in \mathcal{T}} D_t \cdot x_t \quad (6)$$

where g is a positive (scaling) constant and is again estimated by curve fitting the relevant variables using data from several months.

5.1.3 Tariff Formation Problem

We now formulate the exact problem of designing data capped tariffs, using the model expressed in Eq. 1 and the utility function described in Eq. 2. Our goal is to identify a finite set of tariffs which maximizes the balance in Eq. 1, for a given set of per-subscriber coefficients a_n, b_n and c_n. First, we describe the formulation assuming the *deterministic demand* model. Subsequently, we show how this can be extended to the stochastic *logit* model. The *TFP* is expressed as:

$$\max_{\mathbf{p},\mathbf{r},\mathbf{x},\mathbf{q}} \sum_{t \in \mathcal{T}} (p_t \cdot D_t(\mathbf{q})) - C(\mathbf{D}(\mathbf{q})) - G(\mathbf{D}(\mathbf{q})) \quad (7)$$

$$\text{s.t. } q_{n,t} \cdot (U_n(t) - p_t) \geq q_{n,t} \cdot (U_n(t') - p_{t'}), \forall t' \neq t, n \in \mathcal{N} \quad (8)$$

$$q_{n,t} \cdot (U_n(t) - p_t) \geq 0, \forall n \in \mathcal{N} \quad (9)$$

$$\sum_{t \in \mathcal{T}} q_{n,t} \leq 1, \forall n \in \mathcal{N} \quad (10)$$

$$p_t \geq 0, r_t \in \mathcal{L}, x_t \in \mathcal{X}, q_{n,t} \in \{0,1\}, \forall t \in \mathcal{T}, n \in \mathcal{N} \quad (11)$$

Here, $\mathbf{q}$ is the tariff selection vector. Eq.8 ensures that subscribers pick tariffs that maximize their surplus (as prescribed by the deterministic model) and Eq.9 guards against the possibility of selecting a tariff that yields negative surplus (which implies the subscriber leaves the ISP). Finally, Eq.10 forces subscribers to pick at most one tariff. The remaining constraints defined in Eq.11 constrain the feasible ranges for the optimization variables. For convenience, we denote the solution to TFP as OPT(TFP).

The optimization setup for the *logit* model is largely similar. The tariff selection vector, with the associated constraints defined on it, are omitted and D_t is redefined based on the distribution realized by $s_{n,t}$. Given the similarity, we omit a complete description.

Note that TFP contains both continuous (e.g., p_t) as well as integer (e.g., r_t,x_t) variables and this leads to a non-linear optimization problem which usually lack efficient solutions. By mapping it onto the well known Maximum Independent Set Problem (MISP) problem, we formally prove that it is NP-Hard; the proof is provided in the Appendix. Besides, since it is NP-Hard to approximate MISP within an exponential to the number of vertices *multiplicative factor* away from the optimal solution, the mapping indicates the inapproximability of the TFP problem as well. Thus, it is impractical to try to obtain optimal solutions when the subscriber populations are large. A common approach for solving integer programming optimization problems is to develop the *linear relaxation* of the original problem which is more tractable. In the next section, we derive this form and then describe two heuristics based on it. Since the linear relaxation & rounding procedure may deteriorate the quality of the solution of the above heuristic algorithms in an uncontrollable manner, we also present a third algorithm of different philosophy that produces solutions which are provably within an *additive gap* from the optimal one. We refer to the latter as an approximation algorithm.

5.2 Heuristic and Approximation Solutions

To obtain the linear relaxation (LR) form of TFP, we consider $\mathcal{L}$ as an ordered set and convert the integer variable r_t to a binary vector $(r_{t,l})_{l \in \mathcal{L}}$: here, $r_{t,l} = 1$ if the speed-tier of the tariff t is the l-th element in $\mathcal{L}$, and $r_{t,l} = 0$ otherwise. Additionally, we restrict each tariff to be associated with a single speed tier by imposing an additional constraint, $\forall t, \sum_{l=1}^{|\mathcal{L}|} r_{t,l} = 1$. The LR form of TFP, which we denote LTFP, is obtained by relaxing the constraints on x_t and $r_{t,l}$ and allowing them to take on continuous values. LTFP can be solved with computational efficient algorithms (e.g., branch and bound methods), and we denote the optimal solution to this (relaxed) formulation as OPT(*L*TFP). Note that, by ignoring the integer constraints, OPT(LTFP) can often produce infeasible solutions that overestimate OPT(TFP) which is hard to compute. Thus, it offers an useful comparison point for algorithms that yield feasible solutions, and we describe two such approaches in the following.

Naive Algorithm: This heuristic starts by obtaining a solution to OPT(LTFP) and the greedily rounds all the speed tier variables in one step. It operates as follows:

1. Solve OPT(LTFP)
2. For each t, picks the speed tier with the highest (fractional) solution r_{tl}, $\forall l$
3. Solve OPT(LTFP) a second time, but restrict the r variables previously picked to be equal to 1, and zero elsewhere
4. Rounds each of the computed x values to the nearest value in $\mathcal{X}$, and assign each subscriber n to the tariff t', which satisfies

$$t' = \arg\max_t(U_n(t) - p_t), \text{if } U_n(t') - p(t') \geq 0$$

Sequential Rounding algorithm (SR): This heuristic operates by assigning tariffs to the speed tiers one by one, at each step taking into account the subset of tariffs already assigned to a speed tier in previous iterations. Thus, it carries out T iterations, successively building up each tariff, and each iteration proceeds as follows:

1. Solve for OPT(LTFP).

2. Pick the pair (tariff t',speed tier l') with the highest (fractional) solution among all the r_{tl} $\forall t, l$
3. Set $r_{t'l'} = 1$ and $r_{t'l} = 0$ for all other levels $l \neq l'$
4. Restrict the solution to the LTFP at the next iterations to preserve the above rounded (binary) values of r.

After T iterations are completed, all the r_{tl} variables will be restricted to a binary value. Then, we again solve the restricted $LTFP$ and round the computed x values to the nearest feasible value in $\mathcal{X}$ and assign subscriber n to the tariff t', where

$$t' = \arg\max_{t}(U_n(t) - p_t), \text{if } U_n(t') - p(t') \geq 0$$

In practice, both *Naive* and *SR* lead to feasible solutions that *can* be close to the optimal, but this is not guaranteed. Such a property might be unsatisfactory for an ISP diligent about reducing costs (via data caps). To this end, we describe a hierarchical algorithm which provides solutions with tunable approximation ratios. The following description assumes the *deterministic demand* model.

Profit Participation Algorithm (PPA): This algorithm is inspired by the model described in [26] and works by solving OPT(TFP) for a carefully chosen subset of the subscribers. To begin with, PPA defines $\mathcal{Y}$ as the cartesian product of $\mathcal{L}$ and $\mathcal{X}$ i.e., all the speed tier, data cap combinations and denotes p_y as the price associated with $y \in \mathcal{Y}$. Next, it defines a distance metric between subscribers which is given as:

$$d_{n,m} = \max_{y \in \mathcal{Y}} |U_n(y) - U_m(y)|, \ \forall n, m \in \mathcal{N}$$

PPA takes the set of subscribers, their respective data usage(s), and two parameters $\epsilon > 0$ and $0 \leq \tau \leq 1$, and operates as follows:

1. The set of subscribers $\mathcal{N}$ is partitioned such that for n, m in the same cluster, $d_{n,m} \leq \epsilon$. In other words, the clustering assigns subscribers with similar utility to the same cluster.
2. A single "stereotype" subscriber, denoted n_i, is selected from each cluster i. Thus, the set $\{n_i\}$ represents the set of all stereotypes. Note that $\{n_i\}$ is typically much smaller than $\mathcal{N}$.
3. OPT(TFP) is solved for the set $\{n_i\}$. This is feasible even with exhaustive search methods given that $\{n_i\}$ is typically small. Suppose the solution assigns subscriber n_i the tariff (p_t, r_t, x_t). Based on the definition of $\mathcal{Y}$, we can denote as $(r_t, x_t) = y \in \mathcal{Y}$ and p_t to be the price of y (p_y).
4. For each $y \in \mathcal{Y}$ where a price was assigned, PPA discounts the price by a factor that is controlled by τ parameter:

$$p'_y = p_y - \tau \cdot (p_y - cost_y)$$

where $cost_y$ is the cost to the ISP (based on transit & capacity cost) of assigning a subscriber to y.
5. For each (non-stereotype) subscriber n, PPA assigns her to the tariff y', where

$$y' = \arg\max_{y \in \mathcal{Y}}(U_n(y) - p_y), \text{if } U_n(y') - p_{y'} \geq 0$$

The quality of the solution obtained from PPA is controlled by ϵ: large values lead to fewer clusters and a faster, but less optimal solution; but as $\epsilon \to 0$, PPA generates a larger number of stereotypes and the solution approaches the optimal case (at higher computational cost). Note that ϵ effectively bounds the distance between elements in the same cluster. We implement PPA with agglomerative hierarchical clustering [27], which explicitly incorporates a distance threshold. PPA returns solutions within $2 \cdot (\tau + \frac{2 \cdot \epsilon}{\tau}) \cdot N$ of the optimal.

Theorem 1 *If P_{OPT} is the optimal solution of the TFP problem, N the number of subscribers, ϵ is the largest difference in subscriber utility in any cluster, and τ is the discounted factor, then the ISP balance of the PPA algorithm is at least $P_{OPT} - 2 \cdot (\tau + \frac{2 \cdot \epsilon}{\tau}) \cdot N$*

The proof is based on a reduction to the *Screening* problem that is described in [26]; the validity of this reduction is presented in the Appendix □

Notice that for small values of ϵ and N, the term $2 \cdot (\tau + \frac{2 \cdot \epsilon}{\tau}) \cdot N$ is also small, and hence the worst case performance of PPA is very close to the optimal one (P_{OPT}). However, as the number of subscribers (N) or the distance between the elements in the same cluster (ϵ) increase, the term $2 \cdot (\tau + \frac{2 \cdot \epsilon}{\tau}) \cdot N$ increases as well, which deteriorates the theoretical worst-case performance.

Importantly, PPA requires hard assignments of subscribers to tariffs and thus can only be used in conjunction with the *deterministic demand* model. In contrast, Naive and SR are agnostic of the underlying demand model and can be applied to both. To distinguish the two models, we use the Naive-det and Naive-logit (similarly with SR) to denote the combination of heuristic algorithm and demand model. In the next section, we apply the three algorithms described above against our dataset to obtain a set of tariffs which are compared against the bound established by OPT(*L*TFP).

6. IMPACT OF DATA CAPPING

In this section, we evaluate the impact of moving from a flat rate price structure to one with data capped tariffs. The evaluations cover a number of regional cost scenarios, which lead to an understanding of how the impact varies in different regions and markets. Overall, we find that ISPs can extract more value by implementing data caps, but this heavily depends on transit and capacity prices. In the best scenario, an ISP can improve its bottom line by 23% by offering 8 different data capped tariffs with a very small increase (<5%) in subscription revenues. Importantly, we show that setting data caps *naively* can actually lead to a net loss for the ISP. In the rest of this section, we discuss these results in detail; we begin by describing the parameters used in the later evaluations.

6.1 Evaluation Setup

To guide the set of tariffs generated by the algorithms, we constrain the parameters related to speed tiers and data caps as follows. The set of speed tiers, $\mathcal{L}$, is identical to the current offerings seen in our dataset i.e., {24/1Mbps, 30/3Mbps, 100/10Mbps}. We vary the available data caps from 10GB to 200GB, with 5GB increments.

Next, we describe how to extract the utility coefficient parameters, a_n, b_n and c_n which are introduced in Eq. 2. To start, we make the assumption, motivated by the work in [17], that each subscriber, in the current flat-rate offering, evaluates the tariff exactly equal to the price p_t they currently pay for it (Table 1). This is reasonable, since the user would probably have switched providers if this were not the case. Then, replacing the left side of Eq.2 with p_t, yields:

$$a_n = \frac{p_t}{log(b_n \cdot r_t + 1) \cdot (c_n \cdot x_t - \frac{x_t^2}{2})}$$

The coefficients in this equation are determined as follows:

$\mathbf{r_t}$: This is taken as the speed tier currently being subscribed by the user.

$\mathbf{x_t}$: Since the flat-rate plan t allows for unlimited use, i.e. $x_t = +\infty$, we use the expected data usage of the subscriber instead, and we derive this as the *average* traffic volume for the subscriber, over all the months in the dataset.

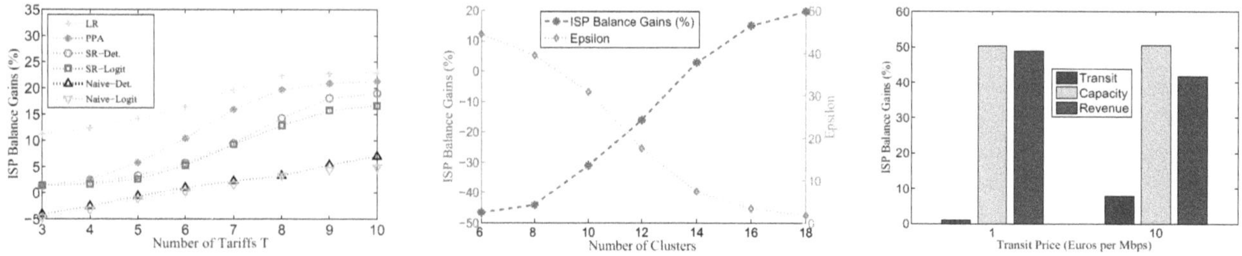

(a) Balance gains for 3 to 10 tariffs.

(b) Impact of clustering on PPA.

(c) Distribution of balance gains.

Figure 4: Data cap pricing balance gains over flat-rate.

$\mathbf{b_n}$: This captures how a subscriber evaluates speed tiers. Large values reflect an indifference to speed tier variations, while low values reflect that the subscriber is affected by changes in speed (e.g., someone that frequently watches video). In our dataset, we suspect users with high traffic volume to have low b_n values and lightweight users to associate with high b_n values. To reflect a range of behavior, we partition the subscribers into four bands based on their average traffic volume, i.e., <10, $10-30$, $30-100$, >100 (GBs) and these groups are assigned b_n values of 1000, 100, 10 and 1 (respectively).

$\mathbf{c_n}$: This parameter captures how much data volume a subscriber may need. We assume that this is bounded by the maximum data usage over the dataset for a subscriber and set it to the largest value (monthly usage) seen over the dataset for the subscriber.

6.2 ISP Impact

We use the notation J^f (J^c) to represent the solution to Eq.1 in a flat rate (data capped) setting. Our main evaluation metric in this section is *gain*, defined as the difference $J^c - J^f$ which is the improvement in the ISPs bottom line when data capped pricing is adopted.

Throughout, we adopt the transit and capacity cost functions defined in Eq. 5 and 6 respectively. Unless otherwise specified, we set the parameters: $f = 0.66$ and $t_p = 1$ as in [24], $c_p = 10$ and $v = 0.7$ as in [13, 25] and $c = 1$ as in [17].

We first investigate the question of how many tariffs are needed. Figure 4(a) plots *gain* as a function of the number of tariffs (T). We find that across all the algorithms (save for Naive), there is an improvement in gain as the number of tariffs are increased until $T = 8$. This can be explained by the fact that adding an extra tariff increases the number of price/byte offerings; this slightly increases the likelihood of some subscribers getting higher utility with the extra offering. However, once T "matches" the heterogeneity of data usage, additional tariffs are unlikely to improve subscriber surplus. While in general, the results obtained by using the deterministic model cannot be quantitatively compared with those obtained using the logit demand model, we consolidate these in Fig. 4(a) to preserve space. We do note however, that the two families yield similar results for SR and $Naive$ (there is no logit equivalent for PPA). In the following discussion, we focus mainly on the results from the deterministic model.

Looking at Fig. 4(a), we find that SR consistently produces more beneficial solutions compared to $Naive$. This is likely due to the differences in how they assign speed tiers to tariffs. $Naive$ performs a "one-shot" assignment, while SR iteratively improves the solution obtained at each stage. Importantly, note that $Naive$, with $T<5$, has *negative gain*, i.e., the ISP does worse *after* instituting data caps. Examining this carefully, we uncover that with $T<5$, most of the plans are (myopically) allocated to the higher (more expensive) speed tier(s) since user utility increases with speed, ignoring all else. However, the higher prices make it less likely for subscribers to find a suitable tariff, and they leave. The ISP can only counter this by lowering prices across tariffs (reducing the revenue). These conflicting factors result in the ISP being worse off with data caps. The key takeaway here is that tariff selection is non trivial: simplistic solutions may not extract value from subscribers effectively. Finally, we see in Fig. 4(a) that PPA and $SR{-}Det$ return solutions that are qualitatively similar and are also approach the OPT(LTFP) solution (labeled as LR), indicating that these are quite close to the optimal solution of the TFP problem.

To understand the intuition about why increasing tariffs improves gain, we examine two tariff assignments in detail. Table 2 enumerates the tariffs selected by PPA for $T{=}3$ and $T = 10$. When $T = 3$, each speed tier is allocated one data cap. In fact, this scenario reflects the system where operators – Comcast, for example – apply a single (uniform) data cap for each speed tier. However, when $T = 10$, a higher fraction of data caps are assigned to the 100/10 Mbps tier. In our dataset, the subscribers in this speed tier exhibited the most variation in monthly data usage (over the other 2). By allocating more tariffs to the tier with the most variation, PPA increases the likelihood of subscribers finding maximal surplus tariffs. The overall gains are dictated by the number of subscribers that are able to identify such tariffs amongst the offerings (and staying with the ISP). Given that PPA is the best performing scheme, we focus the rest of the discussion on the results for PPA with $T = 8$.

Recall that with PPA, the solution quality (and computational complexity) depends on the required number of clusters, which is a parameter to the algorithm. Fig. 4(b) plots this (on the x-axis) against two different terms on the y-axis – *gain* on the left y-axis, and ϵ on the right y-axis (this parameter controls the approximation bound of the obtained tariff solution). When the number of clusters is less than 12, PPA actually returns solutions with negative gain. We believe this is due to the number of clusters being unable to capture the heterogeneity of the subscriber population. However, with larger number of clusters, the extracted tariff solutions have positive gain. The relationship between the number of clusters and ϵ is consistent with this observation. Lower values of ϵ, which determines the tightness of the clusters, force it to find solutions that are closer to the optimal, and this necessitates a higher number of clusters (and hence complexity).

PPA requires only 8 tariffs for the ISP to improve its gain by 23%. This is significant, and comes without requiring any capital expenditure from the ISP. However, in practice, ISPs may not be willing to use more than a few tariffs in order to make their offerings simple to understand. Subscribers may face significant cogni-

Speed tier	24/1 Mbps	30/3 Mbps	100/10 Mbps
			T=3
Cap(GB)	45	55	70
Demand(%)	32.2	7.8	60
Price(€)	21.8	25.32	33.8
			T=10
Cap(GB)	15,40	20, 60	20,25,35,50,80,100
Demand(%)	9.55,17.73	1.82,5	16.36,15,11.82,10,8.18,9.09
Price(€)	21.8,22.65	24.58, 26.55	32.51,33.41,34.1,34.75,35.22,35.75

Table 2: Data cap pricing tariffs when T is 3 and 10 (PPA algorithm).

Region	transit price t_p (€ per Mbps)	transit fraction f (%)	balance gains(%) c_p=0.1 (€ per Mbps)	c_p=10 (€ per Mbps)
NY	0.5	66	10.2	19.6
UK	2	66	11.6	20.8
Tokyo	3	33	10.9	20.2
Sao Paulo	6	66	14.8	24.1
Rural Texas	50	66	26.5	33.4
Sub-Saharan	100	80	36.1	38.2

Table 3: Traffic cost parameters and ISP gains in various markets.

tive dissonance is choosing between a large number of tariffs [28], which works against the ISP. Thus in practice, ISPs may choose to use fewer tariffs (than are optimal) and thus not realize the full possible benefit in order to attract (or retain) customers. A detailed analysis of these interactions is outside of the scope of this paper.

Dissecting the gains: The ISP can improve its gain by adopting data caps due to two factors: (i) by reducing traffic costs (transit and capacity), or (ii) by pushing users to more expensive tariffs (higher speeds and/or caps). While much of the recent arguments offered by ISPs in moving to data capped schemes center on the former, *both* of these factors are important and we find evidence of both even as the relative effects vary by region. We start by examining two extreme cases for transit prices in Figure 4(c), which presents the breakdown of ISP gain in two different markets. The parameters used are as enumerated in the beginning of the section. In the first market (on left) with t_p=1€ and the second market (on right) with t_p=10€. On the left, transit is plentiful and cheap and hence effective transit *costs* are low, 50% of the gain from moving to data caps is realized by lowered capacity costs, 48% is contributed by increased revenue from users going to more expensive tariffs, and only about 2% of the gain is contributed by the lowered transit costs. We contrast this with the scenario on the right, where transit is ten times as expensive. Here, 10% of the gain is contributed by lowered transit costs, and this is for the exact same subscriber and traffic composition. Thus, we can generalize this to say that when traffic prices (transit or capacity) are low, the ISP gains relatively little by reducing traffic volume (which is what caps accomplish), making it more likely that the ISP will look elsewhere to balance the increased costs (e.g., increasing tariff prices significantly for heavy users). On the other hand, when traffic prices are high, the ISP is able to reduce its cost overhead significantly by lowering the traffic. A related observation is that transit (and capacity) costs affects the undesirability of heavyweight users to the ISP. With low transit prices, ISPs are less sensitive to heavyweight users: with the transit cost at 1€, we find 1% of subscribers leave the ISP when data-capped, while this grows to 5.2% when the transit price is 10€.

The transit cost settings used in Figure 4(c) may seem contrived, but in fact, they are very much in line with prices reported today. Table 3 is a compendium of network cost parameters reflecting various regional markets around the world, and were assembled from several sources [24, 29–31]. The second column in the table indicates the unit price for transit traffic, and column 3 represents the transit fraction of total traffic for a sample ISP in the region. The remaining two columns indicate the overall gain with using $T = 8$ data capped tariffs (under two capacity cost regimes); we return to this shortly. Examining column 2, we find tremendous variability across ISPs depending on the size, geography, and the number of available transit providers. For e.g., an ISP in rural Texas recently reported transit prices over 50$ due to a lack of competition in the local transit market [29]. We also uncovered examples of extremely high transit prices in sub Saharan Africa and small island nations [30]. Thus, the cost examples used in Fig. 4(c) reflect prices well inside what can be found today. In the following, we examine transit and capacity prices independently and analyze how gains vary in each case. We do this independently because these prices are not necessarily coupled: some regions may have very good intra-region connectivity, but sparsely connected to other regions, and vice versa. The last two columns of Table 3 summarize the overall ISP gain for two extreme capacity price points.

In Figure 5(a), we look at the impact of varying transit prices on the ISP gains. We fix T=8, c_p=10€, and f=0.66. As expected, when transit prices are high, data caps benefit the ISP by reducing the aggregate traffic, and hence $G(.)$ – the transit cost. When the unit transit price is greater than 1€, the ISP stands to improve its bottom line by at least 20%. The gains are less striking when transit prices drop below this price point. In fact, most markets in the US and Europe today have transit prices that are sub 1€ and in such markets, data capping is not likely to noticeably impact the ISPs bandwidth costs (even if traffic rates decrease). On the other hand, in markets with high transit prices – parts of South America and S.E. Asia, Africa, etc. – moving to a data capped model significantly lowers the traffic costs for the ISP and benefits subscribers as well. This observation is consistent with the fact that data capped pricing plans have existed for a long time in such areas.

In Figure 5(b), we look at the impact of changing capacity prices on ISP gain. While we expect this to qualitatively follow the same behavior as seen with transit prices, the actual costs have minor differences (a log factor, cf. Eq.5 and Eq.6). Again, ISP gains from data capping steadily increase as the unit capacity prices increase, and thus, data capping becomes a more viable tool to manage costs as the capacity costs increase. Unlike with transit prices, where regional prices are sometimes available, capacity costs are much harder to discover (ISPs consider them confidential). Typically, we expect capacity prices to be slightly lower than transit; the latter is likely to have a small margin since it is offered as a service. In any case, our evaluation covers two orders of magnitude in capacity prices, and we believe most markets fall somewhere into this range.

Deterministic vs. logit: Turning now to the *logit* demand model, we first note that the algorithms $Naive{-}logit$ and $SR{-}logit$ perform very similarly to the deterministic case as seen in Fig.4(a). This is because the logit model assigns users probabilistically to tariffs, based on their utility. When computing tariffs for each user, they eventually get assigned to the tariff associated with the highest probability. Hence the users are mapped to tariffs in a manner that largely mimics the deterministic model. One of the salient features of the *logit* model is that it allows us to investigate the impact of competition, captured by the parameter c in Eq.3. In monopoly or duopoly, as is the situation most US markets, an ISP may be able to set data caps (alternatively, set prices) aggressively – without fear of losing subscribers. On the other hand, in markets with a large number of competing providers, such as in most of Western Europe, small pricing tweaks may result in subscribers departing the

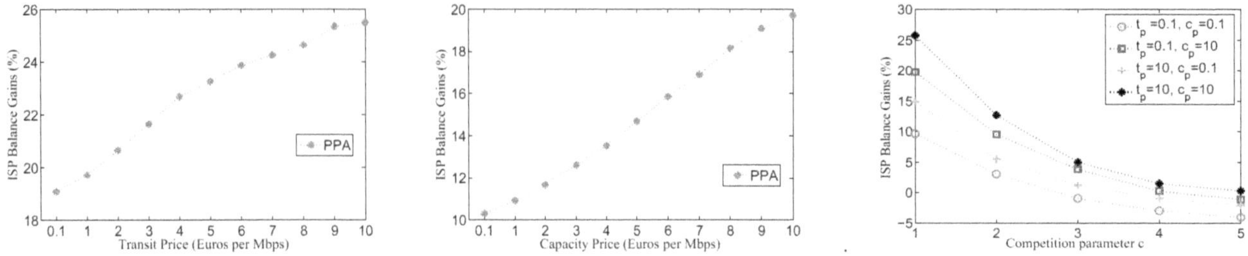

(a) Balance gains for various transit prices (b) Balance gains for various capacity prices (c) Impact of market competition on ISP gains

Figure 5: Data cap pricing balance gains over flat-rate with varying transit price, capacity price, and competition.

ISP and this is likely to make the ISP more risk averse. In Figure 5(c), we examine various levels of market competition for four cost settings. Recall that the numerical value of c does not reflect the number of competitors; it simply characterizes the intensity of competition. As c increases, we find that more subscribers leave the ISP when data caps are imposed and the net impact varies with the cost scenarios. When the traffic costs are high, and as observed previously, the ISP can afford to "shed" customers up to a point. Even with high competition ($c = 5$), the ISP still finds a positive gain with $t_p, c_p = 10€$ and the gain decreases as the traffic costs drop. Thus, overall, the impact of data capping to an ISP's bottom line is also affected by the level of competition in the market. In many cases, ISPs often use incentives such as service-bundling or promotional pricing to retain customers to counteract the increased competition.

While putting these results into perspective, we point out an important assumption in our methodology – the monthly price paid by subscribers (between $21-33€$) goes entirely toward the capacity and transit costs borne by the ISP. In reality, only a small fraction of this is likely to used toward traffic costs, with a much larger fraction is likely to be toward cost factors not easy to uncover – leasing costs, salaries, etc. If the evaluations were to be carried out with more detailed and fine grained cost structures, we expect the economic gains from data capping to be much more striking.

6.3 Subscriber Impact

We now examine data capping from the viewpoint of individual subscribers. Figure 6(a) plots the distribution of the difference in monthly subscription prices (p_t) between a flat rate pricing scheme and a data capped scheme, across all the subscribers. We observe that roughly 25% of the subscribers see a net (small) reduction in their monthly bills. These generally correspond to the lightweight users that pay a disproportionately high cost per unit of data usage in the flat-rate setting. Note that cheaper tariffs associated with the lower end of the data capped plans are likely to attract new customers to the service and increase revenue – a side effect that we cannot model easily from our dataset. Thus overall, data capping can benefit the (potential) subscriber with modest needs by lowering costs. In our dataset, 18% of the users have a significant increase (>2€ per month) in the new scheme. These particular users correspond to the most heavyweight users; and who are willing to pay more for increased speed or data cap (as captured by the utility function). The remaining users are charged almost the same or a slightly higher price with a data capped tariff structure. We do note that some users may choose to modulate their behavior (download less rather than pay more) when faced with steeper charges. However, such behavior is very challenging to model, and we leave that as an open question.

Next, we compare the *fairness* between flat rate and data capped pricing. In a *completely fair* scheme, subscribers would pay proportional to their actual data usage (all subscribers pay same unit cost). Comparing two pricing schemes, the fairer one would exhibit less variance in this unit cost across subscribers. Figure 6(b), plots the distribution of the ratio of price paid/usage over all the subscribers for the two pricing models. As can be expected, we observe smaller price/byte variations among the users under caps. The most visual case is for the heavy users (area in CDF near zero) who shift to the right, since they are forced to pay more for maintaining their data usage or they are capped. The standard deviation of price/byte among subscribers drops by 1€ under caps. Thus, our empirical results validate some of of the existing theoretical benefits of data capping for subscribers [4–7, 10–13].

7. DISCUSSION

In this section, we revisit some assumptions made in our model and methodology and also describe some extensions to our work so far.

Cost model: The profit and cost model we use is relatively simple. Making it more realistic would involve obtaining accurate and fine grained cost structures from an ISP. However, even this might not be quite enough given that there is a great deal of subjectivity in how costs are applied (and over what time frame). To use an example: consider the real estate cost of housing the networking equipment. Some buildings are owned outright, some are rented, and some are obtained using public funds or support (as is the case for national carriers in some countries). Another example is the cost of manning the help desks that users call into – staffed by a combination of salaried full time and temporary personnel. This is often a large expense to ISPs and the outlay depends on the expected volume of service calls. In such cases, the month-to-month amortization is unclear and open to debate. Our simple model avoids such issues and importantly, it captures how the nominal profits/costs depend on subscriber behavior.

User utility: The utility function we use leverages previous work to describe (user) satisfaction entirely in terms of the speed tier and usage allowance. While we believe it to be reasonable, it may not be universal (some users who are extremely price sensitive might not tolerate *any* price hikes). In addition, we consider that each subscriber can pick any speed tier that is offered; this is not the case in reality: rural subscribers may not have access to a faster fiber service and cannot switch to it. Yet another shortcoming of our model is that it assumes users can upgrade/downgrade speed tiers easily; in reality, the switching cost might be non-trivial, or there could be other dissuading factors [4, 9]. Finally, our work ignores the impact of particular overage policies when data-caps

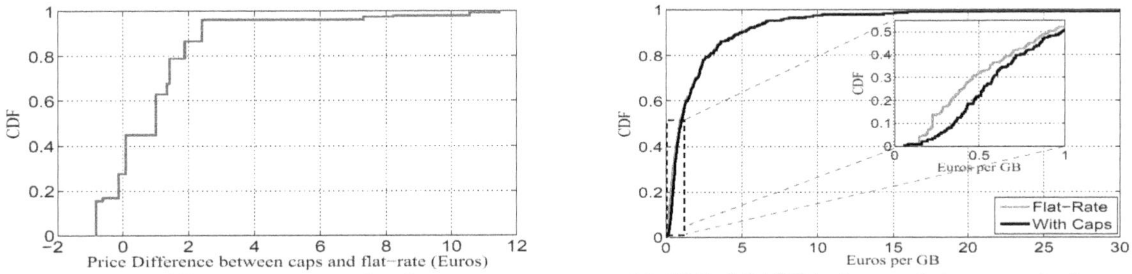

(a) Tariff changes across subscribers

(b) CDF of $€/GB$ in flat rate & data capped schemes.

Figure 6: Impact of Data Caps on Subscribers

are exceeded. We plan to investigate other utility functions and extend our models to account for overage policies in future work.

Alternate pricing models: Our empirical findings hint at two extensions to current pricing models. Recall that subscriber traffic volume correlates with their impact on transit and capacity costs. Given this, it is interesting to imagine time-based pricing models (such as those being discussed in the context of "smart grid") to incentivize users to shift their elastic consumption (file downloads, etc.) to off-peak times. This could reduce the ISP costs (by driving down the peak traffic) and these savings could be passed on to subscribers. This model has been previously studied in a theoretical framework [32], so fine-grained usage data such as in our dataset could provide empirical validation.

8. CONCLUSION

In this paper we investigate the issues surrounding data capping in residential broadband networks. To this end, we develop a methodology that yields a set of optimal tariffs, taking a set of cost components and a population of subscribers. This framework builds upon a simple, extensible model of ISP costs and a model that relates subscribers' utility to bandwidth speeds (speed tiers) and data caps. The developed framework enables to examine the relative benefits, for providers and their subscribers, of moving from flat rate pricing (the predominant model in most western broadband markets) to data capped pricing models, and to understand these benefits (or the lack) as traffic costs change.

We then apply the framework to a novel dataset that captures fine grained, broadband data usage from a set of 260 ISP subscribers. By referencing traffic prices that reflect different broadband markets around the world, we are able to identify the particular conditions when moving to a data capped pricing model is beneficial to an ISP, in the sense of limiting bandwidth costs. Overall, we find that data capping can be an effective mechanism for ISPs to reduce their costs only when transit and capacity costs are relatively high. On the other hand, when these costs are relatively low, data capping is not a very useful mechanism to balance bandwidth costs. In addition, the level of competition directly influences the outcome of data capping; in competitive markets, data capping may not be effective in managing costs as subscribers may leave the service and reduce the incoming subscription revenues. Our work in this paper is a first attempt to enable ISPs or policy makers to obtain quantitative insights of the impact of data capping.

9. ACKNOWLEDGMENTS

We would like to thank Augustin Soule and Pascal Le Guyadec for facilitating access to the data. We also thank our shepherd, Kenjiro Cho, and the anonymous reviewers for their constructive feedback.

10. REFERENCES

[1] Will Netix Kill The Internet?, Dec 2010.

[2] `www.stopthecap.com`.

[3] Public Knowledge Petition Against Comcast. http://tinyurl.com/ofp2azs, 2012.

[4] Andrew Odlyzko, Bill St Arnaud, Erik Stallman, and Michael Weinberg. Know your limits: Considering the role of data caps and usage based billing in internet access service. *Public Knowledge*, 2012.

[5] Daniel A Lyons. Impact Of Data Caps And Other Forms Of Usage-based Pricing For Broadband Access. *Mercatus Center*, 2012.

[6] Soumya Sen, Carlee Joe-Wong, Sangtae Ha, and Mung Chiang. Pricing data: A look at past proposals, current plans, and future trends. *arXiv preprint arXiv:1201.4197*, 2012.

[7] Richard Edell and Pravin Varaiya. Providing internet access: What we learn from index. *IEEE Network*, 13(5):18–25, 1999.

[8] J. Williams. A. Nevo, J. Turner. Usage-based Pricing And Demand For Residential Broadband. *Social Science Research Network*, 2013.

[9] Anja Lambrecht, Katja Seim, and Bernd Skiera. Does uncertainty matter? consumer behavior under three-part tariffs. *Marketing Science*, 26(5):698–710, 2007.

[10] FCC Open Internet Advisory Committee. Policy issues in data caps and usage-based pricing, 2013. Annual Report.

[11] Gregory L Rosston, Scott J Savage, and Donald M Waldman. Household Demand For Broadband Internet. *The BE Journal of Economic Analysis & Policy*, 10(1), 2010.

[12] Andrew Odlyzko, Papak Nabipay, and Zhi-Li Zhang. Flat vs. Metered Rates, Bundling, and "Bandwidth Hogs". In *NetEcon*, 2011.

[13] Wei Dai and Scott Jordan. Design and impact of data caps. In *GLOBECOM*, December 2013.

[14] Parminder Chhabra, Nikolaos Laoutaris, Pablo Rodriguez, and Ravi Sundaram. Home is Where the (Fast) Internet is: Flat-rate Compatible Incentives for Reducing Peak Load. In *HomeNets*. ACM, 2010.

[15] Jeremy Blackburn, Rade Stanojevic, Vijay Erramilli, Adriana Iamnitchi, and Konstantina Papagiannaki. Last Call for the Buffet: Economics of Cellular Networks. MobiCom '13, 2013.

[16] Liang Zhang, Weijie Wu, and Dan Wang. Time-dependent Pricing In Wireless Data Networks: Flat-rate Vs. Usage-based Schemes. In *INFOCOM*. IEEE, 2014.
[17] Vytautas Valancius, Cristian Lumezanu, Nick Feamster, Ramesh Johari, and Vijay V. Vazirani. How many tiers?: Pricing in the internet transit market. SIGCOMM '11. ACM, 2011.
[18] Federal Communication Commission, A Report on Consumer Wireline Broadband Performance in the U.S., 2014. FCC report.
[19] Costas Courcoubetis and Richard Weber. *Pricing Communication Networks: Economics, Technology and Modeling*. John Wiley & Sons, 2003.
[20] Asuman Ozdaglar and R. Srikant. Incentives and pricing in communication networks. In *In Algorithmic Game Theory*, pages 571–591. Cambridge Press, 2007.
[21] J. Bauer et. al. Economics Of Usage-based Pricing In Local Broadband Markets. *Michigan State U.*, 2012.
[22] Ana Amante and João Vareda. Switching Costs In The Portuguese Telecommunications Sector: Results From A Customer Survey. *Concorrência e Regulação*, pages 115–135, 2011.
[23] Daniel McFadden. Conditional logit analysis of qualitative choice behavior. *Frontiers in Econometrics*, pages 105–142, 1974.
[24] Rade Stanojevic, Ignacio Castro, and Sergey Gorinsky. CIPT: Using Tuangou to Reduce IP Transit Costs. CoNEXT '11. ACM, 2011.
[25] Wei Dai and Scott Jordan. Modeling ISP Tier Design. In *International Teletraffic Congress*, pages 1–9. IEEE, 2013.
[26] Kristóf Madarász and Andrea Prat. Screening with an Approximate Type Space. *STICERD - Theoretical Economics Paper Series*, 2010.
[27] Trevor Hastie, Robert Tibshirani, Jerome Friedman, T Hastie, J Friedman, and R Tibshirani. *The Elements Of Statistical Learning*. Springer, 2009.
[28] Barry Schwartz. *The Paradox Of Choice*. Ecco, New York, 2004.
[29] 2014 Transit Prices and Peering Projections. `http://drpeering.net`, Oct 2013.
[30] Global Internet Geography: Executive Summary. `http://www.telegeography.com`, 2013.
[31] IP Transit Pricing Service. `www.telegeography.com`.
[32] Prashanth Hande, Mung Chiang, Robert Calderbank, and Junshan Zhang. Pricing under constraints in access networks: Revenue maximization and congestion management. In *INFOCOM*, pages 1–9. IEEE, 2010.

APPENDIX

Lemma 1 *The TFP problem is NP-Hard.*

PROOF. We prove the NP-Hardness of the TFP problem by reduction from the Maximum Independent Set Problem (MISP), which is NP-Hard. Given a graph $\mathcal{G} = (\mathcal{V}, \mathcal{E})$, where the sets $\mathcal{V}$ and $\mathcal{E}$ denote the vertices and the edges, a maximum independent set is the maximum-sized set of non-adjacent vertices. For any instance of MISP, we construct the following equivalent instance of TFP:

For each vertex $v \in \mathcal{V}$, we create a tariff described by the pair of speed and cap (r_v, x_v), with cost that is independent of the demand and equal to the degree of v (d_v). The price of the tariff is equal to $1 + \frac{\gamma}{d_v}$, where γ is an arbitrarily small positive constant. Thus, the ISP benefits by offering the tariff (r_v, x_v) iff it is picked by at least d_v subscribers. Finally, we create one subscriber per edge $e \in \mathcal{E}$, who obtains arbitrarily high utility from each tariff (r_v, x_v) such that v is an adjacent vertex to e; otherwise zero. The TFP problem asks for determining the subset of tariffs to offer to the users.

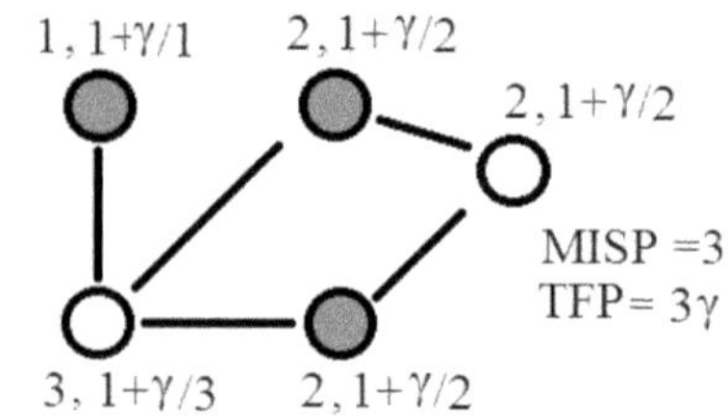

Figure 7: An example of the reduction from the MISP with 5 vertices (tariffs) and 5 edges (users). Vertex labels denote the costs and the prices of the respective tariffs.

Given a solution of value $k \cdot \gamma$ to TFP, one can find a solution of value k to the MISP instance. This is because, this TFP solution specifies that exactly k tariffs of the form (r_v, x_v) are offered by the ISP, each one of them picked by *all* the d_v subscribers corresponding to an adjacent edge to vertex v, who pay in total $d_v + \gamma$. Since, the cost for offering a tariff (r_v, x_v) is equal to d_v, the ISP benefits by γ for each one of the k tariffs that it offers, and the solution value is $k \cdot \gamma$. But, recall that each offered tariff (r_v, x_v) corresponds to a separate vertex v, and these vertices must be non-adjacent, since each subscriber can pick *at most one* tariff. Thus, there are k non-adjacent vertices in $\mathcal{G}$.

Figure 7 describes a simple example. There exist 5 possible pairs of speed and cap (tariffs) with costs $\{1, 2, 2, 2, 3\}$. The ISP balance-maximizing policy is to offer 3 out of 5 tariffs to the subscribers (those that correspond to the marked vertices). The prices per tariff are $\{1 + \frac{\gamma}{1}, 1 + \frac{\gamma}{2}, 1 + \frac{\gamma}{2}, 1 + \frac{\gamma}{2}, 1 + \frac{\gamma}{3}\}$. □

Screening Problem: The "Screening problem" [26] commonly refers to the case that a seller offers a menu of item-price specifications to a buyer or a continuum of buyers. The buyer's item preferences depend on her private type $b \in \mathcal{B}$, while the seller only knows the probability density function $f(.)$ of it. The evaluation of the buyer of type b for an item $i \in \mathcal{I}$ is equal to $V(b, i)$. The seller wishes to find the menu $\mathcal{M} \subseteq \mathcal{I}$ of items to offer and the prices $p(i)$, $\forall i \in \mathcal{M}$ aimed at maximizing her profit: $\sum_{b \in \mathcal{B}} f(b)(p(y(b)) - c(y(b))$, where $y(b)$ denotes the item picked by the buyer of type b and $cost_i$ is the production cost of item i. The buyer of type b will purchase the item $y(b)$ in $\mathcal{M}$ such that: $V(b, y(b)) - p(y(b)) \geq V(b, j) - p(j), \forall$ pairs $(j, p(j)) \in \mathcal{M}$.

Theorem 1 *The TFP problem is polynomial-time reducible to the Screening Problem.*

PROOF. Consider an instance of the TFP problem defined by the set of subscribers $\mathcal{N}$, the possible tariffs $\mathcal{L} \times \mathcal{X}$, the utility functions U and the costs C. Then, the above is equivalent to the special instance of the Screening problem, where we set: $\mathcal{I} = \mathcal{L} \times \mathcal{X}$, $\mathcal{B} = \mathcal{N}$, $f(b) = \frac{1}{|\mathcal{N}|}, \forall b \in \mathcal{B}$, $V(b, i) = U_n(t)$ and $cost_i = C(t)$, where type b corresponds to a subscriber n and item i corresponds to a tariff t. □

Collaborative Consumption for Mobile Broadband: A Quantitative Study

Juan Camilo Cardona‡†, Rade Stanojevic‡, Nikolaos Laoutaris‡
Telefonica Research, Barcelona, Spain‡
IMDEA Networks Institute, Madrid, Spain†

ABSTRACT

Mobile broadband is predominantly priced following tiered plans that involve a certain prepaid *commit volume* and additional metered volume priced at a higher *penalty rate*. An individual's demand, however, may vary wildly from month to month and thus users inevitably purchase packages that are either too small or too large for their needs. By collaborating in predefined closed (*e.g.*, family) or open groups (*e.g.*, through tethering) users can reduce both the amount of paid-but-left-unused capacity or the high penalty rates. In this paper we present a quantitative study of collaborative consumption using data from 40K mobile subscribers and tariffs from ten operators around the world. We show that small 2-person family plans offer modest expected savings in the range of 3% to 14%, whereas getting more substantial savings requires rather impractically large groups of approximately 10 people or more. Going over to open groups, where users can freely trade their data capacity, we characterize the impact of the secondary market price on the user costs and the operator revenues, and show that Telcos might be better off to embrace secondary markets (*e.g.*, let them integrate with billing), and thus have some control on, as opposed to letting them operate unsupervised through tethering. The latter may severely harm the revenues of a Telco, in an uncontrolled manner, especially in densely populated areas.

Categories and Subject Descriptors

K.6.2 [**Management of computing and information systems**]: Pricing and resource allocation; J.4 [**Social and behavioral sciences**]: Economics

General Terms

Economics

Keywords

Cellular Networks; Collaborative Consumption; Data Plans; Mobile Broadband.

CoNEXT'14, December 2–5, 2014, Sydney, Australia.

978-1-4503-3279-8/14/12 ...$15.00.
http://dx.doi.org/10.1145/2674005.2674997.

1. INTRODUCTION

Over the last two decades, cellular networks have been instrumental to connecting billions of people. Mobile broadband currently corresponds to a significant fraction of the cellular operators' revenues (currently $1000 billion, or 1-2% of world-wide GDP) and is projected to be the dominant source of revenues in the near future [37][1]. Mobile broadband retails through tiered plans that involve a predefined volume at a certain *commit rate*, and additional (variable) metered volume at a higher *penalty rate* [35].

As we will see later, the user demand for mobile broadband services is extremely volatile, making the decision process of choosing the 'right' data package non-trivial. Consequently, many users either underuse their quota, or occasionally use more than their committed quota, paying large overage fees. With users on both sides of the fence, those that have unused capacity and those that may need some extra capacity, mobile broadband can be a fertile land for a *sharing economy.* In the recent past, sharing economies have emerged in a number of domains sharing various items or services from cars [13], to houses [1], to books [4], and not surprisingly such trend have been picked up in the realms of mobile broadband by researchers [7, 15, 24], app developers [9, 19, 14] as well as the cellular operators themselves [8, 23, 40]. We can classify mobile broadband sharing systems in two groups:

Telco-driven: A number of operators have devised family plans [8, 34]. Such plans are *closed*, meaning that the group of customers that share their caps is closed/predetermined. In some cases, Telcos have even permitted users to freely sell their leftover capacity in an *open* market to any other user willing to buy it [23, 40]. In both cases, the collaborative consumption is implemented through the billing system of the Telco. By allowing plan sharing, Telcos improve customer retention/acquisition and help customers feel they truly own the packages they purchase.

User-driven: Collaborative consumption can be implemented even without the involvement (or blessing) of the Telco through tethering. This is a typical example of the *sharing economy* driven by the users themselves. Several apps have been developed that allow users to share mobile broadband [14, 19]. The large-scale success of these apps, however, depends on the density of users (per km^2) using them; users in low density areas would have infre-

[1]We have witnessed a similar trend in the landline telecom market in the previous decade, where the revenues from the voice communications have been almost completely replaced by the broadband services.

quent opportunities to buy/sell unused mobile broadband, while those in denser areas would gracefully have more opportunities for efficient sharing.

Although it is intuitive that collaborative consumption is beneficial for users, it remains largely unknown by exactly how much, and at what impact on Telco revenues. Our goal in this paper is to quantify the potential of collaborative consumption of mobile broadband and for this we use real consumption data from 40K mobile broadband customers as well as pricing data from 10 mobile broadband operators geographically spread across developed and developing markets. We begin by asking *"Is there a case for a sharing economy for mobile broadband?"*. We subsequently ask *"What are the benefits that can be expected from family (closed group) plans?"*. We then move to open group plans and examine both Telco- and user-driven approaches. We ask *"How the price of leftover bandwidth on the secondary market impacts user bills and operator revenues?"*. We examine the previous question under different levels of "liquidity" in terms of the ability of users to exchange bandwidth (either through operator supported billing yielding perfect liquidity or through user driven tethering yielding partial liquidity depending on the density of users). We finally ask *"What is the impact of market liquidity on open collaborative schemes"*.

The main contributions of our work are the following:

- We demonstrated that the volatility of user demand makes it hard for the users to pick the 'right' package, effectively leaving significant fraction of purchased packages unused, with occasional spikes in demand that go beyond purchased commit volumes. We show that this holds even if users are able to adjust their contract on a monthly basis using various package selection strategies.

- Looking at the smallest closed ("family") plans involving $k = 2$ users, we see that expected savings are 3-14%. Increasing the group size yields greater savings but the extent always depends on the tariff structure. For $k = 10$ the savings can range from 11% to 45%. Such groups are rather large, however, for most practical uses. Generally the savings achieved through collaboration are higher for tariffs that involve a greater difference between commit and penalty rate.

- We turn to open sharing model and start with full liquidity as realized for example by Telcos that help their users sell their leftover capacity using their billing system. We characterize the relationship between the steady-state supply, demand and the price of the mobile data in such secondary market. Overall users could expect significant savings in the range of 19% to 71%. The exact number depends on the relationship between the commit, penalty, and secondary market rates. Knowledge of this relationship is important for a Telco in order to decide whether it wants to permit a secondary market, whether it wants to control it by setting the secondary price, and also to help the operator to design the tariffs in the presence of such secondary market.

- In the case of user-driven collaborative consumption through tethering, liquidity plays a paramount role. Unlike in the Telco-supported case, it is no longer guarantee that the leftover capacity of a user can be brought to the market. We employ census density maps to estimate the liquidity in one representative European country and characterize the impact of the density of sharing users on the sharing economy. Our results suggest that even in low-density areas of 3 neighbors per user the potential user savings can be significant, in the range of 8-23%, while in the dense, urban, areas the opportunity for sharing via tethering approximates the case of full liquidity.

For both open and closed groups, we report a number of factors that influence the efficiency of sharing. Explicit recommendations on how to choose tariffs, or how to choose partners in closed groups or buyers/sellers in the open groups is out of scope of the present paper.

2. DATA

Here we briefly introduce the datasets used in the rest of the paper.

2.1 Per-user demand

The mobile broadband usage data analyzed in this paper are from a small national European cellular operator. The dataset contains a record for each mobile broadband session with the anonymized user id, timestamp and the volume of the data session in bytes. To facilitate the empirical study in the following sections, we extract the set of all those users who have used mobile broadband at least once every month over a 7-month period spanning the end of 2011 and beginning of 2012. There are around 40 thousand such users and we have a detailed history of their mobile broadband usage over the 7 month period. An important property of the dataset is that mobile broadband in this operator was not metered during the period over which the data was collected, *i.e.*, there are *no* volume caps. This means that the demand generated by users is their natural one, without any bias from pricing, *e.g.*, self-regulation due to volume caps and penalty rates.

We observe some seasonal variability in the data and a relatively small growth of the overall mobile broadband demand. Fig. 1 (left) shows the per-user median and mean mobile broadband demand over $m = 7$ months covered by our dataset, from which we can observe that in the final months of the dataset the overall demand is some 20% larger than in the first months of the considered period. Also, we note that mean is greater than the median by a factor of 5, indicating a skewed distribution in per-user demand.

Denoting the mobile broadband volume of user u in month t by $d_u(t)$, we capture her temporal demand volatility through the ratio between the minimum and maximum of the monthly demand series:[2]

$$variability\_index(u) = \frac{\min_{t \le m}(d_u(t))}{\max_{t \le m}(d_u(t))}. \quad (1)$$

The empirical CDF of $variability\_index$ across all 40K studied users is depicted in Fig. 1 (right). It reveals a large amount of volatility in monthly demand; for around 60% of all the considered users the maximal monthly usage is $\times 5$ or more of their minimal monthly usage ($variability\_index < 0.2$).

Such temporal volatility far exceeds the volatility observed in shared backbone links where statistical multiplexing of

[2]Note that our relatively small sample (7 months) precludes using measures like standard deviation to quantify volatility.

Operator	Tariff 1	Tariff 2	Tariff 3	Tariff 4	Tariff 5	Tariff 6	Tariff 7	Tariff 8	Tariff 9
Vodafone IND	300/100/2	1000/250/2	1500/375/2	2000/450/2	3000/650/2	4000/750/2	5000/850/2	8000/1250/2	12000/1600/2
Telstra AUS	250/20/0.2	700/30/0.2	1000/40/0.2	3000/50/0.2	4000/80/0.2	6000/100/0.2	12000/180/0.2		
Vivo BRA	150/30/0.4	250/35/0.1	500/60/0.1	2000/90/0.1	5000/120/0.1	10000/200/0.1			
Claro ARG	125/49/0.1	512/69/0.1	1000/99/0.1	3000/129/0.1	5000/159/0.1	10000/199/0.1			
Olleh KOR	500/34/.04	1000/42/.04	1500/52/.04	3000/62/.04	5000/72/.04	7000/85/.04	10000/100/.04		
Unicom CHI	150/46/0.3	300/66/0.3	400/126/0.3	500/156/0.3	750/226/0.3	950/286/0.3	1300/386/0.3	2000/586/0.3	3000/886/0.3
E-plus GER	250/10/.05	750/15/.01	2000/20/.01	5000/25/.01					
Vodafone UK	250/3/.1	500/7.5/.015	2000/15/.015						
Etisalat UAE	100/29/1	1000/99/.5	5000/249/.5	10000/449/.5					
ATT US	300/20/.067	3000/30/.01	5000/50/.01						

Table 1: The tariffs for prepaid mobile broadband from 10 representative mobile operators. The compact representation (x, y, z) refers to the cap of x *Mbyte*, price y in local currency and z overage rate in local currency per *Mbyte*.

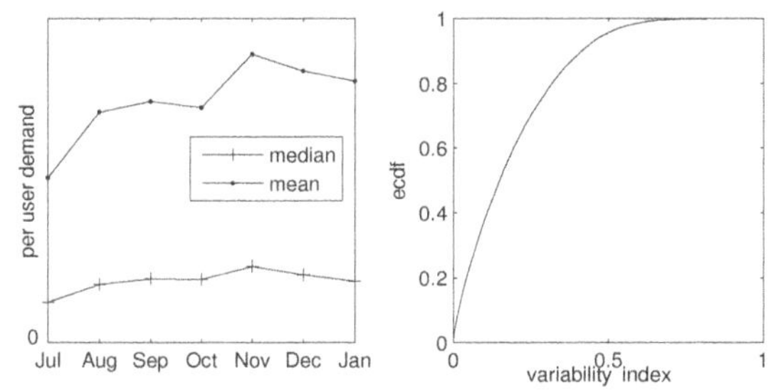

Figure 1: Left: mean/median monthly usage (scale not shown to preserve confidential information). Right: empiric CDF of the ratio between the min and max of the per-user monthly demand.

individual flows makes daily or monthly aggregate volumes almost periodic (off by few percentage points [17]). Interestingly, even individual consumption for utilities like water and electricity [3] appears to be more predictable than mobile broadband consumption.

2.2 Pricing

In addition to mobile broadband usage data, we also collected data on the pricing packages of 10 different mobile operators in 10 different countries across 5 continents (listed in Table 1) [11]. This dataset depicts a wide range of relationships between commit and penalty rates, including offers with low caps and relative high penalty rates, which are usually referred to as pay-per-byte packages. Plan diversity, as will be shown later, plays an important role in package selection and are critical in understanding the potential of collaborative consumption in mobile broadband.

Since we started working on this paper in the autumn of 2013 there were virtually no changes in the tariffs among those 10 studied operators.

3. USER PACKAGE SELECTION

Before we look at the potential of collaborative consumption in the mobile broadband, we will first in this section demonstrate that the high temporal volatility of demand makes the selection of an appropriate plan hard, thus leaving many users effectively (heavily) under-using their package with occasional spikes in demand which go beyond the cap of the purchased cap.

We use $d_u(t)$ to denote the demand of user u in month $t = 1, 2, \ldots, m$. At the beginning of every month,[3] users choose a plan among the set of available plans $\mathcal{P}$. The plan $i \in \mathcal{P}$ is determined by the triplet $(cap_i, price_i, \mu_i)$: the volume with a cap (in *Mbyte*), the committed price of the plan (in \$), and overage price – what user has to pay after the volume cap is reached (in \$[4] per *Mbyte*), respectively. If the plan $i \in \mathcal{P}$ is chosen the charge at the end of the month during which the user consumed volume d (in *Mbyte*) is

$$C(d, i) = price_i + \max(0, d - cap_i) \cdot \mu_i.$$

At the beginning of every month t, the user u has to choose the plan i that matches her demand. If she knew her demand up-front, she could choose the plan that minimizes the charge for the month t, and we use $o_u(t)$ to denote the minimal possible charge and refer to this as the ***a-posteriori optimum***

$$o_u(t) = \min_{i \in \mathcal{P}} C(d_u(t), i).$$

However, the demand $d_u(t)$ is rarely known upfront, and users can use various heuristics that depend on history of consumption in the previous months, to choose the plan during month t based on the estimated demand in that month t. For that purpose, we use the following possible heuristics:

Max rule (MR): in month t the user u chooses the plan i_{MR} that minimizes the charge in the month of the maximal demand prior to t.

$$i_{MR} = \arg\min_{i \in \mathcal{P}} \left(C(\max_{1 \leq \tau \leq t-1} (d_u(\tau)), i) \right). \quad (2)$$

For user u that chooses the plan i_{MR} at the month t the charge is

$$h_u^{MR}(t) = C(d_u(t), i_{MR}) \geq o_u(t)$$

Optimal-expectation rule (OER): in month t the user u chooses the plan i_{OER} that minimizes the expected charge assuming that the demand in month t is equal to the demand in one of the previous months with uniform probability $(1/(t-1))$.

$$i_{OER} = \arg\min_{i \in \mathcal{P}} \left(\frac{1}{t-1} \sum_{\tau=1}^{t-1} C(d_u(\tau), i) \right). \quad (3)$$

For user u that chooses the plan i_{OER} at the month t the charge is

$$h_u^{OER}(t) = C(d_u(t), i_{OER}) \geq o_u(t).$$

We also experiment with other heuristics that output the plan that optimizes the cost, by using the estimate for the next month demand equal to the average and median of

[3] We assume that the billing happens in the monthly cycle. Both shorter (*e.g.*, daily or weekly), or longer (yearly) plans are being offered by some providers, though the monthly billing cycle is the most widely used around the world [35], and hence we focus on them exclusively in this paper.

[4] By \$ we mean local currency.

the previous month's demand, and observe the average costs comparable to MR and OER. Thus we omit them for brevity. Sophisticated time-series analysis is unlikely to provide significant improvements over these simple estimators, since our dataset contains relatively small number of data points (only 7 samples per user). However, the impact of more advanced estimators, remains to be studied in the future.

Remark 1. We would like to note that modeling the user decision process regarding the tariff choice is highly challenging. We settle here for the two intuitive strategies, OER and MR, as two possible ways to model such decision process. Whether such models reflect the tariff selection process (employed by end-users) remains to be validated in practice.

Remark 2. Similarly, modeling the impact that volume caps may have on user demand is a hard problem [22][5][28]. In this paper, we assume that users' demand is invariant and influences the decision on the tariff as well as the overall cost. Alternatively, one could analyze another model in which users adjust their demand under caps paying an implicit (non-monetary) cost in terms of reduced traffic consumption. Models with invariant user demand can lead to higher cost per user with respect to the self-regulation models. However, our base assumption allows us to compare different types of collaborative systems directly, without the need of quantifying the indirect cost experienced by users when they cannot satisfy their original traffic demand.

3.1 User demand vs. capacity

Intuitively, the high volatility of demand combined with large penalty fees, implies that many (rational) users would often, but not always, choose a tariff that leaves them some spare unused capacity as a cushion against the risk of going over the cap and paying large overage fees. We evaluate mismatch between the user demand and the capacity she purchases (under OER or MR), and in Figure 2 we plot the data volume (right) and fraction of users under-the-cap and over-the-cap (left). We observe that in most[5] of the cases the amount of traffic (and fraction of the users) under-the-cap is significantly larger than the traffic (and fraction of the users) over-the-cap, indicating an opportunity to 'offload' the over-the-cap traffic through those users that under-utilize their cap and avoid paying the large penalty fees. In later sections, we will study how sharing of underutilized packages may affect the bill of the mobile broadband users. While over-the-cap volume may appear to be small, the amount of revenues operator could collect from those overage charges is nontrivial, and in the case of OER it ranges from 11% for ATT tariffs to 42% in Vodafone India tariffs. The revenue coming from overage fees is indeed smaller in MR than for OER, as by default customers purchase larger packages and have smaller over-the-cap volumes.

3.2 Heuristics vs. a-posteriori optimum tariff

This paragraph is not directly related to sharing economy, but it does represent an interesting result on its own, and partly answers the question raised by [28] on why users choose 'inappropriate' data plans. Namely, we quantify how much do heuristics (OER and MR), based on the historic demand pattern, differ from the a-posteriori optimum tariff, for the real users with volatile demand pattern.

[5]The only exception is China Unicom, which has extremely low penalty rate, which basically discourages users to purchase large packages.

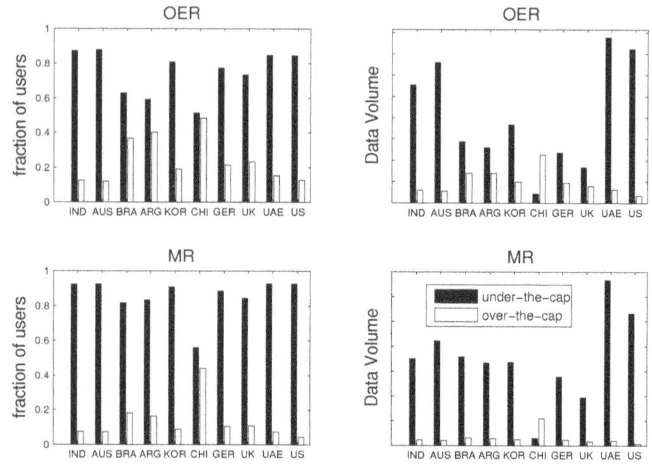

Figure 2: The amount of total unused and over-the-cap traffic (left) and fraction of users under- and over-the-cap (right) for the 10 operators under OER and MR tariff selection. Significant amount of unused packages, could potentially serve all of the over-the-cap traffic.

To compare the cost max rule h_u^{MR}, and optimal-expectation rule h_u^{OER}, against the a-posteriori optimum o_u we use diverse pricing policies, described in Sec. 2 to study the effect of different available tiers and over-the-cap rates. In Fig. 3 we plot the ratio between the average[6] charge based on our heuristic rules (MR and OER) and the average o_u, in the final month of our dataset $t = m = 7$.

From the Fig. 3 we can learn several lessons. First, the relative difference between the history-based heuristics and the a-posteriori optimum largely depends on the structure of the available plans, and specially the relative price per *Mbyte* of the committed cap and the overage/penalty rate. For operators with very large penalty price compared to the price of *Mbyte* in a committed cap, such as Vodafone India or Etisalat UAE, the heuristics perform much worse than the a-posteriori optimum with customers using the OER heuristic paying 70% and 45% more than a-posteriori optimum. For operators in which the penalty rate does not differ much from the committed rate, the cost of the heuristic rules does not significantly differ from the a-posteriori optima, as is the case with China Unicom and ATT for which the difference between the OER bill and the a-posteriorly optima is under 5%. We also observe that the optimum-expectation rule and maximum rule show similar average costs, with OER being marginally better in all of the ten studied policies.

4. CLOSED GROUP SHARING

In the previous section, we showed that demand volatility and diverse commit-to-penalty ratios make the task of selecting an appropriate plan for an individual user hard, leaving many users selecting plans much larger than their needs. One way to address such difficulties is through *collaborative purchase plans* shared among multiple users. The key advantage of shared plans is that the variability of the aggregate of independent demands is smaller than the sum of individual variabilities of its constituents. This effectively

[6]Average over the whole user-base.

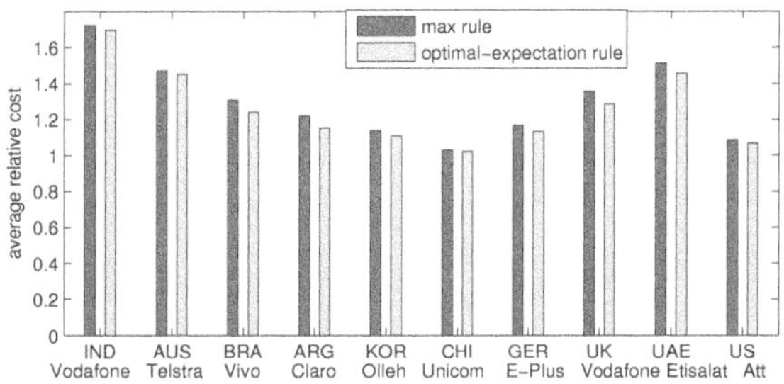

Figure 3: Ratio between the average cost of Max rule (optimal-expectation rule) and average a-posteriori optimum.

allows a group to pick collectively a better suited plan than what members can do on their own. Indeed, there exist several proposals for protocols that facilitate ad-hoc sharing of resources like voice call minutes [29] and mobile broadband [19] between users. Likewise, several operators offer shared plans for families and friends [8]. Our analysis is focused on characterizing the gains from collaboration – to the best of our knowledge, this is the first such empirical study.

The scenario we study is the following. A group G is composed of k users that purchase individual mobile broadband plans. When a user exhausts her volume, she may consume from the volume of any of the other users in the group. In order for such a scheme to work in practice, users must be on a shared data plan offered by some of the operators, or be in close proximity for a significant part of the billing period and thus be able to implement ad-hoc sharing over WiFi or bluetooth [19, 29, 14]. If k users in the group G have chosen plans $I_G = (i_1, \ldots, i_k)$, and generated the demand $D_G = (d_1, \ldots, d_k)$, respectively, then the cost for delivering that traffic is:

$$C(D_G, I_G) = \sum_{s \in G} price_{i_s} + \max(0, \sum_{s \in G} d_s - \sum_{s \in G} cap_{i_s}) \cdot \min_{s \in G}(\mu_{i_s}).$$

Users can purchase plans (for each month t) either in a:
- (1) non-coordinated manner using one of the heuristics described in the previous section, say OER, or in a
- (2) coordinated-OER manner by choosing the tariffs $I_G = (i_1, \ldots, i_k)$ in month t to minimize the expected cost aggregated among all partners in the group.

$$I_G^{OER} = \arg\min_{I_G \in \mathcal{P}^k} \frac{1}{t-1} \sum_{\tau=1}^{t-1} C(D_G(\tau), I_G). \qquad (4)$$

4.1 Setting up groups for volume sharing

There are many ways in which the users can engage in collaborative cap sharing. We briefly describe three dimensions of the problem of group selection that most collaborative arrangements face at some stage.

First, we need to answer how to select the group for collaborative sharing, which can be done in many ways. For example, the group selection can be done based on (1) *location* where users residing at the same location can use short-distance communication to share via tethering; or (2) *social relationships* where users with close social ties collaborate; or (3) *random* where random users collaborate opportunistically.

To evaluate the gains we use the random group matching. In Appendix A we demonstrate that groups formed using the social relationship or home location result in statistically identical benefits as those with random grouping.

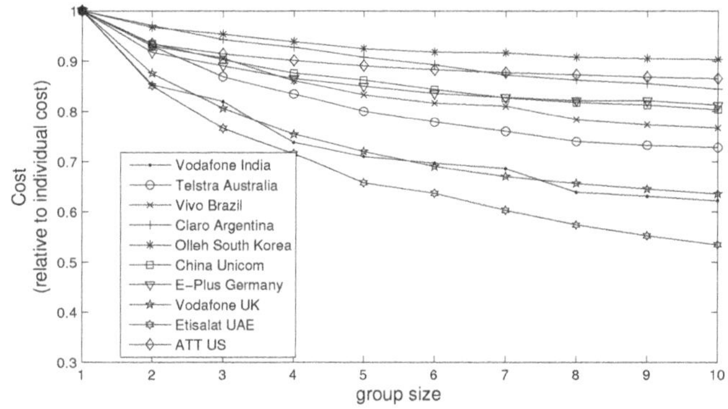

Figure 4: The average cost in the groups with coordinated tariff selection, relative to the cost of individual a-posteriori optima.

The next question would be to decide how large the group should be. Smaller groups are easier to set-up and coordinate, while larger ones are more cumbersome but may provide greater benefits from statistical multiplexing. Finally, once a group is formed, one needs to decide on how to select individual plans – in a non-coordinated manner (simple but sub-optimal) or in a coordinated one (more complicated but efficient).

In the remainder of this section, we study several facets of this design space. We study how the group size affects the cost of the group $C(D_G, I_G)$ compared to the cost of delivering the same demand without sharing the caps $\sum_{u \in G} C(d_u, i_u)$, when the groups are selected randomly. We also evaluate how much the coordination between the users in choosing the next-month-tariff can help in reducing the bill, when the groups are selected randomly. We conclude the section with the analysis of how the demand volume similarity affects the expected statistical multiplexing and costs.

4.2 Effect of group size

Intuitively, larger groups yield more predictable aggregate demand by statistically multiplexing more independent sources. In order to test this hypothesis and evaluate the impact of the group size on the overall cost incurred by the group $C(D_G, I_G)$, we vary the group size k, and for each k generate $N = 10000$ random groups of k members from our dataset, and evaluate the ratio between the average cost per group where the packages are chosen in a coordinated-OER manner (optimizing Eq (4)) in the final month of our dataset ($t = m = 7$), and the average cost of sum of the individual packages when no sharing is in place. We plot our findings in Fig. 4. With $N = 10000$ sampled groups, the standard error in all cases is less than 1% and, thus, the confidence bars are omitted for clarity.

Expectedly, the groups with 2 or more members can reduce the group cost. Having a single partner in the group is likely to bring the average cost of the 2-partner group down for 3%-14% compared to the cost of purchasing the plans individually using the OER and not sharing them $\sum_{s \in G} h_s^{OER}(m)$. For groups of size $k = 2$, the largest reduction in cost (around 14%) occurs with plans that impose high penalty rates (*e.g.*, Vodafone India/UK, Etisalat

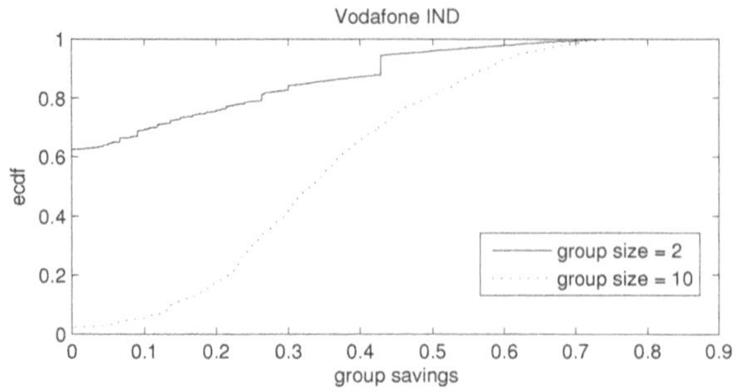

Figure 5: The empirical CDF of (coordinate) group savings in Vodafone India. Group size of 2 and 10 shown. The other group sizes and operators follow similar trend.

UAE and Telstra AUS tariffs). With larger groups, *e.g.*, $k = 10$, the benefits grow more and can range between 11% (for Olleh South Korea tariffs) and 45% (for Etisalat UAE tariffs). Another way to appreciate the gains is to look at the corresponding aggregate cost reduction for the entire group. Figure 5 depicts the CDF of the group savings for Vodafone India tariffs, and group sizes of 2 (pairs) and 10. For the group size of $k = 2$ (pairs), 60% of all pairs would see no benefit in collaborating, while around 20% of pairs could expect the cost reduction of 30% or more by sharing their caps. For larger groups of $k = 10$ partners, the distribution of expected savings is smoother, with the mean and median at around 35%.

While groups of 10 or more partners may bring considerate benefits for the involved partners, they are rather difficult to setup and maintain. With the open sharing analyzed in Section 5 such concerns of group creation and maintenance disappear.

4.3 Intra-group coordination

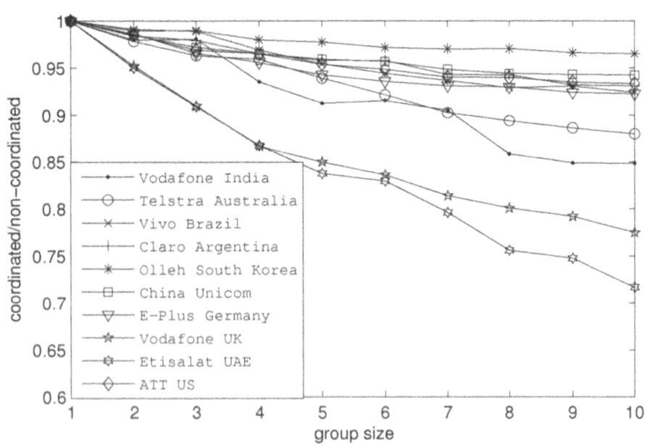

Figure 6: The ratio of the average group cost between the coordinated and the non-coordinated tariff choice. For small group sizes, coordination gives small benefit, which grows for larger groups.

In the previous section, we assumed that once several users engage in collaborative sharing of their caps, they choose their packages in a coordinated manner (to minimize Eq. (4)) based on their historic use pattern. However, if users are not willing to share their history with the others in the group, but rather purchase their packages individually, in a un-coordinated manner (using for instance, the optimal-expectation rule Eq. 3) they can still benefit from sharing, although the benefit of such group sharing is likely to be lower than in the coordinated case. In Fig. 6 we depict the ratio between the average group cost between the coordinated and the non-coordinated plan choice obtained by randomly selecting $N = 10000$ groups with k users from our dataset, and evaluating the average cost of the group with and without coordinated plan selection. We can conclude that coordination brings relatively small benefit (5% and less) for very small groups of 2 partners and brings higher benefit for the larger groups. Indeed, the expected benefit of coordination is the pricing-policy dependent.

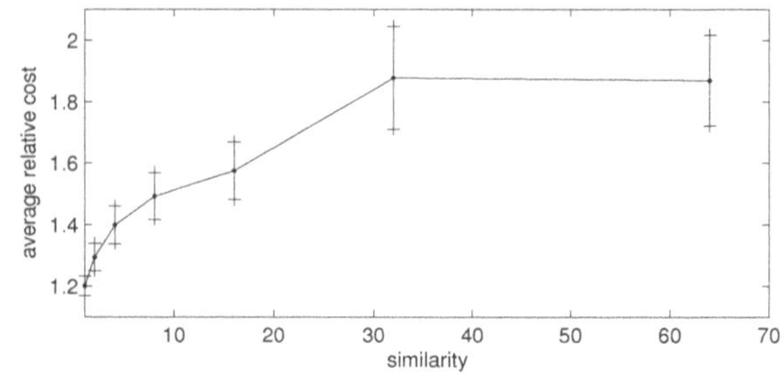

Figure 7: The cost (relative to the a-posteriori optima $\sum_{u \in G} o_u$) of the pairs sharing the cap for different similarity indices. Users with similar demand (low *similarity* index) complement each other's cap better than the users with large difference in demand.

4.4 Volume-based group selection

A natural question in the context of collaborative volume sharing is related to whom should one partner with. Next, we demonstrate that similarity of demand, in terms of total volume per month, should be taken into account when constructing groups. In particular, a group should combine users that consume similar volume across the month because in that case the statistical multiplexing is likely to provide the largest benefit to the cooperating partners.

The average demand per user is very skewed, covering multiple orders of magnitude. For a group G of users, we define the *similarity* metric as the ratio between the maximum and minimum average demand among the members in the group.

$$similarity = \frac{\max_{u \in G} \sum_{\tau < m} d_u(\tau)}{\min_{u \in G} \sum_{\tau < m} d_u(\tau)}.$$

To evaluate the relationship between the demand *similarity* and the impact of sharing the cap on the cost, we select $N = 10000$ random pairs of users from our datasets, and split them in 7 different sets depending on which of the following 7 segments the pair demand similarity falls into: $[1, 2), [2, 4), [4, 8), \ldots, [32, 64), [64, \infty)$. For each of the 7 segments, we evaluate the average cost of the pair sharing the cap in the last month of the dataset, divided by the a-posteriori optima ($\sum_{u \in G} o_u$). We report our findings in Fig. 7 based on the plans of Vodafone India. The other plans and group sizes follow similar pattern and are omitted. From this figure, we can conclude that it is most beneficial to collaborate with the users with similar demand volumes. Note that users with similar demand would produce a low *similarity* index.

We conclude this section reiterating that closed (family) sharing can reduce the bill of the involved parties, with small savings for small 2-partner groups that grow when group has more partners, with similar volumes and with a coordinated plan selection.

5. OPEN SHARING

The close collaborative groups that we study in the previous section, although beneficial for users, could be too restrictive, and may not allow efficient sharing of unused caps. The gain from the closed-group sharing becomes substantial only when the many users partner-up, they generate similar traffic volumes and coordinate the plan selection. Moreover, coordination and the issues related to how the cost/savings should be shared in large groups may be cumbersome. For that reason, we look at a more flexible model, which we refer to as open sharing model (or simply open model), in which anyone with a mobile broadband subscription may buy or sell mobile data according to their demand and capacity.

Open sharing systems are supported by some major mobile broadband operators, like China Mobile Hong Kong [40] and SK Telecom Korea [23], which allow their subscribers to freely resell unused mobile data. Similarly to (closed) family sharing plans, these offers help operators attract/retain customers by allowing them better control and ownership of their packages.

For the customers of the operator that do not enable sharing/reselling to others, there is an option of sharing their unused caps via tethering to users in their close proximity. Several applications, such as Airmobs [19] or Hotspotio [14], allow users to share their data for capacity credit or other type of rewards.

In the rest of this section we first study the open sharing where users are allowed to trade their unused data freely via an operator-controlled market (in Section 5.1) and then explore the potential of the open sharing under the proximity constraint in Section 5.2.

5.1 Telco-assisted open sharing

5.1.1 System model

As we mentioned above, our goal here is to understand the potential of the mobile broadband sharing in which the users are free to resell their unused cap for a fee. We denote with $\hat{p}$ the price per *Mbyte* of mobile broadband on such secondary market. In the case of telco-controlled market, $\hat{p}$ can be either controlled by the operator or by the free market based on the supply and the demand. As we will see, the value of $\hat{p}$, has a critical impact on the user plan selection, and hence on the demand D and supply S of the mobile broadband on the secondary market.

For a user selecting plan i and with data consumption of d (in *Mbyte*), the total cost of their data plan at the end of the month is:

$$C_{TS} = (d, i, \hat{p}, s, b) \begin{cases} price_i + \max(0, d - cap_i)\mu_i(1-b) + \max(0, d - cap_i)\hat{p} \cdot b - \max(0, cap_i - d)\hat{p} \cdot s & \text{if } \hat{p} < \mu_i \\ price_i + \max(0, d - cap_i)\mu_i - \max(0, cap_i - d)\hat{p} \cdot s & \text{if } \hat{p} \geq \mu_i \end{cases} \tag{5}$$

with s we denote the fraction of the unused capacity that the user could sell to others in the trading system. Likewise, b denotes the fraction of the capacity over the cap that the user could acquire from others. These fractions depend on the demand and the supply on the secondary market. If the supply is greater than the demand, $s = 1$, otherwise $b = 1$.

Given the price $\hat{p}$ on the secondary market, and supply/demand parameters, s and b, users can select the plan according to the rules described in Section 3 to minimize their monthly cost. In the rest of the section we use the optimal-expectation rule: users select the plan i^{TS}_{OER} as following

$$i^{TS}_{OER} = \arg\min_{i \in \mathcal{P}} \left(\frac{1}{t-1} \sum_{\tau=1}^{t-1} C(d_u(\tau), i, \hat{p}, s, b) \right). \tag{6}$$

We define of the supply S in the open-sharing market to be the sum of unused caps across all the customers participating in the market:

$$S(\hat{p}, s, b) = \sum_u (\max(0, cap_{c_u} - d_u))$$

Similarly, the demand D of in the open-sharing market is given by the sum of demand on top of the purchased cap across all users:

$$D(\hat{p}, s, b) = \sum_u (\max(0, d_u - cap_{c_u})) \text{ where } \mu_{c_u} > \hat{p}$$

Note that a user under a plan i with a μ_i smaller than $\hat{p}$ does not contribute to D, as these users would obtain their over-the-cap capacity directly from the operator. The overall amount of traffic users can share in this market is simply $min(S, D)$. We distribute equally the amount of capacity exchanged among all users; therefore the fraction of unused/extra traffic users can sell/buy on the sharing market will be respectively:

$$s = \frac{min(S(\hat{p}, s, b), D(\hat{p}, s, b))}{S(\hat{p}, s, b)} \tag{7}$$

$$b = \frac{min(S(\hat{p}, s, b), D(\hat{p}, s, b))}{D(\hat{p}, s, b)} \tag{8}$$

Users participating in the market make individual decisions on which package to purchase based on their consumption, the value of $\hat{p}$, and the parameters s and b (optimizing Eq. (6)). On the other hand, such decisions determine supply and demand. Hence for a given $\hat{p}$, the supply and the demand would self-regulate to stable values $s(\hat{p})$ and $b(\hat{p})$, which solve the system of equations (7)-(8). In general, the smaller $\hat{p}$ result in larger demand (as user purchase smaller packages), while for larger $\hat{p}$ supply on the secondary market dominates the demand; see Fig. 8 (top).

The final charge per user is then

$$h_u^{OER,TS}(t) = C(d_u(t), i^{TS}_{OER}, \hat{p}, b(\hat{p}), s(\hat{p}))))$$

5.1.2 Benefits of trading systems

We use the equilibria supply/demand parameters ($s = s(\hat{p})$ and $b = b(\hat{p})$) to estimate the impact of $\hat{p}$ on the cost of users and the revenues of the operator. By choosing the equilibria parameters, we are analyzing steady state scenarios in which users actually obtain from the system what they expect. Unstable scenarios can occur at the starting phases of the system and continue until users adapt their s and b

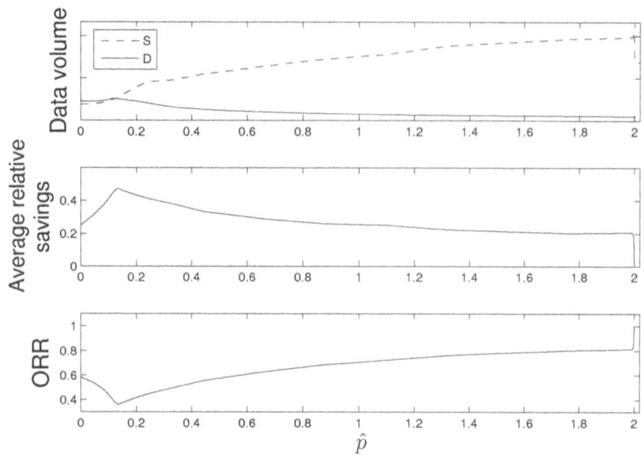

Figure 8: Supply and demand (top), average user savings (middle), and operator revenues ORR (bottom) for varying $\hat{p}$ in Vodafone India tariffs.

to the steady ones[7]. Figure 8 shows the steady state supply ($S(\hat{p})$) and demand ($D(\hat{p})$) for a range of $\hat{p}$ for Vodaphone India tariffs in the last month of our dataset. Also, we report the average savings per user and the revenues of the operator. The reported revenues of the operator are relative to the earnings without trading system:

$$ORR(\hat{p}) = \frac{\sum_u h_u^{OER,TS}}{\sum_u h_u^{OER}}$$

When $\hat{p}$ is equal to the penalty rate (in case of Vodafone India[8] it is $\mu_0 = 2$), each user makes the decision to purchase a cap, which is the same as in the case where there is no secondary market. Hence the $\sim 19\%$ savings that happen when $\hat{p} = \mu_0$ come not from users purchasing smaller packages but rather exclusively from sharing the packages they would purchase if no sharing was enabled (by optimizing eq. (3)). We report the average per-user savings and the overall operator revenue ORR, for $\hat{p} = \mu_0$ for all of the 10 studied operators in Table 2. We observe that the ORR is greater than 80% in all but one operator (Vodafone UK). This means that if the Telco allows sharing through their billing system, but controls the price to be the penalty rate, the impact on its revenues can be somewhat controlled and kept relatively low.

In Vodafone India, a $\hat{p}$ slightly over 0.1282 drives the system to the largest average user savings, which is around 47%. We denote that optimal point with $\hat{p}^*$. This $\hat{p}^*$ is also the one in which $S(\hat{p}^*) = D(\hat{p}^*)$ (i.e. where the supply and demand are identical) and where the relative revenues of the operator are the lowest (near 36%). We report the average per-user savings and relative operator revenue for other 9 operators in Table 2 for $\hat{p} = \hat{p}^*$. From the table, we observe how users under tariffs with high penalty rates, such as Vodafone India and Etisalat UAE, receive large benefits from the trading system while the telco revenues are strongly impacted by it. On the other hand, for ATT and Olleh South Korea plans, which possess plans with relative low penalty rates, operators' suffer a low impact on their revenues even under the $\hat{p}^*$. Additionally, the users in such low-penalty tariffs experience the least amount of savings from the trading system. China Unicom is again an exception for our analysis. The tariff system offered by China Unicom is somewhat atypical with commit rate being cheapest in the second smallest package[9], which creates some unusual dynamics.

Regarding the relative savings per user, the ECDF of per user savings with Vodafone India tariffs for the case $\hat{p} = \hat{p}^*$ is depicted in Figure 9. From the figure we observe that per-user savings are widely distributed with a peak around 38%, which corresponds to a large fraction of users which move from one package to another. In Figure 10, we plot the average relative savings for several groups of customers based on their average consumption for $\hat{p} = \hat{p}^*$. The ways savings are distributed among the customers is very tariff-dependent, and indeed differ from one operator to the other. In general, the heavier the customer is, the larger is her expected savings, even though in some tariffs this is not the case (Vodafone UK and China Unicom). As a large percentage of users have a relative low consumption (less than 200MB), the savings from these users drive, in a large percentage, the global benefits provided by the collaborative system.

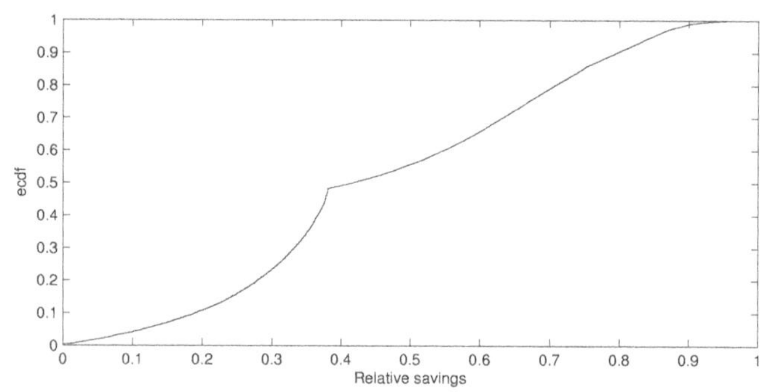

Figure 9: ECDF of relative savings per user with Vodafone India tariffs ($\hat{p} = \hat{p}^* = 0.128$).

5.2 Open sharing via tethering

If the network operator does not enable reselling of the unused data caps, the users can still share via short-range tethering with others in their close proximity. Such proximity constraint may significantly limit the potential of sharing in the rural areas, where the density of mobile users may not be enough to allow meaningful cap sharing. However, in the dense urban environments, the opportunities of finding a buyer/seller match are much more likely. In this section we aim to quantify the potential of the open sharing model under the proximity constraint.

[7] An example of an unstable scenario is when most users select the plan with the lowest cap (usually the cheapest), probably expecting to acquire cheap capacity in the secondary market for most of their demand. This, however, creates a buyer's market, in which capacity is not available in the sharing system; thus, compelling users to obtain capacity under the penalty rate of the mobile operator.

[8] We note that each time we refer to a particular telco, e.g. Vodaphone India, we actually refer to their tariffs not the telco itself.

[9] In all other telcos, the lowest commit rate is in the largest package.

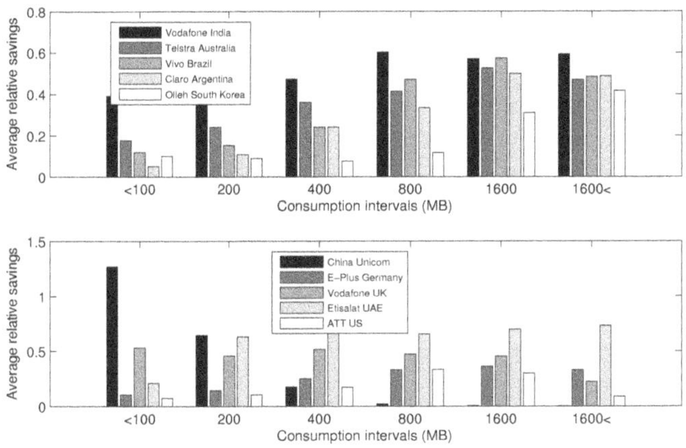

Figure 10: Average savings for users under different consumption intervals for $\hat{p} = \hat{p}^*$.

Operator	ORR $\hat{p} = \hat{p}^*$	Avg. user savings $\hat{p} = \hat{p}^*$	ORR $\hat{p} = \mu_0$	Avg. user savings $\hat{p} = \mu_0$
Vodafone India	36%	47%	81%	21%
Telstra Australia	51%	33%	84%	14%
Vivo Brazil	58%	28%	89%	3.9%
Claro Argentina	68%	22%	95%	2.1%
Olleh South Korea	80%	14%	94%	4.5%
China Unicom	81%	54%	81%	54%
E-Plus Germany	72%	22%	83%	14%
Vodafone UK	51%	47%	68%	32%
Etisalat UAE	29%	53%	93%	5.9%
ATT US	79%	17%	84%	13%

Table 2: Lowest average user cost and lowest relative revenue found in stable systems ($\delta = \hat{\delta} = \delta_e$) for all operators.

The first question we ask is how many cellular users can one expect to communicate with over a short-range channel. To answer that question, we use the census data from the country of the operator we study. For each ward, the census data reports the area (in km^2) and number of people per ward from which we can calculate the density of people per km^2. To estimate the number of people a cellular user can communicate with over a short-range channel, we calculate the expected number of people in the circle with $20m$ radius for each ward. The $20m$ radius was taken as a standard WiFi indoor range. Different technologies would indeed have different ranges, but for the purpose of quick first order estimate, we use the $20m$ range. The CDF of the number of neighbors within $20m$ range is depicted in Figure 11. In this particular country, a cellular user has a median of 3.18, and an average of 4.11 other cellular users in their $20m$ radius. Note that these numbers are rather conservative in that they assume that humans are spread uniformly in the area covered by the ward. In practice both in urban, and especially in rural, areas a large fraction of space is non-occupied (e.g. parks, highways or agriculture land), and even in the populated land, humans tend to be clustered; hence the denominator area in the density calculation is likely much smaller, and the number of proximal neighbors is likely to be larger than what the CDF in Fig. 11 would suggest.

Next, we study the relationship between the density of an area (represented by the expected number of users a user can communicate with) and the potential savings users may expect in the open sharing among their neighbors. For this analysis, we let users select their cap based on their historical consumption, optimizing their bill as if full market liquidity was in place with various $\hat{p}$, but allow them to trade capacity with other users in a near range of them. The number of users within the tethering range is defined by a parameter η we call *density*, which we vary between 0 and 20 following the official census data report. To understand the impact of *density* on the sharing, we employ the following procedure. We take $N = 40000$ users for which we have a detailed history of data sessions described in Section 2. Time is slotted in seconds, and each user tracks the total consumption and spare capacity in the billing circle. At the time of each data session with volume V, user u checks its total consumption. If the total consumption is smaller than the capacity of her package, she uses it; otherwise she picks randomly $\eta =$ *density* other users as neighbors. In case any of them has a spare capacity greater than V, the one with the largest spare capacity responds by sharing it with the user u and adjust its own consumption by $+V$. In case none of the neighbors has enough spare capacity, user u purchases it on the primary market from the operator paying the penalty rate. Users decide on which package to purchase optimizing Eq. (6) for various $\hat{p}$. Varying $\hat{p}$, allows to control the supply and the demand of the secondary market.

For each of the ten operators and each density value, we experiment with several $\hat{p}$ values and report the maximal *total relative savings* in Figure 12. For low densities, in the optimal state the supply is much larger than the demand of the secondary market, allowing users which have an excessive demand to find a supplier with high likelihood. In the case of high densities, the system converges to the case with full liquidity studied in Section 5.1 where in the optimal state the supply of the secondary market is equal to the demand.

From Figure 12, we can observe that the savings of users in environments with average density population (4 people) are in the range of 9-25%. For the highly populated areas, with 20 people per tethering circle, the relative savings increase to 18-48%. The results are encouraging and complement, from an economical perspective, previous endeavors of measuring technical benefits of collaborative systems for the mobile users [18].

We conclude this section with the remark that our analysis suggests that in some cases the operator may be better off (have higher *ORR*) by embracing the sharing economy and assisting it though its own billing system while controlling the price on the secondary market than allowing the users to create their own secondary market via tethering. For example, the operator relative revenues *ORR* of Claro Argentina is 0.95 when $\hat{p}$ equals the penalty rate μ_0. However, when users can choose their own $\hat{p}$, even with the constraint of tethering they can save more than 5% of their bills as long as they have sufficient density of sharing neighbors; in dense areas with 20 neighbors the revenues of the operator could be reduced by as much as 19%. Our results indicate the existence of a fine tradeoff between the tariff structure, the population density and the potential of the sharing economy with and without Telco assistance.

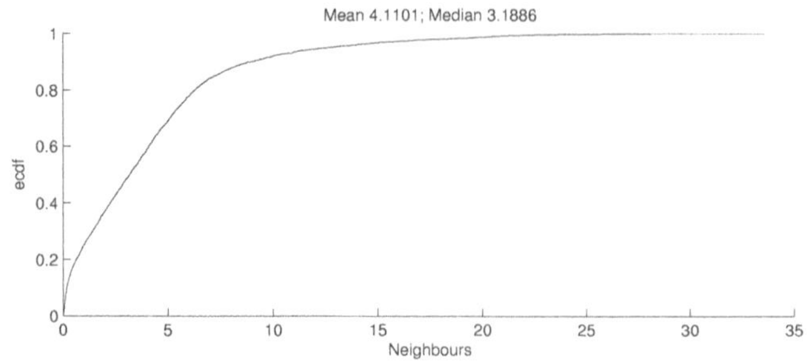

Figure 11: Expected number of cellular users in 20m radius.

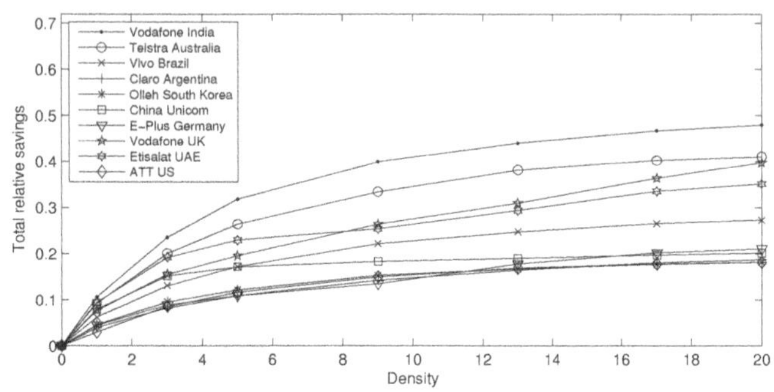

Figure 12: Total user savings (1-ORR) for varying density values.

6. RELATED

Our work is related to pricing and economics of mobile broadband. Recent work has looked into the merits and demerits of usage based pricing (UBP) in cellular networks [2, 20, 26]. Likewise, authors of TUBE [12] suggest time dependent pricing can help in reducing peak-hour congestion. Authors of [30, 31] investigate the existing 3G/4G billing systems and demonstrate a number of loopholes in them. Our contribution is to investigate how volatility (hence, lack of predictability) in demand can lead to sub-optimal decisions in terms of choosing plans. A closely related recent work investigated the notion of 'irrationality' of users in choosing mobile broadband plans – users often pay more than they consume [28] for different services. Our work builds up on the findings to investigate variability in demand and suggest how one can pick close to optimal plans.

A number of authors have analyzed the sharing in cellular networks. In [29] authors suggest sharing unused the minutes and sms and designed a prototype of the system that enables such sharing. In [15, 21] authors apply game theoretic tools to study crowdsoured architectures (including collaborative consumption) for mobile data access. Authors of [24] propose *kibbutz*, a system that leverages mobile link sharing to improve the energy consumption and connection performance of users. We complement these works by providing quantitative insights on the viability and the impact of collaborative consumption in the mobile data access.

There has been recent surge of services that enable collaborative consumption of various resources including apartments [1], cars [13], books [4], etc. Results of our work here suggest that collaboration between end-users can be beneficial for users of mobile broadband, providing economic incentives for technical solutions like Airmobs [19] or Hotspotio [14].

7. DISCUSSION

In this section, we briefly discuss some of the issues that may influence our results.

A major assumption that we rely on is that the user demand is independent of the pricing signal and market structure. This is a fairly strong assumption, since it is well known that pricing signal may have a rather important impact on how much demand one generates. However, we believe that the demand data we use here offers a useful input for a first-order approximation of the demand mobile broadband users put on the network. The effects of the pricing signal on the mobile broadband remain to be studied in the future.

As stated earlier, our analysis is performed assuming prepaid plans, which are the norm in large parts of the world [11]. Having said that, long-term contracts are popular as well and we intend to extend our analysis to such plans. Likewise, mobile broadband prices could vary depending on the technology mobile technology employed (4G/3G) or if they are bundled with other mobile services (e.g. voice or sms). These options can play a role in the choice of a mobile broadband plan, but we do not incorporate such externalities in our analysis. However we expect that mobile communications will follow the trend seen in fixed-line communications where residential broadband has replaced a large part of traditional fixed-line business (voice telephony).

Our analysis is purely economic. In the context of opportunistic traffic sharing (via tethering), such sharing may impact the end-to-end performance (e.g. increased bandwidth from multiple radios [36]), quality of experience (e.g. TCP issues with multihoming [33]), network coverage (e.g. users in close proximity may have different cellular signal strengths) and energy consumption [24]. These considerations are out of scope of this paper.

We believe our analysis can form the basis for designing incentives for risk management with and without user collaboration. Various solution (cost/revenue-sharing) concepts[10] from cooperative game theory as well as non-cooperative game theory could be of great use in designing such systems.

In the context of open sharing, an important element for enabling such system are micropayments. Our largest motivation for this type of systems comes from innovative Asian operators that facilitate the exchange of data using in-house applications [23, 40]. These solutions should include the necessary features to facilitate safe transactions among users. On the other hand, applications could also leverage tethering to provide a similar service [19, 29]. These applications should be enhanced to support micropayment without compromising the security and privacy of users. Solutions along the lines of [39] could be used to eliminate the effect of possible fraud in such a p2p micropayment system.

In this paper, we assume that operators do not react to the appearance of collaborative systems. Although we used a wide range of existing pricing plans to explore different scenarios, finding the effects of long-term strategies from mobile providers under this environment is still an open problem. Operators could, for instance, try to tune their penalty rates or cap structure to discourage the use of collaborative systems, while also minimizing revenue impact. Also, operators with control of the collaborative system could try to find a secondary market price that maximizes its revenues. Since

[10]Eg. Shapley value, Nash bargaining, core, nucleus, etc.

the domain space of possible strategies and pricing plans is enormous, studying these cases in a general way is very challenging (either analytically or empirically) and forms an interesting line for future research.

Recently, it has been recognized that time and the location are two important dimensions, which may influence the value of mobile data [12]. For example a crowded cell in the peak hour may price mobile data higher than a sparse cell over off-peak hours. Such time/location based pricing may improve the efficiency of cellular networks, albeit most existing cellular operators do not distinguish the price of the mobile data based on time nor location. Incorporating time/location in the models we study would be an interesting direction for future research.

8. CONCLUSIONS

Collaborative consumption is an exciting new trend of sharing various goods or services for economic and social benefits. In the context of mobile broadband, collaborative consumption can either be user-driven (e.g. via tethering) or Telco-driven (integrated through the Telco's billing system). We quantified the economic impact collaborative consumption could have both on the Telco and the customers. The methodology we develop can assist the operators to design the tariffs and/or control the secondary market to optimize its revenues in the presence of mobile broadband sharing.

9. ACKNOWLEDGEMENTS

This work has benefitted from a number of discussions we had with Vijay Erramilli, whose input significantly influenced the early versions of this paper.

10. REFERENCES

[1] Airbnb. `http://airbnb.com/`.

[2] J. Blackburn, R. Stanojevic, V. Erramilli, A. Iamnitchi and K. Papagiannaki. "Last call for the buffet: economics of cellular networks". In *Proc. of MobiCom 2013*.

[3] L. Bravo. "Aqualogy". Personal communication. 2013.

[4] Bookmooch. `http://bookmooch.com/`.

[5] M. Chetty, R. Banks, A.J. Bernheim Brush, J. Donner, R. E. Grinte. "You're Capped! Understanding the Effects of Bandwidth Caps on Broadband Use in the Home". In Proc. of ACM CHI 2012.

[6] S. DellaVigna. "Psychology and economics: Evidence from the field". Journal of Economic Literature, 47(2), 2009.

[7] N. Do et al. "CrowdMac: A Crowdsourcing System for Mobile Access". In Proc. of the 13th International Middleware Conference 2012.

[8] K. Fitchard. Att and Verizon shared data plan. `http://gigaom.com/2012/07/18/att-new-shared-smartphone-data-plans-undercut-verizon/`. GigaOM, 2012.

[9] FON. `http://corp.fon.com/en`.

[10] T. Gilovich, D. W. Griffin, D. Kahneman. "Heuristics and Biases: The Psychology of Intuitive Judgement". Cambridge university press 2002.

[11] Google. International Broadband Pricing Study: Dataset for public use. `http://policybythenumbers.blogspot.com/2012/08/international-broadband-pricing-study.html`

[12] S. Ha et al. "TUBE: time-dependent pricing for mobile data". In Proceedings of ACM SIGCOMM 2012

[13] M. Hart, M. J. Roberts, J. D. Stevens. "Zipcar: refining the business model". Harvard Business School Pub., 2005.

[14] Hotspotio. `http://hotspotio.com/`

[15] G. Iosifidis et al. "Enabling Crowd-Sourced Mobile Internet Access". Proc. of Infocom 2014.

[16] A. Lakhina, K. Papagiannaki, M. Crovella, C. Diot, E. D. Kolaczyk, and N. Taft. " Structural analysis of network traffic flows" In *Proc. of ACM SIGMETRICS'04*.

[17] N. Laoutaris et al. "Delay tolerant bulk data transfers on the Internet". In *Proc. of ACM SIGMETRICS'09*.

[18] S. Liu and A. Striegel. "Exploring the potential in practice for opportunistic networks amongst smart mobile devices"'. In *Proc. of MobiCom 2013*.

[19] A. Lippman, H. Holtzman and E. Toledano. "Air Mobs". MIT Media Lab, 2013

[20] D. Lyons. "The Impact of Data Caps and Other Forms of Usage-Based Pricing for Broadband Access". Preprint 2012.

[21] M. H. Manshaei et al. "On Wireless Social Community Networks". In Proc. of INFOCOM 2008.

[22] M. Muraven and R. F. Baumeister. "Self-regulation and depletion of limited resources: Does self-control resemble a muscle?." Psychological bulletin 126.2. 2000.

[23] Money Today. "Smart phones data business, 1GB price". `http://news.mt.co.kr/mtview.php?no=2013020713333217104`

[24] C. Nicutar, D. Niculescu, C. Raiciu. " Using Cooperation for Low Power Low Latency Cellular Connectivity" In Proc. of CoNEXT'14.

[25] A. Odlyzko. "Pricing and architecture of the internet: Historical perspectives from telecommunications and transportation". In *TPRC 2004*.

[26] A. Odlyzko et al. "Know Your Limits: Considering the Role of Data Caps and Usage Based Billing in Internet Access Service". Public Knowledge 2012.

[27] R. Stanojevic, N. Laoutaris, and P. Rodriguez. "On economic heavy hitters: shapley value analysis of 95th-percentile pricing". In Proc. of ACM IMC '10.

[28] R. Stanojevic, V. Erramilli, K. Papagiannaki. "Cognitive bias in network services". In Proc. of ACM HotNets 2012.

[29] H. Pan et al. Sharing airtime with Shair avoids wasting time and money. In Proc. of ACM HotMobile 2009

[30] C. Peng et al. "Can we pay for what we get in 3G data access?". In Proc. of ACM MOBICOM, 2012.

[31] C. Peng et al. "Mobile data charging: new attacks and countermeasures". In Proc. of ACM CCS 2012.

[32] M. Roughan et al. "Experience in measuring backbone traffic variability: Models, metrics, measurements and meaning." Proc. of the 2nd ACM SIGCOMM Workshop on Internet measurment. ACM, 2002.

[33] C. Rossi et al. "3GOL: Power-boosting ADSL using 3G OnLoading" In Proc. of CoNEXT, 2013.

[34] G. Shaw. "Telus announces new two-year talk and text, data plans." `http://blogs.edmontonjournal.`

com/2013/07/15/telus-announces-new-two-year-talk-and-text-data-plans/

[35] S. Soumya et al. "Pricing Data: A Look at Past Proposals, Current Plans, and Future Trends". Preprint 2012.

[36] C. Tsao, R. Sivakumar "On effectively exploiting multiple wireless interfaces in mobile hosts". CoNEXT, 2009.

[37] Telco 2.0 Initiative. "European Mobile: The Future's not Bright, it's Brutal". http://www.telco2research.com/articles/EB_European-mobile-future-brutal-telco_Summary, 2012.

[38] V. Valancius, C. Lumezanu, N. Feamster, R. Johari, V. Vazirani. "How Many Tiers? Pricing in the Internet Transit Market". In Proc. of ACM SIGCOMM, 2011.

[39] B. Yang, H. Garcia-Molina. "PPay: micropayments for peer-to-peer systems". In Proc. of ACM CCS 2003.

[40] ZDNet."China Mobile Hong Kong subscribers can sell unused data capacity". http://www.zdnet.com/china-mobile-hong-kong-subscribers-can-sell-unused-data-capacity-7000024541/

[41] Vodafone India, tariffs. https://www.vodafone.in/3gworld/pages/tariff_plans.aspx?cid=del

[42] Vodafone UK, tariffs. http://www.vodafone.co.uk/shop/internet/dongle/index.htm

[43] E-Plus Germany, tariffs. http://www.eplus.de/Tarife/E-Plus-internet-flats/E-Plus-internet-flats.asp?WT.ac=pk/Tarife/Internet-Flats/T2/130401

[44] Telstra, Australia, tariffs. http://www.telstra.com.au/internet/mobile-broadband/prepaid/rates/

[45] Claro, Argentina, tariffs. http://claro.com.ar/wps/portal/car/pc/personas/movil/planes-claro/planes-claro-control

[46] Olleh, South Korea, tariffs. http://shop.olleh.com/weblogic/EventServlet?pname=EventLTE

[47] Etisalat, UAE, tariffs. http://www.etisalat.ae/eportal/en/personal/mobile-mydata-packages.html

[48] ATT, US, tariffs. http://www.att.com/shop/wireless/data-plans.html#fbid=aE3VuzRgpel

APPENDIX

A. GROUPING BY LOCATION OR SOCIAL RELATIONSHIP

As described in Section 4.1, users can form collaboration groups based on their location or social relationships. Our dataset includes additional data from all users, such as billing information or call registries, which we can leverage to build these types of groups. In this section, we show that the benefits of these groups are similar to the ones from random groups, which we analyzed previously.

To form groups based on location, we use the residence information of our dataset. Users living in the same postal code[11] are placed in the same location group. On the other hand, we use the call registry from the users to build social relationships groups. The call registry allows us to find pairs of users who have called each other at least once. We refer to these pairs of users as peers. We create the social group of every user by combining all his/her peers. Figure 13 shows a histogram of group size for social and location groups we obtained from the 40K users in our dataset. Note that the y-axis is in the log-scale: the number of groups per group size decreases rapidly for each group selection type.

Figure 14 (left) depicts the cost of the coordinated-OER rule for localization and social groups relative to the cost obtained for random groups. We observe how the benefits obtained by group size are similar to the ones described in Section 4.2. We show the results until groups of size five, as we could not obtain a statistically significant number of groups with larger sizes. In Figure 14 (right) we compare the costs for users when coordinated and non-coordinated tariffs are chosen relative to the ratios for random groups. Similarly, the results agree with the analysis of random groups that we describe in detail in Section 4.3.

[11]In the country we analyzed, postal codes have very high granularity, with around 35 people in average per postal-code.

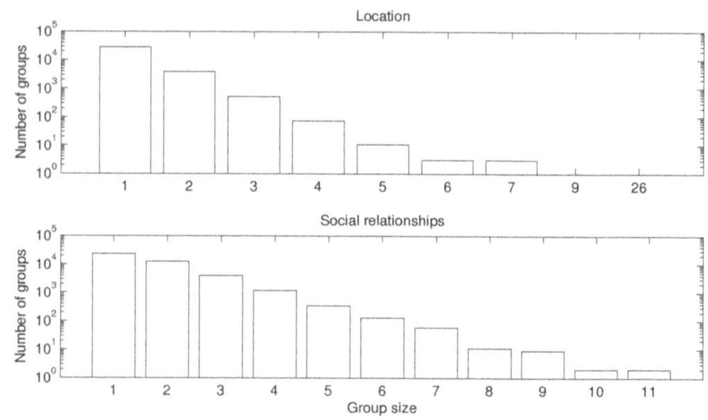

Figure 13: Number of groups of different sizes for social and location groups.

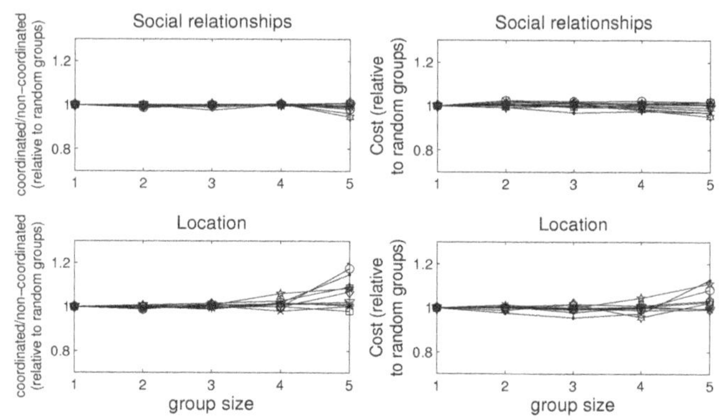

Figure 14: Average cost of random grouping vs. social and location grouping. The value of coordination (left). The impact of group size (right).

User Behavior and Change: File-sharers and Copyright Laws

Arnau Gavaldà-Miralles[†‡], John S. Otto[†], Fabián E. Bustamante[†], Luís A. N. Amaral[†], Jordi Duch[‡] and Roger Guimerà[‡]
[†]Northwestern University [‡]Universitat Rovira I Virgili

ABSTRACT

Though the impact of file-sharing of copyrighted content has been discussed for over a decade, only in the past few years have countries begun to adopt legislation to criminalize this behavior. These laws impose penalties ranging from warnings and monetary fines to disconnecting Internet service. While their supporters are quick to point out trends showing the efficacy of these laws at reducing use of file-sharing sites, their analyses rely on brief snapshots of activity that cannot reveal long- and short-term trends.

In this paper, we introduce an approach to model user behavior based on a hidden Markov model and apply it to analyze a two-year-long user-level trace of download activity of over 38k users from around the world. This approach allows us to quantify the true impact of file-sharing laws on user behavior, identifying behavioral trends otherwise difficult to identify. For instance, despite an initial reduction in activity in New Zealand when a three-strikes law took effect, after two months activity had returned to the level observed prior to the law being enacted. Given that punishment seems to, at best, result in short-term compliance, we suggest that incentives-based approaches may be more effective at changing user behavior.

Categories and Subject Descriptors

C.2.4 [**Communication Networks**]: Distributed Systems—*Distributed applications*; K.4.1 [**Computers and Society**]: Public Policy Issues; K.5.2 [**Computers and Society**]: Governmental Issues

Keywords

File-sharing; user behavior; copyright law

1. INTRODUCTION

Countries around the world have taken opposing steps in legislating against file-sharing of copyrighted content. Within the same month in 2013, while France repealed the ability of its three-strikes law to disconnect users [20], Russia [17] and Ireland [16] both moved forward with plans to require ISPs to block IP addresses and websites hosting infringing content. We have yet to determine the best approach to deal with illegal file-sharing.

The impact of regulation has historically been difficult to evaluate due to the challenges of obtaining longitudinal user-level data. Supporters of laws for digital copyright protection have been quick to point out results indicating reduced use of file-sharing sites and increased digital media sales [6,9], and researchers have compared week-long snapshots of traffic statistics to show the efficacy of such laws [1]. However, such aggregate measures are unable to discern user versus population changes, and snapshot-based comparisons fail to distinguish long- and short-term trends.

In this paper, we introduce a novel approach to model user behavior based on a hidden Markov model and apply it to analyze the evolution of file-sharing activity patterns using a two-year-long, user-level trace of download activity from over 38k users.

We find that, though user activity patterns vary widely, we can identify several clusters associated with heavy, regular and sporadic download activity, based on the model's parameters.

We show how to detect shifts in user download behavior by studying the evolution of these parameters over time: when users change their behavior, this is reflected in the model's output parameters for that user. We apply a sliding window approach to compute the timeseries of usage patterns at the per-country level and study how user behavior changes after major events. We demonstrate this approach's ability to detect changes in user behavior using two known events – the shutdown of one-click hosting service MegaUpload in early 2012 and the NATO attack on Pakistan in late 2011.

We apply this approach to detect the impact of copyright infringement legislation and legal action on user behavior. We focus on the reaction of users to New Zealand's three-strikes law [1] and lawsuits brought in the United States against over 100,000 users. We show that, while these measures appear to result in short-term changes in user behavior, download activity soon returns to levels seen prior to the measure being applied.

Our findings echo what has long been understood by behavioral psychologists – that punishment only yields short-term behavioral changes [14], and suggest the need for positive reinforcement strategies to achieve lasting results.

2. DATASET

We capture the download activity of individual BitTorrent users by studying traces of when they initiate downloads. By analyzing user-level rather than aggregate measures of BitTorrent usage, such as traffic volume [1], our approach allows to distinguish shifts in user behavior versus changes in the population of users.

CoNEXT'14, December 2–5, 2014, Sydney, Australia.

http://dx.doi.org/10.1145/2674005.2675009.

We study the download activity of 38,624 users in 150 countries. This dataset from the EdgeScope project[1] comprises application- and network-level statistics contributed by users of the Ono plugin [5] for the Vuze BitTorrent client [21]. Our dataset includes over 6 million downloads spanning 25 months, from March 1st, 2011 to March 31st, 2013. We select the subset of users from the total EdgeScope population who provide sufficient data to accurately model their behavior, selecting users that downloaded at least 35 files over a time span of at least 5 weeks. We map users to countries based on the ISP advertising the user's IP address. For each user, we record the set of days on which the user initiated downloads, which we interpret as user activity.

3. MODELING USER BEHAVIOR

Given the diversity of users' activity patterns, a key challenge is finding a way to characterize users. Here we propose a generative model of user behavior able to produce activity patterns that are statistically similar to those of real users. We then characterize each user by obtaining the model parameters that best fit the observed behavior of the user.

We consider the simplest possible models for user activity patterns in BitTorrent, namely hidden Markov models. In hidden Markov models, the active/inactive state of each user is assumed to be a Markov process, and the probability of switching between states depends on a very small set of past states [12]. This is likely a crude oversimplification of the complex psychological processes that lead users to change states, but this approach has been successfully used in temporal pattern recognition, from speech and gesture recognition [15] to bioinformatics and email usage [10].

A critical step in designing a hidden Markov model is choosing the best set of parameters to predict behavior. To inform this decision, we plot the auto-correlation of user download behavior: given download activity on a day, we compute the probability of user download activity X days in the future. Figure 1 plots this auto-correlation for different values of X. We note a high probability of activity on the next day and two days later (days one and two), as well as peaks at multiples of seven, indicating weekly periodicities.

Given these patterns, we use activity on seven days prior (α) or one day prior (β) to predict activity on the current day (γ). The top half of Fig. 2 illustrates this relationship.

Considering all combinations of these input values, we select the best resulting model based on Bayesian Information Criterion (BIC) [13] and relative likelihood [4] values. BIC is a measure of how well the data fits the model while attempting to minimize the number of parameters. Relative likelihood computes the ratio of the fit between the best and next-best models. We selected the model with the largest BIC and found a very small relative likelihood value (10^{-10}), which means that the chosen model is much better than any alternatives.

We use a hidden Markov model with two parameters, which we present in the lower half of Fig. 2. Each user has two parameters: a probability of becoming active if currently inactive (p_{00}; $\alpha = 0$ and $\beta = 0$), and a probability of remaining active (p_1; α or β is 1). The figure shows the "state transitions" and their corresponding probabilities based on these two parameter values.

We compute these parameters for the full set of users studied and plot the resulting joint probability distribution of the two parameters in Fig. 3a. This lets us visualize the relationship between both parameters in the population and identify clusters of users with similar behavior. The densest region of users occurs

[1]http://aqualab.cs.northwestern.edu/projects/EdgeScope

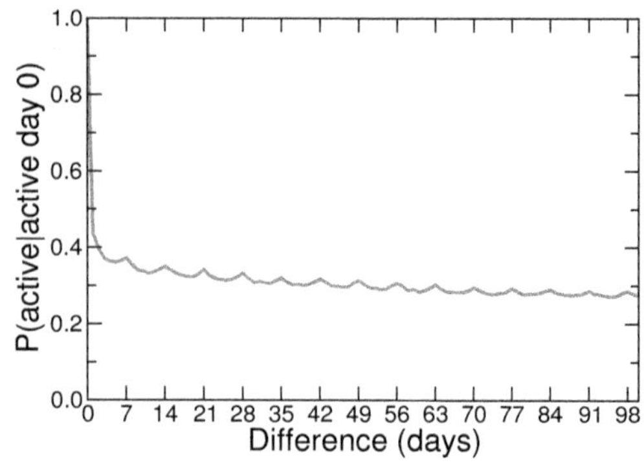

Figure 1: Auto-correlation of download activity reveals weekly periodicities and high probability of activity on the following day.

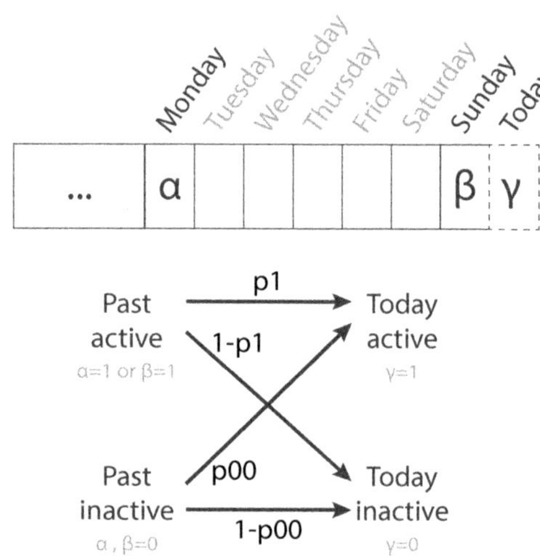

Figure 2: Diagram of hidden Markov model input variables (top) and parameter and state transitions (bottom).

in the lower left corner of the figure, meaning that these users do not often initiate downloads on a day-to-day or weekly basis. We identify three clusters and draw boxes around each in the figure. We identify "heavy" users with both a high probability to connect (p_{00}) and to stay active (p_1). "Regular" users rarely become active (low p_{00}), but when they do they are likely to remain active for some time (high p_1). Finally, we identify sporadic users as those with both low p_{00} and low p_1, who rarely download files. We refer to several of these clusters of users in our subsequent analyses as a way to distinguish the reactions of *different types* of users to the events we study.

We validate the model by comparing macroscopic measures of the real data to those of synthetic data generated from the model. In Fig. 3b we show the joint probability distribution for the synthetic data we generate from the model using parameters estimated from the input data. Visually, the distributions appear very similar; the synthetic distribution includes the same clusters we identified in the real data. We also compare the distributions of several macroscopic measures, such as number of days between downloads or the number of days of sustained activity, to show that the model reconstructs higher-level phenomena present in the input data. For

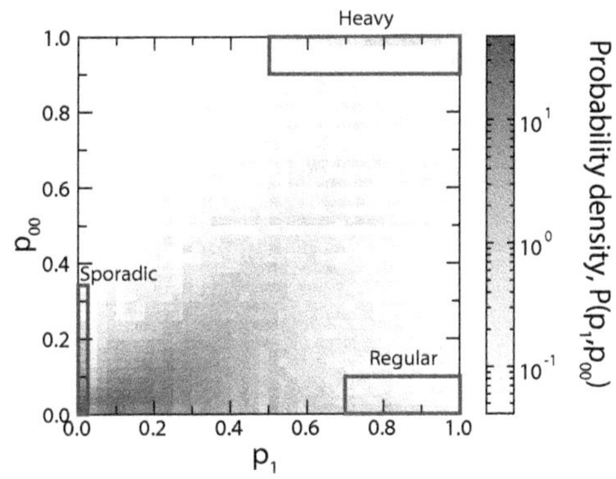

(a) Real data

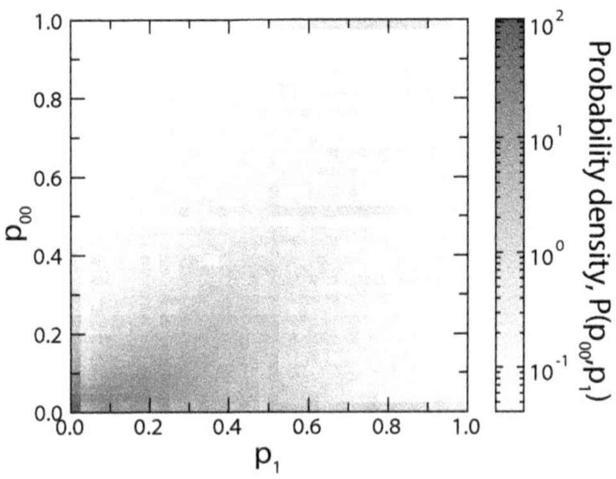

(b) Synthetic data

Figure 3: Joint probability distribution of p_{00} and p_1 parameters for entire sample population (a), and with synthetic data generated from model parameters (b). We identify clusters of users in the real data.

each cluster of users, we find similar distributions for all measures we examine. Overall, this indicates that the model works well to capture behavior across the range of user types we identify.

4. DETECTING EVENTS

So far, we have studied the diversity of behavior as if a user's activity patterns were static. While this analysis yields average behavior, it does not account for temporal dynamics, such as seasonality or changes in the type of content consumed, which are likely to cause shifts in user model parameters over time.

To identify changes in behavior, we now study trends in the population's distribution of model parameters. While it is practically impossible to determine the reasons behind the behavioral changes of a particular user, coordinated shifts across many users indicate the presence of a common cause.

In this section, we first discuss our approach for studying shifts in the population's usage patterns. Then, we demonstrate its effectiveness at identifying changes in behavior through two well-known events.

4.1 Methodology

We compute a timeseries for each user's model parameters, using a sliding window approach to capture the user's recent activity patterns. We select a sufficiently large window (100 days) so that

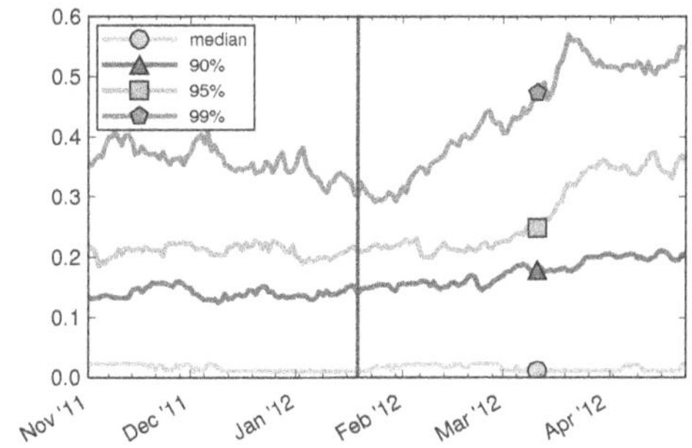

(a) Pakistan

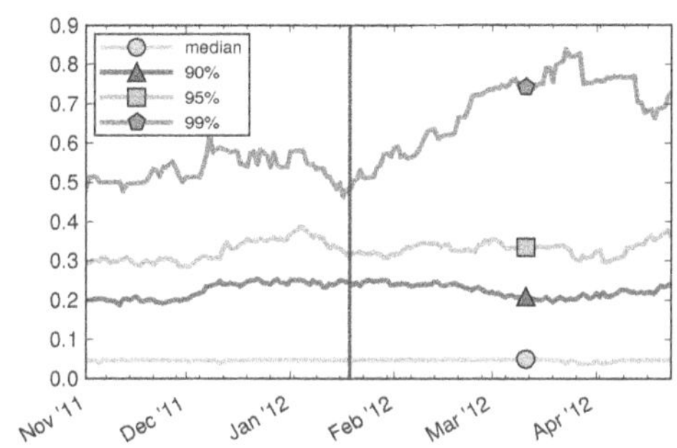

(b) Turkey

Figure 4: Growing activity (p_{00}) following the shutdown of MegaUpload on January 19, 2012 (vertical line). The "median" curve captures activity levels of typical users; the other 3 curves show the same for increasingly heavy users.

we can calculate model parameters for the vast majority of users (over 95%) – even those who are inactive for long periods.

We group users by country and look for shifts in the population's distribution of model parameters that correlate with external events. We verify that the size of each country's user population remains approximately constant over the course of each event studied; this ensures that the trends we identify correspond with changes in user behavior.

4.2 Validation

We validate that our approach is sensitive to both increases and decreases in BitTorrent usage patterns through two case studies of well-known events: the shutdown of one-click hosting provider MegaUpload (January 2012) and the NATO attack on Pakistan (November 2011).

4.2.1 Usage increase after MegaUpload shutdown

We show the ability of our approach to detect increases in BitTorrent usage corresponding with the shutdown of the 1-click hosting site MegaUpload, which took place on January 19th, 2012. Farahbakhsh et al. report that BitTorrent had an influx of publishers [7] seeking a venue to distribute content.

We expect this event to manifest as increases in users becoming active as they turn to BitTorrent to obtain content previously available from MegaUpload. Figure 4 plots country-wide trends of the p_{00} parameter – the probability of becoming active if currently inactive – for Pakistan and Turkey. We plot trends for both typical and heavy users; "median" shows the typical user's value and "90%", "95%" and "99%" plot the trends for heavier users.

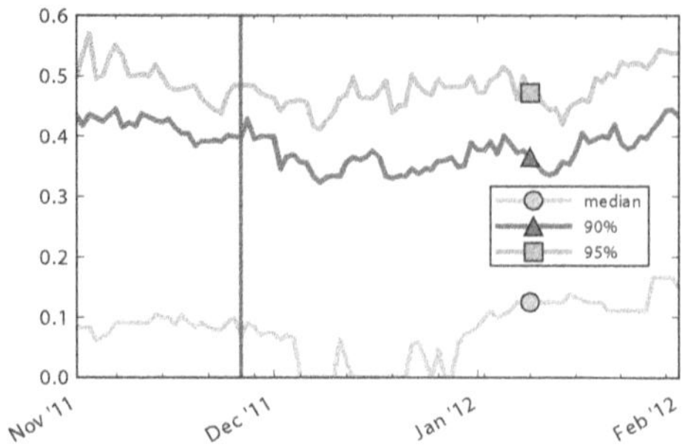

Figure 5: The impact of the NATO attack in Pakistan; trends in distribution of p_1 in Pakistan following November 26, 2011.

In Pakistan (Fig. 4a), we find that the top 10% of heaviest users have increased activity after the MegaUpload shutdown. We observe the heaviest users ("99%") becoming more active beginning almost immediately – within a week of the event. However, we observe a delay in increased usage in the 90%ile and 95%ile users, which does not begin until late February. This delay can be explained by the relative activity of these users; the heaviest users will find out about the MegaUpload shutdown – and change their behavior – the earliest.

In Turkey, only the top 1% of users changed their behavior – in contrast with Pakistan's 10% of users. As we show in Fig. 4b, the "99%" curve shows increased activity after January 19 – but the other curves remain approximately flat in the following months, and we do not observe the time-delayed increase we noted in the Pakistani population.

This case demonstrates the ability of our model to detect increases in download activity.

4.2.2 *Usage decrease after NATO attack in Pakistan*

We also show the ability of our technique to detect reductions in BitTorrent activity through an analysis of usage in Pakistan following the NATO attack on November 26, 2011. The subsequent weeks saw civil unrest and anti-American sentiments throughout Pakistan, both of which could result in reduced use of BitTorrent.

In contrast with the MegaUpload analysis, here we focus on users' tendency to remain active. A reduction in activity will translate to lower p_1 values because users would be less likely to maintain download activity. We plot trends in p_1 for Pakistani BitTorrent users in Fig. 5. As with the MegaUpload figures, the curves show trends in the activity level for typical as well as heavy users.

Within a week of the event, we see a sharp reduction in the activity of typical users – the curve drops to 0 for much of December. This means that half of Pakistani users had no sustained periods of download activity over this month. In contrast, the curves for heavy users do not show significant trends following the event; unlike the typical user, they have not changed their level of activity.

5. IMPACT OF COPYRIGHT LAWS

Both examples in the previous section serve to illustrate our approach for detecting changes in usage patterns, and validated its sensitivity to increases and decreases in user activity.

We now apply our technique to determine whether threats of penalties from file-sharing impact user behavior. We focus on two case studies: the enactment of a three-strikes law in New Zealand and several high-publicity lawsuits in the United States.

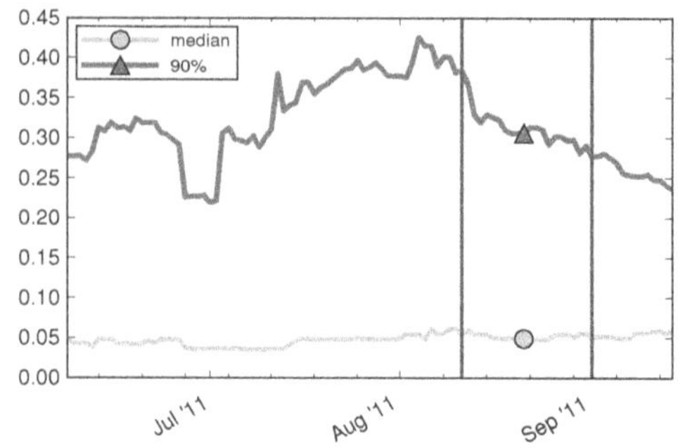

(a) Probability of becoming active (p_{00})

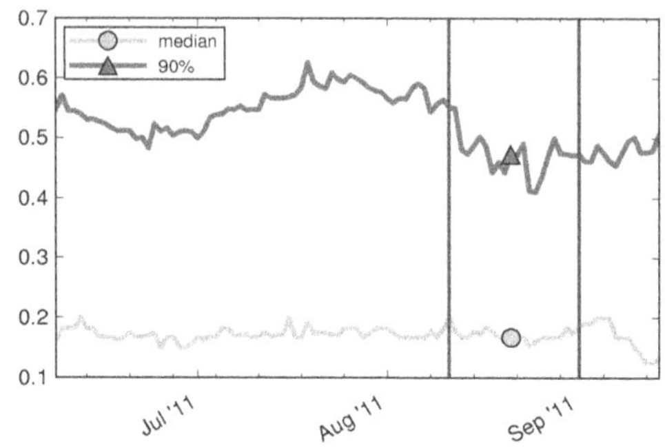

(b) Probability of staying active (p_1)

Figure 6: Trends in New Zealand surrounding the enactment of a three-strikes law. Heavy users ("90%") reduced usage when infringement complaints started to count as strikes on August 11th (left line), but typical users ("median") did not reduce usage until the widely-publicized start date of September 1st (right line).

5.1 New Zealand's three-strikes law

In April 2011, the New Zealand's Parliament passed an amendment to the Copyright Act under which users would receive three warnings for sharing copyrighted content before facing fines of up to NZ$15,000 [8]. The highly publicized law took effect on September 1st, 2011 – though a less-known aspect of the law allowed for infringements to count against users starting three weeks earlier on August 11th [22].

We examine trends in New Zealand users' activity patterns to evaluate the impact of the law on behavior. We plot the trends for both the probability to become active (Fig. 6a) and to remain active (Fig. 6b) to see how BitTorrent usage increases or decreases following adoption of the law. As with the validation studies, we plot the values of typical ("median") and heavy ("90%") users to see how different types of users respond.

We find that heavy users, who are more likely to be familiar with details of the three-strikes law, have reduced activity beginning on August 11th. These users were both less likely to initiate downloads and less likely to stay active for multiple days, indicating a significant reduction in BitTorrent usage.

In the case of typical users, we find that they continue to download content from time to time, but are less likely to use BitTorrent regularly. After September 1st, the probability of

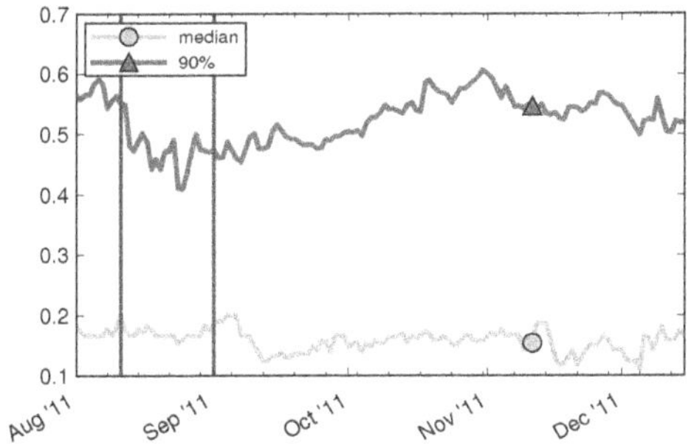

Figure 7: By November 1st, both typical and heavy user activity in New Zealand recovers to the levels seen before the law was enacted. Same as Fig. 6b, showing an additional 3 months.

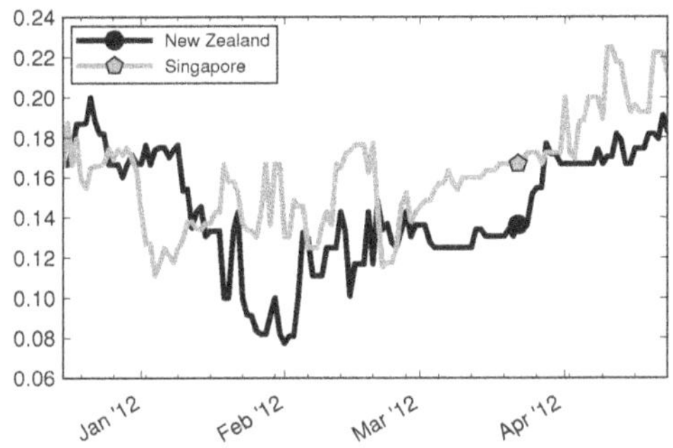

Figure 8: Reduced download activity (p_1) in New Zealand and Singapore during the summer months from January to April.

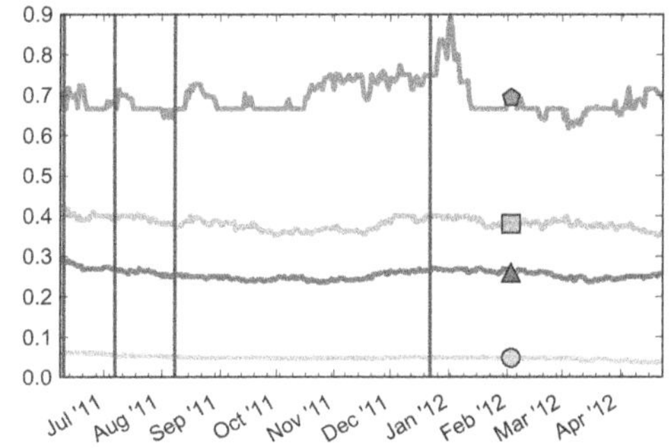

(a) Probability of becoming active (p_{00})

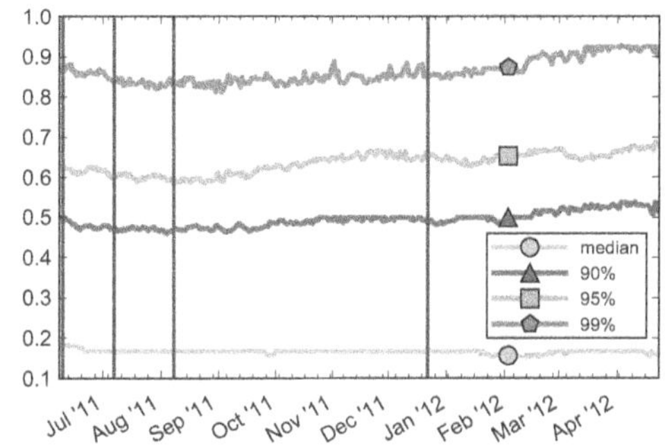

(b) Probability of staying active (p_1)

Figure 9: User behavior is unaffected in the United States in 2011 and 2012, despite several high-publicity events including lawsuits against file-sharers.

becoming active is unaffected (Fig. 6a) but sustained download activity declines by 33% within two weeks (Fig. 6b). This corresponds with the results of Alcock and Nelson [1] of lower relative BitTorrent traffic volume in September 2011 compared to earlier traffic data from January 2011.

Beside short-term impact, we want to study the impact of the 3-strikes law on long-term download behavior. Figure 7 plots the trends in users' probability to remain active over 4 months following the enactment of the law. We find that activity recovers to pre-enactment levels by November 1st. This recovery is similar to that of Swedish traffic volume after the enactment of an anti-piracy law in 2009 [2]. In sum, our results suggest that while regulation has the targeted change on file-sharing behavior in *the short term*, long-term behavior remains unaffected with activity rapidly returning to levels prior to the measure being applied.

Our continuous analysis approach reveals the susceptibility of snapshot-based comparisons [1] to mistaking local variations for global trends. Comparing traffic statistics from a week in September 2011 and a week in January 2012, Alcock and Nelson concluded that the copyright law had a sustained impact. However, our results show that the reduced download activity they observed in January is a local trend and not indicative of a sustained reduction in BitTorrent use.

We show that BitTorrent activity often declines during the summer months,[2] which explains why Alcock and Nelson observed lower BitTorrent traffic volume in January 2012. Figure 8 shows this reduction in activity for New Zealand and nearby Singapore; we also observe this pattern for several other countries in the region.

[2]Perhaps related to school calendars.

We find that New Zealand's copyright law resulted in an approximately 2-month-long reduction in BitTorrent activity. While prior reports concluded that the law had a sustained impact on download behavior, our continuous view reveals the presence of common seasonal trends that explain this results. Following the summer period, we see that download activity returns to pre-enactment levels in April 2012.

5.2 Legal action in the United States

In the United States during 2011, there were several high-publicity file-sharing lawsuits and discussion of laws to combat copyright infringement. We examine trends in download activity during this period to see the impact of these events on user behavior. As with the New Zealand case study, Figure 9 plots timeseries for both model parameters for typical and heavy users. The vertical lines in the figures denote four file-sharing events:

- June 10th: 50,000 BitTorrent users sued last month [11]
- July 7th: ISPs agree to six-strikes law [3]
- Aug. 8th: 145,000 BitTorrent users still being sued [19]
- Dec. 22nd: suits against many users are dropped [18]

Studying the trends in user behavior before and after each of these events, we see that none has any noticeable impact on *typical* users' patterns of activity. The gradual upward and downward trends that reflect the seasonality of BitTorrent usage – for the United States, reduced activity (p_1) from July to September. The p_{00} parameter also declines seasonally, albeit later from October to

December because this parameter is slower to respond to seasonal changes than p_1.

Counter-intuitively, in the case of heavy users we see that reports of lawsuits or threats of legal action against file-sharers (the three earliest events) correspond with *increases* in users becoming active. One explanation for this effect may simply be that publicity surrounding BitTorrent is sufficient to bring heavy users back to the system.

In the United States, we find that neither typical nor heavy users reduce their downloading behavior even while over 50,000 other users are actively being sued.

Overall, these results of the New Zealand and United States case studies suggest that legal threats and copyright infringement laws have at best a short-term impact of reducing file-sharing behavior.

5.3 Discussion

By basing our analysis on a model of user behavior, we get insights that one cannot possibly get by measuring aggregate quantities such as overall traffic. Consider, for example, the passing of the "three-strikes law" in New Zealand (Fig. 6). According to our analysis, heavy users react to the passing of the law by immediately reducing both their probability of becoming active (which implies longer inactive periods) and of staying active (shorter active periods). However, median users only react to the publicizing of the law weeks later, and only respond by reducing the probability of staying active but not the probability of becoming active; that is, they shorten their sessions but they connect with the same frequency as before.

We argue that the benefits one gets from such a nuanced user-based description justifies the complexity introduced by having to define a model of user behavior.

6. CONCLUSION

We introduce a novel approach, based on hidden Markov models, to characterize the behavior of different types of users at scale. We detect shifts in user activity patterns by studying the evolution of the model parameters over time.

We apply this approach to detect the impact of copyright infringement legislation and legal action on user behavior, focusing on periods following the enactment of New Zealand's three-strikes law and some highly-publicized lawsuits against file-sharers brought in the United States. Copyright infringement laws can be seen as punishment strategies puzzlingly looking for long-term behavioral changes. Our analysis shows that, at best, they attain short-term compliance and suggests it may be time to explore positive reinforcement strategies to achieve lasting behavioral changes.

Acknowledgements

We thank the anonymous reviewers for their invaluable feedback. This work was supported in part by the National Science Foundation through Award CNS 1218287 and by a generous Google Faculty Research Award.

7. REFERENCES

[1] S. Alcock and R. Nelson. Measuring the impact of the Copyright Amendment Act on New Zealand residential DSL users. In *Proc. of IMC*, 2012.

[2] N. Anderson. Swedes start buying music; are anti-P2P laws working? Ars Technica, 24 November 2009. http://arstechnica.com/tech-policy/2009/11/swedes-start-buying-music-are-anti-p2p-laws-working/.

[3] N. Anderson. Major ISPs agree to "six strikes" copyright enforcement plan. Ars Technica, 7 July 2011. http://arstechnica.com/tech-policy/2011/07/major-isps-agree-to-six-strikes-copyright-enforcement-plan/.

[4] K. P. Burnham and D. R. Anderson. *Model selection and multi-model inference: a practical information-theoretic approach.* Springer, 2002.

[5] D. R. Choffnes and F. E. Bustamante. Taming the torrent: A practical approach to reducing cross-ISP traffic in peer-to-peer systems. In *Proc. of ACM SIGCOMM*, 2008.

[6] B. Danaher and M. D. Smith. Gone in 60 seconds: The impact of the Megaupload shutdown on movie sales, 6 March 2013. http://ssrn.com/abstract=2229349.

[7] R. Farahbakhsh, A. Cuevas, R. Cuevas, R. Rejaie, M. Kryczka, R. Gonzalez, and N. Crespi. Investigating the reaction of BitTorrent content publishers to antipiracy actions. In *Proc. of IEEE P2P*, 2013. To appear.

[8] D. Greenwood. New Zealand passes 'three strikes' copyright law, 15 April 2011. http://www.zdnet.com/new-zealand-passes-three-strikes-copyright-law-2062208409/.

[9] Hadopi. Hadopi, 1 1/2 year after the launch, 1 March 2012. http://www.hadopi.fr/sites/default/files/page/pdf/note17_en.pdf.

[10] R. D. Malmgren, J. M. Hofman, L. A. Amaral, and D. J. Watts. Characterizing individual communication patterns. In *Proc. of ACM SIGKDD*, 2009.

[11] J. Pepitone. 50,000 BitTorrent users sued for alleged illegal downloads. CNN Money, 10 June 2011. http://money.cnn.com/2011/06/10/technology/bittorrent_lawsuits/index.htm.

[12] L. R. Rabiner. A tutorial on hidden Markov models and selected applications in speech recognition. *Proceedings of the IEEE*, 77(2):257–286, 1989.

[13] G. Schwarz. Estimating the dimension of a model. *The annals of statistics*, 6(2):461–464, 1978.

[14] B. F. Skinner. *Walden Two.* 1976.

[15] T. Starner and A. Pentland. Real-time American Sign language visual recognition from video using Hidden Markov Models. Master's thesis, MIT, February 1995.

[16] TorrentFreak. Irish ISPs start blocking The Pirate Bay, 10 July 2013. http://torrentfreak.com/irish-isps-start-blocking-the-pirate-bay-130710/.

[17] TorrentFreak. Russia's 'SOPA' passed by lawmakers, site blocking begins "in weeks", 21 June 2013. http://torrentfreak.com/russias-sopa-passed-by-lawmakers-site-blocking-begins-in-weeks-130621.

[18] TorrentFreak. Hurt Locker BitTorrent lawsuit dies, but not without controversy, 22 December 2011. http://torrentfreak.com/hurt-locker-bittorrent-lawsuit-dies-but-not-without-controversy-111222.

[19] TorrentFreak. 200,000 BitTorrent users sued in the United States, 8 August 2011. http://torrentfreak.com/200000-bittorrent-users-sued-in-the-united-states-110808/.

[20] TorrentFreak. Three strikes and you're still in – France kills piracy disconnections, 9 July 2013. http://torrentfreak.com/three-strikes-and-youre-still-in-france-kills-piracy-disconnections-130709/.

[21] Vuze, Inc. Vuze. `http://www.vuze.com`.

[22] A. Walls. 'Three strikes' file sharing law coming sooner than you think, 4 August 2011. http://www.nbr.co.nz/article/three-strikes-file-sharing-law-coming-sooner-you-think-aw-98379.

PARCEL: Proxy Assisted BRowsing in Cellular networks for Energy and Latency reduction

Ashiwan Sivakumar[†] Shankaranarayanan P N[†] Vijay Gopalakrishnan[‡]
Seungjoon Lee[*]* Sanjay Rao[†] Subhabrata Sen[‡]
[†]Purdue University, [‡]AT&T Labs - Research, [*]Two Sigma

ABSTRACT

Today's web page download process is ill suited to cellular networks resulting in high page load times and radio energy usage. While there have been notable prior attempts at tackling the challenge with assistance from proxies (cloud), achieving a responsive and energy efficient browsing experience remains an elusive goal. In this paper, we make a fresh attempt at addressing the challenge by proposing *PARCEL*. *PARCEL* splits functionality between the mobile device and the proxy based on their respective strengths, and in a manner distinct from both traditional browsers and existing cloud-heavy approaches. We conduct extensive evaluations over an operational LTE network using a prototype implementation of *PARCEL*. Our results show that *PARCEL* reduces page load times by 49.6%, and radio energy consumption by 65% compared to traditional mobile web browsers. Further, our results show that *PARCEL* continues to perform well under client interactions, owing to its judicious functionality split.

Categories and Subject Descriptors

C.4 [**Performance of systems**]: Design studies; Measurement techniques; C.2.2 [**Computer communication networks**]: Network Protocols—*Applications*

Keywords

Proxy-assisted Browsing; Mobile Web; Energy Consumption; Cellular Networks; Smartphones; Cloud Browsers; Web Optimization

1 Introduction

Along with the spread of higher speed cellular technologies like 3G and LTE, the past few years have witnessed an explosive growth in mobile Internet data traffic (projected to increase 11-fold between 2013 and 2018 [4].) Web browsing is a key activity on mobile devices, accounting for more cellular traffic than any other application, excluding multimedia streaming [24]. There exists tremendous interest in improving user's Quality of Experience (QoE) for the mobile web. Key challenges include the resource constraints of common cellular devices like smartphones and tablets, and the radio access network (RAN). While processing capabilities of mobile devices have dramatically improved in recent years, mobile device battery energy seems likely to remain a major resource limitation for the foreseeable future.

Several factors make current approaches to web downloads ill-suited to cellular networks (§2). On the one hand, web pages consist of hundreds of objects spread over multiple server domains, and downloading pages involves a large number of HTTP request-response interactions. On the other hand, cellular networks involve large round-trip times resulting in substantially longer download times compared to wire-line. The delays are exacerbated since initial objects fetched during the download (e.g., HTML, style sheets (CSS), JavaScript (*JS*)) may need to be processed to identify what objects to fetch subsequently. Higher download latencies and frequent short data transfers in turn leave the radio in a high power state for longer duration, resulting in increased cellular radio energy usage [25].

Some notable prior attempts have been made in tackling the challenges associated with web downloads on cellular networks [2, 5, 6, 8, 21, 35, 36] by leveraging proxies to enhance performance.[1] However, while important first steps, these prior efforts fall short in several ways (e.g., real-world web page design and user interactivity can result in some of these approaches increasing user perceived latencies and radio energy usage [32]), as we describe in detail in §3.

In this paper, we seek to better realize the potential of such proxy-assisted approaches by addressing the question: *what should be the right division of web download functionality between the mobile device and the cloud?*. Our primary goal is to improve user experience by reducing page download times and radio energy consumption over the entire user session, covering initial page download as well as subsequent user interactions with the page. We focus on radio energy consumption, since studies show that the power consumed by the cellular radio interface contributes a considerable fraction (1/3 to 1/2) of the total device power consumption for normal workloads [26].

To this end, we present *PARCEL*, a new proxy-assisted mobile web-browsing system (§4). The key ideas underlying

*This work was done when the author was employed at AT&T Labs

[1]By proxies, we refer to well-provisioned servers with good network connectivity. We also use the terms proxy and cloud interchangeably.

CoNEXT'14, December 2–5, 2014, Sydney, Australia.
Copyright 2014 ACM 978-1-4503-3279-8/14/12:$15.00.
http://dx.doi.org/10.1145/2674005.2675004.

PARCEL are: (i) perform object identification and download at the proxy, leveraging its superior network connectivity; (ii) support interactive operations locally at the client to avoid network communications to the extent possible; and (iii) support cellular friendly data-transfers by greatly reducing the number of HTTP request-response interactions, and by providing the proxy with the flexibility to push objects in a manner that balances latency and radio energy use.

Realizing *PARCEL* requires us to address a number of important system issues. To demonstrate our ideas, we have implemented an initial custom Android-based browser prototype of *PARCEL* using the Webview library, addressing many pragmatic considerations (§5). We discuss how the flexibility of data transfer provided by *PARCEL* may be exploited by proposing multiple scheduling strategies and analyzing the performance trade-off between page load time and radio energy usage (§6).

We validate *PARCEL* through extensive evaluations in live LTE network settings, and compare its performance to both a traditional web browser, and an existing cloud-heavy browser. We also evaluate multiple policies for scheduling data transfers from the proxy to the client within the *PARCEL* framework. Our evaluations employ a carefully crafted methodology to ensure that the performance comparisons are not affected by variability in LTE signal strengths or the web pages themselves (§7).

Our results are promising (§8). They show that *PARCEL* can reduce web-page latencies by 49.6% and radio energy consumption by 65% on average compared to conventional web-browsers. Further, unlike a popular cloud-heavy browser, *PARCEL* continues to perform well with client interactions. Overall, these results indicate that judiciously splitting functionality between the mobile device and the proxy can substantially enhance user browsing experience in cellular network settings, and show that *PARCEL* is a promising step towards this end.

2 Web download in cellular networks

In this section, we discuss why the web download process is a poor fit for cellular networks.

2.1 Modern web-pages and pageload process

Modern web-pages are complex constructs, easily comprising of tens to hundreds of static and dynamic objects (banners, images, style-sheets, multiple different types of *JS* files, etc.) from multiple different domains. An analysis of the Alexa top-500 web pages indicates that 40% had at least 100 objects (20 *JS* files). Further, the individual objects are typically small (a few KB) to moderately sized (a few MB). Across all the pages, the 95th, 80th and 50th percentile of the object sizes were 386, 107 and 18 KB respectively.

Figure 1 depicts the various stages involved in loading a page at a typical mobile browser. The browser first initiates a DNS lookup to resolve the domain address for the main page URL, and fetches the main page from the content web server using the HTTP protocol. It then begins parsing the page and dynamically builds and updates the Document Object Model (DOM) tree (an in-memory data structure to represent the parsed nodes in a page). As it encounters new objects in the page that are not available locally, it initiates new HTTP requests to the relevant servers for those objects. There are inter-dependencies among objects – e.g., downloaded *JS* files have to be executed, which

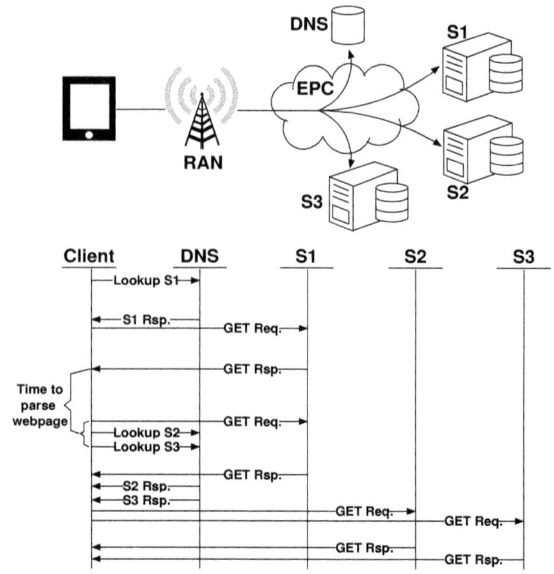

Figure 1: Web-page load process in mobile networks.

in turn may lead to additional new objects (including more *JS* files) being downloaded. The resulting network traffic pattern typically consists of a large number of short data transfers, related to (i) establishing distinct TCP connections per-domain; (ii) DNS lookups to resolve the potentially large number of servers involved; and (iii) a HTTP request/response associated with each object.

Measuring page latencies: We next discuss typical metrics used to quantify web page download latencies. An *Onload* event is triggered by the browser when it has received sufficient objects for rendering an initial version of the page. The time from the request initiation to the time of the Onload event, is referred to as the *Onload time* (**OLT**) of the web page. OLT is a commonly used Key Performance Indicator (KPI) for measuring the latency of the page load process and indicates the initial responsiveness of the page. Note that objects can be requested by the page even after the OLT [33]. This happens due to the presence of *asynchronous* JS files, often used for displaying independent sections of the page like advertisements and chat widgets in parallel to the main web page. We define the time required to fetch all objects required by the page beyond OLT and in the absence of any user interaction as the *Total pageload time* (**TLT**).

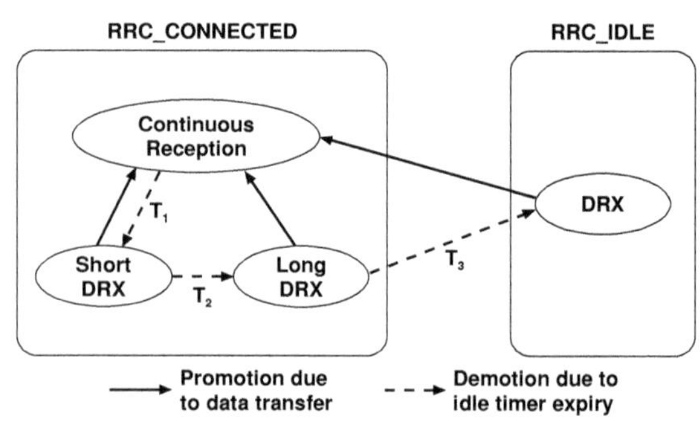

Figure 2: LTE RRC State Machine

2.2 Cellular network characteristics

A key determinant of performance in cellular networks is how the application traffic interacts with the LTE Radio

Resource Control (RRC) State Machine [11, 18] The device consumes very different levels of radio energy in the different RRC states(Figure 2). The device has to be in the highest energy state (*Continuous Reception* or CR in the CONNECTED state) for any data transfer to occur. The Discontinuous Reception (DRX) modes enable the device to trade off some responsiveness for energy savings (different trade-offs for Short and Long DRX) within the CONNECTED state: it actively polls for data transfers periodically and turns off the radio at other times, thereby consuming less power compared to CR, but higher power than the IDLE state. For the radio to transition to IDLE, typically the device has to be idle for > 10 sec. If the device is in IDLE or DRX states, and a packet needs to be sent/received, the device needs to get promoted to the CR state. Research has shown that small data transfers on LTE are very costly and large data bursts are much more energy efficient as a device in the CR state consumes significant base energy even if it uses a small fraction of the available network bandwidth [25].

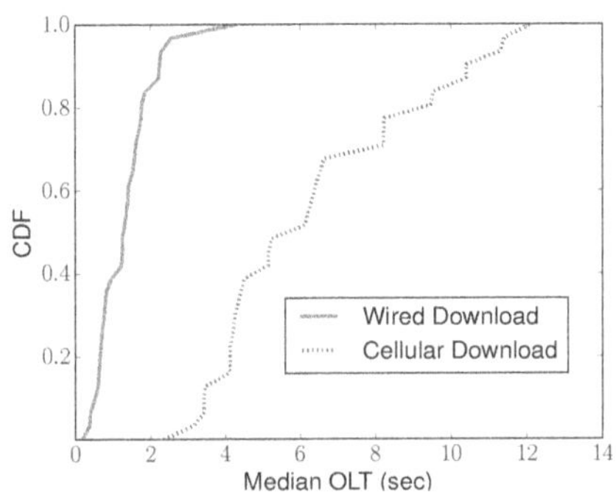

Figure 3: Median OLTs on Cellular and Wired

2.3 Page load performance in cellular networks

The interplay between web-page downloads and cellular network characteristics leads to two key concerns:

• *High latencies:* Figure 3 shows a CDF of the median OLT for a subset of the Alexa top-500 web-pages when downloaded using an LTE network and a wired network. The OLT with LTE is > 6 sec for 50% of the pages, with the maximum being about 13 sec. For the wired network, the corresponding values are 1.1 sec and 4 sec. Web downloads on LTE networks incur high latencies since typical RTTs for LTE are high (of the order of 70 – 86 msec. [18]), and since initial objects fetched during the download must be processed to determine what objects to subsequently fetch. The use of traditional web proxies [9] partially ameliorates the situation since DNS resolutions are performed by the proxy. However, the solution still involves a large number of short data transfers due to the request-response semantics of the HTTP protocol.

• *High radio energy usage:* The typical web download pattern of a large number of short data transfers over several seconds means the device has to stay in CONNECTED state for an extended period of time, frequently transitioning to CR. Because of the energy characteristics of the RRC state machine described above, such a traffic pattern can use up a lot of radio energy.

3 Related Work

There has been interest in the industry [2, 5, 6, 8, 17] and academia [21,35,36] to address the limitations of web browsing in general and cellular networks in particular. The techniques used may be classified as:

Offloading processing to the cloud: Many existing solutions have advocated a cloud-heavy, thin-client approach [6, 8, 36] with the cloud performing most of the compute intensive tasks including parsing and rendering web pages, and *JS* execution. This approach has the potential to reduce CPU usage on the mobile device as well as device CPU energy consumption, since most processing is done on the cloud. However, real world web page design and cellular network characteristics have meant that the performance of these browsers has not lived up to their promise. For instance, recent work [32] shows that interactive user actions (e.g., mouse hover, button clicks) with cloud-heavy browsers incur higher latency and device radio energy consumption than traditional browsers. This is because while conventional browsers execute *JS* associated with the events locally, cloud-heavy approaches require communicating these events back to the cloud, executing *JS* remotely and transferring the results back to the client. Consequently, the total device energy consumption with these browsers may in fact be *higher* than conventional browsers. We present a detailed example in § 8.2 to demonstrate these limitations of cloud-heavy approaches and how *PARCEL* performs better. Our approach with *PARCEL* is not to blindly offload processing to the cloud, but rather determine the right split in functionality between the cloud and the device.

Splitting functionality between cloud and device: Silk [2] claims to run browser functions both on the device and in the cloud. Since Silk is closed source, little is publically known about what functions Silk offloads to the cloud or under what conditions. Moreover, in real-world testing, several sites have recommended disabling cloud-based acceleration in Silk to improve page loading speed [1,3]. A recent position paper [35] suggests off-loading partial logic to the cloud, with the cloud sending back a page that consists of processed and unprocessed portions back to the mobile device. The paper, however, does not provide details on how to achieve this. In contrast, we present a detailed design and implementation, and present comprehensive evaluations of our approach.

Data transformation and compression: A number of browsers [2, 5, 6] offer support for data transformation and compression in the cloud, with the primary focus being to reduce the amount of data downloaded. While useful, these techniques do not address the causes for high page load latencies (multiple RTTs associated with per-object http request response semantics). Further, these techniques by themselves do not lower device energy requirements, and can in fact hurt radio energy consumption since the time for compression and transformation could result in the radio staying in the high energy state for a longer duration [32]. That said, compression and transformation is orthogonal to our work, and can be easily integrated with *PARCEL*.

New protocols (e.g., SPDY): There is increasing interest in devising protocol-based approaches that overcome TCP's limitations. For example, SPDY [17] establishes only one connection per server domain and multiplexes the transfer of objects from that domain. SPDY also eliminates the need for one outstanding request per connection and supports the ability for the server to "push" objects to the client. There have also been proposals to deploy cloud-based proxies that use SPDY between the client and the proxy [2, 5, 35]. The performance improvements with SPDY in the real-world, however, are mixed [16,34]. Inter-dependencies in web pages due to *JS* and CSS and the relative lack of power of mobile browsers implies that all the objects cannot be requested in parallel even though supported by SPDY [16,34]. Further, each server has to explicitly support server push with SPDY. Given that objects are requested across a range of domains, the gains from server push are unclear. Further, the SPDY proposal does not specify how to implement server push in the presence of proxies.

Mobile offload beyond web-browsing Many works [14, 15, 19, 20, 28, 29, 31] have investigated issues around offloading code of generic applications (e.g., compute intensive face recognition applications) to the cloud, primarily to reduce computation time and save device energy. Mobile web browsing has unique issues such as multiple round-trip times associated with data transfer, and is different in that data naturally flows into mobile devices from remote servers, with cloud servers potentially on the data path from the server to the device. Recent work has looked at energy efficient transfer of video streams in LTE networks [27], but web-browsing poses issues quite different from video streaming.

4 *PARCEL* approach and design

We describe the design of *PARCEL*, our objectives behind that design, and how our design addresses the problems with cellular web browsing. We then discuss some of the practical considerations in realizing our design.

4.1 Design Considerations

Our goal with *PARCEL* was to improve user experience when browsing on cellular networks by reducing page load times and radio energy usage, a key component of total device energy consumption. To that end, our key design considerations were:

Minimize per-object HTTP request-response interactions: Traditional browsers involve per-object HTTP request-response interactions. Given the high RTTs of cellular networks, we seek to avoid HTTP request-response interaction with the browser for individual objects.

Responsive and radio energy efficient client interactions: Cloud-heavy solutions that offload *JS* execution to the proxy entail network communication with the proxy to support client interactions. This results in lowered responsiveness and increased radio energy usage [32]. A key consideration in designing *PARCEL* was to handle dynamic page changes and user interaction locally at the client to avoid network communication.

Cellular-friendly and latency-sensitive data transfer: To reduce radio energy consumption, it is desirable to bundle data to and from the client. However, in doing so, it is important to take the page load process into account, and ensure page latencies are not impacted. Our goal in designing *PARCEL* is to balance these multiple considerations.

4.2 *PARCEL* design

The *PARCEL* architecture is designed to meet the objectives listed above. *PARCEL*, as shown in Figure 4, splits the typical browser functionality between a browser installed on the mobile device and a proxy in the cellular network. Like with traditional browsers, when users enter or select a URL, the browser issues a request for this URL to the proxy. On receiving the request, the *PARCEL* proxy does necessary

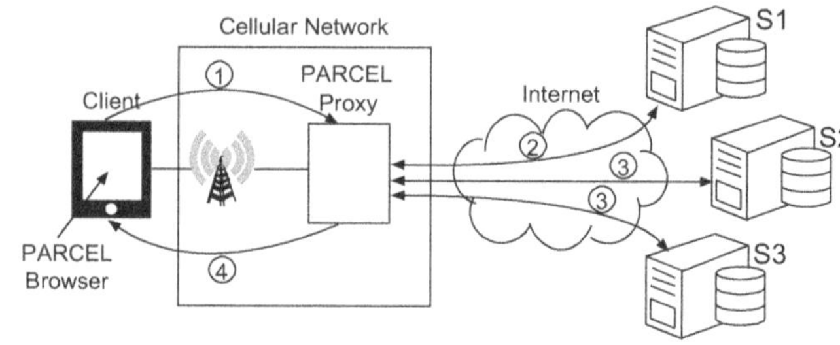

Figure 4: *PARCEL* Architecture

DNS lookups, and requests the URL from the corresponding web server, much like traditional proxies (steps (1) and (2)).

This is where *PARCEL* starts to deviate from traditional browsers and proxies. On receiving the response from the web servers, rather than just forwarding it to the client, the *PARCEL* proxy starts to parse the web page and identify all the objects that are required to successfully render the page in its entirety. This not only includes parsing the HTML page to identify the objects in that page, but also processing all *JS* since these objects may also refer to other dependencies or point to objects that are dynamically identified for this request. The proxy then goes ahead and requests these identified objects without the client requesting them (step (3) of Figure 4). In that process, the proxy may choose to apply any necessary compression and/or transformations (transcoding images, shrinking size, etc) to these objects as they arrive. It then collects all these objects and transfers them to the client.

The client, for its part, receives the main HTML page and all the objects associated with the page from the proxy. It then behaves like a traditional browser in that it parses the HTML files and identifies the objects on that page. Unlike traditional browsers, however, the *PARCEL* browser does not issue requests for these objects since the objects are proactively fetched by the proxy and made available as part of the collection transferred to the browser. The client browser uses the meta-data associated with the collection to identify the right object and use it for rendering the page. As part of this process, the client also parses all CSS files and processes *JS*. While there seems to be repetition of work at the proxy and the client, our design allows for all interactivity to be locally handled by the client browser (and therefore keep it responsive and energy efficient). That said, our design does not preclude optimizations that allow the client to leverage the work done by the proxy as part of its rendering process (like using some of the *JS* processing).

4.3 Benefits of *PARCEL* design

While conceptually simple, the *PARCEL* design addresses many of the important issues with mobile web browsing.

• By sending just the URL request to the proxy and no other requests, *PARCEL* reduces the number of round trips from the client on the higher latency cellular link, thereby reducing page load times. We envision that the proxy will be implemented on a powerful server with lots of processing power, high bandwidth and low latency to the Internet. Consequently, having the proxy identify which objects to download (through html parsing and *JS* processing) allows for fast downloads of these objects (refer Figure 3).

• By getting the browser to just send the URL, we get the client to not continuously use up radio energy. Similarly, by getting the proxy to push objects, we give it the flexibility to

	HTTP proxies [9]	SPDY proxies [5,16]	Cloud browsers [6,8,36]	*PARCEL*
# of TCP connections	many	single	single	single
# of HTTP requests	per object	per object	single	single
Object identification	client	client	proxy	proxy
Interactive *JS*	client	client	proxy	client
cellular-friendly transfer	×	×	×	√

Table 1: *PARCEL* vs. existing approaches.

bundle and schedule object transfers to the client efficiently, in a cellular friendly way.

• Compared to cloud-heavy approaches, *PARCEL* executes *JS* locally which minimizes network communications during client session, and allows for responsive and energy efficient client interactions [32]. Though, cloud-heavy approaches may lower device CPU energy consumption by executing *JS* remotely, this may be outweighed by the radio energy consumed due to client interactions (§ 8.2). *PARCEL* does not incur any more device CPU energy consumption than conventional browsers or proxies, and CPU energy consumption could potentially be lowered by allowing the client to leverage the work done by the proxy.

• The advantages of *PARCEL* above continue to hold even if a protocol such as SPDY is enabled between the client and the proxy since the performance with SPDY is limited by how quickly the (less capable) mobile client issues requests for objects in a web-page [16].

We contrast *PARCEL* with existing efforts and summarize the key differences in the approaches in Table 1.

4.4 Cellular friendly data transfer

Once the *PARCEL* proxy identifies and downloads the different objects on a specific page, it has the flexibility of transferring the different objects to the client in a manner that is cellular friendly. Figure 5 illustrates the different approaches possible with *PARCEL*.

IND: In this scheme, shown in Figure 5(b), the proxy transfers objects to the client as and when it receives the objects. Apart from reducing the energy consumption, this has the potential to significantly reduce OLT because it eliminates the need for the client to make requests and allows the client to start processing HTML and *JS* objects as they arrive.

ONLD: An alternate approach, shown in Figure 5(c), is for the proxy to fetch all objects from the web servers and transmit the data in a single batch to the client. This approach trades off increased OLT (compared to *IND*), for the potential to further reduce energy consumption. This is because, the client can go into idle mode when the proxy is downloading the data and then receive all the data as a single bundle from the proxy.

PARCEL(X): A final approach, shown in Figure 5(d) is to strike a balance between the latency energy benefits. With *PARCEL(X)*, the *PARCEL* proxy does not wait for all objects to arrive. Instead, it starts transferring data to the client when a certain threshold of data (X) becomes available or if the onload event is detected. This allows us to transfer objects quickly to the client for processing while reducing the number of state transitions of the client radio. We explore and evaluate these approaches further in § 8.

4.5 Practical challenges and solutions

In this section, we describe some of the practical challenges that need to be addressed in the realization of *PARCEL* design, and our proposed solutions.

Suppressing object requests The *PARCEL* browser starts parsing the main HTML page as soon as it is received and identifies the objects needed to display the page. If all the objects in the page are part of the received bundle, it can immediately start the rendering process. The browser, however, will not have the entire set of objects when it receives the HTML page with *IND* or *PARCEL(X)*. The fact that some objects are requested after onload can cause the bundle with *ONLD* to also not have all the objects. Finally, in rare cases, the use of *JS* can cause the object URL as determined by the *PARCEL* browser to differ from that by the proxy. In all these cases, the browser has to decide when to request the object because the missing object could well be on flight from the proxy to the browser. Our approach is for the browser to suppress making requests for any objects it has identified as needed but not already available. When the proxy determines that it has downloaded all the objects it sends a notification to the browser of such completion. If there are outstanding objects after such notification, the browser can request for these missing objects.

Determining page completion: In order to send the completion notification, the proxy has to determine when it has completed the page download (traditionally indicated by the onload event). Since this approach would not work for pages that request objects even after the onload, we resort to typical page statistics to make this determination. An analysis of the Alexa top-500 web pages indicates that the inter-arrival time of objects is less than 5 sec for 95% of the objects after onload. Based on this, our proxy implements a simple heuristic where it waits for a short time period of inactivity between the proxy and the server (after onload) and then determines the page complete. In the rare event that the proxy misses some object, the browser can still request for those missing objects.

Client properties and customization Web-pages have browser-dependent code that downloads objects or renders web page differently for different browser implementations. Similarly it could check for the type of access device (smartphone vs. laptop) and send objects tailored for the screen size. In *PARCEL*, since web servers receive requests from the proxy rather than the browser, we need to inform the proxy of the relevant attributes about the client (device) and its browser. e.g., the client sends these attributes (user-agent, mobile device screen information) to the proxy when it connects to the proxy and requests the URL. The proxy then uses this information to emulate the client while downloading the page.

Caching and cookies The *PARCEL* design allows both the browser and the proxy to cache data. However, since the browser does not request for objects other than the main URL, the proxy is unaware of the objects that are cached at the client. Handling cookies and other session objects is challenging for the same reason. One approach is for the proxy to track the object versions sent to the client, which helps avoid redundant transfer of objects. We prefer a model where these proxies are deployed as personalized proxies [12] for each user, running on virtual machines.

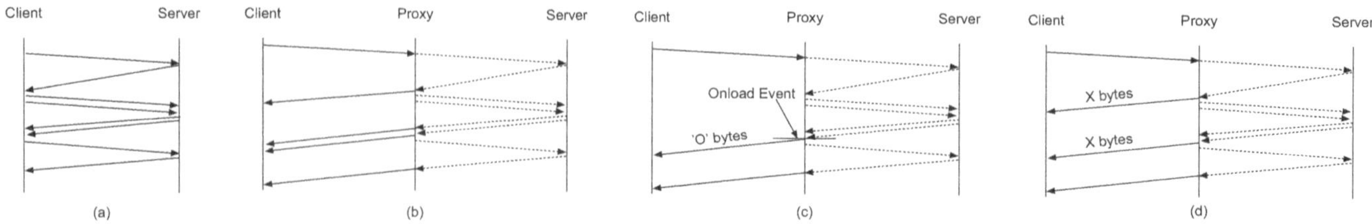

Figure 5: Download patterns of traditional browsers (a) and *PARCEL* with *IND*, *ONLD* and *PARCEL(X)* (b-d)

This allows the proxy to easily mirror the state of the objects (cache and cookies) stored at the client. While proxies could be located in Amazon EC2-like public clouds, they could also be deployed similar to middle-boxes within the cellular networks in the near future. Further, as approaches like CloudRAN [37] get more popular, cellular operators can deploy these proxies closer to the edge and have a tighter coupling with the cellular base stations for optimal energy efficiency. We hope to explore these alternatives as part of our future work.

Handling HTTPS and POST For encrypted pages, *PARCEL* falls back to the traditional way of downloading web pages since the proxy cannot parse and identify objects. However, using personalized proxies where the user trusts the proxy, HTTPS requests can potentially be handled by setting up independent secure channels between the browser and server. The *PARCEL* proxy handles POST requests by relaying them to the server as received from the client. If the POST response from the server is a HTML, the proxy processes the response as explained in § 4.2 before sending it out to the client. For HTTP responses that do not have content (e.g., HTTP 204), the proxy simply forwards them unmodified to the client.

5 Prototype implementation

In this section, we describe the prototype implementation of *PARCEL*. There are three main objectives we seek to demonstrate with our implementation: (a) efficacy of *PARCEL*, (b) real-world performance and energy improvements with *PARCEL* and, (c) how existing software can be reused to build *PARCEL*.

5.1 Proxy implementation

While many web proxy implementations exist, we cannot simply reuse these implementations as *PARCEL* requires the proxy to not only parse HTML files but also process CSS and *JS* (or in essence behave like a browser). To achieve this capability, we use an existing browser (*Mozilla Firefox*), sufficiently extended, to act as our proxy. We used the *JS* server sockets API to implement server functionality in the proxy, which on receiving a URL request from the browser, invokes Firefox to load the page and execute *JS*. Using the Firefox extension framework, we developed an extension that intercepts HTTP responses received from the web server. The interception mechanism helps in bundling and scheduling the responses to the client and in minimizing the impact of rendering of the Firefox process on the proxy's performance. Our extension includes an event listener that detects onload event at the proxy and begins data transfer to the client in the *ONLD* and *PARCEL* (X) schemes.

We use MHTML (a standard HTTP file format) to bundle and transfer data from the proxy to the client browser. MHTML is a low overhead format that allows inclusion of HTTP headers along with the object data in the bundles. Further, MHTML is supported by most modern browsers (directly or through third-party libraries), which enables them to parse and directly render bundles transferred by *PARCEL* proxy. Since browsers implement single-threaded execution of *JS*, we use asynchronous IO in our proxy implementation to decouple the proxy-server path from the cellular path when transferring objects to the client. Further, our implementation ensures that the proxy writes enough data to the kernel buffer and proceeds with execution until a callback is received when the buffer is available.

5.2 Client implementation

While the *PARCEL* client browser differs from traditional browsers in how it requests/receives objects and in the information sent to the proxy, the parsing and rendering process do not change. Hence, our client implementation reuses existing parsing and rendering functionality of browsers while modifying how the objects are requested and downloaded. While it is easier to write extensions for existing browsers to realize *PARCEL* functionality on clients (e.g., intercepting and manipulating HTTP requests/responses using HTTP Channel Observers in Firefox XUL runner framework), support for such extensions is not yet mature on mobile platforms. Hence, we build our own custom browser on top of the Webview library for Android devices. Webview allows us to integrate browser functionality into applications and uses the WebKit rendering engine to render the web pages. In our implementation, the client browser application accepts URLs from the user and sends the request to the *PARCEL* proxy over TCP. Our client also receives the MHTML bundles as part of the response from the proxy and sends them out to Webview for rendering.

6 PARCEL model and analysis

In this section, we present a simple analytical model to provide insights into the trade-offs between the various data transfer schemes presented in § 4.4. Suppose B is the aggregate object size at the time of page onload event. Let us assume that we use n equal-sized bundles and that the proxy sends out the n-th bundle as soon as the onload event occurs at the proxy (We approximate IND as a case with large n). We further assume that the $(n-1)$th bundle transfer was complete before the proxy onload event. We define $s(n)$ to be the download speed between *PARCEL* proxy and client with n bundles. We denote the OLT at the proxy as T_p, which we assume is independent of the number of bundles.

Radio energy We first focus on the radio energy at the time of client onload event. Let us assume that after each bundle transfer, the client always completes CR_{tail} and SDRX cycles. We denote the duration of each cycle to be d_c and d_s. Let us consider the aggregate duration of LDRX cycle $d_l(n)$ before the n-th bundle arrives to the client: $d_l(n) = T_p(n) - \frac{n-1}{n}\frac{B}{s(n)} - (n-1)(d_c + d_s)$. This is from simply accounting for the transmission and state transition time for $(n-1)$ bundles before the transmission of the n-th bundle. Then, we add up the radio energy for LDRX, state transition, and actual transmission to obtain the total radio energy at the time of client onload: $E(n) = p_l d_l(n) + (n-1)(p_c d_c + p_s d_s) + p_c \frac{B}{s(n)}$, where p_l, p_c, and p_s are power consumption in LDRX, CR, and SDRX states, respectively.

For ease of exposition, we assume that $s(n) = s$ for all n and that $E(n)$ is a continuous and differentiable function of n.[2] By solving $E'(n) = 0$, we can find an optimal bundle count n^* that minimizes the radio energy: $n^* = \frac{1}{\alpha}\sqrt{\frac{B}{s}}$, where $\alpha = \sqrt{((p_c - p_l)d_c + (p_s - p_l)d_s)/p_l}$. Then, it follows that the optimal bundle size b^* is:

$$b^* = \frac{B}{n^*} = \alpha\sqrt{sB}. \quad (1)$$

Eq. 1 matches intuition. First, for higher download speeds, larger bundles are more acceptable since there is less penalty in waiting longer. Second, as web pages become larger, using larger bundle sizes ensures the total number of bundles, and the associated state transition overhead is limited. Lastly, α captures relative radio state transition overhead due to radio technology and parameter settings - as transition overhead increases, it becomes important to use fewer bundles and reduce the state transition overheads.

Trade-off between energy and time By simply accounting for the transmission time of the n-th bundle after onload at the proxy, we get: $\text{OLT}(n) = T_p + \frac{1}{n}\frac{B}{s(n)}$. Assuming $s(n) = s, \forall n$, OLT(n) is a decreasing function of n, which agrees with our intuition that OLT is likely better with smaller bundles. On the other hand, from Eq. 1, performance in radio energy depends on various web page and network characteristics. For example, for a 2MB page, with download speed of 6Mbps, and $\alpha = 0.74$ (derived from LTE parameter values obtained as described in § 7), the optimal bundle size is approximately 0.9MB. In our evaluation, we experiment with different bundle sizes and explain the findings using the analysis result (§ 8.3).

7 Evaluation Methodology

Downloading web pages over a cellular network is subject to high variability due to dynamically changing web pages and radio signal fluctuation. In this section, we describe our experiment setup in which we limit the variability in both aspects and ensure fair comparison across different schemes.

7.1 Schemes for comparison

We compare *PARCEL* with a popular traditional mobile browser for Android that we call **DIR**.[3] For the comparison with DIR, we use the IND scheduling scheme for *PARCEL* to help us understand the benefit of *PARCEL* proxy in isolation. We also separately compare different scheduling schemes of *PARCEL* to understand the relative performance benefits due to bundling. Finally, to evaluate *PARCEL* under client interactivity, we contrast its energy usage with a popular cloud browser (we call **CB**) that performs all *JS* execution functionality in the cloud, as we discuss in § 8.2.

Metrics Our primary metrics of interest are *OLT* and *TLT* at the client as defined in § 2. To compute these quantities, we collect packet traces on the device for each experiment. For OLT, we compute the time between the first SYN and the last ACK for all objects required to generate the onload event at the client. For TLT, we compute the time between the first SYN and the last ACK for all objects in the trace. For each experiment, we limit the packet collection for 60 seconds, which we found sufficiently long for all objects of each page to be downloaded with all schemes. Note that we do not include rendering time, which is typically small (median rendering time is 0.436 sec) and is comparable for *PARCEL* and DIR.

Another metric that we use is the *radio energy* consumed by the LTE radio interface for different schemes. We calculate the radio energy using the open source ARO tool [18], which captures the Radio Resource Control (RRC) state transitions and the corresponding energy consumption levels by performing fine-grained simulation on the packet traces collected from the client device using a pre-computed model. We conducted new measurements to generate the model parameters specific to our phone (Samsung Galaxy S3) and experimental location (since power values are device-specific and timer values are periodically tuned by operators) by using the same methodology [18]. However, the relative power hierarchies of the different RRC states (as described in § 2.2) remain the same across all settings. In addition to using the energy model, we also report actual measurements of total device energy consumption using a power meter (See § 8.2). Unless otherwise mentioned we compare the schemes on the **median values** of all the metrics in § 8.1, 8.3 and 8.4.

7.2 Robustness to radio network variability

All experiments were conducted over a production LTE network in West Lafayette, IN, using a Samsung Galaxy S3 phone. To overcome variability in production networks, traditionally experiments are conducted by emulating the properties of the network. But given the significant variability in LTE networks, generating realistic models of latency and throughput for emulation is challenging and such models do not exist currently. Hence we chose to conduct all our experiments in live network settings. We conducted experiments at night, when the cell load is low, to eliminate variability due to other users. Next, we conducted experiments in rounds, where each round consists of back-to-back runs using different schemes for a given web page. This minimizes the effects of changing network conditions for different schemes. Finally, we logged the signal strength and cellular technology for each experiment, and only considered those rounds where all schemes experienced comparable signal strengths. We also filtered rounds where the device used 3G or handed off from LTE to 3G.

To obtain statistically significant results, we needed to collect statistics from tens of experiment rounds for a given web page. However, due to radio signal fluctuation and cellular technology hand-off, we had to filter out almost 50% of rounds. To make our experimental process tractable, we focused on a smaller subset of 34 web pages from the top 500 Alexa global pages (31 US sites), covering a wide range of

[2] An alternate option of considering $\Delta(n) = E(n+1) - E(n)$ provides a similar intuition with more complexity, which we do not show here. Note also that $E(n)$ omits some delay aspects that are constant across all n (e.g., propagation delay), which does not affect the analysis result.

[3] We anonymize the browser to keep the focus on the scientific aspects of our study.

categories like news, sports, photo streaming, business and science. The page sizes ranged from few KB to 5 MB. The median page size is 1.04 MB. To put the time in perspective, it took us multiple weeks to collect more than 20 post-filtered runs for each of the 34 web pages and the different schemes for Figure 9b.

We used the full versions of the web pages in our experiments. These are the web pages downloaded when data cards or tablets are used. Previous work has shown that mobile versions of the pages are optimized for smaller screen sizes; however, they are not significantly different from the full versions from a network communication perspective [25]. Hence, using a mobile version does not solve the problem of increased page load latency in cellular networks and we expect *PARCEL* to provide benefits even with mobile versions of the pages. The relative gains with mobile versions, however, may be different than the full versions.

7.3 Replaying pages to control page variability

Over the course of our experiments, we observed significant variability in the number of objects and aggregate download size for a given web page, even over short intervals of time. When we conducted 10 runs back-to-back during the month of February 2014, we found that 50% of the web-pages in our set had at least 0.5 as the coefficient of variation of the total number of objects. A similarly high variability was observed when considering page sizes as well.

To ensure fair comparisons in the presence of variability in web pages, a bulk of our experiments were conducted using an open source tool called web-page-replay [23] to record and replay web pages. Specifically, we first accessed real web pages from the actual web server(s) and stored the objects in a local server. Then, the same snapshot of a given page was replayed for all schemes in later experiments. Some web pages still showed variability as they had *JS* that requested different URLs (e.g., using a random number or date) over different runs. We modified the web-page-replay code to replace such occurrences with constant values to ensure the same objects were requested for all schemes.

Since both the proxy and the replay server are at the same location, we used dummynet [13] to emulate proxy to server delay. While we used 20ms as the default delay value for majority of our evaluation in the paper, we did conduct experiments to study the sensitivity to different delay values between the proxy and the server (last paragraph in § 8.3). We used the same proxy to server delay for all objects because we wanted to minimize the effect of page and network variability between the proxy and the server and for controllability of the setup. Further, web-page-replay [23] as a tool does not support capturing different latencies to different web servers for objects in the same page, though a recent tool [22] may allow emulation of heterogeneous delays in the future. For realism, we also compared the different schemes using real web servers (without using web-page-replay or dummynet), which captures heterogeneous delays from the proxy to the server. Note that while the mobile device and the proxy are in the same location, the path between the two goes through a production LTE network and is hence representative of a typical data session going through a LTE packet core and the Internet.

To eliminate variability across runs due to cached objects, all comparison experiments were conducted by flushing device cache across runs for both DIR and *PARCEL*. We also disabled proxy caching for *PARCEL* proxy. Moreover, we ignore the first run in each round and obtain the median for the remaining runs to ensure that DNS resolution does not impact our experiment results. Note that our experiments in § 8.2 do consider local device caching only because the focus of these experiments is on client interactions during a user session.

A majority of our experiments focussed on landing pages, though we conducted experiments involving a user session in § 8.2. In general, since a session consists of a sequence of webpage downloads, we expect *PARCEL's* benefits to aggregate over each page download. Even though some objects in subsequent pages of a session could potentially be cached in the device, an approach like *PARCEL* is still important since these pages too are likely to contain content that must be explicitly fetched.

8 Results

In this section, we present results comparing *PARCEL* with DIR (§ 8.1), and CB (§ 8.2), as well as compare variants of *PARCEL* (§ 8.3). All these experiments are conducted by replaying pages using web-page-replay and the experimental approach described in § 7. We also present results with real web servers in § 8.4. Since CB does proprietary data transformations not implemented in *PARCEL*, we limit our comparisons with CB to § 8.2 where we wish to highlight the benefits of local JS execution.

8.1 *PARCEL* vs. traditional mobile browsers

• ***Latency Reductions:*** Figure 6a shows the timeline for an example web page (*taobao.com*) highlighting the cumulative data downloaded at *PARCEL* (proxy and client), and the DIR client. From the figure, we observe that download occurs fastest at the *PARCEL* proxy, followed by the *PARCEL* client and DIR client respectively. This is because DIR incurs the long RTT of the cellular network for each object it requests, while *PARCEL* client sends a single request to the proxy. The DIR curve has a few long flat segments (no objects are downloaded – these are likely because the client was processing html and *JS* to figure out what objects to fetch next) and the gap between consecutive object downloads is long. In contrast, *PARCEL* proxy leverages the better processing power, high bandwidth and shorter RTT to the origin servers, to download the whole page quickly and to transfer the objects to the client faster. Observe from Figure 6a that the time to download all objects until onload event is 6 sec quicker at the *PARCEL* client (OLT is 7.5 sec) when compared to DIR (OLT is 13.44 sec). This result validates the intuition behind a key design element in *PARCEL*: it is desirable to reduce the number of requests from the client, and empower the *PARCEL* proxy early on in the download process to identify and download objects.

Figure 6b presents the CDF of the per-page median latencies (onload and total) across all web pages for the *PARCEL* client and DIR, observed over 40 runs with each scheme. From the figure, we see that *PARCEL* outperforms DIR consistently by a large margin. For 70% of the pages, the *PARCEL* OLT is smaller than 3 sec and the highest observed OLT is 8.8 sec. In contrast, only 10% of the pages have OLT smaller than 3 sec with DIR. Also, the 70th percentile and maximum latencies– 11 sec and 29 sec respectively are $3X$ higher than the corresponding *PARCEL* latencies. We also find that *PARCEL* reduces the OLT by > 1 sec for 90% of

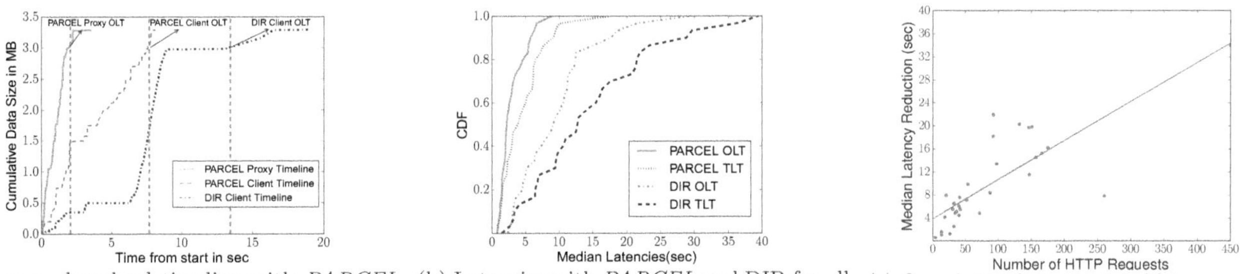

(a) page download timeline with *PARCEL* and DIR for *taobao.com*

(b) Latencies with *PARCEL* and DIR for all pages.

(c) Correlation between total latency reduction and number of HTTP requests.

Figure 6: Effectiveness of *PARCEL* in reducing latency compared to DIR.

the pages, > 5 sec for 60% of the pages, and reduces the total latency by > 5 sec for 80% of the pages.

Figure 6c shows a scatter plot highlighting the correlation between the median total time reduction for *PARCEL* and the number of client HTTP requests (or number of objects) for each page. From the figure, we see that latency benefits with *PARCEL* increases with the increase in number of HTTP requests (correlation coefficient is 0.83). This shows that, as pages get richer and request hundreds of objects, benefits with *PARCEL* will be critical for maintaining a good user experience.

• ***Radio Energy Savings*** Figure 7a shows the RRC states over time for a single download (median run) of an example web page (landing page of *ebay.com*). The black shade represents CR, the white shades represents DRX and the bold red line shows the onload. From the figure, we see that with DIR spends a longer time in CR (active) and DRX (low power tail) states, whereas *PARCEL* reduces time spent in both CR and DRX states, saving energy in both the states. For example, the total radio energy consumed by *PARCEL* for this page is $5.63J$, which is half the energy consumed by DIR ($11.16J$). *PARCEL* benefits from the use of a single TCP connection to the proxy to download the entire page in a single transfer. In contrast, DIR uses multiple parallel TCP connections (6 per domain) to download individual objects. *PARCEL* delegates the effort to identify and fetch objects to the proxy which batches object transfers through the single TCP connection, thereby achieving higher throughput and hence reducing the time spent in CR state. Further, the implicit batching observed by the *PARCEL* proxy helps reduce the gap between consecutive objects transferred and thus reduces the time spent in DRX state. For the example page shown in Figure 7a, DIR observes 22 transitions between the CR and DRX, while *PARCEL* observes only 7 transitions between the states for the entire download.

Figure 7b shows the CDF of the per-page median radio energy consumption with *PARCEL* and DIR for all pages. From the figure, we see that *PARCEL* consistently consumes much lower energy when compared to DIR. With *PARCEL*, the energy usage was $< 4J$ for 80% of the pages and maximum of $8J$. In contrast, the DIR energy usage was $< 4J$ for only 38% of the pages with a maximum of $13J$.

Figure 7c shows for each page, (i) the median total radio energy savings with *PARCEL* for all the pages and (ii) the corresponding median CR energy savings, both expressed as a fraction of the total energy consumed with DIR. From the figure, we observe that *PARCEL* achieves significant energy savings compared to DIR across all the pages. *PARCEL* saves at least 20% of radio energy compared to DIR for 95% of the pages and the savings is at least 50% for 50% of the pages. Further, we note that the savings in the energy consumed in the CR state accounts for at least 50% of the total energy savings for 85% of the pages (the remaining savings are attributed to savings in DRX energy).

Overall our results show that *PARCEL* reduces both the incurred latency and the radio energy consumption when compared to traditional browsers by minimizing the HTTP request-response interactions and delegating the download process to the proxy.

8.2 Importance of local *JS* execution

A key design decision with *PARCEL* was to execute *JS* at the client to ensure responsive and energy efficient client interactions. In this section, we illustrate the importance of this decision by conducting experiments involving the landing page of *ebay.com* and emulating an interactive session where the user clicks on a button once every minute to scroll through different product images. We compare *PARCEL* with DIR as well as **CB,** a popular commercially available cloud-based mobile browser, which executes all *JS* in the cloud and not at the client [32].[4]

Figure 8 top graph shows the cumulative radio energy consumption with *PARCEL*, DIR and CB over the entire user session. Each group of bars corresponds to a particular event in the session. The left-most group corresponds to the first download (FD), while the other groups correspond to subsequent user click events (C1-C4). Each bar shows the cumulative radio (total) energy consumed up to that event for a given scheme. The figure shows that the cumulative radio energy consumption grows significantly with each click event for CB, but remains unchanged with user interaction for *PARCEL* and DIR. This is because both DIR and *PARCEL* request the product images during the first-time download of the page, and store them locally. On a click event, *JS* runs locally on the client and displays the cached images without any network interaction. In contrast, CB issues a request to the proxy on each click event which processes the *JS* and sends back a new snapshot of the page to the client. This network communication required by CB results in radio energy consumption on each click event.

While CB incurs higher radio energy usage, it can potentially lower CPU energy usage compared to DIR and *PARCEL* by not executing *JS* in the client. Figure 8 bottom

[4]We anonymize the browser to keep the focus on the scientific aspects of our study.

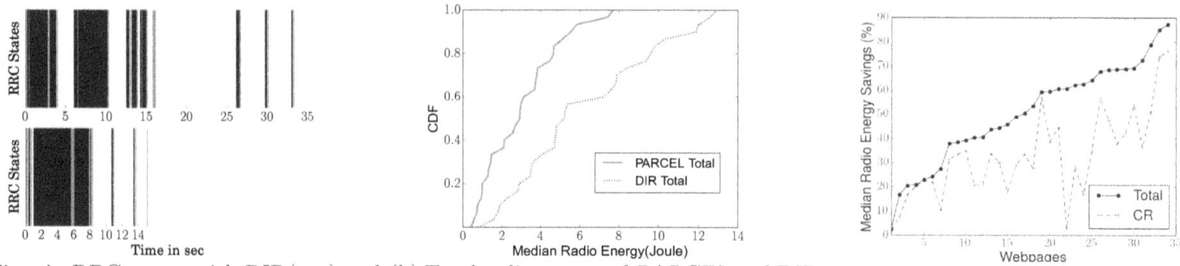

(a) Time in RRC states with DIR(top) and *PARCEL* (bottom) for *ebay.com*.
(b) Total radio energy of *PARCEL* and DIR for all pages.
(c) Radio energy savings with *PARCEL* as a fraction compared to DIR.

Figure 7: Effectiveness of *PARCEL* in reducing total radio energy compared to DIR.

graph provides a more complete picture by showing the total device energy consumption cumulative to each session event. The total energy consumption was measured using a power meter. The screen was kept in the lowest brightness throughout the experiment. The baseline screen power (626mW) was measured and deducted from the total energy consumption. The total energy consumed by CB is indeed lower after the first download (FD), which can be attributed to running *JS* in the cloud rather than the device. However, the total energy consumption for CB increases rapidly on subsequent user clicks, and is higher than not only *PARCEL* but also DIR by the end of the session. In contrast, the cumulative total energy consumption with *PARCEL* is lower than DIR at every point in the session.

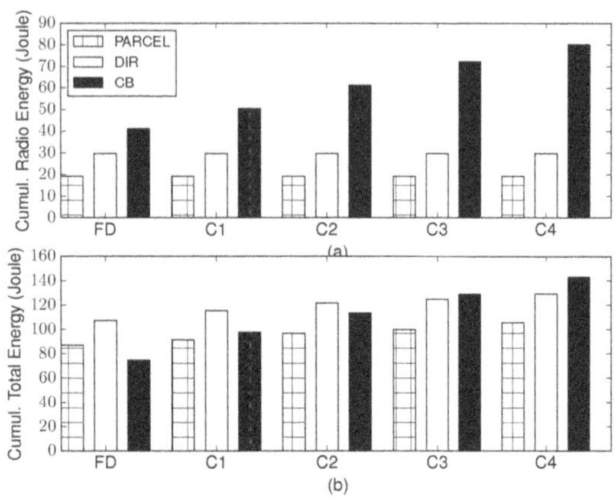

Figure 8: Cumulative radio and total device energy consumption for various schemes over a user session.

8.3 Exploring design knobs within *PARCEL*

One of the design considerations with *PARCEL* is to schedule data transmission to the client by judiciously balancing user latencies and radio energy consumption (See 4.2). In this section, we experiment with different bundle sizes (512KB, 1MB, 2MB) for *PARCEL* (X) and present how they perform in terms of latency and radio energy. We use the same setup as before (§ 7) and results from 20 runs for each page and each scheme.

In Figure 9a, we present the OLT increase for different *PARCEL* bundling variants, compared to *PARCEL* (IND). As expected, all the bundling variants experience higher latency than *PARCEL* (IND), and the amount of increase in general becomes larger with larger bundles, which is consistent with our intuition and analysis in § 6. Specifically, as shown in Figures 9a, *PARCEL* (ONLD) has the highest latency (e.g., the increase is 0.57 sec). For *PARCEL* (512K), the increase is much smaller than other variants using larger bundles (e.g., the increase is 0.11 sec). We also observed similar trends in the TLT. However, we note that all *PARCEL* variants perform better than DIR.

In Figure 9b, we present the total radio energy increase for *PARCEL* bundling variants compared to *PARCEL* (IND). We observe that the trend is not as clear as the latency case and there seems to be no one single bundle size that can minimize the radio energy for all web pages. Specifically, for around 60% of web pages, *PARCEL* (512K) results in less radio energy consumption than *PARCEL* (IND), while the opposite is true for the rest of the web pages. All *PARCEL* variants consume less radio energy than DIR.

We further analyze the results to understand when bundling helps in reducing the radio energy. In Figure 9c, we show a scatter plot of total page size and radio energy difference between *PARCEL* (512K) and *PARCEL* (IND). With larger web pages (e.g., $>$ 2MB), bundling decreases the radio energy consumption, compared to *PARCEL* (IND). Although not shown here due to space constraint, we observe the similar trend when using other bundle sizes. This energy saving is because bundling reduces the gaps between consecutive objects and thus incurs lower transition overhead. Also, transferring larger bundle potentially helps TCP overcome the slow-start effects and achieve increased effective throughput. With smaller pages ($<$2MB), the potential energy saving opportunity is inherently small, and the LTE network variability makes it difficult to identify a clear trend.

Sensitivity of bundle sizes on energy savings As expected, larger bundle sizes increase the client OLT compared to *PARCEL* (IND). The energy results however are more nuanced. For instance, smaller bundle size (512KB) seems to give more benefits than larger bundle sizes. The typical large web-pages range anywhere between 2 and 4MB and we observed download speeds ranging from 4 to 8 Mbps with median of 6 Mbps in our experiments. As shown in § 6, the optimal bundle size is around 1MB for those large web pages. However, we observe that energy saving in practice is largest with a bundle size slightly smaller than the optimal size from Eq. 1 (e.g., 512K instead of 1M). We believe that this is due in part to some of the assumptions we make (e.g., full state transition per bundle transfer, fractional n). Another reason is that in practice the observed download

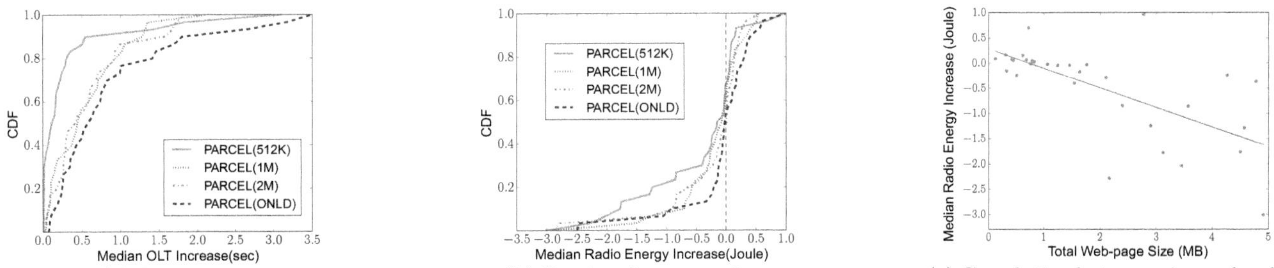

(a) OLT increase

(b) Total radio energy increase

(c) Correlation between size and radio energy increase with *PARCEL* (512K)

Figure 9: Performance of *PARCEL* bundling variants, compared to *PARCEL* (IND).

speed is variable and hence larger bundles are more severely affected by sudden radio signal degradation.

Sensitivity to proxy-server delay We briefly report the results when we use dummynet to vary the delay between the *PARCEL* proxy and our web-page-replay server. In our experiments, we used two round-trip delay values: 20 and 60 ms, representing the RTTs from the client location (Purdue) to the east and west coasts. We observe that with a higher delay, *PARCEL* (ONLD) had higher latency penalty, but provided more energy savings compared to *PARCEL* (IND). Note that in general *PARCEL* (IND) will perform better if objects reach the client close to each other and cause lower state transition overhead. As the delay between proxy and server increases, the object arrivals at the proxy and with IND, at the client are likely to be more spread out, which causes higher energy consumption due to higher state transition overhead.

8.4 Experiments with real web servers

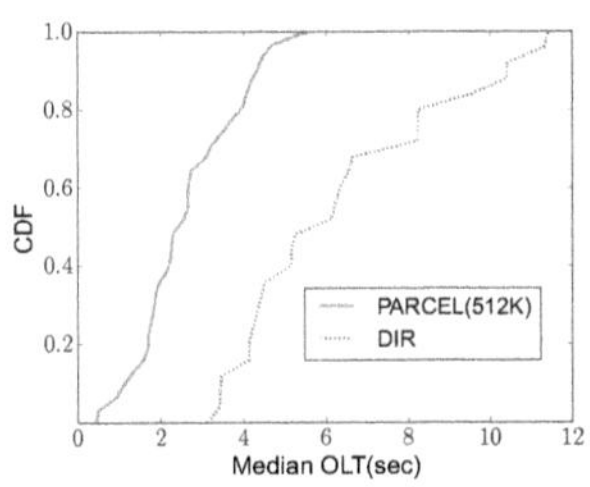

Figure 10: OLT with real web servers

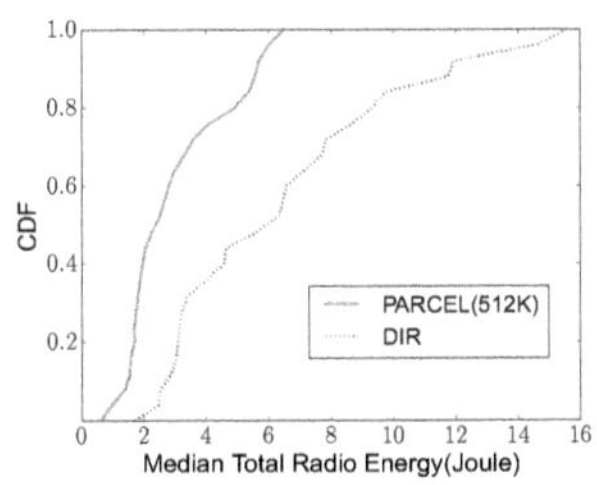

Figure 11: Radio energy with real web servers

The evaluation so far has focused on understanding the benefits of *PARCEL* in a controlled setting, where the pages are hosted on a server in Purdue. In this section, we conduct experiments with pages served from the original domain servers to study the benefits of *PARCEL* in the real world. We use results from 10 runs for each page with each scheme. In Figure 10, we observe that *PARCEL* (512K) consistently outperforms DIR in both onload latency and radio energy usage, which is consistent with our controlled experiment results. For example, the median OLT of *PARCEL* (512K) is < 2.5sec, while that of DIR is around 6sec. We also observe that for 50% of the pages, the *PARCEL* (512K) OLT was one third or less of the DIR OLT. In Figure 11, we observe that *PARCEL* (512K) also reduces the total radio energy significantly compared to DIR. Specifically, with *PARCEL* (512K), the radio energy consumption of all pages is $< 6.5J$, while for around 40% of pages, DIR consumes significantly more radio energy. While we do not show the results, we also conducted experiments with *PARCEL* (IND). *PARCEL* (IND) had slightly lower OLT (0.1sec) and slightly higher radio energy ($0.5J$) than *PARCEL* (512K), but performing significantly better than DIR in both the metrics. The above results confirm the benefits of *PARCEL* in real world settings as well.

9 Conclusions

In this paper, we have shown that judiciously refactoring functionality between mobile browsers and proxies can significantly reduce page load times and radio energy usage in cellular networks. We have presented *PARCEL*, an initial attempt at such functionality refactoring. Distinct from traditional browsers, *PARCEL* moves the task of identifying and downloading objects needed to render a web-page to a well-provisioned proxy. Distinct from existing cloud-heavy browsers, *PARCEL* retains most other functionality including execution of *JS* in the client browser. Our evaluations confirm the potential of *PARCEL*. Compared to a traditional mobile web-browser, *PARCEL* reduces OLT by 49.6% and radio energy consumption by 65%. Unlike cloud-heavy browsers, *PARCEL* continues to perform well on client interactions. While our results are promising, there are many areas for future research as discussed below:

• *Combining PARCEL with page optimizations:* There are many recent efforts at webpage optimization services [7] to be used by web developers to optimize their sites. *PARCEL* can co-exist well with such optimizations, since the *PARCEL* proxy only processes the page to identify the objects and sends the objects received from the server as such to the client without modifying the HTML. Evaluating *PARCEL* in conjunction with such techniques is an interesting direction for future work.

• *Comparisons with other proxy-assisted approaches:* In this paper, we have demonstrated the benefits of *PARCEL* over the CB proxy (§ 8.2) and discussed its benefits over SPDY proxies (§ 4). A quantitative comparison with SPDY proxies is an interesting direction for future research, though we note that previous work [16] has already shown SPDY protocol alone does not outperform HTTP in the cellular setting. A fair comparison is complicated since the most noteable SPDY proxy [5] not only uses SPDY [17] to communicate with the clients, but also performs webpage optimization and data reduction [7], a feature not implemented in our *PARCEL* prototype. Integrating *PARCEL* with such page optimization techniques as described above will facilitate a fair head-to-head comparison in the future.

• *Adapting PARCEL for traffic encryption:* Today 67.2% of the top 151,509 Alexa pages still use HTTP [10] and only 7.25% of the mobile traffic in NorthAmerica is encrypted [30]. However, recent reports do suggest that the aggregated encrypted traffic is increasing throughout the globe [30]. Dealing with HTTPS traffic is an issue not only for *PARCEL* but also for many proxy-assisted solutions([5,6]) that involve web-page parsing. While our current *PARCEL* implementation lets HTTPS traffic follow the normal path without using our proxy, one approach to handling HTTPS traffic is using a trusted, per-client proxy, as we have discussed in the design section (§ 4.5). In the future, we hope to investigate potential issues around personalizing *PARCEL* proxies, and tackle questions around how they must be deployed, placed, and managed. Understanding the cost of running personalized proxies with large number of users is an interesting direction for future research.

10 Acknowledgments

We thank our shepherd David Choffnes and the anonymous reviewers for their constructive feedback and comments. We also thank Oliver Spatscheck for his valuable inputs during discussions. This work was supported in part by the National Science Foundation (NSF) under Career Award No. 0953622 and NSF Award No. 1162333. Any opinions, findings and conclusions or recommendations expressed in this material are those of the authors and do not necessarily reflect the views of NSF.

11 References

[1] The amazon kindle fire: Benchmarked, tested, and reviewed. http://www.tomshardware.com/reviews/amazon-kindle-fire-review,3076-7.html.

[2] Amazon silk split browser architecture. https://s3.amazonaws.com/awsdocs/AmazonSilk/latest/silk-dg.pdf.

[3] Amazon's silk browser acceleration tested: Less bandwidth consumed, but slower performance. http://tinyurl.com/84br5tc.

[4] Cisco visual networking index: Global mobile data traffic forecast update, 2013-2018. http://www.cisco.com/c/en/us/solutions/collateral/service-provider/visual-networking-index-vni/white_paper_c11-520862.html.

[5] Data compression proxy in android chrome. https://developer.chrome.com/multidevice/data-compression.

[6] Opera mini architecture and javascript. http://dev.opera.com/articles/view/opera-mini-and-javascript/.

[7] Pagespeed optimization service. https://developers.google.com/speed/pagespeed/.

[8] Skyfire - cloud based mobile optimization browser. http://www.skyfire.com/operator-solutions/whitepapers.

[9] Squid web proxy. Available at http://www.squid-cache.org.

[10] SSL Pulse. https://www.trustworthyinternet.org/ssl-pulse/.

[11] 3GPP TS 36.331: Radio Resource Control (RRC) (v10.3.0). 2011.

[12] R. Cáceres, L. Cox, H. Lim, A. Shakimov, and A. Varshavsky. Virtual Individual Servers as Privacy-Preserving Proxies for Mobile Devices. In *Proc. ACM MobiHeld*, 2009.

[13] M. Carbone and L. Rizzo. Dummynet Revisited. In *ACM SIGCOMM Computer Communication Review*, March 2010.

[14] B.-G. Chun, S. Ihm, P. Maniatis, M. Naik, and A. Patti. CloneCloud: Elastic Execution between Mobile Device and Cloud. In *Proc. ACM Eurosys*, 2011.

[15] E. Cuervo, A. Balasubramanian, D. Cho, A. Wolman, S. Saroiu, R. Chandra, and P. Bahl. MAUI:Making Smartphones Last Longer with Code Offload. In *Proc. ACM MobiSys*, 2010.

[16] J. Erman, V. Gopalakrishnan, R. Jana, and K.K. Ramakrishnan. Towards a SPDY'ier mobile web? In *Proc. CoNEXT*, Dec 2013.

[17] Google. SPDY: An experimental protocol for a faster web. http://www.chromium.org/spdy/spdy-whitepaper.

[18] J. Huang, F. Qian, A. Gerber, Z. M. Mao, S. Sen, and O. Spatscheck. A Close Examination of Performance and Power Characteristics of 4G LTE Networks. In *Proc. ACM Mobisys*, 2012.

[19] R. Kemp, N. Palmer, T. Kielmann, and H. Bal. Cuckoo: a Computation Offloading Framework for Smartphones. In *Proc. MobiCASE*, 2010.

[20] S. Kosta, A. Aucinas, P. Hui, R. Mortier, and X. Zhang. ThinkAir: Dynamic resource allocation and parallel execution in cloud for mobile code offloading. In *Proc. IEEE INFOCOM*, 2012.

[21] K. Matsudaira. Making the mobile web faster. *Communications of the ACM, Vol 56. No 3.*, 2013.

[22] R. Netravali, A. Sivaraman, K. Winstein, S. Das, A. Goyal, and H. Balakrishnan. Mahimahi: A Lightweight Toolkit for Reproducible Web Measurement (Demo). In *ACM SIGCOMM 2014*, Chicago, IL, August 2014.

[23] Web-page-replay. Record and play back web pages with simulated network conditions. https://www.code.google.com/p/web-page-replay/.

[24] F. Qian, K.S.Quah, J.Huang, J.Erman, A.Gerber, Z.M.Mao, S.Sen, and O.Spatscheck. Web Caching on Smartphones: Ideal vs. Reality. In *Proc. ACM MobiSys*, 2012.

[25] F. Qian, S. Sen, and O. Spatscheck. Characterizing Resource Usage for Mobile Web Browsing. In *Proc. ACM MobiSys*, 2014.

[26] F. Qian, Z. Wang, A. Gerber, Z. M. Mao, S. Sen, and O. Spatscheck. Profiling Resource Usage for Mobile Applications: A Cross-layer Approach. In *Proc. ACM Mobisys*, 2011.

[27] S. Rajaraman, M. Siekkinen, V. Virkki, and J. Torsner. Bundling Frames to Save Energy While Streaming Video from LTE Mobile Device. In *Proc. ACM MobiArch*, 2013.

[28] A. Saarinen, M. Siekkinen, Y. Xiao, J. K. Nurminen, and M. Kemppainen. Smartdiet: Offloading Popular Apps to Save Energy(Poster). In *Proc. ACM Sigcomm*, 2012.

[29] A. Saarinen, M. Siekkinen, Y. Xiao, J. K. Nurminen, M. Kemppainen, and P. Hui. Can Offloading Save Energy for Popular Apps. In *Proc. ACM MobiArch*, 2012.

[30] Sandvine. Global internet phenomena report 1h-2014. Available at https://www.sandvine.com/downloads/general/global-internet-phenomena/2014/1h-2014-global-internet-phenomena-report.pdf.

[31] M. Satyanarayanan, P. Bahl, R. Cáceres, and N. Davies. The Case for VM-based Cloudlets in Mobile Computing. *IEEE/Trans. Pervasive Computing*, 2009.

[32] A. Sivakumar, V. Gopalakrishnan, S. Lee, S. Rao, S. Sen, and O. Spatscheck. Cloud is not a silver bullet: A case study of cloud-based mobile browsing. In *Proceedings of ACM HotMobile*, 2014.

[33] S. Souders. Onload event and post-onload requests. http://www.stevesouders.com/blog/2012/10/30/qa-nav-timing-and-post-onload-requests.

[34] X. S. Wang, A. Balasubramanian, A. Krishnamurthy, and D. Wetherall. How Speedy is SPDY? In *Proc. NSDI*, April 2014.

[35] X. S. Wang, H. Shen, and D. Wetherall. Accelerating the Mobile Web with Selective Offloading. In *Proc. ACM MCC*, 2013.

[36] B. Zhao, B. C. Tak, and G. Cao. Reducing the Delay and Power Consumption of Web Browsing on Smartphones in 3G Networks. In *Proc. ICDCS*, 2011.

[37] Z. Zhu, P. Gupta, Q. Wang, S. Kalyanaraman, Y. Lin, H. Franke, and S. Sarangi. Virtual base station pool: towards a wireless network cloud for radio access networks. In *Proc. of the 8th ACM International Conference on Computing Frontiers*, 2011.

Using Cooperation for Low Power Low Latency Cellular Connectivity

Cătălin Nicuțar, Dragoș Niculescu, and Costin Raiciu
Dept. of Computer Science, University Politehnica of Bucharest
first.last@cs.pub.ro

ABSTRACT

Mobile devices today rely on cellular (3G or LTE) connectivity because it has ubiquitous coverage. Unfortunately cellular links are energy hungry at low bit-rates and have high round-trip times after idle periods. These characteristics punish common mobile applications such as web browsing and streaming, decreasing battery life and user satisfaction.

We present the design and implementation of the Mobile *kibbutz*, a system that improves the performance of cellular links by having nearby users share their links with each other via shorter range wireless links - WiFi or Bluetooth. *Without requiring application specific knowledge, instrumentation, or recompilation*, the *kibbutz* allows multiple users' traffic to be consolidated on a subset of links, leading to reduced energy consumption and smaller round-trip times, while ensuring fairness across different users.

We have implemented the *kibbutz* on Samsung Galaxy Nexus devices and shown that for typical usage applications, collaborating phones consume 25% less energy when listening to radio, experience more responsive web browsing (1.2s faster on average), and 33% faster downloads.

Categories and Subject Descriptors

C.2.1 [**Computer-Communication Networks**]: Network Architecture and Design—*Wireless communication*

Keywords

3G; 4G; WiFi; Bluetooth; MPTCP; tethering; power

1. INTRODUCTION

Mobile devices have become more numerous than the traditional desktop computers, and much of their success is due to the "always-connected" paradigm they enable: users are constantly in touch with the latest news, receive email, navigate and chat while on the move. Cellular technologies such as 3G and LTE are the default choice of connectivity because they have ubiquitous coverage. Unfortunately, they are both energy-hungry and have high latency after periods of inactivity. Indeed, many mobile user forums single out 3G as the usual suspect for high battery drain and suggest turning it off when battery is low; LTE draws even more power than 3G.

CoNEXT'14, December 2–5, 2014, Sydney, Australia.

ACM 978-1-4503-3279-8/14/12 ...$15.00.
http://dx.doi.org/10.1145/2674005.2674983.

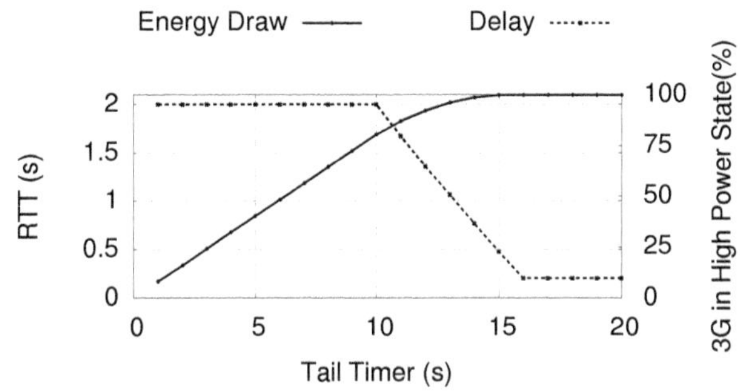

Figure 1: Cellular links offer a fundamental tradeoff between energy consumption and latency after idle

Cellular networks rely on centralized capacity allocation for high utilization of the wireless spectrum and bandwidth and fairness guarantees that are not available in distributed access control such as CSMA. The price paid is the need for signaling between the mobile devices and the network: whenever a device needs to send or receive a non-trivial amount of data, it asks the network for a dedicated channel. Once the channel is allocated, the mobile device draws a lot of energy regardless of its data rate. Signaling is expensive both for the operator as it limits scalability, and for the mobile device, as it increases energy cost and communication latencies. That is why the mobile only releases the channel when the there is no traffic during the *tail timer*, a parameter set by the MNO (mobile network operator).

Cellular connections offer a fundamental tradeoff between low latency on one hand, and low energy consumption on the other: we could achieve low latency if the mobile link were always on, at the cost of quickly draining the device battery. Mobile operators already exploit this tradeoff by altering the tail timer dynamically. In Figure 1 we simulate the impact of the tail timer on the energy consumption and latency for a user browsing the web and visiting a new web page every 12s (details are given in section 4).

In fact, most existing work on reducing the energy consumption of cellular links impacts latency. An active LTE link during idle periods may transition into a more efficient DRX (Discontinuous Reception) state where it alternates between listening to the channel and sleeping; this delays traffic by tens to hundreds of milliseconds but reduces energy consumption. Higher up the stack, Balakrishnan et al. [1] propose to use 3G fast dormancy to allow mobile devices to transition to idle when the likelihood of future traffic is low, inflating the latency when the prediction is wrong.

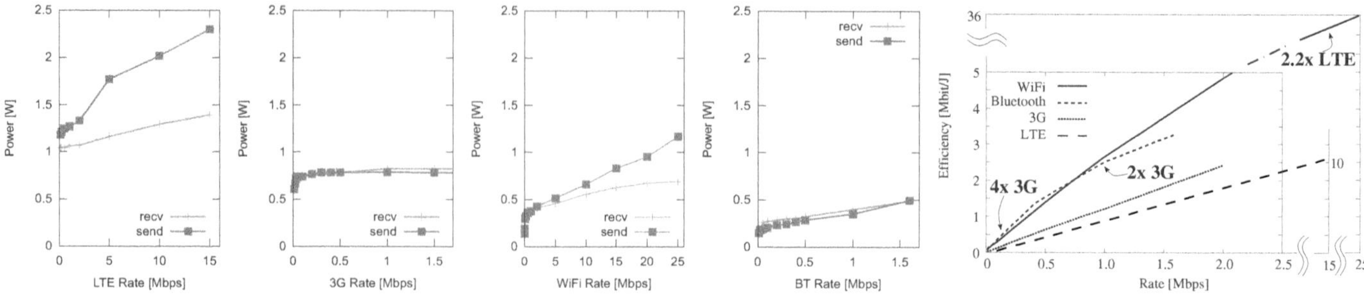

Figure 2: Power consumption of a Galaxy Nexus phone generating traffic at various rates over different wireless interfaces: a) LTE power consumption b) 3G power consumption c) WiFi power consumption d) Bluetooth power consumption e) Receiving efficiency compared: at 150Kbps 3G is 4x worse than WiFi or BT, at 15Mbps LTE is 2.2x worse than WiFi.

Finally, other approaches use application knowledge and explicitly delay traffic to reduce the number of costly energy tails [2].

In this paper we ask the question of how latency and energy consumption can be reduced simultaneously for cellular links. To find a solution, we leverage the key observation that cellular links are only energy efficient when idle or fully-loaded, because lightly loaded links consume just as much power as fully loaded ones. A good solution should try to move these links into one of these two states. Reduced latency will come as a side effect, because traffic will travel mostly "active" links.

Our solution targets groups of nearby devices, rather than individual ones, and it aims to **consolidate cellular traffic onto as few cellular links as possible**, striving to keep a few devices' links fully utilized, and the rest of the links completely idle. In many formal or informal user communities, there are ample opportunities to share connections [3].

Our solution, the Mobile *kibbutz*, enables nearby mobile devices to dynamically share their cellular connections with each other via WiFi or Bluetooth links in a secure and fair manner. When a mobile device uses its cellular link for its own purposes, it also forwards traffic for its neighbors connected via local links. Measurement results show that the added cost of forwarding and of the local links is significantly smaller than the cost of enabling the cellular link of all the devices, so the aggregate energy consumption is smaller.

There have been many previous works proposing connection sharing, including [4, 5, 6, 7, 8, 9], and mobile operating systems are enabled by default with the ability to "tether" traffic. Most of these works focus on bandwidth or minutes sharing, is manually enabled by the user and static. The *kibbutz* also uses tethering, and its novelty is in addressing the key problems related to reducing energy consumption on mobile phones via collaboration:

- Is application agnostic, and the first work that breaks the aforementioned power-RTT tradeoff.
- Provides an algorithm that allows dynamic and continuous changing of roles (multiple times per minute), to ensure that all the devices gain from collaborating.
- Can shift traffic onto different paths seamlessly by using an optimized version of Multipath TCPs.
- Includes accounting mechanisms that ensure users are only billed for their own traffic, and a tit-for-tat mechanism that ensures fairness in energy consumption.

We have implemented and tested the *kibbutz* both in simulation and on Android devices. Our experiments show that the *kibbutz* is very robust, fair, and offers benefits for a wide range of traffic patterns. Android tests shows that unmodified applications can benefit greatly from the *kibbutz*: two devices listening to (different) online radio streams with the *kibbutz* leads to 25% less energy consumption; typical web searches are 1.2s faster on average, and 4s faster in the 90'th percentile; downloading mobile apps takes 30% shorter.

2. MOBILE NETWORKING TODAY

We begin by discussing the basic properties of radio technologies available on mobile devices today (cellular, WiFi and Bluetooth), attempting to understand how they cater for the traffic patterns of common applications.

Cellular connectivity such as 3G and LTE is widely available geographically, being the default choice for devices. Cellular power consumption depends on the state of the connected link: when the link is idle, its power consumption is close to zero. When the device has to transmit or receive a single typically-sized packet (e.g. 1KB), it will transition into a high power state. The transition takes seconds and is expensive energetically because of signaling with the base station. To amortize its cost across many packets, the solution used in practice is for the mobile device to remain in the high-power state for a predefined amount of time after the last packet has been sent (5-10 seconds, depending on the operator). When very little traffic is sent, this tail wastes precious energy, draining batteries. This behavior is widely studied in recent literature [2, 10, 1, 11], and also visible in our own experiments (see Figure 9 left, labeled 'Stand alone'). Any relevant transfers are performed in the high power state (called DCH in 3G, and CONNECTED in LTE).

In our **3G tests**, the transition to DCH state takes about 2.3s up, and 7.3s down for one operator. The sum of these values seems to vary slightly with time of the day, but stays roughly in the 5s-10s region. This behavior has two critical implications for interactive traffic. First, after a silence, a mobile using 3G will have to wait the 2.3s setup time before sending *any* traffic, and second, waste about 3J of energy to wind down. In addition, any amount of traffic with a period of less than 5-7s will keep the radio in the high power state, regardless of the actual transfer rate. In fact, 3G power consumption tends to have a flat response to increasing traffic. Beyond a certain inter-arrival rate, the 3G interface remains in the high power state, and variations in consumption depend only on the cost of moving data through the stack, as confirmed by measurements in Figure 2(b).

LTE networks behave similarly (Figure 2(a)). There are quantitative differences, though: total power consumption is higher, on the order of 1.0-2.5W, while the setup time is a bit smaller, between 0.2s-0.5s for the MNO (Mobile Network Operator) we have tested. We found that DRX is used both in RRC (Radio Resource Connected), and in IDLE states, with a 1ms short timer. Other authors report similar findings [11, 1].

WiFi links offer better throughput than their cellular counterparts, but their coverage is patchy. Most phones use the 802.11 power save mode permanently in order to power down the interface when little traffic is to be transferred, making WiFi power consumption proportional to the traffic rate. In Figure 2(c), we plot the power consumption for different rates, and it is mostly linear for rates above 200Kbps. Part of the linearity of the curve is given by the cost of the software stack, as was recently shown in [12].

Bluetooth links (3.0 in our phones) are only available at a few meters and provide 2Mbps in our tests. On the other hand, Bluetooth power consumption curve is linear with the throughput achieved (Figure 2(d)).

To emphasize the difference in power consumption patterns between the four radios, in Fig. 2(e) we recast the measured data to show the efficiency measured in Mbit/J. The efficiency does increase for all three technologies due to amortization. For 3G the tail end gets used better with increasing traffic, when more bits are handled with the same cost. For Bluetooth and WiFi, powering the circuitry takes proportionally more than the software stack - in Figures 2(c) and 2(d) the line doesn't actually pass through 0. Note that at lower rates, the efficiency of 3G is much worse, due to the long inactivity timer in the DCH and FACH states. Beyond 750Kbps WiFi is more efficient than Bluetooth.

Mobile applications fall in two broad classes. Background apps synchronize periodically with servers, have low rates and waste energy because of the tail timer. Optimizing energy consumption for such apps has been an active research area, with quite a few solutions proposed [13, 14, 2, 10, 1].

Interactive applications can be loosely characterized in other three classes: streaming (VOIP, radio, online gaming, video streaming), web browsing and app downloads.

Streaming apps utilize cellular links inefficiently: they consume little bandwidth (tens to hundreds of Kbps) and have large packet inter-arrival times. Web browsing works in a user-driven closed-loop: a burst of traffic downloading a page triggers a costly energy tail, followed by a relatively short period of silence that allows the radio to go idle. When the next burst arrives, it has to wait for a state transition. Finally, app downloads utilize the full speed of the cellular interface for brief periods. Here, higher download speeds are preferable, but users are limited by the cellular capacity.

Running these apps over cellular links leads to high energy costs and poor overall performance. Ideally, we would like to run all these applications over WiFi-like links that offer energy proportionality and high speeds, but such links are not available all the time.

3. THE MOBILE KIBBUTZ

The key insights from our measurements are that:

- Cellular links offer good interactive experience only when in the high-power state. In this state they draw (roughly) the same power regardless of the traffic load.
- Many mobile applications such as web radio, or web browsing under-utilize cellular links most of the time.
- WiFi and Bluetooth links offer power-proportionality and low delays.

Our goal is to achieve low energy consumption, low RTTs, and fair privacy aware sharing of cellular links, all while maintaining

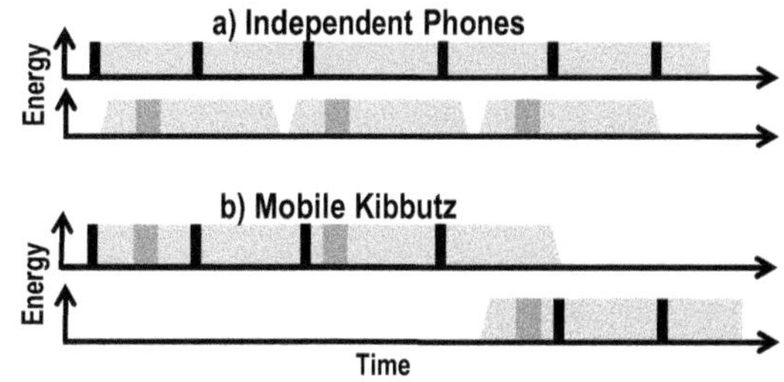

Figure 3: The mobile kibbutz consolidates traffic onto a single link, reducing energy consumption and delay at the same time. Energy consumed by traffic is shown as red and black bars, and wasted energy in gray.

the TCP socket interface to existing applications. To the best of our knowledge, there are no solutions that achieve this goal today.

All existing work on optimizing energy consumption for cellular links trades latency for energy efficiency by *adaptively reducing the tail timer* or *clustering packets in time by delaying some of them*. The first solution works reasonably well for background applications, but it is not applicable to applications that send at low data rates (e.g. radio, streaming). The second solution requires application changes, and only applies to delay-tolerant apps. Even PHY-layer solutions such as LTE's DRX use the same tradeoff, decreasing energy consumption for increased delay.

Our solution is based on the observation that, in most cases, mobile users roam in dense areas where many other mobile users are around (public spaces, transport, office, home). We propose to join nearby mobile devices into a Mobile *kibbutz*, which allows devices to use each other's cellular connection by forwarding traffic along cheaper WiFi or Bluetooth links. By joining the *kibbutz*, devices can dynamically share their cellular connections with the rest of their group for an advertised period. While the advertisement is valid, neighboring devices have a choice between using their own link or the shared link for sending or receiving traffic.

The *kibbutz* allows devices to **consolidate their traffic onto one or a few cellular links**, reducing both energy consumption and delay across all devices. Consolidation brings cellular links closer to the their optimal operating point: one link will be highly loaded while others will be idle. Intuitively, the *kibbutz* saves energy because: a) local links are power proportional and b) the added energy cost of forwarding data on behalf of others is very small compared to the cost of using the cellular link.

The concept is presented in Figure 3. The black user is listening to Internet radio, while the red user is browsing the web. In isolation, both users keep their cellular links busy most of the time (Fig. 3.a), despite the low data rate. In addition, the red user experiences high delays when accessing every single page because his link must transition from idle to the connected state. By consolidating traffic onto a single link we can leave the other link IDLE all the time; this reduces the total energy consumption to approximately half. Additionally, the red user's delay decreases because state transitions are unnecessary most of the time.

Users may leave a *kibbutz* when mobile: we must ensure that connections are not disrupted in such cases. To this end, the mobile devices use MPTCP to dynamically steer traffic over one or a subset of available links. In effect, the *kibbutz pools together cellular links*, enabling many optimization avenues. In the rest of this section we describe in detail the operation of the mobile *kibbutz*.

3.1 Basic Operation

To use the mobile *kibbutz*, a device will automatically connect to other nearby devices. There are a number of technologies that can be used for this purpose:

- **Bluetooth** is the most energy efficient but it only supports point-to-point connections, so it will be difficult to create large groups of devices because of the sheer number of connections required. Additionally, Bluetooth has relatively low speeds (2Mbps in our tests).
- **WiFi hotspot** mode (or WiFi direct) is when one device acts as the access point, and the other as client. This mode is widely supported and offers high speeds. On the downside the setup is asymmetric as the access point will consume more power (200mW on the Galaxy Nexus).
- **WiFi Ad-Hoc** is our favorite technology because it allows true peer-to-peer operation and high speeds; unfortunately support for Ad-Hoc is being phased out of mobile WiFi drivers.
- **LTE Direct** [15] is an emerging technology that uses the LTE band for energy-efficient device-to-device communication and discovery. LTE Direct appears very promising for our purposes but is not yet available.

The mechanisms needed to automatically join a *kibbutz* depend on the local link. WiFi ad-hoc is easiest: a device willing to share a link will send broadcast messages that prospective clients can hear and respond to. For WiFi hotspot mode, a device willing to share its cellular link will become an access point using some predefined SSID. To join the *kibbutz*, prospective clients will simply associate to this AP. Finally, BT devices will set their device names to some predefined values, and devices willing to enter the *kibbutz* will search for other devices and allow themselves to be discovered; unsafe pairing can be done automatically, without requiring user input.

Advertisements. Once the device is connected to a *kibbutz*, it can share its cellular connection with other devices. One simple option is to always share the connection, but this may quickly drain the device's battery. A better option is to share the link only when it is already in the high power state: this way the additional energy consumed to forward the neighbor's traffic is very small and the traffic will experience low delays. Device A will advertise its link when one of its own packets leaves the interface and the interface is not already shared. A's advertisement includes an expiration time t that tells peers when to stop forwarding traffic via A.

The choice of t affects the performance of the *kibbutz*; smaller t leads to more signaling required for advertisements, and it could also lead to frequent switches of traffic between devices, thus negating the energy savings the *kibbutz* can bring. That is why we use an advertisement period equal to the tail timer of the mobile operator – the largest value that guarantees the link will always be in the high power state when used by peers. Sharing an IDLE link would be bad: it costs a state transition and provides increased delay.

The default advertisement algorithm can lead to unfairness: in many cases the whole *kibbutz* will end up using a single device's link. Additionally, it is very easy for a device to leech on other devices' resources, undermining the *kibbutz*. To incentivize devices to share their links we adopt a simple tit-for-tat algorithm: each device keeps a counter for each neighbor indicating the number of times it will allow the neighbor to use its link without the neighbor reciprocating. The counter is decreased when the neighbor first uses the link during an advertisement period, and increased when the device uses one of the neighbor's advertisements. When the counter reaches zero, the link is no longer advertised.

The initial value of the counter must be positive and is a parameter of the algorithm. Larger values are more energy efficient as they reduce the need to switch between links; at the same time they can create short-term unfairness in link usage. We explore this tradeoff in simulation in Section 4.

Traffic Optimization. Each device keeps a list of received advertisements that it can use to optimize different goals as follows:

- **Save Energy:** devices will always send traffic via advertised links; they will only use their own link when no other links are available. This is the default strategy.
- **Maximize Bandwidth:** devices will use all advertised links as well as their own in a bid to maximize their throughput.
- **Minimize RTT:** the Save Energy strategy will also reduce the RTT because advertised links are by design in the high power state which gives small round-trip times. However, the horizontal link used to reach the neighbor also adds precious milliseconds to the round-trip time; devices wanting the absolute smallest RTT might prefer their own link in the DCH state to advertised links.

When device A wishes to use neighbor B's link it will simply route packets via the "local" link to B. B will receive packets on the local link, change their source address and port (i.e. NAT) and place them onto its cellular link. Return traffic reaching B will go through the (reverse) NAT and then will be forwarded to A. In effect B is acting like a mobile hotspot for A - and this is already supported out of the box by most mobile platforms.

New TCP connections will work seamlessly over the new link, without the applications needing to know which link their traffic is taking. As long as these connections finish before the advertisement period ends, everything is great.

However, connections that last longer than the advertisement period will simply be terminated, as they are bound to the IP address of the advertised cellular link. This is a fundamental limitation of TCP: once a connection is created, it is bound to the addresses of the endpoints. Change the addresses and the connection will just die. As 97% mobile traffic runs over TCP [16] and many connections are long-lived, this limitation severely restricts the utility of the *kibbutz*.

Multipath TCP. To take full advantage of the *kibbutz* we use the newly standardized MPTCP protocol [17]. It is an evolution of TCP that allows unmodified applications to use multiple paths in the network through a single transport connection. MPTCP connections are composed of one or many subflows that appear like a single TCP socket to the applications. By default, MPTCP will use all available subflows to send data, favoring connections that have lower loss rates [18]. *With MPTCP, endpoints can add and remove subflows at any point during the lifetime of a connection.* Using this feature we can redirect any connection to use the cellular or neighboring links by adding new subflows. To force the connection's packets via the new subflow there are two options: we can close the cellular subflow, forcing the remote end to use the new subflow, or announce the remote-end that the direct subflow has lower priority. We use the second option because it avoids repeated setup and tear-down of subflows over the device's cellular link. By default, all direct subflows are marked as low priority; subflows routed via neighbors are marked differently depending on the optimization goal.

In the energy saving profile, neighbor subflows are marked as normal priority, thus all traffic will prefer them to own 3G links; these will only be used when all the neighbor links experience repeated timeouts.

In the bandwidth and RTT profiles all subflows will be marked low priority, and transition between the two modes is done automatically: if the application generates enough traffic all subflows will be used thus maximizing bandwidth; otherwise, the MPTCP scheduler will send the packets via the available subflow with the smallest RTT.

3.2 Robustness

All devices prioritize their own traffic over that of the neighbors to ensure good user experience. Implementing prioritization for uplink traffic is straightforward by using priority queuing; on the downlink the *kibbutz* provider (see below) prioritizes direct traffic.

Consolidating many users' traffic onto a single cellular link may exceed the capacity of that link. The MPTCP priority mechanism will always prefer a congested *kibbutz* link to the direct link, but this may result in poor performance.

Another issue appears when the forwarding device moves out of range, affecting the experience of the devices relying on it for connectivity at that time.

To address both these issues we have optimized the MPTCP path selection algorithm for the *kibbutz*: if a high priority subflow delivers insufficient performance (determined by examining the *ssthresh* variable and the number of timeouts currently experienced), the mobile starts using its own low-priority cellular link - in effect it switches temporarily into bandwidth mode - until the *kibbutz* peer link recovers.

3.3 Deployment Considerations

To deploy the *kibbutz*, mobiles need to install a client app and an MPTCP enabled kernel. Our *kibbutz* implementation presented in Section 5 uses Android 4.1.2 and 3.0.5 kernel with MPTCP.

As MPTCP is not widely deployed yet, most servers do not support it, thus we need an MPTCP proxy that speaks MPTCP to the mobiles and regular TCP to the rest of the Internet [19]. The proxy can be a standard Linux box running MPTCP. The service is supported by a *kibbutz* **provider**, usually the MNO, where users are already registered using a unique identifier such as their SIM number. The *kibbutz* provider deploys a proxy in the wired domain, and the *kibbutz* client is pre-configured to route traffic via this server. As the *kibbutz* groups potentially mistrusting users, the provider handles security and bandwidth accounting.

3.4 Security and Bandwidth Accounting

The *kibbutz* routes traffic via untrusted neighbors and it opens new avenues of attack: the neighbors can violate privacy by reading the traffic, can impersonate a server or insert/change/delete content arbitrarily by modifying traffic. Therefore, all traffic routed via neighbors may be encrypted. Another concern relates to providing user incentives to sharing their link: obviously, a user must not pay for traffic forwarded on behalf of another user. Previous work proposes to use digital coins for this purpose [5], as it targets the case where the users have different cellular providers. Our focus is on enabling the *kibbutz* for users of the same operator, and the solution is much simpler: all we have to do is ensure that the operator can properly account for traffic sent by each mobile directly or via neighbors, and traffic forwarded on behalf of other mobiles.

A *kibbutz* user sharing its link effectively acts as a hotspot for the other *kibbutz* users, offloading traffic from their cellular links. We can thus address both concerns above by leveraging existing solutions to offload data from 3G/LTE to WiFi, which are popular with MNOs because they improve capacity and reduce cost. Such solutions encrypt traffic and enable MNO accounting.

Mobile offloading allows the operator to remain in charge of the authentication, encryption, and accounting of the subscriber's traffic [20]. The Extensible Authentication Protocol (EAP) is used to authenticate the mobile device via the WiFi hotspot which relays this information to the relevant MNO servers. The *kibbutz* partner acts as an offloading point from the point of view of the mobile, as the EAP conversation is performed over the partner's own 3G link. Once the authentication process is completed, the *kibbutz* partner knows whether to allow the traffic through or not. The key resulting from the authentication exchange is then used by the mobile device to establish an IPSec tunnel that is terminated in the operator's network. All other policy and charging functions are reused from the existing core. Note that MNOs already have all the equipment required to support mobile data offloading, and mobile devices support the required technologies out of the box. The only downside of such offloading is that encryption is done in software.

One alternative that avoids the overhead of software-based encryption is proposed by the Swedish startup AnyFi [21]. It allows a WiFi device authenticate against its home network even when away from home, by tunneling the authentication, association, and encrypted data through local access, through WiFi in IP encapsulation. This does not require any changes on the mobiles, but requires AnyFi support on the home APs(a back-end) and foreign APs(a front-end). AnyFi is being considered by many MNOs [1] for mobile data offloading as it has the advantage of using the hardware AES present in any WiFi card, and it simplifies authentication for both the user and the network. Adapting this architecture for the *kibbutz* entails only running an AnyFi front-end on the phone that accepts to encapsulate and route traffic from other *kibbutz* peers on its 3G/4G uplink. AnyFi can also be easily extended to tunnel Bluetooth instead, thus enabling secure Bluetooth links.

4. SIMULATION ANALYSIS

In this section we use simulation to understand the basic properties of the *kibbutz* across parameters that cannot be easily controlled in practice. We show experimentally in Section 6 that these benefits can be obtained on real devices.

We have implemented a discrete-time simulator that services scheduled traffic requests from devices. To model 3G power consumption the simulator tracks whether a device is in the high power state, and the tail timer is given as input. Cellular link speed is set to 2Mbps. RTT is measured for each traffic request; it is set to 2s if the device must transition to the high power state, otherwise it is set to 200ms[2]. Finally, the simulator assumes the local links are perfect, having zero delay and infinite bandwidth (BT and WiFi are mostly negligible compared with 3G). The simulator also implements the tit-for-tat algorithm and sets initial counter to five slots.

We have modeled three application classes: streaming models audio and video streaming apps that send traffic every second thus keeping the cellular link up all the time; web browsing is modeled using randomized inter-arrival time with an average of 13s (value chosen by profiling our own browsing habits on mobiles); background traffic such as podcasts, or email and was similarly modeled with an average of 30s.

Energy Savings. To understand the possible benefits of the *kibbutz*, we varied the number of devices and ran the three app types described above. In Figure 4(a) we show the expected energy savings from a *kibbutz*; the numbers given represent the percentage of time the 3G interface stays in the high power state. The best we can hope for is the power to decrease inversely proportional to the number of devices.

[1] private conversations with MNO engineers

[2] RTT for our 3G MNO varies, sometimes wildly, between 85ms and 900ms depending on time of day, user speed, and cell population.

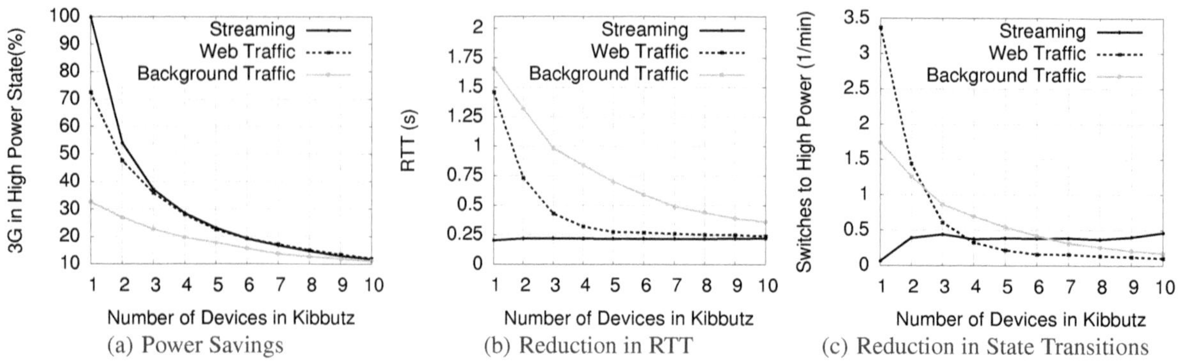

Figure 4: Simulation results for the mobile *kibbutz* with varying number of devices and three classes of applications.

Streaming keeps the radio up all the time if a single device is playing; if two devices are playing in a *kibbutz*, they will each save around 45% of the 3G energy. As more devices join the *kibbutz*, the benefits increase as expected. A similar curve is seen for web traffic; here the baseline is at around 80%, because the radio manages to sleep a little in between two pages. We observe that for these two applications even small numbers of devices make a big difference to power consumption. The story is different for background traffic; here the baseline consumption is only 30%, and it drops more slowly; with three devices it stays at 24%.

How many devices is it feasible to have in a *kibbutz*? Assuming the device density is high enough, the local links will become bottlenecks when many devices join. We have run experiments with two Android devices without any problems. Going to four-five devices is certainly feasible for Bluetooth links as long as aggregate traffic rate is low. Beyond that other costs will start dominating and will produce diminishing returns. With this in mind, it becomes apparent that the *kibbutz* does not bring many benefits for background-style traffic: the messages are so sparse in time that consolidation does not help much, especially for small numbers of devices. It makes sense, then, to only enable the *kibbutz* when the device is active.

RTT Reduction. 3G state transitions induce high delays to packets; our measurements show this delay to be around 2s depending on time of day, for a number of operators. Once the radio is in the high power state, delays are much lower - typically 100ms-200ms. We measured the average RTT experienced by each transfer for each app class, with the results shown in Figure 4(b). The simulated RTT decreases five times for web transfers with three devices in a *kibbutz*. As web transfer is RTT-bound, this reduction is significant and will enhance user experience. Background traffic is less sensitive to RTT, hence the decrease in RTT while sizeable it may not matter that much in practice. Finally, RTT increases a little for streaming apps because the *kibbutz* switches between different links that will have to transition to the high power state. With a single device this is not needed, as the link is up all the time.

Reduced Signaling Costs. Our previous measurements focus on user-centric performance indicators. We also wish to understand how the *kibbutz* affects the network, in particular in reducing the signaling costs between the devices and the cellular base-station needed for state promotions. Signaling is an important optimization target for carriers [13]. To this end, in Figure 4(c), we measured the frequency of transitions to the high power state induced by our three categories of apps. Web and background traffic induce a transition every time a packet is sent when a device is running standalone. In a three device *kibbutz* the number of transitions is reduced tenfold for web-traffic, and halved for background traffic. Streaming will incur a bit more state transitions with the *kibbutz*, because instead of staying always up, the 3G link now toggles up and down whenever the mobile consolidates its traffic with the neighbors.

Effect of the Tail Timer. We wish to understand what effect the tail timer has on the key metrics for users (power) and the network (signaling). The tail timer is the only knob available to mobile operators today. To measure its impact, we vary the tail timer from 1 to 30s and measure the web application when running standalone and in groups of two or three devices.

The tail timer offers a trade-off between power (Fig. 5(a)), signaling (Fig. 5(c)), and RTT (Fig. 5(b)). The graphs show how difficult it is to choose a good trade-off today: one has to go for low signaling and delay or low power, but not both. The *kibbutz* changes the trade-off space: it tames power consumption for higher values of the tail timer, while also reducing RTT.

If we compare the tail timer to the average inter-arrival time between web requests (13s) we get other insights from these graphs. When the tail timer is very low, web traffic rarely benefits from the *kibbutz* because the radio is in the low power state most of the time. As the tail timer increases, the cellular link is up more and this allows the *kibbutz* to consolidate traffic and obtain benefits for both power and RTT. As the tail timer goes beyond 13s, the *kibbutz* only improves power usage.

Dynamic Adjustment of the Tail Timer. There is a wealth of existing research that exploits fast dormancy, a feature standardized by 3GPP [22] that allows the mobile device to demand a transition to the IDLE state, thus reducing its tail time and its associated energy cost. Using fast-dormancy can save energy but it requires that the device knows the traffic pattern of the application [13, 14, 1]. A concrete example is the MakeIdle algorithm proposed in [1] that uses machine learning to infer when it is appropriate to transition to sleep.

To understand how the *kibbutz* compares to these works, we have implemented an oracle that knows the traffic workload and decides after each packet sent whether to transition to sleep or not. The oracle goes to sleep only if the next packet is due after a threshold number of seconds. The threshold takes into account the time needed for the two state transitions, each of which takes 1-2s in our measurements; we set it to 4 or more seconds.

We ran all the simulations shown in Figures 4 with the oracle algorithm and varying thresholds. We found that the algorithm has no impact whatsoever on the streaming app, and the performance is the same as on a standard mobile device. This is because streaming packets have low inter-arrival times and there is no time to sleep. In comparison, a three-device *kibbutz* cuts energy consumption to a third.

The web traffic results are more interesting. With a 4s threshold, the Oracle reduces the time spent in the high energy state from 72% to 17%, but the energy reduction comes at a cost: the average

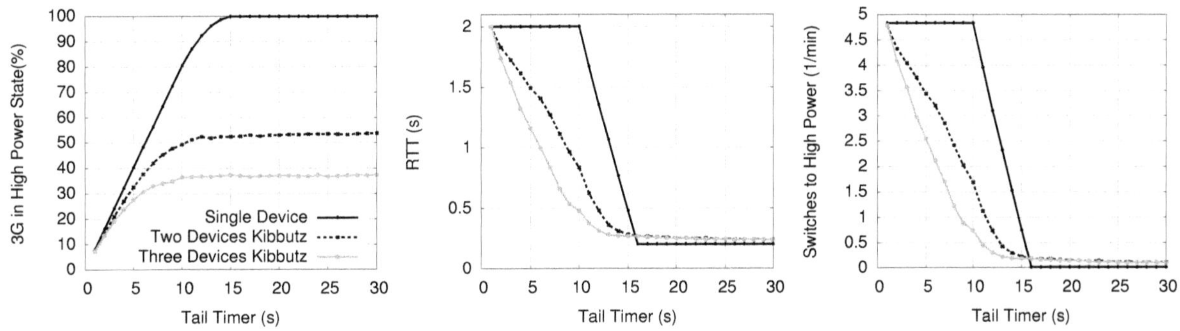

Figure 5: The Tail Timer trades device power fewer state-promotions (signaling) and RTT (web-like traffic).

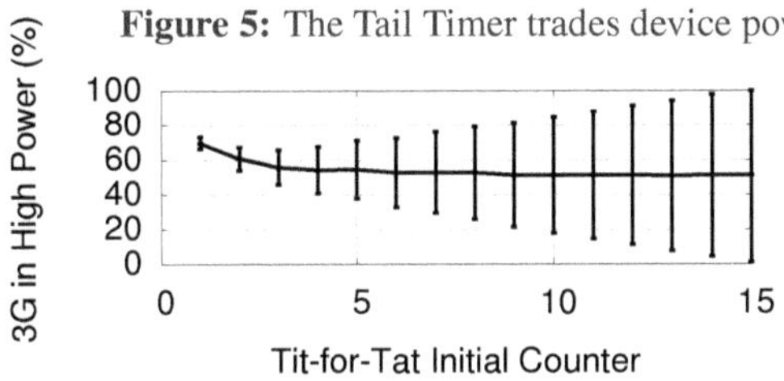

Figure 6: Power consumption distribution for a 5 minute streaming session.

RTT increases from 1.46s to 1.9s as the number of state transitions increases by a third. This should be avoided as it affects the scalability of 3G networks [13, 23]. In fact, carriers are afraid to enable fast-dormancy because of increased signaling traffic[23].

To reduce the effects of signaling, we increase the Oracle algorithm's switching threshold to be the same as the tail timer (10s): this guarantees that the number of state transitions (and the RTT) will not increase. In this case, the RTT and signaling costs stay the same, while the time spent in DCH drops from 72% to 36%. In comparison, a three-device *kibbutz* has similar energy behavior (35% in DCH) but it reduces the RTT to 0.4s and the signaling costs by 50%.

Tail reduction has the biggest positive effect on background apps, decreasing the time spent in high power state from 33% to around 8%. For such apps the *kibbutz* gains are modest: a three-mobile *kibbutz* reducing energy to 22%.

The oracle algorithm provides an upper bound for tail-reduction algorithms, and the actual benefits will be smaller in practice. Nevertheless, this comparative analysis shows that the *kibbutz* excels for streaming like applications, while tail-reduction works really well for background applications—hence the two techniques could complement each other nicely. For web-style traffic, the energy gains are similar, but the *kibbutz* also reduces the RTT and signaling costs.

Fairness. All the experiments shown so far were run for a long period (2 hours); this ensured that all the performance measurements were nearly identical across all devices.

The tit-for-tat counter governs how many times a device will share its connection without the neighbor sharing back. To understand the effect of this parameter we ran the streaming application for a short period of time (5 mins) with different values of the counter. The results in Fig. 6 show that using small values of the counter leads to increased energy consumption because of frequent switching between power states and the tail timer. Higher values of the counter are more efficient, but lead to unfairness: a single device may bear the whole cost of cellular connectivity for high values. Values above five give diminishing returns in average consumption, but increase unfairness. This is the value we used in all our other experiments.

Interactions Between Different Application Classes. We now look at experiments involving different classes of applications, with results given below. A row shows an application class running in a *kibbutz* of two devices with another application class (the column), or in a *kibbutz* of three devices. Each cell lists the amount of time the 3G interface stays up; the baseline is also given on each row. For instance, the Background power consumption drops from 30% to 21% when running in a *kibbutz* with a Web application.

The numbers show that the application mix does influence the results but not dramatically. Also, the savings are shared between the different apps. As expected, the Background class of applications improves the least.

App. Class	Back.	Web	Stream.	All
Background (30%)	25%	21%	21%	17%
Web (80%)	68%	49%	48%	41%
Streaming (100%)	78%	58%	54%	50%

5. IMPLEMENTATION

We have implemented the *kibbutz* using Bluetooth and WiFi as local links. First we enabled the devices to seamlessly route traffic for neighbors with pre-existing Android mechanisms: we created BNEP interfaces using `pand(1)` from the BlueZ[3] suite available on Android 4.1.2 and we employed normal netfilter mechanisms to route traffic and perform Network Address Translation.

The traffic consolidation scheme and the short-term fairness are implemented in a kernel module. We use netfilter hooks to efficiently handle the traffic on every interface without polling. This way, our module knows when the mobile link is up, when we are using a neighbor's link or when a neighbor is using our own link.

The main part of the service consists in "moving" traffic from one link to another, without changing the application. This is achieved using standard MPTCP mechanisms. Upon system startup we set the cellular link to low priority and disable MPTCP for local links. This ensures MPTCP will try to avoid the 3G link when emitting traffic and will never attempt to create flows on Bluetooth links by itself – by default MPTCP creates flows on all interfaces. The module exposes an interface permitting userspace program to declare the local links as "usable". Once a local link (Bluetooth or WiFi) is declared usable MPTCP will consider it. Since the cellular link has low priority, any local links will win the flow selection process, i.e. traffic will move from the mobile link to the local links. Implementing the bandwidth maximizing / RTT minimizing profile is easily achieved by removing priorities and using the default scheduling algorithm of MPTCP. For the energy saving profile, we implemented the bandwidth watchdog by changing the MPTCP scheduling algorithm.

We implemented the upper part of the *kibbutz* as a userspace driver that uses the kernel module and controls the entire process.

[3]http://www.bluez.org/

This driver monitors the local link and the kernel module for advertisements. The kernel module sends up notifications like 'when did A last use our link', 'when did we last use A's link', allowing the enforcement of short-term fairness via a tit-for-tat mechanism, as discussed in §3.

6. EXPERIMENTAL EVALUATION

We have deployed the mobile *kibbutz* on two Galaxy Nexus mobile devices running Android 4.1.2 (Jelly Bean) and tested it with synthetic traffic as well as representative applications. We measure power using the Monsoon power monitor. We ran most experiments using the only cellular operator in our area that allowed MPTCP (it did not remove MPTCP options from packets). This operator offered 3G (HSDPA) at advertised speeds up to 7.2Mbps.

To enable the *kibbutz*, we deployed a Linux box running MPTCP that we used in all experiments. The setup is shown in Fig. 7. Ideally, this box would act like a SOCKS proxy terminating MPTCP connections and opening TCP connections to the real server (Fig. 7.a). For this to work we would need proxy support from Android; unfortunately this is only available over WiFi connections, not 3G ones – this seems to be a policy option rather than a technical one. A work-around is to open an MPTCP-based tunnel to the proxy, and tunnel all device traffic (Fig. 7.b). In this case, the MPTCP-based tunnel is encrypted. This setup works fine, however tunneling TCP connections over (MP)TCP can lead to bad performance interactions that could bias our experiments. That is why we used the third setup (Fig. 7.c) for most of our experiments: here our box also serves content, running stock HTTP and streaming servers.

In most of our experiments we used 3G with Bluetooth as the local link. We prefer Bluetooth as it has has low, symmetric energy consumption across connected devices; RTT is 7ms, less than 9% of the minimum RTT obtained for our 3G MNO. We also tested the *kibbutz* with WiFi connectivity, having one device act as an access point and the other as client. This setup offers better performance at the cost of increased energy consumption; it was used for our download tests. Finally, we tested over LTE cellular link with both Bluetooth and WiFi as local links to understand how applicable the *kibbutz* is.

Below we describe our practical findings. In brief, they confirm our simulation results showing that the *kibbutz* significantly reduces the power costs associated to using the cellular links and their RTTs. We also find that the network represents a large fraction of device consumption: using the mobile *kibbutz* with 3G and Bluetooth reduces total phone energy consumption by 25% for radio and web browsing.

6.1 Basic Functionality

To test the basic operation of the *kibbutz*, we ran experiments where each device runs a simple client that opens a long-running TCP connection and then sends a timestamp twice per second to the server which just echoes it back. The clients measure the app-level RTT and print it.

In Figure 8, the upper curve shows the power consumed by Device1 as it switches its 3G card on and off. The segments at the bottom correspond to the packets received at the server from Device1 or Device2. The upper segment sequence corresponds exactly with the power consumption recorded by the power-meter, confirming the fair behavior of the *kibbutz*. If a device uses only its link, it needs 754mW on average, whereas it only needs 169mW if it uses its neighbor - the upper and lower levels of the power measurement. The average power consumption of Device1 is 480mW. This is a saving of 37% over its maximum consumption if it used only its own 3G connection.

We also tested power consumption with periodic bidirectional traffic of 24Kbps (e.g. VOIP) for all combinations of hardware of interest for the *kibbutz*. In the following table we summarize power measurements in mW for these link combinations: 3G and 4G for the vertical link, and BT or WiFi for the horizontal link. The *kibbutz* server uses its vertical link to route packets from the *kibbutz* client obtained on the horizontal link. In all WiFi experiments we use WPA2, therefore including the cost of traffic encryption (BT is encrypted by default).

Link type vertical + horizontal	*kibbutz* Router [mW]	*kibbutz* Consumer [mW]	Stand alone [mW]	Power Savings
LTE + BT	1095	220	1020	35.5%
LTE + WiFi	1316 / 1080	170 / 320	1020	27.1% / 31.4%
3G + BT	740	191	675	31.0%
3G + WiFi	866 / 630	113 / 323	680	28.0% / 29.9%

When using WiFi as a local link, the energy consumption is higher for the mobile acting as access point. That is why we give two numbers, one when the mobile is also the access point, and one when it only is a WiFi client. As expected, LTE has higher power consumption, and provides ample savings opportunities. Using BT as a local link for 3G is the best choice: using WiFi would not increase throughput by much, and would slightly increase energy consumption. For LTE, using WiFi makes sense as it allows greater speeds. Unless stated otherwise, the experiments in this paper are run over 3G and Bluetooth.

The *kibbutz* reduces energy consumption for all possible combinations of cellular and local links, and the savings for our hardware/MNO setups are of 27% - 35%. These relative gains are for the "best case" scenario with synthetic traffic, that is not consumed by an actual application. Next we show significant benefits can be had even when real apps are running.

6.2 Improving Popular Applications

We four typical applications that depend on network connectivity: audio streaming (e.g. radio, VOIP), video streaming, web browsing and app downloads. While not exhaustive, we believe these capture the main "active" traffic patterns on mobile devices. We consciously focus on active apps, leaving out background apps such as email that generate traffic rarely. We do not expect worthwhile improvements for such apps, especially when we consider the overheads for running the *kibbutz* (measured in Sec. 6.4).

Streaming apps. We installed Apache on our server and VLC player on the mobile phones. For audio streaming we served MP3 files encoded at 48Kbps. The Galaxy Nexus phones consumed 978mW when streaming radio alone, with the screen off. Most of this cost is due to the 3G link. When running a two-device *kibbutz* with both streaming the same file, instantaneous power consumption was bimodal: the device routing data consumed 1047mW (slightly more than standalone), while the other device consumed only 403mW. The two devices traded roles periodically.

The average power consumption for a device in the *kibbutz* was 723mW, 25% less than standalone consumption. **A device streaming radio in a *kibbutz* will last 34% longer than one running standalone**. The savings in absolute terms—around 250mW—are a bit less than half the energy consumed by the 3G radio in the high power state (650mW) which is the maximum gain that can be had in this configuration: the *kibbutz* is working as expected.

For video streaming we served a YouTube clip encoded at standard definition (250Kbps). Here standalone energy consumption was 1819mW - this value includes the cost of the screen, as well as of the GPU used for rendering. Consumption was again bimodal in the *kibbutz*: 1890mW for the forwarding device, and 1205mW

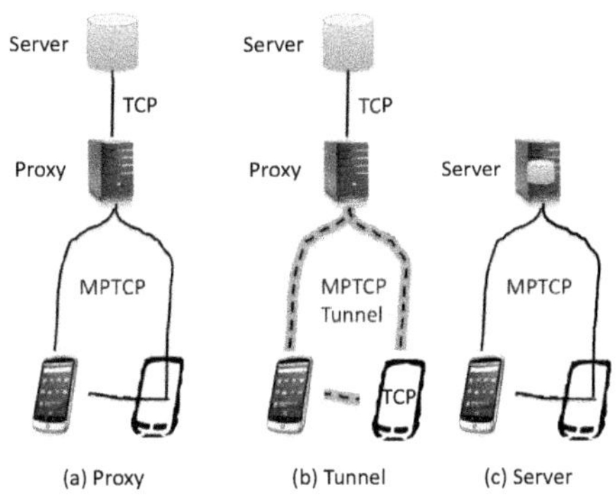

Figure 7: Experiment setup

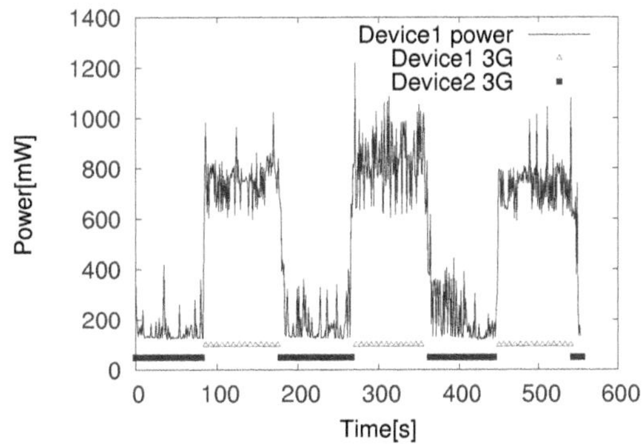

Figure 8: Simple TCP ping on two devices in a kibbutz.

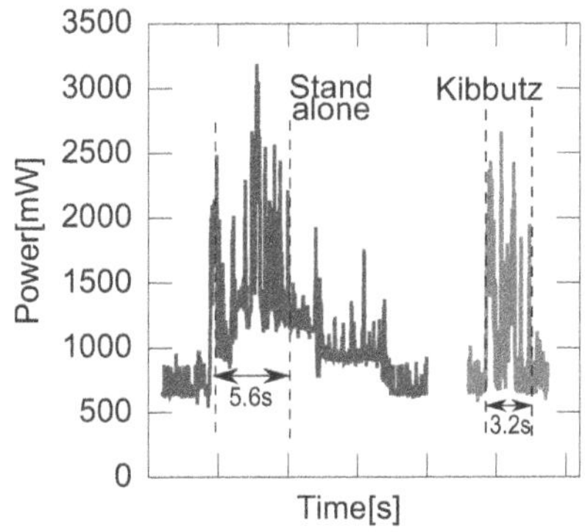

Figure 9: Loading a Google search results page

for the other. Average consumption for devices in the *kibbutz* was 1547mW—15% less than standalone. **A device streaming video in a *kibbutz* will last 18% longer than one streaming on its own.**

Web Browsing. Popular web pages today are optimized to the point where their load times are determined by the RTT rather than the bandwidth. That is why Google has been actively promoting a number of TCP optimizations aimed at reducing the number of RTTs required to download a webpage, including a proposal to increase the initial TCP congestion window to 10 packets [24] and to implement a flavor of transactional TCP called TCP Fast Open [25]. On cellular links, the RTT after idle is very large, dominating the load time. Can the *kibbutz* help alleviate this problem?

Measuring web traffic is tricky. We cannot simply replicate webpages on our server because modern sites link many objects, some of which are dynamically generated and on different sites. That is why we ran two types of web browsing experiments: an MPTCP-based tunnel and emulating web-traffic. The tunneled experiment has a few potential pitfalls: it is prone to TCP-over-TCP performance issues, and it uses a "visual" method of measuring the load time. The emulated web traffic experiments avoid both problems: they give precise timings and avoid encapsulation problems, but may not model web traffic as accurately. Both experiments showed good improvements for the *kibbutz*, which gives us confidence the benefits will appear in practice.

In the tunneled setup (shown in Fig. 7.(b) we repeatedly loaded a Google search page using a single device over 3G, or a device in a *kibbutz* using its always-available neighbor's advertisements. In both cases the screen is on and the device's browser renders the page. To measure delay we use the power meter readings, identifying the peaks of consumption that appear during page load. These are shown in Fig. 9. Downloading and displaying the Google search page takes 5.6 seconds on average, and it costs around 15.9 Joules. When using a *kibbutz*, browsing the same page takes 3.2 seconds and costs 3.9 Joules. **The *kibbutz* loads the search page 2.4s quicker**, just a bit more than the state promotion time measured for this provider.

To emulate web traffic, we analyzed *tcpdump* traces obtained by loading typical pages from several mobile optimized web sites including BBC, CNN, Amazon, and Google search. Most sites exhibit the following behavior: after a DNS lookup, a main index file of 20K-50K is started; smaller transfers of 1K-5K of images, ads, or scripts get downloaded progressively as the main index is parsed; about halfway through, another DNS lookup is made, usually to a CDN server, and more small transfers occur. Most newspapers and google searches include another larger transfer of 20K-50K, with some images. We verified for all the sites used that the browser and the server use HTTP 1.1 with persistent connections, therefore one transfer typically brings in several smaller files. We then generated a random mix of transfers mirroring each of the observed patterns interspersed by a random 10-15 seconds period of silence.

In fig. 10(a) we plot the cumulative distribution for the completion times of 50 web-like downloads as described above. Compared to a standalone user, a **user in a *kibbutz* receives a page 1.2s sooner on average, and almost 4s sooner for the 90%.** The bulk of this saving comes from avoiding the ramp up time when a neighbor already has the 3G active. Web browsing via the *kibbutz* also saves power: a standalone user needs on average 435mW to download the page, the user of a 2-*kibbutz* only uses 297mW, 31% less.

App Downloads. How long does it take to download an average mobile application alone or in a *kibbutz*? We downloaded repeatedly the same 6MB file from our server (this is the average size of Android apps [26]), measuring download time and energy consumption. For a standalone device, the download time was 31 ± 8 seconds. The high variance is due to competing traffic in the HSDPA network we are using. The phone draws 1.3Watts during this download, consuming on average a total of 41 Joules.

For the *kibbutz*, one device generates low-rate traffic using our synthetic client. The other device is running in bandwidth optimization mode, using all links it has available. This *kibbutz* uses WiFi as the local link to ensure the best throughput (the bandwidth-hungry device acted as client, and the other acted as Access Point).

HSDPA dynamically assigns all available cell bandwidth to active users, so joining two users connected to the same cellular basestation in a *kibbutz* will not always increase the total bandwidth available to them, yielding similar download times to the standalone test. If the two devices are in different cells or sectors, bandwidth should always increase.

We confirm this hypothesis by using a different operator for our second device - this operator strips MPTCP options, so we tunneled MPTCP traffic over UDP. Downloading the same file in the *kibbutz* takes 21 ± 5 seconds, **decreasing download time by a third on average**. Counter-intuitively, the *kibbutz* also saves power despite using more network interfaces: the total energy consumed to download the file is 31 Joules, 25% less than standalone.

6.3 Robustness

If a mobile device leaves the area of a *kibbutz*, how will it affect other *kibbutz* users? To answer this question we ran an experiment where one user is downloading a large file via its neighbor. While the transfer is taking place, the neighbor suddenly stops forwarding packets. Figure 10(b) shows the progression of the connection sequence number against time, with the disruption happening around time 14s.

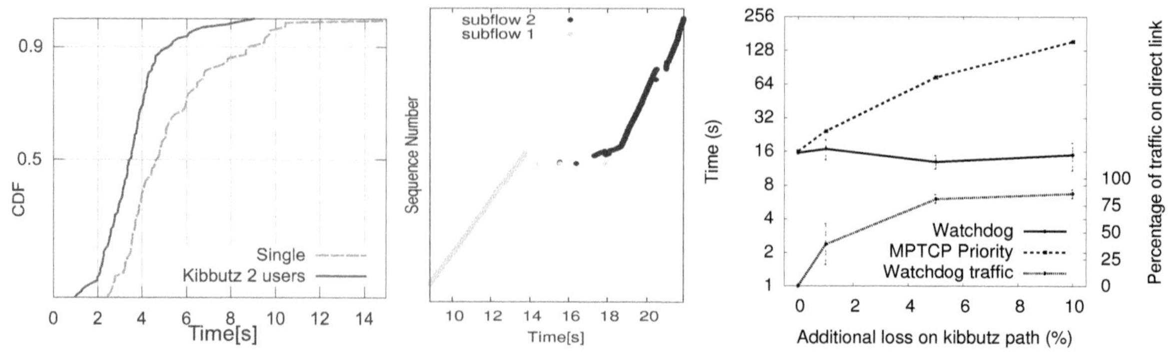

Figure 10: a) Time to load a mobile optimized web page. The *kibbutz* needs 1220ms less at the 50% and 3980ms at 90%; b)The *kibbutz* reacts when a neighbor stops forwarding; c) The watchdog ensures good performance when the *kibbutz* path is congested.

Our watchdog mechanism quickly detects after one timeout that the prioritized path has poor performance, so it starts sending packets via the direct path. After another few seconds—needed for the idle 3G link to become active— traffic resumes via the direct path.

Sudden path blackouts as above will be relatively rare: it is more likely that a path will become worse as the user is moving away from the *kibbutz*, leading to increased packet loss rates. High packet loss rates may appear also when there are too many users are sharing one link at the same time.

To understand how the *kibbutz* fares in such cases, we had one device download a 2MB file via its neighbor which also dropped a fraction of the packets it forwarded. Figure 10(c) shows how the total download time varies as the loss rate varies. Vanilla MPTCP always prefers the path via the neighbor (top curve), which dramatically increases download times when loss rates are high. The watchdog detects performance problems and starts using the direct path, managing to have similar performance regardless of the loss rate. We also show the fraction of bytes sent via the direct path: with no loss all bytes are transported via the neighbor. With higher loss rates, most bytes are sent using the direct link.

These experiments outline the importance of using MPTCP for load balancing across links: single path mobility solutions must commit to a single path, while MPTCP can dynamically choose the best path at any time.

6.4 Kibbutz Overheads

The *kibbutz* brings benefits when there is cellular traffic, but how much does it cost when the phone is idle? We measured how much an idle device running the *kibbutz* software consumes compared to an idle device without the *kibbutz*. We expect higher costs due to Bluetooth networking and receiving *kibbutz* advertisements.

Our Galaxy Nexus phone draws 12mW with screen and all wireless links except 3G off (3G was in the IDLE state). The same phone running the *kibbutz* draws 60mW - the *kibbutz* adds 48mW to the baseline power consumption. We broke down the power usage as follows: starting Bluetooth raises consumption to 28mW, and enabling IP connectivity over Bluetooth (Pan) further raises consumption to 50mW. Finally, receiving *kibbutz* advertisements increases to 60mW.

The *kibbutz* brings most benefits for applications that send traffic at short intervals. Background traffic benefits less from the *kibbutz*: a simple optimization is to run the *kibbutz* when the traffic rate is greater than some minimal threshold. This reduces baseline costs to almost zero, while giving the same benefits for busy applications.

Another question relates to the cost of encryption. It is best if the kibbutz leverages the local NIC's encryption (i.e. WiFi WPA or Bluetooth) in conjunction with AnyFi at no added cost. Without AnyFi (or similar technologies), software encryption is required. We have run measurements to understand how much this costs, and found the overheads to be relatively small. For instance, listening to radio over Bluetooth costs 403mW, and sending traffic via an encrypted tunnel adds a further 100mW. Even with encryption, *kibbutz* devices consume 21% less energy than standalone.

7. RELATED WORK

The importance of cellular links to the mobile experience has long been recognized, and the result is a wealth of research measuring the properties of cellular connectivity [13, 11], and proposing solutions to optimize them ([14, 2, 10, 1] to name only a few). Most of this research has focused on reducing energy consumption of cellular links by adopting one of two high-level approaches. The first approach, discussed in our simulation analysis, includes techniques to reduce the tail timer via fast-dormancy [1, 14, 27].

The second approach uses application knowledge to optimize the 3G link usage; for instance, [28] instruments email clients to batch operations to network and flash memory. Transmissions from different applications are batched by delaying subsets of traffic to reduce the tail energy in TailEnder [2] or to use the cellular link when it is cheapest in Bartendr [10]. Stratus [8] uses a proxy in the wired domain to compress the mobile traffic and bunch it up in time, thus reducing energy consumption. Finally, Catnap [7] also uses a proxy to batch application traffic to allow the WiFi link to sleep. However, these techniques are applicable mostly to background, delay-insensitive traffic: either apps must be changed to take advantage of it, or the system must infer which traffic can be delayed safely which is error prone.

The basic idea of the *kibbutz* is to opportunistically use other devices' links, and this idea is not new, with a raft of work already published including [4, 5, 8, 6, 29, 30, 31]. The mobile *kibbutz* allows energy optimization across many devices, and is complementary to existing works. It offers the biggest benefits for applications that send data (almost) continuously such as audio and video streaming, as well as web browsing. These applications are highly popular on mobiles, yet they are not supported by existing works. Beyond energy, the *kibbutz* significantly lowers the impact of state promotion delays and reduces signaling overhead - to our best knowledge, ours is the first work concurrently reducing power, RTT and signaling cost for cellular links.

PRISM [4] proposes aggregating cellular links of nearby mobiles to increase throughput and network utilization. The focus was on changes to TCP that allow splitting to happen: we rely on Multipath TCP instead which has been carefully designed to work in today's networks [32]. Multipath TCP has been adopted by Apple in IOS7 [33] and MPTCP proxy support is already available from Citrix[34].

Combine [5] proposes aggregating cellular links across groups of mobiles with the purpose of increasing bandwidth and focuses on an accounting mechanism that creates a market to enable bandwidth sharing. CoolTether[6] aims at providing high bandwidth to laptops by leveraging mobile phones in the vicinity, while reducing the energy drain on the mobile phones, but only focuses on HTTP. It uses a gatherer in the mobile domain to "gather" all data for a webpage and then sends it in one go to the mobile device. CoolTether relies on a local mobile device community to increase aggregate download capacity and attempts to even out battery consumption across devices, however raises privacy concerns when the devices report their battery levels to the gatherer.

In contrast, the *kibbutz* targets the case when the mobiles themselves are traffic clients. There is no centralized entity (like the gatherer) in the *kibbutz*: devices take turns in sharing their cellular links, and traffic optimization is completely distributed and seamless. Furthermore, the *kibbutz* is applicable to unchanged applications, and reduces overall mobile energy consumption, not just tethering consumption.

Using radios selectively based on their range vs. energy tradeoff was studied in the context of WiFi/BT in Coolspots [35], also without changing applications. The *kibbutz* extends this to 3G/4G links, and actually uses WiFi and BT as low power horizontal links for peering. Also, the use of MPTCP brings transparency, consolidation, and liquidity for the vertical 3G/4G links used.

Another recent work [36] shows that MPTCP can be tuned to improve energy consumption and performance on devices with multiple radios.

8. CONCLUSIONS

We have described the Mobile *kibbutz*, an opportunistic solution to reduce the energy consumption of cellular links. The *kibbutz* enables one key optimization: **consolidating all traffic** from a set of devices onto as few cellular links as possible. Consolidation increases the energy efficiency of links that are in active use, allowing other links to sleep thus saving energy. Active links will be "always-on", providing low round-trip times and fewer state transitions.

We have implemented the *kibbutz* and tested it on Samsung Galaxy Nexus devices: a two-device *kibbutz* nearly halves the networking related power consumption. In particular, two Galaxy Nexus devices can stream radio 35% longer than if they were running independently. Further, web browsing experiments have shown that the median page load time is 1.2s faster with the *kibbutz*.

Until now, the only knob available to optimize cellular networks has been tweaking the inactivity timers; these allow trading device energy consumption for delay and signaling. The *kibbutz* adds a new optimization dimension that can be exploited: traffic consolidation. We have shown that on its own, consolidation can reduce energy consumption, RTT and MNO signaling **at the same time**. In the future, it would be interesting to see how a network can be optimized by using these knobs simultaneously.

Acknowledgements

This work was partly funded by Trilogy 2, a research project funded by the European Commission in its Seventh Framework program (FP7 317756), and by Mobil4, a research project funded by the Romanian Government (UEFISCDI 11/2012).

9. REFERENCES

[1] Shuo Deng and Hari Balakrishnan. Traffic-aware techniques to reduce 3G/LTE wireless energy consumption. In *Proceedings of the 8th international conference on Emerging networking experiments and technologies*, CoNEXT '12, pages 181–192, New York, NY, USA, 2012. ACM.

[2] Niranjan Balasubramanian, Aruna Balasubramanian, and Arun Venkataramani. Energy consumption in mobile phones: a measurement study and implications for network applications. In *Proc. IMC*. ACM, 2009.

[3] Liam McNamara, Cecilia Mascolo, and Licia Capra. Media sharing based on colocation prediction in urban transport. In *Proceedings of the 14th ACM international conference on Mobile computing and networking*, page 58–69, 2008.

[4] Kyu-Han Kim and Kang G. Shin. PRISM: improving the performance of inverse-multiplexed TCP in wireless networks. 6(12):1297–1312, 2007.

[5] Ganesh Ananthanarayanan, Venkata N. Padmanabhan, Lenin Ravindranath, and Chandramohan A. Thekkath. Combine: leveraging the power of wireless peers through collaborative downloading. In *Proceedings of the 5th international conference on Mobile systems, applications and services*, page 286–298, 2007.

[6] Ashish Sharma, Vishnu Navda, Ramachandran Ramjee, Venkata N. Padmanabhan, and Elizabeth M. Belding. Cool-tether: energy efficient on-the-fly wifi hot-spots using mobile phones. In *Proceedings of the 5th international conference on Emerging networking experiments and technologies*, page 109–120, 2009.

[7] Fahad R. Dogar, Peter Steenkiste, and Konstantina Papagiannaki. Catnap: exploiting high bandwidth wireless interfaces to save energy for mobile devices. In *Proceedings of the 8th international conference on Mobile systems, applications, and services*, page 107–122, 2010.

[8] Bhavish Aggarwal, Pushkar Chitnis, Amit Dey, Kamal Jain, Vishnu Navda, Venkata N. Padmanabhan, Ramachandran Ramjee, Aaron Schulman, and Neil Spring. Stratus: energy-efficient mobile communication using cloud support. 41(4):477–478, 2011.

[9] Rajiv Chakravorty, Sulabh Agarwal, Suman Banerjee, and Ian Pratt. A mobile bazaar for wide-area wireless services. *Wirel. Netw.*, 13(6):757–777, December 2007.

[10] Aaron Schulman, Vishnu Navda, Ramachandran Ramjee, Neil Spring, Pralhad Deshpande, Calvin Grunewald, Kamal Jain, and Venkata N. Padmanabhan. Bartendr: a practical approach to energy-aware cellular data scheduling. In *Proc. Mobicom*. ACM, 2010.

[11] Junxian Huang, Feng Qian, Alexandre Gerber, Z. Morley Mao, Subhabrata Sen, and Oliver Spatscheck. A close examination of performance and power characteristics of 4g lte networks. In *Proceedings of the 10th international conference on Mobile systems, applications, and services*, MobiSys '12, pages 225–238, New York, NY, USA, 2012. ACM.

[12] Andres Garcia-Saavedra, Pablo Serrano, Albert Banchs, and Giuseppe Bianchi. Energy consumption anatomy of 802.11 devices and its implication on modeling and design. In *Proceedings of the 8th international conference on Emerging networking experiments and technologies*, CoNEXT '12, pages 169–180, New York, NY, USA, 2012. ACM.

[13] Feng Qian, Zhaoguang Wang, Alexandre Gerber, Zhuoqing Morley Mao, Subhabrata Sen, and Oliver Spatscheck. Characterizing radio resource allocation for 3G networks. In *Proceedings of the 10th ACM SIGCOMM conference on Internet measurement*, IMC '10, pages 137–150, New York, NY, USA, 2010. ACM.

[14] Feng Qian, Zhaoguang Wang, Alexandre Gerber, Z. Morley Mao, Subhabrata Sen, and Oliver Spatscheck. Top: Tail optimization protocol for cellular radio resource allocation. In *Proceedings of the The 18th IEEE International Conference on Network Protocols*, ICNP '10, pages 285–294, Washington, DC, USA, 2010. IEEE Computer Society.

[15] Qualcomm. LTE Direct: Operator enabled proximity services. `http://www.qualcomm.com/solutions/wireless-networks/technologies/lte/lte-direct`, December 2013.

[16] Aaron Gember, Ashok Anand, and Aditya Akella. A comparative study of handheld and non-handheld traffic in campus wi-fi networks. In *Proceedings of the 12th international conference on Passive and active measurement*, PAM'11, pages 173–183, Berlin, Heidelberg, 2011. Springer-Verlag.

[17] A. Ford, C. Raiciu, M. Handley, and O. Bonaventure. TCP Extensions for Multipath Operation with Multiple Addresses. Rfc6824, IETF, 2013.

[18] Damon Wischik, Costin Raiciu, Adam Greenhalgh, and Mark Handley. Design, implementation and evaluation of congestion control for multipath tcp. In *Proceedings of the 8th USENIX conference on Networked systems design and implementation*, NSDI'11, pages 8–8, Berkeley, CA, USA, 2011. USENIX Association.

[19] Costin Raiciu, Dragoș Niculescu, Marcelo Bagnulo, and Mark James Handley. Opportunistic mobility with multipath tcp. In *Proceedings of the sixth international workshop on MobiArch*, MobiArch '11, pages 7–12, New York, NY, USA, 2011. ACM.

[20] Architecture for mobile data offload over Wi-Fi access networks. *CISCO white paper*, 2012.

[21] AnyFi networks AB. `http://www.anyfi.net`. Accessed: 2013-11-15.

[22] 3GPP. UE "Fast Dormancy" behavior. Discussion and decision notes R2-075251, 2007.

[23] 3GPP. System impact of poor proprietary fast dormancy. Discussion and decision notes RP-090941, 2009.

[24] J. Chu, N. Dukkipati, Y. Cheng, and M. Mathis. Increasing TCP's Initial Window. Internet Draft: draft-ietf-tcpm-initcwnd-08, Work In Progress, 2013.

[25] Y. Cheng, J. Chu, S. Radhakrishnan, and A. Jain. TCP Fast Open. Internet Draft: draft-ietf-tcpm-fastopen-03, Work In Progress, 2013.

[26] ABIResearch. Average size of mobile games for iOS increased by a whopping 42% between march and september. *http://www.webcitation.org/6F2Ifwv44*, 2012.

[27] Pavan K Athivarapu, Ranjita Bhagwan, Saikat Guha, Vishnu Navda, Ramachandran Ramjee, Dushyant Arora, Venkat N Padmanabhan, and George Varghese. Radiojockey: mining program execution to optimize cellular radio usage. In *MobiCOM*, pages 101–112. ACM, 2012.

[28] Fengyuan Xu, Yunxin Liu, Thomas Moscibroda, Ranveer Chandra, Long Jin, Yongguang Zhang, and Qun Li. Optimizing background email sync on smartphones. 2013.

[29] Pan Hui, Richard Mortier, Kuang Xu, Jon Crowcroft, and Victor O. K. Li. Sharing airtime with shair avoids wasting time and money. In *Proceedings of the 10th workshop on Mobile Computing Systems and Applications*, HotMobile '09, pages 6:1–6:6, New York, NY, USA, 2009. ACM.

[30] Narseo Vallina-Rodriguez and Jon Crowcroft. Erdos: achieving energy savings in mobile os. In *Proceedings of the sixth international workshop on MobiArch*, MobiArch '11, pages 37–42, New York, NY, USA, 2011. ACM.

[31] Narseo Vallina-Rodriguez, Vijay Erramilli, Yan Grunenberger, Laszlo Gyarmati, Nikolaos Laoutaris, Rade Stanojevic, and Konstantina Papagiannaki. When David helps Goliath: the case for 3G onloading. In *Proceedings of the 11th ACM Workshop on Hot Topics in Networks*, HotNets-XI, pages 85–90, New York, NY, USA, 2012. ACM.

[32] A. Ford, C. Raiciu, M. Handley, S. Barre, and J. Iyengar. Architectural Guidelines for Multipath TCP Development. Rfc6182, IETF, 2011.

[33] Iljitsch van Beijnum. Multipath TCP lets Siri seamlessly switch between Wi-Fi and 3G/LTE. `http://arstechnica.com/apple/2013/09/multipath-tcp-lets-siri-seamlessly-switch-between-wi-fi-and-3glte/`, September 2013.

[34] Citrix. Maximize mobile user experience with NetScaler Multipath TCP. `http://blogs.citrix.com/2013/05/28/maximize-mobile-user-experience-with-netscaler-multipath-tcp/`, May 2013.

[35] Trevor Pering, Yuvraj Agarwal, Rajesh Gupta, and Roy Want. Coolspots: reducing the power consumption of wireless mobile devices with multiple radio interfaces. In *Proceedings of the 4th international conference on Mobile systems, applications and services*, pages 220–232. ACM, 2006.

[36] Yeon-sup Lim, Yung-Chih Chen, Erich M Nahum, Don Towsley, and Richard J Gibbens. How green is multipath tcp for mobile devices? In *Proceedings of the 4th workshop on All things cellular: operations, applications, & challenges*, pages 3–8. ACM, 2014.

Managing Redundant Content in Bandwidth Constrained Wireless Networks

Tuan Dao
University of California, Riverside
tdao006@cs.ucr.edu

Amit K. Roy-Chowdhury
University of California, Riverside
amitrc@ee.ucr.edu

Harsha V. Madhyastha
University of California, Riverside
harsha@cs.ucr.edu

Srikanth V. Krishnamurthy
University of California, Riverside
krish@cs.ucr.edu

Tom La Porta
The Penn State University
tlp@cse.psu.edu

ABSTRACT

Images/videos are often uploaded in situations like disasters. This can tax the network in terms of increased load and thereby upload latency, and this can be critical for response activities. In such scenarios, prior work has shown that there is significant redundancy in the content (e.g., similar photos taken by users) transferred. By intelligently suppressing/deferring transfers of redundant content, the load can be significantly reduced, thereby facilitating the timely delivery of unique, possibly critical information. A key challenge here however, is detecting 'what content is similar,' given that the content is generated by uncoordinated user devices. Towards addressing this challenge, we propose a framework, wherein a service to which the content is to be uploaded first solicits metadata (e.g, image features) from any device uploading content. By intelligently comparing this metadata with that associated with previously uploaded content, the service effectively identifies (and thus enables the suppression of) redundant content. Our evaluations on a testbed of 20 Android smartphones and via ns3 simulations show that we can identify similar content with a 70% true positive rate and a 1% false positive rate. The resulting reduction in redundant content transfers translates to a latency reduction of 44 % for unique content.

Categories and Subject Descriptors

C.2.1 [**Network Architecture and Design**]: Wireless communication; Distributed networks

Keywords

Challenged Networks; Image Similarity; Redundant Content Reduction

CoNEXT'14, December 2–5, 2014, Sydney, Australia.

http://dx.doi.org/10.1145/2674005.2674988.

1 Introduction

A recent report estimates that there were around 350 million photos uploaded to Facebook and more than 50 million photos uploaded to Instagram on a daily basis in 2013 [1]. While new technologies attempt to increase wireless capacity (e.g., MIMO), users still find that their image/video uploads stall often when using the cellular infrastructure [2]. Moreover, the demand for wireless capacity is likely to be exacerbated when unforeseen events such as natural disasters occur. In such scenarios, the network further gets overwhelmed due to a combination of the physical destruction of the underlying infrastructure (which severely impacts both network capacity and coverage) [3][4] and users generating more content than usual [5]. For example, there was a sudden increase in the number of images related to the hurricane Sandy that were uploaded to Flickr during the hour when the hurricane made landfall in New Jersey [6]. Even disaster rescue teams may upload images/videos to a control center, to allow the center to appropriately distribute resources/help. The higher traffic demands combined with the strapped wireless infrastructure can significantly hinder information delivery in such scenarios [7].

The large volume of images/videos that users attempt to transfer during such events is likely to have significant redundancies in information (photos of the same event taken by different users). For example, Weinsberg *et al.* [7] study the images taken by people in the San Diego fire disaster in 2007 and the Haiti earthquake disaster in 2010. They found that 53% of the images in the San Diego set and 22% of the images in the Haiti set were similar to each other (and in essence contained redundant content). Suppressing transfers of such redundant content can ease the load on the network, and allow unique[1] information (possibly critical) to be transferred with low latency. Subsequently, the redundant content can be lazily uploaded when the network conditions are more benign. Content suppression and lazy uploading can also benefit users in more generic settings (e.g., a flash crowd scenario during a sporting event); users can save on their cellular data plans, as well as the energy on their smartphones. These are likely to be taxed when the available bandwidth is low.

Arguably, the biggest challenge in suppressing the transfer of redundant content is to determine whether or not content generated by disparate clients are similar (e.g., photos of the same event, cap-

[1] In the context of this paper, unique information refers to content in dissimilar images, which contain objects or surroundings that are not covered in other images.

tured almost at the same time). This is inherently hard since the service to which clients are uploading images (e.g, Flickr or a server at a disaster control center) must make this determination *before* a client uploads the image content. Even if any one among a set of similar photos has been previously uploaded, the service has to determine if a *second* photo [2] that is being considered for upload is similar to the one that has already been transferred; if the transfer of the first photo is underway, the process is even harder.

The computer vision community has studied the problem of identifying similar images largely in the setting where the two images being compared are at the same client/server. However, requiring clients to upload images before the service can check for similarity with previously uploaded images nullifies the utility of our framework. Therefore, to suppress the uploads of redundant image content, we leverage the *metadata* used by the computer vision techniques that detect image similarity. Specifically, we have the client first extract metadata from the image it wishes to upload, and upload this metadata to the service. The client then uploads the image content only if the service is unable find any similar images using the uploaded metadata.

This approach however presents a fundamental trade-off. On the one hand, the more fine-grained the metadata extracted by the client from its image, the better the service's ability to correctly identify whether similar images have been previously uploaded. It is important to ensure not only a low false positive rate so that clients do not miss uploading critical images but also a high true positive rate to reduce as much of the redundant content as possible. On the other hand, it is vital that the metadata extraction at the client, the metadata exchange between the client and the service, and the metadata-based lookup by the service all be lightweight. If not, high processing overheads at the client-side or server-side, or large delays incurred in transferring the metadata over the network, can render moot our goal of reducing image upload times by suppressing the uploads of redundant content; the same time can instead be spent to simply upload the image.

To address this trade-off between minimizing the metadata-related overhead and maximizing the accuracy of suppressing redundant content, we break up the photo uploading process into multiple phases. Our goal here is that, when a client is attempting to upload a photo, if no similar image was previously uploaded to the service, we seek to determine this with the least amount of metadata exchange, so that the upload of the image's content can begin at the earliest. For this, the first phase involves the exchange of a very small amount of coarse level metadata between the client trying to upload the photo and the service, which allows us to determine if a more careful comparison is even necessary; if there are no images that match the candidate image to be uploaded even at this level, the client can simply proceed with the upload.

If matches are found in the first phase, we employ a series of vision algorithms and exchange fine-grained metadata to increase the fidelity of the comparison. We first seek to minimize the amount of metadata/processing needed (we combine [8] and [9]). However, this does not adequately ensure that false positives are rare. Hence, we slightly increase the overhead by adding additional metadata using the approach in [10]. While this allows us to bring down the false positive rate, we are still unable to reach a reasonably high true positive rate. Hence, we incorporate a third phase which involves human feedback based on thumbnails (again, we increase the metadata by a small amount) returned from the service; this drives up the true positive rate without introducing additional false positives. In combination, these three phases are able to significantly reduce the amount of redundancy in transferred content and thereby the congestion, while ensuring very low false positive rates and low processing overheads at the client and the server.

Our contributions: In this paper, we propose a framework for identifying and suppressing the transfer of redundant image content in bandwidth constrained wireless networks. A key component of our framework is the aforementioned three-phase approach for metadata exchange between the generators of content (smartphones) and the service which receives the images. The framework allows a client to estimate if the service is already in possession of content that is similar to that in an image being considered for upload. If the estimation suggests that this is the case, the image upload is suppressed and deferred for a lazy transfer at a later time when conditions are more benign; else the transfer proceeds.

We implement and evaluate our approach on a 20-node Android smartphone testbed in various conditions with the Kentucky [11], and an US cities image data set that we put together. We find that our multi-stage approach for uploading images correctly identifies the presence of similar images on the service with $\approx$70% accuracy, while ensuring a low false positive rate of 1%. More importantly, our framework's suppression of uploads of similar content enables the network to tolerate 60% higher load (for target delay requirements), as compared to a setting without our framework. We obtain similar results even at scale, when using ns-3 based simulations. Finally, we also show that the overheads imposed by our framework in terms of bandwidth and energy are very small, therefore making it viable for use.

2 Related Work

In this section, we briefly overview relevant related work.

Improving network performance and reliability during disasters or flash-crowd events: There has been research on the impact of flash-crowd events [12, 13, 14] and natural disasters [3, 4] on network performance and connectivity. Proposed solutions allow the network to adapt and survive in such scenarios [15, 16, 17]. From among these, the work that is closest to ours is CARE [7], which is a framework for image redundancy elimination to improve content delivery in challenged, capacity-limited networks. While the premise is similar, our work differs in terms of how image similarity is detected. In CARE, it is assumed that central infrastructure is unavailable and thus, content is transferred in a peer-to-peer fashion. Similarity detection takes place locally at a chosen node, where the images to be compared are first made available. This node transfers unique images when a DTN (delay tolerant network) relay with infrastructure connectivity is available. In our system, we assume that users have access to central infrastructure; only metadata that is extracted from the images is used for similarity detection. Our goal is to preemptively suppress the uploading of similar images on the bandwidth constrained wireless network. We acknowledge that the authors of CARE were the first to suggest the use of similarity detection in images to reduce content; we believe that our proposed work is complementary to CARE, both in terms of the setting considered and the actual approach itself.

Data deduplication in network services: Orthogonal to our work, data deduplication has been used to reduce storage capacity [18] and bandwidth [19, 20] requirements in systems which involve storing and moving large amounts of data. However, these efforts do not consider content semantics as we do here.

Image similarity detection: Our work leverages state-of-the-art approaches in computer vision for image feature extraction and object matching. Over the last decade, many algorithms have been proposed for robust extraction of global [9, 21] and local key-point [8, 22] features. The bag-of-words (BoW) approach, which had been

[2]We use the terms image and photo interchangeably.

originally used in text document classification, was applied in computer vision for image classification and matching by building a visual codebook from image local key-points [23]. The min-hash technique was proposed by Chum *et al.* [9, 24] to effectively estimate similarity between images represented in the BoW format. Recent work has been focusing on geometry verification to improve similarity detection accuracy [10, 25]. In section 3, we describe in detail how we effectively combine these techniques to create a lightweight, yet accurate image similarity detection system.

3 Efficient, lightweight detection of redundancies in images

Our goal is to determine if there are similarities between images that are to be uploaded by a plurality of spatially disparate uncoordinated clients. We seek to do so with a very low overhead while still sustaining a high accuracy for detecting similar images. We envision that these images are to be transferred over a wireless network to a central server. The server has access to all the images that were previously uploaded to it.

3.1 Our framework in brief

Figure 1 presents an overview of our framework, which can be adopted by any service to which users uploads photos, such as Flickr or Facebook, or even a server at a disaster response control center. When a new image is considered for upload to the server, a small amount of metadata is first extracted from the image and transmitted to the server. The server compares this metadata with that from images that were previously uploaded, and determines if a similar photo is already available. If this determination yields a positive outcome, the photo upload is suppressed for the time being; else the device seeking to upload the image proceeds to do so.

This seemingly simple high-level approach has three phases, with the aim of reducing the overhead associated with identifying similar images. The first two phases form a hierarchical, automated approach for image similarity detection. First, when a client seeks to upload an image, it extracts certain coarse-grained global features and sends these to the server. If the server finds that there is (are) a previously uploaded image(s) with similar features, it invokes the second phase. In this phase, the client intelligently combines state of the art vision algorithms to extract fine-grained local features from the image. A compact representation of these features is then sent to the server. The server performs a further comparison of these features with those in its pre-existing set of images. If there is a further match, it is deemed that similar content exists, and the upload of the candidate image is suppressed.

For all images that pass the first check but fail the second check, the server sends back thumbnails of a small set of the closest matching images in its pre-existing set to the client. In fact, in the scenarios of interest, a small set of pre-existing images may turn out be the closest matching ones to multiple images (being uploaded by disparate users) that are being considered for transfer; in such cases, the server can simply broadcast these thumbnails. If a client device is in the possession of a human user (e.g., a smartphone), the user can look at the thumbnail and then make a final decision on whether or not to continue with the image upload.

Table 1 provides a summary of the techniques used in our framework. In the subsequent subsections, we elaborate on how these techniques are combined to efficiently detect image similarity.

Scope of our work: While our approach is applicable to different forms of rich content, we limit ourselves to image/photo uploads/transfers in this work. Extension of the work to video is possible [26] but will be considered in the future. Further, our focus is the identification/suppression of redundant content in this work. In scenarios such as disasters, it is conceivable that some images are more important than others (e.g., a human in need of rescue versus a damaged uninhabited vehicle). Thus, one could conceivably target prioritizing image uploads based on content; however, we defer studies of such possibilities to the future.

Technique	Usage	Goal	Section
OCS color histogram	In Phase 1: Compare Euclidean distance between color histograms to determine server has candidate similar images	Lightweight, but coarse-grained similarity detection	3.2
ORB local key-points	In Phase 2: Capture distinctive patches on an image; these can be matched to find similar images	Facilitate highly accurate similarity detection; uses image local features	3.3.1
BoW representation	In Phase 2: Compute the Bag of Visual Words (BoW) representation of an image by mapping its key-points into pre-computed clusters	Provide the inputs for computing the min-hash values	3.3.2
Image min-hash values	In Phase 2: Convert a BoW representation into a fixed number of hash values	Reduce communication and processing overhead	3.3.3
Geometry visual phrases	In Phase 2: Add geometry information to reduce false visual word matches	Reduce false positive rate	3.3.4
Thumbnail feedback	In Phase 3: Feedback image thumbnails	Use user input to increase true positive rates	3.4

Table 1: Summary of techniques combined to form our framework

In this work, we assume that if there is no prior image that is similar to the one that is considered for transfer, the image is transferred; else it is suppressed. We do not take into account things like the quality of the image (e.g., resolution), or the coverage (e.g., close up versus wide angle) as criteria for the above determination. Accounting for these factors is a harder challenge; the service will need to delay image transfers, compare all metadata from images that are being considered for uploaded and explicitly pull images from a chosen client based on some criteria (e.g., HD quality image with a close up of a house). Furthermore, the vision algorithms that we use here will not provide such assessments.

Our work primarily targets public services that require the transfer of images (e.g. photos transferred during a disaster to facilitate rescue operations). Our approach can be potentially leveraged in flash crowd scenarios where bandwidth is scarce; for example, an image sharing service can use our approach to provide mobile users an *option* to temporarily point to a similar version of an image (that they seek to upload), which is already available on the server side. A seamless upload and replacement with the user's own image could be done lazily when the network is under less duress; from the user's perspective, such an approach would save both on the data usage (if WiFi was used instead of 4G later) and energy costs that could be heavy due to retransmissions when the bandwidth is poor.

Finally, we do not leverage device features (e.g., GPS location, geotags, camera orientation) to assess if two images could be similar; these features could be useful in reducing the search space at

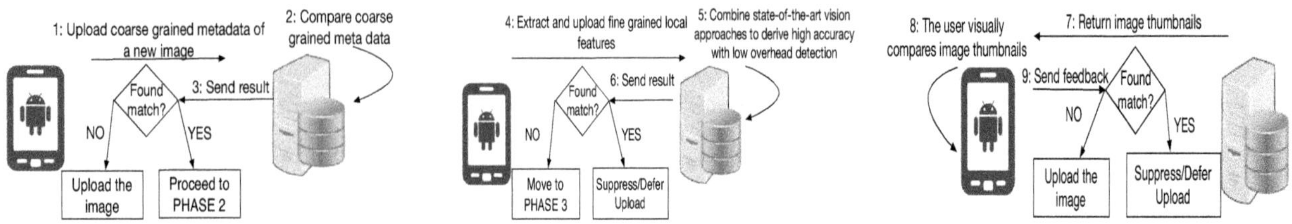

(a) Phase 1: Coarse grained metadata matching (b) Phase 2: Fine grained feature matching (c) Phase 3: Thumbnail feedback

Figure 1: Our framework for determining and suppressing images that contain similar (redundant) information

the server side (e.g., it can compare images that are taken by cameras in close proximity only). Leveraging such features is orthogonal to, and can be used in conjunction with our framework.

How do you determine if content in two images is similar?: Whether or not the content in one image is similar to that in another is a subjective matter; different human users may perceive things differently and with respect to different images as well. Moreover, a general user may choose to upload his image regardless of whether or not someone else has uploaded a similar image. We assume that (i) savings in terms of data usage and energy will incentivize users to suppress their image transfers, especially when the network is congested and, (ii) in scenarios such as disaster recovery, smartphones could be used by the relief crew, who will want to suppress redundant content to reduce congestion and thus, aid relief operations.

In this work, we seek to ensure that if it is highly likely that a typical human does not perceive that two images are similar, they are classified as dissimilar. In other words, our framework must minimize false positives when classifying images as similar. Keeping this primary goal of a very low false positive rate, we seek to eliminate redundancies via such similarity detection to the extent possible, using state-of-the-art computer vision algorithms. We use known data sets (discussed later) to get objective evaluations of our framework; these evaluations show that our framework is extremely effective in decreasing network congestion.

3.2 Phase 1: Use of a coarse-grained global feature

Global features capture the entire content in an image. Examples include the color pattern or the scene pattern in the image. A global feature is represented by a single feature vector. As color is an important image attribute, a histogram of the color distribution in an image is widely used as a global feature for determining if two images are similar.

To construct such a histogram, we use the opponent color space (OCS) [9] to determine image similarity. We use the OCS color space, since it is not very sensitive to illumination (brightness) variations, unlike the RGB space. In brief, there are three components in the OCS space: an intensity component and two opponent colors. The components in the RGB color space can be used to compute the the OCS color components using the following equation.

$$\begin{aligned} I &= (R+G+B)/3 \\ O_1 &= (R+G-2B)/4+0.5 \\ O_2 &= (R-2G+B)/4+0.5 \end{aligned} \tag{1}$$

The intensity component is quantized into 64 bins, while the other two components are quantized into 32 bins. The histogram vector is normalized so as to represent each component with 1 byte; thus, 128 bytes are used overall to represent the histogram. Once these 128 bytes are sent to the server, the server compares the bin values with those of the images that it has in its data set (previously uploaded). If the Euclidean distance of the histogram of any image on the server side and the histogram of the image about to be uploaded is less than a threshold τ_1, the system enters the second phase for similarity detection; otherwise, the client uploads the new image.

3.3 Phase 2: Using fine-grained local features

In the first phase, only the global distribution of colors and intensity were examined. If the server finds matching histograms, in the second phase, finer grained local features are extracted from the image and uploaded as metadata for further comparisons. Contrary to global features, local features are extracted from small patches in the image. When combined together, such local features (called key-points) represent the characteristics of the entire image. Fine-grained local features can be used to detect image similarity with high accuracy. Our approach for using local features consists of the following steps.

3.3.1 Extraction of key-points from an image

As mentioned above, the local features that we compare in order to assess the similarity of images are *key-points*. Key-points are small patches of an image that differ significantly from the surrounding areas (in the image). In computer vision, SIFT (Scale Invariant Feature Transform) is the most widely used algorithm for determining the key-points in images [22]. However, SIFT typically imposes a very high processing complexity and is thus, not a viable solution for resource (battery) limited devices like smart-phones. In our experiments, extracting key-points of a high resolution scenery image (approximately 2 MB of data) with SIFT requires about 30 seconds or even more.

Hence, we choose ORB [8] as our algorithm to extract image key-points, instead of SIFT. Experiments from other research groups have shown that ORB is about two orders of magnitude faster than SIFT while offering comparable results in many situations [27][28]. Each ORB key-point is described by 256 binary digits, whereas with SIFT, each key-point is described by a 128-dimensional vector. The number of key-points depends on the image size, the image resolution and the number of objects in the image. Normally, the amount of data associated with the key-points in an image is far greater than the size of the image itself! Therefore, directly comparing and matching key-points of images is not an option for our framework; this would violate our goal of exchanging a very limited amount of metadata for determining the similarity across disparate images.

3.3.2 Bag of Words (BoW) representation

Instead of directly working with image key-points, we use the bag-of-words (BoW) approach [23] to build what is called a "visual codebook." Any image can be represented as a bag of *visual words*, which is much more compact than simply representing the image via key-points. We describe below how the visual words are determined. For now, we point out that a visual word in the ORB representation is simply described by a 256 bit-vector; each element of the vector is called a dimension. A comparison of the visual words representing two images could be used to determine if the two images are similar. Representing an image by a bag of visual words is performed as follows.

Determining the visual words: First, the ORB key-points of a large set of representative images are extracted. These key-points are all grouped into a pre-defined number of clusters using any good clustering algorithm. In our approach, we use a modified version of the k-means clustering algorithm to partition and group binary vectors [29]. With this algorithm, the input key-points are mapped onto k different clusters based on the Euclidean distance between the key points and the cluster centroids. However, the Euclidean distance is not suitable for binary data such as the ORB key-point descriptors. Therefore, in our framework, we use the Hamming distance instead of the Euclidean distance. The Hamming distance between two binary vectors is simply the number of bits that are different in the two vectors.

The centroid of each cluster is randomly chosen first but is iteratively refined, as key points are added to the cluster; details are available in [30]. With the binary vector representation, in order to determine the centroid of a cluster, we count the number of zeroes and ones in each of the 256 dimensions, for all the data points (key points) that are associated with the cluster. If the number of zeroes is greater than the number of ones, the value of the corresponding dimension for the centroid is a zero, else it is a one. If there is a tie between the number of zeroes and ones, the value of the that dimension for the centroid is randomly assigned as either a "0" or a "1". Each such cluster centroid is then considered to be a visual word in the aforementioned codebook.

When an image is considered for transfer, each ORB key-point in the image is mapped on to the closest cluster centroid in terms of the Hamming distance. With such a mapping, each image is now represented by a histogram of visual words; the number of key-points mapped on to a cluster reflects the *value* of the corresponding visual word in the histogram.

We wish to point out here that the codebook can be pre-loaded onto the clients when our software framework is installed (under benign conditions of connectivity); thus, there is no need to exchange it each time a comparison is to be done across images. In the BoW approach, the number of clusters is generally chosen between tens of thousands to hundreds of thousands.

3.3.3 Reducing detection overhead using min-hashes

Transferring the histogram of visual words constructed as above will incur significant overhead since it would require at least $n * k$ bytes if each component in the histogram can be represented by n bytes and we have k such components. For example, even with n = 2 and k = 50000, this corresponds to 100 KB. To adhere to our goal of having very little overhead of exchanging metadata, we use the min-hash approach proposed by Chum *et al.* [9, 24] in conjunction with the BoW representation.

To define the min-hash function of an image in the BoW representation we do the following. First, if the value associated with a visual word in the histogram is greater than 0, the word is simply considered to be included in a set that is associated with the image. Simply accounting for whether or not a visual word is present in an image (as above) is a weaker representation of the BoW vector, since the number of occurrences of a word is not taken into account. Now that each image is simply represented by a set of words, the similarity of two images with sets of visual words I_1 and I_2 respectively, is defined by the following equation.

$$sim(I_1, I_2) = \frac{|I_1 \cap I_2|}{|I_1 \cup I_2|} \quad (2)$$

The min-hash function approximates the similarity in Equation 2 between two images as follows. Let h be a hash function that maps all members (visual words) of set I (or I') into distinct integer numbers (called labels). The min-hash value of an image I is the minimum from all the hash values associated with the visual words in that image. Formally, for each visual word X, a unique hash value $h(X)$ is assigned. The min-hash value of image I is $H(I) = min\{h(X), X \in I\}$. The client uses M different assignments of labels to the visual words. Specifically, let us say there are N visual words; each is assigned a unique label value $\in \{1, N\}$ at random. This is referred as one assignment or permutation. The client can perform M (different) such permutations and compute the min-hash value in each case. The number of identical min-hash values between two images can be used to assess the similarity level between the two.

permutations	A	B	C	D	E	F	I_1=ABC	I_2=BCD	I_3=AEF
	3	6	2	5	4	1	2	2	1
	1	2	6	3	5	4	1	2	1
	3	2	1	6	4	5	1	1	3
	4	3	5	6	1	2	3	3	1
	Label assignments						Min-hash values		

Table 2: An example of min-hash functions: Four permutations of label assignments are shown.

We use an example from [9] to demonstrate how the min-hash approach works. Consider a vocabulary of six visual words A, B, C, D, E and F and three different images. Each image contains three of these visual words, specifically, I_1 = {A,B,C}, I_2 = {B,C,D} and I_3 = {A,E,F}. For each image, 4 min-hash functions are generated by using different permutations as shown in Table 2. For example, the min-hash of I_1, corresponding to the first permutation (row 1) is the value associated with C and is thus equal to 2. As I_1 and I_2 have 3 identical min-hash values out of 4, their similarity is $\frac{3}{4}$=75%; for the same reason, the similarity between I_1 and I_3 is $\frac{1}{4}$=25%.

Proof sketch: The skeleton of a simple proof for why min-hash approach yields the similarity between two images is as follows. Let $\pi(S)$ be a random permutation on a set S, and let X be the element which has the minimum hash value in $\pi(I_1 \cup I_2)$. Because π is a random permutation, the probability that X is *any* element in the set $I_1 \cup I_2$ is equal for all elements. If $X \in (I_1 \cap I_2)$, then obviously, $H(I_1) = H(I_2) = h(X)$. Otherwise, without loss of generality, assume $X \in I_1 \setminus I_2$; then, $H(I_1) < H(I_2)$. To summarize, two images have the same min-hash value if and only if the element X, which has the minimum hash value, is included in both of them. It is easy to see that, as a consequence, the probability that two images I_1 and I_2 have the same min hash value is equal to their similarity, i.e., $sim(I_1, I_2)$, as defined in Equation 2.

3.3.4 Improving detection accuracy by using geometry visual phrases (GVPs)

In the bag of words representation and the inferred min-hash information, the geometry information of each key-point (for example, the location of a key-point in the image) is lost. To reduce the likelihood of false matches because of the above, we use geometry visual phrases (GVP) in combination with the min-hash values. This reduces the false positive rates significantly.

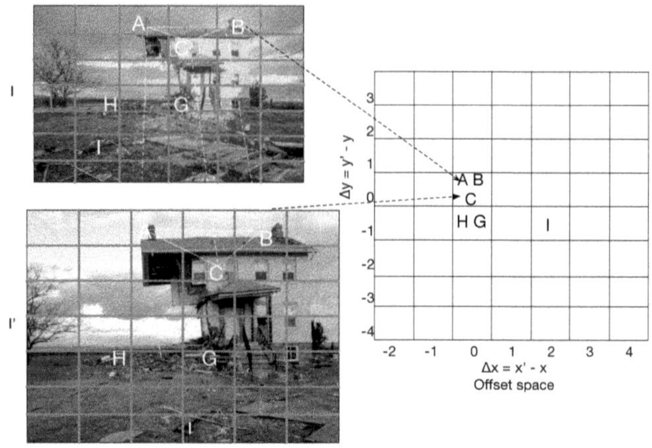

Figure 2: An example of visual phrases between two images

We describe in brief how GVPs are computed and used; more details are in [10]. Towards determining the GVPs between two images, each image is divided into a fixed number of bins (same for both images regardless of the size of the image). In each image, each key-point corresponding to a visual word is then mapped into this offset space and is represented by the co-ordinates $\{x, y\}$, of the bin index to which it belongs; this is referred to as the geometry information. Each pair of equal min-hash functions identify a visual word that occurs in both images. For each of these visual words, the differences in geometry information of the key-points (denoted by Δx and Δy) are computed. If these "difference" values for say L visual words are the same, this implies that these L key-points are likely to be mapped onto the same (corresponding) objects in the two images and thus, are said to form a *co-occurring* GVP of length L. To illustrate, let us consider the example in Figure 2, which shows two different images of a house (found online) that was damaged due to hurricane Sandy. The Δx and Δy values for the key points A, B and C are all $\{0, 0\}$. Thus, these three points together could potentially map onto something common in the two images and this forms a GVP of length 3. Similarly, for the the two key points G and H, the Δx and Δy values are 0 and -1 respectively; thus, these two key points could potentially map on to identical constructs in the two images. This is a GVP of length 2.

Given two images I and I', the similarity score based on visual phrases of length L is defined in equation 3.

$$sim^L(I, I') = \sum_s \frac{\binom{M_s}{L}}{\binom{M}{L}}, \tag{3}$$

In equation 3, M_s is the number of key-points in bin s of the offset space, and thus $\binom{M_s}{L}$ is the number of GVPs of length L in that bin. For example, in bin {0,0}, there are 3 key-points viz., A, B and C; if $L = 2$, the number of length-2 GVPs in the bin is 3, corresponding to AB, AC and BC. Thus, the numerator on the RHS of equation 3 is simply the total number of GVPs of length L between two images. The denominator, $\binom{M}{L}$, corresponds to the maximum possible number of GVPs of length L that can be formed between the two images, given that M min-hash functions are used. Hence, the similarity score between two images is the number of GVPs of length L that are common between them, normalized by the maximum possible number of GVPs length L that can be created by using M min-hash functions.

If the similarity scores between the user's image and a candidate image is greater than a threshold (say τ_2), the images are deemed similar.

3.4 Phase 3: Thumbnail feedback

If at the end of phase 2, if the server finds no matches for the image considered for upload, it invokes an optional phase 3, seeking user input for finally making a decision on whether or not to have the image uploaded.

Upon failing to find a match in phase 2, the server rank orders the images in the candidate set based on the similarity scores with respect to the image being considered for upload. For each of the top k images in this ordered list, a small thumbnail is sent back to the client device; photo sharing services typically generate a thumbnail for every image at the time it is uploaded [31]. The user of the client device can visually compare her image with the received thumbnails and assess whether or not similar images are already available at the server; based on this, she can decide whether or not to transfer the image.

3.5 Handling parallel transfers of similar content

Thus far, we implicitly assumed that an image being considered for upload is compared with images that were already uploaded previously and stored in the server database. However, it is quite possible that in our scenarios of interest, multiple user devices attempt to upload similar images almost at the same time (close to when the event is occurring). Due to the shared access to the wireless medium, these attempts could be proceeding in parallel. If bandwidth is limited, it becomes important to reduce the load especially in such settings; for example, multiple such critical events (people needing to be rescued) could be ongoing at the same time and it is desirable to have (unique) information associated with all such events. The challenge here is to essentially compare such parallel uploads and determine if such attempts are towards transferring similar content.

When a client sends an OCS histogram of a new image, the server inserts an entry (with this information) for the image, into a queue. When there are other parallel uploads, the server not only compares the histogram of a candidate image with that of the images in its database, but also with the histograms of entries in this queue. If there are similar histograms (in either the database or in the above queue), the client is instructed to upload the local features as before. When the server receives the local features of an image, it associates them with the proper entry in the queue. It then compares these local features with the images from the database that were classified to be likely candidates with similar content *as well as* the local features of entries in the queue that are already available (with matching histograms). If there is a match with either, the image transfer is suppressed and the corresponding entry is deleted from the queue; else, the client is instructed to upload the image. After an image is completely received, the corresponding entry is deleted from the queue and the image is added to the server database. We point out that we only use the first two phases in determining if images that are considered for upload almost simultaneously, are similar. When this determination is taking place, only metadata of the images is available at the server side (the thumbnails of such images are not yet available). Since we desire that the decisions on whether or not to upload be quick, we avoid waiting for the complete information towards generating thumbnails and providing subsequent user feedback; this would cause delays and affect user experience. However, recall that the thumbnail feedback in phase 3 is mainly to help increase the true positive rate; thus, for the images considered for upload almost simultaneously, our system still achieves a low false positive rate.

4 System Implementation

In this section, we describe the prototype implementation of our framework. Our prototype consists of a central server which accesses a database where a set of previously uploaded images are stored. A number of mobile client devices generate new images and attempt to upload them to the server. We use the Kentucky image data set (described later in Section 5) to learn the appropriate values for the parameters in our implementation.

4.1 Image server

The server stores the images that it receives in a central database. For each image, it extracts and stores the image's 128-byte OCS histogram and the image's min-hash values as described in Section 3. At the server side, we choose to construct 512 permutations (recall Section 3.3) and determine the corresponding hash values for each image; each hash value is stored using 2 bytes. As one might expect, the larger the number of permutations, the higher the accuracy in similarity determination. However, Zhang *et al.* [10] showed that when more than 512 hash functions are used, the gain in accuracy is at a point of diminishing returns due to an increase in the imposed processing overhead.

For each hash value, the server also stores the geometry information of the visual word that corresponds to that min-hash function (the visual word which is assigned the minimum value by the hash function). Specifically, for each visual word, we store the x,y indices of the bin to which the key-point associated with that visual word belongs, as described in Section 3.3. For each image, we use a 10x10 bin-space as in [10]; thus, the geometry information of a min-hash value consists of 1 byte, including 4 bits for the horizontal bin index and 4 bits for the vertical bin index. Therefore, the total byte count to capture the local features of an image is 1536; this includes 1024 bytes for the min-hash values and 512 bytes for the geometry information. In total, we impose only 1664 bytes overhead for each image, together for both the global and local features. This is less than 1% of the size of a normal quality image taken with a modern smartphone. Our server application is implemented in C++ and uses the OpenCV library [32] to extract global and local features of the images.

Server operations: When a client application is about to upload an image, it sends the OCS histogram of the image first. The server searches its database to find images with similar histograms (the component values are within a threshold τ_1 of the incoming image's histogram) based on Euclidean distance. If such similar histograms are found, the corresponding images are considered as candidates for containing the content in the image to be uploaded; then, the client is asked to transfer min-hash values and the geometry information of its image. If no similar histograms are found, the client is instructed to upload its image.

In the next phase, when the local features of the image are received, the server calculates the geometry similarity score of that image with respect to each of the images in the candidate set according to Equation 3. Here, the scores are based on GVPs of length 2; it has been shown that this provides a good enough detection accuracy when compared to using GVPs of other lengths [10]. If any of these similarity scores is $\geq \tau_2$, the server deems that the content is similar and notifies the client application to suppress the image upload.

Otherwise, the server chooses those images that have the highest similarity scores and sends back thumbnails of these, to the client (a delayed multicast is possible to reach a plurality of clients, but we don't implement this). The human user of the client device can then check to see if the images are similar, and only choose to upload the image if she feels that they are not. We assume that users are objective and suppress an upload if a thumbnail is indeed of a similar image (we discuss our data sets and their objective usability for determining the similarity of images in Section 5).

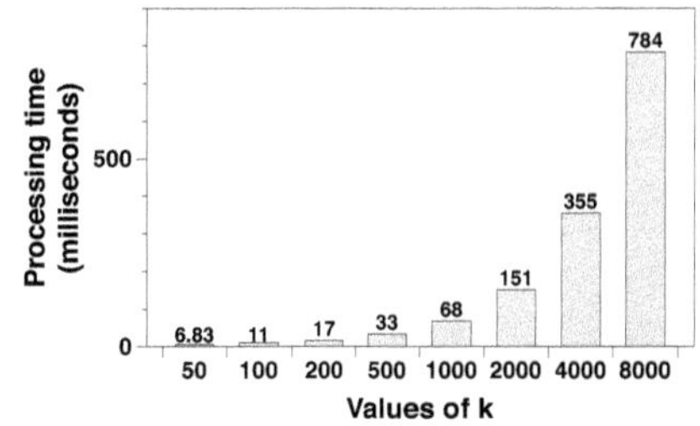

Figure 3: Search time for different values of k with ***knn***

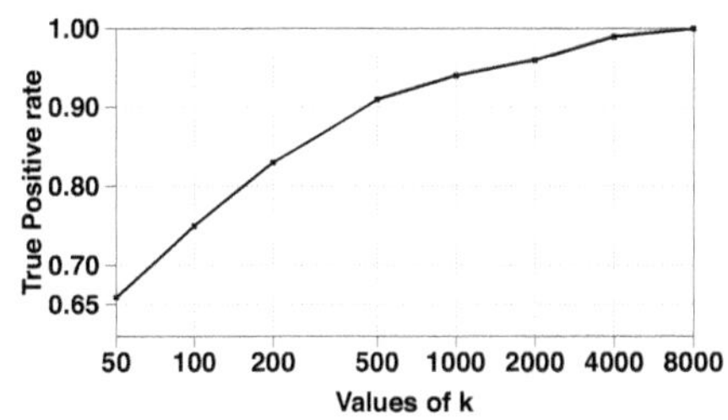

Figure 4: Percentage of images similar to an incoming image found

Fast histogram matching in Phase 1: For each OCS histogram that is received (from the clients), the server needs to find the set of images in its database with similar histograms. The database could potentially contain a large set of images, and brute-force checks are thus not viable. To achieve an efficient search, we utilize the fast "k nearest neighbor" search (***knn***) to find a good approximate set of the candidate images. We use the FLANN library [33] which is freely available for knn search. The histograms of all the images on the server side are grouped into hierarchical clusters. Specifically, based on the histograms, all the images are first grouped into N clusters; each such cluster in turn is recursively partitioned into N sub-clusters and so on, up to a maximum number of iterations. Here, we choose a default value of N=32, as suggested by the FLANN library.

Choosing the key parameter for the **knn** *search:* One important parameter when using ***knn*** search is the value of k, the maximum number of nearest neighbors the library should return. The higher the value of k, the library explores a larger number of branches in the cluster-tree and is thus able to find a larger set of similar images. However the search time also increases.

To determine a good value for k, we conduct an experiment using the Kentucky image set with 10200 images. This set contains groups of images that are similar; each group contains four images (ground truth). We build a test set that consists of 500 images, such that no image is similar to any other image in the set. For each image, we execute FLANN with different values for k, and record the processing times and the number of similar images found on the server. Figure 3 shows the search time (for query processing) for different values of k, and Figure 4 shows the accuracy of the search results in terms of the percentage of similar images that are found for a candidate image (as compared to the ground truth). These graphs show that, if we set k=500, we are able find over 90% of similar images with an expected processing delay of only about 33ms. Thus, we choose this to be the default value in our server implementation.

4.2 Client application

The client app is implemented on Android smart-phones using Java and native C++ code (JNI). Upon capturing an image, our client app is invoked for attempting an upload of the image to the server. The Java code is only for the graphical interface; the image processing code is written in C++ and is linked with the OpenCV library for feature extraction.

Client operations: First, the client application extracts the OCS histogram of the image and sends it to the server. It then awaits a server notification with regards to whether or not there are images with similar histograms in the server's database. If such candidate images exist, the client app extracts the local features, i.e., the min-hash values and their corresponding geometry information, from the image. To calculate the min-hash values, first the ORB key-points of the images are extracted. Next, the client application converts the image into the BoW presentation by mapping the key-points into visual words based on a vocabulary file. The vocabulary file contains the book of visual words (codebook) that is pre-built and preloaded from a set of training images (these are also available to the server). We choose to use a codebook of 20000 clusters. With this, the processing time at the client for each image is approximately 1.2 seconds. With a larger codebook, (e.g., with 50000 clusters) the processing time is around 3.5 seconds. Thus, choosing this larger codebook will degrade the performance of our framework (increased latencies). Furthermore, with 20000 visual words, we only need to use 2 bytes to represent each cluster and this limits the metadata overhead; larger numbers of clusters will increase these overhead costs.

Next, the client reads 512 different hash values (permutations) from a pre-built data file; for each permutation, a unique label is assigned to a hash value and thus, each visual word. It identifies the label of the visual word with the min-hash value for each permutation, and computes the geometry information for the visual word associated with that value. It sends both the min-hash values and the geometry information back to the server (local features).

Pre-installed data on client side: We pre-install a vocabulary file for the BoW processing and a permutation file for determining the min-hash labels for images on the client side. Thus, this information does not need to be exchanged for each image. With 20000 clusters, the size of the vocabulary file is only 640 KB; each cluster centroid of an ORB key-point is just 256 bits (32 bytes). The permutation file contains 512 permutations; each permutation in turn contains 20000 assignments which map each cluster on to a unique 2-byte label value. To reiterate, each permutation essentially re-orders the identification labels to be assigned to the clusters. Thus, the size of the permutation file is $\approx$ 20MB. These files are also available to the server (which essentially provides the software at install to each client). The only time that these files need to be re-built is if there are large changes to the image database maintained by the server.

5 Evaluation

In this section, we describe our evaluations of our framework. We perform experiments on a testbed of Android phones, as well as simulations using ns3 to showcase the performance as well as the benefits of our approach.

5.1 Training and test image sets

We begin with describing our image data sets and how we use them to evaluate the accuracy with which our framework can identify similar images. We use the Kentucky image set, which has been widely used in computer vision, primarily because of the availability of ground-truth information. We also use an image set of US cities that we collected on the Internet as described below.

The Kentucky image set [11]: The image set consists of 10200 images forming 2550 groups. In each group, there are 4 images of the same object taken from different angles; such images match our requirement/definition of similar images.

The city image set: We use the Bing image search service to find one image each for 5000 popular US cities. As these pictures are taken from different cities, there are no pairs of similar images in the entire image set.

We resize and increase the file size of all the images to $\approx$ 700 KB using ImageMagick [34]; this reflects the average size of normal-quality images taken by smartphones today.[3]

Building the training and test data sets: We evaluate the accuracy of our framework by partitioning our image data sets into a training set and test set. We pre-upload images in the training set to the server and evaluate the accuracy with which our framework is able to identify images in the test set (when we try to upload these images) as having corresponding similar images on the server.

We randomly pick 2000 images from the US cities set and 2000 images from the Kentucky set to create a test set of 4000 images. Though images from the Kentucky data set are chosen randomly, we ensure that no more than 2 images are taken from the same group (the aforementioned 4 images of the same object). The remaining images from the Kentucky data set and the US cities data set are used as our training set; this set is used to build the codebook for the BoW representation and stored at the server.

To eliminate biases with a specific test set, we construct 5 different test sets (by randomly choosing images from the Kentucky and US Cities data sets) and the corresponding training sets. By default, the results reported are the average from our experiments with these 5 different sets.

With the above, we essentially ensure that for each image in our test set that is taken from the Kentucky set, there is at least one similar version of the image in the server database; this can be used as ground truth while estimating our true positive rates in identifying similar/redundant content. For each image taken from the US cities set, there is no similar version in the server database; thus, this set is useful in estimating the false positive rates with our framework.

Remarks: We do recognize that the Kentucky and the US cities data sets contain largely dissimilar images. We tried to perform experiments with a large set of images from a disaster scenario (Hurricane Sandy) but had difficulty in establishing the ground truth for the purposes of quantifying true and false positive rates. While we believe that our framework works well in such cases (based on some limited experiments where we tried to upload about a 100 photos and manually checked for similarity), we need a set of volunteer users to categorize whether the images are similar or not; for a large set of images, this was difficult to do. Using the Kentucky and US cities data sets allowed us to evaluate the accuracy of our framework without human involvement in an objective way.

When emulating human feedback based on thumbnails, we again rely on the objectivity possible with the above data sets. If two images are indeed similar (based on the ground truth), we assume that the user will correctly classify it to be the case; if the images aren't, we assume that the user will correctly decide to upload her image.

A training set of images (and a corresponding codebook) for a specific disaster location, can be built by using images of the same location before the disaster *and* images of the same kind of disaster (for example, an earthquake or a wildfire) that had previously

[3]With modern smartphones, the average file size of high quality images can be between 2 and 2.5 MB [35].

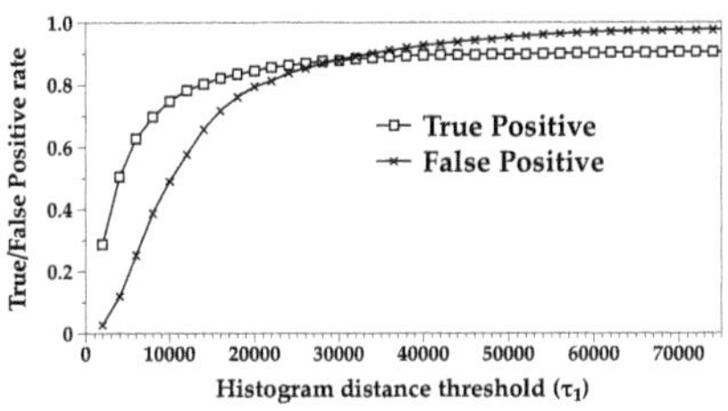

Figure 5: Accuracy with different histogram thresholds

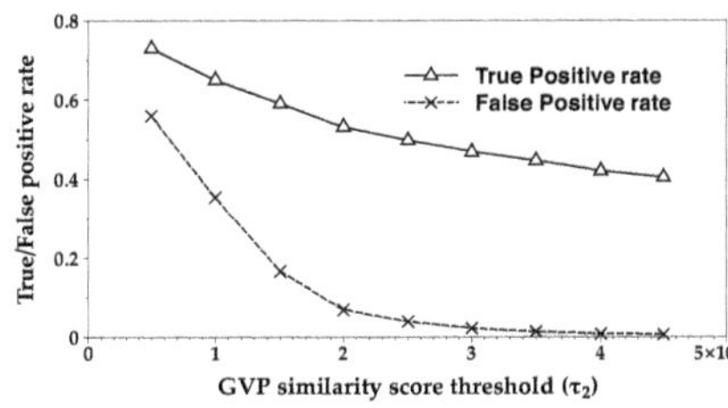

Figure 6: Accuracy with different GVP similarity scores

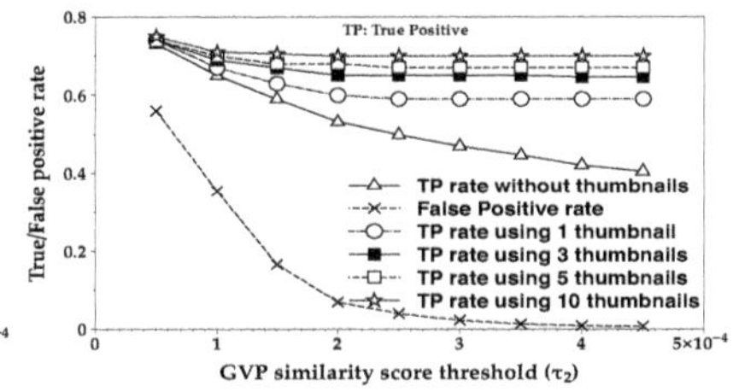

Figure 7: Accuracy with different numbers of image thumbnails

occurred at other locations. A codebook built based on the two image sets is likely to contain key points that are similar to the key points in the images captured at the disaster scene. This determination is based on results from prior research on disaster images; specifically, Yang *et al.* [36] found that images of the same kind of disaster have many similar local features.

5.2 Experimental setup

Our experimental system consists of a server with an associated database; all the images in the training set and their global and local features are stored in the database. We have 20 Android-based smartphones as our client devices; the test images are divided equally among these phones. The smartphones connect to an access point (AP) on a WiFi network; the server is also connected directly to the AP via a 100 Mbps Ethernet cable. To emulate bandwidth constrained settings, we set the network bitrate to 6 Mbps. We experiment with different workloads (upload rates) from our smartphones. Note that we vary the network bandwidth in our simulations in Section 5.8; we also consider uploads using the cellular infrastructure in those studies.

Remark: Unfortunately, we were unable to showcase the performance of our framework via real experiments on cellular networks. Specifically, we do not have a sufficiently large set of phones to create enough load that strained the network bandwidth. Further, we were unable to determine the bit rate on the LTE links and could not accurately characterize the network load; thus, it was difficult to objectively quantify the benefits from our framework. However, in the scenarios of interest (e.g., disasters), we expect that there will be sufficiently large user activity that will strain the capacity of the network [7, 17].

5.3 Accuracy of detecting similar content

Detection accuracy with global features only. First, we examine the accuracy with which Phase 1 of our framework determines if or not the server is in possession of a similar image as compared to one being considered for upload. Recall that image similarity is determined here only by comparing the global OCS histogram associated with two images. Figure 5 shows the true positive rates (correctly detecting similar content) and the false positive rates (wrongly classifying images as containing similar content) with different histogram distance thresholds. If we set a very low threshold (meaning that the Euclidean distance between the histogram of the image to be uploaded and a candidate image in the server database should be very small), we will end up not identifying any similar images; here, the true positive rate will be very low. To increase the true positive rate, we will need to increase the threshold so that we have a bigger likelihood of identifying candidate images in the server database, but this will have the undesired effect of increasing the false positive rate, since some wrong images in the database will also be classified as candidates for similarity checks.

Based on Figure 5, we choose a threshold of τ_1=14000 towards achieving $\approx$ 80% true positive rate; however, this results in a 63% false positive rate, which we seek to drastically decrease with Phase 2.

Improving detection accuracy with local features. In Phase 2 of our approach, the assessment of image similarity is refined by calculating the similarity scores based on GVPs (see Equation 3). Figure 6 depicts the true and false positive rates after this phase, when different similarity score thresholds are used. We observe that with a very low threshold, the false positive rate is very high (images are wrongly classified as similar) but then drops drastically as we increase the threshold. However, increasing the threshold decreases the true positive rate as well, since similar images are discarded for "not being good enough". To avoid missing critical image uploads, a very low false positive rate ($\approx$ 1%) is desirable. If we set a threshold to achieve this, the true positive rate is $\approx$ 47%; this implies that approximately half of the images which have redundant content are detected and are subsequently suppressed at the end of this phase.

Feeding back image thumbnails to further increase the true positive rate. To further improve the detection of similar images, in Phase 3, the server sends back thumbnails to the user for visual inspection (Section 3.4). In our experiments, the size of an image's thumbnail is $\approx$ 11 KB; we believe that this a reasonably small volume of data needed for improving accuracy.[4] Figure 7 shows the increase in accuracy when different numbers of thumbnails are fed back to the user. With 3 to 5 image thumbnails, we find that the true positive rate increases to about 68% (from 47% at the end of Phase 2). Beyond that, we find that we hit a point of diminishing returns; for example, with 10 thumbnails, the true positive rate increases to just over 70%. Note here that the false positive rates do not change after Phase 3 (the human accurately determines if the content is similar or not).

Detection accuracy with parallel uploads. Next, we consider the case where multiple client devices are attempting uploads of similar content in parallel (almost simultaneously). Specifically, we conduct an experiment where three smartphones attempt parallel uploads of an ordered set of 500 images to the server. The database on the server side does not contain any images that are similar to the test images. We manually ensure that the images at the same position in the ordered sets at the three clients are similar; for example, the first image on the first client is similar to the first image on the second and the third client and so on.

First, we conduct the experiment without performing any similarity detection; as a result, all the 1500 images from the clients are uploaded to the server. Next, we implement similarity detection using the process described in Section 3.5. Here, we observe that only 585 images are uploaded to the server. Specifically, 500 images with unique content and 85 images with redundant content are

[4]The overheads due thumbnails are discussed later.

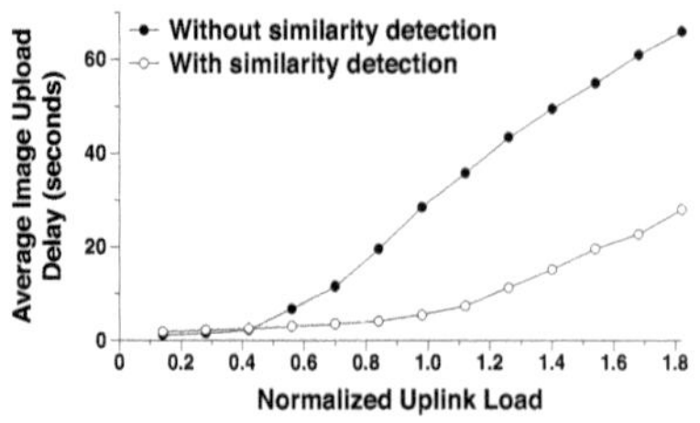

Figure 8: Impact on network load and image transfer delay (Ideal case with 100% detection accuracy)

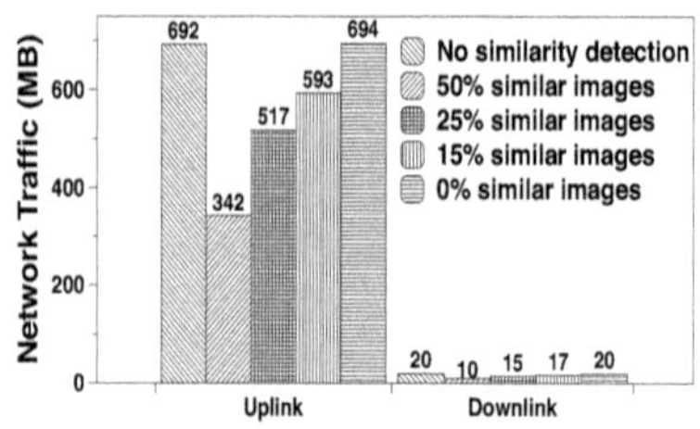

Figure 9: Varying the proportion of similar images at the server (Ideal case with 100% detection accuracy)

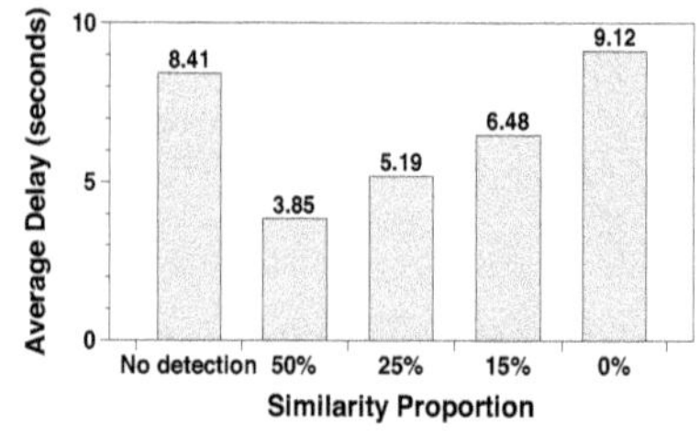

Figure 10: Upload delay with different proportions of similar images (Ideal case with 100% detection accuracy.)

uploaded; this corresponds to a 17% contribution from redundant information.

5.4 Impact of redundant content suppression on network performance

In this section, we seek to understand the impact of redundant content reduction on network performance. Specifically, we seek to quantify the impact on (i) the delay experienced during image uploads (where we can expect a decrease) and (ii) the total sustainable load (where we can expect an increase). We also quantify the overheads due to our approach.

For the experiments in this section, each smartphone sends a test set of 50 images, back to back to the server. The test set consists of 25 images from the Kentucky data set with similar versions on the server, and 25 images from the US cities set. The total size of the test set is $\approx$ 32 Megabytes. Subsequently, we vary the proportion of the redundant content in the test set and quantify the impact on network performance. First, we show the results in an ideal case wherein all redundant content is correctly detected and suppressed; in other words, we assume a 100% detection accuracy unlike what we expect in practice. With our framework, the proportional improvements are reduced by a factor equal to the complement of the true positive rate; we show this later in Section 5.7.

5.4.1 Delays under different network loads

The normalized network load (also referred to as simply network load) is defined as $\frac{n\lambda}{\mu}$, where n is the number of devices in the network, and λ is the load generated per device, and μ is the rate achievable on the transfer link. To vary load, we first fix λ, but vary the number of clients that are attempting image transfers per unit time (n). Each client transfers/suppresses one image completely, before attempting the next transfer. Specifically, we assume that a new image is generated every t seconds. We set $t = 6$ seconds (we have other results but do not report them as they are similar), which implies that a client device (given the 32 MB content volume consisting of 50 images) generates an average load of $\lambda = 0.85$ Mbps. With the wireless bandwidth of 6 Mbps (μ), this corresponds to *each* client generating a *normalized* load of 14% (0.85/6) , on average.

Figure 8 demonstrates the reduction in the delay experienced under different normalized network loads, due to similarity detection/redundancy elimination. The delay experienced by an image is defined as the duration between when the image is generated and when it reaches the server; the delay is computed for only those images that are transferred to the server. Under light network load (e.g., below 40%), sending the images directly without any similarity detection/redundancy suppression is faster! This is because in these regimes, there is no congestion and it is possible to transfer images without much delay; the process of similarity detection adds processing/metadata exchange delays but does not contribute to a reduction in congestion.

However, when the load $>$ 50%, the network transitions into a congested state; this is the regime where redundant content reduction will benefit performance. The figure demonstrates that similarity detection and redundancy suppression allow us to tolerate up to a 100% increase in load. Similarly, at high loads (e.g., at loads $>$ 1.0), more than a 100% reduction in the experienced delay is possible. Note that these results are based on about 50% of the images to be uploaded having similar counterparts at the server.

5.4.2 Varying the proportion of similar images available at the server

Next, we vary the fraction of uploaded images that have similar counterparts at the server. In these experiments, we use `tcpdump` to capture network traffic transferred over the wireless network. We show the results when the normalized load is 0.6; the behavioral results are similar at other loads. The results are shown in Figure 9.

First, the figure depicts a case where the server does not contain any image that is similar to any image being considered for upload. In this case, there is an overhead associated with each image due to the metadata, but this overhead serves no purpose (images are ultimately uploaded). In this extreme case, we find that the performance with our framework is only slightly worse than in the case without it; the upload data volume increases from 692 MB to 694 MB. Second, as one might expect, as the likelihood of the server finding a similar image increases (the proportion of similar images present is increased), the performance with our framework improves in terms of a drastic reduction in network load. The figure shows that when the redundancy in content is about 50%, the decrease in network traffic (because of redundancy elimination) is in fact slightly higher than 50%. The main reason for this artifact is that the reduction in network load also reduces the overheads due to retransmissions of corrupted packets that are typically incurred, if an image is in fact uploaded. These experiments also inherently account for the uplink overheads with our framework; the results suggest that these overheads are extremely low (because the gains are as expected in an ideal setting with no overhead). Finally, the metadata overhead consumed in the reverse direction (from the server to the smartphones) is also depicted; this corresponds to a very small fraction of the upload content volume ($\approx$ 3%).

We also examine the delays incurred in transferring images, while varying the proportion of similar images available to the server. The results are shown in Figure 10. Again, if no similar images are present at the server for any of the images being considered for upload, there is a very slight increase in delay (from 8.41 seconds to 9.12 seconds) due to the metadata exchange and processing. This demonstrates the extremely low overheads with our approach. As the proportion of similar images increase, drastic reductions (54%

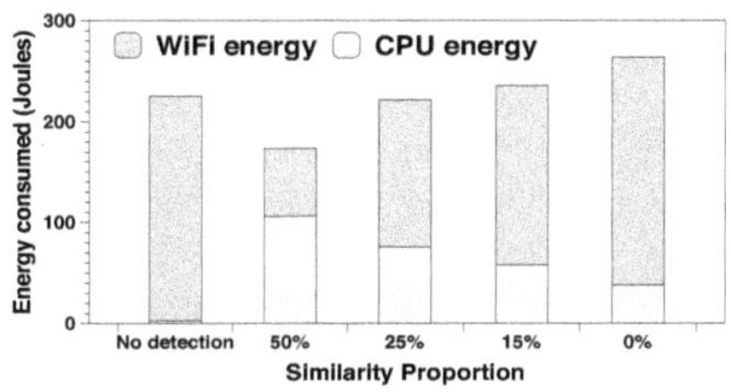

Figure 11: Impact on Energy

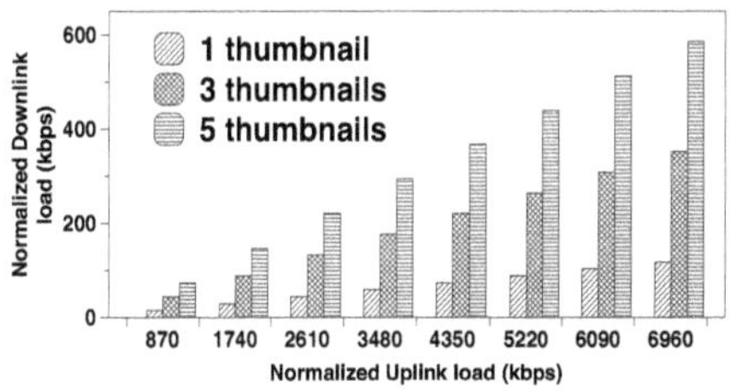

Figure 12: Overheads from thumbnails

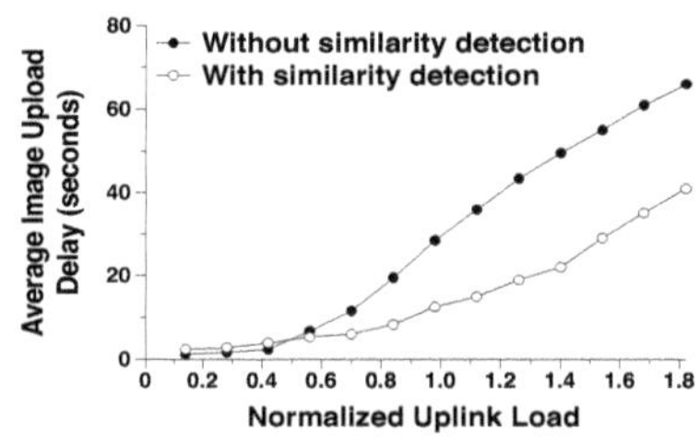

Figure 13: Upload delay with our framework (True Positive rate ≈ 70%)

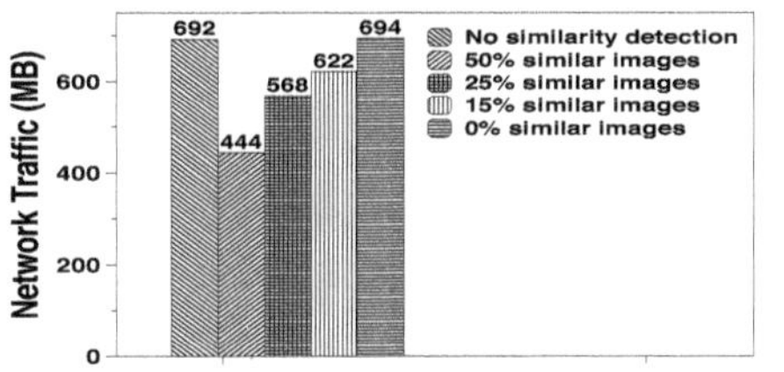

Figure 14: Uplink Network traffic with our framework (True Positive rate ≈ 70%)

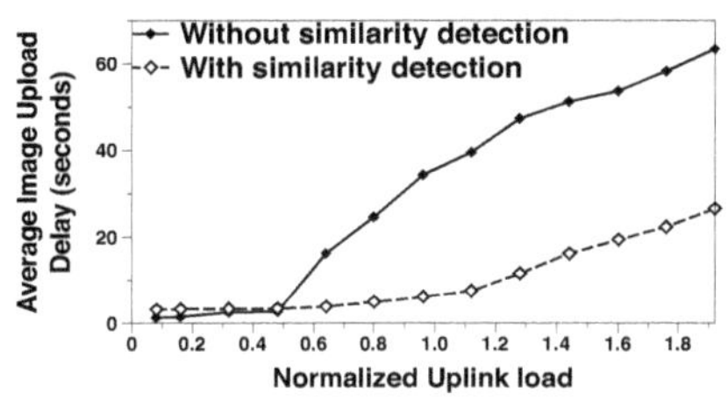

Figure 15: Delay vs load with WiFi (ns3)

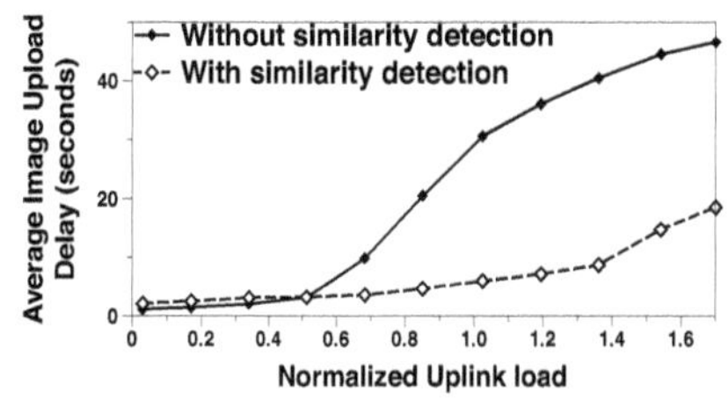

Figure 16: Delay vs load with LTE (ns3)

when this proportion is 50%) in image transfer delays are realized with our framework as depicted in the figure.

5.5 Impact on energy consumption

Our next set of experiments capture the impact of our framework on the energy consumption on the client devices. Specifically, we pay particular attention to the (i) energy consumed due to processing, towards extracting local and global features, and (ii) the energy consumed by the network interfaces due to content/metadata transfers. We compare the energy consumed on smartphones with and without our framework.

We use the PowerTutor tool [37] to capture the energy usage on our smartphones. For clarity, we only show the results with a Sony Ericsson Xperia Arc phone in our test bed. However, we observe similar results on different phones from different vendors as well. Figure 11 shows total energy consumed and the energy breakdown when a set of 50 images is uploaded from the phone. It is observed that our approach only induces a very small energy overhead on client devices when the similarity detection fails in all cases (server does not have any similar images to the ones considered for upload). As the volume of the transferred data is reduced, the energy consumed by the WiFi connection is also reduced. However, the energy consumed due to processing increases (due to the computation of global/local features of the images). The highest difference in energy consumption is between when no similarity detection is deployed and when there are no images with similar versions on the server side; this is about 40 Joules. On today's modern smartphones, the battery capacity is around 1800mAh with a voltage of 3.7 Volts; the above energy overhead only only corresponds to about 0.2% of the battery capacity. Given the large number of image transfers considered from each phone here, the overhead is likely to be even lower in practice and thus, will not adversely affect user experience.

5.6 Overhead due to thumbnails

As our final experiment on our Android testbed, we seek to quantify the overheads incurred in sending different numbers of thumbnails from the server to the smartphone clients. In this experiment, 50% of the images that are considered for uploads have similar versions on the server side. Figure 12 shows the normalized (upload) load and the corresponding overhead in terms of download load if 1, 3 and 5 thumbnails are generated for those images for which the server comes up with a negative result at the end of Phase 2, in our system. It is observed that when the upload rate is increases, the overhead of generating thumbnails also increases. However, even when the generated upload load is higher than the capacity of our link (6Mbps), the overhead of generating 5 thumbnails is still less than 10% of the link capacity. This demonstrates that Phase 3 of our framework is lightweight and is a viable option in practice.

5.7 Improvement in network performance with our framework in practice

Thus far, we have shown the improvements on network performance in an idealized settings where we assume that similarity detection can be performed with 100% accuracy. Next we show the impact on network performance with our framework, using our test set of images. Here, the true positive rate is approximately 70% (as described in Section 5.1). Figure 13 shows the reduction in upload delay if the proportion of redundant content is 50%. Unlike in an ideal case, our framework is able to eliminate ≈70% of the redundant content (given the true positive rate achieved). The figure shows that when the load is high, the upload delay without similarity detection is about ≈44% higher (even though only ≈35% of the data considered for upload gets suppressed). The reason for this higher than expected delay reduction is the same as that in the ideal case. The retransmission overheads due to corrupted packets decrease (to significant extents in cases where the link quality is poor) as compared to a case without similarity detection (when the images actually get uploaded); this in turn further reduces the aggregate network load and thus decreases delay. The elimination in redundant content also allows the network to sustain a higher load. For a target expected delay of 30 seconds, the sustainable load increases by about 60% as seen in the figure. Figure 14 shows the uplink network traffic when different amounts of redundant content are present. For the same reason as above (fewer retransmissions), the reduction in the total (uplink) traffic is typically higher than the proportion of redundant content that is suppressed except in the case where there are no similar images at all (0% of similar images). In this extreme case, all images are uploaded, and there are slight overhead penalties due to our framework.

5.8 Evaluations via simulations

Finally, we examine the impact of our framework on network performance using ns-3 based simulations, which allow us to experiment with different network set-ups and scales.

Simulation set-up: We evaluate the network performance with both WiFi and LTE: (i) In the WiFi set-up, all the mobile devices connect to the same wireless access point (AP) through a 802.11b link, which in turn connects to a server node through a dedicated link of 100 Mbps. All the the clients are initially distributed evenly in a square area of 50x50 meters; the AP is positioned at the center of the area. We use a random walk mobility model for the clients; each client moves at a random speed in a random direction inside the area. The WiFi channel is characterized by a distance based loss propagation model. The channel bit rate is kept constant (but varied in different experiments) to allow us to compute the normalized load. (ii) In our LTE set-up, all the smartphones connect to the same base station (regarded to as an enb node in ns-3) through a LTE network; the base station is connected to a LTE gateway, which in turns connects to the server node via a dedicated link of 100 Mbps. In this set-up, all the LTE clients are initially distributed evenly in a square area of 100x100 meters; the base station is also positioned at the center of this area. We again use the random walk mobility model. The LTE channel is characterized by the default Friis path loss model. Again, the channel rate is kept at a constant value (but varied across experiments) in order to be able to characterize the normalized load.

Impact on image delay time: We examine the impact of our framework with different loads and with different numbers of mobile devices when 50% of the content to be uploaded is redundant, and is correctly eliminated. In all our experiments, under the same load, we observe consistent and very similar results even if the number of devices and data rates are changed. For simplicity, we only show one sample result from our WiFi experiments and one result from our LTE experiments. Figure 15 shows the results with a 54 Mbps WiFi network and 200 smartphones. Figure 16 shows the results with a 15 Mbps LTE network and 50 smartphones. In both experiments, a new image is generated every 10 seconds. These results match those obtained from the real experiments with our 20-phone Android testbed (shown in Figure 8); more than a 100 % improvement in the average network delay is achieved at high loads (> 0.8).

6 Conclusions

In this paper, we propose a framework for detecting similar content in a distributed manner, and suppressing the transfer of such content in bandwidth constrained wireless networks. Such constraints are likely to be imposed on networks during events such as disasters. With our framework, we seek to enable the timely delivery of every unique piece (possibly critical in some cases) of information. In building our framework we tackle several challenges, primary among which is the lightweight decentralized detection of redundancies in image content. We leverage, but intelligently combine, a plurality of state-of-the-art vision algorithms in tackling this challenge. We perform both experiments on a 20-node Android smartphone testbed and ns-3 simulations to demonstrate the effectiveness of our approach in decreasing network congestion, and thereby ensuring the timely delivery of unique content.

7 Acknowledgments

This work was sponsored by the Army Research Laboratory and was accomplished under Cooperative Agreement Number W911NF-09-2-0053. The views and conclusions contained in this document are those of the authors and should not be interpreted as representing the official policies, either expressed or implied, of the Army Research Laboratory or the U.S. Government. The U.S. Government is authorized to reproduce and distribute reprints for Government purposes notwithstanding any copyright notation here on.

We would like to thank our shepherd, Gianluca Iannaccone, for his constructive comments and guidance through the camera-ready submission process.

8 References

[1] "More photos shared daily on Snapchat than Facebook, Instagram combined." `http://bit.ly/1sfog1M`, 2013.
[2] "Apple support communities blog." `http://bit.ly/1iy8gOQ`, 2014.
[3] T. Anthony and M. Moss, "Preparing cities for crisis communication," in *CCPR*, 2005.
[4] C. James, , A. Popescu, and T. Underwood, "Impact of Hurricane Katrina on internet infrastructure," in *Renesys*, 2005.
[5] A. Hughes, L. Palen, J. sutton, S. Liu, and S. Veweg, "Site-seeing in disaster: An examination of on-line social convergence," in *ISCRAM*, 2008.
[6] T. Preis, H. Moat, S. Bishop, P. Treleavan, and E. Stanley, "Quantifying the digital traces of Hurricane Sandy on Flickr," in *SREP*, 2013.
[7] U. Weinsberg, Q. Li, N. Taft, A. Balachandran, V. Sekar, G. Iannaccone, and S. Seshan, "CARE: Context aware redundancy elimination in challenged networks," in *ACM HotNets*, 2012.
[8] E. Rublee, V. Rabaud, K. Konolige, and G. Bradski, "ORB: An efficient alternative to SIFT or SURF," in *ICCV*, 2011.
[9] O. Chum, J. Philbin, M. Isard, and A. Zisserman, "Scalable near identical image and shot detection," in *CIVR*, 2007.
[10] Y. Zhang, Z. Jia, and T. Chen, "Image retrieval with geometry-preserving visual phrases," in *CVPR*, 2011.
[11] D. Nistér and H. Stewénius, "Scalable recognition with a vocabulary tree," in *CVPR*, 2006.
[12] F. Liu, B. Li, L. Zhong, B. Li, H. Jin, and X. Liao, "Flash crowd in P2P live streaming systems: Fundamental characteristics and design implications," in *IEEE Trans. Parallel Distrib. Syst.*, 2012.
[13] C.-H. Chi, S. Xu, F. Li, and K.-Y. Lam, "Selection policy of rescue servers based on workload characterization of flash crowd," in *SKG*, 2010.
[14] A. Koehl and H. Wang, "Surviving a search engine overload," in *WWW*, 2012.
[15] Q. Tran, K. Nguyen, K. E, and Y. S, "Tree-based disaster recovery multihop access network," in *APCC*, 2013.
[16] S. M. George, W. Zhou, H. Chenji, M. Won, Y. O. Lee, A. Pazarloglou, R. Stoleru, and T. A, "Topics in situation management distressnet: A wireless ad hoc and sensor network architecture for situation management in disaster response," in *IEEE Communications Magazine*, 2010.
[17] K. Fall, G. Iannaccone, J. Kannan, F. Silveira, and N. Taft, "A disruption-tolerant architecture for secure and efficient disaster response communications," in *ISCRAM*, 2010.

[18] Y. Zhang, Y. Wu, and G. Yang, "Droplet: A distributed solution of data deduplication.," in *GRID*, 2012.

[19] P. Riteau, C. Morin, and T. Priol, "Shrinker: Improving live migration of virtual clusters over WANs with distributed data deduplication and content-based addressing," in *Euro-Par*, 2011.

[20] X. Zhang, Z. Huo, J. Ma, and D. Meng, "Exploiting data deduplication to accelerate live virtual machine migration," in *CLUSTER*, 2010.

[21] M. Douze, H. Jégou, H. Sandhawalia, L. Amsaleg, and C. Schmid, "Evaluation of GIST descriptors for web-scale image search," in *CIVR*, 2009.

[22] D. G. Lowe, "Distinctive image features from scale-invariant keypoints," *Int. J. Comput. Vision*, 2004.

[23] J. Sivic and A. Zisserman, "Video Google: A text retrieval approach to object matching in videos," in *ICCV*, 2003.

[24] O. Chum, J. Philbin, and A. Zisserman, "Near duplicate image detection: min-hash and tf-idf weighting," in *BMVC*, 2008.

[25] Z. Wengang, L. Yijuan, L. Houqiang, S. Yibing, and T. Qi, "Spatial coding for large scale partial-duplicate web image search," in *MM*, 2010.

[26] A. Sarkar, P. Ghosh, E. Moxley, and B. S. Manjunath, "Video fingerprinting: features for duplicate and similar video detection and query-based video retrieval," in *SPIE*, 2008.

[27] O. Miksik and K. Mikolajczyk, "Evaluation of local detectors and descriptors for fast feature matching," in *ICPR*, 2012.

[28] J. Heinly, E. Dunn, and J. Frahm, "Comparative evaluation of binary features," in *ECCV*, 2012.

[29] C. Grana, D. Borghesani, M. Manfredi, and R. Cucchiara, "A fast approach for integrating ORB descriptors in the Bag of Words model," in *IS&T/SPIE*, 2013.

[30] J. MacQueen, "Some methods for classification and analysis of multivariate observations," in *Proceedings of the 5th Berkeley Symposium on Mathematical Statistics and Probability*, 1967.

[31] D. Beaver, S. Kumar, H. C. Li, J. Sobel, and P. Vajgel, "Finding a needle in Haystack: Facebook's photo storage," in *OSDI*, 2010.

[32] "OpenCV library." `http://www.opencv.org`.

[33] M. Muja and D. G. Lowe, "Fast approximate nearest neighbors with automatic algorithm configuration," in *VISSAPP*, 2009.

[34] "Image Magick." `http://www.imagemagick.org`.

[35] "Apple iPhone 5s reviews." `http://bit.ly/TXPtqr`, 2013.

[36] Y. Yang, H.-Y. Ha, F. Fleites, S.-C. Chen, and S. Luis, "Hierarchical disaster image classification for situation report enhancement," in *IRI*, 2011.

[37] L. Zhang, B. Tiwana, Z. Qian, Z. Wang, R. P. Dick, Z. M. Mao, and L. Yang, "Accurate online power estimation and automatic battery behavior based power model generation for smartphones," in *CODES/ISSS*, 2010.

Trace-Driven Analysis of ICN Caching Algorithms on Video-on-Demand Workloads

Yi Sun[⊗], Seyed K. Fayaz[†], Yang Guo[⊗], Vyas Sekar[†]
Yun Jin[◇], Mohamed Ali Kaafar[*], Steve Uhlig[∘]
[⊗] ICT/CAS, [†] CMU, [◇] PPTV, [*] NICTA, [∘] QMUL
{sunyi, guoyang}@ict.ac.cn, seyed@cmu.edu, vsekar@andrew.cmu.edu
yunjin@pptv.com, dali.kaafar@nicta.com.au, steve@eecs.qmul.ac.uk

ABSTRACT

Even though a key driver for Information-Centric Networking (ICN) has been the rise in Internet video traffic, there has been surprisingly little work on analyzing the interplay between ICN and video – which ICN caching strategies work well on video workloads and how ICN helps improve video-centric quality of experience (QoE). In this work, we bridge this disconnect with a trace-driven study using 196M video requests from over 16M users on a country-wide topology with 80K routers. We evaluate a broad space of content replacement (e.g., LRU, LFU, FIFO) and content placement (e.g., leave a copy everywhere, probabilistic) strategies over a range of cache sizes.

We highlight four key findings: (1) the best placement and replacement strategies depend on the cache size and vary across improvement metrics; that said, LFU+probabilistic caching [37] is a close-to-optimal strategy overall; (2) video workloads show considerable caching-related benefits (e.g., $\geq$ 10% traffic reduction) only with very large cache sizes ($\geq$ 100GB); (3) the improvement in video QoE is low ($\leq$ 12%) if the content provider already has a substantial geographical presence; and (4) caches in the middle and the edge of the network, requests from highly populated regions and without content servers, and requests for popular content contribute most to the overall ICN-induced improvements in video QoE.

Categories and Subject Descriptors

C.2.4 [**Computer-Communication Networks**]: Distributed systems—*Distributed applications*

General Terms

Design, Management, Measurement, Performance

Keywords

Information-centric networking; caching; Internet video

1. INTRODUCTION

Many future Internet architectures incorporate key information-centric networking (ICN) concepts (e.g, [6, 12, 27, 31, 33]). This is rooted in the observation that Internet traffic consumption is largely *content driven*, as users largely care about "what" content they want as opposed to "where" the content is delivered from. This decoupling promises to simplify several aspects of networking today by eliminating complex optimizations required by CDNs, providing intrinsic trust embedded in the content itself rather than network sources, and enabling the network to handle larger traffic volumes.

This motivation for ICN is accompanied, and driven in large part, by the dramatic rise in Internet video traffic volumes over the last several years [3]. In particular, the promise of ubiquitous caching and simplified network traffic engineering that ICN architectures offer have a natural synergy with the quality expectations and bandwidth demands of Internet video workloads. In this context, there are two natural questions that arise with respect to the interaction between ICN and Internet video:

- *How do video workloads impact network-level improvements offered by different ICN caching strategies?*

  The canonical improvement metrics studied in the ICN literature include cache hit rate, origin server load reduction, and the reduction in the overall network footprint [23]. There is a very rich literature on different aspects of caching to optimize these metrics including work on *content placement* to decide which routers on a request path should cache the content (e.g., [18, 22, 36, 37, 43]) and *content replacement* to decide how to manage the cache storage when full (e.g., [9, 42]). We would like to understand the specific placement and replacement algorithms that work well for video workloads and what magnitude of improvement they can offer on video workloads.
- *How do ICN caching mechanisms impact key video-specific QoE metrics?*

  Unlike traditional Internet web workloads, Internet video introduces new QoE metrics that impact user engagement such as buffering ratio, startup latency, and average bitrate [21, 34]. Going beyond the aforementioned network-centric metrics, we would also like to understand how different ICN caching strategies impact these key video-specific QoE metrics.

Despite the tremendous interest in both ICN and Internet video, there has been little work on systematically answering these questions with actual video workloads and using real network topologies. Much of the ICN literature today has focused on generic Zipf-like workloads and on small-scale topologies [44,45,49]. Similarly, most of the Internet video literature focuses on traditional CDN-based delivery architectures [14,21,28,34,41]. Thus, there is a gap in our understanding of the interplay between the design space of ICN content placement and replacement strategies and video workloads and QoE considerations.

This paper bridges this gap using large-scale video on demand (VOD) request traces consisting of over 196 million video requests

CoNEXT'14, December 2–5, 2014, Sydney, Australia.

http://dx.doi.org/10.1145/2674005.2675003.

from over 16 million users from the PPTV deployment in China [8]. We evaluate a combination of seven ICN content placement [18, 22, 36, 37, 43], five content replacement schemes [9, 42], and four different cache sizes (1GB, 10GB, 100GB, and 1TB). For each of these scenarios, we run trace-driven simulations on a country-wide router-level topology with around 80K routers. To the best of our knowledge, this is the largest (in terms of the topology and number of requests) and most comprehensive (in terms of the design space) trace-driven analysis of ICN caching strategies on video workloads.

Running such a large-scale workload on a large topology and a broad range of scenarios raises significant scalability challenges for existing ICN simulation frameworks [10]. We develop a custom request-level simulator called iCache for our analysis that provides almost 50× improvement over state-of-the-art ICN simulation platforms.

Using iCache, we answer the two high-level questions raised above in the context of a popular video content provider (PPTV). Our key observations are as follows:

- Across all strategies, we observe that only very large caches (i.e., 100GB or 1TB) provide considerable ($\geq$ 10%) reduction in the network traffic.
- For a provider like PPTV that already has a substantial server footprint, even with the largest cache size in our evaluations (1TB), the overall video QoE improvement is at most 12%.
- While the best combination of content placement and replacement strategies does depend on the cache size and the metric of interest, the combination of probabilistic content placement (*Prob*) and LFU content replacement (*LFU*) emerges as a near-optimal strategy across all scenarios.
- We also analyze *where*, *when*, and *what* contributes to the improvement and find that: (a) caches in the middle and access portions of the network contribute most to traffic reduction and QoE improvement; (b) requests from highly populated regions without content servers observe the highest QoE improvement; and (c) requests for popular content are more likely to contribute to overall ICN-induced QoE improvements.

Contributions and Roadmap: To summarize, the main contributions of our work are:

- Developing a scalable and extensible ICN simulator that provides up to 50× improvement over state-of-the-art platforms (Section 4);
- Analyzing the impact of video workloads on canonical ICN metrics such as traffic reduction, hit rate, and server load reduction over a broad combination of ICN caching strategies (Section 5);
- Understanding the improvements that ICN caching algorithms offer for video QoE metrics (Section 6);
- A spatiotemporal and request-level dissection of the benefits of the best ICN strategies with respect to network-centric and QoE-centric metrics (Section 7).

In the rest of the paper, we begin with related work in Section 2. We describe our datasets in Section 3. We discuss some outstanding issues in Section 8 before concluding in Section 9.

2. BACKGROUND AND RELATED WORK

In this section, we review the most relevant related work on ICN, ICN caching algorithms, ICN evaluation platforms, and measurements of Internet video. At a high level we find that while there is a rich literature on analyzing ICN and video workloads separately, there is little work on evaluating ICN caching mechanisms *at scale* on real video workload on a large topology. Our work bridges this gap.

ICN vision: The main ideas in ICN are decoupling content names from locations, name-based content routing, in-network caching, and the use of name-based binding for security. Major ICN efforts include TRIAD [25], DONA [33], 4WARD [12], CCN [30], NDN [31], and COMET [4]. Many of these envision content caches on routers to improve user experience (e.g., lower latency) and network performance (e.g., lower server load and congestion). However, these ICN architectures are not evaluated with respect to video workloads, which is the focus of our work.

Design space of in-network caching: In-network caching plays a key role in ICN architectures and has attracted a lot of research along two main dimensions: *content placement* and *content replacement*.
A *content placement* strategy decides where an object should be cached across routers on the request path (i.e., the sequence of routers from the content origin to the requesting client). We study seven specific content placement strategies: (1) leaving a copy everywhere (*LCE*) [19]; (2) leaving a copy only on the immediate downstream router when there is a hit on an upstream router (*LCD*) [36]; (3) leaving a copy on some randomly chosen router along the request path (*Rand*) [22]; (4) constant probability of caching on each router (*Prob*) [37]; (5) the probability of caching on a router is a function of its distance from the origin server and the shared storage capacity of the path (*PProb*) [43]; (6) using centrality-based measures where the router with the largest value of betweenness[1] will keep a copy (*Centrality*) [18]; and (7) a hybrid approach where the probability that a router caches an object is a function of both the router's betweenness and the content's popularity (*Cross*) [48].
A *content replacement* strategy captures how objects are evicted when the cache is full. We consider five such strategies: (1) least-recently used (*LRU*); (2) first-in first-out (*FIFO*); (3) least frequently used (*LFU*); (4) time to live (*TTL*) [42], where an object's time to live (TTL) on a router's cache depends on object's popularity and router's location; and (5) largest item first (*Size*) [9].

Notably, content placement and replacement are fundamentally different from strategies for content staging, which essentially prepopulate or *initialize* the caches. In other words, content placement and replacement strategies together determine the steady state behavior of the caches rather than the initial conditions that may only impact a few initial requests.

ICN evaluation: There are many ICN evaluation platforms such as ndnSIM [10], ccnSim [20], DEC [5], and Mini-CCNx [15]. Unfortunately, our experiences showed that these cannot handle the scale of the workload and the topology we study in this paper. Thus, we developed a custom request-level simulator called iCache. Prior works have also considered trace-driven evaluations of ICN caching (e.g., [23,49]). Our work extends them in three significant ways. First, our evaluation considers a much larger topology and request workload. Second, we consider a broader spectrum of placement and replacement strategies. Finally, we focus on video-specific aspects of ICN.

Video over ICN: Recent work has extended ICN to support video streaming [35, 38], optimized ICN-based streaming on mobile devices [26], and has suggested cooperative caching to improve video delivery [39]. Closer to our work, Fricker et al. [24] found that

[1] Betweenness is a measure of a node's centrality in a network. It is equal to the ratio of shortest paths from all vertices to all others that pass through that node.

Nodes	Edges	Avg. Degree	Diameter	Avg. Path Length
82,726	167,921	4.06	22	8.26

Table 1: Attributes of router-level network topology.

VOD workloads are cacheable at the edge of the network using synthetic traffic and a small, synthetic hierarchical topology. Similarly, Ando and Nakao [11] evaluated the performance of caching on a YouTube workload collected at a campus network gateway. Our analysis uses much larger traces and a real country-wide topology.

Internet video measurement: Several studies have analyzed the content popularity in video workloads (e.g., [13,17,29,50,51]) and suggest implications for caching in CDN and edge proxy architectures. However, they do not consider ICN-like ubiquitous caching. Recent studies analyze the impact of QoE metrics such as buffering, startup delay, and average playback bitrate on user engagement [21,34]. There are also proposals to improve QoE by designing better adaptive streaming protocols (e.g., [32]) and intelligently using multiple CDNs [40,41]. However, these focus on existing CDN-based delivery architectures while we focus on the interplay between ICN and video QoE.

3. DATASET DESCRIPTION

In this section, we describe how we collected the datasets used to answer our two motivating questions. These datasets, a router-level network topology and session-level statistics of video views, were collected from the operational platform of PPTV [8]. PPTV is a leading online video content provider in China. (While PPTV originally started as a P2P delivery platform, today it is a well-provisioned commercial content provider with traditional CDN-style servers and P2P.) PPTV has a user base of more than 227 million users, and its active user base is 49.7% of the total number of Internet users in China. The average viewing time per user per day is more than 2.5 hours, making it one of the most popular content portals in China [7].

3.1 Topology data

To collect a router-level network topology, we instrumented the PPTV client software with `traceroute` capabilities. After PPTV released this instrumented software, more than 150 million users (i.e., 66% of PPTV users) updated their software. Out of the users with the updated client software, we randomly selected 1.68 million users for conducting traceroute measurements. These clients issue traceroutes to other peers, the CDN servers deployed by PPTV, as well as specific IP prefixes associated with Chinese ISPs. To balance the tradeoff between measurement overhead and coverage, we used simple heuristics in choosing the destinations and the time to issue traceroutes. Some examples of such heuristics include avoiding duplicate requests to peers within previously covered IP prefixes and issuing traceroutes when the network is less congested (e.g., early morning).

The topology used in this paper is based on traceroute measurements collected over a 2-month period. Given the popularity and spread of PPTV clients in China, we have a unique high-coverage map of a country-wide network covering 89 ISPs, 6583 PoPs, and all the 31 provinces in mainland China. Table 1 summarizes the key characteristics of the network topology.

3.2 Video views data

We also collected a dataset of *video-on-demand* (VOD) requests from PPTV server logs. Each log record represents the summary statistics of a single video request, which is pushed to log collection servers when the video session ends. There are four main categories of relevant entries:

1. *Client-specific information* such as a (unique) client ID, client IP, client ISP, client location city/province, client's access network type (e.g., ADSL, WiFi, 3G), and client terminal type (e.g., PC, Tablet, Smartphone).
2. *Server-specific information* such as the PPTV server IP and the ISP this server is located in.
3. *Session-level information* such as video name, start time of the request, view duration, and total bytes transferred during this video session.
4. *Video QoE information* such as:
   - Buffering ratio or the fraction of the session time spent on buffering $= \frac{BufferingTime}{TotalViewTime}$;
   - Average bitrate, which is $\frac{TotalBytesDownloaded}{TotalPlayTime}$; and
   - Join time or the delay between the request and video start $= StartTimeOfPlay - RequestTime$.

PPTV shared with us a (uniformly-at-random) sampled dataset over a two-week period with more than 196 million viewing instances involving more than 16 million users. (Due to business considerations, we cannot reveal the total number of sessions.) Overall, these users watched more than 500K unique videos with the total size of unique content views being 137TB. To put this in context, a large 1TB cache can hold $< 1\%$ of the entire content population. Figure 1 depicts the distribution of user access to video content: a Zipf-like distribution with the parameter $\alpha = 1.174$.

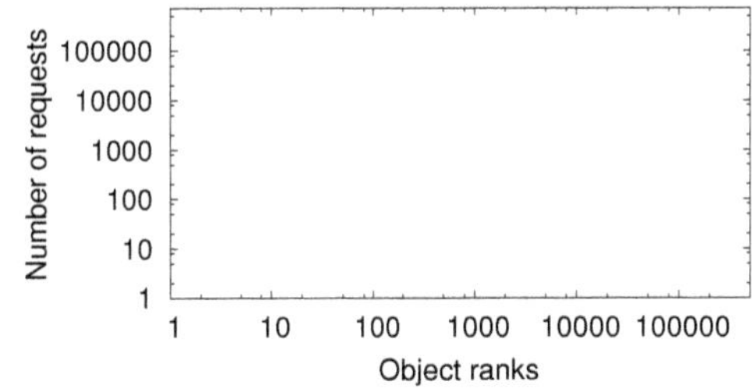

Figure 1: Object popularity distribution follows a Zipf-like distribution.

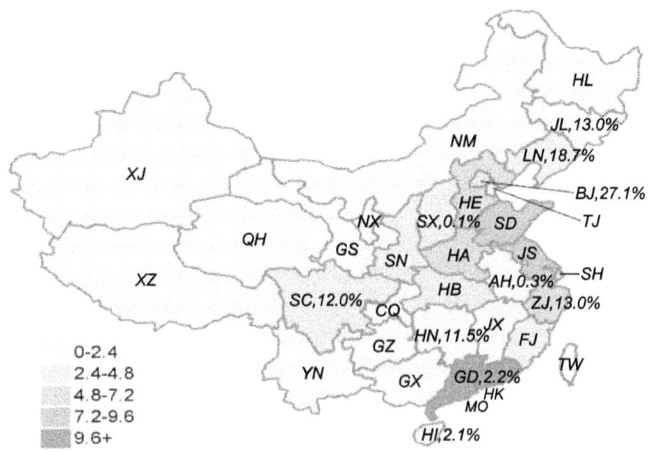

Figure 2: Distribution of incoming requests and number of requests served across different provinces in China. The "heatmap" scale represents the percentage of client requests originating in a given province, and the annotated text with each province is the percentage of requests served by PPTV servers in that province.

Figure 2 illustrates the spatial distribution of content access by PPTV users, showing the percentage of content access and the percentage of requests destined to PPTV content servers on a per-province basis. In Figure 2, darker colors indicate higher content requests, which matches very well with the Internet user population distribution in China.

4. SIMULATION SETUP

In this section, we discuss iCache, our simulation platform (written in C++) for large-scale ICN evaluations.[2] iCache is built with two design goals in mind: scalability and extensibility. First, in terms of scalability, iCache completes simulation of a very large network with tens of thousands of routers, tens of millions of ICN clients, and billions of content-view logs within a reasonable period of time (less than 5 hours). In contrast, existing platforms may take more than 250 hours for a similar simulation. Second, with respect to extensibility, in addition to supporting several existing caching and routing strategies, iCache provides APIs to plug in new algorithms.

We begin by documenting our experiences with existing simulation platforms that motivated us to develop iCache. Then, we describe the main design decisions underlying iCache and validate its scalability, fidelity, and extensibility.

4.1 Need for a new ICN simulation platform

There are several ICN simulation platforms currently in use including CCNx [1], ccnSim [20], DCE [5], mini-CCNx [15], and ndnSIM [10]. ndnSIM is generally considered to be the most scalable ICN platform; e.g., as reported by Afsanyev [10] et al., CCNx, ccnSim, DCE, and mini-CCNx can only support ICN simulations with a few hundred routers, and cannot be used for our large-scale evaluation with 80,000+ routers.

Thus, we originally considered using ndnSIM. Unfortunately, even ndnSIM was not sufficiently scalable for the large-scale trace-driven evaluation we needed to perform. For instance, a single trace-driven run with one content placement and one content replacement strategy took more than 125 hours on a Xeon 2.13GHz machine with 1TB of memory running Linux. This performance is clearly not sufficient for us to practically meet our goal of comprehensively evaluating the design space of content placement and replacement strategies with different cache sizes. With 7 content placement, 5 replacement strategies, and 4 distinct cache sizes, using ndnSIM would roughly take $125 \times 140 = 17,500$ CPU hours.

4.2 Design of iCache

In designing iCache, we make three key decisions:

- ndnSIM does a detailed packet-level simulation carefully capturing every content packet and content response. This leads to a significant number of events in the system and also increases memory consumption at high request rates. As a first step, we simplify the simulation by moving to a request-level rather than a packet-level simulation. One concern is that we may not be able to replicate fine-grained QoE metrics with a flow-level simulation. Fortunately, we use a data-driven extrapolation methodology for computing QoE metrics, as we discuss later in Section 6, that is amenable to a flow-level analysis. Second, ndnSIM provides a complete implementation of all ICN functionalities; e.g., checks for content-level security. These additional features, while relevant for other applications, significantly add to the per-request processing. We simplify the per-node operations and do not implement the content-integrity steps.
- To emulate complex content routing protocols such as OSPF extensions, ndnSIM effectively recomputes each routing table on each cache eviction event. This creates a large number of routing protocol messages and increases the processing overhead. However, for many common ICN routing strategies (e.g., shortest path to servers [23,47]) the routing table does not need to be updated. We, therefore, precompute the routing tables and use them throughout the simulation.
- Finally, rather than a node-centric software architecture, we move to a "tier"-based architecture where we group the same functional modules on different nodes into a single layer such as caching layer, forwarding layer, and routing layer as shown in Figure 3. Unlike other simulators, where each simulated ICN node maintains its own routing, caching, and forwarding tables, this grouping enables the use of global tables that are shared by all routers avoiding redundant entries. In turn, this reduces the memory consumption of the simulation. Furthermore, it improves the locality of memory accesses and thus minimizes I/O operations, and also improves the processing time of each simulated router.

[2]An open-source version of iCache will be available at the following URL: `http://fi.ict.ac.cn/firg.php?n=Member.Source`.

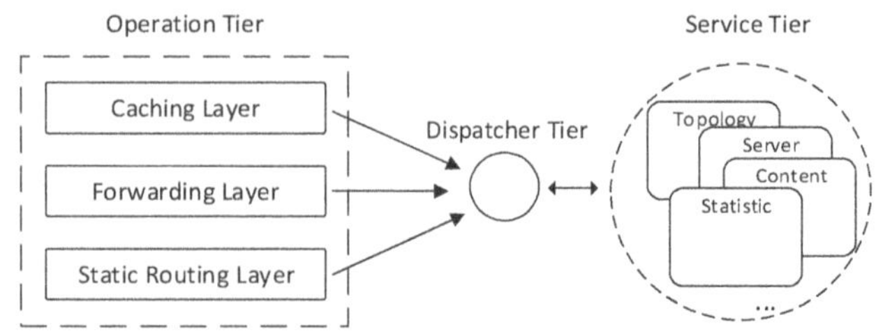

Figure 3: iCache architecture.

Figure 3 depicts the architecture of iCache including three functional tiers (i.e., the operation, dispatcher, and service tiers) as described next. The operation tier provides the core caching and routing functions. The dispatcher schedules the events in the simulation. Finally, the service tier provides a common set of functions such as queries on network topology and content properties as well as collecting statistics.

Here we focus on the operation tier. The *caching layer* implements the functionality of a content cache; i.e., basic operations of individual caches such as content placement/replacement. We have implemented seven content placement and five content replacement algorithms (see Section 5). The *forwarding layer* processes content request and reply messages and implements the basic forwarding functions such as receiving pending requests and forwarding the responses on the correct interfaces of each simulated router. The *routing layer* maintains global routing information of the network. We have currently implemented a name-based OSPF algorithm, which is the basic routing strategy in several ICN architectures [6,31,33].

We record several useful statistics such as the transmission path of each request and the traffic load on each server during the simulation. We process these offline using custom scripts to generate statistics such as cache hit rate, traffic reduction, server load reduction (Section 5), and video-related user experience metrics (Section 6).

4.3 Validation and evaluation

Next, we evaluate iCache on three key dimensions: fidelity, scalability, and extensibility.

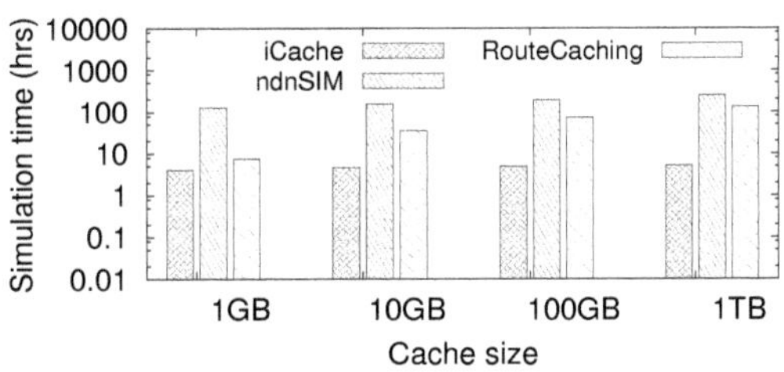

Figure 4: Simulation time of iCache and ndnSIM showing that iCache can provide 20–50× speedup. Note that the y-axis is on log scale.

Algorithm	LoC
LCE	17
LCD	17
Rand	23
Prob	29
PProb	38
Centrality	56
Cross	80

(a) Content placement

Algorithm	LoC
FIFO	108
LFU	233
LRU	140
TTL	184
Size	139

(b) Content replacement

Table 2: Lines of code for different algorithms in iCache.

Fidelity: First, we need to ensure that the optimizations we introduced in iCache do not introduce semantic bugs in the caching behavior. Thus, to evaluate the fidelity of iCache against ndnSim [10], we generated several topologies and content request traces. Due to the scalability limits of ndnSIM, we typically ran this for smaller topologies with less than 100 nodes. Then, we observed that the cached contents of corresponding routers and paths taken by the request exactly match across the two experiments (not shown). This being said, we acknowledge that iCache does not provide all the features of ndnSIM, especially in terms of advanced content routing protocols, security checks, and packet-level behaviors.

Scalability: Figure 4 shows the simulation time of a large-scale simulation on a machine with a Xeon 2.13GHz core and 1TB of memory running Linux. The simulation involved about 80K routers, 16M clients, 500K videos, and 196M content requests (see Section 3), and took ≤5 hours for different cache sizes. For comparison, the native ndnSIM needs 127.1 to 252.2 hours to finish the same scale of simulations. As a point of comparison, we also include a version of ndnSIM with routing pre-computation optimization described above. This precomputation does help significantly, as it drop the simulation time to 7.5-132.9 hours; but this is still almost 2× slower than iCache.

Extensibility: We evaluate the ease of adding new caching algorithms to iCache by counting the lines of codes for the 7 content placement and 5 content replacement algorithm modules written in iCache. Table 2 shows that across all the strategies we did not need more than about 230 lines of C++ code.

5. EFFECT OF VIDEO WORKLOADS ON ICN

In this section, we investigate the effect of the PPTV VOD workload on the performance of ICN and address the following questions:

- How does cache size impact the performance of ICN caching schemes in terms of network footprint reduction, cache hit rates, and server load reduction given video workloads?
- What is the best combination of content placement and replacement algorithms for different cache sizes and across different performance metrics?
- Is there a near-optimal or good enough strategy that is robust across this space of considerations?

5.1 Setup

First, we describe the simulation setup used in the rest of the paper. There are three types of nodes in the iCache platform: servers (i.e., content origins), consumers (i.e., content requesters), and routers. Servers correspond to the PPTV CDN servers. (Note that we do not consider the P2P mode in the evaluations and only focus on the CDN mode.) There are a total of 221 servers connected to the network from the same access points as in the real deployment of PPTV. We assume each server maintains all video contents. Consumers correspond to the PPTV clients observed in the dataset.

Each client is attached to the access router whose IP has the longest prefix in common with it. There are 82,726 routers each equipped with a cache of the same size. As in many previous works (e.g., [23,44,45,47]), we use the shortest paths to populate the routing tables of each router. Each content request is routed toward the closest origin server, and the request is "shortcut" if the content is found on an on-path router.

There are three key dimensions to explore here: (1) *cache size*, (2) *content placement strategy*, and (3) *content replacement strategy*. For (1), we consider four different cache sizes: 1GB, 10GB, 100GB, and 1TB. To put this in context, considering the total volume of different videos in our dataset is 137TB, these sizes of caches can approximately store 0.0007%, 0.007%, 0.07% and 0.7% of contents, respectively. As a reference point, we also consider a zero-cache scenario. For (2), we have implemented seven different content placement algorithms from related work: *LCE*, *LCD*, *Rand*, *Prob*, *PProb*, *Centrality*, and *Cross* [18,22,36,37,43,48]. Finally, for (3), we consider five content replacement algorithms: *FIFO*, *LRU*, *LFU*, *TTL*, and *Size* [9,42]. This space of parameters covers some of the relevant sizes for today's storage caches and represents main proposed caching strategies. In total, there are $4 \times 7 \times 5 = 140$ combinations of these parameters.

5.2 Results

There are three main metrics used to quantify the performance of ICN [23] that we define below. Here the subscript r refers to a specific router and R is the number of routers. Similarly, the subscript q refers to a specific object request and V is the total number of video requests. The metrics are:

1. *Average cache hit ratio* across all routers defined as $HitRate = \frac{\sum_{r=1}^{R} \frac{Hit_r}{Hit_r + Misses_r}}{R}$, where Hit_r refers to the number of requests that router r was able to serve from its cache, and $Misses_r$ is the number of requests that it forwarded upstream due to cache miss.
2. *Total reduction in the network footprint* or the total number of byte-hops saved via in-network caching defined as: $TrafficReduction = \frac{\sum_{q=1}^{V} (HopsNoCache_q - HopsICN_q) \times Bytes_q}{\sum_{q=1}^{V} HopsNoCache_q \times Bytes_q}$, where $HopsNoCache_q$ refers to the number of hops the request would take to reach the nearest origin server, and $HopsICN_q$ is the number of hops the request took to reach

(a) 1GB

	LCE	LCD	Rand	Prob	PProb	Cent.	Cross
Size	0.003	0.004	0.005	0.004	0.004	0.002	0.004
TTL	0.008	0.007	0.008	0.008	0.008	0.003	0.008
LRU	0.008	0.010	0.006	0.006	0.004	0.004	0.008
LFU	0.007	0.003	0.007	0.007	0.007	0.002	0.007
FIFO	0.007	0.010	0.006	0.006	0.004	0.004	0.007

(b) 10GB

	LCE	LCD	Rand	Prob	PProb	Cent.	Cross
Size	0.010	0.011	0.014	0.012	0.012	0.007	0.010
TTL	0.020	0.025	0.022	0.020	0.019	0.011	0.020
LRU	0.013	0.023	0.017	0.012	0.014	0.011	0.013
LFU	0.025	0.014	0.025	0.026	0.025	0.011	0.025
FIFO	0.013	0.023	0.016	0.012	0.013	0.008	0.013

(c) 100GB

	LCE	LCD	Rand	Prob	PProb	Cent.	Cross
Size	0.026	0.029	0.035	0.032	0.034	0.016	0.028
TTL	0.036	0.048	0.046	0.041	0.041	0.023	0.038
LRU	0.034	0.047	0.048	0.043	0.046	0.023	0.038
LFU	0.059	0.039	0.058	0.059	0.058	0.030	0.059
FIFO	0.032	0.046	0.045	0.039	0.040	0.020	0.035

(d) 1TB

	LCE	LCD	Rand	Prob	PProb	Cent.	Cross
Size	0.065	0.070	0.079	0.076	0.082	0.030	0.072
TTL	0.079	0.090	0.091	0.088	0.088	0.043	0.085
LRU	0.084	0.091	0.096	0.095	0.097	0.043	0.091
LFU	0.111	0.085	0.104	0.108	0.103	0.049	0.111
FIFO	0.078	0.089	0.091	0.088	0.088	0.040	0.085

Figure 5: Average cache hit ratio: The cache hit rates are generally low, and the best combination of placement and replacement for 1GB, 10GB, 100GB, and 1TB are *LCD +LRU*, *Prob +LFU*, *Prob +LFU*, and *Cross +LFU*, respectively.

(a) 1GB

	LCE	LCD	Rand	Prob	PProb	Cent.	Cross
Size	1.8	2.1	2.5	2.2	2.1	1.3	1.9
TTL	3.7	3.5	3.4	3.3	3.2	1.4	3.6
LRU	2.6	3.6	2.3	2.3	1.9	2.0	2.5
LFU	3.0	1.7	3.3	3.3	3.2	1.3	3.0
FIFO	2.5	3.6	2.3	2.3	1.8	1.8	2.5

(b) 10GB

	LCE	LCD	Rand	Prob	PProb	Cent.	Cross
Size	5.5	4.9	6.7	6.1	5.8	3.7	5.7
TTL	8.6	10.1	9.0	8.4	7.7	5.2	8.3
LRU	5.7	9.6	7.6	5.9	6.4	4.5	5.8
LFU	10.5	6.4	10.7	10.7	10.2	5.0	10.5
FIFO	5.6	9.3	7.1	5.7	5.6	3.9	5.6

(c) 100GB

	LCE	LCD	Rand	Prob	PProb	Cent.	Cross
Size	12.8	11.9	14.1	13.5	13.4	7.1	13.3
TTL	15.4	17.4	17.3	16.2	15.5	9.8	15.8
LRU	15.0	17.5	18.1	17.1	17.2	9.6	16.3
LFU	21.9	15.0	20.4	21.3	20.3	11.9	21.8
FIFO	14.1	16.8	17.0	15.7	15.3	8.6	15.1

(d) 1TB

	LCE	LCD	Rand	Prob	PProb	Cent.	Cross
Size	23.7	22.1	25.0	24.5	25.0	12.2	25.4
TTL	27.2	26.3	27.6	27.8	26.9	15.4	28.5
LRU	28.6	26.7	28.7	29.3	28.8	16.4	30.0
LFU	33.7	25.3	29.9	31.6	29.9	18.5	33.5
FIFO	27.1	26.3	27.6	27.8	26.9	15.4	28.4

Figure 6: Total traffic reduction (%): The reduction is more than 20% only with cache > 100GB. The best combination of placement and replacement for 1GB, 10GB, 100GB, and 1TB are *LCE +TTL*, *Prob +LFU*, *LCE +LFU*, and *LCE +LFU*, respectively.

(a) 1GB

	LCE	LCD	Rand	Prob	PProb	Cent.	Cross
Size	2.3	3.1	3.5	2.9	3.0	1.7	2.5
TTL	5.6	5.1	5.6	5.5	5.4	1.9	5.4
LRU	5.3	7.1	4.4	4.3	3.1	3.1	5.4
LFU	4.8	2.5	5.1	5.1	5.2	1.7	4.8
FIFO	5.1	7.1	4.4	4.3	3.1	2.6	5.3

(b) 10GB

	LCE	LCD	Rand	Prob	PProb	Cent.	Cross
Size	6.6	7.3	9.3	8.1	8.1	4.9	7.0
TTL	13.2	16.1	14.4	13.2	12.5	7.4	12.9
LRU	8.8	14.9	11.1	8.4	9.8	7.3	9.1
LFU	16.1	9.4	16.3	16.5	16.5	7.2	16.2
FIFO	8.8	14.7	10.6	8.2	8.6	5.4	8.9

(c) 100GB

	LCE	LCD	Rand	Prob	PProb	Cent.	Cross
Size	16.6	18.3	21.9	19.8	21.2	10.9	17.6
TTL	21.9	28.8	27.7	24.7	25.0	15.2	22.8
LRU	20.7	28.4	28.5	25.9	27.7	15.2	22.7
LFU	33.7	24.1	33.5	34.1	33.9	18.8	33.8
FIFO	19.5	27.5	26.9	23.9	24.6	13.3	21.3

(d) 1TB

	LCE	LCD	Rand	Prob	PProb	Cent.	Cross
Size	36.3	40.2	43.8	42.2	45.3	19.2	39.3
TTL	42.0	49.1	48.8	47.2	47.5	24.4	44.7
LRU	44.3	49.8	51.1	49.9	51.3	25.9	46.9
LFU	54.5	47.3	54.3	55.2	53.8	29.2	55.0
FIFO	41.9	49.0	48.8	47.1	47.5	24.3	44.6

Figure 7: Server load reduction (%): The reduction is substantial only when cache size is > 100GB. The best combination of placement and replacement for 1GB, 10GB, 100GB, and 1TB are *LCD +LRU*, *PProb +LFU*, *Prob +LFU*, and *Prob +LFU*, respectively.

the closest location containing a copy of the video content (i.e., either an in-network cache or the origin server).

3. *Reduction in load on the origin servers* defined as: $1 - \frac{NumCachedReq}{V}$, where *NumCachedReq* is the number of requests that were served from *some* in-network cache.

Figures 5, 6, and 7 show the values of these three metrics across the space of 35 caching strategy combinations for four different cache sizes. We reiterate that such a comprehensive evaluation of the design and parameter space would not be possible without the scalability of iCache.

We make a few observations from these results. First, we see that the metrics improve as the cache size grows, and, because of the large traffic volume of videos, we observe significant benefits only with 100GB or 1TB cache sizes. Note that with a 1GB cache on each router, the average reduction of video traffic and cache hit rate of routers is less than 3.7% and 1.0%, respectively, across all caching strategies. However, when the cache size increases to 100GB, the above metrics improve to 21.9% and 5.9%, respectively. Second, we observe a sub-linear effect of adding more cache capacity or a natural "diminishing returns" property, as increasing the cache size by 10× provides less than 2× performance improvement, even with the best possible strategy. Third, we do observe that some of the more "intelligent" content placement-replacement combinations can provide substantial improvements over the vanilla *LCE +LRU* combination; e.g., with a 100GB cache size, we observe that the best strategy is 46% better across all the metrics. Finally, we can see that the optimal strategy can be quite different both across the space of metrics and the cache sizes. For instance, *LCD +LRU* is the best strategy w.r.t. hit rate at 1GB cache, but *Cross +LFU* is the best w.r.t. hit rate at 1TB. Similarly, at 1TB, *Cross +LFU*, *LCE +LFU*, and*Prob +LFU* are the best strategies w.r.t. hit rate, traffic reduction, and server load reduction respectively.[3] We do not yet have a simple analytical basis to explain why the optimal combination varies, and we leave this for future work.

Correlation across metrics and cache sizes: Next, we summarize how *correlated* the different strategies are across metrics and cache sizes. Recall that we have 35 different combinations of content placement/replacement algorithms. Now, for a given cache size and metric, we construct the 35-item vector with each entry denoting the performance of a given combination. Then, given these vectors, we compute the Pearson correlation coefficient between these vectors for different cache sizes and metrics. In Figure 8a, we show the correlation between each pair of metrics for a given cache size. Similarly, in Figure 8b, we show the correlation between pairs of cache sizes for each metric.

First, we see that hit rate and server load reduction are perfectly correlated. This is expected, as higher cache hit rate reduces server load. Second, we find that optimizing the server load reduction

[3] We found it interesting that Centrality performs poorly across different scenarios. We conjecture that in the strictly hierarchical structure of the Chinese Internet, very few routers (located near the core) have high betweenness and are selected for caching.

does not necessarily translate into a reduction in the overall network footprint. This is also expected, since the traffic reduction depends not only on cache hits, but also on *where* hits occur and whether they occur for popular vs. unpopular objects. We revisit this in greater depth in Section 7, where we systematically dissect the benefits of the various caching strategies. Finally, with respect to the cache sizes, we see a natural correlation between similar cache sizes—1GB cache is the least correlated with all other values, and the correlation between 100GB-1TB caches is the strongest.

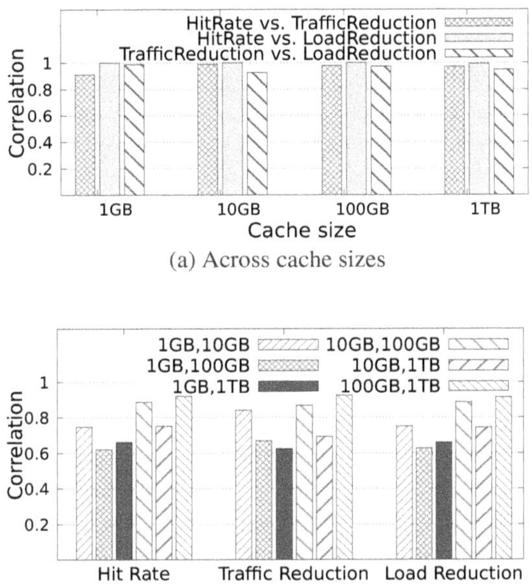

(a) Across cache sizes

(b) Across metrics

Figure 8: Hitrate and server load reduction are most correlated, and similar-sized caches have higher correlations.

Is there a dominant strategy? The previous results show that the *best* strategy varies quite significantly across the space of cache sizes and metrics. Given this diversity, a natural question for ICN deployment is whether there are some strategies that are consistently close to the optimal value, even if they are not always the best. To understand this, we calculate an aggregate performance metric that computes the average normalized distance of each strategy from the best possible strategy for each of the 12 scenarios (i.e., 4 cache sizes and 3 metrics). Specifically, for a given scenario s (i.e., a fixed cache size and metric), we compute a score for a given placement-replacement combination pr relative to the performance of the best combination $Perf^*_s$ for that scenario: $Score_{pr,s} = \frac{Perf^*_s - Perf_{pr,s}}{Perf^*_s}$, where $Perf_{pr,s}$ is the performance of pr on scenario s. Then, the overall score $Score_{pr}$ is the mean across all scenarios.

Table 3 shows this normalized score for the 35 caching strategies and highlights the top three strategies. First, we see that in terms of content replacement, *LFU* is the most dominant strategy. In fact, the top 5 strategies all use *LFU*. Second, looking at each dimension separately may not necessarily indicate the best strategy. For example, for cache placement, *Rand* and *LCD* are the top two strategies, but none of their overall combinations rank in the top-3 strategies highlighted in the table. In particular, *LCD* does not work in concert with *LFU*, which, as we saw earlier, is the best strategy for content replacement. Similarly, we find that the combination of the best placement (*Rand*) and the best replacement (*LFU*) strategies

	FIFO	*LFU*	*LRU*	*TTL*	*Size*	RowAvg
LCE	0.64	0.92	0.66	0.76	0.48	0.69
LCD	0.86	0.60	0.88	0.85	0.52	0.74
Rand	0.71	0.91	0.74	0.82	0.62	0.76
Prob	0.65	0.93	0.69	0.78	0.57	0.72
PProb	0.62	0.91	0.67	0.76	0.58	0.71
Centrality	0.38	0.43	0.43	0.40	0.30	0.39
Cross	0.66	0.92	0.70	0.77	0.52	0.71
ColAvg	0.65	0.80	0.68	0.73	0.51	

Table 3: Normalized scores of each strategy across all 12 scenarios to identify a "dominant" strategy that is optimal or close to optimal most of the time.

(i.e., the best row and column averages) is not the optimal strategy; the global best strategy is *Prob +LFU* with a score of 0.93. The *Rand +LFU* combination is also quite close with an averaged normalized score of 0.91.

5.3 Summary of main findings

Our analysis of the impact of video workloads on ICN caching metrics shows that:

- Cache sizes need to be greater than 100GB to provide significant (22% traffic reduction and 34% server load reduction) benefit for PPTV traffic. Compared with other workloads, video seems to require much larger cache sizes; for instance, prior work suggests that a cache that can store 10M files on each router can bring a 20% traffic reduction of BitTorrent content [47]. We also see a natural diminishing returns property wherein increasing the cache 10× from 100GB to 1TB only yields less than 2× improvement.
- The best combination of content placement and replacement depends on the operating regime and the caching metric of interest. For instance, techniques that optimize cache hit rates or server load, do not directly yield a substantial reduction in network footprint. Therefore, ISPs should carefully select their caching strategies according to their objectives (e.g. optimizing traffic reduction or server load reduction) and their network characteristics (e.g. cache size, hierarchical/flat topology).
- Fortunately, there exists a sufficiently dominant strategy *Prob +LFU* that is close to the best possible strategy almost always. We also find that *LFU* is the dominant replacement strategy. However, the best content placement strategy is not part of the best combined placement-replacement strategy.

6. VIDEO QUALITY OF EXPERIENCE WITH ICN

As discussed in prior work, Internet video introduces new QoE considerations such as buffering ratio, startup delay, and average delivered bitrate [21, 34]. In this section, we study the effect of using ICN on video QoE using the same simulation setup as described in Section 5.1. Specifically, we are interested in understanding:

- How do the ICN caching schemes and cache sizes impact video QoE?
- How do the network-level metrics and the best choices from the previous section translate into video QoE considerations?

6.1 Methodology

To understand QoE improvements of ICN, first, we need a way of modeling the QoE that a client would perceive if its requests were served from a specific in-network cache. In the absence of a real caching deployment, we do not have this directly; thus, we need some way to extrapolate the QoE metrics from our PPTV traces.

Province	Buffering ratio			Avg. bitrate			Join Time		
	SamePoP	SameISP	DiffISP	SamePoP	SameISP	DiffISP	SamePoP	SameISP	DiffISP
BJ	1	1.17	2.69	1	0.85	0.69	1	1.07	1.48
LN	1	1.33	4.01	1	0.92	0.56	1	1.03	1.49
ZJ	1	1.18	3.35	1	0.80	0.47	1	1.05	1.71
...	...	...	...	...	...	...	...	...	...
Others	1	1.17	3.18	1	0.86	0.55	1	1.06	1.52

Table 4: Normalized QoE metrics across different provinces for different server classes.

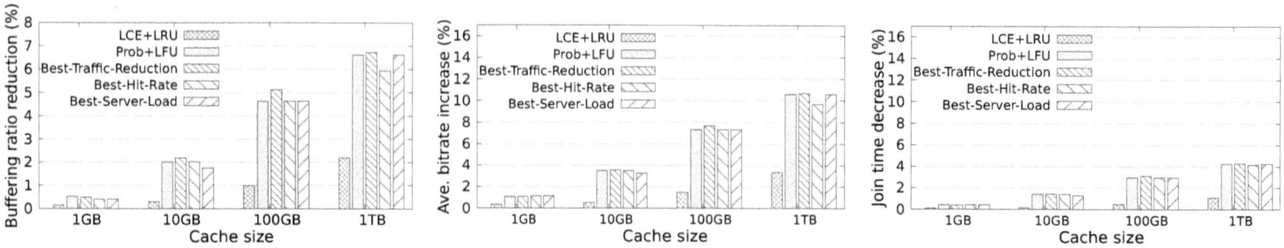

(a) Buffering ratio (b) Average bitrate (c) Join time

Figure 9: Improvement in different QoE metrics for different ICN caching strategies and cache sizes.

Given a specific client-router pair c, r, our extrapolation methodology tries to find requests in the original PPTV traces that share *similar* client and server attributes [41]. For instance, if there is a client c from Beijing on a DSL connection from China Telecom as its ISP, and the router r chosen in the ICN caching case is also a China Telecom router in Beijing, we select all PPTV traces where the client-server attributes match these values and use those statistics to extrapolate the QoE for the hypothetical c, r request. Then, to predict the expected QoE for this hypothetical request c, r, we use the median value over requests with similar attributes. (For all metrics other than buffering ratio, we use the median. For buffering ratio, the median is typically zero, and we use the average.)

Ideally, we would like to pick the requests that match every possible client and server attributes. However, we run into a classic "curse of dimensionality" problem where the data becomes quite sparse as we increase the number of dimensions. Furthermore, for some provinces (e.g., TB for Tibet), client terminals (e.g,. mobile), and client connection types (e.g., 3G), we have only few requests.

Given the above constraints, we take the following heuristic. First, we only focus on the dominant client terminal and connection types; in this case it is desktop clients on broadband connections. Second, we exploit the hierarchical structure of the Chinese Internet topology to focus on three *classes of servers* rather than attempt to match all possible server attributes. (The three main ISPs, ChinaTelecom, ChinaUnicom and China Mobile organize their networks in a hierarchical manner and connect to one another at a higher level. Other small ISPs interconnect via one of these major ISPs.) Specifically, we partition the content-view dataset into three non-overlapping categories based on the locations of the client and the server IPs:

1. *Same PoP (SamePoP):* The client and the server are in the same PoP (point of presence) of the same ISP;
2. *Same ISP, but different PoPs (SameISP):* The client and the server are in the same ISP network but in different PoPs;
3. *Different ISPs (DiffISP):* The client and the server are in different ISPs.

Finally, we use the client location at a province-level granularity. To this end, for each province with a sufficiently large number of requests, we consider the servers in one of the above three categories and obtain the summary statistics. For the remaining provinces that do not have individually a sufficient number of client requests in our dataset, we use the average value across the provinces with sufficient data for each of the three server categories.

Using this extrapolation methodology, Table 4 shows the improvement of the QoE metrics relative to the case of SamePoP for 3 of the major provinces. Due to confidentiality considerations, we cannot show the absolute QoE numbers and normalize the values relative to the baseline of SamePoP; e.g., for SameISP the normalized QoE will be $NormQoE_{SameISP} = \frac{QoE_{SameISP}}{QoE_{SamePoP}}$. Note that for buffering ratio and join time, higher values of the normalized metric indicate worse QoE and for average bitrate, lower values indicate worse QoE. We observe that the QoE is strongly dependent on the distance between the user and the provider. For instance, in the "Others" row the buffering ratio increases by 17% if the server is in a different PoP but within the same ISP; this value grows by 218% for the case of different ISPs.

6.2 Results

Given the above extrapolation methodology, we can compare the QoE provided by a specific ICN strategy relative to the QoE provided by the reference, no-cache strategy. That is, for each request q, we calculate two normalized QoE values based on the values shown in Table 4: $NormQoE_{q,ICN}$ and $NormQoE_{q,NoCache}$. Then, we calculate the difference between the per-request means of these values: $\frac{\sum_{q=1}^{V} NormQoE_{q,NoCache}}{V} - \frac{\sum_{q=1}^{V} NormQoE_{q,ICN}}{V}$, where V is the total number of video requests.[4]

Figure 9 shows this improvement metric (expressed as a percentage). In the interest of brevity, we only consider a few interesting caching strategy combinations from the previous section. Specifically, we consider three combinations: (1) *LCE +LRU*, which is the most basic combination suggested in previous work; (2) *Prob +LFU*, which emerged as the dominant strategy across all scenarios from the previous section; and (3) The best caching strategy for each of the different network-level metrics from the previous section.

We make three main observations from this figure. First, the overall magnitude of QoE improvement is quite low; the maximum performance gap between the largest 1TB cache and a no-ICN scenario is $\leq 12\%$ across all QoE metrics. Second, with small caches $\leq$ 10GB, video QoE improvement is almost negligible. Finally, we see that the more complex caching strategies are more beneficial

[4]For bitrate, the difference is reversed since a higher value is better.

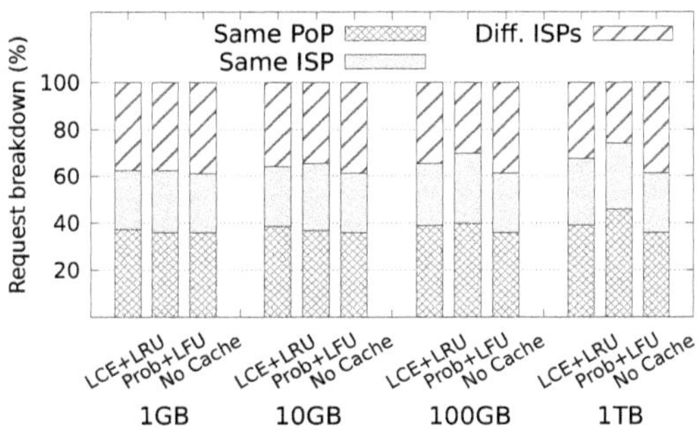

Figure 10: Breakdown of requests served by servers in three different types of locations.

to QoE than simpler strategies. For example, the average relative performance improvement by using the *Prob +LFU* strategy compared to *LCE +LRU* strategy across all the metrics and cache sizes is close to 4×.

Overall, we find that the traffic reduction appears to be the most useful criterion to improve the QoE metrics. This is intuitively expected, as reducing traffic load improves requests locality. As we saw earlier in Table 4, locality directly correlates with improved QoE in our dataset. We also see that the dominant strategy from the previous section (i.e., *Prob +LFU*) is again very competitive, as it is close to the best result in all cases.

To further analyze why the overall improvement in the QoE seems quite low, we provide a breakdown of the number of requests served by the three key categories of (client relative) provider locations in Figure 10. As a point of reference, we also show the corresponding breakdown for the case of no ICN deployment (denoted by No Cache in the figure). For ease of visualization, we focus only on two of the ICN strategies. The figure shows that the current server deployment of PPTV is effectively *localizing* requests; i.e., the fraction of SamePoP and SameISP requests is largely similar at $\leq$ 100GB caches, and only at 1TB does *Prob +LFU* show a visible difference.

6.3 Summary of key findings

After analyzing the effect of ICN caching strategies on video QoE improvement, we find that:

- We see non-trivial QoE improvements only with caches $\geq$ 100GB. Even then, the QoE improvement is quite low $\leq 12\%$ across all QoE metrics even with a 1TB cache.
- The caching strategy that optimizes the traffic reduction appears to be the best strategy to also optimize QoE; the dominant strategy in terms of the caching metrics (i.e., *Prob +LFU*) is again a close-to-optimal strategy with respect to QoE (as shown in Figure 9).
- The QoE improvement seems to be low mainly because of the good coverage of the PPTV servers across popular PoPs/ISPs. This suggests that for popular video services whose server footprint is already spatially diverse, the QoE benefits of ICN will be limited.

7. DISSECTING BENEFITS

In the previous two sections, we studied the aggregate improvement of different content replacement/placement algorithms in terms of network-level and QoE metrics. In this section, we provide a more in-depth analysis to identify *how* and *where* these benefits manifest, so that it can better inform the deployment decisions of content providers and ISPs as they consider ICN-like architectures. Specifically, we are interested in:

- Which network routers (e.g., edge vs. core) provide the largest contribution to caching metrics and QoE improvements?
- What types of requests (e.g., low vs. high popularity) and client locations (e.g., types of provinces) are more likely to perceive the largest benefits?
- At what times of day do we see the most benefits?

In the interest of brevity, we only focus on *Prob +LFU* that we found to be the dominant strategy across caching metrics and near-optimal for QoE.

7.1 Routers contributing to improvement

We identify the (network-wide) top-100 routers with respect to performance metrics (i.e., hitrate, contribution to traffic reduction, and contribution to server load reduction). Then, we characterize these top-100 routers along two dimensions: (1) The relative role of a router in the network (i.e., Edge, Middle, or Core) and (2) Geographical location of the router (i.e., which province). Because we do not have such role annotations in our measured topology, we use the following heuristic for (1). First, we classify a router's role for each request relative to the shortest path between the client and the server. We divide the path into three equal-sized segments: Edge, Middle, or Core, with Edge being the segment closest to the client, Core being close to the server, and Middle being the rest. Then, for each router, we compute its overall role by taking a simple majority vote over all requests the router is involved. For (2), we use a proprietary IP-to-location mapping database [2].

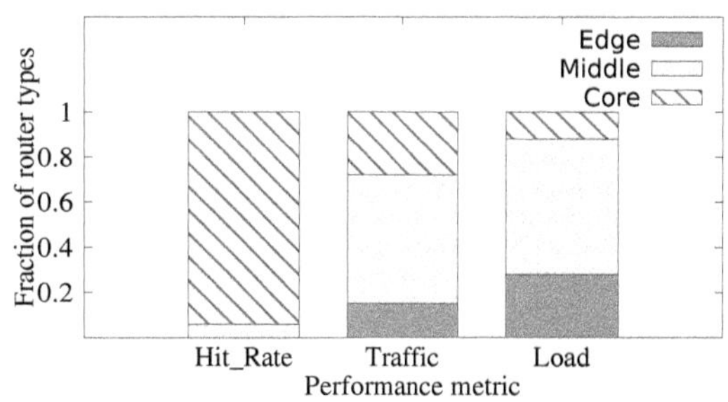

Figure 11: Breakdown of top routers locations.

Figure 11 shows the breakdown of these routers in terms of their network roles. We see that most of the top-100 routers with high cache hit rate are Core routers. This is because the requests of the same content aggregate when going towards the direction of the origin server. However, Core routers contribute very little to reducing the traffic and server load. This observation is consistent with previous work on more general request workloads [23]. We posit that the incentives for real world ICN deployment by ISPs and content providers will likely stem from traffic and load reduction. Thus, we suspect that ICN routers will not be prominent in the network core.

We have also analyzed how these top-100 routers are geographically spread (not shown). We observed two main trends. First, the top routers with respect to traffic and server load reductions are mainly in provinces with a large client population (e.g., HE, SD, GD). This is expected, as the routers in regions with larger populations serve more client requests and thus cumulatively reduce more network footprint. Second, top routers with respect to hit rate improvement are located in provinces with many PPTV servers (e.g., JL, BJ, SC). This is consistent with Figure 11, as a province with more servers naturally has more routers closer to servers. Similar to our earlier observation in Section 6 that the video QoE metrics are

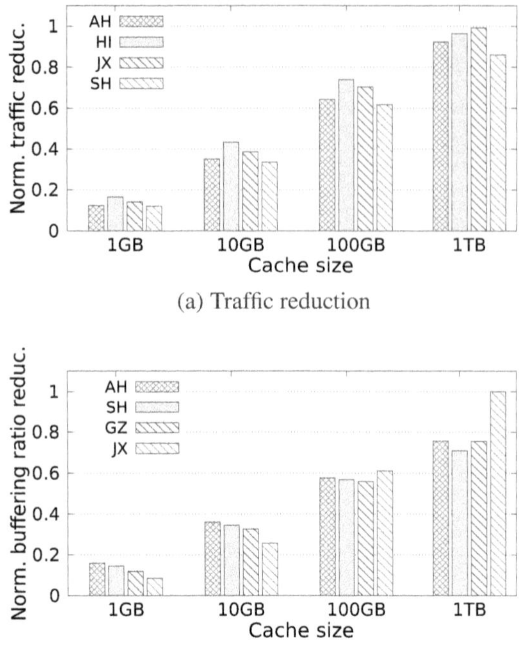

(a) Traffic reduction

(b) Buffering improvement

Figure 12: Locations with best improvement in traffic reduction and buffering ratio improvement.

closely correlated with traffic reduction, here, we saw the routers contributing to most QoE improvements are, to a great extent, the same routers that contribute most to traffic reduction (not shown).

7.2 Request-level analysis

Locations with most improvement: We identify the regions with the highest caching performance and QoE improvements using the traffic reduction and buffering ratio as representative caching- and QoE-related metrics. Recall that each request q is associated with the province where the client is located. For each province, we calculate the average traffic reduction and QoE improvement across requests originating in that province. Then, we normalize these values across different provinces with respect to the province with the highest value such that the best value is 1. While this normalization is because of PPTV's confidentiality constraints, since our goal is to study the relative behaviors across provinces, we believe this is a reasonable choice.

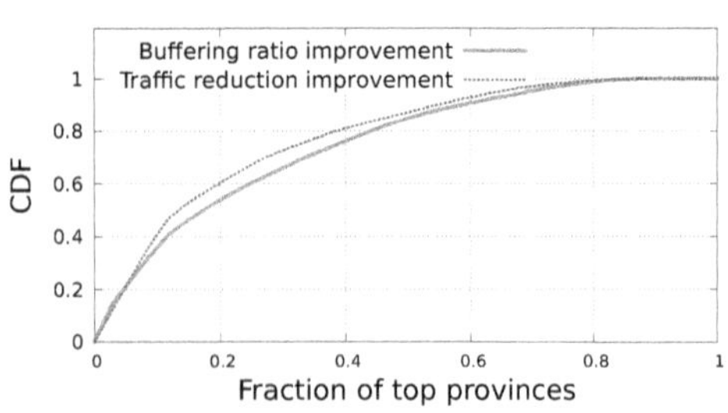

Figure 13: CDF of buffering ratio and traffic improvement as functions of top provinces.

Figure 12 shows the normalized values for top 4 provinces. The top provinces shown in Figure 12a and Figure 12b have substantial overlap, with AH, JX and SH being in common. For QoE improvement, the top provinces tend to be those with few servers deployed (e.g., JX, AH, GZ, SH) (see Figure 2). This is intuitively

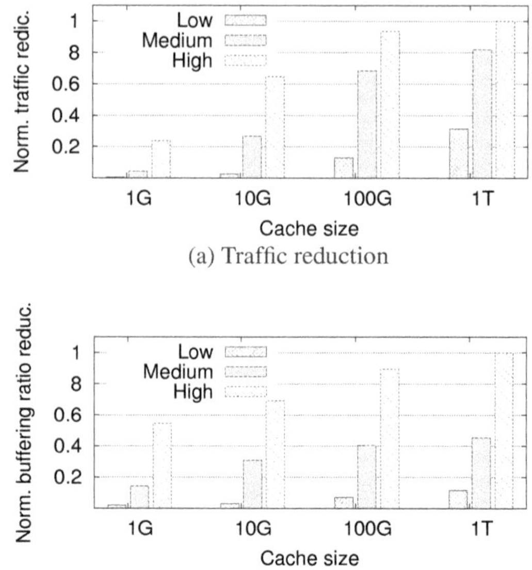

(a) Traffic reduction

(b) Buffering improvement

Figure 14: Improvement in video QoE and traffic reduction vs. popularity of objects.

expected from the earlier observation in Figure 10: Provinces with PPTV servers already localize traffic and cannot substantially improve QoE further.

The previous result looks at the average per-request improvement, but does not consider the volume of requests from a given region. To account for this, we also analyzed how the top-k provinces contribute to the *total* improvement across requests $\sum_q Improvement_q$ for different $Improvement$ metrics. Figure 13 shows the cumulative distribution of improvement of buffering ratio and traffic reduction as a function of top provinces. We see that there is a skewed and diminishing returns behavior: the top-20% provinces contribute about 60% of the total improvement. As discussed earlier, these tend to be provinces with high request volumes but low/no server presence. The above results suggest that ISP deployment efforts may be better invested in such regions to gain maximum return-on-investments.

Request popularity: In Figure 14, we analyze which type of requests receive the highest QoE improvement and contribute most to traffic reduction. To this end, we categorize videos into three popularity bins: high ($\geq$ 10,000 views per day), medium (5,000 to 10,000 views per day), and low ($<$ 5,000 views per day). Then we assign each request q to one of these three bins and, for each bin, we compute the average values of traffic and buffering ratio improvements. Then we normalize these values such that the high-popularity bin using 1TB cache is assigned a value of 1. The result is quite intuitive: popular contents by virtue of higher request rates and cache hits see the highest QoE improvements and contribute most of the traffic reduction. With increasing the cache size, we observe that objects with medium and low popularity also benefit.

We have also analyzed the contribution of the top-k popular objects to the aggregate improvement of buffering ratio and traffic reduction. Here, we observed an even greater skew; the top 0.0014% objects ($\approx$700 videos) contribute 91% of the buffering ratio improvement and 92% of the traffic improvement (not shown).

7.3 Temporal analysis

Finally, we analyze at *what time of day* we observe most of the perceived benefit. (Since there is only one time zone in China, we do not need to be concerned about the effect of different time

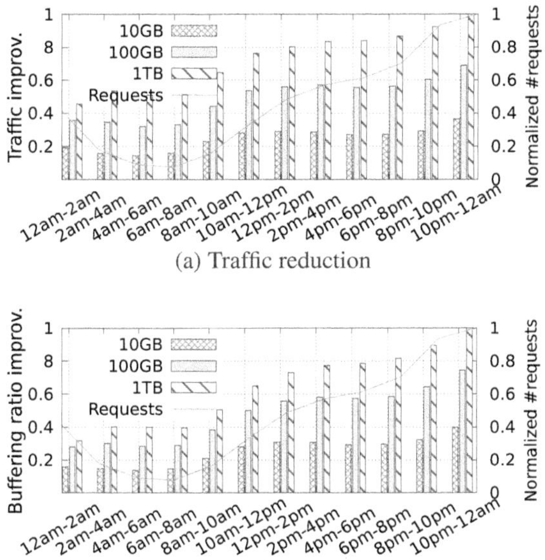

(a) Traffic reduction

(b) Buffering

Figure 15: Time-of-day effects: We can visually confirm that the times of high improvement roughly coincides with high request volume.

zones.) Figure 15 shows the breakdown of the QoE improvement for the buffering ratio and traffic reduction per content-view trace as functions of time on a single day. For brevity, we do not show the other days or QoE metrics since the results are similar. We observe that, on average, most QoE improvement and traffic reduction is achieved in the evening (8:00pm to 12:00am). We can see that these periods are actually the busiest time (i.e., highest number of requests) for PPTV platform. This observation that caching provides the most gain at the time interval with most video traffic provides good incentives for access ISPs, as reducing peak utilization can reduce costs with "burstable billing" schemes that charge based on 95-th percentile usage.

8. DISCUSSION

Cache placement and provisioning: Our evaluation assumes that all locations have the same amount of cache storage. A natural question is the impact of more fine-grained cache placement and provisioning strategies on our findings. For example, previous work has shown that a network-wide cache deployment may not yield substantial benefits [23]. While an exploration of optimal cache placement is outside the scope of this paper, we present some initial results.

We make a performance comparison between two extreme cache provisioning strategies: (1) *Ubiquitous caching*, where every router in the network is equipped with a cache of the same size, and (2) *Access-Only caching*, where only access routers (i.e., one hop away from the client) are equipped with caches. To make a fair comparison between these two strategies, we assume that the total volume of network-wide cache storage is the same.

Our experiments show that the relative gain of ubiquitous caching over access-only caching depends on the cache size. For a very small cache size of 1GB, the gain is as large as 2× for different performance metrics. As the cache size increases, however, the performance gain diminishes. This is consistent with previous results reported in [23].

Origin server placement: As we saw earlier in Section 6, the improvements of video QoE as yielded by ICN caching are quite marginal, at least partially, because of the sufficient geodiversity of PPTV servers. A natural question, therefore, is the sensitivity of our results to the number and placement of origin servers.

To find the answer, we evaluate the sensitivity of our results to the number of origin PPTV servers. The results are shown in Figure 16. In each plot, the X axis represents the total number of origin servers and the Y axis is the gain yielded by ICN caching for the corresponding QoE metric. We show the normalized values on the Y axes to make it easier to compare the results across different cache sizes and metrics. The locations of each given total number of servers are chosen at random from all the 221 PPTV servers.

We observe that as the number of origin servers grows, the effect of ICN caching on improving QoE metrics diminishes because of increasing geodiversity of the content servers. We believe that our results in Figure 9 are representative—Popular content providers today (e.g., YouTube, Netflix) that carry the most amount of traffic, typically, already have a significant geographic footprint [16], if not directly, at least via CDNs.

Request routing: One question is whether intelligent request routing strategies can help; e.g., would some of the less optimal caching strategies we saw perform better under different routing regimes? Extrapolating from prior work, we posit that complex request routing will offer minimal benefits over simple routing [23,46] and will likely not impact our observations.

Other forms of video: We have studied the interaction between VOD workloads and ICN because it is the dominant form of Internet video used today. An interesting direction of future work is to replicate our analysis on other types of video workloads (e.g., live streams).

9. CONCLUSIONS

Even though video and ICN have been considered natural allies, there has been little work on analyzing how video workloads impact the network-level benefits of ICN and how ICN helps improve video QoE metrics. Our work addresses this crucial gap. To the best of our knowledge, our study is the most comprehensive and the largest-scale analysis of ICN-on-video in terms of trace size, topology scale, and the space of ICN caching strategies explored.

Our findings have key implications for providers and future Internet architectures: (1) the benefits of ICN for video workloads with caches smaller than 100GB are marginal; (2) the combined content placement and content replacement strategy of *Prob +LFU* is close to the optimal with respect to improvements in both ICN caching performance and QoE metrics across the entire spectrum of analysis parameters; and (3) a small number of regions without origin servers and with requests for highly popular objects contribute to the most of the improvements. That said, this is by no means the final word in this space, and there are several directions for future work including analyzing other forms of video (e.g., live stream and short VOD), providing a more analytical basis for our empirical observations, and exploring the effects of different ICN routing schemes.

Acknowledgments

The authors would like to thank Alexander Afsanyev for helping us gain an in-depth understanding of ndnSIM. We also thank Stratis Ioannidis for shepherding our paper and Haiyong Xie for insightful discussions. This work is supported in part by the National Basic Research Program (2012CB315802) and the Natural Science Foundation of China (61379133). This work is also funded in part by NSF under award number CNS-1345305.

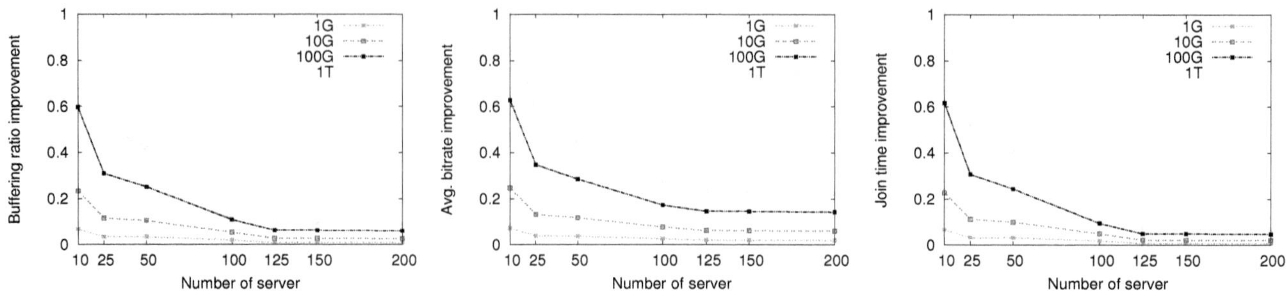

(a) Buffering ratio (b) Average bitrate (c) Join time

Figure 16: Improvement of QoE by ICN as a function of number of origin servers.

10. REFERENCES

[1] CCNx Project. http://www.ccnx.org/.

[2] Chunzhen. http://www.cz88.net/.

[3] Cisco forecast. http://blogs.cisco.com/sp/comments/cisco_visual_networking_index_forecast_annual_update/.

[4] COntent Mediator architecture for content-aware nETworks (COMET). http://www.comet-project.org/.

[5] Direct Code Execution (DCE). http://www.nsnam.org/docs/dce/release/1.0/manual/singlehtml/index.html.

[6] NetInf. http://www.netinf.org/.

[7] PPCloud: Big Data in PPTV. http://www.dvbcn.com/2014/03/18-109253.html.

[8] PPTV. http://www.pptv.com/.

[9] M. Abrams, C. R. Standridge, G. Abdulla, E. A. Fox, and S. Williams. Removal policies in network caches for world-wide web documents. In *Proc. SIGCOMM*, 1996.

[10] A. Afanasyev, I. Moiseenko, and L. Zhang. ndnSIM: NDN simulator for NS-3. http://named-data.net/techreport/TR005-ndnsim.pdf, 2012.

[11] S. Ando and A. Nakao. In-network cache simulations based on a youtube traffic analysis at the edge network. In *Proc. CFI*, 2014.

[12] P. A. Aranda, M. Zitterbart, Z. Boudjemil, M. Ghader, G. H. Garcia, M. Johnsson, A. Karouia, G. Lazar, M. Majanen, P. Mannersalo, D. Martin, M. T. Nguyen, S. P. Sanchez, P. Phelan, M. P. de Leon, G. M. Sollner, Y. Zaki, and L. Zhao. 4WARD. http://www.4ward-project.eu/, 2010.

[13] B. Cheng, X. Liu, Z. Zhang, and H. Jin. A measurement study of a peer-to-peer video-on-demand system. In *Proc. IPTPS*, 2007.

[14] A. Balachandran, V. Sekar, A. Akella, and S. Seshan. Analyzing the potential benefits of cdn augmentation strategies for internet video workloads. In *Proc. IMC*, 2013.

[15] C. M. Cabral, C. E. Rothenberg, and M. F. Magalhães. Mini-CCNx: Fast prototyping for named data networking. In *Proc. ICN*, 2013.

[16] M. Calder, X. Fan, Z. Hu, E. Katz-Bassett, J. Heidemann, and R. Govindan. Mapping the Expansion of Google's Serving Infrastructure. In *Proc. IMC*, 2013.

[17] M. Cha, H. Kwak, P. Rodriguez, Y.-Y. Ahn, and S. Moon. I tube, you tube, everybody tubes: Analyzing the world's largest user generated content video system. In *Proc. IMC*, 2007.

[18] W. K. Chai, D. He, I. Psaras, and G. Pavlou. Cache "less for more" in information-centric networks. In *Proc. IFIP Networking*, 2012.

[19] H. Che, Y. Tung, and Z. Wang. Hierarchical web caching systems: modeling, design and experimental results. *IEEE JSAC*, 2002.

[20] R. Chiocchetti, D. Rossi, and G. Rossini. ccnsim: An highly scalable ccn simulator. In *Proc. ICC*, June 2013.

[21] F. Dobrian, V. Sekar, A. Awan, I. Stoica, D. Joseph, A. Ganjam, J. Zhan, and H. Zhang. Understanding the impact of video quality on user engagement. In *Proc. SIGCOMM*, 2011.

[22] S. Eum, K. Nakauchi, M. Murata, Y. Shoji, and N. Nishinaga. Catt: Potential based routing with content caching for icn. In *Proc. ICN*, 2012.

[23] S. K. Fayazbakhsh, Y. Lin, A. Tootoonchian, A. Ghodsi, T. Koponen, B. Maggs, K. Ng, V. Sekar, and S. Shenker. Less pain, most of the gain: Incrementally deployable ICN. In *Proc. SIGCOMM*, 2013.

[24] C. Fricker, P. Robert, J. Roberts, and N. Sbihi. Impact of traffic mix on caching performance in a content-centric network. In *Proc. INFOCOM WKSHPS*, 2012.

[25] M. Gritter and D. R. Cheriton. An architecture for content routing support in the Internet. In *USITS*, 2001.

[26] B. Han, X. Wang, N. Choi, T. Kwon, and Y. Choi. Amvs-ndn: Adaptive mobile video streaming and sharing in wireless named data networking. In *Proc. NOMEN*, 2013.

[27] D. Han, A. Anand, F. Dogar, B. Li, H. Lim, M. Machado, A. Mukundan, W. Wu, A. Akella, D. G. Andersen, J. W. Byers, S. Seshan, and P. Steenkiste. Xia: Efficient support for evolvable internetworking. In *Proc. NSDI*, 2012.

[28] T.-Y. Huang, R. Johari, N. McKeown, M. Trunnell, and M. Watson. A buffer-based approach to rate adaptation: Evidence from a large video streaming service. In *Proc. SIGCOMM*, 2014.

[29] Y. Huang, T. Z. Fu, D.-M. Chiu, J. C. Lui, and C. Huang. Challenges, design and analysis of a large-scale p2p-vod system. In *Proc. SIGCOMM*, 2008.

[30] V. Jacobson et al. Networking named content. In *CoNext*, 2009.

[31] V. Jacobson, J. D. Thornton, D. K. Smetters, B. Zhang, G. Tsudik, K. claffy, D. Krioukov, D. Massey, C. Papadopoulos, T. Abdelzaher, L. Wang, P. Crowley, and E. Yeh. Named Data Networking (NDN) project. http://named-data.net/techreport/TR001ndn-proj.pdf, 2010.

[32] J. Jiang, V. Sekar, and H. Zhang. Improving fairness, efficiency, and stability in http-based adaptive video streaming with FESTIVE. In *Proc. CoNEXT*, 2012.

[33] T. Koponen et al. A data-oriented (and beyond) network architecture. In *SIGCOMM*, 2007.

[34] S. S. Krishnan and R. K. Sitaraman. Video stream quality impacts viewer behavior: Inferring causality using quasi-experimental designs. In *Proc. IMC*, 2012.

[35] D. Kulinski, J. Burke, and L. Zhang. Video Streaming over Named Data Networking. *IEEE COMSOC MMTC E-Letter*, 2013.

[36] N. Laoutaris, H. Che, and I. Stavrakakis. The LCD interconnection of LRU caches and its analysis. *Perform. Eval.*, 2006.

[37] N. Laoutaris, S. Syntila, and I. Stavrakakis. Meta algorithms for hierarchical web caches. In *Proc. ICPCC*, 2004.

[38] Z. Li, M. Sbai, Y. Hadjadj-Aoul, A. Gravey, D. Alliez, J. Garnier, G. Madec, G. Simon, and K. Singh. Network friendly video distribution. In *Proc. NOF*, 2012.

[39] Z. Li and G. Simon. Time-shifted tv in content centric networks: The case for cooperative in-network caching. In *Proc. ICC*, 2011.

[40] H. H. Liu, Y. Wang, Y. R. Yang, H. Wang, and C. Tian. Optimizing cost and performance for content multihoming. In *Proc. SIGCOMM*, 2012.

[41] X. Liu, F. Dobrian, H. Milner, J. Jiang, V. Sekar, I. Stoica, and H. Zhang. A case for a coordinated internet video control plane. In *Proc. SIGCOMM*, 2012.

[42] Z. Ming, M. Xu, and D. Wang. Age-based cooperative caching in information-centric networks. In *Proc. INFOCOM WORKSHOPS*, 2012.

[43] I. Psaras, W. K. Chai, and G. Pavlou. Probabilistic in-network caching for information-centric networks. In *Proc. ICN*, 2012.

[44] I. Psaras, R. G. Clegg, R. Landa, W. K. Chai, and G. Pavlou. Modelling and evaluation of ccn-caching trees. In *Proc. NETWORKING*, 2011.

[45] G. Rossini and D. Rossi. A dive into the caching performance of content centric networking. In *Proc. CAMAD*, 2012.

[46] A. Sharma, A. Venkataramani, and R. K. Sitaraman. Distributing content simplifies isp traffic engineering. In *Proc. SIGMETRICS*, 2013.

[47] G. Tyson, S. Kaune, S. Miles, Y. El-khatib, A. Mauthe, and A. Taweel. A trace-driven analysis of caching in content-centric networks. In *Proc. ICCCN*, 2012.

[48] W. Wang, S. Yi, Y. Guo, M. A. Kaafar, and Z. Li. Crcache: Exploiting the correlation between content popularity and network topology for icn caching. In *Proc. ICC*, 2014.

[49] Y. Wang, Z. Li, G. Tyson, S. Uhlig, and G. Xie. Optimal cache allocation for content-centric networking. In *Proc. ICNP*, 2013.

[50] H. Yin, X. Liu, F. Qiu, N. Xia, C. Lin, H. Zhang, V. Sekar, and G. Min. Inside the bird's nest: Measurements of large-scale live vod from the 2008 olympics. In *Proc. IMC*, 2008.

[51] H. Yu, D. Zheng, B. Y. Zhao, and W. Zheng. Understanding user behavior in large-scale video-on-demand systems. In *Proc. EuroSys*, 2006.

SoftMoW: Recursive and Reconfigurable Cellular WAN Architecture

Mehrdad Moradi[†] Wenfei Wu [‡] [*] Li Erran Li[⋆] Z. Morley Mao[†]
Bell Lab, Alcatel-Lucent[⋆] University of Michigan–Ann Arbor[†] University of Wisconsin–Madison[‡]

ABSTRACT

The current LTE network architecture is organized into very large regions, each having a core network and a radio access network. The core network contains an Internet edge comprised of packet data network gateways (PGWs). The radio network consists of only base stations. There are minimal interactions among regions other than interference management at the edge. The current architecture has several problems. First, mobile application performance is seriously impacted by the lack of Internet egress points per region. Second, the continued exponential growth of mobile traffic puts tremendous pressure on the scalability of PGWs. Third, the fast growth of signaling traffic known as the signaling storm problem poses a major challenge to the scalability of the control plane. To address these problems, we present SoftMoW, a recursive and reconfigurable cellular WAN architecture that supports seamlessly inter-connected core networks, reconfigurable control plane, and global optimization.

To scale the control plane nation-wide, SoftMoW recursively builds up the hierarchical control plane with novel abstractions of both control plane and data plane entities. To enable scalable end-to-end path setup, SoftMoW presents a novel label swapping mechanism such that each controller only operates on its logical topology and each switch along the path only sees at most one label. SoftMoW supports new network-wide optimization functions such as optimal routing and inter-region handover minimization. We demonstrate that SoftMoW improves the performance, flexibility and scalability of cellular WAN using real LTE network traces with thousands of base stations and millions of subscribers. Our evaluation shows that path inflation and inter-region handovers can be reduced by up to 60% and 44% respectively.

Categories and Subject Descriptors

C.2.1 [**Network Architecture and Design**]: Distributed networks; C.2.5 [**Local and Wide-Area Networks**]: Applications

*This work was performed when Wenfei was an intern at Bell Labs and was supported by NSF grant CNS 1218668.

CoNEXT'14, December 02-05 2014, Sydney, Australia

http://dx.doi.org/10.1145/2674005.2674981.

Keywords

Cellular Networks; Software-Defined Networking; Hierarchical Controllers

1. INTRODUCTION

The current LTE network architecture is organized into very large and rigid regions. Each large region has a core network and a radio access network. The core network contains an Internet edge comprised of packet data network gateways (PGWs). The radio network consists of only base stations. In this architecture, there are minimal control plane and data plane interactions among regions other than distributed interference management at radio access networks and limited coordination for mobility (e.g. no inter-PGW mobility [ ]). All users' outgoing traffic must traverse a PGW and possibly go through the Internet.

This rigid architecture is becoming harder and harder to support new trends of mobile traffic. First, mobile application performance is seriously impacted by the lack of Internet egress points per region. Specifically, as shown by a recent study [ ], the lack of sufficiently close Internet egress points is a major cause of path inflation, suboptimal routing, and QoS degradation in large operators. Second, the continued exponential growth of mobile traffic puts tremendous pressure on the scalability of PGWs. Third, the fast growth of signaling traffic known as the signaling storm problem [ ] poses a major challenge to the scalability of the control plane.

Rather than organizing mobile wide area networks as rigid regions with no direct traffic transit, we argue that cellular networks should have a seamlessly *inter-connected core network* with a logically centralized control plane. The inter-connected core network should consist of a fabric of simple core switches and a distributed set of middleboxes (software or hardware). The control plane directs traffic through efficient network paths that might cross region boundaries rather than exiting to the Internet directly from the origin region. The control plane should also globally support seamless UE mobility and optimize the performance of mobile traffic. For example, mobile traffic routing should be globally optimized; regions should be reconfigured to adapt to its workload.

Such an architecture raises unique challenges in scalability in comparison with data-center networks [,] and inter-data center WANs [,] since the cellular WAN has its own unique properties and challenges. First, the logically centralized control plane needs to control tens of thousands of switches and middleboxes, and hundreds of thousands of base stations in the data plane. A control plane with many controller instances in one data center cannot effectively handle the signaling load (e.g., connection setups and handovers) from hundreds of millions of subscribers distributed throughout a continent. Second, without global network states and a single controller exerting control, it will be hard to perform network wide routing optimization and inter-region handover minimization.

To address these problems, we present SoftMoW, a scalable network-wide control plane that supports global optimization and control plane reconfiguration. SoftMoW makes the following contributions.

- First, SoftMoW *recursively* builds up the hierarchical control plane with novel abstractions consisting of both control plane and data plane entities. Key to our SoftMoW architecture is the controller. It is designed to be *modular* which consists of the network operating system (NOS), operator applications and the recursive abstraction application (RecA). NOS provides core services such as routing and path implementation. NOS does not handle cellular specific functions. Operator specific functions (e.g. mobility management) are implemented as applications on top of NOS. All recursive abstraction functions are implemented in RecA.
- Second, to enable scalable end-to-end path setup, SoftMoW presents a *novel label swapping mechanism* such that each controller only operates on its logical topology and each switch along a flow's path only sees at most one label. This new mechanism reduces the states in the switches.
- Third, SoftMoW designs new network-wide optimization functions such as optimal routing and region optimization to minimize inter-region handover.
- Fourth, we demonstrate that SoftMoW improves the performance, flexibility and scalability of cellular WAN using real LTE network traces with thousands of base stations and millions of subscribers. Our evaluation shows that path inflation and inter-region handovers can be reduced by up to 60% and 44% respectively.

2. SoftMoW DESIGN OVERVIEW

SoftMoW's goal is to design a scalable cellular WAN architecture (both the control plane and data plane) to enable network-wide optimizations. We introduce the components in a SoftMoW network, the design challenges and our solutions.

2.1 SoftMoW Components

SoftMoW does not require expensive, inflexible and specialized devices (e.g., PGWs and SGWs) that integrate control and data plane operations with middlebox functions. SoftMoW does not change the LTE protocols used in the user equipment (UE) and the protocols between UE and base stations. SoftMoW has the following high-level architectural components.

Nation-wide inter-connected core networks. SoftMoW distributes and inter-connects programmable switches nation-wide. The network in one region should have enough egress points through a subset of the switches. An egress point can connect to other regions of the same carrier, other carriers' mobile networks, Internet service providers or content providers at peering points to exchange traffic. This eliminates the internal path inflation problem caused by the lack of sufficiently close egress points and enhances end-to-end QoS metrics by offering better diversity of external paths.

Radio access networks. Radio access networks consist of base stations which are organized and inter-connected into base station group (BS group) with different topologies (e.g., ring, mesh, and spoke-hub) to ensure intra-BS-group fast-path communications. BS groups are connected to core network switches locally. We assume each base station has an *access switch* performing fine-grained packet classifications on traffic from UEs.

Middleboxes and service policies. SoftMoW departs from the centralized policy enforcement at PGWs and utilizes middleboxes which can be flexibly placed throughout the cellular WAN. For scalability, middlebox functions will be mostly limited to edge networks of the cellular WAN. Middlebox instances can potentially implement any sophisticated network functions. The functions can be specific to application types (e.g., noise cancellation function and video transcoding function) and operators (e.g., charging and billing), and security (e.g., firewall, and IDS). A service policy is then met by directing traffic through a *partially ordered set* (also known as poset) of middlebox types. Given the location and utilization of middlebox instances, the controller can implement a poset using various combinations of physical instances.

Controller. The controller enforces a rich set of service policies on subscribers' network access through new global network applications. These applications are based on a global view of the inter-connected core networks, which are not available in current LTE networks or recently proposed cellular architectures such as SoftCell [ ]. Specifically, the controller sets up end-to-end optimal paths for aggregate flows and minimizes the number of inter region handovers.

2.2 Design Challenges and Solutions

Challenge 1: scalable control plane. The logically centralized control plane needs to control tens of thousands of switches and middleboxes, hundreds of thousands of base stations in the data plane. A control plane with many controller instances in one data center (e.g., [,]) will not effectively handle the signaling loads (e.g., connection setups and handover events) from hundreds of millions of subscribers distributed throughout a continent. Also, a flat decentralized architecture where local controllers only communicate with their neighbors (e.g., [ ]) is not scalable enough to support fast and global optimizations. It requires distributed algorithms that involve many rounds of message exchanges.

Solution: recursively build up a hierarchical and reconfigurable control plane. SoftMoW hierarchically constructs a *network-wide control plane* that is *reconfigured* in response to the signaling loads and traffic patterns. The control plane consists of geographically distributed controllers that are organized into a tree structure. Recursively from the leaf level, each controller (except the root) exposes a small number of logical and reconfigurable data plane entities to its immediate parent. These entities aggregate many switches, middleboxes and base stations. To enable global optimization such as routing optimization by ancestor controllers, the exposed logical switches and their interconnections are described as a *virtual fabric* with annotated bandwidth, latency, and hop count information.

Challenge 2: scalable end-to-end path implementation. Our cellular WAN provides connections between millions of UEs and thousands of Internet egress points, the number of routing states in the core network switches is tremendous. One way to implement the routes is to aggregate flows traversing the same path, assign them one label and route on labels (e.g. MPLS). In a decentralized flat control plane, implementing a label-switched path involves all controllers and switches on the path. To do this, each controller has to know the global state. Keeping entire data plane states consistent at each controller or storing them into a central data base is not scalable. In SoftMoW, each controller has a limited summarized view over a set of logical entities to improve scalability, but this makes the state management and path implementation more challenging.

Solution: scalable recursive label swapping. SoftMoW leverages its tree structured control plane architecture. Using a novel recursive label swapping approach, SoftMoW implements end-to-end paths while keeping per packet overhead minimal. An ancestor controller pushes labels onto packets of matching flows traversing its logical and reconfigurable switches. Recursively, these labels will be replaced with local labels by each lower level controllers. At the physical data plane switches, only a local label is pushed onto packets of matching flows, which each represents a local regional path segment. When packets leaving a region, the local label is popped off and an ancestor's label is pushed.

Challenge 3: scalable topology discovery and maintenance. Topology discovery is easy in flat multi-controller settings. Each switch is controlled by one controller instance. A controller sends discovery messages from all ports of registered switches. When a switch receives a discovery message, it forwards the message to the controller. The controller then maintains the link between the source and destination switches and stores link-specific information (e.g., port name, link capacity). In SoftMoW, detecting links is more challenging because each cross-region link is visible to only one non-leaf controller; the non-leaf controller needs to discover it without breaking the abstraction.

Solution: recursive discovery protocol. We design and introduce a novel global discovery protocol allowing recursive discovery of topologies by each controller. Each leaf controller first discovers its own physical topology. Then the parent controller is exposed with a logical topology and can discover the cross-region links it controls. This process continues until the root controller discovers its topology. Controllers at the same level can perform discovery at the same time in parallel. The sequential process only applies to the bootstrapping phase. During normal operations, periodical discovery messages will be carried out concurrently.

Challenge 4: network-wide optimization. SoftMoW's goal is to enable global optimizations for control plane and data plane functions such as optimal routing and inter-region handover minimization. Maintaining and performing optimization with global network states for a country-wide network is not scalable.

Solution: design algorithms on abstract topologies of hierarchical controllers. SoftMoW supports global network optimization without a global network state at each controller. We demonstrate this feature using two important network functions. First, application traffic may have its own requirements on the path (e.g. low-latency path for delay-sensitive VoIP). In SoftMoW, the path is computed by controllers from the leaf to the root. If a local optimal path meeting the application requirements is found, it is used without further delegating to ancestor controllers. We show that the root controller is guaranteed to find an optimal

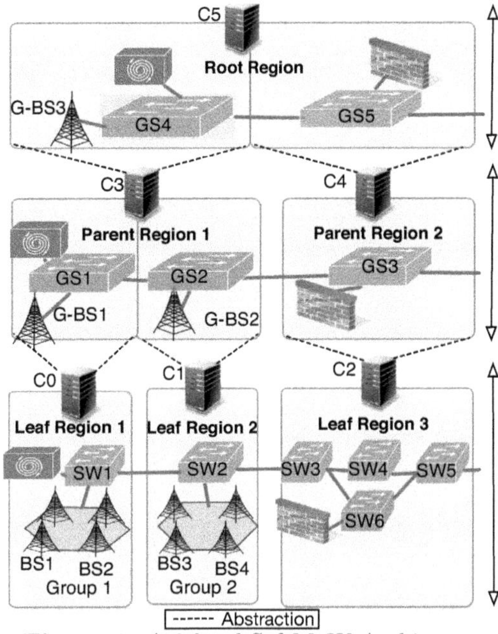

Figure 1: A 3-level SoftMoW Architecture

path in terms of performance metrics (e.g., latency and hop count). Second, an inter-region handover requires the involvement of an ancestor controller, the source controller and destination controller. In this procedure, new paths have to be implemented and in-flight packets have to be diverted to the target base station. To minimize control plane load, SoftMoW performs inter region handover optimization. The optimization is done from the root controller to leaf controllers. We show that the process converges if handover traffic pattern does not change during the optimization.

3. SoftMoW CONTROL PLANE

We first give an overview of how we recursively construct the control plane and the logical data plane, and present the design of the controller architecture.

3.1 Recursive Constructions

As shown in Figure 1, SoftMoW hierarchically builds a reconfigurable network-wide control plane. The control plane consists of geographically distributed controllers that are organized into a tree structure, each controller associated with a level number and a globally unique ID. The topmost node is the *root* controller which can make coarse-grained decisions for the entire network, and level 1 nodes are *leaf* controllers close to the physical data plane. The number of levels, the number of children per node, and the geographical location of each node can be determined based on fine-grained latency budgets of control functions [ ] as well as the density and size of the physical topology.

SoftMoW partitions the physical data plane network into logical regions whose borders can change over time based on traffic and failure patterns. Each leaf region is managed by a leaf controller. In Figure 1, leaf controllers (level-1) discover their physical switches and build the level-1 data plane, and they also abstract some entities for level-2 controllers. The level-2 controllers obtain logical network entities from the leaf controllers, discover their logical level-2 data plane and also make logical network entities. Finally, the root controller (level-3) obtains logical network entities from the level-2 controllers and builds the level-3 data plane. When building these data planes recursively from the leaf level, each controller simplifies its topology and exposes the following three types of *logical* and *reconfigurable* data plane entities to its parent.

- **Gigantic Switch (G-switch)** aggregates a number of physical or gigantic switches and the controller. A G-switch is programmable and characterized by an ID, ports, and a virtual fabric (will be clear in Section 3.2) and flow table. Each port of a G-switch corresponds to border ports of its constituent switches, i.e. is connected to either Internet domains (e.g., ISP) or neighboring regions.
- **Gigantic Middlebox (G-middlebox)** hides physical or G-middlebox instances of the same type and function (e.g., light weight DPI) and their controller. A G-middlebox can be attached to G-switches, and is identified with the sum of the processing capacities and utilization of constituent instances.
- **Gigantic Base station (G-BS)** summarizes one or more adjacent BS groups or G-BSes, and their controller. A G-BS inherits the union of the radio coverage of underlying base stations and connects to ports of a G-switch.

Abstracting the logical region for the parent. To build the first logical data plane (level 2), each leaf controller builds and exposes a single G-switch for all switches, a G-middlebox for all middlebox instances of the same type, a G-BS for one or more adjacent BS groups (will be clear in Section 5.2). Intuitively, a parent's logical region is the union of regions exposed from its children in the tree. Recursively, non-leaf controllers except the root (e.g., level-2 controllers in Figure 1) perform the same procedure on G-middleboxes, G-switches, and G-BSes located in their logical region.

Reconfiguration of logical data plane devices. Each non-leaf controller can reconfigure logical entities exposed from its children. This gives each controller the ability to optimize its descendants' control plane hierarchy and data plane operations without a global state, solely based on its partial view and abstract topology. Any non-leaf controller can initiate a reconfiguration that indirectly causes controllers in its subtree to level-by-level from bottom-to-top interact with each other to modify the exposed logical entities. This new feature enables interesting global applications such as minimizing "east-west" control load in the cross-controller handovers (see Section 5).

3.2 G-Switch Virtual Fabric

To enable global optimization, e.g., traffic engineering and optimal routing, each controller in the tree hierarchy should know a few pieces information about the internal inter-connections behind its G-switches. SoftMoW exposes a virtual switch fabric for each G-switch. A virtual switch fabric (vFabric) is a succinct representation allowing the parent controller to have three pieces of information per G-switch port pair:*latency*, *hop count*, and *available bandwidth*.

Using standard shortest path algorithms, each child controller constructs these metrics by computing multiple shortest paths for each port pair in its topology. Note that, for the bandwidth metric, different port pairs of the G-switch can share bottleneck links. In this case, if the available bandwidth exposed for a port pair in the child controller's data plane changes more than a predetermined threshold, the child controller will recompute new bandwidths, update the vFabric and notify the parent controller.

3.3 Controller Architecture

We design a modular controller architecture as shown in Figure 2. A SoftMoW controller consists of a network operating system (NOS), operator applications and an application called RecA that implements the recursive abstraction.

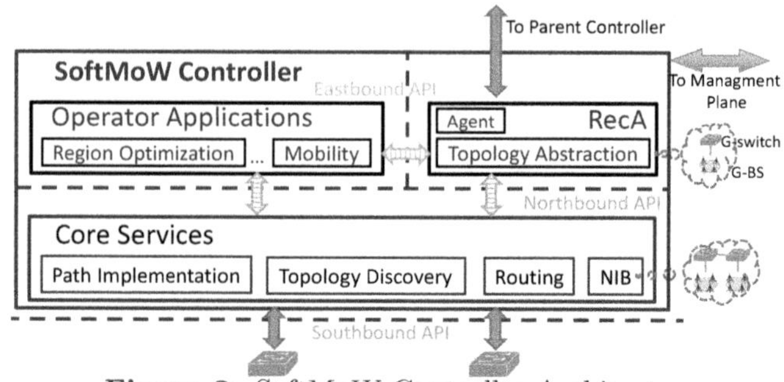

Figure 2: SoftMoW Controller Architecture

Network operating system. SoftMoW expects a number of core services: *path implementation*, *topology discovery*, *routing* and *network information base (NIB) query*. SoftMoW NOS can reuse any existing controller platforms that expose these services through a northbound API. SoftMoW NOS is agnostic of cellular specific functions and other controllers in the hierarchy. NOS communicates with switches (logical or physical) using a southbound API, e.g. OpenFlow API extended to support our virtual fabric feature.

Operator applications. SoftMoW cellular specific functions are implemented as operator applications on top of the NOS, e.g. functions similar to LTE such as home subscriber server (HSS), policy charging and rule functions (PCRF), mobility and new functions such as region optimization and routing optimization. Applications can use the northbound API to get network information (e.g. topology) and set up their configurations (e.g. path setup, sending messages).

Recursive abstraction application (RecA). To implement the recursive abstraction, we design a NOS application called RecA. RecA encapsulates all functions related to the recursive abstraction and provides an eastbound API for operator applications. RecA has two basic modules: *agent* and *topology abstraction*. RecA's topology abstraction module queries the NIB using the NOS northbound API. It abstracts a network topology (including switches, base stations and middleboxes) as one G-switch, a number of G-BSes (border BS groups need to be exposed in a specific way, will be clear in Section 5) and one G-middlebox of each type. The RecA agent communicates with a parent controller (if any). For each logical device, the agent establishes a channel to its parent controller. This way logical devices act as physical ones (e.g., a G-switch acts as a physical switch).

RecA provides the eastbound API to other operator applications. An operator application can register its message type in RecA, and give messages that it cannot handle to RecA; then RecA will send the message to its parent controller as a Packet-In event. The agent also handles messages from the parent. If a message is about path implementation, the agent sends it to the topology abstraction module, which translates the message to multiple messages using the current network view of NIB; if the message is of a type registered by an operator application, it is sent to the application. RecA and operator applications use the northbound API to send messages to logical (child controllers) and physical data plane entities.

Management plane. The management plane bootstraps the recursive control plane. It configures all controllers in the hierarchy via dedicated channels (e.g. assigns IP addresses, and region identifier, and configures the tree structure). The RecA at each controller exports its topology to the management plane. The region optimization applications communicate with the management plane to reconfigure local or physical network devices. The management plane also coordinates UE state transfer during region optimization.

4. CORE SERVICES

SoftMoW core services provided by the network operating system includes the NIB, topology discovery, routing and path implementation. Similar to the NIB in other controller designs [ ], SoftMoW's NIB consists of network devices, device type (e.g. base station, middlebox, switch), links and their metrics. We assume standard mechanisms (e.g. those in [ ]) to gather NIB and maintain NIB's consistency. The NOS has visibility of its own local network topology (physical or logical), does not maintain UE state, is not aware of any ancestor or descendant controllers (may communicate with peer controllers). Now we proceed to present the other three core services.

4.1 Recursive Topology Discovery

SoftMoW presents the first topology discovery protocol in a recursively built control plane architecture. Topology discovery in SoftMoW is much more challenging than in flat architectures. This is because only leaf controllers have direct control over physical switches. Yet each inter G-switch link is physical and is only visible to the ancestor controller of both endpoints of the link.

In SoftMoW, each controller discovers a subset of total links of the physical topology. Data plane switches and links (logical and physical) are discovered sequentially from bottom to top; controllers at each level can discover their (inter G-switch) links in parallel. We now proceed to describe the procedures of topology discovery: *G-switch discovery*, *inter G-switch link discovery* and *Computation of G-switch abstraction*. These procedures are performed by RecA and the topology discovery module. Base stations, middleboxes and links with them as endpoints can also be discovered similarly. If base stations and middleboxes do not implement our discovery protocol, they can also be configured by the management plane.

4.1.1 G-switch Discovery

Similar to physical switches, the RecA agent of each non-root controller connects to the parent controller. After a controller starts, its topology discovery module first discovers all switches (G-switches or physical switches) in its region. If the switch type is G-switch, the controller also performs a feature request to obtain the virtual fabric information. The G-switch device information is stored in NIB. The controllers use the southbound API (e.g., Openflow) to get the G-switch information.

4.1.2 Inter G-switch Link Discovery

Link discovery message. After G-switch discovery, a controller uses inter G-switch Link Discovery Protocol to find the links between its G-switches. For each G-switch port, it initiates a link discovery message, which has a meta data field and a stack field. The link discovery message traverses through the controller hierarchy down to the physical data plane, goes through a physical link, and is reported from the receiving switch back to its origin along the controller hierarchy. The meta data field carries the properties of the traversed physical link (e.g., latency and loss rate), which is filled by the leaf controller on its path. The stack stores the traversed path in the controller hierarchy with the format of (Controller ID, G-switch ID, G-switch port).

Origination path. In more detail, when the topology discovery module in a controller discovers inter G-switch links, link discovery messages are sent out from each port of G-switches (which is actually received by the corresponding child controller). Intuitively, the link discovery message recursively is passed to lower-level child controllers and finally sent out of a port of a physical switch. The initiating controller pushes its ID, the G-switch ID and the port onto the stack. When the RecA agent of a child controller receives the message from its parent, the message is forwarded to the RecA topology abstraction module. This module extracts the G-switch and port from the top of the stack, and maps them to one of its G-switches and its port. Then, RecA pushes its ID, the G-switch ID and port onto the stack. If the controller is a leaf controller, it also encodes meta data of the physical link into the meta data field. RecA calls the northbound API SendMsg(switch, port, msg) to send the message.

Return path. Both topology discovery module and RecA register the link discovery Packet-In message from the lower-level. When a controller receives a link discovery message from one of its G-switches with an incoming port. It pops the stack to get the (Controller ID, G-switch ID, G-switch port). In the topology discovery module, if the popped controller ID is its ID, the link discovery message has been originated by itself, so a new inter G-switch link is discovered. This inter G-switch link is added to the NIB of the current controller. In RecA, if the controller ID is not its ID and the stack is not empty, the link discovery message is reported to the parent by the RecA agent; if the stack is empty, the link discovery message is dropped indicating the link discovery message can not return to the initiating controller and there is no inter G-switch link on the path.

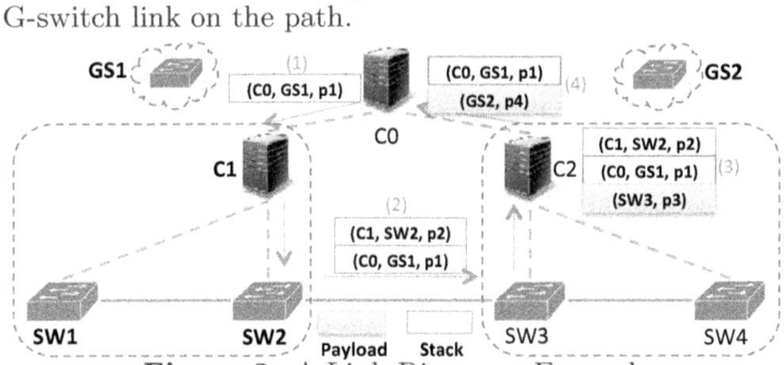

Figure 3: A Link Discovery Example

Example. Figure 3 shows an example of inter G-switch link discovery. The root controller intends to discover the link between G-switch GS1 and GS2 on its logical data plane. The link discovery protocol finishes in 4 steps. (i) The root controller C0 initiates a link discovery message. It populates the stack with its own ID C0 and the G-switch ID GS1 and port number p1. (ii) The child controller C1 receives the link discovery message. It translates the G-switch ID and port number into the physical switch ID SW2 and port number p2. Then, C1 pushes (C1, SW2, p2) onto the stack. (iii) Physical switch SW3 receives the message at port p3 and passes it to its controller C2. C2 encodes the receiving (SW3, p3) into link discovery message. C2 pops the stack and find the controller ID at the top of the stack is C1, which is not its ID. So it translates the (SW3, p3) to corresponding ID and port number of its abstract G-switch, which is (GS2, p4), and passes the link discovery message to its parent C0. (iv) C0 pops the stack and find the controller ID at the top of the stack is its ID. In this way, it finds the inter G-switch link between its G-switches (i.e. GS1 and GS2).

4.1.3 *Computation of G-switch Abstraction*

The RecA application in a controller uses the northbound API topo=GetTopology() to get its G-switches and inter G-switch links, and then it computes one abstract G-switch. In an abstract G-switch, all internal ports (i.e. ports between G-switches) are hidden, and all border ports are exposed. SoftMoW also computes other properties between G-switch port pairs, such as latency, bandwidth and hop count as discussed in Section 3.2. The parent controller requests the G-switch features (e.g. virtual fabric) from the RecA agent in the child controller via the southbound API. G-BS and G-middleboxes can also be computed similarly. We do not go into the details in this paper.

4.2 Route Computation

SoftMoW must provide UEs with Internet access. The routing service computes end-to-end optimal paths through the northbound API (path, match fields)=Routing(request, service policy). The inputs are a routing request and a service policy. The outputs are a computed path and match fields to classify the flow. The computed paths are implemented using the path implementation service.

Interdomain routes. To perform routing, SoftMoW interacts with ISPs and content providers through an interdomain routing protocol (e.g., BGP) at egress points. Similar to a RCP server [ ], leaf controllers run the route selection procedure on behalf of their gateway switches, each keeping a session with an eBGP speaking router in a neighbor ISP. For each gateway switch, leaf controllers select interdomain routes for all prefixes. In addition, the network performance of each selected route is measured (e.g., hops, latency) [ ]. Leaf controllers forward the selected routes to their parent as Packet-In messages, each is associated with performance metrics. The routing module in each controller registers for interdomain routing messages, and puts them into NIB. Recursively, the RecA agent reads the interdomain routes from NIB and sends it to the parent (with translation to the G-switch). This procedure finishes once the root receives interdomain routes from its G-switches.

Recursive routing. When a controller has a routing request from one of its operator's applications (e.g., bearer request), it first checks if its logical region has an interdomain route to the destination on the Internet and the end-to-end internal path satisfies the performance constraints if specified in the request (e.g., latency). In addition, it checks whether the middlebox poset can be met in its logical region if specified in the service policy field. If so, the routing module returns the path and match fields, and then the application implements the path. If no path is found, the operator application delegates the request to RecA agent, which creates a routing request and sends to the parent, where the application in the parent controller registers in the core to get the message and process it. The application also registers for the response in RecA (e.g., to store in local caches). The delegation procedure increases the chance of satisfying the request since the parent has a better global view due to having a larger logical region. We will explain the routing service usage in handling bearer requests (Section 5.1).

Optimality discussion. Each controller might need to compute internal paths to interdomain routes through its own egress points. Using the virtual fabric of G-switches, the routing service can find a shortest path between the logical or physical gateway switches and base stations. We can guarantee a shortest path computed by a controller is the shortest is in the controller's region and its corresponding physical topology. We call such paths **locally optimal**. However, the shortest path in a controller's region may not be the global shortest path in the entire topology. We define shortest paths computed by the root controller in its global abstract topology as **globally optimal**. In general, a controller at a higher level is able to compute more optimal paths compared to any controller in its subtree.

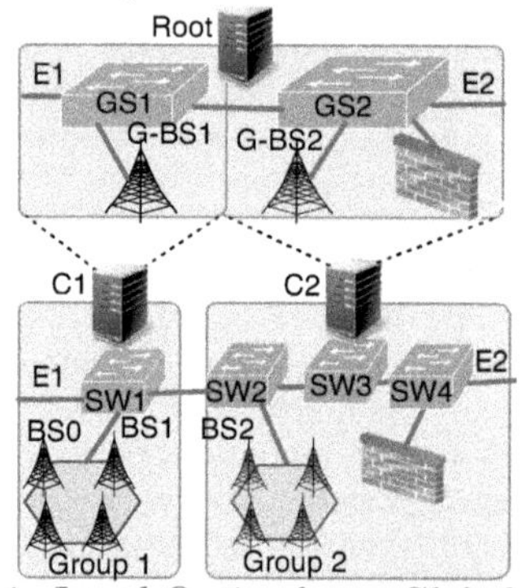

Figure 4: Local Optimal v.s. Global Optimal

Example. Using the interdomain routing messages, we know egress points E1 and E2 are 10 hops away from the address prefix A in Figure 4. The leaf controller C2 receives routing request (BS group= Group 2, destination=A) with the constraint of the maximum end-to-end hop count of 14. C2 computes the shortest path (SW2, SW3, SW4) going through E2 since it satisfies the performance requirement. This path is a local optimal path in C2's region. With the global network view, path (SW2, SW1) is one hop closer to the destination. The virtual fabric of a G-switch contains performance metrics for all port pairs. The root has the virtual fabric of G-switches GS1 and GS2, so it can easily compute the globally optimal path exiting from GS1.

4.3 Global Path Implementation

In SDN architectures where a controller has full visibility of its physical data plane topology [,], path setup is straight-forward. The controller installs a match-action rule on each switch along the path. The match-action rule can match IP prefixes, VLAN tags, MPLS labels or some combinations of them. In SoftMoW, a controller aggregates flows on the same path, assigns them the same label and sets up routing on labels. So the states in switches can be significantly reduced. However, non-leaf controllers do not have full visibility of the physical data plane topology. We present a scalable mechanism that enables non-leaf controllers to implement paths in their abstract topology onto the underlying physical data plane. A northbound API PathSetup(match fields, path) is provided to applications to set up an input path with certain match fields.

In SoftMoW, a leaf controller can simply implement any intra-region paths. Similar to SoftCell [ ], the access switch of base stations can perform fine-grained packet classification and push labels onto packets matching flow rules. Then, switches along the path are programmed to forward traffic based on specified labels. A non-leaf controller does not have control over physical switches, and multiple descendant controllers make partial forwarding decisions; so its path setup is more challenging. Similar to leaf controllers, a non-leaf controller should be able to instruct the access G-switch attached to each G-BS to classify packets and push virtual labels into the traffic, and program its G-switches along any desired path to operate based on pushed virtual labels.

To implement this operation, intuitively, when RecA agent in each child controller receives virtual label switching or packet classification rules, it translates them using its own topology. Each virtual label switching rule is mapped onto internal paths between the egress and ingress ports of the child controller's logical region, and the path computation is performed by the routing module. During the recursive translations, descendant controllers can establish any desired number of internal shortest paths between the ingress and egress points as long as the performance metrics of computed paths comply with the parent's virtual fabric. A descendant controller should be able to push a separate local label on top of the parent's label to establish each local path. Accordingly, the classification rule should be updated for each local path and installed into constituent access switches, each attached to a component G-BS.

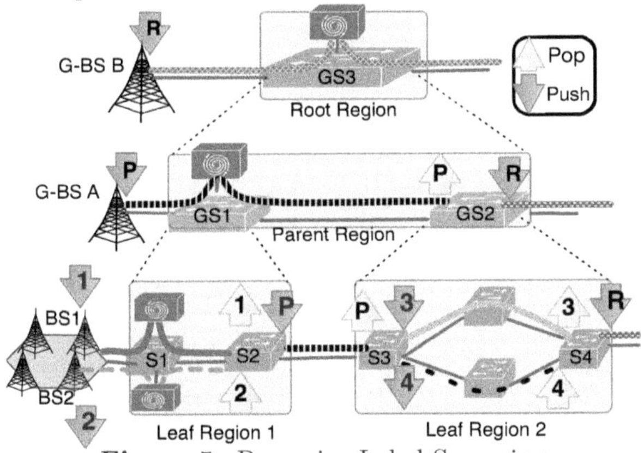

Figure 5: Recursive Label Swapping

High-overhead label stacking. To implement the recursive translations of virtual rules onto physical switches in underlying topology, a simple approach is to recursively stack k labels in the packets where k is the level of the controller initiating the path setup. Label stacking allows a label specified by an ancestor controller to be visible and available in the packets traversing across physical inter-G-switch links detected by the controller itself. Label stacking approach gives the illusion of packets traversing through the region of controllers at different level. When traffic enters a logical region at any level, the controller reads the label in the stack at the same level. This approach is not scalable in nation-wide mobile networks since it increases per-packet overhead due to encapsulating k labels in each packet, which exacerbates the bandwidth consumption as the number of levels in the SoftMoW architecture increases.

Label stacking example. Figure 5 shows logical regions of two leaf controllers, their parent, and the root controller (controllers are excluded for simplicity). The root has a single-path service policy for rate-limiting bidirectional traffic between G-BS B and a destination address prefix. To satisfy this policy, the root pushes label R at access switch of G-BS B and then installs the corresponding virtual rule into G-switch GS3 to forward traffic specified by label R. At the level below, the parent controller receives the rules. Based on its local view, it decides to stack label P on R (i.e., pushes [R P]) onto the packets. It programs the G-switches GS1 and GS2 to process incoming traffic with label P. In this approach, leaf controller 1 should at *least* push the stack [R P] onto each packet at the base stations. This allows leaf region 2 to read P from the stack and perform the forwarding. Then the rest of the network reads label R of the egress traffic from region 2. Intuitively, this gives the illusion of packets traversing up to the parent region at S2, and traversing down at S3. Also, the packet traverses up to the root level at S4. It is easy to imagine an increase in the packet header space and network bandwidth consumption, as SoftMoW levels increases, due to stacking multiple labels in packets.

Scalable recursive label swapping. We propose a novel *recursive label swapping mechanism* eliminating the high bandwidth overhead per-packet. In our approach, each packet has only one label at any given time. We have observed that a label specified by a non-leaf controller only needs to be visible across physical inter G-switch links detected by the controller itself. Thus we instruct controllers to perform *label pop* and *label push* operations. Each controller at the ingress switch (physical or gigantic) of its logical region pops the label (specified by an ancestor who controls the just traversed link) of the traffic. It then pushes an internal label corresponding to each internal path. Finally, it programs switches along each path. At the egress switch of its logical region, the controller aggregates the internal paths by popping their label. It then pushes back the ancestor's label onto packets of the flow. This mechanism guarantees the global coordination between the controller by having the necessary label at each switch while it minimizes the bandwidth overhead.

Recursive label swapping example. In Figure 5, the root adds label R to the traffic group at access switch of G-BS A similar to the previous example. It then programs G-switch GS3 to forward traffic based on label R to the rest of network. In this step, the controller of parent region receives the classification and forwarding rules. Using the push operation, it only pushes its local label P due to the local preference and does not mark the traffic with label R. Using the pop operation, it pops P and pushes backs the root's label R at G-switch GS2 where it loses its control on the egress traffic.

In the leaf region 1, the leaf controller decides to load balance the packets between two rate limiters, so it implements two local paths with label 1 and 2. With the push operation, it pushes label 1 and 2 at access switches of BS1 and BS2 respectively. With the pop operation, these two labels are replaced with the parent's label P at egress switch S2, so the next leaf region can process the traffic. In the leaf region 2, switch S3 is programmed to perform load balancing on ingress traffic from region 1. The leaf controller implements two separate paths by pushing local labels 3 and 4, and popping P at switch S3. These paths are aggregated at egress switch S4. The local labels are popped off and the root's label R is pushed back onto the packets. As shown in the physical data plane, packets always carry a single label denoted with different patterns while many controllers make partial decisions.

5. OPERATOR APPLICATIONS

A key cellular network function is mobility management which includes setting up bearers (a bearer provides network connectivity service to the UE) and handovers. Mobility management is performed by the Mobility Management Entity (MME) in LTE whereas it is done by the mobility application in SoftMoW. The key differences are: (1) mobility application is simpler because of the use of the controller's northbound API which is not available in LTE; (2) it supports mobility better (e.g., LTE does not support inter-PGW handovers [ ]). LTE mobility management has many procedures, due to the lack of space, we only discuss main functions that highlight the differences. Besides the mobility management, we present a new application, the region optimization application, to reduce the handover load of the controllers.

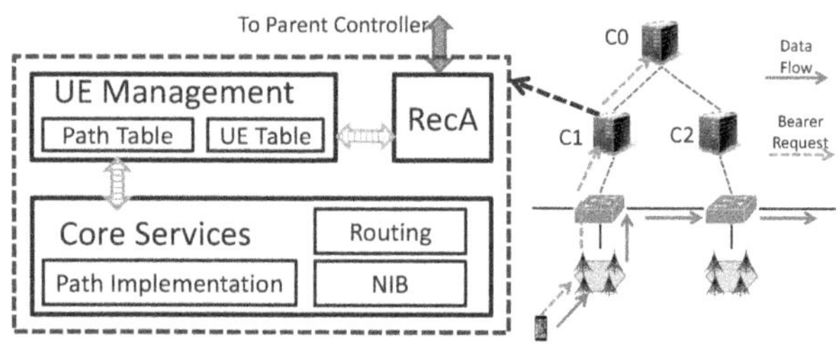

Figure 6: UE Management Application

5.1 UE Bearer Management

In each SoftMoW controller, the mobility application registers for the bearer request message type in the core. It also registers for the bearer response from the parent in RecA. The mobility application maintains two tables (Figure 6): (i) UE table where each row contains a bearer request and a local path ID. (ii) Path table that maps path IDs to the their details. A bearer request can be in the format of (UE ID, BS ID, SRC IP, DST IP, REQ) where the "DST IP" is the destination address on the Internet and "REQ" contains QoS. For example, some UE applications can request for better QoS on the end-to-end latency.

When a UE sends a bearer request to the base station, the request is forwarded to the leaf controller as a Packet-In message. The mobility application receives the request from the core and associates a service policy (i.e., a middlebox chain) with it if necessary. If there is no precomputed path in the path table, the mobility application calls the routing service using the northbound API (path, match fields)=Routing(request, service policy). Then it calls the northbound API (pathID, pathInfo)=PathSetup(path, matching fields) provided by the path implementation service. Finally, the path information is cached in the path table and the mobility application asks the base station to allocate the resources. As discussed in Section 4.2, if the routing service cannot find an end-to-end path that satisfies the bearer request and service policy, the mobility application sends the bearer request to RecA, which is forwarded to the parent controller.

Example. In Figure 6, the UE requests for a path with a larger bandwidth, which cannot be found by the routing service of C1 in its region; the request is sent to the root controller C0. C0 computes the path, stores the UE and path information, and sends the UE bearer response to C1's RecA. The C1's RecA implements the local path in it region, and C1's mobility application registers in its RecA to get the path information. Also, C2's RecA implements the rest of path in its region once it receives the virtual rule from C0.

The bearer state is synchronized between the UE and the mobility application. If the UE becomes idle, its bearers will be deactivated. We add two more fields to the UE table indicating whether a UE is active or idle, and whether the UE request has been handled locally or by the parent. When the mobility application deactivates a bearer, it updates the tables and also asks the path implementation service with the northbound API deactivatePath(pathID, pathInfo) to deactivate its path. If the UE bearer has been handled by the parent controller, the mobility application continues to request bearer deactivation from its parent via RecA.

5.2 UE Mobility

LTE has many handover procedures depending whether the source base station and target base station has a direct connection or not and whether the UE's current associated MME, or the serving gateway needs to be changed or not, etc. Similarly, there are many handover procedures in SoftMoW. We only discuss two main types of handovers: intra region and inter region. The handovers are performed through the coordination of the mobility application, RecA, the routing service and the path implementation service.

The Intra region type is used to handover a UE between a source base station and a target base station when both of them are in the same leaf region. This type of handover is easy, so we focus on complex inter region handovers. In inter region handovers, the source and target base stations are located in different leaf regions. Thus each corresponding border G-BS is exposed by a separate leaf controller. To simplify the inter region handover procedure and allow fine-grained region optimizations, we assume controllers do not aggregate gigantic stations and physical BS groups sitting at the border of their logical region with others in the recursive abstraction procedure. A leaf controller abstracts each border BS group as a single G-BS for its parent, and non-leaf controllers expose a single G-BS for each G-BS located at their region's boundaries. However, controllers can group, abstract, and expose their internal G-BSes and BS groups in different ways.

To handover a UE from the source base station to the target base station in inter region handover, SoftMoW only requires base stations abstracted as a border G-BS to advertise the corresponding *G-BS ID* along with other information periodically through the physical broadcast channel. When the source leaf controller and the UE agree on the handover target, the source leaf controller sends a handover request to its parent. The request contains at least source and target *G-BS IDs* and *BS IDs*. The mobility application registers for the handover request in the core. If the current controller is the ancestor of both the source and target leaf controllers, it starts a procedure to handle the request; otherwise the request is sent to RecA and forwarded to the parent controller recursively. For simplicity, we explain the inter region handover procedure through an example.

Example. To handover a UE from BS1 to BS2 in Figure 4, C1 sends a handover request from (G-BS1, BS1) to (G-BS2, BS2) to the root. The root requests G-BS2 to allocate the resources at the BS2 to the UE. Then, it implements a new path between G-BS1 and G-BS2 to transfer in-flight packets and establishes some paths E2 and G-BS2 for new flows. Once the handover finishes, the root asks G-BS1 to release the resources. It then removes old paths between G-BS1 and E1 as well as between G-BS1 and G-BS2.

5.3 Region Optimization and Reconfiguration

Inter region handovers increase "east-west" control plane load because they require the intervention of at least three controllers: the source and target leaf controllers, and the ancestor controller. Allocating more resources to busy nodes in the controller hierarchy is difficult due to the geographical distribution and also increases the intra-node coordination costs. Thus the regions should be refined to reduce this type of load; each non-leaf controller should reconfigure its own logical region to minimize the inter region handover load it handles. To achieve this goal, the region optimization application changes borders between sub-regions, each exposed by an immediate child controller, based on handover patterns. Handover patterns vary across time-of-day. Thus it is difficult to find static borders using an offline and static approach, so each controller should be able to perform optimizations periodically and on a slow time-scale. In particular, we are interested in minimizing inter region handovers at the root (level L) first because a handover request processed and handled by the root goes through more controllers. Similarly, the controllers at the level $n-1$ have a higher priority compared to the controllers at the level $n-2$. Hence we should run the handover optimization algorithm first at the root. Once the root is done, all controllers at level $n-1$ can run the optimization in parallel, and similarly for the levels below.

5.3.1 *Region Optimization Algorithm*

We now discuss the optimization algorithm for a non-leaf controller which we call the initiator controller.

Handover graph input. When the mobility application processes handover requests, it can log these processing. Then a *handover graph* can be computed, in which each node of the graph is a G-BS and an edge shows the number of handover in the past time window (e.g., several hours) between two nodes. The region optimization application can fetches all handover graphs from the mobility application. The two applications can communicate through mechanisms such as inter-process communication. We do not provide any further details for lack of space.

Example. For a two-level SoftMoW architecture, Figure 7b represents a global handover graph built by the root through aggregating histories. Figure 7a shows the leaf regions' BS group-level handover graph. As discussed earlier, to allow the root to run fine-grained optimization at the site-group level, leaf controllers have abstracted each border BS group (e.g., BS groups 3 and 2) as a single G-BS (e.g., G-BS 3 and 2) and have exposed to the root. However, they have abstracted adjacent internal BS groups all together. A similar rule applies to any other non-leaf controllers.

Greedy algorithm. Using the handover graph, the region optimization application in the initiator controller computes the reconfiguration of its logical data plane by refining sub-regions, each exposed from a child controller. The region optimization informs the management plane about the changes. The management plane performs the actual reconfiguration. In handover-specific reconfiguration, the initiator detaches a border G-BS connected to a source G-switch and then re-associates it with a destination G-switch. The source and destination G-switches are connected through an inter G-switch links (discovered by the initiator). This operation transfers the control of the border G-BS to new descendant controllers in the initiator's subtree. We propose a simple greedy local search algorithm to decide which border G-BS should be reconfigured by the initiator. In our algorithm, the initiator at each step selects a border G-BS connected to a G-switch, which yields the maximum gain. The gain is defined as the reduction in the amount of inter region handovers requiring the intervention of the initiator.

Example. Figure 7b shows the root level handover graph before the optimization showing the root handles 900 inter region handovers between G-switches A and B or the corresponding leaf regions shown in Figure 7a. Based on the gain function, the controller selects border G-BS 3 for the reconfiguration since it gives the maximum gain 200 (=500-200-100). The root associates the G-BS with G-switch GSA.

Constraints. We assume we have the lower bound LB_i and the upper bound UB_i on the amount of control plane loads (e.g., UE arrival) that each G-switch (or actual child controller) can handle. When the initiator picks the maximum gain border G-BS, it avoids reducing the load of a G-switch GS_i to below LB_i or increasing it to above UB_i, assuming the load of each type of control plane events (e.g., bearer arrival) incurred by a G-BS is given.

Termination and Convergence After the above steps, the initiator controller can enter into a new iteration of reconfiguration computation by selecting the next G-BS. The algorithm terminates when there is no more positive gain. *The sequential-parallel approach converges* because the handover optimization at an initiator controller, which is done by refining its logical sub-regions under its control, neither produces nor removes any gains for ancestor controllers except for the initiator itself, and controllers in its subtree. This is because a controller cannot affect inter region handovers seen at ancestor controllers.

5.3.2 *Reconfiguration Protocol*

Region optimization application computes the reconfiguration and sends reconfiguration messages to the management plane.

Finding leaf controllers. The management plane subscribers to topologies changes from NIB and abstraction changes from RecA. Using the topology information and configuration information, the management plane finds the source and destination leaf controllers, and instructs them to fulfill the G-BS re-association request from the region optimization application.

Reconfiguration. At this step, the source leaf controller finds a cut containing switches that are necessary to transfer the border BS group (abstracted as a single G-BS to allow fine-grained optimization) to the target leaf's region. It then communicates with the switches and component base stations to seamlessly add the target leaf controller as their new controller. In this procedure, the source leaf controller sets the role of the target leaf controller to the equal role (e.g., OpenFlow "OFPCR_ROLE_EQUAL"). This role means both the source and target leaf controllers receive all events generated by data plane devices (i.e., BS group, switches, and middleboxes). The management plane instructs: (i) the source leaf controller to handle events generated by existing

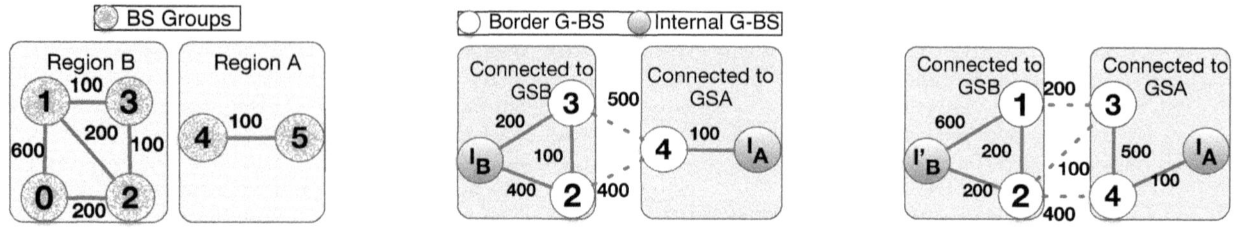

(a) Leaf controllers' graph (b) Root's graph before the optimization (c) Root's graph after optimization

Figure 7: Inter Region Handover Optimization

rules and avoid installing new rules. (ii) the target leaf controller to process all new requests (e.g., handover, routing, UE arrival, and path implementation). To make states consistent, the source controller transfers existing UE states and path information to the target controller in advance. When old communications finish, the source controller disconnects itself from the data plane devices and the new controller gets the master role.

Updating logical data planes. After a successful control transfer at the leaf level, the logical regions are updated from bottom to top in a recursive fashion to reflect new abstract topologies. Recursively, each RecA agent along the path modifies the G-switch ports and the virtual fabric for its parent. Next, the parent automatically discovers new inter G-switch links. Also, the RecA agents need to update, register, or deregister G-BSes. This is because some internal BS groups in the source leaf region become border BS groups, which should be reflected recursively. Figure 7c shows the root's handover graph after reconfiguring G-BS 3. The procedure transfers the control of BS group 3 from the source region B to the target region A. As a result, the new border BS group 1 is separated from I_B, abstracted as border G-BS 1 and exposed to the root. This leads to updating the internal G-BS I_B to I'_B which has lost BS group 1. Also, the target leaf controller might need to treat previous border BS groups as internal BS groups due to an expansion of its region.

6. DISCUSSION

We discuss how a basic SoftMoW can handle the controller, switch, and link failures, and implement consistent paths.

Controller failure recovery. To guarantee the reliability of the control plane, each logical node in the tree structure contains master and hot standby instances. For each node, NIB is decoupled from the controller logic and stored in a reliable storage system (e.g. Zookeeper [ ]). The NIB is shared between the master and standby. The standby uses a heartbeat protocol to detect the failure of its master. Also, each physical or logical (i.e., master and standby) switch connects to both master and standby instances. All messages from a physical or a gigantic switch are duplicated and delivered to both instances. If a master is alive, the standby does not do anything. Otherwise, it takes over the master's work immediately. When the master controller receives an event, it first logs the event arrival in the NIB, and then processes it. When the master fails, the hot standby detects this and immediately checks the event logs and redo unfinished events.

Switch and link failure recovery. When a link failure occurs, the leaf or ancestor controller, which discovered the link, is notified through our recursive discovery protocol. If the failure affects the exposed G-switch and virtual fabric in a way that cannot be masked from the ancestor controllers, changes are reflected bottom up which may cause upper-level controllers to recompute new paths. Otherwise the controller finds affected local paths and implements alternative shortest paths with the same performance.

Consistent path setup. In SoftMoW, path implementations by a controller are pushed top-down. However, the topology updates propagate bottom-up. If we want to provide strong consistency between controllers in neighboring levels, messages needs to be ordered (e.g., paxos, locks) which impacts the agility of path implementations. SoftMoW guarantees eventual consistency. If a failure happens due to inconsistency (e.g., path implementation during topology changes), SoftMoW's controllers recomputes new paths. To guarantee a packet goes through a consistent path during path updates, the new path and packets are assigned a new version number. The packets with the old version number can still use old rules to guarantee reachability.

7. IMPLEMENTATION AND EVALUATION

We prototype the architecture of SoftMoW to show the performance gains of SoftMoW compared with current rigid LTE architecture and evaluate the scalability of our topology discovery protocol. Finally we show the effectiveness of inter region handover optimization using trace-driven simulations.

7.1 Prototype and Methodology

Data plane. We prototype SoftMoW on top of the Floodlight [ ] and Mininet [ ]. Leaf controllers use the OpenFlow protocol to communicate with switches while other controllers interact with logical data plane elements through a custom API similar to OpenFlow. We build realistic data plane topologies using the RocketFuel dataset [ ]. We present the results for a data plane containing 321 software switches. To attach radio access networks, we use our LTE data set. We connect each BS group to an access switch. Each BS group contains at most 6 inferred base stations organized in a ring topology. The minute-level uplink and downlink traffic rates of BS groups is obtained from the dataset. We set the delay and bandwidth of links to 5ms and 1Gbps respectively.

LTE dataset. We collected about 1TB traces from a large ISP's LTE network during one week in the summer of 2013. The dataset covers a large metropolitan area with more than 1000 base stations and 1 million mobile devices. The trace is *bearer*-level. A radio bearer is a communication channel between a UE and its associated base station with a defined Quality of Service (QoS) class. The trace includes various events such as radio bearer creation, UE arrival to the network, UE handover between base stations. From the trace, we compute the uplink and downlink traffic per minute per base station. When a flow arrives and there is an existing radio bearer with the same QoS class, the flow will use the existing radio bearer. Radio bearers time out in a few seconds, so a long flow may trigger several radio

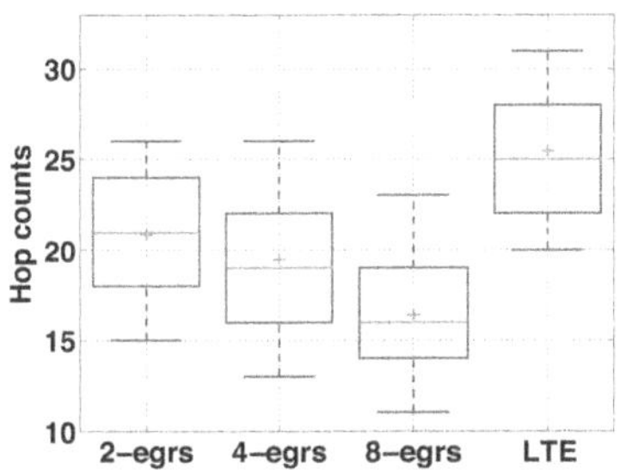

Figure 8: End-to-End Hop Count

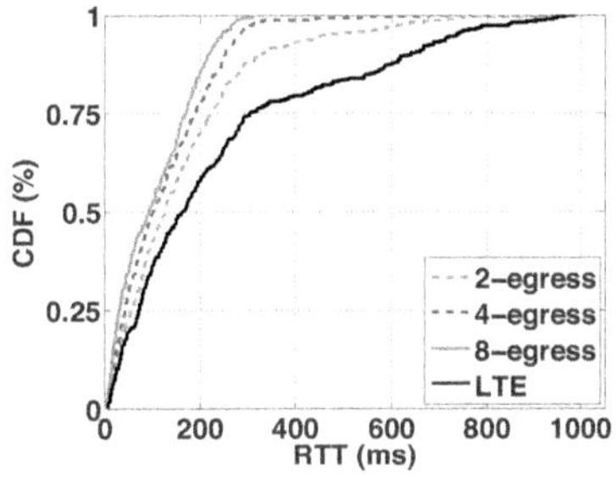

Figure 9: End-to-End Latency

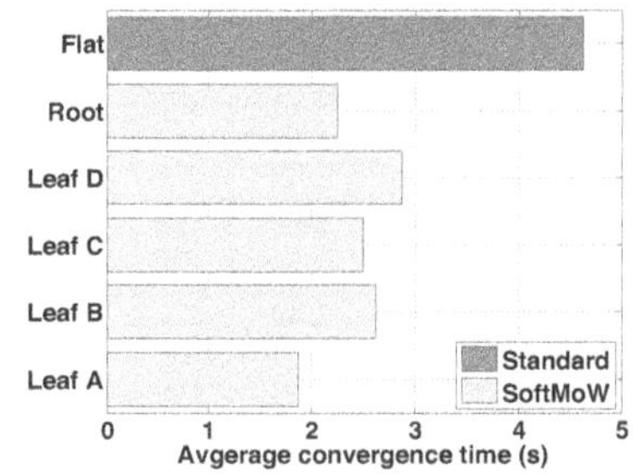

Figure 10: Convergence Time

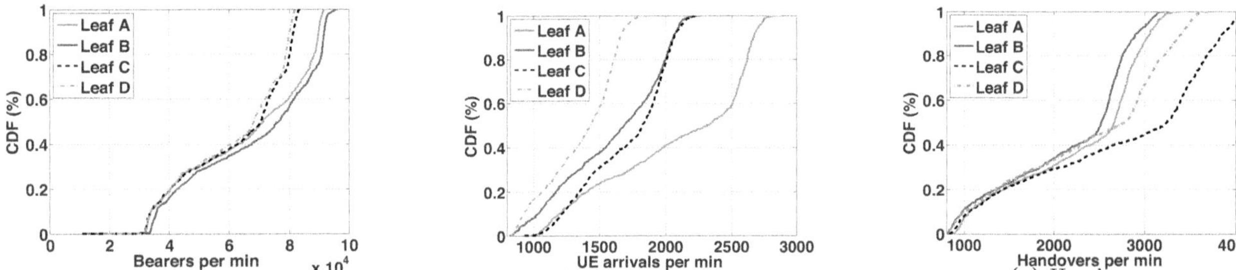

(a) Bearer Arrival

(b) UE Arrival

(c) Handover

Figure 11: Cellular loads on Balanced Regions

bearer creation and deletion events. Because the data set does not contain flow-level information, we use radio bearers to estimate flow activities.

BS group inference. Our LTE dataset does not contain BS-group level information, so we infer BS groups by a simple algorithm. We assume each group has at most 6 base stations organized based on the ring topology. Our algorithm aims to find groups maximizing the weight of intra-group edges in the global handover graph. The optimal solution is NP-hard, so we design a greedy algorithm. In each iteration, the edge with the lowest weight is removed and then strongly connected components with fewer than 6 base stations are computed. We remove the components from the working graph and mark each as a new BS group. Finally, inferred BS groups are partitioned to form approximately equal-sized logical regions with similar cellular loads. We carefully assign a geographical location to each BS group to preserve the neighborhood relationship among them.

7.2 Routing Performance

We first focus on a two-level architecture with 4 leaf regions. We approximately place the leaf controllers in the center of their region. The root controller runs in the middle of the complete topology. SoftMoW's inter-connected core network increases the choices of Internet egress points so that the control plane can compute optimal end-to-end paths. We compare the two-level SoftMoW architecture with an existing rigid LTE region for the same number of base stations. To model egress points, we use iPlane [ ] consisting of traceroute information from PlanetLab [ ] nodes to Internet destinations. To consider routing changes, we replay the hop counts and latencies from multiple snapshots. The root implements internal shortest paths for traffic by taking into account both internal hop counts (from the G-BS to an egress point) and external hop counts (from an egress point to the destination).

Figure 8 illustrates the distribution of end-to-end hop counts as a function of the number of egress points for 11590 destinations on the Internet. We observe the average hop count decreases from 20.83 to 16 as the number of egress points increases from 2 to 8. This is because internal path inflation disappears since the traffic is directed through sufficiently close egress points, and also diversity of external paths improves the Internet access performance. In particular, SoftMoW with 8 egress points can reduce the average end-to-end hop count by 36% compared to LTE network. In addition, SoftMoW can also reduce end-to-end latencies by computing globally optimal paths at the root. Figure 9 depicts the CDF of RTT latency. We observe the 75th and 85th percentile RTT latencies reduce by 43% and 60% when we switch from the LTE network to the 8-egress point SoftMoW.

7.3 Discovery Protocol Performance

In the same setting, we now measure the convergence time of our recursive discovery protocol. The convergence time is measured per controller and starts from the beginning of a discovery period until all links and ports are discovered and become stable. We compare our results to the standard discovery protocol (e.g., LLDP) when a single controller is placed at the root's location and discovers all the links and ports.

Figure 10 shows the average convergence time for different controllers in our architecture and the flat control plane. We observe SoftMoW's controllers detect their topology between 44% and 58% faster compared to the flat discovery by the single controller. We identified the queuing delay at controllers is the root cause of such differences and the propagation delays between the controllers and switches have insignificant effects. The queuing delay is in proportion to the number of ports and links in topology.

Basically, SoftMoW is more scalable and can detect faults faster compared to flat single controller deployments because a large portion of links and ports are masked from each controller. Table 1 shows the leaf controllers on average have exposed 20.75% of total ports discovered in their logical

Table 1: SoftMoW Controller Abstractions

	Discovered			Exposed	Exposed
	SW	Ports	Links	Ports	Ports (%)
Leaf A	55	218	80	58	26
Leaf C	79	250	99	52	20
Leaf B	68	213	87	39	18
Leaf D	98	416	167	81	19
Root	4	230	115	-	-

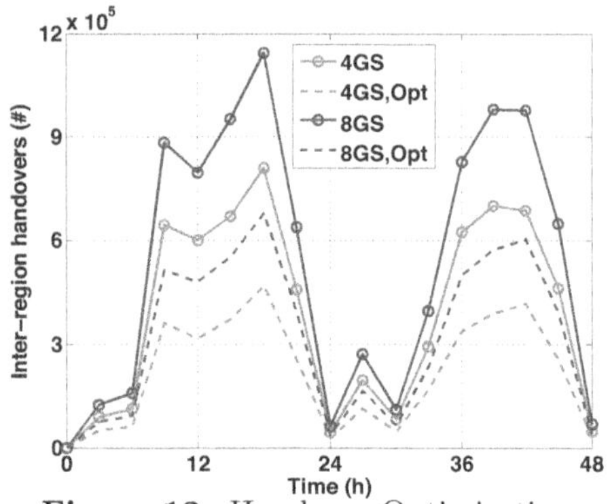

Figure 12: Handover Optimization

region to the root controller. Also, 73% of total links are hidden at the root level.

7.4 Handover Optimization

We characterize the cellular load on the leaf controllers and the effectiveness of inter region handover optimization through network measurement and simulation. We simulate a SoftMoW with two levels. In the first level, we define four and eight roughly equal-sized logical regions, each assigned to a leaf controller. In the second level, the root controller manages the abstract topology.

Cellular loads. Each leaf controller should handle three types of cellular events in addition to exposing logical devices to the root: *bearer arrival*, *UE arrival*, *handover request*. In practice, each type of cellular event can triggers multiple rounds of message passing between the controller and the logical data plane. Figure 11a shows the CDF of bearer arrivals. We observe each leaf controller handles as high as 10^5 bearer arrivals per minute. We use the bearer arrivals as the estimate of the number of packet-in messages received by the leaf controllers. Figure 11b shows leaf controllers receive and process between 1000 and 3000 attachment requests from UEs connecting to a base station in their region, which are triggered when users turn on their device. Figure 11c depicts the aggregate intra region and inter region handover requests processed by leaf controllers that varies between 1000 and 4000 per minute.

Optimization results. Periodically, the root refines the abstract sub-regions exposed from the leaf controllers based on its global handover graph. It strives to reduce the load of inter region handovers, which also improves the handover performance. In the optimization, we avoid drastically unbalancing the three cellular loads on each leaf controllers. Figure 12 shows the number of inter region handovers handled by the root over 48 hours for 8-region and 4-region settings. We observe the number of handover requests increases (i) in peak hours and (ii) by doubling the number of logical regions. The root runs the reconfiguration algorithm every 3 hours by collecting local handover graphs. We assume each GS (i.e., leaf controllers) should not handle more (less) than 30% of their maximum (minimum) initial cellular loads per minute. Given these constraints, Figure 12 depicts the root can reduce the load of inter region handovers by 38.08% to 44.61% using our iterative greedy reconfiguration algorithm.

8. RELATED WORK

Scalable control planes. Maestro [ ] utilizes parallelism to achieve high scalability on multi-core machines. SoftMoW can benefit from the proposed techniques to make logical and physical rule installations faster at each node. HyperFlow [ ] and Onix [ ] are multi-controller designs without any explicit hierarchical structure. Kandoo [ ] improves HypeFlow by leveraging a two-level controller. Unlike SoftMoW, Kandoo cannot be extended to more than two levels and can run specific applications such as elephant flow detection. In contrast to SoftMoW, these systems do not offer sufficient scalability to support continent-wide global applications.

Scalable data planes. To scale the data plane, SoftMoW, PNNI [ ], XBar [ ] hierarchically abstract a given network as logical entities. To control their specific target network and satisfy requirements, each of them offers different abstractions. PNNI's abstractions is designed for ATM networks. SoftMoW is the first complete recursive and reconfigurable architecture with richer abstractions suitable for cellular WAN operators. Unlike XBar and PNNI, SoftMoW builds virtual fabrics for its G-switches to enable network-wide optimization such as routing. In addition, SoftMoW runs a novel recursive label swapping mechanism to minimize the bandwidth overhead and data plane states.

Inter-DC control plane. Control plane architectures for data center WANs such as B4 [ ] and SWAN [ ] are specific to inter-DC traffic engineering. Inter-DC WAN topologies have several order of magnitudes fewer nodes and edges compared to the cellular WAN topologies [ ]. SoftMoW's recursive and reconfigurable abstraction scales the network much better.

Cellular network control plane. Recently, researchers have also proposed flexible control plane architectures for cellular networks. SoftRAN [ ] is a design specific to radio access networks. SoftRAN handles intelligent resource block allocation to optimize utilities. SoftCell [ ] focuses on providing operators with fine-grained policies and compresses data plane rules. In contrast to prior work, SoftMoW handles inter-connected cellular core networks.

9. CONCLUSION AND FUTURE WORK

Cellular wide area networks have become an integral part of our society. However, they are remarkably inflexible and inefficient. This is exacerbated by the continued exponential growth of mobile data. To address this important problem, in this paper, we present SoftMoW, a scalable architecture that is based on on effective recursive and reconfigurable abstractions for both control plane and data plane. We designed a recursive link discovery protocol and virtual fabrics to allow automatic topology construction and support global resource management. SoftMoW optimizes network-wide objectives such as inter-region handover, path implementation, and routing. SoftMoW achieves these goals using novel algorithms benefiting from our scalable abstractions. Our evaluation results show that SoftMoW is very efficient and scalable. For future work, we would like to deploy SoftMoW in a large testbed.

Acknowledgments

We would like to thank the anonymous reviewers for providing valuable feedback on our work and Gordon Wilfong at Bell Labs for helpful discussions on BGP. This research was supported in part by the National Science Foundation under grants CNS-1039657 and CNS-1345226.

10. REFERENCES

[1] Floodlight. http://goo.gl/eXUprV.

[2] iplane dataset. http://goo.gl/JZWdK2.

[3] LTE design and deployment. http://goo.gl/DMKymH.

[4] Managing the signaling storm. http://goo.gl/lkTyb1.

[5] Zookeeper: Wait-free coordination for internet-scale systems. In *Proc. USENIX ATC*, 2010.

[6] P. Berde, M. Gerola, J. Hart, Y. Higuchi, M. Kobayashi, T. Koide, B. Lantz, B. O'Connor, P. Radoslavov, W. Snow, et al. ONOS: towards an open, distributed SDN OS. In *Proc. workshop on Hot topics in software defined networking (HotSDN)*, 2014.

[7] M. Caesar, D. Caldwell, N. Feamster, J. Rexford, A. Shaikh, and J. van der Merwe. Design and implementation of a routing control platform. In *Proc. USENIX NSDI*, 2005.

[8] Z. Cai and et al. The preliminary design and implementation of the Maestro network control platform, 2008.

[9] Y. Chen, S. Jain, V. K. Adhikari, Z.-L. Zhang, and K. Xu. A first look at inter-data center traffic characteristics via yahoo! datasets. In *Proc. IEEE INFOCOM*, 2011.

[10] B. Chun, D. Culler, T. Roscoe, A. Bavier, L. Peterson, M. Wawrzoniak, and M. Bowman. Planetlab: an overlay testbed for broad-coverage services. In *ACM Computer Communication Review*, 2003.

[11] T. A. Forum, M. Ahmed, and J. H. Rus. Private network-network interface specification version 1.0 (pnni 1.0), 1996.

[12] A. Greenberg, J. R. Hamilton, N. Jain, S. Kandula, C. Kim, P. Lahiri, D. A. Maltz, P. Patel, and S. Sengupta. VL2: A scalable and flexible data center network.

[13] A. Gudipati, D. Perry, L. E. Li, and S. Katti. SoftRAN: Software defined radio access network. In *Proc. workshop on Hot topics in software defined networking (HotSDN)*, 2013.

[14] S. Hassas Yeganeh and Y. Ganjali. Kandoo: A framework for efficient and scalable offloading of control applications. In *Proc. workshop on Hot topics in software defined networking (HotSDN)*, 2012.

[15] C.-Y. Hong, S. Kandula, R. Mahajan, M. Zhang, V. Gill, M. Nanduri, and R. Wattenhofer. Achieving high utilization with software-driven WAN. In *Proc. ACM SIGCOMM*, 2013.

[16] S. Jain, A. Kumar, S. Mandal, J. Ong, L. Poutievski, A. Singh, S. Venkata, J. Wanderer, J. Zhou, M. Zhu, et al. B4: Experience with a globally-deployed software defined WAN. In *Proceedings of the ACM SIGCOMM*, 2013.

[17] T. Koponen, M. Casado, N. Gude, J. Stribling, L. Poutievski, M. Zhu, R. Ramanathan, Y. Iwata, H. Inoue, T. Hama, et al. Onix: A distributed control platform for large-scale production networks. In *Proc. USENIX OSDI*, 2010.

[18] B. Lantz, B. Heller, and N. McKeown. A network in a laptop: rapid prototyping for software-defined networks. In *Proc. workshop on Hot topics in software defined networking (HotSDN)*, 2010.

[19] J. McCauley, A. Panda, M. Casado, T. Koponen, and S. Shenker. Extending SDN to large-scale networks, 2013.

[20] R. Niranjan Mysore, A. Pamboris, N. Farrington, N. Huang, P. Miri, S. Radhakrishnan, V. Subramanya, and A. Vahdat. PortLand: A scalable fault-tolerant layer 2 data center network fabric. In *Proc. ACM SIGCOMM*, 2009.

[21] N. Spring, R. Mahajan, and D. Wetherall. Measuring ISP topologies with Rocketfuel. In *ACM Computer Communication Review*, 2002.

[22] Tootoonchian, Amin and Ganjali, Yashar. Hyperflow: A distributed control plane for OpenFlow. In *Proc. INM/WREN*, 2010.

[23] Xin Jin and Li Erran Li and Laurent Vanbever and Jennifer Rexford. SoftCell: Scalable and flexible cellular core network architecture. In *Proc. ACM CoNEXT*, 2013.

[24] K. Zarifis, T. Flach, S. Nori, D. Choffnes, R. Govindan, E. Katz-Bassett, M. Mao, and M. Welsh. Diagnosing path inflation of mobile client traffic. In *Proc. International Conference on Passive and Active Network Measurement (PAM)*, 2014.

[25] J. C. Zuniga, C. J. Bernardos, A. de la Oliva, T. Melia, R. Costa, and A. Reznik. Distributed mobility management: A standards landscape. *Communications Magazine, IEEE*, 2013.

Democratic Resolution of Resource Conflicts Between SDN Control Programs

Alvin AuYoung[†], Yadi Ma[†], Sujata Banerjee[†], Jeongkeun Lee[†],
Puneet Sharma[†], Yoshio Turner[†], Chen Liang[‡], Jeffrey C. Mogul[*]
[†]HP Labs, Palo Alto, [‡]Duke University, [*]Google, Inc.
[†]{FirstName.LastName}@hp.com, [‡]cliang@cs.duke.edu, [*]mogul@google.com

ABSTRACT

Resource conflicts are inevitable on any shared infrastructure. In Software-Defined Networks (SDNs), different controller modules with diverse objectives may be installed on the SDN controller. Each module independently generates resource requests that may conflict with the objectives of a different module. For example, a controller module for maintaining high availability may want resource allocations that require too much core network bandwidth and thus conflict with another module that aims to minimize core bandwidth usage. In such a situation, it is imperative to identify and install resource allocations that achieve network wide global objectives that may not be known to individual modules, e.g., high availability with acceptable bandwidth usage. This problem has received only limited attention, with most prior work focused on detecting, avoiding, and resolving rule-level conflicts in the context of OpenFlow.

In this paper, we present an automatic resolution mechanism based on a family of voting procedures, and apply it to resolve resource conflicts among SDN and cloud controller programs. We observe that the choice of appropriate resolution mechanism depends on two properties of the deployed modules: their precision and parity. Based on these properties, a network operator can apply a range of resolution techniques. We present two such techniques.

Overall, our system promotes modularity and does not require each controller module to divulge its objectives or algorithms to other modules. We demonstrate the improvement in allocation quality over various alternative resolution methods, such as static priorities or equal weight, round-robin decisions. Finally, we provide a qualitative comparison of this work to recent methods based on utility or currency.

Categories and Subject Descriptors

C.2.3 [**Network Operations**]: Network Management; C.2.1 [**Network Architecture and Design**]:

Keywords

Network state; software-defined networking; datacenter network; SDN resource conflicts

CoNEXT'14, December 2–5, 2014, Sydney, Australia.
ACM 978-1-4503-3279-8/14/12.
http://dx.doi.org/10.1145/2674005.2674992.

1. INTRODUCTION

A Software-Defined Network (SDN) provides a network operator with significant flexibility in programming the network. By exposing a simple control plane API, a variety of features can be quickly modified or introduced to the network by implementing software control programs, or modules in a logically centralized SDN controller. It has been argued that such flexibility is vital to support any network with rich and evolving requirements [7].

However, this flexibility is a double-edged sword. While introducing new functionality may no longer be a bottleneck to enhancing the network, we argue that maintaining desirable or predictable performance will instead become the main impediment. Today, many controllers are built in a monolithic manner with tight integration between software components implementing various network functions. As controller complexity grows, it is imperative to enable modular composition of SDN controller modules, where individual self-contained modules can be safely plugged into a single SDN controller. Modular composition would foster an ecosystem where independent software vendors can develop controller modules, and a network operator can pick and choose a set of best-in-class modules to manage the network.

With multiple controller modules, each with a different objective, the onus will fall on the network operator to ensure that these modules operate to meet their local objectives without disrupting global network objectives. Consider the following simple example of two independent controller modules. The first module aims to maintain high service availability and thus generates resource requests to reserve extra link bandwidth in the network. Concurrently, a second controller module aims to minimize use of scarce and costly core bandwidth, and thus generates conflicting resource requests to shift load, or free bandwidth on some of the same links.

With only two modules, a network operator might successfully resolve conflicts using simple static policies, such as prioritizing one module over another. However, the number of potential dependencies between modules grows exponentially with the number of modules and becomes untenable for a single person to manage by hand. Moreover, if modules are implemented by third parties, it may be impossible for the operator to understand module objectives or behavior. Finally, static priority cannot represent a network operator's possible goal of achieving a compromise resource allocation that partially meets the objectives of multiple modules with conflicting requests.

Assuming a network operator has a rough idea of global invariants and desired network behavior, she still needs a mechanism to resolve conflicts in a way that maximizes the value of the network. We argue that resource allocations should be *Pareto efficient*: any change (to a Pareto-efficient allocation) that would increase the benefit to one module would decrease the benefit to another module. Moreover, the ability to adequately consider these alternative allocations should depend not on the expertise of the network operator but rather be assisted by the modules themselves, which can be refined (i.e., implemented) independently.

The primary challenge to resolve these conflicts efficiently is accurately inferring each module's objective function [22], while still maintaining modularity, or loose coupling between the modules and the system [27].

We argue that there is a *family* of appropriate resolution mechanisms, and the choice of which mechanism to use depends on two module characteristics: evaluation *precision* and *parity*. Precision refers to how accurately a module is able to evaluate (in a relative manner) alternative allocation options. Parity refers to how easy it is to normalize the objective functions of the modules, which is useful in order to compare their relative allocation preferences when resolving a conflict.

Consider two state-of-the-art approaches that sit at opposite ends of the spectrum in balancing this trade-off. In Corybantic [22], the focus is on providing the best "value" to the network by maximizing a global objective function among modules. This approach requires both precision and parity; each module must implement fine-grained objective functions to evaluate potential allocations, and these functions must be of consistent granularity across modules.

Statesman [27], in contrast, requires little precision or parity between modules. Modules may request resources on their own time scale, and conflicts are resolved without regard to any objective functions or system performance. Instead, a state manager simply resolves (or "merges") any conflicts such that no global invariants are violated. Despite its simplicity, this approach places the onus on the network operator to manually create the appropriate rules or priorities to resolve conflicts. This deployment scenario may not be appropriate for network operators of small businesses or enterprises, who lack direct visibility and control over the implementation of each module.

Compared to explicit rule-conflict detection, we argue for a higher-level abstraction for conflict resolution among modules. This design is particularly necessary for SDN deployments where modules are implemented by third parties, or re-factored often, and are thus otherwise difficult to collectively tune by hand.

In this paper, we present *Athens*, a revision of the original Corybantic design, but one that sits as a compromise between the Corybantic and Statesman approaches. Similar to both designs, modules in Athens propose different network states. Its key difference is the family of voting mechanisms used as an abstraction to determine the resulting network state. Athens explores the possibility of using a voting-inspired mechanism to provide general, non-rule-based conflict resolution.

Depending on the degree of precision and parity in deployed modules, network operators have more discretion over how conflicts are resolved, and can use a family of mechanisms to automatically resolve these conflicts. At a minimum, modules in Athens only need to compare the relative value of any two proposed network states, and the network operator can employ a base *ordinal* voting method. However, this simple ordinal procedure can be enhanced to use cardinal values or weights to increase the precision of the trade-offs made by Athens, if modules can precisely express a relative magnitude valuation of allocation alternatives.

From our early experience with developing controller modules – applied to both SDN *and* cloud control programs, we observe that there are many practical limitations to providing parity among modules, and that any general framework for combining diverse modules must support flexibility in module parity and precision.

In this paper, we make the following contributions:

- We first develop a framework with the notions of parity and precision to frame the problem and classify existing approaches. We present our system design of Athens with voting based resolution.
- We implement two examples of voting procedures and four modules and evaluate their performance quantitatively using a data trace from a production workload. Our results demonstrate that the Athens framework is guaranteed to select a Pareto efficient allocation among known candidates, and in several cases leads to a Pareto superior allocation over simpler techniques that do not consider preferences.

2. BACKGROUND

In this section, we describe the target deployment scenario for Athens: a shared network infrastructure, comprising of SDN (e.g., HP VAN SDN Controller, NOX/POX, Floodlight, OpenDaylight) and cloud (e.g., OpenStack, CloudStack) controllers.

2.1 Basic framework

The Athens framework, similar to Corybantic, consists of control programs and resource controllers. Without Athens, the control programs would run – with little or no coordination – on top of the resource controllers. The two resource classes we consider are networking resources and compute (i.e., cloud) resources.

SDN controllers. An SDN controller configures a set of networking resources, namely a set of SDN-enabled switches. These switches implement a standard programmatic interface, e.g., OpenFlow [20]. The SDN controller (e.g., [5, 12, 17]) sends commands conforming to this API to control the forwarding behavior of the network. For example, the SDN controller may send commands to a subset of switches that install local OpenFlow rules for packet filtering or performance isolation between different flows. An SDN "control program" decides which commands to send to the switches via an SDN controller. Typically these control programs operate in a tight control loop: reading the state of the network, and reacting (i.e., writing state) upon observing some condition [15, 28]. As described in both Corybantic [22] and Statesman [27], there may exist many such control programs operating simultaneously, with varying complexity. Coordinating these control programs are at the heart of the Athens design.

Compute controllers. In our vision, control programs are not limited to network control but can control other resources as well. For example, a control program might want to instantiate and migrate Virtual Machines (VMs). Frameworks for controlling these "cloud" resources include OpenStack [25] and CloudStack [2]. In fact, the OpenStack network controller is already integrated with the Project OpenDaylight [17] SDN controller.

Like both Corybantic and Statesman, Athens implements a *meta-controller*, which interposes between the control modules and resource controllers in order to resolve resource conflicts. We illustrate these conceptual components in Figure 1, and describe them next.

2.2 Basic operation

Athens, Corybantic and Statesman all follow the model of allowing control programs (blue boxes in Figure 1) to propose changes (red lines) to the underlying infrastructure (blue boxes on bottom), via existing SDN or cloud controllers (green boxes) and providing a means to resolve these requests into an implementable network state.

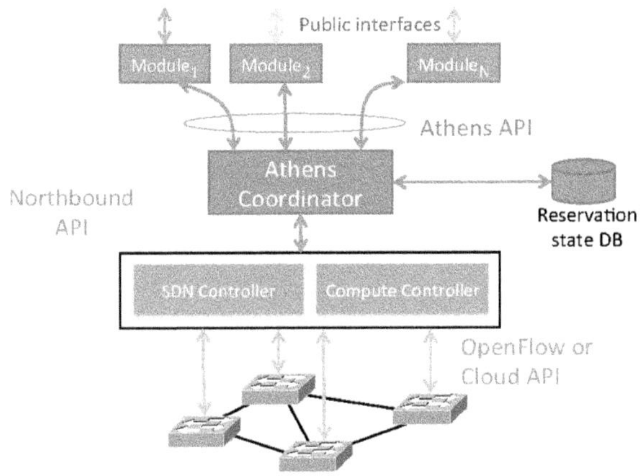

Figure 1: Basic *Athens* architecture, which is very similar to the original Corybantic design [22]

Proposing network states. Consider the example of a program that wants to create two VMs with a minimum bandwidth guarantee between them. It may use the Cloud and SDN controllers to identify one or more racks with available capacity to host these VMs, and an appropriate layer-2 forwarding path (with sufficient bandwidth) between them, respectively. It can then propose a network state in which it has instantiated VMs on each rack, and reserve the desired bandwidth on a path between them. We discuss more concrete examples of network state proposals and control modules in Section 3.

Sequence of operations. Athens runs in a logical *while(true)* loop. Upon any external events, such as a public tenant request (i.e., green arrow in Figure 1), it will run a sequence of operations: (1) collect proposals, (2) evaluate proposals, (3) choose a "winning" proposal, (4) implement the winning proposal. We outline these steps here and describe them in more detail in the indicated sections.

When collecting proposals, Athens will send a copy of the current network state to each controller module (blue boxes). Each controller module synchronously sends a set of proposed changes. For example, if there is a new tenant request, the module may propose an allocation or placement of the resources in that request (see Figure 2 for an example of proposals).

After collecting these proposals, Athens has each module evaluate *all* proposals. The choice of particular evaluation method in the original Corybantic design resulted in a numeric value for each module. Athens introduces a family of such evaluation methods (Section 3.6) for each module to implement. Proposals can also be filtered if they violate a global constraint defined by the network operator or module (Section 3.4). To support these two operations, all modules must therefore implement the Athens API (red lines) of *propose()*, and *evaluate()* or *compare()*. This API is how each module provides "feedback" to the Athens meta-controller about its opaque preferences. The specifics of these operations are detailed in Section 3.

Based on the evaluation feedback, Athens runs a conflict resolution method (can be chosen by the network operator; see Section 3.6) to decide on a winning proposal, and then implements this proposal. This loop continues indefinitely, sleeping until the next event.

We observe that this "forced" coordination between modules and Athens may incur unnecessary overhead. This may be a problem if modules operate at different time scales. In our current implementation, however, we rely on synchronous state updates, where Athens maintains a snapshot of the global state, and pushes this state to modules in each round. In our evaluation, we use an incoming tenant request to trigger an iteration of the Athens control loop.

3. Athens MODEL

The key distinguishing features of Athens are in how modules are written, and how conflicting resource requests from these modules are resolved. Note that we use the three terms – controller program, controller module, and module – interchangeably.

3.1 Programming a module

An Athens module only needs to implement two of the three methods in the Athens API (Section 3.3). First, it needs to *propose* network states that meet the resource needs of a user request (e.g., a tenant requesting a set of VMs) in a way that satisfies the module's objectives (e.g., meet high availability goals by appropriately placing VMs). Proposals are simply changes to the current network state, such as creating a VM or cluster, moving an existing VM, making a bandwidth reservation, or otherwise modifying state (switch links, OpenFlow table entries).

Second, an Athens module needs to implement a method to *evaluate* proposals from other modules. For this method, the module has a choice between implementing a simple coarse-grained comparison, or a more fine-grained rating method. The comparison method, *compare(proposal1, proposal2)*, takes two arbitrary proposals as input, and expresses a preference for one of the states, or indifference between the two. The more fine-grained method, *evaluate(proposal)*, returns a numeric value for a given network state proposal. A module need only implement one of these two methods; if it implements *evaluate(proposal)*, Athens can infer its *compare(proposal1,proposal2)* preference.

We show pseudocode for the implementation of these methods in Section 3.3.

Example: Fault-Tolerance Module (FTM). Consider the Fault-Tolerance module described by Corybantic [22]. This module wants to maximize the average service availability of its tenants' VM instances by minimizing the impact of any single rack or server failure on the VM instances. Specifically, it uses a metric called "worst-case survivability" (WCS) [6]. Its implementation of the *compare()* method would return a preference for the network state with the higher WCS, or a "no preference" if the WCS for each state is identical. Its *evaluate()* method could return a numeric value proportional to the resulting WCS of the state. When proposing a network state, this module has multiple options for how to place VMs in isolated fault domains to increase each tenant's WCS.

Example: Core-Bandwidth Module (CBM). Revisiting the example from Section 1, we consider a module that tries to conserve link bandwidth in the core of the network. This module was illustrated by Corybantic [22] as one that conflicts with FTM. Its *compare()* method would prefer network states that use less core bandwidth. Its *evaluate()* could return a numeric value inversely proportional to the average core bandwidth usage associated with a network state. When proposing a network state, CBM tries to place VMs in the same physical rack or aggregation switch to avoid using core bandwidth.

Example: Guaranteed-Bandwidth Module (GBM). As a more sophisticated example, consider a Guaranteed Bandwidth Module that tries to reserve inter-VM network bandwidth for each tenant's set of VMs. The choice of this module was inspired from requirements of real-world control programs, and is meant also to embody recent research in tenant bandwidth reservations [4, 16]. The goal of these methods is to place as many tenant requests as possible for VM clusters with bandwidth guarantees. Thus, GBM prefers allocations that are likely to fit more such requests by consuming less network bandwidth. When proposing a network state, GBM uses the same implementation suggestion by Ballani et al. [4], which places each request (described in the Hose bandwidth model) in the smallest (lowest) network subtree. Its *compare()* method would prefer network states that use less average link bandwidth. Its *evaluate()* method could return a value inversely proportional to the average link bandwidth usage of a network state.

Example: Switch Resource Module (SRM). Finally, consider a module that manages switch resources, such as entries in a flow table. Unlike other modules, this Switch Resource Module (SRM) does not need to generate new proposals. Instead, it evaluates proposals from other modules: ensuring no switch is overloaded by expressing fixed-size flow table limits as a constraint, while also expressing a preference for proposals that use fewer flow table entries. For our prototype SRM, we assume that it is given adequate information about flow table usage in each proposal (i.e., we assume all-to-all VM communication patterns for each tenant, and that flow paths are assigned within a proposal). We do not consider flow aggregation. SRM's implementation of *compare()* method would prefer network states that use smaller number of flow table entries. To *evaluate()* a network state, it could return a value that is inversely proportional to the total number of entries used in switches if the network state is admitted.

3.2 Example proposals by modules

Figure 2 shows examples of proposals generated by two modules. For illustrative purposes, the examples assume a three level tree topology with four racks; each rack has four physical machines with two VM slots per machine. Each rack thus has a capacity of eight VM slots. We also assume each link has enough bandwidth to satisfy two incoming tenant requests: R1 <5, 100 Mbps> and R2 <10, 200 Mbps>. In other words, R1 requires a cluster of 5 VMs connected by virtual links (hoses) of bandwidth 100 Mbps, while R2 requires a cluster of 10 VMs connected by hoses of bandwidth 200 Mbps.

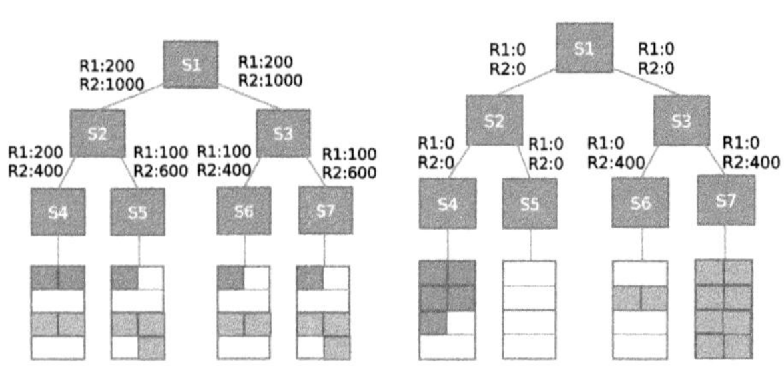

(a) Example FTM proposal (b) Example GBM proposal

Figure 2: Proposed network states by FTM and GBM for tenant requests R1: <5, 100 Mbps> and R2: <10, 200 Mbps>, respectively. Red slots are occupied by R1 and green slots by R2. Numbers beside a link show reserved bandwidth on the corresponding link for each request

Figure 2(a) shows the network state proposed by FTM for requests R1 and R2. Since FTM aims to preserve per-tenant fault-tolerance, it spreads each tenant's VMs across fault domains, shown as red rectangles (VMs of R1) and green rectangles (VMs of R2) in Figure 2(a).

Figure 2(b) shows the network state proposed by GBM for the two requests. Since GBM tries to place VMs of each request in the smallest subtree in the topology, it places VMs of R1 in the subtree of switch S4, and VMs of R2 in the subtree of switch S3.

For GBM, VM placement impacts the reserved bandwidth on each link. In Figure 2, the number beside a link shows reserved bandwidth on that link for each request. Each link divides a tenant tree into two components, and bandwidth needed on this link for the tenant is determined by multiplying the per-VM bandwidth required by the tenant and the number of VMs on the smaller of the two components [4]. For example, in Figure 2(a), the link between S2 and S4 divides R1's VMs into 2 components, with 2 and 3 VMs respectively. Therefore, the bandwidth required by R1 on this link equals $min(2,3) \times 100Mbps = 200Mbps$. Similarly, the bandwidth required by R2 on this link equals $min(2,8) \times 200Mbps = 400Mbps$.

3.3 Implementing the Athens API

Currently, each module only needs to implement two of three methods:

- *P propose(requests)*: return a proposal P representing network state.
- *int compare(P1, P2)*: compare proposals P1, P2, and indicate which proposal it prefers, or "no preference".
- *float evaluate(P)*: evaluate a proposal P, and return a value representing a rating.

Using FTM as an example, we illustrate pseudocode for these methods. Algorithm 1 shows a code snippet of the *propose* method. This method changes the current topology by placing VMs of a tenant's request in isolated racks (fault domains) to increase the tenant's WCS.

Algorithm 1: Pseudocode for FTM.*propose*()

```
def propose(requests):
    newTopology = getCurrentTopology();
    for r in requests:
        numVMs = r.numVMs;
        numOpenSlots =
        newTopology.getNumOpenSlots();
        if numOpenSlots < numVMs:
            return getCurrentTopology();
        openRacks = newTopology.getOpenRacks();
        openRackIndex = 0;
        length = openRacks.length;
        for vm in r.getVMs():
            rackIndex = openRackIndex % length;
            openRacks [rackIndex ].addVM(vm);
            openRackIndex += 1;
    return newTopology;
```

Algorithms 2 and 3 show the implementation of the *evaluate* method for FTM and SRM, respectively. The FTM evaluate method simply returns the average worse-case survivability (WCS) of all tenants if the proposal is accepted. Thus, it favors proposals that result in higher WCS values. The SRM evaluate method simply calculates the aggregated flow entry count that the switches would have used if a proposal is accepted[1]. It returns *constraintViolation* if the resulting flow entry count in any switch would exceed the physical limit. Otherwise, it returns a value inversely proportional to the number of entries, meaning it favors proposals that use fewer flow entries. In both cases, we could implement an accompanying *compare* method by simply comparing the return value or the evaluate method in each proposal, and returning a preference for the proposal with the higher evaluated value.

To be clear, implementing *compare* using *evaluate* is simply an implementation shortcut used in our evaluation to compare evaluation methods. As described before, the assumption is that in a deployment scenario without complete module precision, it is more straightforward in practice to implement a *compare* method relative to an *evaluate* method. And if an *evaluate* method is implemented, there is no need to provide a corresponding *compare* method. This implementation shortcut has limited use, but perhaps can also be useful for providing "backwards compatibility" for using an ordinal comparison instead of a fine-grained evaluate method, even when an *evaluate* method is provided.

Algorithm 2: Pseudocode for FTM.*evaluate*(proposal)

```
def evaluate(proposal):
    numTenants = 0;
    totalWCS = 0;
    for t in proposal.getTenants():
        numTenants += 1;
        wcs = t.getWCS();
        totalWCS += wcs;
    return totalWCS/ numTenants.
```

Algorithm 3: Pseudocode for SRM.*evaluate*(proposal)

```
def evaluate(proposal):
    for s in switches:
        numEntries = s.countFlowEntries(proposal);
        if numEntries > maxNumEntries:
            return constraintViolation;
        totalFlowEntries += numEntries;
    return 1/totalFlowEntries.
```

3.4 Expressing constraints

Global network invariants can be expressed globally or per-module. Each module can be configured with the appropriate invariant by the network operator at deployment time. Currently, Athens assumes that constraints are inviolable. For example, given the modules described above, the network operator may require that all non-trivial allocations meet a minimum WCS of 0.6. FTM can be configured with this WCS requirement, and FTM can filter out any proposed states violating this constraint. For example, the state proposed by GBM in Figure 2(b) will be rejected since it has WCS of 0.1 (detailed calculation in Section 5.1).

3.5 Design assumptions

As in [22], we assume a cooperative environment where modules are neither malicious nor greedy. Protecting against the latter would require a minimum notion of incentive compatibility. A recent explanation of these properties applied to a shared resource infrastructure is provided by Ghodsi et al. [11]. It may be possible to extend our model to leverage their "strategy-proof" allocation mechanism, but we would need to use SDN and Cloud controllers that could satisfy partial allocations. This is because their model relies on being able to allocate, say, a fraction of CPU cycles or a portion of shared memory, whereas our controllers deal with coarse-grained bandwidth reservations, fixed-sized VM slots, etc.

Given these assumptions, a particular weakness of our deployment model is that we rely on each module to not overzealously "veto" another module's proposals. Strategically speaking, a greedy or malicious module can simply claim that every proposal originating from other modules violates a constraint, thus increasing the likelihood of receiving the proposal it wants. In this scenario – which may occur unintentionally due to program errors – we place the onus on the network operator to observe the behavior of the system; a high fraction of vetoes from a consistent subset of modules may warrant investigation.

3.6 Conflict resolution

Athens resolves conflicts by choosing a single proposal for network state, with the goal being to deliver the most value. The practical challenges that we address are that value may be difficult to measure accurately (precision) and consistently across modules (parity).

Our discussion assumes that a single proposal is chosen among conflicting proposals.[2]

3.6.1 Design space

We argue that a network operator must consider two characteristics of the deployed modules: precision and parity.

Precision for a module means that it can accurately discern its space of allocation alternatives. For example, FTM can translate different levels of WCS: if *evaluate(P1)* == 2·*evaluate(P2)*, then the allocation represented by proposal P1 has twice as much survivability as P2. That is, a module can provide a cardinal rank that accurately reflects the *magnitude* of one option over another. A lack of precision occurs when preferences are not tied to metrics; for example, if a module must trade off multiple resource types ([15]) or its decisions are binary (e.g., firewall rules). Even when preferences are tied to metrics, the metrics may not accurately express the actual value of alternative proposals. For example, CBM would prefer a proposal that requires 15% of the core bandwidth over another proposal that requires 18%, but their actual value to the users are unlikely to be strictly proportional to the bandwidth percentages and accurately assessing the actual values for different users could be impossible.

Parity across modules means that their preferences are inherently on equal footing. In other words, their relative rankings of proposals are known or can be easily normalized across modules. An example of this scenario is if all modules can express precise rankings (values) in a common currency [22]. Lack of parity can occur for several reasons. Corybantic [22] proposed using dollars as a common unit to capture the (economic) values or costs of proposals. However, in our experience, we found it challenging or impractical to relate a module's preferences to a dollar amount, such as unused bandwidth or load balancing.

[1]A straightforward extension could weigh entries at different switches based on importance, but we do not consider this scenario in our evaluation.

[2]Here, a conflict does not mean violating a constraint. Techniques exist for both detecting resource conflicts or otherwise merging non-conflicting states. The Athens framework accommodates these techniques, but we do not implement them; we induce conflicts for the purposes of exposition.

On the other hand, if the network operator knows only that fault tolerance is generally preferred to saving power, ranking (*compare()*) may be more appropriate to use instead of ratings/values (*evaluate()*) and the operator can optionally assign (voting) weights to each module.

Given these two definitions, a network operator has to consider three deployment scenarios, depending on the precision or parity of available modules.

Scenario 1: all modules have both precision and parity. In this setting, the operator can plausibly use the Corybantic methodology of using the value of *evaluate(P)* summed across all modules to determine a winner. In this case, the *evaluate(P)* method from each module returns a value representing currency, and the global maximization objective is formulated in these dollar units in aggregate.

Scenario 2: all modules have precision, but no parity[3]

This scenario means that each module can express the relative trade-off of each proposal accurately, but manual intervention must be used to normalize each module. In this case a cardinal voting mechanism can be used to determine a winner. Using this method, an operator also has the option of setting a different number of votes (akin to weighted voting) for each module to express the relative importance of that module's objective.

Scenario 3: not all modules have precision. In this scenario, we cannot rely on a module to evaluate the magnitude of difference, but can instead evaluate a preference between proposals. In this case, we expect modules to implement a *compare(P1,P2)* method to provide a partial ordering over preferences. A collection of these local preference orderings can be used to establish a global ordering using an ordinal voting procedure.

3.6.2 Algorithms

Next, we describe algorithms for each scenario.

Scenario 1: Maximizing a global objective function. This algorithm is described in the original Corybantic design [22]. It selects the proposal that yields the largest sum of *evaluation(proposal)* over all modules.

Scenario 2: Maximizing a set of voter ratings. Illustrated in Algorithm 4, this particular cardinal voting mechanism implements a *cumulative voting* scheme, where every module (voter) can distribute its fixed votes to candidate proposals. Athens invokes a module's *evaluate(P)* method to get its votes.

Algorithm 4: Scenario 2: Cumulative voting mechanism

```
def CumulativeVote(candidateProposals):
    for m in Athens.modules:
        mTotalVotes = 0;
        for p in candidateProposals:
            votes[m][p] = m.evaluate(p);
            mTotalVotes += votes[m][p];
        for p in candidateProposals:
            votes[m][p] = votes[m][p] / mTotalVotes;
    for p in candidateProposals:
        for m in Athens.modules:
            finalVotes[p] += votes[m][p];
    return p with the maximum finalVotes[p].
```

Scenario 3: Maximizing the mutual majority. We illustrate a simplified version of the algorithm used by the Athens ordinal voting mechanism in Algorithm 5. This algorithm implements a *Condorcet mechanism* [19]. The rationale behind choosing this particular mechanism is discussed in Section 3.6.3. One interpretation of the Condorcet mechanism is that it determines a winner as the candidate that would have won the largest fraction of votes in a set of all-pairs elections, conducted by invoking *compare(P1,P2)* for each candidate state pair, for each module. Ties are not counted as victories. Thus, this algorithm has complexity $O(|m||p|^2)$, where m is the set of modules, and p is the set of proposals. This mechanism has several desirable properties for our deployment, including Pareto efficiency and Monotonicity [19].

Algorithm 5: Scenario 3: Concept of Condorcet voting procedure

```
def CondorcetVote(candidateProposals):
    for p_i in candidateProposals:
        wins[i] = 0;
    for p_i in candidateProposals:
        for p_j in candidateProposals:
            if i ≠ j:
                for m in Athens.modules:
                    cmp = m.compare(pi,pj);
                    if cmp < 0:
                        wins[i] += 1;
                    elif cmp > 0:
                        wins[j] += 1;
    return p_i with the maximum wins[i].
```

3.6.3 Other considerations

Choice of voting mechanisms. All voting mechanisms have well-known limitations, formalized most directly by Arrow's impossibility theorem [19]. In Athens, we prioritize the following three theoretical criteria: Pareto efficiency, Monotonicity and Unrestricted domain. We find these properties particularly useful for adjudicating preferences among SDN control modules. The first property guarantees that among all available (i.e., generated by modules) proposals, our mechanism will never fail to select an obvious winner. In other words, if every module prefers proposal A over another proposal B, then B will never be selected over A.

By providing Monotonicity, we guarantee that if any module modifies its local ordering by ranking a proposal higher, that action alone will never decrease the proposal's position in the global ranking. This property is important in our setting if a module's individual choice of ranking can be refined due to new information or other external changes in global state. Finally, the property of Unrestricted domain indicates an ordering that considers all modules' preferences in a deterministic way. One way to view this property is a way to restrict allocations chosen based on the preferences of only a single module, or a random – and thus non-deterministic – mechanism. Adopting this property in Athens eases the burden on a network operator to understand that roughly, a particular set of inputs (modules and their logic for generating proposals) will lead deterministically to a particular set of outputs (winning states).

For our ordinal voting procedure, we considered three classic options: an instant run-off, Condorcet method, or Borda count [19]. We chose the Condorcet mechanism because it satisfies the three criteria mentioned above. For alternative settings, a network operator can freely choose among other mechanisms that satisfy her objectives.

Readers are encouraged to refer to Voting Theory literature [19] for a more thorough treatment of this topic.

[3]We are investigating relaxing the requirement for unanimity, and instead accepting a majority of precise modules.

Inferring cardinality from ordinal preferences. In Scenario 2, we may be able to relax the condition that all modules need to be precise. If a majority of modules express cardinal preferences, it may be more effective to *infer* cardinal rankings from the minority expressing ordinal rankings, and use a resolution mechanism that can leverage the cardinal rankings from the majority precise modules. As we will see in the experiments, the cardinal method significantly improves the quality of allocations. One way to implement this approach is to extrapolate ordinal rankings as a linear cardinal ranking; investigating both the interpolation method and the fraction of precise modules needed is future work.

Establishing a bootstrap. A limitation of a voting procedure is the possibility there is no winner. A simple example is a game like *Rock-Paper-Scissors*, where the collective preferences across voters is circular. We break such ties by allowing the network operator to assign a priority to each module a priori, and select outcomes among ties based on the higher-priority module's preference.

3.7 Refining or generating multiple proposals

One avenue requiring further exploration is an idea of refining proposals, as discussed in Corybantic [22]. Unless a module generates an adequate set of proposals, many mutually beneficial allocations are potentially unexamined. Thus a secondary design goal of Athens is to encourage module developers to express alternatives in a way that will permit reasonable conflict resolution. To maximize satisfactory conflict resolution, each module could generate a set of new proposals (counter-proposals) after it has had a chance to examine the proposals generated by the other modules. Our current implementation adopts a simpler approach for initial exploration of this idea– each module generates a certain number of proposals randomly from the available search space.

We observe that the ability to generate or refine a proposal is logically equivalent to the notion of partial proposals in Statesman [27]. Even if a proposal for network state is rejected, a module can resubmit – or perhaps even submit in parallel – alternative forms of a proposal with varying degrees of partial allocations that it finds acceptable. We defer rigorous comparison of these techniques to future work.

4. Athens SYSTEM IMPLEMENTATION

The Athens framework consists of several software components: the control modules, the Athens meta-controller, a SDN controller and a network emulator. In this section, we present each component's implementation and interaction with other components.

4.1 Implementation framework

The Athens software components are illustrated in Figure 3. In our evaluation (Section 5), a traffic generator injects requests (e.g., tenant VM cluster size, bandwidth requirement, etc.) to the control modules. This injected request is an instance of the "external event" alluded to in Section 2 ("Sequence of operations"), which triggers Athens to iterate its control loop.

We now describe each software component in more detail.

4.2 Control modules

The control modules exemplify SDN control programs one would deploy on top of existing SDN controllers like Floodlight or OpenDaylight. These modules might be written by multiple parties and need only adhere to the Athens API to operate in the framework.

A module must implement either compare() or evaluate() (Section 3.3). At minimum, it must implement compare() for use by the basic ordinal voting mechanism. If evaluate() if implemented, the result of compare() can be inferred.

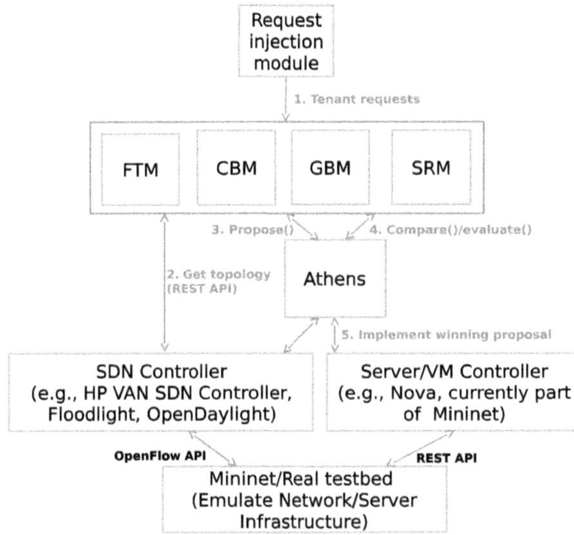

Figure 3: Athens implementation framework

We implement in Python prototypes of the four control programs described in Section 3.1. For each control program we implement all three methods: propose, evaluate and compare.

The controller modules communicate with an SDN controller using a REST API to get the current network topology. The modules also communicate with the Athens meta-controller using its API. As discussed in Section 3, we assume that modules are not malicious, and thus have not yet implemented any safeguards to prevent them from bypassing the Athens meta-controller without permission.

4.3 Athens meta-controller

The meta-controller is at the core of the Athens logic. Its primary roles are (1) to gather suggested modifications to the network ("proposals") from each module and (2) choose and implement winning proposals based on the mechanism chosen by the network operator.

The Athens meta-controller is implemented as a software layer that might be described as middleware between a standard SDN controller and SDN control programs. This means that the meta-controller needs to re-export the SDN controller's northbound API to these programs.

The meta-controller is intended to be used with multiple off-the-shelf SDN controllers without modification. We have implemented support for both Floodlight and the HP VAN SDN controller. It is currently implemented in Python.

Currently, the meta-controller can communicate directly with an actual Server/VM controller or Mininet – a network emulator platform [21] – to implement a network state. We have enhanced Mininet to emulate VM placement, as we describe in Section 4.5.

4.4 SDN controller

The main requirement to interface with SDN controllers is the ability to maintain a common notion of network topology and state. Our current implementation queries the network topology from Floodlight (or the specific controller) using REST APIs, and re-materializes this topology as a Python *networkx* object in the Athens class. A copy of this class object is shared with each module during each proposal or comparison phase. Athens is not limited to a specific SDN controller. Currently available SDN controllers, like OpenDaylight, HP VAN SDN controller, and Floodlight, provide

REST APIs to get network topology information, add/delete flows in switches, etc.

4.5 Network emulation

We can emulate a 3-level tree network topology using the Mininet emulation platform. Mininet creates a virtual OpenFlow network - controller, switches, hosts, and links - on either a single real or virtual machine. The interface between an SDN Controller and Mininet uses OpenFlow.

In order to emulate VM creation and migration, we implement several enhancements to Mininet. Since the out-of-box software does not have a concept of virtual machines, we use Mininet hosts to represent VMs. We also introduce new functions to Mininet so that the Athens meta-controller can modify network state when implementing a proposal. For example, it can thus directly change the network topology, or add/delete/move VMs on racks. Finally, we added a software wrapper to allow the meta-controller (or, in the future, sufficiently privileged control modules) to access these functions via REST APIs.

We also implemented Athens in a real testbed with two OpenFlow-enabled switches and a number of servers attached to them. We use KVM to manage VMs in the testbed and enhanced the interface between Athens and the underlying physical network to make it work with KVM.

5. EVALUATION

We evaluate Athens in deployment scenarios 2 and 3 (Section 3.6.1) using cumulative and ordinal voting mechanisms, respectively. We investigate the effectiveness of these voting mechanisms against alternative allocation approaches. We run our simulations against a production workload trace and provide various metrics to interpret the results. Finally, we investigate the impact of Athens modules generating multiple proposals and discuss an example of using global constraints to assist a network operator to guarantee that certain global properties are preserved.

5.1 Workload

Our workload is based on a trace of tenant resource allocations in a production data center. The trace contains information about the arrival times of these allocations, the various sizes of the virtual machine clusters, and the aggregate bandwidth usage by the cluster. Though we do not have information about duration of each allocation, we deduce the departure time of each allocation from the traffic matrix of the clusters. From these trace data, we model a set of incoming client requests. Each request is considered to be independent, and consists of (1) a set or cluster of homogeneous virtual machines (VMs), and (2) a desired intra-cluster bandwidth quantity between VMs.

We assume that each tenant's bandwidth estimate is the same as its actual usage. While we acknowledge that this is likely to be an unrealistic assumption in practice, we do not believe this assumption changes the high-order result from our experiments. We summarize the workload statistics in Table 1.

Total number of tenant requests:	221
Total number of VMs in all requests:	1767
Max number of VMs in a request:	82
Avg number of VMs in requests:	7.99

Table 1: Workload summary statistics

To further understand the trace, we define a set of tenants as T, with each tenant $t \in T$ having a cluster of C_t virtual machines and B_t bandwidth demand between VMs. We define aggregated bandwidth, BW_{agg} of all tenants, T, to be:

$$BW_{agg} = \sum_{t \in T} C_t \times B_t$$

To get a high-level sense of the production workload, Figure 4 plots the number of live virtual machines and the aggregated bandwidth of all live tenants at any time in the system. As we can see, there is a sharp jump at the beginning of the trace as a large amount of tenant requests arrive, then it stays roughly stable despite some ups and downs as tenants' requests come and go.

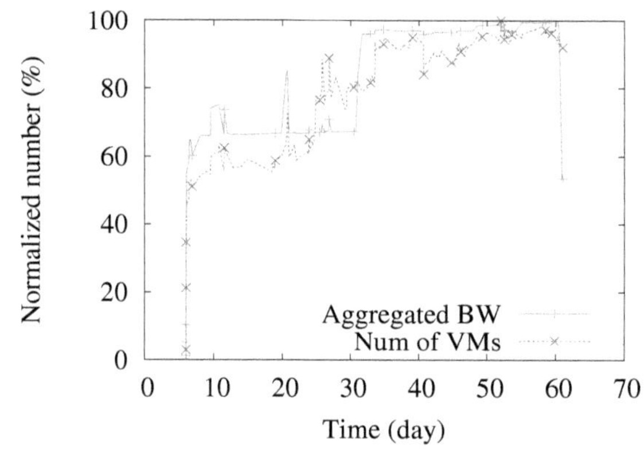

Figure 4: Normalized tenant request in workload trace

Network topology and resource capacity. Our experiments emulate a network with a single-rooted, three-level tree topology: specifically, a 1-8-16 tree with 128 top-of-rack (ToR) switches. Rack capacity is 16, which is chosen such that this topology can accommodate up to 2,048 VMs: large enough to allocate all the VMs in the trace. Unless explicitly noted, we used a network topology and capacity configuration for our experiments such that we had enough bandwidth on all links to accommodate all the bandwidth requests. We chose this somewhat simple scenario to try and separate the difference in allocation quality from the quality of online placement heuristics. In other words, this ensures a more straightforward comparison such that every allocation exhibits the same admitted load. We also ran the experiments with various topology and capacity constraints on links to simulate scenarios where bandwidth was and was not a bottleneck. However, the results were similar enough to omit for brevity.

Metrics. Each control module has its own objective function. For our initial experiments, we plot each of the various metrics separately. While this complicates the task of interpreting the results, this is a necessary exercise also incurred by a network operator absent a global objective function like Corybantic. The aim is to demonstrate that Athens can arrive at something close, without requiring a network operator to define such a complex, or sensitive function.

- **Aggregate core bandwidth.** We define core links as the links from the root of the network topology to the second-level nodes [6]. This metric is the sum of bandwidth used by core links. For the example shown in Figure 2, there are two core links: S1-S2 and S1-S3, and aggregated core bandwidth of FTM and GBM is 2400 Mbps and 0 Mbps, respectively.

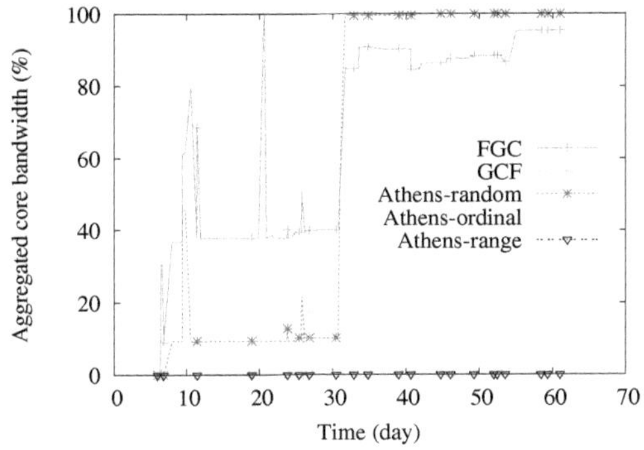

(a) Aggregate core bandwidth (lower is better)

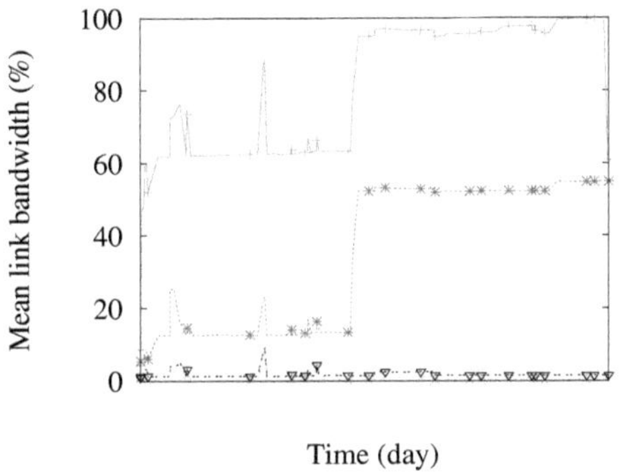

(b) Mean link bandwidth (lower is better)

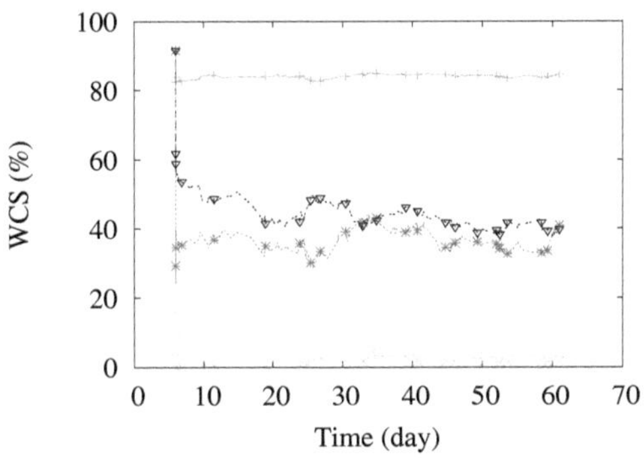

(c) Worst case survivability (higher is better)

Figure 5: Comparing alternative conflict resolution schemes; numbers shown are normalized against maximum value in each metric

- **Mean link bandwidth.** This metric is a proxy for the objective of GBM. This metric is the mean bandwidth used among all the links.

- **Worst-case survivability (WCS).** This metric is the objective of FTM. In our workload, WCS for a single tenant is defined as the fraction of VMs that survive from a single, worst-case, ToR switch failure. This value ranges from $[0, 1)$. If all VMs are on a single host, or under the same ToR switch, this value is 0. If there are two VMs, each on a separate fault domain (i.e., different racks), then this value is 0.5. This metric returns the *mean* WCS across all tenants. As shown in Figure 2(a), WCS of R1 and R2 is 0.6 and 0.7 respectively. Therefore, FTM's mean WCS of the tenants is $(0.6 + 0.7)/2 = 0.65$. Similarly, GBM's mean WCS is $(0 + 0.2)/2 = 0.1$, as shown in Figure 2(b).

Comparing the trade-offs between metrics. To aid with assessing the quality of allocations made by Athens, we devise a "distance" metric as one way to compare the trade-offs made among the modules' individual objectives. This metric calculates the Euclidean[4] distance of a mechanism's allocation from an *optimistic* ideal solution. This ideal solution – likely unattainable – would be to have each metric achieve its best solution – the highest WCS with the least core bandwidth consumed and the lowest mean link utilization. We normalize each of these three metrics between 0 and 1 with respect to the maximum values obtained on that metric, and the distance metric is normalized to the maximum distance in this 3-D unit cube space. The lower the distance from the ideal operating point, the higher the quality of the allocation. We stress that absent a well-defined global objective function, this is only one of many methods with which to capture the trade-off between three metrics.

Alternative conflict resolution mechanisms. We explain each of the resource conflict resolution methods compared in our experiments.

- **Static Priority.** Using this method, one of the modules (FTM, CBM, GBM) is given the highest priority, followed by the other two modules. Proposals from the highest priority module are accepted unless constraints are violated, in which case proposals from lower priority modules are considered. The plots will indicate the order of modules' priority, e.g., "FGC" means we use static priority, with FTM given the highest priority, followed by GBM and CBM. Similarly, "GCF" means GBM is given highest priority, followed by CBM and FTM. Since results of "CGF" are similar to those from "GCF", we omit them for brevity.

- **Athens-random.** In this scheme, Athens selects a random proposal among those that do not violate any constraints, e.g., bandwidth guarantee. This essentially gives all modules equal weight and the modules have equal probability to win. This method is used as a baseline since it uses no information aside from constraints.

- **Athens-ordinal.** Among the proposals that do not violate any constraints, Athens selects the proposal that wins the Condorcet voting process, which is described by Algorithm 5 corresponding to Scenario 3 (Section 3.6.1).

- **Athens-cumulative.** Corresponding to Scenario 2 (Section 3.6.1), Athens selects the proposal that wins a cumulative-based voting process (Algorithm 4).

Global constraints. In Athens, network operators may define high-level objectives as constraints to express global system requirements, and also to prevent any module from abusing the system. This expression is similar in spirit to the invariants described by Statesman [27]. In Athens, examples of global constraints include size of flow table (i.e., maximum number of flow table entries), to make sure that any proposal that overflows a flow table is rejected; minimum WCS, to make sure that any proposal that causes WCS to be below this constraint is rejected by the selection mechanism; and bandwidth guarantee, to make sure that any proposal that violates a tenant's requested bandwidth guarantee is rejected. We examine the use of the flow table size constraint in Section 5.3.

[4]We also investigated using Manhattan distance, but report only Euclidean in this paper as the results are similar.

5.2 Understanding baseline evaluation results

In this section, we compare the allocation of Athens with alternative resolution mechanisms.

Figure 5 plots the three metrics of interest (y-axis) against request arrival time (x-axis). For aggregate core bandwidth, we normalize aggregate core bandwidth of each method by the maximum aggregate core bandwidth. Similarly, we plot mean link bandwidth usage of each method normalized by the maximum link bandwidth usage of FTM.

Before we discuss the details of each graph, we summarize the high-level trends from the graphs:

- The individual modules work as expected and in line with their goals, at the expense of the goals of other modules: prioritizing GBM and CBM (by way of GCF) uses little bandwidth but provide allocations with less than 10% worst-case survivability (WCS); prioritizing FTM (by way of FGC) provides WCS greater than 80% survivability, but at the cost of 20 times more core bandwidth and mean link bandwidth usage than GCF.
- While Athens-cumulative and random achieve a fairly even bandwidth / fault-tolerance balance, Athens-cumulative does this more efficiently, and, in fact, results in a superior allocation across all metrics.

Next, we look into each metric in greater detail.

Aggregate core bandwidth. Figures 5(a) plots the aggregate core bandwidth of each mechanism we evaluated. As expected, GCF has the lowest core link bandwidth usage, while FGC has the highest. GCF is most effective in conserving core bandwidth, which is 0 in this case. Athens-ordinal is more effective in conserving bandwidth usage than providing high fault tolerance because a majority of the modules seek to conserve bandwidth. The allocation outcomes are similar to that of GCF, because there are two bandwidth-conserving modules (GBM and CBM) and also a resource-conserving module (SRM); proposals from the majority preference are more likely to win.

The performance of Athens-random lies between that of FGC and GCF in the first part of the trace and jumps above FGC in the second part of the trace. This is a function of the presence of tenants with large bandwidth demands (Figure 4).

Bandwidth usage of Athens-cumulative is also close to that of GCF, while it provides reasonably good fault tolerance. This increase in WCS is a result of considering potential allocations in which both CBM and GBM would not save significant bandwidth for a particular cluster placement (resulting in fewer relative votes for proposals from those modules), while FTM uses most of its votes to express the correspondingly (and relatively) significant gain in WCS.

Mean link bandwidth. Figures 5(b) plots the mean link bandwidth of all the mechanisms we evaluated. Similar to core bandwidth usage, on average, GCF and Athens-ordinal consume the least amount of link capacity, close to 0% of what FGC consumes. Athens-random consumes about 20-60% of what FTM consumes. Athens-ordinal is close to GCF/Athens-cumulative. The difference among these three schemes is small, and almost negligible.

Worst case survivability. Figures 5(c) plots mean worse case survivability (WCS) among all requests. FGC has largest WCS, larger than 80%. As mentioned above, performance of Athens-ordinal is close to GCF, and the resulting WCS is around 4%. To save link bandwidth or flow table entries, GBM, CBM and SRM tend to put VMs on same rack or close-by racks, so GCF exhibits low WCS: close to 0 in this case. Athens-cumulative achieves notably higher WCS of approximately 40-50%.

Euclidean distance from ideal. The first row of each group in Table 2 lists the average WCS, core link bandwidth, mean link bandwidth, and distance from the idealized allocation described in Section 5.1. As we can see, both of the priority-based approaches arrive at allocations that are closer to the ideal than a random approach. Moreover, using either the ordinal or cardinal (cumulative) mechanism arrive at an allocation even closer to the ideal.

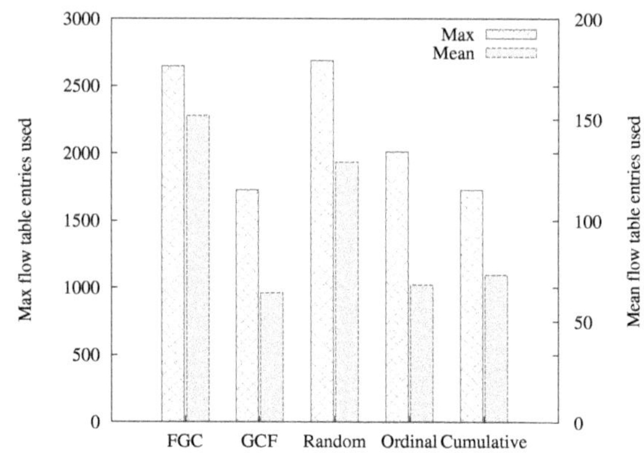

Figure 6: Max and mean number of used flow table entries (flow table size constraint set to 3000 entries)

5.3 Using constraints

In our experiments, we arbitrarily set a constraint of 3000 entries per switch flow table. In our experiments, we found that this resulted in approximately 1% of all proposals being rejected due to (flow table) constraint violation. Figure 6 illustrates the maximum and mean number of flow table entries used in each scheme. The maximum values shown in each column is the largest number of flow table entries used in any switch by the specific scheme, while the mean value is the mean number of flow table entries used among all the switches in the system. FGC and Random consume the largest number of flow table entries while GCF and Cumulative consume the least. We see the same trend for the mean number of flow table entries consumed by each scheme.

5.4 Precise evaluation and more proposals

We repeat a subset of the previous experiments by also evaluating the benefit of the case where modules can generate multiple proposals.

Mechanism	Mean WCS	Core Link BW*	Mean Link BW*	Dist
Static Priority FGC	0.84	0.95	1.00	0.80
Static Priority GCF	0.02	0.00	0.00	0.57
Random	0.41	1.00	0.90	0.85
Random-1	0.42	0.17	0.69	0.53
Random-2	0.48	0.31	0.74	0.55
Random-4	0.43	0.40	0.76	0.60
Ordinal	0.04	0.00	0.03	0.55
Ordinal-1	0.04	0.00	0.01	0.55
Ordinal-2	0.02	0.00	0.00	0.57
Ordinal-4	0.04	0.00	0.01	0.55
Cumulative	0.40	0.00	0.02	0.35
Cumulative-1	0.40	0.00	0.02	0.35
Cumulative-2	0.40	0.00	0.02	0.35
Cumulative-4	0.38	0.00	0.02	0.36

Table 2: Increasing the number of proposals for each voting mechanism; *columns are normalized to maximum usage.

Modules can express cardinal (i.e., numeric) preferences using the *evaluate(P)* method in lieu of the simpler *compare(P1,P2)* method.

The former provides more fine-grained rating of each proposal, but is still a relative comparison. In other words, we do not assume parity, and one module's numeric range can differ from another's. The cumulative voting mechanism implicitly normalizes the ranges.

Each row in Table 2 compares various resolution mechanisms across our metrics (columns) from the full trace run (Table 1). Each mechanism leads to a different way to resolve conflicts over the placement of each tenant cluster. Each entry in the table corresponds to the mean over the duration of the run. The last column has the normalized Euclidean distance metric (from Section 5.1) that we use as a simplistic proxy to assess the quality of resource allocations chosen using each mechanism.

Five rows summarize results from previous sections. The rest are labeled *Mechanism-k* to represent using the specified mechanism, but each module makes k additional proposals to increase its likelihood of winning a good allocation. For example, FTM can propose a range of VM placements with slightly different WCS values to explore placement of a different fraction of a tenant's request within one fault domain (its ideal setting is thus a single VM per fault domain).

For *Random-k*, the outcomes seem to stabilize for $k > 1$; the winning proposal is still selected at random but from a larger set. For *Ordinal-k*, the outcomes also seem to stabilize for $k > 1$. The mean WCS and distance metric are generally the same, but additional proposals provide the opportunity for a small, but 3× decrease in normalized mean link bandwidth usage.

For *Cumulative-k*, we see that Athens more quickly arrives at a more "balanced" compromise, without necessarily needing additional proposals. Regardless of k, the low distance values that the *Cumulative-k* mechanisms incur compared to the other schemes is due to the fact that the mechanism treats all modules' preferences equally. We believe that the minimal impact of increasing k is a function of the workload trace.

Discussion. If a network operator decides to "prioritize" some Athens modules over others, it could do so by providing more votes to that module. Assigning weights in this way seems a natural abstraction for network operators to think about, and using weights with a voting mechanism as opposed to a static priority system yields more opportunities for fruitful trade-offs. Indeed, Table 2 shows that the Cumulative mechanism is Pareto superior to random allocation, and the Ordinal method performs better than both the CBM and GBM priority mechanisms with respect to the first two (column) metrics, with only a slight degradation in the third metric.

Increasing the number of proposals has slightly less impact on the cumulative voting mechanism for this workload. This result is not wholly surprising as, in this case, the range values can be extrapolated from a few proposal values. We hypothesize that if modules happen to exhibit a less "straightforward" mapping of range values (i.e., a linear preference function would be easy to interpolate; one with steps or otherwise piece-wise would be difficult to infer), more proposals would help uncover this irregularity.

5.5 Comparison with Corybantic

In this section, we compare Athens and Corybantic using a scenario similar to the one presented in the original Corybantic work [22]. In this two-module scenario, the relative *global* utility between providing tenant fault tolerance and preserving core network bandwidth is computed using a parameter $\alpha \in [0, 1]$. α and $(1-\alpha)$ are used as weights for the utility function of FTM and CBM, respectively, to derive an implicit global utility function.

As described in the Corybantic work, the purpose behind using different weights to characterize the underlying utility function is

Mechanism	Normalized Mean Utility for various α						
	0.1	0.2	0.4	0.5	0.6	0.8	0.9
Corybantic	1.0	1.0	1.0	1.0	1.0	1.0	1.0
Athens-cumulative-weighted	1.0*	1.0	1.0	1.0	1.0*	1.0	1.0*
Athens-ordinal	0.162	0.221	0.351	0.423	0.501	0.677	0.776
Random	0.185	0.231	0.332	0.389	0.449	0.586	0.664

Table 3: Benefits of Resolving only two conflicting modules by increasing search space; α is as defined in the Corybantic paper [22]. $\alpha = 0.1$ means FTM has a weight of 0.1 and CBM has a weight of 0.9, or $1 - \alpha$. *Indicates rounded up to 1, when using 3 significant digits.

that the relative utility of fault tolerance and preserving core bandwidth can vary for different environments, and perhaps at different times for a single environment. More information about the motivation behind this model are described in [22]. As with the Euclidean distance function used in earlier experiments, this weighted utility function is simply a proxy for a global network objective.

As mentioned in Section 3.6, a network operator can similarly use these weights with the Athens-cumulative voting procedure by assigning a total voting budget for each module in accordance with these weights. We also compare against a random allocation, which does not use these weights, to provide a baseline comparison point.

Table 3 compares the utility delivered by allocations for various values of α. Since we expect Corybantic to provide an upper bound, we normalize the values in Table 3 to the mean utility achieved by Corybantic across allocation rounds.

Athens-cumulative-weighted makes nearly identical allocation decisions as Corybantic. For $\alpha \in \{0.1, 0.7, 0.9\}$, Athens-cumulative makes different allocation decisions on only one, two or three out of over 200 proposal decisions, respectively.

While these results are consistent for this particular production trace, it is possible to imagine other (or particularly degenerative) workload that would make these differences more pronounced.

Perhaps unsurprisingly, Athens-ordinal and Random perform notably worse, as they do not take module weights into account. Athens-ordinal, in particular, is sensitive to skewed weights (i.e., low α), and it performs worse than random for these low α values. This is perhaps, unsurprising, since each pairwise comparison is much more likely to be incorrect when it is oblivious to weights.

6. RELATED WORK

The problem of detecting, avoiding, and resolving rule-level conflicts has received significant attention, most specifically from Frenetic [9, 10] and Pyretic [23]. As opposed to this work, we focus on resolving resource-level conflicts between modules. Merlin [26] and PANE [8] also aim to provide higher-level (relative to OpenFlow) API to coordinate behavior between SDN programs, but these approaches require a network operator to manually resolve module-level conflicts, and thus do not address how to automatically resolve them.

Complementary to our work is the goal of verifying the correctness of an SDN program. Specifically, the goal of ensuring (network-wide) invariants has received a great attention recently [1, 24, 3, 13, 14]. These papers propose either 1) foundationally strong languages to write SDN programs that can be verified by existing verification logic or tools [1, 24, 3], or 2) systems that verify the correctness/invariants of a given network real-time by analyzing flow rules and the network topology [13, 14]. While none of these papers addresses the problem of detecting and resolving conflicts between different SDN programs, we envision that the coordinator or each control module in Athens can leverage these mechanisms, for example, to determine which proposals violate constraints.

The systems most related to Athens are Corybantic [22], which provided the initial design of the system, and Statesman [27]. In Athens, we have extended Corybantic with a more complete implementation, and a guided approach to resolve resource conflicts beyond the single, ideal scenario of global utility functions. Statesman solves a similar problem, but we see Athens as a complementary system, providing a family of resolution mechanisms to aid a system like Statesman to dynamically resolve conflicts between module programs for better system performance. Besides offering a different level of abstraction for conflict resolution, another difference between Athens and Statesman is that Athens explores compromise solutions while Statesman will try and merge states from multiple modules or else pick one module's solution.

Finally, network economists have explored related issues (e.g., [18]) but have focused on obtaining accurate prices, not on software modularity.

7. CONCLUSION

In this paper, we build upon ideas from previous systems [22, 27] for composing modular SDN control programs to provide a framework to automatically resolve resource conflicts between modules. The goal of Athens is to ease the impending challenge facing network operators of data-centers (e.g., hosting SDNs, cloud infrastructures) to coordinate and dynamically manage resource conflicts between a diverse suite of controller modules. We introduce notions of module parity and precision, and provide a framework within which we can classify existing approaches. As opposed to prior designs, Athens resolves conflicts by leveraging well known voting mechanisms and is able to relax requirements of parity and precision from modules, while achieving efficient resource allocations across a variety of metrics.

8. REFERENCES

[1] C. J. Anderson, N. Foster, A. Guha, J.-B. Jeannin, D. Kozen, C. Schlesinger, and D. Walker. NetKAT: Semantic Foundations for Networks. In *ACM POPL*, 2014.

[2] Apache CloudStack: Open Source Cloud Computing. `http://cloudstack.apache.org/`.

[3] T. Ball, N. Bjorner, A. Gember, S. Itzhaky, A. Karbyshev, M. Sagiv, M. Schapira, and A. Valadarsky. VeriCon: Towards Verifying Controller Programs in Software-Defined Network. In *ACM PLDI*, 2014.

[4] H. Ballani, P. Costa, T. Karagiannis, and A. Rowstron. Towards predictable datacenter networks. In *Proc. SIGCOMM*, 2011.

[5] Project Floodlight. `http://www.projectfloodlight.org/floodlight/`.

[6] P. Bodík, I. Menache, M. Chowdhury, P. Mani, D. A. Maltz, and I. Stoica. Surviving failures in bandwidth-constrained datacenters. In *Proc. SIGCOMM*, 2012.

[7] M. Casado, T. Koponen, S. Shenker, and A. Tootoonchian. Fabric: A Restrospective on Evolving SDN. In *HotSDN*, 2012.

[8] A. D. Ferguson, A. Guha, C. Liang, R. Fonseca, and S. Krishnamurthi. Participatory Networking: An API for Application Control of SDNs. In *Proc. SIGCOMM*, 2013.

[9] N. Foster, M. J. Freedman, R. Harrison, J. Rexford, M. L. Meola, and D. Walker. Frenetic: A High-Level Language for OpenFlow Networks. In *Proc. PRESTO*, 2010.

[10] N. Foster, R. Harrison, M. J. Freedman, C. Monsanto, J. Rexford, A. Story, and D. Walker. Frenetic: A Network Programming Language. In *Proc. ICFP*, 2011.

[11] A. Ghodsi, M. Zaharia, B. Hindman, A. Konwinski, S. Shenker, and I. Stoica. Dominant resource fairness: Fair allocation of multiple resource types. In *USENIX NSDI*, 2011.

[12] N. Gude, T. Koponen, J. Pettit, B. Pfaff, M. Casado, N. McKeown, and S. Shenker. NOX: Towards an Operating System for Networks. In *SIGCOMM CCR*, July 2008.

[13] P. Kazemian, M. Chang, H. Zeng, G. Varghese, N. McKeown, and S. Whyte. Real Time Network Policy Checking using Header Space Analysis. In *USENIX NSDI*, 2013.

[14] A. Khurshid, X. Zou, W. Zhou, M. Caesar, , and P. B. Godfrey. VeriFlow: Verifying Network-Wide Invariants in Real Time. In *USENIX NSDI*, 2013.

[15] W. Kim, P. Sharma, J. Lee, S. Banerjee, J. Tourrilhes, S.-J. Lee, and P. Yalagandula. Automated and Scalable QoS Control for Network Convergence. In *Proc. INM/WREN*, Apr. 2010.

[16] J. Lee, Y. Turner, M. Lee, L. Popa, S. Banerjee, J.-M. Kang, and P. Sharma. Application-Driven Bandwidth Guarantees in Datacenters. In *SIGCOMM*, 2014.

[17] Project OpenDaylight. `http://www.opendaylight.org/`.

[18] B. Lubin, A. Juda, R. Cavallo, S. Lahaie, J. Shneidman, and D. C. Parkes. ICE: An Expressive Iterative Combinatorial Exchange. *J. Artificial Intelligence Research*, 33:33–77, 2008.

[19] A. Mas-Colell, M. D. Whinston, and J. R. Green. *Microeconomic Theory*. Oxford University Press, 1995.

[20] N. McKeown, T. Anderson, H. Balakrishnan, G. Parulkar, L. Peterson, J. Rexford, S. Shenker, and J. Turner. OpenFlow: Enabling Innovation in Campus Networks. *SIGCOMM CCR*, 38(2):69–74, 2008.

[21] Mininet. `http://www.mininet.org/`.

[22] J. C. Mogul, A. AuYoung, S. Banerjee, J. Lee, J. Mudigonda, L. Popa, P. Sharma, and Y. Turner. Corybantic: Toward Modular Composition of SDN Control Programs. In *HotNets-XII*, 2013.

[23] C. Monsanto, J. Reich, N. Foster, J. Rexford, and D. Walker. Composing Software-Defined Networks. In *USENIX NSDI*, 2013.

[24] T. Nelson, A. D. Ferguson, M. J. Scheer, and S. Krishnamurthi. Tierless Programming and Reasoning for Software-Defined Networks. In *USENIX NSDI*, 2014.

[25] O. Sefraoui, M. Aissaoui, and M. Eleuldj. Article: Openstack: Toward an open-source solution for cloud computing. *International Journal of Computer Applications*, 55(3):38–42, October 2012.

[26] R. Soulé, S. Basu, R. Kleinberg, E. G. Sirer, and N. Foster. Managing the network with Merlin. In *HotNets*, page 24, 2013.

[27] P. Sun, R. Mahajan, J. Rexford, L. Yuan, M. Zhang, and A. Arefin. A Network-State Management Service. In *SIGCOMM*, 2014.

[28] M. Yu, J. Rexford, M. J. Freedman, and J. Wang. Scalable Flow-Based Networking with DIFANE. In *Proc. SIGCOMM*, 2010.

Scotch: Elastically Scaling up SDN Control-Plane using vSwitch based Overlay

An Wang
George Mason University
awang10@gmu.edu

Yang Guo
Bell Labs, Alcatel-Lucent
Yang.Guo@alcatel-lucent.com

Fang Hao
Bell Labs, Alcatel-Lucent
Fang.Hao@alcatel-lucent.com

T. V. Lakshman
Bell Labs, Alcatel-Lucent
T.V.Lakshman@alcatel-lucent.com

Songqing Chen
George Mason University
sqchen@cs.gmu.edu

Abstract

Software Defined Networks use logically centralized control due to its benefits in maintaining a global network view and in simplifying programmability. However, the use of centralized controllers can affect network performance if the control path between the switches and their associated controllers becomes a bottleneck. We find from measurements that the software control agents on some of the switches have very limited throughput. This can cause performance degradation if the switch has to handle a high traffic load, as for instance due to flash crowds or DDoS attacks. This degradation can occur even when the data plane capacity is under-utilized. The goal of our paper is to design new mechanisms to enable the network to scale up its ability to handle high control traffic loads. For this purpose, we design, implement, and experimentally evaluate *Scotch*, a solution that elastically scales up the control plane capacity by using a vSwitch based overlay. *Scotch* takes advantage of both the high control plane capacity of a large number of vSwitches and the high data plane capacity of commodity physical switches to increase the SDN network scalability and resiliency under normal (e.g., flash crowds) or abnormal (e.g., DDoS attacks) traffic surge.

Categories and Subject Descriptors

C.2.1 [**Computer Communication Networks**]: Network Architecture and Design

General Terms

Design

Keywords

Network Architecture; SDN; overlay

CoNEXT'14, December 2–5, 2014, Sydney, Australia.
Copyright 2014 ACM 978-1-4503-3279-8/14/12 ...$15.00
http://dx.doi.org/10.1145/2674005.2675002.

1. INTRODUCTION

Software Defined Networking has recently emerged as a new networking paradigm of much research and commercial interest. A key aspect of Software Defined Networks (SDN) is the separation of control and forwarding [20]. The control plane is logically centralized and implemented on one or more controllers [13, 18, 3]. The centralized controller configures the flow tables in the various switches that it controls using a de facto standard protocol such as OpenFlow [12]. Each OpenFlow capable switch has a software implemented OpenFlow Agent (OFA) that communicates with the switch's controller over a secure TCP connection. This connection is used by the switch to inform the controller the arrival of new flows, and by the controller to configure the switch's flow table in both reactive (on-demand) and proactive (a priori configured) modes. The reactive mode, which permits fine-grained control of flows, is invoked when a new flow starts and there is no entry in the flow table corresponding to that flow. In this paper, we call the interconnection between a switch and its controller this switch's *control path* or *control channel.*

Since the controller and the switches it controls are separated, it is important that swithes' control paths are not bottlenecks between the switches and their controller. This is particularly important if the switch is configured to operate with a large fraction of reactive flows since each reactive flow requires communication with the controller. If a switch's control path is completely saturated, the switch becomes essentially disconnected from the controller and unable to change its flow tables in response to network conditions or new flow arrivals. The switch may then become unable to handle new flows even though the data plane is uncongested and could have forwarded the flow's packets. A low throughput of a control path can also lead to new Denial-of-Service (DoS) attacks. Malicious users may attempt to saturate the switch to controller channels and stop network operations by effectively making the controllers not reachable.

The load on the control path can be reduced by limiting reactive flows and pre-installing rules for all expected traffic. However, this comes at the expense of fine-grained policy control, visibility, and flexibility in traffic-management, as evidently required in [3, 16]. Alternatively, the control path capacity can be increased by optimizing the OFA implementation. However this is not sufficient to bridge the large gap between control plane and data plane throughputs. A switch's data plane forwarding capacity is typically several orders of magnitude larger than that of its control path. Ideally, one would like to elastically scale control plane capacity. Mechanisms for elastically scaling controller capacity have been proposed [18, 7]. However, they only scale the actual processing capacity of the controller but not the switch-controller control path capacity.

In this paper, we aim to develop new mechanisms that exploit the available high data plane capacities to elastically scale up the achievable throughput of control paths. We propose *Scotch*, an Open vSwitch based overlay that avoids the OFA bottleneck by using the data plane to scale the controller channel capacity. This scaling permits the network to handle much higher reactive flow loads, makes the control plane far more resilient to DDoS attacks by providing a mitigating mechanism, and permits faster failure recovery.

Scotch essentially bridges the gap between control and data plane capacities by building an overlay from each switch to the Open vSwitches that run on host hypervisors (assuming a virtualized environment). The idea is to pool the vSwitch-controller capacities of all the vSwitches and use it to expand the total capacity of control paths. Two significant factors that we exploit are (i) the number of vSwitches greatly exceeds the number of physical switches, and (ii) the control paths of vSwitches running on powerful CPUs with sufficient memory possess higher throughput than that of physical switches whose OFA runs on less powerful CPUs with less memory.

Scotch enables an elastic expansion of control channel capacity by tunnelling new flows to vSwitches over a control overlay. When the control path of a physical switch is overloaded, the default rule at the switch is modified so that new flows will be tunneled to multiple vSwitches, instead of being sent to the central controller through Packet-In messages. Note that when the new flows are tunneled to vSwitches there is no additional load on the OFA since the flows are handled by the switch hardware and stay in the data plane. This results in shifting load from the OFA to edge vSwitches. The vSwitches send the new flow's packets to the controller by using Packet-In messages. Since the vSwitch control agent has much higher throughput than the OFA on a hardware switch, and a large number of vSwitches can be used, the control plane bottleneck at the OFA can be effectively eliminated. Below we use DDoS attacks as an extreme example of traffic that can cause control path overload and study this in detail.

Scotch also uses the overlay to forward the data traffic, and separates the handling of small and large flows. Generally, it is not sufficient to address the performance bottlenecks at any one switch. When one switch is overloaded, it is likely that other switches are overloaded as well. This is particularly so if the overload is caused by an attempted DDoS attack that generates a large number of small flows in an attempt to overload the control plane. If an attacker spoofs packets from multiple sources to a single destination, then even if we spread the new flows arriving at the first hop hardware switch to multiple vSwitches, the switch close to the destination will still be overloaded since rules have to be inserted there for each new flow. To alleviate this problem, *Scotch* forwards new flows on the overlay so that new rules are initially only inserted at the vSwitches and not the hardware switches.

Most flows are likely to be small, and may terminate after a few packets are sent [1]. This is particularly true for flows from attempted DDoS attacks. *Scotch* can use monitoring information at the controller to migrate large flows back to paths that use physical switches. Since the majority of packets belong to a small number of large flows, this approach allows *Scotch* to effectively use the high control plane capacity on vSwitches and the high data plane capacity on hardware switches. The activation of *Scotch* overlay can also trigger the network security tools and solutions. The collected flow information can be fed into the security tools to help pinpoint the root cause of the overloading system. The security tools will hopefully kick in and tame the attacks. Once the control paths become uncongested, the *Scotch* overlay automatically phases out. The SDN network will gradually revert back to the normal working conditions.

The paper is organized as follows. Section 2 describes the related work. Section 3 investigates the performance of SDN networks in a DDoS attack scenario. We use DoS attacks and their mitigation as the extreme stress test for control plane resilience and performance under overload. Section 4 proposes the *Scotch* overlay scheme to scale up the SDN network's control-plane capacity, and Section 5 describes the design of key components of *Scotch*. The experimental results of *Scotch* performance are reported in Section 6. Concluding remarks are in Section 7.

2. RELATED WORK

Security issues in SDN have been studied and examined from two different aspects: to utilize the SDN's centralized control to provide novel security services, e.g., [21, 27], and to secure network itself, e.g., [10, 28]. The SDN security under DDoS attacks is studied in [28]. Two modules are added at the data-plane of the physical switches. One module functions similarly to a SYN proxy to avoid attacking traffic from reaching the controller. The other module enables the traffic statistics collection and active treatment, e.g., blocking harmful traffic. The motivation for our work is to elastically scaling up the control path capacity as the load on the control plane increases, due to either the flash crowds or DDoS attacks. No modification at the physical switches is required.

Centralized network controllers are key SDN components and various controllers have been developed, e.g., [13, 2, 18, 9], among others. In our experiment, we use the *Ryu* [5] OpenFlow controller. *Ryu* supports latest OpenFlow at the time of our experiments, and is the default controller used by Pica8 switch [23], the physical switch used in our experiment. Since Scotch increases the control path capacity, the controller will receive more packets. A single node multi-threaded controller can handle millions of PacketIn/sec [30]. A distributed controller, such as [7], can further scale up capacity. The design of a scalable controller is out of the scope of this paper.

Traffic detouring techniques have been employed to reduce the routing table size, e.g., [33, 17, 25, 26], where traffic is re-routed inside the physical networks. *Scotch* employs an overlay apporach for traffic detouring, which offers better flexibility and elasticity than the in-network traffic detouring approach. In addition, *Scotch* can also help reduce the number of routing entries in the physical switches by routing short flows over the overlay.

DevoFlow [6] has some similarity with our work in the sense that it identifies limited control-plane capacity as an important issue impacting SDN performance. The proposed DevoFlow mechanism maintains a reasonable amount of flow visibility that does not overload the control path.

The authors of [15] investigated the SDN emulation accuracy problem. Their expriments also reveal SDN switches' slow control-path problem, which is consistent with our findings using a different type of physical switch. However, the goal of their work is quite diffent from ours. While they attempt to improve the emulation accuracy, we develop a new scheme to improve SDN's control-path capacity.

3. OPENFLOW CONTROL PLANE BOTTLENECK

3.1 Background

Fig. 1 shows a basic OpenFlow network where all the switches are connected to a central controller via secure TCP connections. Each switch consists of both a data plane and a simple control plane – the OpenFlow Agent (OFA). The data plane hardware is responsible for packet processing and forwarding, while the OFA allows the central controller to interact with the switch to control its behavior. Each switch has one or more flow tables (not shown in the figure), which store rules that determine how each flow should be processed.

When the first packet of a new flow arrives at a switch, the switch looks up the flow table to determine how to process the packet. If the packet does not match any existing rule, it is treated as the first packet of a new flow and is passed to the switch's OFA. The OFA encapsulates the packet into a *Packet-In* message and delivers the message to the central controller (Step 1 in Fig. 1). The Packet-In message contains either the packet header or the entire packet, depending on the configuration, along with other information such as ingress port id, etc. Upon receiving the Packet-In message, the OpenFlow controller determines how the flow should be handled based on policy settings and the global network state. If the flow is admitted, the controller computes the flow path and installs new flow entries at the corresponding switches along the path (Step 2). This is done by sending a flow modification command to the OFA on each switch along the route. The OFA then installs the new forwarding rule into the flow table. The controller may also generate a *Packet-Out* message to explicitly tell the switch where to forward the first packet.

One problem with the current OpenFlow switch implementation is that the OFA typically runs on a low end CPU that has limited processing power. This seems to be a reasonable design choice since one intention of the OpenFlow architecture is to move the control functions out of the switches so that the switches can be simple and of low cost. However, this can significantly limit the control path throughput.

To better understand this limitation, we study a DDoS attack scenario, where a DDoS attacker generates SYN attack packets using spoofed source IP addresses. The switch treats each spoofed packet as a new flow and forwards the packet to the controller. The insufficient processing power of the OFA limits how fast the OFA can forward the packets to the OpenFlow controller, as well as how fast it can insert new flow rules into the flow table. A DDoS attack can cause Packet-In messages to be generated at a much higher rate than what the OFA can handle. This effectively makes the controller unreachable from the switch and causes legitimate traffic to be blocked even though there is no data plane congestion. Note that this blocking of legitimate traffic can occur whenever the control plane is overloaded, e.g., under DDoS attacks or due to flash crowds. We merely use the DDoS attack scenario as an extreme traffic pattern that causes control plane overload.

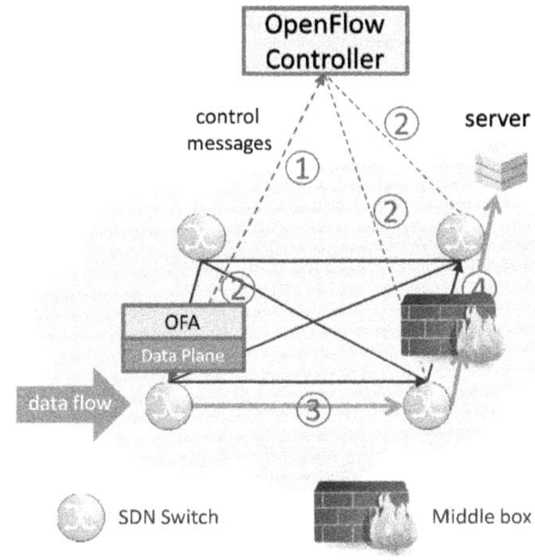

Figure 1: OpenFlow network with the OpenFlow Controller.

3.2 Attack's impact on SDN switch performance

Here, we experimentally evaluate the impact of control plane overload on SDN packet forwarding performance. The overload is caused by an attempted DDoS attack. The testbed setup is shown in Fig. 2. We experiment with two types of hardware switches: Pica8 Pronto 3780 and HP Procurve 6600, with OpenFlow 1.2 and 1.0 support, respectively. For comparison, we also experiment with Open vSwitch, which runs on a host with an Intel Xeon 5650 2.67GHz CPU. We use the *Ryu* OpenFlow controller, since it was one of the few controllers that supported OpenFlow 1.2 at the time of our experiments, a requirement by Pica8 Pronto switch. The experiments are done using one switch at a time. The attacker, the client and the server are all attached to the data ports, and the controller is attached to the management port. We use *hping3* [14] to generate attacking traffic. The Pica8 switch uses 10 Gbps data ports, and the HP switch and vSwitch have 1 Gbps data ports. The management ports for physical switches are 1Gbps.

Both the attacker and the legitimate client attempt to initiate new flows to the server. We simulate the new flows by spoofing each packet's source IP address. Since the OpenFlow controller installs the flow rules at the switch using both the source and destination IP addresses, a spoofed packet is treated as a new flow by the switch. Hence in our experiment, the flow rate, i.e., the number of new flows per second, is equivalent to the packet rate. We set the client's new flow rate at 100 flows/sec, while vary the attacker's attacking rate from 10 and 3800 flows/sec. We collect the network traffic using tcpdump at the client, the attacker, and

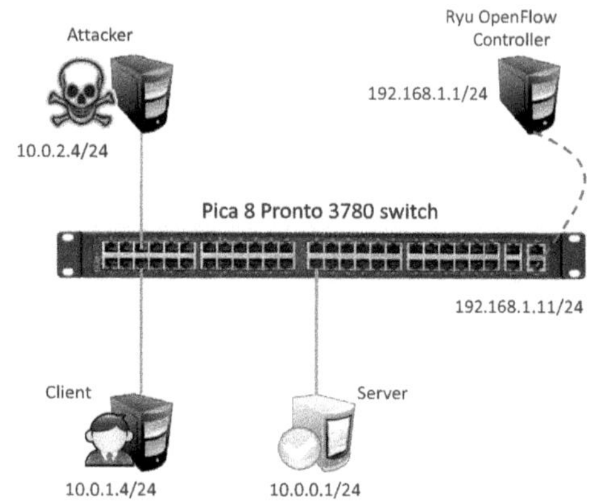

Figure 2: DDoS attack experiment setup.

the server. We define the *client flow failure fraction* to be the fraction of client flows that are not able to pass through the switch and reach the server. The client flow failure fraction is computed using the collected network traces. Fig. 3 plots the client flow failure fraction for different switches as the attacking flow rate increases. We observe that all three switches suffer from the client flow failure as the attacking flow rate increases. Note that even at the peak attacking rate of 3800 flows/sec, and even with the maximum packet size of 1.5 Kbytes, the traffic rate is merely 45.6 Mbps, a small fraction of the data link bandwidth. This indicates that the bottleneck is at the control plane rather than at the data plane. In addition, both Pica8 and HP Procurve physical switches exhibit much higher flow failure fraction than the software-based Open vSwitch, suggesting software-based vSwitch has higher control path capacity than the two physical switches tested in this experiment.

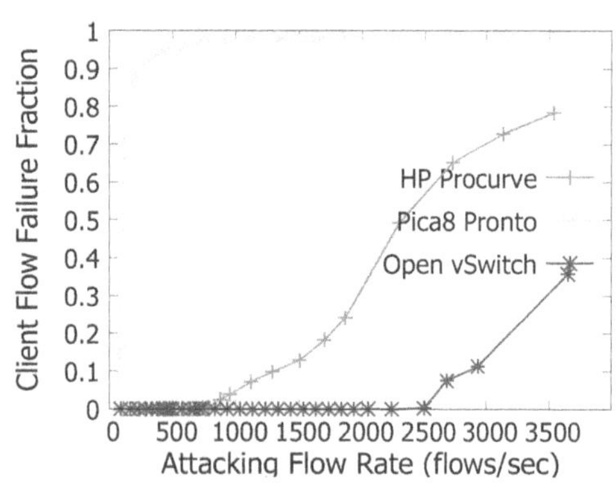

Figure 3: Physical switches and Open vSwitch control plane throughput comparison.

3.3 Profiling the control path bottleneck

We next identify which component along the control path is the actual bottleneck. Recall that a new flow arrival at the SDN switch triggers the following control plane actions: (1) a Packet-In message is sent from OFA to the controller; (2) the controller sends back a new rule to OFA; and (3) OFA inserts the rule into the flow table. The new flow can go through the switch if all the above three steps are completed successfully. Below we use the similar experimental set-up as in the previous experiment (see Fig. 2), with the client generating a new flow per packet towards the server while the attacker is turned off. The network traffic is traced at the server and the OpenFlow controller. We measure the Packet-In message rate (observed at the controller), the flow rule insertion rate (observed at the controller), and the rate at which the new flows successfully pass through the switch and reach the destination (observed at the server).

Fig. 4 plots the Packet-In message rate, flow rule insertion rate (one rule is included in one packet), and the received packet/flow rate at the server. We use the Pica8 switch for this experiment. We observe that all three rates are identical, which suggests that *the OFA's capability in generating Packet-In messages is the bottleneck*. Experiments in Section 6.1 further show that the rule insertion rate that the switch can support is indeed higher than the Packet-In message rate for Pica8 switch.

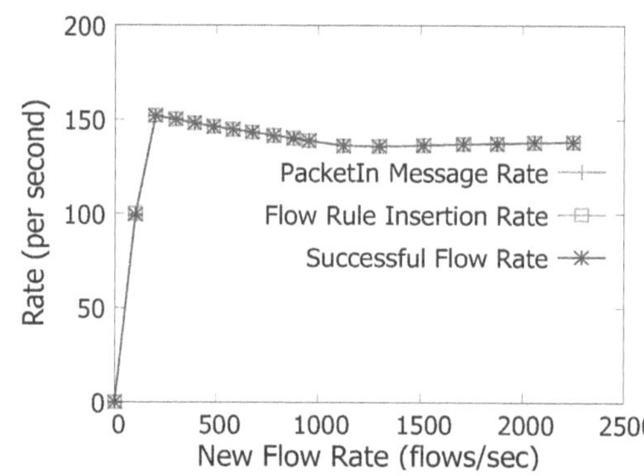

Figure 4: SDN switch control path profiling.

A limited amount of TCAM at a switch can also cause new flows being dropped [19]. A new flow rule won't be installed at the flow table if it becomes full. In the above experiment, OFA's capability in generating Packet-In messages is the bottleneck while the TCAM size is not. However, the solution proposed in this paper is applicable to the TCAM bottleneck scenario as well.

We use Pica8 Pronto switch instead of HP Procurve switch in this experiment and most of the later experiments. Though the Procurve switch has higher OFA throughput (see Fig. 3), we use the Pica8 Pronto switch due to its more advanced OpenFlow data-plane features that it supports, e.g., tunneling, multiple flow table support, etc. Also the Pronto switch can do wire speed packet processing with full OpenFlow support, while the older Procurve switch used in our experiments cannot. We do not intend to compare different hardware switches here, but just to explain the rational for our selection of equipments.

4. SCALING UP SDN CONTROL PLANE USING SCOTCH OVERLAY

We make the following observations based on the experiments as presented in Section 3:

- The control plane at the physical switches has limited capacity. The maximum rate at which the new flows can be set up at the switch is low – it is several orders of magnitude lower than the data plane traffic rate.

- The OpenFlow network running in reactive mode is very vulnerable to DDoS attacks. The operation of SDN switches can be easily disrupted by the increase of control traffic due to DDoS attacks, unless the switch operates very much in proactive mode.
- The vSwitches have higher control plane capacity but lower data plane throughput compared to the physical switches. The higher control plane capacity can be attributed to the more powerful CPUs on the general purpose computers where the vSwitches typically run on.

Our goal here is to elastically scale up the SDN control plane capacity when needed without sacrificing any of the advantages of SDN regarding the controller having high visibility and fine-grained control of all flows in the network. A straightforward method is to use more powerful CPUs for the OFA combined with other design improvements that allow faster access rates between the OFA and line cards. One can also improve the design and implementation of OFA software stack to enable more efficient message processing. With continued research interest in the SDN network control plane [6], these improvements will be likely. However, the significant gap between the control path throughput and data path flow setup requirements will still persist. For example, it may not be economically desirable to dimension the OFA capacity to be based on the maximum possible flow arrival rate given that the peak flow rate may be several orders of magnitude higher than the average flow rate [1]. Another method is to dedicate one port of the physical switch to the overloaded new flows. Whenever the control path is overloaded, the new flows are forwarded to the controller via this dedicated port at the data-plane. However, using a dedicated physical port does not fully solve the problem. The maximum flow rule insertion rate is limited as shown in Section 6.1. The controller cannot install the flow rules fast enough at physical switches when overloaded.

Software based virtual switches (e.g., Open vSwitch) have been widely adopted. vSwitches offer excellent switching speed [4, 8], and high control path throughputs as shown in the previous section. The interesting question is whether we can use vSwitches to improve the control plane capacity of physical switches. *Scotch*, our proposed solution, addresses this question and achieves high control plane throughputs using a vSwitch based overlay.

4.1 Scotch: vSwitch based SDN overlay network

Fig. 5 depicts the architecture of the *Scotch* overlay network. The main component of *Scotch* is a pool of vSwitches that are distributed across the corresponding SDN network, e.g., across different racks in the data center for a data center SDN network, or distributed at different locations for a wide-area SDN network. We select vSwitches at hosts that are lightly loaded and with under-utilized link capacity.

The *Scotch* overlay consists of three major components: (i) *vSwitch mesh* - a fully connected mesh (using tunnels) of vSwitches; (ii) the tunnels that connect the underlying physical switches with the vSwitch mesh; and (iii) the tunnels that connect the end hosts with the vSwitch mesh. The tunnels can be configured using any of the availablel tunneling protocols, such as GRE, MPLS, MAC-in-MAC, etc.; they use the underlying SDN network's data plane.

The tunnels connecting the physical switches with the vSwitch mesh allow a physical switch to forward the new flows to the vSwitches whenever the physical switch becomes overloaded in its control path. The vSwitches can then handle the new flow setup and packet forwarding tasks for these flows. The benefits are two-fold. First, the new flows can continue to be serviced by the SDN network in the face of control path congestion. Second, the SDN controller can continue to observe the new flows, which give us the opportunity to mitigate the possible DDoS attack (more in Section 5.2). The collected flow information can also be fed into network security applications to diagnose the root cause of the control path congestion. For the purpose of load-balancing, a physical switch is connected to a set of vSwitches so that the new flows can be distributed among them. Further details of load-balancing are described in Section 5.1.

The tunnels connecting the end hosts with the vSwitch mesh allow the new flows to be delivered to the end hosts over the *Scotch* overlay. Once a packet is forwarded from a physical switch to a *Scotch* vSwitch, it needs to be forwarded to the destination. This can be done if a path over the underlying SDN network can be set up on demand. But this may not be desirable since it may overload the control paths of physical switches on the path and create other hot spots. Another option is to configure tunnels between the *Scotch* vSwitch and the destinations directly. This, however, would lead to a larger number of tunnels since it requires one tunnel from each *Scotch* vSwitch to each host.

To avoid these problems, we partition hosts based on their locations so that all hosts are covered by one or more nearby *Scotch* vSwitches. For example, in the case of data center SDN network, there may be two *Scotch* vSwitches at each rack. Tunnels are set up to connect the host vSwitches with their local *Scotch* vSwitches.

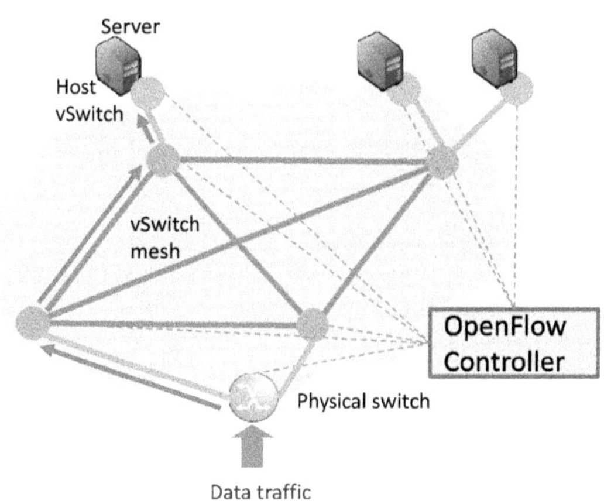

Figure 5: Architecture of Scotch overlay network.

Finally, we choose to form a fully connected vSwitch mesh in order to facilitate the overlay routing. The arrows in Fig. 5 show how the packets are forwarded through the *Scotch* overlay when the *Scotch* is on. Packets are first forwarded from the physical switch to a randomly chosen

Scotch vSwitch. Then they are routed across the mesh to the vSwitch that is closest to its destination. The receiving *Scotch* vSwitch further delivers the packets to the destination host via the tunnel. Finally, the host vSwitch delivers the packet to the destination VM. Since there is a full-mesh tunnel connectivity between *Scotch* vSwitches, a packet traverses three tunnels before reaching its destination.

Next, we use an example to describe how the *Scotch* overlay network scales up the control path throughput, and also illustrate how packets are forwarded if middleboxes are involved.

4.2 An example

Fig. 6 illustrates an example how the scheme works. The OpenFlow controller monitors the rate of Packet-In messages sent by the OFA of each physical switch to determine if the control path is congested. If a control path is deemed to be congested, the new flow packets arriving at the switch are forwarded to one or multiple *Scotch* vSwitches (only one is shown in Fig. 6) (Step 1 in Fig. 6). This allow these packets to leave the physical switch via the data plane instead of being handled by overloaded OFA and going through the congested control path. Details of overload forwarding rule insertion at the physical switch and load balancing across multiple vSwitches are discussed in Section 5.1.

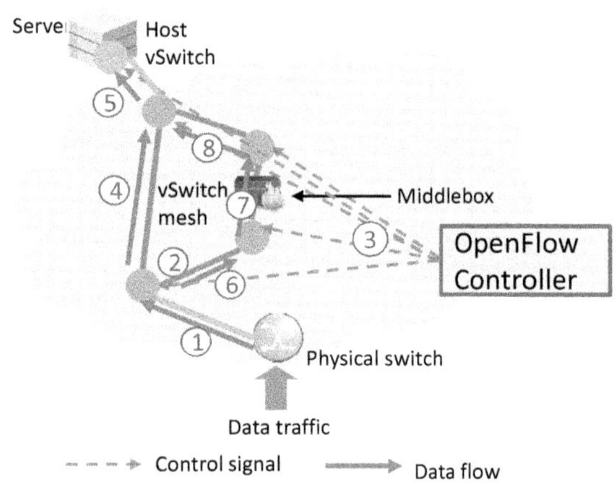

Figure 6: An example showing how Scotch works.

When the packet reaches the vSwitch, the vSwitch treats the packet as a new flow packet. The vSwitch OFA then constructs a Packet-In message and forwards it to the OpenFlow controller (Step 2 in Fig. 6). We configure the vSwitch to forward the entire packet to the controller, so that the controller can have more flexibility in deciding how to forward the packet. The controller can choose to set up the path either from the vSwitch or from the original physical switch. If the path is set up from the vSwitch, the *Scotch* overlay tunnels are used to forward the packet. The controller needs to set up the forwarding rules at the corresponding vSwitches, as done in Step 3 in Fig. 6.

The packets continue to be forwarded on the *Scotch* overlay until they reach the destination (Step 4 and 5 in Fig. 6). If middleboxes need to be passed through, e.g., a firewall needs to be passed through as shown in Fig. 6, the packets are routed through the firewall (Step 6, 7, 8, and 5). Details of maintaining policy consistency is described in Section 5.4. Packets from the same flow follow the same overlay data path.

5. DESIGN DETAILS

5.1 Load balancing across vSwitches

In general, we want to balance the network traffic among different vSwitches in the overlay to avoid performance bottlenecks. Hence when multiple vSwitches are used to receive packets from a physical switch, we need a mechanism to do load balancing between these vSwitches. In the following, we describe a method that implements load balancing by using the *group table feature* offered in OpenFlow Switch Spec 1.3 [12].

A group table consists of multiple group entries, where each entry contains *group Id*, *group type*, *counters*, and *action buckets*. Group type defines the group semantics. Action buckets contain an ordered list of action buckets, where each action bucket contains a set of actions to be executed and their associated parameters.

To achieve load balancing, we use *select* group type, which chooses one bucket in the action buckets to be executed. The bucket selection algorithm is not defined in the spec and the decision is left to the switch vendors/users. Given that ECMP load balancing is well accepted for router implementations, it is conceivable that using a hash function based on the flow id may be a likely choice for many vendors. We define one action bucket for each tunnel that connects the physical switch with a vSwitch (see Fig. 5). The *action* of this bucket is to forward the packet to the corresponding vSwitch using the pre-set tunnel.

5.2 Flow management at OpenFlow controller

Identifying the flows at the controller. In order to manage the flows at the central controller, we first need to make sure that the Packet-In message arriving at the controller from the *Scotch* vSwitch carries the same information as that coming directly from the physical switches. This is mostly true since the Packet-In messages contain similar information in both cases. But there are two exceptions. First, when the packet comes from a vSwitch, it does not contain the original physical switch id. This can be easily addressed by maintaining a table to map the tunnel id to the physical switch id, so that the controller can infer the physical switch id based on the tunnel id contained in the Packet-In meta data. Second, the packet from vSwitch also does not contain the original ingress port id at the physical switch. We propose to use a second label to solve this problem. In the case of MPLS, an inner MPLS label is pushed into the packet header based on the ingress port. In the case of GRE, the GRE key is set according to the ingress port. Note that since the packets need to be load balanced across different vSwitches, two flow tables are needed at the physical switch: the first table contains the rule for setting the ingress port; and the second table contains the rule for load balancing. The vSwitch strips off the inner MPLS label or the GRE key, attaches the information on the Packet-In message, and send them to the controller. The controller maintains the flow's first-hop physical switch id and the ingress port id at the *Flow Info Database*. Such information will be used for large flow migration as described in Section 5.3.

Flow grouping and differentiation. Next we describe how the OpenFlow controller manages the new flows. When a new flow arrives, the controller has three choices: (1) forwarding the flow over the physical SDN network, starting from the first physical switch encountered by the flow; (2) forwarding the flow using the vSwitch overlay network, starting from the vSwitch which forwards the first packet using the Packet-In message; and (3) dropping the flow when the load is too high, especially if the flow is identified as a DDoS attack flow. In general, we can classify the flows into different groups and enforce fair sharing of the SDN network across groups. For example, we can group the flows according to which customer it belongs to, so that we can achieve fair sharing among different customers. In the following, we give an example of providing fair access to the SDN network for the flows arriving from different ingress ports of the same switch. This is motivated by the observation that if a DDoS attack comes from one or a few ports, we can limit its impact to those ports only.

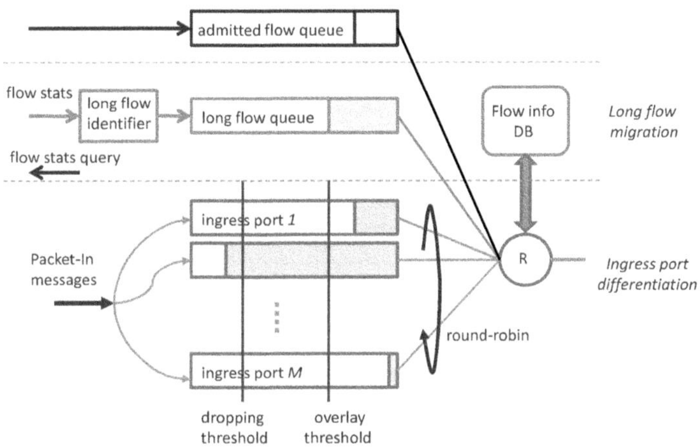

Figure 7: ***Scotch*** **Flow management at the OpenFlow controller for one SDN switch: ingress-port differentiation and large flow migration from the** ***Scotch*** **overlay to the SDN network.**

For the new flows from the same physical switch, the OpenFlow controller maintains one queue per ingress port (see *Ingress port differentiation* at the lower part of Fig. 7). The service rate for the queue is R, the maximum rate at which the OpenFlow controller can install rules at the physical switch without insertion failure or packet loss in the data plane. We will investigate how to choose the proper value of R in Section 6. The controller serves the different queues in a round-robin fashion so as to share the available service rate evenly among ingress ports. If a queue size grows to be larger than the *overlay threshold*, we assume that the new flows at this queue are beyond the control plane capacity on the physical switch network. Hence the controller will route the flows surpassing the threshold over the *Scotch* overlay by installing forwarding rules at corresponding vSwitches. If a queue size continues to build up, and exceeds the *dropping threshold*, then neither the physical network nor the *Scotch* overlay is able to carry these flows. The Packet-In messages beyond the *dropping threshold* will simply be dropped from the queue.

Note that the focus of this paper is to provide a mechanism to mitigate the impact of SDN control path congestion, which may be caused by flash crowds or DDoS attacks. Although our scheme offers high visibility to new flows and the opportunity and mechanism to monitor and handle flows, we do not address DDoS attack detection and diagnosis problems. Existing network security tools or solutions can be readily integrated into our framework, e.g., as a new application at the SDN controller, to take advantage of the visibility and flexibility offered by *Scotch*.

5.3 Migrating large flows out of the overlay network

Although vSwitch overlay can scale up the control path capacity, it is not desirable to only forward flows by using vSwitches since the vSwitch data plane has a much lower throughput than that of physical switches. In addition, the forwarding path on the overlay network is longer than the path on the physical network. In this section, we discuss how to take advantage of the high data plane capacity of the underlying physical network.

Measurement studies have shown that the majority of link capacity is consumed by a small fraction of large flows [1]. Hence our idea is to identify the large flows in the network and migrate the large flows out of the Scotch overlay. Since there are few large flows in the network, such migration should not incur major control plane overhead.

The middle part of Fig. 7 illustrates the operations that the controller conducts for large flow migration. The controller sends the flow-stats query messages to the vSwitches, and collects the flow stats including packet counts. The *large flow identifier* selects the flows with high packet counts, and puts the large flow migration requests into the large flow migration queue. The controller then queries the *Flow Info Database* to look up the flow's first hop physical switch. The controller then computes the path and checks the message rate of all switches on the path to make sure their control plane is not overloaded. It then sets up the path from the physical switch to the destination. This is done by inserting the flow forwarding rules into the *admitted flow queue* of the corresponding switches (top part of Fig.. 7). The rules will be installed on the switches when the inserted rules are pulled out of the queue by the controller. Once the fowarding rules are installed along the path, the flow will be moved to the new path, and remain at the physical SDN network for the rest of time. Note that the forwarding rule on the first hop switch is added at last so that packets are forwarded on the new path only after all switches on the path are ready.

The OpenFlow controller gives the highest priority to the *admitted flow queue*, followed by the *large flow queue*. Ingress-port differentiation queues receive the lowest priority. Such a priority order causes small flows to be forwarded on physical paths only after all large flows are accommodated.

5.4 Maintaining policy consistency

When we migrate a flow from *Scotch* overlay to the underlying physical network, we need to make sure that both routing paths satisfy the same policy constraints. The most common policy constraints are middlebox traversal, where the flow has to be routed across a sequence of middleboxes according to a specific order.

A naive approach is to compute the new path of physical switches without considering the existing vSwitch path. For example, if a flow is routed first through a firewall FW_1 and then a load balancer LB_1 on the vSwitch paths, we may compute a new path that uses a different set of firewall FW_2 and load balancer LB_2. This approach in general does not work since the middleboxes often maintain flow states. When a flow is routed to a new middlebox in the middle of the connection, the new middlebox may either reject the flow or handle the flow differently due to lack of pre-established context. Although it is possible to transfer flow states between old and new middleboxes, this requires middlebox specific changes and may lead to significant development cost and performance penalty.

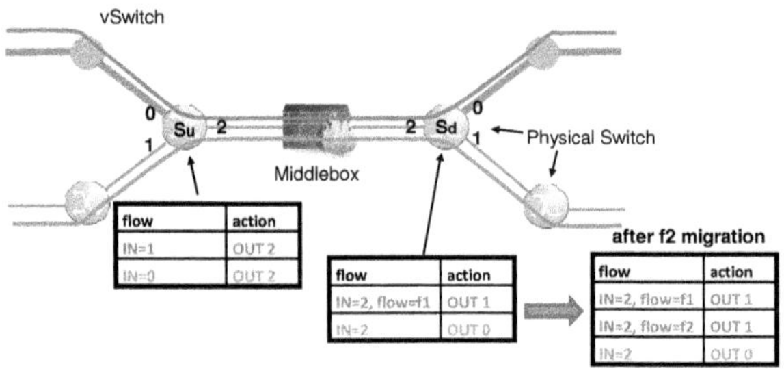

Figure 8: Maintain policy consistency in *Scotch*.

In order to avoid the middlebox state synchronization problem, our design enforces the flow to go through the same set of middleboxes in both the vSwitch and physical switch paths. Figure 8 illustrates how this is done. In this example we assume a typical configuration where a pair of physical switches, S_U and S_D, are connected to the input and output of the middlebox (firewall), respectively. But the solution also works for other configurations, as we will discuss at the end of this section.

The green line on the top shows the overlay path. The vSwitches in the overlay mesh connect to the physical switches S_U and S_D with tunnels. In the case that the physical switches cannot support tunnels to all vSwitches in the mesh, a few dedicated vSwitches in the mesh that are close to the middleboxes can serve as dedicated tunnel aggregation points. The upstream physical switch, S_U, decapsulates the tuneled packet before forwarding the packet to the middlebox to ensure that the middlebox sees the original packet without the tunnel header. Similarly, the downstream physical switch, S_D, encapsulates the packet again so that the packet can be forwarded on the tunnel. The flow rules at physical switches S_U and S_D (green entries in the flow tables) enforce the flows on the overlay path to go through the firewall and stay on the overlay.

The red line at the bottom shows the path for flows that are not routed on the overlay. They can be either elephant flows that are selected to migrate, or the flows that are set up while the physical switches have sufficient control plane capacity. The flow rules for forwarding such flows are shown in red in the flow tables. The red (physical path) rules have higher priority than the green (overlay) rules. Each individual flow forwarded on the physical path requires a red rule, while all flows on the overlay path share the same green rule. In other words, flows without individual rule entries are forwarded on the overlay path by default. This is important for scalability: when the control plane is overloaded, all flows can be forwarded on the overlay path without incurring per-flow setup overhead on the physical switches.

Fig. 8 shows an example of how flows are forwarded. Initially, flow f_1 is routed over the underlying physical network while other flows are routed over the *Scotch* overlay. When an elephant flow, say f_2, needs to be migrated to the physical path at the bottom, the controller adds an additional forwarding rule to make S_D forward flow f_2 to the physical network.

We next examine the impact of different middlebox connection types. In the data center network, sometimes the middleboxes are "attached" to a physical switch. This happens, for instance, when the middlebox is integrated with the physical switch or router. This is essentially combining the S_U and S_D in Figure 8. Since the rules on both switches are independent of each other, we can simply combine the rules on S_U and S_D and install them on the "attaching" switch. Virtual middleboxes that run on Virtual Machines may also be combined. In this case a vSwitch can run on the hypervisor of the middlebox host and execute the functions of S_U and S_D.

5.5 Withdrawal from Scotch overlay

As the DDoS attack stops or the flash crowd goes away, the switch control path becomes uncongested and hence the *Scotch* overlay becomes unnecessary. We then stop forwarding new flows to the overlay at the uncongested switch, while keeping existing flows uninterrupted.

The controller detects such control plane condition change by monitoring the new flow arrival rate at physical switches. If the arrival rate falls below a threshold, the OpenFlow controller starts the *withdrawal process*. The withdrawal process consists of three steps. First, for the flows that are currently being routed over the *Scotch* overlay, the controller inserts rules at the switch to continuously forward these flows to the *Scotch* overlay. Since the large flows should have been already migrated to the physical network, most of these flows are likely to be small flows and may terminate shortly. Second, the controller removes the default flow forwarding rule that was inserted initially when *Scotch* was activated (Section 5.1). The new flow packets will be forwarded to the OpenFlow controller directly via OFA. Third, if any remaining small flows routed on the overlay become large flows, they can still be migrated to the physical path following the same migration procedure.

Note that the *Scotch* overlay is for the entire network, so other congested switches may continue to use *Scotch* overlay.

5.6 Configuration and maintenance

To configure the *Scotch* overlay, we first need to select host vSwitches based on the planned control path capacity, physical network topology, host and middlebox locations, and so on. Extra backup vSwitches are added to provide necessary fault tolerance. We then configure the Scotch overlay by setting up tunnels between various entities: between physical switches and vSwitches for load distribution, between each pair of mesh vSwitches for forwarding, and between mesh and host vSwitches for delivery. vSwitch offers reasonably high data throughput [4]. Recent advancements in packet processing at general purpose computers, such as the systems based on the Intel DPDK library, can further boost the vSwitch forwarding speed [8] significantly. In addition, vSwitch has low overhead to support software tunneling. According to [31], it is possible to do tunneling in software with performance and overhead comparable to non encapsulated traffic, and to support hundreds of thousands of tunnel end points. In terms of configuration overhead, although the

Scotch overlay can be large, configuration is done largely offline so it should not affect operation efficiency.

A vSwitch may fail or stop functioning properly. Hence we need to detect such failures in order to avoid service interruption. vSwitch has a build-in heartbeat module that periodically sends the ECHO REQUEST message to the OpenFlow controller, which responds with the ECHO RESPONSE message. The heartbeat period can be adjusted by changing configuration parameter. The heartbeat message enables the OpenFlow controller to detect the failure of a vSwitch. In fact, several OpenFlow controllers, e.g. Floodlight [11], already include the vSwtich failure detection module. Once a controller detects the failure, the controller can replace the failed vSwitch with the backup in the action buckets installed in the physical switch as described in Section 5.1. The flows that are originally routed through the failed vSwitch will then be handled by the backup vSwitch, which treats the affected flows as new flows. When recovered, the failed vSwitch can join back *Scotch* as a new or backup vSwitch.

We may also need to add new vSwitches to increase the *Scotch* overlay capacity or replace the departed vSwitches. A new vSwitch becomes part of the overlay after it is connected with other vSwitches or physical switches, depending on its role, and is registered with the *Scotch* overlay controller. We do not expect frequent vSwitch additions or failures.

6. EVALUATION

We implement the *Scotch* overlay management as an application on the *Ryu* OpenFlow controller. We also construct a basic Scotch overlay with multiple vSwitches, and form an overlay together with end-hosts and physical switches using MPLS tunnels. Note that attackers, servers, clients, and vSwitches can be anywhere as long as a tunnel can be set up between the physical switch and them. We use experiments to demonstrate the benefits of ingress port differentiation and large flow migration. We also show the growth in the *Scotch* overlay's capacity with addition of new vSwitches into the overlay. We further investigate the extra delay incurred by the Scotch overlay traffic relay. Finally, we conduct the trace driven experiment that demonstrates the benefits of *Scotch* to the application performance in a realistic network environment.

6.1 Maximum flow rule insertion rate

As shown in Fig. 7, the maximum rate at which the OpenFlow controller installs the new rules into the switch, R, is an important design parameter. The larger the R, the better, so that more traffic can be routed over the physical network. However, the value of R needs to be set properly so that all the new flow rule insertion requests can be successfully handled at the switch. We first measure the maximum flow rule insertion rate allowed by the Pica8 switch. We let the *Ryu* controller generate flow rules at a constant rate and send them to the Pica8 switch. The switch OFA installs the rules into the flow table. The generated rules are all different, and the time-out period of a rule is set to be 10 seconds. Throughout the experiment, there is no data traffic passing through the switch.

The *Ryu* controller periodically queries the switch to get the number of rules currently installed in the flow table. We set the query interval sufficiently long (30 seconds), to minimize the impact on the OFA's rule insertion performance. Denote by N_k the number of rules in the flow table at the k-th query, and K the total number of queries. Denote by T the rule time-out period. The successful insertion rates can be estimated as $\sum N_k/(K \cdot T)$.

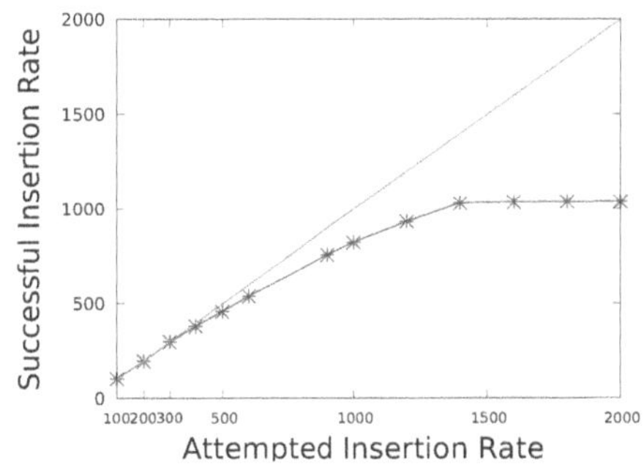

Figure 9: Maximum flow rule insertion rate at the Pica8 switch.

Fig. 9 plots the successful flow rule insertion rate with varying attempted insertion rate. The Pica8 switch is able to handle up to 200 rules/second without loss. After that, some rule requests are not installed into the flow table, and the successful insertion rate flattens out at about 1000 rules/second. In *Scotch*, the OpenFlow controller should only insert the flow rules at a rate that does not cause installation failure.

6.2 Interaction of switch data plane and control path

During the maximum flow rule insertion rate experiment, the Pica8 switch does not route any data traffic. In reality, while the OFA writes the flow rules into the flow table, the switch also does flow table lookups to route incoming packets. These two activities interact with each other. We conduct an experiment where the OpenFlow controller attempts to insert the flow rule at certain rates while the switch routes the data traffic with rates of 500, 1000, and 2000 packets/second. We measure the data-plane packet loss rate at the receiving host.

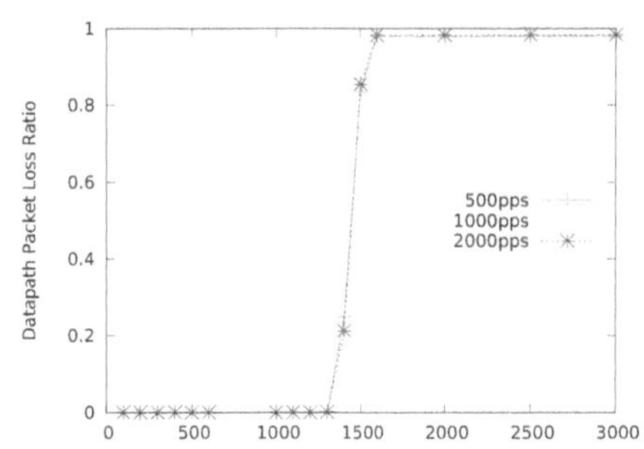

Figure 10: Interaction of the data path and the control path at the Pica8 switch.

Fig. 10 depicts the packet loss ratio with varying flow rule insertion rates. The curve exhibits an interesting *turning point* at a rule insertion rate of 1300 rules/second. The data path loss rate exceeds 90% when the rule insertion rate is greater than 1300 packets/second. This clearly demonstrates the interaction between the data and control-paths. We conjecture that the interaction is caused by the contention for the flow table access, which is confirmed by the vendor [22].

The results from this experiment and the previous experiment help us with setting the right new flow insertion rate at the OpenFlow controller. For Pica8 switch, the flow rule insertion rate is lower. Thus it governs the new flow insertation rate at the controller. Fortunately we only need to do one set of such experiments for every type of physical switches.

6.3 Effect of ingress port differentiation

Here we evaluate the benefits of ingress port differentiation. The experiment setup is the same as in Fig. 2 with the vSwitches added to form the *Scotch* overlay. An attacker generates the attacking flows, while the client generates the normal flows. The normal new flow rate is set at 30 flows/second, while we vary the attacker's new flow rate. Since we are only interested in switch's control-path performance, we generate one packet for each flow with different IP addresses. For this experiment, we turn off the large flow migration functionality and focus only on the ingress port differentiation feature. We set the queue service rate to be 70 flows/second to make sure the rule insertion will be successful and that it will not affect the data path throughput.

Fig. 12(a) depicts the flow failure rate for the attacking traffic and the normal traffic. The *Scotch* overlay management application maintains two queues and each queue receives at least 35 flows/second for rule insertion. All normal flows can be installed successfully. Attack traffic only uses the leftover capacity from the server, with some of the attack traffic being dropped at the OpenFlow controller. Ingress port differentiation clearly segregates the attack traffic from normal traffic arriving at a different ingress port.

6.4 Benefits of large flow migration and adding additional vSwitches

In this experiment, we examine the effect of large flow migration. To focus on the performance of large flow migration, we turn off the ingress port differentiation in the OpenFlow controller application. All flows arriving at the OpenFlow controller will be routed over the *Scotch* overlay. The large flow will be migrated to the underlying physical network. We set the large flow detection packet count to be 10 packets.

The attacker sends out the attacking traffic (one packet per flow) at a constant rate of 200 flows/second. The client establishes two large flows to the server at time 200 and 400 seconds, respectively. Fig. 12(b) depicts the data-path traffic rate going through the vSwitch and the Pica8 switch, respectively. Since the traffic is forwarded to the vSwitch by the Pica8 switch, the data-path traffic rate going through the Pica8 switch is equal to the total traffic rate. The data-path traffic rate going through the vSwitch is the traffic rate routed over the *Scotch* overlay.

The data-plane traffic rate is 200 packets/second at both the Pica8 switch and the Open vSwtich at the beginning of the experiment. This is because the *Scotch* overlay is on and all traffic passes through both the Pica8 physical switch and the vSwitch. The flow size is small (one packet per flow) so none of the attacking flow is migrated to the physical switch.

At time 200 seconds, a large flow of 80 packets/second starts. We see a small bump in the data-path traffic rate of the vSwitch since the large flow is initially routed through the vSwitch. Once the packet count reaches 10 packets, the large flow detection threshold set in the Scotch application at the controller, the large flow is migrated to the Pica8 switch. The traffic rate at the vSwitch comes back to 200 packets/second. The same happens at time 400 seconds when the second large flow of 60 packets/second arrives. Except for a short time period during which the vSwitch traffic rate experiences a bump, the data-path traffic rate at the vSwitch remains at 200 packets/second. The experiment clearly shows that *Scotch* overlay carries the small attack flows that require large control-path handling but relatively a small data-path throughput.

Next we investigate the benefits of additional vSwitches to the *Scotch* overlay. The experimental setup is similar to the large flow migration experiment except that we add one more vSwitch as a *Scotch* node. Fig. 12(c) depicts the data-path traffic rate at the Pica8 switch and two vSwitches, respectively. Here the data-path traffic rate is 100 packets/seconds since the attack traffic is carried by two vSwitches. The large flow arriving at time 200 seconds is first routed through vSwitch 1 and then migrated to Pica8 switch. The second large flow arriving at time 400 seconds is routed through vSwitch 2 at first and then migrated to Pica8 switch. The two vSwitches, however, split the attacking traffic. The *Scotch* overlay's data-path and control-path overall capacities are doubled by adding one more vSwitch. In general, we can scale up the *Scotch* overlay's data-path and control-path capacity by adding more vSwitches.

6.5 Delay of vSwitch relay in Scotch

As in any Peer-to-Peer network, *Scotch* overlay incurs both extra bandwidth and delay overhead. There have been extensive studies on the bandwidth overhead caused by the extra traffic of the overlay network, e.g., [32]. Such overhead is in general tolerable. Also in our case, *Scotch* is turned on only if the control path is congested. The alternative would be to drop the new flows, which is clearly less preferrable.

We conduct experiments to evaluate the extra delay overhead caused by *Scotch* overlay. Without considering the middleboxes, when *Scotch* is activated, packets are first sent to a randomly selected vSwitch for load balancing purpose. Packets are then forward to the vSwitch close to the destination host. The later vSwitch finally forwards the traffic to the destination. The extra delay comprises of both propagation and processing delays incurred at both the vSwitches and the extra physical switches along the tunnels. Since the load-balancing vSwitch is randomly selected, the propagation delay on average is doubled when packets are forwarded on the *Scotch* overlay.

We conduct two delay measurements with and without *Scotch* overlay. In the first experiment, a client periodically sends ping messages to a server via the Pica8 physical switch. In the second experiment, the ping message is detoured to two vSwitches in sequence before reaching the server; each vSwitch represents a vSwitch in the *Scotch* overlay. There is no direct link between the vSwitches; instead they are connected via the Pica8 switch. Hence the packet has to traverse through the physical switch multiple times when it is forwarded on the overlay. Note that we ignore the host vSwitch in both experiments; including it would add a small

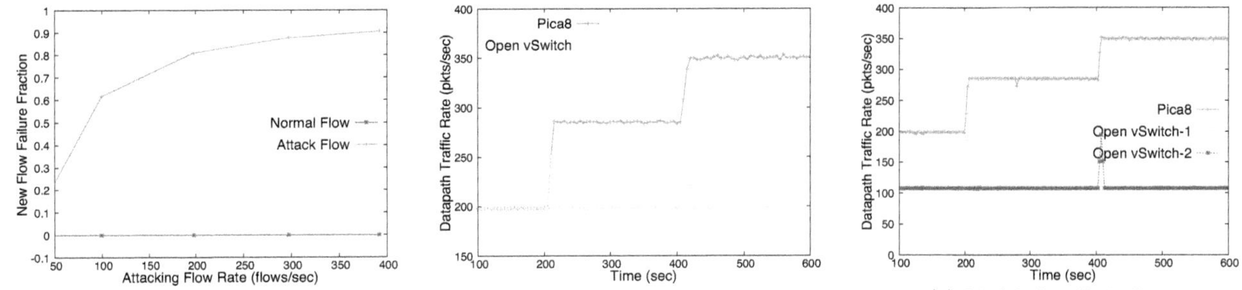

(a) Ingress port differentiation (b) Large flow migration (c) Multiple vSwitches

Figure 11: (a) New flow failure fraction with ingress port differentiation (b) Data-path traffic rate at the vSwitch and the Pica8 switch with large flow migration (c) Data-path traffic rate at two vSwitches and Pica8 switch with large flow migration.

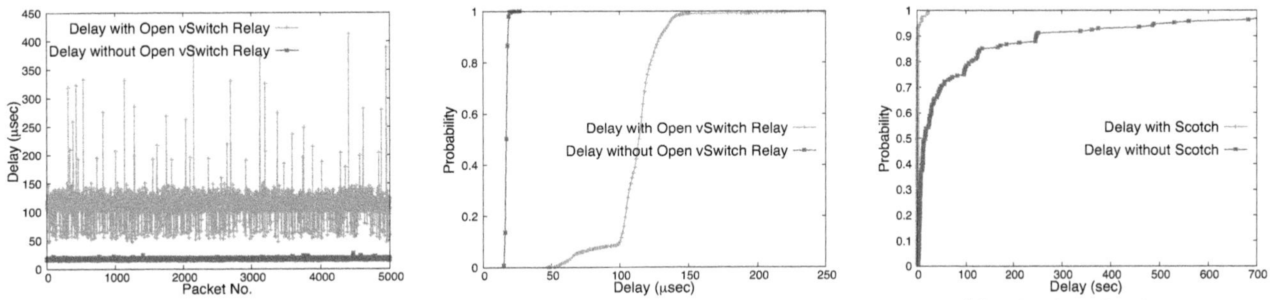

(a) Measured delay (b) CDF of delay (c) File downloading

Figure 12: (a)(b) Delay with and without vSwitch relay (c) File downloading delay with and without Scotch.

additional delay for both cases but not affecting the comparison. For the convenience of measurement, we run both the client and the server on the same physical host in order to avoid clock synchronization problem.

Fig. 12(a)(b) shows 5,000 measured delay samples and the CDF from the experiments. The delay without overlay is very small, around 17 microseconds. The delay with overlay is on average 113 microseconds. The delay with the vSwitch relay is more volatile, with the standard deviation of 22 microsecond. This indicates that packet processing done by a vSwitch software has larger variance compared to a hardware switch. However, given that the overall delay is still very small, well below 1ms, we believe this satisfies the requirement of most applications in the data-center scenario. If *Scotch* is employed for a wide-area network, the extra switch processing delay should be negligible compared to the propagation delay.

6.6 Case study with data center traffic trace

Finally we conduct a case study with real data center traffic traces [24]. We select the packet trace collected from a university data-center (EDU1 in [1]). The packet trace is collected at a switch inside this data-center. We use Tcpreplay [29] to playback the first 30 minutes of the trace, and send the traffic toward a sink node via the Pica8 switch. To study the benefit of *Scotch* on applications, we set an Apache server that serves out a small file of one Kbytes. A client periodically (every ten seconds) attempts to fetch the file. Both the file download traffic and background traffic go through the same physical switch. We measure the file downloading time for both with and without *Scotch*, and report the results in Fig. 12(c).

As reported in the study [1] (Fig. 3(a)), the number flow rate is slightly greater than 200 flows/sec, which is right above the loss-free control path capacity of the Pica8 switch. Without the help of *Scotch*, 3% of file retrieval fails. For the successful file retrievals, the average downloading time is 71.4 second, with the standard deviation of 133.9 seconds. In contrast, with the *Scotch* overlay, the control path capacity is greatly improved and the client always manages to retrieve the file successfully. The average downloading time is shortened to 0.8 second, with the standard deviation of 3.3 seconds. This result shows that *Scotch* improves the file downloading performance significantly. Note that without *Scotch*, the worst downloading time is 711 seconds. Looking at the tcpdump trace, we notice that due to the control path congestion, it takes multiple attempts to successfully install a flow rule into the switch. Since the expiration time interval for a flow rule is 10 seconds, a flow rule may be timed out before a TCP connection is succesfully set up. This causes the application to make multiple retransmissions before the download succeeds.

7. CONCLUSION

To mitigate the bottleneck of control path of SDN under the surge of control traffic (e.g., due to flash crowds or DDoS attacks), we present *Scotch* that can elastically improve the control plane capability of SDN by using an Openflow vSwitch overlay network that primarily carries small flows. *Scotch* exploits both the high control plane throughput of vSwitches and the high data plane throughput of hardware switches. It enables the control plane throughput to scale linearly with the number of vSwitches used.

While achieving the high control plane capacity, *Scotch* still preserves high visibility of new flows and flexibility of fine-grained flow control at the central controller. We experimentally evaluate the performance of *Scotch* and show its effectiveness in elastically scaling control plane capacity well beyond what is possible with current switches.

8. ACKNOWLEDGMENTS

This study was done while An Wang was a summer intern at Bell Labs, Alcatel-Lucent. It was supported in part by NSF under grants CNS-0746649 and CNS-1117300. The authors thank anonymous reviewers for their constructive comments. Yang Guo would like to thank Muralidharan Kodialam for helpful discussions.

9. REFERENCES

[1] T. Benson, A. Akella, and D. Maltz. Network traffic characteristics of data centers in the wild. In *IMC*, 2010.

[2] Z. Cai, A. L. Cox, and T. S. E. Ng. Maestro: Balancing fairness, latency and throughput in the openflow control plane. In *Rice University Technical Report TR11-07*, 2011.

[3] M. Casado, M. J. Freedman, and S. Shenker. Ethane: Taking Control of the Enterprise. In *ACM SIGCOMM*, 2007.

[4] G. Catalli. Open vSwitch: Performance improvement and porting to FreeBSD. In *CHANGE & OFELIA Summer school*, 2011.

[5] Ryu: Component-based software defined networking framework. http://osrg.github.io/ryu/.

[6] A. Curtis et al. Devoflow: Scaling flow management for high-performance networks. *Proc. of SIGCOMM*, 2011.

[7] A. Dixit, F. Hao, S. Mukherjee, T. Lakshman, and R. Kompella. Towards an Elastic Distributed SDN Controller. In *HotSDN*, 2013.

[8] Packet Processing - Intel DPDK vSwitch - OVS. https://01.org/packet-processing/intel-ovdk.

[9] D. Erickson. The Beacon OpenFlow Controller. In *HotSDN*. ACM, 2013.

[10] A. D. Ferguson, A. Guha, C. Liang, R. Fonseca, and S. Krishnamurthi. Participatory networking: an api for application control of sdns. In *SIGCOMM*, 2013.

[11] Floodlight. http://floodlight.openflowhub.org.

[12] O. N. Foundation. OpenFlow Switch Specification (Version 1.3.0). June 2012.

[13] N. Gude, T. Koponen, J. Pettit, B. Pfaff, M. Casado, N. Mckeown, and S. Shenker. NOX: Towards an Operating System for Networks. In *SIGCOMM CCR*, 2008.

[14] hping3. http://linux.die.net/man/8/hping3.

[15] D. Y. Huang, K. Yocum, and A. C. Snoeren. High-Fidelity Switch Models for Software-Defined Network Emulation. In *HotSDN*, 2013.

[16] X. Jin, L. E. Li, L. Vanbever, and J. Rexford. Softcell: Scalable and flexible cellular core network architecture. In *ACM CoNEXT*, 2013.

[17] C. Kim, M. Caesar, and J. Rexford. Floodless in seattle: A scalable ethernet architecture for large enterprises. In *SIGCOMM*, 2008.

[18] T. Koponen et al. Onix: A Distributed Control Platform for Large-scale Production Networks. In *OSDI*, 2010.

[19] K. Krishna Puttaswamy Naga, F. Hao, and T.V. Lakshman. Securing software defined networks via flow deflection, 812383-US-NP.

[20] N. McKeown, T. Anderson, H. Balakrishnan, G. Parulkar, et al. Openflow: enabling innovation in campus networks. *SIGCOMM CCR*, 2008.

[21] A. K. Nayak, A. Reimers, N. Feamster, and R. Clark. Resonance: Dynamic access control for enterprise networks. In *Proceedings of the 1st ACM workshop on Research on enterprise networking*, 2009.

[22] Personal Communication with Pica8.

[23] Pica8: Open networks for software-defined networking. http://www.pica8.com/.

[24] Packet trace at a switch in a data-center. http://pages.cs.wisc.edu/ tbenson/IMC10_Data.html.

[25] S. Ray, R. Guerin, and R. Sofia. A distributed hash table based address resolution scheme for large-scale ethernet networks. In *ICC*, 2007.

[26] A. Shaikh and A. Greenberg. Making routers last longer with ViAggre. In *NSDI*, 2009.

[27] S. Shin, P. Porras, V. Yegneswaran, M. Fong, G. Gu, and M. Tyson. Fresco: Modular composable security services for software-defined networks. In *NDSS*, 2013.

[28] S. Shin, V. Yegneswaran, P. Porras, and G. Gu. Avant-guard: Scalable and vigilant switch flow management in software-defined networks. In *Proceedings of the 20th ACM Conference on Computer and Communications Security (CCS)*, 2013.

[29] Tcpreplay. http://tcpreplay.synfin.net/.

[30] A. Tootoonchian, S. Gorbunov, Y. Ganjali, M. Casado, and R. Sherwood. On Controller Performance in Software-Defined Networks. In *HotICE*, 2012.

[31] The overhead of software tunneling. http://networkheresy.com/2012/06/08/the-overhead-of-software-tunneling/.

[32] Yang-hua Chu, S. Rao, S. Seshan, and H. Zhang. A case for end system multicast. In *IEEE Journal on Selected Areas in Communications*, Oct. 2002.

[33] M. Yu, J. Rexford, M. J. Freedman, and J. Wang. Scalable flow-based networking with DIFANE. In *SIGCOMM*, 2010.

Providing Reliable FIB Update Acknowledgments in SDN

Maciej Kuźniar
EPFL
maciej.kuzniar@epfl.ch

Peter Perešíni
EPFL
peter.peresini@epfl.ch

Dejan Kostić
KTH Royal Institute of Technology
dmk@kth.se

ABSTRACT

In this paper, we first show that transient, but grave problems such as violations of security policies can occur with real switches even when using consistent updates to Software Defined Networks. Next, we present techniques that are effective in ameliorating this problem. Our key insight is in creating a transparent layer that relies on control and data plane measurements to confirm rule updates only when the rule is visible in the data plane.

Categories and Subject Descriptors

C.2.6 [**Computer-Communication Networks**]: Internetworking—*Routers*; C.4 [**Performance of Systems**]: Reliability, availability, and serviceability

Keywords

Software-Defined Networking; Reliability; OpenFlow

1. INTRODUCTION

Software Defined Networks (SDNs) enable flexible network configuration by allowing a centralized controller to manipulate forwarding rules in switch flow tables. The controller reacts to events such as topology changes, traffic engineering decisions, and failures by computing and installing the new desired network state. This process is referred to as the *network update*, and involves issuing commands to the switches to install the new set of rules and reconfigure the network. The network update process is complicated and if not conducted carefully, may lead to transient problems such as black holes, forwarding loops, link overload, and packets reaching undesired destinations. There are many approaches that guarantee some correctness properties [3,8,9,11]. These all split an update into many stages, and rely on knowing when a particular rule modification was applied at the switch(es) before issuing further modifications. This necessitates positive acknowledgments confirming rule modifications.

CoNEXT'14, December 2–5, 2014, Sydney, Australia.

http://dx.doi.org/10.1145/2674005.2675006 .

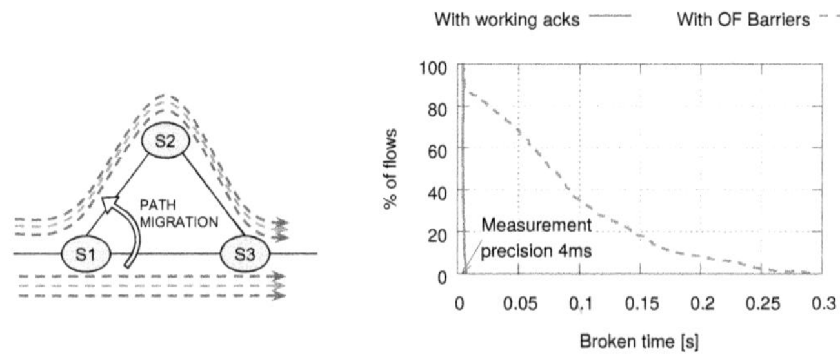

(a) (b)

Figure 1: Consistent network update using a hardware switch. Despite theoretical guarantees, for most flows switch S1 gets updated before S2 and the network drops packets for up to 290 ms. Using our system eliminates this problem.

Unfortunately, in OpenFlow, currently the most popular SDN protocol, there is no mechanism with a sole purpose of acknowledging rule modifications. Instead, there exists a Barrier command with a more general functionality.[1] However, studies [12] show that OpenFlow switches do not satisfy the specification in this crucial for correctness aspect. We further verify that this happens even to the latest-generation switches [7]. This may lead to transient but grave network problems.

To demonstrate the magnitude of the problem, we prepare a small end-to-end test: We set up a network in a triangle topology with the hardware switch S2 and two software switches S1 and S3 (Figure 1a). We preinstall paths for 300 IP flows between hosts H1 and H2 going through switches S1 and S3. Then, we perform an update that modifies the paths to S1-S2-S3 in a consistent manner, such that a given packet can follow the old rules only or the new rules only [11].

Despite using consistent updates, some flows drop packets for an extended period of time (Figure 1b). A detailed analysis shows that the switch sends the barrier reply up to 290 ms before the rule modification becomes visible to data plane traffic. Other switch models not only reply to barriers too early, but also reorder rule updates across barriers [7].

The consequences of this observation have great impact –even though provably correct in theory, *none of the consistent network update techniques work in practice with buggy*

[1]According to the specification, after receiving a barrier request, the switch has to finish processing all previously-received messages before executing any messages after the barrier request. When the processing is complete, the switch must send a barrier reply message [1].

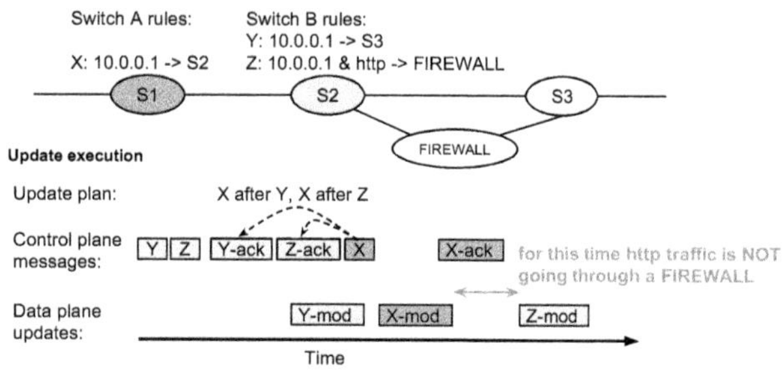

Figure 2: If switch B does not report data plane updates correctly, the theoretically safe update that adds rules for trusted and untrusted traffic from the same host turns into a transient security hole.

switches, and all systems that build upon these techniques are unsafe as well. In particular, buggy behavior may lead to security violations, broken bandwidth guarantees, or black holes – an example of the first is depicted in Figure 2. If the issues that we bring up here are not addressed (*e.g.*, by adopting one of our schemes) the SDN deployments that are increasingly taking place in enterprises are in jeopardy.

While an incorrect barrier implementation may be just a temporary problem and not a fundamental limitation (one of the tested switches does implement barriers correctly), we see three main reasons why it should be immediately addressed. First, there are many solutions that rely on barriers and it cannot be expected that all switches in a network will correctly function. Second, even after five major revisions the OpenFlow specification is unclear – it does not explicitly state that the commands must be applied in the data plane, instead it may be understood that the barrier enforces control plane-ordering only. This in turn means that, unless there is a high pressure from customers, vendors will have no incentive to provide data plane-level confirmations, and therefore the problem might not disappear in future switch generations. Finally, we argue that controllers need acknowledgments of each rule installation, rather than only high level barriers [10]. Therefore, we go one step further than just fixing barriers, and the solutions we propose provide such fine grained rule update acknowledgments. Providing this functionality entails a few challenges: i) handling heterogeneous switches, ii) dealing with the variable delay in installing rules in the data plane, iii) ensuring low overhead.

In this work, we introduce a transparent layer below an SDN controller that provides reliable acknowledgments for rule modifications. In particular, when using our scheme, the controller can never receive an acknowledgment before a corresponding rule is installed in the data plane. Our contributions include proposing various methods, including data plane probing schemes, that achieve the aforementioned goal depending on switch capabilities. The effect of applying one of these techniques is visible in Figure 1b: no packets get dropped. Moreover, we explain how, at the cost of a higher overhead, such a layer provides barrier-like guarantees to the controller working with switches that do not implement barriers correctly.

2. SYSTEM OVERVIEW

We have two main requirements in mind when designing our system called RUM (Rule Update Monitoring). First, it needs to work with existing switches and take into account their capabilities and limitations. Second, the system should provide reliable barrier commands in a backward-compatible way without requiring any modifications to the existing controllers and switches. However, it should allow the RUM-aware controllers to benefit from fine grained acknowledgments.

Acknowledging rule modifications. The first goal of the system is to provide reliable rule modification acknowledgments to the OpenFlow-speaking controllers. We design RUM as a transparent layer between the switches and the controller that intercepts and modifies the communication between them similarly to FlowVisor [13] or VeriFlow [5]. In contrast with these systems, RUM plays a more active role in the interception, as it can buffer, rate-limit, remove or add messages. To allow easy deployment and transparency for controllers that are not designed to work with the fine grained acknowledgments, RUM adapts existing OpenFlow messages to convey successful modifications (such notifications are not available in OpenFlow). Depending on the required precision and available switch properties, the techniques (Section 3) rely only on the control plane communication with the tested switch, or may install additional rules and involve the neighboring switches.

Providing reliable barriers. To provide reliable barriers, RUM intercepts all barrier requests and replies. After capturing a barrier request, RUM holds off sending the corresponding barrier reply and following messages from the switch until it can ensure that the switch completed all pending operations. An ability to correctly acknowledge commands issued to the switch is therefore the key to reliable barriers. Additionally, when working with switches that reorder modifications across barriers, RUM buffers all commands that the controller sends after the last unconfirmed barrier. It releases them to the switch after acknowledging the barrier. The barrier layer uses standard OpenFlow barrier commands and is therefore transparent to any controller.

3. DATA PLANE ACKNOWLEDGMENTS

RUM aims to acknowledge rule modifications as soon as the new rule is active in a switch data plane, but not sooner. Because different switches have different limitations and capabilities, we discuss several possible solutions to the problem at hand.

3.1 Control-plane only techniques

The first class of techniques uses control plane information only and requires modeling the switch behavior.

Using OpenFlow barrier commands. Relying on barrier messages is a natural way to receive acknowledgments in OpenFlow, therefore, we present it as a baseline. A switch must send a barrier reply message only after it finishes processing all previous commands. However, our measurements show that some switches respond to a barrier immediately, before the modifications were applied to the data plane, and as a result the data plane is often between 100 and 300 ms behind what may be assumed based on barrier replies [7]. This confirms previous measurements [12] indicating that barriers cannot be trusted and should not be used as rule update confirmations.

While one can imagine using other OpenFlow commands instead of barriers (*e.g.*, using statistics requests), we believe such an approach does not solve the underlying problem —

the reply from the switch is still based on its control plane view and/or it does not have enough temporal granularity (*e.g.*, flow statistics might be updated only once per second). Therefore, in the rest of this section we introduce techniques that still rely on the barriers, but take into account the data plane delay.

Delaying barrier acknowledgments. The first technique relies on experiments prior to deployment. If the maximum time between the barrier reply and the rule modification being applied is bounded and can be measured, RUM waits for this time after receiving a reply before confirming earlier modifications.

The main drawback of this method is that it requires precise delay measurements or overestimation. We observe that in practice the delay depends on many, often difficult to predict factors and therefore providing strong guarantees is difficult [7]. For example, if the data plane is typically delayed by up to 100 ms, but there are cases of a 300-ms delay, one needs to always wait for 300 ms. Even then, in hard to predict corner cases, the delay may reach several seconds, which is impractical to use as the upper bound. Therefore, waiting for a timeout after each barrier has a negative impact on update performance and rule modification rate.

Adaptive delay. Adaptive timeout improves the performance of the previous technique, but requires even more detailed measurements to develop a precise switch model. Based on such models and knowing the rate at which a controller issues modification commands, RUM estimates when a particular rule modification will take place in the switch. Thus, the timeout is adjusted accordingly. However, this method requires building detailed switch performance models, which is difficult [7].

3.2 Data plane probes

The basic idea of data plane probes is to inject special packets into the network and use these packets, as well as special probing rules, to monitor which rules are active in the data plane. There are two aspects of OpenFlow barrier commands: (*i*) a switch should respond with a barrier reply after it processed all previous commands, and (*ii*) a switch should never reorder commands separated by barriers. In practice some switches violate either the first of these properties (because they process commands in the control plane, but push the rules to the data plane later), or both. The two techniques presented in this section are design to work correctly with such two classes of switches.

3.2.1 Sequential probing

If a switch violates only the first barrier property (responds to barriers too early) two modifications separated by a barrier are never reordered in the data plane. Therefore, a strawman solution follows each real rule modification with a barrier and an additional rule installation for probing. By the time the probing rule is determined to be active (*i.e.*, it forwards a probing packet), the original rule must be in place as well.

Implementation-wise, the probing rule matches only the specially selected probe packets and has a high priority so that no other rule can override it. The probing rule sends the matching packets to the controller. RUM then repetitively injects probe packets (using a PacketOut message) into the switch forwarding pipeline and when the probe arrives back to RUM, it means that the probe rule is installed and therefore the corresponding real rule is active as well. Finally, after probing rule is confirmed, it is no longer needed and can be removed.

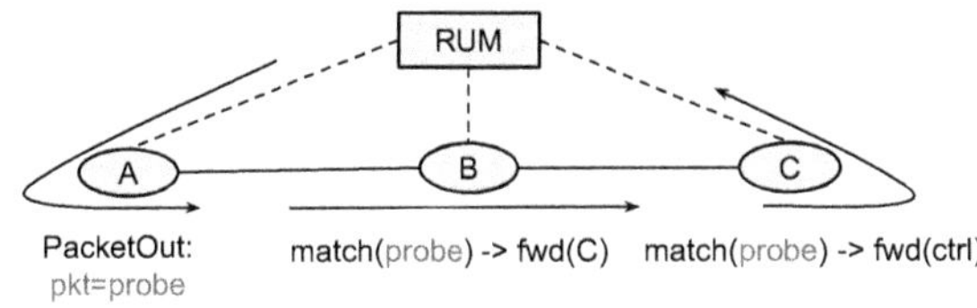

Figure 3: Probing the data plane at switch B. The controller (RUM) sends a probe packet from switch A to switch B. If B installed the probing rule, it forwards the packet to switch C which sends it back to the controller.

There are, however, technical details of the strawman solution that make it impractical and require improvements. First, from the correctness perspective, it assumes that the PacketOut processing and probe rule matching are performed in hardware. Unfortunately, this might not be the case – rules sending packets to the controller are often kept in software and may start forwarding traffic before the previous hardware rules are pushed into the data plane. As such, we modify our solution to use hardware-only probing rules – we use two additional switches[2] as depicted in Figure 3.

Second, inserting one probe rule after each normal rule is prohibitively expensive. Instead, we notice that a single probe rule installed after a batch of several rule modifications acknowledges the whole batch at the same time. This way the probing overhead gets amortized over more rules at the expense of a longer acknowledgment delay. Moreover, the probe rules can be optimized even more – instead of installing a new probe rule for each batch and then deleting it, we use a single probing rule which rewrites a particular field in the packet header (*e.g.*, ToS or VLAN) with a version number of this probing rule. Then, we just update the rule to write the new version number to the probe packet header. RUM recognizes the last version of probe rule based on the probing packet headers it receives back.

Multi-switch deployment. The approach described so far requires setting up different probe rules matching different packets for each probed switch, because otherwise forwarding the probe packet on the next switch will interfere with probe collection on that switch. We overcome this problem by choosing two header fields H_1 and H_2 to be used by probing. These can be any rewritable fields in a packet header. Additionally, we reserve two special values of H_1; we call these values *preprobe* and *postprobe*. In our solution, all switches install a high priority probe-catch rule that sends all packets with $H_1 == postprobe$ to the controller. We also install one probing rule per each switch. It matches packets with $H_1 == preprobe$ and rewriting them to post-probes while also storing the per-switch unique probe rule version in H_2 ($H_1 \leftarrow postprobe$, $H_2 \leftarrow ver$). To do the probing, RUM sends a probe packet with $H_1 = preprobe$ inside a PacketOut message through switch A towards switch B as depicted in Figure 4.

This technique comes with two sources of overhead. First, a switch needs to install the probe rules which reduces its usable rule update rate. Further, the probe rules are probed by data plane packets, which affects the neighboring switches'

[2] In principle, switches A and C can be the same switch. We keep them separated for the presentation purposes.

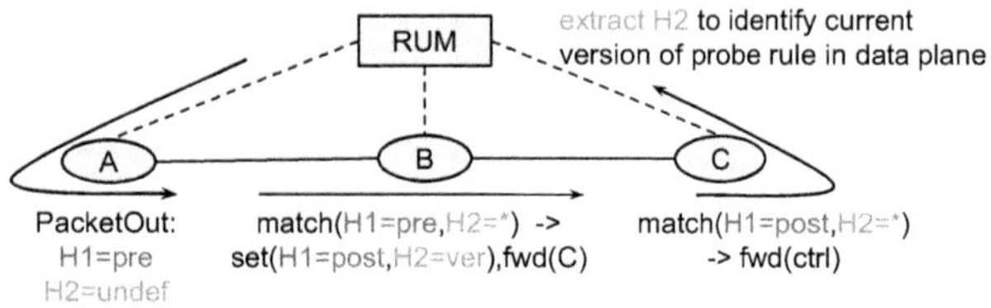

Figure 4: Network-wide probing solution. There are two rules preinstalled at each switch and only the version of the probing rule is updated over time.

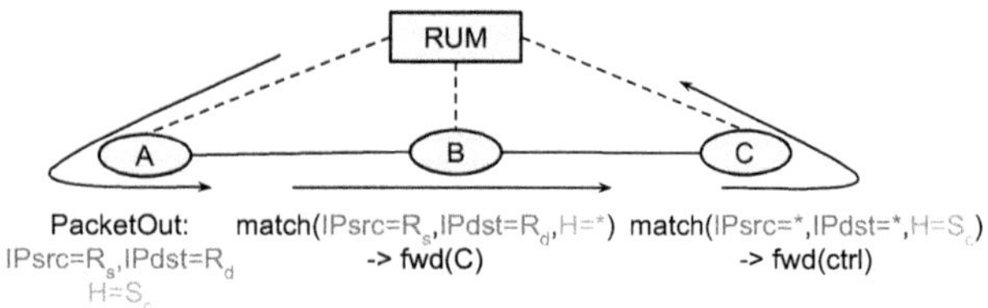

Figure 5: Probing for a rule matching IP packets with source R_s and destination R_d. A probe packet matches the tested rule at B and a send-to-controller rule at C.

control planes though the PacketOut and PacketIn messages. Thus, there is a trade-off between notification delay and the usable update rate.

3.2.2 General probing

The final strategy addresses the problem of switches that reorder rule modifications despite the use of barriers. In such a case, confirming that the last update took place is insufficient to acknowledge all previous updates. Specifically, it means that we cannot rely on probe rules described previously. Instead RUM needs to confirm each modification separately, where a modified rule may match an arbitrary set of header fields.

In this strategy, we need to reserve a header field H that is not used in the network, meaning that all normal rules have it wildcarded and no packet has it set to a value used by RUM (*e.g.*, VLAN, MPLS or ToS depending on the deployment). At the beginning, each switch i gets assigned a unique value S_i of field H. Each switch i then installs a high priority probe-catching rule that sends all packets that match on $H == S_i$ to the controller. Figure 5 shows a scenario where RUM confirms the installation of the rule that matches packets with an IP source R_s and IP destination R_d and forwards them to switch C. Assuming the action of the probed rule is to send the traffic to switch C, we use switch C with its probe-catch rule matching on $H == S_c$ to receive the probes. To create the probe packet, RUM computes an intersection of the probed rule on switch B and probe-catch rule on switch C. In our example, the probe packet has $IP_{src} = R_s$, $IP_{dst} = R_d$, $H = S_c$ and arbitrary remaining header fields. This probe gets injected through any neighbor of switch B (*e.g.*, switch A). As soon as the tested rule gets installed, the controller observes the probe packet coming from switch C inside a PacketIn message. The same method can detect rule deletions (probes stop arriving at the controller) or rule modifications (probes reach the controller from a different neighbor of B or have header fields modified to new values in case of header rewriting rules).

Overlapping rules. The previous, simplified description does not take into account the fact that there is more than one rule installed at a given switch. When creating a probe packet for a particular rule, RUM needs to take into account other rules such that the probe does not get forwarded by any other, already installed rule. In particular, probe generation needs to address two issues.

First, the generated probe packet must not match any higher-priority rule which overlaps with the probed rule. While finding a probing packet that hits exactly the tested rule is NP in a general case, others [4,17] show that in practice the problem can be solved quickly for real forwarding tables. Second, the generated probe packet must have a different forwarding action (*i.e.*, either a different output port or a different rewrite action) than the lower-priority rule matching the probe when the probed rule is not installed yet (otherwise we cannot distinguish if the packet was processed by the probed rule or the lower-priority rule). Note that as a special case, we can probe for rules dropping packets if there exists an overlapping lower-priority which does not drop the packets (a common case of ACLs and forwarding rules combination). If no suitable probe exists, RUM falls back to one of the control plane-based techniques. For example, if the probed rule is fully covered by higher priority rules, or if it covers other, already installed lower priority rules that have exactly the same actions, probing cannot reveal when the rule got installed.

Reducing the number of switch-specific values. This technique relies on using a header field and values that are unused by the live traffic in the network. Because there may be few such fields and values, it is essential to reduce the number of required values. However, to prevent the tested switch from sending the probe directly to the controller, each two adjacent switches need to have different identifiers. Thus, instead of using a network-wide unique value of S_i for each switch i, one can solve an instance of the vertex coloring problem for which there are well known heuristics [15].

4. PROTOTYPE

We implement a RUM prototype that works as a TCP proxy between the switches and the controller. The switches connect to the proxy as if it was a controller, and the proxy then connects to a real controller using multiple connections, impersonating the switches. This design allows us to modularly compose RUM as a chain of proxies to add functionality and freely replace components. For example, a barrier layer built on top of the acknowledgment layer is just another proxy. We implement the proxies using the POX platform.

In the current implementation we assume IP-only traffic and rely on the ToS field for probing. Because there are only 64 ToS values, we need to periodically recycle them in longer experiments. Moreover, we assume that the rules do not overlap,[3] and therefore, selecting a probing packet degrades to using the same source and destination addresses as in the rule's match.

While the OpenFlow specification lacks messages to confirm that a rule modification was successfully applied, it defines error messages used when something goes wrong. We reuse an error message with a newly defined (unused) error code for positive acknowledgments. Alternatively, one could potentially add vendor-specific messages to the protocol.

Finally, the hardware switch we use does not support priorities but takes the rule installation order to define the rule

[3] Except a low priority drop-all and high priority probe rules

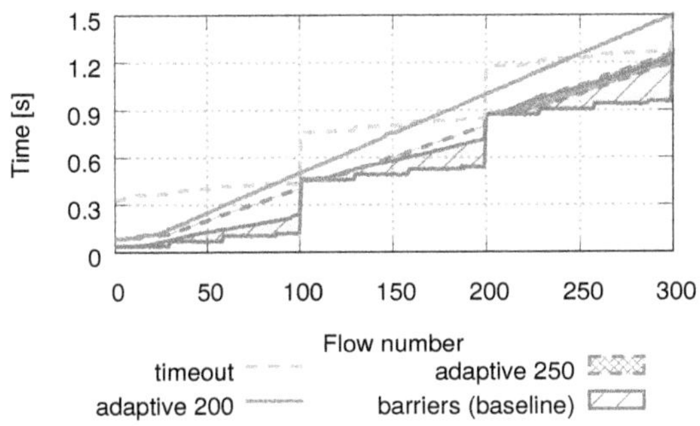

Figure 6: Flow update times when using control-plane only techniques. The reliability depends on correct estimation of the switch performance.

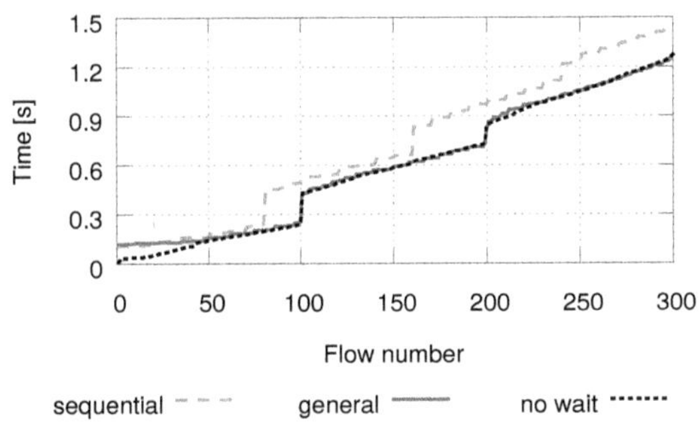

Figure 7: Flow update times with probing. There are no packet drops and the overhead of the general technique is negligible compared to the best achievable update time.

importance. Therefore, we carefully place the low priority rules early, and make sure that other rules do not hide the high priority ones.

5. EVALUATION

We evaluate RUM in the same end to end experiment as presented before, and using a hardware OpenFlow switch (HP 5406zl) that incorrectly implements barriers.[4] Further, we use low level benchmarks to analyze the properties and trade-offs in our techniques. Admittedly, these are just small scale experiments. However, a large scale test would require a testbed built of hardware switches because emulators use software switches that perform differently than the real ones. We do not have access to such a testbed.

5.1 End to end experiment

We first show that the presented techniques solve the dropped packets problem described in Section 1. The setup is as in Section 1 and we send data plane traffic at a rate of 250 packets/s per flow (75000 packets/s in total). We use the previously described control plane-only techniques and in Figure 6 plot the times when the last data plane packet following the old path and the first packet going along the updated path arrives at the destination. The area between the two lines visually represents the periods when packets get dropped.[5]

[4] The precise characteristics can be found in [7].

[5] If the delay between the two packets is lower than our measurement precision, we plot a single line.

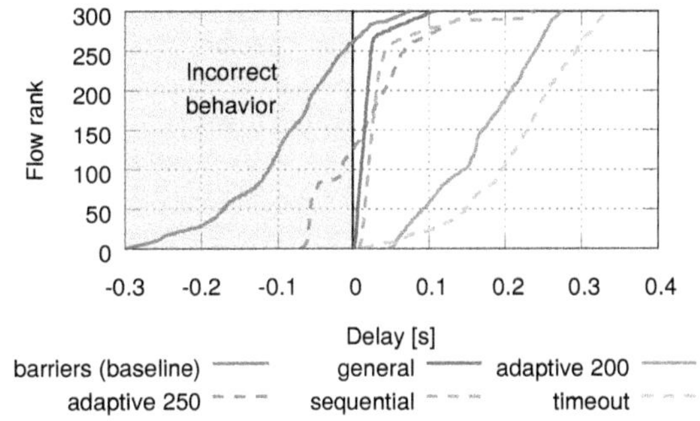

Figure 8: Delay between data plane and control plane activation. Using barriers leads to incorrect behaviors, control plane techniques increase the update time and the data plane techniques strike a balance.

An update with barrier messages is the fastest, but because the barrier replies are arriving too soon, rules at switch S1 get updated before rules at switch S2 are in place, which leads to extensive periods of packet drops (a total of 6000-7500 packets got lost in each of multiple runs of this experiment). The three visible steps in flow installation times are an artifact of the way how the switch synchronizes the data and control plane [7].

Using a 300-ms timeout solves a packet drop problem, but increases the average time it takes before a flow starts following a new path from 592 ms to 815 ms. Finally, while the 300-ms timeout is sufficient when there are up to 300 rules in the switch flow table, it becomes too short when the table occupation grows [7].

Based on the measurements, we set the adaptive timeout to assume that a switch performs 200 and 250 rule modifications per second. We see that the technique offers a stable performance over time, however when flow table occupancy increases and the assumed update rate is overestimated (250), the acknowledgments arrive too early and the network starts dropping packets.

Figure 7 shows the results of the same experiment but when using the data plane probing techniques, which guarantee no packet drops. For comparison, we plot the result when all flow modifications are issued at once to all the switches (*no wait*). It shows the shortest update duration one can get, limited only by the slowest switch update rate, but also offers no theoretical consistency guarantees. The *sequential probing technique* requires additional rule modifications (we modify a probing rule after every 10 real modifications). This fact is noticeable, because the data plane synchronization steps [7] are more frequent which hurts the update performance. On the other hand, the *general probing technique* does not require additional rule updates, but only sending and receiving data plane probes. If probing up to 30 oldest flow modifications at once, every 10 ms, the flows get updated almost as quickly as the lower bound.

We originally send packets belonging to each of the updated flows every 4 ms and observe no drops. To verify that there are no transient periods shorter than 4 ms when packets are dropped, we randomly select a single flow ten times and send traffic for the flow at 10000 packets a second. Once again we observe no drops.

Barrier Layer Performance. To validate the overhead of a full barrier layer, we rerun the same experiment with our reliable barrier layer introduced before and sending a barrier after every 10 flow modifications. When a switch does not reorder modifications across barriers, the total update time and the particular curve of flow update times is the same as for the normal sequential probing technique. On the other hand, if the switch can reorder modifications and RUM needs to buffer them to ensure correct ordering, the overhead is big and the total update time is twice that of the general probing technique. Understandably, this time increases even more (up to 5 times) if the barriers are more frequent (up to a barrier after each command).

5.2 Low level benchmarks

After observing that RUM achieves its main high level goal - allowing for reliable network updates with consistency guarantees even on unreliable switches, we analyze how changing variables in each technique affects various aspects of the update.

The setup in the next two experiments is the same. Initially, there is a single, low priority drop-all-packets rule at the switch. Then, a controller modifies R rules in the switch in a way that at most K modifications are unconfirmed at any time. When a modification confirmation comes, the controller issues a new update. Meanwhile, we send data plane traffic matching the modified rules again at a rate of 250 packets/s for each rule.

Data plane delay. First, we measure when packets matching a particular rule start arriving at the destination (data plane activation) and when the controller receives a confirmation that the rule was installed (control plane activation). In Figure 8 we plot the delay between the data plane and control plane activations for various techniques for $R = 300$ and $K = 300$ (send all rules at once). All values below zero mean incorrect behavior and positive values cause a delay during an update. Thus, the ideal behavior would be a vertical line at $x = 0$. We see that, as mentioned in the introduction, barrier replies arrive even 300 ms before the rule gets applied. Using a 300-ms timeout fixes the correctness problem in this case, but is very inefficient – for the median the update wastes 230 ms on each barrier. The adaptive timeout technique achieves very good results, however, it requires precise models, otherwise the delay can fall below zero (possible inconsistencies). Finally, both probing techniques never incur a negative delay and, accordingly, are within 70 ms and 30 ms after the data plane modification for 90% of modifications.

Impact of probing rules. A technique that relies on installing probing rules to confirm that previous modifications took place requires finding a balance between the frequency of such confirmations and measurement precision. In this experiment we issue $R = 4000$ modifications and vary the number of modifications after which RUM sends a probing rule, as well as the number of allowed, unconfirmed modifications (K). Table 1 shows that the usable modification rate (rate of real modifications, not counting probes) is proportional to the number of rules probed at once and is usually close to the expected rate. When the number of allowed unconfirmed messages is low compared to the number of rules confirmed at once, the controller does not receive the confirmations quickly enough to saturate the switch.

Number of probes a switch can process. Sending data plane probes requires a switch to process two types of messages. First, an injecting switch receives a PacketOut and forwards a probe packet to the required port. Then, the receiving switch gets the packet, encapsulates it in a PacketIn message, and sends it to the controller. In the previous experiments, we used software switches as sending and receiving switches. Here, we instead benchmark the performance of a real hardware switch. We measure the PacketOut rate by issuing 20000 PacketOut messages and observe when the corresponding packets arrive at the destination. Similarly, we install a rule forwarding all traffic to the controller and inject traffic to the switch to measure the PacketIn rate. The rates are 7006 PacketOut/s and 5531 PacketIn/s, averaged over 5 runs. Both of these values are sufficient to allow RUM to probe the rules frequently.

Probing frequency	$K = 20$	$K = 50$	$K = 100$
after 1 update	51%	51%	51%
after 2 updates	64%	68%	68%
after 5 updates	74%	86%	86%
after 10 updates	76%	93%	94%
after 20 updates	74%	95%	98%

Table 1: Usable rule update rate with the sequential probing technique (normalized to a rate with barriers).

Finally, our additional experiments show that processing PacketIn requests in parallel with rule modifications has minimal impact on the rule modification throughput—new rate is over 96% of the original rate without any other messages. Similarly, processing PacketOut messages in parallel with rule modifications decreases the rule update rate by at most 13% for the ratio of PacketOut messages to rule modifications up to 5:1.

6. RELATED WORK AND CONCLUSIONS

SOFT [6] identifies inconsistencies in the way OpenFlow switches respond to commands, but cannot ensure that the rules are installed in the data plane.

To the best of our knowledge, our work is the first to look at the network update consistency from the practical point of view, using the real switches. There is a large body of work that guarantees particular properties during an update [3,8,9,11,14], but they all assume correctly-functioning switches. We show that this assumption does not hold and propose a workaround that allows the aforementioned solutions to work correctly.

ATPG [17] is a system that determines and injects packets that exercise all rules in a network. It is however an end to end solution designed to work on a coarser granularity than RUM. Its main goal is testing network correctness in a stable state, not during an update.

Oflops [12] is a study that benchmarks switches in a controlled environment and reports some of the problems we describe in this work. In contrast, we propose a solution to these problems.

Finally, there are efforts to build switch models [2, 16]. This work can be help RUM to better estimate timeouts and optimize the probing.

7. ACKNOWLEDGMENTS

We thank the anonymous reviewers who provided excellent feedback. The research leading to these results has received funding from the European Research Council under the European Union's Seventh Framework Programme (FP7/2007-2013) / ERC grant agreement 259110.

8. REFERENCES

[1] OpenFlow Switch Specification. `http://www.openflow.org/documents/openflow-spec-v1.0.0.pdf`.

[2] D. Y. Huang, K. Yocum, and A. C. Snoeren. High-fidelity switch models for software-defined network emulation. In *HotSDN*, 2013.

[3] N. P. Katta, J. Rexford, and D. Walker. Incremental Consistent Updates. In *HotSDN*, 2013.

[4] P. Kazemian, G. Varghese, and N. McKeown. Header Space Analysis: Static Checking for Networks. In *NSDI*, 2012.

[5] A. Khurshid, X. Zou, W. Zhou, M. Caesar, and P. B. Godfrey. VeriFlow: Verifying Network-Wide Invariants in Real Time. In *NSDI*, 2013.

[6] M. Kuźniar, P. Perešíni, M. Canini, D. Venzano, and D. Kostić. A SOFT Way for OpenFlow Switch Interoperability Testing. In *CoNEXT*, 2012.

[7] M. Kuźniar, P. Perešíni, and D. Kostić. What you need to know about SDN control and data planes. Technical Report EPFL-REPORT-199497, EPFL, 2014.

[8] H. H. Liu, X. Wu, M. Zhang, L. Yuan, R. Wattenhofer, and D. A. Maltz. zUpdate : Updating Data Center Networks with Zero Loss. In *SIGCOMM*, 2013.

[9] R. Mahajan and R. Wattenhofer. On Consistent Updates in Software Defined Networks. In *HotNets*, 2013.

[10] P. Perešíni, M. Kuźniar, M. Canini, and D. Kostić. OpenFlow Needs You! A Call for a Discussion about a Cleaner OpenFlow API. In *EWSDN*. IEEE, 2013.

[11] M. Reitblatt, N. Foster, J. Rexford, C. Schlesinger, and D. Walker. Abstractions for Network Update. In *SIGCOMM*, 2012.

[12] C. Rotsos, N. Sarrar, S. Uhlig, R. Sherwood, and A. W. Moore. Oflops: An open framework for openflow switch evaluation. In *PAM*, 2012.

[13] R. Sherwood, G. Gibb, K.-K. Yap, G. Appenzeller, M. Casado, N. McKeown, and G. Parulkar. Can the Production Network Be the Testbed? In *OSDI*, 2010.

[14] S. Vissicchio, L. Vanbever, L. Cittadini, G. Xie, and O. Bonaventure. Safe Updates of Hybrid SDN Networks. Technical report, UCL, 2013.

[15] D. J. Welsh and M. B. Powell. An upper bound for the chromatic number of a graph and its application to timetabling problems. *The Computer Journal*, 10(1), 1967.

[16] M. Yu, A. Wundsam, and M. Raju. NOSIX: A Lightweight Portability Layer for the SDN OS. *ACM SIGCOMM Computer Communication Review*, 44(2), 2014.

[17] H. Zeng, P. Kazemian, G. Varghese, and N. McKeown. Automatic Test Packet Generation. In *CoNEXT*, 2012.

Author Index

www.ingramcontent.com/pod-product-compliance
Ingram Content Group UK Ltd.
Pitfield, Milton Keynes, MK11 3LW, UK
UKHW051412290926
15471UKWH00009B/1558

9 781450 334396